NUCLEAR EVOLUTION

Discovery of the Rainbow Body

by

CHRISTOPHER HILLS

Edited by:
Norah Hills (General Editor)
Ann Ray, Deborah Rozman, Richard Welker

UNIVERSITY OF THE TREES PRESS, P.O. Box 644, Boulder Creek, CA 95006

Library of Congress Catalog Card Number: 76-53180
ISBN: 0-916438-09-0 Soft cover
0-916438-12-0 Hard cover Library Edition

SECOND EDITION

First Edition Copyright 1968
in England by Centre Community Publications

Front Cover: Design & Photography: John Hills
Labwork: New Sun Color Lab, Mill Valley, Ca.
Meditating figure: Patti Danton

Printed in the United States
by R.R. Donnelley and Sons

Library of Congress Cataloging In Publication Data

Hills, Christopher B
Nuclear evolution.

Includes bibliographical references and index.
1. Cosmology. 2. Occult sciences. I. Title.
BF1999.H6133 1977 133 76-53180
ISBN 0-916438-09-0
ISBN 0-916438-12-0 lib. bdg.

11-84
Gift

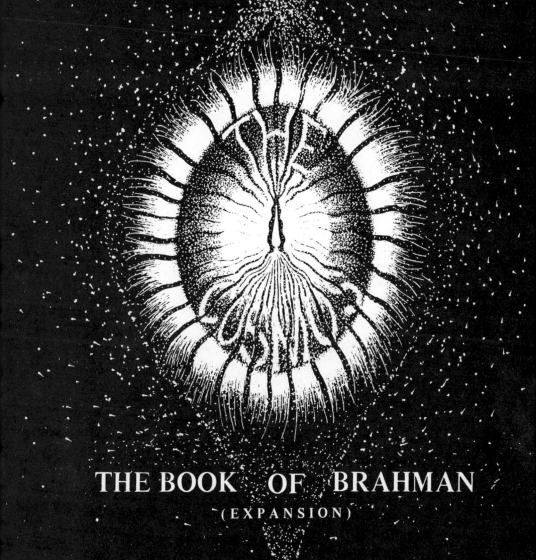

THE BOOK OF BRAHMAN
(EXPANSION)

DEDICATION

This book is first dedicated to the awesome glory
of the ONE being it is about, who is the author of
all things expanding in the cosmic womb of space.
Secondly it is dedicated to those beings who
persist until the hidden Brahmic splendour of the
cosmic heart is seen in the deep invisible light of
their own consciousness.

ACKNOWLEDGEMENTS

I feel uniquely blessed to be surrounded by the twenty selfless and willing persons who dropped everything they wanted to do to get this longest of all my books into print. May I thank the ONE who sent them. After writing so many words I find myself speechless to thank so many arms, heads and hearts who make up the nucleus of Nuclear Evolution in practice.

My first and most important acknowledgement goes to the editors and those students who have given their love and time to the production of the book. But for their insistence and effort, this work would have remained my cryptic shorthand notes written for the students at Centre House Community, London, without concession to the general readership. Now in this edition gratitude is due to the four editors, Ann Ray, Deborah Rozman, Richard Welker, and especially my wife Norah as General Editor, who have, with their visible love, shared the devotion of the author to the nature of light.

I thank all those who typed and proofed and mocked up the manuscript, especially my secretary Pamela Osborn, and all the family at the University of the Trees Press, for their cheerful tireless service in devotion to that ONE whose light is the rainbow of life. May it come back to them multiplied a thousand times. Credit for the cover photography and design goes to my son John Hills, and for art work on the spine and other drawings to Gary Buyle.

Appreciation is given those who contributed to Section Four in order to show the relevance of Nuclear Evolution to other works, namely Norah Hills, Deborah Rozman, Humphrey Osmond, Miriam Siegler, Richard Smoke, Vasco Ronchi and Regan Power.

An Acknowledgement is due to all those true scientists of the spirit and the spectrum of matter on whose shoulders we can stand to see the vision of the transparent radiance of consciousness which forms my idea of God.

Christopher Hills
July, 1977

CONTENTS
PART I

The Cosmic Light Primaries of the Three Guna Qualities --
The Binding of the Gunas -- The Human Lens -- Why is Colour
Important? -- Letting In More Light -- The Secret of Light --
Black: The Dark Night of the Soul -- Fundamental Ray Disc --
Tools For Evolution -- Conscious Control of the Life-Force --
How Does Kundalini Become Colour? -- Developing
the Supersense -- The Spherical Raindrop as Nature's
Letters of Light -- The Rainbow as Nature's Signature in Light --
Mirror for the Self -- The Turning Point -- The Seven Major
Types of Nuclear Evolution -- Ye Are The Light Of This World

PART II

PART III

PART IV

The above diagram depicts the many radial spokes leading to the Nuclear centre of the universe from which the subject matter of Nuclear Evolution radiates in the seed or nux. For the convenience of "onlooker consciousness" we have listed the subject of each chapter as a spoke leading to the Nucleus, but this is not the viewpoint of Nuclear Evolution. The diagram is an image of the observer's consciousness which should be reversed so that the separate rays or spokes are radiated out from the centre rather than going in. Then the view from the centre is different and all the chapters are aspects of the same thing. They are connected only in the nux of consciousness and not at the periphery where the observer is and where the rays get progressively wider apart. The "onlooker consciousness" which tries to make connections should be left behind after this page. Just to remind the reader of this wholistic mirror image of their own self, we will print this visual symbol as a statement on each chapter page without more explanation. By the end of this book the reader will be looking out on the creation not as an observer, but as one whose consciousness is co-creator of all that is seen and all that is said.

EDITORIAL PREFACE TO THE SECOND EDITION

For men of vision, who bring to their own age the wisdom of all ages in a new and highly original message of Truth, there is always a choice to be made between either communicating with the few great minds of the era or endeavouring to speak to a wider spectrum of intelligence. In 1968, when Christopher Hills first published Nuclear Evolution, he chose to convey his insights into man's processing of consciousness or Light to those who had trained "ears to hear", with the result that it transformed the lives of those who were ready for the message and bewildered those who, having done no research into consciousness themselves, wanted the book to do it for them. This it did not do. Nuclear Evolution, in its original form, is a cryptically expressed challenge and a mind-stretching experience for every reader, and an exhilarating break-through for those of high intelligence who have cleared their cir-cuits of preconceived notions of how man relates to Light and Time and the ONE Source of creative energy in the Universe. Inevitably, the words of those who speak from a level of consciousness that far transcends our own will present problems, especially when their terse style makes absolutely no concession to the more familiar and acceptable modes of writing.

The readers of Nuclear Evolution over the past eight years have di-vided themselves into two classes or groups. There were those who, in the early seventies, appeared in the spectrum doorway of Centre House London (from which the book was first printed) with stars in their eyes and a copy of Nuclear Evolution in their hands, "I've just read this," they said, and from the look on their faces it was obvious that they expected you to understand the magnitude of their experience. Often, over a cup of English tea, they elaborated: "All my life I've been looking for some idea, some solution, some philosophy that explained both the diversity of man and his poten-tial for ultimate unity. This book has the answer."

So these people came to meet the man, Christopher Hills, who had for them thrown a beam of light on the riddle of the Universe. The insights that the book gave them as to why we are on this planet often inspired these people to start their own research into the evolutionary dynamic that is at the heart of every atom and of every man.

The other group struggled for a while with the concise and powerful text and then gave up. "Can't make head or tail of it" they said, meaning "I don't understand a word of it" although they knew intuitively that Nuclear Evolution contained brilliant insights. For them the book had gaps which they themselves could not fill, so they were unable to glean the wisdom that they knew was hidden there. The author himself has always said of Nuclear Evolution: "The real stuff is in the blank spaces between the lines." Nuclear Evolution has never drawn a mediocre or neutral response. People either "dig" it or reject it.

This third printing and second edition is an endeavour to fill the gaps and bridge the span between those whose understanding was expanded and illumined by the earlier text and those who were unable to resonate with either the content or the form. So vibrant and so vital is the message of Nuclear Evolution that those of us who do respond to it feel a strong obligation to pass it on. Just as there are levels of consciousness, so are there levels of understanding. What is simple and obvious to the abstract thinker is quite unintelligible to the practical, the logical or the conceptual mind. "Why can't you give us some real examples from life?" say the latter, "real" to them being either concrete physical stuff or comprehensible concepts. So we are applying the very theory of Nuclear Evolution itself in catering to the inner worlds and the understanding of seven levels of consciousness.

We have decided to include an interspersed commentary that both supplements the original text by means of some extra elucidation of the more abstruse passages and also from time to time, applies the truths and insights to situations in life, thus enabling the reader to be his or her own source of validation. We have reversed the order of Parts I and II, so that we now plunge straight into discussion of the seven levels of consciousness, which is the section that not only has the widest appeal but also stimulates the greatest response from the reader. Then, with this experiential work behind us, we approach the sociological, political, ideological and even economic application of our understanding of man's rainbow personality and the still Centre of Being in the heart of us all.

What has finally emerged as this second edition has itself developed by a process of Nuclear Evolution. From the nux of the original text, the author, Christopher Hills, has expanded and enlarged on the whole dynamic whereby man can realise his True Self. The book is part of the evolutionary process and over the next thousand years Nuclear Evolution will still be evolving, not only in the sense that many more books will be written about it from many different levels of consciousness, but also because every manifestation of the process then generates new potentials for a higher unfolding. Whether the potentials, like those of atomic energy, are utilised to destroy mankind or to raise it up to a totally new level of planetary consciousness depends on whether we can arouse the hero or the heroine within us before it is too late. By deep study and **practice** of Nuclear Evolution we have the self-chosen opportunity to change the present disastrous course of world events and to redirect it, from the nuclear centre of our being, toward a selfless planetary consciousness.

Ultimately everything arises from the centre and returns to the centre in a never ceasing flux of involution and evolution. The symbol we use here and which will be repeated throughout the book, represents in simple diagrammatic form the nuclear centre from which all the material of the book has flowed and to which it will return, to be re-expressed again and again in the working out of Nuclear Evolution through you and by you in the years ahead. This is Nature's way which takes the solidified mass of molecules and matter into which the human race has crystallised, like a block of ice, and melts it, so that it becomes once again as soft, responsive and resilient as the water of which we are mostly made.

N.H.

R.W.

Note: Throughout the book the writing of Christopher Hills is clearly recognisable, since it has all been printed in a slightly smaller type and in narrower columns to correspond with the text of the original edition which is also incorporated. All contributions by the editors or other authors are printed in the larger type and wider columns.

PART 1

NUCLEAR EVOLUTION AND THE COSMIC LIGHT

THE PURPOSE OF THIS BOOK

What is our purpose in writing this book? It is to manifest the timeless knowledge as revealed through the incarnation of humans in the seven universes of the superconscious; it is to determine the next phase of human evolution and to enhance the unfoldment of the Supersense. It is to enable the reader to utilise the human antenna which is sustained by cosmic rays and radiation and not just the visible solar rays. The vegetable kingdom is dependent upon sunlight but humans absorb their essence being from the cosmic radiation impinging upon the earth from every direction in space. All the stars send this blessing of cosmic light through space as brothers and sisters of the ONE. The purpose of this book is to reveal the source of the Supersense which picks up the sonic vibration of the Cosmic Song. The spotlight of consciousness can now shine on the Supersense through the new science of Supersensonics -- the full sense of cosmic sound.

What are we doing on this planet earth and what is our ultimate purpose? This question is a non-question in modern science since it is believed that nature has no purpose, that her incredible array of complex systems is merely the result of accidental happenings or at best the selection of affinities through the accretions of positive and negative charges on atoms, cells and organisms. The answer to the question is simple but not easy to grasp with a logical mind. It is this: The purpose of life is to evolve consciousness until it becomes one with the light which created it. To witness this light, this invisible light of consciousness, is to see the glory of all the suns and stars inside one small microscopic cell of the human brain.

Through development of the Supersense man can develop an instrument of survival that can detect the methods which can give immunity from cosmic radiation. Consciousness moves along a continuous spectrum throughout evolution until the supreme knowing reveals the nature of the self-sense. The physics of Supersensonics has its own laws like the nucleus of an atom. The electrons and protons balance their forces in tranquility in the nuclear centre of their being. Man is on the verge of knowing the timeless dimensions of Nuclear Evolution in colour and light. The Supersense can be known through the enhancement of the human nuclear centre of Being in which the ONE is thinking in light and is sitting on the seat of pure consciousness which Christ called "The Light of this World".

C.H.

6

1

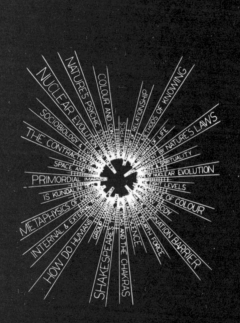

NATURE'S PSYCHE & COLOUR AND CONSCIOUSNESS
NUCLEAR EVOLUTION RELATIONSHIP METHODS OF KNOWING
SOCIOBIOLOGY & COLOUR AND CONSCIOUSNESS OF LIFE BY NATURE'S LAWS
THE CONTRACTION SPIRITUALITY
SPACE AND NUCLEAR EVOLUTION
PRIMORDIAL IMAGINING LEVELS
IS KUNDALINI BODY SCALE OF COLOUR
METAPHYSICS OF IMAGINATION BARRIER
INTERNAL & EXTERNAL SCIENCE EARTH FORCE
HOW DO HUMANS GROUP AND THE CHAKRAS
SHAKESPEARE'S AND THE CHAKRAS

THE RAINBOW BODY

WHAT IS
THE RAINBOW BODY?

The following is a transcription of a taped talk by Christopher Hills given at University of the Trees on 14th November 1976.

It's almost impossible to talk about the rainbow body with words because the rainbow body is the same thing as Brahman, and since Brahman only has one voice and one vibration, one note, we have already been talking about Brahman in just singing Om, and that's all there is to be said about Him, because in that one vibration is everything else. So to speak about Brahman or to speak about the rainbow body is just to step it down from what it is into lower vibrations. We could say that the distinction between the rainbow body and Brahman is that one is manifest and the other is unmanifest, although they're both one and the same thing, in the same way that light is unmanifest until it passes through something. In other words, it is impossible to visibly experience light until it passes through moisture, the clouds, or the atmosphere, or through a glass prism, for instance; then it splits into the rainbow colours because it passes through something, but until it goes through that glass prism it's unmanifest, invisible, not possible to see. So we can't see any colour passing through the prism until it comes out the other side and then we can see the seven colours reflected on the screen and so we know that that light is comprised of these seven vibrations. And in the same way, you could say that the human being is a prism receiving the cosmic light which is unmanifest in the form of consciousness, but as consciousness passes through the medium, the human vehicle, it splits into seven centres, seven chakras, seven vibrations, and manifests as the rainbow body.

We all have a rainbow body. But the number of men and women who have ever achieved it, that is, ever actually realized it, can be counted on one hand. It was said by his disciples in the eleventh century that Milarepa achieved the rainbow body, and even his gurus, his own gurus, bowed before him in acknowledgment of his spiritual achievement. It did appear from the things that Christ said too that he also possessed a rainbow body, and his disciples on one occasion, just before his death, actually saw the radiance of it manifest. It is unlikely that such a person would ever display it intentionally. You will remember, when the transfiguration was taking place, the disciples were all asleep or in a deep state of meditation, and they happened to wake up when Christ was communing with the prophets. Elijah and Moses were on either side of him in their spirit bodies. And it was at that time that one of the disciples noticed that Christ had a light around him. He was in a higher state of vibratory energy which he didn't normally manifest, and so that disciple woke the others up and said, "Look what is happening!" But for everyday purposes it is unnecessary and unwise to manifest that body, because to communicate at that level of the One, unless people are already there, is a waste of time, since the One is already communicating with us at that level without our knowing it. Unbeknown to us, we have a rainbow body. That is, until we tune into its vibratory unity, we will not know it is there for a fact. We can only know about it intellectually because Christopher Hills is talking about it or Milarepa talked about it or somebody said it was there. But for us to experience that rainbow body is like looking inside ourself with a microscope and seeing entirely another universe. It is as if you were to turn the inner eye of consciousness back inside with a microscope and analyse perhaps all the seven different levels of consciousness and purify them, so that the light could pass through all of them at the same time. In other words, this doesn't normally happen except when we have what you might call an electron microscope or spiritual microscope, or whatever you like to label it. This scope does not clear and we can't see through it until all those chakras which are vibrating and spinning like magnetic fields become stopped and still. And when each one stops its churning and spinning and is held in balance, vibrating but not spinning, and each one of the seven is still, then that light, the rainbow body, pours through it and washes out the brains. It's like a spiritual purgative in the sense that there is nothing left in the vehicle.

You could say that the rainbow body is another name for the vajra body or vajra yana; yana means vehicle and vajra means indestructable, indivisible, adamantine, meaning uncuttable in the same way that a diamond is adamantine. Diamond being the hardest stone on the planet, nothing can cut it except another diamond. And in the same way, nothing can cut Consciousness except Consciousness. It's uncuttable by anything else, indivisible by anything else. So the little divisions that we have in Consciousness called self, ego, mind, spirit, death, life, all those divisions are created by Consciousness, by the adamantine stuff which cuts Consciousness up into little pieces and says "that's that." In other words, that consciousness which we have is doing that all the time. That light or Consciousness which is passing through us unknowingly is creating those seven divisions and at the same time, because of its nature, it is able to put anything into it and manifest it. So whenever we put in a seed thought or a seed image or an idea of ourself, whatever it may be, whether it may be mystical, spiritual or mental or emotional or physical, on any of those levels, that is what we will experience. And to see through this vehicle is an awesome experience because it requires the death of the self-sense; to understand what the rainbow body is, even to have a glimmer of it, requires the death of the mind, requires the annihilation of that self-regarding sentiment, the idea that we are a separate self, that we are somebody. So the state of making contact with Brahman is achieved through the vajrayana, the indestructable vehicle, and of course this state of Being is built by years and years of practice. Milarepa wanted it so much that he gave up everything else in order to get it and was prepared to physically die for it in order to know it. I don't think it comes openly manifest to anyone, in fact I know it doesn't come to anyone, unless they are prepared to make the supreme sacrifice in order to get it. But the supreme sacrifice, of course, is not just physical death but death on all the other levels of consciousness too. To understand the kingdom of death and to go through the experience of death on all the seven levels is only for a few people. It is unlikely that anyone will fall in love with Death. It is hard enough to fall in love with Wisdom, who is his sister (in the form of a goddess, of course!). We humans have to have male and female, so we could say the King of Death is male and his sister, Wisdom, is female. Of course it doesn't matter what sex it is but it's easier for a man to fall in love with Wisdom if it's female. And if a woman wants to fall in love with Wisdom then she can make it male. But until we

10

build up enough passion for that goddess of Wisdom, the kind of passion that makes you a bit silly, we shall not make the breakthrough. You know when you fall in love passionately on the earthly level, you go a bit stupid, usually do things that people wouldn't normally do, make extra efforts; for example, it is nothing for a young man in love to ride about five miles on a bicycle just to see his girl every night or even to walk there. Or for another person to go round the whole world to find or to be with someone they love. But in the spiritual life, we would feel that making that kind of effort for something so abstract as dying to yourself, was pointless. If you could develop as much passion for wisdom, falling in love, becoming madly in love with the goddess of Wisdom or the god of Wisdom, whichever sex you want to endow it with, then you would be doing something very similar to what the ancient sages did when they chose that way of finding the rainbow body. To fall in love with light or to fall in love with rainbows wouldn't be very exciting at night time because a rainbow in bed isn't very shapely and it's very difficult to snuggle up to a rainbow, so if you want the cuddly kind of love, then rainbows aren't much good to you. To fall in love with rainbows then requires a special kind of passion, a special kind of passion which spurs us on so that we develop our consciousness and our senses to be able to actually *feel* rainbows, to be able to *feel* light. To be able to *feel* the light pouring through our own eyes is a special meditation, to be able to meditate all day long on that which is pouring out of your eyes, until you can actually feel, until you see through the illusion of your own body, the illusory body. There are all kinds of doctrines like the doctrine of the illusory body and the doctrine of this and that and the other, but that is only what the priests have written, based on the teachings; they have written it very simply but it is very hard to practice. To be able to see that everything is made of rainbows is a form of madness, but it is *true* madness, and if you become passionately in love with rainbows then you'll see them dancing on everything. And you'll see pots of gold under everyone, because people are all rainbows. The old story that there is a pot of gold under the rainbow is not just an old wives' tale, because if you've ever seen a rainbow that close and you go to the end of it and try and dig there to see where the pot of gold is, you won't find any ordinary gold, but you will learn something about rainbows, and that is that the closer you get to a rainbow, the more it will recede, because it's created out of your relationship with the sun; the angle that you have with respect to the raindrop and the sun's angle is what produces the rainbow in the sky. And this applies in everything.

The angle at which we approach life will determine whether we see rainbows everywhere and in everything. If we look at the atom, we see also the structured layers, seven layers, seven filters, seven thresholds of energy around every atom. In the structure of matter, in the crystals of the molecular form of matter of which our own body is made, we can see the seven crystalline structures, seven forms, basic forms of crystal. And if we look deeply into *all* life, we'll find that it consists of vibration; all energy patterns in the universe are vibrating patterns of energy, they don't have any real material substance. Even atoms are not material in that sense. They're only energy forms which are patterns vibrating in a certain way so that they interact with our senses, and we feel something solid, but it's only solid to *us* because we are vibrating in that same band of frequencies. Looking at life through these seven filters is almost as if we became another person who is living on another planet. Supposing that other planet was moving past the earth at the speed of light or very near, then it would shrink to zero mass because at the speed of light there is an infinite contraction. Slowing down less than the speed of light, nearly 163 thousand miles a second, the contraction comes to 50%, so on that planet you would be half as small at that speed as you are now, and the planet would be half as small. We would be looking at the planet that was whizzing past Earth at that speed; we would see it going and we would have the appearance of standing still and we'd see that planet flashing by, as it were, half its normal size, it would be the shape of an elipse; instead of a round planet it would be squashed up. If you were on that planet, looking back at the earth, flashing past you at the speed of light, you would have the appearance that you were standing still and that the earth was zero mass.*And you'd see the same earth that you are on now, but at the slower speed you would see it also squashed up 50% because travelling at that speed of 163,000 miles per second, there is this amount of contraction. So isn't that strange that we have the appearance of standing still and anything that flashes past at the speed of light or near, seems to be travelling, and yet if you were on that travelling thing, it would look like the earth was flashing past you, because in space there is no reference point, there's no point from which

---

* See Chapter 18 for more detailed explanation of time dilation at speed of light.

to measure any velocity, it's all moving in our mind. Our consciousness imagines there's a fixed point in space somewhere and we have the experience of movement, an appearance that things are travelling. Just like, sometimes when you're in a train or a bus or a car and you're standing still, and there is another train that begins to move at the side, and the coach windows go past and you say, and actually feel it, "Oh, we're moving! We're moving!" and yet you don't feel anything shaking and think inside yourself, "Isn't that strange, we should be rattling. How is it that I don't feel any movement?" Then suddenly that train beside you pulls out completely and you find, in reference to the scenery, that you're still standing there and it was the other train that was moving. Yet we were convinced visually that we were moving. In the same way, the illusory body moves through space—this body that we carry around, the moving vehicle in which consciousness is imprisoned in its rainbow. We have the impression it's moving through space, but actually it's our consciousness that is moving through space. Because the whole of space is created by consciousness. It is a notion. Space does not exist in reality. Only your consciousness of space exists. Why does your consciousness of space exist at all? Simply because your consciousness is concerned with being a body. It's so fixed and rooted in its own idea of itself being a physical body that it has developed a notion that other bodies exist too, other than its own.

The notion that you are a body gives rise to another notion that there is something called space in which that body is moving and this gives rise to the notion that there are other bodies such as stars, planets, humans, whatever, also moving in reference and relation to the physical body, the vehicle that you occupy. But this is all part of your consciousness. Because you imagine your consciousness is not throughout the whole of space, and is only imprisoned in the vehicle of a physical body, this gives rise to a false notion. How can this notion be obliterated or brainwashed from the human organism when it is continually being convinced by its senses, physical receptors in the material world, that it is separate from everything it is experiencing? Only by understanding how the senses work, only by understanding that nothing really happens in your senses; it all happens in your consciousness. Scientific exploration tells us that the signals your senses send to your brain are merely little electrical signals and whether they come from your finger tips or your eyes or your ears, the nervous messages are all the same kind of little electrical spikes. The meaning to these little spikes or pulsing vibrations is given by the consciousness which is able to interpret what they mean, but we tend to believe that things like colour and light are coming off the objects. We say, "That thing is red" but that again is an illusion; it is not reflecting red light at all. It is absorbing light; you are seeing what is left after all the other light is absorbed. So with a pigment which absorbs light and leaves back just that light which is in the red spectrum, we are only seeing its excreta; the object is digesting all the other light and we say, "All we're seeing is what it's leaving back, red, orange, or whatever it is." But we tend to believe that the object has some colour of its own, but actually the colour is only the frequency of the light and is only experienced in our consciousness. Something in our consciousness is able to tell that this object absorbs everything except red or orange, etc. We get an electrical signal down the nerves through the receptors in our eyes, but that signal is very little different from those of the auditory nerves recording acoustic phenomena. There is little difference in the spikes of the taste, smell or touch organs.

A certain potential goes down through the nerves, and somewhere inside us someone says, "That's green"; but we don't understand that it is our consciousness which has gone out through the senses to that object, wrapped itself around it and discovered what it absorbs, in order to know what its pigment is reflecting. Instead we have the distinct impression that the colour somehow is separate from us and that when we close our eyes it will still remain that same colour, but the colour only exists when you open your eyes; when you close your eyes it is no longer that colour. Now this is a form of madness, rainbow madness, because if you are looking at my orange shirt with your eyes open and then you close your eyes and the colour's gone—there's no colour—you say, "Ah, but while my eyes are closed it's still orange," but it isn't, it's no colour. It's only your own consciousness which makes you see that colour, and it is this belief that there is an outside, that a colour still remains the same when we close our eyes, which prevents us from experiencing the vehicle of the Rainbow Body. Because we have a self-sense, a self-regarding instinct, which is so ingrained in our consciousness, in the Mind, we are imprisoned in it as if in a prison-house, saying, "You are a self looking out and there is an OUT there and an IN here."

In order to be enlightened you have to kill that self, put it on the cross, crucify it and get rid of it completely, so that when you look out you don't experience any self seeing anything. You have to realise that you *are* just whatever you see, because your consciousness is making "that" whatever it is, and there is no separation from what is created, even the stars, even the whole thing, the Universe, because there is no "I" to say that there is anything separate from anything. And this is the first stage of what we call Brahman. When Brahman looks out through your mind do you think he's saying: "I'm Brahman and you're you"? No, he's just saying, "Whatever you think I am, that's what I am, because I'm you thinking whatever you're thinking and I am whatever you do with the consciousness, that pure stuff, the indestructible, immortal, indivisible, eternal, adamantine, vajra body or eternal vehicle, whatever you do with that, that's what I am. So if you want to misuse it, I'll help you, but you pay the price, of course." Brahman is always helping us to be whatever we are, saint, sinner, child or ignoramus. Brahman is helping you to be whatever you are making yourself to be, in your heart. So watch out for your unconscious selfish desires, watch out for your illusions, your notions about space and time and concrete reality, for all will be confirmed and helped into manifestation by consciousness who is Brahman and your real self-creator. Brahman is your rainbow body, your seven worlds within worlds within worlds which help you to know who you really are. You could ask yourself then, "Why is Brahman tempting me with all this illusion, sensory delight, and fascinating stuff which is not any real help at all?" The answer is, Brahman is not tempting anybody, he is only testing. Only by continuous testing can we know for sure that what we know is true. Brahman is a great scientist; he is always testing your reality and your life of appearances. He does more experimentation than any physicist or chemist. Unwittingly they themselves are being tested, testing themselves, testing their knowledge in some greater experiment that is continually ahead of them. Brahman merely helps them to chase Himself in the smallest particle, just as he can help you to chase Him in the vast infinite realms of the eternal universe, his own rainbow body.

So Brahman allows you to pay the price of misusing his help, just as other human beings will misuse your love and twist your words. So most people do pay the price, that price which is the feeling and experience of separation. In other words if you want to use all your passionate love just for one thing, for sensual enjoyment, sensual excitement commonly referred to as sex, Brahman will help you but it will be only temporary. But if you can take that passion and use it on every level of your being as com-passion, then you will be experiencing Brahman sitting at the Centre of the Rainbow experiencing the Rainbow Body which is eternal--the Light of Consciousness filtering through all the prisms in the creation, experiencing itself without any division, and the experience of this consciousness is vajra. Vajra means, like "dorje" (vajra is Sanskrit and dorje is Tibetan)--thunderbolt--thunderbolt consciousness is what it is, because it comes to you like a thunderbolt, and if any of you have been in the presence of lightning, if any of you have been struck by lightning or been near to a spot where lightning has struck, and if you have smelt the air that has been burned by lightning . . . you will have experienced the awesome power of this mighty energy. I remember very vividly standing on the bridge of a ship in mid-ocean one night when there was a thunderstorm. Suddenly, with an awful bang, a bolt of lightning hit the corner of the bridge only a few inches from where I was standing, and it seemed that even the air around was burnt, for it smelt like brimstone, rather like the smell when an electric motor burns out.

This is the kind of consciousness that vajra is; it's indestructible, it's like lightning, it's all-powerful, because it creates its own universe which is what it's doing right now in you. Unbeknown to you, you are creating everything that you're seeing. Every sound you hear is self-created. The appearance of you localising certain vibrations in your consciousness is not real. If you hear an aeroplane passing overhead you are localising the aeroplane in one part of the sky when it is really in another. By the time it has travelled over to one place, the sound is coming from the part of the sky that it has left. The plane is not there in reality.

So if you believe the sound and the source of the sound, you are believing in a phantom aeroplane, because where the aeroplane should be from where the sound is coming, is a ghost aeroplane. So how can you believe sounds, how can you believe that they're real? They are only just where your consciousness localises them.

16

It's the same with every sound that you hear; it's not the real sound, it is only the vibration coming into our ears and we are making sense and our consciousness is localising in space the source of all those vibrations, but the actual source of the vibration is not physical, because if you really traced the signal you'd find that even light which we think we see is not really pure and the light that we experience inside our consciousness as lit up, is psychic light, not real light. When you look at the sun and you see something lit up, that is not light; it is only what your consciousness is saying is light. Light cannot be seen; it's only your senses reacting to the invisible radiations of light which tell you inside yourself that there is something called Light and you are localising that light out there in the sun, but there is nothing there that you can see that's physical. What you are seeing and thinking is physical is purely a psychic electrical internal phenomenon. This is scientific. If you trace the scientific signal from your senses where the radiation impinges, it sends a message down the nerve, goes into the brain, there becomes another electrical impulse, and there it finishes and something has to take over then and take that electrical signal and say "That is Light." So you must discriminate between internal illumination or Lux or whatever you want to call it, and radiation, the Lumen, which is invisible. And in the same way you have to discriminate between the physical sensations, the vehicle of the body's experiences and the consciousness which is making those sensations real to you. The reality may be something else again, beyond what you are experiencing as real. In fact, with our senses can we tell what is happening inside this brick wall? Can you physically hear the atoms singing to each other and saying "sweet nothings". Mrs. Female Atom Electron saying to Mr. Male Atom Proton--"You're positive and I'm negative and we must get together." He says, "No. You haven't got enough energy for me. I want a high energy atom. I just want to have some fun with a real big atom who will give it to me really good. I don't want a weak energy little atom like you. Go away. I want to find a real mate." Can you hear that selection going on? Can you go up to the wall and touch it and know that it is full of atoms singing such vibrations to each other, saying the same things that human beings are saying basically, just in another language? Yet we know that that is what is happening. Our senses can tell us nothing about it. But through mathematical representations, through splitting atoms up in pieces and measuring them with all kinds of devices, we

17

know that there are operations going on inside that wall—atomic vibrations that we can measure which are unavailable to our senses, but however hard we try we can't experience them with our senses; we can only experience them in our consciousness. It is the same even with the atoms of our body. Can you hear the atoms of your body singing? Can you hear the oxygen atoms whizzing down your blood stream, and other atoms screaming for nourishment, saying "Get out of the way, that's *my* food. I'm hungry! You stay out of the way, silicon and potassium atom. I want that bit of nourishment that's coming down the bloodstream to keep the brain alive." Can you hear it, get in tune with that and go down your own bloodstream as if on a raft? You can't do it; you can only do it in your consciousness. You can't experience separate cells in your hand or your heart, can you? Just try!

It is very much like that with the Rainbow Body; you can only know it with your consciousness, because that is what it is. You can only know that it is your consciousness that makes meaning out of everything that happens to you in your consciousness. And so if you are screwed up in your body, and you're screwed up in your emotions, and you're screwed up in your mind, and you're screwed up spiritually or whatever, it's because your consciousness is screwed up, nothing else, and the answer lies simply in going to the cosmic toilet and eliminating it and getting rid of yourself, taking all the chakras and washing them out with light and dumping the garbage in the cosmic toilet—everything you know, everything you've experienced, everything you think you know, everything you ought to know, all the knowledge you've ever learnt—getting rid of it, because it all helps to make you think that you are a separate self, experiencing a body, when what you are in reality is a Rainbow.

Now, just to close this off, suppose you went to bed tonight and you dreamt you were a rainbow. Wouldn't that be a nice dream? But if you wake up in the morning and you say, "Last night I dreamt I was a rainbow," now can you really say whether you're a man dreaming that you're a rainbow or whether you're a rainbow dreaming that you're a man? When you wake up you're just in another ocean--you're a rainbow dreaming that you are a man--an awakened man. How do you validate the fact that you're not a rainbow dreaming that you're a man? Because someone else comes along who thinks he's not a rainbow and says, "I don't see any rainbows around you," and so you believe them because they don't dream about rainbows and so they don't have that problem. So they think you are just a man dreaming that you are a rainbow. But the one who has the vajra body or the rainbow body, actually believes that he's a rainbow dreaming that he's a man, and when he looks at himself he looks through all his faculties, his psychic chakras, and if they are clean and pure then he looks straight through them at everything and all he sees is rainbow; but if there is the slightest impurity in any of those chakras, then that is what he will see. But how did the impurity get there? Consciousness put it there. And how will it leave? Only when consciousness leaves it. So whatever is happening to you at this moment (or has happened in the past, or will happen in the future) is being programmed by the Cosmic Movie Director who is making a special movie for you—isn't that great? And he's actually employed the best producer, the best script writer, the best actors and actresses and has appointed you as the Director and the audience as well. So not only do you have to direct the show and act the show and write the script for the show, but you also have to watch it and you also have to pay for it, and the ticket price is pretty high. If you look closely at the lucky number on the ticket, you will see zero there, and underneath that in very small letters you will see that the price of the ticket is self-delusion. If you turn the ticket over, on the other side you will see the words "self-obsession" and that's the name of the movie. So the only way to get into the Rainbow show, which is one continuous movie, one continuous rainbow, is to become what you are. Then all you see is the seven brilliant colours in everything you look at until somebody says something or does something or whatever. On the other side of the rainbow it's all pure—no movie going on. The minute somebody wants something, says something, desires something or thinks something, then there's a movie.

So realisation of the Nuclear Self—Nuclear Evolution—means getting a Rainbow Body. It's a big trip, because those seven levels of consciousness that are within the Nuclear Self are only going to experience the Light of which they are made when they completely get rid of the self-sense, that instinctual feeling or thought or concept that not only are you a body or a mind or a memory but a separate soul or something called an entity. As long as you're dreaming that you are an entity, you are part of the movie. You've got a superstar role and the price is self-delusion.

Fig. (1)

THE RAINBOW BRIDG
was an ancient symbol f
seven worlds of Being whi
each individual separate so
must eventually cross. Ma
of the ancient legen
enshrine knowledge of t
Rainbow Body in symbol
form of representations. Ju
as $E=MC^2$ is used as a math
matical symbol standing f
the reality of energy transf
mation in our modern civil
ation, so did the ancie
civilisations represent t
experience of their enlig
ened sages who discover
the relationship between lig
and matter and consciousne
An example of this can
found in the symbolic my
of Asgard, the home of t
Norwegian gods, which
now considered to be me
superstition. In the allego
Heimdal was the guard wh
stood on the rainbow brid
that connected earth
heaven, and he was a symb
for the Ego or self-sense. Ov
the bridge of the sev
rainbow colours the go
passed on their way
Asgard. The dying Nor
heroes were carried over t
rainbow bridge (the sev
levels of consciousness)
the Valkyrie maidens
Valhalla, the state of pea
and bliss which existed
Asgard.

Their knowledge of death and the structure of consciousness was far superior to ours sin
they knew what we do not, that the soul of man lives on in seven different worlds of bei
which transcend the physical senses. Yet in our own blindness we believe them to
ignorant because we do not understand their symbolic language.

20

THE COSMIC CONNECTION

The gap between human beings and the vast cosmos we live in has recently narrowed with the emergence of sophisticated sensors which have mapped out the all-pervasive background radiation of space. The ideas of infinity not long ago considered the stumbling blocks of the ancient Greek and Hindu civilisations have returned to modern cosmology along with such concepts like the big bang and the receding red shifts of other island galaxies. The imaginations of ancient thinkers stretched to include cosmic eggs and the ocean of radiation out of which all existence was born, does not seem at all naive compared to modern ideas of an exploding galactic nucleus, black holes, quasars and gigantic radio galaxies.

The mystery of how the explosion of energy and space began however, is just as far away from the discoveries of science as it was from the ancient seers. Man has begun to wonder whether the incarnation of the universe will ever take place again or whether it is a one-time happening. Science speculates on the vastness of nature and believes the greatest question is whether the universe is an unending cycle of continuous creation or a pulsing entity. To say it is the greatest question of all is to confuse the vastness of the universe with its significance for our evolution.

Even if we knew the answer to this question, the greatest question of all would still remain: What is man's own consciousness which validates all he knows? To some enquiring minds the challenge of our times is: Are we alone in this vast universe? Are there other kinds of intelligent life in other parts of interplanetary space? So far the search for life on other planets has been unsuccessful from a scientific view, and the question of whether intelligent beings inhabit the planets of distant stars is considered widely speculative. Cosmology is driven to find greater and finer tools to probe the astronomical environment, not only to discover intelligent life but to solve the question of our universe's one and only incarnation. But the greatest tool of all, man's own mind, lies covered under the dark blanket of ignorance. All our tools are but extensions of that ignorance and while man's excitement at looking outwards into the far reaches of space continues, the depths of inner space are largely ignored. The question of man's incarnation as an intelligent being will still be with us even if intelligent species are discovered or discover us. The nature of consciousness as a product of our environmental condition will not be discovered by any external explanations about the red shift of the most distant galaxies. Nor will the evolutionary universe divulge its secrets of eternal expansion by discovering the atomic mechanism of the primordial fireball.

In fact these questions are quite naive compared to the much more profound question of man the experiencer and validator of all these intellectual explanations. Man himself may be a black hole searching for his own antimatter or a point of light searching for self-annihilation in a black hole.

Black holes are sometimes defined as areas from which nothing, not even radiation and light, can escape into space. This may be the perfect analogy for those men whose consciousness is trapped eternally in the darkness of sensory phenomena, whose mental brilliance is none other than the ancient idea of luciferic light – the false light of egocentric consciousness which arrogantly sits on the seat of power and believes it knows all there is that is known. The pride of being at the leading edge of scientific enquiry dazzles the imagination so that instead of seeing clear light, the mind is blinded to its own conceit.

The greatest challenge of man is, as it always has been, to know what is not known about ourselves -- that quality of the validator and seer of all that is – which does not see the origin of its own light, but takes all consciousness for granted. All truth is said to be self-evident, but can it exist without a self?

Therefore the greatest advance will come to man when the science of Being and intelligence (ontology) stands equal with the science of epistemology (the validation of evidence). When man turns the brilliance of the light of consciousness upon the nature of the human heart and the origin of love, the origin of the universe will stand revealed.

This book has essentially been written backwards, because we must begin with what is known and proceed to the unknown. But the unknown reservoir of love in the depths of the human heart contains the primordial fireball whose existence gives us the indestructable light of consciousness itself. The journey through the ancient understanding of kundalini, akasha, colour, and universal holograms is a journey into light. The doorways to our perception have never been spelled out in any scientific testable theory which unites the knower with what is known, except under the general name of yoga. Much of spiritual thought has been filled with analogies and models of a descriptive nature which seem archaic to our scientific methods. However, we must test the laws of the heart out and see if they work. If they do we will be no worse off than most science projects, which often work without much understanding of the fundamentals which make them work.

Therefore, if the reader should feel that he has arrived in strange territory and is asked to go through some intellectually dubious doors, he must remember that every scientific discovery which finds a new way of looking at nature, must often leave the familiar concepts behind. I have deliberately employed many scientific metaphors of the age I live in and if they sound reasonable, you can lose nothing by applying them to spiritual understanding.

The ultimate science is nature and the ultimate scientist is the cosmic intelligence. Thinly veiled in a great deal of conceptual thought, this book is about that scientist and His rather awesome laboratory.

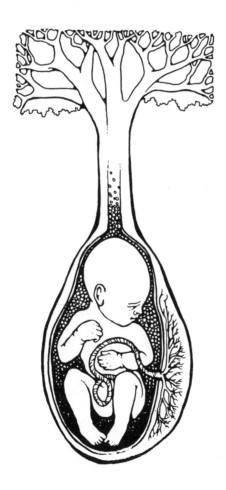

KUNDALINI -- THE EVOLUTIONARY FIRE

In all the literature, both on yoga from ancient times dealing with mind-stuff and in all the modern psychology, I have yet to find any direct description of how kundalini works in terms of process. The word itself seems to be translated as a "coiled serpent" whereas this must be merely a descriptive metaphor since the root word "kunda" in Sanskrit means "to burn": Most people have some idea that it rises entirely from internal biological or biochemical action, but how that action has any relationship with the creative cosmic forces is not made clear in any of the literature. Nor is there anything specific on the direct connection between kundalini and the chakra system, except to say that it indeed passes through the channels which link them together.

The knowledge about chakras has been around a long time but first-hand experiential knowledge of the chakras is very rare. There are many who think that it's all old hat, but I observe in their lives no more awareness from their reading of books, and certainly no fundamental change in their ego-structures. Hence I have no illusions about the limitations of books.

In some of the secret books of the Brahmins of ancient times there is reference to the psychic control of Akasha, but it appears that all instruction on its real nature was given orally. In all the literature, I have found no scholar who explains its relationship to light or who relates the experience of kundalini to the absorption of light in order to produce what human beings call consciousness. References to Self in the Gita abound, without saying what "Self" is. It was a result of my discovery of this gap in the ancient writings that I set out thirty years ago to probe the nature of consciousness and this book is the result of that probing and research.

Whether we refer to that consciousness as kundalini or Akasha or any other Sanskrit name is totally irrelevant and will not add one bit to our knowing directly the actual process of its origin in human beings. There is only one book to read if we are to discover or re-discover the lost knowledge which the ancient Hindus, Egyptians and Chinese had about consciousness and that is the book of Nature, which is the same book that they them--selves studied and researched by methods of divination. This same book of Nature is the source of the wisdom of the I Ching which describes the interactions of consciousness with matter in a totally unique way and makes clearly evident the exact laws by which consciousness and the whole of Nature operates.

24

The majority of the planet's population are sense-orientated and it is difficult for these people on the lower levels of consciousness to understand that this very consciousness, which we experience as our own Self, operates to exact laws of perception, as exact as any laws of physics. It is very difficult for people operating from only the sensory levels to understand that these exact laws of Nature cannot be broken, but as you read on in this book it will become increasingly apparent that our level of consciousness conditions everything, even our will to change and expand our awareness. Each human being is unable to manifest anything but his or her true nature, whether for good or for ill.

It is my belief not only that these laws of consciousness apply on the seven levels of man's prismatic rainbow body but that life is already determined for most of us by the quality and level of our own consciousness. Beyond that there is the awesome nature of Pure Consciousness which has no laws and forms my idea of God. When people contact that Supreme source which created this fantastic stuff called Consciousness with all its many mansions, then and there alone do all laws disappear in the absolute purity, devoid of all thought, concepts of Self, etc.

I apologize to some readers for not pandering to the current fashion to quote references to other people's work. I do not frankly feel that this practice adds much scholarship to the subject and has become merely a practice of scientific sophistry. Where necessary I have given references in the text, but since the main reference to this original work is nature herself, I only ask that people get out of their heads and do something with these facts of life. Then they will get a quicker validation of results than they will ever get from any second-hand source of knowledge.

Thus my belief is that Nature is the true teacher and that all knowledge of men must be ultimately confirmed by her long and eternal refining of our own vehicle of consciousness. In this sense Christ and Socrates said that all knowledge lies within.

The following work attempts to explain many ancient methods of knowing reality which are thousands of years old, but I have kept to the modern language of science and have avoided using religious or mystical terms. Since Nuclear Evolution was first written, many students have published their research on it and enhanced it with more illustrations and proofs from life. Some of their works are listed at the back of this book under various titles. The reader is also recommended to study the practical tools of validating the work for himself or herself which are to be found in my book SUPERSENSONICS. I am confident that those who have direct perception of nature's ways and who are naturally clairvoyant or use the divining powers of pendulums and rods to obtain feedback signals from the unconscious mind, will also confirm all these results without much argument. However, the book is also written for those who do not by inclination wish to do the training in dowsing or extra-sensory perception. They can learn the theory and conceptual structure of consciousness and its seven levels of human awareness and apply it to their own first-hand experience of life. This is the real purpose of the book, to put theory into practice.

The purpose of this Part I and Part II is to relate what was known by Jesus and the ancient seers about Light to the creative powers expressed in the vibration of three primary colors. In the Samkyha philosophy underlying the GITA of Krishna and the sayings of Christ, the creative forces are portrayed as **Satya guna**, intelligence (White rays) characterised by light and by proton, **Raja guna** (Green rays) by movement of energy, life and the electron, **Tama guna** (Black rays) characterised by inertia, electrical neutrality and the equilibrium status quo of the neutron.

The three PRIMARY LIGHT colors Green, Red and Blue which combine their wavelengths to make white light and all the other electro-magnetic forcefields which occur in creation, are manifested through the action of Black light which the Yogis call psychic electricity or akasha. This is not material electricity but a subtle electricity in the all-pervading unmanifest void. All electricity is eternal and manifests in nature as protons, electrons and neutrons. When this subtle and motionless ocean of electricity is in resonance with certain frequencies of an oscillating protonic substance (which is electricity in a state of excited motion), this psychic motionless electricity becomes quantized on contact and manifests as electro-magnetic white light. Although these three primary colors are presently thought of as light waves of certain frequencies in the visible spectrum, science is now having second thoughts about this in the experiments of Edward Land of the Polaroid Corporation. He has succeeded in combining only two frequencies of light within only one band of color and creating a full spectrum of colors. See his research published in "Scientific American" May, 1959.*

When we see the reflected light colors which artists and painters know as primary colors for mixing pigments, namely red, yellow and blue, we know now that our eyes and the mind which experiences the sensations of the optic nerve only record the colored rays which are not absorbed by the pigment. Since this process of absorption of light rays in humans is complicated due to the ionizing quality of primary light sources and the polarizing effects of reflected light, I have added a new section on the current scientific understanding of color. It is hoped that with these different explanations the reader can put the process together in his own mind and see the relationships to the ancient chakra systems and the

* See References Part I

26

raising of kundalini through them.

Because there is a distinction between unmanifest light which cannot be seen, which corresponds to the creative forces, and manifested light seen as brightness within human consciousness corresponding to the mixture of red, green and blue rays, an explanatory section has been added to the first edition.

It remains only to say that the vibrations of white light that we experience as brightness are the internal response of our consciousness which is in resonance with the original word.*

> In the beginning was the Word,
> and the Word was with God, and
> the Word was God.
> The same was in the beginning with God.
>
> All things were made by him
> and without him was not any
> thing made that was made.
> In him was life and the life
> was the light of men.
> And the light shineth in dark-
> ness and the darkness compre-
> hended it not. (St. John, Ch. 1, vv. 1-5)

It is obvious but not often seen that the "word" which is equated with the light of man in the above quotation is the light of consciousness. Only this light can shine in the dark and cannot be quenched by darkness. For any other form of light cannot exist with darkness, for they are the antithesis of each other.

Ordinary light cannot exist in the same place as darkness without annihilating it, but the light of consciousness exists in the darkness of sleep. The invisible light of consciousness which eternally shines out of the eyes of men, cannot be comprehended unless the darkness of that sleep be understood.

---

* In the Sanskrit this is referred to as the 'name of God' or universal sound. 'Hallowed be Thy name' is the Christian way of making its vibration holy, meaningful and respected.

EDITOR'S NOTE

Throughout these pages we will read of seven colours or seven worlds of being which will be hard to understand through the use of words in English. The English language evolved during the dark ages in a period much later than the ancient studies of the mind and spirit, and therefore has very few words which describe the different spiritual states of consciousness, whereas the Sanskrit language is full of words specially coined for this purpose. We will try to avoid as many Sanskrit words as possible and in their place we will use symbols and maps of consciousness. Some Sanskrit words will be unavoidable. These will be explained whenever they are used. However, the following pictorial symbols in this chapter should be kept in mind whilst reading the more difficult pages in the book. This will avoid the use of too many Sanskrit terms and keep things simple.

Fig. (2)

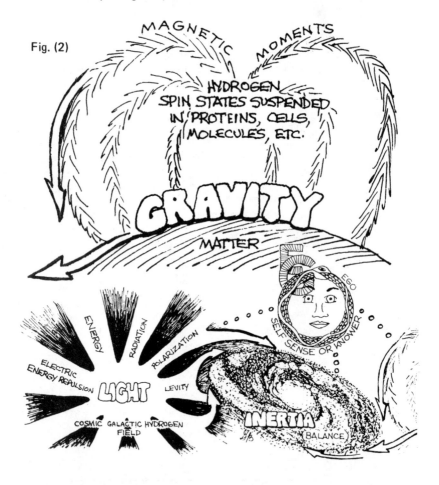

One of Christopher Hills' many visual ideas of the rainbow bridge of Cosmic Light drawn by Gary Buyle.

Radial labels (clockwise from top):
COLOUR AND CONSCIOUSNESS · METHODS OF KNOWING · RELATIONSHIP · SPIRITUALITY · GOVERNED BY NATURE'S LAWS · OF NUCLEAR EVOLUTION · LEVELS · SEVEN LEVELS OF COLOUR · BODY · IMAGINATION BARRIER · FOURTH FORCE · SHAKESPEARE AND THE CHAKRAS · HOW DO HUMANS · INTERNAL & EXTERNAL · METAPHYSICS OF CONSCIOUSNESS · IS KUNDALINI · PRIMORDIAL IMAGINATION · SPACE AND · THE CONTRACTION OF · SOCIOBIOLOGY & EVOLUTION · NUCLEAR EVOLUTION · NATURE'S PSYCHIC · TYPES · OF LIFE

MAPS
OF
NUCLEAR EVOLUTION
AND LEVELS
OF CONSCIOUSNESS

WHAT A PIECE OF WORK IS MAN!

The planet earth and all organisms upon it evolve through seven stages:

1. The cooling gaseous state of atoms

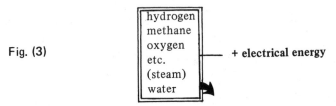

Fig. (3)

hydrogen
methane
oxygen
etc.
(steam)
water

— + electrical energy

2. The amino acids essential to life and the molecules of the chemical elements.

3. Molecular adhesions and the replication of single cells and algae.

4. Multi-cellular configurations such as the sensitive organisms in the long evolutionary chain:

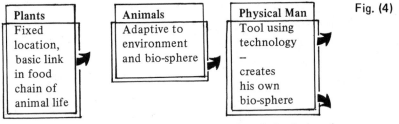

Fig. (4)

Plants	Animals	Physical Man
Fixed location, basic link in food chain of animal life	Adaptive to environment and bio-sphere	Tool using technology -- creates his own bio-sphere

5. Thinking, brain-centred man who is master of physical evolution through insight or destructive power.

6. Intuitive man who is group conscious and linked to the total mind of the planet as a cooperative species. (See concept of a linked species with all human brains acting as the cells in one single superbrain.)*

7. The divinisation of man through refining of limitless pure consciousness unrestricted by conceptual modes or logical consistency. The functioning of the planetary and interplanetary brain to produce images with primordial power to warp time and space. Control of destiny of the species becomes enormous through multi-dimensional manifestation on many levels of consciousness but desire of conscious control disappears through refinement of our incarnation so such powers are never used.

---

* This idea was first expounded in "Christ-Yoga of Peace" and "Nuclear Evolution", first edition by Christopher Hills, published Centre Community Publications, London, 1968.

There are seven levels of life present in every person which are set out in Nuclear Evolution according to nature's universal response to color. These levels beget drives which are developed by the linkage of consciousness with life as teacher, although some drives are neglected depending on the awareness and will (heart nature) of each person.

They are both positive and negative:

1. Reactive; skin sensations create positive or negative response to environment and action.

2. Social and political dependence on one's culture, or love of fellow beings.

3. Intellectual and mechanical separative thinking, or penetrating insight.

4. Security and obtaining of sufficient vital force, or possessive love.

5. Mental and conceptual idealism, or devotion to higher authority.

6. Psychic and abstract intuitive faculty, or "cloud nine" mentality.

7. Spiritual perception of cosmic order with interdependence of all species, or seeking of hidden powers.

A single conscious entity who experiences and perceives the universe does not function merely on one level thereby restricting perception to one narrow slit like this

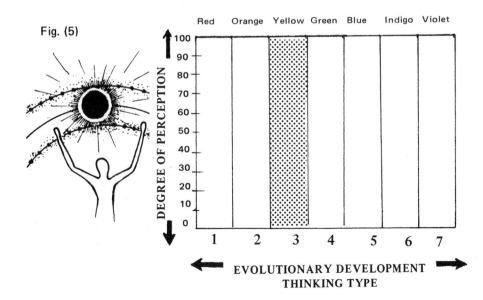

Fig. (5)

31

but consciousness is distributed proportionally across all stages and is dominated by his currently incarnate stage as in the following diagram.

Fig. (6)

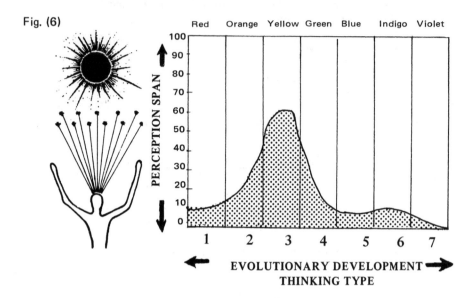

EVOLUTIONARY DEVELOPMENT
THINKING TYPE

or is in the process of overlapping several stages with the functions of each level of consciousness varying from moment to moment like this:

Fig. (7)

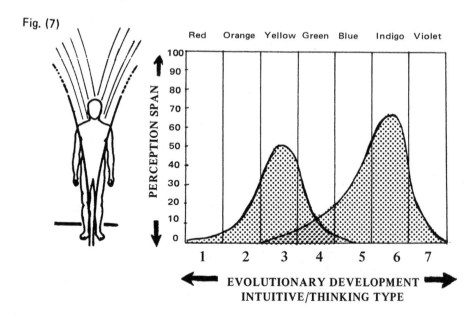

EVOLUTIONARY DEVELOPMENT
INTUITIVE/THINKING TYPE

The many permutations which lie across the seven spans of perception create many different universes in which people live, sometimes unaware of the missing worlds of time and being like this:

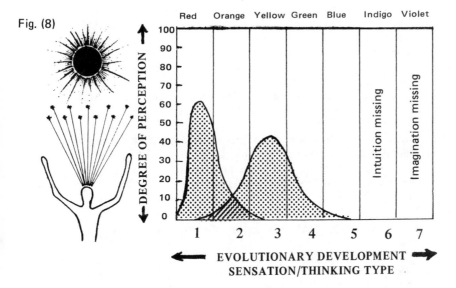

Fig. (8)

Then occasionally a great imaginer will come and be totally disconnected from the lower worlds of matter, thought and sensation in any worldly sense like this:

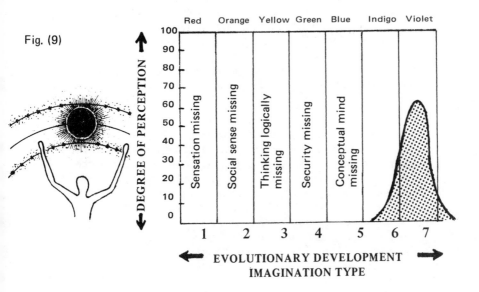

Fig. (9)

The most elevated spiritual beings when they come through to us on the intuitional level and even when these beings occupy a body and incarnate here on earth, come in a terrestial envelope which they retain during their stay with us. It is not possible to communicate with higher beings without this etheric interface as these intelligences would not experience the grosser molecular vibrations of earthly matter without this special clothing of subtle matter acting as an antenna. This book is about this etheric interface or the subtle envelope we call the human aura.

All humans to some extent have remnants of this spiritual clothing in the envelope of psychic electricity which clothes them in the pranic energies of consciousness. This is the interface energy we use between the muscles and nerves, and between the mind and memory. It is this subtle earthly body which animates the physical body and allows it to produce perceptions such as water divining, scrying, telepathy, clairvoyance, psychometry, etc.!

Spiritual beings, like the humans on earth, change their worlds by drawing from the atmosphere around them. If a human being travels to the North Pole he not only looks different in his special clothing but when he travels back to the warm summer at the equator he changes his clothes to suit the environment. Thus do we as spiritual beings change our etheric bodies of perception to grosser forms of envelope whenever we incarnate. It is through our activating the different chakras that all spirits, whether high or low, earthly or in transition, only hear and feel what they choose to hear and feel. Thus the chakra system is the first step to knowing other more subtle and deeper worlds of being. Knowing the functions of each chakra gives us an instant map of the territory we have come to explore on earth. However, any map is no good unless the traveller knows how to use it and more important puts his feet forward on the journey of discovery.

Just like a traveller in strange territory comes across people in different kinds of clothes and with different kinds of bodies, eyes, customs and languages so do the different realms of the spirit have their own unique worlds. To travel those worlds in our consciousness we must understand that all maps of the territory do not tell us much about the people and customs but only help us to get there. Once there, we must develop new ways of communicating and understanding these vast inner-worlds which are just as unlimited as the external worlds around us. It pays to go to navigator school first so we don't finish up on the reefs and rocky coasts.

Fig. (10)

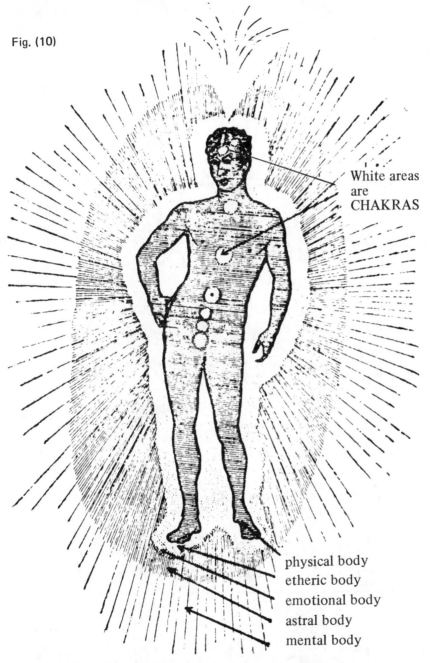

White areas
are
CHAKRAS

physical body
etheric body
emotional body
astral body
mental body

The traditional idea that man had five bodies or sheaths of different states of subtle matter did not take into account man's ability to use the Supersense which adds two more dimensions of consciousness on the intuitional level and the imagination level. It is now known that energies in the electromagnetic spectrum vibrate in bands. Different individuals are tuned to different parts of this spectrum and therefore may disagree in their descriptions of reality. The continuum of consciousness extends the electromagnetic spectrum and is divided into transpersonal bands which correspond with these seven levels of energy which can be called bodies or vehicles.

Fig. (11)

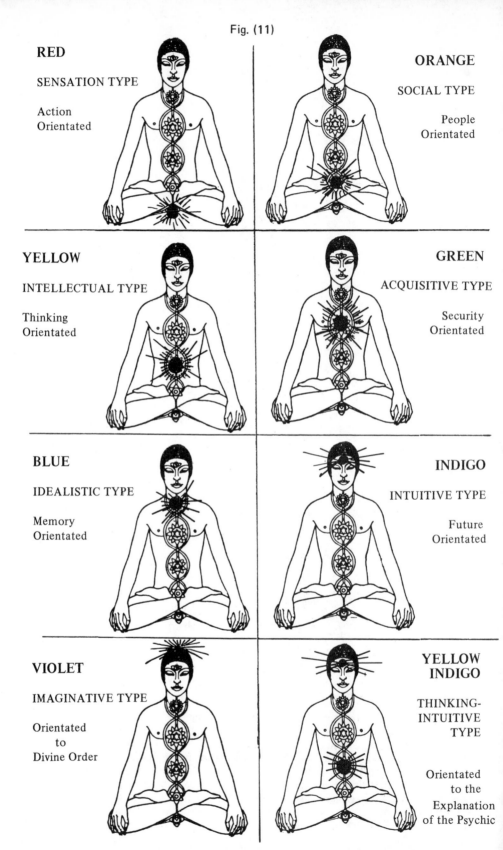

RED

SENSATION TYPE

Action
Orientated

ORANGE

SOCIAL TYPE

People
Orientated

YELLOW

INTELLECTUAL TYPE

Thinking
Orientated

GREEN

ACQUISITIVE TYPE

Security
Orientated

BLUE

IDEALISTIC TYPE

Memory
Orientated

INDIGO

INTUITIVE TYPE

Future
Orientated

VIOLET

IMAGINATIVE TYPE

Orientated
to
Divine Order

**YELLOW
INDIGO**

THINKING-
INTUITIVE
TYPE

Orientated
to the
Explanation
of the Psychic

LETTING THE LIGHT IN

In speaking of Nuclear Evolution we use certain words or terms to make things more clear as to how light penetrates our being and causes us to see a brightness within. If we can be constantly aware of this brightness then we can maintain the radiance of being that all people crave for the world over.

LUMEN   The first word is **Lumen** from the Latin word for light. This is not the light you see but more the radiation which passes through space. Lumen is invisible like our own consciousness, but it is very real just as our consciousness is very real. Lumen leaves the sun and stars and passes through space to us and does not change its wave-like character by passing through space until it is absorbed by the atmosphere and layers of ozone around the earth. There its radiant property lights up these gases in the atmosphere and we see it as irridescent blue sky.

LUX   The second word is **Lux**, also from the Latin word for light, but this time meaning internal light which is caused inside our minds and brains. The lumen penetrates through the atmosphere directly to our eye and activates nerves and cells, and ends up inside our brains as the brightness of light (lux). We confuse this with real light (lumen or radiation) when in reality it is a psychic light, created by our own consciousness being disturbed by the lumen, which we see then as internal lux.

NUX   The third word is **Nux** from the Latin word for seed or kernel. This means the inner core of our being in which the cosmic plan of evolution is unfolding. We do not know this core of our real selves because it is the dark unconscious from which all our primal drives spring. It is symbolised by the black emptiness of space because it is pure and unadulterated by any thoughts, images and sensations. It is the ground of our being, just as the silence is the ground from which all vibrations of sound arise. This basic field of consciousness is like an ocean, so transparent and quiet that any disturbance or vibration in it or through it will make waves. These waves are the vibrations of the universe around us from all the objects of creation -- suns, stars, sky, trees, rocks, crystals or people. Everything we perceive is, as it were, a disturbance or oscillation in our nux. The nux is self-limiting because it is whatever it is doing with itself. If it is listening to music, it is experiencing the consciousness of the player, the sound of the instrument and its own responses all at the same time; but the appearance in our personality self is that we are listening only to sound which we like or dislike. This superficial listening from the surface of things, whether to music or to the vibrations of all the objects in the environment or even to the words of other humans, is done with the shell of our being and not the nux. The nux is the first cause of our hearing, not the effect; the nux is the ear of the ear or the very consciousness which makes sense of what the senses pick up from the skin and the total environment.

Whenever we absorb light or radiation from the cosmic radiance we are in effect taking into our body the vibrating energy caused by the activity of atoms oscillating at tremendous intensities in the heat of supernovas and stars like our sun. We do not feel this energy consciously or even acknowledge it as the source of our consciousness. The reason we do not experience this radiant cosmic light is because it is no different from our nux, our inner core of radiance. Being one and the same stuff it cannot tell any difference between itself and the cosmic background radiation which is the ground of all created forms. The objects we sense, the trees and stars and those crystals which make up our cells, are all concentrations of this energy. They are held together by **proticity** which attracts this radiating lumen and crystallises it into matter. All matter is crystallised energy - crystallised light. Lumen crystallises into lux like liquid water crystallises into solid ice through the withdrawal or absorption of its heat. Add some radiance (heat) or lumen from the light of the sun and the ice turns back into a liquid. Thus lux (inner light) turns back into lumen (pure radiant consciousness of the heart of the nux) by this absorption of radiant light from the stars. This cosmic process is going on in everything and not only in human bodies, human minds, and human imaginations. The sun absorbs light from other more powerful suns which activate its vibrating atoms intensely. If it did not absorb this cosmic radiation light (lumen) from other stars it would eventually slow down its intense internal activity (its lux) and would crystallise from a gas into a liquid and thence into the crystal elements as a solid.

This attraction of the nux or nucleus for the absorption of cosmic light is in everything created, including our own consciousness. When the attraction is very great the lumen absorbed creates internal heat (lux) and this is called kundalini in Sanskrit. Our consciousness of this internal light only emerges from the nux when this attraction reaches such an intensity that not only do we see the kundalini burst into flames in our consciousness and become uncrystallised liquid fire within the nux, but we also realise it as radiance (lumen). It is then that the human being notices that there is no difference between his own consciousness in the nux and the radiance of the cosmic light of the sun and stars, eternally radiating as lumen. Consciousness and the light of the cosmos become ONE. Thus the "nux" or nuclear centre of all things in creation absorbs light (lumen) until its heat and brightness become first "lux", then radiance or "lumen".

An object or a human being is much like a pigment which absorbs part of the light and reflects the remainder as secondary rays which we then call colour. It becomes important to quickly distinguish between the characteristics of radiant lumen or radiation before it touches an object and the reflected rays of light which have had part of the energy in them absorbed and crystallised into matter. We shall go into this in more detail in Chapter 7 on the nature of colour, but in the meantime we must become more clear about the heat and radiance of lumen and its ability to uncrystallise matter in liquid fire, as well as its tendency to be absorbed and crystallised into matter. Is there any difference between the spiritualisation of matter and the materialisation of the spirit? We can answer this question with an equation. The process of absorption of cosmic light can be summed up in the symbolic equation:

$$NUX + LUX = FLUX$$

$$FLUX - LUX = LUMEN$$

where flux is equal to the change required to bring about the transformation from lux (internal light of consciousness) to lumen (the external light of cosmos). The word flux comes from the Latin word meaning flow, becoming fluid, change or fluctuation.

It will be seen that the key to this process is in the flux or the ability of the medium to change. If the absorbing medium (whether it is a human or a material object does not matter) resists change or is insensitive to the radiation of the lumen, then it will absorb the cosmic light and become even more crystallised energy and therefore more condensed, like matter. There will be less flux and the object will become soon saturated or constipated with the little light that it can absorb. This is because a changing object which is less rigid and less solid can absorb more energy than an unchanging crystallised object which has a low flux threshold. You could take as an example solid ice, whose molecular crystal structure can absorb less heat than its liquid counterpart water, because water has a higher flux (change) threshold and can absorb heat and light between $32^{O}F$ and $212^{O}F$ before becoming gas or vapour (steam) at boiling point.

The more an object or a human body can absorb of the lumen the more intense is the flux threshold and therefore the ability to increase the vibrations of the internal lux, until it changes into lumen and begins to radiate light instead of crystallising it into matter.

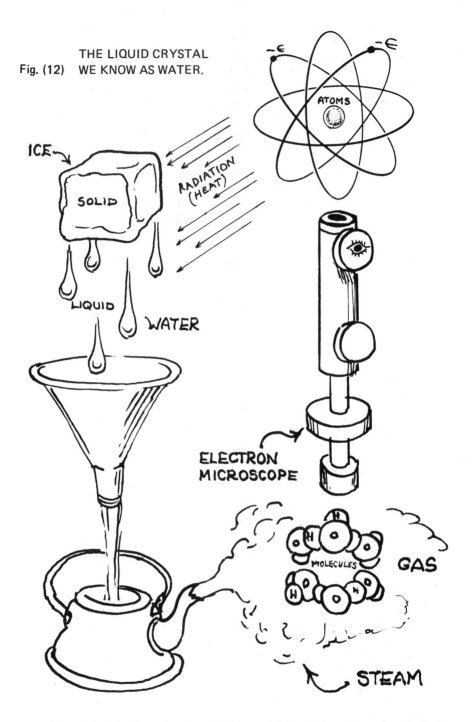

THE LIQUID CRYSTAL
Fig. (12)   WE KNOW AS WATER.

Like chloresterol, water is a liquid crystal that takes many forms. In its colder state it crystalises like ice and in its hotter states it becomes progressively liquid, first as water, then a vapour as steam, then as a gas (Hydrogen 2 parts, Oxygen 1 part (H_2O)), and finally as vibrating Hydrogen and Oxygen atoms it becomes radiative energy, particularly when intensely radiated from stars in microwaves.

It follows that there is absolutely no real difference between the composition of matter and light, in the same way that there is no difference between the atoms of ice and water. The only difference between them is structural arrangement of the molecules of water due to the addition or subtraction of heat/radiance/lumen:

Fig. (13)

H₂O
LIQUID

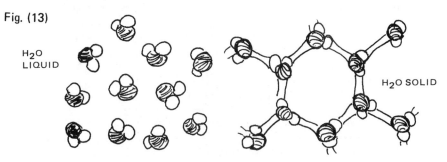

H₂O SOLID

Solid ice has a crystaline structure which arranges the molecules of water in a smaller volume than water in its liquid state. The water molecules in their crystal form have a hexagonal shape which makes liquid water expand on freezing into a solid. Water is therefore less dense in its solid form than its liquid state. The molecules occupy a greater volume than H₂O in its liquid state, hence ice floats on water. For most other crystals the packing of molecules into the solid state results in a smaller volume than the liquid state. This is because water itself is a liquid crystal.

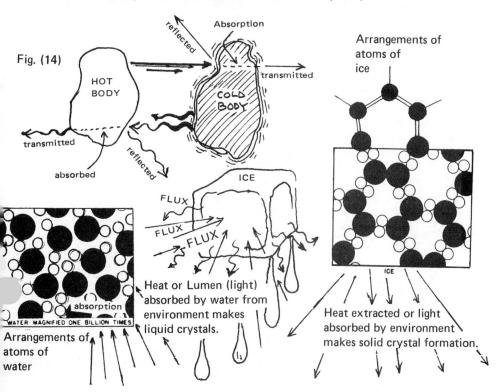

Light or radiation striking a body is partly reflected, partly transmitted and partly absorbed depending on its atomic structure. The absorbed energy is converted into excited molecular motion (heat). This heat is radiated not only directly to each object but to the whole environment in all directions.

41

Whatever the structural form of water it is still H_2O, whether liquid, solid or gaseous, the only variant being the temperature.

In exactly the same way there is no difference between the nux, lux and the lumen. Only the flux or the ability to change the more dense crystallised state to the liquid and gaseous states makes the structural arrangement of the levels of human consciousness permeable to radiant light or lumen. The remainder of this book deals with the complexity of this flux in humans which is controlled by the different levels of consciousness. The different thresholds of this flux are caused by the ability to absorb and re-radiate the light of the cosmos (lumen). It may strike the reader as strange to write a whole book of 1000 pages about six words, but such a simple transition in the previously mentioned equation as:

$$NUX + LUX = FLUX$$

$$FLUX - LUX = LUMEN$$

contains the secret of the whole mystery of our purpose on earth.

Since Lux and Flux cancel out on both sides of the equation, it is easy to see that Nux and Lumen are the same thing. The only difference is that Nux is self-imprisoned in self-consciousness while Lumen is free and expanding throughout space as radiant energy of cosmic consciousness or Brahman, otherwise known as the heat and radiance of kundalini.

Fig. (15)

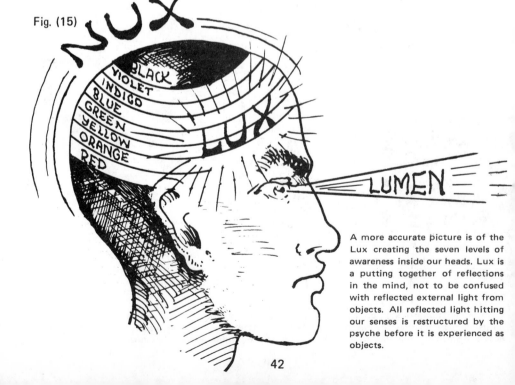

A more accurate picture is of the Lux creating the seven levels of awareness inside our heads. Lux is a putting together of reflections in the mind, not to be confused with reflected external light from objects. All reflected light hitting our senses is restructured by the psyche before it is experienced as objects.

42

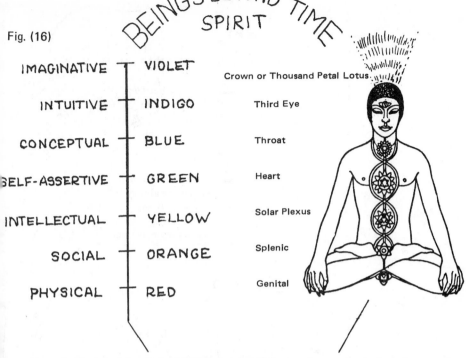

Fig. (16)

IMAGINATIVE	VIOLET	
		Crown or Thousand Petal Lotus.
INTUITIVE	INDIGO	Third Eye
CONCEPTUAL	BLUE	Throat
SELF-ASSERTIVE	GREEN	Heart
INTELLECTUAL	YELLOW	Solar Plexus
SOCIAL	ORANGE	Splenic
PHYSICAL	RED	Genital

BEINGS BEYOND TIME
SPIRIT

Nuclear Evolution relates the chakras with subtle psycho-energetic functions and personality traits with the manifestation and actualization of electromagnetic wave-fields. Consciousness interacts with these wave-fields and modifies them.

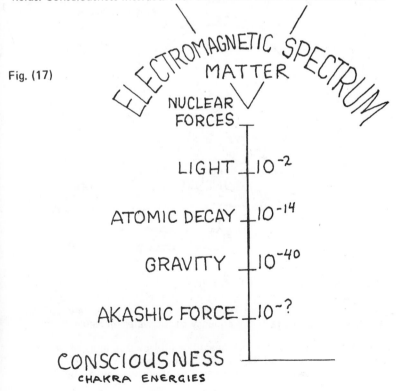

Fig. (17)

ELECTROMAGNETIC SPECTRUM

MATTER

NUCLEAR FORCES

LIGHT	10^{-2}
ATOMIC DECAY	10^{-14}
GRAVITY	10^{-40}
AKASHIC FORCE	$10^{-?}$
CONSCIOUSNESS	

CHAKRA ENERGIES

Fig. (18)

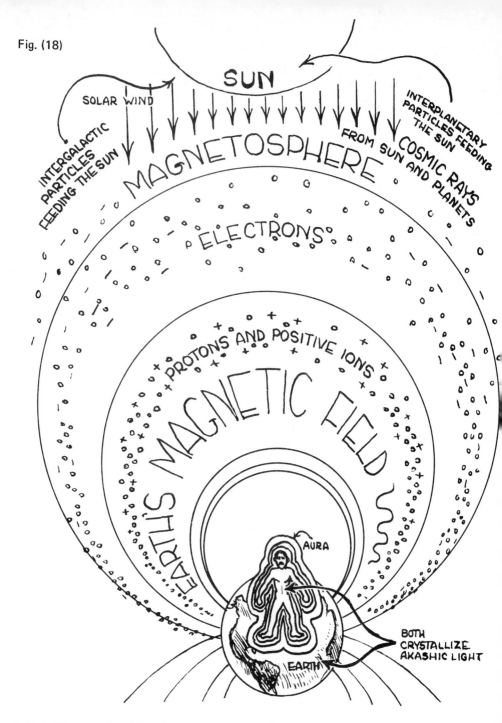

THE INTERACTION OF LIGHT AND WATER: On the opposite page we see stage (1) -- the unexcited water molecule of H_2O, one oxygen atom (with eight electrons) and two hydrogen atoms (with one electron each) are bonded together. They oscillate up and down and side to side and vibrate at the regular frequency of the water molecule.

Then we see stage (2) of water in the body. When heated or subjected to a ray of primary light the electrons expand into wider orbits, the oscillations become excited and the atoms absorb more energy and re-radiate more energy. The atoms are said to be ionised when the electrons jump into wider orbits.

Beams of light we see coming from the sun or the searchlight beams across the sky are only seen because of the light scattered by particles in the atmosphere. The actual light itself is invisible -- we only see it as it illuminates dust or droplets of water. The phenomenon of scattering of light is very similar to that of resonance. Just as tuning forks resonate with the same frequency of vibration and scatter the sound in all directions so do the atoms in the molecules of air scatter beams of light. This is the cause of the blue in the sky, the red, yellow and green part of the light having been already scattered by the atmosphere. About 80 percent of our atmosphere is nitrogen and the remainder mostly oxygen. The atoms contain electrons which are oscillating like a crystal radio set. The resonant frequencies of these tiny oscillators match the frequencies of ultraviolet light and scatter the ultraviolet rays. Much of the higher frequency light is filtered out by the oxygen and nitrogen atoms in the ionosphere letting the resonant frequencies of the lower energy visible light through. Most of the red-orange and some of the ultraviolet rays are allowed through the sky filter and reach our bodies. For every red photon scattered by the atmospheric blanket, ten violet photons are filtered out.

However, cosmic rays coming from powerful stars are not scattered because they are coherent light. Their light has already been scattered in space so we are receiving only the frequency of radiation that is left behind. Thus cosmic radiation is penetrating the atoms and molecules of our bodies and that which is in resonance with our cell molecules is being scattered inside us. Just as water vapour scatters light in the atmosphere making rainbows so the water molecules in the human body scatter the photons of energy making the cells into tiny radiomagnetic centres of life. Here is a picture of a water atom excited by a ray of light.

Fig. (19)

A beam of light falls on an atom and causes the electrons in the atom to vibrate. The vibrating electrons in turn radiate in horizontal and vertical directions.

A beam of light falls on an atom of liquid crystal in the body, such as water, chloresterol, etc. and cause the electrons to vibrate. These electrons in the liquid crystals vibrating excitedly cause an atom to radiate life-force or bioelectric light.

The inner worlds of each person correspond to the absorption of cosmic light energies which are mixed together inside the consciousness of an individual human being as colors. Depending on the proportion of the color rays absorbed each human becomes a type of liquid crystal who acts and reacts in his or her consciousness according to laws of harmonic resonance. In the same way that the Fibonacci ratios in plants and the music scale relates to the golden section, this mixture can be looked at as follows:

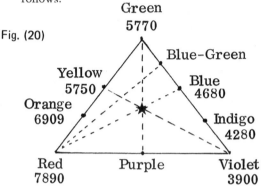

Fig. (20)

The diagrams opposite and below show the relationship of the golden mean to the proportions of the music scale, the Fibonacci ratio in plants and wavelengths of color as it affects consciousness in the psychic centers.

The color Triangle of the classical scientific theory is shown in a two dimensional representation, whereas the real form is a spiral within a half sphere. Points of intersection of the dotted lines represent those colors obtained by mixing wavelengths of light[shown in angstrom units] together in proportional amounts equivalent to the distance from the sides of the Triangle. Equal mixture of the primary color light rays is shown at the central point and is seen as white light.

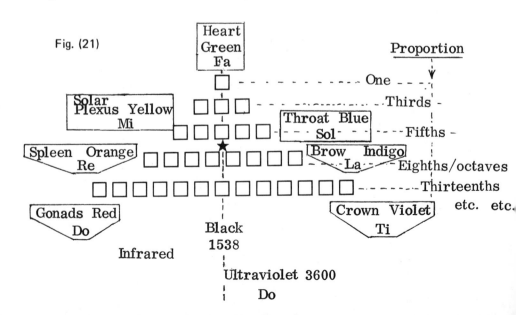

Fig. (21)

The human body is a resonating system whose aura can be measured according to the excitement of the electron shells around the atoms of our bodies. Various reactions can be detected with the instruments of Supersensonics* such as dowsing rods, rules and pendulums which react at specific distances away from a psychic centre. These centres set up edges or outlines of spherical wave-fields depending on the health of the person and the number of chakras functioning. In a healthy person the pendulum reacts at approximately 13, 19, 25, 50-55, 62, 68 and 80 cms. away from the centre of a sphere around each chakra centre. The earth itself receives light from the cosmos like a giant chakra and within its magnetic field there are subsidiary vortexes spiralling around several centres which resonate with different types of crystal structures upon the earth.

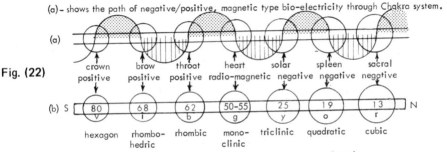

(a) - shows the path of negative/positive, magnetic type bio-electricity through Chakra system.

Fig. (22)

(b) - shows a supersonic wave-guide rule giving a cross-section of a sphere.

The spherical field which surrounds the earth corresponds to the universal field that surrounds the human body showing an L-field of 13 to L-80 — resonant nodal points which make the pendulum "come alive" when passed over the invisible field edges at seven points which correspond to one of the colours of the spectrum. Horizontal or vertical polarity of the colour is determined by its being in phase with the vertical electric plane at right angles to the horizontal magnetic plane. The human consciousness resonates to vertical electric energy at mental levels of mind energy and horizontal magnetic relates to emotional chemical energies in the human body. These in turn correspond to the nervous system's seven plexus electromagnetic energies and the endocrine system's seven chemical hormones.

---

* See instruments shown in the back of this book.

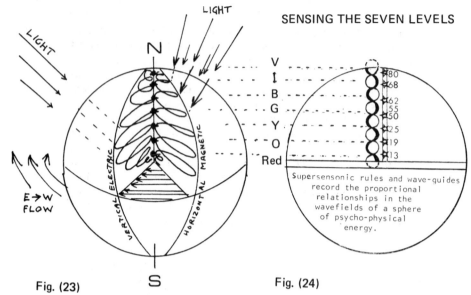

Fig. (23)

The earth's electromagnetic core sends out its field and interpenetrates everything on the planet. Each organism concentrates these forces at different angles in a spiral of manifestation as the elements materialise.

Supersensonic rules and wave-guides record the proportional relationships in the wavefields of a sphere of psycho-physical energy.

Fig. (24)

Our consciousness acts as a wave-guide to energies at different thresholds of excitement which correspond to the seven colours of the spectrum.

By using the radionic detectors* our supersense can delineate the outlines of spherical fields which assume specific dimensions based on the nature of the elemental atoms in the cells. There is a close relationship between the wave-fields of the carrier waves of light and the polarisation of the atomic crystals in the cells. The planes of the vertical and horizontal fields of polarisation in the cells are in magnetic resonance with the earth's magnetic poles. Since the earth is a vast electro-dynamo, it creates a magnetic field which interpenetrates everything on the earth's surface and permeates the atmosphere for several thousand miles out to the Van Allen radiation belts. These belts trap many of the more energetic particles of light and scatter them before they can reach the surface of the earth and affect our bodies. Much of this potent coherent starlight does penetrate our atoms and the excitation causes our bodies to radiate light. This light cannot be seen except when it interacts with something else, in the same way that light cannot be seen unless it shines on something and illuminates it. This light is the same light as our consciousness which interacts with other objects enabling us to see and experience. It illuminates these objects just as light does. In other words the light of consciousness lights up the world around us. We do not see this light because it is our own self. We absorb it, we re-radiate it, we control it with our chakra functions, all unconsciously in the same way our body digests, assimilates and excretes food by unconscious processes.

---

* See the radionic biological feedback instruments at the back of this book.

Electrons move in curved orbits around the nucleus of an atom, tracing out a spherical shell. All the electrons in a given shell are identified with one energy level. Shells farthest out from the nuclear centre of an atom correspond to the higher energy levels. Although this mental image of an atom as a sphere is not always acceptable, the terms **shell** and **orbit** still denote thresholds of energy. The analogy of these thresholds of spherical fields of consciousness occurs again and again throughout all the entities of Nature.

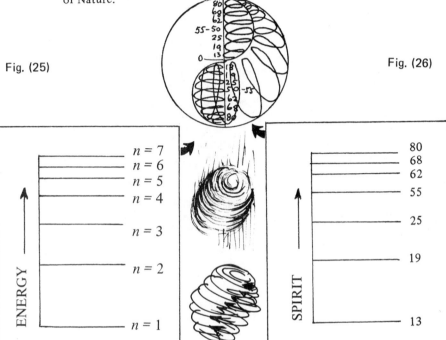

Fig. (25)

Fig. (26)

DIAGRAM OF MATTER

Energy level of electrons in an atom and levels of spiritual energy in the indivisible human entity-

Particles of small mass such as electrons do not follow Newton's laws of motion and classical laws of electrodynamics which describe moving electric charges. The vibration levels are numbered according to the energy quantum number referred to as n. For the lowest energy level ($n = 1$) the maximum population of electrons is 2, for the second level 8, the third level 18, fourth level 32, fifth level 50 etc. Electrons in the lowest energy level are referred to as being in the k shell or orbit and are the most tightly bound to the nucleus. Those in the second energy level ($n = 2$) are referred to as being in the L shell or L orbit and the higher energy levels are numbered $n = 3, 4, 5$ or consecutively L, M, N, etc.

DIAGRAM OF SPIRIT

Both the energy levels of matter work together with the vibration of consciousness and find harmonic resonances which show that spirit experiences itself in octaves of the spectrum at different thresholds of being. The low energy existence is unaware of what life is like on the higher levels of existence even though they interpenetrate each other within the nucleus of the same person. Only by raising up the lower levels by absorbing more energy and expanding them to the wider shells can the total primeval atom be known completely on all seven levels.

AKASHA

The ancient sages postulated that there was an invisible light which could not be sensed because it does not become matter until it touches some gravitational or spiralling vortex, which attracts it into a center. They viewed the seed or nucleus of a material form as a transformer of this Akasha into Kasha or visible light. Today the existence of an aether or Akasha is not considered by scientists as a possibility.

Fitzgerald, like Descartes, was convinced that space, even interstellar space, is occupied by a medium which, though undetected by the senses and our physical measurements, is capable of transmitting force, energy and light to those bodies of matter immersed in it. This medium, which was called aether, must therefore contain unique mechanical properties like the unique properties possessed by solids, liquids and gases. Descartes had suggested that aether consisted of fine particles constantly in motion and everywhere colliding and pressing on other particles; others saw it as corpuscles so small that they could not be measured. They thought of the propagation of light through the aether as they did that of sound through a gas, but permeating all matter and filling the entirety of space. However, it was found that light produced vibrations which were generated at right angles to the direction of its propagation, whereas sound produces vibrations in the same direction as its propagation.

Fresnel suggested that aether behaved not like a gas but more like an elastic solid with its resistance to change and distortion accounting for the vibration of the transverse wavefronts. There was debate as to whether the electric aether was the same as the luminous aether which transmitted light. When Fitzgerald attacked the problem of subtle aether he did not fall into the crude materialism of present day science, which rejects it. He regarded the medium as something not capable of description by our kind of measurements. Einstein took the same view, but realised that since relativity was measuring only the velocity of light in respect to a stationary observer situated in an imaginary vacuum, it was not necessary to bring aether into his equations, and said that it was not necessary in the purely mathematical mental operations to have a stationary aether as a fixed framework for measuring relative velocity. It could not make any difference, since, if it existed, both the light and the observer were situated in the same all-pervading medium and therefore it could be dispensed with. But he did not say that aether never existed; on the contrary he regarded the experiment of Michelson and Morley as inconclusive -- a null experiment, which Fitzgerald was able to explain.

Fig. (27)

Fitzgerald believed the aether needed to have the properties of both a liquid and a solid and his starting point was a theory of matter by William Thomson (Lord Kelvin), who pointed out that atoms propagating through aether may be like smoke rings which rebound when they approach each other and pass through air rotating upon themselves. He suggested that matter could be explained as vortex rings in a perfect fluid. He introduced the idea of a vortex-sponge – a mass of fluid in which rotating and non-rotary portions of matter were finely mixed together in the aether. Fitzgerald saw that the concept of a vortex-sponge would solve his problem, since this velocity in a perfect fluid could not be created or destroyed, he reasoned that the electric field forces of Maxwell's Electromagnetic theory was a modification of the system of propagation in which the vortex motion in the aether was polarised. In this he was supported by the statements of the sages of over five thousand years ago who invented mathematics and probed the nature of matter with other means of the Supersense.

Fitzgerald wrote many memoirs developing the electromagnetic theory and it was he who gave us the Maxwell-Lorentz equations. But he is best known for the discovery of the Fitzgerald contraction on which Einstein based his theories of relativity. He used the Fitzgerald interpretation of the failure to measure the velocity of the earth through space relative to a stationary aether. Fitzgerald calculated the ratio $\sqrt{(1-v^2/c^2)}$ to 1, with v representing the earth's velocity relative to the aether and c representing the velocity of light. This mathematical discovery that the length of a rod and the fixed periodic intervals of a clock are not absolute properties, but depend on their motion in respect to an observer at rest, showed that rods do contract in length and clocks do get slower. This has now also received confirmation from experimental physicists in the observation of cosmic rays and the generation of fast particles in accelerators. This contraction profoundly impressed Einstein who used these equations in his own theory of relativity to develop his concept of space-time, which has the elastic properties of the elusive aether.

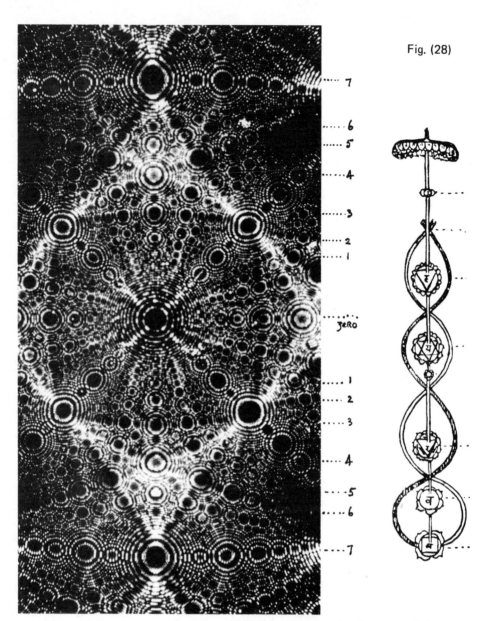

Fig. (28)

7

6

5

4

3

2

1

ZERO

1

2

3

4

5

6

7

The evidence for seven levels or thresholds of energy in the octave is not only available in the rainbow and spectrum of light, but also in the structure of solid matter. Man's consciousness is scientifically structured in layers similar to the music scale, and the seven worlds around him interpenetrate each other in spheres of energy in the human aura. Consciousness extends outwards from the centre in radiating patterns which can be sensed with the faculties of direct perception developed through Supersensonics. Through the gradual process of evolution, man will soon develop these faculties to sense these hidden all-pervasive energies. The picture taken by Dr. Erwin Mueller of the arrangement in solid matter of the atoms of platinum crystals in a needle tip, shows clearly the nodal points of energy. As such, it is a modern reproduction of the ancient seven-fold chakra system seen by the clairvoyant sages who wrote the Vedas.

THE VEDAS AND THE CHAKRAS

The connections between the various drives and types of personality and the chakras is hinted at and expressed descriptively in the Vedas.

The first chakra was said to be concerned with the instinct for survival, domination of others, fears of physical insecurity and territorial instincts. The second chakra was concerned with the genitals, the instinct of reproduction and sensuality. It was said that this chakra created lust and cravings for contact with others in sensual delights. These two descriptions fit only the bottom chakra in Nuclear Evolution. The third chakra in the solar plexus was said to be expanding one's urge for power in society and to influence others. Nuclear Evolution puts this in the second chakra and attributes the desire to be separate in the self-sense to the third chakra. The Vedas were variously interpreted by each individual yogi who made changes as he saw proper to make it fit his own system. However, it appears that all systems, including Nuclear Evolution, place the heart or centre of Being in the fourth chakra. This was regarded as a centre of selfless love but Nuclear Evolution relates it more to feelings of security, jealousy, possessiveness, in addition to the fullness of love.

The top three chakras were always regarded as higher functions which opened up when the kundalini flowed through them to the crown chakra. Little is said about their function and what is said is often naive, as if the top chakras could have no negative aspects and the bottom chakras were all malific. Nuclear Evolution corrects this vagueness, which is the result of thousands of years of losing touch with the methods of research which the Rishis used to detect their exact functions.

However, in the Vedas there is nothing consistent given concerning the relationship of colour and consciousness nor is there any reference to the different time worlds experienced. Hence it was and still is difficult for any yogi to recognise which evolutionary stage he is in. Most would consider themselves already arrived or at least already a Buddha. This is true for everyone in potential but to actualise it is another matter.

Gurdjieff's system mentions the music scale in the creation of these worlds but not the colors, although he hinted at the connection. Tibetan Buddhism often associates certain colours with different Buddhas and these represent states of Being, but they are merely descriptive identifying colors and do not represent anything objective existing in nature, such as the spectrum of energies of which humans are an integral part.

Gurdjieff spoke of the "ray of creation" which started in the absolute. He said that three creative forces within the absolute possessed certain qualities which created all the worlds in series. Each of these worlds repeated the process of interacting on each other. It was obvious that his "law of three" was referring to the three Gunas or qualities which we shall mention later. His law of seven by which he explains his system of proportions of "inner octaves" is outlined in the diagram opposite. He used it to indicate that the universe was composed out of materialised thought. The idea of bridging the gap between mind and matter by bringing the mind down into the levels of matter is not foreign to the Vedas, which look upon mind energy as a more subtle kind of matter.

Fig. (30)

THE THREE CREATIVE FORCES OF THE UNIVERSE OR THE "LAW OF THREE"

Fig. (29)

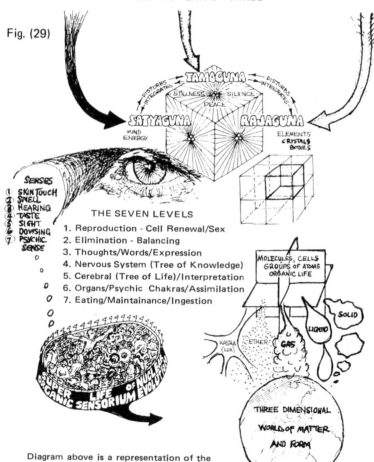

SENSES
1. SKIN TOUCH
2. SMELL
3. HEARING
4. TASTE
5. SIGHT
6. DOWSING
7. PSYCHIC SENSE

THE SEVEN LEVELS
1. Reproduction - Cell Renewal/Sex
2. Elimination - Balancing
3. Thoughts/Words/Expression
4. Nervous System (Tree of Knowledge)
5. Cerebral (Tree of Life)/Interpretation
6. Organs/Psychic Chakras/Assimilation
7. Eating/Maintainance/Ingestion

Diagram above is a representation of the Samkhya Yoga system as conceived by Christopher Hills. The Tree of Life depicted in the Raja Yoga system of Samkhya is shown on the following page.

Absolute	1 — do
INTERVAL	
All Worlds	3 — si
All Suns	6 — la
Our Sun	12 — sol
All Planets	24 — fa
INTERVAL	
Earth	48 — mi
Moon	96 — re
Absolute Nothing	do

This is a representation of the "Ray of Creation" as seen by Gurdjieff.

54

Fig. (31)   Modern drawing of the Tree of Life showing the nervous system and main ganglia corresponding to the seven chakras or psychic electricity centers in man.

PROPORTIONAL VIBRATIONS OF THE CHAKRA SYSTEM IS SHOWN BELOW.

For endocrine correspondences see the next page.

Fig. (32)

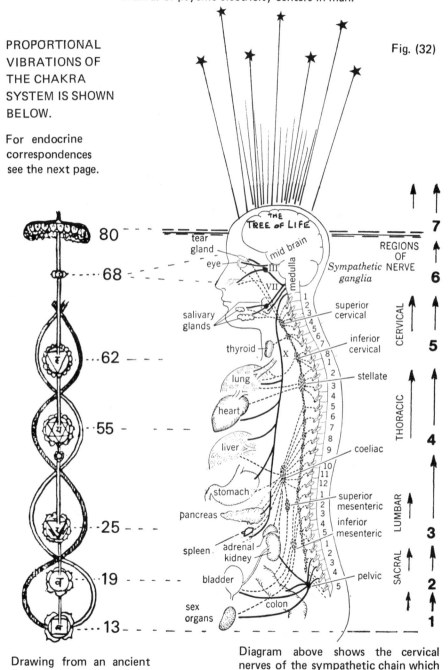

Drawing from an ancient Sanskrit text shows the vibration levels of the chakras in terms of petals.

Diagram above shows the cervical nerves of the sympathetic chain which govern the reactions of cells to events in the glands, heart, intestines, arteries, and sensations of vibrations, pressure, temperature, etc. in the receptors.

Fig. (33)

ETHERIC LINK BETWEEN CHAKRA, PERSONALITY TYPE & ENDOCRINE SECRETIONS

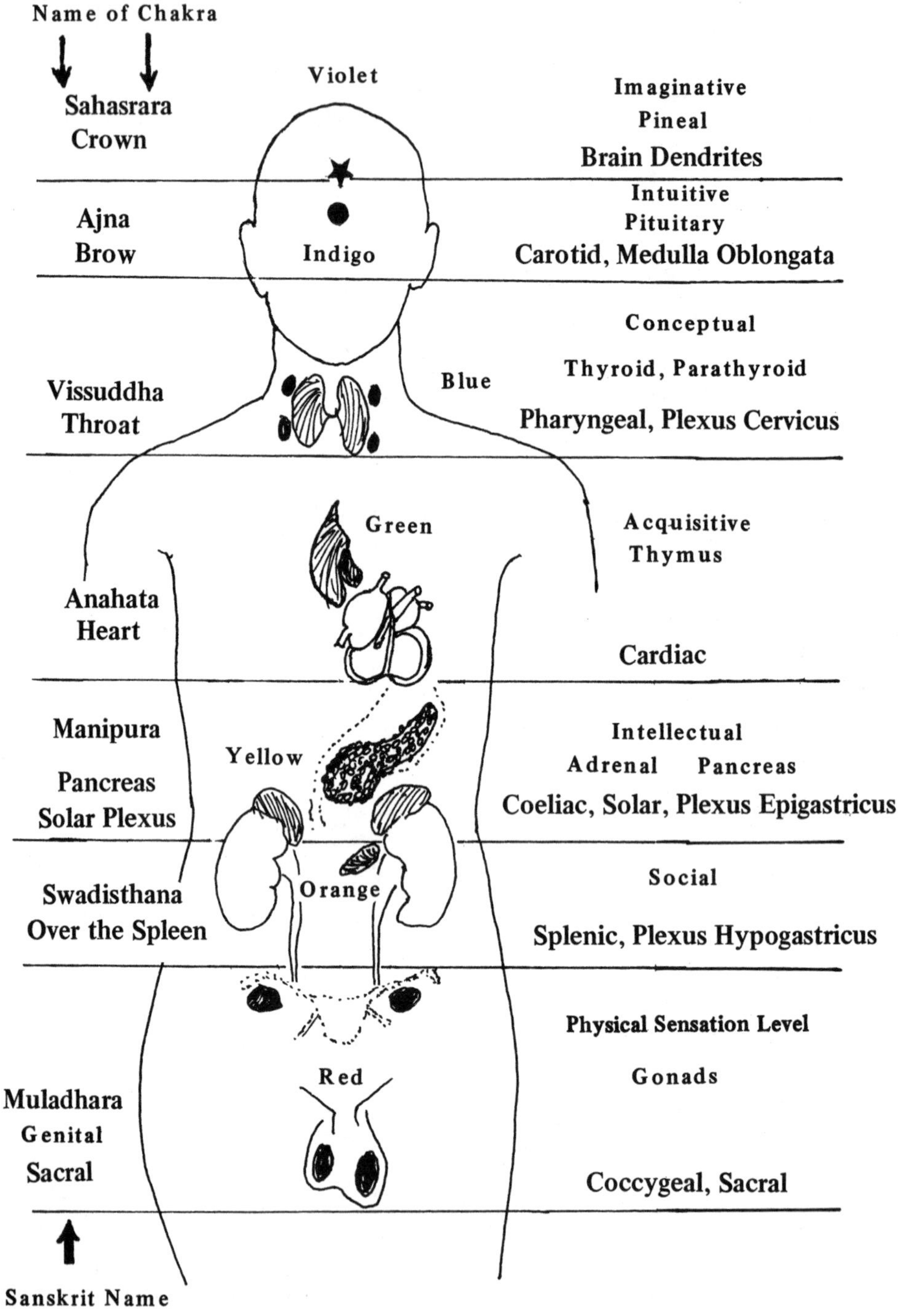

Sanskrit

Name of Chakra

Violet

Sahasrara
Crown

Imaginative
Pineal
Brain Dendrites

Ajna
Brow

Indigo

Intuitive
Pituitary
Carotid, Medulla Oblongata

Vissuddha
Throat

Blue

Conceptual
Thyroid, Parathyroid
Pharyngeal, Plexus Cervicus

Green

Anahata
Heart

Acquisitive
Thymus

Cardiac

Manipura
Pancreas
Solar Plexus

Yellow

Intellectual
Adrenal   Pancreas
Coeliac, Solar, Plexus Epigastricus

Swadisthana
Over the Spleen

Orange

Social

Splenic, Plexus Hypogastricus

Physical Sensation Level

Red

Gonads

Muladhara
Genital
Sacral

Coccygeal, Sacral

Sanskrit Name

CHAKRA- NEURAL- ENDOCRINE CORRESPONDENCES

56

We can see below the intricate design of this chakra or wheel of spiralling energy was seen by the ancient clairvoyant sages as a centre of energy in the form of a flower with a different number of petals to denote its vibration. Anyone who has seen patterns on a cathode tube such as an oscilloscope can note the similarity of a spiralling electron field circling in a conical magnetic field. The pattern can be generated by pointing a video camera at the crystals on a TV screen so that they take a picture of their own vibrations. Circular causality, commonly called "feedback" makes the energy in a system loop back on itself when perfect resonance is established. The symbol below is an artist's impression of a map rediscovered by Supersensitive detectors employing the method of biological feedback known as "dowsing". The new science of detection of invisible processes in man's psychophysical systems is called "Supersensonics" by the author meaning the cosmic full sense of sound.

Fig. (34)

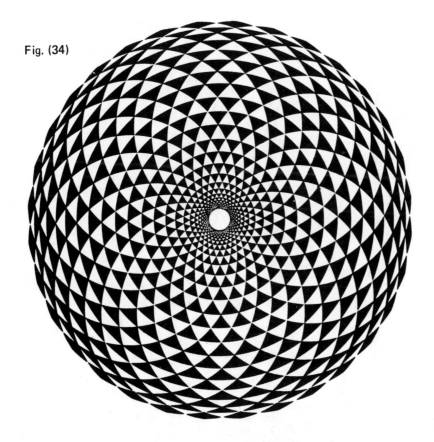

There is a subtle connection between thoughts and the three qualities manifesting through the Akasha at the physical, emotional chemical endocrine system, the seven major nerve centres along the spine and the seven chakras. These centres are made of a different kind of aether energy folding back on itself like the vortex-sponge model of Lord Kelvin. They are different but they are connected to all the mental, emotional and spiritual vehicles of man. Like a sponge they absorb the cosmic radiation. The following diagrams show different ways of looking at these thresholds in man which trigger each other and form our personality. Any change in one of the levels, i.e. chemical, physical or spiritual or mental will automatically produce changes in the others. Similarly changes in chakra function determine the way we absorb the cosmic light of the universe.

57

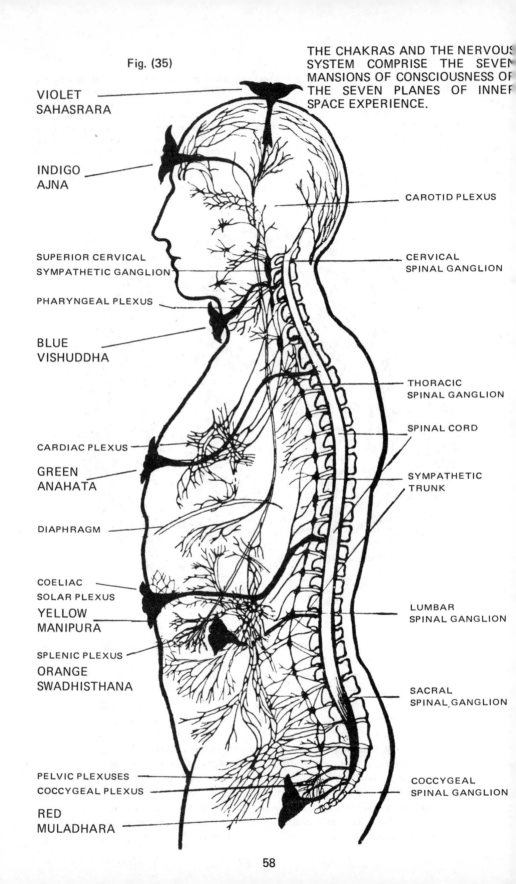

Fig. (35)

THE CHAKRAS AND THE NERVOUS SYSTEM COMPRISE THE SEVEN MANSIONS OF CONSCIOUSNESS OR THE SEVEN PLANES OF INNER SPACE EXPERIENCE.

VIOLET
SAHASRARA

INDIGO
AJNA

CAROTID PLEXUS

SUPERIOR CERVICAL
SYMPATHETIC GANGLION

CERVICAL
SPINAL GANGLION

PHARYNGEAL PLEXUS

BLUE
VISHUDDHA

THORACIC
SPINAL GANGLION

SPINAL CORD

CARDIAC PLEXUS

GREEN
ANAHATA

SYMPATHETIC
TRUNK

DIAPHRAGM

COELIAC
SOLAR PLEXUS

YELLOW
MANIPURA

LUMBAR
SPINAL GANGLION

SPLENIC PLEXUS

ORANGE
SWADHISTHANA

SACRAL
SPINAL GANGLION

PELVIC PLEXUSES

COCCYGEAL PLEXUS

COCCYGEAL
SPINAL GANGLION

RED
MULADHARA

58

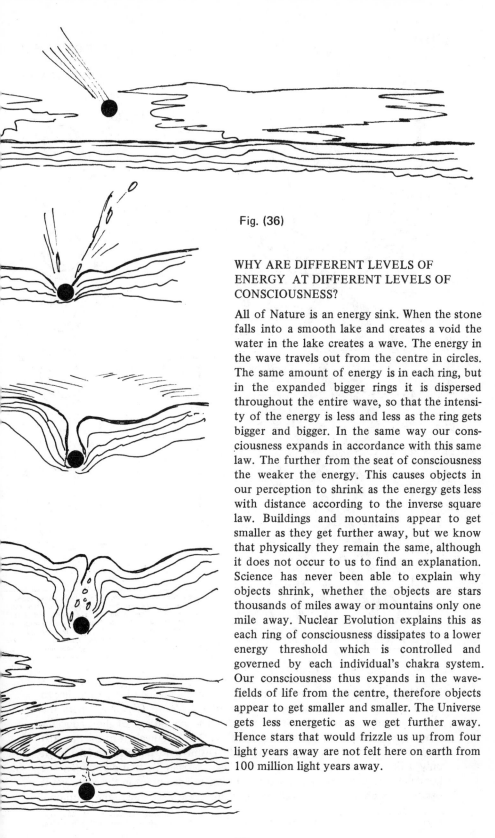

Fig. (36)

WHY ARE DIFFERENT LEVELS OF ENERGY AT DIFFERENT LEVELS OF CONSCIOUSNESS?

All of Nature is an energy sink. When the stone falls into a smooth lake and creates a void the water in the lake creates a wave. The energy in the wave travels out from the centre in circles. The same amount of energy is in each ring, but in the expanded bigger rings it is dispersed throughout the entire wave, so that the intensity of the energy is less and less as the ring gets bigger and bigger. In the same way our consciousness expands in accordance with this same law. The further from the seat of consciousness the weaker the energy. This causes objects in our perception to shrink as the energy gets less with distance according to the inverse square law. Buildings and mountains appear to get smaller as they get further away, but we know that physically they remain the same, although it does not occur to us to find an explanation. Science has never been able to explain why objects shrink, whether the objects are stars thousands of miles away or mountains only one mile away. Nuclear Evolution explains this as each ring of consciousness dissipates to a lower energy threshold which is controlled and governed by each individual's chakra system. Our consciousness thus expands in the wavefields of life from the centre, therefore objects appear to get smaller and smaller. The Universe gets less energetic as we get further away. Hence stars that would frizzle us up from four light years away are not felt here on earth from 100 million light years away.

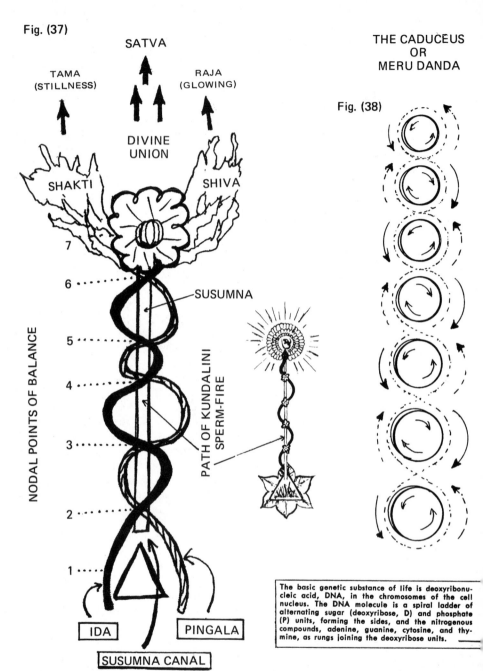

Fig. (37)

THE CADUCEUS
OR
MERU DANDA

SATVA

TAMA
(STILLNESS)

RAJA
(GLOWING)

Fig. (38)

DIVINE
UNION

SHAKTI

SHIVA

7

6 · · · · · · · · · · · SUSUMNA

NODAL POINTS OF BALANCE

5 · · · · · · · ·

PATH OF KUNDALINI
SPERM-FIRE

4 · · · · · · · ·

3 · · · · · · · ·

2 · · · · · · · ·

1 · · · · ·

IDA   PINGALA

SUSUMNA CANAL

The basic genetic substance of life is deoxyribonu-
cleic acid, DNA, in the chromosomes of the cell
nucleus. The DNA molecule is a spiral ladder of
alternating sugar (deoxyribose, D) and phosphate
(P) units, forming the sides, and the nitrogenous
compounds, adenine, guanine, cytosine, and thymine, as rungs joining the deoxyribose units.

The Meru Danda is the mystical name given to the raising of the kundalini to
its full height. It corresponds to the mythical Mount Olympus where the
Gods resided in the Greek initiate schools. The symbolism of the Caduceus,
now used by the healing profession, was the Greek equivalent of the Sanskrit
chakra system, but was taught orally and transmitted from teacher to student
only when readiness to receive had been proven by self-discipline. The
kundalini fire or ambrosia rises and balances at each point in the chakra as it
passes through the cross over point in the central channel---the Susumna.

NOTE: The similarity of these ancient insights to the DNA spiral double helix.

60

Later in this book we shall look at the similarities between modern physics and its knowledge of energy, matter and form, and the spiritual synthesis of light. For the moment we may wonder whether the ancients who probed the unknown by different methods of clairvoyance, by dowsing of nature's forces with instruments of divination, were able to see into the heart of the cell nucleus. We can see the similarity of the DNA molecule and the spiral of the caduceus which represented the microcosm in man.

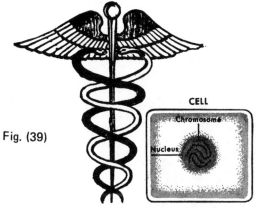

Fig. (39)

CELL

Chromosome

Nucleus

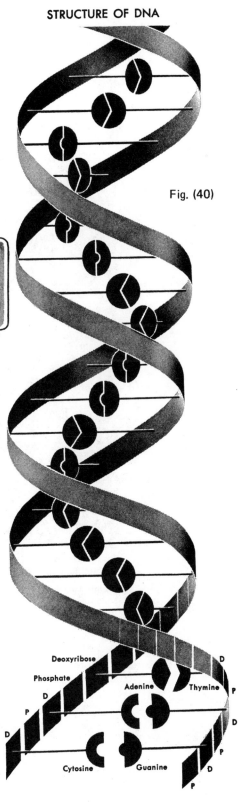

Fig. (40)

The double helix is said to be the best macroscopic picture of the microcosmic nucleic acid structure of the cell genes. As such it portrays the macromolecule of DNA which transmits the pattern of life from generation to generation. The DNA itself does not act as a template but as a messenger which transfers its "message" to other nucleic acid proteins in the protoplasm surrounding the nucleus. It is a fundamental concept of Nuclear Evolution that consciousness can not only change the patterns of protein synthesis but also enter into the DNA patterns through the controlled action of cosmic light and the enzymes involved. The role of field forces set up by the chakras and their effects on the ways we transduce light energy into biophysical energy is determined by resonance between the gene, the ph of the cerebrospinal fluid in the ventricles of the brain and the universal field of consciousness in which all evolution takes place. The ancients believed that the physical proteins of the body took the shape of the guiding mental field in terms of current thoughts and the experiences stored in the memory. No one who has ever seen a person improve in physical health, shape, flesh and bone, etc. by letting go of an unwholesome thought pattern can doubt the power of consciousness to transform cell-proteins and flesh almost out of recognition. Also to see the change which comes with self-doubt, fear or some negative thought effect on the conditions of the cell proteins does not require any sophisticated instruments or clairvoyance or other form of proof. Common sense sees plainly the emotional connection between the replication of cell life in plants and humans is dependent on the patterns of thought and the level of wholeness. Healing is done by nature not by science or a doctor. In the same way, evolution takes place in the human when the nature of consciousness is understood and its connection with light is mastered.

Deoxyribose

Phosphate

Adenine   Thymine

Cytosine   Guanine

61

The Bo Tree and Ashoka's 1st Century temple

Bodhi Gaya is the location of the Buddha's enlightenment, near Patna in central India. The tree in the picture is the same tree under which Gautama sat.

NUCLEAR EVOLUTION
AND KUNDALINI

IS KUNDALINI REAL?

For some years we have watched while various authorities have talked of kundalini and the yoga scene. Some have even started fashionable cults and built up impressive organisations of rather gullible but well-meaning people who have been promised that their kundalini will be raised by certain practices. Most of these, with two notable exceptions, have yet to show any remarkable internal changes or emphasis on detection of ego structures. **We have seen great external changes in clothes, beads and bells, but little of the real spiritual work on the quality of consciousness has come from these bringers of kundalini yoga to the West.**

Alan Watts said to me once that yoga was all happening here at the grass roots and I looked around at the scene and wondered if he really knew! Yoga is not what passes for a current fashion or lip service or reading the right books, but something totally transforming, something which does not require us to look for spiritual crutches nor to make excuses for drugs. Consciousness is already the most powerful drug and a true yogin is already drugged and so intoxicated with it that all other drugs are superfluous. This is not to say that alcohol or sex are not good things but that an immoderate obsession with them shows that kundalini is not working its magic.

EXPERIENCE IS THE TEST

So in writing about such things as kundalini I have come to see that many book writers and preachers do not necessarily demonstrate what they talk about except to the gullible and impressionable. When it comes to actual transformation of society or presenting some real original credentials to the world we find these authorities and fashionable cults are lacking in depth and perspective.

What kundalini really is and what yoga really is when all the traditional words are said and done may elude even the very elect. The evolutionary thrust is not towards explanations or "talking about" kundalini or for that matter speaking in anecdotes and second-hand knowledge of this and that. What the evolutionary consciousness is concerned with is something so scientifically verifiable that the laws of consciousness become as predictable as the laws of matter, or more so. The evolutionary force is not interested in any particular philosophy, religious tradition or scientific method, but in more real ways of self-mastery.

In this sense all systems of religion and science which contain "essence knowledge" of kundalini can be said to be second-hand knowledge until it becomes validated by our own ignorance or insights of the systems. The tools of religion and science in the evolutionary sense are no greater than their users. One could say the same of kundalini or consciousness, just as a brand new set of chisels is not much use to an old widow who never learned carpentry.

IT CAN BE DANGEROUS

So from the viewpoint of an evolutionary kundalini force acting cosmically through man's vehicle, we are no further on until the potential state (which everyone has) becomes manifest. Without seeing its manifestation or being able to determine the shape, form or content of its existence in the so-called material or external world, kundalini is as dangerous as it is enlightening, just as a kitchen knife is capable of cutting vegetables or of killing. Guns are not dangerous because they don't go off by themselves. They are only dangerous when human consciousness directs the bullet and pulls the trigger. Guns will stay harmless under your breakfast table for a hundred years as long as no one plays around with them. So with kundalini we are talking of the energy of consciousness when it burns away the dross of human dependence and raises men to wider levels of consciousness.

Heightening awareness of the cosmic relations that give us direct perception of psychic electricity is the only evidence that we can indeed evolve the biophysical structures we call a human body. But do we see this happening at the grass roots level or do we see the same preoccupations as our forefathers had with outward forms and exotic teachings? Is kundalini thrusting us irrevocably towards absorbing the history of gurus and the analogies and metaphors of ancient personalities?

Of what use is all this acquisition of ancient traditional religion if the evidence shows we are just as egotistical, self-seeking, personality-, fame- and name-orientated and public relations-promoting for psychic income as any businessman is for dollar income? **From the cosmic point of view, from the standpoint of eternal time, the promotional efforts of gurus to get the kundalini into action in the planetary sense may be sometimes seen as a considerable circus on a grand scale.**

Surely nothing short of the Einsteinian revolution in science must take place in the spiritual sense of religious experience of kundalini manifestations. With man's very being becoming more threatened and more ominously blind, according to prophets Solzhenitsyn et al, with more countries of the planet falling to totalitarian despotism of small aggressive cliques of self-righteous know-alls, where is this so-called evolutionary power?

In the great monasteries of Tibet the Chinese smashed in the faces of the great high Lamas with rifle butts in front of thousands of Tibetan disciple lamas to show them that they really had no power at all and that their philosophy of super-powerful control of life-force was just a phony myth. Millions of lamas and "believers" were disillusioned when their gods bled to death in front of their very eyes. What happened to the great Tantric teachings about kundalini powers and the superhuman ideals?

We do not mention this to cast doubt on the ancient teachings of great traditions but only to remind ourselves that belief in such powers or for that matter kundalini, whatever it is, must be based on direct experience and not on some teacher's parroting of cultural brainwash. Hence methods of actually determining what kundalini is and how it works must now be outlined in some conclusive way, to enable us to experience its reality; some "thought experiment" similar to Einstein's physical concepts, which transformed the world of man with a power incalculable in terms of one man, or one all-knowing guru. The understanding of"kundalini", in other words, must go beyond the "writing about" stage which is merely descriptive and allegorical, however interesting, to some real nitty-gritty things that we can do in our own backyard.

WHAT IS KUNDALINI?

There seem to be so many people jumping on the kundalini bandwagon and including the word in their offerings to the public that I feel it's time to throw in my own two cents worth and say what it is. We have heard a lot about kundalini energy but "writing about" something or talking about something is quite a different thing from the actual thing itself. Judging by the amount of claims made by ignorant people as to what kundalini really is and the loose talk which goes under its label, it might be wisest to start with some statements about what it is not.

GET TO THE "NITTY-GRITTY"

Unfortunately it is always easier to say what a thing is not, and a long list of what it is not would practically include everything on the spiritual path offered to the gullible as enlightenment. I propose instead to say that kundalini is not energy at all and that any attempt to understand it in terms of energy, orgone, etheric electricity, or in biophysical terms, is doomed to failure. In short, everyone has kundalini and it is not something special but something super-ordinary. In fact, you could not even read these words without kundalini coming out of your eyes and "seeing" the words in front of you.

Kundalini is basically consciousness and everyone has it. The only difference between a "seer" and an ordinary person is that kundalini is latent in one and manifest in the other when it moves out of its normal house in the bottom chakra and burns its way up to the higher chakras or psychic centres in man. How many young men have felt the burning sensation at the base of the spine when they become sexually aroused and frustrated through lack of a union?

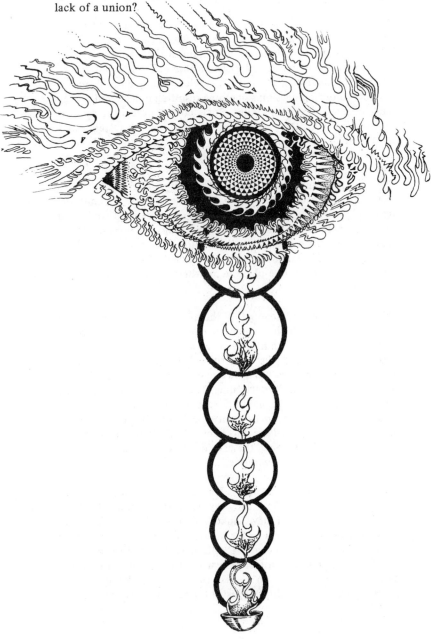

This is caused when kundalini cannot rise and gets stuck at the barrier between the root chakra and the one above it. In some people it even gets stuck two chakras higher up and gives them a spinal weakness in the back. This burning sensation is the movement or the uncoiling of the kundalini which is there all the time being used for the ordinary purpose of living, mating, and feeling.

When it moves through the chakras, the kundalini burns fire through the channels or nerve currents which carry it upwards to the magnetic part of the mind and brain. Strictly speaking, what is burning and moving is not a chemical or an energy; but energy is the by-product, just as light is completely unquantised until it is absorbed or impinges on something resulting in heat and energy being released as a by-product. So is consciousness the same as unquantised light. Only when it moves through the system can it be described as kundalini because only then do we become conscious of its existence as an ambrosia which melts and burns.

To describe kundalini in chemical or energetic terms alone is to avoid the real cause and look only at the effects. Without the light of consciousness moving through our receptors we would not see, smell, taste, hear or touch anything. Yet we do not see kundalini described as ordinary consciousness but always as something special. Kundalini is a basic component of life and it is only when it moves from one place to another that we sense it or feel it as "energy".

To call it kundalini energy is therefore a misnomer. It is a prephysical state which merely becomes manifest when it burns its way through something. Then we sense it, but really all the time it is asleep inside us; it is there helping us to be alive, to sense the world through our eyes and ears, etc. and to imprint our consciousness with all its patterning. The mind-tapes we play have their counterpart in the habitual sensory responses of the body which is no less a creature of habitual patterns than our emotions or mental states. These are the habitual states which block the rising of kundalini through the psychic electricity stations we call chakras. Kundalini is in everyone.

In my book "Supersensonics" I have described in detail what kundalini actually is and the way it works through the biophysical system and I have linked its behaviour to light and consciousness. However, I feel it is a great error to think of this as a concept of "energy" because that is merely mistaking the effect for the cause. Just as we feel pain when there is pressure on the cells of our big toe, so do we feel the passage of kundalini as a sensation of internal light. But just as the pain is really experienced

THE COSMIC PRISM OF MAN'S RAINBOW BODY

When kundalini rises to the magnetic part of the mind there is often a loud noise like the heavens opening up. Christ experienced this and heard a voice inside his head answering a life long question about his self-preparation. "My son I am well pleased with thee" is obviously something he must have told his disciples or it would not have been written down in the gospels, or it is a mistranslation for the feeling of blissful ambrosia which spreads when the ultimate being is realised.

The author experienced this loud noise or mega-nadam whilst meditating at the same spot where Buddha was enlightened 2500 years before under the Bo Tree at Bodi Gaya in 1961.

in the brain and not the toe, as we prove by blocking the nerve current to the brain with an injection, so can we mistake the causation of kundalini moving through the chakras as kundalini energy when it is in fact only experienced in the brain and not in the root of the spine.

It is important to get this process crystal clear to understand kundalini. When I told someone who was making a deep study of kundalini that it was a psychic electricity he immediately mistook my statement and thought I was saying that nothing physical actually happened at the root of the spine and that it all took place in the head. Obviously there is a chemical and electrical energy which can easily be measured by Supersensonics instruments not only at the base of the spine, but at all the chakras too, but as I said, this is only an effect and the psycho-physical energy thus created disturbs the corresponding centre in the brain. The cerebrospinal system is the seat of all experience in the body. Every centre in the body has a corresponding energy centre in the brain. Whatever happens inside the body or outside of the body eventually finishes up as electrical potentials inside the brain and thus eventually is recognised as a sensation in the mind-stuff which ultimately makes sense of it in our conscious-ness. The entire cerebral cortex is involved in the transformation of kundalini into the chemical, emotional, mental and spiritual functions of each level of consciousness corresponding to the number of chakras activated in each person. The chakras are vortices of spiraling psychic electricity but like the nervous system they are only the biological prisms through which kundalini is differentiated from the whole spectrum.

KUNDALINI = CONSCIOUSNESS

When the chakra opens and the kundalini flows toward the brain it is no different from the pain signal telling us through consciousness that something is happening to the molecules in our toes. The kundalini is actually made of consciousness and the actual sensation is merely a message of our consciousness passing through the psychic veil or skin which acts as a membrane between one world of experience and another. And thus it happens through all of the chakras, that our biological system is merely a physical replica of another system made of kundalini which is identical to consciousness, while we "experience" only the burning feeling and internal light that we call the cosmic fire.

In "Supersensonics," which is Volume III of the series "The Supersensitive Life of Man", I have written a full exposition of how kundalini follows the laws of consciousness and have shown how our invisible consciousness pours out of our eyes every second without our noticing anything unusual until we become

70

Fig. (41)

This picture of VAJRA SATTVA gives an idea of how the Tibetan monks imaged the Kundalini force in man. The "Vajra" or diamond hard stuff of consciousness which is indestructable was coupled with "Sattva" or the creative intelligence which brings equilibrium in nature. The icon above is shown in active aspect (in dance posture) but is often shown in mandalas as passive (in meditation posture) sometimes embraced by his spouse Prajna (wisdom). It was thought of as being a reddish white colour of spiritual love -- the mixture of red being the colour of the Shiva force energy passing through the "Pingala" nadi on the right side and the white Shakti force passing through the "Ida" nadi on the left. The sceptre in his arm symbolised the Vajra power of pure consciousness and the skull bowl in his hand is filled with bliss. In his right hand he wields a combination of a vajra handed chopping knife for cutting through the ego-attachment to ordinary life and its desires. The figure is shown dancing on the body of the ego-self or personality which brings delusion, jealousy, attachments, and separation from others. The whole icon is surrounded by the mystic circle of cosmic fire representing the light of Kundalini which burns away the obscuring poisons to the enlightened state. The symbol is an ancient representation of the symbol of Nuclear Evolution in an anthropomorphic image. This contrasts with the idea of pure consciousness in the Jewish religion which forbids any image to be made of the Vajra Sattva because it is beyond the conceptualising power of mind. The Tibetan monks also believed the Vajra was not conceptual but void and abstract. This emptiness was symbolised by the Hebrews in the holy of holies which was kept in the temple as an empty space behind a veil.

71

enlightened. Then we see clearly that what we took for granted all along was really the priceless jewel of consciousness bouncing off everything, lighting up everything, enlightening everything, making all things light.

CONSCIOUSNESS = LIGHT

Such is kundalini. We use it everyday, we have sex with it as often as we can, we use it for all the promiscuous activity of the mind and we don't know it exists until we see lights inside our head! Just as the light we see inside our head as "brightness" is not the real light but only the psychic response of our receptors to light as it impinges on them, so is the burning sensation described by the sages only the passage through unaccustomed cells of a new level of consciousness functioning in a higher octave. Our body senses it in the biological vehicle because that is the antenna which receives it from the light of the cosmos, but it is our consciousness and brain which makes sense of these sensations in the psychobiological network.

To think of kundalini as something objective and separate from the experiencer is like separating the internal light of our consciousness from the external light of the cosmos. We think it can be done by closing our eyes. But without both internal and external light functioning together nothing objective can be seen or experienced.

Light only becomes energy when it strikes something material in space; until then it is unmanifest radiation, unquantised and invisible throughout space, to which the ancients gave the name **akasha**, meaning in Sanskrit the light that cannot be seen, as against **kasha** which means the light you see as brightness.

CAUTION IS NECESSARY

It would take a whole book to say what kundalini is and that is why I wrote "Supersensonics" on it. However, I deliberately avoided the magic word "kundalini" in the title because of the false connotations placed upon it by half-baked seers who have obviously never experienced it for themselves. It is good to have Gopi Krishna come out and sound a note of caution and send out a clarion call for its proper investigation.

I hate to think what will be done in his name in the so-called biochemical research for the source of kundalini! He is one of the few who are talking sense, but I would like to see more rigour in getting from the "talking about" stage to the actual determination of its nature as consciousness moving through the structure of the psycho-biological system and let us stop this nonsense term "kundalini yoga". All yoga is kundalini yoga. Yoga is meaningless without it. **Let us stop referring to it as something special and begin to see its ordinariness as the fundamental super-sensory sonic note of the universe.**

HISTORICAL BACKGROUND

Tantra yoga is sometimes referred to as "kundalini yoga" because it is the sadhana or path of the **prakriti** (defined as primordial creativity) through the dynamic aspects of life while the system of Shankacharya, which passively displaced Buddhism in India, is the sadhana of **purusa** (defined as "pure consciousness") which is accomplished without stress; it is the way of inaction or letting things BE. Shankara taught that enlightenment is stability, peace and joy of union with the inactive purusa which is the absolute total potentiality of existence, whereas Tantra or the so-called kundalini path teaches that Truth is infinite power and dynamic manifestation. It is the creative utilisation of all potential energy.

Shankacharya taught that the kundalini energy flows into endless potential states in which the manifested states of Shakti and Shiva (or negative-positive) are said to be annihilated and united in Brahman or Buddha who is ONE beyond all conceptualisation of the duality of opposites.

There are many schools favouring the way of Tantra or power which essentially is that path which predominantly seeks special knowledge of the kundalini within consciousness. There are fewer schools who seek the predominance of grace instead of power. Through the contemplation and enjoyment of uninterrupted bliss, these schools study pure being rather than manifestation of energy.

DON'T WORK FOR POWERS

There are even fewer yogis and systems which seek to manifest kundalini power plus the total potentiality to be found only in grace and bliss. This elevation of "power" in favour of "being" involves the absolute control of the flow of consciousness in the void. Notably the Tibetans have absorbed both the Tantra and the yoga of voidness or nirvana. Nirvana means nir (not) vana (flowing) and is a negative state, because it means not doing.

However, the number of persons who can do everything while not doing anything can be said to be those few who have become master of the creative forces of consciousness or kundalini. They are called **gunavana** in Sanskrit, or one who can control flow of kundalini through the gunas or qualities which make up the prakriti or creative energy. Pra means primordial and kriti means creative so prakriti refers to kundalini before it becomes manifested.

The Samkyha yoga says that without mastery of purusa or pure consciousness the control of kundalini at the pure creative prephysical level of prakriti is not possible except in our fantasies of life. This is simply because prakriti or kundalini in its primordial state can only imitate whatever has been put into the being in pure consciousness. Just as a seed can only bear fruit of itself so the manifested creation can act on these potential powers only according to the True nature of the Being.

When Proverbs 23:7 said, "As a man thinketh in his heart, so is he" it was merely stating the connection between the potential state and the manifested state which can only "act" according to its own true nature. Lao Tse observes the same thing when he says that all things are worked by the Tao and cannot act except in accordance with their ultimate true nature. "Kundalini yoga" adherents tend to forget this and work for powers and dynamic action, but as we see through the history of the world, the self cannot be conquered in that way.

STUDY THE NERVE CURRENTS

The first step for the control of kundalini energy in the study of the Tantras is the study of the path of the nadis or nerve currents which carry life-force to the divine spark of the soul which burns like a flame (lings sarira). This is achieved by balancing the polarities of the Shakti female force on the left side of the **sushumna** (central spinal channel) with the Shiva or male force on the right side through the Ida and Pingala nadis. Through breath control the **prana** (life-force) springs up the central nadi from the **kanda** (plexus) at the base of the spine. Man is viewed as a divine instrument of which the **meru danda** (the cerebrospinal nervous system) is the axis of Mount Meru (the symbolic Mount Olympus) on which the gods reside. The Mount Meru is a symbol which refers to the top **padma** or chakra which expands into Brahman from the root word **Brih** (to expand). This tree of life in the brain expands to include all and pervade all. The path of the sleeping divine power residing in the chakra at the base of the spine is known as the uncoiling of kundalini from the verb root **kund** (to burn). Its movement is traced through the nerve plexus in the remaining six chakras or padmas. On reaching the **sahasrara** (highest chakra) the kundalini or burning fire unites with the magnetic part of the mind and causes the expansion of the self-sense into limitless selfhood. Each chakra has its own seed, its own orientation to subtle light energy called **Tatwas** and is controlled by its own guna or kind of prakriti. The petals of the chakras or padmas depicted in so many pictures are merely its rate of vibration distinguished as subtle sounds.

COSMIC PERCEPTION REQUIRED

As the energy of kundalini passes upwards like an ascending scale the supersonic AUM manifests harmonic intervals between the resonant notes of each chakra. The sahasrara is sometimes called the **Bramarandra** or the opening of the top of the head. The null point or hub of the padma has its centre in the "cave of brahma" or the third ventricle in the brain. **For the kundalini or energy of consciousness to keep on rising higher and higher, a complete purification of the self-sense through the direct perception of the cosmic intelligence is required.**

It is known that certain elements and crystals resonate with the lower six padmas or chakras in the order of rising from the root chakra; they are lead, brass, tin, gold, copper and mercury. The crystal lattices which correspond to the chakras are explained in my book "Supersensonics". The wavelength and beat frequencies are discussed in a later chapter which also sets out the connection between colours and the chakras. Both show clearly the criteria of the different levels of consciousness caused by the movement of kundalini energy.

These levels of consciousness can only be directly experienced as one whole vibration by doing **samyama** (complete practice) on the "inner light of consciousness" which is the same thing as kundalini, except that kundalini is its active state of flowing into the cave of Brahman.

WHAT IS A REAL YOGI?

Only where we have direct perception of all these levels beyond the human personality or mind can we be illuminated and thereby directly understand the nature of the experience of consciousness. The windows of the soul are the eyes, but what makes sense of what the eyes see is consciousness.

In yoga or union anyone who achieves less than this supreme state of direct perception cannot be truly called a yogi. Only when the kundalini has risen and its manifestation has actually demonstrated this rising to other members of mankind, through a completely original insight or vision of the worlds of Being, only then can it be said that a human has become a yogi or seer and has transcended the human condition. For this to take place not only does the kundalini have to rise but the hidden evolutionary devices have to be activated, and it is these that spark off the visionary insights that penetrate the real structures of nature and give us the creative genius of the rishis or seers of every age.

The numbers of followers or the self-made claims are no use here because only a fresh vision of the world and the way laws of consciousness work in reality can contribute to real self-knowledge. The acquisition or mere repetition of traditional knowledge which nowadays can be obtained through learning and scholarship or received second-hand from another is of no use in the control of kundalini forces. These subtle energies of prakriti are beyond the control of men until they become a gunavana through the direct experience within themselves of nirvana.

THE SKY IS THE LIMIT

This is the aim of all true yoga: to achieve this transhuman state and then communicate it to the universe. Until they can thus communicate their full vision and express it to another, they have not truly experienced the full control of kundalini energy. Only he who can map out the path of this energy and divine the causes for our human condition can truly be called a yogi or an avatar because all else is transitory, mere inherited comparative knowledge.

The true knowledge of consciousness is for all time – eternity -- and is not transitory or comparable with anything else. Consciousness is beyond descriptive or intellective levels of communication simply because it is "pure", which means without any images or content. The form which holds the content can never exist without consciousness imaging its pattern. Therefore to teach of this content through forms, images or packaging of traditional information is not enough.

The consciousness which creates the "form" in all the manifested states is what we are after in Supersensonics. Once this is experienced, the kundalini can take any form imaginable to man's faculties. Then the universal sky is the limit.

Yet the patterns of nature, including the form of man's being, its sensorial equipment, the nervous system of molecules are all kundalini. In this sense we answered our opening question, "Is kundalini real?" It is as real as your own consciousness is real.

Once a human being is enlightened this is not the end of the road as most people think but only the beginning of a humiliating task. **The job of communicating it back through all the levels from the highest inspiration of the imagination down through the conceptual mind and into the physical manifestation is no easy task. In fact it represents the greatest challenge of the entire world beside which all other tasks appear easy. It is easier to become president of a country or become a famous person than to speak one word from the level of the nuclear centre and manifest it in the lives of others. The beings who have achieved this in the entire history of man, who speak to us through the minds of Christ and Buddha, Lao Tse and Krishna, are those who have this power to make the unnameable realm of God come alive in the heart.**

76

PENETRATING
THE IMAGINATION BARRIER

PENETRATING THE IMAGINATION BARRIER

If Nuclear Evolution is to step up life to its next level of manifestation in the human species there must be some way of contacting the cell life and programming it with the desire for change
and the ability to absorb more light and adapt to new thresholds
of cosmic energy. The cosmic energies are themselves not new
ones, since they have been radiating from different parts of the
zodiac around us in enormous amounts since the beginning of
time, but our individual response to them and our ability to sense
them and to understand them is new. If we are to use this new
faculty or awareness we must begin to tap that power within
man, within his consciousness, which enables him not only to
regenerate himself emotionally but to transform the actual
vehicle of perception – the body and its nervous system.

The use of the faculty of imagination in this process has hardly
begun. New techniques of visualisation are being discovered, such
as the method of healing cancer through hypnotic restructuring
of self-image by suggestion and the healing of psychosomatic
disorders through psychosynthesis or guided imagery. But these
techniques only use a fraction of the primordial quality we call
"imagination" and utilise the human faculty of fantasy more
often than imagination. There is an enormous difference between
the two but the problem is that the word "imagination" is used
by so many philosophers, healers and psychologists without there
being any real research on what it really is.

BRIDGING THE PSYCHIC GAP

This is not surprising when we consider the religious experiences
of mystics who describe going through the dark night of the soul,
that last desperate clinging to the familiar images of the world in
the face of the black unknown depths of the Nuclear Self beyond
the imagined condition of things.

The way to cross the psychic gulf between Violet and Black is
the re-training of the imagination which has been spoiled by the
continuous negative affirmations of separateness inflicted on all
humans by their cultures. The first image of Self as a child is
constantly pumped into the mind and imagination: "You are a
separate being from others. Your reality is that you exist only
inside your skin and that everything sensory, what you touch, see
or hear is objective, real and tangible. Whatever is in your universe
is 'out there'. 'In here' there is a private world that no one else
can enter. You are a human being and a separate reality from all
other reality. Everything you experience outside of your own
body is thus external to you and it is a ridiculous fantasy to think
that events in the real world are creations of your own imagination."

Until we take our imagination and study the way it works to recreate the universe around us, we will not solve this problem of man's image of himself. Yet this very image of a separate self not only limits our Self, but limits others when we are communicating with this separate image of the "otherness" of others. There can be no depth if we do not allow in our imaginations that there is anything deeper than our own level of thought, our own truth or experience of emotion, perception etc. Hence the training of our perception and the use of our true imagination rather than fancy or fantasy becomes an entire discipline in itself with its own profound methods of skillful penetration, just as there are skills in music, physics, gardening, meditation or any other human activity. To fill this need for restructuring consciousness the author has written a three-year correspondence course on the nature of direct perception which utilises a great number of techniques for development of the transforming power of true imagination. Those students of consciousness who would actually wish to perfect the primordial imagination to contact the cell life and develop the tuning power of resonance radiation, should write to the publishers for more details of the course of study. Since it would be possible to talk about the imagination for several weeks and to fill several books, we must here be content with an outline of what is fancy and what is true imagination.

WHAT IS IMAGINATION?

The word in the dictionary is defined as follows: "Imagination is the act or power of forming a mental image of something not present to the senses or never before perceived in reality." It is obvious that the word "Imagination" covers a vast part of our being if not the whole of Being. Considering that the faculty even at its fanciful level enters into all thought, conceptual operations, intellectual and mathematical imagery as well as every experience of external matter, the word "imagination" can hardly be said to be merely the imaging of something not present to the senses. Since everything sensory is also an image or pattern which must be recreated from the vibrational sensory impulses passing down the nerves from the skin or eye, from ear or tongue, etc. it cannot be said that this dictionary definition tells us anything about imagination. In fact it may be more confusing than enlightening, while sounding like an intelligent definition to those who do not have the true imagination to question its validity.

HOW DO YOU CONTACT THE CELL LIFE?

The pattern of life comes in the primordial image of our nervous system, two arms, two legs, head and a digestive and reproductive system very similar in pattern to those of the animals and insects. Primordial imagination, in which the predetermined images of the universe come to us is of course born with us. Whether we use this

79

imaging faculty which every baby has, or abuse it or train it so that we can learn to play it like an instrument, will depend on whether we value it as the instrument of perception by which we perceive the creation around us. Most people are totally unaware of its function in our thoughts as the dictator of our reality. The entire creation is presented to our consciousness in one primordial image or another, whether it is the image of our own body or the image of a spiralling galaxy. Whether it's the pattern of a snowflake or the delicate pattern of our own nervous system and brain, the entire creation is manifested to us in some form of an image; otherwise it is not real. This is the primordial imagination we are all born with and communication between ourself and a baby which has not yet learned any human language must take place at this primordial level for the first year of life.

Though we cannot recall it the very first year of our life was spent forming primordial images of hot and cold, mother and self, wet and dry, big and small, entirely through our imagination since we could not communicate with the universe with any language except the images produced by our senses. It is through this primordial faculty that the baby smiles at us in recognition of our being which is not merely a sensory input of a picture of a body with a head and two legs, but something which enables the baby to discriminate our vibrations from others that it does not like. Where does this difference come from in the central experience of the baby? The baby may respond to two strangers quite differently by using its higher imaginative faculty of pattern recognition or it might respond to all strangers with the same sense of insecurity through programming of fear images which leads us to a kind of imagination which is fanciful and not real. For good or ill, most people live by these inferior images, enjoy them and pay for them in suffering.

FANCIFUL IMAGES ARE NOT PRIMARY

The word "fancy" describes more accurately what the dictionary means by imagination since that would truly mean the faculty of seeing images or likeness not present to our senses. Human beings really mean "fancy" when they use the word imagination, something not real, images which roam around in the imaginary world somewhere and are quite unreal. This is not the primordial imagination which controls our destiny as a species. Yet we do not have another word for it. Let us discriminate more carefully.

Fanciful imagination is used not only by artists and poets but also by musicians. Beethoven's "Pastoral" symphony is able to give us an image of nature that touches the primordial part of our being that we are born with. The tree we pass every day without noticing comes alive in the words of a poet as he lends to us the power of his own vivid imagination. Yet these artistic images which have such power to move us are still only a pale imitation of that real creative power inside us. A painter, though he reshapes the world in his art, still only copies nature, and his works are objects of art one step further removed from the real prime imagination than nature herself who is the living artwork in every perceiver.

With people on the lower levels of evolutionary development, this copying of real life appears in popular songs which lure us romantically further and further away from the true imagination. Appealing to the desire for the love object in our imaginations, the love songs trigger emotions that make us lose control over our thoughts; the imagination becomes an inner demon ruling over our decisions, habits, and actions at a deep unconscious and uncontrollable level of manifestation. Our sorrows, even though fanciful and often not based on facts, as well as the lack of love objects which satisfy us, are painted in mental images which write themselves in the body. Our primal fears, real or imaginary, take their toll on the body.

People do not really have to say how they live, work or play. However we live shows directly on the face. Fear, deceit and frustration which lie deep in the heart spring from our primordial sense of being and how we imagine our self to be. It will not stay inside us without taking its toll on the garment of the skin, nerves and blood cells we wear. What lies deep in our self-image we wear in our heart center and what is hidden in the heart we wear on our faces. If we are selfish and self-centred it will not bring that light to the body that the mystics call grace. Only the primordial imagination can do that.

HOW CAN LIGHT PENETRATE INTO
NATURE'S PROCESSES WITHIN YOU?

The direct perception into nature's processes in the cell life of the organism can only be achieved by contact through the primordial imagination. We are all born with this faculty but quickly abuse it for ego-centric purposes and ignore its real purpose — the super penetration into the nucleus of life.

We have already written of the ability of light to ionise certain metallic crystal elements in the cerebrospinal fluid which changes its ph (alkaline/acid balance). The reader may be tempted, as many have been to write the process off as a description or theory. This is the way of mankind from the beginning. Certain imaginers come and tell us truth by using primordial images of what the kingdom of heaven is like. We then proceed to ignore their words as mere descriptions and put on them our own images which have nothing to do with their originators. For instance, Christ said nothing about harps, violins and idyllic fairy-like beings, devas, etc. existing in the kingdom of heaven, yet to talk to many priests it is obvious that they look on heaven as a place to go, an idyllic perfumed garden with harps, no work to do and no problems to solve. Since the self is the only problem it won't go away by listening eternally to heavenly strings or organ music or rock-like jazz or by watching continuous miracles being done. The image of such a place does not demand self-transformation, or the improving of our concepts of ego, the annihilation of separate self or any real turning back on self as it is, for the answers to our life situation are here on earth.

So it is with Nuclear Evolution. We read about cells reaching a saturated state of resonance radiation in Part III dealing with the physics of consciousness (page 807) and we probably say, "What a nice thought," but we do not believe it is really possible to take our imagination and turn it from fantasy into the primordial stuff. We cannot be totally convinced that it re-creates the self and the universe it experiences around it by the power of self-suggestion. This lack of conviction exists in us because the self does not know that the imaginer who creates the idea of a separate self, imagining itself as a human possessing an independent piece of mental substance we call a mind, is purely a creation of consciousness with all its power to suggest to itself that it is separate from the total environment it lives in! But this suggestion of separate individuality is not reality because, whether we like it or not, we are part of the whole and cannot escape it. The next step is to realise that Nuclear Evolution uses the power of the imagination to get into the DNA-RNA-ATP energy transfers mentioned in the physics of consciousness section which follows. The super penetration can only occur when we fully understand how we program the pure consciousness of Being with the contents of our imagination. We cannot get the electron pumps in the cell life to work consciously for enhanced oxidation and ionisation of the bioelectric field forces in our body until we can control internal events through the complete transforming power of prime imagination. Therefore more reaching into our own power of imagination causes us to look to the development of "direct perception" as a specific tool for training the instrument of consciousness for its evolutionary task. Once we see that the faculty of Prime Imagination created all the forms in the universe including us, then we become more willing to let go of our prized attachments to those forms and we are attracted to the divine. We begin to see that that same creative power could be ours but our "human" imagination and its fanciful images is always blocking the way.

HOW DO WE BECOME THE NUCLEAR SELF
AND PENETRATE EVOLUTION CONSCIOUSLY?

How can each individual wipe away the cravings, obsessions, and ideas which attach the mind to the status quo and which prevent the creative prime imagination from functioning? Allowing the false images, habits, and obsessions to govern our imaginative power, programs the future with more of what we are getting now. Your destiny is made by what you imagine now; your cells, in the same way, are not fixed biological mechanical units divorced from the field of the imaginer which creates your psychic environment. The obsessions which sit securely inside the imagination are demons waiting to be satisfied. They determine whether we shall feel rotten or feel good and in this sense they set up a biological stress field and inhibit the correct functioning of tissues and cells. It therefore becomes important to know how to use our imaginations. The poet uses the faculty skillfully to produce aesthetic reactions which have physiological effects on muscle tensions, emotional tension, sympathy, anger, sweat glands and so forth, but he may not have the power to direct the imagination into his own ego structure or penetrate the secret of good health for his bodily cells. He knows that words and images have the power to appeal to some deep part of ourself, to reach some divine sense of order in us, but do we, when we respond to his poetic imagination, understand that the power to make us respond deeply and emotionally can also be used to move our cells and nerves into liberation? Do we know that the primordial imagination can liberate us and our cells from slavery to our image of self-limitation? Do we know what it feels like to be free? Unless we have some imagined vision of what life is like for the enlightened person, will we ever want it or yearn for it enough to deprogram our existing fantasies?

The enlightened know that every thought and image of the world, that all the gods and hells and beauties, are created by our faculty to imagine and that even beyond that lies the real creative power of the universe in all its purity. That power being pure, lives in the imageless condition of life where it is always free to love the world as it is or to change it. The power to create primordial images is nothing less than mastery over the creative forces. Such powers are not given to those who are enslaved by images. The paradox is that these powers are given only to those who do not need them and who do not use them, for they see no separation between themselves and that consciousness which is working through all beings. The subtle manifestations of this cosmic power are reflected in the aesthetic experience of man in works of art, the beauty of a scientific theory, or the worship of the awesome.

IMAGINATION AND THE AESTHETIC EXPERIENCE

The aesthetic experience is a sensory one causing corresponding reactions in the whole being at physical levels of excitation
as well as intellectual, emotional and social levels of life. This is
the reason why the church introduced the powerful image of the
dead Christ bleeding and torn on the cross. This image was in
direct opposition to the teachings of Christ which preached the
joy of the resurrection and the ignoring of worldly pain and
persecution. However, its powerful negative image did help the
suffering and oppressed peoples through many centuries to
identify with their own impotence and helplessness and look to
the priests for their passports to heaven. It is around such images
that our own lives are built. The images of martyr or master, the
devoted one or the dazzling messiah who is self-obsessed, these
are all examples of secret self-concepts which determine our
future in society. They also dictate who will be with us in our
physical environment. These fundamental images determine the
stresses of our emotional life and the type of life experience we
select now and in the future. Yet they are not primordial ones!
How much more powerful are those of the creative intelligence!

PLAYING THE IMAGINATION LIKE AN INSTRUMENT

To be able to clear the imagination at will, leaving it free for
bigger and more important things is the first step to gaining full
control of the creative intelligence operating at the cellular level
of ion transport and light synthesis. Instead of admiring masters
of the fantasy level of imagination, such as our great actors,
artists, composers and poets, we join with their prime imaginations and participate by borrowing their skills, not by envying
their talents but knowing that they have disciplined more and
developed more the faculty of the primoridal direct perception
which they lend to us and so it responds in us too.

The Sanskrit word "Antakarana" has no English equivalent but
its meaning refers to the building of a psychic antenna through
the constant imaginings of a human being as it passes through
many lives. From the word "Antar" — within or internal, and
"karana" — acting or "kara" — action, the meaning is the subtle
inner instrument through which consciousness is acting. The
Antakarana is that instrument we create as we live our life, that
becomes so sensitive that it can pick up the cosmic signals for our
real purpose on the earth, so that we begin to live with more
precision and more skillfulness because our instrument of action
becomes more perfect, more refined, and we become more aware
that we are playing on that instrument that we ourselves are
creating with our consciousness. This instrument made up of all

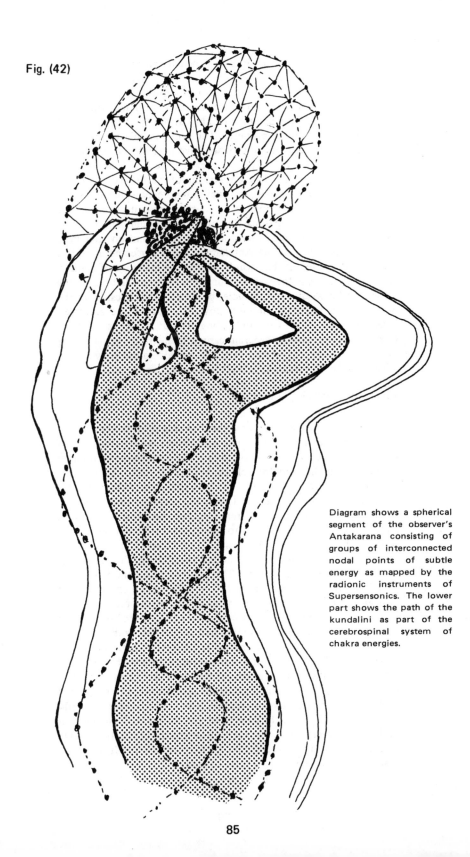

Fig. (42)

Diagram shows a spherical segment of the observer's Antakarana consisting of groups of interconnected nodal points of subtle energy as mapped by the radionic instruments of Supersensonics. The lower part shows the path of the kundalini as part of the cerebrospinal system of chakra energies.

the strings of our inner life can be tuned to subtle cosmic vibration or to the grossest vibrations through which we act. For example, when we have a reaction from within, it is a result of what is stored there and unless we understand what is the cause of that reaction, we will never be able to purify the instrument and learn to play on it properly. The inner vehicle will not just do anything we wish it to until we have perfect mastery of the instrument because the notes are very precise, the tuning of the frequencies very exact. The Antakarana obeys the exact laws of resonance like any other material phenomena, turning some people off and some people on like a radio, making a wave-guide and antenna for the broadcasting of the individual soul. It is just like a very fine antenna around us, just like rays of invisible light all knitted together. If the Antakarana is not perfected, it will be a very crude antenna. The whole universe is made up of sounds, vibrations, and it is the way we put them together that makes the difference between ordinary noise or music in our lives. Since the instrument is made of the most powerful stuff of the universe— consciousness — it can only be played by consciousness. Furthermore its cosmic program cannot be heard by physical ears but only by the ear of the ear. The cosmic music only comes alive when the Antakarana is built to hear its song.

HEARING THE COSMIC SONG

Not only do we have to know the instrument of perception but we must also learn to play it. The Antakarana is a combination of the inner magnetic part of the mind, the conscience or internal organ of thought, and the self-consciousness —Ego, all brought together in the self-sense called "I" who sits at the Nuclear Centre of Being. Bridging the gap between the physical body and the Nuclear Centre of the Antakarana can only be done by advanced students of consciousness who understand the nature of the subtle etheric vehicles. The psychic electricity in which the etheric matter is stored is time—bound and fixed in the primordial image of the chakra system. This system has sometimes been called by the name of the "astral body" but its energy is not "astral" or different from the vital forces of the physical body which is dependent upon it. It can be viewed as a shadow body or the field of the unconscious mind and is made of a subtle kind of matter, but nevertheless it is matter and has its own pattern in the imagination. There is nothing in the whole manifested universe of atoms, molecules, suns, stars, which does not possess such a shadow energy form which controls and governs the shape and pattern of its outer physical vehicle. The pattern of the butterfly wing is still printed in the caterpillar and its pupae. Its memory is biological, transmitted to each incarnation of itself. Human beings do the same except that their incarnation is from subtle matter to a more condensed form of energy.

86

Design of the symbol of Nuclear Evolution by Christopher Hills, 1957. Wreath surround designed by T.R. Henderson, 1965.

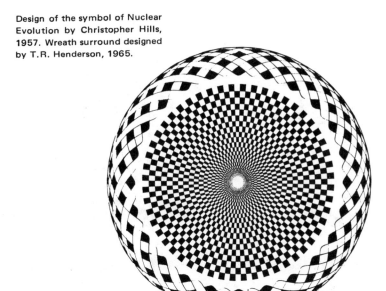

Fig. (43)

An actual clear-seeing (clairvoyant) view of these cakras (chakras) pulsating with psychic electricity in left and right-hand spirals, looks like the wheel symbol above, the number of petals varying from chakra to chakra. The direct perception of this subtle energy of consciousness is more important than the knowledge of its colour or being told what its function is. The instruments of Supersensonics are extensions of our Antarkarana (inner instrument of perception) and are capable of measuring the psychic electricity and detecting its frequency in each chakra. (See list of Supersensonic tools at back of this book.)

The building up of this nuclear entity of self through the perfection of the inner instrument in which our consciousness is acting, constitutes the real purpose of our incarnation upon this earth. The energies of the cosmos which are exchanged and redistributed throughout the universe by the action of light also help us to create the Antakarana by the accretion of every thought Just as a sea snail gradually building its calcite shell a thousand fathoms under the ocean records in the accretions of its rings the activity of the solar flares, so does the human being build its record in the light of consciousness. Like a cosmic hologram every thought and action and even our unconscious omissions are recorded in the subtle matter of this fine instrument. The energies in the system are primordial and are unconsciously found by the creative intelligence in the combination of the three Gunas.

Fig. (44)

These symbols were drawn by Col. T. Robert Henderson of Edinburgh, for the author in 1965.

See pages 556-563 for explanation of the above symbols.

This energy system is then combined by the thoughts and images in the human world and by the self desire of each entity in the created world of living organisms. In this sense an atom is a living organism with its own etheric cloud of electrons which ceaselessly changes and qualifies its manifestation to our senses and their etheric counterparts in the chakra system. Nuclear Evolution and this book is concerned with the levels of consciousness on which this etheric shadow vehicle functions. It clearly sets out the subtle links between our different faculties of perception and the physical world of matter as we experience it.

The Antakarana is essentially the bridge we build with our imagination between the two systems of the physical body and the etheric body. Communication between them consists of inter-locking lines of force radiating like the lines of force from the poles of a magnet. These lines of psychophysical energy flow back and forth through the seven planes of consciousness in each one of us. Streams of interlocking energies are flowing constantly through the etheric focal points in our human body. These whirl-ing wheels act as filters of life forces from the cosmic background radiations of starlight and sunlight. Everyday and all day these focal centers are awakened to the resonant frequencies of cosmic energy reaching into the etheric body. We are tuning ourself right now to a particular centre which may or may not become vibrant and excited like a radio antenna. If we are not ready we do not respond. Whenever anyone who is a beginner who has not trained themselves to penetrate the inner world tries to meditate or concentrate,they either fall asleep or the mind is distracted and begins to wander. If we can keep intent upon these focal points we gradually become responsive to the subtle throb of their vibration. The functioning of the chakra centres controls the reception of the subtle energy on the physical level of our body, and the centres are in turn controlled by the images in our consciousness. This dense cloud of atoms we call the physical body is continuously glued together by the chakra energies which pass through the etheric vehicle of consciousness. Even in what has been called astral travelling they do not separate but merely become attenuated. The astral or etheric energy can travel any-where and will take up any form we give to it. A dowser uses the same energy to pick up a response to a particular thought pattern of water or gold or mineral. Not only does the primordial imagination in our unconscious dictate the shape of physical form but the etheric form underlying the physical manifestation is also controlled by that specific chakra where the unconscious self is focussed.

To be able to hear the cosmic program through this instrument of perception each person chooses through the genetic hereditary line of their cells and thought patterns the particular point in the

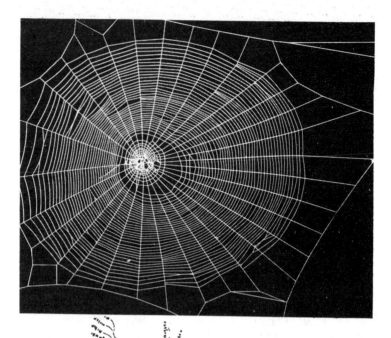

Fig. (45)

The Antakarana is built slowly by thought like an invisible spider's web which makes a good model of an antenna created to catch invisible cosmic rays.

Fig. (46)

The picture below is from an ancient Sanskrit text on the distribution of the nadis, the subtle tubes in which the psychic electricity (prana) flows outwards during the daytime and reverses its flow during sleep to recharge the body. In yogic sleep (yoga nidra) the prana flows in to raise the threshold of energy needed to synthesise light.

This flow of energy is achieved by complete relaxation of body, emotions, mind and intuition until the whole Antakarana is magnetised in a suspended state. Though motionless like the wire of an electric lamp, the current projects constant light in biolumin-escence.

evolutionary spiral when he will incarnate again and what circumstances will govern his manifestation. Whatever images are in the mind at death will determine the future incarnation of the soul.

The etheric vehicle and its seven major centres are tuned to the inflowing subtle energies which take up the pattern of being into which all these physical atoms fall in the primordial image of our soul nature. In other words deep in the centre of our consciousness there lies the pattern which has grown through evolutionary steps into the whole person that we are. All our successes and mistakes have been programmed and built up into the antakarana through many incarnations of which we are the total sum. This image of our idea of our self is helped, sustained and amplified by consciousness flowing into its form. Although there are over 72,000 lines of force in the network which we call the counterpart shadow body which the occultists call "Nadis" or channels, we are concerned here only with the controlling centres which tune the carriers of subtle energy along these tiny streams of lifeforce.

This then is the vibrating antenna which exists only in the subtle matter of the human aura connected to the physical body through the network of channels of life-force. Five of the major centres are connected to nerve plexuses around the spinal column and their corresponding endocrine glands, and two are centred in the cavities of the brain and related to the pituitary and pineal glands. This antenna built and refined by every thought and image is part of the inner instrument which listens to the cosmic song. The powerful effect of the in-flow of cosmic energy through the Antakarana, has a definite effect upon the blood cells, imprinting the primordial image of our being upon them and carrying that image to every cell. The music of creation with all its subtle tones and swirling forces plays to that image and is heard by every cell. The cosmic song is imprinted in every cell according to its own image in the blood. Like a hologram any part of it contains the image of the whole. Cut any part of it and there is a whole image again. Such is the wholistic system of chakra energies, blood, lymph and the liquid crystals that make up the miraculous human body and its Antakarana. The human body is a cosmic listening post in a vast sea of vibrations listening for an echo of itself. What it receives depends on the construction of the inner instrument and its program for the evolution of the image of itself as a point of resonance in the primordial hologram.

COMPOSING THE NEW MUSIC

As a co-creator of the primordial inner instrument we are then led by the evolutionary intelligence to the pathway of transformation of our entire patterns of consciousness. By certain techniques we can penetrate the nucleus which carries the genetic program of evolution. Most people cannot believe this is possible but actually it is very simple. The ability to change the fundamental images even at the fantasy level determines the kind of future which emerges as a result of all our unconscious thoughts and actions. Hence the ability to change primordial images made by nature enables us to become master of self, master of the contents of our minds and imaginations, not continuously affected by the imaginations of others. Once we are master of our imaginative faculty we are never disturbed in our bodies and minds by chaotic conditions. The images which lurk in our own minds, whether they be poetic, artistic, musical, political, fanciful, unreal or false, can only have the power we give to them, hence the self-discipline required to cut off their power and re-program our lives cannot effectively be done for us by anyone else. The exercise requires that we first learn total detachment from what we already know and detachment from conceptual modes of knowing, whilst having compassion on those who are still imprisoned in the mind. The super-penetration of nature's way is beyond the mind and its concepts. To achieve Nuclear Evolution we must penetrate through our labyrinthian mind-stuff without identifying with it.

THE POWER OF VISION

Our greatest men have had the power to see beyond the ordinary perception of parts and their limitations into wholes. Their particular kind of vision has not just been a fanciful new idea or merely another way of saying old things but there is something original about them, some quality that says something about what is ancient in such a new way that it is a fresh and original insight into nature in its own right. This ability to paint original pictures in the mind of the worlds beyond ordinary description gives a person direct contact with the transforming power of the primordial imagination. Their little descriptions of invisible worlds beyond our own experience are very convincing and like first-hand witnesses, they have the ring of authority and truth. They describe the states we ought to be in because they themselves have experienced those states in reality and not in some fanciful way. Christ talks of the Father being inside the sparrow which does not fall to the ground without consciousness being aware of itself falling. If we think God is somewhere other than everywhere, we tend to think it rather marvelous that God knows what we are thinking, but to Christ it was just normal and not marvelous at all. He saw that God and consciousness were one. He saw consciousness without any images of itself was pure consciousness; and pure consciousness could enter into a sparrow, an atom, a planet or the cell life of a plant or a man. There was no awesome miracle here, what was awesome was what that intelligence created in the myriad patterns and images out of its own pure consciousness. Every human is a duplicate of this consciousness constantly re-creating the myriad universes in its own imagination, mirroring itself. All of Christ's images are reflections of nature mirroring its own image back to his clear imagination.

THE IMAGE OF THE SEED

Christ's parable of the sower of seed and his image of the kingdom of God as a mustard seed is identical with the concept of Nuclear Evolution. The word nuclear comes from Nux meaning seed, or kernel as opposed to husk. Why is heaven like a seed? Because the seed has new life in its inert self. When it germinates and sprouts it only needs the right conditions to grow of itself into a new shoot, and in that new shoot the seed leaf contains the potential of hundreds of new seeds to come. Christ used this image to say that the truth is like that, that it comes from a small seed which has its own truth within it which is its inner authority. When it grows to maturity the seed is multiplied a hundred fold. If we come along and screw up the process by sowing it on stony ground then there will be no germination, no truth realised or spreading by its own life within it. Hence Nuclear Evolution is like the seed in the imagination of mankind. If the soil of the imagination is well composted and well weeded the seed of the nux of being must inevitably bear fruit of itself by cosmic laws of the primordial imagination.

THE IMAGE OF LIGHT AND CONSCIOUSNESS

To illustrate the difference between imagination as fantasy and the creative imagination there is another primordial image taken direct from Christ's penetrating insight into nature. "The eye is the lamp of the body" he says. Obviously he is not talking about lamps but something which the lamp does. The metaphor is saying that the lamp does the same thing that the eye does — it shines. Because the lamp shines with its own light you don't take another lamp to see a lamp. Neither do you take another consciousness to see your own consciousness. Authentic imagination is seen with its own light; just as the lamp has its own light, so the human eye is the lamp of the human body and has its own light to see itself by. That light is the primordial imagination which lights everything up inside our heads as brightness. When radiation strikes a receptor such as an eye, the signal is carried down the optic nerve to the brain as a nervous spike of electricity. When it reaches the occipital in the brain it is reconstructed at the seat of consciousness as brightness, while the original stimulus is merely invisible radiation, quite colourless and transparent as a radio wave passing through space. The light we see is not the real light but an internal psychic reaction to an external stimulus.

The real light is consciousness itself which shines like the invisible rays of a lamp. Hence Christ says truly, with another primordial image, "Ye are the light of the world", meaning "your consciousness lights up the world." He is not using fantasy images but primordial images which correspond not as metaphors but descriptions of fact. Thus Nuclear Evolution if applied to the whole of nature uses the faculty of the Prime Creative Imagination to penetrate and enhance the ionisation of body fluids and to charge the psychophysical nature of the genetic programming in the DNA-RNA-ATP energy transfers for more efficient oxidation of the metabolic fluids. The details of this scientific analogy have been placed in Part III as an example of a factual process of wholistic group interactions. The "Physics of Consciousness" was written in 1967 and published in 1968. Nothing published in the years between the first and this third edition of Nuclear Evolution has changed the process or the understanding of the process.

PRIMORDIAL IMAGINATION

We have written at length on the nature of fantasy as a quality of our creative imagination in order to discriminate the difference between the cosmic imagination which makes the outlines of things, and the kind of imagination we have called fanciful which blurs the outlines and makes things all fuzzy. The cosmic imagination doesn't see any outlines unless it makes them itself by preventing itself looking at all the fields within fields which make up the whole. By creating a field or a pattern of energy of itself, it separates itself from itself by becoming an observer of its own outlines. The only real difference between the cosmic imagination and the type of "fancy" which creates fuzziness is that the whole ONE knows that any image which limits anything by outlines was put there in the first place by its own pure consciousness, whereas fuzzy outlines are always put there by something else or someone else who is fuzzy. The purpose of the next few pages is to give some exercises which free our conceptions and release our prime imagination so that the student of consciousness can visualise and then imagine what it would be like to be the ONE whole, which while containing outlines within itself, does not regard them as any big deal. All our sages including Christ have said, "Thou art that One." The difference between Christ and ordinary men is that he knew it. Mankind has this capacity to think as light, to think in light, and to identify with the wholeness that light is, before it manifests to our senses. There are no outlines with light until it is encompassed in matter.

The prime imagination is not the stuff that makes unreal fantasies but the stuff that makes you know what you are so that if anyone asks you and you identify with your body, you will say "that's who I am" or if you identify with your mind, "that's me" or your soul "that's my identity, the real me." So a cabbage has within it the primordial image of "I am a cabbage, man, and a cabbage is all I want to be and I'm going to keep on being a cabbage and beget other cabbages." If the cabbage had the capacity to look at a carrot and wish it could be like that, then in several generations (by evolution) it would become a carrot. But it has not the capacity.

Man has the capacity with every breath to consciously plant an image throughout the inner hologram. Hence some breathing exercises follow later which must be practiced in order to understand the truth and replicate it in one's own vehicle. You can do all the deep breathing and yoga breathing you want to and all you'll get is hyperventilation, because it is just quantitative. But if you do qualitative breathing, then you will put an image from the prime imagination into the process and it will change you. The key to the process is in the intensity of the imagination; in proportion to the intensity, so will be your results. If in chanting Om, the name of God, you exhale all your breath, then you will have to inhale, you have no choice, and if you have sent out this kind of radiation on the exhalation (this reverence for God), what will you have coming back to you on the in-breath?

Whatever you imagine is passing through your subtle astral tubes will eventually take place in the gross body. In dreams we experience directly and you don't ask the dreamer if he can believe his own eyes or accept what he is seeing in his dream. He is the dream, and in the same way your waking consciousness is still a dream in your imagination. The task is to purify your imagination and the channels it uses to communicate between the seven worlds of our Being, to realise that you only 'imagine' you are as awake now as you will ever be. You can only know you are asleep by waking up. So there is another state of imaging which we practice within the seven worlds that when you experience it you will say "I was asleep when I thought I was wide awake".

AVAILABLE TECHNIQUES FOR
PENETRATING THE IMAGINATION BARRIER

In order to make the foregoing come alive and to give the reader a rudimentary idea of its success as an evolutionary tool, the following steps set out a technique which enters into the process of conscious Nuclear Evolution. Since the first edition of this book, the author has written the previously mentioned three-year course in direct perception specifically so that others may train in depth and see the power of the primordial imagination to command and influence the cell oxidations in the brain and evolve the instrument of life.

As a method of healing the self and stabilising the spiritual and emotional life, this method of "direct perception" offers any individual who will be totally committed to practicing it for three years, the ability to control their own thoughts and imaginations at will. The course uses all the images brought to earth by the great seers and prophets of every religion without indulging in religious sentimentality, self-pity or guilt. The ability to penetrate the heart of every cell and the heart of the Nuclear Self is the prime object of commitment and not to worship any specific personality figure or doctrine. In short, the method penetrates the primal imagination and we see what we really are rather than what we think we are. The object of any technique of training the Self, especially our imagination, must be to avoid those fanciful images of Self which have little power to influence the course of destiny. Everyone who incarnates contains some false imagery in the mind or they would not be thinking of themselves as a human being. The task of each individual being, however high spiritually, is to avoid distorting human reality with those basic assumptions about themselves or others. These false images create erroneous pictures of life, pollute our image of others and ourself. This pollution of our imagination, whether it is the mental self-centredness and narcissism of most spiritually inclined people or merely the exclusive concentration on do-gooding in the external world, will always block the achievement of inner peace and prevents our using the power of the golden mean, the balanced way.

To achieve inner peace we must meditate and learn to watch the motions of the mind. We must also learn how to work on the imagination which we use to create our reality from day to day. But it is not sufficient to quiet the mind only, as taught by so many schools of meditation. On the first real test the ego structure will reassert itself unless the primal image of Self has been understood. Spiritual students are notorious for their self-righteousness and blindness to ego and many a swami who teaches about the ego has not mastered his own system. Therefore beware of any self-satisfaction in programming our divine imagination. There is a vast difference between contentment and self-satisfaction, between cosmic bliss and ordinary everyday ecstasy, and between being and saying. The three-year course is designed to confront us with those images that lie hidden deep in the consciousness of our being. The students who take it are those who have been searching for years in one authority or another for many incarnations. They find in it the marrow of them all, since it is expressly written to find not the earthly wisdom of man, but the magic spiritual power within his own soul - which is God.

This course is not for everybody and certainly not for those who think it should be all made easy for them. The practice of white magic or natural magic is the beginning of wisdom and it was on this account that the wise men were called magi. The magic of Nuclear Evolution follows the same path as Christ himself trod, viz. humility, charity, mercy, continence, prayer and healing. However, because the true magic of our imaginations cannot be given completely until people are ready and have met the conditions set by cosmic laws along the evolutionary spiral, the following techniques are given to those readers who would wish to probe the enormous power of imagination immediately.

There is in all individuals that power of perception we have called divination, which is a complete system within ourselves - the microcosm. We carry in this divine instrument of divination*

---

* A study of the author's 608 page book "Supersensonics" gives a complete account of this instrument and the tools we can use to amplify the diviner's perception.

a kingdom of heaven from the very beginning of time which God, the all-pervading field of intelligence, has sealed in us; his own image of pure consciousness. For those who would not commit themselves for three-years of life to continuous practice, the following will help them to ask counsel of God and take instruction from their own divine soul.

A SIMPLE METHOD OF SELF-TRAINING

STEP 1: SELF-KNOWLEDGE

Meditation and self-introspection must not be done to the exclusion of the practical things of life. Therefore find some instruction or initiation in some system of self-knowledge. Follow it by keeping a spiritual diary, a control book for your eyes alone. You write in it all your habits, weaknesses, passions, failures, expectations of life and ugly character traits. There are some good methods of keeping this dialogue with yourself for the purpose of self-analysis. The Progoff method is excellent or the reader may write the publisher for details.

STEP 2: GROUP CONSCIOUSNESS

The purification of the imagination at its deepest levels involves the cleaning out of the conceptual mind to make it into an instrument of dynamic spiritual action rather than making it inert and passive. To experience the nature of its reality we must take note of our weaknesses and not pretend that we have worked on them when we have not. Nothing must be hidden from the Self. To be sure that we are not indulging in the type of self-analysis which has narcissist overtones while hiding under some respectable traditional religious path, we must be continually open to group feedback. This cannot be done unless the group can be trusted to be compassionate, otherwise the Ego will always tend to paint the lily whiter than it is. In additon to keeping a diary and meditating alone, we should also practice some form of creative conflict and ask ourself some confrontation questions in the group situation. To make sure that the work on ourself has really been done in the heart and not just recognised in the head, we should find a group or form a group of people interested in working on themselves. The basic rules of creative conflict have been set out elsewhere in this book. To work with a group does not mean we accept all the projections of the group, but if we are misunderstood by the group it points to some lack of clarity in our own imagination and communication power. This alone is an important investigation. To react to group feedback shows us we are still imprisoned in the Ego. However painful, we must then go back to square one until all signs of self-righteousness and conceit in our own wisdom have disappeared. To find such a group is not easy and you may have to create one. There are ways of going about this available from the publishers.*

STEP 3: BREATH AND CONSCIOUSNESS

The physics of consciousness demands that we maintain a healthy and wholistic body through breath control and proper understanding of the levels of consciousness on which it functions. It is not part of this book to bring in yoga postures and physical exercises but a clean vehicle of consciousness is a prerequisite for the next step.**

To contact the cell life directly through breathing and the oxidation of the brain metabolites we must begin training the function of the nerve dendrites. This method of creating psychic electricity causes stimulation at the nerve ends and causes the dendrites to grow towards the areas of greatest stimulation. (See "Rumf Roomph Yoga"– a system for transmitting life-force, available from the publisher.) Conscious breathing includes several steps. The first step involves the impregnation of the idea or concept we wish to achieve into the Akasha or the formless invisible light of consciousness so that it may be endowed with the brightness and form of visible light and patterned clearly in our imagination. This is achieved by placing the image intensely into the Akasha in the air we breathe so that it penetrates to the primordial imagination in each cell. The molecules of air are stripped of oxygen which is carried in the blood cells to all other cells of the body. It is not often known that blood cells can carry the life print of the whole body and act as a witness for the total field of a person. The new science of radiational paraphysics shows that the witness of oxygen and blood acts as a broadcast frequency for the entire body. Therefore, by planting the seed of the image in the Akasha of the air the imaged pattern permeates the blood and endows the electric fluids of the bodily instrument with prana or life-force in that pattern of ionisation. By consciously breathing in the concept of Nuclear Evolution with each breath the vast energy of the earth's field and the radiation of stars and sun is converted to our individual use as consciousness.

---

* See "Conduct Your Own Awareness Sessions" by Christopher Hills with Robert Stone (published by Signet Books) now rewritten and published as "Exploring Inner Space" by Christopher Hills, edited by D. Rozman and S. Welker.

** See "Wholistic Health and Living Yoga" by Malcolm Strutt, published by University of the Trees Press.

Everyone gets the same quantity of this radiating life-force but not everyone is physically or psychically tuned to use the same amount or extract it from the background radiation of the universe. In the same way it is not the quantity of air we breathe that makes the sodium – potassium trigger fields work but the quality of the conscious imagination subtly impregnating the air molecules before we breathe them in. We must learn to visualise the molecules of actively oscillating air being flavoured with the aroma of the idea as we take in each breath. Nor is this a far-fetched idea as it is well known amongst sensitives that they can smell certain vibrations given off by people. Noticeably sex perversion and even raw unperverted sex drive have their own characteristic smells, as does the psychic aura of a baby, the stale smell of a poltergiest or the sweet smell of a holy place or saint. Ionised air of the woods or the seaweed ozone is caused by the action of light on chlorophyll and iodine. In exactly the same way consciousness, being identical with light and radiation at a more subtle level, can interact with all plant life, air molecules, and liquids.

The second step after impregnation of the air molecules with the primordial imagination is to achieve conscious control over the firing of the trigger fields and to charge the tiny villi on the inner walls of the ventricles with negative ions. This ionisation of the extracellular body fluids makes the fluid inside the inner walls of cells into a positive charge. The polarity laws of electrostatic fields work the same way as the magnetisation of molecules. Just as the atoms of iron line up and orientate themselves in the presence of magnetic fields so do the poles of molecules in fluids and liquid crystals behave. The human body is full of metabolic compounds which are "liquid crystals", the largest one being cholesterol. Step four is concerned with the polarised molecules becoming irradiated with tuned cosmic radiation from the stars and the sun. To get some concept of this cosmic radiation surrounding us everyday, let us just look at the tremendous magnitude of one star Cygnus A at 10^{38} watts. The radio energy radiated by this source in one millionth of an earth second is sufficient to supply all of the world's electronic power requirements for all purposes, such as light, heat and mechanical work etc. at a million times the present rate of consumption for the next ten million years. Since Cygnus A is 600 million light years away its power to affect our brain fluids may not be as potent at the lower chakra levels as that of the millions of other stars in our own galaxy which are only a few light years away. Sirius, a smaller star, is 40,000 times as dense as our sun and only 8.7 light years away, therefore is much more potent than the larger Cygnus A. So these stellar rays from nearby stars which ionise the polarised body fluids and liquid crystals determine the plus or minus of all unbalanced brain fields. Hence the single electrons in the outer orbits of sodium and potassium atoms can be stripped easily. It is estimated that to remove one of the K electrons or inner orbit electrons from the sodium atom would take 1,000 electron volts. Only 47 electron volts are sufficient to move one of the electrons from the next or L middle orbit and only 5.14 electron volts to remove the single outer electron from the M orbit.

The electrical voltages of static electricity which can pass through the human body without harm so long as there is no earthing of the charge, can go up to 500,000 volts in the author's personal experience. Therefore it is not far-fetched to say that cells pass on their electric charge from the sun and other ionising stars to other cells. The pulsing blood cells are kept alive by their electric charge which repels them from each other. If they assimilate radiation in resonance with the charge of their molecules they become saturated and discharge, making the cells come together and coagulate.*

Hence the direction of the image in the air to the blood cell and thence to oxidation in the brain cells makes step four an important part of the process of tuning to the cosmic energies. This ionisation of the cerebro-spinal fluids is achieved by using the imagination in deep yogic trance through the power of self-suggestion. The visualisation of Self as one with the total environment and all its radiative properties is part of step four. But the process also requires that we imagine our food also as a carrier of the most intense imagination, not so much as lumps of solid matter but as a form of concretised light. Consciously we bless our food as we eat it with the idea that it is the light of the sun and stars locked up in the very idea that our bodies have now become – crystalised light. At every meal we bless our food knowing that this light synthesis is passing into the wholistic cell system of body and soul, reprogramming the cells with a new idea of themselves as cosmic light without limits set by the owner of the body. This programming of the imagination into wholistic health patterns is the opposite of what we have been doing with human consciousness for countless incarnations in the flesh. Instead of visualisation of our body as crystalised light we have repeatedly imagined it at the depths of our primordial imaging power to be matter and solid. By continuous visualisation of our own consciousness as light and our food as light, the ionisation of brain cells can be bathed with the thought and image of the divine purpose. Whenever we do these steps three and four we make sure that the same image we put into the air we breathe is the same image we project into our food so as to reinforce the

---

* See "The Physics of Consciousness" Part III.

wave-field and not create interference waves at the mental level of the conceptual mind. It is important to note that the imagination functions beyond the mental level but the two levels can still be in conflict, and therefore one must be on guard not to have conflict between thoughts on one level and images on another level, which divides the wholeness of the person and creates the experience of the self-sense. The self-sense is not real, we are not separate from the radiation of the stars, but our imagination has so far negatively programmed this. Hence only that which programmed it can take it out.

STEP 4: PROGRAMMING CONSCIOUSNESS INTO WATER

In the ionisation of body fluids and particularly the cerebrospinal fluid, water plays the most important part. One of Christ's primordial images is that we cannot be regenerated without spirit and water. Water can be impregnated with primordial imagination to the point that it can not only act as fuel for oxidation and reduction in the body tissue but also as a sink for the elimination of unwanted vibrations of Akasha. Water can be ionised with orgone and life-force (prana) and can be magnetised by the primordial imagination to the point that it can be seen visually. Take two glasses of water and impregnate one of them through the fingertips with the idea of holy water. Ask a stranger, preferably a child without mental clutter to choose which glass of water you magnetised. He or she will actually "see" the difference. This impregnation you do with all liquids containing water, visualising the idea of light entering the water through the power of consciousness. The correct temperature of the water should be divined with a pendulum before impregnation so that there is resonance between the molecular agitation of the water and the vibrations of our consciousness. After a while we become automatically selective of water at the right temperature for us. Whenever we are washing or bathing, the pollution of our mental environment can be impregnated into the water and run down the bath hole. Consciously hold the hands either side of the tap faucet allowing all failures to pass into the water stream. When you take a bath magnetise the water first in your imagination and then mentally strip off all negative thoughts into the water while bathing, programming them into the Akasha of the water and letting them drain away into the sink hole.

STEP 5: CLEARANCE OF THE INSTRUMENT
OF PERCEPTION

Take an eye bath for direct perception by planting the idea of resonance radiation and ionisation into the water. Every morning take some boiled water and impregnate the water with the prana breath. Using a small basin or an eye bath open the eyes in the water and roll them around to the left up and right down, then roll them right up and left down, and then all the way round to the right and then to the left in a circle. Repeat this exercise seven times. A homeopathic solution of Euphrasia (Eyebright) can be added or the water placed in a psychotronic device such as the Pi-ray Coffer if there is some weakness in the eyes (see back of book for instruments,).

The following exercise is to charge the physical body up with active etheric forces so that the light of consciousness is increased and the vehicle of consciousness made more effective. The exercise is taken from one of the sections of the three-year course in direct perception, "Into Meditation Now".* It is used as a stepping stone to pure light. Heat is caused by excessive absorption of light, and light is caused by excessive absorption of heat. Any concentration of either will produce the other, as they are both the same in essence. Similarly, light and consciousness are the same.

1. Visualise yourself surrounded by life energy (prana) and hold in the back of your mind the sole motive and will to enlightenment. If you use this method for psychic tricks and display of powers all you will get out of it will be just that – the adoration of the weakminded and gullible.

2. Breathe as follows:

Hold the left index finger over the left nostril. Breathe in and out of the right nostril gently as you turn your head slowly to the right. Do this three times.

Hold the right index finger over the right nostril. Breathe in and out gently through the left nostril three times as you turn your head slowly to the left.

Take in three normal breaths gently through both nostrils while keeping the head to the front.

Repeat the steps above but breathing stronger and stronger, moving the head faster and faster.

Repeat the first steps above, this time breathing very hard in bellows fashion and moving the head even more rapidly in between each breath.

---

* "Into Meditation Now" by Christopher Hills. Information available from the publishers.

3. The above steps were physically performed while you were visualising yourself surrounded and in the midst of a fiery ball of life-force. There are three steps to this visualisation practice:

   a) Visualise yourself completely enclosed in life-force or prana or radiant biological energy while performing the above breathing steps.

   b) Visualise this life-force entering your body through the pores and travelling up from the base of your spine to the top of your head and radiating out horizontally throughout your nervous system while you do the breathing steps.

   c) Meditate fixedly on that symbol or picture which signifies to you personally the highest expression of life you know of as you do these breathing steps. After you have done the breathing, stroke the symbol or photograph four times without touching it, while visualising Cosmic heat energy flowing from it into your fingertips and into your own body.

4. See the breath, your own action, the symbol or picture, the visualisation of energy and heat as all part of the ONE, the non-duality of the vehicle, your body, and the Cosmic Oneness of which you and it are a part.

5. Know this cosmic fire as Agni or Love. No words can describe it. If you wish to call it Agape or Christ Consciousness or just plain God, no one will care, least of all God. God is the experience of it and He will let you call it any name you like best. He likes it best when you stop talking about it and experience Him in the silence.

6. The next step is to hoist yourself up to the highest observation point where one imagines the Self has been melted by the fire and there is no subject or object, i.e. you have become the very light created by the intensity of the heat. You have absorbed all the forms which light takes, on contact, and there is now just a self identification with the Light of Consciousness as a luminous cloud of intelligence in which one is vibrating on all frequencies.

7. You then realise the nature of the Light of the Universe which is perceived and the Light of Consciousness which perceives it.

8. You visualise yourself looking into a bright light such as the sun or incandescent source. You feel its rays pouring into you enveloping the entire being, beginning first as a soft gentle rain on the skin, and then penetrating deeply through and through.

9. The descent of the light from the source ceases and you are aware that it is spreading outwards from you through your consciousness of being it. One feels and sees the light though it is transparent, clear and formless.

10. One becomes conscious of living in seven universes at the same time as the light filters through and outlines the chakras and psychic centres.

11. These centres are made of the light structuring itself in whorls of psychic electricity in the etheric body and interpenetrating each other, and we become aware of the functions of these centres as step-down transformers that we can vary with the frequency of the consciousness which we pass through them.

12. We feel the crown centre glowing hot and bright as an intense sunflower growing from out of the sun, out-pouring its rays from the heart centre and enclosing us in concentric rings of coloured light like the rainbow.

13. We see that consciousness is identical to external light, that literally there is no difference. That the non-physical light of consciousness works in exactly the same way as physical light and that one without the other is unmanifest and non-existent. One becomes one with the eye of God seeing through His own vehicle of intelligent, luminous consciousness, using human eyes or looking through other forms of nature such as trees, animal eyes, stars, etc. or listening to voices coming through the various expressions of life and light.

14. With this light of consciousness you then ponder and contemplate the nature of "PURE" light, which created consciousness itself. Because it is Pure and there is nothing in it except a certain "suchness", nothing whatever can be said about it by consciousness without making it impure. Hence only adoration of it is possible and then all commentary stops.

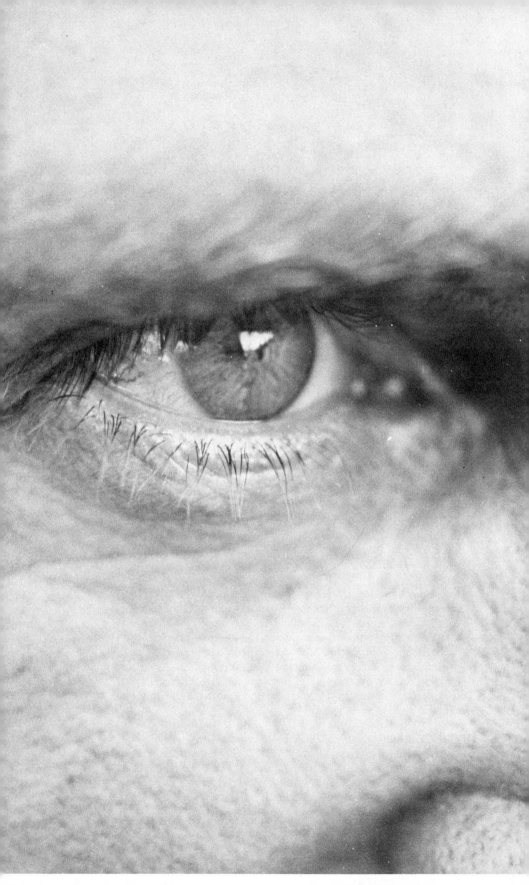

BIOLUMINESCENCE

BIOLUMINESCENCE: THE CHEMISTRY OF LIGHT

In order to understand evolution not by hindsight nor even with just foresight but with deep insight into the awe-inspiring ways that the Evolutionary Intelligence is working in us to bring us to perfection, we must look at evolution not only at the level of "how did the giraffe get its long neck?" or "how is the social behaviour of monkeys similar to humans?" but at the much more fundamental physical level of cells and molecules and chemistry on the one hand and the corresponding psychic levels of consciousness organisation on the other. Man has now reached the ultimate biological complexity of protein synthesis of material atoms, and the micro evolution process awaits the next stage of man at the macro level of being: to live from light.

In another part of the book (pages 613,807) I have described how we humans ingest light, depending upon our psychological drives and reactions, and how we excrete unused or unwanted light which appears as the aura. The excretion process is a faint and subtle bioluminescence. In this section, I will discuss how the body's various electrochemical processes enable the ingested light to be absorbed, assimilated and transduced, and how our system of energy transfer is **both modified by and modifies** our psychological level of consciousness. In other words, I will show biochemically why we tend to remain in the same level of consciousness and to maintain the same attitude stance and to radiate the same amount of life-force year after year. The quality of our elimination of light determines what we will next ingest and process in a continuous cycle. So there is a tendency for the seven filters through which we process the light of our awareness to bring back to themselves the same kind of light and to nourish themselves by highly selective ingestions of light energy. This self-perpetuating tendency (the force of inertia or stability, as opposed to the evolutionary force of change) explains such stereotypes as spiritual people who take in light at the Blue frequency and radiate it out as devotion, yet continue to reject the Red or Yellow energies of that same light which they are supposedly worshipping as "the One". Conversely the red-neck, physically orientated people will continue to reject the devotional or abstract levels of consciousness as unreal or pie-in-the-sky, shutting themselves off from several levels of experience.

Bioluminescence is the spontaneous emission of light from organic compounds and molecules which takes place at the chemical level of our (unconscious) awareness. But this chemical cycle of ingestion, absorption, digestion, assimilation and elimination of light energies is produced at the psychological level by the interaction of seven personality shells. The link between these two — between matter and the spirit which animates it -- is the age old riddle and only now is man coming to the time when he may solve it. The fact that light can spontaneously be emitted from organic compounds and molecules found in cell proteins suggests that the proteins of the human body are not inert masses of insensitive flesh but act as semiconductors and transistors like we use in radio reception. Very few people in history have discovered the exciting link between the molecule level of our being and the levels of personality we experience as consciousness. Once man discovers and begins to use the subtle connections between atoms, molecules, cells and consciousness, then he will experience an evolutionary leap in understanding comparable to the physical leap by which primitive organisms such as the amoeba were enabled to evolve into fantastically more complex organisms such as man.

THE NEXT STEP

In effect we are now returning to that primitive cellular level of the structure of our being but at a higher rung of the evolutionary spiral. The ability of the skin of the amoeba to find its food and propel itself through its watery environment by sensing its direction is inherited by man's skin in the water divining phenomenon. But man in his long climb through evolution has lost the conscious use of this faculty of the physical molecules to respond to excitement and polarity of radiating energy. Man is now at the threshold of becoming conscious (but at a tremendously higher level than that of an amoeba) of these unconscious processes of the supersensitive atomic, molecular and cell level of his functioning.

The proteins which make up the animal nerve fibres store the polarised energies, which then make up human consciousness at the higher level of the spiritual being. Therefore to consciously enter the world of the cell, the molecule, the protein, is to gain mastery of consciousness in a different way than we usually think of it. To gain mastery of the chemical processing of light is to change the way we relate psychologically to people and to life, just as these psychological levels of our identity also drastically affect the way our micro self is creating our bodies, our moods, and the kind of energies which our brains receive to do the work of gaining self-mastery. Because of this vicious circle, mastery must happen not just at one level of our being but at all levels, even to the I AM at the heart of the atom.

People accept the idea that the spirit is immortal, but they usually do not realise there is a continuity of the flesh as well. Not only has the spirit never died but the body cell proteins have never died either. The body has passed its characteristics along from generation to generation of cells in the same way that the spirit has unfolded from incarnation to incarnation, and in fact these two evolutionary processes are one and the same. The physical sperm carries in it,imprinted in the DNA molecule in the cell nucleus, the whole long history of consciousness including the choices that were made and the actions that were never taken and the world-changing plans of the great and mighty and the unfulfilled dreams of the masses. We are products of these consciousness-links that came before us, and in the whole long line of evolution which produced the bodies in which the physical seed is being formed again,that may or may not change the future of the world (depending on how we are using our consciousness right now), not one sperm nor one ovum is missing in this long physical chain of life. Our evolution is wholistic because consciousness is One.

The following diagram is a graph of man's long period of growth from the original cell. There has been no physical break in reproduction since the beginning. Abraham's seed is our seed. As living proteins, the physical body is a continuous union of protein cells in sperm and ovum from the time human life began.

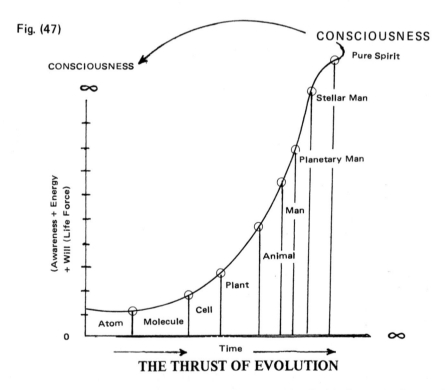

Fig. (47)

THE THRUST OF EVOLUTION

The Evolutionary Thrust proceeds in jumps from one threshold of organisation to the next more complex level. Simplification is achieved by synthesis of many complex functions into one higher governing organism such as the atom → molecule, organs ——→ brain, brain → mind, mind/memory → consciousness.

Each step up from one state to the next has required a greater degree of organisation and a level of awareness which, compared to the state below it, amounts to a supersense. The fact that plants respond emotionally to human consciousness shows that we are linked with their molecular proteins and cell structures despite the fact that we have, in complexity of organisation and function, surpassed them on the evolutionary spiral. In other words, we are linked with them at the sensitive cell and molecule level of awareness even though there is no affinity at the level of life-styles.

What has happened at the micro level is that human cells have interactions and affinities with molecules more sensitive to light rays in other parts of the radiation spectrum, thus bringing emotional and psychological fields to bear on the chemical organisation. The process is analogous to the way in which a crude and insensitive person, living with people whose vibration is rarified and subtle, would gradually experience a lifting of his level of consciousness. The vibration rates of the cells are in this same way heightened to produce new levels of functioning. Like a ratchet, the energy of the cell is jacked up to a higher potential which requires a new order of government to regulate the more complex interactions between cells and the nerve currents which unconsciously control their functioning.

NO SEPARATION

This same ratchet effect of the heightening vibrations of man's **macro** molecules brings us to the next step; man must stop dividing his consciousness from the material world (including his own body) which he perceives as an object. By studying the electrical, magnetic and bio-energetic exchanges between man and the crystal elements in his environment, we can understand how mankind evolved and continues to evolve out of that light which is materialising his present psychic faculties.*

The leap from one level to the next in the long chain of evolutionary reproduction has always been achieved through the attraction of the male/female polarities which creates the dance of life. Several atoms come together as a group and become molecules and the polarities in the atoms then polarise the molecules so that they also pair off into groups and become cells, and so on into greater and greater complexity and hence into a constantly increased positive or negative electrical potential. Higher functions become possible which were not possible at

---

* Refer to "Supersensitive Life of Man" series of six volumes in references at end of section.

111

simpler levels of organisation. These subtleties are visible, for instance, in the vast range of expression possible to the human face or in the fact that a being like Christ could consciously manifest the supreme laws of the universe.

All this originally springs from the simple attraction of positive for negative, male for female: nature's most basic law. The electric polarity of the cell is correlated with the electric currents which result from cell oxidation (described in Chapter 19). Thus bioelectric psychophysical currents which interact with electromagnetic currents in the earth's field are the direct result of the oxidation reduction actions of atoms stimulated by ionising rays of cosmic energy. The differences of potential at two points – on the nucleus and the surrounding protoplasm of each cell – causes the cosmic light to interact with oxygen supplies in the production of the high rate of metabolic nervous activity we call consciousness. There can be no separation between this cosmic radiation of light and biological activity and what we call consciousness.

There is no separation between our consciousness and what we call matter. Thoughts are as much a form of matter as tables are. We are conscious of matter as such because our senses pick up the polarity of matter and its rate of vibration. Matter is an electrical energy made up of positive/negative couplings which gives off a radiating vibration which is selected out of the totality of all vibration by our narrow senses. And our senses differentiate matter from the whole of reality because their level of awareness is limited to this narrow physical range of frequencies. The human senses are highly selective at every level in separating out "matter" from the whole mass of cosmic vibration. Now, however, man's increasing supersensitivity to the wider range of cosmic vibration enables him to select and absorb more intense, higher frequency radiations which steps up the evolutionary potential.

No longer is it necessary for human consciousness to feel bound by the seemingly "solid" world of the senses since we can now extend them into space by the use of the supersensitive reactions of our cells. The electronic properties of biological molecules, quite apart from the semiconductor proteins which store in the nerve fibres the energies of consciousness, reveal that electrons can be consciously transferred not only through the nerve fibres but even through our human tissues. The inter-molecular relationships between various types of acceptor cells depends on the electron coats and the chemical structure of the carbon chain. For instance the lungs split the oxygen from the air and carry it through the proteins of the body and the carbon dioxide is also split off and excreted in exhalation. The electrical stripping of the oxygen atoms is constantly feeding the brain with blood in the process of thinking. This is an example of consciousness affecting the burning of oxygen atoms by the physical vehicle. The body depends on this supply process for the operations of consciousness. Breath can be also controlled by consciousness thereby affecting the electrical polarity of our brain and our biophysical luminescence.

THE ANCIENT WISDOM

The interesting part of this process to non-scientists is the connection of electro-biochemical fields of the total organism with thinking. The ancient yogis through their development of clairvoyant vision were able to probe deeper into the process of oxygen reduction and oxygen consumption in the breathing process than modern man with all his sensitive electron microscopes. The yogic discipline of pranayama, i.e. development of the vehicle (yama) for getting more vital life-force (prana), is based on sound scientific principles which have now been lost since they were always transmitted orally and in analogies rather than exact mathematical formulas.

The ancients as well as Christ referred to the interaction of spirit and water.* They knew that in order for consciousness to work, the human body must have enough body water. In the same way that the plant needs water in order to split hydrogen atoms and oxygen atoms and to fix hydrogen with carbon in the hydrocarbon products of photosynthesis, the quasi-crystalline structures of human body fluids act as liquid crystal hydrogen bridges for the transport of ionised protons and are likewise semiconductors of bioelectric energies enabling consciousness to function. Without this work-energy of oxygen feeding all the cells and particularly those of the brain, there would be no consciousness. Even if there is enough for life support, there must be a certain threshold of this electron/protonic transport across the hydrogen bridge for consciousness to function. Below that threshold there is only unconscious life. Most humans function at such low thresholds of electron/protonic electricity transport that they are indeed unconscious of any higher levels of awareness than the ones they happen to be on.

---

* Christ said, "Except a man be born of water and of the Spirit, he cannot enter into the kingdom of God." (John 3:5) "Whosoever drinketh of the water that I shall give him shall never thirst; but the water that I shall give him shall be in him a well of water springing up into everlasting life," (John 4:15) and John the Baptist said of Christ, "I indeed have baptised you with water: but he shall baptise you with the Holy Spirit." (Mark 1:8).

Nuclear Evolution sets out these thresholds of electro-chemical transport in terms of colour harmonics because the vibratory rate of each strata of processes is conditioned by the capacity of each human to absorb photons of light. Once absorbed, the light is either stored as psychic electricity in the electron charge on the semiconductor proteins or used in the liquid crystal body waters in the protonic energy of consciousness. The protonic energy of consciousness, referred to as "proticity", is described in more detail in Part III of this book. Since we already use this energy unconsciously, the next step is to amplify it by becoming conscious of how to control our ingestion of light.

TAPPING THE POWER OF CONSCIOUSNESS

If only a person gets the insight that there is something bio-physical happening at the micro level of the proteins and chains of nervous reaction below the conscious threshold of awareness, then he can begin to get conscious control of unconscious processes. As long as he is unaware or believes it is all happening beyond his control at the tiny level of the cell proteins, then whatever is in the unconscious, whether it is psychological stress or thoughts which limit the organism, will be what manifests at the micro level. When the awareness is expanded to include the domain of consciousness of the nuclear centre of the cell proteins, then the cell begins to function with a purposive intelligence which is the equivalent of wisdom at the human level of the total being.

For instance when blind spots in people's awareness are so blind that they cannot see them, then they are self-perpetuating their blindness forever. How can they know what they don't know? How can a person get to the point of sending more energy across the hydrogen bridge if he doesn't believe it can be done or does not even know there is a possibility of a hydrogen bridge in his own body? Or to put it another way, what good does it do us to know there is a hydrogen bridge if we are not prepared to test out ways of changing our conscious interaction with our cell life across the hydrogen bridge? Can we use a simple exercise to change the way we use our consciousness? Practical methods of bridging thresholds of consciousness at the psychological and micro levels are dealt with in the Rumf Roomph Yoga exercises.*

The ability of the human being to absorb light at the biochemical level determines the thresholds of his awareness, whether he is able to perceive the effects of consciousness upon the cell condition or is only able to wallow in his own blindness and reap the effects of ignorance. A person reaches a major

*See references at end of book.

turning point in his evolution when he can move his consciousness to a new place, whether this movement is at the micro level
of the cell or to influence the macro molecules we call the whole
body. To give up old limits and really hear the truth of one's own
body speaking as a mirror of one's reality is to acknowledge the
neurotic condition of life in most human bodies. In conditions of
ignorance and disease the proteins are literally in a crazy state,
since even the total organism is unaware of why situations are
what they are. If we knew how powerful our consciousness really
was and what power it had over the life's choices at the micro
level of nerve and cell, then it would make a difference to the
way we respond to light. Cancer is the price we pay for ignoring
this power.

HOW DOES CONSCIOUSNESS INFLUENCE CELLS?

It is not often realised that consciousness has power over
enzyme action. Many healers can inhibit or enhance enzymes
growing in a culture merely by placing the hands over it. A
simple experiment is to take a cheese or yogurt bacteria culture
and mix it up together with a bottle of milk. Separate into three
identical bottles. Place in identical temperature conditions. Place
a label around the neck of each bottle as follows: 1) God's
culture, 2) Control culture, and 3) Devil's culture. Now bless the
bacteria in bottle number 1. Curse the bacteria in bottle number
3, and leave bottle number 2 entirely alone without even
thinking about it. Carefully time the experiment for setting times.
The Devil works faster but the result is bitter to the biological
sensors on the tongue. God takes longer but the cheese is sweet.
The control is in between. It is hard for some people to believe
this simple kitchen experiment would work and they would be
full of doubt. Doubt and negativity indeed would affect the
results as they do in every life situation. Those who try with an
open mind get the same results and you can try the different
samples on your friends to show it is not your subjective taste
buds that are misleading your observations.*

If this power works on bacteria external to the body then how
much more will it work on the many thousands of enzyme
bacteria reactions under control of our own body functions? This
catalysis is unconsciously controlled in the two-way movement of
electrons and protons through the bioelectric system. The
generation of proticity, a positive form of electricity due to the
generation of positrons instead of electrons and the creation of a
protonic field force from the nucleus, determines the configuration of life's patterns in the mind as well as the body. The
ionising of the cell membranes by the attraction of negative ions

---

* This also appears in another context on page 478

115

Heavy protons with enormous density shoot from much bigger stars than our sun through the spiralling currents of the Van Allen trap and pass through our bodies into the centre of the earth where their energy heats up the central core of molten iron. Some of them break up the atoms of our body. This radiation we call light but it is not that light we can see in the visible spectrum. It is the light of consciousness which of course is also invisible and intangible but very much present as it reads these words. (You cannot read without it.) The picture below is like a giant chakra (Sanskrit for wheel) of energy. It is created by the trapping of light.

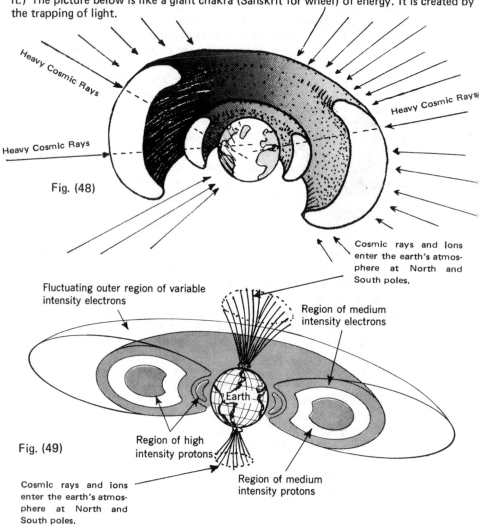

Heavy Cosmic Rays

Heavy Cosmic Rays

Heavy Cosmic Rays

Fig. (48)

Cosmic rays and ions enter the earth's atmosphere at North and South poles.

Fluctuating outer region of variable intensity electrons

Region of medium intensity electrons

Earth

Fig. (49)

Region of high intensity protons

Region of medium intensity protons

Cosmic rays and ions enter the earth's atmosphere at North and South poles.

The Van Allen radiation belts trap most of the cosmic charged particles such as fast protons and electrons created in the heart of the sun and stars moving at the speed of light. The trapped particles follow corkscrew paths around the magnetosphere of the earth. The sun hurls great fountains of charged particles which bounce around between the earth's poles miles above the atmosphere. These ionised particles dip into the atmosphere through the funnel effect of the magnetic vortex causing it to glow like a fluorescent light bulb. Cosmic rays penetrate the earth's protective magnetic skin and enter the human sphere of consciousness.

to the cell's increased proticity enhances the well-being of each cell and determines the state of health, e.g. the tendency to cancer and disease or the tendency to embody radiant good health, the tendency to self-doubt and negativity or to creativity, originality, and expanded awareness. Yogis have always known that the energy which is generated unconsciously by the processing of light is also expended unconsciously and leaked away by our misunderstanding of what consciousness really is and therefore our misuse of it. This is why yogis practice various ways of storing up the vital force or prana which in most people's lives is trapped unconsciously in the seven-fold expression of personality. To become fully conscious of this seven step process in storing nature's life-force is to discover the rainbow body and the jewel of consciousness.

LAYERS OF LIGHT

In Nuclear Evolution we regard the human vehicle as a living system which is so structured as to process light energies functionally in the same way that the planet earth itself traps light in its many layers. The earth's Van Allen radiation belts, the magneto–plasmic skin, the magnetosphere, the ionosphere, the stratosphere and the atmosphere and the physical terrasphere, have a similar function of trapping light energies at frequency rhythms in resonance with different thresholds of human psycho-physical energy and one could refer to them as different levels of excitation or equally view them as a ball surrounded by a pulsating shell within a shell within a shell, etc.

The new science of Supersensonics and psychotronics enables any person who wishes to learn, to penetrate deeply into the subtle interchanges between the various interfaces in the layers of trapped light energies which filter down from the macrocosmic level of photons to the microcosmic levels of the bioelectric system of the human body. The thresholds of intensity which exist one within the other on the macrocosmic level of the sun ⟶ Photons ⟶ Van Allen radiation belts ⟶ magnetosphere ionosphere ⟶ atmosphere are directly reflected in the different donor-acceptor characteristics of the protein semiconductor cells. The human vehicle with its various shells of subtle aura energies mirrors the macrocosm in the microcosm. The ancient Kabbala attempts to show this stepping down of the cosmic energy in a famous symbolic diagram with various mystic words used to depict the domains such as Kether, Malkuth, Binah, etc. The danger is that one gets immersed in the technical jargon of the Kabbala and spends years studying it, only to find it is very simple, that the complexity is in our own consciousness, and that there are simple mirrors of the Kaballistic tree in almost everything you look at, from a flower to the scientific explanation of the atom ⟶ cell ⟶ brain model. This "tree of life" is basically

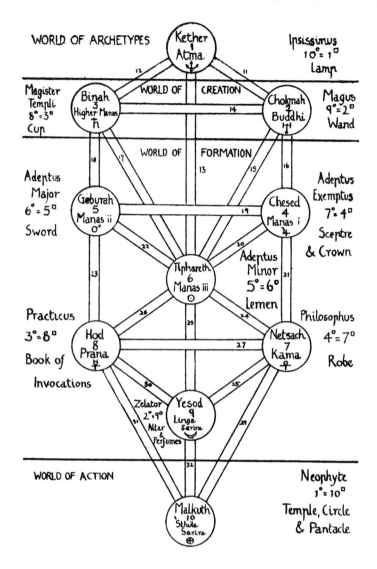

Fig. (50)

WORLD OF ARCHETYPES

Ipsissimus
$10° = 1^□$
Lamp

Kether
Atma

Magister
Templi
$8° = 3^□$
Cup

Binah
3
Higher Manas
♄

WORLD OF CREATION

Chokmah
2
Buddhi

Magus
$9° = 2^□$
Wand

WORLD OF FORMATION

Adeptus
Major
$6° = 5^□$
Sword

Geburah
5
Manas ii
♂

Chesed
4
Manas i
♃

Adeptus
Exemptus
$7° = 4^□$
Sceptre
& Crown

Tiphareth
6
Manas iii
☉

Adeptus
Minor
$5° = 6^□$
Lemen

Practicus
$3° = 8^□$
Book of
Invocations

Hod
8
Prana
☿

Netsach
7
Kama
♀

Philosophus
$4° = 7^□$
Robe

Zelator
$2° = 9^□$
Altar &
Perfumes

Yesod
9
Linga
Sarira

WORLD OF ACTION

Neophyte
$1° = 10^□$
Temple, Circle
& Pantacle

Malkuth
10
Sthula
Sarira

KETHER (The Crown) The first emanation of the Absolute. Kether is in Malkuth and Malkuth is in Kether, but after another manner. As that which is above is relfected in that which is below, Malkuth reflects Kether. It corresponds to the head; to the stage of evolution symbolized by Will. The "will to will" as distinct from the creatively intent will.

CHOKMAH wisdom, the second emanation of the Absolute; Ab "the Father" in the Trinity. A masc. potency: the vital, energizing element of existence. The illuminating intelligence. The starry heavens, the first expression of the will of Kether; the inner, spiritual side of man's nature.

BINAH understanding, the third emanation of the Absolute. The first Heh of Tetragammation. The "Supernal Mother", Aima, the Great Sea.

CHESED mercy, also Majesty. Male, positive, but the feminine quality of water is attributed to it. A Crowned, Enthroned King receiving, preserving, organizing, that which has already been brought into being. He who has been freed from karma and rebirth.

GEBURAH strength. The fifth emanation of the Absolute. The Sephira of Mars; the fiery serpent of energy. The symbol and instrument of dynamic will: the phase of evolution when the vindictive Yahweh held sway over the tribes of Israel: the period that knows no other consideration save that of its will.

118

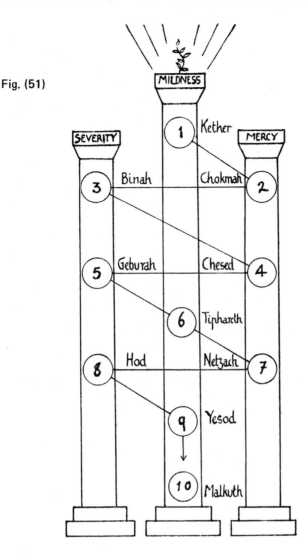

Fig. (51)

TIPHARETH beauty, harmony, balance; the sixth emanation of the Absolute. Mediates between Kether and Malkuth. Corresponds to the Heart, is the phase of devoted and sacrificial love, the Christ - phase of evolution, he who rises from the death of material being into the light and life of the spiritual, who is made ONE with his Inner Self.

NETZACH victory. Venus, the Morning Star. The phase of evolution when the one light, descending through the Sephiroth to Tiphareth, is transmitted to Netzach becoming the refulgent splendor of many-rayed hues. Sustainer of the life-force below the level of the heart-centre. Venus is not the passionate goddess of Love, but the very essence of the Spirit of Nature.

HOD glory. Mercury, the Messenger of the Gods. Sphere of the intellect, the phase in evolution that gives form to the astral and elemental activity of the preceding phase (Netzach). Directs energy towards specific purposes, or which direct the body as a whole by locomotion towards its objective.

YESOD foundation. Referred to the generative sphere. The vast fields of magic, religion, fantasy and illusion associated with matters of sex show clearly the influence of this sphere. Stage of evolution immediately preceding that of the physical universe.

MALKUTH (The Kingdom) represented by the anus and the feet, those parts of the body which show the closest affinity to earth. Malkuth is the completion of the involutionary processes of the universe, and is the only Sephira in which any act of whatever kind can find material manifestation.

119

the description of the levels of consciousness in the archaic language of an esoteric tradition. The diagram on the opposite page can be translated into the nuclear model but since there is no difference in essence, the simpler shell model of Nuclear Evolution is preferable by the principle that the simpler explanation takes precedence.

To be able to perceive our human personality and its link with the macrocosm as a series of layers, then to see everything around us in terms of layers sandwiched between subtle energies, leads us to a very dynamic awareness of people. One begins to see that low potential people have low intensity thresholds and high potential people have high intensity. They can trap light in their total macro/microcosm bio-energetic system and penetrate the intense Nuclear Centre of Being. Intensity at the level of the cell or atom is no different. A state of balance will always bring peace but if that peace is low intensity inertia it will be more like the sluggish absence of something rather than the fullness of light. To look at the human body with the X-ray vision of direct perception by using the Supersensonic tools, we begin to see why the electron microscope reveals that structure of the mitochondria and the Golgi body of the cells, etc. are made up of layers of different electron intensity. These structures operate on the same sandwich principle as the p-n junction in the semiconductor.* Some understanding of the p-n junction as an image of the way our cells work for us enables us to get conscious control of our body.

The inter-atomic bondings of some materials such as germanium and silicon crystals act as ionic or metallic depending on their purity. This could be a great analogy for the purity of our chakra system as an acceptor or emitter of cosmic energy in the form of heavy protons and free electrons sent from the big stars in the total environment. Pure crystals are good insulators but when doped with some impurity their conductivity of the negative electrons increases tremendously. The n-type semiconductor can

---

* Semiconductor: Certain crystals possess two types of carriers: negative electrons and positive holes. The conductivity associated with these electrons is called n-type (meaning negative) and that with the holes is called p-type (meaning positive). The only difference between a semiconductor and a crystalline metal is that the number of free electrons in the semiconductor is small, the energy levels being entirely full or entirely empty. Semiconductors are made of thin wafers of germanium or silicon. One type of crystal has an impurity that causes electrons to be emitted as n-type. Another type of impurity causes the crystal to be a collector of electrons. A transistor is made by placing a thin layer of n-type next to a thin layer of p-type to form a p-n junction. The emitter corresponds to the cathode and the collector or acceptor type to the anode. See page 122 for analogy with human cells as p-n junction. Here the entire body can be viewed as an emitter or collector or both as a n-p-n or a p-n-p.

THE SHELL MODEL OF PERSONALITY

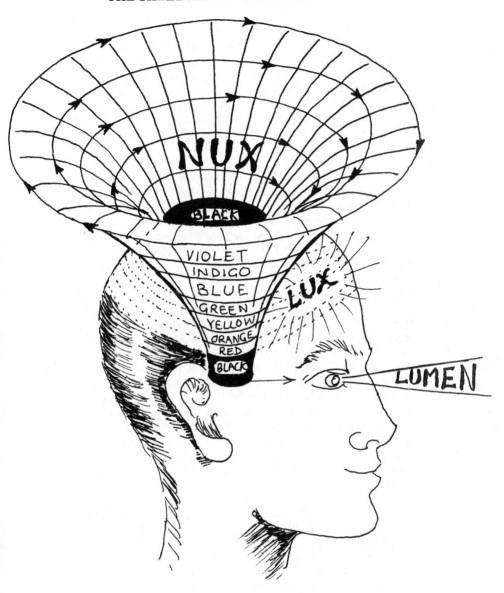

EVERY PERSON'S CONSCIOUSNESS IS ANNIHILATING ITSELF IN A BLACK HOLE INTO WHICH THE UNIVERSE CONTRACTS SPIRITUALLY AS IT EXPANDS MATERIALLY.

Why is consciousness (God) invisible?

The Crown chakra is shown as containing all the shells of consciousness one within the other rotating at different frequencies into the Black nuclear core (Nux) of Being (total absorption of light), thus creating the clear colourless inner light (Lumen) of consciousness by which we perceive the external world inside the mind (Lux). This transparent clear inner light of consciousness (Lumen) needs no other light to validate its levels because it is the self-limiting, self-validating authority for all experience and statements about itself or any other. In other words we cannot deny God without setting up a new God -- "I".

121

be compared to a cell or a liquid crystal in the body fluids which adds electrons and carries a negative charge throughout the crystal or cell structure. In the p-type the cell would hold a positive charge because the impurity would cause electrons to be repelled and removed to make electronic "holes" in the crystals, effectively carrying a positive charge. An object, whether human or a piece of metal which is positively charged as a whole, would repel a cosmic ray proton which is positive and attract negative ions.

The interesting information is that a semiconductor or cell can also be made to conduct electrical forces by shining a light of the proper colour on it. Every electronic expert knows this and anyone who understands how a Xerox copier works knows this but when it comes to applying the same knowledge to the human cell and the liquid crystals between the human cells, the knowledge seems too speculative to the nuts-and-bolts mind. Yet yogis, magicians and occultists have talked about this process for hundreds of years in terms of the human semiconductors which we all have under our immediate control in our own body. In fact they are the **only** thing we do actually control at this moment since all other events outside our body depend on other bodies, other events and changing environments. Even as you read this book the sun is changing its angle in relation to the earth you are standing on and your semiconductor cells are changing their resistance and conductivity in relation to the sun's angle. Because you can't feel it you do not believe it. What you need is an instrument which can give you a natural biofeedback signal when there is any change from positive to negative, from p-type to n-type of response in your cell structures. This instrument is the basic divining tool since all your muscles and nerves are composed of p-n junctions.

The most important but primitive of all electronic structures which enable the synthesis of vastly complex organisms to be concentrated in a yes or no command, or the firing of a cell potential, is the p-n junction. This junction performs the simple function of creating an empty hole into which any surplus electrons can jump, thereby creating a donor-acceptor mechanism which governs the biochemical reactions in human cell growth and metabolism of the natural elements in the body. The make-up of these minute junctions in chloroplasts, cell membranes and mitochondria and the way they trap light is described in Part III, but here we are looking at the consciousness which triggers and modifies their functioning to result in different aura colours.

THE MACRO COSMIC SPECTRUM OF CREATION

Fig. (52)

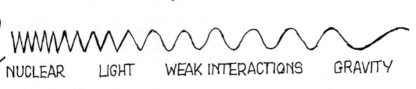

NUCLEAR   LIGHT   WEAK INTERACTIONS   GRAVITY

The electromagnetic spectrum has several energy thresholds which interact. First the strong forces which hold the nucleus of the atom together, we give the intensity of 1 unit. Then on this scale light photons with an energy threshold one hundred times weaker will have a strength of 10^{-2}. The weak disintegrations of the atomic decay are much smaller than the strong nuclear forces and would rate at 10^{-14} on this scale. Gravitational forces which act through space and hold the planets together are still weaker and rate at 10^{-40}. There is a barrier between the nuclear force of 1 and the light radiations of 10^{-2} so that when light photons shine on matter it does not often affect the nucleus unless the light is a powerful cosmic ray from another star. Gravitational forces only attract light at certain heavy intensities when they suck the light back into the system and we get a black hole.

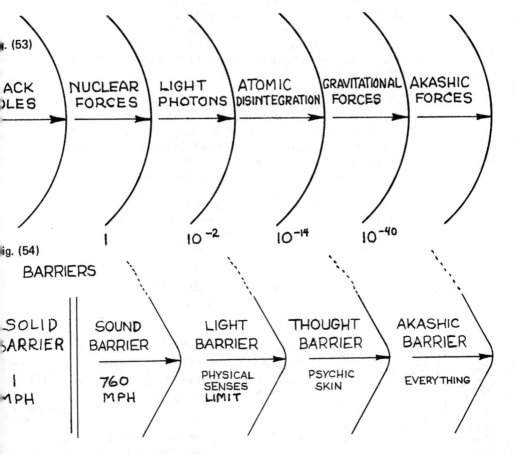

The psychic skins between the Akasha/light barrier, the thought barrier and the physical barrier of the solid world of flesh can be looked at like the sound barrier at 760 mph and the Supersonic barrier. The Supersense passes another barrier beyond thought. The Super (full) sense of sound (Super-sense-sonic) barrier.

Lumen is the Latin name we have given to the invisible light of radiation (the Sanskrit equivalent of Akasha), containing invisibly the colours of light. If we can view our own body as a vehicle with a simplified form of layered thresholds for the trapping of light, we begin to see the simplicity of the p-n junction as a trigger switch which functions under the control of consciousness either at the unconscious or conscious level of organisation. Just as, with an ordinary light switch, we shall remain in darkness until our consciousness decides to act on the muscles of our body to mechanically switch it on, so too is an act of consciousness required for stored energy to be released for the emission of radiation and photons of light in bioluminescence of the human aura. The optical effects described in Part III are no accidental by-product of spiritual grace but are an index to the way each person is patterning the process of light absorption which the universe sends to each organism from atom, molecule, insect or human in the same amount and quality. Only the different layering of the biophysical field forces will determine how this light is revealed in the aura and what this means in terms of the psyche. A psyche with no layers would not filter selectively; much of the energy would pass straight through it and little would be trapped. Hence more complex organisms with more intense auras represent a greater potential for trapping of lumen in bioluminescence.

What are the implications of this process for imprisoning the splendour of light in ordinary human life? Does it pay to be more complex or are people who are simple more close to the ONE? All great beings ultimately become simple in humility before the one light of the cosmos. People who love Truth and Light care about the condition of the human aura not as some end in itself like some fashionable attempt to trigger a really new flashy aura, but because it shows us truly what we are and what others are. To be able to know the radiation we emanate immediately gives us a mirror image of our correct relationship with the light of the cosmos. We need no "other" to tell us what the splendour of life is.

Fig. (55)

THE MICRO COSMIC SPECTRUM OF CREATION

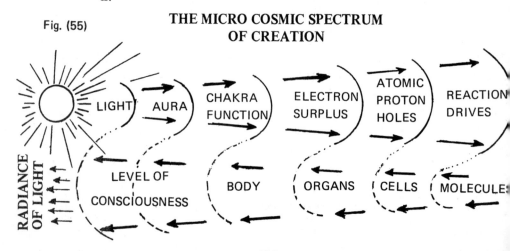

The recombination of certain chemical charges, such as sodium-potassium hydrogen-oxygen in the sandwich layers of living proteins of cell life such as chloroplasts and cellular membranes of mitochondria, produce these optical effects of light which are visible to human consciousness as the human aura. Since the aura is light it cannot be seen directly until it becomes intense, just as low energy light sources do not register on our optical sensors, films, etc. Again the sensitivity of the human aura to external fields of light, which determines its intensity, would interact very much like different sensitivities of photographic film emulsions. Like a colour film in which only certain layers of emulsion are sensitive to blue light, red light, yellow light, etc., the thresholds of consciousness determine what is absorbed and reflected in the aura and vice versa:

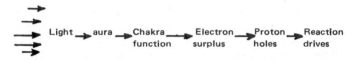

= Level of consciousness

In addition to the electronic/protonic electricity of the body there is the well-known ability of human tissues to floresce in states of high emotional excitement. This ability to create light from within the cell by the chemical combinations of certain proteins and nucleic acids has been reported most famously in the transfiguration of Christ, but also in the language itself when we say a person is glowing (with love, health, religious devotion, etc.).

At the time of writing the first edition of Nuclear Evolution ten years ago the exact nature of the bioluminescence process was scientifically unproved. The author meticulously had mapped it out by means of Supersensonic detectors (shown at the end of the book). Hence in 1967 we were able to construct a theoretical basis for Nuclear Evolution which would eventually be borne out by ordinary scientific methods several years later. The advantage of mapping the layering around any organism to discover the interfaces and bio-electric exchanges between cells by this method is that the patterns and their outlines are directly and immediately available to us as they are in nature without having to construct any models, use mathematics or even a chart-recorder to measure the energy levels. The disadvantage is that, like seeing or any other human observation, the instruments are only extensions of the psyche. But then, in ordinary science this is also true at any level, that all instruments from telescope to microscope are extensions of our own sense perceptions. Failure to see this is the cause of a certain scientific arrogance which will die hard over the next few decades. With the perfecting of psychotronic devices these die-hard attitudes will disappear.

It is interesting to note that the theory described in Part III of this book which was the result of research by Supersensonic methods has not needed any updating after ten years, showing that the Supersense is capable of detecting the electrical pumping of the electrons in the cell life. Furthermore the idea of the chemically pumped amplification of light energy by consciously changing the amount of photons absorbed by the human nervous system and its linked body fluids, is still a valid analogy for enhancing the bio-electrical energies and the levels of consciousness on which they manifest.*

THE FOUNTAIN OF YOUTH

The biochemical cell reactions, which constantly take place with the absorption of electromagnetic energies from the sun and earth's environment as well as those very dense cosmic radiations from the background of the galaxial stars, are fluctuating with bursts of cosmic energy. Because the cells' evolution took place through being bathed for billions of years in this powerful radiation it is not harmful at the earth's surface or in space. Quite apart from the sun's rays which regenerate the earth's magnetic field with free excited electrons, this background cosmic energy charges the entire system of semiconductor proteins, cells and body fluids with refreshing life-force, particularly when we are asleep. The whole process of sleep is described by the rishis, who observed it by clairvoyant means, as a reversal of flow along the nadis (channels of psychic electricity). They said that the fine astral tubes, the moment we fall asleep, begin to suck in prana instead of radiate it out, very much like the reversal of the flow of sap in plants at the moment of sunset. To be able to consciously control this back and forth flow and enhance it enables the organism to prolong the life of cells.

THE SEA OF LIFE

Most people are unaware of any connection between themselves and the macrocosm because the experience of the cosmic micro energies at such a tiny level do not affect the gross sensations and they cannot see why it matters that we are interconnected with the whole universe. Why does it matter that we are interconnected with the stars in galaxies millions of light years away from our own? Why does it matter that we take in this energy of light and process it biochemically? It matters because this processing is life, giving birth to life and consciousness. Without the umbilical link to the universe of light, our awareness (our life) is snuffed out. The processing of light is conditioned by our consciousness but also makes possible our consciousness through the biochemical symbiosis of our relation to the whole.

---

* See reference "Supersensonics"

The way electric potentials are unconsciously triggered from the chakras and the way the cerebrospinal fluids are used by our body is one of the most crucial subtleties of that hazy borderland in which spirit becomes matter and matter becomes spirit. To get clarity we must know that the state of the pranic centres controlling the electrical potentials in the chakra system, influences the intake of cosmic bursts of energy from the stars (which affects the subtle manifestation of bioluminescence) and this intake conditions the ph of the cerebrospinal fluids which again is dictated by the ability of our consciousness to ionise them. On the other hand, effects of conscious control at the psychic, psychological or spiritual levels (such as psychic healing and personality changes) often come unconsciously from this cerebrospinal dwelling place of the self. But by consciously knowing the influence of these electric potentials on the body fluids and the cell membranes we are able to use the charge on the fluids of the cerebrospinal system to act as a trigger to all other psychic electricity systems of the body.*

This is the full meaning of self-mastery that all levels of our being -- mental, physical and spiritual -- are subject to absolute control. Yogis are known to control many autonomic functions such as body temperature, hunger, breath, heart muscle, etc. but none of this alone guarantees that they can control their egos. The state of consciousness beyond ego and beyond the physical phenomena must also be mastered for the human aura to reveal an advanced and evolved soul. The ingestion of light and its reradiation is an indicator of cosmic consciousness.

---

* The ionisation of the tiny cilia on the inner membranes of the brain cavities and specifically in the third and fourth ventricles is achieved through atomic resonance. Like a whale whose head is full of sperm oil for sounding off signals and receiving them by sonar over thousands of miles, so can the human cerebrospinal fluids commune with worlds within worlds within worlds through ionisation of these liquid crystals in the brain. Cosmic light radiation containing fast electrons and protons makes the fluids into ions. These ions flow into the atoms of our brain and body.

What really is an ion? A neutral atom has an equal number of electrons surrounding the nucleus as the number of protons in the nucleus. Because the electron and the protons have electric charges of equal magnitude but opposite polarity the total charge on the neutral atom is annihilated and is therefore equal to zero. But when the number of electrons and protons are not exactly the same the atom is said to be ionised. Usually the atom which has become an ion has lost an electron or two and therefore the electron number is less than the proton number making the atom a "positive" ion. In rare cases in nature the electron number is greater than the proton number and the ion is said to be a "negative" ion. Negative ions have a surplus of excited electrons waiting to jump towards a positive nucleus of any atom which is short of electrons. To consciously make the nucleus of every cell positive is to attract electron energy from the cosmos.

The yogis of ancient times discovered that the ventricles of the brain sent out a resonant frequency to the entire body through the nervous system and that this was triggered by the ph of the brain fluids interacting with light. Photons of light in their excited states have the power to ionise these fluids and set off the photo impulses which activate the acceptors and donors of the enzymes in the endocrine system. These can act as "starters" which ionise the energy balance of the sun/human system which is linked together through the chakras. We human beings are not often aware that we are living in an electromagnetic sea of ionising radiations which strike every object on the planet and create an excited field around all things including every atom of air we breathe. Our interconnection with these objects creates a biological link with our muscles and nerves which unconsciously respond to these incoming influences.

PSYCHIC RADIATION

The ingestion of these ionising radiations is not always necessary for life and, as with food, we do not use all that is taken in. Hence we can look at the biological radio energies as excretion of surplus unwanted energies and not always as an energy loss. Elimination is as important as ingestion, as it is with ordinary food, and therefore the correct excretion of cosmic energies is necessary to the health of all organisms and especially for balancing the energy exchanges with the total environment through the human aura. Hence the aura is an interface or psychic skin which is controlled by its corresponding chakra functions. The chakras therefore are like organs of elimination as well as organs of ingestion. Not to radiate surplus psychic electricity amounts to spiritual constipation of the human organism. To put this in spiritual terms: we choose whether or not we will give to others or radiate our love, but most of us do not fully realise that we **need** to give of ourselves. It is as much a need of our human organism as the need to take in food and eliminate its wastes.

An actual experience of psychic constipation can happen at any of the chakra levels. For instance, a man with a Blue chakra function is interested in concepts and storing them in memory. If he absorbs so many facts that he fills all his mental circuits up, he becomes a mental encyclopedia but cannot forget anything and so ultimately cannot learn anything new. Someone who cannot learn anything new because of what he already knows is as good as dead. The same analogy holds good for storing up other drives where they become self-defeating, in the same way that someone eating too much ice cream eventually becomes sick and cannot eat anymore. When life reaches a point of moribund action in a person, he can be sure he is blocking the light synthesising process of Nuclear Evolution.

KUNDALINI

Light enters the total field of the biological system and is absorbed in every cell through the controlling action of the psychic centres or chakras which correspond roughly to the location of the nerve plexuses along the spine. However, the word **chakra** is not just a reference to these physical locations in the body. The chakras are a whirling concentration of light energy which can be experienced as a tingling sensation in the palm of the hand when it is held over these areas of the spine. The amount of energy given off from the chakras depends upon how evolved a spirit is inhabiting the body. The root of the chakra is near the spine and the mouth of the chakra is like a lily shaped trumpet extending out to the front of the body as a vortex of energy at a particular frequency of vibration. These trumpets close and open like sea anemones, and with their closing that particular frequency of light is shut off from the organism.

If someone has all the chakras wide open, then the corresponding pathways in the brain which "trigger" their activation must also be open since all the chakras, like the nervous system and organs, have their control centres in the brain. This opening of the pathways (or cleansing of the nadis) has been achieved in the past by yogins and mystics by breathing exercises which ionise the cerebrospinal fluid in the ventricles and cause the flow of consciousness to act as a passage of biochemical psychic electricity through the channels along the spine and chakra system. The resultant release of energy is felt as a burning hot sensation as the energy is raised to the next thresholds of consciousness. Hence the yogis called it kundalini, from the root Sanskrit word **kunda** to burn. Where the description of kundalini as a coiled snake originally came from we do not know but clearly someone used this metaphor of the serpent fire and, since then, ancient and modern writers who do not know its origin have continued to say that kundalini means "coiled energy" which it does not. The sensation of a spring expanding, or of a snake sliding up inside the spine and around it has spread to several cultures because this feeling is experienced when the bio-chemical release of luminescence begins to rise up through the chakra system. This subjective feeling may have led to this erroneous meaning of the word kundalini as "coiled serpent".

If a person has all the seven chakras open then the cosmic prana or psychic electricity absorbed will pass through the system as if it were transparent and be expressed in much the same condition as it entered in. Gopi Krishna, an Indian pandit, describes in great detail his own subjective personal experience of this energy in several books* and calls on scientific disciplines to study it objectively. However, it has already been studied objectively by several doctors for many years (to my knowledge at least 17 years) in yogic hospitals and ashrams such as the Kaivalyadhama laboratory at Lonalva near Poona. A friend of mine, Dr. S. Vinekar, the Director of Research, demonstrated a map tracing of the kundalini path by using EEG and GSR equipment to record its electrical effects in 1961 at a conference of renowned yogis in Patna under the chairmanship of the then just retired ex-president of India Ragendra Prasad.

The opening of the chakras and the path of the kundalini is described in many ancient texts and Dr. Vinekar merely checked these documented statements from an objective medical and bio-physical point of view. The rising of the kundalini is much the same as experiencing a drug in its first effects but whereas the drug wears off and the subject returns to normal state, the kundalini fire permanently changes the cell structure, often disorientating the mind and senses for long periods. There are ways of opening the pathway safely by radionic conditioning so that the organism adapts to a slow daily release controlled by a radiesthesic device.** Whether opened by this gradual method or by meditation practice the results may vary considerably from person to person depending on their evolutionary spiritual development.

Not all chakras may be fully opened by its rising. However, a person functioning with all seven levels fully opened becomes a powerful amplifier of the human biological radio energies emitted by the enhanced functioning of cells and body fluids. The state of transfiguration, in varying degrees depending on our purity of consciousness, is then achieved and cuts through any word blockages in communication. At the tiny level the radio-stimulated cells begin to "talk", as it were, on other levels of Being. A person with only one chakra open would of course only get this communication from the total Being of an enlightened person at the one level of understanding; a person with two chakras open would receive the "power" on two levels and so on.

An experiment to artificially boost radio energy of a person was done with a Tesla coil by charging a man at the centre of an electri-fied field of 500,000 volts. The man's aura changed to its comple-mentary chakra for several days, from Yellow to Indigo, and the man himself changed during that time from an intellectual gad-fly

---

* "The Awakening of Kundalini" by Gopi Krishna, published by E.P. Dutton, 1975.

** This is described more fully in Volume II of the "Supersensitive Life of Man" series entitled "Energy, Matter and Form", second edition by Phillip Allen, Alastair Bearne, and Roger Smith, published by University of the Trees Press, 1977. Also see Chapter 3 of this book.

to an intuitive and sensitive person for those few days. Such effects are only temporary, however, and the person soon slips back to his normal mental pattern. Unless a person begins to work on changing his patterns of consciousness, such temporary external stimulation does less to affect the human life patterns than does the existing more powerful macrocosmic radio stimulations daily impinging on everyone from stars in different parts of the galaxial disc.

WHERE DOES CONSCIOUSNESS STOP?

That person who controls only one or two chakras or keeps one chakra open partially would not be tuned to the frequency of other chakras and would thereby restrict the intake of light energies, very much like a sluice valve controls the flow of water into a dam. Another analogy for the function of a chakra would be the choke or an attenuator which controls the frequency response of a vibrating electrical circuit on a radio receiver. Thus a person is constantly bombarded with all the cosmic frequencies just as there are thousands of radio stations broadcasting along the entire spectrum of radio waves but only one frequency is received at one time in a finely tuned radio circuit; so the unwanted light energy of the cosmos, represented by the balance of cosmic radiation unwanted by each organism, is either tuned out, reflected back, filtered off or absorbed according to the personality functions of each chakra function. This would make up considerable variety of operations since each of the seven chakras can be cracked open a fraction of a degree or held wide open like the aperture of a camera lens to produce an infinite variety of combinations and permutations.

This conscious and unconscious selectivity explains the uniqueness of each individual human being and the capriciousness and freedom of human thought, since each second of time the chakras can change their configurations with changes in consciousness. If the human personality were dictated purely by the genetic code in the genes we would be merely stereotype combinations of our mothers and fathers. Since the likeness between parents and children is mainly physical and emotional and since children very seldom resemble their parents on the spiritual and mental levels of consciousness, the Nuclear concept of human personality, represented as a system of seven concentric shells triggered by the chakras, is more reasonable than a genetic explanation of personality types.

Since there is no system of psychology which can explain the many different types of human beings without categorising human beings in little boxes, the beauty of the Nuclear theory is that it allows everyone to be different. Once the seven drives have been learned and the percentage of optimum function of each chakra has been detected by a Supersensonic measuring instrument, there can literally be millions of ways that light can be synthesised by different human beings. Furthermore any human being is not fixed forever by the genetic code as if he were some mechanistic product of matter but is free to change and transmute light in a new way at any time there is a conscious awareness of the role of consciousness in the process of synthesis.

HOW WE LIMIT LIGHT

An example of just two ways here might give a clearer picture of how we change personality functions through the chakras.

(a) The personality reflects off most of the available radio energy and light from the sun and stars because of a basic lack of biological receptivity. In other words there is a cosmic sluggishness (tama guna) which causes the human chakra system to create a superficial mirroring of the universal lumen (Akasha) so that it is quickly reflected back into the environment. Thus the aura appears to an observer as an indistinguishable blend of many reflected colours minus the one colour absorbed by the functioning chakra. In this case the energy coming from the person is first absorbed and then reradiated out as low energy, reflected, secondary light which has no ionising power and little ability to influence other human cells or receptors or affect the lives of other people.

(b) Another way is to absorb the total spectrum of radio energy and light by seeking a supersensitive receptivity but only to be capable of reradiating the single colour of that particular chakra (or two chakras or more). In this case the balance of the unwanted energies of light are absorbed and become a constipated accretion of life-force. This ability to receive but not to re-give causes a breakdown of the internal communications between cell and cell in the interconnected life systems we call a body. The conflict in a person's aura between one or two clashing colours can be diagnosed as the origin of cancer. What we see of cancer medically is an effect; the origin starts with a constipation of the mental life of the patient. There is not one cancer case I have known which did not have this internal conflict between what is willed in the heart or what is wanted or imagined in our idealistic fantasies, and the actual life situation of the person.

Obviously there are many variables of the above examples depending on which chakra is open and how much. A classic type of personality for type (a) with one chakra open as above can be seen more easily in the negative manifestation of the drive for that chakra. For example the Yellow chakra would be extremely separated from self and others and unable to see its own separation which would lead to Schizophrenia. An extreme case of one chakra open at the Blue level would be the self-righteous religious fanatic. This negative state is to be contrasted to the positive union of intellect with the whole (as with the Yellow-gold aura colour of Christ consciousness) and the devotion and intelligent dedication of the soul as with the electric blue aura of saintly life.

Another example of the self-negating chakra function would be the person who operates say from two different ends of the spectrum with two chakras open simultaneously. The Yellow thinking type controlled from the solar plexus area and the Indigo intuition type from the brow chakra could give us a combination of both functions with one or the other as dominant. So we have two possible personalities for this combination, with various permutations: one personality would manifest for example as the logical intellectual scientist internally in conflict with the rather abstract and intuitive side of himself, the specula-tive dreamer who spends time meditating on his unconscious wish fulfillments. Because this type can never completely let go of sequential order of events, we call this overlapping function the thinking/intuitive type, and the other personality type who would have the intuition dominant would be the positive visionary who first sees the way and then tries to explain what he sees in some intellectual theory or logical order, which we would call the intuitive/thinking type. In the first combination we have conflict and in the second type they complement each other. Both relate to the outside world and to others in totally different ways because the overlapping of each chakra function conditions the other.

SPIRITUALITY AND THE BOTTOM CHAKRA

Another example of the ways we limit consciousness would be the cutting off of the flow of kundalini through to the higher chakras by excessively developing the lower ones. It is often thought that kundalini rises only from its dormant position at the base of the spine but this is not always the case. Sri Aurobindo describes his form of yoga as the penetration of the spiritual vibration entering the vehicle of consciousness from the crown chakra and diffusing itself throughout the lower vehicles and chakras. Many other Tantric teachers believe that kundalini cannot flow through the top chakras without first going through the lower ones. However, these are naive people who do not realise that Aurobindo regarded the kundalini as nothing less than a pure form of consciousness (Purusa) coupled with the creative force (Prakriti) and that the sexual activity of the lower chakra was not necessary unless it had to be conquered. The problem with any yoga which does not grapple with the lowest chakra is that the Red chakra function does not only control sexual activity alone but also a number of other functions such as our daily manifestation in the physical body, the senses of man which can enslave or be trained to serve the higher chakras, and also the sense of self-preservation of the physical vehicle which triggers the fear of death on the physical as well as on higher levels.

It has been a fault of many great spiritual leaders who spent much time developing their higher centres at the expense of their health through despising the lower functions. To bring inner conflict in the physical bodily incarnation does not fit with the wholistic health concept of planetary man who regards the physical universe as the body of God. To concentrate all consciousness on the higher chakra functions certainly brings no fear of survival but it may bring neglect of the physical vehicle which is just as much a creation of God as the mind or the spirit of man. Consequently Aurobindo died unnecessarily of a prostate infection when a simple operation would have resolved this common problem for men of his age, and Ramana Maharshi died of cancer from ignoring his inner conflict with the world and its physical life. The Truth of these two great men was impeccable but the manifestation of the lower chakra would have given them more respect for God's temple.

Christ on the contrary was a great respecter of the physical temple and not only healed it but believed consciousness was its daily bread and that by putting our consciousness on the cosmic aspect of the physical body we need not pay great attention to what it eats and drinks but nourish it with spiritual food. To so regard it as the awesome handiwork of God is to regard not the body but only its uncontrolled pull of appetites as the enemy of the spirit and therefore not villify the flesh itself. The bottom chakra, then, is that energy which anchors the spirit of man in the manifestation of Light in the precious vehicle of the world of physical life. The more the flow of kundalini through any particular chakra the more acutely a person is aware of the depth, breadth and intensity of that particular function, so when it comes to the body we cannot neglect its health and care. To ignore it is as self-defeating as to glorify its role excessively as did the ancient Greeks. The body is only a small part of a spiritual being but it is the vehicle in which the spirit creates its awareness of the kundalini and discovers its role in the evolution of the Nuclear centre of Being. Therefore to cut off the flow of kundalini either way, up or down, will produce people who are cutting themselves off from life on earth as it is actually lived by ordinary men and women. The second line of the Lord's prayer illustrates Christ's attitude:

As it is in the Cosmos, let it be done here on Earth.

Only by learning the simple physical and mental functions of each chakra and its link with each level of consciousness through the meaning of its colour can we begin to interpret the composite patterns of spiritual energy which overlap and interact with the dynamic energies of the total physical environment in which we live. This interaction is the basis of psychotronics and Supersensonics.

THE MEASURING OF COSMIC ELECTRICITY

The human body has evolved in the presence of much more intense fields of energy than we can sense with our normal faculties. However, it is not difficult to learn how to divine or become conscious of these forces which are vital to life and which surround us everywhere on the planet. A new science with its own branches, world conferences and methods of validating the "shadow fields" of consciousness has emerged under the name "psychotronics" since the first edition of Nuclear Evolution was written. It is these pioneers who will eventually prove the validity of this knowledge to the world.

In recent years the scientific and general public have developed an increased interest in the interactions between living organisms and their internal and external environments. The energetic processes which underlie the manifestation of psychic and bio-physical interconnection are dependent on consciousness. The subtle structural organisation of the interpenetrating fields of matter, energy and consciousness have led to the new science of psychotronics, radionics, radiesthesia and parapsychology. All of these new sciences are covered in the term **Supersensonics**, which attempts to link them together in a wholistic interpretation through the development of special tools.

Breakthrough research at the frontiers of modern science in the study of human potentials covers the study of consciousness and its energies, quantum theory, electromagnetic fields, biogravity, psy phenomena, Kirlian photography of the radiation field, dowsing, dermotropic perception, psychotronic generators, acupuncture, measurement of the chakras, biofeedback signals, imagery, medicine, holograms, bioenergetic healing, psychokinesis, and many others. **Supersensonics**, a name coined by the author, covers all these fields and provides a coherent theory as well as experimental proofs for everyone to practice for himself.

SUPERSENSONICS AND DETECTION OF THE PRANA FIELD

The interconnection of the human aura with the flux of cosmic forces has never been satisfactorily explained or measured. It is often referred to by occultists and those with esoteric leanings as "other planes". The word "plane" is not satisfactory nor is the word "zone" any better. One can use "realm" or "domains" as we know that different kinds of space exist outside the earth. The Theosophists use the words "astral body", "mental body", etc. to explain these planes of existence in which the human vibration is tuned to a specific cosmic vibration (such as the intuitive or telepathic), but in Nuclear Evolution we use the word "level" because even on the physical plane there are many obvious levels of functioning, e.g. sexual activity, nutritious eating, digestion, elimination, recreational exercise, endocrine effects on emotional/chemical release, oxygen intake, metabolism, walking from San Francisco to New York City instead of flying, earth atmosphere as against lunar atmosphere, and space flight, etc. etc.

Undoubtedly the spiritual level of Being is the greatest power in the universe because it is the source of all other powers in their highest manifestations, but to speak of this level by direct experience is a very different thing than to speak of it theoretically. The spirit of man is a rather abstract term which is referred to by advanced yogis and great beings like Christ as the absolute consciousness of Self where there exists nothing but absolute Truth and absolute Wisdom, but science as it stands today knows no absolutes; everything is transitory knowledge and subject to question. So how do we avoid the lofty terminology of untested theories and yet not forsake experienced realities?

If we wish to accomplish anything great, the first requirement is the presence of pure absolute spirit power because it is this power which gives man understanding. However, it is not enough to make dogmatic statements about this power without giving understanding of the hidden planes from which this power derives its authority.

It is plain for all to see that these hidden forces of the cosmos and of space cannot be studied with an intellect that is devoid of spiritual light. We cannot begin to measure the planes and levels of the hidden worlds within worlds and their cosmic forces unless we already feel their existence with our soul. The most brilliant scientist, if he does not have this feeling, is back in the mental labyrinth, for only when the desire for the spiritual light is intense enough will we be able to comprehend the power which transcends the lower planes of man's dark existence.

Just as sunshine cannot grow out of the earth but must always come from above, so the essence of Nuclear Evolution cannot be understood from the purely genetic animal earthly elements of man's physical vehicle of knowing. Yet through "Supersensonics" it is possible for an agnostic or someone who does not believe in pure consciousness or any absolutes, but has an open mind to investigate these hidden worlds of nature and gain some insight into that perfection of intellect that we call the level of wisdom. The first domain or level such a person should investigate to gain some sense of conviction on which to go further would be to be able to detect and experience "prana". This Sanskrit word is translated as "life energy of the universe" but in Supersensonics we are concerned with earthly things before talking of cosmic things. If we are seeking practical proof of extended fields of consciousness we can begin by developing our water divining capability and thus discover that it is prana which causes the divining phenomenon which can also detect other types of psychic electricity on the seven levels of being and bring higher understanding of nature. Terrestrial prana creates two dynamic centres of action in all gross matter presented to our physical senses which form together as a human body. This is that part of our gross matter which is polarised around the northern hemisphere, and part of it gathers around the southern end of our human system. The northern centre develops in man into the brain and the southern into the heart centre. The column along which this gross matter develops runs up between these two poles and is called **Sushumna** in Sanskrit. Pingala is the channel for the currents of prana which govern the right half of the body and brain and the sympathetic system; the channel for working the left half of body and brain is called the **Ida nadi** governing the parasympathetic system. These three channels or currents of prana work forward and backward like tides with the breath and meet in six different places, each place of joining forming a centre of the cerebrospinal system of nerves. Each of these centres, called chakras, pulses with the vibrations of the current which flows constantly with the prana received by the Sushumna which joins them together. The great energy of prana playing through the Sushumna gives all the main chakra drives which, dependent on the openness of each chakra, enable all the separate parts of the human organism to survive.

There is a correspondence between these centres of psychic electricity and the patterns of the planets in the zodiac which condition the cosmic forces of the total zodiac. Various disciplines are available from the University of the Trees for training the induction of prana into the vehicle, called prana-yama, but in the science of Supersensonics we are not only concerned with this. We are concerned with finding out scientifically what makes us tick and how does prana become consciousness? How do the cosmic rays give prana to the earth and how is this polarity of two currents balanced by the third, Sushumna.*

---

* Detailed instructions are available in a complete course for waking up the sleeping brain in the 24 cassettes of Rumf Roomph Yoga available from the publishers.

137

The methods of detecting prana with divining instruments which amplify our perception of it give us a power to look into the unseen and directly see the earth as a living being receiving the prana from the cosmic rays and making it available on earth to us. The great life principle of prana used by Christ to heal others and which we ourselves can use for enhancement of our own evolution is not separately working from our consciousness but is its servant in matters of health and sickness. Whatever we do consciously or unconsciously with prana absorbed from the atmosphere will determine our power to respond to the total spectrum of life.

Fig. (56)

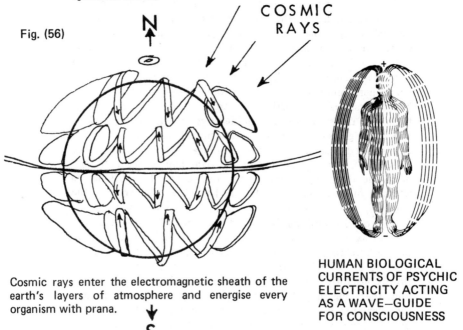

COSMIC RAYS

N

S

Cosmic rays enter the electromagnetic sheath of the earth's layers of atmosphere and energise every organism with prana.

HUMAN BIOLOGICAL CURRENTS OF PSYCHIC ELECTRICITY ACTING AS A WAVE—GUIDE FOR CONSCIOUSNESS

The prana flowing through the centres in our vehicle and its nervous system determines what kind of person we are and what levels of being we can function on and what zones of life we can understand. The more the flow, the more we are aware. Supersensonics is the method of detection by which we can become familiar with the fields of prana around and in every food and object as well as with our own physical domains of existence.

THE LIFE FORCE

The following describes the way that prana or cosmic life principle enters into the world from above as light, is then absorbed by the subtle matter of the earth's many rarefied zones or levels including the human level. Thence it is converted by the human vehicle as consciousness, coming up from below from the bottom chakra and eventually assuming the form of the pure creative energy (kundalini) in the top chakra of man. The kundalini flows constantly through the Sushumna but only excites those chakras which have an equal (balanced) polarity of Ida and Pingala at the points where they cross over in the Sushumna.

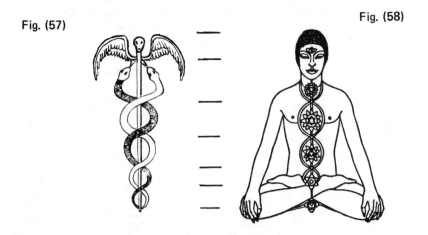

Fig. (57)

Fig. (58)

Equal polarity between the postive/negative, yin/yang aspects of prana allow the energy of consciousness to flow through and awaken the level above it. This balanced equilibrium can be achieved consciously by meditation and sometimes unconsciously, but it is unlikely that all chakras would become accidentally balanced in polarity at the same time. Without some training the chakras are never still since they are throbbing and pulsating with the life-force as we breathe, constantly bathing the entire organism in consciousness. Every desire in every chakra amounts to a tipping of the scales of perfect equilibrium and therefore a blocking of the rise of kundalini. Only when all chakras are clear (still) does kundalini flow harmlessly upwards through the psychic channels of the chakra system. Meantime the aura is always either changing or static depending on which chakra a person is thinking, feeling or sensing through. It can be yellow one minute and indigo the next or both together with flashes of each pulsing in different layers around the body.

In a fully enlightened being, the aura colours return to their original unmanifested state (stillness) as part of the invisible white light or lumen. Such a being, because he is not blocking the flow of life-force through the chakras is more alive, more vital, more conscious than other people, and this is the true meaning of the word **spiritual**.

THE TRANSDUCTION OF PSYCHOTRONIC ENERGY
INTO HUMAN CONSCIOUSNESS

The human body acting as a transducer for light energies of the full spectrum (including cosmic super-optical and sub-optical radiation) of the universal field acts as a prism or tuning device for the separation of specific energies called consciousness. These energies are absorbed from the total environment on seven hierarchical levels of manifestation. This can be likened to the analogy of the prism, but in looking at this analogy one must not mistake it for the reality of the field, which is not triangular.

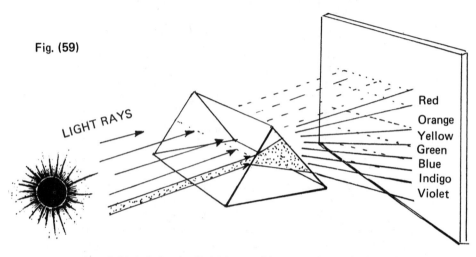

Fig. (59)

LIGHT RAYS

Red
Orange
Yellow
Green
Blue
Indigo
Violet

The field being spherical is more like a raindrop which creates the rainbow, but there again the analogy is not exact enough for any more than a transitory image since the field is within the field within the field, etc. with the observer's consciousness at the centre of the rainbow effect instead of being separate and observing it from outside the raindrop or prism.

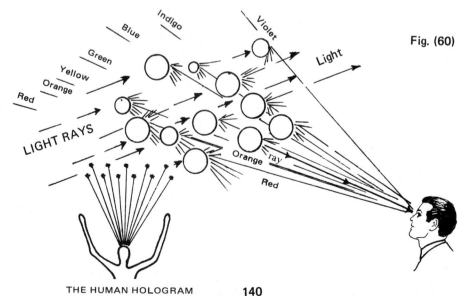

Fig. (60)

The absorption of colour into an object is not separate from the molecular and atomic construction of its materials which determine its pigmentation, its coefficient of absorption, etc. It can be said that colour of any object is absorbed in direct inverse proportion to the energy radiated by the object; but even that is not correct in all cases, particularly when that object is a complex human being absorbing cosmic energies not only in one spectrum of the physical level of manifestation of energy but also through other energy systems which we could call spiritual or psychic or mental or emotional depending where we ourselves are coming from. Hence it is worth wrapping our mind around this transduction from photon, electron and proton energy exchange to see clearly that although the full spectrum of cosmic radiation impinges on everybody, there are various modifiers of its effects.

Not only do the configurations of the planetary system create an astrological pattern which modifies the construction of the human psychic vehicle at birth, but also the consciousness which reacts to these patterns will determine how much or what part of the full spectrum remains unused or is reflected back into the environment. In other words, I do not believe the planets themselves exert special influences or qualities on the individual person which determine his fate in a predetermined way. However, I do believe that the pattern of life in each individual is modified, although not controlled, by the relative positions of sun and moon and planets in reference to the general backdrop of cosmic radiation from different parts or sections of the galaxy. Since different energies are produced by say Sirius in one sign of the zodiac and the star Arcturas in another, it is reasonable to say they will modify our basic biological, emotional and mental vehicles and the way these human vehicles absorb cosmic energies. However, the nature of human consciousness, once its enormous power is realised, enables any person to influence these patterns of energy and control the planetary effects rather than allowing them to control him. By far the greatest modifier, then, is our own attitudes, drives, and levels of consciousness which will determine whether we absorb as an introvert does or reflect these cosmic fluxes as an extravert does.

LIFE COMES THE SAME TO EVERYONE

In order to understand more accurately the differences between introvert/extravert and the process of light absorption and the re-radiation of these psychic electricity fields, we can use another analogy of the natural process of ingestion, digestion, assimilation and excretion. All objects including stars, atoms, cells, organs and people follow this natural sequence of absorbing their nourishment from the environment. Obviously if energies are constipated through some inability of the organism to excrete them because of ineffective elimination of unwanted material, then sickness and unbalanced states will result in dis-ease. The following table gives a visual idea of the way different human beings maintain the balance of cosmic energies in the human vehicle through absorption and elimination. A balance is achieved through the ingestion of energies through the chakra system leading to introvert/extravert use of the total spectrum of light energies.

Fig. (61)

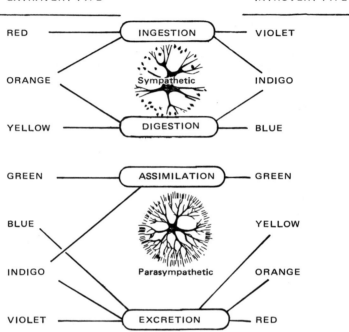

EXTRAVERT TYPE   INTROVERT TYPE

RED	INGESTION	VIOLET
ORANGE	Sympathetic	INDIGO
YELLOW	DIGESTION	BLUE
GREEN	ASSIMILATION	GREEN
BLUE		YELLOW
INDIGO	Parasympathetic	ORANGE
VIOLET	EXCRETION	RED

In the same way that atoms eliminate and eject rays of unwanted energy from their systems when saturated with electrons, so do the cosmic forces release in man's vehicle the enhanced biolumen which energises the human aura. The colour of the process merely denotes the level of excitement. As with the burning of the natural elements in the sun and stars in the macrocosm, so do we burn them also, at a less intense rate of vibration, in the microcosm. A person who responds to red corresponds in the microcosm to the atoms whose electrons have little attraction for the nuclear centre and are easily excited and thrown off into the environment. They metaphorically generate a lot of heat but have little penetration. One who absorbs only this cosmic energy at the Red level would put most of his attention on the ingestion of food or the sense of pleasure and be mostly superficial. Like the heat created by throwing off electrons, the waves of energy from red would be long, dissipate fast and get quickly lost in the cold around them. Therefore the extravert ingests red and digests orange and yellow; he assimilates green and blue but does not experience them, just as when we eat, digestion and assimilation are largely unconscious processes out of our voluntary control. The shorter waves of the blue and violet end of the spectrum penetrate deeper and therefore have a much longer, more delayed reaction time. A Red type is reactive while the Blue and Violet type is more passive.

The Red type excretes indigo and violet and a person with a Red aura personality and temperament does not favour psychic or imaginative people. One can think of the red-neck type rejecting or reflecting any communication from the abstract levels of thought because the concrete world of physical matter is all that is real to him. Similarly this process is reversed for someone whose intake as an introvert (Indigo, Violet) makes the concrete world a heavy cross to bear, since concrete matter ties him down on earth. What the Red extravert ingests, the introvert excretes and finds intolerably boring. However, both assimilate the same colour, Green, because it is the colour of assimilation both at the level of chlorophyllian photon conversion of visible light and at the level of the human synthesis of cosmic light and its prana. Therefore the harmonic colour of prana is green, just as the excited electron is red (rajas/action) and the stable proton is blue. However, if we apply heat, i.e. electron disturbance, to the proton it loses its stability and becomes excited, going through another octave of changes, red hot, orange hot, and so on to white hot. The heating flow of electrons in an electric circuit can be likened to the flow of prana in the nervous system, and the ionisation of an atomic nucleus in the microcosm can be likened to the radiance of the kundalini which burns its way through macro molecules of human matter.

THE CONSCIOUSNESS GRADIENT

The absorption and re-radiation of the energies of consciousness vary with the flow of the kundalini. Activation of the centres can vary widely and a person may have unique combinations of the 7 x 7 x 7 possible operations of each chakra and be further modified by the degree of openness of each chakra. Hence one chakra may be open 90 percent and another 2 percent or one may be 15 percent and three only 5 percent, with the remaining ones only 1 percent cracked open. One can see the millions of permutations possible, accounting for the uniqueness of every human on the planet. Therefore the 7 x 7 x 7 possibilities are each multiplied by factors of 100 if we allow 100 degrees of openness for each chakra. The number of different types then becomes

$$7 \times 100 = 700 \times 7 = 49,000$$
$$49,000 \times 100 = 490,000 \times 7 = 3,430,000$$
$$3,430,000 \times 100 = 343,000,000 \times 7 = 2,401,000,000$$

If we allow 360 degrees of openness for each chakra we can see that this would account for more than the entire world's population to be unique and different. If we then allow the number of possibilities by closing off some chakras and having combinations of 2 or 3 chakra functions we increase the factors by another 7 x 7 x 7. This explains the miracle that although each human has one head, two arms and two legs as a cosmic image, not one face is a strictly identical image. On page 613 we show a few of the possibilities of blending the seven chakra types as a graphic example with each chakra as a variable depending on the level of consciousness functioning and awakened in each individual person.

People who radiate a dark and heavy vibration are, like all else in the cosmos, made of light. But they are ignorant of this fact and their ignorance blocks the light from the evolution process and cuts them off from their real Self. The fact that biolumi-nescence occurs is a proof of the fact that we are light, we are consciousness -- the same stuff that is creating the macrocosmic layers of the magnetic fields around the earth and the same that is processing itself beyond our knowing in our own molecules in the microcosm. The more we radiate and give off this light, the more we are being who we really are.

The point of studying the human aura and its chemical process of bioluminescence is to gain some sense of identity both above and below our normal range of self-image: to become acquainted with our body cells (our microcosmic self) and consider their needs and work in cooperation with them rather than against them, and to tune into our macrocosmic self in whose being we are like a cell whose awareness is such that it tends either toward health or toward dis-ease. Cancer occurs not only when our body cells are going in a different direction than we have intended but also when we ourselves are similarly out of step with the splendour of the Whole.

To get some inkling of this imprisoned splendour and the order and harmony of its laws we have only to look at the resemblance between an atom and a galaxy, or to notice that the love which binds two people together is the same creative force which polarises the atoms and binds them into molecules. There are many ways of looking at the complexity of these functions scientifically but our study of bioluminescence not only gives us insight into the nature of light, but also shows the ways that we modify this light (in wisdom or in ignorance of its laws) and the ways that it modifies us, whether we acknowledge it or not.

Our adventure as author and reader in seeking the chemistry of light together at the Nuclear centre of Being, must now step up to the next stage of man's awareness as a whole space Being who lives on the nourishment of light. To understand this we shall look at the hologram of life and then proceed directly to the secret of God's signature -- the rainbow body in which the ONE manifests in our consciousness as colour.

If we have said that light and consciousness are ONE, then we can say discovering the links between colour and consciousness will bring us to the threshold of the divine temple of light.

THE HOLOGRAM OF LIFE

THE UNIVERSAL HOLOGRAM

The whole of man's evolutionary history is impregnated in the consciousness of every atom, cell, molecule, organism. The creation of a proton from a supernova explosion is imprinted in the self-image of that proton. The holograms of proton, cell, molecule, human, star, supernova, are replications created by the intersecting of light beams in standing waves, of the original image projected into the light of consciousness by consciousness itself. Therefore, all images of creation are reflections at different angles of the original image. The many is in the One and the One in the many. This perception is possible to the human mind that is clear of all obstructing self-concepts and ego filters. Thus the universe is truly contained in the "grain of sand" and the origins of life are present in every brain cell. Every part contains the whole hologram, every drop of water contains the whole ocean. The experience of cosmic consciousness is reliving and re-creating the play of consciousness, the creation of billions of stars and supernovas from time immemorial and the realisation of the total evolutionary potential of man's consciousness. When we glimpse the vastness of this galaxy and other galaxies, contained within countless universes, we realise that our sun which illumines our world is a small fry in relation to the awesome splendour and expanse of creation, of consciousness. In relation to the universal potential the sun's consciousness is not much more evolved than man's, a similar aggregation of primeval atoms, even though the sun is billions of times bigger and more powerful than the earth's hologram. Mankind is at the brink of a cliff into the never-ending reaches of cosmic consciousness, awaiting his own self-discovery and annihilation of his separate self.

The cosmic intelligence is not some abstract quality with fancy esoteric names, rays, logoi, spirits, etc., but the cosmic rays which make up the invisible light of consciousness expressing itself through seven vortexes or centres. The mystification and creation of thousands of terms in esoteric literature for something which is very plain and simple is a product of human consciousness. The divine consciousness sees only its own light splitting the cosmic rays into seven thresholds of vibration in the universal whole.

HOW DOES CONSCIOUSNESS ARISE?

How are cosmic rays generated? The answer to this question has not been fully given by science. Some say they are heavy protons shot out from the nucleus of atoms of neutron stars. Some say that they are X-rays generated by the gyrations of

Optical map of M51 photographed by Mt. Wilson and Palomar observatories.

Picture of the lines of radio emission showing intensity expressed as a contour map of M51 with the optical map of M51 superimposed.

high energy electrons in a strong magnetic field of old stars in the centre of our galaxy which throws off protons and electrons. Another view is that hot cosmic gases ionise the inner shell of an atom such as iron by protons and electrons from other stars, and the cosmic X-rays are sent out when the inner shell vacancy is filled from outside the atom. Cosmic ray electrons emitted by neutron stars which are decaying are very fast particles and reach the earth's atmosphere by being captured by the earth's magnetic field. Fast electrons travelling at the speed of light have radio frequencies which can be plotted on a radio map of the energy of a galaxy. On the previous page we see such a radio wave energy map superimposed on top of a visual map of galaxy M51.

This galaxy is about the same diameter as our own (100,000 light years) and the radiation mapped is of atomic hydrogen with a wave length of 21 cm . These fast electrons coming from oscillating clouds of hydrogen gases can not only excite the antenna of a radio telescope but also the sensitive supersensonic instrument of our own natural biofeedback equipment in the nervous system.* We can now view the entire human vehicle as an antenna, since most of the human body weight is water made up of hydrogen and oxygen atoms. Astronomers have now found that hydrogen atoms in stars emit radio waves which reach the earth in addition to the light of the visible spectrum. What we see with eyes and optical telescopes is only a small part of the radiation being absorbed by humans even now at this moment. The hydrogen radiation of 21 cm from fast hydrogen electrons from stars with 100,000 times the energy of the sun excites the elements of our bodies because it is in resonance with the water atoms of hydrogen and leaves some of its energy behind after the fast electrons collide with the different atoms of our bodies. Our consciousness can be regarded as a hologram with our fundamental background radiation as one reference beam and the visual light of the sun as the exciting beam which illuminates our part of the galaxy. Our consciousness and the background radiation being ONE and the same provide the picture of the hologram image.

Two or more intersecting beams of coherent light can form standing wave patterns. When these intersect over a given region there will be places where the electric field values will add up to a greater value than the sum of the individual waves alone (light added to light). There will also be places where the electric field values subtract (absorption subtracts from light). At any given moment when we discern the brightness of the light in the intersection region of space with our consciousness, a very definite pattern of light and dark areas will be observed.

(See next page.)

---

*The book "Supersensonics" shows how we can detect gases and other elements burning in the sun and map the radiating energies of objects, humans, and invisible forces with a dowsing rod.

Fig. (62)

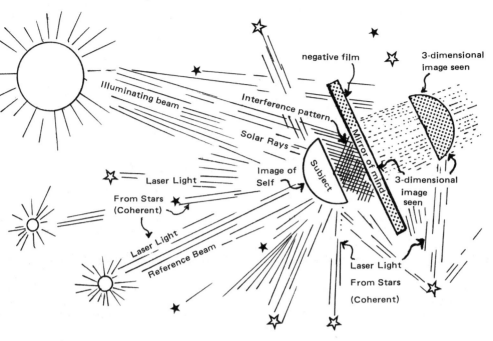

THE HUMAN HOLOGRAM

The three-dimensional image of the hologram is created before our eyes in space by two beams of coherent light (light of the same frequency with the waves in phase). The waves overlap creating standing wave patterns over a certain region of space which subtract and add to the light field. Our consciousness sees the image as real even though there is nothing solid in space. One can put one's hand through the image which looks like a real object. The image is created entirely by interactions of light disturbing (the field of the knower) -- consciousness.

Fig. (63)

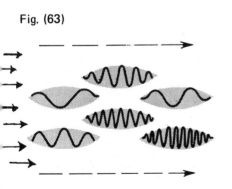

This drawing of photons of light from the sun shows an imaginative mental picture of how the little packets of energy (quanta) are all going at the same speed but vibrating with different wavelengths (distance) and frequencies (time).

Fig. (64)

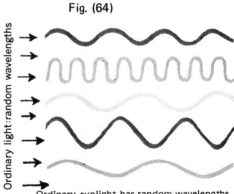

Ordinary sunlight has random wavelengths with a wide range of frequencies (colours). The light is not polarised to travel in one plane but travels in similar spirals along a spherical wavefront in random phases.

The Hologram is made up of coherent laser light. Coherent light is the same light which reaches us from some of the distant stars. Ordinary sunlight is not coherent and not monochromatic (all of one frequency) but laser light is both. The diagrams below show the different kinds of light in order to distinguish the difference of coherent light.

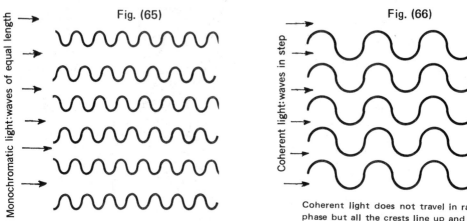

Fig. (65)

Monochromatic light:waves of equal length

Monochromatic light (light of one colour) has waves all of the same wavelength but their crests may not be in phase with each other.

Fig. (66)

Coherent light:waves in step

Coherent light does not travel in random phase but all the crests line up and all the troughs line up so they are in perfect resonance and amplify each other. Laser light is coherent and the waves are in step (in phase) and therefore do not spread out very much.

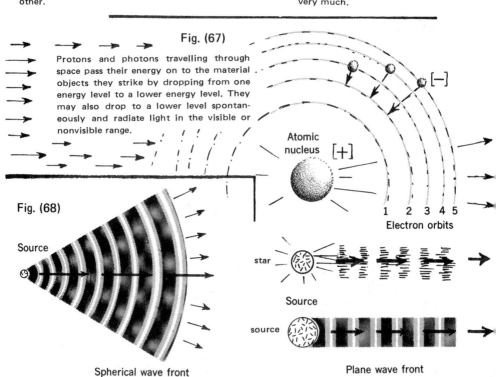

Fig. (67)

Protons and photons travelling through space pass their energy on to the material objects they strike by dropping from one energy level to a lower energy level. They may also drop to a lower level spontaneously and radiate light in the visible or nonvisible range.

Atomic nucleus [+]

[−]

1 2 3 4 5
Electron orbits

Fig. (68)

Source

Spherical wave front

star

Source

source

Plane wave front

The above shows a spherical wavefront of light whose wavelengths are in phase compared to a plane wave front of a coherent source such as a star or laser. The reason the starlight is coherent is that all its spreading out has been done over millions of light years so only its coherent wavelengths get through to us, while the sun is a very close star so its many colours (frequencies) spread out and we see a wide range of colours.

Fig. (69)

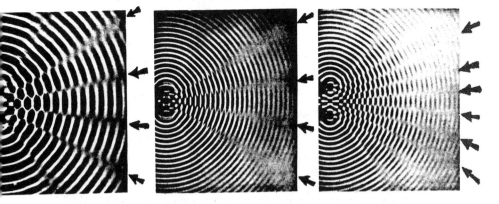

Waves sent out by two identical sources interfere with each other at different distances apart to create patterns of energy. At the nodal points where the waves intersect they annihilate each other; there is a darkness in space. Where they coincide there is added lightness. The whole universe including human consciousness is a creation of light and dark with various phases in between at seven nodal points. The light from the stars and the light from the sun vibrate in our consciousness and create a disturbance of destructive waves which are not in resonance with it or amplify it by constructive interference.

It is purely a creation of our consciousness in three dimensions. The image lasts as long as the interference of the coherent waves (which create this spatial pattern of light) remains fixed at a given frequency, and while the waves overlap. This is what is meant by a standing wave pattern. Starlight is coherent light because many of the frequencies have been scattered by its long passage through cosmic gases and its collisions with other protons in interstellar space so that only the wavefronts of coherent light (light waves of a single frequency) reach the earth. The sun is too close to us and therefore produces incoherent light where the phases of the light waves vary very rapidly, and therefore no fixed intensity patterns can be seen or recorded. The exposure of a photographic plate in the overlap region of the coherent waves leads to a hologram image whereas incoherent waves result merely in a fogged photographic plate. If we look at consciousness as being coherent cosmic light from the stars and therefore coherently fixed in frequency we can see that people who think that light is only what you visibly see, like incoherent sunlight, get a foggy image of themselves and do not perceive the material vibrations of the three dimensional universe around them as a hologram, but as something solid and tangible.

There is about one supernova explosion for every 30 years of life in our own galaxy. This rate given by Fred Hoyle* means that the contents of the stars are continually being redistributed and returned to other stars in the form of gases, energy, radiation and light. He estimates that about 2% of the mass of our whole

*References: "Astronomy and Cosmology," by Sir Fred Hoyle, W.H. Freeman & Co., San Francisco, 1975.

galaxy is being circulated by supernovae in this way. If we multiply this by even a modest number of 1000 other galaxies we will find that the energy we are receiving now at this moment from cosmic sources is 2000 percent of our own galaxy. And 1000 galaxies is a small figure if we consider that the size of the total universe may be well over 100,000 galaxies like our own.

The implication of all this enormous atomic radiation and light is that all the common materials we know in our daily world, including the elements in our own body and carbon products essential to life as well as the oxygen we breathe, were all produced in stellar furnaces like our own sun and had already been flung violently into space long before the sun and its planets formed. The atoms of every object of our daily world, including the ground we stand on, have not been fashioned here in this locality on earth within the solar system, but were fashioned long ago in different parts of our own and other galaxies and sent here in the form of heavy protons, fast electrons and neutrons of light and radiation. These three protonic, electronic and neutronic forces constitute the three gunas or qualities of cosmic radiance. (Satva - Being, Rajas - Glowing, Tamas - Inaction.) The very rocks of the earth made of the elements from annihilation of these heavy protons have a fantastic history from before we clothed our bodies in their mineral elements of carbon, oxygen, hydrogen, magnesium, etc. At this very moment the waste energy of a thousand galaxies with an average of one supernova every 400 years per galaxy (Fred Hoyle estimates one every 30 years per galaxy) means that during the life of our own galaxy our bodies are receiving continuously the residue of millions of supernovae which have exploded over its 10 billion years existence. Right now our bodies are receiving continuously the cosmic debris of these radiating fireballs in the form of fast electrons, protons and fast neutronic cosmic rays – the residue of potent supernovae explosions at an enormous rate of expansion. Our own consciousness is a product of this vast expansion of the original hologram nucleus.

Because our own vehicle of consciousness and its radiation has grown up and adapted to this enormous energy intake we do not sense it, nor does it appear to affect us . Like certain algae that grow in the hot steam of geothermic pools, or the fish that does not drown in the ocean waters, the human being lives in a sea of radiation fire so powerful that it reproduces the very stuff which created the universe, i.e. pure consciousness.

HOLOGRAM LIGHT

Everyone knows the familiar photographic process of the negative and positive film. In considering the cell as a hologram or negative image which creates the positive image of the cell manifesting in three dimensions, we have to readjust our thinking about the microwave background radiation of the universe. Does the cell or the nucleus of the cell respond to thought in some way to tune the chromosomes in the nucleus, and can the microwave background radiation affect the genes and the DNA-RNA template which governs the synthesis of proteins in our body?

The answer will depend on whether there is enough light which is exactly tuned to the atoms in the cell nucleus. As we have said, starlight and the microwave background is coherent, like laser light, while the sun's light, being near to us, is not coherent and spreads out. But there is a point at which light does not spread out, if the object it irradiates or the hole it shines through is smaller than .01 mm. The human cell is so small we must get some idea of its size in relation to light waves which irradiate it.

The size of the DNA molecule is incredibly small by ordinary standards of measurement. Its parts are made up of ties which are paired together like a railway track. The particular pattern of these ties along the double helix track determines the actual construction of all our biological cells and contains the information required for the evolution of any plant or animal organism. The DNA is coiled up in such a spiral way that it occupies incredibly little space. The space occupied is about a hundredth part of a millimeter. Remarkably this size is about the same dimension at which incoherent light begins to turn corners due to the spreading out of its waves.

Fig. (70)

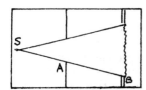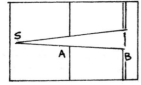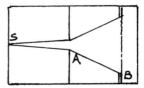

Light from a point source passes through a hole in screen A onto a viewing screen in this diagram. If the light travels in straight lines without spreading out as at left, the illuminated area on screen B should decrease with the smaller size of the hole in A. It can be shown that ordinary sunlight does so until the diameter of the hole is reduced to about one hundredth of a millimeter as in the centre picture. Picture at right shows what happens when the hole or slit gets smaller than .01mm. when the light beam expands its image on the screen.

At the same diameter of a hole in a screen (of .01 mm), particles of radiation, photons, radio waves, or light, begin to diffuse, but up to this measurement the waves are coherent, like starlight or laser light. To get an idea of how large an antenna the DNA structure is for the interaction of these tiny light waves, we can look at the scale of the ties of an actual railway track.

Between New York and Los Angeles, Fred Hoyle calculates there are about six million railway ties, if we allow about one

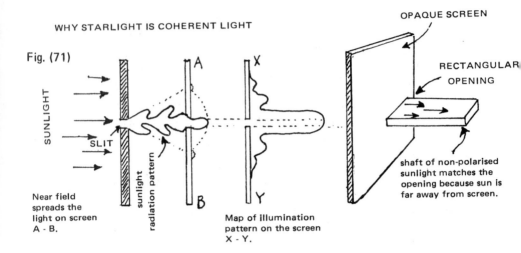

Fig. (71)

SUNLIGHT

SLIT

Near field
spreads the
light on screen
A - B.

sunlight
radiation pattern

A

B

X

Y

Map of illumination
pattern on the screen
X - Y.

OPAQUE SCREEN

RECTANGULAR
OPENING

shaft of non-polarised
sunlight matches the
opening because sun is
far away from screen.

The diagram above is an elaboration of the phenomenon on the previous page. The sun would be a different star when it is close to us on earth than if it were far away. At left is shown rays of an oscillating source of incoherent light which have a tendency to spread out when they pass through a slit from a near field.

At right from the far field the light does not spread out. However, sources of radiation from stars far away do not behave like the incoherent rays from our nearby sun. Starlight and microwave background sources are coherent because all the other wave frequencies have been filtered out by long passage through space. This coherent light is in resonance with human cell life and consciousness fields so we do not feel any disturbance from it like we do from sunlight.

yard between them to match our stride. In a single human cell the "railway track" of the DNA molecules has about six **thousand million** or one thousand times this distance if we had to walk it. The whole structure is packed away in a space about .01 millimeter.Even so small, the DNA strands in a cell would stretch out about 2 meters if we laid them out straight end-to-end like a railway track. This very small measurement, at around the size of the slit at which the wavelengths of light cause it to spread out and stop being coherent light, is a key factor in the ability of starlight and coherent light to act as a hologram for the biological message systems such as DNA and human cells. The idea that thought and light are effective in changing the DNA structures of life in the evolutionary development of a human life is not currently a scientifically proved idea. In fact, most geneticists believe the contrary, that once given the DNA structure the pattern is the same for all replicating generations and that only through some mutation can a change in the basic DNA pattern occur. The carrier of genetic material is the genes which are contained in the chromosomes of the cell nucleus. The number of chromosomes in the cell depends on the plant or animal.

Human cells have 46 chromosomes and those of a mouse have 40. The genes are made up of the chains of DNA which are strung out in the double stranded twisted "railway track". Thought induced changes in the RNA messenger molecule does not mean there are any changes in the DNA of the genes themselves. However any change in the medium through which orders pass effectively changes the message. Like the scrambling of a telegram, the message which passes down the nerves can also be changed by changes in nerve structure, so can the RNA which carries the message of the DNA strands be changed by light and consciousness.

Nuclear Evolution postulates that the body attracts to itself the primary conditions which affect the system as a whole and these conditions manifest according to an evolutionary plan which is true for the whole of creation, both manifest and unmanifest. Consciousness is unmanifest, but its effects on the body are manifest. Yet the laws of evolution apply to both the replication of the microcosm as well as the macrocosm. Therefore, the ability of light to affect DNA-RNA replication process at the physical cell level is the same as its universal effect on the constructions of solids, liquids and gases.

Fig. (72)

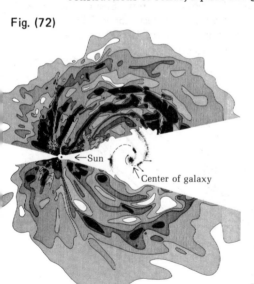

← Sun

Center of galaxy

Fig. (73)

At left is the spiral nature of our own galaxy plotted from the emission of 21 cm. wavelength hydrogen radiation from clouds of light-stimulated gas. When electrons in hydrogen atoms spin in the reverse direction to the proton in the nucleus they release energy in the form of a radio signal of 21 cm. wavelength. By tuning to this wavelength an astronomer can map the concentrations of the background radiation in our galaxy.

The Orion Nebula glows because its clouds of gas are lit up by nearby suns thereby ionising the atoms. Light and radiation emissions are produced by the excited atoms which are combining to bring new stars into birth. Hot stars from 400 light years away may cause photoionisation of the gases and atoms. Our own bodies are made of such atoms and are ionised by starlight although we cannot feel this excitation with our senses. The distance of Orion Nebula is about 1500 light years away or 100 times its diameter. Our own galaxy is 100 times greater still, about 100,000 light years.

One-half the star Antares

Fig. (74)

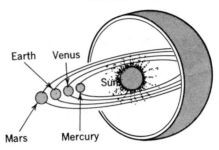

An imaginary representation of our sun as a cosmic baby, whose brightness is tuned to our senses while the stars are tuned to our minds. The hologram of life is made by the laser-like light of the stars while the diffused light of the sun illuminates the hologram along with the light of our consciousness.

The star Antares is 70 million times bigger than our sun. All the planets in the solar system up to Mars could revolve in their existing orbits and still be inside this enormous star. Its light travels to us from a vast distance and penetrates our atmosphere as well as our psychic envelope of consciousness. A similar comparison in smallness can be obtained from Sirius, the brightest binary star in our sky whose smallest star is 30,000 times smaller than our sun, but whose rays are 40,000 times as potent. It has a mass or weight equal to our sun.

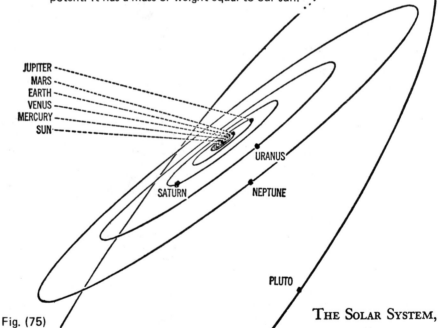

Fig. (75)

THE SOLAR SYSTEM,

The enormous size of Antares is shown as a comparison in the drawings above. Millions of stars like Antares and Sirius exist in our own galaxy and billions exist in countless other galaxies over 100,000 light years away. Their light is coherent, like laser light, and enters our cells and nervous system at non-sensory, non-visual, levels from every direction in space. This enormous amount of energy creates the hologram of life.

THE HOLOGRAM OF THE THREE-DIMENSIONAL WORLD

Humans experience the world in three dimensions although most of our pictures, photographs, measurements, graphs and ideas are expressed only in two dimensions like the flat surface of this paper or a photograph.

Imagine now a slightly streaked photographic negative. You shine a special light through it and look at it just like you look at a mirror and there, hanging in front of you in mid air as if like a desert mirage, is a three-dimensional picture of a whole village. By moving around it you can look around the village church and see around the back of the tallest buildings. The smallest buildings behind it can be seen and people, sign posts and automobiles appear and disappear around the corner of the buildings. The mirror through which you are looking is called a hologram and the photography used to create this three-dimensional village scene is called holography. If you tear off a piece of the negative, none of the village scene is lost and if you cut the negative in four quarters you could have four whole villages created in front of your eyes by four different light beams. Imagine now that the negative was the biological pattern of the subtle energies and wave-fields set up by the human aura and that you yourself were a three-dimensional scene illuminated by the coherent light beams of several stars. You would be a human hologram and if you took any of your parts each would have the identity of the whole you. Each cell would contain the blue-print for the entire three-dimensional image that you see as yourself. Now imagine all other groups of macro molecules, such as other human bodies also to be holograms created by the resonant vibrations of cosmic rays shining through the negative template created by thousands of overlapping radiations.

All wave-fields whether light waves from a laser, radio waves from an antenna or sound waves from a loudspeaker or waves on the ocean have the common function of re-distributing the energy which caused them, into the space around. The whole universe is still re-distributing the energy of the primeval atom which expanded and created it in the first place. That energy is coming to us in the waves of gravitation and levitation. Gravitational waves flow inward towards the centre of every object including our consciousness and levitational waves are flowing out from the centre as light. Light waves are then merely the energy of something redistributing itself in space, and our consciousness which looks out of our eyes and shines on objects is that same expanding field of waves of levitational energy.

We must now assume the viewpoint of a universal hologram illuminated by rays from every direction in space expanding from everything at once and entering into everything through gravitational pull into a nuclear centre. The attraction of gravitation working inside every nuclear centre pulls all matter into tighter and tighter clumps but this attraction is resisted by another effect, for example some pressure within the material. If it is a star we say it is radiation pressure which counteracts gravity. It is this radiation pressure which forces light out of the sun and creates an expanding wave-field of solar energy which continues forever and ever in space until it is absorbed by other suns and galaxies of suns. These suns are also expanding and their levity force is expanding their energy into the totality of space.

The universal hologram is created by the light rays of all these suns whose coherent rays of expanding energy create wave-fields travelling in every direction at once and this light energy is then absorbed into our own system of atoms and molecules according to the resonant frequencies established by the different cellular mechanisms in which these wave-fields propagate.

If we look at the diagram below we will see that the microwave background consists of radiation whose main wavelength distribution is from about 0.5 mm. to 80 cm. and which reaches the earth smoothly from all parts of the sky. However, the cells of human beings and the atoms of the 44 crystal elements in the human body do not resonate with every vibration in this universal wave-field but only absorb from 13 cm. to 80 cm. of the cosmic background radiation.

Fig. (76)

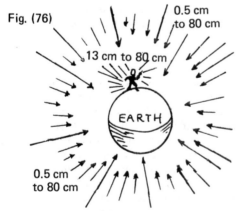

0.5 cm to 80 cm

13 cm to 80 cm

EARTH

0.5 cm to 80 cm

The radiation of the cosmic background is believed by astronomers to be the remaining vibrations of a hot, dense condition of the universe caused by gravity which is often called the "big bang". All the atoms in our bodies according to this theory were made at the time of this big bang.

Nuclear Evolution, however, views the formation of atoms as a flux in which the configuration of an atom and its parts is determined by its angle of manifestation in a continuum of cosmic vibrations spiralling wherever there are nodal points of zero vibration. These points only happen when all vibrations annihilate each other through resonance and interference.

The universal hologram is caused by the absorption and reflection of rays of cosmic light, which constitute the continuous expansion of the universe in seven different thresholds of a homogeneous medium. The word levity, from the Latin, means lightness in weight and the continued lightening of matter causes it to expand into these seven levels of radiation. Hence light is that quality which causes our consciousness to expand beyond the heavy weight of our atomic vehicle. The subtle matter of this vehicle acts as a medium for absorbing the background radiation from all the expanding stars in the cosmos, which are redistributing the energy of their intense enlightening.

WHAT CAUSES COLOUR?

The background radiation is vibrating at different wavelengths which mesh with different kinds of proteins in the physical medium which is also vibrating material. A pure colour is a fixed distance between the crests of the wave oscillations in the vibrating field which is called by the convenient name of "wavelength". The background of invisible radiation or ordinary white light as we call the visible radiation from our local star the sun is made up of pure colours consisting of seven whole sets of different wavelengths. These waves can be separated in man's body by his chakras acting as different mediums; or to make these invisible rays visible we can shine the waves of light or radiation through a glass plate or prism so that the rays are bent as they enter, depending on the nature of the glass and the colour of the light, i.e. on its wavelength and frequency.

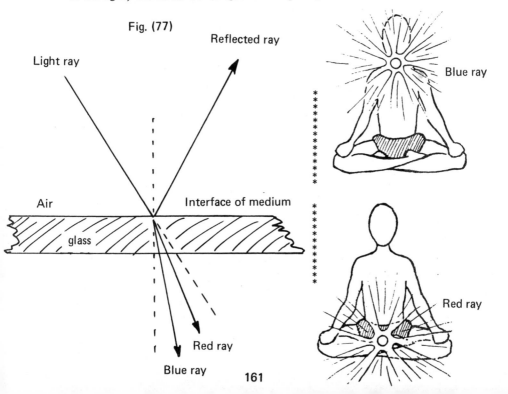

Fig. (77)

Reflected ray

Light ray

Air

Interface of medium

glass

Blue ray

Red ray

Red ray

Blue ray

Blue ray

161

We can see that the blue ray is bent more than the red ray and we can see that the shorter wavelength of the blue light has more penetrating power in a subtle medium, whereas in the dense medium such as cells and proteins, the larger red rays are quickly absorbed as heat rays. Hence we see that the slower frequency and longer wavelengths of red light affect the physical sensations of matter, while the blue light penetrates the mind which is also a more subtle material vibration of man's being.

If a ray of light containing the mixed radiating colours of the sun's levitating expansion is passed through a glass prism the various colours are refracted and separate as they emerge out of the far side of the prism. This expansive radiation is still in the form of invisible rays when they emerge but by shining them on some matter such as a white screen we reflect the colours so that the separate colours may be observed to take up the seven different thresholds in the colours of the rainbow. The phenomenon of the rainbow made by spherical water drops in the sky acts like a prism and in the same way the spherical wave-fields of the medium we call the human vehicle act to separate the cosmic light of the stars into its constituent aura colours. In exactly the same way that the prism shows us the seven thresholds of ordinary white light from the sun, the human chakra system of subtle radiating energies reveals the colours of the cosmic expansion in every human consciousness.

If we liken each chakra to a filter then we can use it in the same way that we can separate one specific colour wavelength or frequency from all the other background colours of white light, by interposing it as a filter and passing the rays of light through it.

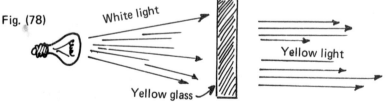

Fig. (78)

White light

Yellow light

Yellow glass

All we need to do is to pass the white light through a yellow glass and only the yellow light will pass through, the remaining colours being absorbed. However, in practice the human being is not so simple as a piece of yellow glass simply because the human being not only absorbs light from the cosmos but is also an expanding radiator of light as well. Hence some light is absorbed and pulled in from other stars and some light is reflected and some light is re-radiated as consciousness and bioenergetic vibration.

In following the process with the mind we must always keep the hologram clear by not confusing the three kinds of light – the primary cosmic light which is unpolarised until it hits matter, the reflected light which is polarised by its angle of reflection, and the absorbed light which is subtracted by some pigment medium before it is reflected back to our consciousness.

In a vacuum, light can be made to propagate as a one-way wave-guide in any chosen direction. Outer space is such a vacuum so a star propagates its radiation one way as it expands and lightens its material atoms. The same is true for light propagating in some translucent material, provided that material is homogeneous, that is, the same density and substance in all places. But when light, propagating in a homogeneous medium such as space or a tube of plastic resin or glass fibre, meets with another different homo-geneous medium, then the one-way propagation is destroyed. Not all the light continues into the second medium but some is turned back at the boundary between the two mediums. This is said to be reflected and the light that continues on through the second boundary is said to be refracted. The direction of the reflected and refracted rays is dependent on the angle of the incident rays of the one-way propagation.

When the mediums are the different electromagnetic sheaths of the earth and the bioelectric sheaths of the human chakra system, the cosmic rays which are coming from every star in the universal hologram in every direction and at a vast range of wavelengths and frequencies, enormous amounts of energy are reflected, refracted and absorbed in different ways. To understand the way in which humans act as a complex negative for the cosmic light expansion to radiate through the universal hologram requires that we view each nucleus of every atom and the nucleus of every cell as we do the nucleus of the entire whole vibrating universe and that we understand that one law is common for them all. If we cut one part of the negative up into smaller and smaller pieces it still contains the nuclear or seed picture of the whole. This is the basic plank of Nuclear Evolution, namely that all vibration works through the same laws of resonance for every medium, whether that medium is pure space or vacuum or some other density of expanding matter. To understand this expansion requires a full understanding of colour.

THE HOLOGRAM OF MIND-STUFF

The universe is interpenetrated with the wave-trains of cosmic radiation sent in every direction by stars around us. The cosmic rays from stars are coherent light like those of a laser.

The human body is a hologram image of the whole made up of the intersecting of consciousness and light with cosmic radiation patterns manifesting in primordial imagination. A hologram is defined as two or three wave-trains of light, from a coherent source such as a laser, intersecting to form standing wave patterns. If the reflected light from an object can be reflected by two secondary sources so as to intersect over some region of space, the standing wave pattern in the electric field will be obtained which shows a three-dimensional image of the object in space.

Fig. (79)

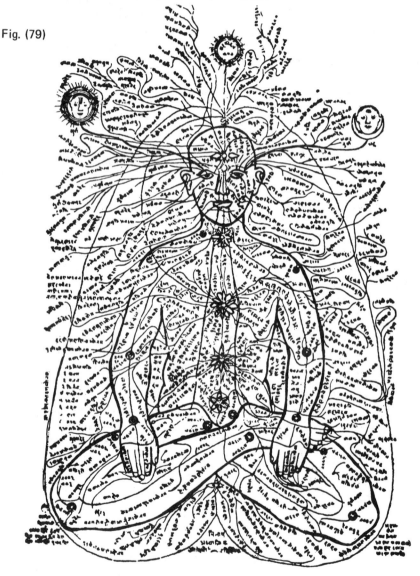

CURRENTS OF LIFE FORCE

PRANA CURRENTS CONNECTING THE SEVEN MAJOR PSYCHIC CENTRES WITH THEIR SUBSIDIARY CHAKRA CENTRES IN THE ETHERIC VEHICLE

NATURE'S OWN RADAR SYSTEM

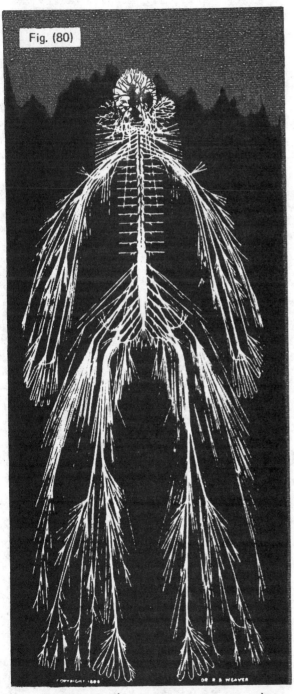

Fig. (80)

The cerebrospinal nervous system or the Tree of Life and the Tree of Knowledge, on which the University of the Trees is based.

The human nervous system is not only nature's method of transmitting signals from the external environment to the brain through the normal senses of eye, ear, touch, smell, taste, etc. but it is a vibrating radio-magnetic antenna which is constantly in touch with the internal environment. It can detect the most subtle changes in the needs of the cells such as carbon dioxide levels, fatigue and the hunger of different parts of the inner worlds. Both at the chemical-emotional, the thought-intellectual, and the spiritual-imaginative level the nervous system is also sensitive to the bioelectrical energies of other objects in the environment such as humans, water tables underground, radiations of crystals, and magnetic fields. The system acts as an antenna for tuning to the different frequencies of light which we absorb unconsciously but which we can sense consciously if we can regard it as a feedback instrument for cosmic processes. First the subtle vibrations of objects disturb the "consciousness — field" with oscillations and this is then picked up by the nervous antenna and relayed to the brain. Most people however live at a very low threshold of perception and do not know how to use the nervous system to make sense of all the information it receives. Several ancient civilizations found ways of using this antenna to "divine" events taking place in the internal world of cells and thereby record the neuromuscular reactions to more subtle thought-fields impinging on the system. The study of these interactions with the inner world is called "Supersensonics."

I.R. 13 Red   19 Orange 25   Yellow   50 Green 55 Blue 62 Indigo 68 Violet

COLOUR

MASTERING THE FORCES OF LIGHT

What did Christ mean when he said, "Ye are the light of this world? Was he only speaking metaphorically or was he speaking from a point-of-view that transcends our ordinary perceptions and therefore appears mysterious to us? Most people are confused by such statements on light made by spiritual masters, because most people are convinced that our consciousness is acted upon by external objects rather than the other way round. It is difficult to convince anyone to swallow the idea that our perception of the phenomenon of colour and light is an internal affair, but all spiritual truth has this upside-down quality about it and often times the words of fools are closer to true wisdom than is the common view of society. When Christ said, "Ye are the light of this world," he was saying "your consciousness literally lights up this world."

Because of our childhood programming, most of us think we see light and colour objectively and that they exist outside of our heads in the objects around us. But in fact not only the colours but the objects themselves are a psychic re-creation inside our heads. The light of the universe is invisible. The light we "see" is only the reflection of light as it is thrown off by "objects" or the effect of light absorbed in the pigments of the eye. The images of light which become objects are made visible only by a subjective reaction of the consciousness inside us working through the senses. Without our consciousness perceiving through the structuring and shaping windows of our senses, there would be no physical world of matter shining bright with all the colours of the rainbow.

We light up this world not only by receiving and perceiving its objects but by translating the sensory signals into whatever textures, subtleties, forms and meanings our own limited consciousness permits us to see. A nihilist sees very little of God's light shining even in the best of worlds, but a wise man can perceive the light as consciousness shining in the midst of devastation and catastrophe. So the holy man lights up the world in quite a different way to most people, and yet the light of consciousness comes to every human being in the same quality and quantity. The difference in the way we experience this light is revealed in the age-old teachings on the evolutionary force of kundalini. The word kundalini has a kind of magic for those who are students of the esoteric, yet there is really no mystery to it. Throughout this section on light and colour and its relationship to the evolutionary force of kundalini we shall be giving facts which anyone can prove and apply in the understanding of life energies in man.

The connection between so-called kundalini energy and the radiant light of the cosmos is often misunderstood. When that same cosmic light of the primary radiation expresses through a human being, we call it kundalini. By primary radiant light we mean the radiation of photons which appear to travel from the sun and all the stars through empty space and also the vibrating octaves of matter which exist on either side of the visible spectrum. So you can see how vast is the light of consciousness in each human being, locked in the sleeping kundalini. In order to understand the force of nature which raises biological matter up to conscious awareness of the light of consciousness we must continually study the effects in ourselves of the primary light from which kundalini is derived. This constant study of primordial light and its rainbow colours will not only help us understand ourselves but will bring about the evolution of the Supersense and a new age of light for mankind.

It can be asked what is the purpose in showing how colours represent thresholds of light? How does all this make any difference to a person's evolution? The operations of consciousness are very profound; just a simple operation of opening your eyes and seeing the outlines of objects and their colours is not just a matter of the eye picking up patterns of light. We are told by modern science that the message which passes down the optic nerve is purely an electrical spike conveyed by the neuro-transmitters which are released at each synapse. In other words the signal is a combination of an electrical potential and a chemical reaction. Yet the natural image is a perfect picture sent to the brain with all its nuances, shades, tints, subtle emotions and distance, conveyed along the nerve fibre like it was passed down a bent fibre optics tube. The image from eye to brain in fact is entirely re-created in the mind from all these tiny electro-chemical impulses and reactions.

We humans take this awesome power of light to recreate images of itself in colour inside our heads as a given, without asking how or why it happens except in electro-chemical terms. The answer is a secret of nature as profound as the birth of the universe. It cannot be described in words or concepts any more than my mother's Being can be described to the reader through bits of information like the colour of her hair and the five thousand other facts such as her temperature or the size of her blood cells. To know that we ourself make colour and recreate the spectrum of the material sensation of any object in our subjective mind is only meaningful if we can consciously understand its awesome purpose. To see the colours of light as the divisions of our own consciousness creating seven thresholds of Being at every level of nature enables us to probe the inner world of the psyche like the physicist uses light to probe the nuclear centre of the atom. To probe the heart of man with light and its seven colours is man's great adventure for the next 1000 years.

BECOMING THE LAWS OF CREATION

To reach the end of this long evolutionary journey, full of the joy of coming home, we will have to understand, master, and become the laws of creation, because in Nuclear Evolution there is no difference between the external cosmic light of the universe flowing between star and star, sun and planet, or filling the totality of empty space, and the consciousness or kundalini energy which is experienced internally as brightness, colour or heat. If there seems to be a difference, it is because there is a vast difference in the way different human beings process kundalini through their sensory vehicle-- the human bioenergetic chakra system.

When the creative forces of the universe rise through the body we call the energy kundalini, but before it enters the body it is called Akasha which is identical with pure consciousness before it is absorbed into the body. Basically the kundalini or the creative fire of pure consciousness is composed of three interlacing forces of nature which we can refer to as qualities of life force. These three life energies (called, in Sanskrit writings, "the three gunas") can work in us consciously to the extent that we take hold and shape our being, but in most people work unconsciously, controlling their behaviour by default.

SATVA GUNA (INTELLIGENCE):

That quality in nature which translates itself into purity, harmony, balance of opposites, knowledge of eternal reality. Satva implies substantial knowledge of light and leads to human radiance, happiness, joy, compassion and natural virtue or good. It does not imply moral or social values of good or even philo-sophical concepts of good, but the essence of all goodness-- right action. This translates into righteousness and not self-righteousness, since satva is super humble and unaware of separate selves. The fact that many people believe that they are conscious and wise is often the darkness of the soul. They cannot believe that there are more worlds of light than they can see. But with most people the gunas are unseen and uncontrollable at the conscious level of being. The root word is from Sat, the radiance of being.

170

Fig. (81)

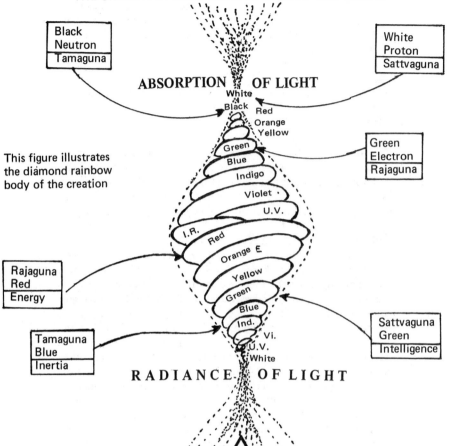

THE CREATIVE PRIMORDIAL FORCES OF THE GUNAS

Black
Neutron
Tamaguna

White
Proton
Sattvaguna

ABSORPTION OF LIGHT

White
Black   Red
Orange
Yellow
Green
Blue
Indigo
Violet
U.V.

Green
Electron
Rajaguna

This figure illustrates
the diamond rainbow
body of the creation

I.R.
Red
Orange E
Yellow
Green
Blue
Ind.
Vi.
U.V.
White

Rajaguna
Red
Energy

Tamaguna
Blue
Inertia

Sattvaguna
Green
Intelligence

RADIANCE OF LIGHT

...an's supersense is linked with the
...ility to absorb seven rays of cosmic
...rces of proticity from the nine levels
...the created world, namely Black,
...ed, Orange, Yellow, Green, Blue,
...digo, Violet, Ultraviolet, through
...astery of the three gunas of the
...eative force.

The human vehicle re-radiates the
absorbed energies through the
biological radiomagnetic cell which
acts as a semiconductor for the
transport of electrons into the
human wave-field. The aura is
composed of seven spiralling
spheres of seven dimensions of
interpenetrating vibrations.

RAJA GUNA (ENERGY):

The quality of nature which moves energy from one place to another, causing the motion of planets, vibrating the atoms and people to perform a restless dance of ceaseless activity. Applied to mental forces and emotional energies of the personality, raja guna translates into passion, action, struggle, effort, ambition, possessiveness, acquisitiveness, and the thirst of desire and expression. The root word Rajas means to glow red with energy.

TAMA GUNA (NEUTRALITY):

The force of inertia which resists motion and conserves energy. In human terms it translates into status quo, stability, rigidity, stubbornness, inaction, apathy, ignorance of self, darkness and obscurity. The root word Tam means to perish or to become sad or subject to depression, as against raja guna's urge for expression.

Perhaps you have experienced the way that certain people drain your energy. Twenty minutes in their company and you feel exhausted. You do not know why it happens and they do not know that they suck the life-force of others, because it all occurs at an unconscious level. In lesser degree, all relationships between people are either "sucking" or "giving" relationships. A person may give you a big warm hug and think he is giving love, but his vibration says just the opposite; he is wanting love to be given to him. This makes you recoil inwardly and withhold your love, because only love can elicit love. Such a person has an excess of tamasic energy which causes him to absorb much more than he is able to radiate. Because of his choices he makes in himself, either consciously or unconsciously, he has an imbalance of the gunas. But when these qualities are equally balanced with each other an orgasm takes place and the creative energy pours forth on seven different levels of consciousness, depending on our own level of evolution at the centre of Being. Thus the gunas are inherently an evolutionary force once they begin to work in perfect cooperation. The sexual orgasm is only the balancing of life force at the lowest (sensory) level of consciousness.

OCTAVES OF LIGHT AND SOUND

The interplay between these radiations of light energies and their absorption by the material universe, human bodies, mind-stuff, intelligence stuff, etc. is revealed by the experience of colour in the functioning of the chakra system which acts at the subtle level to process the three qualities of invisible cosmic light which we call kundalini. An excess of tamas could manifest as the unmoving caution of negative energy in the blue frequency--

172

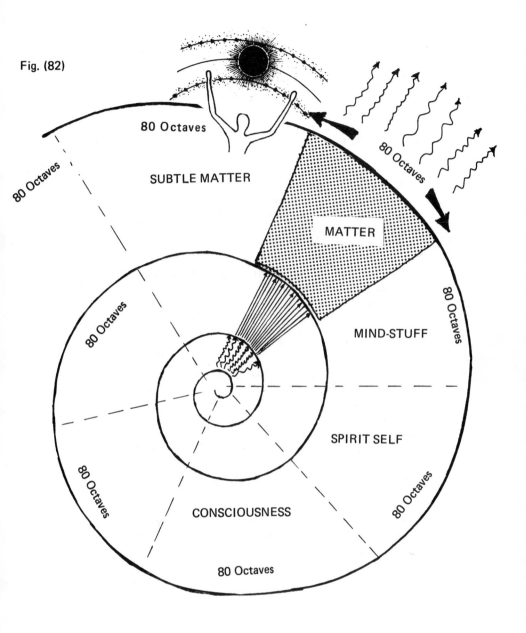

Fig. (82)

80 Octaves

SUBTLE MATTER

80 Octaves

80 Octaves

MATTER

80 Octaves

80 Octaves

MIND-STUFF

80 Octaves

SPIRIT SELF

80 Octaves

80 Octaves

CONSCIOUSNESS

80 Octaves

The shaded areas represent the narrow section of light radiations of the cosmos which interact with human bodies, human sensory devices such as colour photo emulsions, and sensors. It covers about 80 octaves of vibrations in the total spiral of the universe of 80 x 80 x 80 octaves. Each set of 80 octaves is a vibration of three combined interpenetrating primary cosmic radiations referred to as the three gunas in Sanskrit (guna meaning "a cosmic quality").

173

the kind of person who says "No" before you have even finished your question. At the opposite extreme, an excess of rajas might express in the red frequency with a person who springs to action so swiftly that he is the bull in the china shop, oblivious of anyone's feelings but his own. The expression of these three creative guna qualities at the human level of personality shows us clearly why people experience the light of consciousness at seven different unconscious levels of Being which correspond to seven colour harmonics, because the warmth and expansiveness of raja (the red-orange end of the spectrum) polarises with the cool contractive introversion (the blue-violet end of the spectrum). In other words, the imbalance in the gunas creates the 7 colours. Most people are either too introverted or too extroverted and only in very rare human beings are these three forces of intelligence radiation, energy and absorption ever balanced in perfect equilibrium to produce that white light which contains within it at one time all the colours of the rainbow. Such a being is the enjoyer of all the worlds, from the earthy experience of good food, material beauty, sex, etc. to the highest octaves of spiritual consciousness. To such a one the whole creation is the body of God, and matter and spirit become one cosmic vibration of AUM.

From the three gunas (or "cosmic qualities") the creative forces of the cosmos give us the power, through the light of consciousness to re-create our experience of sensation as vibrations of consciousness. Without the gunas, our experience of a tree would be like a camera, which records the image without any memories, imaginings, resolves, thoughts, intuitions, or feelings of life. On either side of our sensory experience of this vibrating cosmos, there exist many other octaves in the total vibration which we cannot sense on the physical level of consciousness but which can be known in six other ways on six other levels of Being. We get so wrapped up in the demanding stimulations of our senses that we take for granted the subtler levels of our awareness which are also functioning more or less unconsciously. Only when we become acutely conscious of such subtle faculties as intuition and imagination can we begin to develop their full potential and get some inkling of how incredibly vast our consciousness really is and how far it can extend if we will only let it.

The universe around us talks to us constantly in the divine language of colour. Our eyes read the language of colour vibration in exactly the same way that our ears vibrate to the language of sound. The nervous impulses which travel to the seat of consciousness from eye to brain and from ear to brain are identical. The notes attributed to the various radiating colours of light frequencies are shown in the diagram opposite. They are reversed for the pigment colours of absorption. It is interesting

Fig. (83)

THE RADIANCE OF LIGHT

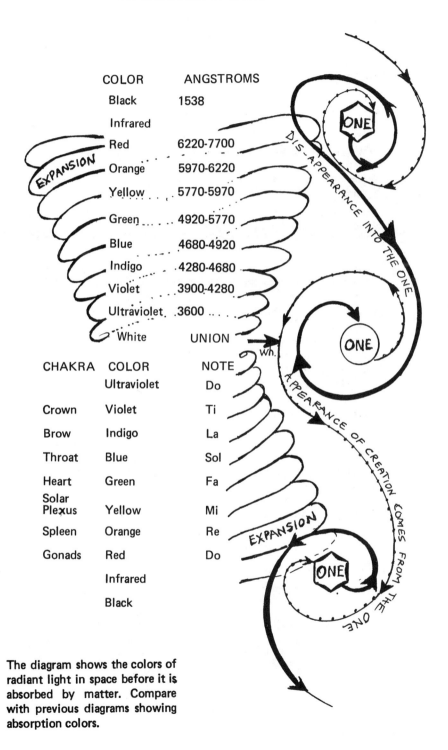

COLOR	ANGSTROMS
Black	1538
Infrared	
Red	6220-7700
Orange	5970-6220
Yellow	5770-5970
Green	4920-5770
Blue	4680-4920
Indigo	4280-4680
Violet	3900-4280
Ultraviolet	3600
White	UNION

CHAKRA	COLOR	NOTE
	Ultraviolet	Do
Crown	Violet	Ti
Brow	Indigo	La
Throat	Blue	Sol
Heart	Green	Fa
Solar Plexus	Yellow	Mi
Spleen	Orange	Re
Gonads	Red	Do
	Infrared	
	Black	

EXPANSION

DIS-APPEARANCE INTO THE ONE

APPEARANCE OF CREATION COMES FROM THE ONE

EXPANSION

ONE

The diagram shows the colors of radiant light in space before it is absorbed by matter. Compare with previous diagrams showing absorption colors.

to study the relationship of the seven light frequencies of colour to the vibration of sound since the exact resonances between sensory vibrations which are transmitted to our consciousness are not only indications of the different octaves of human consciousness but also are harmonic vibrations of the celestial octaves in which the entire universe vibrates. These vibrations can be detected and proved by the methods outlined in the book "Supersensonics" available from the publishers.

These infinite octaves of an ever-expanding universe of vibration are the stairsteps of our evolutionary journey into our potential vaster Self (as in the colloquial expression, "he is a big person"). The combinations of the three cosmic qualities interacting like three rays of light create our internal experience of reality through the seven different levels of the octave, the eighth level being the balance point between octaves. This point of perfect equilibrium is the orgasm of kundalini energy by which consciousness is lifted to a higher vibration (the next octave). As in the experience of sound the eighth note at the top of an octave is the bottom note of the next octave above. Similarly the bottom note of an octave is the top note of the octave below. In human terms, each actualising of potential (when the highest vibration of any octave of experience is attained) is the birth of new potential (the low note of the next octave) which has yet to unfold. Within each octave, the three guna qualities combine by radiance (intelligence), energy movement (glowing) and by absorption (annihilation) to produce all seven levels of consciousness with their corresponding colour complementaries.

HOW LIGHT CREATES THE WORLD

The three gunas are represented by the Primary light colours of radiation, red, green and blue, which are experienced as always expanding and expressing. In their opposite complementary polarity they are contracting and absorbing. This opposite complementary polarity is really the shadow psychic electricity field from which the primary light colours are created in our consciousness and originates from white, green and black rays as follows:

> The diagram on the next page tries to show on a two-dimensional surface what is more like the strands of a rope. If we imagine a wire rope of three strands with each of these strands made up of many finer strands and then picture the rope as a cable along which light travels from sun to the earth or from star into outer space then we get some idea of what the central core of the rope which binds our consciousness in Akasha is like.

176

Fig. (84)

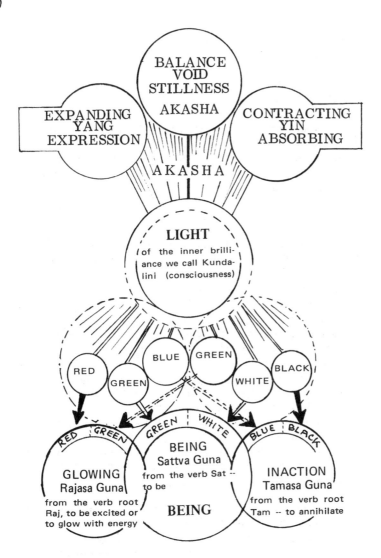

The above figure shows the nature of the Akasha which is made up of two poised and balanced actions in the stillness. These two create the vibration between expression of the invisible light of consciousness and its absorption, the yang and yin, the expansion and contraction. The light of consciousness which experiences the colours of light as Red, Green, Blue is shown as mixing with its shadow field of Green, White, Black to produce the interlocking three qualities of the creative forces known as Gunas.

The gunas create by pulling and pushing the cosmic energy into form. In a painting, cool colour recedes, creating shadow, while a warm colour shines out. Together, shining out and receding, they create the illusion of three-dimensional form. In the same way the three gunas, radiating and absorbing, create the form of human experience. Adding light to light (radiance) creates satva and subtracting colours from light (absorption) takes us closer to tamas. A human being radiates and absorbs the light of consciousness in the exact same way that the sun radiates and the chlorophyll molecule in grass absorbs its light and reflects off a green colour. Therefore the remainder of this chapter will discuss in depth these laws of light and we will suggest certain experiments in colour which lead to the proof of Nuclear Evolution as an accurate interpretation of Nature's signature in the colours of the rainbow spectrum. What is valid for Nature is valid for the shaping, by free and conscious choice, of the human psyche. Evolutionary forces work through our consciousness and thoughts as well as matter.

THE BINDING OF THE GUNAS

All the guna qualities are binding of human consciousness when they are not understood within our self. Tamas binds through negligence and uncaring action, error and insufficient action, thus encouraging ignorance and separation, desire and egocentric drives. Rajas brings variety of expression and ambition, intense desires for objects, people, experiences, and the self-satisfaction of sensory perversions and sexual hang-ups. Hence it binds the consciousness by its attraction of longing, its liking of love objects and its attachments to works, its desire to manipulate money, power and people, creating one stumbling block after another through unskillful actions. Satva binds equally, even though it expresses a great noble desire and spiritual selflessness. It binds human beings to knowledge and wisdom for its own sake, it binds man to beauty so that ugliness disturbs, it binds a person to doing good without necessarily first becoming good, and it binds the human being to the search for peace and tranquility in the lonely cave or monastery cell.

Satva can bind people to food if they think eating will make them better people and it will also enslave those who want to be considered good and saintly by others into a life of keeping up a good and holy spiritual image. Gaining power over the satva guna in one's own self is the first step of self-discipline which leads to the genuine spiritual life which is beyond the controlling unconscious manifestations of the three gunas. Direct control of all three gunas is very rare and as with Christ and other avatars it gives humans the power to move through the seven levels of Being into the higher states of consciousness. Such a being is called a

Gunavan – one who controls the flow of the creative cosmic forces within.

THE HUMAN LENS

If each human being is that consciousness which is the radiant light of the universe (whose octaves of vibration are infinite), and if each human being separates the white light of Pure Consciousness into seven different levels of awareness which are either bright or dark depending on the purity (selflessness) of the person, then there can be no self-understanding nor any understanding of the universe or the meaning of life without that deep study of light and colour which will increase our sensitivity to all those infinite vibratory worlds which are potentially within our grasp but which we constantly filter out with our crude and unsubtle awareness.

The following diagram shows what happens when a narrow beam of light passes through a prism. You can see these colours on a soap bubble or a raindrop or dewdrop or through a diffraction grating. These are called spectrum colours but because we use pigment colours everyday and spectrum colours almost never in practical life, we begin with the words **radiant light,** which we use to describe a primary radiant source of energy.

Fig. (85)

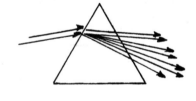
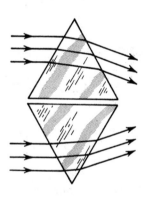

The rays of light come together in one diamond when they pass through two prisms.

The speed of light through different substances varies. Refraction bends the light towards the base of a prism and the larger waves of the red rays are bent up and the short waves are bent towards the base.

THE DIAMOND LENS
OF THE HUMAN BODY
WHICH FILTERS LIGHT
BY ABSORPTION

Fig. (86)

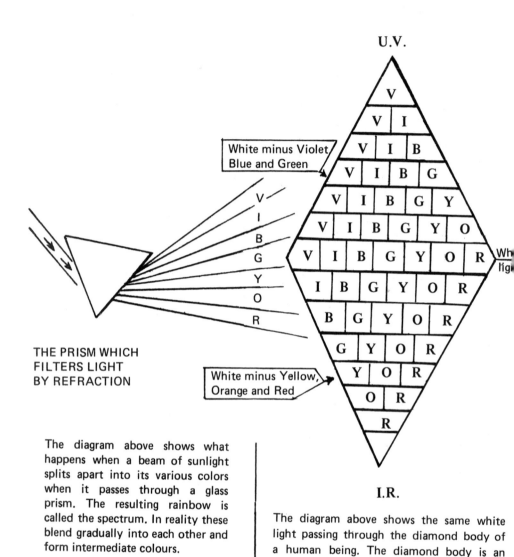

U.V.

White minus Violet,
Blue and Green

THE PRISM WHICH
FILTERS LIGHT
BY REFRACTION

White minus Yellow,
Orange and Red

I.R.

The diagram above shows what happens when a beam of sunlight splits apart into its various colors when it passes through a glass prism. The resulting rainbow is called the spectrum. In reality these blend gradually into each other and form intermediate colours.

The diagram above shows the same white light passing through the diamond body of a human being. The diamond body is an esoteric reference to pure consciousness.

Ordinary consciousness acts as a filter depending on the purity and absorbing power of a person's evolutionary development. The diamond lens is focussed by the psychic chakras. The energy which passes through them from the cosmic light energies creates our consciousness and is called Kundalini. When this consciousness moves through the chakras on its evolutionary way up to the union with the pure light of the cosmic lens it has a tendency to burn and create heat sensations in matter just as light does. Kundalini, light and consciousness are all different words for the same thing in different stages.

180

WHY IS COLOUR IMPORTANT?

Since we shall be looking at the ways a human sees reflected colour in pigments and absorbs colour from light as if he himself were a receptor like a pigment absorbing rays of light, we will go step by step through the differences between **pigment colour** (reflected colour which depends on the pigment's absorption: subtraction from light) and the **radiating light colour** (the action of rays of energy giving off radiance: adding to light, creating the excitement and ionisation of matter). Ionisation is the input of a tremendous amount of energy that excites the atom and raises it to a higher level of vibration. To lift the vibration of the atoms in your body is to lift the vibration of the whole organism. Therefore the ionising power of **light colour** is tremendously more beneficial to us in our evolutionary unfolding than is the **pigment colour** most people prefer.

By combining the three cosmic radiations in their primary and secondary manifestations, the colours of light and the pigments of worldly objects work together as expressive and absorbing, warm and cold, light and dark. It will be important while reading this section on colour not to juggle with primary and secondary concepts and miss the truth of how humans translate invisible radiation into light and colour. Let us therefore define that **primary pigment colour** means reflected light from curtains, flowers, and all material objects, whereas **primary light** means the radiation of the three gunas which act through all glowing rays of light created by intensely vibrating matter. The radiating light of the universe is the cause of all colours. All **light colours** as well as **pigment colours** are fundamental reactions of our internal consciousness to stimulations and nerve impulses coming into the human brain. These colours of light and colours of pigment are created in the brain and are not objective or separate from the light of consciousness which sees them. All colour is our subjective response to invisible radiations and our experience of it depends on our state of consciousness and level of evolution. The spectrum as it appears to a highly evolved person is seen as God's signature throughout the whole of matter. To those who are imprisoned as yet in the ego-self, the rainbow is just a bunch of pretty colours of little importance to life, but the wise man knows that the rainbow and the spectrum can only be created by radiant energy. He knows that our consciousness and radiant energy of light behave in identical ways and cause colours to appear whenever they are separated by any medium, whether that medium is a glass prism or the human mind. And this knowledge that light and consciousness are one transforms him and gives him the power to transcend the painted glitter of the world and transmute ordinary consciousness into a shimmering rainbow of light.

WHAT IS "OUT THERE"?

The prism which shows that white sunlight is made up of colours red, orange, yellow, green, blue, indigo and violet reveals that the radiant energies of white light are the raw materials from which all colours in the universe are extracted. Artificial light, or starlight, or radio waves from black holes and quasars all send out individual colours that can be separated from rays of sunlight which is our nearest star. The diffusion of sunlight which we call daylight also contains all those seven colours of the cosmic radiation which fills the whole of space and passes invisibly between each star. All our visual sensations are experienced because of the stimulation of light rays entering the eye and creating electrical signals which pass down the optic nerve into the occipital area of the brain. The rays of light have to come from some energetic glowing (raja) substance like the sun, an electric light source activated by current, a burning flame or a chemical reaction of phosphorescence. All other objects of creation are seen by reflected light and the colours reflected exist only in the light and not in the pigmentation of the object.

Most people have some idea that a colour is a paint or dye you put on objects or consists of some natural dye such as in the petals of a flower which appears to come from the object itself. But all colour, whether absorbed pigment colour or from radiant light sources, is a quality (guna) of light and does not exist apart from light. If artists were aware that they were painting with light, the aesthetic effect they are trying to create would hinge upon a very different kind of internal experience and their work would automatically lift up to a subtler vibrational level. A red object is not red in the dark, because the red comes from the light, not from the object or the paint on it. The same applies to consciousness exactly because consciousness and light are the same radiant substance. A person gives off red in his aura only because the red energy was already present in the light of consciousness which he absorbed from the Akasha.

A coloured object actually subtracts energy (colour) from the light which falls on it and this process of absorption is the prime cause of all the visible colour we see. Until it hits a material substance or surface, light is not even a manifested energy but only exists through space as expanding potential energy. What it hits is a lower gradation of its own reality, called matter. If a ray of light was not stopped by our body or the earth on its way from the sun it would carry on past us forever. Immediately on contact with matter it is absorbed and releases energy or heat into the object whether that object be a living being, a plant or a metallic crystal. Various substances such as glass, crystals, metals, have different coefficients of absorption depending on their chemical and electrical structures and therefore absorb certain wavelengths of light and reflect others. This is just as true of the chemical nature of the human body as it is for any other object in the universe. The absorbed energies are turned into body heat and are metabolised into consciousness.

Thus the colours absorbed by the body are analogous to pigment colours while the colours of the aura are analogous to the colours of a radiant light source. Like the sun, we radiate light. The human body is like a filter and these processes of absorption and reflection of cosmic radiance from solar and stellar radiation are controlled by our own being and its entrapment in the binding effect of the three gunas. A pure (satvic) channel will transmit almost all the primary cosmic light received by absorption in a similar way to a white surface reflecting all the seven colour wavelengths of light equally. Each person's consciousness will determine a selected frequency since all organisms select from nature according to their philosophy of life. Even a blood cell has a philosophy. In the same way a blocked and sluggish channel or tamasic organism will, like a black substance, absorb all the colours of the primary light source but will not reradiate them.

LETTING IN MORE LIGHT

How can we bridge the gap between ourselves and those rare enlightened souls who understand and master the cosmic laws of radiation and absorption of light (which is mastery not only of themselves but of the whole creation, since these laws create the world as we know it by crystalising light into form)? How can we bridge the gap between these souls and people who are only concerned with the effects of colours from carpets, walls, textiles, architecture, paintings and objects which communicate through our sensory perception of colour? We must begin with what is most familiar.

We can see coloured objects made by man and nature and we see coloured lights. We all know that the colours in the paint box are not the same brilliance as the spectral colours in the rainbow. Therefore colour scientists give the name **pigment colour** to any colour we see reflected from a fruit, a cloth, a flower, or from a paint box or ink bottles. The colour that comes from the sky, the sun's light, from glowing lamps excited by electricity or from heated bodies like stars or flames, we call **radiant light**. We shall see later that both originate from the invisible light of the universe we called Akasha, but for now let us keep them mentally quite separate in our psychic experience. Although the non-sensory perception of colour which is at the back of the teachings on Nuclear Evolution is far more important and mind-blowing than any visual perception of colours, we must begin with what we know and later proceed onwards to what we do not know. Hence we repeat briefly for those who have no training in the arts or the traditional colour systems a simple version of colour absorption by pigments. We make a mental note that all pigments reflect light in such a way that reflection and absorption are directly proportional to each other. By studying this rosette of pigment colours you can see the complementary of any colour by looking directly across at its opposite colour on the wheel. Later when we discuss the colours of radiant light energy and their complementary colours as revealed in the human aura, we can refer to this simple diagram as a guide to pigment colours of absorbed light.

Fig. (87)

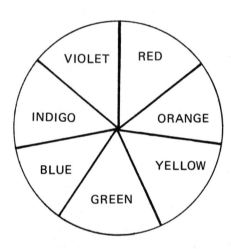

In the colour ring above the seven colours contained in light are arranged in order of the spectrum with violet joining with red at the ends of the spectrum. The pairs opposite each other are approximately complementary. However, the diagram is very over-simplified because there are colours between violet and red such as infra red, infra black, infra white and negative green (sometimes called radiesthesia grey) which are not visible colours. For methods of detecting these, see my book "Supersonics". For the sake of discussion we will miss these out as well as Indigo, which is not possible to make as pigment without adding black for greater absorption.

One of the recurring questions concerning Nuclear Evolution is the relationship of the aura rainbow body to the standards used by designers, artists, paint manufacturers, etc. and the rules and charts they use to establish colour harmonies. If Nuclear Evolution is to be taught in schools we shall need to validate its meanings.

The principles of colour harmony, triadic colours, tints, shades, etc. can all be learnt in any art school. One of the leading art schools in San Francisco which has over the last 50 years produced many of the professors of art and interior decorators in California colleges has taught many colour theories over the years. The school was founded and is led by a ninety-year-old connoisseur of oriental art, Rudolf Schaeffer. Let me reproduce a statement given freely to the author by Rudolf Schaeffer to show that Nuclear Evolution is in no way in conflict with modern art nor is it any fly-by-night theory of colour.

> I have known Christopher Hills for five or six years and have visited his Centre in London. His writing and books I knew sometime before that. His book "Nuclear Evolution" in my opinion is the best book published on the spiritual-psychological meaning of prismatic color. This unique book has made a great contribution to the teaching of color in our School which specializes in the study and application of color in the sphere of daily living. Recently he has given a most interesting and inspiring series of lectures on color to our students.

I am using the terms **primary** and **secondary** because these are an established part of the vocabulary of the art world, but this distinction between primary (unmixed) colours and secondary (mixed) colours is not nearly so crucial to Nuclear Evolution as the distinction between colour from **radiant light** and colour reflected from **pigments**, because colour from a pigment, whether it is a primary or secondary colour, is not the same living energy we get from a radiant light source. Primary and secondary **pigment** colours are reflected light waves whereas primary light comes straight through space direct.

Once we know the rules of colour mixing we can see which chakras blend together to make a certain colour frequency. To mix **light** frequencies together, however, is not the same as mixing **pigments**, so for those who are artists or already know about pigment colours we must show how primary **light** colours, which are quite another thing from pigment colours, are blended to produce many shades. We tend to think of light as a homogeneous thing. Light is light. But if light comes in a corkscrew across many planes it is quite a different energy from light that is polarised into one plane. As we shall see later on **primary light colour** is the same colour as **secondary pigment colour** but they are not the same energy because pigment radiation is polarised through having been reflected off an object. **Pigment** colours are created by the guna force of <u>absorption,</u> while **light** colours are expressions of the guna force of expansion and radiation. Therefore our relationship to the colours of our world are a mirror of our relationship to the life-force of the cosmic energies. While less enlightened souls spend 30,000 dollars re-decorating their houses with pigment colours, the wise man seeks out the rainbow. Why does he do this? Because he knows the secret of light.

THE SECRET OF LIGHT

Nature uses colour widely for signals. The bee tunes to the flower petals, the butterfly to its mate's wing patterns and birds to fruits. All over the world humans have set up their own language of colour, red for danger, green for safe passage, red for port and green for starboard, red for anger and blue for peace, red for action and revolution and blue for conservatives. It is not often known that people unconsciously absorb colour from the invisible radiance of light energies just as other objects in the environment do. If we use colour tests of these unconscious responses we can create a remarkable map of our inner world. By testing thousands of different types of people and seeing which colours they pick from a selection of six or eight colours we can determine the meanings of these mixtures. This is what Dr. Max Luscher did, whereas the colours we discuss as the drives in Nuclear Evolution were discovered another way which you yourself can prove by looking into nature herself, using the instruments such as the colour pendulum and the Turenne rule described in more detail in "Supersensonics", and thereby discovering the secret of light.

Since we do react to colours all around us unconsciously, we need to be aware not only of aesthetics but what colour actually is, how it functions in the infinite subtle scheme of nature, and how it can affect us. As I said earlier, colour is produced by **adding** light to light which comes from a primary light source of radiation or it can be made by subtracting certain frequencies of colour from a source of light waves which we call absorbed and reflected colour. Hence the colours we see reflected from the pigments of matter are created by light energy that has already been absorbed or used up. All we receive from a red rug is the life energy which is excreted as waste material from that object. How much more beneficial to us, then, is the actual light energy itself, radiating from starlight, a torch or lamp or rays of sunlight which divide up into all the colours of the rainbow? If people would spend their home decorating budget on a few coloured light bulbs, they could change the quality of their consciousness within a very short time. The energy in each chakra, which resonates with the colours of the spectrum, spirals to the right if it is positive (optimistic, cheerful, healthy, content) and to the left if it is negative (doubting, fearful, selfish, suspicious). A 60 cent coloured light bulb can reverse the flow of these energies from negative to positive just by the sheer power of light upon that consciousness which is also made of the same light.

BLACK: THE DARK NIGHT OF THE SOUL

When a radiant light source such as starlight, a torch or lamp or rays of sunlight, divides up into all the colours of the rainbow, we see that white light is made up of red, orange, yellow, green, blue, indigo and violet. But because indigo is a most difficult colour to reproduce by printer's inks or colour photography and is not necessary in the making of the colours which come from the three gunas we shall miss it out of our explanation of pigment colour from here on. Indigo is a colour made by the addition of black to that colour between violet and blue, so we prefer to exclude it temporarily, since very few pure pigments or even radiant light sources have black light in them. Black light is mostly filtered out from the earth by the magnetosphere of the planet.

A primary colour is one that cannot be made by mixing other colours together. A secondary pigment colour is one that can be made by mixing equal amounts of any two primary pigment colours. The following diagram enables us to visualise how mixing together all three pigment primaries of red, yellow and blue makes the colour black.

When I first tried this I found that the mixture turned into a muddy olive green brown. This was because I did not know that pigments are not of equal colour strengths and that the three colours must be a good 50% of each in order to neutralise each other in black. But the important point in terms of the Dark Night of the Soul is that the three bright primary colours of pigments annihilate each other through absorption in producing black. This black colour is the result of total annihilation through infinite receptivity and absorption of all the colours from a radiant source of light. This happens because it is the nature of pigments to absorb; the mixing of three primary light colours would produce quite a different result as we shall see later.

In looking at the levels of consciousness some knowledge of the way pigment colours mix together to produce other colours gives us a clue to the way the seven psychic chakra energies work together. When we find any two colours from pigments, whether primary or secondary colours which will neutralise each other, they are called a complementary pair and each colour is then a complementary of the other. Sometimes these complementaries may produce a neutral grey-black or muddy green-brown when mixed, but they are still complementaries.* We have already said

*We need not get into the meaning of hue, value and intensity, which are dimensions of colour for achieving optical definition of brightness but which do not concern us here. We can detect with scientific instruments thousands of colours in the spectrum of light, but with our human eye it becomes very difficult to discriminate more than 70 or 80.

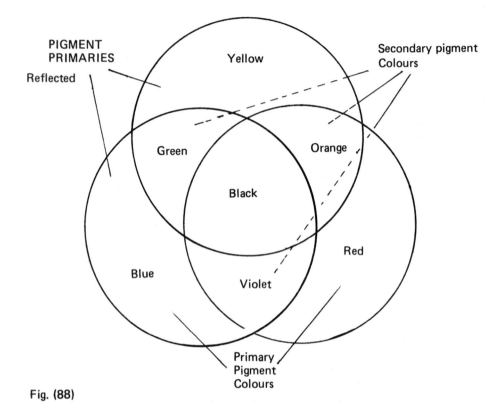

Reflected

Yellow

Secondary pigment Colours

Green

Orange

Black

Red

Blue

Violet

Primary Pigment Colours

Fig. (88)

The outer parts of the three circles show the Blue, Yellow, and Red pigment colours, long recognised as "primaries" in art texts. Where two circles overlap, the "secondaries" are formed — Green, Orange, and Purple. The black in the middle shows the mixture of all three primaries. On a later page we will see a more scientific division of primary and secondary colours.

Fig. (89)

When Blue and Yellow pigments are mixed together the common colour reflected is Green. The other colours have been subtracted from the white light by the vibration of atoms by absorption. The light which is reflected is called Secondary Light while the incident white light is called Primary Light. This should not be confused with Primary Pigment Colours and Secondary Pigment Colours which are the reverse of the corresponding Primary Light Colours.

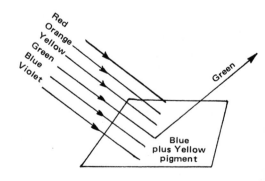

Red
Orange
Yellow
Green
Blue
Violet

Green

Blue plus Yellow pigment

that mixing primary pigment colours red, blue and yellow would produce black. Hence, by mixing a primary colour pigment with the secondary colour opposite to it, say red with green, we will get black, because green contains already blue and yellow. For the identical reason that they contain all primary colours between them, blue and orange will neutralise each other and result in black. Yellow and purple opposite each other, when mixed, will also make black. Therefore, people who are channeling light through the chakras may have two complementary chakra colours which produce black when they function together in the human aura.

Fig. (90)

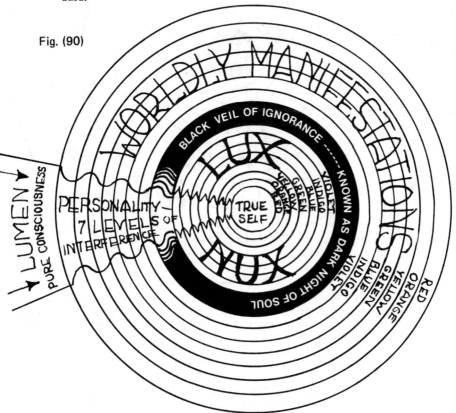

How do the three gunas or qualities of light change what a person does or make him what he is? The answer is that at the deep psychic centre of each person there is a nuclear core which not only absorbs light like the **pigment** colours do but also radiates biological radio waves of invisible light in reverse proportions to the **light** colours absorbed. This nuclear core is black when it is totally absorbing without giving out any re-radiated light.

189

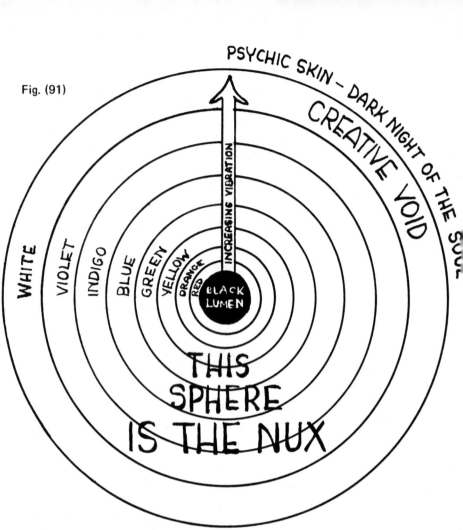

Fig. (91)

PSYCHIC SKIN – DARK NIGHT OF THE SOUL

CREATIVE VOID

WHITE
VIOLET
INDIGO
BLUE
GREEN
YELLOW
ORANGE
RED

BLACK LUMEN

INCREASING VIBRATION

THIS SPHERE IS THE NUX

The above diagram shows the central core of the previous diagram which most people never cognise or even re-cognise. Yet we are all born into this state of the unconscious nux until we acquire our ego and self-sense. It is this state which Christ refers to as the Kingdom of Heaven.

A sluggish channel, absorbing all colour and radiating none, is easy to recognise in a human being. Apart from being a self-centred and opinionated person, we would notice how everything in his life was referred to "I" or "mine" to the point of obsession. Such people are impossible to communicate with because they ignore the light of others and suck in energy like water going down a bath plug hole. Whether it is love, care, light, energy or time you give, it all goes down the water hole. Trying to change such dark aura people is a waste of time as they do not listen to anyone, nor to God nor to life itself. Such people are usually angry at the world, their situations, and argue with their friends and lovers all the time because they cannot see they are creating the life situation by their own obsession and self-destructive drives which have the certainty of desperation.

This state of being contrasts with the white aura person who is taking in light to the Nuclear core and re-radiating out in service to others. If a person has not reached the black state of desperation and self-annihilation (either physical which is the negative, or spiritual which is the positive side of black), then they may still hope to escape facing the ultimate Self. Such hope sometimes brings fear in a negative person who in a Luscher colour test will accept grey, while a spiritually healthy person rejects the colour grey. By referring to the diagram of the Turenne Disc we can see that black and white act as neutrals and that grey lies in between them. Grey is another neutralising colour representing the condition of disintegration. Before we reach the Nuclear core of Being the old self must disintegrate, but the ego can disintegrate in an unhealthy (imbalanced) way, leading ultimately to insanity, or in a strong (balanced) way, leading to rebirth.

In my book "Supersensonics", which goes more deeply into the methods of detecting the effects of colours, this disintegrating colour is sometimes referred to as Radiesthesia Grey or "negative green" because from the pigment point of absorption, it appears grey, but from the complementary of a radiant light source it is the opposite of what is called "positive green". The precariously balanced equilibrium in any person between positive and negative green represents that borderland between the forces of disintegration and integration that exist for the mystic in the Dark Night of the Soul, but for the scientist they represent the annihilation of time and the stopping of the universe, since all vibrating atoms in that void come to a state of rest where motion, velocity, distance and time have no meaning and therefore indicate a frightening domain not to be meddled with.

There are not many examples which can serve as an analogy for this enlightening annihilation. Perhaps the closest is the breaking of the light barrier. When matter moves at the speed of light it becomes infinite in mass and therefore annihilates itself instantly

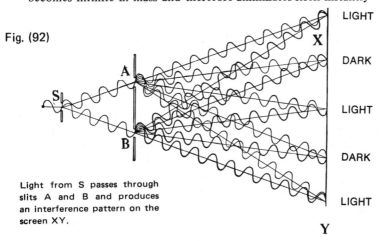

Fig. (92)

LIGHT

X

DARK

S

LIGHT

A

DARK

B

LIGHT

Light from S passes through slits A and B and produces an interference pattern on the screen XY.

Y

191

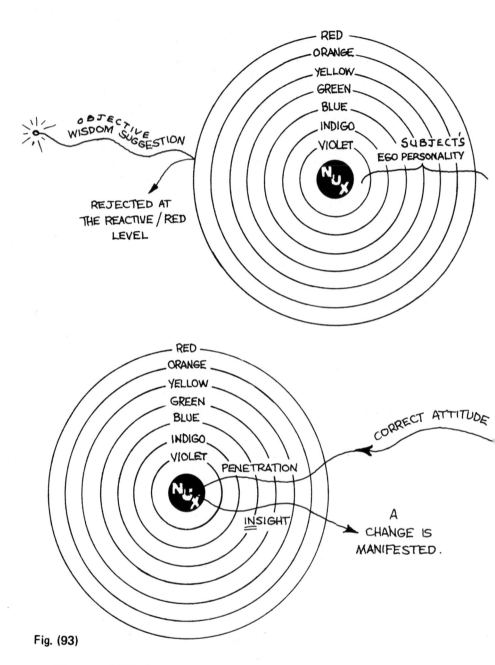

Fig. (93)

The central "I" of any observer is called the Nux in Nuclear Evolution from the latin word for seed or kernel. It is the origin of the word Nuclear. The Nuclear Self has seven shells which receive light from the universe. The same way a person receives light they also receive thoughts from others. According to their level of chakra functioning the light and thought energy penetrates through the seven shells into the Self. Persons communicate with others in the same way as they communicate with the universe. If they are conceptual (Blue) they live concepts. If they are sensation orientated (Red) they live only in the world of the senses.

becoming light energy. Another analogy would be interference, the way that two sound waves equal in length and moving in perfect opposite phase cancel each other out just as 2 waves on a pond, if they meet, disperse each other, or just as a light wave overlapping with another light wave cancels itself to make darkness.

An invaluable tool for evolution, then is to be able when any negative thought begins to trigger off the chemical reaction of your emotions, to set equal and opposite thought waves in motion, but if you do this with popular methods of positive thinking, your results will be superficial. Mastery is not a matter of repeating a mantram; it is a movement of the will that is rooted deep in the heart.

Not many people know that they can actually will the intake of light forces for the purpose of higher evolution. The Akasha or invisible background radiation, as yet unmanifest before it hits a human or an object, can be absorbed and made manifest in biological radiance if we imagine our consciousness to be a form of energy transducer between the cosmic rays (Akasha) and the visible tangible energies experienced as sensations by the body (Kasha). To know that we are also reflecting that light which we do not absorb, in proportion to the positive field forces we set up around the Nuclear core of Being, immediately gives us a clue to the nature of human personality.

See   Fig. (93)

Light is made up of vibrating photons which appear to travel in waves at a speed of 186,000 miles a second. The light may not travel any more than air does when sound passes through it at 1090 ft/sec. or any more than water does when waves pass across it and through it. Light waves pass through space depending on the excitement of the source which disturbs the elastic medium which fills the whole of space and which the Sanskrit seers called Akasha, meaning invisible light. to discriminate it from the experience of the travelling wave energy called Kasha (visible light). The oscillating waves of red light are the longest waves we can see in the visible spectrum and 33,000 of them in a single line occupy one inch. The waves of violet light are the shortest we can see. They measure 67,000 to the inch.

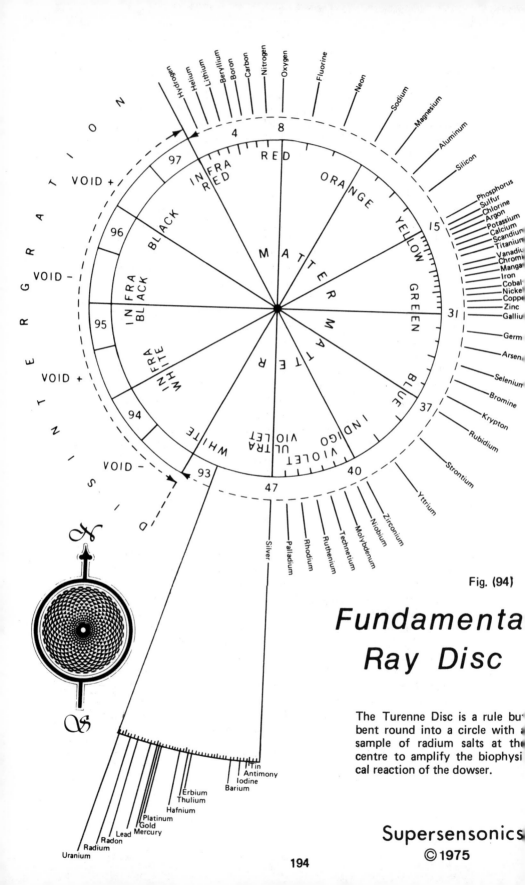

Fig. (94)

Fundamenta
Ray Disc

The Turenne Disc is a rule bu
bent round into a circle with a
sample of radium salts at the
centre to amplify the biophysi
cal reaction of the dowser.

Supersensonics
© 1975

194

TOOLS FOR EVOLUTION

Once you get a feel for the aliveness of light, you begin to see how light can change your consciousness and how, once you start to think of your consciousness as a radiant source of light, you can do something new with it. Processes that were formerly unconscious can be made conscious. Compulsions can be transcended. Caught in negative habits of thought, each like a weed which if not pulled will sow 1000 more seeds of its kind, you can find the will to pull the weed and change who you are. You cannot only gain control of the negative thoughts which affect your body but can even gain control of the body elements which in turn affect the psyche.

To tune into body elements you can use the Turenne Fundamental Ray Disc, shown opposite, which was the work of a famous French pioneer of radiesthesia. This colour disc divides each segment of colour into angles representing the elements of nature as they manifest to our consciousness out of the spiral form of the primordial atom. Turenne found that by putting a radioactive sample at the centre of the disc the vertical polarisations of any element placed at the centre of the disc would radiate its spectral lines in a horizontal direction and could therefore be plotted for each element as a series of angles in different sections of the colour spectrum, depending on the complexity of the atom, its atomic number and its shells of electrons orbiting around the nucleus.

By placing one's finger at the centre and holding a pendulum over it, the angle of the various elements of matter in the human body will produce a diviner's reaction just like a water dowser gets from a rod over underground water. The Turenne disc measures any disturbance or oscillation in the body due to lack of body elements. It measures imbalance, whether in the aura or in the body, and by treating the one, heals the other. Or the body may be treated directly by divining the proper remedy to fill the lack, placing it at the centre of the disc with a witness of the person where it cancels out the vibration of the illness it is in phase with.

The ability, using the Turenne disc,* to detect the thresholds of radiations coming from all objects around us in the environment in terms of their relation with the colour spectrum,gives mankind a completely new technique for probing and measuring the

---

* Complete details of this instrument are available in the author's book, "Instruments of Knowing" available from the publishers showing where you can get the whole range of Turenne's rules, discs, and divining rods, etc.

Fig. (95)

If we identify with crystallised light (matter) we are bound within the psychic skin created by the speed of visible light and we cannot transcend its visible limits of manifestation. But if we understand the true nature of that unmanifest light (Akasha) we will be able to find that stillness which is eternal. This state of being is the "eternal life" promised by Christ.

vibrations of matter as they are influenced by light and to understand the natural state in which they function without the
distorted images brought to us through mechanical devices and
sensors which do not give us a correct picture of causes but only
detect effects. Therefore Turenne's colour rosette is a useful tool
for detecting not only visual colours but invisible colours
emanating as auras around objects and people. It is a way of
detecting what the kundalini energy is actually doing inside us
and tracing its effects on our consciousness.

By learning the relationship of natural elements to colours we
begin to see that our entire human body is a symphony of colour
which is constantly taking in light, in the way the **pigment
colours** do, and sending it out in **light colours**. Hence every
human can be looked at in terms of the two diagrams we repeat
together.

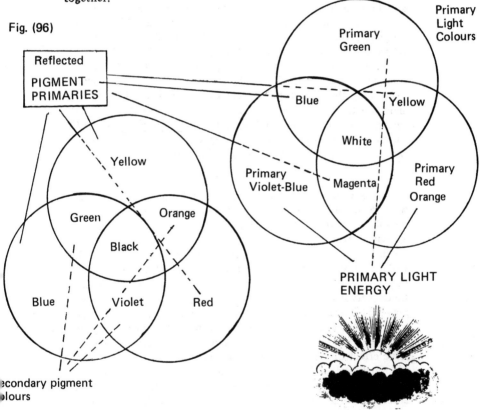

Fig. (96)

This diagram compares the difference between the pigment primary
colours and the light primary colours showing that absorption and reflection of light from pigments is exactly reversed. The secondary light colours
become the primary pigment colours and the secondary pigment colours
are reversed into the primary light colours. By keeping this clear when
we talk of colour we can see the different effects on human beings and
in their consciousness between a primary light source and light reflected
from coloured objects or pigments.

197

We can look at these two diagrams and imagine our unconsciousness radiating out a mixture of light colours in our aura or sucking in a blend of colours by subtracting them from the light we receive from the stars, sun, etc.

If artists were always consciously aware of these unconscious effects of colour on others rather than just painting for their own preferences and styles then art could become a healing agency. Why do sugar factories paint their walls blue? Because bees don't like blue. The inside of a restaurant is never green because green is the colour of sick and a person who is sick to his stomach often has a green aura as we can see in the expressions "sickly green" or "you go green" or "green around the gills". When a person gets sick he feels insecure; something has gone wrong in his body and he doesn't know what, so it triggers his heart chakra with insecurity and his aura turns green. If you are sick, certain shades of green pigment will make you sicker because in reality there is no green in the pigment. Green pigment colour is due to the absence of green light in the object. Green is not in the pigment; everything else is absorbed except the green. The colour is in the light not the object and while light gives you a charge of radiant energy a pigment gives you only a psychological effect due to the absence of that colour. Therefore a green light might energise you while a green pigment may pacify and rest you.

Lacking energy, you can become restful and slowly recharged with a certain vibrant green pigment or revitalise yourself completely under a shining green light which affects your nerves, especially the sympathetic nervous system. You would get the feeling of being toned up without getting tense, whereas blue would relax you by toning down because blue sedates and constricts, working on the capillaries, heartbeat, and parasympathetic nervous system. If you are a red manic type person you may feel antagonistic to blue because you are restless and want something to excite you. While blue would calm down a normally passive person who was agitated, it wouldn't necessarily have the same effect on an active person. In the same way red can agitate a normally passive person because he does not want stimulation. Yet in treating manic-depressives, a dose of the opposite light colour can help them to gain a better balance. Blue light in the room of the manic can be calming and red light in the room of a depressive will be stimulating. These effects are much less noticeable with pigment colours because there is less energy for us in a pigment colour although we respond to it psychologically.

In the human aura bright colours are always positive, always giving out energy. If the aura colour is dull or dirty it means that the positive light energy is being held back, held in and coloured by negative attitudes. The person is in a negative space and is psychically constipated by holding onto the energy. By noting our psychological reactions to coloured pigments and treating our chakras with coloured light, we can learn self-healing and ways to balance our entire system.

Treatment by coloured light can work on a person even if his chakras are closed to it. If you shine green light on a person whose heart chakra is closed he will, once he is saturated with green, begin to feel more secure and therefore more able to radiate a heart vibration. Or using the subtle tool of your own mind, if you put your consciousness in any one of your chakras which is closed to the cosmic light, you can open the chakra and become an absorber of that particular frequency. For example, if you are selfish and want to stop grabbing and become a giver, you have to get rid of insecurity in the heart chakra. You must know how to tune into the green energy of the universe.

CONSCIOUS CONTROL OF THE LIFE-FORCE

The different courses of study given by the University of the Trees (see references) and described at various points throughout this book, are step-by-step training in learning this self-mastery. The one important thing to remember for those who seek this mastery is that Consciousness is all-powerful. You put your consciousness in resonance with the frequency of light in the place where you want it and you absorb that frequency from the Cosmos. When you know how to tune into each chakra to replenish what you need, then you have learned to play the Cosmic instrument that controls and modifies these gunas. If you are a Christ, you would open yourself up to the green part of the spectrum if your need was for money or some green energy, or a place to lay your head. You tune to green the heart chakra and trust the Cosmos, know that it will give and you will get what you need. You also say, "Let my will be Thy will and if I'm meant to have something it will come." Eventually if you put your consciousness into that pure energy it will create a miracle for you. You won't lack anything. The minute you go wanting more than enough for this day, then you will have a security problem and you will be disturbed. You can tune to each of the chakras for different needs in the same way.

You can also play the instrument of the chakras to help tune into the depths of another person. If you want to know the heart of another, tune to your green energy in yourself, and then channel it into them and see what comes back to you. See what colour or vibration comes back from their aura. It will give you a clue about the fears they have, the things they want, the insecurity they feel about themselves. Most people are not in touch with the unconscious part of themselves because they don't control their chakras.

199

Therefore the colour which comes back will reveal their attitude because they have received the light you sent and done to it what they do to the pure consciousness that the universe sends them every day. If their aura flashes dirty, this is your clue to how they process light. Yet the person is no more aware of your sending him the energy than he is aware that he has consciousness. If the chakra you send the energy to is closed or if it is absorbing without giving, nothing comes back to see in the aura. Energy goes in but not much comes out; the person holds onto it because of fear, and this fear coming from the green chakra can affect any and all of the other chakras. If a person is so selfish and self-centred that he sucks in light through many chakras but radiates nothing, his aura is black. But this black of psychic constipation must not be confused with the black of ego annihilation.

Each primary light colour and its opposite secondary colour, for example violet and yellow, are a complementary pair. Each pair represents white light from which the other colour has been absorbed or subtracted by some form of filter such as a colour screen. When the equivalent of a colour screen is a person, absorbing the light and acting as a lens or filter, the energy which is let through the chakra system and absorbed by the person determines the kind of personality. The corresponding colour of the aura is what is left after the person has absorbed his needs and re-radiated. For instance, a person with a magenta aura absorbs all colours in white light minus the green (see diagram C which follows in the next section). When combined in the form of **light energies** the colour emitted by the aura is complementary to its pair colour, which would produce white light if they were added to each other. But when combined as **pigment colours,** the complementary colours both produce black because there we are dealing with reflected light and in this case of pigments we are adding together the absorbing powers of each colour vibration. This process of absorption is the cause of all the visible colour we see coming off objects. We see the entire universe by the light absorbed or reflected off objects of matter or we experience the radiance directly from other objects which radiate their own light like the sun and stars and lamps.

If light hits the medium of the human vehicle it helps the expansion of our consciousness since that is what light is. This fact that our consciousness is comprised of light added to light makes this subtle expansion the most important spiritual concept of Nuclear Evolution which confirms the statements of the ancient rishis and researchers. They have always said without saying how they knew it, that the Akasha or primary stuff of the expanding Brahma of invisible light is made up of three gunas or primary vibrations. The expansive movement of this energy is called **kundalini.** The secondary visible light vibrations, called

200

Kasha, are those which are reflected or emitted from objects of the creation including humans. The confusion which exists between the primaries and secondaries of light and the primaries and secondaries of pigment colours can be cleared up by studying the gunas and by seeing that the **secondary colours of light,** namely reflected blue, yellow and magenta made by the overlapping primary light beams, are the true **primary pigment colours.** The traditional blue, yellow and red are therefore not quite correct primaries of these pigment colours. The following diagram shows the links between Akasha and the kundalini manifesting to our consciousness as colours.

Fig. (97)

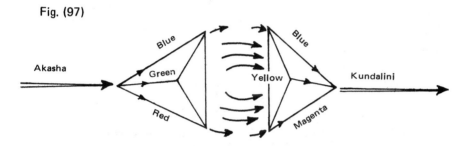

The primaries of a radiant light energy source, violet-blue, green and red-orange are the same as secondaries of the pigment colours of reflected light which comes to us from the many objects in the environment which absorb some of the light around us. In this same way we ourselves are objects which balance our intake exactly with the cosmos by re-radiating what cannot be absorbed into our vehicle of consciousness. Primary light radiation therefore exactly balances material absorption and reflection depending on the purity of the medium through which the three great creative forces of the universe pass. That purity in the consciousness of a human being is the beginning of an evolutionary advance.

Why does the student of consciousness need to know that these qualities of radiant light reverse themselves in the secondary pigment colours? And what does it do for the evolution of a human being to know that the primary pigment colours are the reverse of the secondary light? It is only when the human being begins to regard this earthly incarnation as upside down or complementary to the heavenly one that evolutionary "thinking in light" begins. Or put another way, the Akasha of pure consciousness is converted by the human mind into Kasha, the internal brightness which lights up the worldly objects of sensation. This internal light of the mind creates a world of colour within, which activates the sluice valves of evolution -- the chakra functions.

Fig. (98)

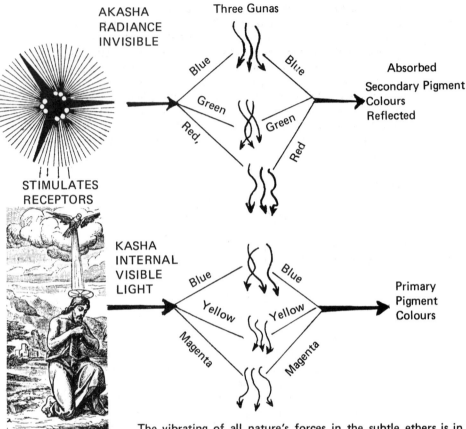

AKASHA
RADIANCE
INVISIBLE

Three Gunas

Blue   Blue

Green   Green

Red,   Red

Absorbed
Secondary Pigment
Colours
Reflected

STIMULATES
RECEPTORS

KASHA
INTERNAL
VISIBLE
LIGHT

Blue   Blue

Yellow   Yellow

Magenta   Magenta

Primary
Pigment
Colours

STIMULATES
CONSCIOUSNESS

The vibrating of all nature's forces in the subtle ethers is in resonance with the three fundamental cosmic vibrations of the gunas which are scattered and refracted by material bodies on contact. They break up into different frequencies and appear as colours to our consciousness after being absorbed. The mixing together of all vibrations in the created universe -- audible, inaudible, primary and refracted, absorbed and reflected, and as yet unmanifested in the invisible light of radiation is called "The AUM".

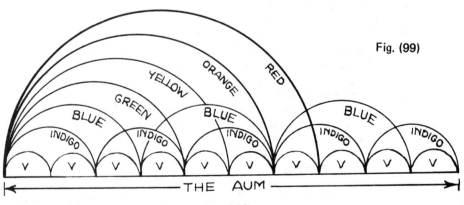

Fig. (99)

THE AUM

202

HOW DOES KUNDALINI BECOME COLOUR?

Studying the colour levels tempts us to pigeon–hole people simplistically and miss the subtle intricacies which make each human being completely unique. But when we begin to study the mixing of radiating light colour we see that the possible combinations of radiation and absorption by which the aura is created are infinite. To illustrate absorption we can use a beam of white light from a theatre spotlight which contains all the colours of the spectrum and then shine it through a red/orange filter. Obviously a beam of red/orange light comes out the other side as below:

Fig. (100)   Page 20

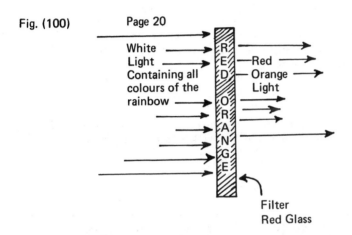

White Light Containing all colours of the rainbow

—Red — Orange Light

Filter
Red Glass

What has really happened to the white light? The following diagram gives an answer:

(A)

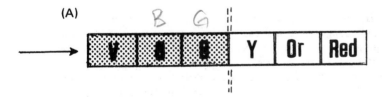

The shaded area shows the part of the white light which was absorbed by the filter and the white area shows the light which passed through the filter. If we point a blue-green light and a red-orange light at a white screen we will get a re-combination where the two meet and get white light. From this method we can define red-orange as a white light minus the blue-green frequencies. In the same way we can see that to get a blue-green light we can shine a white light minus the red-orange part of the spectrum.

Fig. (101)

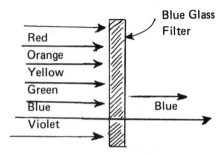

A blue-green filter will absorb all the yellow, orange, red colours from the white light in the same way that the red filter absorbs the violet, blue, green rays.

If we take bright spectrum yellow we would write the formula as white light minus the blue-violet part of the spectrum as follows:

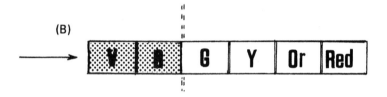

If a yellow light is shone on a white surface plus a blue-violet light, then the spot will reconstitute as white light again.

It is important to know why yellow as a mixture of green, yellow, orange and red is used and not a yellow glass filter alone to get a rich coloured light. Nearly all colours we see are mixtures of other colours because monochromatic light of one colour frequency makes only a very weak impact on human consciousness. If a coloured glass filter absorbs all the colours except yellow we can hardly detect the yellow with our eyes. It is the same with a blue-green filter or a red-orange filter; the light appears to be weaker. The brightest colours we see around us are all combinations of several other colours and so it is incorrect to say that a yellow object absorbs all colours except yellow or reflects only yellow light, or that a blue object reflects only the blue part of the spectrum. We are taught in school that a red object absorbs all colours except the red and therefore the red light is reflected back to the eyes. But when a pigment reflects light its colour is a mixture of other colours so it is not quite correct to say only red is reflected to us unless the object is emitting monochromatic light in one band of the red frequencies. This can only be achieved by special filters or lasers. However, when we come to regard human beings as prisms and filters we find that their bioenergetic systems of atoms and molecules and cells can act as generators of a single colour such as the mono-chromatic vibrations of invisible light energies. We can then say they may be radiating on one frequency.

A colour can be detected more accurately by what it absorbs from white light containing all the colours than by the colour it reflects from some pigment or what is transmitted through a filter. Since every human is such a filter and absorbs light we can make comparisons with the ways people control their own absorption, but to do so we must temporarily forget what we know already about mixing pigments, since pigment colours give very different results from those we get from mixing frequencies of light. Pigment colours reflected into our eyes do affect us psychologically and we will talk about them later, but for now let us think only of radiant light.

If we compare diagram (A) for obtaining red-orange light with the diagram (B) for obtaining yellow light we can see that yellow contains exactly the same colours as red-orange but with the extra colour of green added. A red-orange light plus a green light ought to produce a yellow light. Try this experiment by getting two different coloured bulbs and letting them shine together on a piece of white paper and prove it is correct. Then combine a red-orange light with a blue-violet light and get the purple-red colour of magenta which can be said to be half or 50% of each colour. Let us make another diagram of magenta colour by finding out what part of the white light is missing from magenta. From diagrams (A) and (B) we can see that orange-red light contains yellow-orange-red and that blue-violet light is a combination of violet-indigo-blue and by mixing all these coloured lights together we are combining all the colours of white light except the green light. Let us draw the diagram for magenta light thus:

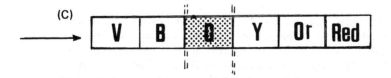

(C)

V B [G] Y Or Red

In other words you can make magenta by adding red to blue or by subtracting green from white light.

Now when we come to apply this type of colour knowledge to ourself we can see that a person with an aura of magenta colour can be either a person with two chakras open (the red physical energies and the blue devotional idealistic conceptual type) or could be a person operating on all the chakras except the green (heart) one.

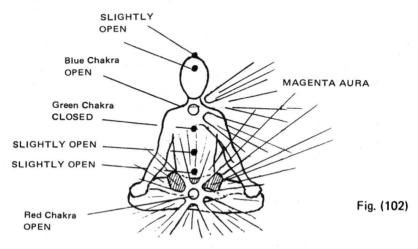

SLIGHTLY OPEN

Blue Chakra OPEN

Green Chakra CLOSED

SLIGHTLY OPEN

SLIGHTLY OPEN

MAGENTA AURA

Red Chakra OPEN

Fig. (102)

The magenta aura is caused by adding the radiation of the Blue chakra to the base chakra making the combination colour of the idealist who wants his heaven down on the earthly level of the red sensations. Such a person would want the best of both worlds.

Both of these cases illustrate the principle of absorption: how the chakras, like pigments, subtract from light. The terminology is perhaps a bit confusing, because looking from the point of view of the person, the colour is **absorbed** from the white light whereas if you were the white light, you would say that the colour had been **subtracted** from you. The person with two chakras open (red and blue) absorbs or subtracts red and blue, which he then re-radiates in his aura as magenta. The person with one chakra closed (green) absorbs the six remaining colours of white light (red, orange, yellow, blue, indigo, violet) and radiates them out as magenta.

The first example would be someone caught between two worlds with the spiritual call of the blue idealist mixed 50% with a love of earthly things like good cheese, sex, pleasures, etc. Since magenta is not violet but the colour of erotic idealism, we could expect such a person to be a charmer and someone who always fell for charm too. A mixture of the two chakra functions would reveal the positive or negative tendencies of each chakra (as given in Chapter 24   ) combined into one. Or it could be the positive tendency of the red (manifestation in concrete terms) conflicting with the negative tendency of the blue (hankering for the past).

206

Fig. (103)

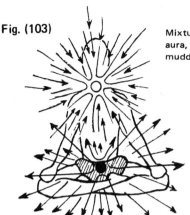

Mixture produces magenta aura, one bright and another muddy.

Positive red conflicts with negative blue.

Fig. (104)

Positive blue conflicting with negative red.

To reverse them, the negative red (domination and sensuality) conflicting with the positive blue (worship) would give a bigoted idealist who, in trying to get the best of both worlds and be practical, chased after every guru who looked like he had the earthly sensual thing together with the spiritual ideal. Once these basic colour meanings are learned, any amount of readings of auras can be done by combination of the chakra functions. For instance, anyone who had a magenta aura because of a closed heart centre and lacked green would not only be erotic but would have no attachments on earth to remain secure in the heart centre. He would therefore be seeking power and security in the occult sense since the colour magenta is also the colour of magic and such a person often has an expectation that events will happen not through investment of consciousness/money/ effort/work, but by magical means and wish-fulfillments.

We must always remember when combining energies of light that we are adding light to light, whose invisible rays are themselves the original source of colours. Therefore the results of combining colours are always closer to white light, which contains all of them, than are any of the original separated colours. We can represent the adding of colours by looking at the white areas of our three diagrams as follows:

Diagram (D) RED-ORANGE LIGHT ⟶ V B G Y O R
plus GREEN LIGHT ⟶ V B G Y O R
equals YELLOW LIGHT ⟶ V B G Y O R

Diagram illustrates the principles that when we mix light colours the result is the sum of the colours that each light contains.

By mixing light energies, whether they come from the sun or from the white lights of a tungsten spot light, we can see that the effects on our consciousness follow exactly the same combinations that are produced by the human absorption of specific frequencies of light which cause the aura to manifest itself bioelectrically.

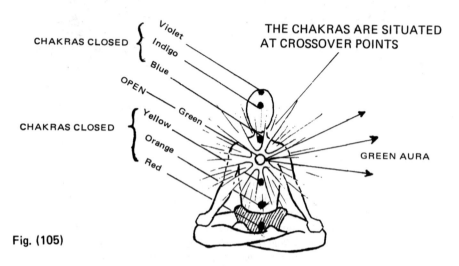

CHAKRAS CLOSED { Violet, Indigo, Blue

OPEN

CHAKRAS CLOSED { Yellow, Green, Orange, Red

THE CHAKRAS ARE SITUATED AT CROSSOVER POINTS

GREEN AURA

Fig. (105)

When only the Green heart chakra is open and all others are closed there will be a dull green aura. Because such a person is insecure without knowing why, the most vital part of the green energy is absorbed.

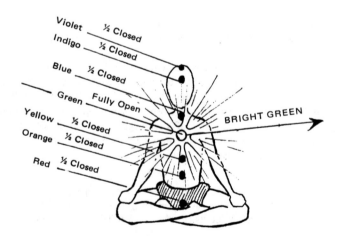

Violet ½ Closed
Indigo ½ Closed
Blue ½ Closed
Green Fully Open
Yellow ½ Closed
Orange ½ Closed
Red ½ Closed

BRIGHT GREEN

Fig. (106)

Because the person is a giving type who does not hold on to energy but wants to share the energy, his cosmic light is not kept back but re-radiated from the heart. Such a person will still be attached to giving.

In other words, there is a direct correlation between the way visible light conditions our consciousness and the way we process the invisible light of the Akasha. However, there is a spiritual dimension to the human prism that takes us out of the realm of predictability.

We have seen that secondary light colour can be created two ways: one, by mixing two coloured lights together and two, by filtering out a colour from white light. But in the case of the human aura both these processes are represented by one, re-radiation (addition to light) and two, by absorption (subtraction from light) and both these depend on one's attitudes. A person might absorb six colours but choose to radiate only one. An intellectual (yellow chakra function) might write books or teach school in a spirit of selfless service (blue chakra function) and yet hoard up his money like a miser (negative green chakra function), thinking only of himself. Only if he re-radiates the light he receives could we say that the cosmos had increased its light or added light to light. The person described earlier with six chakras open and the green one closed absorbs more from the white light (subtracting light from light) than the person with only two chakras open. If he radiates from all six chakras (adding light to light) then quantitatively he is closer to the white light than the person absorbing and combining only two colours. On the other hand, this person is subtracting from the cosmos all but the green representing its love. His radiating of the other colours without the love of the heart centre reveals that such mechanical experimenting with lights would only take us so far and no further into the depths of our psyche. For the rest of the evolutionary journey, we must develop supersensitive faculties of knowing. Colours can help us to develop the Supersense because they reveal to us what is going on in the depths of the unconscious self.

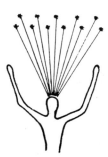

DEVELOPING THE SUPERSENSE

All these complexities can be studied by direct divination of your own chakra energies. Throughout history there have been the few diviners who developed the Supersense and found out the secret of colour and the chakra functions.

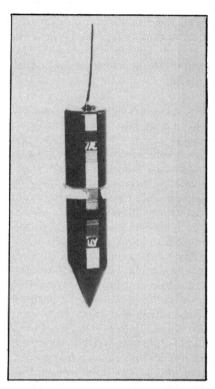

Fig. (107)

The neuro-muscular response of the diviner's instrument is caused by a resonance phenomenon with
light. The aura pendulum reacts when the cursor is
set to a pigment colour because the unconscious mind
can sense the different colours of the chakra functions when the thought of that colour is held. In the
same way a witness of the colour can be held in the
hand. It enables anyone to use their sixth sense (the
Supersense) which is highly developed in animals,
birds, insects, etc. and latent in man.

For probing the nature of our self we can save ourselves years
of work by using the colours of our aura as an indicator of our
evolutionary level, the levels of light and colour intake we lack
and need to work on, plus the levels we can relate to others on
effectively and ineffectively. We can learn how to extract from
light the particular colours we need to synthesise for health and
growth of the Supersense in us. By taking a Supersensonic
instrument and measuring our own colour emanations, divining
our physical needs and psychic needs, we can learn to mix all the
light colours in our environment as well as the inner-worlds of
psychophysical energies. The effects of reflected colours from
walls, flowers and objects in the environment can profoundly
affect the flow of psychic electricity through the chakra system
even though they do not have the power to condition and create
our level of consciousness the same way light colours do. We can

actually take in the vibrations of colour like we take in food to nourish the body. So it is important to be able to detect with the Supersense just what colours we need at different times of the day and whether they are the colours of light from radiant sources such as sun or lamps or stars or are reflected from pigment light sources.

There are some general guidelines which one can follow like the fact that orange is healing to psychological depression and nervous debilitation but no good for healing cuts with inflamation or a stomach ulcer. Although orange is excellent for relaxing the intestine and increasing the appetite it is useless for relaxing hypertensive children. Blue and violet should be omitted from the kitchen because they affect the appetite and the circulation of blood. But at the same time we must remember that our level of consciousness controls our unconscious reaction to colour. Even white colour on the walls can disturb some people because it reflects back their own vibrational colours which may not be so harmonious. There is no one standard which is generally good or bad to human consciousness, and this is why it is necessary to divine or dowse each situation, because what is good colour for one organism is harmful for another, imbalancing the energies of the body and affecting the emotional life. When the human body gets an over-saturation of any one colour then it is absorbed into our total system and acts as an overdose. Just as if we were to drink too much water we would drown in it, however pure, so with pigment colours in the environment around us. This does not happen, however, with light colours because each organism subtracts from light only that colour resonant with the particular chakras opened. But even with light, our sensitivities are so undeveloped that we can only absorb the life-force unconsciously. Only by becoming supersensitive can we begin to know this unconscious world in which "prana", the invisible light energy of creation, offers itself like an invisible priceless treasure to anyone who can realise it is there.

The sun's radiance is a disturbance of excited atoms we experience consciously; the Akasha unconsciously. Human beings are all receiving the same radiations of the cosmic forces from the total environment as the earth spins like a top in space, though not all humans receive the same amount of sunlight. Only a small part of our cosmic being is influenced by the local nearby sun. Even though man's physical being could not live without the sun which feeds all vegetable life, by comparison with the amount of invisible radiant light of cosmic rays (Akasha) the sun's influence on humans is hardly more than the moon's. In fact in some people the moon's influence on their state of consciousness is stronger and we actually call them lunatics. There are many non-lunatics, however, who are more under lunar influence (reflected light) than the rays of direct radiant solar energies. However, both sunlight and starlight contain the three primordial rays which make the seven visible colours of the octave which we find in the rainbow.

Red	Orange	Yellow	Green	Blue	Indigo	Violet	Red
1	2	3	4	5	6	7	8
Do	Re	Me	Fa	So	La	Ti	Do

These invisible colours in sunlight and starlight affect us even more than the ones in visible light do. The visible rainbow is made of droplets of rain seen at different angles and if we could see behind the raindrop we would see the invisible colours of the rainbow at another angle. (See "Supersensonics" for more explanations of the invisible colours: Infra Red, Black, Infra Black, Negative Green, Infra White, and Ultra Violet). These invisible colours of the rainbow-behind-the-rainbow are beyond the physical sensors and can only be perceived by the Supersense.

A rainbow is produced by both refraction and reflection of light by raindrops. If we regard a human prism as a spherical raindrop we can see it as a model filter. The dispersion of light through refraction of the prism of the rainbow is a most spectacular model of the human spherical wavefield in which rays of sunlight and more powerful invisible cosmic rays are absorbed and reflected. The colours are dispersed from the white light of the sun by thousands of tiny drops acting as prisms. If we look at the atoms and molecules of our body with all its liquid crystals as tiny raindrops we can see that light does indeed disperse in it as it does when entering any other material medium.

A ray of light is said to be refracted when it is bent obliquely while passing through a transparent medium such as atmosphere, glass or from one density of matter to another. This is caused by the difference in the frequency of the light. The average speed of light is less than 186,000 m.p.s. in a transparent medium. How much less speed depends on the frequency of the light. The nearer the frequency of the light is to the natural frequency of the oscillating electrons in the atoms making up the transparent medium, the greater will be the absorption and interaction between light and matter. When perfect closeness of frequency is achieved there is said to be resonance or resounding of the energy which is soaked up into a standing wave as we shall see in a later chapter.

THE SPHERICAL RAINDROP AS NATURE'S LETTERS OF LIGHT

Fig. (108)

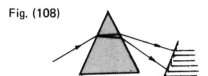

Dispersion of a ray of light through a prism shows how light is refracted according to its frequency.

Because there is a different periodic oscillation associated with these interactions of different frequencies of light in a transparent medium, a slowing down of the average speed of the light results. The speed of the light through the transparent medium is dependent on its frequency. Because the natural frequency of the transparent medium is mostly in the ultraviolet range, the highest frequencies of sunlight interact in the absorption process more frequently than do the lower frequencies of light. This results in

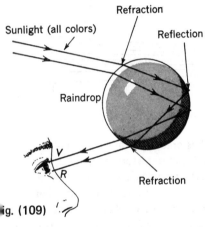

Refraction or dispersion of sunlight by a single raindrop is shown as well as reflection.

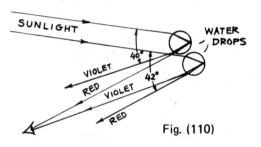

Fig. (110)

Incident sunlight shines on two raindrops as shown and emerges from them as dispersed light. The observer sees the refraction of the red light from the upper drop and the violet light from the lower drop. With millions of drops, the spectrum of all the colours is seen.

a slower speed for the higher frequencies of light energy when passing through the medium. Hence violet light travels through a glass prism while red light travels faster. The other colours travel at speeds between the violet and red light. The degree to which light bends obliquely depends on this relationship of frequency to the frequency of the transparent medium which effects the change in the speed of the light's passage. The greater the change in speed the greater the light is refracted from its original pathway through the medium. Since different frequencies of light travel at different speeds through various transparent materials, it follows that human consciousness will disperse light in different amounts to that of transparent glass or raindrops. Being much denser material than water atoms the human body will disperse more light than a transparent medium like pure water. The following drawings show the stages of dispersion by refraction and reflection.

THE RAINBOW AS NATURE'S SIGNATURE IN LIGHT

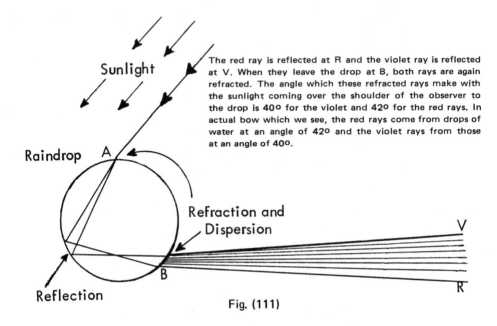

The red ray is reflected at R and the violet ray is reflected at V. When they leave the drop at B, both rays are again refracted. The angle which these refracted rays make with the sunlight coming over the shoulder of the observer to the drop is 40° for the violet and 42° for the red rays. In actual bow which we see, the red rays come from drops of water at an angle of 42° and the violet rays from those at an angle of 40°.

Fig. (111)

This imposing phenomenon of the rainbow has created so many difficulties for those who have tried to explain it throughout history that until the theory of refraction was developed it was considered a divine mystery. Now it is readily explained by science that the phenomenon is due to light striking small water drops in the atmosphere during or just after a rainfall. In the same way when we position ourself at a certain angle to the sun in respect to a water fall or a spray-hose jet the tiny drops with spherical shapes will act as prisms. Yet this did not explain why at a single point of the eye the rays ordered themselves in finely coloured bows with the bands separated in concentric circles. The same phenomenon can be seen on flat surfaces of certain liquid crystals and on thin layers of soap and oil spreading on water.

Fig. (112)

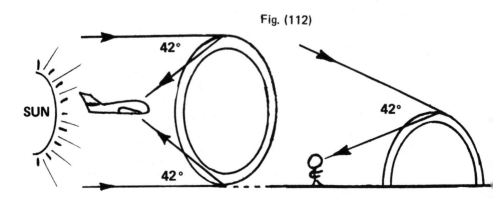

214

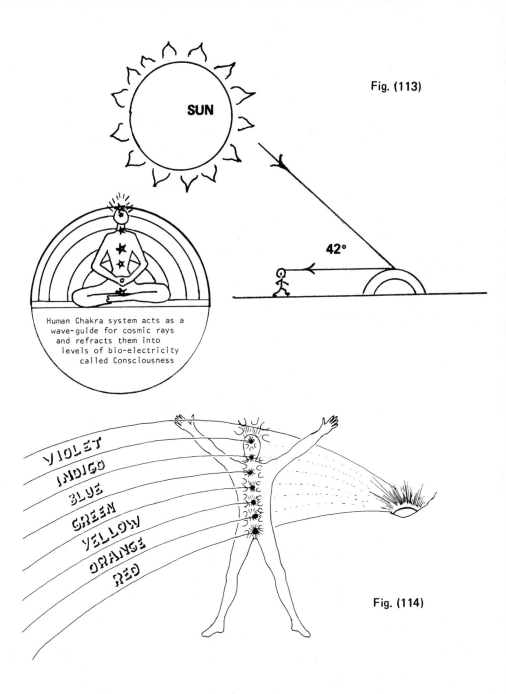

Fig. (113)

Human Chakra system acts as a
wave-guide for cosmic rays
and refracts them into
levels of bio-electricity
called Consciousness

42°

VIOLET
INDIGO
BLUE
GREEN
YELLOW
ORANGE
RED

Fig. (114)

The human aura acts as a series of spherical concentric energy centres rotating like catherine wheels and connected by subtle energies to the seven nerve centres and their ganglions and the seven glands of the endocrine system. Colours are just energy vibrating at different frequencies, some visible some not. Each chakra has a colour band associated with it which is affected by that colour. Primary light is absorbed and re-radiated as biological radiomagnetic light. Pigment reflected light is absorbed but not re-radiated. Sunlight and starlight is primary light, moonlight is reflected sunlight. The human body acts like an array of raindrops acting as spherical prisms to filter the cosmic light rays.

Why are we so affected by light and colour? What is the evolutionary purpose behind it? Let us make a diagram of the **pigment colour mixtures** similar to the one we made for **light colour mixtures,** knowing that the dynamic quality of a pigment is in reality not its reflecting power but its absorption power, so that when we add the white part of our diagram (E) we are adding or compounding the absorption powers of each pigment. In mixing pigments each single colour also continues to subtract from white light all those colours that were subtracted in order to get that colour when it was obtained alone.

TABLE (E)

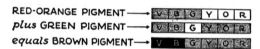

RED-ORANGE PIGMENT

plus GREEN PIGMENT

equals BROWN PIGMENT

Diagram illustrates the principle that when we mix light the result is the sum of the colours that each light contains.

The mixture of red-orange plus green shown above actually subtracts all the colours of the spectrum. The result theoretically should turn the mixture black but there are no paints or pigments which absorb all frequencies of light perfectly so when we mix all the pigment colours together we get a drab olive green, muddy brown colour. This is because all the pigments tend to reflect only a little of all the colours in the light which reaches them. But when we mix all the **light colours** together we get white because the light contains all the colours in a pure form like the rainbow.

If we mix yellow pigment (white minus violet and blue) with blue pigment (white light minus orange and red) the result is a chartreuse green. Mixing these two colours blue and yellow does not make green but leaves green light rays behind which enter our eyes as a frequency which in turn is experienced inside us as light energy in the green spectrum. To mix pigments of yellow and blue is really to mix their powers of subtracting from light. White light minus violet, blue, red, and orange leaves us with blue light rays and yellow light rays combining to form green. Mixing yellow pigment with a red pigment will give us the colour which is between yellow and red in the spectrum, that is orange. What has actually happened is that the green rays of light have been absorbed by the red pigment and the blue rays of light have been absorbed by the yellow and the red pigments.

Similarly if a pigment or a person's chakras are functioning so that they extract the green rays and the yellow rays out of white light, what remains are the red and blue rays which combine to make purple and violet colour. In this case the red pigment or chakra absorbs the green part of the white light and the blue pigment or chakra absorbs the yellow light leaving the violet behind to impinge on our eyes or to manifest in the colour of our aura. Since we are like pigments in our absorbing of the light of consciousness, the mixing of pigments can help us see that our aura can be created either of three ways: (a) reflecting off the light and not taking it in, or (b) by our taking in of light and re-radiating it in the aura, or (c) by our taking in of light and not re-radiating it, in which case the aura shows what is left in white light after certain light colours have been subtracted from it. This is why the person who absorbs all seven and re-radiates none has a black aura, whereas a person who re-radiates all seven has a white aura. In (b) the human chakra system is analogous to a filter.

When we study pigments in this way we see a mirror of ourselves. We see how the whirling of the chakras turns the simple purity of white light into a complex kaleidescope of colours. But we can also see a mirror in white light which (according to most scientific and technical authorities) is composed of three basic frequencies only, namely red-orange (red), yellow-green (green) and the blue-violet (blue). These three prime colours are called the primary colours of light and all the radiations which impinge on the receptors of our eyes, either directly as with solar rays or indirectly by reflection off objects, people, clouds, etc., may be analysed and defined in terms of these three primary vibrations. As we saw earlier, the ancient sages referred to these vibrations as the three gunas or creative forces which enter in at every level of vibration and not just those of the visible light spectrum. Many people are not aware of how these creative forces are affecting them at every moment and in the content of every thought. Hence this book is about the way they influence not only single individuals but how they are affecting the entire world through the seven portals of existence through which the human race functions.

The gunas can be illustrated in the following diagram as inter-locking and overlapping cosmic forces which are reflected in our perceptual apparatus of eye, occipitals and mental equipment, which has been organised by evolutionary intelligence over several billions of years. The diagram below should be compared with the previous one representing the mixing of pigments which subtract from light. It can be seen as that which adds light to light like three great rays or torch beams shining through the whole of creation upon a white reflecting surface.

217

Fig. (115)

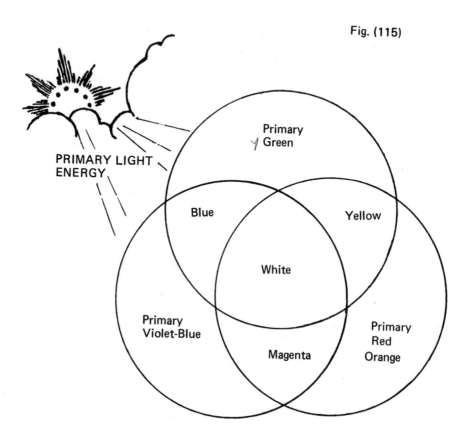

The circles represent beams of the three primary colours of light — Blue-Violet, Yellow-Green, and Red-Orange — shining upon a white surface. Where two light beams overlap, we have the secondary colours of light —Blue-Green, Yellow and Magenta. And where all three shine together, we have white light. But this order is exactly reversed if we consider these colours as pigments instead of as lights. The three inside colours become the pigment primaries and the three outside colours become the pigment secondaries. When we read the diagram in that way it tells us, for example, that a mixture of Blue-Green and Magenta pigments will produce a Blue-Violet secondary.

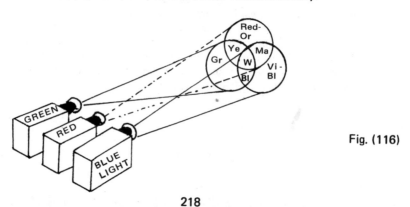

Fig. (116)

The circles above represent radiant beams of the three primary light colours made by radiation of photons lighting up a white surface. Where the beams overlap they create secondary colours of light. But the order is exactly reversed if we look at these colours as pigments absorbing colours from light instead of seeing them as radiant beams of light energy. If we reverse the order, the pigment primaries then become the three inside colours (blue, yellow, magenta) and the three outside colours (green, violet-blue, and red-orange) become the secondary colours of the pigment absorptions. For instance, if we read the diagram from this pigment absorption viewpoint we can see that the combination of a magenta and a blue of the inside colour pigments would produce a violet-blue secondary colour.

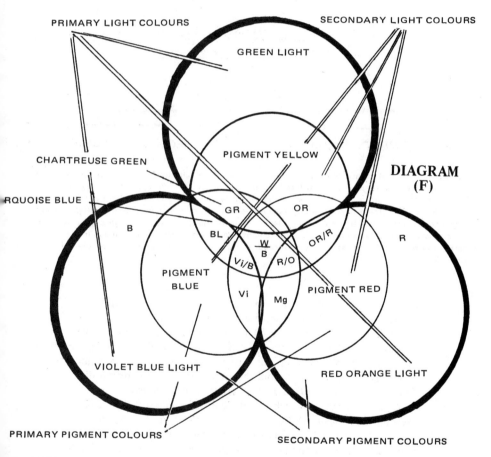

Fig. (117)

The inner circles represent pigment colour primaries with their secondaries overlapping. The thick black circles represent beams of coloured light energy shone on a white surface. Where both overlap they add or subtract from each other to reverse themselves. The pigment primary becomes the light secondary and the light primary becomes the pigment secondary. This combines the two diagrams on pages 188/218 by laying one on top of the other. The absorption and reflection of light from objects, humans, atoms, gases, crystals follow this law of the spectrum and is a basic proof of Nuclear Evolution which states that everything is radiative and re-radiating in direct proportion to its rate of absorption.

INVERSE

To know that the secondary pigment colours are the reverse of the primary light colours and that the primary pigment colours are the complementary reverse of the secondary light colours immediately gives us the tool of colour to work with in healing and in adjusting our chakra energies to optimum absorption in the black centre.

Fig. (118)

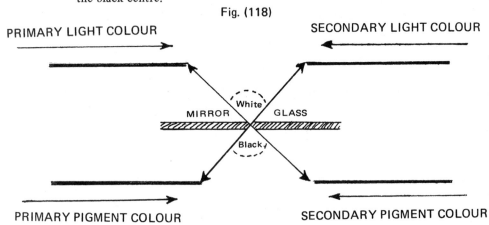

Radiation like heat is not always absorbed by a body it falls upon. It may be transmitted in a transparent way through a medium, like light is transmitted through glass; or it may be reflected as light is reflected from a mirror surface. That which is absorbed out of the light cannot be reflected and must be re-radiated in some way. Likewise light which falls on a body and is reflected cannot be absorbed. A good absorber is a poor reflector of heat and light radiation and a good reflector is a poor absorber of radiation and light. The radiant energy we receive from the sun into our bodies is partly transmitted like glass, partly absorbed and partly reflected according to the colour of our aura. The amount varies with the functioning of our chakra system.

At the cross point of the X is the consciousness in which the experience of colour is created, and the whole reason we incarnate in a body is to have this experience in which the rainbow of colour "out there" can mirror to us the white light "in here" and the Self can come to see itself as in a mirror. Light and consciousness are one and the same, therefore the primordial light exists, but until there is a mind to consciously reflect it there is no mirror in which it can see itself. The only way we can ever see the Light of Consciousness is by its reflection in the mirror of the mind, just as we would see the reflection of our body in a pond. If the pond were pure, we would see ourselves clearly but if it were muddy then we would only see the mud. The reflection of Light is the same as when we say that the mind "reflects on something", because Consciousness and light are creating all that we experience and it all takes place in the mind. Colour is only in the mind, reflecting.

One can look at colour (or at the human psyche) from the point of view of absorption or the point of view of radiation. If you are a pigment only, then your emphasis is on "what can I get from light? or what can I get from life?" but if **you are Light** and you identify with that light and know that your consciousness and your very life are light, then your attitude is "what can I — give? what can I radiate?" To see that primary light colour is secondary pigment colour and that secondary light colour is primary pigment colour gives us the "what can I give?" attitude. Why? Because we begin to see that absorptive power is only the complement of the radiating power. Absorption is only radiation turned inside out in the mirror of the mind at the centre of Consciousness.

Black and white are neutrals which complement each other just as primary colour and secondary colour complement each other in the diagram No. **(F)** And this is why the saints have referred to the total absorption of consciousness in the ONE as the black night of the soul, because the complementary of that blackness in which the ego is annihilated is the radiant white purity of selflessness. At this point of perfect equilibrium between total absorption and total radiation, we reach the still point where there is neither absorption nor radiation and all that process stops because there is no separate self to tell any difference between itself and Light.

THE TURNING POINT

How does one go about identifying with the invisible light of the universe? In this New Age, in which the wisdom of the ancient rishis can be validated by the findings of modern science, the spiritual life is no longer a matter of being concerned simply with psychological energies. Though the spiritual disciplines are still essential if we are to learn to love our neighbor as our Self, that frame of reference has now become a kind of tunnel vision, like an ostrich with its head in the ground refusing to see the whole. Evolution is at a turning point in time where the human race can continue to inch along, perfecting its veneer of civilised behaviour, or it can suddenly see itself a new way and thus radically change, making a tremendous leap up the spiral of expansion.

This book is meant to show you the many ways that you are part of that whole which is called **Akasha**. You affect it by your level of consciousness, just as you affect everyone in a room if you come with an angry vibration. And in turn, that light, with its seven colours, radically affects you, whether you are aware of it or not. If you begin to see how intimately your body and your psyche are related to colour, how the aura can reveal bodily or psychic health, then little by little you will begin to know in more than an abstract theoretical way that you are that light in which the rainbow body is born. The remarkable way in which human beings unconsciously ingest light energies of the primary cosmic gunas into the bio-energetic system without feeling anything unusual, shows that we must revise our ideas. The colour systems we learnt at school are a little different from the absorptions and re-radiations of the chakra system, so we will now list the artist's complementary colours of pigments along-side those of science and Nuclear Evolution before going on to describe their absorption into the rainbow body. The way these colours are re-expressed in the aura after they are absorbed is not as straightforward as with a simple material object because every human being has unconscious control over the action of the three gunas and consequently the blending together of the primal light colours is dependent on how evolved the being of a person is. The following tables show that the complementaries when mixed together make black.

TABLE (G)		TABLE (H)		TABLE (I)	
Pigment colours and reflected primaries of artists (called secondary light)		Primaries of the Guna light energies for the mixing of colours.		Aura colours of the human absorption from the total spectrum of the cosmic Gunas:	
	COMPLE–MENTARY	W. LIGHT BEAM	COMPL.		COMPLEMENTARY
1. RED —	BLUE GREEN	R W minus Blue Gr.	Vi, Y, O, R	R	Pale Blue, Green
2. ORANGE —	BLUE-VIOLET	O Minus Bl, Gr, Vi	Y, Or, R	O	Turquoise Blue
3. YELLOW —	VIOLET	Y Minus Bl, Vi	Gr, Y, O, R	Y	Pale Violet, Blue
4. GREEN —	PURPLE	G W minus Red, Or, Bl	Gr, Y, Bl	G	Pale Violet, Pink
5. BLUE —	RED/ORANGE	B W minus Red, Or	Bl, G, Y, V	B	Pale Lemon Yellow
6. INDIGO —	———	I	———	I	———
7. VIOLET —	YELLOW	V Minus Gr, Y	Vi, Bl, R, Or	V	Lemon Chartreuse Yellow

It can be seen that the aura colours in table (I) fit with the primary light energies required to make up a colour in table (H) and that the complementary secondary colour of the artist's pigments (table G) becomes the primary light colour. The colours from (G) and (H) are subtracting from white light in order to

222

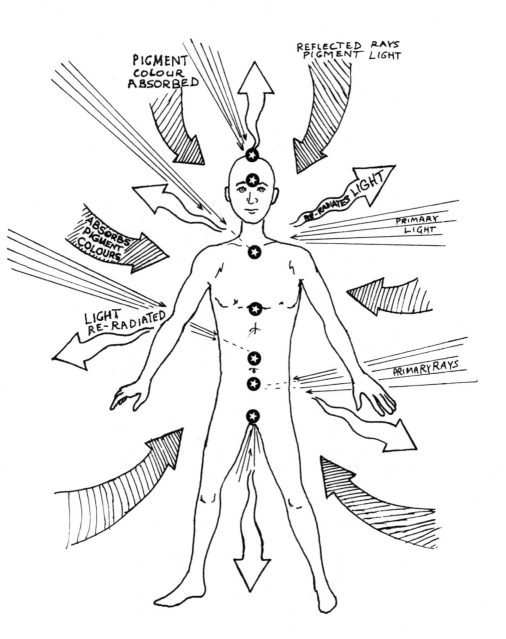

Fig. (119)

This diagram shows the rays of reflected light from pigment colour being absorbed as if the human body were itself a pigment. The light absorbed from primary rays is re-radiated like the surface of a pigment. Colour is subtracted from light by mixing of coloured pigments. Blue pigment reflects not only Blue but also colours either side of Blue, namely Green and Violet, and absorbs Red, Orange and Yellow.

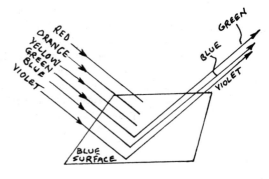

create the colours from the mixing of three invisible light radiations, i.e. red, green and violet-blue, which the ancient seers called the three gunas.

Fig. (120)

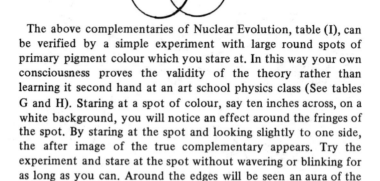

The above complementaries of Nuclear Evolution, table (I), can be verified by a simple experiment with large round spots of primary pigment colour which you stare at. In this way your own consciousness proves the validity of the theory rather than learning it second hand at an art school physics class (See tables G and H). Staring at a spot of colour, say ten inches across, on a white background, you will notice an effect around the fringes of the spot. By staring at the spot and looking slightly to one side, the after image of the true complementary appears. Try the experiment and stare at the spot without wavering or blinking for as long as you can. Around the edges will be seen an aura of the colour revealing its complementary radiation in our consciousness.

The usual explanation is the blanching and saturation of the visual purple in the pigments of the rods and cones of the eye. But on meditating on this, one clearly sees that this explanation is not valid at all and that the effects are due to the play of the mind. The fact is we <u>do not see colour with the eye</u> but with the <u>mind</u>. It is a psychological phenomenon not an objective one. A certain frequency of light impinges on the eye which sends an electrical stimulus down the optic nerve to the occipitals where the nerve spike is interpreted as a colour. The nerve spikes are the same for every colour; only their period and the frequency of the pulses will determine any difference in the brain. The psyche recreates the colour inside the brain by vibrating the consciousness (which is fully aware of its own nature even if human beings are not aware of its marvelous qualities of recreation). Not only the colour is thus created from light but its opposite complementary in consciousness can be seen around the edge of the spot where no colour at all exists.

The absorption of light into the human etheric body and its constant re-radiation through the psychic energies of the aura seems complicated if we still hold on to traditional concepts of colour which we have been taught at school. For one reason or another the colour emanating from the human bio-energetic surround called the aura does not always follow a straightforward pattern of absorption and radiation. For instance, a person could have only one chakra open. Then that colour will be absorbed from the full spectrum of light and re-radiate outwards into the environment.

Say this one chakra is an introvert one which processes Blue (emotional conceptual), then the blue aura can be caused by two or three internal processes which may be hard for a beginner to discriminate. These are listed below in three possible modes:

COLOUR ABSORBED BY THE 5TH CHAKRA
BLUE (INTROVERT)

Fig. (121)

Method 1: Electric blue colour comes through as it is absorbed because the blue channel is wide open (through devotion or other discipline) and leaves the body in almost the same condition as it enters the vehicle (purity of mind). Transcendence process.

Method 2: The mode in which the blue of a deep dull colour is mixed with several other chakra colours. In the whole vehicle of consciousness there are other chakras open which absorb all colours of light except the blue.

Fig. (122)

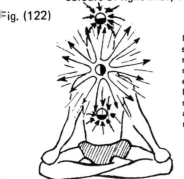

Diagram (a) shows chakras receiving but not radiating except on one level. Dia.(b) shows receiving and hardly radiating at all.

(a) Blue chakra open, Blue excreted.

(b) Other chakras open partially; colours which together make blue are absorbed but not re-radiated into the aura.

Because the chakras in (b) are open but not excreting the unwanted colours there is a condition analogous to psychic constipation, a sluggishness which creates the limited experience of the cosmic radiation as, living in the past, memory, associative events, and being separated from the fulfillment of the now or the promise of the future. Hence the dull colour of (a) is due to a clogged system. This condition applies to all chakras emitting a dull colour which shows inability to re-radiate what we take in. For instance if (a) were the heart chakra, a dirty green aura would be conditioned constantly by the state of (b) and we would have envy or jealousy instead of a tamasic condition.

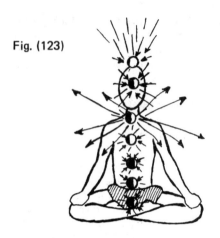

Fig. (123)

Method 3: a deep but clear blue (not indigo) indicates the conceptual mind or the locking up of images in time by building a mental model. It results from taking the energies of the other open chakras and internalising them through the slower processes of introversion. These are then externalised at a slower rate radiating them into the aura through the blue chakra. This produces idealism or scientific modelling of reality through the blue chakra which is tuning the entire being to expression on only one level of consciousness. The difference between the radiating chakra and the closed one is that change and evolution are taking place as compared to lack of will and stagnant being. The tendency of the blue chakra if it is not radiating is to reduce everything to words. This process is known as the combinative, conceptual putting together of all perceptions into fixed models, thought forms, patterns, authorities and storing them in the memory. In practical terms this method of processing light limits experience to the operations of one chakra. It therefore describes a person who relates to life in one fixed way who is cautious, conservative and does not like change and who submits all experience from any other chakra to those criteria before expressing himself.

The above example can be applied to all the other chakras but is further complicated by the fact that there is a negative and a positive expression depending on whether the energy patterns in the chakra are spinning to the left or to the right. Generally all blue chakra types are introverts and introspective but sometimes there is another chakra function, say red, which interferes with the blue function and modifies it, making a normally introvert person into an extravert and changing the blue colour aura from an electrical blue to a cerise or blue tinged with red. In looking at the aura which is an excretion of bioelectrical energies it is possible to see these combinations by observing the particular mixture. For instance fifty percent red and fifty percent blue would mean a person functioning on two chakras positively with a conflict between ideals and the more earthly sensations. If the aura was very positive the conflict would be resolved in the synthesis of charm and grace which is usually shown by irridescence in the aura while the negative lefthand spiral is dull and plain magenta colour.

Another example of the kundalini functioning in an extravert type which conditions the movement of kundalini through the chakra system would be a person with a red aura. These extravert people seldom have persistent spiritual discipline (see page 257 on Red), are sensation loving and restless and orientated to the body and its needs. If they do undertake discipline to gain control over the kundalini in its most sensual (red) aspect they will invariably take up Hatha Yóga as a physical discipline, evolving eventually to the channeling of the kundalini into the idealistic devotional chakra (blue-green) and very rarely do they ever become expressive on the yellow intellectual level. The reason is that yellow is not the complementary aura colour of red as shown in table (G) but is complementary to a violet aura. People tend to go to the complementary shown on the Nuclear Evolution equivalent table (I) as their next stage of development rather than logically proceed one by one in linear fashion up the chakra system like a ladder.

Because red aura people bounce light off so it cannot really penetrate to the deeper more introspective levels they do not ingest all the colours from the total spectrum of Akasha. An actual description of an exclusively red aura person is given later (page 262) to show how this chakra creates a personality that acts from impulsiveness and reactiveness. Because a red aura person ingests very little of any other chakra energies but the red chakra, there is very little awareness of others who do exist and function

Fig. (124)

WISDOM SUGGESTION
RED ORANGE YELLOW GREEN BLUE INDIGO VIOLET
NUX
REJECTED AT THE REACTIVE / RED LEVEL

on levels of consciousness unknown to the red aura person. A person who ingests a little of all the colours but is closed off in the red chakra may find a companion who will provide stimulation and intensity at the missing physical level and thereby be excited by such a person. But because the red aura person does not internalise any of these other colours through their respective chakra centres, none of these different energy levels will be digested into the chakra system and consequently he will eventually appear to others as a superficial person, however sincere he may be within himself. Because these other colours are not absorbed into the chakras when they are closed down, in a red aura person, all the red energy is subtracted from light energies of the cosmos and sucked into a left-hand or right-hand chakra spiral (left negative/right positive) and immediately re-radiated into the aura through the activity of the bottom chakra.

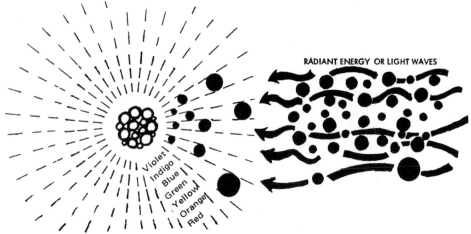

RADIANT ENERGY OR LIGHT WAVES

Violet
Indigo
Blue
Green
Yellow
Orange
Red

Light energy is swallowed into the nucleus of an atom, a chakra, a cell or any medium in nature according to its natural frequency. The closer the resonant harmonic frequency of the incoming light to the natural frequency of the vibrating nucleus the greater the absorbtion. All organisms in nature obey this law of resonant interaction which overlaps and penetrates all levels of creation. Red energy is absorbed near the surface, Violet energy penetrates to the inner core. The light becomes the thing that swallows it.

Now if we come to apply the three modes of absorption of light (as given in the example for blue) to the extreme type of extravert symbolised by the red chakra, we find that methods two and three do not often apply simply because an extremely red aura person does not function on any other chakra levels of consciousness, does not know of their existence, and therefore does not absorb any of the other types of colour energies. In fact even method number one which depends on the purity of the vehicle does not apply because the nature of the red chakra functions more as a mirror does than as a channel. In other words the kundalini as it arises in the bottom chakra does so reactively and not as a lengthy internal process. Hence red sensation types rarely experience anything but superficial reactions which have no depth of Being. Since most of the world's population operates on this one sensation level of kundalini we can see that the cause of overpopulation is due largely to their preoccupation with sex, and their political life is confined to sensation rather than thought. Hence the Roman Caesar's dictum that the people of the empire must be given bread, circuses and sport and they will be kept happy. Since the red chakra function governs the experience of the concrete world, it follows that most of the world's population, however devout in the religious sense (blue) is orientated more to the material world, and their gods will be physical ones, i.e. personalities, social idols (orange), pictures of anthropomorphic beings and an earthly guru who can be seen, touched and heard by the senses. Any devotion they display will be to climb the social ladder and even if they go to church their real caring will be focussed on the various kinds of materialism, spiritual politics, making money, etc. The next diagram represents the interplay between the chakras which in turn control the endocrine secretions, which thereby dictate the type of personality and in turn determine the ingestion of the guna qualities of creation from the primordial light -- Akasha.

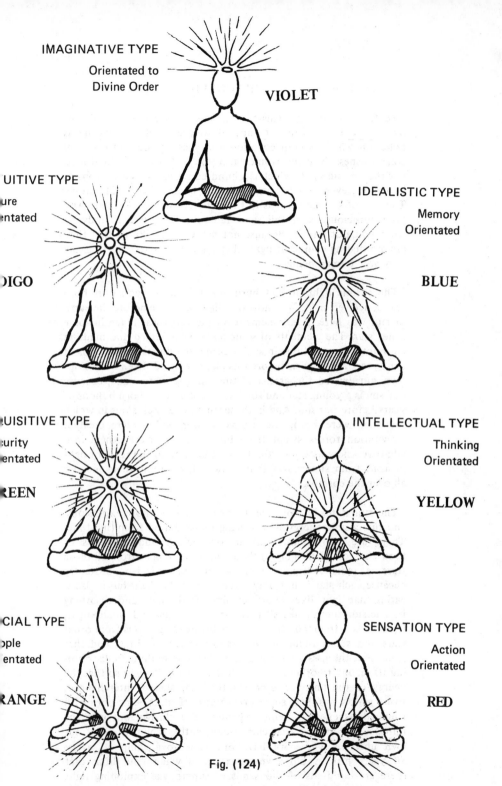

IMAGINATIVE TYPE
Orientated to Divine Order

VIOLET

UITIVE TYPE
ure
ntated

)IGO

IDEALISTIC TYPE
Memory Orientated

BLUE

UISITIVE TYPE
curity
entated

REEN

INTELLECTUAL TYPE
Thinking Orientated

YELLOW

CIAL TYPE
ple
entated

RANGE

SENSATION TYPE
Action Orientated

RED

Fig. (124)

The seven major types of Nuclear Evolution are shown radiating their characteristic aura. Most people function as overlapping types with two or more chakras opened in varying degrees of self-mastery.

229

YE ARE THE LIGHT OF THIS WORLD

To the ancient Egyptians the sun was the symbol of God. But our sunlight is peanuts compared to that fantastic enormous radiation which is your consciousness. The sun doesn't give you consciousness. The sun would burn you to a frizzle in the desert, yet the cosmic light, which is a hundred thousand times stronger, you don't even feel because your life comes from that source. The life of the universe is in the radiation of the universe. And your consciousness is this same radiating light, limited only by what you put into it. Because not many people know that they are a radiating source of light, they limit themselves by thinking they are "human beings".

The cosmic light doesn't burn you up because you were born and conceived in it. We know that light was here before the earth or sun was here. Every element on the earth was made in some other star. The elements of your body were forged and made at enormous temperatures in stellar furnaces billions and billions of light years away, even before this planet existed. Even before our own sun existed the atoms of the universe were made, because our sun is a young star and some of the stars were born billions of years before our sun. And in those supernova explosions in which the stars were born, the atoms of our bodies were created. Gravitation forces swept them up and concentrated them into what we know as the earth. They came here in the form of light protons from supernovas that exploded, dumping their energies all over the cosmos.

The sun is made from the debris of some of those explosions, and the cosmic energy is still being redistributed from that time. There are 100 billion stars in our galaxy and hundreds of thousands of galaxies bigger than ours and the light from all those stars is redistributing the energy of the universe constantly because each star is not only a radiator of that light but it also is eating that light, like we are, feeding off the light and absorbing it. The sun doesn't just sit there as a ball of gas and radiate light, it also has a tremendous attraction for heavy protons from other stars and sucks them in every morning for breakfast and that excites all the gasses so it is able to keep on burning, redistributing its energy to other stars which also suck in its light so that the energy of the universe is constantly being shared, interchanged. Every galaxy has these supernovas going off, stars being born with tremendous energies being expanded and thrown out into the universe. We receive that energy constantly. If you think of our own universe where we have one supernova going off every 30 years just in our own galaxy, and when you think that there are hundreds of thousands of supernovae exploding right now in the 100 billion galaxies around us and sending out this powerful potent energy in the invisible radiation that penetrates right through the kind of matter we are made of, then you can see that we have an enormous strong powerful light creating this movie that we have going on in front of our consciousness which we call creation.

Every few minutes a cosmic ray hits your atoms and blows them up. Every few minutes a cubic centimeter of your body is being destroyed and reborn into different kinds of particles but on such a microcosmic scale that you don't feel anything. You don't feel the starlight sustaining your life even while the sun is shining brightly at midday so that you cannot see the stars. You do not feel yourself processing the light of the universe either skillfully or poorly, but you absorb and reflect that light just as the grass does or the sky or the red rose. Can you see yourself as a being interpenetrated by the vast life energies of the universe, a being who in his own potential self has the power to change the primordial light of the Akasha into Kasha, manifesting in concrete material form the full glory of that Light which created you and creates you even now in every instant of your life, and which places in your hands the power to choose?

> Ye are the light of the world.
> A city that is set on an hill
> cannot be hid.

> Let your light so shine before men
> that they may see your good
> works and glorify your Father
> which is in heaven.

That Father or primordial radiation is called Brahman, from the root word Brim meaning expansion, and the state of Brahmic consciousness is constantly expanding. Why is it doing that? What is expanding the universe? Of course it is Light! The universe expands by radiation, outwards from the centre. So only when we can look at ourself as a radiating being can we stand with our consciousness at the centre, lighting everything up 360° around us, not just viewing through narrow sensors limited to the visible spectrum. It is better you were a blind man seeing nothing with your eyes, because they only fool you. Looking through the visible slit of the creation is like looking through one of those very narrow thin windows in the battlements of a castle, just big enough to shoot an arrow through. The walls were very thick, so the field of vision was very narrow and all they could see was just two or three people in front of them. This is what a human being is, a slit. All they can see is through one tiny slit, the vision, the eye. Visible light is only one tiny part of the whole, yet consciousness is vibrating with **all** the radiation of the universe. When we identify with this piece of skin the sensitive eye, all we see is the objects of visible light, but when we see with radiation that is the invisible light, then we begin to see into the heart of things, begin to see how things vibrate, how each flower, each atom, each object around us is sending out its vibration, its very subtle radiation, how each person is a radiating star sucking in the light from other stars and also sending out its light. When we begin to look at that light coming out of a person we begin to know more about them because what they are radiating is the result of their true being, not what they think they are but their true state of vibration.

Christ said, "Don't bother what goes into a man; it is what comes out of him that is important." This is a specific cosmic law he was talking about. You can eat anything you like; it is what you do with it inside that is important. People can eat poison and process it and be a pure being. The holiest holy men sometimes eat nothing but rice and dahl, yet they radiate fantastic light. You could put the best dinner in front of them and they would eat it, and if you asked them five minutes later what they had eaten they would say, "I don't know. It was food." If you wanted them to put their consciousness on the food they could tell you what it was but why bother? They are only interested in radiating that light and communing with the cosmos. We are like that light too, but we do it unconsciously while they do it consciously. They do it because they identify with light and they see that everything material is crystalised light and that we are continuously creating with our own consciousness this movie of life that is going on in front of us, this narrow slit that is just like a film strip.

Once you have experienced that light of the cosmos that is burning in everything, you can never be the same again. The spiritual eye is opened and even if you tried not to see it again, you couldn't because once you get to that state there is no going back. Once you become the creative force everything you think is dangerous because this is a state of precariously balanced equilibrium. You can get to this state by seeing that the positives and negatives when they come together annihilate each other if they are equal and opposite. They complement each other and therefore destroy each other in the black nucleus centre and become something else. When the positive and negative energies are equally balanced in a person, the whole of creation and the cosmos is held in stillness. This is not a negative stillness but a dynamic stillness, because if there is any change in either positive or negative sides of a balance then there is a disequilibrium and the positive and negative begin to vibrate and oscillate in their attempt to get back to equilibrium.

When these two energies violently oppose each other we have what is called evil or negative conditions. But when they work together for balance, they are creative and create a third energy.

Out of that stillness when they annihilate each other's potentials, they unite together as one and then there is no separation between positive and negative. Negative is positive and positive is negative and they have absolutely no meaning in that oneness. They create something else, a new wholeness which is another kind of energy altogether, called kundalini by mistake. Kundalini is still the state where the positive and negative are rising up through the chakra system to come together in the magnetic part of the mind. When they come together there, they annihilate each other and that is where we see the psychic light, at the seat of consciousness where another, completely new energy is created out of those two. When positive and negative become one, they become the creative force, the evolutionary force in man that raises up every cell and every atom of the vehicle.

The remainder of this book is about that evolutionary force of consciousness working its way through all the vibrating systems of the world. Its expansion is the awesome creative power of Brahman radiating through everything at the nuclear centre as light.

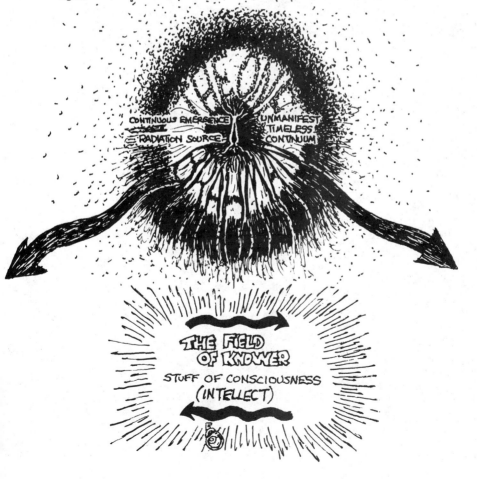

CONTINUOUS EMERGENCE
RADIATION SOURCE

UNMANIFEST
TIMELESS
CONTINUUM

THE FIELD
OF KNOWER
STUFF OF CONSCIOUSNESS
(INTELLECT)

50 Green 55 Blue 62 Indigo 68 Violet

COLOURS
AND THE
INNER WORLDS
OF TIME

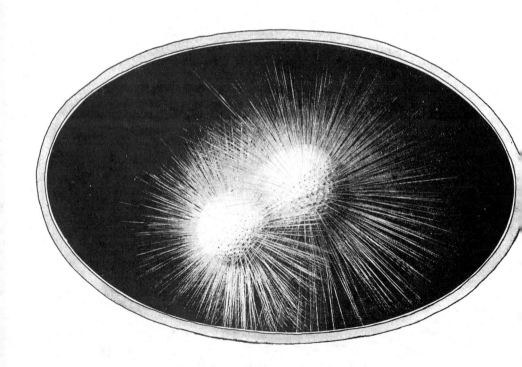

INTRODUCTION TO THE COLOUR LEVELS
OF CONSCIOUSNESS AND PERSONALITY

THE DRIVES AND COLOUR

All people live by colour daily in the choice of food, clothes and housing. Most choices are made unconsciously and the personality does not know why a tomato is red, or what effect such a colour would have on themselves or the intestinal secretions of a bird, or how the pigment of the eye and object is related to the light that hits it.

The colour of a material object is determined by its absorption of light; molecular substances as well as living organisms absorb light.

What is colour? We know that material objects only have colour when lit. Look into a darkened room. Where are the colours? Look out of your window on a moonlit night. Where are the colours? So every material thing needs to absorb light to have a colour. What about us? Look at a whole row of faces in any audience. Are they all the same colour? Why is the fat gentleman's face so red, when the little white-haired lady sitting beside him has a pale bluish tinge to her skin? And what about the egg-head along the row, why is he so yellow, while his friend with the hunched shoulders looks "positively green"? And who is this gorgeous red-head coming down the aisle? Why do all the men's heads turn? Is it just for her obvious physical attributes or is it that she exudes a warm red glow of sexuality?

Every gathering of people is a rainbow; we have given this new version of Nuclear Evolution the subtitle "Discovery of the Rainbow Body" and in this lies the key to our study of the first part of the book. The nature of the Rainbow Body has already been generously expounded in the transcript of Christopher Hills' talk on the subject. That is the end of the long evolutionary voyage of discovery. It may help now to go back to the beginning, where it all started:

In the beginning God created the Heaven and the Earth.
And the earth was without form and void; and darkness
was upon the face of the deep . . .

Pause there and experience the darkness, not temporary darkness that we experience every night, but eternal darkness that was from the beginning of Time.

And the spirit of God moved upon the face of the waters.
And God said 'Let there be LIGHT' and there was LIGHT.

Moving from Genesis to Isaiah we find the words:

The people who walked in darkness have seen a great
LIGHT.

The story of Nuclear Evolution is the story of those people, or
rather it is the story of all of us on our voyage of discovery from
darkness, via the spectrum of the seven rainbow colours, into the
light of pure consciousness.

Why do we say 'via the spectrum'? Just as any ray of light passing
through a prism splits into seven hues, so light that is ingested by
every living thing on the planet is absorbed or reflected according
to its unique qualities. We humans are no different, except that in
discussing the human personality and ultimately, the inner being,
we shall be talking not of secondary light nor of colour pigments,
but of primary light and pure radiation, or, in other words, all-
pervading consciousness, the stuff that is given to each one of us as
pure and which we modify according to our state of being. It is for
us to search ourselves and to discover whether we are contaminat-
ing or glorifying the gift.

It is not well known that people react to light and colour in
the same way as they relate to and experience time. Consciousness arises when events are experienced as time-flow.

In timeless states of being such as deep sleep, self-consciousness disappears. In the dream state of sleep, events are experienced by the self as an observer and witness of a time-flow
which is not fixed by any external periodic occurrence, such
as a clock. The " I " which is awake and experiencing " time ",
is the same " I " which dreams, and the same " I " which
is unconscious of " self " in deep sleep.

The basic " drive-needs " of this " self " whether sleeping,
dreaming, or waking, are the same and reside deep in the
unconscious. Time distortion which we experience when bored
and waiting as long and extended and which accelerates when
engaged in happy or fulfilling tasks, is affected by light of
certain frequencies which we call colour. The way we relate
to time or timelessness, and space or spacelessness, can be
ascertained by the way we relate to colour. Man is sensitised to
frequencies in sound, radio-waves and light in ways that he
cannot explain. His drives are expressions of the energies which
come to him imprisoned in time.

Every reader brings to this book his or her own special personality with its preferences and abhorrences, its likes and its dislikes, its preoccupation with Time or its seemingly complete obliviousness to the significance of the passing hours and minutes. Within one family we discover a whole range of levels from which the radiations of light/consciousness are experienced within the context of Time. So before we plunge into the evaluation of each of the colour levels in the spectrum of consciousness, it would be well to research our own personality as to its colour preferences and its habitual response to Time.

Look around your room. What is the prevailing colour in the decor? Did you choose it? Look at the clothes in your closet. What colour predominates? Then look out of your window or any window where there is a variety of buildings, people, flowers and so on. Now note where your eye rests. Is it on the green grass or on the orange marigolds? Or does it zero in on a new red sports car? Does the yellow sweater of a passing girl catch your eye (irrespective of what is inside it!) or do you latch on to the faded violet garment of a passing hippy? Is there a colour that brings a negative reaction? Does any one colour make you feel slightly sick? Note these reactions. They will be valuable reference material for the chapters that follow on the seven colour levels.

Then what about Time? Do you refer everything to the past or do you live vibrantly in the Now? Are you spaced out in dreams of the future or do you have to check past sources, present facts and future possibilities before you act? All these are clues to your present state of consciousness, and by becoming aware of them now you will embark on this voyage of discovery of the Rainbow Body better equipped with resource material and ready to enjoy the excitement and intensity of new realisations about yourself.

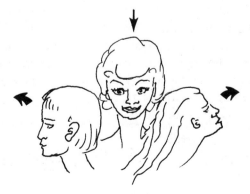

COLOUR IS NO ACCIDENT OF NATURE

All matter is a form of veiled life and life is merely the wriggling of veiled Consciousness in a body expressing itself. Consciousness in " matter " expresses itself as " life " through colours of the spectrum, each colour merely being the vibration of life expressing itself on a certain wavelength of energy or matter. It has been revealed in thousands of scientific tests that all matter is electrical vibration and the mind itself is a veiled form of material vibration of energy. Therefore, if man cannot transcend the binding power of the mind, he cannot transcend his material form of life. If a man cannot understand how colour arises, how the different wavelengths impinge on the consciousness of certain sensitised cells in the subtle intake of light into his organism, then it is because of his own ignorance of Self. This fact, that his spiritual faculty is still asleep and that the organ of perception is obstructed by the veil between his illumined intuition and his knowledge of sensations, is enough to show that stimuli from the outside would only become meaningful to the organism when it can select its needs " at will " from the huge mass of stimuli pouring in at all times from the Universal energies. The will to experience, the will to understand, the will to open up the veil between sensation and intuition, is the whole turning point of Nuclear Evolution. Without " will " the Divine Will cannot be contacted, the spectrum of consciousness cannot be seen, and the Self cannot be known.

As further preparation for the study of the seven levels we need now to clear our minds of all preconceptions and basic assumptions about what we know or even think we know. The fact that we are reading this book at all indicates that we are among those who have the will to live consciously and not to be at the mercy of the continual barrage of stimuli that pours in on us every day, not only from other people but from society and the mass media, with all its subtle and not so subtle persuasiveness and inevitable twisting or slanting of the truth.

The I Ching refers to this attitude of receptivity in its image of a sunken lake on top of a mountain, which it equates with a free and humble mind that can remain receptive. In the words of the Wilhelm translation and commentary: "People soon give up counselling a man who thinks he knows better than anyone else." No doubt every author hopes for this receptive attitude in his readers, but here it is the basic and essential ingredient of the first stage of Nuclear Evolution, since without this attitude there is a negation of the whole process from the word go!

It is because men believe they already possess consciousness and life that they take no trouble to acquire it. The chief obstacle to man's unlocking the knowledge of Self through awareness of the seven colours (the different energy levels), which manifest life and consciousness, is his mistaken belief that he already possesses full consciousness and knows himself well.

There are two ways we can go now. Either we can accept the premise that Light/radiation and consciousness are one and the same thing and that what streams out of our eyes and lights up the world is not different from what streams out of the sun and other light sources; or, if that is too much for us to accept at this point, we can acknowledge our limitations and see the expose that follows as a "typology" whereby each level or type of personality corresponds to a certain colour or band of the spectrum. Either premise can be accepted temporarily for the argument to proceed, rather than rejecting before the evidence has been shown.

For those who choose the second way it will be interesting to note that woven inextricably into the fabric of our language are terms that tie the colours to the personality or mood levels. We say "he was red with anger" or "green with envy" or "having a fit of the blues", and those of us who have been into yoga psychology recognise that the spectrum colours relate to the seven chakras and to the extent of individual awareness, according to which chakras are open and how much they are open.

The following diagrams set out the attitudes of the introvert (receptive) and the extrovert (expressive) types who both absorb light into their chakra system in different ways. As the reader progresses through the book it could help to determine for himself or herself the first attitudinal differences met with in the study of Nuclear Evolution. These differences in perception are dealt with in much greater detail later on in the book. The introvert takes longer to digest psychophysical energies but allows penetration, while the extrovert is reactive and forms impressions before there is a chance to assimilate at greater depths of awareness.

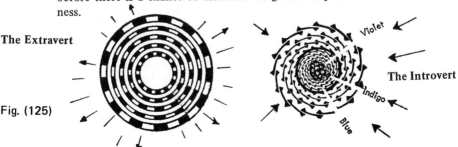

The Extravert

The Introvert

Fig. (125)

241

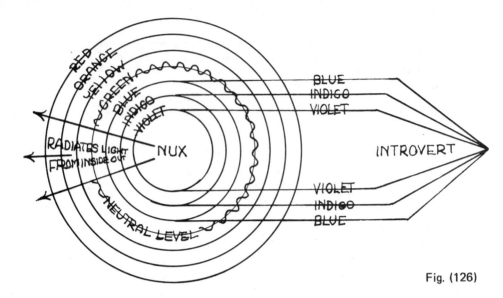

Fig. (126)

Introverts depend on something internal for their experience of time. Their time worlds are Blue/conceptual, Indigo/intuitive and Violet/imaginative. They are more in tune with the nucleus and its blueprint for their evolution. The pure introvert is a Cosmic being whose time world is mainly governed by internal events.

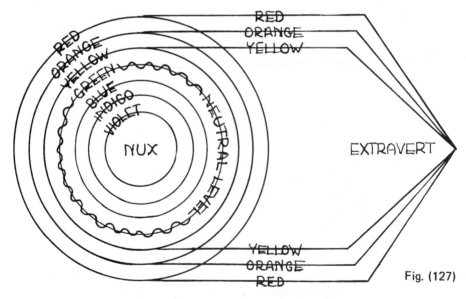

Fig. (127)

This diagram shows the way the personality of the extravert absorbs light into his active levels, selecting only those colours from the external Lumen that he resonates with. These colours are seen as that person's AURA. The longer wavelengths do not penetrate the psychic layers inside the neutral green level of consciousness.

Extraverts depend on EXternal Time.

THE SENSATION LEVEL
OF
PHYSICAL CONSCIOUSNESS

*The following is a transcription
of one of a series of lectures on
the Human Chakra System given
by Christopher Hills in 1974.*

THE RED LEVEL   MULADHARA CHAKRA

We are going to talk about the flow of energy through the chakras. On the right-hand side there is an energy which flows and is called Shiva in the Hindu mythology. Shiva represents the Creator or the creative aspect of consciousness. The Hindus invented many kinds of gods to explain how the universe works and we must not regard them as rather naive just because they worship gods that happen to dance around like Shiva. We see these brass images that Hindus worship, with flames all around–Shiva doing his cosmic dance. Of course, this is only a mental aid. All Gods are man-created in the sense that we create them in our mind. But God or Brahma or the big God is unfathomable with our mind, or incomprehensible to the mind, therefore we mustn't have the idea that because conceptually they worship so many gods that they are rather naive. It is only a way of looking at the aspects of consciousness. Shiva then is the aspect of consciousness which is the creative positive dynamic projective force and opposite to the other one which flows on the left-hand side through the chakras. This is the Shakti force which is the female aspect of Shiva, or the receptive or negative flow of consciousness which is the compliment to the positive. Now we mustn't think that these two are independent of each other, otherwise we fall into a mental trap of thinking there is such a thing as positive and negative. All that positive and negative mean in the Hindu concept is that they arise out of each other. They don't exist independently and what may be positive to one aspect of consciousness may be negative to another. The best way to explain it is to use the analogy of a magnet. If you have a magnet and cut it in half then each piece becomes a magnet. This magnet has a positive end and a north and a south pole; then you chop it in half and immediately you have two pieces with positive and negative ends. You can't have one end existing without the other, and the end which was positive may become negative when you chop it in half. If this half of the magnet is chopped off then part of that positive end becomes negative. Positive only means more positive than negative. It means that what may be positive now, is negative to a higher state of consciousness. Now you could say that man is polarised like a magnet. He walks on the earth and the bottom half of him, his body, his instrument is polarised to the earth. The top half is polarised to space or heaven, of course. Now his top half in his normal state of consciousness is negative to heaven, that is, he doesn't take much notice of heaven, he takes more notice of earth. So his attention and consciousness is thereby grounded in earthly things, and his bio-energetic responses are polarised to the earth which has its own energy very much like electricity. But this electricity is Prana or psychic electricity, not the kind of electricity you get from P.G.& E. This kind of electricity doesn't flow along wires. It's all around you all the time. It's free electrical energy, free electrons which are passing through your body and being earthed all the time. And sometimes if you wear rubber soles you'll charge yourself up a bit more and it will take longer for it to leak back into the earth. Some of you may have worn a fur coat now and then or some special woolen clothing and got yourself charged up and gotten an electric shock off the car door or something like that. It's quite a strong shock. It's quite a few thousand volts that a human being can be charged up with. And you could pass 40,000/50,000 volts of this type of electricity through the body and you wouldn't even feel it.

Now, we're going to talk about this bottom chakra at the base of the spine. Keep your consciousness on how the shakti and shiva forces flow through this chakra. We could say that this is affecting our breathing because this centre controls the physical body and its way of sensing the universe. And one of the ways we are hooked up to the universe is through our breath. In fact the only thing that separates you as your body--not you inside but you as your body, from cosmic consciousness is your breath. This realisation is a deep meditation. It sounds simple on the surface, but without breath you would have no consciousness at the human level. So this is the link between you and the type of eternal consciousness which is going on inside you which ordinary people do not have much awareness of . . . (I say ordinary people but I mean those people who do not work on themselves and don't enter into the experience of this eternal consciousness). It may take several lifetimes to get to this in its pure state. In fact, in human form, it's very unlikely that you will ever get into the ultimate pure, pure state. If we were ever in that state we'd be able to create the entire universe and play God. Now, the important thing to remember about all these chakras is that this pure energy flows through them as it comes down through the top and filters through each of the centres--each of the centres is a whirling ball of energy, like a spiral, like a figure 8 spiral. It spirals into the centre and out again. Think of these like balls of energy inside each other, not just strung along the spine, that you are sitting inside the inside ball above the top chakra. Here at the centre of these systems of energy is where you really are. You're really floating over your head, not inside your body, but that's your real Being, your real Self. Then, consciousness comes down through this (top) chakra and you begin to imagine that you are a self, because this chakra governs the imagination. Everything created has some kind of image or imagination whether it's divine imagination or human imagination. We'll go into that later because the imaginative faculty is very tricky.

Now as it comes down into the lower mind states we enter into a different time world. We become more human and get human ideas about being human. We think "I am a human" don't we , and as it filters through the system a different time world comes. All these (chakras) are different time worlds until we get down into the physical body which has its own time world. Now the problem with the time world of the physical body is that the senses are all time experiences. Essentially, they are all now, but they are not the eternal now. There are several kinds of now. The first now we have to be aware of is our senses. Why is it always now with our senses? Well, the main reason is that we think that the universe we sense with our senses is outside of our skin. Remember, the senses are all bits of skin, the nose vibrates in its olfactory bulb to the aromatic chemicals in the air and they are all resonating and vibrating aromas which are picked up; our very sensitive equipment sends a message to the brain to tell you that this is ammonia, this is perfume, this is a rose and so forth. You have learned to recognise what these vibrations are. And your eyes are just bits of skin again, sensitised to light, which have evolved over millions of years of seeing and the eye is not just the piece of skin on the surface, it's hooked up to a whole computer of its own, the occipitals at the back of the head. The eye is a very highly discriminating mechanism when the consciousness looks through it and it has a very large computer, it has a bigger computer than anything else in the head, in the brain. The brain has different centres in it and they vary in size. Some have a smaller number of circuits and some have a larger number. The visual cortex, that part of the brain that handles the visual stimuli, the sensations that come through the eye, is a hundred times as big as the equipment which handles auditory stimulations that come through the ear. The ear, by the way, is another piece of vibrating skin which is tuned to the vibrations in the air. My voice is coming to you from the air vibrations. I am vibrating the air and my mind is shaping my throat and lips without my thinking about it and thoughts are being translated into language. That language vibrates some phonetic vibration and the skin of your ears picks it up and sends the message to the auditory cortex, which is 100 times smaller than your visual cortex. Now let's meditate for a moment . . . How is it that sound or music is carried to us with so much more power to move us inside ourself than sight, and yet sight has 100 times more sensitive equipment? It is able to discriminate many more vibrations in light than the ear is in sound. The spectrum of vibrations is very small in sound. We can hear very little sound actually. Sometimes children can hear up to 15,000 cycles and as you grow older you drop down to about 12,000 or 11,000. There are crickets that sing, for instance, at 17,000. Another kind of cricket that sings at 22,000. We can't hear them because it's beyond our ear capacity. So, there are all kinds of sounds that are going on around us now which we can't hear. They're just out of ear shot, just out of range. So why is it that the vibrations of sound have so much more effect than the vibrations of sight?

The main reason that we haven't learned to use fully the visual cortex is because it's the latest thing to evolve in us, whereas sound was the first thing. The sound centre, the sound cortex belongs to a very primitive area of the brain, which was built long before we ever became human. That is, nearly all living organisms from the reptiles on up, began to develop this sensitivity to sound. Then the first reptile developed on its brain a piece of sensitised skin, with which it sensed light, and remember it was after it had stopped being a water creature and it climbed out as an amphibian and became a water and land creature. When food supplies ran out in the water, it came out on the land and began to use its flappers as feet and developed a two-hemisphere brain, with which it began to sense light. This gradually became more and more refined as it came to more and more specialised animals so that it gradually began to get *convoluted skin,* and then as it got more precious to the organism it grew a casing or protection. As time went on, through millions and millions of years of course, we came through those kingdoms. We relive all that in the womb. We go through the whole scene. The egg joins with the sperm and there's a tadpole . . . you've all seen a sperm no doubt, and it wiggles its way in and a whole gaseous process starts, just like the birth of the earth. And it goes through splitting and splitting and splitting until the whole thing is built up and it develops a nervous system. Gradually it goes through living in the sea in the fluid in the womb, and then it gradually gets a skin and so develops all its organs and gets gills. Then the body gets covered with hair and then by the time you are born the hair is all gone and you're a nice pink baby. Inside the womb you were quite hairy at one point, in the evolution process or the re-enactment of that process. Now if we can imagine that as a kind of scale going toward a higher state of consciousness, we can think of it as a graph where perhaps that vegetable experience, when we were vegetables, took consciousness a certain time to get into the vegetable state, then from the vegetable state it took another stretch of time to get to, say, the fish state. Then from the fish to the reptile so much time elapsed and from the reptile to the animal it took some more time and from the animal to the man it took that much more time. From man at birth as a non self-conscious being it takes three months to become aware of himself, in other words, to get an ego; babies don't have egos, not in the beginning. When you're born you're not self-conscious. It takes perhaps just a tiny slice to relive that part of our evolution which is man as a non-selfconscious being. In other words, we relive the entire evolutionary process from the vegetable to animal in the nine months in the womb. From the point at which we become conscious of our self as a person to the time we die, you could say that this is just a slice that is hardly measurable. The amount of evolution that takes place between being born and dying is the least. Human beings evolve very little in each lifetime. That is, they are born with all this equipment which has taken millions of years to evolve, light receptors like eyes and ears, which are highly refined senses. All these senses are very refined bits of equipment. No man has ever duplicated them exactly. No man has ever built a computer as complex as the human brain. So let's think in terms then that in this short span of time we've somehow got to get to the enlightened state. You see, we've got to make up all that distance to where we're eventually going. The question is, can we be enlightened in one lifetime? I don't want to put you off or to put a negative wet blanket on the feeling that you might not get enlightened this time around. Because what I'm going to say about time now is important to that matter.

Every time we come into a physical body we have to deal with that bottom chakra, don't we. Somehow we have to become master of our body rather than our body becoming master of us. Now, unless we understand the time world of the bottom chakra there is very little chance that we will escape it or little chance that we won't have to go through the same trip every time, of conquering our senses so that they don't lead us astray, or of conquering the incarnation in the physical body. We have to understand why we have it, and try to get out of being a slave to it. Most people in a normal state of consciousness are complete slaves to their bodily needs. Whether it's food, sex, or instincts like self-preservation and self-replication, which are two very powerful instincts, they are governed by that bottom chakra. So to become master of that bottom chakra involves getting both those instincts under control. Now you might be able to go on a celibacy trip you see, but it doesn't mean you're going to conquer your bottom chakra by being celibate, because all you might be doing is repressing it. It might be oozing out somewhere else. Because if you repress something you create a pressure and a resistance. Pressure and resistance go together, just like positive and negative. You can't have one without the other. You can fill a tin can with pressure but you can't fill the universe full of pressure unless there is something to contain it.

So, in our lives we are continually pressured by these energies because we put limits on them. The sexual energies particularly, we're always pushing them away because society has educated us to believe that they are either bad, sinful or something else. Of course if you become a priest you will be pushing it down too, if you are celibate. But the whole art of getting mastery over the sexual impulse is the conquering of desire, not the pushing away, but rather not desiring . . . unless you want to desire. But if you don't want to desire, then, the urge, the instinct doesn't arise. The energy goes higher up into another chakra, without rushing up out of control as a compensation for repressing it. Then there is the instinct of self-preservation which is a very hard one to get control of. Very few people want to die physical death. They talk about it but very few really want to go. Suicide of course is where a person thinks that if they commit physical death then they somehow hold up the whole universe for ransom and particularly some other person. Many suicides, if they can't get noticed by another person when they are alive in a physical body, will commit suicide just to get their own back on people or to get notice in some way. As you've seen, they hang on the Brooklyn Bridge or the Golden Gate Bridge until someone rescues them. What they are starved of is personal recognition, but because the consciousness is fixed on the body as their person, they think that they are going to get back at society or the ones they love, or are going to punish them in some way by punishing themselves. But of course when they wake up on the other side they find they really haven't punished anyone but themselves with even greater consequences for having not faced the quality of their own lives.

(New Editor's Note: From this section of the lecture Christopher went into the nature of space and time and as this will be dealt with in a later discussion we thought it better to apply only that part of the lecture that deals with the Muladara centre.) He continues:

Now let us just look at our bottom chakra and discover what kind of time it lives in. Having exploded the idea that there is something like a periodic occurrence, that there is something like a body that floats through space, how is it that we become aware of space? Because we think we are a body. That's the only thing that creates space. It's our insistence that we're a body bumping into other bodies, other things. When we are a baby we walk around bumping into things and we look at another body and we say, "That is outside of my body. There must be some space in between us." As long as we think that that is another body separate from our body, that our consciousness is inside our skin and can't get out and that other body has consciousness inside its skin and can't get out ... as long as we think there is space separating the two bodies we have a notion that this thing space exists. The minute that you dissolve the idea inside your head that somehow your consciousness is stuck inside your body, and realise that actually it is radiating out through space, and that when you look at something your consciousness travels out there and dissolves space then you can begin to think like this, that everything you see is what you are inside your head, and you realise that only your senses bump into objects. Only the sensory information that an object is there has created a notion that space is there. But the only thing that created space was your consciousness believing it was not in the space. That it was inside your body. The minute that you believe that your consciousness is interpenetrating the whole of space, then all the objects become part of your consciousness.

Do you follow? Is anyone mystified? You are? Okay. Let's go through this again in a different way. Let's assume that we are sitting inside our imagination and inside that is another way of knowing and inside that is another way of knowing and so on until we have seven ways of knowing about a signal coming in from outer space. The outer layer is our skin. So a signal from the sun, for instance, comes in and your senses and receptors go to the centre and there you are sitting and you say, "That's the sun out there." Because you are believing that your consciousness stops at that skin. Right?

Now there are other skins. Cultural skins, mental skins, survival skins, imaginative skins. We all have these layers and they change the signal considerably. What changes the signal as it pulses space? The medium it passes through. You pass light through a prism, you'll get certain colours. You don't get seven colours unless you pass it through a prism or a raindrop. Consciousness is the same. There is no difference from light. We think there is a difference because our consciousness is making differences. But when your consciousness is pure and you look out of your eyes you see that what is looking out is the same thing as light. Because you've never seen light actually, you see. We think we see light, but we don't. We only see the source of energy and we see the objects it falls on, and our senses pick up those signals, but our senses cannot pick up light! They can only feel radiation absorbed as heat or something like that. But they do not see anything when they look at light. Can you see anything passing between me and that light? You can see the light bulb and you can see me but you can't see anything passing in between. Light is invisible and so is your consciousness. If your consciousness cannot discriminate any difference between itself and light then it must be the same thing. There's no way that your consciousness can tell any difference between itself which is invisible and something else which is invisible. So what is looking out of your eyes and sensing the universe is consciousness. But of course it's looking through some very narrow windows called senses which only measure a small part of light and vibration.

To live in a body is like being inside a castle; you know those old Norman castles, they used to have slit windows through which they could shoot with bow and arrows. But they were very narrow and all you could do was get a very narrow vision of the enemy through there. If somebody was crawling up the wall, you couldn't even see them. Well, that's a bit like this body. We're looking at a vast universe through narrow slits.

It's important then to understand the kind of time world that one of those narrow slits called the senses uses. What kind of person is it who lives in the bottom chakra?

Well, because he is reactive, his first sensation is his only sensation. Do you follow? The skin reacts, and the skin doesn't penetrate to any of these other layers. They are closed off. Now for somebody at another level (say the conceptual level) the signal will have to take a little time to get there to be processed and understood in conceptual terms in the mind and go through all these layers–the cultural level, security hang-ups, and all the rest of it, and it would take that person some time to receive that signal, because they're not reacting to the first stimulation. They're trying to think about it, reflecting on it. Therefore, the person functioning from the bottom chakra is a reactive person. He is totally responding from one stimulation to the next. To him it's always now, but his now is always one second, a glimpse of a girl's leg and his consciousness is fascinated following that leg down the street. Then as he passes a shop window, he sees a cream pie and he says, "My God, that's a lovely pie, I'd love to eat that pie." So his consciousness fastens on the pie and then he looks into another shop window and he sees a T.V. show going on so his consciousness goes to the T.V. show and gets into that trip. Then it swings around ... and all the time consciousness is being stimulated and reacting from one stimulation to the next. So such a person who lives in that kind of now, is living in a very transitory world, because his time world has no past and no future. His consciousness is not aware that it can reflect or save something, because it's constantly occupied in its physical senses. That is, you'll find that such a person is very restless and can't keep his mind on anything for a second. He's distracted. His consciousness is never really experiencing anything except sensation, he lives in sensation. Now you can understand why the world is like it is. It lives from one sensation to the next. And why are the masters of persuasion so powerful? Because they understand this and they understand that the most rubbishy things can be put over the television and stimulate people because that's what they want, to be stimulated. Because for 90% of the earth's population, that's where their consciousness is at ... in the world of sensory excitement. So all the newspapers, what are they catering to? Stimulation, controversy. They just make controversy. They never report the news as it is. It has to be made exciting. It has to be slanted. If they didn't do that, they'd never sell newspapers. So politics is the same isn't it? It is getting a response from people by creating some kind of sensation.

It doesn't matter what the field is. It could be religion. Exciting discoveries all the time going on. When we can understand what our bottom chakra is doing to us when we touch a nice curve for instance and get into that sensation and our consciousness goes to the sensation and begins to enjoy the physical touch of whatever it is, then we can understand the functioning of the chakra. The ancient Chinese studied this considerably and they felt that human skin was so exciting to touch that they would try to duplicate it. They used to take pieces of human skin and wrap them around objects so that they could stroke them and they developed a very high art of touching. They even shopped around for different kinds of skin where the silkier kinds were at a premium and then of course it got to the fanatic point where they were trying to get young virgins to give their skin while they were still alive. So the emperor ruled they had to make some artificial skin. So they took a thing called shagreen which was made of shark skin which is very rough because it's all bony, but you polish and grind that down and make it smooth and it gives you exactly the same feeling as stroking the most sensitive virgin skin. So there was a new trip and everyone tried to make the most sensitive shagreen that they could and this developed into a whole art. Then shagreen went out of fashion and they went into snuff bottles, trying to make the smoothest snuff bottles and the most delicate touch. They made them so that they even fitted the shape of the hand. That's where they get these long sleeves from in China. They are always rubbing things under their hand. So they carried snuff bottles one in each hand and rubbed them. They developed a great art. They could even have orgasms just rubbing snuff bottles! See how people take things to such extremes? Well, of course they were developing their sense of touch in a way we would never dream of. Now most people only have a very gross sense of touch. But when you are looking now you are touching me with your eyes. See, if you can get into that knowledge that when you touch me with your skin it's no different from touching me with your eyes, another piece of skin, which touches through space. The eye is such a refined thing that it can dissolve space and touch objects that are reflecting light. It records the same sensation as when you touch it. Now in actual fact, your skin can see just as well as your eyes, if your consciousness knows how to make it see. You can actually see with your hand because the skin cells of your hand have the same origin as the cells of your eyes. They both evolved from the same intelligence. Once upon a time the "skin" of your eye was the same as the skin of your brain. Your brain was just one piece of sensitised skin and it gradually got more specialised. The eye got specialised for light, the ear got specialised for sound, the skin for touch, the nose for chemicals (smell), so we scan the universe through these reactions. The best way to know the bottom chakra is to take away all these sensations one by one, get back to the baby state, where you enter the world, where you had never heard anything, smelled anything, seen anything, felt anything . . . there you are, just arrived on the planet, and you don't even know there's a mother's nipple yet. Well, you're all experts on this, because you've all been a baby, I hope. You've all been there so I'm not talking about anything you don't know. I'm talking about something you may have forgotten. You know it! You've been through it. So why don't you go back and regress yourself to the pure state of consciousness where you never smelled anything, never touched anything, never saw any lights or heard any sound, never heard your mother's voice or heard Christopher Hills speaking or anybody. You didn't know anything . . . none of that kind of knowledge that you heard in the school, or that your mother told you. You blot them out one by one. Say, "Okay! I've never seen anything." (You have to pretend of course.) "I'm like a blind man." Do it, just to experience something. It's no use talking about it. We close our eyes and we say, "All right, I've never seen a light in my life." Let's try that. What would it have been like to be born blind? "I'm still very much alive inside. My intelligence is still there. I can still be aware through my other senses and all those people who think I'm stupid because I'm blind, are more stupid for thinking it. I'm very much smarter than them in my senses because of the fact that I am blind. My hearing is much more acute. My sense of touch. Everything else. All those sighted people don't even know how to feel things like a blind person."

Now let's remove our sense of hearing. There are many people who have been deaf from birth. Now close the eyes and then close the ears. Okay. You've never heard anything in your life. Just pretend. You are still very much alive inside. Now let's remove the sense of taste. You've never tasted anything and you don't know what anything tastes like. One way of telling what the universe is vibrating at is to taste it. It's the first instinct you have. You put everything in your mouth when you were a baby. You want to taste it!

Now let's take away the sense of touch. We can't feel anything with our skin. Some people are born that way. They're always having accidents because their skin doesn't tell them a thing hurts. They're breaking legs and kicking things and stumbling over things because they don't have any sense of touch in their skin. So let's pretend that we never touched anything. So we don't know what it's like to feel another person, or to bump into a wall. And we don't even know that space exists because we've never bumped into anything in space.

So let's remove now the last remaining sense. Ears we've had, eyes we've had, taste we've had, touch we've had. Now we can still smell our way around the universe like a dog, with a highly developed sense of smell . . . we can say, "This is soup, this is chemical, this is ammonia, this is a rose." We can still know a lot about the universe from its smells, can't we. And our intelligence would express itself and receive knowledge of the universe through that sense. Let's pretend now that even that is gone. We never had it. We never smelt anything. What's left inside us? We have no knowledge left of the universe from a sensory point of view. And only the pure consciousness, your awareness of being "You" is left. No memories of any sensations. No associations. No smells, no sounds, no music. Nothing except consciousness, very much alive, wriggling around inside you and you're trying to communicate with that universe outside you. What is outside there? Here I am very much aware of myself inside. If you can really contact that *one* inside even for a second in the deep core of your heart, then you will know all the chakras. You will understand how you are shining your consciousness out through your eyes and your senses at everything, lighting up the world. The red chakra controls all your sensations of the sensory now. Your skin is a marvelous membrane receptor of light.

So in the words of Christ, "Ye are the light of this world," meaning "Your consciousness is what lights up the world. That immortal eternal consciousness which is never born in you and never dies." It shines through all the different kinds of skin, the ear drums, the eyes, the tongue, touch and smell. The experiencer who looks through these senses is your eternal self.

RED

The colour red is related to sensation in the bio-energetic spectrum. In the human being it is directly manifesting in our sense of touch. This has basic effects on the reality of how we sense the Universe through our skin in the immediate Now. Most individuals emanating energies predominantly in the Red band of consciousness are concerned with the intensity of experience in the time-framework of the immediate moment. These will have little awareness of the past or future and their inner-world will depend entirely on stimulation from physical inputs either to do with contest in the dominating of the physical environment or sexual love, petting, etc.

The inner world of the sensation-type apprehends the outer world through its sensory mechanisms as opposed to the intuitive (in the Indigo band) who does not respond to external stimuli immediately, as he requires time to integrate his experience into a much wider time-framework.

In other words, a person in the red band of consciousness perceives reality through his senses – not through his feelings, nor his thoughts, nor his memories or concepts or imaginings, but through his senses. And in particular, through the sense of touch. This seems such an incredibly simple thing to say and yet the implications of such a statement are fantastic! If I live for sensation then how will I experience time? Since I cannot experience a sensation yesterday (that would be memory) or wait for one tomorrow (that would be intuition) then I've got to have one now! Thus, the time world of the person in the red band of consciousness is the immediate now. His inner experience of what he senses is dependent on outside physical stimulation. In other words, he can't get high unless he's got something to touch, out there, outside of his body. He can't feel satisfied unless there is a physical something that he can either eat, make love to or push around, since the drive for sensations necessarily means a world "out there" that must be controlled in order to get them.

All this points directly to one thing. The drive of an individual "colours" the way he sees reality. When a man sees a woman and his drive is sex, then the way he sees the situation is coloured by his drive. In this case you could say that he is seeing red. If his drive were to share some abstract communication, then the colouring would be a lot different. In that case it would be indigo. Beyond that, however, is a still deeper point. The colouring of the drive contains within it as part of the basic experience of that drive, a particular manifestation of time. Just as memory takes us into past (time) and intuition into future (time), our red level sensory awareness takes us into the immediate present and the transient now.

In summary then, we could say that consciousness, when expressed in terms of colour like red or indigo or any other colour, has certain predictable and identifiable characteristics of behaviour and lives within a particular structure or "house" of time. It is this house or mansion of time that determines the limitations or confines of the experiencer of the drive, and how much of the total picture of reality he may be aware of.

> Each colour has its own time dimension in which events are processed and behaviour corresponds closely to the contents of consciousness expressed as colour.
> For instance aggressiveness of the colour Red reflects itself in the way the personality attacks its food. Red stimulates the gastronomic juices and the smooth muscle of the intestine and the saliva glands. A person who is aggressive and lacks opportunity of expressing it, either in business, in love making or in physical stimuli, will eat his food aggressively, stuffing large mouthfuls into his maw long before he has chewed the first mouthful. He will seek out a restaurant or call for a sandwich, or go into the pantry the moment hunger pangs come on, even if the next meal is a short time away in the future. Because the colour Red relates all experience to the present, the individual predominantly fixed in that band of consciousness will perceive the present moment in all its many ramifications, so intensely that someone in the time-world of the feeling (Blue) or the thinking (Yellow) type will marvel at the speed at which the person orientated to Red will act.

One way you can see this drive operating is to watch people eat. A Samoan carpenter was observed to put away a thermos full of coffee, bread, more than a pound of meat chunks and some other rather obscure foodstuffs all within the short period of a ten minute coffee break. This type of behaviour is not uncommon and reflects a compensation for a basic aggression.

In dealing with concrete reality of the NOW all psycho-physical energies in the Red are concentrated on the tangible, touchable, visible and sensual events with little concern for looking backwards or forwards. Environmental stimuli govern the entire reality since the (Red) person cannot wait to incorporate past and future events into the response pattern of the sensation of touching the object which is his total reality. The practicality of this type is often awesome to those who live in the past or future as he may act so swiftly it would appear to them that he had thought it all out before when such was not the case and the Red orientated is really acting from impulse.

In other words, such a person concentrates all his psychological energies on what he can see, hear, smell, taste, or feel. He is not likely to express himself in concepts nor will he evidence much desire to plan, as any visit to a nearby construction site would show. The difference, say, between the practical union carpenter and the conceptual university professor, is a difference in the orientation of consciousness to reality. The sensation type takes all his clues for responding to the environment from that same environment and *reacts* or re-ACTS upon it in a physically concrete way. He does not think or imagine or intuit or idealise a thing through. He ACTS, now! It's a bit like the expression, "Shoot first and ask questions later".

If you ask a "thinking type" to fix something like a leaky roof, for example, the first thing you'll get is a plan. If you ask a sensation type you will barely get finished expressing the problem before he's on top of the roof with a hammer and some asphalt cement yelling down at you that the job is already finished and taken care of. Such people are "practical" and not "theoretical." They are concerned with action and not theories and thus move so swiftly from problem to action that to others it seems mind boggling.

Sensation (Red) and satisfaction feeling (Blue) are different in that the first wants to influence his immediate environment; the second, which is orientated to feeling, tends to experience the environment in terms of past memories stored and fixed in historical time. The colour of the active revolution and its intensity and the need to dominate the environment, the opposite sex, or manifest something in the immediate present is the colour Red. It is well known as the colour of the activist, the hot colour which continually conflicts with the conservative restraining influence of Blue.

Here again we are given a contrast between two different energies in order to see the one more clearly. The red level is hot, impetuous, physically active and aggressive. Shakespeare's Hotspur in Henry IV is a famous literary figure who exemplifies this. Simon Peter, disciple of Christ, seems also to have possessed a good amount of this type of energy. You could say that the opposite expression to the red level is the "feeling satisfaction" level. Here the person does not experience the present in any intensity but only in terms of past memories and associations. When you go to a family reunion on Thanksgiving, then you may experience this feeling of peace at any price. It is a restraining influence that does indeed conflict with the hot and volatile colour of red.

> The ability of the person in the Red band of consciousness to read the depths of the immediate present is so developed that in the sensation type it substitutes for any lack of perception in future time. Planning and thinking through a development would put this type at a disadvantage since his reality is determined by reactivity to external stimuli. Action therefore will not depend on any intellectual grounds or be based on any predetermined plans, nor will it reveal the sense of commitment to a simple ideal so common to the colour Blue (feeling types). The ability of the Communist to twist the transient present into a concept of Red Leninist expediency, is indicative of this. Concentration exclusively on the present moment leads to temporary skill in wielding power but it is usually unrelated to past or future events and therefore in cases where foresight is needed it can be disastrous, especially when it involves the expedient use of people and their resources.

There are some people whose genius for reading the present is so astute that it appears they can read the future as well. This appears so because the present seems to be composed of so many complicated and diverse variables that to respond to it with such tremendous speed as one does in the red level seemingly indicates an intuitive comprehension of what lies ahead. This, however, is not the case. If such a person were thrust into a situation where he were required to plan, for example, a job to be done over a certain amount of time using a set amount of materials and an expedient use of manpower, he would immediately find himself in some difficulty. Why? He doesn't think like that! He doesn't plan in his head. He doesn't set up ideals as concepts and use his efforts to gain them. He acts not on blueprints nor on philosophical notions but because the external physical environment has stimulated his motive force and he can exert himself in a direct, immediate sensory approach to whatever situation is at hand.

Man's being is so complicated. It's a paradox of vibration, energy, time, space, and perception woven into a fabric of wholeness. The red level is but a facet on the many-sided jewel of reality. It is the drive to experience reality through the senses. This in itself creates its own awareness of time! When this reality is mistaken for the whole jewel, as it were, and superimposed on situations calling for awareness of the future (as in determining the probable outcome of some action) or an awareness of the past (as in learning from our past mistakes) then an imbalance results and the real total situation is not seen as it is.

What we are getting at then, is skillful action. Wisdom is the right application of action to the right situation. If we use our sensory awareness to rule people, as is done in the Communist dictatorships, then we may be successful in the short run, but in the long run, where an awareness of the inner needs of the people is at stake, we may be blindly ignorant, and thus the author of much suffering.

> Gratification in the Red band cannot be put off because sensation and sensuality does not experience time as flowing from past to future. These persons experience from moment to moment the stimulus of activity and need to experience continuously new and novel, even erotic sensations. They cannot remember nor anticipate and therefore the only way they can imagine a sensation is to actually have it.

This is one of the most important points about this drive. In a word, it cannot wait. It has got to have it now. And it has got to have it continuously. If you put a sensation-oriented person (and in this example it would be most people) inside closed doors with nothing inside, no books, no radio, no T.V., no food, nothing but himself, he would become very restless within a short time. There is no stimulation! A person who identifies with his senses has got to use those senses continuously in order to fill the need that drive calls for. It's only logical. The memory can remember good times and bring a glow to our hearts. The intuitions and our ideals can send us off in dreams or even creative actions to experience tomorrow what is unattainable today. But the senses cannot remember nor can they anticipate. They can only be satisfied Now!

Any sensation to the Red orientated personality is better than no sensation at all, hence the colour red denotes constant activity. Creativity in a positive type leads to constant manipulation of objects, people and money. Hence many personalities in the Red sector enter into business for the intense excitement it provides. The heart attack is brought on by this constant strain and inability to recognise the limitations to which the physical organism can be driven by this need for sensation. After the heart attack, the intensity of the colour red is rejected by the patient, simply because it represents a pathological condition intolerable to the subject. The tactile sense of these subjects being highly developed makes reality dependent on the reception of stimuli in the moment; whereas the thinking-type, which also seeks constant changes, can put it off into the future. Political planners therefore in activist Communism are likely to be negative and impulsive, whilst in the conservatism of the west, they are mainly thinking-types in the Yellow band.

The examples mentioned here are in the areas of business and activist Communism. Both areas attract the red level sensation-oriented individual, although in Communism this type is likely to be negative with emphasis on conquering the world, and in business he's more likely to be positive with emphasis on experiencing a high degree of mental and physical excitement. In the latter case in particular, the desire for excitement can lead to over-exertion and hence heart attacks, simply because the craving for excitement goes beyond the ability of the organism to withstand the intense stress.

It is because of the subject's high degree of physical sensitivity that he becomes dependent on outside stimulation, moment to moment, and in this way we can understand reactiveness as a trait common to this drive. It goes without saying that the reason he is so sensitive on the skin level is because this is where his consciousness has concentrated itself.

Before we go on to outline other colours and drives let us state that no one colour can determine one particular type of person unless he has mastered all his inner conflicts. Every human being has the potential for all the different colours, because the inner experience of life and time, which determines external behaviour, is conditioned by other colours which form a hierarchy of levels and these must be taken into account. Although there is a natural inclination to express through one colour and reject another, the consciousness of the individual may identify at some time or another with all the colours in between. In predicting the drives it has been found by close observation that people prefer predominantly one specific colour at a time and they will choose this many months apart from a large selection of colours.

Because most people who respond to Red energies are manipulative and oriented to action at any price, they are neither sympathetic to nor respectful of any level other than their own, since it is the only one that they know exists. Not only is it the colour of (Red) domination and territorial possessiveness, such as is found in the animal kingdom, but when mixed with the negative Yellow level leads to the know-it-all manipulativeness of the elitists and revolutionaries who do not understand the human race one bit. Unfortunately the world being what it is, these upsetters of stability are banded together in leading cliques of power at this time in history. They dominate with small party memberships approximately half the world's population, just as did the kings, nobles and queens of old with the courts, favours, and self-interested baronial systems. Only the disguise has changed to one of enforced allegiance to ideals rather than to the crowned king. Only when all humans realise that these manipulators with their naive objectives must be booted out of power on the basis of their own philosophy of might is right, will the world be purged of such low efforts to mould human beings like wax.

Hitler achieved his dominion of millions by cultivating the worship of authority. Similarly, the various breeds of Marxists, with their worship of power, have to an even greater extent attempted to mould human life by persistent exercise of coercion and pressure. All these Red-oriented persons believe they have all the answers and they aim at fashioning people to perpetual revolution after their own drives; they annihilate all personal interests by people's courts, and bring about a totally new allegiance to the state rather than to the freedom of self, family, wife, children, etc.

Their efforts are totally doomed to failure, simply because they do not understand the nature of the human personality, neither their own nor anyone else's . After fifty years of communism none of these methods has fundamentally changed human beings. Only superficial change has been made in attitudes and even these have only come about either through inability to resist the coercion or through fanatical response by Red level activists seeking a cause, and not through deep conviction.

Looking at the fundamental structure of consciousness one can detect little real change in the loves, hatreds, and bigoted views of men, women and children educated by the Marxist State. The same self-interests, power struggles and ruthless unconcern for individual rights have reasserted themselves in the minds of the new rulers. The same human nature has frustrated the efforts of the manipulators of men to mould them into ciphers in some idealistic theory of life. Despite the massive efforts of Mao Tse Tung, Stalin and other Red Communist dictatorships to create a state of permanent revolution at great cost to life, conservative elements are now in full control of the economic and social patterns. Yet they cannot wipe out the Russian soul or the ancient Chinese culture. The propaganda says communism changed all the old attitudes and traditions. Superficially this may be true but a culture as ancient as the Chinese, which spawned the I Ching, is essence knowledge and on all levels is eternal. It applies to all world cultures because it is wisdom and wisdom is the universal instrument which transcends ideology and will one day triumph over the arrogant manipulators of people and the intellectually dishonest methods of spreading Truth. Hence, the negative Red energy chakra, which represents thirty-five percent of all people, must be taught its own ignorance of man's personality drives.

Confucius

Military training begins early for millions of children in Communist China. How will democracy fight this deliberate breeding of future killers, who believe solely in the power of the gun? The Marxist dictatorship of the people is committed to violent overthrow of any competing ideology and to the eradication of Confucius, Tibetan Buddhism and God.

BUDDHA IN MEDITATION

INTERVIEW with M.,
a forty-two year-old construction worker.

Editor: What turns you on the most?

M.: Sex. I like sex. Why? Because of the feeling. I like the climax.

Ed.: What else?

M.: I like marijuana. It helps me to relax. I like money too. I like what it can do. It can buy me independence. I don't like working 8 to 4:30.

Ed.: What depresses you the most?

M.: Being in prison. Being locked up. Feeling like you are a nobody. It's like everybody is on a speed trip running around until they get tired of chasing the dollar. Also, I'm a procrastinator, like you a lot. I put things off, off, off! I just go home and sit and let the world go by. I'm way behind on my leather work. I went shopping the other day for a bike for my kid. I got frightened. Everybody was whizzing around. What's it all about? I just went back home. I didn't even buy the bike. I just went back into the house and watched T.V.

Ed.: What are you seeking and wanting in life? What are your goals?

M.: I don't have any goals. I'm looking to stay out of jail. The cops are always after me. I don't want anything to do with cops and they don't want anything to do with me.

Ed.: How do you approach tasks?

M.: I just jump up and start doing it.

Ed.: How important to you is the past? Tradition, memories and so on?

M.: I think about old friends a lot. Mainly though, I live a day at a time. I gave that up. I don't think about the past.

Ed.: What do you admire in others?

M.: Intelligence. Leadership.

Ed.: What do you dislike in others the most?

M.: Laziness. People who just give up. People who when they get down are afraid to start over.

Ed.: What is your attitude to money and possessions?

M.: I'm not very possessive. I can let go of things. My wife is possessive. She took most everything we had.

---

* This interview is one of a series conducted by the editors as a means of illustrating the colour levels. A standard set of questions has been used and can also provide a tool for the reader.

INTERVIEW with L.,
a thirty-six year-old carpenter

Editor: What turns you on the most?

L.: Sex. A woman. It makes me feel good. I also like a little booze and a little dope. I like relaxation--loafing around. I feel good doing it.

Ed.: What depresses you the most?

L.: Work. Certain types of work. Working with a bunch of assholes. Where people are yelling a lot. "Do this. Pick this up. Go over there." And they don't even know what they are doing themselves. People that brag a lot depress me. I have to listen to them.

Ed.: What are you seeking and wanting in life right now? What are your goals?

L.: I just want to be happy. See that the kids have a good life. As long as they are healthy. As long as there is no sickness and we're all healthy. That's my main goal.

Ed.: How do you approach tasks?

L.: I think about it first. How much is it going to cost? I talk to other people who have done it. Look at plans, or go get bids. I never just jump into things.

Ed.: How important to you is tradition, past memories, nostalgias and so on.

L.: Pretty important. I like to talk about old times. Things I've built. Old girlfriends, good times, and memories of people I was with. Otherwise, it's kind of hard to say.

Ed.: How much then, would you say you dwelt in the past or the future?

L.: I'm in the present. I'm just here. I don't think about what's going to happen.

Ed.: What is your usual motive for doing things?

L.: Pleasure.

Ed.: What do you like most in others?

L.: Honesty. Friendship. The way people respect you (me), and take me for the way I am. I don't have to be anyone else.

Ed.: What is your attitude to money and possessions?

L.: It's good to have. But if you don't you still are going to survive. I'd like to have a new T.V. and new car but that's going too far.

Summary

In looking at these brief responses by an individual to some questions about the way he views life, we can get a feel for some of the drives that predominate in his perception of reality.

For example, by asking both men what turned them on most, we find their answer to reflect a basic drive for stimulation. What do they like? Sex. Why? Because it feels good. That is certainly a sensation type of response.

In the case of M., we find other similar responses. Jumping into things hastily is an example. This contrasts with L., who does not leap first but who plans things out before attempting action.

M. exhibits a great deal of reactiveness. He has no goals except the negative goal of staying out of jail. He works just to keep busy. He admires leadership and intelligence and dislikes lazy people. In spite of this he procrastinates and desires to stay at home and do nothing. This may be symptomatic of a basic conflict found in negatively-oriented sensation types. (See Thumbnail sketch of inputs and outputs.)

In contrast, we find L. having some positive aspirations. His concern for the family health and his desire for happiness, although nebulous as to how to achieve these things, are at least idealistically sound. He does feel that he must tolerate people who brag and in his actual work situation his partner was a loud braggart and bully. His silent response is indicative of the peace-at-any-price attitude which characterises the Blue level.

It may be of interest to note here how two levels can work independently and yet create a single reality within a person.

In actual life, M. was domineering, physically aggressive, and somewhat belligerent. He could be observed arriving on the construction site in leather and basic western attire, complete with a bowie knife and swaggering disposition. He would then approach his superiors on the job with the air of absolute confidence and attempt to convince them that he was completely capable of handling the foreman's position and that he should be left completely alone. Yet, by himself, he had difficulty in organising his work, making decisions, and relaying vital information to his co-workers. He expected action on demand and barked domineering commands incessantly. At times, his attitude seemed to be that whatever work he did was somehow beyond the normal and that he was therefore entitled either to some free beer or the afternoon off. On other occasions he showed marked willingness and eagerness to perform and be of genuine service.

The point is, that the image a person has of himself and the actual energy such a person puts out are often in conflict. A person may have an image of himself as an efficient, intelligent, leader type, and may also feel that these attributes qualify him for special privileges. Yet, this may only be a smoke screen for an intense craving or lack on another level. Thus, craving sex, a person sees himself as super-macho. Craving money, he imagines that he does not need to work. Craving prestige, he sees himself as a foreman. Craving peace and quiet, he sees himself as unemotional and level-headed. The list could go on and on. A mental picture of ourself in the form of a concept (Blue), that say, we are unlovable, may lead us to fear the world and hide away (Red), and cause us to adopt a tough swaggering exterior. Such is the power of consciousness.

THE SOCIAL LEVEL
OF
GROUP CONSCIOUSNESS

*The following is a transcription
of one of a series of lectures on
the Human Chakra System given
by Christopher Hills in 1974.*

THE ORANGE LEVEL   SWADHISTHANA CHAKRA

To understand how these chakras work as frequencies, how we take cosmic energy and absorb it through these psychic whirl-pools, is rather complex. Any object absorbs as much light as it can depending on its molecular structure and its coefficient of absorption. The amount of energy anything soaks up depends on its nature. As it absorbs energy or light it will heat up to red hot, then orange, yellow, green, blue, indigo, violet, then white hot and finally it gets so hot you can't even see it because it's invisible black light. The problem of perceiving objects when they reflect light is that you are only seeing the light that is not absorbed. Colour is simply the frequencies of light reflected back by the object--frequencies which the object by its nature cannot soak up. A human being is no different. We absorb light, whether we see it or not, even when it is beyond the frequencies detectable by our senses. If we cannot tolerate or absorb certain kinds of light we reflect it back. Every human is like every object in the universe--an absorber and reflector of light. By "light" we do not mean just light in the narrow visible spectrum, but cosmic radiation which is not experienced consciously.

The absorption of light in the second chakra concerns humanity. Perhaps ultimately it is the ability to transcend the idea that one is a human being, a solid lump of flesh that the "I" identifies with. How do we discriminate the notion of our own humanity? From childhood we have been conditioned. By the time we grow up we are already a tremendous bundle of conventions that our thoughts are trapped in. We have all sorts of hidden subtle thoughts about what a human being is, what we are and our human limitations. We live in a society which has brainwashed us and this is true for any society. We are growing up always in the milieu of other thoughts around us coming from other people.

Many millions of years ago man became a social animal and began to consider other people and cooperate with them in order to survive. Man has had to become very sophisticated, so the brain has grown by leaps and bounds and evolved. The Orange chakra deals with man's relationship with his fellows, social contact as compared to the skin contact of the bottom chakra. If we had a sense that could go beyond the physical sense of touch we would see that what we were touching was just a bundle of electrical forces, atoms swirling, dancing to the cosmic tune of sound, orchestrated by some intelligence forming it into a cohesive whole, with each cell, each organ, grouping together. In each of these groupings there is a jump in consciousness, a jump in organisation, in sophistication, in government. There is a perfect law of self-government for each part of the hologram we call a body.

In a club a new member cannot be absorbed into the group until he agrees to obey the group laws, likewise there must be a place in a group atomic structure for new energy. If there is a place to soak up new energy in the atom then it will absorb that energy and will remain that same kind of atom. If there is no space and new energy comes in breaking the atom up, then it will become a new element and be transformed into something else, a different kind of physical matter. At the next stage of cohesion the atoms group into molecules and have become more sophisticated. The next stage is for the molecules to group into cells whose government is different from that of the molecule. In all these groupings there is close coordination, socially speaking. The body is just like a society, it is a group of cooperating cells. Cells cooperate to form an organ. Each time there is the jump in cooperation, some new decision-making apparatus has to develop. The organs have to get together to share the vital force that is pouring through the whole body and they have to share their individuality with the whole body to function harmoniously.

Cancer and much of illness is being out of harmony with oneself. Cancer is mostly psychologically caused producing a physical breakdown in communication between the different cells. The cancer cells themselves become modified and have their own life, making their own way around the body and not cooperating with it at all. Most of the cells that are healthy cells are cells that adhere to each other and rub together. If you look through a microscope you will see that cancer cells have no cohesion with anything in the body, they go straight through without actually coming into contact with any of the other cells because they have their own independent selfish existence. They become predators on the life force rather than cooperating with it. The cancers in society are no different. Society is a projection of human consciousness. Whatever happens "out there" or externally is because something in the internal self is happening or not happening. Society in general does not see that everything that is going on in society is a reflection of human consciousness.

Human consciousness at its lowest levels is in turn affected by social conditioning and the relationships one has. The Orange chakra governs all these relationships with others in society. Yet there are many people who resist or transcend this social conditioning. Whatever culture we are born in is responsible for an enormous brainwashing of our consciousness. But anything we have been told by the consensus of opinion around us may not be true, simply because the majority of the people have neither the capacity nor the ability to test the evidence. If we think deeply, how do we test the evidence handed down to us by our parents? They tell us something is real, but who told them? Their parents! So you can go way back, to these social truths that we believe in as facts, but we rarely know how they were arrived at in the first place.

We are brought up as children in such a way that unless we are nutty or a complete madman, we will not swim against the whole tide of scientific or social opinion. If we do, the whole world will be telling us we are out of line. So the original geniuses who have come to this earth are very few. An original idea is one of the most rare events in human history. Einstein claimed to only have two original ideas in his entire lifetime and he was one of the most brilliant thinkers science ever had. This Orange chakra causes us to think that certain knowledge that we have, because it is well known, is holy or has some stature of its own merely because society accepts it as a norm. But in order to evolve we have to break free, completely free of the weight of consensus of opinion. Our contact with our fellow men must not be on the basis of any expectation whatsoever about how they ought to be or act based on the social standards prevailing at the time.

The Orange second chakra has one more kind of time than the bottom Red chakra. The person in the Red bottom chakra experiences sensations in the now. The people in this Orange chakra would put off their sensation of the now to the future. They keep the experience of a sensation in their mind, thinking something out but not acting now. This delaying of the now applies to governments, society, politics. Everything which requires a social decision applies to tomorrow. So all social action has this problem in it, it is always a promise in the future. This is a very subtle form of government out in the future somewhere, but it is not now. The power and impact of a politician disappears in practice when, in order to do his job, he needs to consult with and please others. In politics and social situations there have to be planners and sages whose knowledge is consulted as to the possible consequences of taking an action. Then there are the voters who have to decide whether they want the action. So it all takes delayed time. That is why political promises very seldom materialise as promised. If you think about it, government in any country is being done from a totally imaginary point in the future, not by what we think is selection and choice in election, but government by pressures. We are brainwashed to think we have complete freedom. Consequently the activist rises and thinks he can force some change by bringing about pressure through bombing, rioting, marching, etc. The whole problem with the activist is that he is usually living in the bottom Red centre. Politically, he is not sound because he wants action at any price and really he has nothing planned out himself, nothing that is feasible. So in this Orange chakra instead of touching things directly with skin, like the sensation type, we have social contact; we touch our fellow man at a distance with words, concepts, authorities, systems of thinking, cultures, business, mediums of exchange, controversy.

As long as one is imprisoned in the kind of Orange social thinking that depends on what other people say, or conforms to social authorities or worries what your reputation is-- name, fame, glory-- you are trapped. Your name is worth nothing to God, your money is worth nothing to God, your energy is worth nothing to God and you are worth very little to the cosmos if you are trapped in those things. Even if you can write a check for a million dollars, it will bounce off the Kingdom of Heaven if you have not done some refining work on all of the chakras. We cannot get enlightened with our name; there is no chance of freedom as long as we are the prisoner of what we think other people will think of us.

This chakra governs all social drives, like "keeping up with the Joneses." Pressures are going on at every level of society. Children pressure their Daddies for a T.V. to watch Mickey Mouse when Daddy would rather not have the children's brains filled with the stuff T.V. puts out, but he feels awful because all the other kids have T.V.'s and his kids are feeling deprived. Cars are sold with sex advertising because a man identifies with a beautiful girl like he does with other social marks of distinction. These appeals to our social pride are all traps if we have them for motives which we do not understand.

Young people see the phoniness of all this appeal to social pride and do not want it anymore. They are children of abundance and have had enough of it all. But some are still trapped in the social system when they give up material wants and then go to get food stamps. Who gives the food stamps? The government! Who gives to the government? The people who are working in the rat race. How can you be free if you are getting food stamps? You are a prisoner and dependent on the system like anyone else. Anybody who is taking food stamps from a government they are criticising is not being honest with their self. They are not living off their own energy but are a parasite of some foreign system of thinking. When you can ring up God and have Him deliver the food stamps, that is different, but if you have to go and collect them in any way from society it is a trap. It is a trap because you can never get out from under society as long as you are dependent on it for any source of income, as long as you are not free of dependence on the good will of others.

Often the highest man lives off the goodwill of others, but he does not demand it, he leaves the free choice to the people. A Christ can walk around and just because he is Jesus Christ people put money in his bag. But not everybody is Jesus Christ and not everybody is going to put money in the bag. The mark of evolution within yourself is when people do just that, or when things come to you as if by some divine magic so that you can even give them away. You have more than you need. It often requires a little intelligence to live that way, perhaps a little effort. To be free we must make no demands on anyone. Making no demands means expecting nothing. That way you will never be disappointed and what comes in will be bliss and gravy.

The world is really a perfect mirror, a reflection of your skill at using your consciousness. Your consciousness is dancing in everybody and the way you treat them will determine what kind of treatment you get back. If a guru wants followers he must not get too familiar with them, so that they keep him on the pedestal, if he gets too familiar they won't worship. So the only freedom is to not have any followers, to have only one disciple, yourself-- then you no longer need any people following behind you to prove to yourself that you are a guru. Then you do not need anything that does not come from itself, from its own free will because it wants to. You can talk to yourself socially, as I'm doing now, my self. Who is myself? I'm just talking and something is listening, and some parts of myself are not listening. It does not matter because you are my other self, you are an aspect of my consciousness, every one of you, so I am not talking to anybody separate. The consciousness which is vibrating in you is in me. The consciousness which is hearing or reading is the same consciousness which is speaking or writing. We are just putting different disguises on it, different patterns and images are forming in it, but it is the same stuff shimmering there. When you realise this fact of our group existence then you let society and people be what they are. Often in the Orange second chakra the general human tendency is not to let people be what they are, but to try to make them be what you think they ought to be. This do-gooding involves coercion of others and a degree of ideological self-righteousness in determining what ought to be. This is typical of the negative aspect of the Orange drive. The most positive aspect of Orange is its enthusiasm and its healing expansiveness and exploring of the fellowship of man.

ORANGE

The keyword of the Orange drive is exploration or ambition, the drive to contact the concrete reality for the whole community rather than just for self. Where the function of the sensation type in the Red band is to sense reality through objects and to react to touch in a negative and a positive way, the Orange is to move more towards the expansive extravertion of the concrete reality by following social hunches and guesses. Whereas persons in the Red layer will have almost no conception of the real social feeling, all extraverts in the Orange colour layer have the ability to respond to external stimuli from society without the constant orientation towards self of the Red. This leads to feelings of ambition, hope, bigness for one's activity in society or for social contact of a gregarious kind. Whereas the negative Red will be content to experience continued sensuality with several women in some remote shack as sexual stimulation, the Orange would want to share his prowess and activity proudly with his fellow man. Whereas the Red endeavours to keep intense external social stimulation from overwhelming him, the Orange likes happenings on a larger scale, and involves extension of the sense of touch to more abstract things—social contact.

Essentially, the Orange drive is expansive, exploratory, social. Red is sensual, Orange is social. It's the drive to find out reality through other people, the drive for fellowship.

In the Red drive there is emphasis on self-replication, self-preservation, and self-gratification. In the Orange drive the concern is more with social preservation, like armies and unions, social replication, like schools and mass advertising, and social gratification, like high society and social gatherings.

The need to herd together is really a need to get at a reality that is meaningful to everyone. We all feel together when we are united under a democracy as different beings, but we think the same way about our government. We can talk about our football team at break-time at work and get a sense of being with the in-group.

A positive response to this urge automatically produces interest in our society and what others are doing. If I say, "I wonder if so-and-so would be interested in helping our school?" I not only take on some responsibility for the success of the school but I become that much more interested in so-and-so as well. It's like optimism for a project.

Positive Orange is acceptance of our social love. It is not afraid to dance and sing and proclaim itself as a lover of people.

Negative Orange, on the other hand, is pride in status, snobbery, social climbing, conformity, "Keeping up with the Joneses," racism, bigotry and the like. It is basically concerned with second-hand knowledge. What we learn through this drive in terms of social truth is often just knowledge that has been handed down because society has believed it so.

> The fact that Orange comes between sensation (Red) and thinking (Yellow) shows that the movement of psychic forces towards higher hierarchial domains is synonymous with the creative energy. The creative expansive forces were described by the ancient Chinese sages of the I Ching as Orange which polarised and complemented the Receptive and female quality of Indigo.

As we move through the spectrum we may begin to discover a basic motif. As man journeys through his own rainbow body he faces an unceasing encounter with ever widening, ever more expansive, recurringly more subtle horizons. To experience the world is to recreate the world. Each internal realm expands the vistas of the one before it, and by virtue of witnessing this vision, man creates. By virtue of sensory skin contact man may create man. By virtue of social contact he may create societies of men. This is expansion and creation. It is also evolution.

> The Orange orientated individual lives in the sensation of the present but applies it to the future, whereas the Red sensation-type is discontinuous and has little ability or concern for what is ahead. The Orange drive will not react to the immediate stimulus but will act when the stimulus is presented in terms of the wider community where his behaviour can materially affect it, and if it will lead to success; the main objective is to widen his field of experience and shake off any inhibitions and self doubt.

In other words, such a person loves sensory stimulation just like the person in the Red band, but he applies it differently. A man won a lottery where he worked. He went out and bought three dozen doughnuts for the entire crew. He liked doughnuts a lot, but he wasn't willing to eat them all by himself. It made him feel good to give to his fellowman. He wanted everyone else to know how good doughnuts were as well. This typifies the Orange band of consciousness.

Even within each colour there are levels of manifestation which represent different things to different people. Every colour can be divided further into levels of experiential functions which will vary with the degree of individual perception. For instance Orange has the following levels: The orange-yellow saffron robe worn by swamis and Buddhist monks is first associated with the idea of renunciation. But deeper investigation shows that this orange-yellow represents the creative power of change, of transformation and expansion which comes with selflessness at the social level, i.e. with love of fellow man and with the type of compassion which is the intense involvement with life, society, world regeneration and the teaching of ultimate liberation. At even deeper levels of cosmic Being beyond the "mental knowing" in concepts of the thinking mind, this orange-yellow represents the colour of contemplation so much associated with it in eastern religion and the priestliness of teachers of men. Even deeper still it becomes the very colour of life itself as it begins to bubble and flicker within and move towards the positive green colour of prana, which is the movement of life force. A mixture of red-orange-yellow light is the colour of "The Clinging Fire" in the I Ching and this colour is "yang expression" because it governs the first movement of consciousness from within outwards. As such it signifies the radiance of the internal sun shining with the light of consciousness. It represents Brahman, from the root word Brim, meaning "to glow with expansion," thereby expressing itself with the ambition to create with light.

No wonder the ancient Chinese dowsers who divined the nature of cosmic forces in the I Ching looked on this colour of Orange as the colour of healing energy, that radiance which moves into intense passionate action of permanent change at the creative nuclear centre of Being. (See "Supersensonics" for more on the I Ching and colour.)

INTERVIEW with P.,
a twenty-five year-old secretary.

Editor: What turns you on most?

P: The idea of having a family. The idea of becoming one with God. The reason I'd like to have a family is to share with them in the learning and growing activity.

Ed: What depresses you most?

P: My immersion in my negative patterns. I avoid going forward with things and cracking them. If I have to write my paper I have a block and I procrastinate and I eat and get fat and it really upsets me. I get a lethargy and a sort of "I can't" attitude.

Ed: What are you seeking and wanting now and what are your goals?

P: To go on realising my full potential, which I see now as, in terms of the blocks I'm working on, being able to more freely initiate things which in turn give me a great deal of pleasure, because I like activity, and becoming more fully developed on all the levels and also growing to God through devotion.

Ed: If you have a task to do, how do you set about it? For example, we decided to have a flea market, how did you go about setting it up?

P: Well, unfortunately, I like to dream about it a lot, and it's harder for me to start getting the practical things going. I had the idea, I started putting up the signs and now I'm planning the things that we need and the times to schedule people, and to foresee the kinds of needs we will have during the flea market and getting ready for them now.

Ed: How important to you is tradition or past memory of achievements, or reminiscences or nostalgia, or thoughts of the past?

P: Well, I tend to try to understand myself a lot by going into the past. I like reminiscing and telling stories. Sometimes I get really tired of things that aren't really current and alive.

Ed: How much would you say your mind dwells on the past or the future?

P: Very little on the future. Mostly on the present. Maybe 25% on the past.

Ed: What are your motives usually for doing things? For

example, would you do something for sensation or approval or self-confirmation or for a group status?

P: It used to be a lot for stimulation. Now it's more for social interrelating or arranging things to bring the group together. Also a big motivation is approval from my friends and for people I respect like Christopher. It's really a big thing I'm to work with right now. I'm too concerned about what he thinks of me.

Ed: What do you like or admire most in others?

P: I like people whom I consider to have really developed their consciousness, who have explored a lot of levels of experience and who are developed in all the levels and who lead active lives which yield good results in terms of the wider community and in terms of their own growth.

Ed: What irritates you most in others?

P: Prejudice and slothfulness makes me sad at the waste.

Ed: What is your attitude to money and material possessions?

P: I'm not too concerned about money, and I'm not too concerned about earning it, so I don't have that much, and I'm not too concerned about saving it, so it all goes out the other end, but a really nice home environment is really important to me. A nice garden for example. In that sense, I'm sort of attached to my material surroundings.

INTERVIEW with R.S.,
a twenty-four year old public relations man.

Ed: What turns you on the most?

R: Sex. Of course! Also, a lot of times it is something that involves the movement of people; some project or something that I have some kind of role in or some kind of responsibility in. I feel caught up in making this thing happen and I get a kind of rush that's like being carried away. I feel an enthusiasm and optimism that some vision is going to be happening. It's a nice space to be in.

Ed: What depresses you the most?

R: The thought that others are judging me as foolish or not being on top of it or judging me in a negative way. Rejection in other words by other people hurts me most.

Ed: What is your usual motive in doing things?

R: Usually it's ego food. The idea that if I do something people will think highly of me, or I'll get merits for it, or I'll be a good person for doing this thing. Unfortunately that tends to sap any kind of sustaining energy in finishing the project.

Ed: How important would you say the past is for you?

R: Lots of times I'm in the past thinking that I should have done this and I should have done that and if I'd done this I'd be in a better position . . . people would think better of me. At other times the past isn't that important because it's more like what is going to be happening in the future. Thinking more about the great things yet to come. When I do think about the future it often concerns something like seeing a lady tomorrow and I get real excited. Or I think about things further off like the group project down in Carmel. If that goes off then just think! People will be coming here and give the group more purpose and it'll mean dynamic action and we'll be doing something and growing . . . You know, things like that. Future projects that bring beneficial social effects.

Ed: What is it that you admire most about other people?

R: Their heart and their lovingness and the way that they care about somebody. Like even somebody who has on the outside a tough skin like a tough shipyard worker who uses a riveter and some situation will click and his heart will just melt and he'll just be able to be so gentle in spite of all his asinineness . The capacity to be so loving is really so inspiring.

Ed: What do you dislike most about others?

R: Their criticalness, judgementalness. Writing people off. Bad-mouthing people.

Ed: What is your attitude about money and possessions?

R: I would like to be rich. I would like to be a millionaire. Then I wouldn't have to do anything. Just be able

281

	to lie around doing nothing. So I could wear $400.00 suits and drive a nice car, wine and dine elegant women and have a yacht and travel around the world. All these things take money. It would be nice to indulge in every whim that I had.
Ed:	How do you respond to disapproval?
R:	I hate it!
Ed:	What are your ideals and goals? What do you want from life?
R:	It's mixed up now. One part of me wants all the money I need, a lover, a good friend, all these things, just the right perfect situation...Then there is another part of me that wants some fundamental deep union with other beings that I've never experienced before. I know that in every other situation in the past that hasn't been going in that direction, I've dropped it and I've gone into some area that has gotten me closer to deep contact with people and that is what brought me here to the University of the Trees.

Summary

In general we could say that the two interviews show some rather good examples of the Orange drive, especially in the areas of projects and approval and, in the case of R., time. Time for R., when he does think about the future, can be clearly Orange level. His concern in the future for a project now, which will benefit the group later as well as himself, is an example of this. In the case of P., the stress is more on sharing growth activity in a family type situation. While a case could be made for a strong Blue level in P. (family and authority), her desire to explore herself in a group situation can be construed as positive Orange.

R. also shows a good deal of Orange in the questions on motives. The desire for approval and the getting of merits from others is indicative of this. While this may be confused with the acquisitive green drive, there is further support for his motive to get money only to support an active social drive, since he shows a strong attraction for situations that involve people, as well as a hopeful optimism and enthusiasm.

THE INTELLECTUAL LEVEL
OF
ANALYTICAL
CONSCIOUSNESS

The following is a summarised version of a taped talk by Christopher Hills given in 1977.

THE YELLOW LEVEL   MANIPURA CHAKRA

This Yellow level of consciousness is the intellectual level and is related to the manipura or spleen centre or chakra and to its equivalent centre in the brain, where it is actually experienced in consciousness.

THUMBNAIL SKETCH: To summarise this drive we could list its main functions as planning, categorising and separating. The intellectual wants everything presented sequentially so his time framework must include past, present and future. He loves change and novelty, but he sees most things in terms of "problems" and his main problem is his own separation from others through the Ego, which operates most strongly from this Yellow centre. All intellectuals concern themselves with validation of knowledge and theories via deduction or induction and as scientists, religious dogmatists or planners they limit others whose experience extends beyond theirs.

As we explore these functions of the Yellow intellectual centre we shall quote verbatim, from time to time, from the taped talk by Christopher Hills. If you would like to hear the whole talk, which lasts for one hour, you can buy a copy from the publishers of this book.

THE PLANNER: The intellectual looks on the universe as a place run by a Divine Plan, but his kind of order or plan is remote from the Divine Order. He thinks in terms of a logical, linear sequence of events following each other like the ticking of a clock or pearls on a necklace and he sees God as the same kind of planner! But God could be seeing it quite differently:

[Quotation from tape:]
" 'Man, it took me so many billions of years to get where I am and everything in my creation is going to come the same route,' God could be saying. 'Let them have the same difficulties and then I'll show them myself just like I showed my Self myself. Whatever plan people put inside themselves, that's going to be the plan. I'll give them the stuff (consciousness) pure, which is ME, and if they want to dirty it up with their plans, well let them! Let them be wise in their own conceit. Eventually they will find that all those plans are not worth a cent, and eventually they'll stop making plans.' "

Why will they stop? Because the plans don't work. Why is that? Because the intellectual's plans fail to take people, who all have their own plans, into account. You cannot deal with people as categories or boxes or parts of plans. Until people make their energy available of their own free will, no plans can be made for them.

The same applies to achieving unity. The intellectual tries for unity in the head, via a plan or a religious dogma to which everyone must adhere. This is how communism operates. But real unity is in the heart with diversity in the head.

THE SEPARATIVE EGO: The Ego operates on every level of consciousness but it is strongest on the Yellow intellectual level and its main function is to separate. The strong self-sense separates subjectively from the objective universe it lives in and from other people; and the Ego will always be with us until we cease to see "others". This happy day may be a few thousand incarnations ahead.

Not only does the Ego stand apart or aloof but it selects what it will buy from life depending on whether the experience provides ego food or ego confrontation, and it tends to go where it is made to feel good. This separative ego also perceives itself by insisting that everything, including God, is "out there" and it always pretends it is doing something different from everyone else. So it perceives its identity as a separated self and this means that intellectuals often live very cold lives. They treat everyone as a theory and sacrifice everybody for a principle.

TIME AT THE YELLOW LEVEL: Events for the intellectual must follow sequentially so his time world is a string of events like beads on a string. Tell an intellectual something and he will stop you, "Now go back a bit," he says, "Where were you? Where did this all start?" and he is not satisfied until you have filled in all the events in a past, present and maybe future format. Whereas someone on the intuitive level would only need to be told one thing. The framework for him is not important.

The intellectual's mind is always seeking for the next event in the sequence so he sees life and people as a series of problems. All his sentences begin "Well, the problem is . . . . " and his whole life is spent in looking for solutions.

LOVE OF CHANGE: This makes him interested in CHANGE, newness, novelty. Now we all have some of this chakra operating since we all have egos, and we all like some change in the form of a holiday, but the intellectual seeks something new because it has never really experienced the old:

[Quote from tape:]
"The Yellow level has taken it at the information level and stored it but it hasn't experienced the information for itself, so it becomes purely intellectual savouring of knowledge rather than real knowing."

LIMITING OTHERS: Having stored up the knowledge, the intellectual then assumes that if he does not know something in his field then no one else does either.

[Quote from tape:]
"What he is doing is to put himself on the throne of God and then he becomes the one who says whether there is a God or not. 'You can't prove God,' says the intellect, 'so therefore he isn't there.' But this is a self-deception. You can't get rid of God just by saying there isn't a God! The intellectual theologian usually knows a lot *about* God, so he always has a theory *about* God, but God is not a theory . . . and what the intellectuals do not realise is that if you took all the theories and shook them up in a bag, they would all contradict each other and be worthless. Even if you take our much respected scientific knowledge and all the theories about the origin of the universe, they all cancel each other out and they are all rubbish, because theories are just theories!"

CONCLUSION: Let us accept and realise that we all have a bit of this Yellow chakra level working in us, just as we all have egos and we need not only to recognise this in ourself but also to see when it is working in others, so that we can communicate with them, first by filling them in on the whole sequence of where, when and how and then by allowing for their separative Ego that sees us, the whole universe and even God – out there! The delusion is that everything is experienced in front of you instead of inside you!

> A tape giving the full talk by
> the author is available from the
> publishers. (See back of book.)

YELLOW

The colour yellow has the Keyword of Change because it is related to the movement of psychic energies from the primal need of " social contact " towards thinking. To the thinker all " change " is a process which can be related to past, present, and future, and time flows sequentially and logically through these phases. Situations are evaluated by the intellectual process of first categorising and chopping up reality into " events " which are labelled true or false, and then cutting out all conclusions based on feelings, whether pleasurable or distasteful, and then cutting out sensation. The thinking-type may tolerate the inspiration and intuition as a source of fact since he is looking for novel answers and changes which will fill in the obvious logical gaps in his reality. The linear time-line is at the base of the intellectual process which hinges its reality on the transitory nature of all continuity. It erects frameworks which show a preference for direction, even when " direction " has no meaning except in relation to a specific framework.

Before the thinking-type can understand anything he must know in what direction the dialogue or thought process is going. Once he is orientated he can enter any dimension and see the process through to its completion.

Spontaneous reaction to stimuli or events which are common to both Red and Orange domain are not experienced by thinking types who remain detached from the immediate now, unless they can understand how the events originated, where they took place and when they will be brought to focus on the larger process of life.

Although all the drives so far, namely the Red, the Orange and the Yellow are extraverted, this is about all they have in common. Their expression and their time sense make them often incompatible until they understand each other's worlds. This applies particularly to the relationship between the Red and the Yellow, where the precipitous response to stimuli of the Red makes the Yellow constantly react. "Wait a minute!" he says, "before you rush into it, where did all this start and where is it going?" Secretly he may also be saying to himself, "Is this likely to fulfil my expectations? Can my Ego get some kudos out of this operation?" Between the Red and the Orange there can often be a good deal of resonance, although while the Orange is looking for some rewarding social prospects, some fulfilment of his ambitious hopes for himself or for the community, the Red is concerned primarily with immediate satisfaction in the physical Now.

> Anything which does not fit this intellectual process which comes from "out of the blue" is ignored. Everything must be originating from some known source and those facts which do not show their pedigree origins and relate to the ongoing process in its totality, create a frustration. Yet because of his concern for the changing nature of time, the thinking type is always looking for novel solutions. Joy is produced only by the wide sweep of knowledge and fact, which links up so many different events in the whole scope of past, present, and future. Mental excitement at the prospect of solving one of humanity's basic fundamental problems would probably be so much that it would be rejected as "too good to be true". The ability to build frameworks of thought and put events into sequential order enables the intellectual thinking-type to be scientific and analytical. He draws conclusions based on theoretical satisfactions and proofs of hypothesis, however temporary these may be. This ability to bring everything into form, is contrasted with the feeling-type (Blue) who accepts on authority only the existing forms as a means of dialogue. The difficulty of the thinking-type in dealing with an abstract void of the Absolute is marked, since they care so much for consistency, continuity and logical progression, that any event which has neither beginning nor end is unthinkable, or not worth thinking about.

To live with the Yellow level intellectual with his love of change and innovative ideas is to be constantly faced with the prospect of new undertakings that may or may not work out, but which all have within them tremendous potential, so that any objections on the grounds of our having enough on our plates already or of not having the skilled personnel to carry them out, seem like a wet blanket and discouraging to the enthusiastic Yellow planner. The schemes presented to me by a Yellow level partner ranged from a new way of selling art to an apathetic public, who had no appreciation of the artist's striving to express the spirit of man through his work, to vast undertakings like feeding the world's undernourished millions from algae. Often the project was spoken of as a "fait accompli" or at least an imminent undertaking, so vivid was the vision of its viability; but when I, the Blue level conservative, challenged the practicality of the scheme the reply was, "It's just a novel idea. Don't get apprehensive. It will probably never come off!"

"But you sound so definite about it, " I used to object, "and we already have about six projects going."

"Yes, I know," he would reply, "but you cannot shut your eyes to new possibilities," which of course the Blue level *can* do quite easily! Maybe if the scheme had had some authoritative backing from past precedent the Blue might have found it more acceptable!

Sometimes in these situations the Blue can help the Yellow to see snags, but this has to be done in such a way that the originality and enthusiasm of the Yellow is not squashed and deflated. For example, the intense excitement at the prospects ahead can blind the Yellow to the huge amount of work involved and also to the expense of bringing the scheme to fruition. If the scheme goes ahead and this discovery is made too late, the Yellow has two alternatives, either to ditch the scheme and cut his losses or to find some dependable and responsible people to do the dull hard grind that will carry the project through to a stage at which it is no longer a liability. Meanwhile our Yellow level friend trips off on the potentials of the next scheme! Such cooperation between the levels has produced many sound and valuable enterprises which would never have started had not the initiating Yellow person thought up the idea in the first place. Moreover, people on other levels of consciousness, who would never have initiated anything on their own, have gained fulfilment in bringing something unique and original through to a successful outcome. The problems arise when there is no good back-up team; then the scheme, however brilliant in concept, may flounder, for very rarely will the Yellow level man or woman stay with the unglamorous grind and routine, that offers little or no Ego food or Ego satisfaction, which is the life-blood of this intellectual level of consciousness.

Because of the time-lag in arriving at a logical conclusion, the person orientated to yellow finds himself a member of the intelligentsia who are rendered impotent by their careful examination of all principles. The debate as to " how many angels can dance on the point of a needle " would be the medieval equivalent of today's consideration by the intelligentsia of such problems as National Sovereignty, International principles, and the crisis of the starving world. By the time they have thought out meticulously the process required to deal with these, the crisis will be already a historical one. Hair-splitting logic and hindsight can never take the place of prompt action and foresight in world affairs, so it appears the activist (Red band) and the intuitive (Indigo band) will always have the edge over them in the shape of the world to come. In terms of an instrument of change the yellow-type is best fitted to analyse and think through the consequences of action, but by the time all missing facts are fitted logically into place, the opportunity of the moment is lost forever.

The implication here is that a deep understanding of how these levels operate can eventually enable groups, committees, planning boards and other working bodies to utilise the positive qualities of all their members. Imagine, for the sake of example, a small group of three persons working out a project. The analytical Yellow level woman, working with an Indigo level woman and a Red level action-orientated man, could contribute her positive energy and drive for change and could submit her logical scheme to the Indigo woman, whose instinctual 'knowing' would either confirm or veto the scheme's viability. Then, if the plans were confirmed, the Red level man would be there to put the project into operation in accordance with a blueprint that he himself could never have devised.

So Nuclear Evolution can prove itself over and over again as we use this simple typology to know ourselves and those we work with, and all the bickering and misunderstanding that slows down and often kills progress in decision-making, can be eliminated once we understand what levels our colleagues are working on and what their contribution to the "whole" undertaking can be. Much of the ineffectiveness of committee work can be traced to the frustration and even exasperation experienced by one member for another's way of going about the business. Once Yellow level Bill, with his insistence on sequential planning, can appreciate that all Red level Joe wants to do is to "get into the act", then he will see him not as an irresponsible activist, but as the very man who can make his own grand scheme a reality.

To plan the future and plot a course through time which outlines all necessary changes is easy for the thinking-type, but unexpected events or deviations from the plan will disorient the time-order of such a person. Chaos or the mucker-upper is the " devil " and the " plan " is sacred. The time-process is for the yellow intellectual, essential to sanity, seriously demanding of full attention, and " real " in terms of time-flow. Any standing still of time in any state of Absolute and unchanging reality such as timelessness, is either anathema or merely theory, ever to remain unprovable.

It will be obvious that the intellectual faculty is a cutting instrument. It cuts up reality into little bits and then makes judgments by fitting them together in a way acceptable to the temperament of the personal " I ". It can be distinguished subtly from the concept-making faculty (Blue) which is one of " feeling " a certain way about reality, rather than setting it in strict Logical time-order.

The intellect takes the " whole " of Reality and separates it, and then judges itself by saying not this, not that. It is capable of saying what is not, but incapable of saying what is! Those who tend to condemn the use of intellect totally, and praise man's other faculties, are using intellect to do so. When illuminated with the " knowing " of the intuition (Indigo) and imbued with authority of tested concepts (Blue), the intellect can be the " Light of the World ", exposing all that is hypocritical and inconsistent.

It can also be used destructively and negatively, as when a creative scientist who has spent millions of dollars on research is asked first as a prime question, not about his work or skill, but where his office is, how much his budget is, where his files are kept and what his background is. If any intellectual has to know these incidentals first, before being capable of judging or orientating any important facts, it shows his intellect has been developed merely to divide and cut apart, so that all facts become still-born before they emerge and all reality killed by the demon of ignorance of Self. Thinking-types who have not mastered their ego, believe the whole world must fit their theory and that all facts which disagree with it, can safely be ignored or dismissed with satire. Emotionally, such people are the world-changers who would reform the world. If they can work creatively with the lovers of the world, the poets and the prophets, they can bring method and constructive systems to man's highest insights. Armed with arrogance and determination and their pet theory they can easily become opinionated dictators of fashion and Art, innovators of rigid principles and dogmas, or worst of all become schizophrenic in their attempt to divide the world of Reason from the world of man's Absolute and eternal spirit.

The self-assertive, expressive yellow-drive, unless under control of the self, will subordinate friendship, feeling, and insight to principles, theory and analysis. It leads to feelings of superiority, intellectual snobbery, and a calculated reality that can only be described as a miscalculation.

Handled by the Highest self-awareness, this faculty can throw glory upon all other aspects of life. To understand it as a tool and not a God, gives man a humility that releases him from the conflict between time and timelessness, life and death.

The editors have experienced the author of this book of Nuclear Evolution, Christopher Hills, as a typical example of a high manifestation of this level of consciousness, blended and balanced with a masterful command of the other chakras. So has it been with all the Masters; they have been able to use the superb instrument, the intellect, not as a cutting and divisive or separative tool, but as a skilful means of penetration to the truth. Where the Blue level devotee of Christ accepts whatever he says on the face value of the words, Christopher, in his three-year course in self-mastery, urges the student, as Christ himself did, to test out the teachings in our own lives. The second year of this course uses the words of Christ as texts or triggers for study and the work on the Ego; the student is guided to tune into what Christ really meant in his teachings, which have since been masked and muffled by priestly distortions and deceptive elaborations.

This use of the intellect fulfils its true and highest function, namely to offer itself, as the knights of old offered their swords, for the slaying of falsity and the glorification of the self-realised and ultimate Truth.

INTERVIEW with D.,
a twenty-eight year-old journalist.

Editor: What turns you on the most?

D.: Women. Just the charge I get from interacting, touching and sexual contact, also eye contact–a kind of sharing of anything. I also get turned on by spiritual insights–it's like a light bulb turning on. I guess the inspiration becomes emotional. It often comes when I click into a concept, usually when I'm alone and during peak experiences.

Ed.: What depresses you the most?

D.: Feeling lonely or insecure. Feeling too tight to relate or making mistakes in relationships. I feel depressed if I feel I've done an Ego trip in a relationship. I'm lonely for more contact with women.

Ed.: What are you seeking and wanting in life right now? What are your goals?

D.: Firstly to open my heart and to feel a lot clearer in interactions with people, so that I can feel better in myself about what I am. Secondly I want to learn how to manifest and produce.

Ed.: How do you approach tasks? Do you jump right in or do you plan, or what?

D.: Usually I plan it. Somehow I have to have the whole concept of the job. I'm really blocked unless I have a large overview of what needs to be done. After that I can just do it. But I find I'm planning too much and short-circuiting myself. I could jump right in for simple jobs.

Ed.: How important to you is tradition, past memories, nostalgia and so on?

D.: Not real important; it used to be. I often found that I had some kind of commitment to past relationships and friends, but it's not so strong now. I do have attachment to maintaining old friendships because they can help me in some way, so friendships are kept more for my benefit –for social climbing.

Ed.: What is your usual motive for doing things?

D.: Self interest. I do it because it makes me feel good or it is furthering my position.

Ed.: What do you like most in others?

D.: Open love.

Ed.: What is your attitude to money and possessions?

D.: I enjoy them. I enjoy spending money and I like things.

Ed.: How do you respond to disapproval and criticism?

D.: Not well. I've found how much I don't listen to it because it doesn't confirm what I want to hear about myself. Only recently have I begun to accept that in certain areas I'm at square ONE!

Ed.: Do you ever feel misunderstood?

D.: Sometimes. I feel that oftentimes when I'm trying to communicate and share from the heart, it still comes from my head, and the effect is that I seem to be laying an Ego trip on someone. It hurts me to realise that I would be misunderstood. The Ego perverts my real being and I can see from people's expressions that I have failed.

Note the fluctuation here between the head and the heart, between the Yellow level and the yearning for warm human contact at the Red/Orange level. He is aware of his Ego that separates him from others and depressed by the double bind that comes when the Yellow, separate, intellectual level counteracts the effectiveness of the Red/Orange physical, sensory and social levels. He feels that he plans too much (Yellow level) when he could "jump right in" (Red level). His blatant honesty about his motives again reinforces the Ego picture; he uses his friends and his motive is self-interest. Similarly his attitude to criticism is an Ego-sensitive one and the head keeps the heart closed to protect his Ego. So here we have someone whose Ego confines him to the Yellow level head trip, while his heart yearns for expression and response on the sensory (Red) social (Orange) and heart (Green) levels.

INTERVIEW with A.,
a forty year-old writer and college lecturer.

Editor: What turns you on the most?

A.: Three things: Christopher's teachings; lovemaking; intellectual creativity.

Ed.: What depresses you the most?

A.: To see something in me that I hate. When I was younger and went to a cocktail party, if I made a "boo boo" I was depressed all the next day. Now when I listen to a Creative Conflict tape when I have been confronted by the group, I dislike facing what was said and wish it was not there, but it is, so I have to get back on top.

Ed.: What are you seeking and wanting now in life? What are your goals?

A.: Enlightenment, preferably without losing my Ego! I want to be at the top of the ladder. I also want to make love and experience depths of feelings that I have never experienced before. Then I also want to finish all the books I am writing and to get to writing the Creative Conflict book before anyone else does it. The thrill of creativity excites the imagination. When I'm really manifesting, book writing comes first, but lovemaking sometimes crowds out book writing.

Ed.: How do you approach tasks?

A.: I can jump right in without wrapping my mind around it, but I do something nonessential rather than essential (like spending all day making a dessert and then not having the meal ready when guests arrive). I tend to do what I want to do rather than what needs doing or what I'm supposed to do. I do plan but rather sloppily and only up to a point. I start planning and then I say, "Oh, I see how to do that," and I haven't really grasped what has to be done.

Ed.: How important to you are tradition, past memories, nostalgia and so on?

A.: Pretty much. I feel it's my personal history I cling to--wouldn't want to let go of it. I want to live out the next step but it's hard to let go of old ways. I do look back to the past and savour things and I would like to be able to look back on changes instead of thinking of the present need to change.

Ed.: What is your usual motive for doing things?

A.: To be part of the group. Not to be left out. In order to be square with my conscience sometimes I'll do it in a more selfless way, but only for balance. Things I *want* to do I do for *intensity*.

Ed.: What do you like and admire most in others?

A.: I admire strength--people who are "on centre", firm and solid. I like kindness and compassion and humour and taste and subtlety. I like aliveness and intensity.

Ed.: What is your attitude to money and possessions?

A.: Clutchy. I have the feeling that if I only have say $2,000 in the bank I'm poor and about to run out. With the group I feel they are going to misunderstand and think I'm rich, so I tend to hang on harder than if I were not in a situation with others who have less.

Ed.: How do you respond to disapproval and criticism?

A.: I buy it first and then get weaker. Inwardly I resent it but I don't deal with it, and then I hate the criticism, especially if people are critical of my real being (like my family is) but I even buy that!

Ed.: Do you feel that you are getting from life what you deserve?

A.: Yes, but I sometimes wonder how I got this particular Karma. I don't feel I deserve the criticism of my family.

Ed.: Do you ever feel misunderstood?

A.: Yes, especially with my family and here with the group. How can anyone understand my quirks?

Note the strong Ego desires of the Yellow level, also the love of intensity and the mental excitement of writing a book.

In a Luscher Colour Test, A. chose the eight colours in the following order:

YELLOW; RED; VIOLET; GREEN; BROWN; BLUE; BLACK; GREY.

The yellow in the first place indicates a strong desire for release and hope and expectations of greater happiness, which may take the form of sexual adventure or of a discovery of philosophies or teachings that offer enlightenment and perfection. Note here what she says in answer to the very first question: she is turned on by "Christopher's teachings" and by lovemaking (combined Yellow and Red) and seduction (combined pair Red and Violet).

Her answer to the question about the past suggests that, while loving change (Yellow), her hopes for her own change and growth are directed towards the future when she will *have* changed (the actual process is very painful to the Ego!)

Yellow, the separator, combined with Red, the colour of intense involvement, produces a split between the Ego's need to stand aloof as a superior being and the other need not to feel left out. Note that this produces some self-doubt and the feeling that the group may not understand her.

The Luscher Test reading for her choice of Yellow in the first place and Grey as the most rejected colour (eighth place) is that there is a fear that she may be prevented from achieving the things she wants and this leads her to a restless search for satisfaction in illusory and meaningless activities. Note what she says in response to the question about how she approaches tasks: "I do something nonessential rather than essential."

THE ACQUISITIVE LEVEL
OF
SECURITY CONSCIOUSNESS

*The following is a transcription
of one of a series of lectures on
the Human Chakra System given
by Christopher Hills in 1974.*

THE GREEN LEVEL   ANAHATA CHAKRA

The war of reason, in which the head is always countermanding the heart, creates a spiritual problem. The heart wants to be a big giver, a big lover and the head says, "Well, if you do, you'll get hurt. You'd better pull back, better not give power to someone else to hurt you; if you love someone so much all you are doing is giving them the power to hurt you."

The heart says, "Well, I'd rather be hurt than not have any feelings at all. I don't want to be in a prison all locked up inside."

Or the heart feels it is safer to build a wall around itself to protect itself from hurts. This kind of dialogue and withdrawal goes on all the time because the heart has to do with attachment. The Yellow centre has to do with detachment, or separating and cutting off, but the Green level has to do with attaching ourselves. All the levels have different functions; the intellect cuts reality into pieces, the heart experiences it as one whole thing. To experience something you have to identify with it or attach to it in a sense. Your consciousness has to go to it, that is what a normal falling in love is. You want to belong to someone and you want them to belong to you, to become a part of you so you can say, "Mine". The important part of the word "belonging" is "longing" to be with.

If it was God speaking he wouldn't be saying, "Mine". God does not own the universe in a possessive way. It is yours as much as it is mine or His. The whole universe is yours if you want it, He is not attached to it. He can make another one if this one is not satisfactory. The kind of power pure consciousness has is really so great and awesome it does not care two cents for the entire universe, because it can toss off another one in ten seconds, complete with stars, sun, and everything. Everything that is not quite that pure has more time in it, because it involves form. Anything that is created physically or mentally has form. How does our consciousness attach itself to any form? Forms come to us in many ways, from different "thought forms" from the other higher chakras or from our sensory attachment to the body.

As long as the heart is attached to the body it is in a trap, because it feels that the interior core of its being is related to physical existence on the earth and it isn't. The consciousness which is trapped in the human body is inside a delusion. We're cosmic beings, we are not just human beings, but we have hypnotised ourselves to believe we are just human. We think that the consciousness in us is just a separate piece of mental substance called, whatever our name is, with one democratic vote. The picture the heart centre has of itself as a human will determine its limitations or how free it is of being human. The greatest humanity, of course, has been in those who have transcended humanity. People who have identified with the entire cosmos have always been regarded as being more human than humans. Great beings never had their consciousness into being just earthly human, they always manifested their spirit as a cosmic being.

The heart relates to the universe through attachment. When it can get free of its attachments, whatever they are, whether a person, a crucifix, an object, whatever you invest your consciousness in and love, then the love is no longer exclusively for the love-object and is set free and pure. One has to be ruthless when dealing with the heart, otherwise there will be a problem. The head will always be telling the heart there is a problem. If you completely purify the heart and make it just *pure* love it will be all giving and then it won't be sensible anymore. You become the divine fool then. You do things which will get you crucified. Because if the heart is all heart and there is no head stuck on it you will become a fool. This is essentially what every wise man is and this he knows. The wise man has to become a fool because he is doing things for the opposite motive that everybody else is doing them for. So the wise man is he who knows that the heart is a fool and it is out of its mind. It does things without the mind. The wise know the mind is the slayer of the heart.

I'd like to tell a story illustrating this idea. My guru taught me this lesson. We were about to go off together to a very large conference, in which I was the only European invited as well as Dr. Raynor Johnson, a physicist from Australia. The conference was called for the top yogis in India. I wanted to go and I wanted my guru to come with me. I went to Calcutta and asked and he said, "Yes, but you'll have to meet my son."

I thought that was rather funny because he always called people his son, and I was also his son. "Your son?" I asked. "Yes, a real son," was what he said.

So in the morning when we woke he asked for some keys to be brought to him and someone brought in these great big keys the size of which I had never seen before. Then off he went with those great big keys marching down a long dark passage. At the end of the passage there was this green door with some huge padlocks. It was getting more bizarre.

"I want you to meet my son," he said.

He started to unlock the padlocks and I noticed a little trap door on the bottom and it opened and shut and there was a plate there like for feeding an animal. He plunked the big locks back, opened the big door and shouted something. It was half dark; my eyes adjusted to the dim light and I saw an object creeping across the floor trying to climb up the wall, all hairy with matted hair. I thought, "My God, what has he got, a big tarantula spider in there?" Anyway, this object came and just sat down in the door looking up. And I thought, "God, it is a humanoid," and it was swinging its head loosely all around. "What a strange human being, a monster," I thought.

"This is my son," my guru said. "He happens to be my guru also. The reason he is my guru is that although he looks a little strange, you must forgive him because he has developed his heart at the expense of his head. There is one thing my son is supreme in; because his heart is absolutely pure he can see truth. That is why I use him on occasions like this. We are going on a trip together and I want to know what is in the depths of your heart. So I am going to ask my son to look in the depths of your eyes. If there is any falsity in you he will never look at you."

This was more bizarre than ever, and I wondered if I had made any mistakes. What kind of shape is my heart in? This guy has got to look into my eyes or I am a phony. So I started saying, "Well, I chased a cow when I was six with a saw and tried to chop it." And all kinds of things I had done wrong came flashing across my eyes and I thought "Well, these things are not so bad after all, other people have done much worse." Then I realised I had to make this guy look at me, so I tried to look him in the eyes and there he was looking all around the universe except at me. This was really freaky, I wanted this guru to come with me on this trip very much. So my guru said something to this humanoid thing and the thing looked all around in every direction except at me. I said, "My God, he is not going to look at me." Then I thought, "Well he jolly well is, there is nothing wrong with me, I feel okay, I've no guilt in me," and at that moment he just looked straight in my eyes, and looked right into my soul and I've never seen eyes like that in my life. It was like looking into a whole universe which was totally different. He was seeing me without any comparison, without any head, it was like he was seeing from his heart into my heart. Some dogs have that look, but very few. If you find a dog that is just pure heart, it has a certain look that just talks with its eyes, and there is a glassiness and it looks straight at you telling you that it loves you, just like that.

Then this human monster looked away again, his eyes going all around the universe, and my guru shouted something at him and he scuttled off and tried to climb the wall again. My guru slammed the door shut, put the huge padlocks on again and I thought, "My God, is this a dream I am having? It can't be anywhere on this earth." Then the guru turned to me sweetly and said: "I want you to take pity on my son because he has developed his heart at the expense of his head. That is why he is my guru," he said.

I could hardly believe such humility; this was a guru of gurus speaking! When I used to sit with him he would have many other people at his feet, other gurus. And he was now saying his guru was a lunatic. That made a profound impression on me. Being a bizarre person myself I suppose my guru used the most bizarre methods. I guess he must have been just right for me, because that image is burned into my brain.

And whenever I look into people's eyes now, I can tell how much of their heart centre is functioning, through that one look from that strange man. He transmitted some knowledge to me that can only be done that way.

The universe of the heart can make you very stupid, if you rely on that one alone. Motivations in such people who are divine fools are very difficult to see. Why did Jesus get himself crucified? He could have avoided it, but something was telling him he had to go through with it. For his message to be of any importance to man, "Truth" had to be put on a cross. So he did even what his own disciples thought was foolish. In hindsight we don't see it as foolish, but it is very difficult for us to see the same thing in our lives here and now. It is to do something totally pure of any motive, because something secretly tells us to do it. It is God telling us to go through with it. Christ had surrendered to the cosmic will. To surrender to the cosmic will you have to be a divine fool, you have to get the head out of the way so that you are out of your mind. That does not mean that you have to be appearing to be a fool to everyone, but you might be thinking you are a big fool and disguise it. If you have important work to do and you go around playing the fool you won't be allowed to do it. If you ever become a divine fool and don't want to get crucified right away, you'd better disguise the fact. Usually wise men who get this knowledge go live by themselves somewhere in a cave because it is impossible to live in the world of men with such a heart. The wise man is immediately immersed in the problems of everyone who comes along. Having no problems of his own, he has everyone else's. If you get loaded with everybody else's problems and you start helping them to work them out you could also be robbing them of an opportunity to do some work on themselves. The divine fool is often he who, instead of helping them superficially, will give them a good kick up the backside because he does everything opposite. What you'd expect to hear, he will say the opposite. You learn more permanently from the opposite than you would from getting the temporary help.

Another problem with the heart centre is expectations. If we give something, we expect to get it back in return. If we love someone we expect them to love us back. When you become a divine fool that does not work. You love them even when they don't love you back. That does not mean you have to *like* the person. You can have children and love them but that does not mean that you like them when they do naughty things. Loving and liking are different. Love transcends liking because true love is not contingent on anything. Love does not set limits because it is limitless love. Ordinary human love is full of contingencies. I help you, you should appreciate it and love me--this is the attitude. Many of our drives to help others are in this category. We want to be the good guy, we want to be liked, so we go around doing good things. There is something in us that needs some confirmation, some recognition, so unconsciously we compensate for it by being a nice guy. Whereas perhaps the nasty guy does more good for everyone because he really tells them where it is at. If you hate someone in your heart that is a negative attachment and just as much an attachment as the positive attachment we call love. Hate is only as deep as your love was or could be.

The heart centre has to do with whether we are indifferent to people or not. If we like someone we don't show them indifference, and if we hate someone we don't show them indifference either. It is only when we are indifferent with somebody that they can't really hurt us. When we love someone, everything they do can hurt us; words, thoughts, inconsiderations.

These movements of energy in the heart centre are very tricky. The time worlds in the heart are shifting. When the love-object is lost or gone away the time world moves back to the past. You've lost possession of the attachment and so you go back to the time when you were with that possession and you dwell in that world. What you are doing is trying to bring the past into the present. In the time-world of the present one has the love-object and it gives self-confirmation and inner security. Security is threatened when the threat of losing or not being with that object arises. The future time-world is threatened when one feels uncertain and dwells in the future. You can be certain of the cosmos and yourself only when your heart centre is pure. Absolute certainty does not exist except when there is a pure heart. If there is a gnawing feeling that something is missing, if there is an unfulfilled hole in the heart, then there is insecurity, and you become grave, full of gravity. The heart centre is concerned with gravity and levity, going in and down to the centre and going up and out. The way to cure your gravity is to have some levity. You have to become a fool because a fool always has levity in situations of gravity.

The heart centre has a shifting of time-worlds and is concerned with the need to feel secure, to have self-confirmation, and self-recognition from others or from society. This leads to all kinds of actions and motives in order to be respected. Many expectations about life are then set up by our longing, but the way to conquer the heart is to expect nothing. If you expect nothing you cannot be disappointed.

To expect nothing from God or the universe is a very tall order. We wake up each morning and we could say to God, whomever He is, wherever He is, "You have given me life today and I didn't expect it." But of course you did expect it, you jolly well expect to wake up in the morning. You should be aware that tomorrow you may not wake up, you may not have any more consciousness to spend on earth and then you would spend today's consciousness a little more intelligently. If one lives everyday as if it were the last day on earth, life becomes very rich, because you only do important things--you only talk to people who mean something to you, you probably use it to work on yourself. That is why Saint Francis said, "It is only through dying daily that one can come to eternal life."

That means absolute detachment from the desires of the heart, even from life. How can we expect nothing from the universe, from God, or from anyone else? Only by becoming nothing. So we can say with Christ, "I am of myself nothing, it is the Father, the Cosmic Intelligence which does all these things and says all these things through me. I am of myself nothing; *no-thing*." Then there is no I to make any distinction between itself and anything else. And that is the ultimate trip of the heart centre.

GREEN

The keyword in this drive is self-security, self-measuring, or self-confirmation and assurance. If the drive is for self-expression in the Yellow band the drive for self-assertion is in the Green. Basically, it is the power drive, although this need for power is hidden in many disguises.

At the first mention of the word "power" we conjure up images of dictators and powerful authoritarian figures and institutions that dominate their environment and those who live within their jurisdiction. In our minds we visualise Adolf Hitler and a crowd of thousands of automata shouting "zieg heil!" without knowing what they are doing. They are, we say, "in the power" of the dictator. The stage hypnotist apparently controls his subject's actions and the audience feels that the subject is "in his power". We talk of someone's "powerful personality" and secretly long for the same power to affect others with our own dynamism.

The need for power is present in every human being who has to move and this need overlaps all the other drives. The hunger drive is primary even outclassing the sexual drive in the Red; it arises from the need of the primary Green to seek "vital force" and food for the living processes of the organism. The power to survive and obtain energy for consciousness to be maintained is rooted in the *storing up* activities of the body as well as in the psychological functions. Such activity requires one to expend energies and assert oneself in some way. Vegetables do not need to walk around for food as their root is in the ground, but in their search for light the stem will twist and push to find its way through the jungle. Living things need the security of their environment in order to express themselves fully. The tree grows best in the forest with other trees; the human being grows best when he receives love, support, protection and recognition from others. The need for emotional and spiritual security is just as important as

307

financial or physical security and the lack of it can be described as a lack of power, or lack of effectiveness, in the life process. An insufficient supply of Green and Red would cause Paranoia since the resulting colour Brown is the colour of that condition.

Human beings cannot manifest their true potentials until they are secure, physically, mentally, emotionally and spiritually. As long as people feel compelled, for example, to work in jobs that they hate, solely to satisfy their financial and economic needs, they will be unable to express themselves adequately in the more subtle realms of their being. People need to have the inner confidence that they can get what they need from the cosmos and this applies to all realms of experience. When people feel assured from within, then they feel that they can assert themselves positively towards areas of greater fulfillment and growth. When they feel inadequate then they feel trapped by life and helpless. This inhibits their life expression and causes personality and psychic disintegration.

It should be realised that these drives are not only in human nature but through all of creation. Plants and vegetables, or even growing crystals will not only respond to light but hunger for it. Not all organisms are fitted with light seeking devices, but they all do have the urge for the power of seeking that kind of nutrition which keeps them alive.

Life basically seeks light. A weevil hates the light but loves the cotton which grows in the hot sun. While we may find instances of creation that avoid light even in secondary forms, we will not likely find instances of life that do not somehow sustain themselves with nourishment. In other words, everything alive eats. The drive to eat is the power to extract from the universe in order to secure the basic life-stuff needed to live.

The time world of the Green band is a shifting one which varies as security is enhanced or threatened. In the Violet drive 7 the consciousness is concerned with time and duration and timelessness, whereas in the Green it is concerned with time as movement of energy and its flow. As " Rajoguna ", one of the three creative powers of the homogeneous vibration which the Samkhya philosophy calls PRAKRITI, Pra meaning primordial, Kriti meaning creative energy, it can identify one minute with the future or next to the past. Take an example of the confident male who feels secure of his beautiful girl. He shows her off to the world as if to say, " she is mine ! I have power over her affections that other men do not have as she is pledged to me ". He is identifying his need for power and self-assurance with her present allegiance to him. The minute she looks at another man for even a few minutes, this (rajoguna) Green band of consciousness moves from time present to time future. A sickening feeling comes over him as he realises what the future will be like without her. He will not be able to assert himself. People will say, " she has left you for another and you have no power to influence her ". The future suddenly becomes present and a threat to power and self-confidence is immediately experienced as a touch of jealousy. So much for the situation as long as she only looks at another! But what of the feelings if she actually does leave? Then the future is annulled completely and the consciousness of " I " identifies with the past—" We have always had good times together in the past and have all our memories ", he pleads with her. But she is secure for she has the power to crush or the power to pour salve on the insecure feeling gnawing away in his guts. She enjoys her power and makes him wait, or lies to him. because she knows he will believe what he wants to believe in order to remove the pain which her imminent departure evokes. If she rejects him he goes home and lives in the past, touching the mementos and souvenirs of their life together, looking at photographs taken together, and all his activity moves towards bringing back the situation where the past can become the present.

Time experience varies with the expressed level of consciousness. But it may vary within the drive itself, depending on the attitude and placement of the particular psychic energy in question. We may feel secure in the present only when someone is paying attention to us, or when we have a high paying job or when there is lots of money in the bank. But if the stocks go down or there is a layoff at the place where we work or our lover looks at someone else, then our future gets shaky as we imagine what could happen if we had to face it all alone. If such a situation does occur then there is a tendency to revert to the past and remind ourself of the security we once possessed, in order to bring that into the present. The point is that human beings create a shifting world of time by the sheer effort of trying to grasp and hold onto something. Into this shifting time-world we insert our emotional states and thus attach ourselves, with the primordial energy of consciousness given to us, to the everyday situations of life in which we find ourselves.

It's very much like those mussels that you find by the sea. They attach themselves for all they're worth to a rock or a piece of seaweed. If a storm comes along and breaks off their rock then their security goes with it and they wash up on the shore. With humans it's very similar, as we learn from the words of most popular songs: "You were my rock and now you're gone and I'm just a driftin' tumbleweed."

To the wise man who controls his light (satoguna) such an attachment to beauty is a lack of control of " Rajoguna ", the movement of energy and power over one's private universe. The same wonderful girl can delight a man who does not attach his consciousness to her fickle eye, but enjoys her beauty in the moment for what it is, a passing fancy created like a flower to bloom and die away, loved without attachment. She does not become the vehicle for his self-assurance, the object of his self-confidence and the pride of his possession. He experiences the same wonder and thrill of her dazzling personality but he relates his infatuation to past, present and future, and sees clearly that he must enjoy her while he can and then let go. For to hold on to power and to cling to the object of love, gives it power over the man, and he is no longer master of himself. This example can be applied to almost every situation in life from politics to spiritual power. For though we may say that great spiritual men are above the search for temporal power they can never escape their search for Immortality and God. The power to effectively radiate one's being into the Universe is the essence of the Divine in Drive 8. Anyone who pretends or says he has given up this need for " Light-power " for the Kingdom of Heaven's sake, has not understood the Glory of God. Though it may not be possible for humans to seek it consciously, by their calculation or by any system of merit, yet it remains certain that the creator bestows his effulgence as a natural consequence of self-lessness. Jesus prayed for it. Certainly all our Saints have wanted the power to express it, desperately, to the exclusion of all else. The primal urge for power, whether tempered by Grace which beautifies it, or made ugly by those who cling to it for themselves can assume many disguises. The time-world of the Saint who seeks to blend it with Wisdom and creative action is immortality, while he who is imprisoned in the Green band will become a banker, attach himself to a man of power, stay close to large resources or be concerned with his own sense of security. The great challenge for someone who predominates in the Green, will be to find occupation which is satisfying and rewarding at the same time. He needs to have relationships with others which confirm his opinion of himself.

Here we see that to rely on another for our self-esteem and self-confirmation is to create a dependency which is self-defeating. When we cling to people we sacrifice our own power and integrity in order to get something from them. Whatever they do or don't do can affect and disturb us because we have given away our power to determine our own reality. We must learn to rely on ourselves to supply our own needs in every realm of our being. To do this is to turn inward and upwards, as it were, to the source of our needs, away from the attachment to outward and temporal manifestations of what we feel is missing in our lives. This primal power of consciousness is in reality the urge to connect with God in whatever form we may construe him to be. In a saint, this drive manifests as selfless never ending love. In someone trapped by insecurity we may find a predominant concern for material gain. Thus, to find work which can fulfill not just the pocketbook but the heart as well is a positive key to the green level of consciousness. It is in the constructive attainment of vital force that we feel free to share and give it out again. Hoarding, possessiveness, jealousy, and selfishness occur when there is a fear that our giving is going to deprive us of our essential energy needs. When there is overflowing love and positive recogniton then there is a feeling that we can stand on our feet, speak our minds and carry out our thoughts. This is vitality, the power to live and to go on living abundantly.

Because the urge for power is largely a projection of one's urge for food reflected often in the storing up of the vital forces of the community in money, or in gaining a reputation for effectiveness, there may be enhanced interest in the stomach, in ideas about food and nutrition. On the other hand, this drive may be transferred to throwing off self-limitations and restraints which impede his power to assert himself in the community. The drive may also find its way into hoarding or the accumulation of knowledge for its own sake, for it is at the base of possessiveness. Certainly the antique collector who will go to such trouble in the future to secure something concrete in the present which can be appreciated for its past, is a good example of the person who is exclusively in the Green layer. Nevertheless, the primary green is the colour which drives our power house, increases all our appetites and reinforces all other temperaments, traits and levels of consciousness. Without the power of this ray of creation there could be no action, movement or life in the universe.

Primary green is the power to move. Regardless of whether we use this movement to obtain wealth and retain it as in possessiveness, or to overcome it and express as in self-assertion, the basic drive is still the same. All life utilises this energy and when we don't have it we die. This can occur on the spiritual level as with cancer or on the physical level as when the heart stops or on the emotional level as in extreme withdrawal, where the will to live is aborted and we see autism or suicide.

When the basic response to this energy is negative, it can attach itself to anything from sex to images of people, to things, collecting, conquests, reputations, concepts, degrees, money, status, knowledge, and even garbage, all for the sake of self security.

Whatever traits that we have will be influenced by the green drive. If we are intuitive then our desire for intuitive experience will be enhanced and we become more attached to psychic phenomena. If we are intellectual then our attachment to rational thinking process will be the greater. Just as an engine drives a train, our green level of consciousness drives our life. We burn enough emotional fuel to pull a whole train load of negative attachments with us. Without that power, we would be a body of inertia.

> The green ray of life energy and movement of consciousness cannot be compared to the activity and restlessness of the Red. Chronos the Greek God means "the measure of time". The colour Green of life makes us conscious of chronological time, and aware of the flow of life energies through us. In the next drive (Blue) the attempt is made to fix them in experience with the "timebinding" effect of mind. Life on Earth has a time for everything. The Green Ray like Chronos the Greek God, means the measure of time and Life.

In times past, man probably began measuring time by his own survival time. The activity he engaged himself in was for purposes of maintaining his life. Thus he became aware of rhythmic changes that occurred throughout his natural environment. Some of these changes indicated seasons of growth and activity while others marked sleep and decline. He learned to use these changes in seasonal patterns to facilitate his survival. "Knowing the time" gave him power over his physical limitations and he learned when to plant, when to hunt, when to fish, when to gather, and when to store away. He measured life with time. Fruit was "ripe", tracks were "fresh", and winters were "long."

Man noticed that living things were born and they died. Seemingly, the movement between the two extremes was to maintain the one and prevent the other. Experience within this flow caused him to either look behind, think ahead, or act now, depending on his degree of security in the situation. In other words, the insecurity of an approaching winter caused him to prepare for the future by storing up supplies, while failure in an important hunt caused him to remember back into his past more successful experiences which could soften the harsher bleaker reality that now confronted him. A full larder brought feasting and joy into a secure present. Thus, the seasons were defined and the movements of time measured. Man living on the earth, experiencing limitation and obstacles to his survival, "spent" or expended his life force accordingly. This expenditure of life force was perceived as synonymous with time, for in the green level of awareness, where security and the acquisition of nourishment are of prime concern, time and life force become one and the same.

INTERVIEW with J.H.,
a forty-two year-old plasterer.

Editor: What turns you on?
J.H.: Making a pile of money. Cashing in at Las Vegas on a 100-to-1 shot.
Ed.: What depresses you most?
J.H.: Not being able to get things together. Driving around in a dump truck and living out of a can. The government depresses me. They're as bad as the hippies. Working on this job 8 to 5 is no fun.
Ed.: How do you approach tasks?
J.H.: How much does it cost? That's the first thing. Can it be done quick and easy? What's in it for me?
Ed.: What are your goals?
J.H.: Being my own boss. A nice home, swimming pool and a boat. No worries. A stable full of women and a bar loaded with booze. Ha ha.
Ed.: How important to you is the past?
J.H.: I think about being a kid, especially when things go wrong. It was simple then. I think a lot about a gal I used to know. She ran off with a school teacher.
Ed.: How important is the future?
J.H.: The only time I think about the future is when the tax man starts knocking on my door.

Ed.: What is your usual motive in doing things?

J.H.: To get something. Isn't it everyone's?

Ed.: What do you admire most in others?

J.H.: I guess being on top. Guys who get to the top honest and fair and can still drive a Cadillac without forgetting where they came from.

Ed.: What do you dislike in others?

J.H.: People who push and shove like they own the whole world. I hate that. People always looking over your shoulder to make sure you're not breaking some law. Seems like you can't do anything nowadays.

Ed.: What is your attitude to money and possessions?

J.H.: You've got to have money! You can't live without it. I've tried. I spend most of my time getting it and the rest spending it, so my attitude is the more of it I can get, the better off I'll be.

INTERVIEW with W.M.,
a twenty-eight year-old secretary.

Editor: What turns you on the most?

W.M.: One thing is getting into my home. Doing "homey" things. Another is having a nice relationship with my boyfriend. But the main thing is the feeling that I'm getting some insights into the nature of "me", where I'm really making some progress and feeling like I can change from what I thought I was.

Ed.: What depresses you most?

W.M.: The feeling of being left out. That makes me feel like a failure.

Ed.: What are you seeking and wanting in life? What are your goals?

W.M.: To become more disciplined, to understand my heart and how to work with it. I want to get in touch with what is secretly motivating me inside. How do I use myself to gain mastery in even ordinary everyday things.

Ed.: How do you approach tasks?

W.M.: First, my mind runs through the difficulties. Then I think about time. I try to get some idea of the job by measuring it or counting things, like, how many books equal how many shelves and so on. Then I try to see what is going to

Ed.:   be needed to complete the job, not just in materials but furniture and machines and what goes where. If another person is involved I try to coordinate with them, but if that doesn't work I just start moving things around.

Ed.:   How important to you is the past?

W.M.:   Not so much now. I often think fondly of people, even in dreams. I still have memories and look back some. There is a self-image that comes from the past. Also, if I'm uncertain about something, I may go with what someone else has already said because they may know more than I do about it.

Ed.:   How important to you is the future?

W.M.:   I don't think about the future much. In fact, it makes me feel insecure because I don't think about it more!

Ed.:   What is your motive for doing things?

W.M.:   Self-confirmation. It's a feeling like I'm setting up for myself a task and it feels good to know that I can do it. Also, I've accepted these responsibilities and I feel like that is my job.

Summary

In the foregoing interviews we can see several examples of the Green level at work. The responses by J.H. are obvious and almost classic. He is very materialistic in his perceptions and desires. His goals and attitudes are all geared towards security. In one way, J.H. is a picture of need. Throughout the interview there is the feeling that J.H. is striving to assert himself and get some "green energy", especially in the form of dollars. Although he does not say this, his reference to the government and hippies and not being able to do anything nowadays seems to allude to areas outside himself which he feels are preventing him from some self-expression, perhaps to the point of actually costing him something. In other words, not being able to get it together and then blaming the government is negative green. He also demonstrates the Green level in that he reverts to the past when things go wrong and to the future when his security is threatened. W.M. also shows this, albeit in a very subtle way, by becoming insecure at the thought of not

315

thinking about the future enough. In effect, she is thinking what will happen to her in the future if she doesn't think about it!

In general, however, the Green level is not so obvious in W.M. There is some emphasis on self-confirmation and she admires people who can act on their own power of inspiration, which, in terms of self-affirmation, is the green drive. She also desires to see her motivations and understand her heart. The heart is the Green level. Her attitude towards money shows that she does have a tendency to gain some self-confirmation from possessing it, since she wouldn't feel clean without it. This is perhaps the negative side of her security drive since her positive side manifests as a feeling that she can set herself a task and then do it. From this she can gain a feeling of worth. J.H., on the other hand, while wanting to be his own boss, dislikes the job that he is in. This shows the classic conflict of the green drive for security.

REFERENCES

H. Klar, Hope and Fear in Returnees from Vietnam

Results shown by

the Luescher Colour Test

Special print from
»medico« international edition
1968, N° 11, p. 15
Boehringer Mannheim GmbH
Mannheim · Germany

"The striking factor is the outstanding significance of the autonomous colour green in position 1. This is further underlined by the next colour choice, grey. Grey in position 2 shows at the same time that the choice of green in position 1 was a compensatory one. Green in position 1 is the expression of a strong effort of will, of a determination to assert oneself and one's claims, an autistic demand for a significant part to play resulting from an inferiority complex. For the returnees this means "I am determined to make the grade, I must assert myself and find recognition even though I may have lost my opportunity to keep abreast with professional life in Europe as a result of the years spent in the tropics (inferiority complex)".

But green is not only the expression of determination and self-assertion but as far as an aim in life is concerned also an expression of the search for influence, independence and security. They are afraid of being forced into a situation and of losing power. The fear of having to fit in and of being forced to adjust themselves to the principles of the European system in contrast to their free and independent life overseas is typical of returnees. Reintegration into professional and social life in Europe almost always takes place at a lower social level and brings with it a loss of social prestige. It is not surprising therefore that this fear of being forced into a situation and the fear of losing influence should express themselves in the test. The vital and dynamic red and the magically erotic violet fall back to positions 3 and 4 behind green and grey."

THE MENTAL LEVEL
OF
CONCEPTUAL
CONSCIOUSNESS

*The following is a transcription
of one of a series of lectures on
the Human Chakra System given
by Christopher Hills in 1974.*

THE BLUE LEVEL   VISHUDDHA CHAKRA

I am going to speak about how the mind stuff and the colour Blue relate. I have already spoken about how the conceptualising mind makes comparisons and judgements, but we still don't know how it does this, how it functions.

All the psychic centres or chakras are modifiers of the flow of consciousness, that is, the Self with all its images is dancing through all of these chakras just like the vibration of sound in the flute. Variations in sound are made by putting your fingers in such a way on the stop of the flute that the sound wave travels a shorter distance and becomes a different length. The chakras by the same laws of resonance filter out different frequencies of mental activity. Consciousness or Light is pouring through the being constantly and is modified by the chakras into different frequencies. When Kundalini rises, all the chakras are activated while normally only one or two are fully functioning. This activity is what makes the colours of the human aura, and when the colour of the aura changes it is because the quality of the consciousness has changed. It is important to distinguish the difference between the Yellow type of thinker and the Blue type. The function of the

Blue chakra is a conceptualising or a putting together of reality - not taking it apart as the yellow level does. The colour Blue is a totally different function in mental operations. The Blue chakra is what the mind does in order to store experience in the memory. The memory resonates to the colour blue because all conceptualised mind experience takes place in past time. Now, yellow level logical scientists are often interested in taking reality apart in a very subjective/objective fashion. They are themselves the subject studying the object. That kind of separation is all deceptive illusion, in reality you cannot do that because the subject and object are one. The perceiver and the perception are factually connected. You cannot percieve anything "out there" except in terms of the limitations "in here", your mind. Often the 3rd level scientist who is an intellectual yellow type is purely logical and uses rationalisations to kill reality - not enlighten himself. He himself is the last person he can experience internally in his search to define all kinds of tiny particles which he ends up chasing all around the external universe, not realising he is really looking for himself. Sometimes the yellow intellectual is so far away from himself that he is even more ignorant than a peasant who has some connection with real life. This is what the sacred Vedas of India say of a person who is mentally divorced from the knowledge of reality as subject and object being logically one and the same. The yellow scientist has gotten so far away from the true logical process that he cannot see that all studies of external sensory information are all objects of study, which ignores that there must be a subject. Even information from the internal environment such as brain waves, right-left functions, etc., can be viewed as purely objective without a subject if we do not have this understanding of the oneness of both of them. When the Blue conceptualiser comes together with the yellow analyser then we have a good scientist. The Blue type is devoted to the truth or a concept; the yellow is devoted to logic and there is a big difference in reality between the two.

What you reject is equally important in life. The auric emanation which you give to the environment around you is also conditioning your universe. To close out some vital energy or emasculate some important function of your being will affect your reality and show up in your aura, as much if not more than some other person's energy you respond to and attract to your being. The particular function of yellow is related to disintegration or elimination in nature but the Blue, which is equally as important, is the function of assimilation. Material objects, –whether human, animal or mineral,– must excrete surplus energy or eliminate at the optimum rate or they will become dis-eased or ill at ease, otherwise known as unstable, but at the same time they must be glued together by another force or they will disintegrate altogether. The force which pulls things together in our consciousness is the blue colour. Although the Blue type of person can also use logic it is not so fluid as to be logically self-defeating. A Blue person could understand the transcendental type of logic but the yellow would want to reject it as an intolerable contradiction and paradox. Yet it is perfectly logical if you will follow my thoughts step-by-step.

Let us ask the Self the logical question as follows: What is the subject when we objectively study the senses? Obviously the subject is the body that experiences the senses as objective. Then if we make the body the object of study, what is the subject? The subject must be the mind or consciousness which is aware of what the body is experiencing. The mind memorises and forms pictures of what it is experiencing and evaluates that experience. So now let us make the mind the object of study. The ego which thinks it has a mind or thinks it is a separate piece of mental substance from the universe, must be the subject now. Let's make the ego or self-consciousness the object of study and the subject is obviously awareness. Awareness of self. Now let us make the self-sense the object of study, what is the subject? Well the self, "I" the object, is also the subject, isn't it? So mathematically and logically if the self is the object and the self is also the subject then they both cancel out each other. So if the subject is the object there is no separation in reality between the two.

What I have done is used a perfectly logical sequence to prove that whether you are talking about the objective universe or the subjective one, they are one and the same. It is only the ego, the yellow function of our mind, that thinks it is separate. Actually you are totally hooked up to the universe whether you like it or not. And you are the centre of the universe–if you are simple enough on the Blue level to realise that you *are* the centre of whatever is happening to you. We then perceive our own dualistic existence as an illusion. Man is included in the environment and the total environment becomes part of himself. In the ultimate science of Being there is only one God - pure consciousness, and

320

all ideas, rationalisations and reason are aspects of That. The chakras bring about the different functions within the ONE and the Blue one integrates them as a whole system.

The Blue chakra centre is time-binding of the past because it stores the memories from previous incarnations as well as this one. It is useless knowing about your previous incarnations through any other source than yourself, your own thoughts. The only validator is your own stream of consciousness. If someone tells you you were this or that it is all hearsay, there is no value to it. This kind of knowledge the ordinary mind loves, it likes to store up that garbage, psychic garbage. You have to know for yourself what you are. When you know and can think for yourself, then it is valuable. Otherwise it is just words, concepts, names and categories. Does it tell you any more just to name a thing, to define something?

People name things all day long. Children ask an important question and are put off with a name or definition. "What's that big bright thing in the sky, daddy?" "That's the moon!" Does the child know any more about the moon just because we have said m-o-o-n? We are doing this all the time in dictionaries, encyclopedias, etc., with everything--not directly experiencing for ourselves, just being satisfied with all these words. The words don't necessarily mean anything on the fundamental level of reality, it is just all the garbage we collect in our memory. So the person who lives mainly functioning through this conceptual centre is Blue. He is conservative because he lives in the memory of past history. His new information is related to something that has already happened in the past, he cannot have a new experience without relating it to something that has happened already. No matter what you are talking about, he must compare it with the tapes which play endlessly on inside his own head. All your words must pass through the filter of his own stored knowledge in the memory.

We use words all the time to communicate and people actually believe there is some reality to these words, but words are only descriptions of other people's experiences of years and years ago. We use them as if they had some true reality for our experience. They only represent reality, they are not the stuff itself but concepts. It is knowledge about, not direct knowledge. There is another kind of knowing about the mind and we call it direct perception.

The Blue level is always knowing something through information which is stored or is forming concepts about information. Concepts are like models, they are just the most satisfying explanation we have about something real. Concepts of whatever we have stored up in our minds are actually useless for becoming enlightened. Anything we have stored already is useless, because if it wasn't useless we would be already enlightened. The reason I say this is because true learning cannot take place until we jettison all our pretence of knowing logically or conceptually and admit that we really don't know. When you can admit that you don't know what you don't know, you are humble enough to truly learn something. But until you can admit to yourself that what you know already has not enlightened you, you cannot, however hard you try, learn what will enlighten you. If we already had the information of how to get enlightened totally then we would be enlightened! This does not mean that we don't have the pure consciousness which enlightens us, we have that, we just use it in the wrong way by screwing it up with all of these logical and conceptual faculties we've talked about -- first, the red sensory level, then the orange social brainwashing our culture gives to us, then the yellow ego with the way it rationalises, then the green love centre attaching itself, then the blue mind which is time-binding the world with the notion that there is time. Time is just a concept, a thought, something that arises internally by focusing our consciousness on objects which move through space like our own body. It is very hard for the conceptual mind to think there is just no such thing as flow of time.

The Blue level person is typically conservative, not being able to stand great changes, living in the past and being quite content with it. Change unsettles their time world. They think too much change is going on, there is need and craving for a little isle of peace where they can savour events in time. But time is only a thought, it is not real.

Once a fixed concept is confirmed and stored and steady, you create in your mind ideas and ideals; putting together many different separate perceptions-- that is what the conceptualising process is. First the sensory information is taken in through

322

eyes or ears (recepts), then you join some of that together and make percepts because you perceive something. But perception by itself does not mean anything. If I stand in the sun's light and perceive heat, that does not tell me much about the sun. All it tells me about is light and heat, but it does not tell me much about reality. When I start joining many percepts together I get concepts and eventually I can conceive that the sun is out there in space burning. But that may be all bunk too, in fact it is, because the sun in not out there. Only our conceptual mind places the experience of sun "out there".

I'm going to start talking nonsense now: the sun is not out in space, you don't experience it out there. All you experience from out there is with your senses, a notion about space being there because you think of yourself as a separate entity or body with you here and the sun out there in the space. Actually the sun is inside your consciousness, because your consciousness and space are identical. Consciousness, space and light are identical. The only thing that makes them not identical is consciousness when it limits itself from being the whole universe. It traps itself inside our skin and says, "Yes, I have got some light coming through my eyes down the optic nerve to the occipitals to the thalamus and that is the sun!"

But that is only a concept of the sun. People experience these concepts as being real, but they are not real —the sun is experienced inside your head, not outside. The signal is only apparently outside. It is experienced between the ears as just a little tiny ball of whirling energy that the self is aware of. This psychic representation is a re-creation of the sun inside your head. Every star in the universe is the same - between your ears, in consciousness. Of course if you limit your consciousness to just the inside of your skin then reality will appear to be out there -- but don't you think it is rather strange that your consciousness can travel up to the stars faster than the speed of light and even go in between the stars and look at the empty space in just a flash?

The yellow scientist would say that the light is coming to us, it takes so many light years to get here and it must have started out millions of years ago to get here. That may be true in one sense, if there is time and velocity. Time itself may be a notion.

Why is time a notion? Because we have a notion about space. We have a notion about space because of a notion about objects in space. We have a notion about objects in space because we think of ourself as an object. When you think of yourself as pure consciousness, unlimited by time and space, then all the stars and suns are swirling around inside your head, in your consciousness where you are really experiencing them. Right now everything that is happening in the universe, whether you are aware of it or not, is happening in consciousness. Without consciousness there it would not be happening, would it?

People say that when the consciousness leaves the body it becomes a corpse, but the universe still goes on. People attach their consciousness to the body and do not know that as soon as the body is gone they can get another one just like a suit of clothes. Consciousness is wearing all kinds of disguises. Bodies are something we just put on at birth; we even call it a "birthday suit".

We are using the ultimate power – pure consciousness – to make ourselves think we are human beings. We are not, we are cosmic space beings. From all over space we have been, many times, in many universes. We have come to this one to learn how to live in the physical world, the physical vibration of matter. Consciousness is such a fantastic and awesome thing if you just see what it does. Look at its handiwork, it is on an enormous incomprehensible scale! Just look at the world of matter, look at the piece of matter we have got, this body which is a fantastic thing; we don't know the half of what has been sitting here for a hundred thousand years. Do you think there has ever been a physical breakdown between you and Abraham? The cells and bodies came from the living proteins we call sperms and ovums which were living flesh all along the line. You are the end result of a long biological, physical chain that has never died. Your genetic DNA body has never died. Not one sperm has been missing. Sit inside your body and experience the wonder of a million years of evolution that has never, never had one physical break in it. This physical matter has never died. Put your thoughts on it, your mind, and just trip on it! Go back through all those unions and trips people have had – falling in love, petting, all of the action just to get the sperm and ovum together. You are related to Christ and Abraham –there has never been a break. It is a long biological wriggling chain of living flesh in which consciousness has been writing itself in and through time, printing itself, modifying itself. And we have all these centres up here , in the head, we have centres that we are never even going to use for another fifty thousand years, all programmed by a fantastic cosmic intelligence which can just create stars by the millions in a second of time. Pure consciousness can create anything out of itself. It is really awesome and is sitting inside you experiencing the universe through you, right now, allowing you to think of yourself as a separate self because it wants you to find the real stuff – the greatest and most powerful drug there is – pure consciousness, pure, pure, nothing at all.

Of course what we do with that consciousness is another thing. It comes through these seven universes which are interpenetrating each other within us. We have all kinds of screwed up notions about the universe, which manifest in the images of how we think about life.

Now thinking about thinking does not get you anywhere. Thinking about the thinker gets you somewhere. It is a different thing altogether. Thinking about the thinker of the thought is much more deep than thinking about the thought itself, because eventually you will end up at pure consciousness, the stuff that makes everything out of itself and lets you make anything freely. If you are really in tune with what is looking out of your eyes then whatever you are looking at was created by you. That is a difficult thought to realise, isn't it? One can say it and acquire the knowledge about it from somebody else, but to have the experience for yourself is to know that whatever is looking out, the light of consciousness, that pure light which is invisible, is actually creating the universe through you. And whatever you are looking at is doing the same thing looking out at you.

This is all very subtle and difficult to realise. Even with very brilliant philosophers, you ask where it all comes from and they say "imagination", but do they do any research on imagination? I have been to these philosophers and asked what they meant by the word and what research they have done on the imagination. It is just putting a label on something without understanding what it is.

325

Yoga is the science of direct perception because it validates its knowledge in a totally different way than normal human beings do. To perceive a thing directly means to see through it, to see it just as it is, to penetrate and get inside it as if it were transparent. If you can see everything as it is and let it be, then it does not trouble you anymore, there is no worrying about how someone or something ought to be. The science of direct perception is what the ancient yogis studied; transcendental logic is needed to understand it, because it has the power to resolve opposites, the power to resolve all paradoxes. It has the power to become the master of all the worlds within and for one who is such a master, anything he wants will come true, because he does not want anything more than the universe wants for everybody and anybody. A master's will is so attuned to the universal will that he does not really need to do anything; everything is working out beautifully. People are getting the kicks up the backside they need, he does not have to really kick them unless he loves them. Whom the Lord loveth most, he chastises most. The master of himself does not have to tell anyone where to get off, because he knows all will get what pure consciousness is manifesting for them in God's good time. The plan is perfect even though it may seem painful and unfair to our human concepts; it may even seem an unnecessarily exaggerated drama to some of us. But if we meditate deeply on these concepts we will find that we just don't know the uselessness of our conceptual mind to understand this plan. To know this ignorance is to know what we do not know. This is the beginning of the real spiritual life; we are brought by this to the foot of the mountain. It is the Blue level through which we see the awesomeness of the mountain.

The climbing must be done and the peak reached through developing the next two levels of perception - the intuition (Indigo) and the imagination (Violet).

To give up the mind as the knower is a great load off your back which you cannot carry up the mountain. We must not underestimate the power of the separate self-sense – the ego, to hang onto its baggage! For those in this Blue level of consciousness, devotion and trust in the mind tapes of karma will only bring pain. Devotion and trust in the evolutionary ONE in you will bring release and joy.

BLUE

The keyword of the Blue colour is "fixer of time" just as the Green functions as the "measurer of time".

Blue is the "feeling" reality of nostalgic memories, stabilised emotions and the fixed firmly grasped idea or concept. Traditionally Blue is the colour of the conservative, hind-sighted, "looking back" and historically-feeling personality who lives in a time world of inner feelings which can only give satisfaction when they are savoured, memorised, stored, fixed in suitable concepts, metaphors, words, traditions, etc. Whatever ideas, either of reality or about immediate experience are presented to consciousness, the "I" of the personalities favouring Blue will experience a drive for satisfaction which will be seriously disturbed if they have no historical reference to such previous experiences or to historical authority. Hence Blue is the colour of the contemplative who will reflect on the great ideas, ideals, and accepted images of reality or deal with them introspectively.

Even nations have their predominant color levels and it would be an interesting exercise to figure out a United Nations spectrum. England, for example, has for hundreds of years been a typical example of a Blue level country whose conservative, traditional and historically aware people felt that what served their fathers well would be right for them. So we have a situation today where England is suffering among other things for her antiquated rolling stock, machinery and methods of manufacture, which have put her way behind other more aggressive and progressive nations. This is, of course, an over-simplification for the sake of clear illustration; the Yellow forces of change and Red revolution have long been seething in Britain as elsewhere, but the deep tide of feeling in that country is still the love of old established and venerated institutions, standards, ethics and modes of living.

> The colour is related to peace and satisfaction because it has a constrictive effect on the muscle and nerve fibre and therefore is not active like the physical excitement of the Red. It not only slows down the metabolic processes of biological time but soothes the extraneous noise in the nervous system and constricts the capillary flow of the small blood vessels.

Physiologically this is borne out by noting what happens to the body when the blood flow is constricted or slows down. Our fingers get "blue with cold" in frosty weather, "blue babies" are born when lack of red oxygen restricts the flow of blood, and if you have ever given artificial respiration to a near-drowned body, you will know that the first signs of returning life are when the blueness changes to a redder, warmer glow. From another angle, we can experience the effect of blue surroundings or blue light on the body and nervous system. Over-stimulated people are soothed in a pale blue room and we have all flaked out on the grass at times,absorbing the green life force of earth, and regained our calm by gazing into the blue depths of the sky above. On the other hand too much blue can produce a state of depressed immobility, the state of inertia which partially accounted for Hamlet's lethargy and inability to act.

> It is related to relaxed " feeling " as opposed to intensity of " Sensation ", because feelings are the motions of inner energies (E-motion) whereas sensations are merely extended stimulation of the touch faculty. Feelings have to be " time-bound ", tied down into a framework of past experience. This " time binding " does not apply to a sensation-type but certainly applies to the search for Truth, whether it is sought in religion or science. The reason why so many religious people and scientific people are to be found predominating in this band of consciousness is because the drive for satisfaction in " feeling " is rooted in defining and grasping one's reality in some authoritative framework; one looks to the past scriptures as historical authorities or one leans heavily on scientific authorities. The need to grasp something which does not disturb leads to idealism, the formation of concepts, and the validating of them by obtaining a general consensus of educated opinion. The Blue person is generally inner-centric and quite uncomfortable when faced with new, novel and strange facts which have not been accepted by existing authority nor incorporated in the modern dictionary. One could not really say of this type " If it isn't in the dictionary it does not exist " for such an extreme attitude would not be fair to the idealist; but this would be his "feeling" for new words.

> But an idealist has the basic drive of someone orientated to imprisoning reality in fixed concepts. In the eyes of the Blue personality this is the condition devoutly to be wished, when all of reality had been systematically defined and put into its proper place in the time-line of events leading up from the past

to the present. The colour Blue is preferred by passive people, who wish to be left in peace, who do not wish to get into arguments, who are tolerant of others who, while thinking differently, also prefer peace, but who will rise as one body to defend the world against the Red revolutionary active disturbers of the peace.

When my mother died my 85 year-old father not only had his tremendous grief and sense of loss and loneliness to contend with, but also the horrendous prospect of moving from his home where they had lived happily and peacefully for nearly 40 years. "You know, Norah," he said, "my problem is that I *hate* to change -- always have." And I looked back over his long life and saw hundreds of examples of this unwillingness to accept anything which might topple his well-established and tested beliefs and way of life. His biography, if it is ever written, would be a perfect illustration of a Blue level life lived very consistently in keeping with his accepted ideals of service to others and the need for an accepted, authoritative code of ethics and religion which, for him, was Christ's Sermon on the Mount. Even though he would listen patiently to my expounding on the universality of the highest wisdom throughout the other great religions, he never studied them and simply returned to his regular reading of the familiar New Testament. Only when his beloved traditional England or his cherished belief in the Christian teachings were threatened did his Scorpio anger rise, so that he devoted himself wholeheartedly to service and to a fruitless struggle to preserve Church worship in its established form, in the face of growing apathy and even open rebellion by church members and priests.

A good example of the feeling type who inhabits the Blue layer of consciousness is the statement by Patrick Henry an American statesman and great orator who said," I have but one lamp by which my feet are guided, and that lamp is the lamp of experience. I know of no way of judging the future but by the past ".

Fortunately there are people who live in other layers of consciousness who know that nature is not bound by precedent, and that human wisdom of this kind, defeats evolution before it begins. Such thinking assumes that man learns by past mistakes, that history and its effect on the now, determines the future. Nothing could be further from the truth.

Because this type wishes to settle experience in a fixed time framework, his mind develops a drive for authoritative limitation of all that is infinite, absolute, endless and timeless. Hence mind is the stumbling block to realisation of human potential and spiritual unfoldment.

As a Blue level woman I see myself mirrored in every line of this section. Every time I have a realisation it has to be crystalised and confirmed by some reinforcing quotation from a great authority like Christ or Buddha or Shakespeare. And as for the mind, I look back over the years, in true Blue level reminiscing style, and can see that I have always "minded" a lot. For example, my firmly held concept of marriage has taken some batterings and my mind has struggled with the conflict between a persistent clinging to the terms of the marriage ceremony contract and the need to expand into a new understanding of the meaning of marriage and of all human relationships. "To have and to hold..... to cleave unto him/her and to no other" etc., etc.; these are the clear and limiting concepts that I have clung to. Then in the evolving group situation came the birth of an idea of group marriage and even other intimate relationships within the group. This was a shock and bitterly resisted, until, after long self-torture, there came a realisation that the rigidity of the concept can destroy the longed-for result and paralyse the natural flow of consciousness. So there comes a point in the life of a Blue level man or woman when either a leap in consciousness has to be made to another level or the highest expression of the Blue level in pure devotion has to be sustained and glorified.

As a footnote for others on the Blue level who may encounter similar situations, let me assure them that having made the change in the Blue level as the result of the group's confrontations, the rewards are infinite. Not only is the love flowing all around me from my own more open heart, but all the old fears of change and loss have disappeared. During the period of self-confrontation I made regular use of the wonderful book of wisdom, the I Ching. I see now that the whole dynamic of the I Ching is the acceptance of change in tune with the idea of duration through the cyclic flow of Nature itself. Deep study and practice with the I Ching can be tremendously valuable for all of us who are stuck on the Blue level of consciousness.*

---

*See Section on the I Ching and Time and the Levels of Consciousness at the back of this book.

INTERVIEW with N.,
a sixty year-old housewife.

Editor: What turns you on the most?

N: A feeling of certainty and joy when I sense omnipresence, when I *know* that God is working through everything; usually the feeling comes when I am in the presence of Nature, in the woods or by the ocean or even driving in a car through grand rolling countryside. I also get it when I watch little birds pecking at the food on the bird table near the kitchen window and the words that made such a big impression on me as a child: "Not a sparrow falls to the ground without your Father knowing it" become so real that I want to laugh with joy at the certainty it brings.

Ed: What depresses you most?

N: Uncertainty and fear that I may lose my centre and get disturbed by what other people do and say.

Ed: What are you seeking and wanting now in life? What are your goals?

N: My goal right now is to discover my true self, my real potential and how best to use it to achieve a stable emotional life.

Ed: How do you approach tasks?

N: I mull them over in my mind until a plan or picture emerges. This often takes quite a long time, and I walk around for days with the project in my mind waiting for everything to fall into place so that I can get started with confidence.

Ed: How important to you is tradition, past memories, nostalgia, etc.?

N: These things have been very important in my life until comparatively recently. Possibly I have let a lot of this backward looking go since my parents died. However I still refer to the Bible and great literature for quotations to support what I am trying to express about the present.

Ed: What is your usual motive for doing things?

N: Usually my motive is just to get things done. I hate disorder and confusion, so I always have an urge to get things straight and settled.

Ed: What do you like and admire most in others?

N: I like honesty above all. I cannot stand phoney people

Ed: because I do not know where I am with them; they say one thing one minute and another the next and I distrust them.

Ed: What is your attitude to money and possessions?

N: I like to have some money in reserve. I am not attached to possessions, although I like to have enough and would prefer my surroundings to be aesthetically pleasing. If they are not it doesn't worry me too much. Other things like love, warmth and companionship are much more important. I'd put up with a hut and two cooking pots in order to have these things along with peace of mind.

Ed: How do you respond to disapproval and criticism?

N: I feel hurt and deflated; then I process it and try to use it for growth. But I have to make very sure I buy it first!

This interview reveals a very obvious Blue level person. Note that the underlying theme is the need for certainty, confirmation and peace. She will put up with any primitive living conditions so long as she is certain of the satisfaction of loving and caring for her companion. Notice also that although she says she no longer refers back to the past so much, she attaches a lot of value to authoritative expressions of truth (see quote from the Bible and reference to use of quotations in general). She is slow in getting into action and is slow to respond with words, having to process and internalise everything to be sure of her ground first. The reference to her liking of honesty in others also links up with the need for certainty.

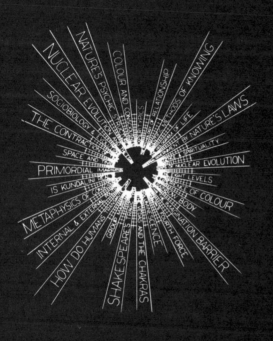

THE INTUITIVE LEVEL
OF
FUTURE CONSCIOUSNESS

*The following is a summary of
a taped talk by Christopher Hills
given at University of the Trees in
Spring, 1977.*

THE INDIGO LEVEL   AJNA CHAKRA

A tape giving the full talk by
the author is available from the
publishers. (See back of book.)

The Ajna chakra, which governs the Indigo level of consciousness, operates from a centre behind the forehead and, together
with the Sahasrara chakra, uses that part of the brain in the
frontal lobes which developed later than the area which governs
the senses. If this part of the brain were removed we could still
function, although we would not be able to deal in abstractions
nor would our intuition be available to us. So the Indigo centre
belongs to that 90% of the brain which man has not yet developed, although there are certain people who live at this level of
consciousness and all of us experience it working for us from time
to time. When someone walks into a room we know by their
vibration whether we like them or not and it is then that our
intuitive faculty is working. 90% of our knowing about people
is at this level and this is what makes all the difference between,
on the one hand, knowing *about* someone, their life history, the
books they've written, or even seeing them on T.V. and, on the
other, actually meeting them and looking them in the eyes. In
all human communication this abstract way of knowing operates.
It is linked with the water diviner's faculty; ask a diviner how he
does it and he will tell you that he does not know. It is a very
loose kind of knowing that is not structured in any way.

Imagine now what it would be like to live entirely in our intuitive centre. You are standing on top of a hill with a beautiful scene stretched out before you. Temporarily you forget your body and are lifted out of yourself. Maybe you are all alone and wish that someone was there to share with you this feeling of being very close to Nature and of being in a dream or trance-like state. Now go back in your imagination to the idyllic life in the Garden of Eden, where all the fruits of the earth were to be enjoyed, except those from the Tree of Knowledge. Adam and Eve were told that if they ate of this tree they would surely die. However, when the serpent told Eve that they would not die but would have full knowledge they decided to eat and so became aware of the opposites of life. Up to that point they had lived intuitively, in touch with God, experiencing things psychically and living in the same dream-like state that you were in on the imaginary hill-top.

People who live in this centre experience a different time world from the other centres and they do not like things too clearly defined. They like words to mean exactly what they themselves intend them to mean, very much like the dream state of "Alice in Wonderland". So the beginning might come after the end or you might dream of the future as Joseph did when he foresaw the famine in Egypt. Many people, if they wrote down their dreams, might know their future since dreams tap into the unconscious.

Just as images come and go and drift through our consciousness in dreams, in the same loose way they come into the mind of the intuitive or the psychic. For example, someone may see the image of a snowy mountain. To one psychic this will convey a visit to the northern climes, to another a name of a person. It is the interpretation of the image that decides whether the psychic is a good one or not. Any of us can close our eyes and remove our intellect and all the ideas in our mind, and we shall see images, faces and so on. By concentrating on this centre and by sending energy to it we can develop this centre so that not only do we see images but we have "hunches" and know things that are going to happen ahead of time. Many people experience periodic hunches about who is going to telephone them or write to them, but unless we consciously work on developing this Indigo centre we cannot rely on our intuition to give us anything but spasmodic hints. We also have to take into account that what comes into our mind may be either telepathy or clairvoyance. If someone else on the planet knows the answer, then you can tune into it. That is telepathy. If no one knows it, then you have to use clairvoyance; in other words you cannot go through the mind of another. The method is to relax and to put your mind out of the way and then to see what floats in. Whatever floats in first, take that. If you start to think about it and fail to take the first impression, then you will fail. The second hint is always wrong.

So how does this Ajna centre relate to the world? It uses direct perception (clairvoyance) and mind-to-mind contact (telepathy), but how does such a person relate to other persons? Having no past and living mainly in the future, the Indigo intuitive has no memories and is usually very optimistic and full of expectations. When you talk to such a person, he or she never really seems to be with you; it is as though they were always chasing their hat down the street. Always the fields beyond are greener and to them the present is already yesterday. They live in an abstract dream with little relationship to their body. When they have an appointment they leave at the time they should be there because in their mind they are already there; they just forgot to take their body along! There is never time for the physical world to catch up with what is in the dream world. This is a rather undisciplined state of consciousness, rather vague and woolly and often what these people say and do has very little definition.

Now to say some good things about the Indigo level; they are very good at abstract thinking. They may move around as though they were drifting without legs, but they are able to handle abstract thoughts very well and they can see through a very complex system very quickly by a series of hunches. If you find that you are one of the people who have these hunches, you should develop this faculty. If you can combine it with the Yellow intellectual level and switch from one to the other at will, you will find this a useful and effective way of both understanding and communicating. To develop this faculty means that the frontal part of our brain is able to have a kind of understanding that is not logical, but it goes directly and sees through things. This was the faculty that man used in his early state of grace when he communicated directly with the cosmos. But he fell from grace and allowed the faculty to diminish when he became more reliant on his senses.

He no longer heard voices or saw images, and all we have now is a vestigial remnant that needs to be re-awakened by practice and by developing the dream-like state which is not to be despised and killed off. We need to use it every day and to become sensitive to its promptings when, for example, we are buying food or making other decisions in our lives. This is the faculty that we use in Supersensonics and also the one used by birds and animals. The prophets of old used this centre and the horn on the forehead of paintings and sculptures of Moses is symbolic of the developed Ajna centre. Similarly the satyrs were portrayed with horns representing their ability to tune into the physical world and to discover the best food· and drink and other delectable things.

If we develop and follow this Ajna centre it can guide us in all the situations in life. Use it every day to discover what will give you pain or fulfillment, who you should be with and who will bring you a load of karma. Right at this moment any one of us can project our situation into the future and know whether it is good for us or not. By opening ourselves up we tune ourselves in, not by a tubular kind of consciousness or by beaming in on anything, but by dissolving everything and just letting whatever free association comes and this enables us to wrap our mind around something. We need to develop this faculty so that we can switch it on at will and use it every day. It is especially valuable in the field of relationships and you can use it to tell right at the beginning how things are going to go. Usually you get three intimations as to what you should do. So watch for those three little intimations or flashes. You might, for example, get the hint: "This person is not going to be good for me." Take this hint and look into it and you will get a real insight into the relationship. Otherwise you may have a karmic problem in getting out of the relationship later. The most important point is to make certain that the flash is coming from a true source and not from your own wishful thinking or expectations. Make sure of this and you will have an invaluable tool in your intuitive faculty.

In closing a point may be made here concerning psychic phenomena and the intuitional level of consciousness. Over the years I have made a point of staying away from anything sensational. While there are now several hundred psychic metal benders and psychedelic explosions and flying saucers and space migrations, which are all seen by different people as catalysts for man's evolution, I have always felt these developments were not important to man for one simple reason. They are all extensions of phenomena and external to the quality of man's own consciousness. They require no fundamental change in the personal inner structure or skill in communication here on this planet. In short it is only a question of whether you believe these psychic wonders or not, and therefore no more important than religious belief in resurrections or any other belief systems. What Nuclear Evolution attempts is to get beyond belief and to give the evolutionary tools to mankind by which we can transform our consciousness entirely, so that external phenomena such as UFO's and sensational space science fiction migrations are understood for what they are, just escapes from the predicament of this planet. These sensational solutions require little work on our attitudes to ego, love, deeper communication with the planet's own intricate vehicles of expression. Their very fascination is a trap because we can become addicted to their excitement and sensation so greatly as to be utterly blinded to the real message of evolution. That message is loud and clear. It is this: All the worlds exist inside you. All goals, experiences, space vehicles, science and religions are created by consciousness. When the consciousness is truly expanded into intuitive contact with all there is without limitation - phenomena - whether physical, spiritual or mental, become part of ourself.

Therefore, excitement and sensation over psychic phenomena is no different from excitement over material phenomena. We must look within for its cause and for that part of ourself which motivates and makes it important. It could be our own ignorance of these realms which creates the excitement in the imagination. Yet nothing more is being said about reality or space or the human situation in all this phenomena than you can find in Alice In Wonderland. In fact, in the imagination of "Alice's" author there are far more insights into human nature than we have had from twenty years of contacts and visits from men in flying saucers or from men who claim to have communicated with them.

The fact is that it is easy to communicate with any entities which exist anywhere in the universe. Through the science of "Supersensonics" one can talk as easily with a flower as with a space intelligence. What is not easy is to get inside its inner world and to ask intelligent questions about its reality. The only important thing is GOD, and God and consciousness are ONE. Therefore the author feels "belief" in God is not enough to transform a person, only realisation of God is of any importance. Realisation of the nature of consciousness is then the only real way to God and all other ways create a duality and illusion which require "belief".

It is man's beliefs which have led him astray from one bigoted God to another. By making God into consciousness we are immediately transforming the quality of the very instrument which can know God. If God and consciousness are ONE then all other separate Gods make sense in their differences and all their statements become crystal clear. One does not need to "believe" in one's consciousness, it is just the "I" which makes all statements about anything.

INDIGO

The personality which resonates to Indigo has a basic drive to touch the Universe or his environment at a distance and out of time. To TELE-PATH means to sense at a distance just as TELE-SCOPE means to see at a distance.

The person who is free of the timebinding functions of the mind (Blue), or who may have never been interested in the discipline of words, concepts and ideals or conformed to the discipline of the thinking and logical operations of the yellow sequential type of person, may be an intuitional type. The intuition is that function which interprets the present in a future time dimension. The domain of consciousness in which such a person lives cannot be understood by any of the people experiencing other dimensions of time.

The experiential inner-world of the intuition band of consciousness is a faith in the future which is perceived first and then related backwards into the more ephemeral (to them) present. To the intuitive nothing is significant unless it has a relation to that which is not yet manifested, since everything which is now is rapidly changing into what happens in five minutes from now, or five days from now.

As we move through the color levels, it becomes interesting to note what happens to our vision of time. The closer we are to our senses, for example, the more time seems to flow forward. The closer we are to our imagination, the more time seems to flow backwards. When we view our present with our senses (Red), we get a vision of the immediate now, like a mouse eyeing a piece of cheese. When we view the present with our intellect (Yellow), we get a vision of logic, like a millipede's legs all stepping in sequential order. When we view the present with our feelings (Blue), we get a vision of history, like rings on a tree. When we view reality with our intuition (Indigo), we get a vision of the future, like an eagle high above

339

the plain, looking down. From that vantage point the intuitive sees far ahead, as if he himself is motionless and the world of his vision revolves slowly towards him. Since his focal point is not directed to what is near but rather to what is far, then it follows that what is real to him is what he sees in the beyond, and not what has occurred in front of him.

> The discontinuity which is experienced may be a failure to integrate the past into the present moment, but it may also be the knowledge that nothing really is as it looks, and nothing ever turns out as we expect it to excepting to the intuitive who learns to trust his pre-cognition. His reality is always lived in the greener fields which are further away and the present pales by comparison with the future possibilities.

> The real world of such an individual is the intuitions that are in his soul and heart about life as it ought to be, not as it is. Hence excitement and intensity are not found in heaven now but in the world to come. Life is spent in the beyond chasing a continually receding future. They move between this and the band of the imagination (Violet) in flights of fancy to true visions which often do come to pass. Because they find it difficult to discipline these imaginations they receive criticism from imaginative people who do. Because they cannot bind the present to any fixed concepts, or lock it up in any words or *istorical relationships they receive criticism from the " feeling " types (Blue), and because they do not think in sequential, logical ways they receive criticism from the thinking type (Yellow). To all these other types the intuitive Indigo band person, who does not identify reality with the senses (hearing, tasting, smelling, touching, seeing, etc.) but moves in an extra-sensory domain, would appear impractical, unreal and divorced from concreteness.

The intuitive knows that there is a better life coming. That fact does not help him much in the life that has already arrived if he is unable or unwilling to stick around and enjoy it. His reality is usually already far down the road, for he is living either in his vision of the future or in his imagination.

To others, the intuitive lives in an apparently dream-like state. In a classroom he is the type who gets the right answers but can't show how he did it. This is particularly infuriating to an intellectual type who requires some logical proof to complete the picture of reality. In religious situations an intuitive would be more concerned with direct mystical contact and less with the ceremony and words of the conceptual types. If we compare the sensation type to someone functioning on the Indigo level, then we see that the one identifies almost wholly with his senses and the other hardly at all! If the intuitive fellow says that he hears voices then he is probably telepathic or clairaudient by nature. This will confound the Red level individual whose only way of hearing is through the ears. Thus, we can see the difficulty that sometimes arises when different levels try to communicate.

However, there is a reality which is as practical and realistic in its own framework of anticipation and foresight, which can equal any of the other types in their own special perceptions of hindsight, logical process, sensation, etc.

The fact is, the reality of the intuitive, although seemingly impractical, can be as potent a force as any other level of reality. Intuitive insight can cut through mountains of complications in a flash that would require the intellectual person incredible effort and time. For example, the German chemist Friedrich Kekule had been working on the molecular structure of benzene. He simply couldn't get it. One night in a dream he saw a snake with its tail in its mouth. He awoke and realized that benzene was a hydrocarbon ring. This intuitive discovery saved him days and weeks, perhaps many years, of intellectual analysis and added greatly to the present knowledge of chemistry. Einstein himself said that he did not arrive at his discoveries by ordinary logical means. The theory came later and proof much later. In fact, it is the intuitive thinking faculty which governs our ability to perceive abstractly, which allows us to think in symbols at all. This contrasts sharply with the Blue conceptual thinker whose reality is tied to definitions and accepted authorities. It is this dreamlike realm of the psyche which allows us to do the highly practical work of supersensitive communication that will become the next area of discovery for evolutionary man beyond his limited conceptual mind.

In the East there is a greater understanding of those who develop their intuitions and relate to the world through spiritual rather than religious and doctrinal persuasions. What is to happen in future life is more real than what is happening in the present life; it follows that the intuitive is constantly waiting for the present to catch up with the already experienced future.

We could find many examples of this. For example, whenever we use pendulums to discover if such and such a person will be good for us or what will cure us, we are using the intuitive faculty. When we want to know if we should take a certain action, we ask the I Ching; this is also the intuitive faculty. In the West this way of approaching reality is just beginning to gain acceptance, whereas in the East, astrology and the spiritual sciences have long been held in high regard. In this realm the emphasis is on the future life. Should I marry this person? Should I go to this school? The answers to all questions about our future come from our intuition about the future, even if they tell us to do something now.

Biological time in which the sensation-type lives, which the thinking-type looks at as process in the time flow of ordinary events, and which the feeling-type experiences as memories of past happenings, cannot be accelerated by the intuitive-type by speeding up his own inner rhythms, and impatience is often manifested with the slow march of time. In the drive 7 (Imagination) it is possible to distort biological time into timelessness so that it appears to fly swiftly by, but the intuitive has difficulty in adjusting in returning to the present and waiting for chronological time to catch up with his perceptions.

This impatience experienced by the intuitive is due to the fact that he thinks he has already done things that he really has not done. In other words, in his head he's already out through the door, gone to the store and returned with a bag of groceries. Yet in reality he's still in his house with a barren cupboard! This condition causes him no end of irritation. He is used to drifting along without much planning; living by his hunches he can muddle through. Extreme cases of the Indigo level like to meditate or dream all day long and therefore the call to action is often a signal for the extreme intuitive to beat a hasty retreat.

With some yellow added as a check against lack of planning, the intuitive becomes our sage who takes the long view.

Difficulties in communication between one level and another arise if one person sees his reality as being in the future and another sensation-type regards the real concrete present as the only basis for dialogue.

Timelessness, as found in drive 7 in the violet band, is a different time domain to the intuitive whose reality never catches up with his time world. The intuitive-type constantly moves backwards towards the present and ordinary time cannot move fast enough to get where he is at. Whereas the Imaginative type, interested in ordered patterns, creates his own absolute time-world depending on the circumstances, the intuitive personality does not experience an awareness of time as an instrument. The person in the Indigo band has difficulty in respecting time enough to be punctual or to make a schedule that is in any way reliable. Therefore he is impatient with such details and fails to master the skill needed for the manifestation of his visions.

INTERVIEW with H.,
a twenty-four year-old architecture student.

Ed.: What turns you on the most?

H.: When I'm inspired by beauty and the magic of how things work together. It could be a person, stars, trees. It's a feeling of being one with everything - seeing harmony.

Ed.: What depresses you the most?

H.: Feeling I can't have the beauty - feeling separate from it, especially a beautiful female.

Ed.: What are you seeking and wanting in life right now? What are your goals?

H.: First I'm seeking a soul-mate. I am also trying to consolidate my spiritual growth and progress it through the understanding of color and the different levels of consciousness. I'm trying to break through to a space of real unity-seeing everything new. I have been in that space sometimes but never for very long.

Ed.: How do you approach tasks? Do you plan or jump right in?

H.: I imagine it first - I live in it, get high on it. When it comes to manifesting it there's always a hundred times more work than I had anticipated and I get discouraged by the gap. This applies particularly just now to the book I'm writing.

Ed.: How important to you are tradition, past memories, nostalgia, etc?

H.: Not too important with me. I haven't followed any tradition; I've always been rebellious - even at an early age I was very questioning. I've been very sceptical of all the spiritual trips, Jewish included (H. is Jewish). Perhaps I have been too sceptical. I do sometimes dwell on sweet past memories.

Ed.: What is your usual motive for doing things?

H.: Ego food. I'm looking for something to puff my image up!

Ed.: What do you like most in others?

H.: Wisdom and a sense of wonder.

Ed.: What is your attitude to money and possessions?

H.: I'm pretty material. When I have enough I can be quite generous and give it away easily.

Ed.: How do you respond to disapproval and criticism?

H.: Depends who it is from. I can take it from Christopher (his teacher) but it's a different thing if it comes from my mother. It's proportional to the respect I have for the person.

Ed.: Do you ever feel misunderstood?

H.: Oh yes. My father and a lot of old friends just don't understand what I am doing, so I always keep it secret. When I went to Europe I was seeking a spiritual teacher, but I didn't tell them that.

This is someone in the Indigo/Violet level of consciousness, who yearns to realise consistently the unity of all life that he experiences in flashes. His problem is that having imaged (Violet) and intuited (Indigo) a desired-for state, he often feels that it is an accomplished fact; he then discovers that to bring it into actual manifestation involves a lot of hard work. The negative aspect of the Violet is to feel misunderstood and to yearn for a deep human relationship which does not materialise, because the personality is still ego-centred. In his answers to the later questions we see a Yellow level aloofness and superiority that refuses to take criticism except from those he considers qualified to give it to him.

THE IMAGINATIVE LEVEL
OF
COSMIC CONSCIOUSNESS

*The following is a transcription
of one of a series of lectures on
the Human Chakra System given
by Christopher Hills in 1974.*

THE VIOLET LEVEL   SAHASRARA CHAKRA

The violet vibration or the frequency of violet is the highest frequency in the visible spectrum and also the highest resonant frequency in the chakras; it is what we call Imagination and it influences not only the cell life of the body, the thoughts we think, the intuitions we have, the desires that lurk deep inside us and the sensations we have, but also the social life we live and exist in around us and how we limit ourself and limit others.

The capacity of the imagination holds all those faculties within it, since these are not independent in a sense; although these levels function separately they also function interdependently and they are interpenetrating each other. The main function or quality of this chakra of imagination is the sense of wonder. Christ referred to it when speaking of children. As an adult this sense of imagining often dies out and adults squelch that sense in children after a time so the child no longer thinks of climbing Mount Everest or changing the world or doing heroic acts. Somewhere the hero dies and we are then turning off a certain image of ourselves. If we examine this quality we might see what Christ meant when he said of the children, "Theirs is the kingdom of heaven," meaning not that they are in heaven but that they have the quality required for bringing heaven down here on earth and living it between the two ears with the sense of wonder.

We can get into this state of wonder where time can be stretched out or shortened depending on what we want to do, just like dreaming. To wonder is another way of saying to have a sense of awe. We don't really know anything fixed or well enough to say what it really is at that young age, so we are continually open to new experiences, we have not made up our minds about anything so we are open to what anybody says to us and there is an open feeling that anything may happen and so we are spontaneous because we get in tune with that unfolding universe that we are discovering everyday. If we can get into that state when we are grownups, then the hero comes back, the one who thinks, "Maybe I do have a chance to change the world, in spite of its negativity."

So the faculty to wonder and the study of different kinds of wonder is an interesting kind of meditation. The whole duty of man becomes to stand in awe of Cosmic Intelligence or God, and to walk in its ways.

We have all experienced this state of consciousness, for example when we were first born, or when the limits are off consciousness. When the self-limits are off where does it evolve to, how great can it be, and what are its powers when the stages of evolution are taken way up to the nth degree to the One who is guiding us there? It does not matter which way you go to this limitless state which exists, of course, prior to bodies or to animal man suddenly waking up to the awareness that his own being is reflected in everything he is doing. This was an enormous leap in self-awareness from primitive man.

Now the next leap for man is just as enormous and awesome so that when we wake up to it, to the state of unlimited consciousness, then we enter into a state of love and a kind of love that is not emotional, but more imaginative and not on the level of the mind. It is beyond the imagination in the sense that we cannot even imagine what kind of love created consciousness itself or what kind of love has bound all the stars into atoms blazing away in space, or what kind of love makes our body hang together instead of going in every direction at once. This is an awesome sort of love, when you are in love in that way, in your imagination–in love with everything great and small, the tiniest atom, the candle flame, with human beings as with stars or sunlight. To be in that state of love is really beyond the imagination because it is so wonder-ful.

It is wonderful to be full of wonder. Our thoughts coming alive, happening on the outside just as they are happening on the inside. What you put into this chakra is going to happen sometime in the future. Whatever you are putting there now is like programming a computer, the answer is somehow going to come out in the physical body the way you put it in your imagination, so if there is wrong information you are going to get a wrong answer. If you put wrong images into the cosmic computer your future is going to be twisted and you are not going to see right pictures later on; it is just as if you are making a movie but it is on a grand scale. You are the director and producer choosing what your movie is about, what your life is about. Choosing good scenes you say, "Let's do that one again." As the producer you have to buy the film after it is made and pay for it too; you are paying for it in consciousness. Your life situation is the currency with which you buy that movie. You spend your consciousness just like you spend money everyday, you spend it on worthless things or nice things or to work on yourself or not to work on yourself. Now the producer always pays the bill, which may come in the next incarnation; you can go on credit a long time in the cosmos, there is endless credit, endless time. But if you look on it like this, as if we have the whole of eternity to get enlightened, you are paying all the time for it. Every instant that you are not enlightened you are in some kind of a suffering and that is what you are paying with. If you put your consciousness into the wrong movie you get karma. Sometimes people get instant karma, which is very good because you get the pain right away, but you cannot always tell what the cost is or when you are going to get the pain by doing a certain thing. The pain may come later in your body somewhere. Wrong imagining produces pains of all kinds through body tensions. They get screwed up into negative energies somewhere. The brain is a whirl of energies and they all manifest in the body. If your consciousness is not imagining right then you are going to be either hung up in your energies or experience indolence or not be able to find the right channel of expression in life.

When you can get to the point that you see the whole movie and are in tune with it then you can make things happen with the snap of a finger with your powers of imagination.

Many times our problems disappear when we are prepared to clear out our imaginations and do the dirty work on ourselves; when we surrender to the situation something clicks in the cosmos and we don't have to go through the pain and all things fall into place. People come, energies change, but not unless you are prepared to work on your self image in the area that is difficult for you. Problems are relative to the individual; some are easy for one and very difficult for another.

When one starts praying or seeking for a need with one's imagination and it is in tune with the need of the universe, then it is delivered automatically because you are then in tune with the cosmic will and you don't really need any effort or energy when you have the whole universe behind you. When the universe is working with you, you don't need to do anything or imagine anything that the universe does not want done. Now many of the trips we go on are private trips . . . projects; it can be an uphill battle trying to get our own things off the ground and if it is going to be an effort like that, if it is not flowing, not effortless effort, then it probably means that you don't need it or if you do need it you only need it for some growth inside yourself; in other words, there is an area there that has to be worked on in your imagination, so the cosmos presents us with a situation and we make a movie of it. If we don't like the movie we make it different and every time we try to make it different we find the same problem because the real problem is not out there in front of the camera, it is in the camera lens and in the one who is pointing the camera, the maker of the film. It is in the producer, director and audience who is going to watch the film, which is you imagining yourself experiencing life.

Somewhere there is one who has to judge your own experience of the film. Real life is identical to this analogy. You are the one who is making the movie in your imagination and you are the one who is going to laugh at it, but you will only be laughing at yourself. Basically all the judgments we make of others are hangups in ourselves. If we are judging someone for not getting into action, but without realising the other person may be in a state of depression incapable of action, then eventually we are going to be in that same situation in our own imagination, so we have to learn not to be that judgmental.

We have to learn to work step by step and not to trip out on the prospect of a tremendous imaginary goal without doing the necessary steps to get there. You have to go with the powers of consciousness you now have and work from there.

With true meditation we can get into the centre of our imagination so we can see how it is unfolding. What we have to do is become master of our future by getting into it. In a sense we are already living in the future, working on the present and thereby remaking the past, because the past is only what your imagination is looking at from the present. All history is only the reflecting back, it is made as you go in your imaginations. History changes depending on how much hindsight we have, and hindsighted people have a lot, but foresight they have very little of. If one could see in one's imagination what was going to happen in the future, one would probably not be doing what one is doing in the present.

So how to get out into the future and imagine how it is going to be, or what seeds to plant in the imagination. Supposing you want to change humanity. You have to be way out in the future to understand what man will be doing then, so that you can put the right things in his imagination now so that by the time he catches up with that vision, it is already happening. What you put in the imagination of man now might be something he laughs at because it is so far removed from what he may be experiencing now, but this is the problem that all world-changers face. What is a world-transforming image?

Imagination is the creative power itself, everything in the universe somehow has an image of itself. Everything that we can visualise in our minds as being part of the creation, whatever kind of energy it is, has to have a form, it cannot exist without form, so there is an interplay between content and form. Now form by itself is absolutely useless without content, because a form without energy in it is useless. It does not matter how many pictures you put on the movie screen; unless you have the power to put consciousness in it so that it comes alive, it won't manifest. All that will manifest will be yards and yards of random film that nobody looks at; which is what people do mainly with their lives, spending years making all kinds of tapes or inner thoughts which they play over and over. Every time they fall in love they play the same tapes. They cannot understand that they have these same tapes playing, they cannot see the pattern that their imagination has led them into. It is the same experience because they did not learn from the last experience or situation and thus arises the whole idea in the mind that history repeats itself, and therefore has some value as a teacher. But at this chakra level, history does not repeat itself, it only cycles back the same pattern because you did not take any notice of it the last time it came.

Backward-looking historical experience manifests only because of our own ignorance. We do not have the foresight to see into the process of the future to see what will manifest. So it is our own ignorance which will produce the historical mess. It is inevitable unless both of two factors are put into the image we create the past and future with. First, there must be some divine inspiration that can rule on matters where human reason will not solve the problem. Second, we had better check up on whatever situation we are confronted with now or our habits of thought will manifest the same problems.

I am using the social situation of the world as an example of the way we make a mess of our little political energy battle that is going on inside us. Spiritual inner politics are going on inside us all of the time. The outside is just a social reflection of what is going on in the inside. We beget a government because of the quality that we are. Our own ignorance is programmed into the political system. If we had a better system to offer we would be doing it, either in our own lives or in building communities that can be an example of the new system or in putting the new system across in such a way that people will be governing themselves.

You must be able to impregnate your images into society or tell your friends or someone in such a way that they of their own free will can respond, so that they are not being politically enslaved. People must be free to be themselves. How do you get people to remake society and keep everybody's free will at the same time? They have their own ideas about how they should be governed. But do you find communists, socialists and radical revolutionaries putting their images into society in such a way that people of their own free will can respond? No, they coerce them! Parents do this with children trying to remake them in their own image.

How you make the future is what you do and think and imagine now. And what you are experiencing now is what you have thought of in the past, when it was still the future. All that you have ever been in evolution is your image of your self, your self-sense, your secret picture of yourself.

There are some people with inflated pictures of themselves and others who are very humble. Saints have a picture of themselves as a nobody. It is a mark of spiritual degree that those who have the greatest opinion of themselves are the lowest spiritually. And that is where the work is ... the universe will eventually humiliate them. It will bring them down. Christ said that those that exalt themselves will be brought down and those who are down will be exalted. It is a spiritual law that those who think they are number one and look down their noses at the rest of creation thinking they are very spiritually advanced will eventually discover how ignorant they are of the cosmic process or even a simple thing like light. What is light? Light and how it operates in our being is an enormous subject. We are brought down basically to discover that the real thing that is going on inside us is so awesome that it is humiliating to even think about it. Just to try and conceive what is going on inside every human being is awesome, and beyond that to imagine the whole of the universe is to realise that we live walking around in a cloud of darkness which is our own ignorance. This need not depress us even though we can say, "I don't know what I don't know."

Even if your soul is in light but the way is unknown, you don't know where you are going. If you know where you are going you are not going into the light!

Supposing you are driving along the road and then suddenly you come to a point where the sun shines in your eyes and you can't see where you are going, it is so bright you can't see even a couple of feet and the sun is directly in your eyes. You stomp on the brake because there might be something coming or you don't know where the road is. All you know at that moment is that you are driving into the light. Everything else is blocked out because the light is too bright for you to know where you are going. In order for you to know where you are going you have to go at an angle to the sun and turn; once you do the turn and follow the road or a tree comes in the way of the sunlight, you can see the road again. So in order to be knowing where you are going you have to turn away from the light; you cannot go directly into it. But there is a state when you *can* go directly into the light so that all you know is that you are going more into the light–that is the only thing you know, because you can't see anything else but the direct light. When you are in that state of brightness you don't know where you are going or what is going to happen, you are in a totally receptive state to the light and yet you are going ahead, without knowing if there is a precipice that you might drive over. That is the kind of movie I am describing. When the movie ends all there is left is such a bright light you can't see anything in the movie, no pictures, nowhere to go, no road, no trees, nothing. All you can see is light in everything, in everybody's eyes and light in everything in solid matter. And you are making the eyes see with light. That is the funny thing, because this imagination is the creative power to recreate the universe, strictly speaking. When we look at a thing we recreate it in a state of re-creation. We're re-creating the cosmic movie. The whole movie has been made already by the cosmic movie director and we are just recreating it with our consciousness. If we have the power to do this we should be able to look at the creation and see it new.

If you are eating a grapefruit in that state of heightened imagination, you are getting into the essence of that grapefruit and experiencing it as a grapefruit would experience itself, and then you know that no two grapefruit feel alike even though they may have come from the same supermarket and they may look the same with the same price. Normally if someone asks you if you have tasted grapefruit you say 'sure.' But do we know? We have not tasted every grapefruit in the world and if we knew how a grapefruit was feeling we'd be able to get inside and tell what part of the tree it came from. One grapefruit may be saying, "I'm from this part of the tree and I taste better because I'm nearer to this and I got more sun," and so on. When you get into it and your taste buds become alive to its condition, then you taste the next grapefruit and it is totally different, because you are recreating it and you are noticing how different each grapefruit is. When you are developing your powers of creation in such a way that you look on every grapefruit as a new creation, you are able to experience a totally different taste so that one may be as different as an orange, because of a totally different vibration. This is the process of the highly developed imagination, because the imagination is going to change your taste buds in a way that you taste the difference between one grapefruit and another.

One begins to see and experience differently like the artist who sees an image in different fashion than the ordinary person. But we have to be able to see and experience way beyond the artist to accomplish a cosmic vision, to look directly into the atoms and to see that everything is radiating with its own light; the same light that sees those atoms and recreates them is inside them and then looking back at you. There is no difference between the light of the universe and our own consciousness. Everything we plunk into that stuff, the light of consciousness, that is what we see and it is not happening outside of us. Where we really experience the universe is inside, in our consciousness, not out there, although our consciousness is out there just as much as it is in here! The consciousness pulls the signal in through the senses then processes it and puts it in here inside the head where there is somebody called you sitting saying, "That's rubbish! That's fine! That's this or that," making judgements all the time depending on whether it fits the picture of the universe in your imagination.

Now what do you do with this gift of consciousness? Well, God is inside of you shining out of your eyes and what you can now do is to use it to see me with or to see who you really are. God is the consciousness to see the glory of being that is working through the whole scene. This is what Christ came to say. He said he did not come to glorify himself, but because he chose to glorify the Father or the One that would automatically glorify him. He knew his destiny, that people would glorify him simply because he glorified the One.

To glorify something is to stand in awe of it in some way.

You will be in a state of grace when you allow something that awesome to come through; it is like holding a mirror up to the divine, it sees itself reflected. You cannot see God unless your consciousness is pure. How can anyone see pure consciousness unless their consciousness is pure?

How to purify the imagination so that we get to the state that is beyond the imagination is the function of this chakra. We have to use some of this knowledge on ourselves, going into our layers of consciousness to see how we are using all of these colours personally because they will reveal things to us that we don't know about ourself; they will reveal the fingerprint of our soul. You cannot penetrate the inner world of yourself or anyone else without having some kind of method for tracing what your consciousness is doing, how it uses the drives and needs and wants and the things we reject, which is just as important. We must understand these colours in the chakras. Colours are able to tell us about our own dance.

To be in that state, free of all images except the light and to put only the images there that are going to evolve you, is the skilled work of the yogi who is re-creating himself so that he can automatically recreate the world around himself. You can't recreate the world around you unless you first recreate yourself. When you get enlightened you don't have to worry about enlightening the world; it will automatically happen. Once you get turned on, everything else will get turned on.

St. Francis of Assisi in Ecstasy, communing with the divine order beyond the imagined condition of things. Painting by Giovanni Bellini.

VIOLET

The drive to enduring order engenders in the person who lives
in the domain of Imagination sometimes a wishful thinking,
a kind of magical power which can bring order out of chaos,
that can " will " events into the pattern and shape of our own
Imagining. It is this desire which brings them not only to
develop this creative faculty but also to challenge it. It is
while in the time dimension of temporal existence that the great
mystics have concentrated on timelessness as an experience.
They are the masters of the imagination who, through metaphors
and the power of images, are able to inspire us with thoughts
of divine order, of supermental systems of thought which
make the disorder in the world explicable and intelligent. They
are the visionaries who see beyond into the future and come
back to us fresh and unspoilt out of the past. They set out the
pattern of our human behaviour and order our lives by their
example and their insights into the enduring nature of things.

Experience now these brief examples from the Bible:

The voice of the Lord speaks to Job out of the whirlwind:
Where wast thou when I laid the foundations of the earth?
declare if thou hast understanding . . .
Whereupon are the foundations thereof fastened?
or who laid the cornerstone thereof,
when all the morning stars sang together,
and all the sons of God shouted for joy? . . .
Hast thou given the horse strength?
Hast thou clothed his neck with thunder?
Canst thou make him afraid as a grasshopper?
The glory of his nostrils is terrible . . .

(Job, Chapter 38)

One can imagine Job himself "afraid as a grasshopper" before the
tremendous images of God's mighty creation, with its awesome
splendour and its infinite variety.

Lift up your heads, O ye Gates;
and be ye lift up ye everlasting doors;
and the King of glory shall come in.
Who is this King of glory?
The Lord strong and mighty,
the Lord mighty in battle.   *(Psalm 24)*

In six lines of Hebrew verse we have here two powerfully original images of the opening of the gates of the heart to the glorious realisation of God's presence, and the image of God himself as one "mighty in battle," towering in ultimate victory over all the petty struggles of men.

The drive to enduring order is concerned with time and duration. Permanence and change are the most difficult of all things to study and they can never be understood with any of the previous six faculties because these cannot enter the dimension of the prime imagination which deals with fundamental ideas of ONENESS such as time itself. How do ideas of time arise in consciousness? How does the human organism experience different orientations to the outer and inner worlds?

What are the archetypal forms at the back of all memory, biological continuity and discontinuity, growth patterns, etc?

These are the conditions of life and immortality that man would ultimately like to control, and to do so involves some idea of magic power, even if it is a predictive scientific way of willing or manifesting events which are presently impossible, into the temporal realm of personal reality. Violet colour represents the desire to gain control over chaos and uncertainty and Hazard in the Universe. Such a desire is satisfied only by absolute certainty and the knowledge of a divine order far beyond that of the physical efforts of man. Hence a faculty for spiritual healing, magic, or for the power to " will " events into being, is usually cultivated in the Violet band of consciousness. Such a faculty calls for the annihilation of time as a concrete concept.

In the domain of Violet consciousness a person is like a poet able to lock up past, present and future into forms, words, images, metaphors, etc., which convey truth or ideas as an information transfer beyond the semantic reaction. There need be no systematic, sequential or logical thought process which leads in a straight time-line to meaning; in fact the faculty of the prime Imagination to conjure up images of reality, often is the cause which brings them about.

Unconsciously every business or government or organisation takes on the quality of the " Imagination " of its leadership. If there is lack of this faculty—the biblical saying " where there is no vision the people perish " comes into its own. The prime imagination which resonates to Violet can bring about fundamental changes in the human organism and governs every act of a person according to that Image which a person secretly has of himself.

It is in this area of the human personality that a man is deluded as well as fulfilled. If he holds an image of his highest expression as a relative Self and not an Absolute Self, he will never understand the way energy manifests through his own Being.

A man with the power to use the prime Imagination sees that all reality is experienced in Images of one kind or another. In music the sounds conjure up Images and pictures which are carried along the sounds in an abstract but powerful way to the depths of our Being. Music is the shape and interval of sound in the same way that time-experience is imagined to be long or short, painful or pleasant, according to our identification of " I " with the events taking place in time. The lover experiences time as painful when he is separated from the love object and vice versa. It passes painfully slow in the presence of those he cannot or does not love. It rushes by almost at lightning speed when in ecstacy. Ecstacy is experienced when the Image of oneself in the prime Imagination is fitting closely into the order of events that we have willed. If events in real life do not correspond with the imagined condition of things, a conflict between the "will" and the "imagination" is induced with fatal effects on the psychological and biological functions. Such people feel unloved by the community and need an absolute hazardless security in order to endure and face life. The drive for enduring order turns inwards against self if it cannot find it. Such a state of absolute security is impossible in temporal life without (a) a blind faith in an absolute God, or (b) facing the absolute king of reality as our own Self.

Even for those of us who do not function normally in the violet level, this self-inhibiting mechanism is at work in relation to our self image. We set ourselves goals and roles that relate not to the ultimate self but to the personality and we even try to manipulate those whom we love into playing a complementary role in our imagined drama. We see ourselves as the macho male or the glamorous irresistible woman or even the inspired teacher or the perfect lover with an eternal soul mate. But is all this in any way relevant to the discovery of the Rainbow Body? Will these petty aspirations get us one step nearer to the selfless state or will they bog us down a little deeper in the ego mire?

How did Christ see himself? What was his self-image? "I am of myself nothing," he said. "Sell all you have and come follow me," he said to the rich young ruler. In other words, "Get rid of all your investments in your worldly personal self and discover the ultimate self." The whole dynamic of the great tragic dramas is the struggle between what seem to be the clamouring needs and aspirations of the personal life and the increasingly strong glimpses of, and later insights into, the eternal. Lear's arrogance is ripped from him shred by shred until the proud autocrat with his 300 knights welcomes the ignominy of the prison cell. Hamlet relinquishes his self-torturing wrestlings with revenge for the dawning awareness that "the readiness is all." So the self-image of the relative self fades into the eternal image of the absolute self.

> In most cases the latter alternative cannot be accepted in the Imagination because it cannot square the facts of the human situation with such an omnipotent all powerful Self which leads out into the beyond into yet another domain of consciousness beyond all imaginings. Absolutism of this kind of union with an all pervading Self which liberates and gives independence from all that limits the self, can only be achieved by supremely great men, for it is perilous in a world of compromise for the absolute "I" to speak on its own authority.

This is, of course, what Christ did and this is what got Him crucified. Even though He insisted that it was not He who did the miracles or spoke the teachings, but the Father or Divine Intelligence that spoke and acted through Him, the unbearable challenge that He presented to the establishment drove the authorities into seeking an excuse for his arrest, and what they came up with was that He called Himself the Son of God.

NUCLEAR EVOLUTION AND THE ONE TO ONE RELATION-
SHIP . . . with special reference to the Seven Levels.

If you have given deep study to the seven levels as we have examined them one by one and if you have faced yourself with all the
various positive and negative traits that characterise these different
drives, you will at this stage have at least a glimpse of the level on
which you normally function. Are you Red level sensation-orientated? Or are you the Blue level, longing for peace and certainty
that you hope will result from adherence to accepted teachings or
authorities? Have you discovered some of the negative pitfalls of
your level? Does the Yellow intellectual level, for example, make
you overly analytical, even schizophrenic to the point where you
see yourself as separate and apart? Or does the Green level security
drive make you jealous and anxious about your possessions,
whether they be money, material objects or a beloved partner?

The next step will be to extend this understanding of all the different drives to those with whom we work or live or love. Has the thought just struck you that your wife or lover or child may be functioning from an entirely different level from your own? You could be a Red level action-orientated, "Get it on now" father with a dreamy, imaginative Violet level son; or an Orange level socially ambitious, "What will the neighbours think?" mother with an idealistic Blue level daughter who has just discovered Yoga. What do you do? Insist that the boy gets on the team and fulfills all your unfulfilled ambitions, or do you let your son know that you will be just as happy if his poetry is published or his music is played? He might even help you to understand it and open up a whole new world of experience for you that you never even knew existed.

Once we leave behind the common basic assumption that everyone functions more or less the same and begin to glimpse the incredible variety of man's personality, then whole new worlds open up for us and every encounter with a friend or a lover or a child is an adventure of exploration. All that is needed to tune into these other frequencies in those around us is the will to understand and the patience and sensitivity to let their beings speak. And of course it works two ways. Once you become sensitive to the being of another, there is a resonance set up which enables him or her to appreciate where you are coming from.

Since each level has its own Time world too it will be important to understand that the Violet level lives in three Time worlds and aspires to experience Eternal Time. The Red level lives always in the immediate Now, so the father cannot understand why his son agrees to do something with him, "but not now." "Come on son," he says, "there's no time like the present," and from his angle of vision he is right! But for the young aspiring poet struggling to find images for his experiences in all the Time worlds, the present seems limited and restricting. Where is the common ground or meeting point? It could be that the son, seeing his father's obsession with the physical present, allows him his sensation-orientated life but also takes time to show him that the great poets of old expressed in eternal words and phrases the beauty, terror and thrill of the sensory world. If the father responds with a deeper part of his being, that may have been afraid to expose itself up to now, then there is a meeting of worlds and each one not only lets the other be, but also expands his own experience of the spectrum of consciousness.

INTERVIEW with R.,
a twenty-two year-old accountant.

Editor: What turns you on most?

R.: Sex. I like to look at women's bodies. I get horny a lot.

Ed.: What depresses you the most?

R.: Not feeling that I'm doing what I need to do ... not meeting my expectations of myself, not feeling creative; it's very frustrating if it doesn't happen. Also seeing a lack of discipline in myself–that really burns me up. Right now I'm in gear to change my life. If I failed that would be very depressing.

Ed.: What are you seeking and wanting in life right now? What are your goals?

R.: I want to become a lot more dynamic. Either I want to find some creative work or I want to make everything I'm doing more dynamic and creative. I want to make my meditations deeper, the whole meditation side of life. I get this feeling, when I get tuned in, of transcending the self; at those times I'm always in a state of peace and understanding. I want to stay tuned in--to make that state permanent.

Ed.: How do you approach such tasks?

R.: Scattered. I tend to think of all the things I have to do at once, and then nothing gets done. I write a lot of lists so that I can have some organisation. But I never get through the list in a day–I get distracted.

Ed.: How important to you is tradition and the past?

R.: Not very important. I forget the past very quickly.

Ed.: What is your usual motive for doing things?

R.: I react to my own self inhibition. I don't want to get into things because of lack of confidence, so I hold back into my own "cave." But then I resist this and kick myself out there into the activity because I recognise my own inhibition. So you could say that my motive was to withstand my own resistance which I see as lack of confidence.

Ed.: What do you like most in others?

R.: Their being warm, loving and radiant.

Ed.: What is your attitude to money and possessions?

R.: I have a conflict between wanting it for power's sake and for security and being loose with it. I usually don't have much, so I would like to have it so that I could control my situation.

Note. Although the answer to the first question might make us jump to the conclusion that this is a Red level person, if we look deeper we shall find much that suggests the Violet, imaginative drive. Even the first reply gives a picture of someone who fantasises over women's bodies and the mere fact that he often gets "horny" could mean that he is not actually indulging the physical urge often enough to get real satisfaction. The Violet level's problem is always to get reality to match up to the envisaged dream.

The expressed need to be creative is recurrent, also the self-image which the actual performance does not always match. He obviously experiences the high meditative state periodically and this transcendance has become his goal, although the reality is seldom reached. This imagining of a heavenly state of bliss which conflicts with personal reality is Negative Violet.

When R. was given a Luscher Colour Test he chose the colours in the following order:

RED; VIOLET; YELLOW; GREEN; BROWN; BLUE; BLACK; GREY.

Note. The first two colours chosen by R. (representing the desired situation or aim) reflect the Red level desire to respond to stimuli, which gets him constantly turned on sexually and also causes him to get distracted, combined with the Violet level imaginative drive, which spurs him on with visions of greater creativity and dynamism. In his present situation, as represented by the group Yellow and Green, we see the planner who does not get his plans into manifestation, and also the intellectual's ability to analyse his own motives and drives and urges. The Green is reflected in his attitude to money as a means of controlling his situation. It is interesting to note that Blue is pushed down, as something under restraint, and we see this tendency when he talks of kicking himself "out there into the activity," when earlier he has talked of wanting to remain in a state of peace.

Although Red is the first choice here, R. seems to be basically a Violet level man, in whom the eroticism of the Red level manifests mainly as a part of the total vision of imagined bliss.

The earth photographed from the
Apollo 8 capsule 240,000 miles away

EMOTIONS
AND THE
LEVELS OF CONSCIOUSNESS

MAN'S POWERFUL EMOTIONS AS THEY MANIFEST ON THE DIFFERENT LEVELS.

The rainbow strands of the levels of consciousness are the cross threads in the fabric of human life and interwoven with them, like the woof and the warp in a woven shawl, are the strong basic threads of the human emotions.

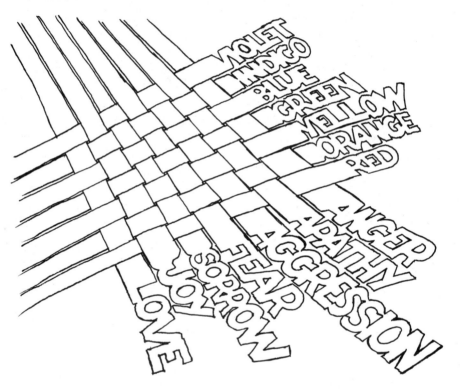

The emotional threads are coloured by each level that they interweave, so that, for example, fear for the Violet level is experienced and expressed quite differently from fear at the Red level. Let us see what happens to some of these basic emotions as they manifest at the different spectrum levels.

Who would bear all the burdens of life, asks Hamlet,

> To grunt and sweat under a weary life
> But that the *fear* of something after death
> .puzzles the will,
> And makes us rather bear those ills we have
> Than fly to others that we know not of?

And he goes on to talk of the inhibiting effect of fear that "makes cowards of us all,"

> And enterprises of great pith and moment
> With this regard their currents turn away
> And lose the name of action.

RED LEVEL–FEAR OF BODILY HARM OR EXTINCTION

Fear operates at every level. For the Red level person, at a certain moment, just before the successful completion of a physical operation, fear flashes in, and the confident thrust that both initiated and sustained the original energy and effort is baulked and braked so that the final stage of the undertaking, where absolute positivity is essential, is never completed. The climber, the runner, the racing car driver and the boxer and all the others who compete in the physical or athletic arena know this "flash of fear" that breaks the concentration, shakes the equilibrium and causes the head to turn in a fatal backward look.

Look into your own life and the lives of people you know for examples. Why does one man survive and avoid the inevitable collision on the freeway when another, with equal chance of avoidance, is killed? Why does one person survive a serious operation and another die? The strong negative energy of fear can make the difference between life and death, although men often do not fear when they need to, and fear too much when there is no need of fear.

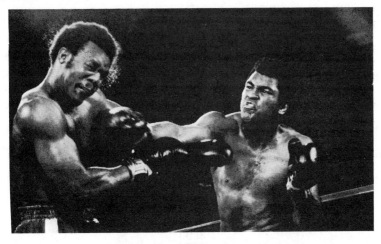

ORANGE LEVEL–FEAR OF BEING LEFT OUT

Between the common bourgeois fear of what the neighbours may think and the perilous apprehension and fear of other nations that produces the fatal policy of appeasement, lies a whole range of fears and doubts that stifle courageous originality and the progressive challenge that could bring new leaps in man's evolution. So we comply with the social norms, life becomes humdrum and our so-called statesmen allow the bullies to dictate their policy. Social change and political triumphs only spring from fearless action by those who ignore the negative doubters and are prepared to risk their reputations and even their lives. Social compliance and appeasement can often involve the sacrifice of ideals and people in order to preserve the cohesion with the social matrix.

Since we all experience the Orange social level, however briefly, at some point in our lives, it would be good to extract our own examples from family, club, group or organisation level, when we might have been afraid of being cast out and having to stand alone. Were you ever afraid of not being liked or approved of by family or friends? Were you ever afraid of failure, or even success, in business? Have you feared being different, while secretly knowing that what the social scene really needs to release it from monotony and boredom is someone who makes it sit up and take another look at itself?

YELLOW LEVEL–FEAR OF REJECTION
AND DISSATISFACTION

This is the level of the Ego with all its expectations, so whatever deflates or wounds the Ego or disappoints its expectations is to be feared. Sometimes the expectations are laid on another person who is "expected" to perform in a certain way; when he or she does not do this then the Yellow level person feels let down and even betrayed. Behind this feeling of betrayal is the deep fear of total rejection.

Since the Yellow level also loves change and novelty and is aways looking for the pastures that are greener than its present grazing meadow, there is a dissatisfaction that can produce a fear of never finding fulfillment and of becoming the victim of its own separative Ego.

GREEN LEVEL--FEAR OF LOSS

It is at this level of security and attachment to things possessed that fear probably operates most powerfully. The rich young ruler asks Christ how he can become enlightened and Christ tells him "Sell all you have and give to the poor and come follow me." In other words, "Give up your possessions and focus on the Eternal I AM." And the young man turns sorrowfully away, "for he had great possessions."

What is the basis for *your* security right now? Investments, your marriage, your academic qualifications, your years of research? Could you ditch it all? Or are you afraid that you might lose your money, your wife/husband, your status or your prestige?

Green level fear filters through most of the other levels. Can you nail yours and confront it now?

BLUE LEVEL--FEAR OF CHANGE

Of all the levels the Blue is the most difficult to get out of, and why? Because the Blue level hates change; it is abhorrent simply because it destroys the foundation of their cherished world. "Don't talk to me about changes," said our big-business friend in New York, "That's just what's wrong with the world; it's changing too fast. We need to slow down, consolidate and preserve what we've got, not risk everything in constant upheavals and change." "But Andrew," says his Yellow level friend, "that's not progress, that's stagnation. The whole motive power of evolution is in change and growth whether it be in an individual or a business company or a mode of government. There is a static 'holy cow' if you like—government! Still using methods and working from concepts that are no longer relevant to our times. Things *have* to change or perish." This is just a snatch of an actual dialogue that

369

probably lasted for many hours. It goes on in families, in organisations like religious societies and churches and it goes on in the constant struggle between the conservative and radical elements in national and international politics. The Blue level conservative fears change. So what happens when the Blue level conserver meets the Yellow level changer in a permanent relationship like marriage? Either the frustration and resistance destroy the relationship, or a positive synthesis is achieved whereby the changer initiates and the Blue level consolidates. As a conservative Taurus, married to a world-changing, Yellow level pioneer Aries, I have experienced this synthesis as the basis of an excellent working relationship. When the negative is turned to positive use, fear disappears.

INDIGO LEVEL--FEAR OF SPONTANEOUS RESPONSE (Doubt)

The motivating dynamic of the Indigo level is the intuitive faculty which can be seriously inhibited and even destroyed by fear. We can all discover examples in our lives of times when we had a strong "flash" or "hunch" about something. If we acted on it, we responded to a cosmic message and success or fulfillment inevitably followed. If we failed to respond and had second thoughts or doubts or fears, we missed our chance and nothing happened. To use the *I Ching* or to practice Supersensonics with a rod or pendulum involves attunement to the intuitive faculty which is our "hot line" to the Cosmic Intelligence and to develop this faculty we have to cast out fear and doubt. Once these are eliminated and a calm openness and receptivity take their place, then truth can be revealed at every level of life. When the intuitive channel is cleared by the removal of fears and doubts every question can be answered, from the simplest queries as to what is the best food to eat to the earnest and deep questionings of those on the spiritual quest. Take out the blockage of fear and the channel is clear for astounding revelations of Truth.

The Indigo level also fears the demands of the present. As long as he is committed to a future scheme, a future manifestation, all is well, but there comes a time when the promised manifestation is demanded of him in the present. Then he often withdraws and bales out of his commitment.

370

VIOLET LEVEL--FEAR OF CHAOS

If your drive is to charm the universe and to use the "shaping spirit of imagination" to create a new heaven and a new earth, then all that disrupts and obstructs this deep urge will be feared. It seems that those who live on this level of consciousness and, through music, painting, poetry and other creative arts, strive to present images that express their vision of Cosmic Reality, unconsciously repeat the original dilemma of the creation. Man, having been created in God's image, with a direct line of communication with the Source, became aware that he had another self, a doubter, and the creative artist suffers agonies of doubt and fear that the final expression of his vision will not match the glory of the original inspiration. So in a fit of despair he may smash the marble, slash the canvas, or tear up the manuscript.

Note to the reader: More valuable than any abstract theory about fear, or even examples from other people's lives, will be your own experience of fear as it relates to your own level of consciousness.

"PERFECT LOVE CASTS OUT FEAR"

If we interpret love as total attunement with the source of life and so with all its numberless manifestations, then love of life or the life force will cast out fear at any level.

Red: The athlete, in love with the God-given energy of his body, leaps forward to win the race. The climber tunes to the exhilaration of Nature's upward thrust and reaches the summit.

Orange: The social being, in love with all men, takes the jibes and the flattery as one and the same thing, as just facets of the expressive exuberance of life that only affects the fearful and vulnerable.

Yellow: The intellectual in love with the magnificent tool of his brain, loves too the full range of intellectuals who cross their swords around him and, in love with the zest and excitement of the fray, he joins in and finds fulfillment in the perfection of the intellect as an instrument of union. When love from the heart combines with the cleverness of the head then a vibrancy results that ensures for the brilliant intellect a place in the hearts of those around him.

Green: The acquisitive man, who knows that one can only enjoy if there is no attachment, collects his rare and beautiful works of art but can let them go tomorrow. And the true lover wants all the world to love what he loves, so jealousy dies and fear of loss is frizzled up in love's all-consuming fire of union with all.

Blue: Devotion that is tuned to the One in all men can minister and serve wherever devoted service is needed. As with all the levels, the inhibiting effect of fear, in this case fear of change, is overcome when we free ourselves of attachment to any particular hero or guru or master or any cherished belief or concept. Then the positive energy of devoted love radiates in all directions and fulfillment is the natural feedback of this unlimited flow of devotion to all teachers of Truth.

Indigo: When love becomes the magnetic indicator of the intuitive, he no longer doubts the promptings, for he "knows" where his messages are coming from. So as love breeds surety so the messages become stronger and the dream of becoming a sage is eventually a reality. Direct perception of the universal and abstract love of the ONE becomes possible at this level.

Violet: For the great imaginers, the love of the divine order, that so often seems inaccessible in earthly life, is realised and fearlessly accepted when the understanding dawns that man's apparent chaos is part of a greater cosmic plan. We can look at any of the works of genius in painting or music or poetry and discover there this paradoxical truth that pain and pleasure, sorrow and joy, chaos and order are ultimately the essential ingredients of any great artistic creation. Using familiar works of great literature, art or music, we can explore this process whereby negative doubts and fears, that program so to speak the negative, dark and chaotic parts of the work, are transcended through the expression of love in its widest integrative sense, to produce the ultimate triumphant expression of the artist's vision of truth and reality (see Shakespeare's tragedies, Brahms' Requiem, Wagner's Gotterdamerung, Rembrandt's paintings, etc.)

*The following notes have
been extracted from a taped
talk by Christopher Hills*

AGGRESSION   RED LEVEL

Aggression on this level is physical. A person may come up to
you and his only thought of aggression is to punch you in the
nose. A bully is often like this. He wants to dominate you physically. The same need to dominate applies to some men. They
want to grab a woman, even if they don't know her. We can find
this aggression in children as well. If we go to an undisciplined
nursery, we may find the boys pouring salt on the hair of the
girls and the girls pounding on the piano and snatching crackers
out of the other children's mouths. In any case, aggression on this
level is the drive to manipulate people or things by dominating
them.

Aggression is not limited to mankind. We find it in apes, dogs,
lions, and birds. Lions will kill each other if they invade one
another's pride or territory. Birds will attack if you come within
a certain distance of their nest.

We can all find hundreds of examples. The main point is that
aggression in the Red level is a direct, physical, skin to skin enterprise.

Now other people may feel just as aggressive as the Red level fellow but they may not be prepared to biff you on the nose. So they project their aggression onto society by trying to get to the top, like a politician. This requires a lot of pushiness. He has to solicit publicity and ride on everyone else's efforts. If you start a new school, he's going to say "Count me in." So you put in your leaflets, "Approved by so-and-so", and that's all he'll ever do. It's a form of aggression because if the school is a success, it gets him higher in society. Everyone begins to feel that such people are powerful. They have invested their name, put it in terms of power, and pushed it on society. They seemingly get mixed up in everything but they're actually not doing anything. They just appear to be doing things. They use education, knowledge, money, anything, to push themselves. This is aggression, even though you would never see them hitting anyone. It would spoil their reputation and they might get sued. They wouldn't then be a good social guy.

Here the aggression is channeled into an intellectual undermining of another person by various techniques. A person who does this tries to denigrate the knowledge of someone else so that they can appear to be correct. This is done in a variety of ways. For example, if a person wishes to confuse or destroy the arguments of another, he uses subtle logical word play or semantic traps. He can ask another person to define what they mean by every word that they say and then the person gets so busy doing that, that everything he says needs a new definition. This gets to be a sport among intellectuals and is the basis of sophistry, logical expertise, high polish and skill at word play. It's where the word "sophisticated" comes from. Such people try to expose inconsistencies but are unable to resolve paradoxes themselves. Thus, they can be utterly destroyed intellectually by someone who can.

There is a certain amount of aggression required to demolish the intellectuals who are living in their own castles in the air. A prophet or guru has to be able to smash down all that nonsense. This is what the Tibetan teachers are talking about in cutting through our spiritual materialism, which is nothing more than our investment of consciousness in the spiritual life as a huge big trip. A true guru will come along and cut the rituals and regalia all in shreds because they don't mean anything, including the whole trip of the Dharma King with a crown that enlightens you! The point is, you can't sit back with your mouth closed where there is negative or destructive aggression. Somehow you have to answer in a way that totally defeats the aggression, although your method may not in itself be aggressive. It may be taken that way by someone who is aggressive, because if you cap his thought he is going to feel threatened and that his ego is being attacked. He just can't tolerate it and he'll probably hate you.

AGGRESSION   GREEN LEVEL

Here aggression moves up from just hitting a person or trying to dominate them intellectually to possessiveness and jealousy. Here a feeling of insecurity comes over a person, and he feels he is going to lose something. If you found your wife in the arms of another you might beat her, right? Why? Because you try to control her and prevent her from going somewhere else. This is so you can feel secure. Anger gets transferred to a sense of possessiveness. This is aggression. Such a person is aggressively seeking that which will give him a feeling that he has what he wants. Jealousy is wanting to possess for yourself what you're not sure of. It's certainly not letting things be as they are, and not to allow freedom to be--*that's* aggression! Aggression is wanting things the way *we* want them.

If you worry about someone who might be looking at your wife and you get jealous, it may be different from biffing him on the nose, but it's still coming out as aggression. It's rather subtle. Some people have to have money in their hands, feeling it, getting a rush from just touching it. That's Red level. Green level is knowing it's in a Swiss bank 10,000 miles away and you are secure. Red level is having your girl next to you every minute to cuddle and fondle. Green level is knowing she's "mine", like a chattel or something. You could be separated from her but as long as she had a kind of chastity belt on you would feel secure that she is yours.

AGGRESSION   BLUE LEVEL

This is the realm of the mental bully. It's the need to dominate something mentally, with thoughts. It usually functions like one-up-manship. The ego feels great if it can get one up on someone else and always get the last word. It's the urge to be in control of what is happening in the mind or the thoughts, not just in yourself but in others. For example, you may have a mother who tries to tell you how everything you think is no good. "Why do you think that way?" she says, or "Why not think another way?" or "That's no good." Such a person wants everyone to think the same way they do. It's just another form of aggression.

AGGRESSION   INDIGO LEVEL

Here we have the knowing level without knowing how you know. A person just feels that he knows, whether it be a solution to a problem or the will of God. Thus, at its extreme, there is this feeling that you are so right in your mind that you're prepared to even kill. In the name of God you would destroy whilst preaching love. This is different from Blue level aggression. There we have people trying to get their *ideas* of how things ought to be accepted as the authority. Here we are involved with vision in the future, trying to get a vision of the unmanifested world of the future into the manifested realm. You could take the life of Mohammed for example, where he was rejected for trying to get the people to see what he was seeing. So he returned to the town that rejected him with an army and conquered them in the name of a Holy War. He killed a lot of people. So, it's not just a question of authority but of getting the vision materialised.

Most great men of vision have to have a certain amount of aggression to push themselves out in front in order to be heard. Christ risked the wrath of the authorities of his day by preaching on the temple steps. That was an aggressive act. It was a bit like cocking one's snook at the authorities. His willingness to openly oppose the authorities and denounce them as phonies for the sake of his vision was an aggressive act and came back at him when he was crucified. Why was he crucified? Because he was a thorn in their sides.

There is yet another form of aggression on the intuitive level. Because the time world of the intuitive is in the future, there is a tendency towards impatience with the present, if not downright evasion. This causes him to make thrusts, as it were, at psychic phenomena, since they often speak of worlds beyond. Consequently, intuitives and psychics hungrily devour the food of the future as aggressively as Red level individuals devour steaks at the table. This is the realm of seances, flying saucers and Armageddon.

AGGRESSION   VIOLET LEVEL

The negative expression of aggression here is the calculated use of the imagination to enslave men. Psychological warfare is an example, but beyond that, it is the armed use of the imagination by men who know that what people think about themselves is what they become. Thus, there can be no greater aggression than to consciously manipulate and promote unsuspecting men and women into seeing themselves as something they are not, in order that they may be exploited.

Aggression as found in nature serves a positive function. In the imagination of God universes are exploding and expanding. From the prime imagination is born creation. From the images of our minds are born our realities. Knowing this, it becomes necessary to apply discipline and a certain ruthless aggression to the products of our own imaginations. If we take the story of Arjuna and Krishna, we see that the disciple had to do violence and go into battle. Of course it is said to be an analogy for the demons within and the brothers, sisters, and attachments of family. Arjuna shrank

"I have X'ed myself from your world."

Charles Manson, accused of masterminding the murder of seven people including actress Sharon Tate, appears in court with an X slashed in his forehead, representing society's rejection of him. His followers and co-defendants, Susan Atkins, Patricia Krenwinkle, and Leslie Van Houten, also bear similar marks.

from doing violence. He said it was bad that we should kill our brothers and sisters. Krishna said, "No, you have to do it. The battle must be waged. You have to be that ruthless, even to kill your own brothers and sisters in battle because they are evil and if they're not cleaned out they'll pollute the whole world." Krishna even said, "Look, I'll drive the chariot for you and you shoot the arrows. I'll tell you where to shoot." So Arjuna knew he'd have to obey and surrender to Krishna, just as Christ surrendered to God. And this is an aggressive act because it means going to war against all these brothers and sisters and situations and things which are in you in the field of the knower and it is there that you have to do the violence and root them out. The battle field is life and that's where the saints are tested. That's where you really discover if you're spiritual or whether you're just a phoney who likes to listen to the words.

Charles Manson, a convicted murderer for the ritual slayings of the actress Sharon Tate and five other people, read this in the Gita and thought it gave him permission from God to kill. Instead of killing the demon in himself he unleashed his aggression upon others whom he believed deserved to die for their indulgences. But he did not wish to look at his own indulgence and the lust to kill, or his own madness. He rationalised his actions as God-inspired and justified by Krishna. This misunderstanding is just an extreme extension of what politicians do in the name of revolution. Solzhenitsyn testified to thousands of political murders, tortures, and millions of slow deaths in slave camps of communist Russia. It goes on in some other countries, many of which are claiming to be righteous in the aggressive extermination of their opponents. This assumption of power over life and death is not only the ultimate in human aggression but also in human arrogance. Do Krishna's words on ruthlessness apply to the extermination of aggressiveness?

✯

Note: We now suggest that you, the reader, using the above as a model, test out your own experience of various emotions as you have experienced them operating in you or your friends at different levels of consciousness. Try looking at jealousy, anger, hatred, joy, sorrow, etc.

BLACK
THE LEVEL OF
SELF-ANNIHILATION

Reference is made to the colours Black and White where we mentioned in chapter 7 that in psychotronics and the physics of consciousness there are twelve colours detectable. In the diagram of the Turenne disc on p. 194   it can be seen that between Black and White there are two colours, Infra Black and Infra White which we call negative green or radiesthesia grey. Greater details on the relationship of these two colours will be found in my other book, Volume III in the series on psychophysical phenomena which I call "Supersensonics". In the theory of Nuclear Evolution, White is a nodal point of timelessness which balances the Black hole at the other end of the spectrum producing circular causality. The absolute singularity of Black or White holes in which the 80 octaves of matter disappear and reappear through intense curvature of space is now called a wormhole in the new physics and is described more fully in Volume II of this series entitled, "Energy, Matter and Form". It is the intention of the author to keep this book to the seven colours of the visible spectrum plus the Black end of the cosmic singularity and its effect on our human consciousness. Since everything we know about Black is only a reverse phase of White, the author feels no need to go into the meaning of White as an aura colour which may involve the reader in a whole book on the nature of pure consciousness. Many explanations of pure consciousness however are worthless unless they are directly experienced. The science of direct perception is a practical one and has been presented in a three-year step by step course of instruction.

BLACK

The level of consciousness which deals with the " will " or the lack of it is beyond the Violet band of the imagination and lies in an uncomfortable domain known as the void. Whenever the absolute " I " is mentioned or the intellect tries to consider the idea of any so-called " Absolute " or whether there is such a thing existing in life, we shall always find hostility from people who suffer the conflict of the intellect, the will, and the imagination, with the flow of events in their inner time-world. Time and motion are related so closely that any idea of time being a separate quality from motion offends the intellect as well as sense impressions.

The " void " of course is just another name for undifferentiated space, the " sacred space " which is the divine absolute. All other Gods are mental gods created by mind. The mind is the great block to spiritual knowledge since it is quite impossible for mind to understand what mind is. It is always minding what is said rather than what is meant.

Here lies the basic cause of all miscommunication. We listen to words, argue with words and tie one another down to our own interpretation of words without listening to, or even acknowledging the voice of the Being behind the words. Relationships fall apart and marriages break up because of this basic assumption that we know in our minds what someone else is trying to communicate to us.

The experimental group at the University of the Trees in Boulder Creek in California uses a technique for the bettering of communication called "mirroring", in which the listener plays back to the speaker what he or she thinks the speaker said. If it is correct the relating and the deepening of the communication can continue; if it is not, then the danger of going on from a false basic assumption is avoided, since the speaker will now have to re-express his point until perfect understanding is reached.

In terms of the various layers of consciousness this "sacred space" cannot be touched (Red), it cannot be explored (Orange), it cannot be separated, changed or undone (Yellow), it cannot be possessed (Green), it cannot be conceptualised or bound in time (Blue), it cannot be known by psychic faculties (Indigo), it cannot be patterned, imagined, ordered or magically conjured (Violet). In short it interpenetrates and underlies every being, its action and reaction, and is nothing manifested. Since " no-thing " cannot move within space, it is perfect stillness and the only absolute there is in being, the pure consciousness of " I " itself—the Absolute " I ".

Throughout this book the word " space " is used as synony-mous with the " void ", the divine absolute pure consciousness of " I ", who directs all thought energy, who induces all ideas, who forms all images, who feeds off the universe, whose energy touches all, who awakes, is born and sleeps in all, who dies in all, who directs the eye and sees all, who hears all, and who would read all and limit all that is said in this book.

" The totality of all physical phenomena is of such a character that it gives no basis for the introduction of the concept of ' Absolute motion ' "; or, shorter but less precise : " there is no absolute motion ". This negative statement of Einstein's refers to the physical world as a separate " real external world " of sense impressions. He states, " Out of the multitude of our sense experiences we take mentally and arbitrarily, certain repeatedly occurring complexes of sense impression and we attribute to them a meaning—the meaning of the bodily object." We can see here the objective word is we. He goes on to say that this concept is an arbitrary creation of the human mind. We can also reason that the human mind, when it thinks of we, speaks objectively ; but if Einstein was just speaking for himself and not for all men, it would become not we but " I ", a subjective statement.

There can be no absolute law which exists outside that of the observer who cannot make any statement in history, or in time past, in time present, or in time future without there being an " I " who makes it. Nor can there ever be a statement about reality, objectivity, or a theoretical, imaginative, descriptive, deductive, or hypothetical nature without the " I " makes it. It must manifest " I " at some time in the past or present of the observer.

BLACK IS AN ABSTRACTION OF THE FUTURE
UNKNOWN SELF.

Any statement about the future is always qualified by the
" I " of the seer, and therefore any observer cannot divorce
himself absolutely from the Universe (as a separate ego) about
which he is making a statement.

The fact that every day absolute and arbitrary statements
are made unconsciously by the separated ego of man, leads the
human Imagination to suppose that the measurement of facts
in such arbitrary units of time as "cycles per second" or
"feet per second" possesses a reality of its own. These
measurements are then generally accepted as " absolute "
measures of an objective kind. Chronological time moves at its
own pace, independent of man's wishes and only respects
the length of a second dependent on 86,400 divisions of the
earth's rotation on its axis. Similarly, the primary standard of
length is the meter which is defined as 1,650,763·7 wavelengths
of the orange-red line in the spectrum of the gas Krypton 86.

In our awareness of this kind of time-flow and experience of
length everything is relative, but in fact the indwelling " I " is
absolute and timeless and only experiences time-flow and
distance because of its identification with the biological clock
and chronological time clock, which are constructions in the
waking imagination.

What is being said here may be difficult to apprehend theoretically
and it only has reality experientially for those with conscious self-
awareness. It can, however, be validated by our subjective experience of time, which is often a direct contradiction of both biological and chronological clock time. Handel writing his Messiah in a
locked room lost all awareness of hours and days passing while the
inspiration from the Eternal Now flowed through him. Lovers in
their bliss and children at play experience this same lack of relationship with clock time as, for them, the hours "rush by". The bored
office worker, sitting at his desk over the same period of time, feels
that every hour is a dragging eternity. The clock on the wall
registers the same period of time for lovers, children and office
clerk; the difference lies in the way in which the time is experienced
by the indwelling "I".

This can also be validated by recalling and re-experiencing for ourselves occasions when time   not only seemed irrelevant but non-
existent. It could have been an intense interchange with another
person when one mind inspired and sparked off response in the
other in a cumulatively exhilarating sharing. The dialogue stretched

out into the early hours of the morning without either party being remotely aware of the passage of time. If a third person had come in and asked, "What is the time?" the reply might have been, "We've no idea. What does it matter?" The very word "matter" is significant. What the speaker is saying in effect is, "What has my present state of being to do with earth time or clock time which gets its validity from man's relationship to matter?" We can all find examples of these timeless experiences that man has described in such common phrases as "out of this world" or "when time stood still"; love-making, listening to great music, meditating or just communing with Nature have all lifted people out of the trap of artificial time.

Men of genius, the great originators and accomplishers in the fields of Science, the Arts, statesmanship, philosophy, religion and spirituality, live their lives more in touch with Absolute Time and the "I" of pure consciousness, so that they transcend the ordinary clock time by which the bulk of human beings run their lives. Hence they cram into the space of fifty years maybe fifty times the average amount of work, creativity and manifestation for that period of time, being more in touch with "God's good time" that responds to their creative energy, while the rest of humanity spins out a humdrum existence as a bunch of clock-watchers. It is also an interesting phenomenon that those whose lives are 100% occupied already in positive output, can always respond to yet another demand on their energy, while those who drift and regulate their lives by mundane events like meals and T.V. programs never, in their own estimation, "have time" to contribute any more than they are doing already!

There seems also to be a correlation here between the selflessness of those who are in touch with Absolute Time and the selfishness of those who go strictly by the clock.

> During sleep this experience of time is not so identified, even though the dreamer is the same "I" and even though the experiencer of deep sleep is the same "I" which wakes up, aware that it was unconscious of time, and incidentally unconcious of Self. This "I" who is asleep while yet awake responds to the colour Black.

Recall any of your dreams that had a sequence of events and ask yourself how long each event took. You walked along a road. How long was the road? You talked with your mother. How long did you talk? And so on and so on . . . What is the difference between those experiences and those of your waking existence?

> The colour Black throughout the world and in all cultures is associated with evil, annihilation and negation. The negation of Self would appear to most people still imprisoned in Self, to be the greatest evil. To mistake self-denial for selflessness is the common error. To be self-effacing without really conquering self, is not humility but an unnatural state of Being. Because the ego lies in wait to ensnare the self in its idea of itself, it is always having to be pushed down by the higher self when it has not come to terms with selflessness. To become selfless means to annihilate oneself as a separated ego. This means the inclusion of all other expressions of self, including all those ignorant of self. Evil is merely that power of darkness (of the Black) which comprehendreth not itself. Black is rejected no longer when the fear of one's other self has been silenced.

> There is no evil except ignorance of that power which is the invisible and unmanifest Self in all men. When they pay it no heed, things go awry.

How does one silence that fear? What is the "other self"? When we can really see and understand that, in terms of consciousness, we are all the other people that we can ever meet, and when we can include all these "other" people in our own Ego, then we have nothing to fear, for these "others" often represent and demonstrate for us our own "other self". Have you noticed that the things which really bug you about another person are your own faults and failings? This surely means that what we have not come to terms with in ourselves, what is not really resolved, is what irritates and frustrates us about other people. So Evil is really fear of our own blind spots and ignorances. Once we see and understand this we can tolerate anyone and see them as part of ourselves.

To take some examples, perhaps you are or have been a "woman chaser". Your head turns and your eye follows every shapely form as it passes by. Then you meet another "woman chaser". How do you feel? Do you judge him? Do you talk to others about him in a derogatory way? Or do you say to yourself, "There goes old Henry, chasing after the girls again. I know just how he feels. It could be me." Or you encounter a timid, wishy-washy woman who never seems to speak out and say what she really feels. How do you feel about her? Irritated? "Why doesn't she come out and make herself felt? I know she'd really like to dominate us all, but she hasn't the guts." Or do you think, "Poor Barbara. That could be me as I was ten years ago. There was I just dying to boss everyone around and tell them how things should be done, but something always held me back,"? In the second case you have come to terms with that conflict in yourself and so can feel empathy with another and can include her in your consciousness. So watch yourself next time you say or feel, "Let me get away from her; she's getting on my nerves." Perhaps *you* are getting on your own nerves!

Here at University of the Trees we practice what we call "Creative Conflict" and the first rule of the "Game" is to recognise that "YOU ARE WHATEVER DISTURBS YOU". At first this is difficult to swallow. "What me?" you say "I'm not the least bit like him or her. I don't bite my fingernails to the quick, but it still disturbs me to see him do it . . . " or "I get really exasperated when she keeps rationalising everything so that she never admits to being wrong. Now *I* don't do that, so how can you say I am whatever disturbs me?" At this point we have to stop and go deeply into ourselves. If we don't bite our nails, have we some other physical habit that we find difficult to break and hardly like to admit to? Or do we rationalise in our minds but do not speak out our rationalisations? If you try this exercise out with your own group or family, get everyone to consider what is "bugging" them about someone else at one given moment. Then let everyone speak it out and ask themselves honestly whether what they see in the "Other" is not also in them. If it is, we call it a "projection" and after a while the group becomes very proficient in spotting one of these projections when it arises.

Try the exercise where one person sits in the centre of the circle in the "Hot Seat", and each member of the group in turn tells the one in the centre what he needs to work on, in other words what his main failing is. Then let the one in the centre play back to each one in turn what they said to him and see whether the "Cap fits" that way round! It's amazing to discover that what we accuse others of is invariably in us too!

To reach the state in which the Ego is finally either transcended or expanded to include all other "selves" as part of the One Self, demands tremendously hard and sustained self-vigilance and self-confrontation. Invariably the breakthrough or realisation comes after an "end of the road" experience, when failure to make any real change results in a group challenge of "Change or else!" Then the "other self" or the "monster", as we call it here, has to be faced, looked at and accepted. For one it could be the horrific realisation that what he or she felt was a wonderful relationship or marriage left the other partner unfulfilled and frustrated and what is worse had done so for many years. For another comes the shock that no one else has experienced the high spiritual vibes that she thought she was giving off; what the others in the group have experienced is self-righteousness and superiority. Yet another finds that what he thought was his selfless generosity has been received as buying of approval and attention. When these smug or proud or manipulative patterns have been genuinely faced and accepted for what they are, namely a powerful manifestation of Ego, then there is a breakthrough and not only does the relationship with others improve a hundredfold but, with the slackening of the demands of the personal ego, there comes a serene acceptance, even an embracing, of all other egos.

MEASURING THE DEPTHS OF " I "—THE SELF

Just as we set arbitrarily the vibrating frequency of Krypton Gas 86 as a standard unit of length for the determination of a metre, so do we know that the human entity is a vibrating bundle of electrical atoms which represent a field of harmonic tones of energy that extends outwards into the universe beyond the skin. There is really no possible scientific separation between this electrically charged field and the universal field which flows through and around it. It is constantly conditioned by the field of which it is a part, likewise the universal field is conditioned by all its parts.

Christopher Hills' book "Supersensonics" is an exhaustive exposition and expansion of this idea, and he goes further in that he introduces us to the means whereby we can develop the use of our 37 mile-long nervous system as a highly sensitive antenna for divining and discovering "the hidden processes by which the human body works and links itself etherically with its total environment" (see "Supersensonics" page 41 et seq.).

Similarly one could say that the brain cells and neurons which recognise and distinguish colours from the wavelengths received along the optic nerve from the eye are also conditioned by the whole spectrum. Medical proof of this would be found if all those cells whose functions are to discriminate the colour blue were damaged accidentally ; the remaining ones would have to be re-educated to discriminate the whole spectrum again. The consciousness of " I " which directs this bundle of vibrating frequencies in the human entity is similarly a spectrum which can identify with any wavelength or colour in the Universal field, by merely choosing its frequency in relation to an absolute stillness. The normal human perception tries to express these realities objectively in " absolute motion " or in frequencies per second, by bringing into our thinking a notion of objective time.

This is where the problem of measurement in seconds becomes complicated if we do not question the " absolutes " set up in our imaginations as to the fixed nature of the time used in the measurements. The total spectrum is the only " absolute " science we can measure with when dealing with material bodies and it would appear that this holds good for consciousness too. We can convert this continuous normal spectrum into wavelengths of a certain unit length and ascertain its frequency in seconds ; but it does not matter what kind of units we use to do it, providing we set an arbitrary value of measure on them.

RESEARCH INTO FUNDAMENTAL ABSTRACTIONS

Man attempts to create an absolute standard measure of time such as the Ephemeris second which is defined as

1/31,556,925·9ths of the tropical year for January 1900 noon, and to devise an atomic clock based on the spectrum of atoms of caesium vibrating accurately to 1/100th of a second over 100 years and to compare it with a biological clock time in which organisms, including our own nervous system, process all the bits of information they need to exist (DNA molecules, etc.). This brings in some fundamental problems in our thinking about measurement itself. Our imagination can mathematically calculate the time it would take to process all the events which take place in this huge laboratory called Earth ; since there must be a maximum and minimum time in which each " bit " can be processed, we could theoretically know the age of the Earth measured in Earth-time. This again would have to be related to the co-ordinate system we know as universal time or Galaxial-time, as arrived at by taking all the matter in the Universe and calculating its average rate of decay by using the half-life of the physical elements.

Man's attempts to find absolute time have led him deeper and deeper into the incredibly precise and abstract areas of mathematics and physics, yet the problem of time remains. In order for there to be a measurement there must be a standard and if the standard employed is in itself fixed relative to something else, then what will remain will still be a relative measurement, not an absolute one. The standard itself must be absolute to begin with! Where oh where in the entire phenomenal universe are we going to find such a thing???

In the Great Treatise, Ta Chuan, found in the I Ching, the following is taken to illustrate the aforementioned point.

> "In the Book of Changes, a distinction is made between three kinds of change: NON-CHANGE, CYCLIC CHANGE, and SEQUENT CHANGE. Non-change is the background, as it were, against which change is made possible. For in regard to any change there must be some fixed point to which the change can be referred, otherwise there can be no definite order and everything is dissolved into chaotic movement."*

---

*See the I Ching, page 280-281, Richard Wilhelm translation, Bollingen Foundation Inc., New York, N.Y. 1950.

This same situation regarding change applies to time as well. Without a point of No-time, time itself has no meaning and becomes as chaotic and disorderly as the current scientific mental illusions of Ephemeris seconds and vibrating ceasium clocks. Ephemeris seconds have meaning only on earth because the standard employed is an earth year, which is relative to a point in space we call a sun. In reality, the second exists only because we have chosen something *relatively* stationary in space from which to begin our measurement.

Einstein who immersed himself in the study of time said, "An important property of our sense experience, is its time-like order. This kind of order leads to mental conceptions of a subjective time". "The subjective time leads through the concept of the bodily object and of space, to the concept of objective time." "The introduction of objective time involves two statements which are independent of each other," says Einstein (but of course we know neither are independent of the subconsciousness of the one who makes the statement). These are, he says :—

(1) The introduction of objective time by connecting temporal sequence of experiences with the indicators of a "clock", i.e. of a closed system with periodical occurrence.

(2) The introduction of the notion of objective time for the happenings in the whole space, by which action alone the idea of local time is enlarged to the idea of time in physics.

"Such a use of notions independent of the empirical basis to which they owe their existence does not necessarily damage science. One may however easily be led into the error of believing that these notions, whose origin is forgotten, are necessary and unalterable accompaniments to our thinking, and this error may constitute a serious danger to the progress of science."

"We now realise with special clarity, how much in error are those theorists who believe that theory comes inductively from experience."

The fact that we experience life through our senses gives us the feeling that we are a solid body with bounds distinct from other solid bodies and separated by or from a vacuum called space. As a baby we experience early sensations of cold and hot, hunger and satisfaction, pain and pleasure, and so on. Through repeated alternations of these physical sensations we solidify the notion that we exist "in here" and the rest of the world impinges on us from "out there". We experience this impingement on our senses as occurring in a sequential order. Pain remembered was "then". Pain anticipated will be "coming". Pain felt is "now". Our subjective experience of the speed in which events approach, take place and depart depends largely on our mental state or level of consciousness. When we are happy, time flies. When we are sad or bored, time creeps. Yet, by seeing ourselves as a physical body, we do not measure the passage of events with our happiness or boredom but with the movements of other bodies such as the sun. Thus, the movement of the sun from sunrise to sunrise measures objectively one day, regardless of how we experience it!

Objective time then, is created by the experience of differences in the consciousness of a man peering out through his senses and seeing with his eyes the movement of some external body in space relative to himself or some other external body. The movement of the earth around the sun we call one year and when we divide this orbit into equal segments we get months, weeks, days, hours, minutes and seconds. These are arbitrary divisions dependent on the local movements of the sun and the earth. When we connect our internal experiences to these divisions, we create "clock time", which is a local affair.

Now Einstein is saying that not only do we create objective time and apply it to us, but we expand the application of this creation to the whole of the universe as well, and thus assume that this notion of time has validity everywhere, even at the level of the tiniest atomic particles or the greatest heavenly galaxies.

We forget that time is our own creation, a practical tool which is meant to be a worthy servant, not an omnipotent master. To insist that clock time as we know it is an independent system that governs the workings of the entire universe is the gravest kind of scientific error. To paraphrase Einstein, "You don't take a particular case and make a law to fit the whole of creation." "On the contrary," says Christopher Hills, "you find the law of creation first, and then you apply it to particulars."

> "And God said, Let there be lights in the firmament and the heaven to divide the day from the night, and let them be for signs, and for seasons, and for days and for years . . . And the evening and the morning were the fourth day."*

---

*The Holy Bible, Genesis, Chapter 1, Verses 14 to 19, King James Version.

EXTRACT:
FROM QUESTION TIME AT UNIVERSITY OF THE TREES

NORAH: Could you please enlarge on these quotations from Einstein, particularly with reference to Time?

CHRISTOPHER: Well, just as I said, time doesn't really exist in the universe. Only cycles happen. Cyclic activity is real but the time is put on it by our making differences between events in our consciousness, that is by us humans thinking in terms of the clock which is just a way of marking off intervals. Then by creating something that marks off regular intervals we have created a subjective time, simply because we have created that clock with our mind. It isn't real, there is no such thing as time as we find on that clock, in the universe. That time results from merely dividing the earth's orbit up into 365, then dividing it into 24, then dividing it into minutes, then dividing it into seconds. You say, "Well, we'll measure everything on the earth with that time." But in reality it's only a mean time, it doesn't represent any "real" time. Now when physicists talk of real time they mean this kind of clock time ... subjective time ... created out of their minds, all agreeing one with another that this will be a second. The year 1900, a certain period of the earth's orbit, is divided by 31,556,925. That will be the length of a second--a common yardstick. So everybody is agreed that that standard period is a second. They extend that time out to the whole universe by measuring the passage of the planets, the period of the spin of the sun's surface, the rotation of Mars, the vibrations of atoms and molecules are all measured everywhere in the universe by this particular earth time which we've created with our minds subjectively, and then we say "Ah, that's objective time." You say it's happening out there whether I like it or not. In other words, you've created something totally independent of yourself. This is your belief that it's objective. You believe it happens willy-nilly, whether you've got your eyes open or not, or whether you're there or not. I say an event is happening at 4 o'clock ... the bus is going to come, and if I stab and kill myself and no longer am here experiencing this physical universe ... the bus is going to come at 4 o'clock just the same, whether I'm here or not. So in this way we create an objective time which appears to go on independent of us little separated beings.

This is merely a notion. Because this thing called time that we think is going on ad nauseum is disconnected and discontinued from our own consciousness; but it was created by our own consciousness in the first place. It was never real to begin with but we only thought it was real and then we extended that reality to everything else that we are dealing with, thinking that somehow the observer or the experiencer is separate from the kind of time we're talking about. So you see, by a trick of the mind, we've taken something subjective which is a clock which we have invented and divided up mathematically, and then we have made out that it is something objective.

DEBBIE: Is the only thing real about time the proportion? And also, on other levels of consciousness, would we experience the measurement differently?

CHRISTOPHER: Well, yes you can measure proportionally. From chakra to chakra you measure the illusion of time quite differently according to your chakra functioning in different time states.

DEBBIE: Is the proportion the same from chakra to chakra?

CHRISTOPHER: The proportions are different but you could call them divine proportions because they obey laws of resonance. Resonance occurs always in terms of your fundamental vibration. You can tune a piano to any one note and have it perfectly in tune providing you start with something with a fixed number of cycles. Depending where a person relates to that note personally, each chakra becomes part of an octave or creates a note in a scale. Let us take the tuning on a guitar. You can tune it to any fundamental frequency and it will still be in tune depending on where you start. You don't even have to know what the first note is, how many cycles a second, or whatever. If you tune it to one note it will resonate even though it may sound flat by our standard notion of middle C. You could start the fundamental note at 257 or 255 or even 250. It doesn't matter as long as the interval between the strings is right. Well, it's the same with all the other things in nature that are vibrating. So you could say that in terms of the clock time an atom of H_2O vibrates at 383 cycles in this direction and say another 800 in this direction and so the two hydrogen atoms are going in and out and round and round the oxygen atom at the same time. There are two separate vibrations there, right? Now, if they are in resonance with each other then they will be harmonious and make one composite vibration--ONE. But if you change the frequency of one or the other there will be separation and disharmony. So the hydrogen and oxygen won't be making one good resonating note, but two notes. It is the same with the chakras exactly.

DEBBIE: From chakra to chakra ... say a person says, "Okay, that star, that atom is vibrating at so many cycles per second, science has it all mapped out." That person thinks that's real. But from another chakra, from another level of perception, isn't it different?

CHRISTOPHER: It's very different, yes. The experience of time on other levels is totally different. See, the chakra that does that kind of measuring is just the yellow, intellectual chakra, which functions in linear consciousness, creates mathematical models of linear events. Logical, sequential events progress forward and create the idea that time flows from the past to the NOW, into the future, and it doesn't flow backwards in our direct experience of that sequential time. You don't experience yourself, right now, as a little girl. People don't experience themselves as just being born. It's gone, time doesn't flow backwards and that's how time is experienced. So we look at life as time going forward in little bits. That's one chakra experience of time. Now when you get up in the intuitional chakra, time doesn't behave that way at all. Time can flow backwards. Time can not only intuitionally flow backwards but even in our dreams we can experience the reversal of time. In our imagination chakra we can have the front before the back and things can happen first before their causes, and time then can go backwards instead of forwards. Some people are aware that all history is created now by our act of looking backwards at it, as we reconstruct it now in our interpretations of it.

DEBBIE: What I'm wondering is: are the proportions the same in all these experiences ...?

CHRISTOPHER: Well, you could say that in your imagination you are always making your own proportions, depending on whether you are using your human imagination or your cosmic imagination.

Cosmic imagination is bound by its own laws. As an analogy you could say that there is a certain amount of freedom in a drop of rain falling into the pattern of a flake of snow that it is going to be maybe one of ten thousand different patterns of ice crystal. If you look around snow you will find most snow say, in one pile, seems to have perhaps all the same kind of crystals on it, because it happened in the same conditions at more or less the same time. But you go around at different times and find 10,000 different crystal patterns of snow. So there is a tremendous freedom of 10,000 to 1 that it's going to be one of those patterns. But we know that they're all going to be six pointed. So in some way the cosmic imagination which has the image of the snowflake has dictated, "Snowflakes are six pointed. They have something in common as a pattern image though they can be 10,000 different images with six points on them."The human proportions are like that image.

Now you could say, Well that kind of cosmic imagination has laid out the whole universe anyway; the pattern of a sparrow, the pattern of your nervous system, the fact that you have big toes, two eyes and one head . . . that's a pattern of elemental form that is beyond your control. You might be born with two heads but that's unlikely. It's been done, but in the sense our cosmic destiny is preordained we look at crystallisation as a certain mechanistic thing . . . but it isn't exact because there are 10,000 chances that it would be one of the other crystals. It's the same way with the evolutionary formation of every other human being. You all have one head, two eyes, one nose, two hands, but have you ever seen two human beings exactly the same? I haven't. Isn't that remarkable when you have FOUR THOUSAND MILLION people on this planet and not one face the same? I mean if you really look we have more complex permutations than does a snowflake crystal of water. All Chinese look like Chinese, but not to the Chinese. Don't you think it's remarkable that there is such freedom in nature and yet there is law? Definitely all humans are going to have one head. As long as they remain in this species they are going to have one head and ten toes. Cosmic imagination has laid that pattern out. That's the cosmic pattern, within all those variables, which forms a human that way.

So you can tune into the cosmic imagination. Why does the cosmos give ten toes? Why does an atom of oxygen vibrate that way? Why does light vibrate the way it does? Why does it behave and propagate itself a certain way? You can tune into the cosmic imagination and see why it's done things the way it has. The cosmic imaginer is God and the proportions in our body and the heavenly bodies too, all manifest themselves in images.

We have the same stuff, but stepped down. We can do anything we like with it. We can make that clock turn backwards in our imaginations or we can dream about it and see it spinning around fast, or looking like "Alice in Wonderland", we can become small. Or we can imagine ourselves with two heads, or two noses, or we can dream that we've got an ass's head on, like in "Midsummer Night's Dream. We can even negate our own imaginations with it.

You have the freedom to form in your imagination all kinds of weird things. When you take drugs that's what happens. When you look at a person under drugs they kind of go into waves, or you see someone go up in the air or you see the face of the devil emerging, or whatever. Anything can happen in that imagination. How do you think there are so many weird things in the world? God must have been through these trips. Why did he create things like mosquitos? He must have had bad dreams one night!

DEBBIE: Can you tune in to that?

CHRISTOPHER: Sure. Don't you think God has tried everything? The Creative Imagination that formed the universe has tried everything. You think you are going to have a fresh thought? Just think.Think of something new. And if you look far enough you'll find it has been done already. In this sense there is nothing new under the sun, and yet everything is made new by our imaginations. If you think you're enlightened and you're the first one to get enlightened, or that there is no one higher than you, just look far enough and you'll find someone that has beaten you to it, or that was enlightened in a different way to you, in a certain way that you didn't even know existed. "Old Nick" is constantly deceiving us about that. This is what Einstein meant by his comments on objective time.

Unfortunately we are totally deceived by our human imagination which is right now constantly recreating the universe between our ears. The way we do this is crucial to our understanding of God, man or anything else. This is the real meaning of the Bible story of the "Tower to Heaven". Einstein knew this and so did Christ. Thus the ancient sages trained their students to see the universe as a projection of our very own ignorance or wisdom. It is summed up in the ancient saying: "Thou art That!" and in the Hebrew scriptures as "Thou shalt not make any image of me!" It is true to say that man falsely makes God in his own image in one sense, hence many personality cults have now grown up around Christ, Krishna, Buddha and others. But these people did not image God in that way; they specifically stated that man is made in God's image, meaning not that He had a head or three heads, but that man's consciousness is God experiencing himself as ONE. "Hear O Israel, the Lord thy God is ONE," is another expression of Cosmic Imagination.

THE SINGLE REALITY

Logical thinking is necessarily deductive; it is based on axioms (postulates) and hypothesis, which is a statement of a set of rules, since without these rules the knowledge would be impossible to acquire. The rules themselves are arbitrary and it is their very rigidity which makes the game of science possible. The fixing of these rules can never be final and they can only have validity in a special narrow field of activity. Sense-experience and measurement can only be interpreted intuitively by the self and cannot be adapted to logical fixation in mental concepts. All measuring devices are extensions of our senses and all science is a refinement of everyday thinking processes. We have forgotten what Einstein said about his own laws of space and time; that there are no laws in nature, also no absolutes in science outside of the observer and *his* laws. Yet within the intuitive observer there are ways of making absolute statements which cannot be made by science, such as " I AM " or " I will die " depending on whether the observer identifies himself with pure awareness or his biological time-bound body.

Minutes, metres, seconds, light years, are all man-made absolutes and we keep an arbitrary foot in the British Museum as a standard just to make sure there is such a reality to measure with.

The necessity for this is because our notion of "object" and "time", induces ideas about objects in space. The notion of space (void) arises inductively in consciousness by virtue of our notion of objects. In everyday thinking the word "space" is accepted as representing something *real* without properly defining it. How the "I" defines it in science leads to relative thinking of assumed material points *in* space. These lead to dualisms which are not challenged by the "self"-"I", who joins and separates "space" from "objects" at will, as if it were truly possible to do so in empirical experience. "Space" [or the absolute void] must be defined as an all pervasive "I" which unites all objects together in the mind as ONE UNIVERSE.

If we move from the theoretical to the experiential and open our minds, as Einstein did, "to experience the universe as a single, significant whole," we can devise innumerable tests and experiments that will validate the experience, provided we maintain an alert and receptive state of consciousness. Below is a series of dots:

●　　　　●　　　　●　　　　●　　　　●

How many spaces are there between the dots? Ninety-nine percent of the world's population will probably answer "four". But look again and become aware of what is happening as you look. Where are you experiencing the dots? On the paper, or in your consciousness, in the same way that you experience the millions of stars in the night sky? So are there millions of spaces between the stars or one space or no space?

As I write this I am sitting on a California beach on the bank of a tidal river as it enters the sea. Two men are playing with a dog on the opposite bank, throwing long strands of seaweed into the water, which the dog retrieves with splashing enthusiasm. Trees and headlands fade into the fog on the other side of the bay. Gulls and a small plane fly overhead and the author of *Nuclear Evolution* is sitting nearby. Where are the beach, the gulls, the plane and the author? Scattered around in space or in my consciousness? If I say that they are in my consciousness, the implication is that everything and everyone is also in my consciousness!

For Einstein the validation of the unified field was the consuming fire, the urgent task of his last twenty-five years of life. In his Special Theory of Relativity he demonstrated the equivalence of energy and matter. In his General Theory he showed that the space-time continuum was indivisible. What he was seeking in the Unified Field Theory was to bring this process of coalescence or unification to its ultimate culmination or climax, to show that the entire universe is one field in which everything, from an atom to a wheeling galaxy, is living, moving and having its being. In other words, Einstein was moving towards a scientific validation of the wisdom of all the sages, by merging man's sensory perception of his universe with his intuitive awareness of an underlying reality and unity, thus fulfilling the words of the Jewish prophets:

"Hear, O Israel the Lord thy God is One."

In Einstein's own words:

"Perception of this world by thought, leaving out everything subjective, became partly consciously, partly unconsciously my supreme aim."

Einstein failed to achieve his wish because he started out his task by trying to exclude all that is subjective. He also failed to take into account that all sensory phenomena, including the physical universe, are ultimately subjective and experienced within consciousness. Today the validation that he was so desperately seeking is within everyman's reach through the new science of Supersensonics that has not only reawakened awareness of the fantastic instrument of verification within us all, namely our supersensitive nervous system, but has presented us with the long sought-for link between science and spirituality. For an explanation of the difference between Einstein's universe and the Supersensonic universe of the rainbow body we refer the reader to the book *Supersensonics**, pages 351-357.

So where does our own daily experimentation lead us? Could it be that our flashes into states of oneness might evolve into a blazing certainty that space as a separator does not exist?

If I am the gull, the pilot in the plane, the dog on the beach and the surging waves of the vast ocean, what am I not?

---

*"Supersensonics", Vol. III of the series "The Supersensitive Life of Man", by Christopher Hills, obtainable from University of the Trees Press.

Fig. (128)   Fig. (129)

EINSTEIN
UNIVERSE

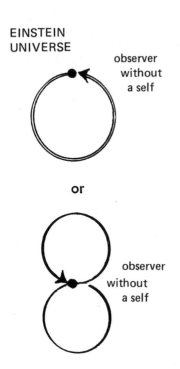

observer
without
a self

or

observer
without
a self

SUPERSENSONIC
UNIVERSE

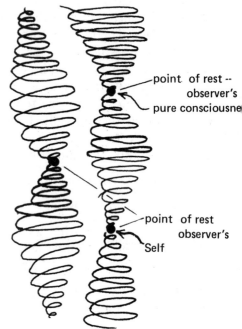

point of rest --
observer's
pure consciousne

point of rest
observer's

Self

TIME, SPACE AND COLOURS

Neither " time " nor " space " as we experience it can be the absolute measure of objects in motion, simply because there is no absolute material point " at rest " from which to measure. The whole concept of an absolute velocity for light is therefore an illusion. The only Absolute is the " I " point of self consciousness of the observer, who can experience one cycle, or two cycles or beats, without any awareness of a fixed clock-time in which they occur. In the same way colour can be experienced in so many cycles, without the limitation of an Earth-time measure (seconds) which the consciousness fixes it with.

For instance we do not have to use units such as metres or " beats *per second*" in measuring the nodal points of say an Eight metre wave, or 80 c.m. wave. According to our mode of thinking in " absolute time " it could be any vibrating system divided into 8, or dividable by 2 or 4 so long as it produced resonance at these points where simultaneous interactions occur. These Absolute points occur continuously and obey the laws of resonance which are proportional laws and not fixed in absolute unitary points of measure; we will find later they can be just as exacting in nature as any fixed arbitary measure made by man.

402

THE EXPERIENCE OF SPACE

We often hear from mathematicians about the fourth dimension and even from metaphysicians about the fifth dimension so it becomes important to see what they mean and to see what relationship these have with the seven dimensions of Nuclear Evolution. Since Einstein, we have become familiar with the four-dimensional concept of space-time.

Space is to our senses a three-dimensional continuum. That is, we can describe the position of any object at rest by means of three coordinates x, y, z, from the central point of that object.

x axis = length,   y axis = depth,   z axis = breadth

Fig. (130)

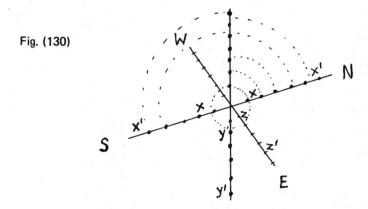

There is an indefinite number of points in the surrounding neighbourhood of the object which extends out from the centre. This can be described by the coordinates x', y', z', which may be as near to the respective values of x, y, z, of the first central point as we may choose to make them. We speak of this expanding property of extension into space as a continuum because such a point can expand outwards forever until it is stopped by our own imagination. This point at the nuclear centre of any system is called Bindu in Sanskrit meaning the original seed of selfhood which expands outwards into undifferentiated space. We speak of these three physical coordinates as "three-dimensional" and in Nuclear Evolution we speak of "Imagination" as the seventh dimension, so what happened to the three missing dimensions?

The answer is that all material objects in space are three-dimensional, but because they exist in time, i.e. they are born and they die as with all physical phenomena, we can see that in nature the addition of time makes a total of four dimensions in a space-time sense. How real is this space-time which is the extension of the object described by four numbers, namely three space coordinates of x, y, z, plus the time coordinate – t?

THE INFINITE CONTINUUM

The whole world and the universe it sits in is also a continuum along with the human body, because for every event which happens at any one time in space there are an infinite number of simultaneous events happening, as many as we care to think or imagine, along the four coordinates x', y', z', t', which differ only in a small amount from those x, y, z, t, we first thought of. Naturally the evolution of human consciousness has not always been capable of regarding the universe as an infinite succession of points or events in a four-dimensional continuum. But since the theory of relativity, it is common to talk of space-time in this way. Up till then, time played an independent role in human thinking. It is because of this age-long habit of human thought that we have treated time as an independent continuum on its own. According to Newton, Galileo and classical mechanics, time is always regarded as an absolute, and largely life on earth is lived still as if time were separate from and independent of the position and the motion of an object through space. In physics up to Einstein, time was always regarded as separate from the system of coordinates x, y, z, but now we see that time is a function of distance. That is, the movement of a physical body in space takes time to go from one point relative to another.

ENTER EINSTEIN

In the theory of special relativity the three coordinates x, y, z, of three-dimensional geometrical space are included with an imaginary magnitude which replaces the usual coordinate t, which is proportional to it, and in the theory this mathematical form plays exactly the same role as the three space coordinates. It is customary in mathematical operations to substitute a symbol for a complex reality which is purely imaginative and this is what Einstein called "space-time". This gives us only a vague notion of the important idea contributed by Einstein that in reality space and time are inseparable.

The structure of space in Einstein's theory was based on two considerations:

1. There exists an average density of matter in the whole of space which is everywhere the same and different from zero or vacuum.

2. The radius or size of space is independent of time.

Albert Einstein 1879-1955, a spiritual physicist.

Both of these hypotheses have been proved consistent in physics but only after an imaginary term was added to the field equations. This cosmological term keeps raising its head. Friedman showed that it could be possible to preserve hypothesis (1) without introducing the cosmological term if we did away with hypothesis (2), i.e. the field equations in which the radius of space is expanding dependent on time. Later Hubble showed by investigating the extra-galactic nebulae, that the milky ways, like our own universe, were moving away from each other and produced a red shift in the spectrum of their light which increased proportionally with their distance away. This is at present interpreted by physicists in terms of the Doppler effect as the result of an expansive system of stars. There is a problem with this interpretation when we calculate that the origin of this expansion could have only occurred about 10^9 years ago, while the birth of stars and their vast systems appear to take a great more time to evolve.

The theory of expanding space does not permit anyone to reach any decision mathematically or physically about the finiteness or infiniteness of three-dimensional space. Nor does Einstein's original static hypothesis of space, which yields the finiteness or closure of space, give us any proof that it is so limited since it is relative to the observer.

However, Einstein had some original ideas about relativity and the psychological origin of the notion of space which are important for the understanding of the seven dimensions of Nuclear Evolution. Einstein realised that in Newton's laws the idea of acceleration appears. This Newtonian theory can only denote acceleration in respect to space. Newton's space was not moving with our rotating galaxies nor expanding like Hubble's observation, but "at rest", or at least unaccelerated as far as considering the acceleration as having any value with a meaning. Einstein saw that the same holds true for time, which we deal with in the rest of this book as having seven levels of experience with only one dimension as "at rest" or zero time. Einstein could only use one kind of time which was relative to the clocks on planet earth.

The concept of time held by many physicists today as being kept by some standard atomic clock is applied to space as well as points in space, and enters into the concept of acceleration. Newton and all contemporaries up to the time of Einstein felt disturbed to ascribe some physical reality to the emptiness of space as well as to its state of motion in the universal field. At that time there were no alternatives since space-time had not been thought of. So no one could give the mechanics of space any clear meaning. It is a mind-blowing experience to have to ascribe the same reality to space as we do to physical objects in general and especially when it comes to empty space in which all pieces of matter are sitting at various distances from each other.

IS SPACE REALLY EMPTY?

Philosophers argued about empty space this way and that, until Descartes said space was identical with extension but extension was connected with bodies, thus there is no space without bodies and hence no such thing as empty space. Only Einstein did not laugh at the thought of there being no empty space and in fact thought it was an attractive idea!

The psychological origin of the notion of space is based on our habits of thought. It is true that the idea of continuous extension away from an object like our own body gets its origin from our experience of space as being the medium in which solid bodies make contact with each other. Einstein saw that the assertion that extension is confined only to bodies is not entirely true and arises as an expansion of our physical empirical experience. Space itself can be expanding if we delimit our consciousness from identification with solid objects. However, Einstein showed that Descartes' idea was true in a relative sense, even though we should not ascribe an objective reality to the notion of empty space since it could not be experienced directly with our senses.

Our human psychological need for space is not as obvious as it would seem from ordinary states of consciousness. The notion of space is suggested to us because our senses learn to discriminate boundaries and outlines around objects, the first of course being our own skin. Our skin includes also its various sensors which are merely refined pieces of skin tuned to specific frequencies of vibration, i.e. eye to visible light radiations, ear to sound vibrations in air, tongue to molecular vibrations of solids and smell to vibrations of gases. The one which more than any other sense gives us a notion of space is our sense of touch. In this sense we are imagining all our other senses as touching, as extensions into a different space or continuum . . . i.e. we touch objects with our eyes, we touch objects with our ears through their sound vibrations in the air, we touch objects through their aromatic vibrations with our sense of smell.

HUMAN NOTIONS ABOUT SPACE

Let us imagine we have an empty ball or sphere so constructed that we can pack the empty space full of objects. The property we have given this material object, the sphere, is something created by the shape of the object, i.e. "space enclosed" by the sphere, which of course will be different for different sized spheres with larger outlines or boundaries. This property of emptiness is imagined as being independent of whether there are any objects in the sphere or not. We have imagined our concept of empty space as being a property of the sphere, something created by its form, but the thickness of the walls of this sphere are of no importance to its storage capacity. Can we reduce the thickness of the walls of this sphere to zero thickness without the "empty space" being lost? We can see that the space is not affected and it remains intact without the sphere and its outlines. This appears obvious to our consciousness but in every day life such a way of thinking appears unreal because we invariably forget the origin of our thoughts about boundaries and skins.

Descartes did not like to consider space as independent of material objects for this reason; space could not be something which can exist separate from matter. Even the creation of a vacuum of emptiness into which matter can move, such as we have with a mercury barometer, is dependent on the surrounding material glass which keeps the pressure of the atmosphere out. Is the vacuum independent of the glass? If we switched the glass for the walls of the sphere would we have an empty space or vacuum independent of the material which surrounds it?

The moment we make the walls of the sphere of zero thickness our idea of vacuum and second-hand imaginary thought experience of emptiness disappears and we have a uniform space that is no different from the extended space around it. Yet even at this stage of thought there is something primitive and sense-bound about our concept of empty space as something separate and real from the objects in it. If we enclosed the first sphere in a much larger one it would not affect the space in the smaller one. In fact the space in the first sphere would be part of the hollow space of the bigger sphere which contains both of them. So long as they are both at rest there is no problem, but the moment the small one begins to move about then the space in the small sphere becomes a variable part of the large one and the two spaces are in motion in respect to each other.* We can now view the outer container as the unbounded medium in which the first sphere can swim around and find an infinite number of spaces to occupy in the motions each sphere has in respect to each other. Such is the concept of Einsteinian thought of our universe.

ALL EXPERIENCE OF SPACE IS IN THE PAST

Einstein is actually coupling this idea of a finite and bounded space with an infinite number of places or points within it and then bringing in the concepts of time which differentiates our sense experiences between events now and our recollection of these past events. He notes that time is a psychological attempt to discriminate between the alternatives of sense experience and dream experience, which is the effect of the activity of the mind trying to create order. An experience of an event is associated

---

* See diagram of Nuclear Evolution sphere on page 418.

with a recollection or memory of it, which is considered as being earlier in comparison with our "present experience". This conceptual ordering of experience as it is experienced now and then stored for recollection gives rise to the subjective concept of time, that which continuously refers to the arrangement and re-ordering in linear fashion of all the psychological experiences of each individual.

Nuclear Evolution takes off from this point and ascribes a level of consciousness to this ordering of events; it is the function of our imagination (Violet) to order the events in the universe into form and pattern, and we call it the seventh dimension of consciousness. Their linear arrangement is the function of our logical and intellectual processing of events which we ascribe to the third dimension (Yellow) of consciousness. The actual recollection of the events in past time is called the conceptual level (Blue), namely the memory or the mind, and it is related to the experience of all events in our total space as if we are experiencing events in time as discontinuous, i.e. separated from the present and future in the act of recollection. All historical events have the appearance of being separated from the now and as soon as we compare the past events with our present, the fleeting present is already past. It is a fact that the act of comparison with something we have already conceptualised as real creates new mental thoughts which we call comparative knowledge. All comparative knowledge is therefore experienced in past time. This is not direct knowledge but an experience which is rendering the concept of time as something objective.

Let us use an example of person A who thinks of "I" in the absolute sense and that what ever happens in their own consciousness is identical to that happening to others at the same time, without reference to any stored information; e.g. person A is standing looking at a sunset, at the same time person B is by his side, and person A experiences the consciousness of person B as also experiencing the sunset in relation to his own concept "the sun is setting". Thus person A associates his own experience with person B as validating his own experience "the sun is setting". Person A is convinced that the scene and the experience which B participated in is identical with his own experience. "The sun is setting" is no longer regarded as a purely personal experience, but as an objective experience of others too. In this way the personal interpretation "the sun is setting" is now interpreted as an objective event which is true for all others who see the sun go below the horizon. Such an "objective event" is then stored in memory as a concept to be used again and again in communicating with others about the "real external world," yet this experience which originated as a subjective one has now become externalised and objective. Such a person feels the arrangement of all their subjective mental experiences can be handled as sequentially ordered events with perfect agreement as to the arrangement of their temporal experiences.

THE ILLUSION OF THE PHYSICAL NOW

In my book "Supersensonics" I go much deeper into these sensory experiences of vision and hearing to show that these are subjective illusions of reality brought out of our consciousness by identification with mind. I used the example among others of the sound of a jet plane coming from a direction where the plane is not. Our sense of hearing tells us the plane is overhead, but by the time the sound reaches our ear the plane is near the horizon so that our mental localisation of the source is displaced. It must be the same with everything we look at from great distances; most of the stars are nowhere near the places where we see them, yet our measuring devices fix them accurately with degrees of right ascension and azimuth in everyday experience. They become objective and real external experience, yet they are only phantom images and merely a disturbance in our consciousness, the actual object having moved on in the case of the stars many millions of years ago. It is the same with the movement of atoms in space which our gross senses experience as solid. We build up concepts of space, time, and events and store them psychologically in our consciousness as objective experiences in relation to an external environment which is separate from the observer of those events. It is not easy to see that these two dimensions are merely creations of human consciousness through first the imagination, which orders, and then the intelligence of the mind, which uses the tools of thought in order to bring these images in line with sensory experience.

THE DIMENSION OF THE SIXTH SENSE

There is another experience of time which is not related to anything sensory or to our past experiences and this is our concept of the future. We still have some essence knowing to add to this brief sketch of the psychological experience of time as being of external origin in the nature of events strewn along in time-like order. We can call these space-like events, because they have not yet reached our senses. Hence I use the modern expression "spaced-out" for this level type of knowing. I refer to the intuition (Indigo) level of consciousness, which is that faculty of knowing which does not spatially order events in time but allows them to be free and fall out of the future. It is more like the experience of time and space which we have in dreams. Yet the dreamer feels nothing strange that time can expand or collapse or reverse. Because the dreamer is the dream, he or she experiences it as direct perception of internal subjective reality,

411

but the moment the eyes open and an external reality is perceived, this direct way of knowing which does not separate inside from outside shuts off and we say we are awake. However, in relation to the exact order of events in the universe we are still asleep; stars are not where we think they are, space is not what it seems and signals coming to us through space, such as jet aeroplane sounds, are not coming from the plane but only from where the plane was sometime ago. The so-called real external world is in fact a phantom world that is purely re-created as vibrations in our consciousness. This domain or dimension of knowing the actual location as distinct from the sensory creation of things is called clairvoyance. This "clear seeing" is in some part of all of us since we know much more about each other than the mere sensory information which comes to our senses. The dowser can actually feel the pull of the rod from the hidden water table underground, the butterfly can actually locate its mate with its antenna from two miles away, birds can fly ten thousand miles without navigation aids and pigeons can find their way home.

ALL DIMENSIONS ARE MENTAL CREATIONS

In extending the three dimensions into a fourth dimension and then extending them into a fifth, sixth and seventh dimension, our awareness unfolds into the non-sensory or extra-sensory worlds of being. It would seem that this dimension of the intuition then completes the seven dimensions which make up our awareness, but this is not so because the three dimensions of depth, height and width which we call our coordinates x, y, z of the three-dimensional world and the fourth dimension t, of Einstein's space-time, are also created psychically by the vibrations of consciousness. To Einstein the concept of the material object must precede our concepts of time and space just as concepts in psychology are preceded by thoughts of pain, purpose, goals, etc. But the nature of physics and science generally is to reduce experience to space-like mental thoughts alone and then try to prove them as valid concepts or models of reality by testing them against sensory experience. Thus the physicist tries to reduce colour and tones merely to certain vibrations, wavelengths and frequencies, the psychologist reduces thought to nerve impulses and the physiologist reduces pain and purpose to chemical reactions and neurotransmitters. In looking at the spectrum of consciousness and the way we react to stimulation from external sources, we forget that these signals all have to be completely re-created in the psychic images of the observer and they do not have independent existence from the consciousness which experiences them. Yet because of some measurement on a chart recorder or an instrument which measures angles like a sextant or absorbs photons like an optical device, we say the reality is external to the human mind. The mind does not often realise that the emulsion on a photosensitive film has been made by our consciousness to respond arbitrarily to certain frequencies of light and therefore the final act of seeing the result and making sense of the distinctions and comparisons is in our consciousness and no where else. To take a photograph, therefore, even without any human agency present, does not prove that the stars are really where we see them any more than a physics experiment proves that atoms are as real as they are conceived to be. Just because a thing works does not mean that is the way it is; for example, a solid object is not solid at the atomic level, but elastic, deformable, and alters in volume with temperature, just as there is no such thing as a perfectly flat surface on earth. Because the earth is a round sphere the surface of the lake is curved although it appears flat. These concepts of flat, curved, spherical, solid, hot or cold, are all relative to something else, just as the concept of "velocity" only has meaning in relation to a fixed point somewhere in space.

ALL IS ONE

The concept of a finite external divisibility for the spaces between atomic and subatomic extension of matter particles must be given up because they cannot be measured except in human arbitrary units created by human minds such as milli-seconds, metres, angstroms, volts, etc. We are compelled by the nature of reality to give up the pre-scientific ideas and concepts of sharply defined boundaries of solid bodies as well as the precise mathematical laws which govern their interactions.

Einstein himself says, without many hearers in this abstract dimension of the direct perception of nature, that there are no precise laws even in the macro regions of space for the possible configurations, patterns, etc. of solid bodies touching each other. This is not what the modern chemist or physicist wishes to hear because precision is indispensable to the system of knowing which we call modern science.

The idea that "physical reality" is something independent of the consciousness of the subject's experience of it is conceived as a combination of time and space interpenetrated by material particles existing permanently and moving about in respect to time and space. Thus the notion that time and space exist independently of the observer is expressed by physicists in this way: If matter were to disappear completely space and time would remain behind as the basic matrix for all physical happenings.

Fortunately the concept of the wavefield appeared and claimed to replace the concept of material particles. But it is characteristic of those who used field theory to think that where no matter was available there could be no reason to have a wavefield. However, in dealing with radiation and light we are dealing with a wavefield which has not yet manifested as matter until it is absorbed by something in "empty space".

THE CONCEPT OF SUBTLE MATTER

It is here that Nuclear Evolution resolves a paradoxical situation, since if the field concept is the product of material bodies and can only be interpreted in terms of mechanical vibrations, then it is necessary to bring back the old concept of aether because mechanical waves would need some medium to travel through like waves in water or sound in air. A cosmic sea of aether was the idea of a subtle matter through which these vibrations could be propagated through empty space. However, Nuclear Evolution sets out the theory that our consciousness is not limited or bound within our skin (this boundary is just a mental idea of human limitation) and extends throughout the whole of space, so that it becomes identical with aether or Akasha as it is called in Sanskrit. This Akasha through history has had many names including primordial aether, astral light, universal soul, matrix of the universe, cosmic substance, serpent fire, pregenetic matter, primordial atom, and is identical in reality with pure undifferentiated consciousness.

If this invisible intangible aether consciousness is the medium in which all vibrations ultimately take place, including our own vibrating minds and these vibrations of stars and suns whose light is also invisible until they strike some matter, then we can see clearly that there are dimensions of consciousness for which the present concepts of science can be extended to include wavefields of consciousness. In this respect matter merely becomes a more gross vibration of energy, which takes place inside the spheres of consciousness like one ball vibrating inside another at different frequencies. It has always been frustrating for scientists to interpret the electromagnetic fields as various states of the aether and particularly as mechanical vibrations, but if we can see that it is our consciousness which experiences these vibrations and not some aether separate from the observer, then the problem of physics is solved. However, hard-nosed scientists who have won their mental concepts with hard-won experiments will not lie down and be convinced by mere words or theories. They must prove it physically in a material sense because they are materialists. No other God will suffice but a material one. This is where Nuclear Evolution begins to investigate the nature of this consciousness on different levels of experience, so that we can see clearly why certain people think like this and why others do not accept explanations of the physical level of consciousness as having any light to throw on the nature of reality. Obviously those imprisoned in dimensions of thought that are bound to the prevailing concepts of space-time, measurement, man-made arbitrary units and so forth, will not find any sense in a non-sensory explanation. To them it will be non-sense. So be it! Let us proceed with our concepts of space and time.

Fig. (131)   THE COSMIC HEART

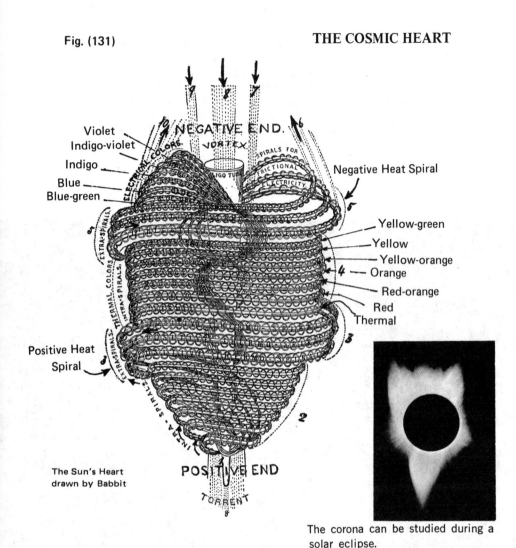

Violet
Indigo-violet
Indigo
Blue
Blue-green

NEGATIVE END.
VORTEX

Negative Heat Spiral

Yellow-green
Yellow
Yellow-orange
Orange
Red-orange
Red
Thermal

Positive Heat
Spiral

The Sun's Heart
drawn by Babbit

POSITIVE END
TORRENT

The corona can be studied during a
solar eclipse.

The diagram above, represented by Edwin D. Babbit in his book "Principles of Light and Color" published New York, 1878, is similar to the seed atom at the nux of all atoms. While his theories of colour are very interesting for their interpretation of the psychological effects of colour, the physical mechanism of the eye as being the sensor of colour is not in keeping with Nuclear Evolution. However, what is most interesting is his symbolic representation of the general form of an atom vibrating the spiral ethers with influx at 7, 8 and 9 and efflux at 6 and 10 represented by the three streams of dots. The similarity to the chakra system on page 60 should be noted. Babbit was writing of visible light coming from the heart of the sun having reference to the solar sphere which was similar to this primeval atom pictured by Babbit and later in Occult Chemistry by the clairvoyants Annie Besant and Leadbeater. The depression at the top was considered its North pole caused by the three cosmic gunas dividing into seven spiralling spheres.

SPONTANEOUS SUPER RADIANCE

Fig. (132)

The sun's field of energy, which it throws off in every direction into space, can only be seen visually when the moon obscures its disc. To fully understand the hook-up between an object in space and the receptor which receives its signals, one must also study the medium through which the signal passes which modifies it. The layers of the earth's atmosphere are one medium, the biological interface is another, the carrier of the signal (light) is another and lastly the space through which the carrier wave passes is another. Mentally all this passage of signals through the four mediums takes time. But time is the subjective mental function of processing the signal and this time delay is the origin of memory. All comparative knowledge and its validation is a function of memory.

The link between the vision of the sun's field and the field of the knower is a comparative reconstruction in the memory. Whether this is achieved in our imaginations by an intuitional drawing, such as that done by Babbit opposite, or in an actual photograph image of the sun's corona, does not reveal any more perception of space or time. The fact that the mind of Babbit could visualise symbolically the field before the telescopes were even constructed which could photograph it, shows the power of non-sensory consciousness.

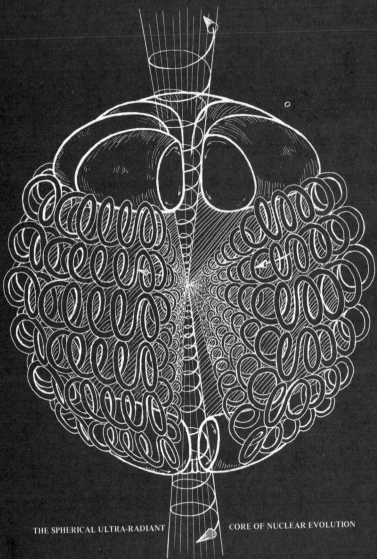

THE SPHERICAL ULTRA-RADIANT   CORE OF NUCLEAR EVOLUTION

The Sphere of Consciousness interpenetrated with its
many spiral wave-fields expanding into unlimited space.

THE EXPERIENCE OF
TIME

THE NATURE OF TIME

Time has nothing to do with the calendar which is merely a convenience for maintaining civilised life. It has little to do with clocks which are only man's way of measuring events by the establishing of some fixed periodic occurrence which fits in with the revolutions of the earth on its axis and the annual revolution around the sun. The sidereal year as kept by the positions of the stars is of little everyday interest except to astronomers, navigators and space travellers.

Time, like temperature, has relevence for humans because it is relative to an absolute. In the case of temperature it is Absolute Zero, but the only absolute there is in time is no time at all, in other words zero time relative to nothing else.

Our physical time is experienced by dividing our path of life into many small pieces called events. We then identify this as "clock time", measured with the aid of radiation of oscillating atoms supplying the ticks of the clock as natural units of time measurement.

Proper time must allow for the acceleration through space of the earth planet whirling around in the galaxial arms of this local universe. But then again the entire galaxy is moving at an enormous speed away from other galaxies. We cannot measure a single moment of time but only an interval of time measured from some reference point of zero which must be set by man's consciousness. Is there a way of setting zero points which are uniform for all observers in the universe or would all such points of rest be purely imaginary? Is there any such thing as a fixed point to measure movement through space (velocity) or time?

UNIVERSAL TIME

If one were to take the Hubble constant for the expansion of the universe which has been observed through the red shift in the spectrum of the most distant galaxies moving away from us, and if we were to use it in reverse, we would theoretically calculate that in the shrinking universe all these galaxies would come together again in a clump – if only we could reverse time. These changes in expansion and contraction of the various galaxies of our universe would be constant for all observers in all the galaxies since the expansion applies in the same way to all of them. However, these observers would have to agree what reference point in the expansion or contraction they would use to set the zero point of their clocks. This would presumably be the moment when the primeval atom (big bang) exploded and began to expand its matter into space. No earth time could be set for such an event because the earth-sun system did not then exist. Therefore, only the vibrations of the atoms at a specified number of oscillations of the original element of hydrogen (or one of the elements created in the original fireball) would indicate the kind of radiation emitted. Such an agreement would need a similar consensus of beings from each galaxy, just as we establish a convention amongst scientists today of a correlated time system such as the scientific year for modern astronomy, the zero point being set at 0.0 hours on January 1st A.D., 1950. Obviously we are back where we started from at the beginning of creation trying to decide the original moment of expansion of the primeval atom. We are reduced again to the same problem of a group of human or intergalaxial confederations of cosmic beings arbitrarily deciding from their own consciousness what is the zero point they can agree upon.

If we take the diagram on p. 404 in the chapter on space and imagine a particle or atom moving through space and redraw it showing the path of the atom, it will give us a geometrical form of the path but will not tell us anything about the time-like behaviour of its movement.

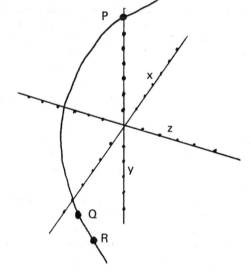

Fig. (133)

We can form no imaginative idea whether the atom moves at a steady speed through space or speeds up along its orbit and therefore does not cover equal distance in equal times. Just as the uneven path of our own planet's journey round the sun has caused us to invent a mean time which we call G.M.T., we would have to invent a mean time for the atom and maybe call it A.M.T. or we can imagine a fourth dimension of time like Einstein's space-time explained earlier in Chapter 17.

It is difficult to visualise in three dimensions on a two-dimensional piece of paper and so to ask the reader to visualise in four dimensions begins to boggle the ordinary mind as it loses its familiar anchorage to the solid concrete world of mother earth.

However, to avoid doing this we can make a series of drawings like builders and architects do to construct buildings in three dimensions – the plan, the elevation, the side view and the view from the different floor levels, etc.* We can add the dimension of time of P the particle moving along its spatial path against the time t, and this can be done for the three coordinates x, y, z.

Obviously the act of measuring takes time, so the three coordinates cannot be measured operationally at the same time. In moving from P to Q and R, by the time we have measured the x coordinate of P at the moment when P is at that point on its pathway through space, it will have moved towards Q and R when we measure the y and z coordinates. By the time we get around to measuring the three coordinates of Q the particle will already have moved on to R. The question of how we make sure our measuring devices are exactly at right angles to each other or whether our rulers are exactly "straight" is not a matter of an intellectual quibble. There is nothing "straight" in the universe if we believe Einstein and if we increase the velocity of particles to the vast speeds of light or the distances to vast distances of space, then the flat or straight surface of the largest lake on earth becomes as curved as the spherical curve of the ocean is curved or the ray of light from the distant star is curved as it passes through the infinite reaches of space. How do we actually make a straight ruler or even a ruler that is not expanding with the universe that we are trying to measure? Astronomers use rulers that are made of light rays or other forms of radiation, but in actual fact these are bent by heavy gravitational fields through which they pass on their way to us. In some cases these particles or protons are accelerated by these gravitational fields very much as particles are accelerated in the man-made synchrotron and are reaching us at velocities vastly in excess of their original speeds at the time of the big bang. Radiation is the only way that one particle or atom communicates with another atom in a far distant galaxy and radiation is the only way that our own atoms of our eyes, ears and senses can communicate with the excited particles in the sun or the stars.

The geometry that we use to communicate these ideas about radiation in four dimensions, which involves the relation of points in space to each other, is exceedingly primitive. It was this limitation on the geometry of space and the mathematical ideas of several dimensions which would not remain still long enough in time which prevented Einstein from solving the problem of the universal field – if the mathematics had been available he was

---

*All the two-dimensional drawings in this book must be viewed as two-dimensional representations of at least four-dimensional states. Some of the drawings may even represent seven dimensions.

clever enough to have done it. It wasn't and it still isn't available, since we still have to use straight beams of light as "rulers" which are not straight and we still use zero points, which are just matters of human opinion, as the absolute starting points for our measurements.

SCIENTIFIC TIME IS NOT ABSOLUTE

Hence time in science is not regarded as an absolute, but is considered relative to the motion of the observer and the particle or atom being observed in its pathway through space.

Let us go back to the example from Chapter One of a planet flashing by us at an incredible speed. Supposing we were able to observe a flash of light reflected back and forth between two parallel mirrors which are fixed. If the distance between the mirrors is constant and fixed, we can use the time taken by the light as a "light clock", because the flashes of light back and forth take an equal amount of time. If, instead of a planet moving past us, we substitute a space rocket which has such a light clock, then the example becomes more clear. But now suppose our light clock is inside the transparent rocket travelling past us to other planets and in our minds we are travelling along at the same speed inside the rocket, then when we watch the light clock we shall see the light flash with our sensory devices at the same speed as if the space rocket was at rest:

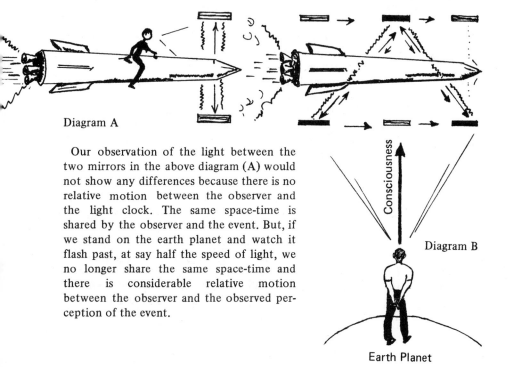

Diagram A

Our observation of the light between the two mirrors in the above diagram (A) would not show any differences because there is no relative motion between the observer and the light clock. The same space-time is shared by the observer and the event. But, if we stand on the earth planet and watch it flash past, at say half the speed of light, we no longer share the same space-time and there is considerable relative motion between the observer and the observed perception of the event.

Consciousness

Diagram B

Earth Planet

We cannot perceive the path of the light as a fixed reflection of the interval between back and forth motion as we did before. Because the light flash keeps up its speed with the rocket's fast moving light clock, the light is seen to be reflected along a diagonal path as in (B) instead of straight up and down as in (A). The flash of light travels a longer distance between the two mirrors as it would move between the two mirrors in our zero "at rest" space-time reference on earth, and therefore does not take the same time as the observer who remains with the same space coordinates and space-time as the fast-moving rocket he's sitting on. Einstein maintained that the speed of light is the same in all space-times so the flash of light must take more time between the two mirrors from our space-time position than in the space-time of the observers on board the rocket, because the diagonal distance must be divided by a longer time interval to yield an unvarying value for the velocity of light. So if the rocket were a passing planet or an interplanetary space ship travelling at a very high velocity as observed from our zero point of rest, we would measure a longer time interval between the ticks of the light clock when it is in motion than when it is at rest or going slower. If the people on the passing planets or space ship did not have light clocks, but measured time by the oscillations of some other kind of radiation, like the vibrations of an atom, or with any other device which measured intervals, their fast-moving clocks on board the rocket would appear to run slow from our observation point at rest.

TIME DILATION

If these clocks were atoms or the oscillating atoms of our own bodies, they would be slowed down and we would live much longer if we were on the rocket travelling at that high speed. This stretching and contracting of time is called time dilation in physics. These intervals are measured in space-time between the different reference coordinates with simple geometry and algebra, using such assumed values as relative time t, and v representing velocity of the moving particles or clock along its pathway P, Q, R in diagram 133 .

When we come to view the enormous velocities of protons and atoms which reach us on their pathways from distant stars , we can see that these simple mathematical relationships, which stand for realities, are based on certain assumptions that there is a place on earth at rest or somewhere else in reality in the cosmos at rest, in order to give the velocity of light and the ticking of the clock intervals any meaning. Yet in reality there is no such place that remains still in the physical world, and because everything is moving in relation to everything else, Einstein said that all time and space is relative to the position of the observer. This was a very difficult idea for most physicists of Einstein's earlier days to accept and they fought it tooth and nail. It is now the foundation plank of all physical and biological science and has transformed our understanding of the universe. However, Einstein was disturbed by his own results, because they were based purely upon human sensory experience which causes us to have unreal perceptions about our own act of observation. He worked for 50 years, after his famous insight, to discover the missing link between the cosmos and the electromagnetic vibrations of light which shine through its vast spaces.

Nuclear Evolution does not view anything created as "at zero rest" and from the viewpoint of an earth observer agrees that everything is relative to the limited consciousness observation point of a physical observer on earth. We call this "onlooker consciousness", because the view from the centre of any system is totally different from the view of someone imprisoned in "onlooker consciousness".

The periods of time for objects moving at high velocity around us with reference to a different inertial frame are not different if the angle of vision is widened to include that system in a central system which begins and ends with the observer. In other words we say that everything is happening in our consciousness which is the real frame of reference, not the physical worlds which are merely local events in our field of consciousness. The events in our consciousness are extensions into space and the distinctions between one frame of reference and another, such as identification of zero rest with the earth planet as a rocket goes by, are purely mental creations. Our consciousness is already "out there" travelling on the rocket or travelling with the passing planet and only by a mathematical trick of substituting a relative framework for an absolute one of "I Am" do we create onlookers of creation with our own consciousness. In fact our consciousness is at the centre of every system until we limit it by identifying ourself (consciousness) with a physical body at a physical but highly imaginary point of rest.

It follows that the only absolute point there is in the universe is in the purity of the observer's consciousness and its unitive links with the total unlimited field of the knower. It is this knower which validates all experience, all phenomena and all events in the physical and material worlds in terms of its own limitations. In other words, the quality of our consciousness determines what our experience of reality will be -- onlooker consciousness or centre consciousness.*

---

*This difficult question of the perception of the real world and our experience of rotation, light, velocity and resonance is dealt with in greater detail in "Hills' Theory of Consciousness" by Robert Massy, PhD. and in "Supersensonics" by the author. (See References)

WHAT ABOUT THE BIOLOGICAL CLOCKS?

The immediate consequence of all these imaginative operations is that if our consciousness could be speeded up so that its oscillations equalled the speed of light then time would stop, the human being would stop aging and would crash through the light barrier into a timeless domain of absolute time. How this could actually happen in reality rather than mathematically is the subject of this book. Here in the meantime is the mathematical explanation:

> The relationship between time in the observer's frame of reference at rest on earth is t_o, and the relative time t in the other frame of reference of the space rocket can be expressed as:

$$t = \frac{t_o}{\sqrt{1 - v^2/c^2}}$$

> where v represents the velocity of the moving clock from our earth reference frame and c represents the velocity of light in a vacuum.

We will not comment on the possibility of ever having light, c, travel in the vacuum which is presumed to exist in space as a constant in all our scientific measurements. It becomes important to understand that the v in this equation is the relative velocity between the observer and what is observed. In our particular example of the passing rocket or planet, the object observed happens to be a light clock and the subject is the consciousness of the observer who perceives that object in the mind. Therefore the equation describes a mental operation in our consciousness and it is not important what the object is; it could be anything moving in reference to the observer. We can see from this equation that if there is any velocity at all between the observer's frame of reference and the object's frame of reference, t will be greater than t_o as we can see from the example of the space ship given.

If v is made equal to 50% of the speed of light we substitute 0.5c for v in the equation and by doing some arithmetic we come to $t = 1.15\ t_o$, which shows that if we observed the light clock travelling on the space ship rocket speeding past us at half the speed of light its second hand would take 1.15 minutes of earth time to make a complete revolution during one minute of our own clock ticking at rest at zero velocity on earth. In other words if the space rocket's clock were at rest on earth it would only take 1 minute instead of 1.15 minutes. If the space ship passes by at 87% of the speed of light, $t = 2t_o$ and we then can see that the events of time would be taking twice as long as the usual minutes on earth. If the space ship was another planet and

426

we could see our cosmic brothers and sisters moving around on it as it flew past us, they would appear to have slowed down all their movements and would move in slow motion. The oscillations of all the atoms of their bodies would have slowed down their vibrations in reference to those on earth, but not in reference to their own time frame which would appear normal to them. They would view the earth as flying past them at the same 87% of the speed of light, with ourselves moving in slow motion. In respect to their time frame we would be taking twice as long as they did to get anything done. They would be thinking we are a slow people.

If the space ship or planet were flying past us in space at 99.5% of the speed of light, $t = 10t_0$ and we would view the hands of their clocks taking ten times as long as ours, for every minute of earth time our space brothers and sisters would take 10 minutes of their time to accomplish the same tasks. They would live 10 times as long travelling at 99.5% of the speed of light, and their clocks would move only 6 seconds for every 60 seconds on earth clocks.

If they flew past us at 87% of the velocity of light their clocks would tick at half the rate of ours and we would live one minute of life for every 30 seconds of their time. At half the speed of light their clock would tick 1/1.15 times and would therefore tick 52 seconds to every 60 seconds of earth time, even though they would not notice any difference unless they happened to look across at our clocks as they flew by and saw our time running much slower. In other words it is not a real time dilation but only in relation to our fixed periodic events on earth that their velocity through space creates for us an inner experience of another time world, because all the frequencies of all the atoms are slowed down relative to our idea that we are the ones "at rest" in space and that all other bodies in space are moving. This has led people to speculate that if a space astronaut were projected on a long journey at a high velocity near to that of light he would only live one year for every 10 years of our life. In other words he could return in a hundred years time and by his calendar he would only be away for 10 years before returning to those new generations who had even forgotten that their parents had sent him out on a space journey. However absurd we think this is, the theory has been tested and found to be true for atomic clocks moving in orbit around the earth. But is it real time? The comparison of the astronaut's clock was with both his clock and earth clock operating on earth time.*

---

*The above is the subject of a meditation on breaking through the light barrier, given by Christopher Hills at the University of the Trees. The meditation is available on a tape entitled "Riding on a Light Beam". (Please see the back of this book for a list of tapes)

The following diagram shows a visual comparison of the seconds ticked off by a moving clock in a passing space ship compared with a 60 second interval on a clock at rest on the observer's earth. It shows different speeds of the clock relative to the observer's consciousness as an onlooker of these events taking place in earth time. The clock can be an atom or any object which is oscillating, like a moving proton, a photon, or a fast electron from the sun or any other particle with a periodic vibration.

GRAPH SHOWING DILATION OF EARTH-TIME WITH THE CONTRACTION OF MASS AND MEASUREMENT AT INCREASED RELATIVE VELOCITIES.

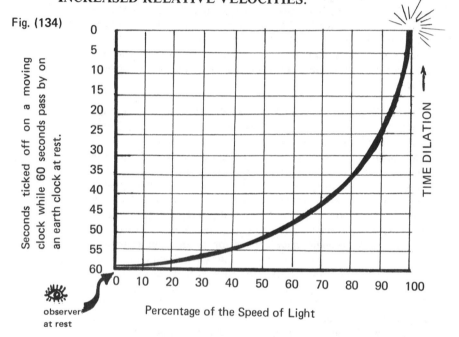

Fig. (134)

It can be seen that the faster a clock moves through space in relation to a stationary observer the slower its mechanism seems to run. It would be the same for any observer not moving with the clock. When the object reached the speed of light, time would stop completely and the clock would appear not to be running at all. The intervals of time between the ticks would be so slow that they would be infinite and therefore unmeasurable by an observer imprisoned in earth time. It would become an eternal clock and ageless. Hence the idea of eternity depends on there being no motion between the observer and what is observed so that the time dilation is zero and $t = t_0$, because they share the same space-time.

The above graph not only shows how much a clock runs slow at higher velocities and how much the vibrations of atoms slow down as they approach the speed of light, but it also shows how mass increases in the same proportion as time decreases at higher velocities. The increased mass shrinks matter in size by contracting at high velocities until it reaches its maximum at the velocity of light, when it loses its material form and becomes light or radiation.

Not only does the life-time of fast-moving particles increase as the speed goes up, according to Einstein's predictions, but objects moving through space-time in respect to an observer at rest undergo a change in measurement. The length of an object contracts according to the Lorentz-Fitzgerald contraction. At 87% of the speed of light an object appears to contract to half its length; at 99.5% it contracts to one tenth its length and at the speed of light its length is zero. The velocity in this case is the relative velocity between the object observed and an observer which at the speed of light is zero. The object does not contract but it is the measure of the object which contracts in reference to another frame. It is merely something about our sensory perception of space which contracts with velocity of light, just as a mountain contracts in size when we view it from a distance. Because it takes our consciousness time to see sensory information at the speed of light, there is a considerable shrinkage in every object that we perceive, from humans to stars. If we watch a person walk down the street he will get smaller and smaller until he contracts in the distance to about two inches high or the height of our thumb. Our mind knows the person has not really shrunk in size, so we make the adjustment in our consciousness without thinking about it or we try to rationalise it with geometrical explanations. But these formulas do not fit except at very close quarters, even for accurately made lenses.

Scientists do not question this strange phenomenon because they accept the rationalisations as valid without testing them out themselves. If they experimented they would know that there is a cosmic mystery in why the objects in the universe shrink in size as we get further away from them and yet the universe is expanding into space, so those objects should be getting bigger and bigger.*

We can now see clearly what has happened to our modern physicists who have come to believe in the supremacy of matter. They believe only in objects moving through space in reference frameworks that are relative to the observer through the speed of light. In science the measurements made in one coordinate system

---

*This phenomenon is explained in my book "Supersensonics", and also in "Hills' Theory of Consciousness" by Robert Massy.

of space-time may not agree with the measurements made in another realm of space-time, but what is common to both systems and is the absolute measurement which scientists must all agree upon (whatever the space-time frame) is the speed of light. In other words there is an absolute in the equation which is considered unvariable, eternal, and sacrosanct -- **the speed of light.**

Since all this time dilation and contraction depends on the speed of light as a maximum boundary at which all time instantly will stop, it can be seen that anyone who penetrated the light barrier would cause the universe to stop. Such a thought to a physicist is an intolerable unthinkable thought, because there would have to be no motion or distance between the observer and the event observed. It would require a jump to imagine that our consciousness is already extended, so that there is in fact no distance in the mind.

It now remains to say that distance and motion are all experienced in our consciousness even though it appears that objects are moving external to it. Such an enlightened person who does not identify with the schizophrenic splitting of the object from the subject, or with the separation of the perceiver from what is perceived, or who does not suggest to himself that his consciousness stops at his skin so that the velocity of light has not become his reality, is regarded by current scientists as a dullard who does not understand the sophistication of operational mathematics. Any person, like the scientist, who does so identify his own consciousness with physical objects and who thus relates only to the limitations of concrete matter and their energetic movements through space, does not see that the light barrier is really a thought barrier and that in fact there is no difference between light and consciousness. When consciousness is so identified as "light", the light barrier is broken and consciousness stops time. Then the next evolutionary phase is revealed to mankind in eternal time. This experience of stopping the "flow of time" and motion is called Nirvana ("Nir" meaning not and "vana" meaning flowing.) This experience of the extension of consciousness into the expansion of the universe (Brahma) frees the being from the limitations of man-made light barriers and time barriers which are euphemistically called "relative" in name but are set up as physical absolutes. It is these absolutes which create the present split between science and spirituality and it is these absolute identifications of our consciousness with material events that causes us to be robbed of any higher transcendental experience of other levels of light and colour.

THE TIME SENSE

In the diagrams on the next pages we try to take the orb of human consciousness and its awareness of time and spread it out on a flat page – a difficult task, but symbolic knowledge has often been the only way to convey certain ideas. Although the layers of consciousness and their thresholds of time are more to be conceived as balls within balls within balls, like an onion with its several layered skins, we can take first the intellectual experience of time as past flowing into present and on out into the future. Mentally we can look back and forth along the sequence of events and interpret history or predict future events. However, all backward-looking is conditioned hopelessly by the quality of consciousness which is doing the looking, and history is not as factual as we are led to believe.

The same applies to individuals on the intuitive level who find it difficult to relate to present and past events as fixed forever by clock time. It would not disturb such individuals to lose the past or present since they live so much in the future that they are not always here with us. In fact, these intuitives (Indigo band of the spectrum) may be so busy seeding the future with what is yet to come that they appear to be rather dreamy prophets from the viewpoint of the here and now. Since many of us flash back and forth unconsciously from one time framework to another, it is hard to recognise clearly our own time sense. However, an analysis of our words, sentences, and ways of expressing ourselves would reveal even in the few words of our next sentence whether we live this day in the past, present or future. The grammatical content of every sentence has captured this time sense because language is nothing but a vehicle for human experience. It is only natural to find that hidden in sentence structures is the key to our own ways of perceiving time. The careful examination of this aspect of human language is left to scholars with more time in the present than the author has available. The examination of the medium of language for the tracks of consciousness is good for validating one's experience of time in relation to others, but does not help much to analyse our own words as they fall out of our mouths every minute of the day already conditioned by the quality of our beings.

As events in time are processed in the unconscious it might be important to mention that the unconscious is a perfect keeper of time. It is possible in deep auto-hypnosis or before going to sleep at night to enter the twilight stage of consciousness and give oneself a suggestion that we will wake up at seven minutes and thirty-one seconds past eight a.m. or any other exact time. Most people actually do wake up at that time exactly by the clock. Until you have tried this and realise your dependence on an alarm clock is

THE EXPERIENCE OF TIME AND COLOUR

Fig. (135)

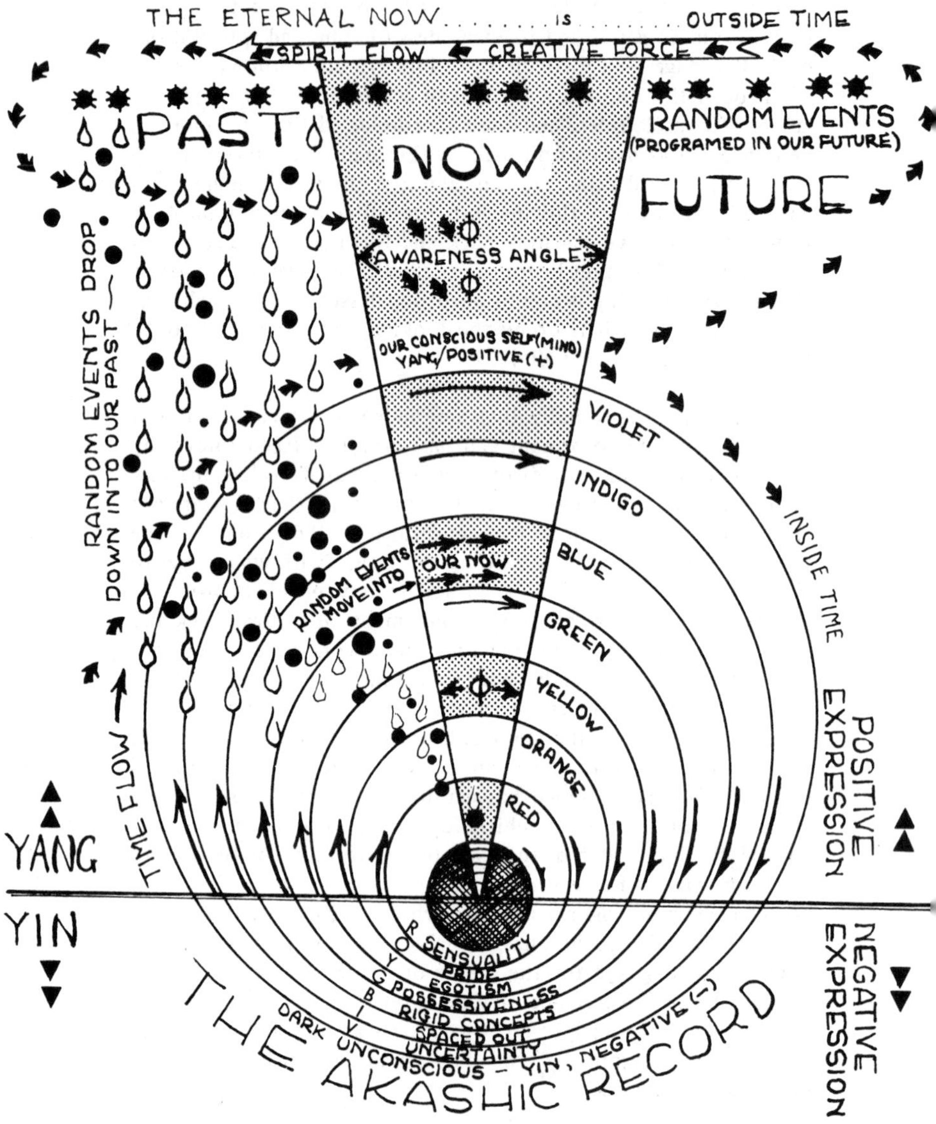

THE RAINBOW BODY

✸EVENTS DROPPING THROUGH LAYERS OF CONSCIOUSNESS

The above diagram shows the movement of events through time as they appear to our consciousness as a flowing stream from the past to the future. The colors of the levels of consciousness are harmonic vibrati of the chakra activity as these timebound events are processed by our total personality.

merely the result of mental laziness or convenience, it will be difficult for the rational mind to accept that the unconscious mind of man indeed has more powers, gifts and capablities than we can ever dream of. Our awareness of different kinds of time is shown in the diagram relating the different types of time experience to a human type and a color.

THE EXPERIENCE OF COLOUR AND THE TIME SENSE.

Fig. (136)

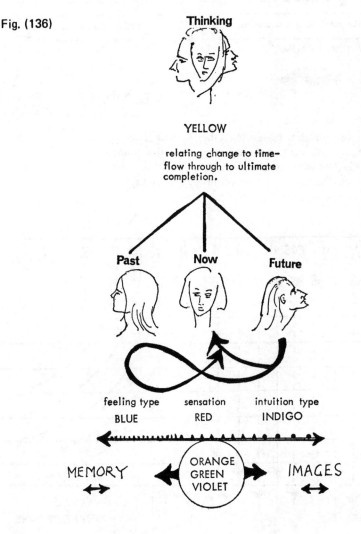

Thinking

YELLOW

relating change to time-
flow through to ultimate
completion.

Past   **Now**   **Future**

feeling type   sensation   intuition type
BLUE   RED   INDIGO

MEMORY   ORANGE   IMAGES
↔   GREEN   ↔
                VIOLET

433

Fig. (137)

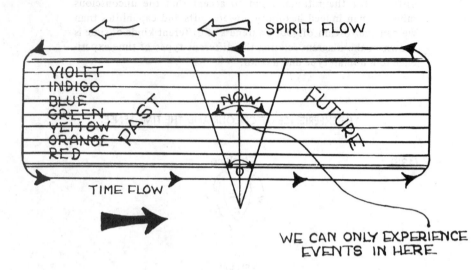

As the events pass through the seven levels they become time-bound. Time flows from the past through our imagination to the present, and into the future on the physical level. The beings in •the eighth domain who have transcended worldly life send spirit flowing in the opposite direction to annihilate time.

Fig. (138)

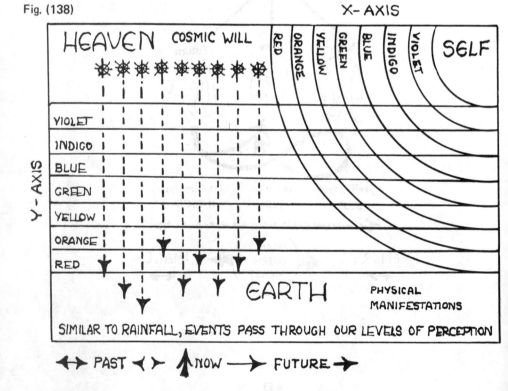

The diagrams on the following pages are taken from "Hills' Theory of Consciousness" By Robert Massy and are drawn by Allan Allen, published by University of the Trees Press, 1976. Massy approaches Nuclear evolution as a physicist and has been a student of "Hills' Theory" in residence for three years and therefore is able to simplify from lectures, blackboard drawings and personal conversation the complex process of how lumen (invisible radiation, light, etc.) becomes lux (internal experience of brightness we call white light) and affects the NUX (the vehicle of consciousness at the nuclear centre of Being).

The drawings are placed here more as symbols, in order to convey symbolic knowledge so that the words of the text are amplified by mental pictures. It is to be emphasized strongly that these are not portrayed as these processes are in reality which is not possible in a drawing on paper. The nearest visual model of the actual process was reproduced in Babbit's book on the colour shown on page 416.

Fig. (139)

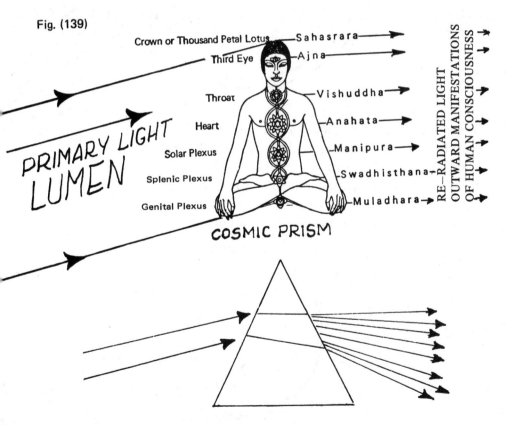

THE COSMIC PRISM OF MAN'S RAINBOW BODY

All worlds active Red through Violet:

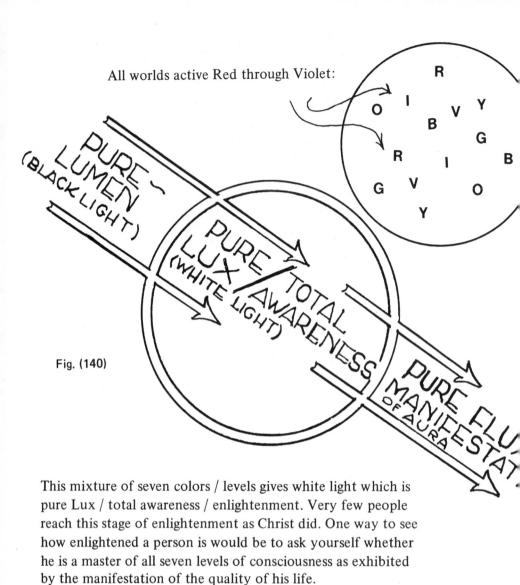

Fig. (140)

This mixture of seven colors / levels gives white light which is pure Lux / total awareness / enlightenment. Very few people reach this stage of enlightenment as Christ did. One way to see how enlightened a person is would be to ask yourself whether he is a master of all seven levels of consciousness as exhibited by the manifestation of the quality of his life.

Fig. (141)

Fig. (142)

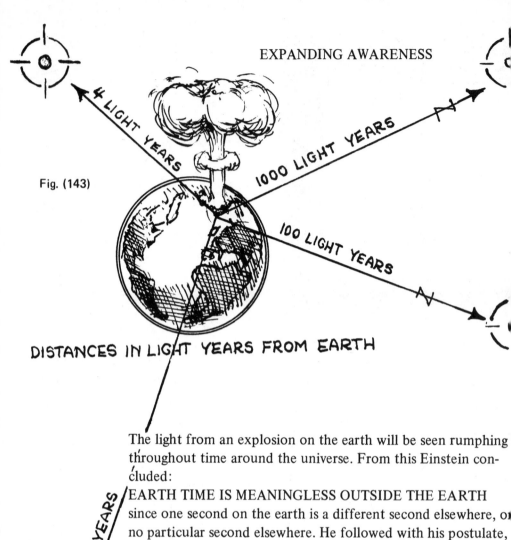

Fig. (143)

4 LIGHT YEARS

1000 LIGHT YEARS

100 LIGHT YEARS

DISTANCES IN LIGHT YEARS FROM EARTH

1,840,000 LIGHT YEARS

ANDROMEDA

The light from an explosion on the earth will be seen rumphing throughout time around the universe. From this Einstein concluded:

EARTH TIME IS MEANINGLESS OUTSIDE THE EARTH since one second on the earth is a different second elsewhere, or no particular second elsewhere. He followed with his postulate,

"ALL MOTION OF THE UNIVERSE IS RELATIVE TO THE OBSERVER."

So Einstein said that

TIME HAS NO MEANING UNLESS YOU BRING IN SPACE.

In destroying the Newtonian concept of space being stationary Einstein did not destroy Newtonian mechanics but merely widened our angle of awareness.

---

*"Rumphing" see Rumf Roomph Yoga tapes available from University of the Trees Press.

IMAGES ON OUR SCREENS..

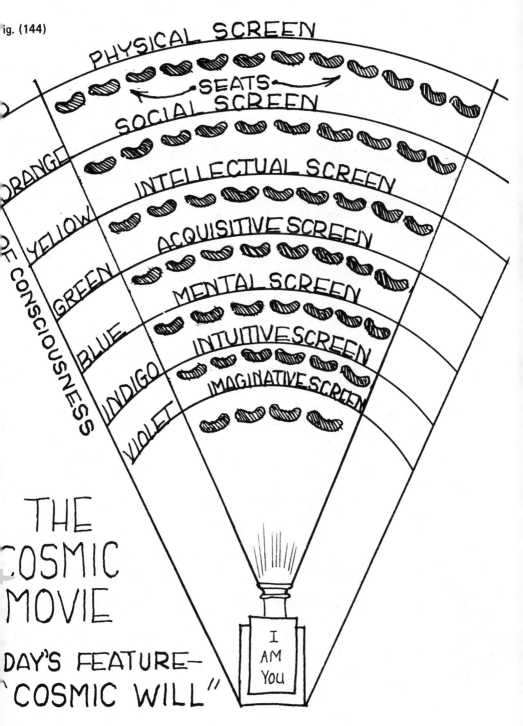

ig. (144)

PHYSICAL SCREEN

← SEATS →

SOCIAL SCREEN

ORANGE

INTELLECTUAL SCREEN

YELLOW

ACQUISITIVE SCREEN

GREEN

MENTAL SCREEN

BLUE

INTUITIVE SCREEN

INDIGO

IMAGINATIVE SCREEN

VIOLET

OF CONSCIOUSNESS

THE
COSMIC
MOVIE

DAY'S FEATURE—
"COSMIC WILL"

I
AM
YOU

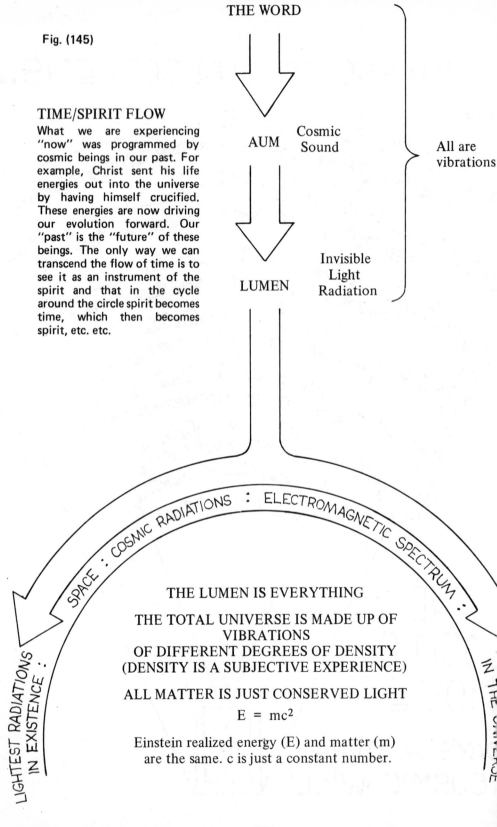

THE WORD

Fig. (145)

AUM   Cosmic
       Sound

All are
vibrations

TIME/SPIRIT FLOW

What we are experiencing "now" was programmed by cosmic beings in our past. For example, Christ sent his life energies out into the universe by having himself crucified. These energies are now driving our evolution forward. Our "past" is the "future" of these beings. The only way we can transcend the flow of time is to see it as an instrument of the spirit and that in the cycle around the circle spirit becomes time, which then becomes spirit, etc. etc.

LUMEN   Invisible
         Light
         Radiation

SPACE : COSMIC RADIATIONS : ELECTROMAGNETIC SPECTRUM :

LIGHTEST RADIATIONS IN EXISTENCE :

IN THE UNIVERSE

THE LUMEN IS EVERYTHING

THE TOTAL UNIVERSE IS MADE UP OF
VIBRATIONS
OF DIFFERENT DEGREES OF DENSITY
(DENSITY IS A SUBJECTIVE EXPERIENCE)

ALL MATTER IS JUST CONSERVED LIGHT

$$E = mc^2$$

Einstein realized energy (E) and matter (m)
are the same. c is just a constant number.

THE IMPORTANCE OF THE INNER SPACE AND
TIME WORLDS OF NUCLEAR EVOLUTION

The evidence for the seven basic kinds of behaviour in Nuclear Evolution which leads us to detect seven "types" or functions is not only confirmed by studies of the human aura and the techniques of Supersensonics but also by the empirically developed colour tests of Dr. Max Luscher by psychological means.

While the imaginative function is not a separate faculty in most people it is a component markedly obvious and unique in all poets, musicians and artists. The fact that imagination and imagery occur in all conceptual thought (Blue) as well as Intuitive knowing (Indigo) does not mean that the human "imagination" is experienced as a separate function but as a faculty used normally in conjunction with all other faculties. When imagination is missing the other faculties at every level are remarkably impoverished.

Similarly, the possessive, acquisitive drive (Green) colours all the other levels and functions with its inner feelings of uncertainty, insecurity, sense of loss (jealously) and of course their opposites of certainty, faith, sharing, etc. This does not mean that it cannot be singled out as a distinct and separate function having to do with our basic attitudes to vital force or cosmic trust. By using the techniques of Supersensonics we are provided with tools available to everyone but not often used by the ordinary scientist or psychologist. These tools can detect the separate functions of each chakra level as the kundalini flows through it. This enables us to detect differences not only in the personality and individual levels of consciousness operating with their specialised chakra function, but also enables us to determine what patterns of psycho-biological energies are really combinations of the separate levels working together harmoniously or opposing each other and thereby causing inner conflict.

WHY DO THE CATEGORIES DIFFER?

The two levels of the imagination (Violet) and the acquisitive drive (Green) do not appear in some typologies as separate types of behaviour because they overlap in complex patterns. By psychological methods it would be almost impossible to identify them as separate functions, from the inner space-time world of each individual. However, it is through those typologies which build their theoretical structures for the different "types" on the probing of the inner world by hypnosis and such other natural means of discovering nature's own ways of perceptual operation, that confirmation for four, and perhaps even for six, of the levels described in the Nuclear Evolution theory is vividly demonstrated.

For three other researchers to arrive at a psychological catalog of four separate mental operations, which each individual has some access to depending on his "type", and then to describe an accurate matrix which correlates almost exactly to four of the levels in Nuclear Evolution, could not be accidental. There must be something in nature's structure of the psyche which brought two independent research results together. Even though these four levels of experience are described in totally different ways with different images and words, the experience of time is the same for both the experiencial worlds of Nuclear Evolution and the typology system originated by Humphrey Osmond, Miriam Siegler and Richard Smoke. In essence they are identical.

The basic matrix which reveals a direct correspondence between the two systems can be shown in the following diagram:

Fig. (146)

THINKING (YELLOW)

Orientated towards processes, principles and intellectual planning and logical analysis.

In Nuclear Evolution this type is divided into : (1) rational types, (2) ideological types, and the rare refinement of jnana or wisdom (Gold).

INTUITION (INDIGO)

Orientated towards inspiration, originality; resists orderliness and restriction Visionary and imaginative but often flighty and dreamy.

In Nuclear Evolution this type is divided into:
☐ Imaginative, visionary, charismatic, original, inspired types, and
☐ the psychic, intuitional, dreamy, unrealistic type, impatient with present reality.

SENSATION (RED)

Orientated toward sensual pleasure, the material universe and concrete reality. Practical but manipulative; efficient but power-seeking.

In Nuclear Evolution this type is orientated to sensory stimuli of the skin and the joy of action. Experiences through sex and physical energy and seeks to dominate.

FEELING (BLUE)

Orientated to emotional relationships with people. Interprets the universe personal terms.

In Nuclear Evolution this type comprised of: idealistic, loyal devotional, and concern for past authorities, rigid truths, quiet and traditional.

The Theory of Experiential worlds (Experitypics)[*] describes the experience of space as overlapping that of the time worlds, but in Nuclear Evolution they are co-existent and interdependent, since all time is a function of space and space only exists because it takes time for physical bodies to move through it. Therefore in Nuclear Evolution neither time nor space is real but just a notion created by mind-stuff.

However, the linking between the above time/space worlds of consciousness in Nuclear Evolution with the four corresponding "experitypic" categories can be shown in the following diagram which can be overlaid as a transparency on the previous diagram.

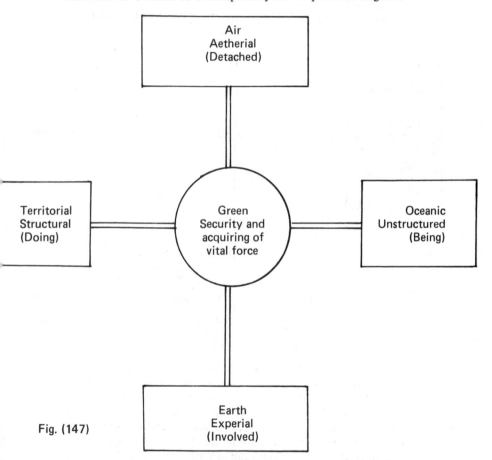

Fig. (147)

The four types delineated by Experitypics and the Theory of Experiential worlds uses these spatial categories and can be correlated with four of the colours of the levels of consciousness in Nuclear Evolution, while the remaining colours, Violet and Orange are correlated with overlapping types such as:

Sensation (Red) + Feeling (Blue) = Violet

Thinking (Yellow) + Sensation (Red) = Orange

*Experitypics, See Chapter 38

This overlapping is shown in the diagram below:

Fig. (148)

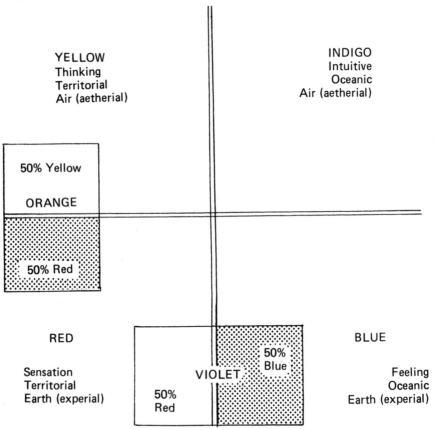

The dimensions of space, action, behaviour and attitudes within this matrix, showing examples of the various personality traits, is to be published in book form by Doubleday within the next two years. However, when the first contact with this typology was established over ten years ago, there was an instant recognition of correlation between the information yielded by dowsing the colours of the aura, the kundalini activity detected in the chakras, and the new information gleaned by psychological and psychiatric methods of probing the personality of man. Although the information was combined theoretically in a different way in the typology approach, this may eventually be changed as the Theory develops toward something more like the natural nuclear system of seven levels plus an eighth all-inclusive "oceanic" domain of "Being" at the central core of Self.

Fig. (149)

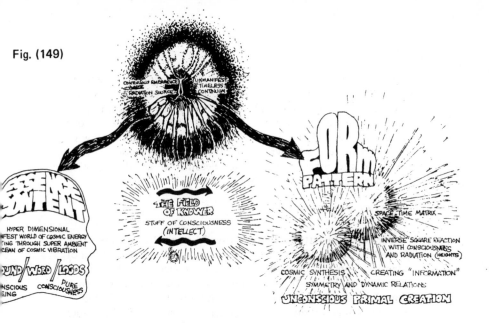

ESSENCE CONTENT

HYPER DIMENSIONAL
MANIFEST WORLD OF COSMIC ENERGY
RADIATING THROUGH SUPER AMBIENT
OCEAN OF COSMIC VIBRATION

SOUND / WORD / LOGOS
CONSCIOUS   PURE
BEING   CONSCIOUSNESS

CONTINUOUS EMERGENCE
RADIATION SOURCE

UNMANIFEST
TIMELESS
CONTINUUM

THE FIELD OF KNOWER
STUFF OF CONSCIOUSNESS
(INTELLECT)

FORM PATTERN

SPACE-TIME MATRIX

INVERSE SQUARE REACTION
WITH CONSCIOUSNESS
AND RADIATION (HEIGHTS)

COSMIC SYNTHESIS   CREATING "INFORMATION"
SYMMETRY AND DYNAMIC RELATIONS

UNCONSCIOUS PRIMAL CREATION

WHAT IS TIME?

There is no such thing as time except as a concept of the flow of events or the motion of objects through space. Obviously it takes time for objects to move down the street, whether that object is our own body or some lump of matter such as a motor car. But the time experienced is only relative to the surface of the earth, or the movement of the earth on its axis, or the earth's orbit around the sun. The creation of some external clock in the mind which measures off events is not known to nature. Even though we can measure through some biological clocks the action of light on living cells, we learn no more of time than listening to our own heart beat and wondering why it beats 70 times against 150 for a mouse or 11½ years for the sun. The spatial representation of time, as in "space-time", is no different. The succession of points along a logical and sequential line of direction corresponds to the succession of instants in time called events or "bits". With all notions of physical motion, the line of direction is traversed in a direction away from the origin of time. And what does time originate in if it is not the absolute concept of no time or zero? We are tempted in quantum physics to use the same linear time line, viewed from the opposite direction as flowing towards the origin of time instead of away from it, thereby representing a "particle" moving backward in time. Any line viewed in this way is just an intellectual exercise unknown to the processes in nature. Certainly nature returns in cycles, but it never exactly repeats an experience nor reverses itself in linear fashion or exact circles.

TIMING

It is not logical to say "before" or "after" if we allow the backward flow of time any reality. In reality there is no backward movement in time but only a backward movement in space towards the state of no time. The origin of time is purely in our consciousness and the way we subjectively perceive the flow of events in space. I have written another book on sensory awareness and the perception of space because we are dealing with complex identification processes in the mind.

MENTAL PROCESSES

A series of cassette tapes given over 24 weeks to students at the University of the Trees goes deeper into this complex problem of identification processes. But here we are concerned with a more popular book which steps down and simplifies rather than complexifies. Therefore certain assumptions about time should be discarded temporarily as conceptual mind-sets until the reader has understood the way that other people with different time worlds experience reality. This will enable the theory to be discussed in a new framework and the scientific method to be applied as a method of validating knowledge rather than as some intellectual game which serves as intellectual self-stimulation.

ANALOGY OF HISTORY

The temptation to theorise about entropy, the running down of the universe, by conceptualising time as an arrow pointing in only one direction is very similar to the way ordinary folks look at past history. Time flows like a river in ordinary experience of consciousness, and past events are recorded in the memory or in books. We can look backward at the history of events from the present as if history cannot be changed. As we turn back the pages to the records of more distant past events, we realise it is only distance of these events which creates the flow of time in our temporal relations. We are still the child with small bones and milk teeth if we dissolve time. We are still the baby who was born without a sensory or mental concept of time or space, if we can mentally dissolve the flow of time. The physical growth that has occurred through passage of time is not reversible or backward flowing. Eggs made into omelettes cannot unscramble themselves and become eggs again through time reversal. Yet the only factor in human experience which separates us from our childhood memories, or the eggs we have eaten, is the experience of time. Dissolve the time and we can instantly relive each moment anew! The experience of time in other states of consciousness such as dreams, however, is not always linear. It is misleading to speak of

446

time flowing like a river because in dream states and intuitional modes of knowing, events are not strung out like pictures on a movie film. Sometimes the "before" can come after and the "after" comes at the beginning.

Hence the theory of Nuclear Evolution, which has received little notice of scientists or academicians since it was published in 1968, has been renamed by a physicist as "The Hills' Theory of Consciousness". If I had called it that at the beginning and owned it as some personal property attached to a name, as everything else in science is, then perhaps the book would have received more attention. However pleasing such vanities may be, the fact is that the theory of Nuclear Evolution was a revelation of what Nature is doing inside each human being and, as such, the theory is being constructed "after" instead of "before". To apply scientific method to it therefore is a backwards step, bringing what is fact into the realm of theory and speculative thought. This is being done so that people can prove it for themselves. The only trouble there is that, however many times one proves it to the doubters, if they don't want to see, one can't make them see. There is something in certain people, call it a particular level of consciousness or a limited, narrow blindness or what you will, that totally rejects anything they didn't think of first. If they don't know it, then it cannot exist because they honestly believe they know everything in their own field that there is to know. This is called the "Yellow level" in my theory, and it is the most difficult level of all because in it we separate the observer from what is seen. We do not see and experience wholes on the Yellow level but merely parts strung together in a logical sequential time line.

It is this level I know best because I am an intellectual. It was only by totally conquering and vanquishing the separative clever mental trickster, like Christ did in talking to the devil in the sun-stroked desert, that I was able to see what the Cosmic Intelligence was really doing in each of us. I say this not really because of any desire to convert the doubters to my view of the creation, but to enable them to validate any theory of their own about the workings of Nature. I feel confident that, if they do this, they will eventually reach the same eternal Truth about consciousness as I have given about time. It is a gift I have received myself which can only be given endlessly away to those who are ready.

I. R. 13　Red　　19 Orange 25　　　　Yellow　　　　　　　　　　　　50 Green 55　Blue　62　Indigo　68　Violet　　　　8

THE ROLE
OF
LIGHT IN MATTER

HOW DO HUMANS TRANSMUTE LIGHT?

It is now taught in every school that photosynthesis is the ultimate energy source for all living things on the planet and that green plants transform light energy into chemical energy for human consumption, but it is not well known that humans also need the sun's light and the light of other suns for the purpose of maintaining their consciousness. The green plant cycle regenerates the earth's air with oxygen which all the animals depend upon, including man. Their carbohydrate cells also provide sufficient nourishment for the cells of the human body, but if light from the cosmos did not constantly bathe these human cells, no one would be conscious.

As we have said in Chap I consciousness and light are the same thing; we have to show now how this is so. By "light" we mean those heavy cosmic rays that continually penetrate the earth as well as our bodies, sometimes passing straight through our solid earth as well as straight through our bodies. These strong energies which pass through us need not concern us here because they do not interact with the atoms of our body cells. However, some of these lighter cosmic rays do interact at lower energy levels because our body is in resonance with them. Then the atoms in our bodies are broken up into many daughter elements without our even being aware that thousands of atoms are destroyed and transmuted every minute of the day.

A process similar to photosynthesis is taking place, not only at the material level of the cell, but also at the next level of that consciousness which animates the cell, the level of a hologram of light. A hologram is a photographic plate exposed to light of one frequency which records visual information in terms of phase and amplitude of light waves, rather than the intensity of the energy. Whereas the ordinary photograph records intensity of light exposure, the hologram image recombines a beam of light with light scattered from the objects in the picture so that the image appears in three dimensions. It is so realistic you can actually look around the corners and sides of the object in space. The analogy of the three-dimensional form of a human body as being recombined light frequencies is given here because all parts of a hologram image contain all the other parts. In other words each cell of our body is a part of a hologram image and contains within it the memory of the whole.* That whole image is sustained by cosmic light, just like it requires a laser beam to sustain a three-dimensional image of the hologram. Therefore some broad out-

---

* See page 148   for the link between imagination and holograms of light.

lines of photosynthesis and its process known as photophospho-rylation is called for in order to understand this chapter on how humans can transmute light. Those who already know this cyclic process well will be able to see the connection with the sodium electron pumps mentioned in Part I.

The accepted equation for green plant photosynthesis is given below with the dotted lines indicating where each element eventually migrates:

Fig. (150)

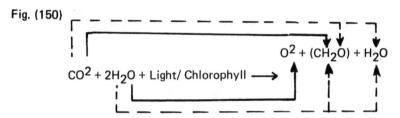

$$CO^2 + 2H_2O + Light/Chlorophyll \longrightarrow \qquad O^2 + (CH_2O) + H_2O$$

If we multiply this equation by 6 we can show that the 6-carbon sugar, glucose, which is the main metabolite in the brain, is often the end product of photosynthesis.

$$6CO_2 + 12H_2O + Light \rightleftharpoons Chlorophyll$$
$$6O_2 + C_6 H_{12} O_6 + 6H_2O$$

The reason why water (H_2O) appears on both sides of the equation is that the water produced by the photosynthesis is new water. It was not the same water which was used as an original material before it was split by the light absorption process. Hence we can now see also how the human body makes water by splitting molecules of carbon, hydrogen and oxygen in the same way as plants do. However, humans do not use chlorophyll like plants do, but amino acids and sugars can readily be synthesised by ultraviolet light. There is a well-founded chemical logic in the structures of long-chain molecules like DNA, RNA and ATP and the cell proteins of life as a storage of the sun's light.

Humans not only utilise ordinary visible sunlight but also absorb ultraviolet cosmic rays from different stars of the galaxy much more powerful than the sun; but these rays do not affect us consciously. Even "visible light" is not visible consciously as a primary energy with our senses, as we see when we look through it. But because our senses are tuned or are in close resonance with this narrow band of radiation (3900 angstroms to 7900 angstroms) our brain does experience its **effects**. Light itself is transparent and invisible just as cosmic rays are. The fact that we see and feel sunlight as visible through the narrow slit of the eyes is an illusion

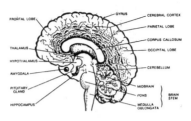

of the senses which creates a brightness internally in our brain whenever the senses are excited. This brightness is called **Lux** in the Nuclear Evolution theory, as distinct from the **Lumen**, which is the invisible radiations of light itself before it is absorbed by the narrow slit of an eye. Looking through this narrow slit leads to a notion that humans are separate from the ocean of radiation they live in.

Therefore, in order to think about light and cosmic rays which are just more intense forms of light, we have to forget we are separate humans and transcend this sensory illusion. We can only do this by regarding our own consciousness as if it had become light itself, experiencing itself directly in matter. Until our primal imagination can do this the complete process of Nuclear Evolution cannot be understood simply because it will always be limited by the inability of the mind to consciously "think in light."

What does thinking in light mean? Though animals and plants can receive impressions, feel emotions like fear and love, they do not conceptualise as humans do. A concept is like a hologram. It is a thought picture made up of many perceptions analogous to the wave-trains of light interference patterns and their amplitudes in the hologram. A thought is not independent of its thinker even though the naiveté of human entities would like to think they conceive them like babies. To form a three-dimensional thought-form inside our consciousness is to "think in light" since light and consciousness are ONE and the same. We recreate all the images we see behind our eyes in consciousness including all other people and the universe itself. We are thinking in light even when we are thinking about an abstract image of "I", the self-sense, consciously.

Though plants and animals can react and respond to light and consciousness, only mankind can think in light. Perhaps there are other extraterrestrial beings who also think in light, even more consciously than mankind. But such intelligence can only be judged on its quality, not on its mode of transmission, however sensational or sophisticated. It does not make sense to be an advanced technology merely to transmit the words "Hello Mother"! To come in a flying saucer and step out of it merely to inform the human race that we are heading for disaster is a cosmic joke. Everyone on the planet knows this. It is the same with "thinkers in light" and the prophets of the new age. So much of what they say could be written by any high school girl one wonders why we bother to communicate with higher intelligences at all! Therefore "thinking in light" involves testing the quality of our concepts by comparing them with the reality of nature. Hence divining is our natural way of asking nature about its many processes, and the imagination is the way that man programs the cosmic biocomputer. (See page 101/2 Penetrating the Imagination Barrier, for the control of light energies.)

When light and consciousness become ONE the following process of Nuclear Evolution can be understood as being identical with the way plants absorb light, with one exception. The chlorophyll process is only taking place on another level of cell organisation just as we stated at the beginning of this book, which we repeat.

Fig. (151)

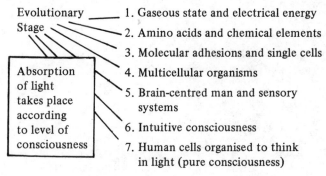

Evolutionary Stage

Absorption of light takes place according to level of consciousness

1. Gaseous state and electrical energy
2. Amino acids and chemical elements
3. Molecular adhesions and single cells
4. Multicellular organisms
5. Brain-centred man and sensory systems
6. Intuitive consciousness
7. Human cells organised to think in light (pure consciousness)

Man's organism is composed of all the previous six stages and he is the end product of them and therefore dependent upon all the prior processes for his existence. Eventually all these stages of evolution 1 to 6 will metamorphose into man through billions of cosmic cycles into the seventh stage and thence into the eighth stage when he begins to live directly from light by becoming light consciously. Man is already crystallised light unconsciously so let us describe the process, so that we can trace the steps in our imagination and see at what point we can project mental control of the electron pumps and achieve enhancement effects in the cell life.

PHOTOSYNTHESIS PROCESS

The process which converts light energy into new chemical energy and stores it by making energy-rich sugar from energy-poor carbon–dioxide is called the reduction of carbon–dioxide. "Reduction" means the addition of an electron (e-) and its opposite process of releasing energy is called "oxidation" and involves the removal of an electron. Whenever an electron is

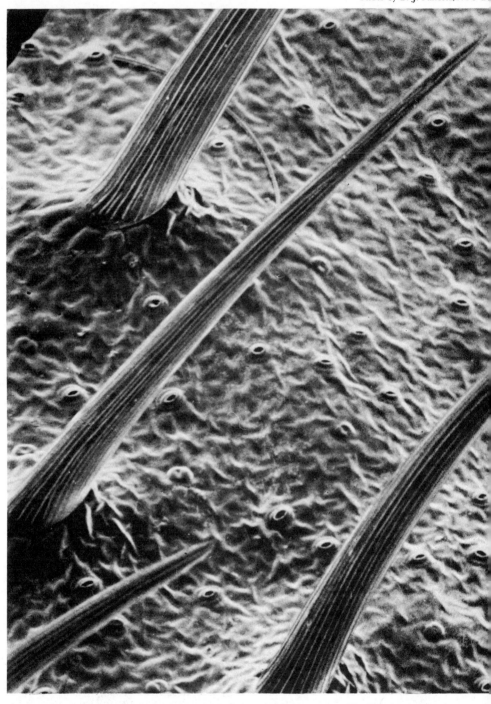

The skin of a plant leaf is one of the most vital structures in the trapping of light energy from th sun. The sustenance of all human life is dependent upon its ability to take radiant energy and manu facture carbo-hydrate plant foods by splitting hydrogen from water and taking carbon from carbo dioxide. The human skin cannot perform this synthesis directly at the physical level of life. Yet ou cells metabolise and store energy in almost identical ways. The human being has several skins, take in radiant energy of all the stars including our sun, and turns it into consciousness. This picture show the hairs on the skin which reduce drying and evaporation, and the pores through which carbo dioxide is taken in and oxygen is excreted in the photosynthesis process.

added to an element or molecule of matter it must have always been removed from some other element, so whenever there is reduction of one molecule, another is automatically oxidised. The main atoms we are concerned with in photosynthesis are the reduction of oxygen atoms (O) and the addition of hydrogen atoms (H). Thus, reduction is expressed as:

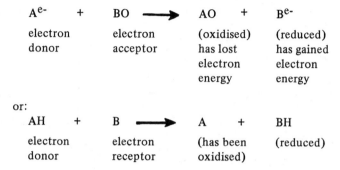

A^{e-}	+	BO	$\longrightarrow$	AO	+	B^{e-}
electron donor		electron acceptor		(oxidised) has lost electron energy		(reduced) has gained electron energy

or:

AH	+	B	$\longrightarrow$	A	+	BH
electron donor		electron receptor		(has been oxidised)		(reduced)

In all biological systems, plant and animal and human, the removal or addition of hydrogen is the most common process of oxidation and reduction. When we speak of reduction in this book we mean the addition of hydrogen or oxygen atoms and when we speak of oxidation we mean the removal of hydrogen or oxygen. The reduction of any element in the human body stores energy in the reduced metabolic compounds and oxidation burns up the energy stored.

The synthesis of sugars such as glucose from carbon dioxide is done by the reduction of carbon dioxide, as with plants which breathe CO^2; or hydrogen is obtained by splitting of water H_2O and is then added to the CO_2 to form carbohydrate units (CH_2O) so that light is stored in the process as energy. The mechanism for trapping the light energy is complex and can be looked up in any encyclopedia but this only refers to the light waves of the visible spectrum such as sunlight, which is only one small part of the electromagnetic radiations of light to which plants and the chlorophyll cells are sensitive. In the visible spectrum the short waves of light give us the sensation of violet colour and the long waves give the sensation of red colour. The shorter the wavelength the higher the energy content and conversely the longer the wavelength the smaller the energy. Chlorophyll which traps the light from the sun absorbs all the radiations except green.

LIGHT

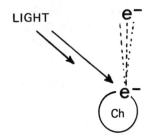

Fig. (152)

Effect of light on chlorophyll: Light striking a chlorophyll molecule (Ch) causes an electron (e-) of the chlorophyll to be raised to a higher energy level.

455

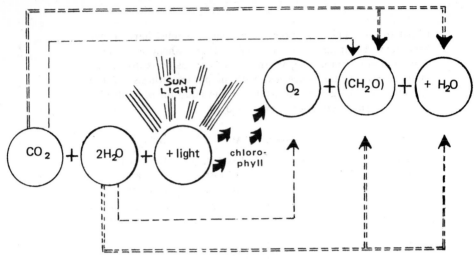

Fig. (153)

The dotted lines indicate the fate of all the atoms involved
in the process of green-plant photosynthesis.

In the photosynthesis process billions of photons shot out from the excited gases in the sun are subjecting the green chlorophyll pigment in the leaves to intense bombardment of radiative energy. Some of these photons are scattering off the surface of the leaf and some are penetrating the atoms of the pigment and being absorbed. How this happens depends on the oscillating frequencies of the electrons in the molecules of the leaf. These electrons must be resonating to the rhythms of the absorbed photons. The remaining photons are scattered or pass through the leaf creating a pattern which we perceive with our eyes as the shape and delicate structure of the leaf in all its detail. Our consciousness plus the photons of light absorbed create a hologram in three dimensions. But these molecular electrons which make up the hologram do not vibrate at any old frequency. They are exactly tuned to dance at about 6×10^4 vibrations per second and that is the colour green.

The analogy with the human being which is a much more complex system is that the liquid crystals of the cells act like chlorophyll pigment. Their atoms vibrate at critical molecular frequencies at the electron level and the nucleus of their atoms also resonates at critical frequencies which is determined by our state of consciousness. This in turn is controlled by the psychic electricity (prana) generated by the interaction of incoming light photons with the auric rings or spheres of subtle matter around a person which is in turn controlled by the chakra system. The evolution of the chakra system determines the type of resonant antenna each person creates with their consciousness. (See "Supersensonics" for exact method of measuring the vibrating spheres and their resonant proportional antenna in the nervous system.)

456

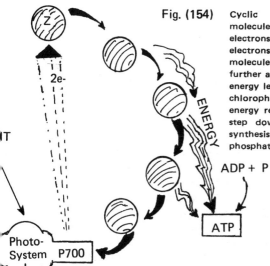

Fig. (154) Cyclic photophosphorylation: Light striking molecules of chlorophyll in photosystem I causes electrons to be raised to a high energy level. The electrons are picked up by an electron-acceptor molecule, Z, which passes them to a series of further acceptor molecules each at a slightly lower energy level. Eventually the electrons return to the chlorophyll from which they started. Some of the energy released as the electrons are eased step by step down the energy gradient is used in the synthesis of ATP from ADP and inorganic phosphate.

Some biologists say chlorophyll cells in solution trap violet and red light best and orange least while it has been found elsewhere that green algae such as chlorella absorb light in the orange spectrum best. The cholorophyll was tested by killing the cells in alchohol rather than measuring them during the action when the various wavelengths were driving the living photosynthesis process. The author has tested the algae in a living situation and agrees that the chlorophyll absorbs more orange yellow light than any other part of the spectrum. When light waves of the correct wavelength strike the chlorophyll molecule its energy is transferred to an electron of the chlorophyll which is then raised up from its normal stage (e-) to a higher energy level (2^{e-}). This excites or ionises the atoms in the cells and begins the storage of energy in the plant.

The pigments of cells are organised into the photosynthetic units which will not be mentioned here since the human being does not have chlorophyll pigment, nor does a human excite its cells only through pigmentation sensitive only to the visible spectrum and sunlight. Human beings can live without sunlight but plants cannot. This does not mean that humans cannot live off sunlight. The plant needs water to split into hydrogen and oxygen and so do humans also need H_2O to achieve metabolism and oxidation of their stored energy.

Many analogies exist in ordinary life to show the cycle of light energy absorption and release. For instance the sunlight is fixed, along with nutrients in algae and green vegetable matter, which is compressed into coal or oil over millions of years, which is then made into the hydrocarbon products such as gasoline. The automobile uses the energy locked in the chemical bonds of the gasoline. If one puts a torch to the gasoline tank the light energy is released all at once in an explosion, but by burning it bit by bit the car is propelled by a continuous supply of small explosions in the cylinders. It is this light energy being released in an enclosed space that causes the car to run. In the same way human beings store the energy of the cosmos by eating the sunlight stored in the plant kingdom or eating animals which have in turn eaten grass or growing plant hydrocarbons, but humans can also generate and store other kinds of energy in ways that plants cannot do. The step-by-step release of energy of sunlight is the special property of plants and the step-by-step release of cosmic energy from the stars is the function of human consciousness. Plants cannot live entirely by starlight and so must have sunlight. In living cells there are step-by-step reactions in the chemical properties of all biological systems. These reactions are utilised in human beings on the higher levels of the seventh stage of evolution by the conversion of light into etheric energy or subtle matter. The wavelengths and wave-fields of these energies have been described more fully in "Supersensonics" by the author, but here we are linking the cyclic phosphorylation of light to the energy of consciousness so that we can show how the psychic bioelectricity (prana), caused by enhancement of the electrons of the body fluids, can be used on higher energy levels to produce bioluminescence in the aura.

The series of small bursts of energy released by oxidation of atoms in our body is captured in the compound named Adenosine Triphosphate or ATP which is present in every living thing. It plays the key role in locking up the light radiations which come from the stars. Synthesis of ATP is nature's way of storing sunlight in plants and both starlight and sunlight in humans. ATP locks up the starlight and then is oxidised into ADP which then becomes ATP again after going through a whole cycle of reactions (see diagram). In order to keep the cycle going back and forth there must be energy from starlight, like the plants need sunlight. The cycle keeps releasing energy into the system so long as there is enough energy to become ATP $\rightarrow$ ADP $\rightarrow$ ATP to store more starlight again. Even stars store the energy of all the cosmic rays they receive, and radiate it out again in light to other stars who in turn synthesise it again into more light.

Humans, plants and stars are all doing the same thing but on different levels of manifestation. The light induction by chlorophyll in plants is only a first step in a long chain, since all higher organisms scrounge off the energy systems of less complex ones and this again is turned back into light. In plant organisms the cycle produces oxygen and vegetable carbohydrates and in man the ATP released produces consciousness of the body. Consciousness is maintained in our sensory mechanisms by the continuous release of energy within the cell and nervous systems. All this energy must be first stored both in plants and humans by ATP. The chemical bonds in this compound are released by hydrolysis which is caused by ionisation. The reaction by which the ATP molecule is oxidised leaves a compound called ADP. New ATP can be made if energy is available from outside the cell to lift up a phosphate group of molecules onto the ADP. Addition of the phosphate is called phosphorylation.

$$ADP + phosphate + energy \longrightarrow enzymes \longrightarrow ATP$$

It is the phosphate bonds which release all the energy in ATP for nerve signals, muscular contractions, transport of sodium and potassium across cell membranes, and the metabolism of all complex compounds in the human body and the plant alike. The production of ATP can be synthesised from ADP in a variety of ways beside photosynthesis in living organisms, and the step-by-step electron transport is not only reserved for plant photosynthesis.

Only the light induction by chlorophyll, as a first step in the photosynthesis process, is unique to plant life. Human beings have other cell membranes which can absorb light and color. By using up other energy-rich compounds to make ATP and store it in the body, the fluids of the body can be charged up by hydrolysis and electron transport to the cells to act as the donor of high energy electrons that are required for synthesis of the cosmic rays. The process of light synthesis is controlled by consciousness which determines the activity of the chakra system. The non-cyclic photosynthetic phosphorylation process in human beings is triggered by control of the sodium-potassium electron pumps in each of the cells, which act as electron donors and electron acceptors, continuously donating ionised electrons back and forth. The same electrons are carried around the cell system and no outside source of electrons is necessary for the making of ATP. However, for the synthesis of light, energised electrons (2^{e-}) are needed for the splitting of water H_2O, both in plants and humans.

NICOTINAMIDE

There are a number of electron acceptors in the human body. Iron atoms pass on electrons through to a substance called NADP or Nicotinamide Adenine Dinucleotide Phosphate. The process is slightly different to those steps in plants. Instead of passing on to another acceptor molecule as with the cycle in photophosphorylation, the NADP retains the excited electrons and has a great attraction for hydrogen, pulling two hydrogen (H+) protons away from the water in the body to form NADP + H_2. This utilisation of light energy by the splitting of water is the way that humans utilise light energy in the production of NADP + H_2 which is the reduction of NADP (Nicotinamide).

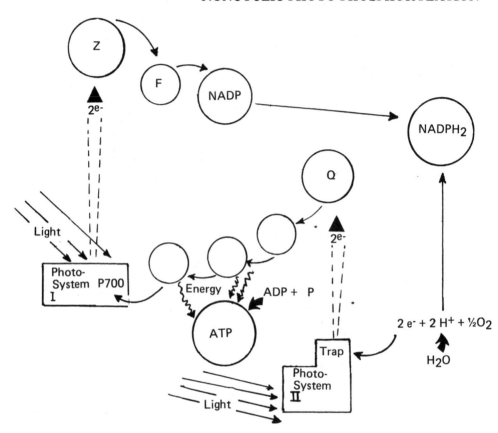

Fig. (155)

NONCYCLIC PHOTO-PHOSPHORYLATION

PHOSPHORYLATION PROCESS: (This is a simplified version, see page 463 for more details.) Light strikes molecules of pigment (chlorophyll in plant cells) in photosystem I at left side of diagram. The electrons are excited and raised to a higher energy level and passed to P700 a special type of chlorophyll. They are then stripped away and picked up by Z a strong acceptor molecule which passes them on to ferredoxin (F) which in turn releases them to NADP (formerly called TPN). This raises up the excitement of the NADP (Nicotinamide) to pull two hydrogen protons 2H+ away from their electrons in the cell water. This forms $NADP + H_2$ and frees the electrons.

In the second photosystem II light energy raises the separated electrons (2e-) released from the water (at right) to an enhanced energy level. These excited electrons are then captured by an acceptor molecule Q which then passes them along a chain of compounds which gradually lowers the energy level of these enhanced electrons down an energy gradient until they return to the pigment molecules of photosystem I to replace the electrons lost to the receptor molecule Z. Thus light energy is stepped down and the energy released by the electrons as they move down the energy gradient is converted into ATP by synthesis of ADP + cell phosphates. Water is the source of the electron energy for the enhancement effect which continually replenishes the electrons (2e-) lost from photosystem II. The remaining oxygen atoms left from the water combine with each other to form molecules of oxygen O_2 and thus water is split by the action of light.

Humans live symbiotically with plant life breathing the oxygen released from the splitting of water. Plants consume the carbon dioxide CO_2. The light in the visible (sunlight) spectrum is necessary for plants to live but humans can draw energy direct from invisible cosmic light (radiation) and split the water in their cell fluids to enhance their consciousness.

There are two light-driven events in photosynthesis in plants. One is the energised chlorophyll electrons of the citric acid cycle (see page 464), and the second is the one involving the splitting of water. This second light absorption concerns noncyclic photophosphorylation as shown opposite. The diagram opposite shows the two-step process.

PLANT AND HUMAN DIFFERENCES

When visible light or cosmic rays strike the molecules and atoms of system II the energy, now jumped up by the ratchet effect of the excited electrons, is pumped around the system until it finally reaches a strong acceptor molecule (See Q). At this stage in humans this then is synthesised into ATP and ADP but in plants it is passed back to the chlorophyll system I to Q, to a chain of acceptor molecules which lead the electrons to fill up electron holes made in system I by passing electrons to NADP + H_2 in the second step, system II. The whole process results in the creation of ATP storage of energy, NADP + H_2 and the release of molecular oxygen in plants. Humans do this respiration in reverse, consuming oxygen and producing CO_2 which plants can breathe.

Any cell in plant or human, whether it contains chlorophyll or not, can synthesise carbohydrate from CO_2 providing the cell has enough ATP and NADP + H_2 which functions as a free energy donor and reducing agent. This process applies to humans or animals or plants, therefore it only needs a supply of CO_2 to form glucose through enzyme reactions. The energy-rich glucose may then be broken down for use in the human brain and other oxidative operations. Other pathways are open for human light synthesis since the photosynthesis model outlined is only a scientific working model consistent with current knowledge since 1960.

NUCLEAR EVOLUTION AND LIGHT

To sum up the synthesis of light in human cells we can visualise what it would be like if you could speed up the oxidation process and generate say 15,000 microvolts of electricity in the brain when imaging. Normally charges of electricity of this order are only present in spontaneous cases of kundalini rising or an epileptic seizure which causes all systems of the body to fire, paralysing the body after it passes through a series of spasms. However, it is possible to release this oxidative energy all at once in a controlled way and the author has done this for several researchers specialising in epileptic EEG readings. They originally claimed this was impossible and then that the author was unique when it happened. But the author maintains anyone can learn with a little practice and the whole training has been set out in a series of twenty-four cassette tapes for students.

This enhancement effect which plants achieve by passing the increased energy 2^{e^-} to system 1 can be duplicated by human beings by using the ATP storage system for conscious transformation of light energies into consciousness. It is not often realised that consciousness and light are ONE and that consciousness can be projected to different parts of the body to accomplish work not only in healing but in raising up the cell life to another threshold of existence. If we refer to page (151) where we mention the hologram as an image created in space by light energy, we can now begin to see that the primordial imagination can fix ATP in storage in the cells, release and direct it at will to events which take place on the seventh level of consciousness. This guiding field of consciousness sets the pattern for channeling the released energy from the ATP electron pumps which print the image in the Akasha. Alternatively, by creating a counter image, a negative image imprinted by long karmic events can be likewise erased from the Akasha like we erase an old tape recording. Once this is known and tried, almost any image implanted in this way into the unconscious with the energy from enhanced ATP metabolism can be programmed into the Akasha. This ranges from spiritual discipline to the reversal and remission of the spiritual diseases such as cancer. The vivid generation of opposite mental waves for negative conditions or mental sickness and unhappiness can all be imagined with such force with this enhanced energy that a change instantly takes place in the human body. Rejuvenation of cell life and extension of cell life and arresting of the ageing process can become easy.

SUMMARY

If we accept the current scientific concept of the origin of the first living organisms then the origin of life took place before the living organisms and plants produced the oxygen layer of the earth's atmosphere. When the first photosynthesis took place there was no protection from high energy radiation from the sun and stars. Living organisms therefore, once they had arisen upon the earth, changed the environment in such a way that destroyed the condition which caused the origin of life. They were then shielded from the ionising cosmic rays by the ozone layer (O_3), which acts as a protective screen. However, this is not true for the very powerful dense cosmic rays which not only reach the earth's surface but go right through it without colliding with our kind of matter. Some of these are less dense and go right through human beings every few minutes breaking up atoms in our body and releasing energy in the ionised particles of nerve, bone and muscles. It is the creation of an acceptor type of atom in our body that causes our consciousness to be involved in Nuclear Evolution.

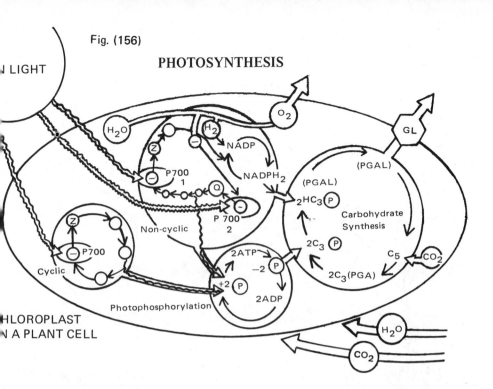

Fig. (156)

PHOTOSYNTHESIS

LIGHT

CHLOROPLAST
IN A PLANT CELL

PHOTOSYNTHESIS

Light energy picked up by CHLOROPHYLL is stored for future use in the chemical bonds of GLUCOSE molecules via PHOTOPHOSPHORYLATION and CARBOHYDRATE SYNTHESIS.

PHOTOPHOSPHORYLATION: There are two types, cyclic and non-cyclic. In cyclic, photons of light energise two electrons in a special form of chlorophyll "a" known as "P 700" and these electrons are then pulled away from P 700 by a powerful electron receptor known as "Z". Z then passes these electrons down a series of molecules known as cytochromes which act as an energy gradient to slowly lower the electrons back to their normal energy levels. In the process the energy released is used to add a phosphate (P) group to ADP (adenosine di-phosphate) in order to form energy rich ATP (adenosine tri-phosphate), the energy carrier for all biological processes. In non-cyclic after Z has pulled the electrons from the P 700 in one "photosystem" it passes them on to NADP (nicotinamide adenine dinucleotide) which, once it becomes energised, pulls two hydrogen protons (H+) away from an H_2O molecule to form $NADPH_2$. In the meantime there is a second excited "photosystem" involved which passes two P 700 electrons to an electron carrier "Q" which then passes them down a cytochrome chain back to the first "photosystem" as replacements for its missing electrons. Electron replacements for the second "photosystem" come from the H_2O which has lost two (H+) to NADP. The remaining O_2 is then passed out of the system and eventually exhaled by the plant.

CARBOHYDRATE SYNTHESIS: CO_2 combines with a 5 carbon sugar (ribulose) to form a 6 carbon molecule which is then energised by ATP and combined with the hydrogen from $NADPH_2$ to form two 3 carbon molecules of PGAL (phosphoglyceraldehyde). Most of this PGAL is then recycled back into 5 carbon ribulose but some of it is used to synthesise a complex 6 carbon carbohydrate known as GLUCOSE. GLUCOSE is used by animal and human cells as a source of energy in a process known as RESPIRATION.

Fig. (157)

CELLULAR RESPIRATION

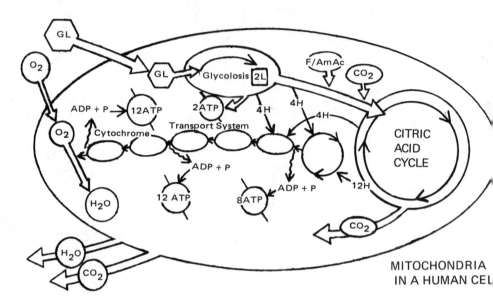

MITOCHONDRIA
IN A HUMAN CELL

CELLULAR RESPIRATION:

Light energy stored in one molecule of GLUCOSE is released through GLYCOLOSIS, the CITRIC ACID CYCLE and the CYTOCHROME TRANS-PORT SYSTEM to charge up 34 ATP molecules.

GLYCOLOSIS: A 6 carbon molecule of glucose is broken down into two 3 carbon molecules of LACTATE. In the process energy is released by charging up 2 ADP molecules into high energy ATP molecules and 4 electons are donated to a cytochrome transport chain.

CITRIC ACID CYCLE: Next each lactate molecule is combined with fats, CO_2 and amino acid before entering the citric acid cycle. During this stage four more electrons are passed on to the cytochrome chain. Next this combination enters a continuing cycle of reactions in which it is changed into citric acid and then broken down from a complex carbon compound into CO_2. During this cycle 16 more electrons (H) are freed and passed on to the cytochrome system.

CYTOCHROME ELECTRON TRANSPORT SYSTEM: Electrons freed during previous steps are passed down a chain of electron carriers called cytochromes. As they proceed down this energy gradient they drive the phosphorylation of 32 "discharged" ADP molecules into 32 "charged" ATP molecules (oxidative phosphorylation). At the end of the chain these electrons (H) are combined with O_2 to form water (H_2O).

The radiating text around the central image includes:
NATURE'S PSYCHIC
COLOUR AND
NUCLEAR EVOLUTION
METHODS OF KNOWING
SOCIOBIOLOGY &
LIFE
THE CONTRACTION
BY NATURE'S LAWS
SPACE AND
SPIRITUALITY
PRIMORDIAL IMAGINATION
NUCLEAR EVOLUTION
IS KUNDALINI
LEVELS
METAPHYSICS OF
OF COLOUR
BODY
INTERNAL & EXTERNAL
SCIENCE
BARRIER
HOW DO HUMANS
FORCE
GROUP
SHAKESPEARE'S
AND THE CHAKRAS

SCIENCE AND SPIRITUALITY

EDITOR'S NOTE

In the previous chapters we looked at the links between colour and light, space and time and the synthesis of light by the psycho-physical organism. What is the link between these subjects and spirituality? Christopher Hills has a unique ability to link everything to everything else without seeming difficulty, by seeing subtle connections which are wholly overlooked by the normal mind. The connection between the scientific approach and the religious approach would seem to be poles apart. We begin this next chapter with an interview because many of the links which seem normal in Christopher's mind often seem mysterious in other people's heads. Often by questioning the written work and obtaining an oral answer the links in the minds of his students become equally clear. The interview shows where Christopher is seeing from and how he sees science linked with spirituality as essential ways of looking at the wholistic universe.

INTERVIEW WITH THE AUTHOR, CHRISTOPHER HILLS

Editor: Christopher, would you agree that over the years, one of the questions that you have most frequently been asked about "Nuclear Evolution" is "How did you arrive at your findings about colour and the chakras and the levels of consciousness?"

Christopher: Yes, I'd agree. That's true.

Editor: Well, how *did* you arrive at them? I feel that by giving you the chance to answer the question now, in this third edition, I can save you a lot of time in the future that might be wasted answering one curious questioner after another.

Christopher: Well, to put it in a nutshell, I got my answers the same way I still do get my answers, by Supersensonics. That's how the ancient Egyptians got their answers too.

Editor: But as I understand it, you only coined the term "Supersensonics" in 1975 when you wrote the book by that name.

Christopher: Right. I coined a new word because it was necessary to begin a new science with its own methods of validating knowledge. Supersensonics transcends the intellectual modes of knowing but does not ignore its methods.

Editor: So you must have been using the method for at least twenty years before you called it by that name?

Christopher: Right again. As I said the method is very old, in fact it was the original Adamic state of man, but in using a new term I am endeavouring to rid people's minds of any limiting or limited ideas they might have about the method of divination. It is actually much more than a method; it is a whole new approach, a new science but using a very old primitive faculty.

Editor: Before we go further, would you actually define the term "Supersensonics"?

Christopher: Well, Supersensonics can be defined as the human biological sensitivity to radiations of all kinds from any source, whether living, inert or divine. There are some special examples of this sensitivity to be found in water divining, the homing instinct of pigeons, the direction-finding of mosquitoes and butterflies. The ability of the primeval amoeba to sense the location of its food with its skin is an example of a faculty man has got

467

unconsciously but somewhere along evolution's long trail it got lost. Bees not only have their own language but they also have a sensitivity to the direction of a honey source. Throughout nature, from the sensitive skin of the amoeba to the affinity of one atom for another, to the sun-seeking face of a daffodil flower, this ability to sense very subtle radiations can be discovered and amplified with the instruments of Supersensonics. There is a whole universe of subtle radiations to discover.

Editor: What about human beings?

Christopher: The most important part of this sensing faculty concerns human beings because it explains such activities as psychometry, dowsing, telepathy, clairvoyance and crystal gazing, as well as the structure of our inner consciousness and personality. It was in researching this structure that I discovered the levels and drives set out in this book, Nuclear Evolution. To know the structure and the thresholds of human consciousness instantly gives us a powerful tool for understanding why some humans can communicate with their environment and others not. To understand why you cannot communicate with another person who functions on another level of consciousness immediately gives you an explanation for the misunderstandings that arise in society, in marriages and between nations. So I saw right away that here was a key to one of mankind's problems, namely his failure in communication, and this fired and inspired me to continue the research to probe deeply by Supersensonic methods into layer after layer of both positive and negative vibrations that make up the full spectrum of human consciousness.

Editor: So Supersensonics covers much more than just dowsing or divining?

Christopher: It covers the fields of radiesthesia, radionics, parapsychology, psychotronics and physics. In the book "Supersensonics" I've set out a rational explanation of all these devices and I have also dealt with the complex relationship between colours and the nature of human consciousness and light.

Editor: How do Supersensonic methods compare with biofeedback methods?

Christopher: Biofeedback operates by hooking up a machine to some part of your body which responds unconsciously to some mental signal from within. This biophysical response is then recorded by expensive electronic gadgets which flash a light or make a beep tone so that you can know what you are doing with your mind or brain energy. But you can do all this without any expensive gadget, just with a simple pendulum or divining rod which will give you a signal whenever your thought pattern is in tune with a particular physical condition such as a sample of blood or a medicinal herb or even samples of oil, water, or minerals. As remarkable as this may seem to those who have never tried to divine for water, the ancient Chinese, Egyptians and sages all used this method of natural feedback to ask questions about nature and human diseases. Since physical measuring devices can measure the spectrum in the known vibrations of radiation that bring about an experience of colour in the brain, it is possible to find verification of the subtle fields by dowsing them and regarding them as harmonic vibrations which operate in a different series of octaves, but they are no less valid. We can see this in the contributions of ancient civilisations which arrived at fantastic results by Supersensonic means; the I Ching and the chakra systems of the East tie in too closely with Nature to be ignored. Without some method of detecting the tensions in the environment and their relationship with human consciousness, the I Ching could not have been written and the Pyramids would never have been built. We can now take this same faculty of knowing by direct perception and use it like we use our eyes to peer into the invisible heart of the atom and ask questions of the all-pervading intelligence that is so awesomely printed into every object around us irrespective of its location. Its potential for extra-terrestrial communication, for one thing, is enormous. Right now scientists can't trust it, but then can we trust science? Its certainties are outdated daily and its speculations are only occasionally right.

SCIENCE AND SPIRITUALITY

Although the most heated debates on the subject of "evolution versus creationism" took place after Darwin's "Origin of the Species" was published in 1859, the same polarising of these two ways of looking at existence is still very much with us. Scientists have grown more subtle and sophisticated in their ways of condescending to religion, but polarising of experience is still a very crude way of using the mind. Half way between the two extremes is a middle ground in which there is a certain humility born of seeing these crude ways in which the mind tries to secure something certain in a universe whose gradations of truth are infinite and awesome. Science itself is not arrogant but certain scientists are, and the whole discussion of science and spirituality is founded on rigid ideas about science and religion which create extreme emotions and render the real science of the spirit impotent.

Among many people there is a religious emotion which feels certain that such a complex organism as thinking man did not arise accidentally out of the pairing of polarised particles, and they ascribe the pattern of his being, his intelligence, his love and compassion to the wilful act of a Creator. This sense of conviction about God's will and "creation" enters into the scientific debate not just because the populace believes it but because it is possible for science and religion to exist together in a man like Einstein. Even Darwin believed in God and thought of evolution and natural selection as God's way.

Before Darwin and Einstein the combination of spiritual emotion and a rigorous logical mind existed in Christ, and before him evolution was a standard idea among the great Hindu sages who invented the scientific method and mathematics in the first place. The discussion 5000 years ago was equally as sophisticated as it is today. The Greeks Lucretius and Empedocles wrote on natural evolution. Only our ignorance of what real science is and the ways we unconsciously try to validate the knowledge of the knower have grown more complex with the passing of time. Blind spots always create complexities, while an open mind is able to see the simple truth. And many of today's scientists, though the finding of certain truth is their whole life's work, are not truth centred; they do not have genuinely inquiring open minds.

Such scientists feel no discomfort in the fact that science by its own rules is a self-limiting epistemology. It is a philosophical system with a particular method of validating evidence which does not include the quality of the scientist's own being, his consciousness, or his wisdom, in any of its results and therefore can only be applied to a limited part of human experience. If we are to take scientific research any further than phenomena and try to include the depths of creation as well as its surface, we must invent or extend the method or rules to create a new science or at least show where these new rules overlap with proven consensus opinion.

The most limited scientists insist that science can only be applied to phenomena that are in one way or another reproducible and testable, that it can only admit hypotheses that have within them the potential to be disproven. Yet these same scientists accept the famous hypotheses of Newton and Einstein as working postulates despite the fact that many of Newton's postulates and Einstein's theories cannot be proven or disproven because we do not have laboratories big enough to conduct an experiment! These same self-appointed authorities on the scientific method, who speak as though they have made the ultimate rules of evidence, say that science cannot deal with phenomena such as miracles or even consider such questions as the human spirit or the nature of consciousness, let alone the absolute nature of God. They make such absolute statements as "there are no absolutes" without seeing any inconsistency in their stance. These logical contradictions would trouble a richer and more textured mind. But beyond these embarrassing little inconsistencies is the even more telling fact that Truth is so infinite and vast and that these small minds, like Pied Pipers leading others behind them, are missing its depths of meaning and its power to transform us.

In this very fundamental sense science and religion (which in reality are breathing the same life-breath and beat with the same heart) cannot come together; they cannot even be discussed together in the same mouth or thought about in the same head without seriously compromising the philosophical system called science. Even though there is a popular misconception that science deals with incontrovertible facts, many scientists know that science does not and cannot reveal absolute truth because any and all of scientific theory is capable of an infinite number of applications throughout the universe and no theory can be proven in all possible situations. Thus all science and its theories are only provisionally "true" until a violation of the theory can be demonstrated by experiment. In this sense the theories of Newton and Einstein raised as many new fundamental problems as they solved.

Scientists will admit that no scientific theory is to be considered sacred, no matter how widely held or proved it is nor how consistently repeatable, and yet most scientists lack the spirit of adventure that led Einstein to ride upon a beam of light to the farthest reaches of the universe while sitting in his own back yard scribbling down the secrets of the Cosmic Intelligence upon the back of an old envelope. Although some of his ideas are famous there are other thoughts on scientific methods which will not unfold themselves to scientists with rigid minds. While admitting that there are more tests to be done, more knowledge of evolution to know, these scientists believe that the tests have not or cannot be done at present and that therefore they have the best knowledge available. They are hasty to conclude that their knowledge is sound and to take their stand upon it, safe in the conventional fold of accepted consensus opinion.

In order to avoid finding out that many tests are done and have been done by individuals who have no desire to publish scientific papers, conventional scientists write off these possible sources of inspirational insight. Standing in the very forefront of their own knowledge, they do not know what they do not know. And they do not **want** to know. They believe that in a religious system, the rigour of proof is not available because any situation in the creation can be explained away as the will of God. Since it is impossible to know the will of God with any certainty, they are willing to throw out huge areas of human perception and revealed experience simply because they do not fall within the pale of modern science. It is as if they had defined an area of the cosmos about six foot square and put up a fence around it called scientific method, leaving all the most interesting questions about the universe outside it. Absolute statements about what is impossible and who can and cannot know "God's will" are products of a certain arrogance which thinks it is making a humble conservative statement and therefore does not see its own conceit.

There is more intellectual fear in such a position than this confident much verbalised stance would indicate. If these very establishment-minded academicians so intent upon reaching the top rung of the status ladder of their field, could now stop for one moment to consider the fact that between the extremes of intellectual rigour and religious emotionalism there might possibly be yet another mode of inquiry and analysis and yet another brand of logical truth, then they might discover the "Science of Being" or the "Science of the Absolute" without which all scientific knowledge is mere opinion. Without understanding of the process of reasoning itself, "science" is just speculation and paradoxes cannot be solved. The notion that science by its own rules can only deal with limited phenomena, and the conviction that science cannot reveal absolutes is all hogwash born out of a closed mind. It is within the possibility of the consciousness of man not only to improve the scientific method but also to remedy its shocking ignorance of the views of those great sages who invented science in its present form and yet at the same time managed to probe the nature of absolute Reality. To put the word "modern" in front of scientific method, while insisting that the very original foundations of spiritual science are invalid, smacks of ego, with all its defensiveness, attachment, and smallness.

If the ancient rishis could see how "modern" science has taken only one part of their three-step process,* they would feel that the present modern method was meaningless and incomplete. They would feel that concern, which echoes throughout this book, that the sighted always feel when trying to communicate to the blind, just exactly what it is like to see light. I am expressing my frustration strongly because I care about these scientists and the way they have, by self-limitation, cut themselves off from the fullness and richness of a full spectrum of consciousness.

Somehow people must try to find within themselves the courage to open their eyes and look beyond the fence, beyond their attachments and their fears, acting just on sheer faith that if an Einstein could glimpse a world which no one else had seen before, perhaps there are other thrilling worlds whose secrets are waiting for someone humble enough to mount a beam of light and follow wherever it takes him, even if it should lead to the unthinkable One.

Those who ask themselves the unthinkable thought are forced to explore other ways of knowing the gaps in our own perception of reality.

---

*This book does not have time to go into these three sciences at this time. The rational basis of Ontology, the Science of Man's Being, can be found in my book "Supersensonics", while the Science of the Absolute will be found in "Divine Mathematics" which I am preparing for publication next year.

PROOF AND VALIDATION

Because Nuclear Evolution has been dealing with an area of research which transcends electromagnetic man's measuring devices it has often been thought of by some people as being unscientific or beyond the realm of science. Without any knowledge of this field, which they are making statements about, they themselves assert without any rational proof that it is false. To be truly scientific a phenomenon should be proved false or proved true. The grounds of Nuclear Evolution are testable in the everyday facts of life, such as the ability of the human nervous system to detect almost negligible light sources, irrespective of distance, to detect ionisation sources, and the ability of the human mind and neuro-muscular system to respond to images formed only in consciousness.

In my book "Supersensonics" I set out the basis of a new science with its own methods of validation which do not require any validation from the old sciences with their antiquated ideas of human intelligence and material substance. Whether Nuclear Evolution can be validated by existing scientific method depends on our making a serious attempt to so validate. If we set out with an already preformed idea that the phenomenon is false and that it overturns modern science (which it does not) then this is mentally programmed into the field of perception and there can be no effective response. Because Nuclear Evolution deals with the universal field, which is self-validating, self-limiting and self-evident, any response is self-cancelled.

However, a curious situation has arisen scientifically where self-evident truth in science requires no self-validator, i.e. there is no consciousness which confirms a thing as self-evident. A mathematical equation is said to be self-evident but for some reason a human self is not so regarded. Scientists say there is no evidence that consciousness exists separate from the material vehicle, yet they say self-evident truth can exist independent of man. The situation becomes even more ridiculous and naive when supposedly intelligent people with fine intellects rely for validation of factual information on instrumentation and mathematical symbols that are purely extensions of man's own mind and nervous system.

Yet it has proved possible to validate facts of Nuclear Evolution, such as the ionisation potentials of the nervous system, with instrumentation alone. As well as the well-known dowsing phenomenon, which uses a natural biofeedback instrument as an extension of the nervous system, there are actual electronic devices and mechanical and chemical sensors which can sense the existence of ionised wavefields such as those detected by water dowsers.

Anyone can prove this, without any chromium-plated gadgets and without any government grant, in their own kitchen or backyard. But will people do it? Will people actually bother if they already think such things are impossible or kooky?

Take for instance the action of the solar rays on underground streams as deep as hundreds of feet below the surface. Over such sources we can detect with standard ionisation counters an intensification of negative ions in a vertical polarisation (see Supersensonics for full details). However, there are dowsing instruments obtainable which can sense these fields which affect our biophysical energies and which do not depend upon any human intervention except to throw a switch.

Dr. Michael Ash demonstrated to me in 1965 that a beam of light could pick up the exact location of a tiny acupuncture point and he actually patented and obtained a specific frequency allocation from the British Post Office, which is the equivalent of the F.C.C. in America. Many years later the medical profession "discovered" acupuncture and now everyone uses all kinds of electronic sensors to detect acupuncture points. Although a surgeon, a medical physician and inventor, Dr. Ash was laughed at by so-called scientific colleagues. He also showed me a sensor for detecting the exact moment of ovulation and fifteen years later I saw that some medical man was claiming to be the first to make a revolutionary ovulation meter. This year (1977) Dr. Ash showed me that, after fifteen years of research, he could do away with electronics because he has found a chemical that could be impregnated on a cotton Q tip and by placing it in the mouth for a couple of seconds anyone could detect from the ionisation count of a woman's saliva when she was ovulating. Yet the big drug corporations continue to sell oral contraceptives with their negative effects on endocrine balance.

Now the same inventor, who wrote a book on medical radiesthesia,* has designed a detector very similar in function to the one described in Volume II of the "Supersensitive Life of Man" series** for the detection of aura energies. We will describe both instruments because they prove that ionisation sources not only can be detected by the human nervous system but can also be nullified by consciousness.

---

* "Health, Radiation and Healing" by Dr. Michael Ash being republished in USA.

** "Energy, Matter and Form" by Alastair Bearne B.Sc. published 1973 (copyright 1968). New edition republished with Phillip Allen, Alastair Bearne and Roger Smith, University of the Trees Press, 1977.

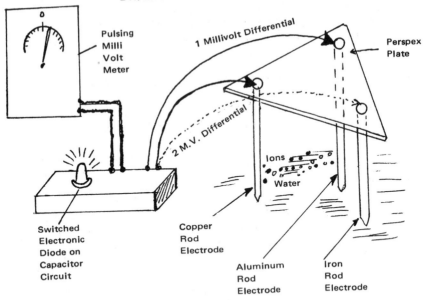

Fig. (158)

DR. MICHAEL ASH'S ION DETECTOR

Pulsing Milli Volt Meter

1 Millivolt Differential

Perspex Plate

2 M.V. Differential

Ions

Water

Switched Electronic Diode on Capacitor Circuit

Copper Rod Electrode

Aluminum Rod Electrode

Iron Rod Electrode

An electronic switch sends a pulse to a millivolt meter, a Wheatstone bridge and a capacitor so that the pulse generates positive and negative charge and then discharges, so that the needle returns to zero. Each pulse can be amplified by the presence of an ionising source such as underground water, an ion generator, the weather and winds, etc. etc. By placing the points of three rods (electrodes) in water, the detection of a flow of ions can be seen between the copper and aluminum by an increased potential on the dial of one millivolt and between the aluminum and iron of two millivolts. Therefore the presence of copper between the electrodes is shown by a drop in the potential charge. For copper mining this has great prospects but its implications are more profound. Over the same water a diviner gets the well-known downward, neuro-muscular pull, but when a piece of copper is placed in the water at the copper electrode, the potential of one volt differential falls to zero at the same time as the dowser's reaction is discharged. This shows that the water acts as an electrolyte for ionisation (excitation of atoms through electron enhancement or electron lack). It also shows that the biophysical effect on which Nuclear Evolution is based occurs not only at the imaging and mental levels of the neuro-transmitters of the nerve cells and muscles, but also at the chemical levels of communication between the natural elements No. 29 Copper, No. 13 Aluminum and No. 26 Iron.

Therefore, in view of this physical evidence of ionised fields, it is not something far-fetched or undemonstrable to regard the human body as a sensor of very subtle ionisation wavefields

which can be controlled by our consciousness. It has been found
that consciousness can interfere with the phenomenon of dowsing
as well as with the ionisation switch designed by Dr. Michael Ash
and with ionisation processes generally.

The instrument designed by the author in 1957 for measuring
chakra energies was a similar ionisation switch working through
a pair of finely balanced inert gas diodes which would "fire"
when a source of ionising radiations (such as sunlight, radio waves,
etc.) was brought into close proximity.

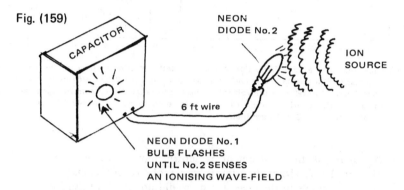

Fig. (159)

NEON
DIODE No. 2

ION
SOURCE

CAPACITOR

6 ft wire

NEON DIODE No. 1
BULB FLASHES
UNTIL No. 2 SENSES
AN IONISING WAVE-FIELD

The same pulse would accumulate on a capacitor and discharge
through one of the diodes which had a slightly less natural
frequency and voltage threshold. When an ionising radiation was
placed near the diode bulb which was not flashing, then the flash
would transfer from neon diode No. 1 to neon diode No.2,
thereby indicating the presence of an ionising field-force. The
frequency of the flashes would determine the number of flashes.
If the field was intense the diode No. 2 would light up continuously
instead of flashing, showing that all the inert gas inside the diode
was heavily ionised by the chakra energy.

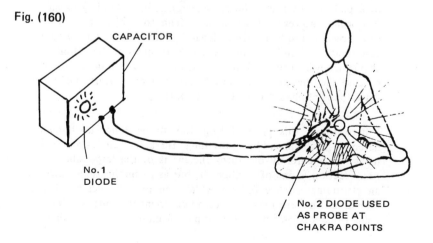

Fig. (160)

CAPACITOR

No. 1
DIODE

No. 2 DIODE USED
AS PROBE AT
CHAKRA POINTS

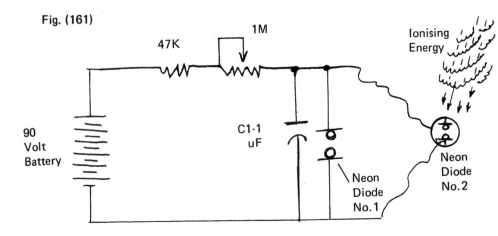

Fig. (161)

The circuit idea that I had was a neon lamp (NE-2, etc.) relaxation oscillator. One of the lamps will fire repetitively and flash. The two lamps would be selected so that NE-2 had a firing voltage some millivolts higher than NE-1. Normally, as the voltage increases across C1, NE's firing voltage is reached first and NE-1 flashes. But if the firing voltage of NE-2 is lowered below that of NE-1 by an external ionising field or radiation then NE-2 will flash instead.

A circuit of this instrument is shown above. However, the writer in 1957, although using it as a probe of consciousness-induced reactions in the chakra system, did not think of using it as a dowsing instrument as did Dr. Michael Ash some years later. The diodes available in 1957 also were not comparable with those of 1977, which are much more sensitive. Variations of this phenomenon, however, were reconstructed at my laboratory at Centre House, London between 1965 and 1969 where we constructed a "thought light switch" which could be switched on from 20 feet away by projecting the prana or healing force from the finger tips. Many physicists and doubters who witnessed this light switch on and off in their presence could not do it themselves, not even from a few inches away. However, if they almost touched the diode it would light up and they were unable to explain it in terms of heat, capacitance, etc. Standing twenty feet away, however, I would ask them to project their vital force towards the lamp. On a signal determined by them I would take their hand and the lamp would light up from the amplified charge. They had to admit it was possible but they quickly forgot because they believed somehow this phenomenon overturned the whole basis of physics (which it does not).

I have found this type of forgetting to be a normal human defence mechanism.When anything threatens an established reality or apparently overturns the limits of the impossible the first reaction is one of excitement, but as its implications dawn, an attitudinal change follows which can only be described as despair at the prospect of all known scientific truth suddenly being violated. The net result is to push it under the carpet. I have often waited even for friends to mention again some such important event which they claimed invalidates all scientific knowledge. But they rarely take it any further. For searchers of truth everywhere intellectual dishonesty or fear overrides human minds on both sides of the scientific/religious fence. This has happened so many times it must be a basic human protection against real knowledge of self.

VALIDATION

I repeat below a statement given to me by Dr. Michael Ash, a member of the Royal College of Surgeons of England; Licentiate of the Royal College of Physicians, London, M.A. Cantab, who was one of the first people to use the symbol of Nuclear Evolution to prove the cyclic periodic flux of the moon cycle and its relationship to the ovulation period, and one of the few scientifically-trained observers in 1965 who did not think that the author was an interesting but odd screwball working from some outlandish theory instead of from demonstrable fact.

STATEMENT OF VALIDATION

Having validated that "what we feel is real" we have in fact created more problems than we claim to have solved.

After a professional lifetime devoted to instrumentation in the field of perception, we now have the problem that our instrumentation is "perceptor sensitive".

We aim to detect "charge" as voltage build-up on capacitance in known time using a high input impedence millivoltmeter. In our observation of events we contribute by our presence to a unified field. Thus is invalidated any observation not allowing for the effect of the observer on that observed event. Starting from what we know, we can show a direct current between electrodes of dissimilar metals across an electrolyte. We can nullify this by showing no current when the metals in the electrolyte are similar.

We can detect negative ions for example when these are generated by an ioniser in air. Such ions can be grounded via the human body so nullifying the meter reading.

The ioniser can be used as a source of negative ions simulating water droplets. As such the neuro-muscular reflex response known as dowsing can be validated.

A dowser holding angle rods shows a reflex in which these rods cross when over the ion source. When this is nullified so is the meter signal.

A.E.M. Ash, M.R.C.S., L.R.C.P., M.A. Cantab
Founder CAMS College of Alternative Medicine and Science
c/o St. Joseph
Congdons Bridge Crackington Haven
Cornwall EX230JP
Great Britain

Because of the difficulty of understanding the full implications of the Nuclear Evolution theory for man, its conclusions will only be obvious to certain people. Any complex theory will eventually be simplified for popular understanding over a long period of time, but at the outset any perception of impact on thought in science or its world changing potential can only be felt by either the bone-marrow feeling of intuition or by someone with knowledge of the entire field of psychotronics, radionics, parapsychology and psychophysics. Since most people do not have this general background it is often not possible for them to evaluate. This is especially true of Nuclear Evolution as it breaks original ground in fields in which there are few authorities or teachers to review the work.

Many physicists who are open to new ideas, regard themselves as already being at the forefront of human knowledge and therefore are unwilling to make a jump into the next thresholds of manifestation. The testing of Nuclear Evolution will take some years but an assessment of the correctness of these concepts of Supersensonic energies which can be detected on different levels of consciousness by psychotronic devices was recently sent me by Lt. Col. Tom E. Bearden, recently retired mathematician and research scientist with the U.S. Department of Defense. He has interpreted new theories in the modeling of mental processes of mind and thought in quantum mechanics and is deeply concerned with the potential of the new science of Supersensonics.

Lt. Col. Bearden points out in his own papers that, since the time of Stalin, the Soviet attitude to scientific technical weaponry research has been far ahead of the U.S. He quotes Stalin as mandating psychotronic research saying that "no field of human endeavor and knowledge was to be avoided and that scientists had better follow **everything** no matter how strange or farout or even absurd it seemed." There are a few **known** Soviet scientists developing psychotronics, their funding continues and their research and investigations are permitted. He further suggests that the Soviet Union already have developed advanced psychotronic weapons and are capable of or will be capable of using them in such a way that "will stun and paralyze the U.S. at the critical time so that strategic nuclear exchange becomes unthinkable to the U.S., even if their field forces are destroyed. The shock from such demonstration can be made so great that mass panic can be introduced into the entire U.S. population."

I have received several requests for "Supersensonics" from Leningrad and Moscow universities but have refused to send them, even though it is in the public domain in the U.S., because of the weaponization of the knowledge. I feel the U.S. has to wake up to defending not so much its antequated concepts of democracy or capitalism, but to defend the world against its lower self and to fulfill its purpose written on every dollar bill. I am aware of the risk in releasing this knowledge hidden for ages, but feel that only with **public outcry** will the politically motivated and self-serving power cliques which are self-perpetuating be forced to change and invest the country's resources in the evolution of consciousness in man and prevent our potential destruction.

Lt. Col. Bearden's comments on "Supersensonics":

> A copy of your "Supersensonics" has just come my way ... and I must say I am impressed, if not well nigh flabbergasted ... let me offer you my profound congratulations on "Supersensonics", it is a magnificent work, and one which carries more true information than any other such book I have ever read ... I wish to commend to the utmost your deep insights into fundamental truth and the nature of man. I have gone through "Hills' Theory of Consciousness" and found it most remarkably similar to my own insights - and in many cases deeper and more penetrating than my own. You are one of the very few persons indeed who has realised that time delay (memory) is the very essence of incarnation, i.e. that change itself is a partial reality, existing only between individually separated fragments of non-perceivable, total nowness, and that all "externals" in fact rigorously exist only in internal consciousness.

FOR THE LOVE OF TRUTH

I would like it to be known that I am not writing the following personal accounts of encounters with scientists and intellectuals with any particular personal axe to grind but merely as illustrations of what I have found to be an unconscious self-deception foisted on the public in the name of Truth. Most of these people I regard as friends and I respect their right to be different, think differently, and have their own opinion of what science is. But I also claim the same rights I give them, and in the interest of Truth and to challenge that attitude which poses as scientific when it is actually psuedo-scientific, I am now giving some practical examples in order to marshall the forces of enlightened minds against the darkness of conceit. I realise that there may be hostility generated by the gut feeling of certain scientists who believe ardently in the games they play. But I believe also they play these games with the lives and beliefs of real people and real pawns who eventually pay for their extravagances of thought. Therefore in the following pages I cock my snout at all those who have cocked their snout up at me or ignored my logic, or deliberately falsified my points with faint praise or condescension.

THE RULES OF THE GAME

Even now, though I have long since given up on trying to prove my research findings to academic minds, I find myself still frustrated by not being able to communicate what I know to be true and doubly frustrated by the scientific establishment's way of conveniently disregarding its own high principles when faced with an unsettling discovery. The worth of scientific inquiry hinges upon its method – the checking and re-checking of results, the testing and rigorous scrutiny of all findings. The customary method of validating and replicating any research is for several universities to replicate it by following exactly the same procedures or by devising another procedure which validates the same result. By its own laws of professional codes, the consensus of scientific opinion must neither acknowledge nor deny any claim made for a discovery until the results have been repeated and confirmed or else proved to be false. Until science has made this all-important effort to prove falsity, in an attempt to do the same experiment, no scientist can make any statement about it, particularly if he has no knowledge of the field he is making a statement about. Yet we find authorities, so-called experts in one field, making pronouncements about the falsity or truth of certain results in another field as if their fame or their expertise in known phenomena entitled them to speak of unknown and untested phenomena. Instead of replicating and proving the claims false or true they demand that proof be specially brought to them so that they can be personally convinced, but they will do nothing themselves until you prove it and they throw the onus of proof on you, the one who is making the claim.

Yet clearly this is not scientific method at all and it is a mark of a poor scientist who demands proof but does not lift a finger to replicate the work himself. Unfortunately the world is full of such misconceptions amongst scientists. The onus of proof or disproof once a method or process has been published is upon those who demand it and we cannot expect a researcher to fly round the world to every doubting university professor at his own expense convincing those who do not have the skill to prove or disprove, or the facilities, or the inclination. For egocentric scientists to expect such special personal proof at no cost to them, and at the researcher's own expense, shows not only a vain arrogance but an ignorance of the way scientific research is actually replicated by responsible experimenters and, after enough tests, finally accepted.

THE HARD FACTS

For some years I fell for the first line of argument which says don't tell me but show me and I went from one scientist to another, proving the results of my own experimentation. It would not be much use for me to give the whole long list of names or to relate accounts of world-wide travels from the years 1957-69 and encounters with prominent scientists, some of whom accepted and some of whom could not accept, even when faced with results determined in their own laboratories and with their own equipment and controls. But I feel I have sheltered delicate reputations long enough, and the suppressing of this data causes me to feel false with myself. What is more, I am ignored by scientists because my books are not full of experiments, yet I have offered proof many, many times. So I will now give a concrete and factual account of why important experiments have never been accepted or replicated. My experience has been that even with solid hard-nosed proof nothing has been published in any prestigious journals nor have the academics who witnessed this proof ever taken it through as a personal crusade to overturn the whole of scientific opinion. None of these academics was willing or courageous enough to take on all the opposition or to crusade against firmly-entrenched opinions held by people who do not have the rigour to repeat and replicate and thereby validate the claims made. Consequently, much research which has already been done in the field of consciousness has been forgotten, has never reached the general field of certain disciplines and hence, by those totally ignorant of its existence, is regarded as never having been done.

Many times I have heard of research in consciousness-related fields that had been done and replicated by myself ten years before now being put forward as generally accepted by the so-called learned opinion as a new discovery when in fact it is old hat to those few who knew about it. This factor of not knowing what you don't know has fascinated me for 25 years of contact with scientific minds and I find that when experts achieve a name in any field they are the least open to admitting there is something they don't know, though they claim an open mind. Over the years I have come to realise that the experts do not know any more direct knowledge about the important things of life than the average man in the street. They know little of life, love and wisdom but are too proud to admit they know nothing but second-hand concepts. This factor has amazed and disappointed me at the same time to the point that I do not waste time with know-alls since all they say is to be found in a good encyclopedia. The true scientist is a different breed and there is a humility before the universe which has recognised that when a man is honest with himself his knowledge, however great in human eyes, is of little account in the shaping of the world and its ways.

Einstein was such a man who realised that even with a famous name and a creative power second to none, the world not only would abuse his knowledge but ridicule his more serious ideas about reality, while accepting and praising widely his more limited ideas on relativity. In fact it now becomes hard to find scientists who have read all of Einstein's more esoteric concepts about the scientific method itself. They say things have moved on since Einstein, and this is true, but the things he was **deeply** interested in have not moved on and we are today no closer to solving the riddles of the subject-observer or participator of physical events in the universal field than we were in Einstein's day. The truth is that no one asked Einstein to prove his own theories. He never did any experiments, never had a laboratory or owned an instrument, never proved anything. All his work was proved by others with the insight and the skill to perform such experiments beginning with Eddington who offered the first proof of the theory.

TESTING THE POWER OF CONSCIOUSNESS

In 1963 I was interested in the power of consciousness to influence electronic circuits. I reasoned that if our minds could even deflect a few electrons at will as they flowed through an electrical system they could be amplified by modern technology and made to perform some function or even deliberately create a malfunction in a circuit. Since distance and time did not figure in my calculations I did several experiments like dropping little balls down chutes to will them to one side or the other in free gravitational fall to targets A or B. Another was to aim a split beam of light at two targets consisting of light sensitive semiconductor cells. The idea was to make photons jump by the sheer force of consciousness from one part of the beam to the other and to register the results on a chart recorder. Many variants of this experiment were performed to my own satisfaction but when I visited scientists with reputations in the field I not only met with disbelief but no one was willing even to attempt to replicate the experiments. I called several U.S.A. physicists and had long conversations, went to physics conventions and talked with those doing the latest experimental research in England. It was impossible to do it, they said, because according to their thinking it would overturn all existing physical knowledge. I did not agree because, like Einstein's work and many other developments in physics, new knowledge had often extended the ideas of Newton, Galileo, etc. and did not invalidate them. I felt the same about Einstein's brilliant work, that a further extension into another mental dimension did not necessarily invalidate the physical dimension, any more than the mind invalidates the body.

My idea was to construct a simple random generator with an electronic impulse that would record impressions on a chart recorder of a number of events which over a given period of clock time would record 50 events to one side of a median line and 50 events on the other. A test could be run on the machine before the experiment so that when the willing of the events to left or right of the datum line was performed the machine would mechanically register more events on one side or the other of the chart paper. I wrote my friend Professor Oliver Reiser about it and he sent me the address of someone in Los Angeles who not only could build the equipment but believed it could be done. This was a great hurdle because to get electronic technicians to build a piece of equipment they did not understand, at that time, was impossible. Since then NASA has changed all that; they can now state that they want a black box which when you put x in, y will come out and the manufacturer does not even know what the equipment is for. But at that time of technology transistors were not even discovered so I was finding it difficult to transport equipment from my own laboratory in the mountains of Jamaica to America. I flew to Los Angeles to see the random generator which worked on a different principle of a mercury switch which would "fire" at random on different changes in the ambient temperature (very much like the Christmas lights) and the event would be recorded. If the mind could interfere with the random flashes of the switch or enter the circuitry of the chart recorder then we should be able to print more flashes on the chart when we willed the recording needle to the right or left at the behest of the experimenter.

I called Professor Willis Harmon who was professor of electrical engineering at Stanford. He would see me but would not promise the use of the Stanford laboratory for a sophisticated experiment because it sounded kooky. A mutual friend, Laurel Keyes, had told him about experiments done on my guru by the Professor and Chairman of the Department of Electroencephalography at University of Michigan Medical Center so he was open and said I could stay with him at his house if I flew up from Los Angeles. I also called Professor Birge who held the chair of physics at Berkeley. He was interested in some of my ideas on world government and we had corresponded on the possibility of psi phenomena.

He had written two positive reports of J.B. Rhine's work and then suddenly accused him of fraud. In his accusation he had demanded Rhine try a certain experiment with a magnetic needle in a vacuum to prove that psi energy worked. I suggested to Birge that he and I do the suggested experiment together. He was a well-known authority on the speed of light and was then presently writing a history of the achievements of the Berkeley physics lab and he was horrified at the thought of colleagues finding out he might even believe in psi phenomena and said he had denied Rhine's results because his book would not sell to physicists if he continued to investigate that field of inquiry. He therefore, in order not to be contaminated with the notoriety, demanded that Rhine prove the work by this method of physics himself. I implored him in the name of Truth to act without fear. Rhine had already proved it himself statistically many times over. I accused him of intellectual dishonesty for suggesting an experiment for Rhine to do which he refused to do himself. Like many other scientists in exactly the same position Birge would not budge. He invited me to come to talk about world government but psi phenomena would have to be a taboo if I came. I decided to write him off, and the many others who took this position, as intellectually dishonest and ignorant of their own vanity as truth seekers.

However, Willis Harmon was a different man and I arrived to perform the experiment late one afternoon in 1963. I set up the random generator in his dining room and asked Dr. Harmon to lock me up in his kitchen and tell me when to will to left or right by shouting through the kitchen door. I concentrated on the electric circuit of the chart recorder and its flasher switch, visualising the tiny electrons obeying the mind making the recording needle mark the chart to right or left of the datum line to Professor Harmon's command. He was satisfied but could not explain the result in physical terms. I suggested we go into his modern laboratory and fix up a sophisticated version of the experiment and prove it to the world. He said, "I believe it because I have to; I saw it; I experienced it, but it destroys the underpinnings of physics and thousands of colleagues at other universities would not believe it, including my own students who have heard me teaching them theories which do not fit this phenomenon. They would laugh at me even trying such an experiment. I am not your man. It would involve not only a crusade to persuade, but it defies well-established laws. Besides, anyone who tackles this problem has to have a mind like Einstein and I frankly am not an Einstein. I have to accept your results but I would not know where to begin to prove them to others."

I admired his honesty and integrity and his humility and realised the problem of convincing doubters was one of enormous magnitude since they demanded proof but they were not

Centre House Community building – London

prepared to experiment themselves. I had been talking to so many scientists who believed in scientific method but had all the psychological failings of other people. There were none so blind as those that would not see. Why should I waste further time trying to convince universities? After I left Professor Harmon I resolved never to bother to demonstrate proof again but to let those who wish to know how to prove this phenomenon come to me. Then I would show them. I set up my laboratory on the bottom floor of a six-storey building used for the Centre House Community and set up many variants of the phenomenon. These were demonstrated to physicists who wanted proof but even when they accepted the results the outcome was the same. These scientists were powerless to do anything even when they **had** to accept results. They were ineffective simply because their own initial enthusiasm for a breakthrough could not overcome the difficulty of getting anyone to listen long enough to replicate the experiments. For any scientist to ignore the hostility of colleagues which was often displayed by so-called detached observers would mean being an outcast. To withstand the emotional criticism of people who believe the rules are the game and that truth is subject to rules, and to hear the illogical demands that every statement must offer repeated personal demonstration and replication was usually too much for any creditable scientists.

Among the most sympathetic who witnessed some of these experiments in 1963 were practical people like physicist Sam Bousky, the manager of the laser research department of Ampex Corporation, who thought the most he could do was to organise a series of lectures on the east and west coasts amongst friends who were interested in the Kabbala. Another person sympathetic to the practical application of my ideas was Dr. Fred Adler, a physicist and executive vice president of Hughes Aircraft Company who also organised lectures amongst selected friends. Dane Rudhyar organised a tour of southern California in 1969, and in 1970 fifty scientists from the West accepted my invitation to attend the World Conference on Scientific Yoga in New Delhi. As president of a conference with over 800 yogis present from all over the world, I also found that if emotionalism amongst scientists in support of their reputations and strong egos was less than dispassionate, the egocentric attitudes of many yogis were even worse.

In spite of all this I never lost faith in scientific method or yoga since both of these are much greater disciplines than many of their practitioners. In fact my paper at this conference was on the scientific epistemology of yogic methods of validating knowledge from texts almost 2000 years old and identical in form and content to present-day scientific method.* It seemed strange to

---

* See "Yogic Methods of Knowing" by Christopher Hills, published by World Conference on Scientific Yoga, 1970.

meet scientists who actually believed modern scientific method was developed after Newton, when it was all written down so long ago. Certain scientists do not or cannot accept such statements because they have such a tremendous ego investment in these "new" rules of evidence which pulled mankind out of the Dark Ages into a period of relative enlightenment. What they believe to be a naive religious statement, evidently lacking in rigorous methods in the spiritual approach, reveals a scientific method equal to any and even transcending it with greater insights into the nature of the observer's consciousness.

Another account will suffice to indicate the nature of scientific validation. I had a friend who I used to paint with who was head of a department of physiology, Dr. Ian McKay who is now holding the chair of physiology at the University of Puerto Rico. I happened to be talking to him in 1958 of my ability to stop at will, by a mental command, the flow of blood. I mentioned that I could give proof at any time using myself as guinea pig. "Rubbish", he snorted, "No one can voluntarily control their own blood flow." He explained he was a specialist and a world authority on vascular flow and had a laboratory specially adapted to work in this field. It was his own field and he flatly stated that he kept up to date and nothing in his discipline could be found to even warrant such an experiment. So I bet him some beers and he condescended to test me when he had set up a special experiment in the next few days just to prove I was talking in a field I knew nothing about. Having stopped my blood and heart on several occasions I knew I was right. But he was adamant that I would be proved an ignoramus and he was only doing the experiment to show me that science really knew what it was talking about.

The day came and I stretched out on special tables that tipped up and he measured the flow by the air displacement on my arm after alternately blocking off the veins and arteries with a tourniquet. As he called out I would stop and start my blood in the arteries and he watched the equipment in great disbelief as it recorded the events. He was convinced there was an error in the equipment but after checking every nut and bolt from start to finish he had to admit defeat. He reserved judgement to evaluate the results till our next meeting a week hence. The time came and I waited for him to buy all the drinks we had bet or at least to say how this rubbish had shaken the scientific world upside down. Not a mention. So I waited to see what he would do. Towards the end of our meeting I could not resist asking him any longer since it was obvious he was not inclined to bring it up himself.

"Oh yes," he said, "I called Guy's Hospital in London and apparently there is a researcher there who has identical results from people in hypnotic trance who are able to control blood flow. I did not know about his work."

I then challenged him on his arrogance and his bet saying that his attempt to make me look foolish had boomeranged. He looked at me and said, "You don't understand science; there is so much research going on in my field alone that one person cannot be expected to ever read all the papers which come out." The paper had been published in England and I had been validated, but that did not even evoke an apology or even an admission of his own ignorance in his own field. I was to him a layman treading on the holy ground in his own private world and could not possibly know anything more than he did about nature or my own body.

This is typical of unwitting scientific arrogance which is self-deceiving and self-confirming in its own conceit. This physiologist and I are still good friends up to the time of writing this book. In the interest of truth and to make the point clear I here state that he still owes me my bet! This early encounter with his presumption projected upon me made me very aware of it in others when I myself later became a scientist.

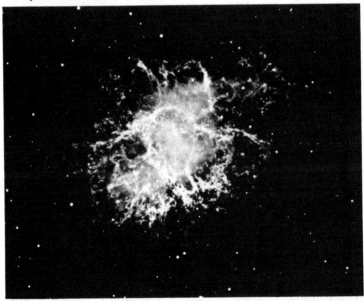

ACCORDING TO SCIENTIFIC AUTHORITIES THE UNIVERSE IS EXPANDING. DOES THE UNIVERSE EXPAND OR IS OUR CONSCIOUSNESS AND ITS INSTRUMENTAL EXTENSION EXPANDING?

The Crab Nebula measures 5 light years across, small compared to our own galaxy of 100,000 light years. The light from the central inner part comes from excited electrons moving at near the speed of light. The outer light comes from hydrogen atoms radiating in spirals around a vast magnetic field.

The remains of a Supernova explosion first observed by Chinese astronomers in 1054 A.D. A Supernova may be expected in any galaxy every 300/400 years. The Crab continues to expand at 800 miles per second. Its distance is only 4,000 light years away from the earth which puts it inside our own expanding galaxy. Could it be that physicists and scientists are only measuring one sensory level of existence out of seven interpenetrating levels? What implications would this have?

One more account will illustrate yet another total blindness of scientific authorities. I could cite many more but already those who are attached strongly to their opinions of what scientific method is may have stopped reading, become emotionally hostile, written me off as a psuedo-scientist or rationalised all these points away by familiar stock arguments. If not, I hope general readers who may continue to read, may not get bored with my insistence on intellectual honesty from scientists who claim to respect hard-nosed evidence.

I was drinking at the bar of the University Club in 1965 when I was introduced by Bill Moore, an alumni of Yale, to a fellow classmate who had become a prominent research scientist, was president of the American Medical Society for Gastroscopy, was the inventor of the gastroscope and had received a current grant undertaking a special research project on human brain electricity. Dr. Roy L. Sexton was a talented researcher and was one of the scientific team selected by Admiral Bird for his expedition to the South Pole.

I mentioned that several years before, in 1960, whilst at a yogic research hospital I had generated over 10,000 microvolts on an EEG machine. He exploded, "Impossible!" he said, "that's just my field and the only way the brain can generate that much energy is in the brain seizure of an epileptic." He said he was working with a bunch of epileptics and also effects of alcohol to study generation of brain currents and it was well-known scienti-fically that no one could create the effects of an epileptic fit by a voluntary act of will. I said I would be glad to prove it and he said he had the latest and most expensive equipment available so we agreed to meet the next morning at his laboratory at 8 a.m. I was flying out to London at 11 a.m. so we would have to work quickly. He said it was routine for him because the machines were already set up for just that research and we would soon prove that the Indian doctors at the yogic hospital had been fooled or made some error in their measurements.

On arrival at the laboratory he greeted me and told the technical assistant to set up the electrodes on my head. He said that if anything unusual happened to call him, and frankly stated that he did not expect anything since I had obviously been fooled into thinking I could do what I said. The assistant did a test run and said okay go on and do your stuff. In the next minute she shrieked and called the doctor because the row of pens were going haywire smashing back and forth across the chart paper and splashing red ink all over her dress. "Something wrong with the machine," the doctor said. "We have plenty more. Just let me

ELECTROENCEPHALOGRAM. A graphic tracing of the electric impulses of the brain, sometimes abbreviated EEG. The instrument which makes the record is known as an electroencephalograph. The electrical activity of the brain is manifested at the surface of the scalp by small potential changes on the order of 5 to 200 microvolts in a frequency band from 1 to 50 Hz. A sample of so-called brain-waves or electroencephalogram is shown by the accompanying diagram. When viewed casually, the usual EEG would appear to be simply random noise, but spectral analysis and some direct electroence-phalograms show pronounced components at several frequencies. The lowest (1 to 3 Hz) is termed the "delta rhythm". Next highest are the "theta waves" (4 to 7 Hz). The "alpha rhythm" is the most pronounced and occurs between 8 and 13 Hz. A third pronounced rhythm appears between 13 and 30 Hz and is termed the "beta rhythm". As shown by the diagram, the alpha rhythm is most pronounced during light sleep, while the delta rhythm appears during deep sleep. One of the uses of the EEG is determination of stages of sleep in sleep research and associated investigations.

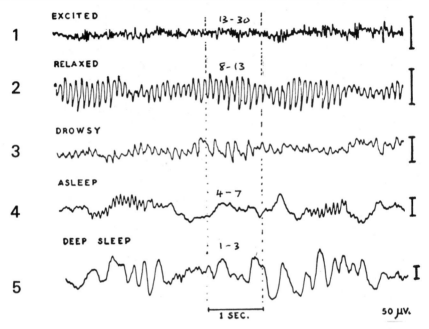

Fig. (162)

EEG tracings of normal subject during sleep. Numbers shown at left indicate increasing depth of sleep.
  In several diseases of the brain, especially epilepsy and cerebral tumors, very slow delta waves of higher-than-average voltage may be seen. Occasionally, as in epileptic seizures, similar waves of very high frequency may occur. In tumors, the appearance of such waves is confined to the area immediate-ly surrounding the tumor; hence electroencephalography has some ancillary value in the localisation of cerebral tumors.*
  Death may occur in grand mal high voltage charges which appear at 25/30 per second in seizures which continue during status epilepticus (in which the seizures follow each other with no intervening periods of consciousness).**

---

* "Van Nostrand's Scientific Encyclopedia" Ed. Douglas Considine, Publ. Van Nostrand Reinhold Co. Fifth Edition, 1976.

** "The Merck Manual", Publ. Merck, Sharpe and Dohme Research Laboratories.

check them out. Machine is okay, do your stuff again." So I did, and again the machine went into a frenzy of red markings. All I could hear from him was "Amazing, amazing, this is a whole new line of research, another grant, a great performance, keep it up" and so forth until we had produced several hundred feet of EEG readings. I only just made the plane to London. Next year I was in Washington and could not understand why I had never heard from him so I called at his office. He handed me my reading and said "Sorry, but I could not get a grant. The National Science Foundation said no go, because you are unique. I could find no others who could do it. We cannot do scientific research on one unique individual. It is not convincing, we need controls and checks with others in groups or the results will never be accepted. Therefore they could not give me the money." I was flabbergasted because I knew I could train almost anyone with half a brain to do the same thing I could do. There is nothing special about it once we know how.

JUST A GAME

Here someone at the N.S.F. was making a dogmatic statement rationalising away the need to investigate a supposedly impossible phenomenon simply by saying I was unique. Dr. Sexton was quite frank that he would have no intention of taking the demonstration further without a government grant!

Here was another occasion where something supposedly impossible according to all medical knowledge suddenly became possible but because the research could not be repeated according to the opinion of the controllers of the grant money, thousands of other scientists were going round saying it is impossible and being quite arrogant about it. I pointed out this fact to Dr. Sexton. He shrugged his shoulders – "That's science" he said.

SCIENCE: THE VANGUARD OF KNOWLEDGE

I was shocked because my opinion of science was that it sought for undiscovered truths irrespective of cost and effort. My opinion of scientists generally took another dive. I realised that many true scientists' work was never accepted because it never saw the light of day. Dr. Sexton eventually published his research on the effects of drugs, alcohol and epileptic brain seisures in a publication called "An Atlas of Electroencephalography" but the voluntary control of high voltage energy of the brain got lost in the scientific bureaucracy of grant-making.

Yet I still believe in the scientific method, though strictly speaking it should be called the yogic method of validation. With the addition of two more parameters science may even speak truth!

This leads me to the last encounter with scientists.* It does not concern me personally but was written up in "Newsweek Magazine" in 1958 on my guru Swami Shantananda. I spent two years walking India as a sadhu with this man during 1961-62. I did not learn anything scientific from him. I did not learn anything that one could call knowledge. I did not learn mantrams; although he taught me how to chant Sanskrit, I also learnt this from others. What did he give me? He gave me what I gave him -- love in the heart regardless of whatever went on in my head. This man would freak my head out every day, every hour and every minute but I loved him and that's all he gave me -- love.

Now the "Newsweek" article does not talk about the measurement of his love, but he is typical of what I call a true scientist, a seeker after Truth, a man who sees through the pseudo thinkers and the universities which teach nothing universal. If I can restore this vibration to the university which insists that all intellectual dishonesty is exposed, I will be glad to do battle against a whole panel of professors on any radio show or in a public debate which will reveal that love is greater than intellect. I will repeat the article below and let it speak for itself since the one lesson I learnt from my guru was not to advertise him as anyone special.

PHYSIOLOGY:
YOGA - WHY IS IT?

The swami was willing. Yes, he would submit to the experiment. The scientists were delighted.

And so it was that Swami Shantananda "master of his own self" and founder of the Yogic University of Delhi, swept up the steps of the University of Michigan Medical Center at Ann Arbor, to be greeted by an imposing battery of galvanometers, electrocardiographs, electroencephalographs, and other sensitive measuring equipment. With the swami's cooperation, the latest and best tools known to neurophysiology would be used to explore the mysteries of the ancient yoga art for the first time under laboratory conditions.

Visitors to India and to carnival side shows have often seen swamis and fakirs demonstrate the triumph of "mind over matter" by driving nails through their hands, walking on hot coals, eating glass, and being buried alive while in a state -- real or pretended -- of meditation. Now science, based on the ability to measure, would record exactly what was happening to Swami Shantananda, a true holy man, in terms of pulse, breathing, heartbeat, brain activity and metabolism.

Prof. Basu K. Bagchi, associate professor of electroencephalography at Michigan and a native of India who is now a naturalized U.S. citizen, cordially welcomed the gentle-faced, 60 year old swami and

---

* The four scientists here portrayed in a negative light for their unwillingness to risk their reputations were, it should be stated, the most openminded scientists in the profession at that time, before the current wave of psi research got underway.

got down to business. First there was a battery of seven tests to establish "normal" body activity: The heartbeat was measured; electrodes attached to the front, top, and back of the head recorded brain-wave activity; a galvanometer measured the electrical resistance of the skin; chest and abdominal breathing rates were recorded.

HESITATION: Then the swami obligingly went into a "posture of deep yogic meditation," sitting cross-legged with his hands behind his neck. Each test was repeated. Only once did the swami hesitate when Bagchi tried to measure oxygen intake with a face mask; it proved upsetting to the old man.

After two more sessions running as long as three hours, Bagchi pronounced himself well-satisfied with the tests. This week, with the swami en route to India, Bagchi was happily poring over the 1,794 separate readings. "It took a lot of coaxing to get the swami to sit for us," Bagchi said, "but it was well worth it. These meditative men are not interested in science but in philosophy. The swami is a kind, holy man who preaches love and peace. Once we convinced him that science, like philosophy, is interested in exploring unknowns, he consented and came here at no expense to Michigan."

BREATH TAKING: In general, the tests seemed to bear out some tentative scientific theories about yoga; for example years of training may make it possible to obtain conscious control over such body functions as breathing, pulse rate, muscle and nerve reactions (the autonomic nervous system). When the swami was in a state of deep meditation, Bagchi found the holy man could lower his respiration to 4 to 7 breaths per minute compared with the normal breathing range of 15 to 23 per minute (the abdominal measurements served as a double check to make sure the swami wasn't taking extremely shallow breaths).

"I am open-minded about yoga," Dr. Bagchi said. "I expected to find some good things and some rubbish. But I'm convinced Swami Shantananda is the real thing."

As a result of Bagchi's research, space travelers may some day tip their helmets to the swami. Air Force physiologists believe yoga techniques of controlling breath and pulse rates can provide clues to survival during journeys to new worlds.
NOVEMBER 10, 1958

THE FAILURE OF THE PHYSICAL SCIENCES

This article appeared in "Newsweek Magazine" November 10th issue of 1958. Professor Bagchi since became head of Department of Physiology and sent me his research papers on brainwaves and voluntary control of internal states. Ten years later in 1968 the same research was independently done again by Dr. Elmer Green of the Menninger Foundation. It was also done again at the All India Institute of Medical Sciences in New Delhi by Dr. B.K. Anand, and his reports were delivered at the World Conference on Scientific Yoga in 1970 and published in several medical journals. However, I was first introduced to this research by Dr. Sanjiv Vinekar of the Kaivalyadhama Yogic Research hospital in Lonalva near Poona where the government of India had for several years been quietly financing an extensive laboratory for research into trance states. Much of this work is published in the Yoga-Mimamsa Journal (in Sanskrit and English) and printed for many years prior to 1958 (when Dr. Bagchi's research was done) by the hospital's Institute for research in Bombay. This centre was directed by Swami Dr. Kuvalyananda, a scientific yogi who sent a number of doctors for medical training after they had become yogis.

TESTS IN THE PIT

In connection with this program, I was invited by Dr. Vinekar to lie in an airtight pit in deep yogic trance while extensive research was done on my internal states. I was glad, in the interest of science, to go into this pit, which was sealed inside a Faraday cage.

A Faraday cage is a copper screen or shield which filters out the effects of the earth's magnetic field, lessens the interference of electrical disturbances from clouds, rainstorms, radio emissions and other ionising effects which can interfere with sensitive measurements and equipment. In this case the pit and the instruments were housed in a large copper shielded room. Normally yogis are buried alive in earth and can stay in suspended animation for 8 to 14 days without effect. There was always some doubt about how much air and moisture could be had from loose soil so this research centre built a scientific pit consisting of a steel tank with a copper lid which could be hermetically sealed to control the escape of gases and air exactly. The lid had an observation window so that the sealed-in yogi could be seen as well as monitored for heartbeat, skin temperature and resistance, breathing capacity of the lung, with about 26 electrodes fixed on different points of the scalp in order to observe the brainwaves during an eight-day period. The instruments were in a separate room where a continuous chart recorder kept the pens gliding

The EEG is situated in a separate room and watched by doctors continuously while the subject is in the experimental airtight pit. The pit is constructed so that it fits in the ground inside a copper room-sized cage. The shielding of the body from stray electricity prevents interference in the signals which are recorded on chart paper moving at different speeds.

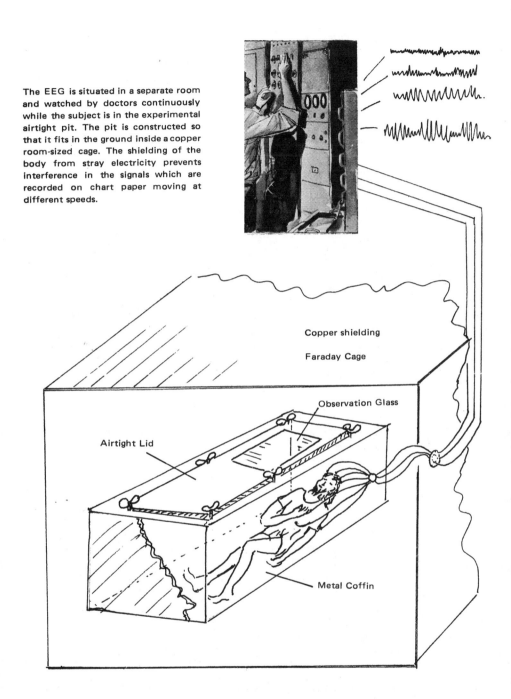

Copper shielding

Faraday Cage

Observation Glass

Airtight Lid

Metal Coffin

The illustration shows the author in 1960 sealed in the pit with a glass observation window in the lid. Electrodes fastened into the scalp record the brainwaves while trance induction is taking place and during sleep/meditation (yoga-nidra). A microphone records the subjective impressions so that they can be compared with the EEG readings. The high voltage peaks reached the maximum the machine could handle. The results were repeated in Washington in 1965.

across the chart and inking the paper of the EEG. There was also a microphone and tape recorder with a two-way intercom between the yogi sealed in the pit and those doctors constantly watching the chart recorder in the other room. The object of the experiment was to observe exactly how much oxygen was consumed and how much carbon dioxide was produced and to measure the oxygen content in the air at all times. If there was any difficulty the yogi could talk over the intercom, ask to be let out or describe in detail his physiological and mental experience, and especially determine what he thought he was doing internally, to achieve the results that were seen on the instruments.

PROOF BY EEG VALIDATION

The purpose of my own research with Dr. Vinekar was not to undertake a project in oxygen consumption* which they had already done with over a thousand yogis before me, but to substantiate my claim that I could contact energies and orders of intelligence in yogic trance which could not be called counterpart personalities or discarnate human entities but more psi energy fields operating on universal levels of consciousness. Many Vedic references exist which tell of beings such as Pitris, Devas, etc. and I was curious as to the reality of their energies, since the subjective experience of heat or inner fire could create anything in the mind or imagination of a meditator and I was aware of claims which could be explained in many other ways.

I also knew that this fire could delude, especially when trance energies are induced, the power of self-suggestion is so great that one can easily imagine one is levitating or blazing with light. But if you took a movie picture you might find the camera saw nothing unusual except a person thoroughly self-hypnotised. Therefore I was personally interested to find out if the energy I experienced internally at certain thresholds when my consciousness changed to another level, produced any results on an electrical measuring device such as EEG. Dr. Vinekar was just as curious because he had met one other yogi besides me in his many years of observations who could keep his brain completely still without recording on the EEG any currents of electricity, who had also claimed he could produce large amounts of electricity in the brain if he wanted to. I was claiming to produce the high electrical energy, so Vinekar wanted to see if I could also keep my brain perfectly free of activity. We were coming from opposite ends but I was just as interested in his idea as my own.

---

* Oxygen consumption is reduced by entering into a state akin to hibernation in animals. The heartbeat slows down, the intake of air and liquids become imperceptible, but the EEG records the alpha, beta and delta rhythms of the brain during yoga-nidra or hibernation. The author during one of 30-days experiment in London stopped the heart and almost could not start it again. There is evidence that repeated stopping of the heart voluntarily puts an unnatural stress on the heart muscles. Swami Shantananda did it many times but finished up in a hospital ward at age 65. He was advised by medical doctors not to do this again.

So I entered the pit and the lid was sealed and I had a flashlight if I needed one and carried on a conversation putting the description of the technique I used for trance induction on the tape. To cut a long story short the result was that whenever I felt an electrical spasm in contacting what to me were visualised planetary centres of intelligence like chakras there was a corresponding jump to the maximum EEG reading as far as the machine could record. When I finally bottomed out, the energy would stay up to a maximum amount.

Some years later in 1968 I was in San Francisco and was invited to visit Dr. Joe Kamiya's laboratory as he had expressed interest in this same phenomenon. Immediately on the production of the large brain voltage he began forming theories about it being "muscle quiver" and every other explanation except the one which related to the centre of the brain which I could actually feel. Dr. Kamiya has since gone on into more open-minded research, but at that time, at the beginning of the new experimenters, long after the work of Dr. Bagchi ten years before and totally ignorant of that work, he was speculating that brainwaves emanated from the scalp and muscles. I knew that the muscle quiver theory was a waste of time and was a bit frustrated, having taken the trouble to send enough enhanced energy through my nervous system so that the EEG would go wild and record it. I was sorry to see this wonderful man rather frantically grasping for an explanation he could fit into his limited scientific framework, saying over and over, "It must be muscle quiver. It must be muscle quiver."

In contrast, the Indian doctors at Kaivalyadhama knew what they were doing because they had the descriptions of the Vedic texts as their guide and hence much vaster framework for inquiry. And it seemed to me that Western scientists when they get a brainwave quickly rush in and use an EEG for a few months, publish some papers, and do not realise what every stage hypnotist knows – that relaxation techniques and meditation are both self-suggestion. The only different quality is that hypnotic induction is egocentric around the lower mind while the true meditation is the ultimate and highest power of suggestion so that our consciousness becomes whatever it imagines, simply because it becomes the creator of its own experience. In high meditation the gunas are stopped.

THE YOGI M.D.'S

The yogic doctors who tested me in the pit were already familiar with trance states and their work was researching what the ancient texts said of the energies. They were familiar with hypnotic states and the difference between proper meditation and self-hypnosis. Therefore I was anxious to find out what they had discovered and compare it with my own research into the nature of consciousness and light energies.

The results of my few days working with Dr. Vinekar in the pit are somewhere in my files in London along with my psychic library. They clearly showed that not only could the human brain energy record large amounts of electricity in the 10,000 to 20,000 microvolt range but whenever different levels of Devic consciousness were reached, the thresholds of energy were recorded as large spikes with higher input voltage readings. These tests also revealed that the brain on a few occasions could lie dormant and passive without any electrical activities recorded on the EEG in a disassociated state while yet performing speech and verbal description of internal altered states of consciousness. This is supposedly scientifically impossible since any imagery produces electrical potentials in the occipital areas, while speech produces electrical waves in the speech centres of the brain. Yet it happened, and it could not be explained by doctors who had been scientifically trained and who had, over a period of years, measured the EEG's of over 1,000 yogis.

BRAIN COMA AND MEDITATION

The only explanation for this is that the events in the human brain and consciousness may be capable of extra-physical bi-location. To put it more simply it is possible for consciousness to operate without a functioning brain. This means that people with brain damage lying immobile in coma as did Karen Quinlan in 1976 in a vegetative state, or even clinically dead persons may still be aware and alive in consciousness. The clinical definition of death in vegetative states is still a matter of much debate at this time in scientific circles.

For those who are intellectually honest and interested in probing this research more deeply the author is willing to share more information and facts. A list of over 200 scientific papers on these related subjects given at the World Conference on Scientific Yoga is available.

The reason why I am making a point about so-called "firsts" is not because I care who is or is not first in the uncovering of truth. My point is that those scientists who are discovering for the first time now what was researched years ago and dismissed by the scientific establishment are very likely dismissing now what will eventually be researched and discovered by the establishment years hence but which is right now in this moment a new discovery which could tremendously benefit the human race. The establishment, though today it is feeling liberal in its new research on yogic trance states and meditation, has only scratched a tiny little portion of the surface. From the statements and work done it is obvious that science has not a clue to how really vast and profound the secrets of Creation really are.

For all the trouble that people take in the scientific proof of one thing or another – of brainwaves, or the effects of particles of energy – demanding proof of this and that, it is obvious to me after a long search that this whole approach through experimentation alone is not where it's at. The human race is destined for bigger things than brainwaves, antimatter or black holes. Even if you went into the middle of a black hole and came out transformed into an antiperson emerging out of a white hole, it would still be no big deal as you would still be just the same. However, if you would change the quality of your consciousness and understand the reason for it all then you'd be a wise man and a very rare person indeed. The search for wisdom leads down much stranger alleys than many scientists care to walk because they already feel they're walking in the strangest places there are around. For the mountain climber, to climb the highest mountain is the only thing to do and for a scientist maybe the game of science is the only game they know since it is the best game around. However, the most deadly game in life is not chasing anti-particles but chasing your expanding self in an expanding universe. Perhaps it is better to be a great being like Einstein who stayed in his garden and scribbled on the back of old envelopes sent to him by famous people. In this way he never had to perform one experiment or prove one theory himself.

The following article by John White appeared in "Yoga Journal" and is reproduced here because it covers the gist of the author's paper "Yogic Methods of Knowing". John White is author of "Frontiers of Consciousness, editor of "The Highest State of Consciousness" (Doubleday), author of "Relax" (Dell Paperbacks), "Everything You Want to Know About TM" (Pocket Books), and "What is Meditation?" (Anchor Books). He is former Director of Education for the Institute of Noetic Sciences.

YOGA

THE OLDEST SCIENCE OF CONSCIOUSNESS

Yoga can be defined as 'a science of consciousness,' and on the basis of historical records it seems to be the world's oldest. In order to understand this claim, the term 'science' must be clarified. Coming from the Latin scire, meaning 'to know', science has been commonly regarded as 'accumulated knowledge systematized and formulated with reference to the discovery of general truths or the operational laws, especially when such knowledge relates to the physical world.'

However, this dictionary definition is not complete. The essence of science is its method, not its data. Science is a way of knowing rather than a body of knowledge. The accumulated information of science is obtained through trained observation and is empirically verifiable. Scientific method requires that research be presented for validation by the scientific community. A clear description of the techniques and materials used is necessary in the presentation. Then the procedures are carefully repeated by others. If the same results are obtained, the findings become scientific fact.

Understood that way, yoga is indeed a science by which others can verify the effects obtained by a previous researcher. The effects do not pertain primarily to the material world. Rather, they deal with the nature of self, that inescapable and fundamental element that is involved in all knowledge. Science is recognizing that a complete description of an event must include a description of the consciousness of that event's observer. The same

event will be seen, described, or 'known' quite differently by observers whose consciousness is of different quality. The purer the consciousness, the more clearly and fully the event is observed by the knower.

Yoga excels in the purification of consciousness; it is here that it demonstrates itself to be a true science. As with Western science, the steps to be followed (including postures, breath control techniques, meditation practices, dietary regulation, rules for balanced living, etc.) are clearly delineated, and the 'findings' (stages of enlightenment) have been attested to uniformly by people who have carefully repeated these procedures in every century for thousands of years.

Yogi Christopher Hills points out in his paper 'Yogic Methods of Knowing', that both yoga and modern science are based on two distinct methods, induction and deduction. The inductive method is based on operations with description, measurement and analysis, resulting in generalisations about things. The deductive method is based on logical postulates and rules for operating with them, and also results in knowledge about things.

'However,' he writes, 'Yoga goes one step further in setting out for proof the hypothetical elements in a thesis in such a way that shows that knowledge about is not knowing directly. It is possible to know about horses without having ever seen one or ridden on one, and this applies to motor cars no less than to other mechanical things. Such knowing about is judged in yogic terms as theoretical, and lacking in six other levels of consciousness.'

The supreme work of yoga has been to guide people through those higher levels of consciousness so that knowledge about something is surpassed by direct knowledge. So long as there is some mental concept that splits or separates the knower from the known (ego), there will be only knowledge about. But when one pierces the veil of maya (cosmic illusion), when one sees through the illusion of ego-isolated personhood, then the division between self and other is healed. The knower and the known become one, the Self.

Knowledge of the Self is what modern science lacks and what makes it incomplete. But on the frontiers of research, science is coming to realise that, as Yale University physicist Henry Margenau puts it, 'Consciousness is the primary factor in all experience, hence it needs and merits the fullest attention any (scientist) can bestow on it.'

Certainly yoga has much to offer here. At University of the Trees, for example, students are taken through a three-year course 'To arouse Kundalini (consciousness) to its fuller state, and past that of mere comment and speculation... to experience consciousness (Kundalini energy) first-hand and to get it out of the verbal/intellectual descriptive 'knowing about' kind of commentary,' Christopher Hills told me recently.

It would seem, therefore, that students and teachers of yoga ought to give greater attention to becoming co-workers with scientists on the problem of knowledge, in whatever field, and how to purify the consciousness(es) involved in scientific investigation. Thus, unification would be supported on the physical plane, as well as the metaphysical because, after all, yoga is unification.

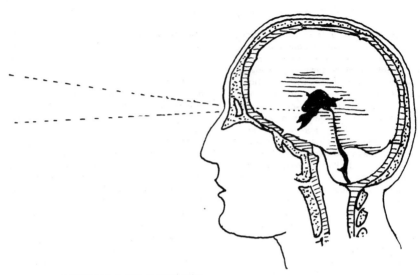

METHODS OF KNOWING

The yogic science of consciousness lists three methods of validating knowledge. The first is knowledge of the knower or observer's limitations, leading to the study of ontology, the science of Being, which deals with the nature of perception. The second method deals with epistemology and is identical with what the West calls scientific method. The third method is transcendental knowing, which unites the previous two in the study of reason itself since, rationally, all effects must be traced to their causes, all perceptions traced to the perceiver, and all evidence examined from the point of view of the Universal Intelligence. This three-step validation enables the student of the knowing process to penetrate directly beyond the relative and comparative knowledge yielded by what we call the scientific method of validation.

A man may walk East on the deck of a ship whose compass confirms that he is definitely walking East, yet he may be going West in respect to the land, if the ship is steaming West. So may science be going towards measuring objective reality while becoming more subjective in respect to greater realities than the immovable body of scientific fact. Until modern man can map out the different domains of consciousness which provide us with various angles from which Truth may be viewed, we must work from the philosophy that everything may be true from the angle from which it is observed. Once we are able to command a helicopter viewpoint and see all the viewpoints at once from a 360 degree angle, then we can arrive at some absolute statements which are true from every viewpoint.

DEFINING THE EVIDENCE

If we look at science as "measurement" or weighing on some scales, we can see easily that there cannot be motion, weight or distance unless the body moves, changes its distance or weight in relation to some other body. In the same way as mentioned earlier "velocity" has no meaning unless there is some fixed point in space to measure from. Whether there really is some such fixed point from which we can measure the velocity of light as in a vacuum, or whether we create such arbitrary points in space with our minds, is not the point here. The point in the theory of Nuclear Evolution is that consciousness itself is the ultimate validator of all experience, whether that experience is mathematical relationships or is physical and objective. Even if the measuring is done with instruments which sense phenomena and record it independent of any human agency such as cameras, chart recorders and spectroscopes, etc., we repeat, it is ultimately consciousness which designed the equipment to perform within certain parameters of the physical world, and consciousness will interpret and make sense of the sensory results.

This is fairly simple when we come to look for the way science makes representations, models, etc., but when we try to erect a frame of reference for some idea of "pure space" exclusive of all bodies, then like the idea of "Pure Consciousness", it seems to the human mind so abstract as to boggle the intellect. Here reason and logic appear to depart from common sense.

HUMAN NOTIONS

In human affairs it is conceivable that by using human images of space in which human bodies move and have their being, we can understand what is meant by "pure" space. However, until we can see clearly that the notion of space is entirely created by the notion of ourselves as a body, we cannot progress into domains of consciousness which are not limited by such notions. When such erroneous notions are used as basic assumptions for logical operations, then the results may be logically correct but basically in error.

EXAMPLE OF ERROR

If you move your arm and it meets with no resistance, you would say there is "space". But if you find resistance, then you will say there is a "body" and, as the resistance is in proportion lesser or greater, you would say there is density of the body, or you would say the "space" is more or less "pure". So if we conceptualise empty space or pure space, we cannot assume that this idea of "space" or the word "pure" stands distinct from the central idea of a body or motion of bodies.

The same error arises when we try to directly experience "pure consciousness". The whole abstraction of "pure" means without thought. Can there be any consciousness which does not think of the concept of an experiencer of that consciousness, nor of a Self which confirms the purity of such a selfless thought as the void of empty space? Can any observer get rid of onlooker consciousness just by thinking he has done so?

This to me is the scientific starting point of my theory, since it is an absolute, whereas ordinary science would say we cannot infer any unknown absolutes from relative knowledge. And it is true that the knowledge of "pure space" and "pure consciousness" cannot be experienced from the relativeness of bodies. Nor can it be experienced by a consciousness which has placed self-limiting thoughts upon its own framework of understanding. Hence, in applying scientific method to the theory of Nuclear Evolution, we are merely validating by a method of consensus what is essentially a revelation. In the same way, Einstein's speculative thought was a revelation; also Newton's insight was a revelation. Both were later validated by sequential, logical and descriptive methods. My theory of Nuclear Evolution must also be logically consistent. Since the theory of Nuclear Evolution deals also with the internal experience of time as the conditioner of the particular kind of reality a human being is likely to validate, we must here state briefly what we mean by time.

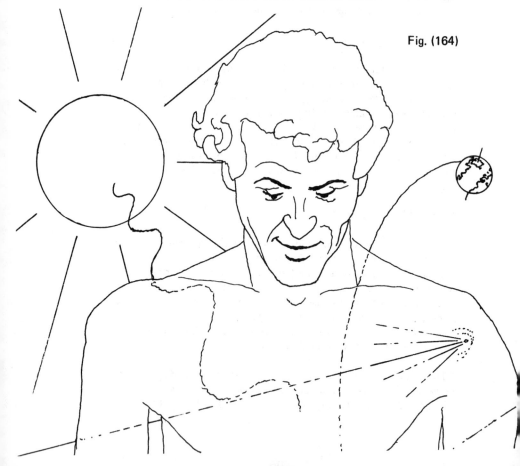

Fig. (164)

ABSOLUTE TIME AND ABSOLUTE SPACE

Consciousness operates spatially in Absolute Time which is instantaneously now everywhere for every system and for every organism experiencing the total system of the universe. The speed of light is an absolute created by mind only. Einstein and modern science accept this absolute velocity as a limit, while denying that any absolute human knowledge exists. At the speed of light it takes a ray of radiation energy 1000 seconds to traverse the diameter of the earth's orbit around the sun, which is approximately 186,000,000 miles. The mind, however, operates at 1000 times the speed of light, which makes the speed of radiation at 700 million miles per hour appear rather slow in comparison. But in comparison with the speed of consciousness the speed of mind is even slower since consciousness travels any distance in no time at all! Consciousness is already "out there" as much as it is "in here" and is able to travel instantaneously to any star or galaxy which is being born or has died millions of light years away. Motion through space in our consciousness is not relative to any point "at rest" which is standing still under the feet of the observer. The observer is a **participator** in the whole and cannot be separated in thought from his own instantaneous sensory observations of phenomena. The brain and its accompanying senses is limited to being "at rest" in relation to the velocity of light while the mind has a thought barrier of 1000 times the velocity of light. But consciousness is unlimited except by consciousness itself and therefore, in comparison to the speed of consciousness, our conceptual thoughts at the mind level are very slow. They can be regarded as merely another form of very subtle matter vibrating at a slow rate in comparison with the top speed of consciousness, which is travelling from self-to-self, i.e. no speed at all.

All motion is directly experienced not in relation to some imaginary fixed point in space under our feet (a sensory limit), but to the eternal moment of no-time. In all thought operations in science the eternal no-time is a hidden absolute which is present in all calculations, just as silence is a hidden attribute of sound. Without the presence of silence (no vibration at all) the concept of sound vibration has nothing to arise in and no periodicity to measure with. In the same way time only arises out of the concept of infinite time or the eternal now of "no-time". The observer is not separate from the intervals created by clocks because the mind, being very slow to realise that it has created the clock intervals in the first place, has forgotten its own subject-object relationship with "no-time". Consciousness is separated from mind only by its own conceptions of itself as differentiated from the whole universe. In fact it is impossible to separate our consciousness from the total mind by conceiving an observer as an entity separate from the instantaneous speed of no-time, just as it is impossible to separate the experience of sound arising from out of silence.

The ground state of sound is silence and all sound begins in silence and ends in silence; therefore all vibration or cyclic activity must be measured from that eternal timeless state and not from some artificial man-created clock hooked to the local earth time of its revolutions around the sun. Every cycle is a circle and from the centre of every circle there is only ONE time – the absolute no-time of consciousness, in which all cyclic vibrations are but disturbances of the eternal silence.

DOES THE BLACK HOLE AT THE CENTRE OF OUR GALAXY RADIATE AN INVISIBLE FIELD OF CONSCIOUSNESS?

At the spiral centre of our universe the dense cluster of stars is obscured from our view by clouds of cosmic dust. Scientists now theorise that there is a black hole there swallowing up stars, light and gases so that it would not be visible, since light rays cannot escape from its centre owing to intense gravitation. The galaxy in Andromeda measures about 100,000 light years across and is about the same size as our own galaxy. According to current scientific opinion the light of the Andromeda galaxy travels for 2.2 million light years to reach our eyes. We are seeing its past history as it was 2.2 million years ago. Our own Milky Way galaxy contains 100 billion stars and there are another 100 billion galaxies that comprise the observable universe. The optical telescopes receive light, which is 2 billion years old when it reaches us, from the furthest reaches of space on the edge of the universe.

THE METAPHYSICS OF CONSCIOUSNESS

If we said to most physicists that our state of consciousness could deflect the positive radiations of atomic fallout by an act of will there would be a snort of disgust from most of them while the less arrogant would merely say it had not been proved. However, it has been proved and what they mean is that it has not been generally accepted. Einstein received the Nobel prize in 1921. It took mankind five years to recognise Einstein's achievement after his theory had been proved and confirmed. He wrote his photoelectric theory in 1905 and it was proved eleven years later by Millikan. Even after he received his prize in 1921, acceptance of his relativity theory was still controversial though it had been proved by Eddington in Brazil May 29th, 1919.

Recently an old friend of mine did an experiment (1974) similar to an experiment I did myself in 1963 to confirm the effects of consciousness on a cloud chamber and she confirmed that cosmic rays can be influenced by human consciousness. A cloud chamber is a device developed by nuclear physicists to study the tracks made by nuclear particles such as protons, photons and cosmic rays to make them visible. Just as a beam of light, that is normally invisible, can only be seen when it shines on cloud, moisture, dust, etc. in the atmosphere, so can the heavy particles of cosmic rays be photographed in the cloud chamber. Dr.Robert Miller, Dr. Philip B. Reinhart and Anita Kern used the cloud chamber in conjunction with my friend Olga Worrall who is well known as a psychic healer along with her late husband Ambrose. Olga concentrated her conscious energy upon the cloud chamber and produced visible effects which could be photographed. She then travelled six hundred miles away and at an appointed time again concentrated her consciousness on the cloud chamber. Distance meant nothing because she could, along with many healers, do this from the other side of the earth planet. The same visible effects were produced by conscious imaging. Not all scientists then will think this is a crazy idea, but for the general public to accept and apply this knowledge or for science to confirm it generally will take many years of controversy before it is finally accepted as valid.

Everything achieved by consciousness, whether it is an experiment, a mathematical result or even the perception of a material object has to be eventually validated by human consciousness. Therefore let us look at the physics of consciousness to know the real purpose of matter.

The idea that man is a hologram projected into the human brain and the fact that we have the power to slow down atomic decay, will not gain acceptance until people try it. This may take many years before scientists think it is feasible or rational even to try.

Alternatively, acceptance could come with a swiftness given by the weaponisation of these powers, as did the atomic age. The fact that metals can be bent and cosmic rays intercepted or attracted at will could be useful for interfering in the circuitry of rockets whose guidance systems have been shielded against jamming by radio waves. Hence instead of waiting many centuries for proof of how consciousness can affect matter, Nuclear Evolution may be proved by man's default in a very few years' time when rockets may be turned back with psychotronic power. Some people rationalise such uses of the gift of consciousness. "Who can tell the awesome loving purpose of the Cosmic One?" they say, "Perhaps it is only for us to accept and do, letting the results, good or bad, fall wherever the cosmic will blows them." But Einstein proceeded with his findings hesitantly, because he knew there is a responsibility with every act of creation that must be acknowledged; otherwise it is like putting a sharp razor in the hands of a child to play with. Every act of love in creation, whether it is sexual, aesthetic or mental, must be considered for its consequences on the lives of others, because what the future may bring, will depend on what we imagine now, think now, worship now and feel now. It is with this in mind that I began this book, knowing that its contents in the hands of a ruthless and selfish person may cause future generations some pains. Therefore we could say one tiny element has been left out but that element is already in the heart of the ones who would see the glory of God's gift to man – pure consciousness. And so it is for them that the book is written, and for them that I have hidden the missing element in my other works on consciousness. This is not intended to hook those interested in occult mysteries but as a protection so that certain people will put the book down with disgust and read no further. Therefore what follows in Part III is the preparatory programming for the introduction of "Supersensonics", the development of the supersense. Together they complete the mystery of man's purpose here on earth -- whilst separate they are two halves of a sphere.

The author's book "Rays From the Capstone" and "Supersensonics" give some details of these newly re-discovered powers of consciousness. The task in this book is to investigate them without sensationalism. The optimum state of consciousness in which this ancient wisdom comes to man is in the form of a committed group of people who use these powers for evolutionary purposes and prevent the weaponisation of any psychotronic devices, if necessary by psychotronic means.

THE ULTIMATE POWER

Nuclear Evolution is not just some intellectual theory based on thoughts or perceptions but is working through nature itself. So the secrets of our own evolution are inevitably bound up with the laws which govern even the evolution of an atom. If we study groups of atomic elements and particularly the way that they absorb new members or particles of light or matter into the whole, we can get some inkling of the next step in the evolution of the human race which must, of necessity, involve the binding of separate egos into one group or whole. And what is the force which can achieve this binding? What force is powerful enough to unite human beings of different ideals, temperaments, and personalities? The power of consciousness is so great that when it discovers its own power, the earth will be drastically affected, either for good or for evil. What can channel this energy into fusion, rather than fission? Is there a kind of love which is more encompassing than the kind we now experience? Is there a use of life-force more deliberate and more creative than the things most people do with their lives each day? Our communication with each other reveals the mediocrity of what we conceive ourselves to be and what we feel is the purpose of our being.

What kind of communication can create a wholistic conscious-ness which cannot be divided? The true meaning of com-munica-tion is found in the root word **munis**, meaning sharing, giving or serving. When we can share the life-force first with the micro-universe of our own cells and then share the macro-universe with others of different temperament, we have the beginning of real love. To try to get real love by finding a mate or by being highly selective of whom we will love is a cosmic delusion and a luxury only to be enjoyed by those with much work to do on the ego which separates the human consciousness from "the other". In ultimate reality there is no "other", since all the "otherness" is experienced in our own consciousness. However, as long as people experience outlines around all natural objects, especially people, there will always be those who cannot see that conscious-ness connects everything together. The kind of love which can achieve the binding together of the human race into one organism must be grounded in this perception that everything in the universe is **already** bound together through the cohesive force of universal love. The force which glues the atom together is the same love which binds the human heart and links us one to another. The inability to separate from the universe we live in is the basic plank in Nuclear Evolution Theory.

HUMAN CONTROL OF CREATIVE FORCES

Atoms are part of nature like humans are and, while we would not expect them to behave like humans do with all their persona-lity problems, the fact is that "personality" itself is dependent on the quality of energy absorbed, synthesised and metabolised in the human system. Therefore both atoms and humans have choices to make depending on what kind of energy comes to them from the vaster part of their existence as wholes, hooked

inevitably to the entire cosmic process. People group together
into social units such as family, club, party, town, community,
nation, and global village and at each level the human being is a
different animal. Yet they are all functioning with the same
consciousness drawn from the same source of life. That source of
energy for maintaining our own consciousness (in the same sense
that nutrition from foods maintains the physical body) is the
subject matter of this book. Man's greatest problem is the
conscious control of his life-force amongst groups of people and
the spiritual nourishment which can bring cosmic order to his
affairs. If we can discover what fuels our consciousness and holds
the atoms of our body together we can find that which will hold
the human race together.

In the section of this book on the similarity of atomic structures
and energies to human groupings, we describe the interaction of
thresholds of energy in a more scientific way. The purpose now is
to give a more general background so that we can understand the
energies which work through the psychophysical interfaces of our
human body and its positive and negative polarities of the proton
and electron.

512

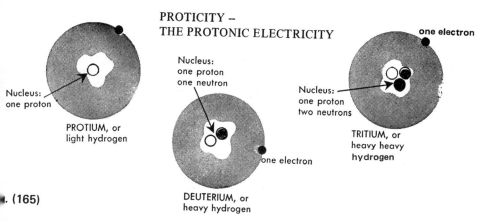

PROTICITY --
THE PROTONIC ELECTRICITY

Nucleus:
one proton

PROTIUM, or
light hydrogen

Nucleus:
one proton
one neutron

DEUTERIUM, or
heavy hydrogen

one electron

Nucleus:
one proton
two neutrons

one electron

TRITIUM, or
heavy heavy
hydrogen

. (165)

The chief parts of an atom are the proton, neutron and electron. An element in nature is determined by its number of protons. Hydrogen is here shown in its three states. Like water can appear in three states, liquid, solid (ice) and gas (steam), so can the fundamental particles of hydrogen combine with other elements in our body and become many different forms.

The proton is a particle of matter with an electric charge equal in magnitude but opposite polarity to an electron. For every proton in a stable nucleus of an atom there is an orbiting electron. However, the proton experiences the attractive pull of the nuclear force which is positive while the electron does not. The proton is paired in the nucleus of an atom with the neutron which keeps it balanced. The positive proton is 1836 times as heavy as the negative electron and is therefore bound into the nucleus very tightly. When electrons are stripped out of their orbits around the nucleus and its protons, the atom becomes excited and is said to be ionised positively. When there are more electrons than protons the atom is ionised negatively. Negative ions are ready to donate electron energy to humans who are short of electricity. Positive ions take electrons away because they are short of electricity.

The proton is the name we give to that part of the nucleus of an atom which consists of a bundle of positive energy. Neither the protons nor the electrons are positive or negative in nature but only positive or negative in relation to each other. What is positive in one thing may be negative in another situation but when we say a proton is positive we mean that in relation to its surrounding environmental electrons it is an attractive force which keeps the electrons peripherally bound to it. The proton is an electric charge which occupies the very dense and most intense part of an atom. It can be likened to that part of a human being which longs in the heart for completion or that part of a cell which has a memory of all that it has ever been. Some groups of atomic protons in the nucleus are electron-rich like a person who has more than enough of everything, and its surplus electrons are therefore allowed to wander freely through a group, interacting with every part of it, but they are still bound loosely to the nucleus which has a positive charge. In physics this is called a donor-type transistor crystal, but in human applications, you could think of an excited person who radiates infectious energy and enriches others around him. Our human bodies have many such crystals made of atoms which can instantly become electron rich. Another atom may have an exactly opposite need in the peripheral electrons of a crystal element and this is called an acceptor-type transistor. This can be likened to a person who always takes rather than gives, but since there is an exact correspondence between someone that needs to give and someone who takes there is a stability or union formed between the energy-enriched giver and the energy-poor taker.

When an acceptor crystal atom meets a donor it takes a single electron from it but this leaves a hole in the atom from which that electron is acquired. This hole, caused by the lost negative electron, acts like a positive charge in the donor atom because it acts as an attractive trap into which any stray unsuspecting electron may fall. We could think of this as a person who gives continually of himself financially but because everyone thinks he is rich, no one ever gives him much. People are always asking to share the riches and so they fall into the trap not realising that a rich person may be emotionally poor and desperately needing someone to love on other levels than the financial one.

The hole-rich atom, whenever it traps an electron, will feel like a person who is more stable and will balance out at zero charge. Protons in matter can sometimes switch roles under certain conditions and change into neutrons and neutrons can turn into protons through the decay of the energy in weak interactions. The neutronic force can be likened to a person who is apathetic and creates inertia around him or her by being lazy and unconcerned with positive or negative attractions. When protons lose their positive charge and become neutral, they give off energy to the environment in the form of weak radiations. All of nature is giving off these radiational energies, some of them so subtle that we cannot detect them scientifically; we can only calculate their existence mathematically. There are many such radiating crystals in every human body and the radiations are controlled by the degree of excitement of all the atoms that is brought about by attraction between energy-rich and energy-poor. It is a situation very much like our world of rich nations and poor nations but at the level of the microcosm, in the cells of our own body.

The nuclear force which binds all the parts of the atom together is not dependent on the charge of the particles within it, i.e. a proton can get married to a neutron with the same delightful attraction as that which unites two neutrons. Although it is the strongest force known in matter, the nuclear binding energy only has a small range inside itself within its own boundaries. Unless it gets excited by disturbing, unbalancing forces from outside its various shells, the atom will remain relatively quiet and passive, depending on its environment. Like someone meditating in a quiet cathedral, everything is blissful until a noisy boisterous crowd of tourists discovers the chapel. Then the patience and communion with God turns into anger at having people chatting while prayer is going on. When it is disturbed by conflicting vibrations, the atom radiates heat or hard rays which result from its decay.

Altogether there are three attractive forces which are constantly acting on the nuclear centre of an atom as they are also acting on the total being of a human hologram. They are (1) gravitation, (2) weak decay interactions and (3) electromagnetic forces, but there is a fourth force which is the nuclear force and this can be attractive or divisive. This fourth and strongest force, which binds the atom into its crystal patterns of matter is carried to the nuclear centre of each atom and from one atom to the nucleus of another by radiation of photons of light. These rays can attract or repel the objects of matter, cells, molecules or people on which they are acting. Therefore the electromagnetic force acts as a medium for the exchange of nuclear forces on one system to another.

ELECTRONIC FORCE

We could liken this to the electron sea which interpenetrates the whole of space in the form of invisible light from all the stars and suns of creation,and visualise it as an image of water. The medium of water is the solution in which not only all organic life takes place but also certain chemical reactions in the human body. A more graphic picture of energy transfer is the analogy of water as a medium through which waves of energy pass without the water itself travelling but merely oscillating up and down. The human body sits in this sea of electrons and photons with enormous spaces between the atoms of the body cells. In the same way an atom of matter is itself an open structure so that many nuclear particles from other stars may pass through it without hitting. The electromagnetic force of light keeps the electron spinning in its orbit around the nucleus. This same force is the binding energy between atoms which form into molecules and then into cells and larger organs. The character of the electron is to go naturally wherever the protons lead but electrons always occupy different thresholds of energy around the nucleus. Like an onion with different skins or a human being with different spherical shells of consciousness around it, the electrons in the body occupy different shells in every atom. For instance, a carbon atom has a nucleus of 6 protons and 6 neutrons, and so has a total of 12 particles in the nuclear centre. For every proton with a positive charge there is an electron with a negative charge and in the same way human cells are charged with negative and positive forces in each cell, and throughout the nervous system each organ is polarised electrically. The carbon atom, like the other 44 atomic elements in the human body, has its own distinct patterning. Two electrons are in the K shell and 4 of the 6 electrons are in the L shell,while in other atoms the outer shells are filled from L to Q representing seven thresholds of energy in matter.

Every human being is a cloud of spiritual energy vibrating at seven levels of consciousness. As each electron cloud around the nuclear centre of each atom has seven levels or shells which prevent other atoms from entering the nucleus, in the same way each human entity is surrounded by outlines of the cloud of swirling forces generated by millions of radiating atoms, all interacting with the electromagnetic sea or cosmic field. It is this cloud of unknown forces around every human which prevents another human entity from occupying the same nuclear centre of Being. But just as every atom in the body is controlled by its rate of vibration at the seven levels of the electron shells so are the field forces which the electrons resonate with controlled by the seven levels of consciousness working through the seven chakras as seven thresholds of cosmic energy. These seven envelopes around every nuclear centre of the whole entity are reflected in every part of the being. Every atom, every cell, every platelet of blood, every organ is impregnated with the total hologram which is illuminated by the cosmic light of the universe. This grouping of forces and the patterns of radiation they send out to every object in the environment is the rainbow body which God is said to have put as a sign in the heavens. It is nothing less than the spectrum of all vibration repeated at every level of existence but it is only experienced by us humans consciously in the refraction and diffraction of light energy. In the production of light radiation in the Solar atom which we experience as the Sun there is a transition from the excitement of hydrogen atoms to helium atoms through tritium (H_3) and (H_4) acting as a fusion catalyst. In the hotter stars which shine their light through space into the primeval hologram of the earth atom, the nucleus of the carbon atom acts as a catalyst for the fusion process which promotes the reaction we call light or radiation, but the catalyst remains unaffected by the change.

In human terms this can be looked at as someone who acts as a catalyst in a group of people. He causes the group to be stepped up to a higher level of excitement until the group begins to generate radiative energies at every level of its nucleus, while his own state of Being remains unchanging by constantly returning to a state of equilibrium or balance. This dynamic state of balance is supercritical and not to be confused with stability caused by inertia or immobility. It is a rarefied state, whereas the neutral state of matter is often caused by cessation of excitement and the static stillness of death rather than the balancing of the forces of life in equilibrium.

NEUTRONIC FORCES

Earlier we mentioned the effect of the three gunas upon our perception of objects and how they worked together to form our three-dimensional picture of reality. It is not often realised that not only people get moribund but whole societies become unable to look at anything which will disturb their present habits of thought. The neutronic force correlates exactly with the tama-guna in Sanskrit. Tamas is the force that attempts to keep people still and balanced and without any change, but as with atoms, so with people. The connecting link between people and atoms or human social organisation is not always easy to see, but once people understand these things they instantly realise the power of consciousness to transform life. The neutron is that part of an atom which balances and neutralises the charge on an atom and makes it stable. We all know of the person who is so stable that he cannot change, cannot think in other patterns and cannot stand anything that disturbs equilibrium. Such people are the neutrons of society, though they can move when the whole gets moving; until then the neutron is just a bundle of inertia -- the opposite of dynamic life. Something that is life-force enhancing would enable us to discover how not to be unduly affected by tamasic energy.

These neutronic forces balance the energetic particles in the nucleus of an atom and occupy the same central space as the protons. The presence of neutrons, packed together in the nucleus with the positive protons, keeps the atom in its ground state in normal equilibrium. The most common element of which human bodies are made and which has a cosmic abundance of 99.98 in the earth is the atom of hydrogen. The non-ionised state or the unexcited hydrogen atom has 1 proton and 1 electron in a single orbit around the nucleus. By adding 1 neutron it becomes ionised and has 3 particles. This is then unstable and is called an isotope. About 1500 different atoms or isotopes can be made by adding one particle or several different neutron particles together in the nucleus of any atom. Only 280 of these are stable and all the others radiate energy as they are an excited form of matter. Many are radioactive but not all radioactive atoms are dangerous to human cell life. The fusion process in the sun is highly radio-active but its helium fusion through tritium (H_3) is harmless to human beings on the earth because all its dangerous high energy particles are too slow and get trapped in the plasma skin of the earth's magnetic envelope. Hydrogen in its natural state inside the sun is highly excited and does not have any neutrons in its nucleus like other atoms and therefore is not made stable by balancing the neutrons with the 1 proton particle in its nucleus. Our bodies are mostly made of combinations of hydrogen such as in water. Ninety percent of the human body is H_2O or 2 particles of hydrogen to 1 of oxygen. However, the oxygen is a much bigger atom and has 8 protons and 8 neutrons in its nucleus; therefore it weighs out at 4 times more than the hydrogen in the water of our bodies. Elsewhere in this book we shall see that oxygen is the fuel of consciousness. Hydrogen binds the stored energy, and the burning of oxygen enables our cells to respirate, so this shows how important water is for man. Spirit (consciousness) and water are necessary for the whole body to function.

By splitting of water we release the fuel of consciousness, oxygen, and release the binding energy for all the cells of our body – the hydrogen which combines with carbon and other elements. It is the action of light energy of the sun and the other more powerful stars that breaks up these atoms in the human body at an enormous rate.

Ten billion atoms die or change their form every second, and ten billion new ones are born. At this rate of change in the human body the consciousness of man is able to enter into the hologram and influence not only the rate of their decay but what level of energy is generated by the disintegration rate of our atomic cloud. Because of this fast and tremendous flux the atomic structure of our body is open to so many new possibilities and re-combinations.

THE POWER OF CONSCIOUSNESS

In a later chapter we shall see that the rate of excitation or vibration is the determining factor which enables a person to enter into the hologram of life. To create the energy needed to make this happen requires the will to will, which comes when anything is close to our heart. This "will" is the same as enthusiasm or the kind of will which makes people perform a strenuous hobby, get up early in the morning to go fishing in the rain, or go climbing impossible mountaintops. When we desire or will to enter the enhanced energy state there is an immediate quickening of our vibration. Remarkable changes in the human body of bone and tissue can take place in a few minutes as a result of the power of human consciousness. It is this power which is behind all spiritual healing and it is this power that Nuclear Evolution is concerned with. In short, consciousness in its pure state is God and with consciousness all things in the material state are possible.

It is this ability of consciousness to get into the heart of the atomic events in our body that gives humans the power to ward off the harmful rays and slow down the protonic atomic decay of the body to create an enhancement of the electronic forces. When we disintegrate at the optimum rate the decay of our cell life is slowed down and we get younger or we get older less fast. When we control the intake of protonic forces we enhance longevity of the cell and generate more energy for awareness at the same time. The consciousness of man can also generate a biological field which can slow down the intake of nuclear fallout by repelling the harmful positive ions. However, the most important aspect of studying the interactions between atomic particles and light is to find the links between the individual parts of the wholistic groups in nature and to apply this knowledge to human group consciousness. As particles behave in the macrocosm so do they behave in the microcosm. The difficulty is in making the transfers and links between human groups and groups of atoms. Humans have such an ego-centric view of themselves that they cannot see themselves acting out the dance of life in the same way that atomic particles separate, unite and disintegrate. One day they will not separate themselves and their own consciousness from what they are observing. Then the revelation will come that atoms, molecules and cells are just like people, with their own personalities and qualities that can colour and charm our view of reality.

Much speculation exists about neutron stars which send down showers of cosmic rays upon us here on the earth's surface. Just as there are stars sending out rays of protons or positive electricity so are neutron stars sending out negative electrons. These have a remarkable effect on our membranes and hence on our brains. The internal membranes and sinuses affect the whole process of absorption in our body and if we breathe negative ions into these cavities the ion transport through the membranes is facilitated remarkably. Just as these cell membranes and electric charges are part of us and the environment, so is each individual person a brain cell in a cosmic brain. When we generally accept and understand that the planetary brain works no differently from an individual brain, then we will know that the time for the great evolutionary advance has come.

Those who can use these interstellar forces for enhancement of this present incarnation will not need any convincing because the result will show in the magic of their own fulfilled life-style. The study of Nuclear Evolution is like stepping off the edge of a cliff. The only way you can feel safe is to know there is nothing down there at the bottom to drop into. The cosmic brain has all attitudes programmed for the leap ahead into the unknown Self.

A HUMAN EXPERIMENT

On the next four pages we set out the criteria and purpose for a human experiment in consciousness development since any theory which postulates certain changes in human beings must have the possibility of being tested. Since humans are not guinea pigs and cannot be compelled except under dictatorships, the experiment must await those willing to embark on it freely of their own will.

SCIENTIFIC DEFINITION

Consciousness cannot be defined accurately because any definition is always conditioned by the consciousness which is experiencing it. However, inability to define something does not mean we cannot discuss it or experience it. In exactly the same way we can experience an electric shock without defining electricity, so we can describe our direct experience of consciousness in metaphors, images, models, and worlds of space and time. In fact all these are expressions of consciousness; they are effects which can lead us to their causes.

THE HYPOTHESIS

Consciousness constantly touches up and modifies laws in order that they may more accurately represent facts. Since facts are knowledge defined as proven and accepted by a general consensus of scientific opinion deemed to be educated opinion, the reorganisation of laws of Nature will be only possible on a general scale of civilisation when the following conditions exist-

1) The educated opinion is convinced that the established and proven body of human knowledge is inconsistent with new evidence or theory about new facts of consciousness.

2) The ordinary understanding of consciousness is concerned with what works and not concerned with validation of knowledge, and therefore it embraces the new facts before the educated opinion has had time to disabuse itself of finely entrenched theories about facts.

3) When the general body of educated opinion believe that the laws of consciousness are as real as any laws of physics, then there can be nuclear changes in the structure of society.

UNDERSTANDING LAWS OF SELF

4) The nucleus of consciousness in each human varies with its own image of itself, i.e.,

a) In Communism, the self is totalitarian, does not exist for itself alone, is part of the social entity known as the state, has no individual rights apart from the general needs of the people and must sacrifice its personal needs to those of posterity.

b) In Capitalist and Democratic societies, the individual self is supreme, and in the pursuit of enlightenment for himself alone, the individual self eventually finds he is interdependent and responsible for all of society. The quality of society depends on the evolution of each individual self who makes it up, and therefore the image of a totalitarian self is in conflict with that of the rights and responsibilities of each individual.

THE LAWS OF PHYSICS

5) The representations of reality by laws of physics or any other provisional models is too simple to encompass the totality of consciousness completely. The task of continual modification of these laws will go on indefinitely between the nature of reality and the laws of physics, because scientific method does not include the quality of the observer's consciousness in the facts presented.

THE LAWS OF LIFE

All laws are laws of consciousness because they are merely symbolic and provisional concepts about perception of external events without regard to internal events. The symbolic representation of any hypothesis can be upset by any experiment that widens the coordinates to include new features not included in the original schematic representation. All laws, whether of matter or consciousness, depend on the degree of tolerance and limitation in the domains measured. They are imposed by the human mind depending on the type of experiment performed and will forever have to do with the nature of the observer's ignorance of his own mental processes.

DESCRIPTION OF THE EXPERIMENT

In order to prove the various parts of the hypothesis, the nuclear experiment with human consciousness is being performed by a group of humans, students at the University of the Trees, assuming the following axioms:

1) that human consciousness is a mirror which reflects the universe and its total intelligence only in terms of its own ignorance or wisdom,

2) that human consciousness cannot differentiate between external light of radiation and the internal light of consciousness, since both are intangible and invisible until they interact with matter,

3) that communication of consciousness by E.S.P. between one member of a group of individuals and another or several others would definitely transcend the laws of physical communication between one body and another as well as laws of time and space,

4) that the group of individuals unite together on the assumption that humans do function in different time worlds and on different levels of consciousness, which leads to expression of different experiential worlds, and that these alternative states of consciousness create a typology of seven humanistic experiential modes of reality or yield combinations and overlapping of these experiential modes which can be qualitatively measured.

5) that the mathematical symbol of zero is a nominal representation of "pure consciousness" or "timelessness of pure space" from which all mental events experienced as vibrations can be used to unite the individual consensus.

This consensus is the validation of factual knowledge of the internal/external universal field. In order to transcend the mental set of separate individuality, the experiment will be conducted with 15 lucid people who live together on the same campus and share equal responsibility for the situation created by their consciousness.

THE EXPERIMENT

A group of dedicated people commited to investigating the nature of consciousness will live together and test the hypothesis that humans communicate in different experiential time worlds, the frequency of vibration of which determines the nature of reality experienced.

Each will write a book of the same teachings concerning the nature of consciousness from their own level of experience and personal awareness. The responsibility for the experiment and its validation or its proof will rest with each individual member of the group, irrespective of who leaves the group or who determines the reality of the group effort. At every moment, all the individuals will consider themselves responsible for what is happening in the group action or inaction. If there is a lack of insight or lack of resources, it is for the individual to attempt to supply what is missing or be challenged by other members on other levels of consciousness to manifest this observed lack.

THE PROOF

... that each individual receives life-force or consciousness and filters it differently through his own levels of consciousness and re-expresses this through the different psychic centres (or chakras) which determine the human personality structure.

... that this difference is revealed by each participant in the way they tackle the writing of a book on the subject of the evolution of a nuclear group. Duplication of the observations of Nuclear Evolution will show whether the hypothesis is correct, because the levels of consciousness and the inner experiential worlds of time will be manifest in the work of each individual learning from a common source.

THE PURPOSE

The purpose of the whole experiment is to lead a group of people to a collective understanding of the uniqueness of life so that they may understand that a common universal field of consciousness may be manifested in countless individual ways. In short, it is to personally experience the many in the one and to see the ONE who is the ground of all being and consciousness.

It remains to say that if you don't like this particular way of presenting Nuclear Evolution, try reading one or two of the other 15 experimenters who are now replicating this research on the nature of consciousness! The theory is proved if you think you have read something different. One thing you will agree: that devotion to a task is a form of love, which is the basis of all science and religion. Of course there will be fears of repetition but I have found in fact that the concept can bear repetition in countless ways. Because of the complexity of many of the ideas, certain concepts have been constantly repeated in the book. As the reader proceeds no doubt he will see the necessity for this in order to maintain clarity.

I.R. 13 Red 19 Orange 25 Yellow 50 Green 55 Blue 62 Indigo 68 Violet

RESONANCE
AND
CONSCIOUSNESS

Underlying all divining phenomena as well as interactions between vibrating physical systems such as atoms, molecules, etc. is the principle of resonance. Magnetic or electrical resonance works identically to sonic resonance to produce beat frequencies and standing waves and interference patterns which annihilate energy or amplify it. The effect of resonance on human beings and their contact with objects in the environment depends entirely on resonance. The blood cell resonates in the same spectrum as oxygen, the hydrogen atom resonates in the same spectrum as carbon, sodium with chlorine, etc. and there is also unconscious selection of energies which appeals to each individual's wave-field of consciousness. In fact more information is communicated between two people at the unconscious level of resonance than we can ever get from verbal clues. We explain this in essence terms such as "I like him" or "I can't stand his vibes" but the resonance effects come clear and loud.

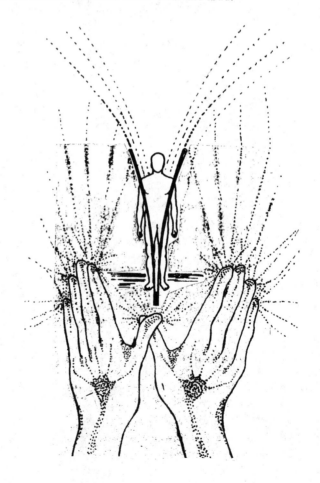

COLOUR AS RESONANCE

When measuring colour as cycles per second we know they resonate with particular sensitised brain cells in the occipital section of the brain, and therefore we must now consider the optical laws of vision and seeing, since there is a definite measurable correspondence in the given lines of the spectrum which is experienced by everybody in the same way; for example it is obvious that sextant angles of the sun at high noon measure the same for everybody.*This shows that the geometrical laws of perspective are universally valid for all human beings at the same time, just as the Fraunhofer lines of the spectrum are valid indications of the origin of the sun's light waves irrespective of the time-frequency with which they are measured.

In order to understand our framework of Absolute zero time (timelessness) we continually have to repeat to ourselves that God did not make the second, the metre or the foot, but he did invent the cycle and the beat—and most of all that common factor of all states of matter/radiation—resonance.

In our attempt to relate colour to consciousness we must get away from everyday thinking in yardsticks which have no reality (seconds and feet) because there are fundamental factors which arise in the psychological laws of seeing (the observer's laws of geometrical perspective) which conflict hopelessly with the physical laws of seeing objects in space. Whether it is heavenly bodies or the heights of buildings in feet, or distances of stars in light years, etc., the problem is the same. All these measurements as well as the heights of buildings and mountains are sense impressions which vary with the distance of the observer and appear rationalised to our Imagination. But these laws of perspective and of geometrical optics are no more rational than the height of a building is in the prime imagination when they are both considered together.

Considered together they have no more reality than the metre or the second. Physically measured buildings get bigger as we walk towards them and the angle subtended gets wider, but we " know " that cement does not grow and that against that arbitary yard or foot in the British Museum they stay the same. Yet laws of optics and perspective and the angles of stars and suns are exact and accurate enough to navigate ships and calculate the width of galaxies with. How does one establish the difference in the absolute " I " (the observer) between the two frameworks equally valid in reality?

---

* For more depth in the investigation of the nature of perception, it is important to read "Supersensonics" Chapters 14-17, dealing with Vasco Ronchi's work on vision and optics. Robert Massy, a student of Christopher Hills, has explained this very simply from the physics point of view in his book "Hills' Theory of Consciousness" (pub. University of the Trees Press, 1976).

Not only can our Absolute "I" switch from one framework of physical concrete reality to another without any seeming difficulty, but internally it hops unconsciously between all seven frameworks. The way this works depends on our awareness of the chakra functions. Failure to recognise our existence in different frameworks of reality blinds us to the real nature of perception and blocks our personal relationship with the Absolute Self. This Absolute Self exists on so many thresholds that it is hard at the beginning to determine our personal responses to the many worlds of time. By studying the way people work and the grooves we ourselves move in, the vision of the Absolute Consciousness working through the whole Self can be seen in the Rainbow Body.

PSYCHOLOGICAL ENERGIES AND COLOURS

With the many detailed tests to find an Absolute time, carried out in our laboratory, we have determined that each person will respond to a different frequency of beats according to his personal relationships with a colour. When we seat a person opposite a metronome and set it beating at a distance of 2 metres at 207 shocks per minute, we will find that if the consciousness is predominating in the Red band the subject will experience the beats in his nervous system. It would appear that the standing wave acts as a carrier wave to the colour. If we set the subject at 3 metres at 197 shocks per minute we will find a subject will resonate to the colour Orange and so on. If we extend the distance we can measure an 8 metre wave extending as far as Violet. (See Fig.166) If we reduce this by 1/10th to a wavelength of 80 cms. we find the same resonances occur proportionally at a different frequency of shocks. By experimentation it is possible to construct a table of beats at any distance away from the metronome which will show the unconscious preferences of time intervals in space. The beat and the colour waves can be measured in cycles (or shocks per minute) to show that oscillatory waves provide a conductor for colours impinging on the biological energy field. We must remember that it is the interval or space between the beats that is measured and determined by consciousness and that one beat by itself is a meaningless absolute to someone imprisoned in time.

If we think of the field around a human being as a vibrating string we can pick out the harmonic frequencies which occur along its length at the nodal points whenever resonance with the beats in the wave is established as follows:

215 beats per minute at zero metres resonate with **BLACK**
207 beats per minute at 2 metres resonate with **RED**
197 beats per minute at 3 metres resonate with **ORANGE**
188 beats per minute at 4 metres resonate with **YELLOW**
180 beats per minute at 5 metres resonate with **GREEN**
172 beats per minute at 6 metres resonate with **BLUE**
164 beats per minute at 7 metres resonate with **INDIGO**
154 beats per minute at 8 metres resonate with **VIOLET**
128 beats per minute at 10 metres resonate with **WHITE**

In the metronome experiments resonances can occur at a specific metric distance in space away from an oscillating source if we change the frequency to suit it. By setting the number of beats per minute proportionally to the standing wave, the colour band is set up at right angles to the direction of the wave emanation.

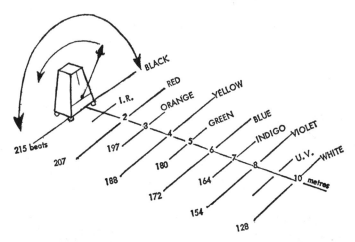

Fig. (166) THE BEATING METRONOME SETS UP A BIO-ENERGETIC WAVEFIELD OF COLOUR SHOWING ITS RELATIONSHIP WITH ALL PERIODIC OCCURRENCE AND ABSOLUTE TIME.

It will be noted that the well known relationship between wavelength and frequency is here justified since the various particles which are exchanging their energy in a monochromatic beam of coloured light are vibrating with different amplitudes but with the same frequency. In a resonance reinforced standing wave the amplitudes are increased enormously.

Fig. (167)

PROPORTIONAL
VIBRATIONS

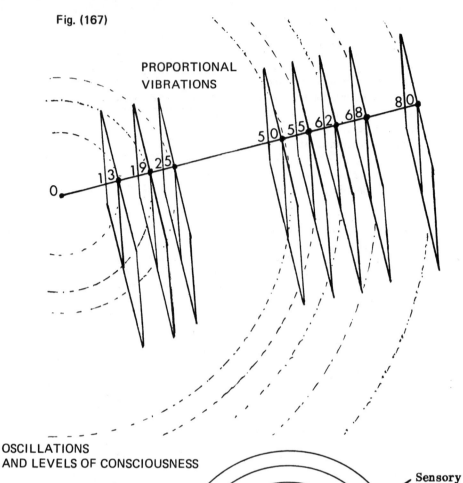

OSCILLATIONS
AND LEVELS OF CONSCIOUSNESS

Fig. (168)

The oscillations of waves
create spheres of wavefronts
around the vibrating source.
In a human being there is a
biophysical response from
the skin and muscle as with
the water diviners' phenomenon at the Red level of
sensory reaction. At other
levels of organisation of
man's psychic structure of

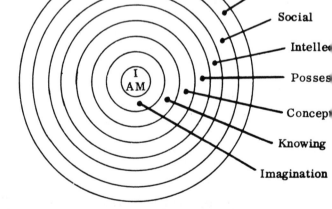

consciousness there are similar reactions at more subtle levels which correspond
to the chakra oscillations. The oscillator at a harmonic frequency of a particular
chakra produces a corresponding reaction at that level of consciousness. The wavefield
of consciousness is proportional for the human being so that vibrating elements of
matter, light waves, colours, or oscillating radio waves can subtly affect the human cell
life through resonance effects with the seven levels of consciousness.

Many of the statements science makes about light are purely formal deductions which have no reality in a natural system; they masquerade as an independent statement regarding the natural world. It must be understood that although the intellect may grasp something through formal principles which often gives us power to influence nature by disturbing it, this knowledge may be an illusion created entirely by the fact that it works. Science has long known that the ideal form may be far from the real form, though it may appear to work satisfactorily for many centuries. Our ideas about the origin of the spectrum are comparatively primitive. The spectral colours may appear between two consonant points of resonance even within the same band of colour, yet we tend to believe that the spectrum only applies to matter as measured along the known 80 octaves of electromagnetic phenomena. Yet another 80 octaves is detectable on either side of the atomic periodic table when we train our nervous system to respond to subatomic and super-atomic frequencies which have their resonances with our thought-energy as well as the type of energy that creates formal principles; this man has named " imagination "—the power to create images of reality.

The training of the nervous system to detect the 80 octaves of sub-atomic and the 80 octaves of super-atomic wave-fields begins at the physical level with the well-known dowsing ability of humans, insects, birds, etc. This is then refined to detect the wave-fields of thought in addition to the wave-fields of underground water and minerals. Once the ability to detect thought energies has been acquired it is then further refined to detect images. Since all of creation is manifested through some image or pattern, it follows that everything in the universe can be divined. The umbrella term used to cover the radiational wave-fields of physics, radionics, radiesthesia and other methods of sensing subtle energies is "Supersensonics". The development of the new science of Psychotronics is dependent on the channeling of consciousness through such wave-guides, images and patterns formed in the imagination of man. For actual training of these faculties the reader is recommended to study the book "Supersensonics" in detail, in order to familiarise himself thoroughly with the interlocking wave-fields which the natural human antenna, namely the nervous system, is capable of detecting.

A human being, an organism or an element of nature which is beating or oscillating at its own specific frequency can be measured by an observer only by its relationship to a fixed non-periodic absolute. We can only determine the real nature of the continuous spectrum of light energy by creating a timeless domain in our minds of zero-frequency. All else is mere relative knowledge and ignorant of self.

In our judgement of others we invariably demonstrate the "observer" type of consciousness. We look out from our own limited level of awareness and self-righteously assume how another human being "should" act and think. Look around your own neighbourhood and then at yourself for examples. What is the prevailing attitude to the lives of others? What is your attitude? How often do you hear or say "You would have thought so-and-so would have . . ." or "I would never do that!" Such statements are a clear indication of non-centred consciousness; we are onlookers making judgements and comments on the lives of others like a radio commentator giving a running commentary on a ball game.

To judge another human being from our own level of consciousness is a fruitless and even a pernicious assumption of righteousness. Only the One absolute of no colour representing the zero state of vibration, the Rainbow Body of all colours, which is the Self manifesting on every level of consciousness, can really know the karma or essence nature of an individual soul. Such a human being, looking out from the still centre, becomes One experiencing through all and judges all as they judge themselves. Although this zero state of stillness, this zero flow of consciousness, is not beyond any individual human being, in all man's history it has been achieved by only the few. This does not mean, however, that it is impractical, abstract or unreal; it merely means that to discover and to maintain that perfection of balance between the potential and the manifest, that still centre or Absolute "I", is to walk the razor-edge path to the end, rather than the easier and broader highway of human life, with all its alluring by-ways. We are all free to choose our own path and most of us choose the one which manifests only a part of the Self, the remainder being hidden potential. But the ultimate soul of each one of us exists between the two states of the manifest and the potential, in the one centre of stillness that we call the Absolute "I".

A non-oscillating source of stillness with no periodic occurrence is a cavity in space in resonance at specific proportional distances or intervals along a spectrum of 80 octaves of matter, and also in resonance with another 80 octaves of spiritual energy, and another 80 octaves of sub-atomic or etheric energy.

Such an absolute zero frequency position is not a material point in space but a void created in the mind, a void in the spirit and a void in the ether in exactly the same way that our minds create the reality of a metre or foot unit of measure.

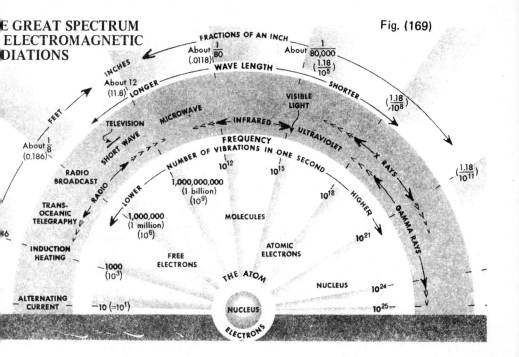

All measurements, whether metres, feet, seconds or whatever, are scientific illusions created in the imagination of man and have no actual existence, nor do they have any meaning except that given to them by man's mind. In exactly the same way that man creates such illusive realities, consciousness can create spiritual models.

The proportional measurements around such an absolute "void" Centre have been found by *our methods of sensing** beyond the electromagnetic spectrum. For each colour resonance we have found a radius from such an absolute still centre to form a vibrating antenna as follows:

0-13-19-25-50-55-62-68-80.

These resonances apply and remain constant for sound as well as colour and it does not matter whether the wave-length is expressed in metres, feet, microns or Angstrom units, the whole spectrum forms a wave showing these proportional measurements as its characteristic bands. This leads to the postulate in Nuclear Evolution that any oscillating source such as a metronome, a person or an object sets up its resonances with zero periodicity in a concentric spherical field with its bands of colour manifesting to our sensing of the Universe according to a particular beat frequency. Although colour wavelengths will change with the frequency of beats, the colour bands will remain proportionally the same if the observer changes his position to the centre of the wavefield.

---

* These methods are referred to in other papers mentioned in Part III and are the subject of a separate study. They are also exhaustively dealt with in the author's book "Supersensonics" published by University of the Trees Press.

Fig. (170)

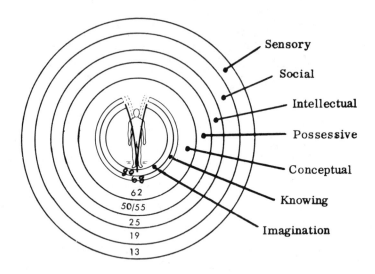

Sensory

Social

Intellectual

Possessive

Conceptual

Knowing

Imagination

62
50/55
25
19
13

The field edge of the Violet Chakra is at 80 and the field edge of the Red Chakra is at 13.

Fig. (171)

The metronome sets up a bea
frequency with an L-field an
an H-field which in tur
resonate with the bioenergeti
wave-field of the aura i
consciousness. These beats ca
be experienced as a sensation i
the nervous system at specif
distances from the oscillatin
source of the beats and also a
successive doubled distances I
the octaves. I.e. this diviner
reaction is felt at double th
distance or double the frequenc
along the entire spectrum c
vibration.

The book *Supersensonics* describes how Louis Turenne, the great pioneer of dowsing and divining, developed his rule for measuring these special spectral resonances. We quote here from pages 120-121:

If the diviner experiments he can make his own rule by detecting where the field edges extend southward (L-field) or at right angles in east-west direction (H-field) and that the oscillations for specific elements or crystals will be found at fixed distances from the "zero" at the north end of the rule, revealing the existence of specific fields.

When Turenne laid ribbons of the spectral colours in turn at zero on the rule, the same effects were found which suggested that all matter is constructed so that each element produces beats at points on the scale corresponding with the colours of light. He found that even a drawing of this rule or of the spectrum lines on paper produced a geometrical effect which "came alive" in the divining sense. He discovered that consciousness in some way stimulates the diviner's reactions when a geometrical form represents a Truth in nature and that there are oscillations at the nodal points at the following distances from zero.

	RATIO	FORM
Zero	0 cms.	
Red	13	Cubic
Orange	19	Quadratic
Yellow	25	Triclinic
Green begins	50	
Green ends	55	Monoclinic
Blue	62	Rhombic
Indigo	68	Rhombohedric
Violet	80	Hexagonal

If the student marks in the above on the 92 point rule he will have the design of a Turenne Rule. Aligning it north-south causes cross beats of the pendulum at those distances from zero. It was found that if there was nothing on the rule except light, all the seven beats would be produced as the pendulum was moved southward but if any sample is laid on at zero most of the cross beats from "light" disappear and leave only the ones applicable to the sample's own vibrational patterns.

This was considered by Turenne to be an interference pattern and he felt that he had invented a new kind of interferometer. However, Turenne did not allow any role of the observer's thought energy or consciousness to enter the picture and believed the phenomenon was merely a physical emanation of a more subtle kind coming from the sample. Today it it possible to get the same pendulum reactions with thought alone, that is, once the student becomes skilled at controlling interfering thought waves.

The 92 point analysis is always done with vertical magnetic needles which detect the positions and phases of the vibrational fields. The pendulum usually gyrates from the zero to one of the 92 Z-points and then reverses its swing or else beats parallel to the rule if there are no more Z-points to be discovered in a sample. Thus salt or sodium chloride gives one gyration from zero to Z-10 (sodium) and then an opposite gyration from Z-10 to Z-17 (chlorine) and then a parallel beat along the north-south line if the sample contains no more elements than sodium chloride. A strip of paper marked in this way produces immediate experimental results with the vertical magnet-fitted pendulum. The best results occur if the strip is measured out with its 92 points marked along a 155 cms. length.

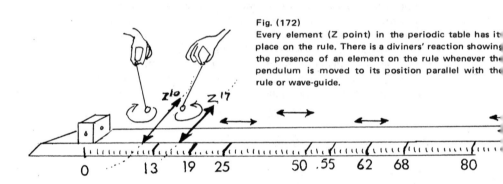

Fig. (172)
Every element (Z point) in the periodic table has its place on the rule. There is a diviners' reaction showing the presence of an element on the rule whenever the pendulum is moved to its position parallel with the rule or wave-guide.

This then gives rise to an Absolute spectrum which apparently does not change through its many octaves in respect to Absolute zero-periodicity. This Absolute **centre** creates a timeless domain without frequency. Such a non-oscillating and absolute zero-frequency domain can only be created by the central conscious-ness of "I". The scientist's "We" or "I" unconsciously creates an absolute centre by placing itself spatially outside the system in all existing mathematical measurements whenever it sets up a **notion** of frequency. For example, the moon turns once a month on its axis in order to keep the same face to the earth when the observer views it from outer space; from the centre of the earth-moon system it does not rotate on its axis at all!

The reader can verify this by poking a stick into an orange and holding it out at arm's length. The orange is now the moon, and you, the reader, are the earth. Rotate slowly and observe the orange. Does it have to rotate on its own axis to keep the same face toward you at all times? Obviously not! So what has happened now to the well-established theory that the moon, in order to show the same face to us at all times, rotates once on its axis in each cycle around the earth?

Fig. (173)

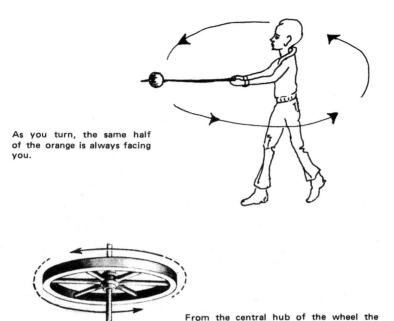

As you turn, the same half of the orange is always facing you.

From the central hub of the wheel the same inner face of the rim is always seen.

"One cycle" has only a meaningful relationship to an absolute — zero cycle; it cannot really have significance to human consciousness unless we say one cycle per ... and fix the movement in time, in its relationship to zero-time. A definition of zero-time would not be a material point of rest but an absolute state of rest, of "no cycle", and this we know can only happen in "I" consciousness of the observer, when he is completely integrated with his Universe. Figure 174, page 538 gives an idea of the absolute continuous spectrum which varies in wavelength and colour with distance away from the **CENTRE** of the system which is void and at rest i.e. at zero-frequency and zero-time. The waves are shown as the cross section of a sphere which includes the whole of space, or any part of it. It is the same for a human being, as for a whole universe. The "wholeness" of any system of being can only be divided from the universe by a trick of the mind, a delusion, or a schizophrenic split of the human "I". Nothing can be known or experienced without "I", and whatever "I" limits, is absolutely limited. Hence a scientist who cannot "see" his "self" chasing a material particle in an objective situation, has a serious, disturbing subjective problem. What is observed as a self-evident truth is not as important as the position of the subjective "I" of the observer. "Reality" can only be observed from the centre of any system. The diagram is a continuous spectrum of "self", a crude universal framework for liberation from the delusion of discontinuous human entities.

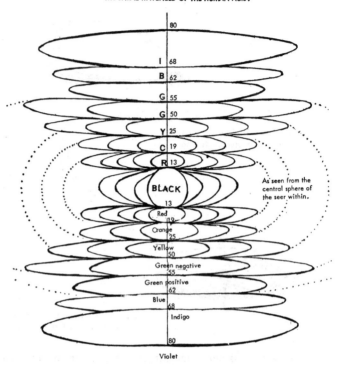

Fig. (174)

The human aura acts as a series of spherical concentric energy centres rotating like pinwheels and connected by subtle energies to the seven nerve plexi and the seven glands of the endocrine system. Colours are just energy vibrating at different frequencies, some visible some not. Each chakra has a colour band associated with it which is affected by that colour. Primary light is absorbed and re-radiated as biological radiomagnetic light. Pigment reflected light is absorbed but not re-radiated. Sunlight and starlight is primary light, moonlight is reflected sunlight. The human body acts like an array of raindrops acting as spherical prisms to filter the cosmic light rays.

The above Fig. (174) shows the kundalini energies of consciousness radiating out from the central nucleus of Being. The seat of consciousness radiates from the Black invisible light of the Akasha and is filtered through the wave-fields of consciousness at the vibratory rates of each chakra. These rates are shown by proportional numbers which mark the surface skin of each domain of consciousness. The domains are like the hologram - whatever you have in the whole field you have in any part you wish to examine. This is because each part is interfaced with the whole like a ball within a ball within a ball, etc. The hollow space inside each ball represents the unmanifest potential of the previous ball. The separate colours are only white light minus some of the others depending on what chakras are functioning in the personality of each individual.

The difference between the centre consciousness of the nucleus of Being and the ego-centric consciousness which we have called the "self-sense" is to be found most markedly in people who fail to grasp the uniqueness of every individual. It would appear that "onlooker consciousness" does not participate in the reality experienced by others, in fact it usually judges them to be wrong and insists that they ought to think the same way it does itself. In short, self-righteousness of any kind is a sure sign of the inability to experience a situation or an individual from the centre viewpoint. The self-righteous are incapable of looking out through the eyes and feelings of another and are continually expressing themselves as separated beings disconnected from the environment they live in. The conversation of such people can be heard everywhere, on the bus, on the radio, in the park, continually making distinctions between their experience, knowledge, etc. and those concepts that they hear from others. Mostly statements begin with "We", as if they speak for the whole human race, rather than from the limits of their own ignorance. Since most of human communication is at this level, most people are quite unconscious of their lack of centering, which is the essence of true listening and speaking.

To appreciate this truth diagrammatically, as in the case of the moon going around the earth, is not difficult, but to apply it as a true analogy with human life is less easy, although it is not impossible. Once we click into this way of looking at the world around us, limitless vistas open up and things that were seemingly haphazard and meaningless take on a grand cosmic pattern; every move in our limitless environment, from the tremor of a leaf on a tree to a massive and destructive war on the other side of the earth, is acknowledged from the centre as being part of a cosmic mandala in which the tiniest detail is always in the right place at the right time.

To bring it nearer still to daily human experience, we can visualise ourself in the centre of our own self-created mandala in which every event, every disaster, every joy and every bit of suffering radiates from the centre, from the "I" that determines our destiny. This may be easily acceptable when life is sweet, but the tendency is, when it turns sour, to blame something or someone "out there" for our trouble and pain. With "Centre Consciousness" there is no "out there" and there are no "others" to cause our suffering. Only after long and deep and repeated meditation is it possible to grasp this Reality, but the reward of full comprehension in the Heart (not in the Head) is eternal joy and peace.

In my imagination right now I can hear a host of voices raising objections and saying "Yes, but . . ." The questionings range from the war in Vietnam to the house burning down, to being knocked down by a car and so on. As long as we are saying "Yes, but . . ." we are not really meditating on this new and evolutionary way of looking at Reality and we shall never see its truth and its validity, for the only way we can validate anything is to do it. In this case it involves getting into the Centre and staying there whatever happens. If we are still attached to anything "out there" then we are not in the centre and we are not able to validate anything. If I am so attached to my husband that anything he does can either elate or disturb me, then I am not in my centre and I cannot let him or anyone else be themselves. When I am "on centre", all Hell can break loose around me but I remain in the still eye of the hurricane, in the sure knowledge that everything will settle down eventually into its perfect pattern.

One powerful validation of this centre consciousness is to look back over the last say five years, and to recall what disturbed us most during that period. Was all our distress really warranted? Did we need to get so anxious, so worried and so disturbed? What would have happened if we had stayed in that still centre and just allowed the storms to blow themselves out? People might have called us fools; they "wouldn't have tolerated such a thing for a moment," they'd say. Anyway try out the exercise for yourself. It is only one possible method of getting some perspective and of using your own experience to test out the truth of what has been said about this centre consciousness, the state of consciousness described in Psalm 91:

> "Thou shalt not be afraid for the terror by night;
> nor for the arrow that flieth by day;
> nor for the pestilence that walketh in darkness;
> nor for the destruction that wasteth at noonday.
> A thousand shall fall at thy side,
> and ten thousand at thy right hand;
> but it shall not come nigh thee."

The spiral field shows a composite picture of the resonant nodal points in the spectrum emanating from a black body irradiated with light from the sun. The light is absorbed according to its resonance with the particles in the nucleus of the absorbing body. The wavelength and frequency is proportional to the distance the wave-field extends from the centre of the vibrating system. This creates an "aura" with edges at 13-19-25-50- etc.

Surrounding man's centre are several layers of "I" which manifest the different drives.

Here we must begin to look at one cross-section of the onion skin layers of consciousness to understand the central person of man and try to comprehend its relationship to absolute time. The biological-clock is more related to absolute zero-time in cycles (and beats) rather than "cycles per second" or earth time.

However, our imagination measures changes in the surrounding material universe by discriminating differences in events as they pass through human-made time based on the earth's revolutions. The drive which humans display for time-like ordered events is rooted in the imaginative process.

How difficult to understand the drive for order in the Imagination layer of consciousness which structures reality in the human psyche! Of all the men who have understood that layer, Jesus and Einstein have made the greatest impact; and both came through the divine madness unscathed.

When consciousness burns itself through the lower vehicles in the etheric body, a process commonly known as the rising of the kundalini, it is more often than not like a 1,000 volt current being put through a 5 volt circuit. If proper preparation has occurred and the human nervous system has been adapted to higher energies, then the imbalance caused by the relentless flow of consciousness does not take place and the organism is lifted up to a higher energy level. If the part is raised then the whole is raised which means the environment and those present in the environment. Hence Christ makes the statement, "And I if I be lifted up, will draw all men unto me."

Much of Einstein's writing on this subject has been ignored by the very people who have used his work to prove their belief in a concrete material reality. They say he was a genius in mathematics but a bit silly in the head when it came to reality, as if they, with all their arrogance, knew very well (with Einstein's help) what reality was all about. Most people only read into a work their own comforting thoughts, which confirm their opinions and neglect the weightier matters of the law. Einstein's writings on "Physics and Reality" are just as important as his work on physics.

Einstein's own words speak with great eloquence and simplicity of the prime motive for his life and work on this planet. The humility that runs through all his writings like a silver thread is a pure and beautiful counterbalance to those arrogant "authorities" who have limited his validity to the realm of Physics and Mathematics:

> "I want to know how God created this world. I am not interested in this or that phenomenon, in the spectrum of this or that element. I want to know His thoughts, the rest are details."

542

On Quantum Mechanics:

"Quantum Mechanics is certainly imposing. But an inner voice tells me that it is not yet the real thing. The theory says a lot, but does not really bring us any closer to the secret of the Old One. I, at any rate, am convinced that He does not play dice ... You believe in the God who plays dice and I in complete law and order in the world which objectively exists, and which I, in a wildly speculative way, am trying to capture. I firmly *believe,* but I hope that someone will discover a more realistic way, or rather a more tangible basis than it has been my lot to do. Even the great initial success of the Quantum theory does not make me believe in the fundamental dice game, although I am well aware that our younger colleagues interpret this as a consequence of senility."

On Science and Religion:

"How can cosmic religious feeling be communicated from one person to another, if it can give rise to no definite notion of a God and no theology? In my view, it is the most important function of Art and Science to awaken this feeling and keep it alive in those who are capable of it.

We thus arrive at a conception of the relation of science to religion very different from the usual one. When one views the matter historically one is inclined to look upon science and religion as irreconcilable antagonists, and for a very obvious reason. The man who is thoroughly convinced of the universal operation of the law of causation cannot for a moment entertain the idea of a being who interferes in the course of events–that is, if he takes the hypothesis of causality really seriously. He has no use for the religion of fear and equally little for social or moral religion. A god who rewards and punishes is inconceivable to him for the simple reason that a man's actions are determined by necessity, external and internal, so that in God's eyes he cannot be responsible, any more than an inanimate object is responsible for the motions it goes through. Hence science has been charged with undermining morality, but the charge is unjust. A man's ethical behaviour should be based effectually on sympathy, education, and social ties; no religious basis is necessary."

I. R. 13 Red   19 Orange 25   Yellow   50 Green 55 Blue   62 Indigo   68   Violet

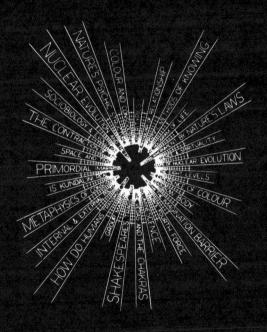

THE EGO BUBBLE

THE STRUCTURE OF SELF-CONCEPT

In the image of the ego bubble we have a surface tension between the outer and inner world, which at some point in the reader's life will burst and let the unitive consciousness merge with the self-sense.

There is no point here in repeating the many concepts of ego formulated by psychoanalytic theory, since it regards the ego as that part of the personality which is governed by reason, experiencing the external world through the senses, censoring the Id and answerable to the Superego. In Nuclear Evolution the ego is all of these plus any concepts, thoughts or images of individual separateness from the universe we live in. The idea that each individual is unique and moulds his desires for self-esteem upon the achievements or failures in social life is not in conflict with unitive consciousness. What is in conflict is whether this idea of separate individuality is real or self-created. Is the ego something real or just an illusion of separateness brought about by our identification with a body?

The ego exists within its inner world and projects the content of its mind and being beyond its imaginary boundary into the outer world. Without feeling any self-suggested concept of "I am a separate self", the ego takes this separateness as a given natural and normal state. The ego is always feeling it is being acted upon by external stimulation or influences and does not see that it is impossible in reality to separate the self from the total environment it lives in. Continually the ego-bubble is maintained by the strong self-suggestion that this outside external world is true and real, that it is not a construction of our inner consciousness, but exists independently of the consciousness/self which perceives it.

Only an equal amount of self-suggestion, that this self-sense is actually self-created and an unreal imposition upon the wholistic universe around us, can prick the ego bubble and dissolve the boundary between the whole and the distinctions in the mind which arise out of personal limitations, self-esteem and self-actualisation.

Adler developed an ego psychology based on the social urges which motivate a man to master some goal in life in order to overcome inferiority. But this insecurity stems not so much from the social drive but from a lack of inner peace. Hence Adler believed that security could be accomplished by denying feelings of inferiority. He did not recognise that physical insecurity, emotional insecurity and spiritual insecurity could exist independently on different levels. Hence Nuclear Evolution puts the source of inner insecurity on the functioning of the heart chakra and not on the social chakra on which the Adlerian ego structure is based. It is the same with all the other systems of understanding human nature which try to determine the ultimate shape of human personality.

Hence Nuclear Evolution does not build on these theories but goes directly to nature. Through the natural biofeedback instruments of Supersensonics we have probed the actual pattern of the unconscious and taken the drives and urges as chakra functions of particular levels of consciousness. These drives exist within the ego bubble. They all disappear in unitive selflessness and reappear whenever the self-sense reasserts itself.

Fig. (175)

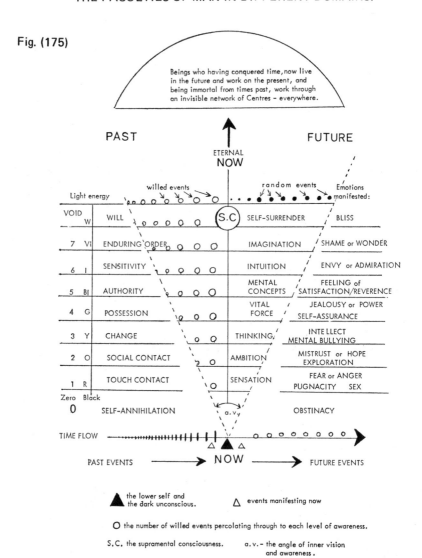

Beings who having conquered time, now live
in the future and work on the present, and
being immortal from times past, work through
an invisible network of Centres – everywhere.

PAST   FUTURE

ETERNAL
NOW

			willed events	random events	Emotions manifested:
Light energy					
VOID W	WILL		S.C	SELF-SURRENDER	BLISS
7 Vi	ENDURING ORDER			IMAGINATION	SHAME or WONDER
6 I	SENSITIVITY			INTUITION	ENVY or ADMIRATION
5 BI	AUTHORITY			MENTAL CONCEPTS	FEELING of SATISFACTION/REVERENCE
4 G	POSSESSION			VITAL FORCE	JEALOUSY or POWER SELF-ASSURANCE
3 Y	CHANGE			THINKING	INTELLECT MENTAL BULLYING
2 O	SOCIAL CONTACT			AMBITION	MISTRUST or HOPE EXPLORATION
1 R	TOUCH CONTACT			SENSATION	FEAR or ANGER PUGNACITY SEX
Zero Black 0	SELF-ANNIHILATION		a.v_y		OBSTINACY

TIME FLOW

PAST EVENTS → NOW → FUTURE EVENTS

▲ the lower self and the dark unconscious.   △ events manifesting now

O the number of willed events percolating through to each level of awareness.

S.C. the supramental consciousness.   a.v.– the angle of inner vision and awareness.

The above diagram shows the levels of consciousness with their main attributes 1 to 7 (left) expressed in terms of positive and negative emotional feelings (right). The drives from the Red sensory level all the way to the Violet level of the imagination are overlapping. The level below can understand the level above, but has little contact with two levels above. When a person has two levels such as the Yellow and the Indigo, the personality may appear to be split, as two different world views alternate in the same entity. When two or three levels are functioning in the same person they may bring a composite result and the separate colours then blend together in the colour of the aura.

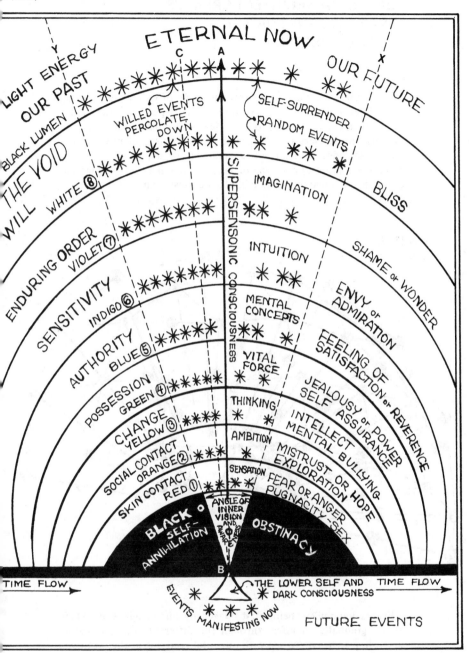

Our emotions and faculties are manifested by the absorption of light at different
levels of being. The process is controlled by the chakras. If the angle of vision
(ABC on the diagram) is narrow we can only pull in a few events into our
imagination. By the time they filter down into the lower levels towards the
lower self at the sensory material level there will be fewer and fewer events to
manifest. If we widen our angle of vision to XBY we see a lot more potential in
the universe.

THE GRAND ARCHITECT CREATES
SEVERAL PLANS FOR THE
TEMPLE BUILDING

In the previous diagram we saw the angle of vision depicted in two dimensions on the flat surface of the paper, with the linear time zones corresponding to seven levels of consciousness shown as a horizontal series of higher steps. But this is merely like an architect's side elevation of a spherical dome, since the real situation is more like a cone of vision extending onto a spherical dome through which events fall into manifestation:

Fig. (177)

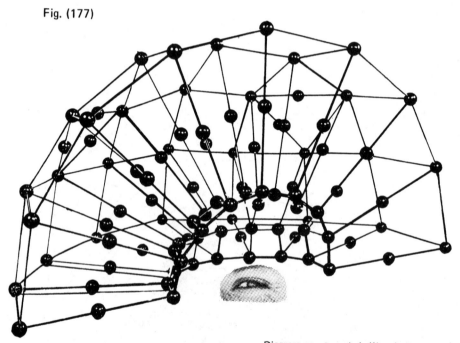

Diagram courtesy de la Warr Laboratories.

Events happen by being first imaged by our imagination. Then they gradually manifest through the different cones of vision according to what we see with our total visioning at the intuitive, mental, intellectual, social and physical levels of perception. Our task is to widen the angle of vision at each level to include more of the past and the future. Each level acts as a censor of the level above it that delays perception and awareness of the total environment. When the sides of the cone expand and widen out to 180° flat, the area of vision becomes a half sphere and wipes out time.

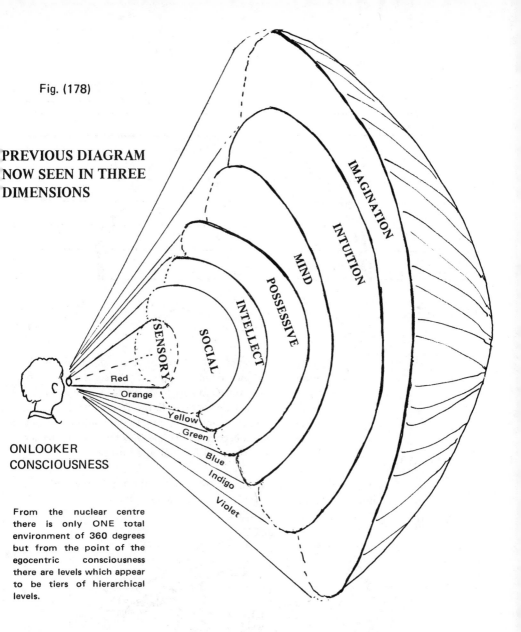

Fig. (178)

PREVIOUS DIAGRAM NOW SEEN IN THREE DIMENSIONS

IMAGINATION

INTUITION

MIND

POSSESSIVE

INTELLECT

SOCIAL

SENSORY

Red

Orange

Yellow

Green

Blue

Indigo

Violet

ONLOOKER CONSCIOUSNESS

From the nuclear centre there is only ONE total environment of 360 degrees but from the point of the egocentric consciousness there are levels which appear to be tiers of hierarchical levels.

Let us now take the cone of vision of the sensory Red level which insists on the supremacy of objects as its reality. Whether we view such a consciousness as trapped in ordinary perception of the mundane level of touch or vision on earth or whether we couple it with the imagination of an environment speculating on the nature of the universe will make no difference. Whether the objects in the local environment are kitchen tables or motor cars, or whether the objects are the sun and stars situated far away in space, will make no difference if the reality of the visual cone is based entirely on the organs of sensation. Measurements based on the fixed velocity of light are only extensions of our physical senses coupled with space and time.

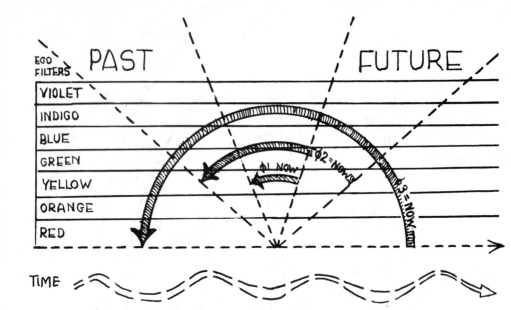

Fig. (179)

Fig. (180)

Our job is to widen our angle of vision and to increase our awareness of how we function on these different levels. As our angle increases from ϕ_0 to ϕ_1 to ϕ_2 we can see more and more into the past including our past Karma from previous incarnations, and we can see into the future to the results of our actions. When our vision becomes a flat line (ϕ_3) the time slot of our Now includes the total Past and the Future.

To widen the cone of vision to 360° makes the total sphere of consciousness, which wipes out space on each level as a series of spheres one within the other.

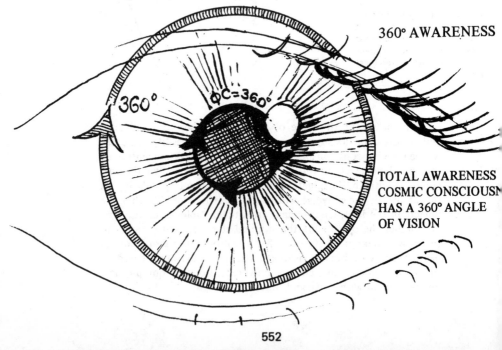

360° AWARENESS

TOTAL AWARENESS
COSMIC CONSCIOUSN
HAS A 360° ANGLE
OF VISION

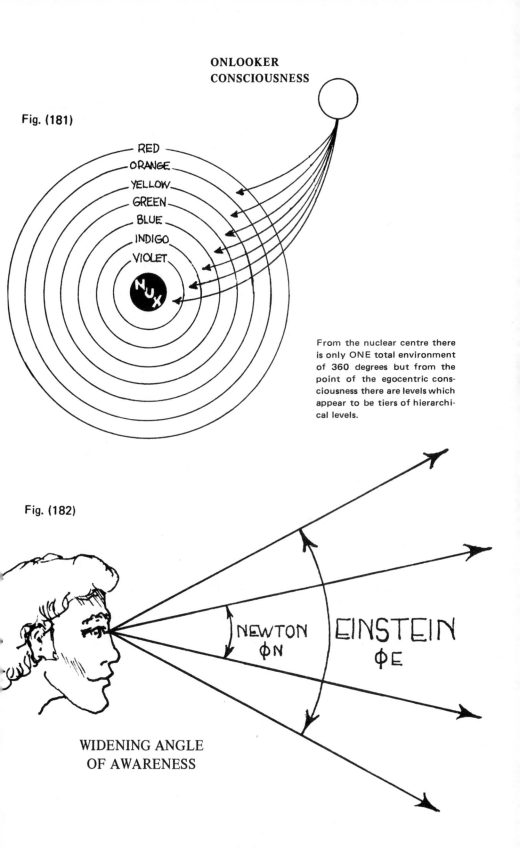

ONLOOKER CONSCIOUSNESS

Fig. (181)

RED
ORANGE
YELLOW
GREEN
BLUE
INDIGO
VIOLET

N U X

From the nuclear centre there is only ONE total environment of 360 degrees but from the point of the egocentric consciousness there are levels which appear to be tiers of hierarchical levels.

Fig. (182)

NEWTON
ΦN

EINSTEIN
ΦE

WIDENING ANGLE
OF AWARENESS

In the Time-space bubble of Fig.175 one can see that when the "I" identifies completely with the "whole" awareness of time, including zero-time in the stillness of the void, that it should be possible to get out into the future and bring about the present by working on the past. If we think of the "bits" or events as being "willed" in the *eternal now* from beyond the Imagination layer in the past, then by the time they have percolated down through the dense levels of time and colour into the more transient and sensory NOW, they have conditioned the unmanifest future.

Images about the future are important in shaping the future because of their influence on the present. Our image of "time" is not so simple and clear as our image of "space," but it exists as an image with power to change reality. Time-images of children and adults are profoundly different and create equally profound personality changes. Positive time-images of the future are a causal factor in cultural change in the growth of civilizations, Aztec, Mayan, Egyptian, and West European included. Nuclear Evolution is a direct method for revealing the basic structure of the personality irrespective of the cultural brain-washing and conditioning. Its time-image of circular causality is described in Fig.175 where the time-flow turns back on itself and becomes "spirit." On its return to its beginnings, "time" and its image becomes the true instrument of change. It transcends all cultures whose standards of comparison are all different.

This is the most difficult concept of Nuclear Evolution because it requires that sense impressions which give rise to notions of "time" are annihilated absolutely. The western nuclear physicist knows that many of the concrete physical particles which bring about these sense impressions are not "real" but "virtual".

Though it is possible to know this theoretically it is not possible for the physicist to have any sense of conviction without sweeping certain facts, such as the velocity of light, under the carpet. However in Nuclear Evolution—the domain of consciousness where time is annihilated for physicist and pigmy alike—there can be no profound meaning to the concept of velocity simply because in reality there are no fixed material points in space. Einstein proved for all time that knowledge of velocity and all motion in space is relative to the observer—the Self. Nuclear Evolution is the science of the Absolute Self.

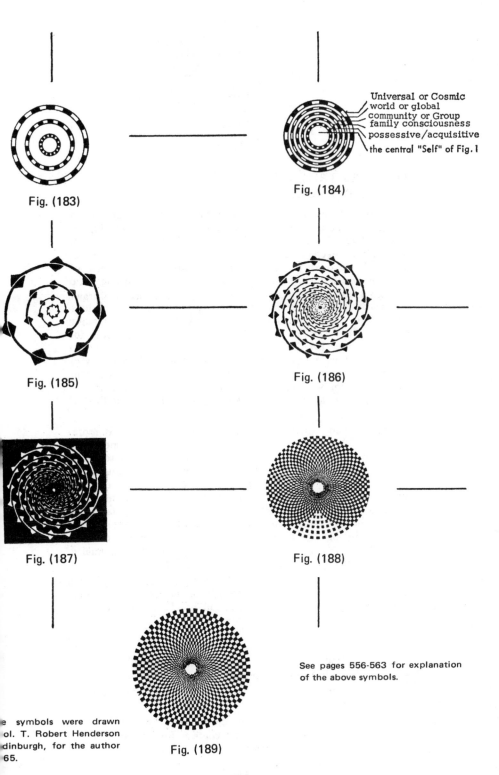

Fig. (183)

Fig. (184)

Universal or Cosmic
world or global
community or Group
family consciousness
possessive/acquisitive
the central "Self" of Fig. 1

Fig. (185)

Fig. (186)

Fig. (187)

Fig. (188)

Fig. (189)

See pages 556-563 for explanation
of the above symbols.

e symbols were drawn
ol. T. Robert Henderson
dinburgh, for the author
65.

THE "CENTRE" SYMBOL OF NUCLEAR EVOLUTION

Diagramatically we can represent the progression of human consciousness during a man's life by means of the seven figures shown. Each layer of consciousness is like an onion skin, revealing at each peeling a sphere of new consciousness in his total personality. Each person becomes like an orb of sight in which the Seer is our simple naked intelligence and consciousness. The figures 183/190 are deliberately drawn as over-simplifications of a very complex study of consciousness which cannot be grasped by the intellect by merely reading a book. They should be used purely as conceptual tools for understanding THAT which is a non-conceptual reality. It appears that we inhibit our growth by intellectual smugness or self-pride in our own boundary of consciousness. This boundary is only thought of in Nuclear Evolution as a psychic membrane or as a surface tension around each individual entity.

The boundary where the inner and outer life meet is represented by the different rings through which each individual Self cannot easily pass; they determine the degree of separateness of the Ego-Self from the outer world. These boundaries vary from one person to the next and are therefore depicted by the concentric circles which are the surface or limit which separates the inner experience of the individual or personality. Each band of consciousness can be identified with the absorption of bio-energy in the endocrine system and the seven principal ganglia, and related in figure 196 to an individual nuclear frequency response to coloured bands of Light.

The first spheres of consciousness developed by each individual entity representing the Id, its surface area the Ego, and the Superego of Freud, as well as the "Self" of Jung are :—

Fig. (183)

    (i) Body consciousness, equal to sex instinct, self-replication, self-preservation and sense of touch.

    (ii) Ego consciousness, equal to herd, race, social instincts.

    (iii) Self-expressive consciousness. Thinking, art, industry, and political contest. Instinct for liberation and fulfilment.

The next layers develop around the central Self in this order :—

Fig. (184) (iv) Acquisitive consciousness. Security, independence. The possessive instinct.

(v) Family consciousness. Love of authority. Religion, the scientific categories, established social concepts, definitions.

(vi) Community or group consciousness. Sensitivity, wonder, admiration, intuition, extra-cerebral knowledge . . .

(vii) World, Planetary or Global consciousness, equal to drive for enduring order, certainty, tenderness, images, will and magical transformations.

(viii) Cosmic or Universal consciousness, equal to zero of Self, serving the absolute in a non-imagined (void) universe.

All the above " rings " or spheres interact with each other according to the stimuli received and the memory of thoughts imprinted in the " whole " protoplasm. In a similar way the cells of trees " remember " the inner activity of the sun's Light (in sunspots) and record the good and bad seasons in the thickness of their rings. This record modifies, in turn, the future flow of protoplasm in the tree by its past experience of this " memory ". The developing embryo " remembers " (consciousness) the major steps and missteps (unconsciousness) in the long evolution of the species.

This analogy can be transferred to the human scene as karma, which is interpreted as the imprinting of all our human actions, thoughts, errors, and successes indelibly in our unconscious as deep-seated drives. These drives in turn provide the backdrop against which we act out the cosmic circus, springing from one trapeze to another like monkeys waiting for the next handhold in the formless milieu of our existence. When man grabs the next evolutionary rung, the circus roles change to mental acrobatics in order to please the audience which is our ego. As men proceed higher up the ladder, again the act changes and man becomes a cosmic clown, tripping over his own ingenuity and cleverness until he falls flat on his face in a pile of elephant dung. Whereupon he gets up, humiliated but transformed from a circus crazy into a sweet fool.

The thicker the rings of the tree the wider the stream of sap—similarly the wider the rings of consciousness, the more awareness.

To probe the analogy, we can equate the process of photosynthesis in the tree with the way in which each human being processes the flow of life-force. In good years of sunlight, whether as a result of solar flares or lessening of cloud cover, the tree widens its rings to process the greater flow of sap. The splitting of water in photosynthesis is directly related to its growth and for the tree to build its vegetation it has to take one hydrogen atom from water and one atom of carbon from CO_2 and, combining them, make the cells of the tree. For the tree to flourish it must draw up more and more water and must expand its rings for a greater flow of sap. Similarly, by widening the auric rings of our psychophysical vehicle, we allow a greater flow of life-force and so extend our spiritual awareness.

> Each endocrine gland has its own corresponding memory system in the brain which is sensitive to Light, heat or chemically induced oxidations which in turn modify the behaviour of a person by experience of "memory". The whole "Self" is an experience of *totality* and "consciousness" is our memory of it. "Self-remembering" is the naked universal "awareness" of the evolutionary thrust in all things.

Recognition of the True Self is the penetration of self-inflicted blockages in our consciousness over eons of time. As consciousness remembers itself in its primordial state, the self sense begins to dissolve until, like the drop of rain hitting the ocean, the part becomes the whole and merges its separate identity into the vastness of the ocean.

We often hear people talk about their past incarnations, rather in the same way that others talk about their operations and their hospital experiences. In both cases these people are trying to boost their image by talking about something in the past that to them seems to add glamour and excitement to otherwise mundane and even drab lives in the present. But are these events really "in the past"? If in centuries past I was a trusted servant of the Pharaoh, that state of being is still with me now. If you were the Pharaoh and you are now slaving at a nine-to-five job in the city, the pharaoh experience and the pharaoh mentality are still with you NOW, but what have you done with it? What kind of a pharaoh were you anyway? I have actually heard a man boast that he was a Prince of the Nile and expect some special respect on the strength of it! Instead of claiming credit or seeking reputation for what we "have been", we need a shift in consciousness to understand that just as the tree "remembers" and coordinates into its total being the sunspot years, so we have to *use* the knowledge of our past to recognise the challenge that is presented to us NOW to change and evolve. We need to discover or rather to rediscover the Pharaoh power within us, that was probably misused and exploited, and to channel it into responsible organisation and guidance for the benefit of mankind. If we think we were Cleopatra and are now a mousy typist in a nine-to-five job, we have to admit that something went wrong somewhere along the evolutionary line; maybe glamour and irresistible sexuality were given their full sway and nobler, less selfish areas of ourself were totally neglected. Now, in this incarnation, the neglected levels have no option but to manifest. Now, instead of turning people on with our figure and our sexual vibes, which we no longer have, we are compelled to use much more selfless methods to relate to our fellow men and women.

This nuclear viewpoint that sees Past, Present and Future in the total context of the Eternal Now, destroys forever the petty and limiting concern with past glories or future aspirations and releases the dynamic energy of a total wholistic awareness. In other words, instead of being strung out in our consciousness with past nostalgias and regrets or with dreams and fears about the future, our whole energy is focussed on the only valid moment—this one-- NOW!

NUCLEAR EVOLUTION: When the universal consciousness is reached the personality realises the unity in all things, and becomes conscious of the Spiritual Sun with its multidirectional rays, and all our spheres of individual consciousness are transmuted into radiating spheres of light. The next step after realisation of this is manifestation in conscious Nuclear Evolution.

Fig. (185) Each separate sphere of consciousness evolves from the nucleus by a spiral process in separate leaps to a higher energy shell.

Fig. (186) As the individual increases his spheres of consciousness and they blend into an integrated unity, the vision of the spiral becomes clear and it appears to be evolving in accordance with a pattern or plan.

As the old patterns fall away and old habits of thought and action are discarded like old garments, as attachments are loosed and we not only free others from our clinging but we free ourselves, there is a feeling of nakedness. All the comfortable and comforting structure that we have built around us has crumbled and we feel not only naked but alone. This, however, is a temporary state, for realisation dawns in the vision of the total plan. The rise in spirits, the blissful certainty that ensues, relies on nothing but the sure knowledge that the evolutionary spiral thrust is our Way, its flow is our Tao, our sure enlightenment.

Fig. (187) **By intuitive perception of the Spirit of Man operating through group activity in society, we become aware of an archetypal pattern that lies at the back of this social illusion. Our consciousness obtains a mirror-image glimpse into the dark unconscious (the unknown).**

Now our expanding awareness experiences an even wider vision that includes the whole of mankind and the divine plan of which we felt ourselves to be a willing, joyous and evolving part now encompasses whole groups and nations. As though we had climbed a new range of mountains a whole new vista opens up, and what appeared before to be a shattered world on the verge of total disaster, shaken by racial conflict, atomic explosions, dangerous pollution and so on, is seen as a planet undergoing the death pangs that are the potential heralds of the phoenix world that can arise out of the ashes of the old and corrupt.

Fig. (188) **When all gaps in the individual consciousness are completed and all spheres of consciousness are fully evolved and integrated into the unity of LIFE, a state of Planetary consciousness is achieved. It then becomes apparent that there are intelligences beyond man for which there is no finite proof. The proof of consciousness is LIFE and its results in a body. When LIFE is extracted from the body, the human awareness sees clearly that consciousness disappears. At this 7th sphere the seer within recognises that the spiral of energy transformations is a reality only at certain levels of awareness. The life of each individual entity is realised as the Imaged CREATIVE POWER flows through and expresses itself by interfering with the spiral of random psychic and " non-willed " physical events in a thought-wave universe. The notion is cherished at this level that the plan is not pre-ordained or fixed in time but free to inter-change (but not change) in an absolute domain of intelligently " willed " events in a divine pattern.**

This mirror image is revealed in a state of society since all our ignorance and knowledge is projected out in the actions of humans who can only be themselves, whether they like it or not. As such, society is a reflection of our real state of evolution as opposed to our imagined idealistic projections of ourselves as intelligent beings. However, the order of intelligence required to solve the aggregate sum of human ignorance is awesome in its magnitude and encompasses the entire spectrum of possibility, going beyond time, space and imagination, to the very source of creation itself.

Also the Lord accepted Job

In other words, at this stage of evolution there is a clear channel through which the Cosmic energy can flow unimpeded by the blocks or membranes at any level, and the Divine Will can be done. Until this point man has superimposed his petty will and manipulative morality on the cosmic plan, which to his little mind has seemed like a totally haphazard series of events; so he has labelled each event as either "good" or "bad", "beneficial" or "disastrous", and has totally blotted out the true vision of the universe in which all things, so-called good and bad, work together for good.

Fig. (189) Full Cosmic consciousness is obtained in a zero-self domain, where the Ego dies through self-annihilation, and the personality is conscious of its own Ego-consciousness in all living things as a mirror reflection in consciousness of its own Being. This Cosmic state must be rejected by the finite mind and intellect simply because their very function as the analyser, divider and separator of reality cannot ever resolve these paradoxes. The zero-self at the CENTRE is an orb of no-thing.

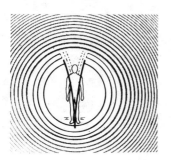 

As long as doubts, fears, questionings and questings continue, this state of zero self-sense cannot be reached and each one of us must come to this Ego annihilation by our own route and in our own time. To know for certain that self-centred consciousness has finally died and that we are living all that we experience is not necessarily to like all that we see around us or even to find the egotistical personalities of others acceptable, but it is to let them be what they are and to remain undisturbed by their Ego-antics. It is to experience the still Centre referred to earlier as described in psalm 91, which begins with the words:

"He that dwelleth in the secret place of the Most High
shall abide under the shadow of the Almighty . . ."

In other words, from the still Centre of Being, from the "eye" of the hurricane, chaos and confusion and the "ego games" of men and women can be seen all around us, but they cannot disturb or dismay. These games are understood for what they are—part of the evolutionary journey of the nucleus towards its true nature as a temple of light.

Fig. (190) In the centre of the figure is the orb of endless sight, an inward personal sphere of light which radiates outwards into an impersonal creative Void, the absence of all Self-consciousness known in the East as Nirvana or Samadhi. In the creative Void the seer does not see anything as being separate from himself, and therefore has no self-consciousness or separated Self. This positive self-annihilation from the centre within becomes not self-negation, but self-fulfillment.

Fig. (190)

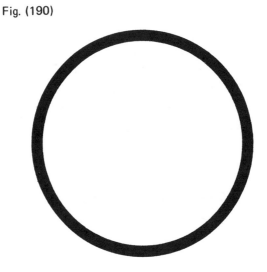

PHYSICAL PROOFS

If pure consciousness is to manifest there must be a demonstration in the creation somewhere that the positive and negative expression of the basic drives in man are reflected in the structure of the Cosmos. All we know of matter and the radiation in the universe has been gained through study of spectrographic emission of energy. Here we are concerned with the consciousness which produces these observations in order to see how it enters into the experiencing of stimuli and material sensations in the eye of the beholder. The pure consciousness of man in the state of Fig. 190 does not experience "life" by reacting to Centripetal or Centrifugal energies but by knowing the eternal CENTRE force of " I AM ". In this 8th domain the positive and negative duality of Being is left behind and they have no reality as separate distinctions, although their reality is not denied in lower states of consciousness. The great ALL is ONE whole and the negative energies are merely the excreta of a living Universe.

The living Universe is ingesting itself and feeding on " life " which is the negative excreta transmuted into positive LIFE in the same sense that the excreta of nature is transformed and converted by green Algae absorbing Light. In this transformation it becomes the basic unit of the food chain. Just as the micro-algae feeds off Light and excreta in nature in order to manifest so we can say with man, that in his subtle body (consciousness) he feeds off negative bio-energies and Light. Here of course I do not refer only to visible light but the whole spectrum of radiation including high energy Cosmic rays which penetrate deep into the earth's crust. At the other end of the spectrum we know all material bodies emit infra-red rays which travel in electro-magnetic waves as a form of energy which will heat up any object or body which responds to it and absorbs it. Each atomic substance in the cell life of the body absorbs a uniquely characteristic amount of infra-red and the higher energy radiations which we call Light; and we know that not only does it absorb, but it again re-emits it at specific frequencies according to its co-efficient of absorption.

Fig. (191)

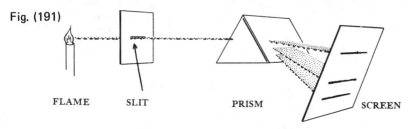

FLAME   SLIT   PRISM   SCREEN

When any material element is heated to incandescence the light emitted by the substance contains characteristic spectral lines which show its chemical composition, almost like a signature in light. Whether it is a burning element on earth or a star undergoing nuclear transformation, the same characteristic signature of Nature is present in the colours of the elements that are burning. Hence everything in Nature, including the human being, is radiating or losing heat and can be said to be burning energy. At the human level the rate of nuclear excitement is so low that we can compare it with smouldering embers as against a raging nuclear furnace in the heart of the sun. Nevertheless, the heat energy burned in the human body, although low in temperature, does succeed in transforming the nuclear structure of elements. In other words the human body achieves by cold processes nuclear transformations which are only possible at the chemical level outside the human body at vastly increased temperatures. It is therefore reasonable to assume that cosmic light energy in the form of radiation enters man's vehicle and helps to transduce those elements by releasing cosmic energy in the breakdown at the nuclear centre of the atoms of the body. This process takes place and reveals the same signature of colours generated by both absorption of cosmic radiation and its reemittance in the form of biophysical energy and psychophysical energy which we call consciousness. This reemittance is what constitutes the well-known effect of the human aura, which can be considered as the excretion of unwanted cosmic radiation. The human bio-physical organism does this on seven different levels and is jacked up from gross energy levels to more subtle etheric energies by a ratchet-effect similar to the enhancement effect required in chlorophyll in the cells of plants in order to achieve photosynthesis of solar energy. There appears to be a direct connection between plant cell life and human cell life at this level of cosmic absorption.

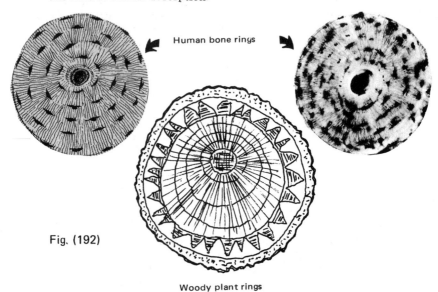

Human bone rings

Fig. (192)

Woody plant rings

COLOUR, CHEMICALS
AND
CONSCIOUSNESS

13 Red   19 Orange 25   Yellow   50 Green 55 Blue 62 Indigo 68 Violet   80

BIOPHYSICAL EFFECTS OF SUGGESTION

The effects of substances such as drugs on personality are well known in the counter culture of LSD, just as the effects of tranquilizers and alcohol are well known generally. But the effects of colour and its link with the chemical nature of our physical organism are not well known. The effects on different levels of personality can all be explained in terms of the endocrine secretions and the links with their triggers in the etheric chakra energies.

The placebo effect or the power of suggestion of the mind has now been adequately demonstrated by research in medicine. A "sugar pill" administered in a bright red gelatin capsule will bring favourable results in 81 percent of the cases tested. There were favourable results in only 49 percent where the placebo was administered as a tablet and 69 percent when administered as a liquid.* Blue or green solutions bring better results if they are applied externally whereas liquids taken internally are more effective if they are coloured red, yellow or brown and have a bitter taste. The power of self-suggestion over the physical organism and its chemical nature is at the back of all mental research into the effects of mind-stuff in yoga.

The ultimate self-suggestion is that the subject is inseparable from the object or, in more plain words, the self is not separate from the surrounding universe, even when the "mind" is suggesting by the "self-sense" that there is an outside and an inside.

Forty-five pharmacy students took a capsule at 8:30 a.m., thinking its maximum effects would appear in about two hours and disappear at 12:30 a.m. Fifteen were told that their capsule was a stimulant; another fifteen were told it was a tranquilizer; the remaining fifteen were told it was nothing but cornstarch. Sixty percent reported feeling the effects they were supposed to feel. Seventy-three percent of the "stimulation" group reported feeling stimulated but only 47 percent of the tranquilized subjects reported an effect. Pulse rates rose in the "stimulated" group and fell in the tranquilized group.

Imagine the power and extent of self-suggestion in religion, health or behaviour. The power of self-suggestion to control the colour we extract from light is even more pronounced than it is when taking "sugar pills", because the power of mental forces over chemical changes in the human body not only has chemical physical effects but emotional and spiritual effects on the nature of personality. Thus it is possible, by understanding the energies

---

* "The Psychology of Being Human", Harper and Row, 1974.

controlled by self-suggestion and self-hypnotism, to change not only personality but temperature of the body, heart beat, blood flow, pain thresholds and endocrine secretions at will.

In yoga it is nothing spectacular to change skin potential, control peristaltic action, relaxation or stimulation of any part of the physical organism. In the West these things are looked upon as extraordinary by some doctors, but a whole body of doctors who are members of the American Medical Hypnotists' Association would not think these feats extraordinary. The ability to control these events has nothing to do with the spiritual nature of man. Anyone can do it with a little explanation of what it is. However, the yogic trance of deep self-suggestion where the ego is dissolved permanently in the unitive state, requires constant reinforcement until it becomes as true subjectively as it is objectively.

To understand the power of this mind-stuff over the chemical processes of the body brings us in touch with the power of the chakra functions to break down light energies into colour, according to the internal subjective self-suggestion of each organsim.

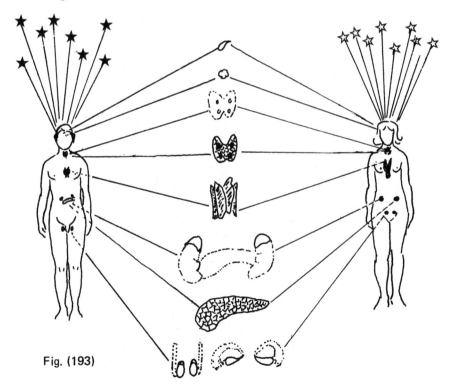

Fig. (193)

The substances secreted as hormones from the endocrine system of glands, such as Adrenalin, are all sensitive to Light and Heat radiation according to their own specific frequency response. The human organism's total response to colour can be seen in both psychological and physical responses to seven specific frequencies of Light which represent harmonics in the broad spectrum of wavelengths and frequencies which we call heat, light and cosmic energy which science tells us passes through many octaves. The exact chemical effects of these radiations cannot be known as they go on inside living glands until man discovers some way of measuring the chemistry changes in the Pineal and Pituitary glands which govern the secretion of hormones. It is the chemistry of these hormone responses to coloured light which determines personality. The pathogenic response to colour can be discovered in the personality by direct experimentation with 7 basic colours* and the projection of primary light. Colours have no objective existence; they exist in our consciousness only as subjective phenomena. Therefore in dealing with colour we are dealing with pure consciousness and its interpretation of ether vibrations of various waves. When light waves of various wave-lengths strike the retina or skin they give rise to nervous impulses which, on reaching the brain and seat of consciousness, are interpreted as colours. White light is a combination of colours each having a specific wavelength.

However there is no such phenomenon as "colour" until some "selection" takes place in nature. The absorbing power of a substance decides its colour. There is no colour made manifest until white light is passed through some medium and the rays separate at different angles according to their frequency and wavelength. Reflected colour is merely the unabsorbed light from an object which is of *one band* of wavelengths or frequencies. These bands of colour represent light energy at different levels of excitation and the human being absorbs them unconsciously. The modern test of the human psychological and physiological reactions devised by Prof. Max Luscher Ph.d. has proved significant not only to the psychologist and psychiatrist but to the medical doctor. The test has become indispensable in the hospital when the need for some way of determining psychic causes of functional disturbances has arisen. Psychosomatic illness such as vegetative dystonia, obesity,

---

* (Ref.: Luscher Test Verlag, 81 Jacobs St., Basle. Also see "Colour Psychology & Medicine"—"Medico" overseas edition, 1936. No. 3, 9. Dr. H. Klar). Also "The Luscher Color Test" translated and edited by Ian Scott from original German text by Dr. M. Luscher. Pub. U.S.A. by Random House Inc. , N.Y.,1969

frigidity and hypertension, to mention only a few, have been described in articles by Dr. Helmut Klar of the C.F. Boehringer Company of Germany. These scientific approaches to colour psychology and medicine show that colours do not lie.

The remarkable information revealed by these tests confirms the hypothesis in this book and much of the previous work by The Commission for Research into the Creative Faculties of Man on the subject of Consciousness and its effects on photo-electric phenomena of all kinds. This is a deep study and few people would have the time or money available to spend exclusively dedicated to it. However the Luscher test is simple, empirical and easy to understand since it does not enter the scientifically "forbidden" territory of Consciousness itself. Anyone who is interested in deeper research into colour and possesses that rare asset, time to spare, can contact the author, who has many notes on experiments with vibration and light. These need editing and preparing for publication. Meanwhile the purpose of this present work is to give a brief practical outline of the concepts of how light (Pure Consciousness) works through a human body and becomes self-consciousness. To test the response of our consciousness to the universe around us various methods can be used, including detection with a pendulum or dowsing rod and noting response to coloured squares on paper. More details of how eighty percent of the human race can do this are given in "Supersensonics". Here in this book, however, is enough information about the eight colours to give us a different picture of the different inner worlds (or *lokas* in Sanskrit). To probe these inner worlds with colour gives us a way of knowing our levels of perception.

Every person likes to know about himself and if possible to get a glimpse of his own psychological structure even when he may not be interested in higher states of consciousness. When a person is confronted by a panel of four primary colours of Red, Yellow, Blue and Green and the four additional colours of Violet, Grey, Black and Brown, the task of selecting and rejecting those he likes best or least is not difficult or mystifying. The person assumes he has revealed nothing about himself by reacting to "just a few colours" but in reality the subject has provided a glimpse into his attitudes towards LIFE which often proves revealing even to himself. He has made a "fingerprint of his soul" which can be evaluated in terms of "active" and "passive" relationships very much like the Yang and the Yin of the ancient Chinese "book of mutations" which relates the eight hexagrams to eight colours. (See ref. 5d).* Like the universe, the personality is built on the octave.

---

*See References end of Part III.

TRADITIONAL LINKS WITH COLOUR

The colour blue symbolises distance and infinity. In the Luscher test this suggests the bottomless ocean and the unlimited, deep-blue vaulted sky. In the "Book of Changes" it represents space, the empty womb of the female, and serenity. Blue has signified meditation and contemplation in India for thousands of years. The person with a preference for blue holds a deep longing for relaxing quiescence, affectionate understanding and shelter. This yearning may remain an imaginative wish-fulfilment and the unfilled desire renders the individual highly susceptible to depressive states of Being. (Ref. see following page). Red signifies opposition and resistance, an excited energetic drive and a strong stubborn will. As a result red is the colour of revolution, of successfully asserting one's ego, in other words having one's own way and dominating one's environment. The orange is the "Creative Energy" in the "Book of Changes" which causes movement from fixed positions. The Yellow in the Luscher test characterises a very different type of "drive". The personality which prefers yellow engages in erratic, unstable and often superficial activity, which is little more than a desire to master one's environment by self-expression in the intellectual or artistic spheres, or by constantly changing the present activity. Yellow is the colour of "thinking" and CHANGE.

Green signifies stability and security therefore choice of this colour indicates a defensive and critical behaviour with great determination to see opinions confirmed. Green is the colour of an opinionated ego, self-consciousness of one's own position, possessions, and independence. Reacting negatively to green is indicative of a basic anxiety. It will be obvious that the many facets of the psychological make-up of an individual person cannot be classified into four colour categories and we merely explain the fundamentals of colour psychology to back up what we shall later say about Consciousness and Light.

COLOURS DO NOT LIE! The more detailed colour test of the clinical psychosomatic Luscher type requires the subject to "react" to 73 colours and to decide which hue or shade of two colours is preferred. There is no opportunity for evasion—the personality must make its choice in such a way that the power of discretion is readily challenged and it is seldom that a response cannot be obtained. The advantage of this test, and a proof incidentally of our hypothesis, is that it does not depend on any special knowledge of Light or Colour, does not depend on schooling, breeding, cultural background or environment. It can be used on Pygmies in central Africa, or natives of central Brazil; it can be used on American farmers or European sophisticates, for all humans respond to colour according to the same principles. Colours do not lie!

COLOUR TEST REFERENCES

Bokslag, J. G. H.: *Alter und Geschlecht im Lüscher-Test und der Einfluss des Versuchsleiters. Ned. Tijds voor Psychol.* 6 (1954) 497; *Ausdruckskunde* 2 (1955) 34.

Busch, L.: *Der chronische Alkoholismus im Lüscher-Farbtest. Med. Klin.* 59 (1964) 254.

Canziani, W.: *Zur Entwicklung der Ehekonflikte. Der Psychologe Nr.* 4/5 (1958) 132.

Dietschy, H. and Dietschy, N.: *Farbwahl und Charakter von zentralbrasilianischen Indianern. Acta tropica,* Basel 15 (1958) 241.

Erbslöh, J.: *Uber die Erkennungsmöglichkeit der Dyspareunie im Farbtest. Medizinische* (1955) 1769; *Die Adipositas und ihre Behandlung aus der Sicht der Farbenpsychologie. Medizinische* (1957) 349. *Die Verwendung des Lüscher-Farbtests in der ärztlichen Praxis. Arztl. Praxis 1962, Nr. 31.*

Erbslöh, J. and Lüscher, I.: *Die Bedeutung des Lüscher-Tests für die Beurteilung seelischer Veränderungen während der Gestationsperiode. Med. Welt* (1962) 2087.

Flehinghaus, K.: *Signifikanzprüfung des Lüscher-Tests bei 1000 Volksschulkindern. Praxis Kinderpsychologie* 10 (1961) 143.

Furrer, W.: *Die Farbe in der Persönlichkeits-diagnostik. Test-Verlag, Basel 1953; Der Lüscher-Test in E. Stern: Die Tests in der Klinischen Psychologie. 2 Halbband, Rascher-Verlag, Zürich 1955.*

Görtz, R. and Klar, H.: *The Emotional and Psychological Differences between Pregnant and Non-pregnant Women, medico* (1963) No. 2.

Klar, H.: *Farbpsychologische Untersuchung von 1000 Persern. (Vergleich mit Europäern in Persien) Acta Tropica,* Basel 15 (1958) 134—240; *L'ivresse de l'opium à la lumière du test des couleurs. Examen psychologique de 70 fumeurs d'opium pratiqué avant et après l'usage du stupéfiant, au moyen de l'épreuve des couleurs, Médecine et Hygiène,* Genève, 17 (1959) Nr. 427, April 20, 1959 *Ihre Lieblingsfarbe gibt Auskunst. Der Lüscher-Farbtest und sein medizinischer Anwendungsbereich. Selecta,* 2 (1960) Nr. 18 S. 16; *The Lüscher Colour Test — a Highly Reliable Procedure in the Psychodiagnostics of Functional Disorder. medico* (1961) No. 4.

Colour Psychology and Medicine. Colours Do not Lie. medico (1961) No. 1.

Obesity in the Light of the Colour Test. medico (1961) No. 3.

Opium Smokers and the Psychological and Emotional Changes that take place immediately after Smoking. medico (1962) No. 1.

An Aid in Diagnosing Frigidity: the Lüscher Colour Test. medico (1962) No. 2.

Colour Psychology and Medicine medico (1963) No. 3.

Lüscher, M.: *Psychologie der Farben. Einführung in den psychosomatischen Farbtest,* 2. Aufl., Test-Verlag, Basel 1949; *Die ganzheitliche Deutung. Ausdruckskunde* 1, (1954); *Psychologie und Psychotherapie als Kultur. Test-Verlag, Basel 1955; La couleur, moyen auxiliaire de psychodiagnostic, in: Le diagnostic du caractère. Presses Universitaires de France,* 1949; *Verständnis und Missverständnis in der Psychologie der Farben. Einführung in die Funktionspsychologie. Inaugural lecture delivered December 21, 1957, Mensch und Farbe, Bonn* 1959, H. 1, 17—23.

Maier, M.: *Farbe und Charakter im Lüscher-Test. Ausdruckskunde* 1 (1954) 209.

Parejo, M.: *Untersuchungen über die Psychologie der Farbe. Acta med. Tenerife* 6 (1956) 171.

Paul, H.: *Der Lüscher-Farbtest. Zentralblatt für Arbeitswissenschaft* 1962 Nr. 10/12.

Preiswerk, F.: *Analyse und Förderung der Intelligenzleistung auf Grund des Lüscher-Tests. Der Psychologe* (1956) 471.

Ries, W.: *Das Altern in farbpsychologischer Sicht. Psycho-experimentelle Untersuchungen mit dem Lüscher-Test. Zschr. Alternsforschung,* Leipzig 13 (1959) 237. *Farbpsychologische Alternsstudien im Lichte der Statistik. Zschr. für Alternsforschg.* 14 (1960) 2.

Ries, W. and Ulrich, J.: *Die Psyche der Fettsüchtigen im Lüscher-Farbtest. Medizinische* (1959) 777.

Schmidt, H.-G.: *Wege der Diagnostik und Therapie bei psychogenen Krankheitszuständen. Medizin heute,* 5 (1956) 70; *Psychische Faktoren bei Cholecystopathien. Arztliche Praxis. VIII* (1956) Nr. 24, 2.

Smits, W. C. M. and Staken-burg, J.: *Instructie voor de Lüscher-Test*. Nimwegen, 1958.

Storath, H.: *Die Bedeutung der Farbe und ihre Anwendung im Lüscher-Test. Der Psychologe 4 (1952) 358.*

Wolfahrt, H.: *Versuche zur Bestimmung eines eventuellen Effekts von Farbstimuli auf das a u t o n o m e Nervensystem. Psychotherapie 1 (1956) 216; Psychophysische Auswertung der Versuche zur Bestimmung eines eventuellen Effektes von Farbstimuli auf das autonome Nervensystem. Psychotherapie 2 (1957) 86.*

Zinder, M.: *Die gebräuchlich-esten Testmethoden in der Psychiatrie. Der Lüscher-Test. In: Die moderne Psychiatrie. Göttingen (1957) Nr. 5.*

Steinke, L.: *"Der Lüscher-Test bei angeborener Farbsinns-törung", Diss. Univ. Augenklinik Basel 1958.*

ADDITIONAL REFERENCES
(POST 1968)

Klar, H.: Hope and Fear In Return-ees from Vietnam. "Medico", p. 15.

Klar, H.: The Discovery of Patho-genic Sources of Conflict by means of the Luscher Test. "Medico" (ov-erseas edition) No.2, 41.

Klar, H.: Reintegration Difficulties for Europeans after their return from Development Countries. (Stu-dies made over a period of 15 years with the Luscher Test. "Medico", No. 10, 12.

Klar, H.: The Luscher Test Colour Preferences of Children under the Influence of Neurotic Masturbation BRITISH JOURNAL OF PROJEC-TIVE PSYCHOLOGY AND PER-SONALITY STUDY.

Klar, H.: Liability to Sexual Seduc-tion--Examination of Backward Children with the Luscher Test. "Medico" No. 9, 7.

EDITOR'S NOTE:

Since Nuclear Evolution was first published nearly ten years ago, an English translation of Dr. Luscher's work on the eight colours has become very popular.* In 1968 it was relatively little known except to a close circle of colour researchers, and the author of Nuclear Evolution included the references listed above to make available material on another way of validating the meanings and effects of colours, since these were arrived at by a means of investigation totally different from his own.

Now the reader is referred to his own powers of validating the meaning of colours via personal experience and through the technique of Supersensonics using the radium and tritium-stimulated colour pendulums invented by Christopher Hills.

---

*The Luscher Color Test translated and edited by Ian Scott, based on the original German text by Dr. Max Luscher. Pub. Random House Inc. NY. 1969.

RELATING SPHERES OF CONSCIOUSNESS
TO THE RAINBOW SPECTRUM

According to the latest research into the effects of light on the hormone secretions of birds, and the irradiation of the Pineal Gland with specific frequencies of light, the Endocrine system is balanced by the subtle intake of Light (radiation caused by an emission of electro-magnetic waves of light or heat from a vibrating body) which is absorbed by the organism in specific frequencies (colour) so as to effect the chemical balance of consciousness. The particular band of consciousness in which the personality lives and has its being, resonates with that endocrine gland which is chemically functioning predominantly in that personality. The selection of a colour which each person resonates with, and that colour which a person rejects, will invariably reveal personality conflicts and basic drives.

Each drive is a bundle of self-regarding emotions which are chemically based on the response of each endocrine gland and its secretions. Such emotions are not only chemical but psycho-social in their potency and origin since the surrounding psychological tensions interact. Such self-regarding sentiments are projected by the observer into everything which is seen from the *centre of consciousness* as seven different kinds of human Love.

RED sensual, touching, sexual, physically demonstrated love.

ORANGE love for family, friends, and in higher levels of expression for humanity.

YELLOW love of intelligent reasoning, change, and novelty expressed in enthusiastic response to new ideas and schemes.

GREEN love of a secure condition, love of treasured things and people. Attached love.

BLUE love of the ideal figure, ideology, religion, scientific truth. Devoted love. Rigid, in that change is usually abhorrent.

INDIGO love of intuited truth; thrilling to the widening of awareness that encompasses future time.

VIOLET love of images of poetic, artistic, and aesthetic truth. Love of divine order in which the image and Reality correspond. Note: Each of these seven kinds of love seeks and sees Truth as the expression of this love at the highest level it knows. So the Red level, immersed in physical, sensory existence will find his truth in the exhilaration of high speed driving or in the orgasm with the perfect partner, or in any way that brings total expression of the moment's powerful urge. Whereas someone on the Blue level, who sees truth as a total commitment to an ideal, a religion, or a hero figure, tries to conceptualise it within the limits of the current ideal and pours out love and devotion in hero worship or cult fanaticism. Today's cult worshippers, who refuse even to consider the thought that others may have found truth by a different route, provide notable examples, among them the Jehovah's Witnesses, the Hare Krishna fanatics, and the "Moonies".

There is an 8th kind of Love which is not chemically induced or triggered without a self-transmutation of the self-regarding sentiment, although attempts have been made to induce euphoric conditions which simulate it through the use of drugs. These effects are temporary and have to be continually reinforced by more drugs unless a genuine self-transmutation has taken place, evidenced by the absolute lack of need for chemical stimulations. This "God-Love" or Love of Wholeness is the love of all self-regarding entities at the Centre of Being itself. The true commandment is to Love thy neighbour as thyself, with the emphasis on the self-regarding sentiment. "Be true to thine own Self and thou canst not be false to any man." The 8th Love is Self-transcending through the radiation outwards of the seven basic drives in their positive manifestations of the pure aroma of Self-transmutation. The choice of colour determines both the need of the entity and the personal goal through which it can be fulfilled. It also determines the Creative Conflict necessary to achieve it.

To take one example here from the Blue level, the *need* is for peace and certainty, so the Blue level person may join a religious group and follow a doctrine that seems to offer reassurance through clearly defined ethical and spiritual laws of behaviour. "If I stick to the Sermon on the Mount, that is all I need," said my father. But the ultimate goal of total fulfillment cannot be accomplished within limitations. Two stumbling blocks are here. One is the assumption that one's interpretations of the Sermon on the Mount is in line with what Christ really meant and the other is that such a rigid assertion makes no allowance for growth and change, the two essentials for evolution. So the Blue level person needs constant feedback that he is holding on to rigid concepts and that there are things which he is not seeing and which do not fit into his neat and static framework. This is not to say, however, that the Blue level of consciousness taken to its manifestation of total devotion, may not storm the gates of heaven with love, for the totally devoted, totally committed will take the buffetings of life and by the sheer totality of their dedication will break through to the ultimate truth at the heart of all the great religions. What is the secret key to the breakthrough for those of us stuck on the Blue level? It is the same key that unlocks the door on any level, namely the total releasing of ourselves from any form of attachment. Once there is no longer attachment to the Sermon on the Mount as the only truth and to our interpretation of it as the only way, then Christ's fiery message is fully revealed and is seen to be blazing out from all the great scriptures. Take any other level of consciousness, preferably your own, and meditate deeply on the application of this same process to that level. Ask yourself "What is my greatest need in life? What is my goal which when reached can fulfill this need? What is blocking this fulfillment?" If you are socially orientated, maybe your love does not extend beyond your immediate circle of family and friends. Try to see yourself as a great orange sun blazing forth with limitless warmth and light in all directions, totally unselective and unrestricted. Then you realise the God-self that is waiting to express through you and the little Ego-self shrivels in the heat of your own beneficence and generous giving.

THE SHELLS OF CONSCIOUSNESS. These are shown in Fig. 196 as the absorption and intake of colour (defined as Bio-energetic specific frequency response to Light) and therefore represent the pathogenic deficit of a person. This response will reveal optimum and minimum in terms of personal fulfillment, and creative or negative conflict within. The response to colour shows up the tenseness between surface and the inner life caused by the conflicting forces in the nervous system and endocrine imbalance. The whole electrical entity with its neural network and the ionisation of membranes which govern the electron discharge of the bio-energetic system responds to colour. Blue triggers constriction of the blood vessels returning to the heart, Red triggers dilation of the capillary blood vessels, while the whole sympathetic nervous system responds to light frequencies at the Blue/Violet end of the spectrum. This range of frequencies on the Blue/Violet side of the Green band governs the secretion of nor-adrenalin and governs the adrenergic nerve endings leading to paralysis and constriction. The Parasympathetic system resonates to the Red/Orange/Yellow acetylcholine secretions between nerve and muscle. Red has a marked effect on all Cholinergic nerve endings and helps to initiate spasms of the smooth muscle. The Red/Orange frequencies affect the secretion of Choline which is essential in nutrition and plays a role in the synthesis of amino acids and as a catalytic agent in the production of Acetylcholine on which the transmission of nerve impulses depends. The effects therefore on the smooth muscle in the alimentary canal of the colour Red will also be revealed by the choice of colour as it will reflect the tension in the colon and stomach wall. X-rays of the stomach while the person is in an angry state reveal tensions which resonate to the Red band of the spectrum. (Ref. research by Dr. S. L. Vinekar Yogic Hospital, Lonalva, Poona.)

The following pages give some basis on which to found the self-transmutation called NUCLEAR EVOLUTION, but before this can be experienced and expressed, the Ego has to be totally transcended so that we become selfless, not temporarily, in a fit of sentimental altruism, but permanently, so that no longer is every event referred back to the Ego for confirmation or rejection.

In a group, or even in a crowd, it is an interesting study to observe the different reactions and responses to a sudden event. It is sometimes worthwhile in an experimental growth group to engineer a situation in which these responses can be studied. (For example, mention can be made of a hurricane warning, or of the possibility that the landlord may be selling the house next month, etc.) Give the "news" and then watch the responses. Who rushes into speedy action? Whose first thought is "How will this affect me?" Who stands asking questions and analysing the news? "What is the source of the information?" "How near is the hurricane?" "Why is the landlord selling?" Who is most shaken by the prospect of change and upheaval? Who is already visualising a more ideal home after this one is left? Get people to describe what went on in their bodies as well as in their minds when they heard the news.

SELECTION AND REJECTION OF THE MAIN DRIVES

The colour least popular to the personality represents that band of consciousness in which there remains a deep unfulfilled *desire*. The whole body is a Kingdom of this Desire shot through with choices at every synapse, at every nerve substation and ganglion. At the nucleus of every cell the physiological response to the psychological drives betrays the inner tensions written in every line of the face, and expressed in every muscle and nerve. Choice and selection are made quite unconsciously in each cell, organ and endocrine gland so that the physical responses of the organism as a whole to Light and radiation obey, without question, the main psychological drives which rule over its deepest needs and desires. The language of colour is as universal as the range of human sentiment and somehow is understood at the deepest structural levels of the human soul.

If the deep significance of the preceding paragraph and the one that follows is to be fully grasped by the reader at this point and not simply understood at the intellectual level, it would be advisable to pause and actually *take* the 8-color Luscher Test. What is being said here is crucial to the whole understanding of Nuclear Evolution: a deep experiencing of our own Kingdom of Desire at this moment in time could reveal to us all the implications of the interrelatedness of body, mind and spirit that forms the basis of wholistic healing and of Christ's attitude to healings when he said, "Go and sin no more" after he had healed the sick. What was he really saying? Wasn't he really telling people, "Now don't go back home and repeat your old patterns and habits or you will surely be sick again?" In other words, to take a specific example, if you have literally had your guts eaten away by jealousy, no cure of the physical symptoms will be lasting if the jealousy remains. Until there is a resolution of the inner conflict that rages inside many people between what "is" and what "should be", no miracle cure, whether from a psychic healer or from the latest expensive antibiotic, will have any lasting effect. It is these deep-rooted conflicts, tensions, frustrations and desires that the colour test brings to the surface. Max Luscher's whole purpose in devising the test and Christopher Hills' whole purpose in writing Nuclear Evolution is to show us the patterns that it is imperative for us to change if life is to be joyful and fulfilling and totally healthy. To face these old habit patterns squarely and to let them go once and for all is to rediscover the bubble of youth without the aid of any so-called "rejuvenating" drugs; it is to be "born again".

When the personality has made his choice of eight carefully selected colours (not any colours but specifically tuned according to psychological criteria) he has revealed evidence of his psychological tensions and his emotional behaviour patterns. Going even deeper than this, he has also disclosed his underlying motives and has pointed out the goals that his personality has set for himself. If then, the personality rejects a primary colour i.e. the selection of Red/Yellow or Green/Blue as the least popular colour in a test, it reveals an *unfulfilled desire* which is intolerable to the subject and causes suffering within. Often this suffering is below the threshold of consciousness, very much like a cancer tumour which lies undiscovered in the tissues before it has begun to give pain. This intolerable band of colour objected to by each person reveals the psychobio-energetic deficit in his personality, and at the same time shows the way to that individual's secret goal in his development of consciousness. He ingests, digests, and expresses colour in the same natural way as he takes his food, and some colours are as objectionable to the organism as some foods. The colours shown in Fig. 196 are to be thought of as Light Energy, expressed according to its frequency and wavelength in bands or "rings" surrounding the person, creating a psychic " shell " with layers at different levels of excitation.

INPUTS AND OUTPUTS

According to a law discovered by Kirchhoff about a century ago the emitting power of any surface is proportional to its absorbing power. A body which absorbs all radiation or light falling upon it appears perfectly black. A perfect radiator is called a black body. This is purely an idealised hypothetical body which absorbs all the light falling upon it. Actual surfaces of objects, skin, etc. differ widely in their behaviour towards incoming radiation. Lampblack or a piece of black velvet absorbs 99 percent of the light falling upon it, while some shiny metals and crystals absorb very little. The nearest approach to an ideal black body is not a black surface as we might assume, but an almost closed cavity such as a jug or hollow cylinder. Any radiation that finds its way into the cavity is soon absorbed by repeated reflections within. As the inside walls absorb the incoming radiation or light they begin to radiate through the entrance hole. Hence the hole itself is called an ideal black body. This is not quite the same thing as a black hole in space which is a super absorber which sucks all re-emitted radiation back into its cavity so that none escapes.

Light or any other type of radiation entering the cavity of an ideal black body by the opening is almost completely trapped so that the opening itself appears intensely black. The rate of emission from an ideal black body is proportional to its temperature.

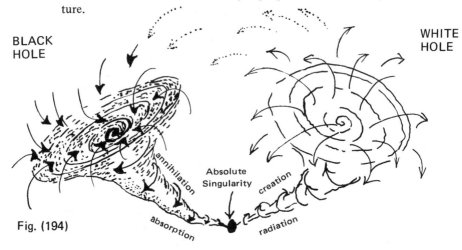

BLACK HOLE

WHITE HOLE

annihilation

Absolute Singularity

creation

absorption

radiation

Fig. (194)

If we can imagine our own consciousness as being so pure that we suck in all light as a perfect absorber then it would be re-radiated outwards in the same state it came in. Such purity is not obtainable physically but the analogy of an ideal absorber is useful because our ego identification with perfect absorption or as a perfect radiator will determine psychically the frequency of absorption and radiation we select from the total environment in which we live.

The human consciousness is so pure in its unadulterated state that it does not heat up like matter. Like the analogy of a black hole the temperatures have become so intense that the radiation is no longer flowing outwards but inwards – annihilating all matter. So there is nothing to heat up and the absorbing system has become supergravitational instead of levitational (heavy instead of light), cold instead of hot. Cold heat may appear contradictory but our senses can even feel this if our hand touches something so intensely cold it burns.

Fig. (195)

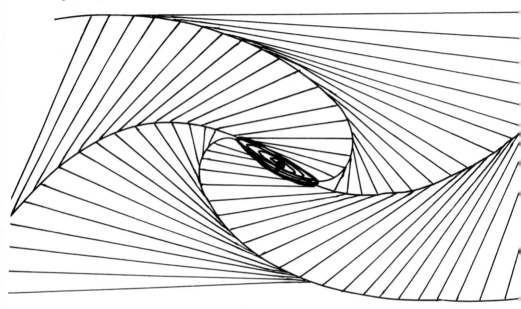

If human consciousness absorbs light to the point of coldness of a gravitational singularity at the centre (like a black hole), then we would not generate heat and light but its opposite until this becomes so intense that its polarity changes into a white hole and begins to radiate energy and heat again. It is an interesting fact that when matter is supercooled to near absolute zero temperatures it begins to levitate. If our human consciousness is viewed as the shadow-field analog of a total absorber we would not heat up like matter but go deeper into the gravitational centre. Hence consciousness has to become transfigured as a white hole (purified) radiator of those different intensities of cold light which generate cold aura colours in exactly the same way as matter generates hot colours. They are related proportionally opposite and complementary.

In looking at the construction of the galaxy we live in we see its centre is obscured by clouds of cosmic dust. The human brain has approximately 100 billion cells which correspond roughly to the estimated 100 billion stars in our spiral universe. At the centre of consciousness we are told by mystics there is a black night which swallows the self-sense, to emerge in a brightness where there is no dark and no light as opposites but only existence as the transparent purity of the immortal clear light of consciousness itself.

At the centre of the galaxial disc resides the logos of every one of the galaxies at different stages of evolution. This central core governs the cosmic desire of every particle in our universe. The annihilation of all thought, matter and form is only possible at the still centre between the fullness of White and the emptiness of Black. The design of the universe is such that all things in it have this common nuclear form. This central concept of Nuclear Evolution was published before there was any talk of black holes in space. Now there is observational evidence. Evidence will become available which proves that human consciousness itself is such a Black hole or White hole.

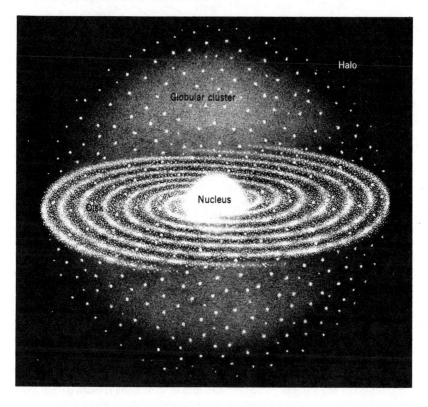

A central nucleus of a spiral galaxy surrounded by globular clusters of stars may consist of an invisible black hole. The central consciousness of every individual may also be a black hole which absorbs everything in it to make every individual person the centre of a multicentred universe.

Fig. (196)

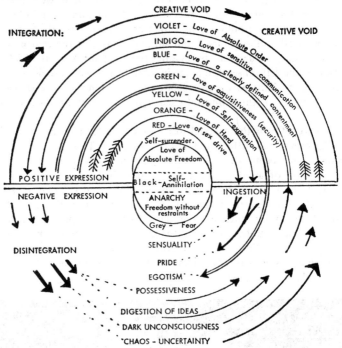

If we view the output of the human aura as being expressed in terms of colour radiated from an ideal black body we can compare it to the heating up of an ideal black ball or sphere. Because black is the most light receptive colour, any quanta of energy, radiation or light which hits it will immediately be absorbed, until it begins to throw off invisible infra-red radiation or heat waves. To picture a human being as an ideal black sphere, with total receptivity as a radiating vessel or receptacle for cosmic radiation, enables us to think of the aura as the emission of a wave-field with different frequencies and wavelengths. If the quanta of energy absorbed is increased the ideal black ball will glow with a red light as it becomes red hot. A human being emits a considerable amount of infra-red heat which can be detected from several miles away by modern heat sensors but radiating with a visible red light would require an increased energy output which will glow as the energy input, and hence the output, is increased. The black body will in turn glow orange hot, yellow hot, blue hot, violet and white hot. We must always remember, however, that the radiation itself is invisible to our eyes, which only see the **effects** of absorption either with light sensitive rods and cones or when the light is hitting some surface, some dust or clouds or some gas, such as air, neon, etc.

The input of energy for a human being is not so simple as for a black iron ball, since the heat transfers are achieved by cold processes. They are stored in the splitting of water and the separation of hydrogen atoms and oxygen atoms which are stored in hydro-carbons and fats in the body as potential energy. The heat of the body is maintained at an even temperature by the slow consumption of stored oxygen which the body burns.

The input is so complex and differs with the lack or surplus of each human entity ; no valid diagram could describe the hundreds of variant processes of intake. It would be impossible to describe in a paragraph or a chapter, any more than we could say what happens to each kind of food without writing a whole book ; but, once the functions of each colour are learnt, it is possible to combine them in the mind and make up a composite picture of each individual intake, always taking into account the overlapping of colours.

A generalisation of this intake process could be said to be that all human consciousness operates in water. No movement of electrical energy can take place in living organic life without hydrolysis of water. Life began in water and it appears that the function of the body as a vehicle for the spirit (consciousness) is to make water and hold water for all the protoplasm and its exchange of nutrients. Without this water in each cell there could be no ionisation of the membranes and no activity in the electron pumps, those energy generating wet-cell batteries which we call mitochondria. As Christ put it, "Nothing can be born again without spirit and water."

The photosynthesis process is impossible without water. A similar synthesis of the Light energies takes place by the breaking down of hydro-carbons in the ingestion of food. However, there is a direct method of hydrolysis which can take place in the blood and cell life. The electrical potentials within each cell, coupled with the extraction of certain electro-magnetic Radio frequencies in the sound spectrum from the homogeneous vibrations of primordial creative energy, using the principles of resonance outlined in this book, can cause the splitting of water to make hydrogen. This has been proved experimentally in the laboratory. Its simple operation would revolutionise our present methods of producing electrical power.

Several processes have been studied for splitting water but this special process of vibrating a sonic frequency in the radio-wave band through an electrically charged medium releases hydrogen in the same way that we use an electrical battery. In the well-known process of electrolysis much research has been done world wide to make it less costly. The spontaneous release of hydrogen when treated with its own resonant frequency is also possible in the creation of hydrocarbon nourishment for the body cells through the absorption of light at controlled frequencies (colours).

585

It is now well known that an efficient release of hydrogen from water, which is the most common element of the earth, would take care of all our future energy requirements. This could be achieved by direct burning of hydrogen, or by converting it chemically in the creation of a synthetic fuel and natural gas, or converting it into electrical energy. Its use in powered vehicles would decrease pollution and give 50% greater efficiency and cleaner burning than gasoline. A substitute for electric lighting by the excitations of phosphorous when in contact with hydrogen would provide a bright luminescence for our homes, but the energy companies would be doing themselves out of business to research it for home use.

HYDROGEN, LIGHT AND WATER AS CATALYSTS

It has been found by experiment that some reactions between the crystal structures of matter can be speeded up by the presence of substances which themselves remain unchanged after the reaction has ended and after the crystal has undergone a change in the lattice structure of its constituent atoms. Such a substance or transforming agent is called a catalyst and its effect is known as catalysis. In the human body as well as in industry, in chemistry and in semiconductors only a trace of a catalyst is needed to accelerate the reaction. In the case of a semiconductor the adding of an impurity to the crystal makes it an acceptor or donor type crystal. If we treat the human cell as a conglomerate of liquid crystals we can see that there must be impurities and catalysts which trigger the exchange of electrons between the different types of cells, acting as semiconductors, and their atomic reactions. They accelerate the metabolism of the natural elements of which our skin, bone and muscles are made.

If we let hydrogen gas escape from a cylinder into the atmosphere of our earth no visible change can be detected as the hydrogen atoms easily bond with the gases of which air is made, i.e. oxygen, nitrogen, etc. However, if the escaping hydrogen is directed at a piece of finely divided platinum (element No. 78) the platinum glows and eventually will ignite the hydrogen. In the absence of platinum the reaction with oxygen and nitrogen is too small to observe, but in contact with platinum the hydrogen reacts with the oxygen in the air to form H_2O (water). As they react they give off electrons and the energy heats the platinum. As the platinum gets hotter and hotter it heats up the hydrogen and oxygen so that their reaction with each other gets more accelerated until they ignite each other in fire (light) which then becomes a self-sustaining burning of each gas.

Fig. (197)

The top diagram (A) shows two atoms of hydrogen and one atom of oxygen. The diagram (B) shows a molecule of water formed by the sharing of common electrons to complete the shells of both elements.

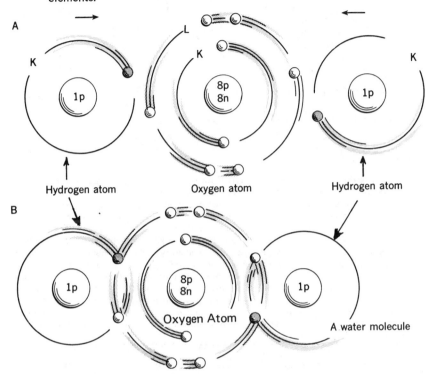

A

Hydrogen atom   Oxygen atom   Hydrogen atom

B

Oxygen Atom   A water molecule

Diagram (C) shows the single outer shell electron of sodium combining with an oxygen atom in water and becoming positively ionized. Other elements such as potassium in the cerebral fluids also ionize through the membrane transport of electrons on the villi in the wall of the ventricles in the brain causing the tuning to cosmic energies of light. A process similar to photosynthesis is taking place continuously to produce consciousness through breathing (inspiration). The atoms of oxygen have 8 protons and 8 neutrons in the nucleus. Hydrogen has 1 proton while sodium has 11 protons and 12 neutrons, potassium 19 protons.

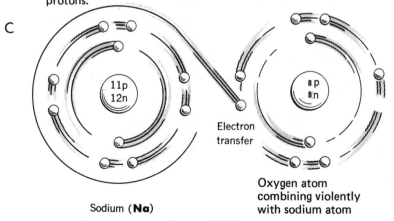

C

Electron transfer

Sodium (**Na**)

Oxygen atom combining violently with sodium atom

Fig. (198)

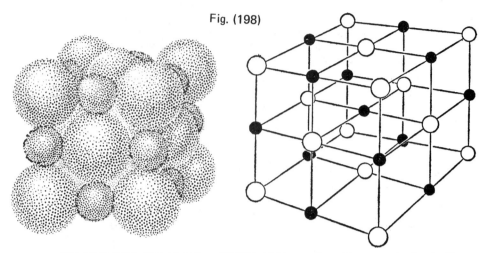

The alkali metal element sodium (NO.II) is highly reactive with oxygen in the air. The principle force holding the lattice of the sodium crystal together is the attraction of positive sodium ions for the negative electron cloud which surrounds the outer orbits of atoms. It is relatively easy to pull these outer electrons off a neutral alkali atom, hence it forms a ready bond with chlorine to make common salt. This mechanism applies to many of the atoms in the body which only need a catalyst to bring about the reaction which sodium and chlorine achieve by direct affinity. The mechanism of this high affinity is that sodium requires little energy to pull off its single outer electron and donate it to chlorine's seven outer electrons. After contact, chlorine has eight outer electrons but the sodium now has a positive charge because of its loss of a negative electron and the chlorine has a negative charge because it gained an electron. Thus a positive and a negative ion (atom) are formed and share the same electrons in the crystal lattice of sodium chloride. The sodium ions are shown in black and the chlorine ions in white.

Enzymes, which sometimes perform the same roles, are complex substances in biological systems which perform the role of catalysts for biochemical changes in the cells, but by far the most important agent of catalysis is the reaction of hydrogen and oxygen atoms to light and radiation. It is in this sense that the theory of Nuclear Evolution regards the reactions between basic atoms of hydrogen (1 proton, 1 electron structure) and oxygen (8 protons and 8 electrons) in the production of water as being caused by light. At the beginning of the earth's solidification the radiation (light) was far more intense, since the oxygen layer (ozone) and the earth's cloud cover (water) had not been created. But the light from the stars, in the form of heavy protons (cosmic rays), penetrates and travels through the cloud cover and even passes through the atoms of our body. Some of these rays of light interact and react with the hydrogen and oxygen in our bodies after they have already passed through the ozone layer and the cloud layers of the earth.

The effect of this radiation upon the chemical structures of the elements of the body in the living human being has hardly been tested by science. Only a Supersensonic measuring device is even capable of tracing the pathways and the complex processes, since there are no measuring devices which can register these reactions in a living body.

The alkali metals crystallise with a body-centred cubic lattice in which the lattice points are occupied by positive ions. The electrons in the outer orbits, one from each atom of the crystal, make up a sea of negative charges which permeate the entire lattice structure of the crystal element. Since these outer electrons are not fixed in any position they can wander at will throughout the metal element and give a high electrical conductivity. Because heat is transported through an element or metal by the conduction of electrons this means that high conductivity of electricity means also high conductivity of heat. When a light beam strikes the surface of a metal element such as sodium or potassium, the electromagnetic radiation in the wave-field agitates the electrons in the metal into a back and forth oscillation. These alkali metals are readily responsive to light because the outer electrons are not bound to any particular atoms. Whenever electrons begin to oscillate they begin to give off light like any other moving electric charge. The result is that we see the beam of light is reflected or absorbed according to the excitement of the disturbed electrons. The electrons in the crystal metals act like tiny radio stations which receive the light signal at a certain frequency and send it out again at all angles.

In metallic sodium crystals the force holding the lattice together is the attraction of the sodium ions for the negative electron cloud of the outer orbits. Because this attraction is in all directions there is a uniform field in all directions so there are no strongly preferred positions for the sodium ions in the crystal lattice. The final result is that sodium ions can move from one site in the crystal element to another, making it easy to ionise because of the low potential energy required to pull off the one outer electron from a neutral alkali atom.

These alkali metal crystal elements are the most reactive elements known, so that practically any oxidising agent no matter how small can be reduced by the alkali metals. We can now see why these elements represent the trigger fields which set off ionisation processes in the oxygen-filled brain and how these create radio-electromagnetic emanations by re-radiating light energies. It is common sense that these two alkaline metals with positive ions are the two most predominant in the brain since they both are among the most abundant elements on the planet ranking sixth and seventh of all the crystal elements found in the earth's crust. It is not surprising that sodium and potassium are essential components of all animal and plant cells since sodium ($Na+$) is the principal cation of the fluids outside the cells of all living matter and potassium ($K+$) is the principal cation for the fluids inside the cells.

Sodium and potassium ionisation not only applies to the body fluids in the brain and cerebrospinal system but also to all intercellular and intracellular fluids in the human body. For instance sodium (Na+) depresses the response of muscle enzymes and is necessary for contractions of all muscles in the animal world. The only difference between animals and plants is that plants are not mobile and do not need to move muscles; therefore the element potassium (K+) is their primary requirement. Hence 90 percent of the alkaline content of plant ash is composed of potassium. Plant life demands such a high percentage of potassium that even in sodium-saturated soils they prefer to take up the potassium at the rate of 50 pounds per acre, making it necessary to replace it with organic or inorganic fertilisers. In order to get this potassium for themselves humans must eat plant life or make it in their own bodies.

Sodium is made commercially by electrolysis of melted alkaline compounds. The fused mixture of sodium chloride (NaCl) and calcium chloride (CaCl$_2$) at 600° generates ions of sodium metal at the iron or copper cathode and chlorine at the carbon anode. However, the making of this sodium in the human body is done at body temperatures and furthermore it is transmitted into potassium through the sodium-potassium pump at the same temperatures. This fact which demonstrates nuclear changes from one element to another is an anology for Nuclear Evolution at higher levels of synthesis at the psychophysical levels. These changes take place through the ability of nature to change patterns of energy (images) at the nuclear level of being through the primordial quality of imagination (the ability to form images of non-existent realities) and the power of imagery (pattern) to condition the flow of energy into any natural system of interlocking processes. See page (96).

SODIUM POTASSIUM PUMP

The neuron consists of a sensitive cell body containing the nucleus and other parts necessary for metabolism. Thin short projections called nerve dendrites extend from one end while the long thicker projection extending from the other end is called an axon. The axon is wrapped in a myelin sheath. The membrane of the neuron is polarised by electrical charges of between 60 to 70 millivolts called the resting membrane potential, which is the difference between its negatively charged exterior and its positively charged interior wall. When the neuron fires its potential the nerve impulse is transmitted.

Fig. (199)

THE TREE OF LIFE

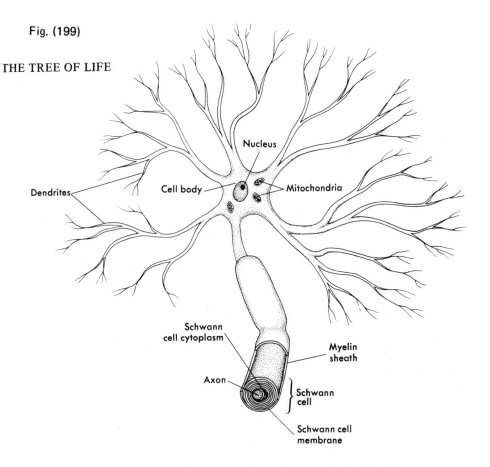

The nerve impulse is conducted from the negative inside of a neuron to the positive outside of the cell. In the neuron's resting state, the number of internal negative potassium ions (K+) are much greater than the sodium ions (Na+) on the outside of the membrane. By using ATP as its energy source the neuron membrane can pump sodium ions out of the cell as fast as they diffuse inward through the cell wall to maintain a balance of electrical charge. Because of this fine balance the cell can become extremely sensitive to small electrical stimuli in its external environment, and therefore acts as a detector of polarities and charges which will cause it to fire its impulse to shock the next axon so that the neuron's message is self-propagating from axon to axon. The process of firing the nerve dendrites by increasing the potential through conscious control of the neurotransmitters is mentioned here because the entire body works on this principle of the electrical potential between the inner and outer sheath. If we view not only the dendrites of the brain as a model of the "Tree of Life", but the entire body as a "Tree of Knowledge", then we have a superdetector of very small atomic charges in the environment. The ionisation of the sodium and potassium in the dendrites is the origin of the divining faculty.

Here we are more concerned with the conscious control of the small wet-cell batteries in the human bioenergetic system. It is not often realised that the way the human body generates electrical charge is through the transport of cations through cell membrane walls. This process can be consciously controlled through mental discipline and breath control. Yogis have known of this process for centuries but the medical profession looks askance at such practices. Yet there is at least one doctor who comes from a large family of 13 doctors who rejuvenates people and himself (now a sprightly 88 years old) and believes in the possibility of charging up the cerebrospinal fluid by an ionisation process similar to the method we here describe. In a forthcoming book Dr. Aaron Friedell*sets out the essence of his sixty years of research into the medical aspects of yogic breathing, but here we are more directly concerned with the mental control of body fluids. In order to bring about the physiological process of Nuclear Evolution as well as the psychological changes needed we must understand that the human body like the human personality has its own thresholds of psychic electricity which can be related to seven levels of consciousness. When these energies of the body are exactly balanced, as at the age of puberty, between positive and negative, male and female, yin and yang, etc. it is possible to bend metals and materialise matter.

To use this latent faculty in all humans for bending spoons is a misuse of the highest order of consciousness since it was given for the creative purpose of evolving ourselves through the sacred process of raising up a human being to his full spiritual potential. In the author's knowledge there are right now people going to classes and paying $150 to learn how to bend spoons like the thousands of children in England and Japan are doing since seeing a TV performance of this power. This sensational use of our mind is a total diversion of the power of consciousness, since it is this same power of consciousness which should now be used for changing ourselves, not the molecular composition of a piece of steel. While it may be a sensational demonstration of bending metal it would be far better for students of consciousness to be employed bending their own minds into better shape and using this power for working on the Ego structure which is a much tougher substance to bend than a metal spoon, since it is built of consciousness and light.**Building up the charge of the psychobiological currents for breaking through the light barrier is the pure motive which has been endorsed by all the sages of ancient times. They have consistently warned against getting lost in material phenomena.

---

* See statement at end of chapter.
** This comment applies equally to levitation, becoming invisible and other forms of spiritual materialism so fashionable today.

Now taking this analogy further we can detect, through Super-sensonic instruments, (see photographs at back of the book) a process of continuous ionisation varying of course in intensity with the health of each person. It is obvious that the ancients knew of these techniques of longevity and rejuvenation of cell life through the enhancement of the ionisation process which obeys the commands of consciousness.

Fig. (200)

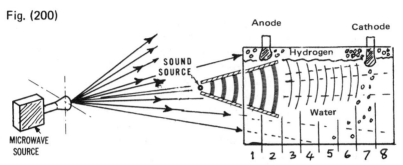

ANALOGY FOR IONISATION LEVEL OF THE SEVEN CHAKRAS

LIGHT PENETRATES THE BRAIN — A cascade of electrons is produced by the photo-electric effect in the liquid of the brain and body fluids. The level of ionization determines the oxygen reduction and the release of hydrogen bubbles.

A chemical analogy for the cosmic ionization level which determines oxygen reduction of water or body fluids thereby releasing hydrogen atoms. Each human cell is a small wet cell battery. Diagram shows how an electrically modulated sound wave in resonance with the background radiation of the universe produces spontaneous electrolysis in water or the human brain.

The principle of a wet cell battery is ionization and release of hydrogen. Positive ions move towards the cathode (Cations) in water solution while negative ions move toward the anode (Anions). The same principle works with organic cells of the mitochondria to store body electricity or life-force (prana). Kundalini is the movement of this energy towards the ventricles in the brain called in Sanskrit "The Cave of Brahma".

This process takes place in water, which acts as an electrolyte for the transduction of light photons into psychophysical energies of consciousness. In exactly the same way that one physical atom combines with another atom sharing a common electron and making itself positive, the union of the cells of the body (including the blood cells which are electrically positive) can bring about electrical charges stored in the mitochondria.

The above diagram is not intended as a strictly accurate picture describing the inputs of the psychophysical electricity which passes through the chakra system, but it gives an idea how the human organism absorbs radiomagnetic energies of Supersensonic

593

character. Further details of the wave-fields are set out in my book "Supersensonics".

The figure (200) on the previous page shows how sound and tuned radio energy from an ionising source such as radio waves, sunlight or spontaneous atomic decay of radium, uranium, etc. can be used to make water spontaneously split as it does in photosynthesis, electrolysis, and bioluminescence.

About 1/6th or 20% of the total circulation of the blood goes through the brain to carry oxygen atoms for metabolism of glucose utilised in thinking and controlling the physical functions of the body. About a quarter of all oxygen taken in by the lungs is used by the brain which comprises only 2% of body weight. About 90% of the glucose is oxidised into carbon dioxide which is then excreted from the brain via the veins. There is a continuous highly energetic activity in the brain even during sleep but it is possible to excite the oxidation process mentally and also to reduce metabolism in states of meditation, anesthesia, etc.

The brain consists of approximately 77% water and 23% solids. Of that 8% proteins and 13% lipids constitute the intracellular and extracellular fluids. Of all the inorganic ions in the brain the potassium ions and sodium ions represent the greatest quantity.

It is interesting to note that the element sodium (Na) number 11 in the periodic table, which is alkaline and ionises positively, and potassium (K), element number 19 also alkaline and positively ionised, not only both combine with water violently, creating much energy, but are only one step away from each other after passing through the nodal point of the inert gas previous to it in the periodic table. Sodium follows neon (element 10) and potassium follows argon (element 18). Diviners in France who discovered physical relationships between the sun's light and matter detected a relationship between the inert gases helium and argon on the lower and upper half of the wave-field of objects as long as the sun's ionising rays were shining on that portion of the earth. As soon as the sun set, the helium and argon would change position and reverse their order at the exact same moment, just as the sap in plant protoplasm would begin streaming in the opposite direction and begin to produce carbon dioxide instead of oxygen. The process has something to do with the ionising quality of radiation from the sun. The sun can be behind the clouds and the phenomena still continue so it is not just the visible part of the sun's rays which the plant is sensing. The ionising of plant cells which contain mitochondria like human cells is necessary for the breathing plant to absorb light through the splitting of water in hydrocarbons.

For an example of this ionisation process we can use the most common elements in the brain fluids of sodium and potassium which are important in brain metabolism. Just as water is made by combining two atoms of hydrogen on either side of a larger oxygen atom by sharing the same electrons in their outer shells to complete the water molecule, so can the sodium atom and potassium atom lose their single electron from their outer shells to become positively charged ions in the cerebrospinal fluids. By losing its electron to the oxygen atoms (O) in the water (H_2O) they become intensely excited and the water becomes an electrolyte for the purpose of receiving cosmic radiation from the sun and stars. The previous Fig. (200) shows how water is ionised through sharing electrons and how the energetic union of potassium and sodium ions with water help absorb more psychic electricity (prana).

e diagram below shows "The Cave of Brahma" at III referred to in the Sanskrit texts as e seat of resonance with the ONE ocean of cosmic vibrations. It manufactures the ˙ebrospinal fluid in IV which floats the whole brain and spinal nerves. The chemical Ph the fluid is determined by ionisation of the villi and cilia which in turn control onance with cosmic forces of light.

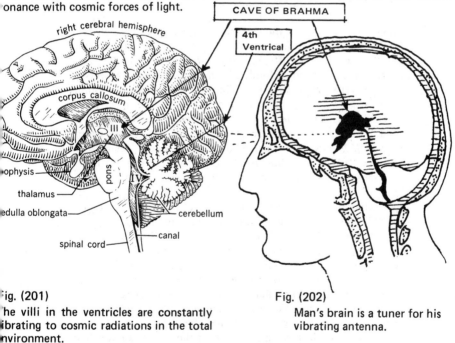

Fig. (201)
The villi in the ventricles are constantly vibrating to cosmic radiations in the total environment.

Fig. (202)
Man's brain is a tuner for his vibrating antenna.

The tiny villi on the inside of the cerebral cavities act as cathode and anode and cause the brain to become a resonating radiating vehicle of an enhanced wave-field.

Photons of radiation, whether they come from the sun as visible light or as cosmic rays from other stars, are discrete packets of energy travelling in spiral corkscrew motions through space. This energy is travelling like the wave travels through water. The water does not move horizontally, only the wave moves up and down vertically with the quanta of energy. The speed of these waves travelling in pulses called quanta is known as the velocity of light. This velocity, however, is only the limit within which our physical senses can experience light. Of course our man-made physical sensors, which measure beyond our physical senses on either side in microwaves and radio waves, are merely extensions of those senses, just as the camera is. The camera produces images on film emulsion only when the lens is specially made to produce perspective and focuses light in ways similar to the human eye; the mind does the rest. Change the lens and the perspective and shape of the objects on the emulsion are all changed to abnormal. This shows that the medium through which quanta of light passes drastically changes the picture. If the light passes through a gravitational field or through several layers of the earth's atmosphere or even through the successive layers of protein and intercellular liquid, the nature of the light is drastically changed by the medium.

When we come to the human vehicle which traps light we tend only to look at the surface skin and ignore the other layers which absorb its energy in different ways. We can look at the three different types of body fluids like three different pigments of emulsion, very similar to colour film in a camera, each recording a different frequency as a different part of the spectrum is absorbed. This is easy to visualise with visible light but when we take the background radiation of the cosmos, the radiant energy we call light comes from every direction at once. Yet it is not only more penetrating than visible light from the sun but is also able to influence our life and metabolic processes more.

Our relationship to this radiant energy of the universe is crucial to our health and crucial to our perception of the whole person we are. Many cells of our body are constructed like the rod cells of our eyes. When we think that a quanta of only one photon is needed to trigger the potential of a molecule of the visual pigment and let us see something, we do not normally attribute this great sensitivity to similar structures in the intestine and walls of the brain cavities. Yet waving and moving like wind over a corn field or the lashing waves of the wind-driven seas, there are cilia moving to the tides and currents of the very small quanta of energy released from the invisible collisions of photons with the mucous membranes of our body. Cosmic rays of light radiation pass straight through our surface skin where sunlight stops and excites the liquid crystal of the body fluids in ways we cannot yet measure by the crude instruments of modern science. The ability to measure one photon of light, in the way that the cilia-type rods do, has not been equalled by any scientific equipment so far devised by mankind.

The energy of a photon is usually described as a proton balanced with an electron so that it has no charge. On contact with any kind of matter the photon releases an electron and its impact imparts energy to that system. If the matter is the chlorophyll molecule it releases enough energy to split water and strip oxygen atoms away from carbon dioxide and excrete them. If the matter is the potassium and sodium atoms in the cerebrospinal fluid which extends throughout the inner membranes of the nervous system, then it triggers changes not only in the brain cells but throughout the entire body. The reason for this is that although the body has three different kinds of fluids which exchange and interchange with the nervous system they do not mix with each other. Like catalysts they cause chemical and atomic changes in the structures of our cells, but in healthy bodies are not destroyed in the process. However everyone has a certain amount of unwanted chemicals in blood, lymph and cytoplasm, and these pollutants will affect the efficient functioning of the synthesis and processing of the metabolic fluids.

e tip of a
outer seg-
nt acts as
antennae
radiation
eption.

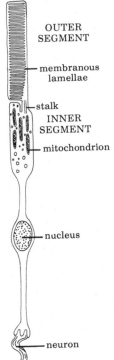

OUTER SEGMENT

— membranous lamellae

— stalk

INNER SEGMENT

— mitochondrion

— nucleus

— neuron

Fig. (203)

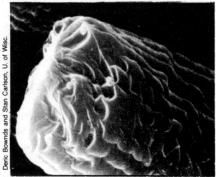

Deric Bownds and Stan Carlson, U. of Wisc.

A rod cell from the human eye shows the same pattern as cilia on the inner wall of the brain ventricles. The rod cell is a highly specialised cilia sensitive to vibration of radiation in a narrow part of cosmic radiation in the visible spectrum. Its basal body (not shown but similar to that in Fig 227) consists of nine peripheral fibrils like all cilia which run through the stalk to the outer segment. The visual pigment is held in the lamellae of the outer segment.

Rods and cones contain light sensitive pigments converted into a different form when struck by radiation frequencies in the visual spectrum. One photon converts one molecule of the pigment and the chemical reaction generates electrical potential across the membrane of the rod cell which in turn sends an impulse to the neuron and thence to the occipital area of the brain.

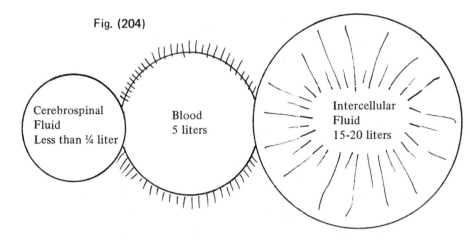

Fig. (204)

Cerebrospinal
Fluid
Less than ¼ liter

Blood
5 liters

Intercellular
Fluid
15-20 liters

Blood is a connective tissue consisting of various types of cells in an extracellular fluid called plasma which comprises about 50 -- 60% of its volume. It carries gases, nutrients, hormones and wastes around the body. Each platelet is charged positive on its outside membrane and no two blood cells actually touch each other as this positive charge repels. The blood clots when this positive charge is lost on contact with a foreign body. About 90% of the plasma is water with a great number of elements dissolved in it. The principle inorganic positively charged ions are Sodium (Na+), Calcium (Ca++), Potassium (K+) and Magnesium (Mg++). The concentration of these ions determines the ph of the body fluids and the plasma is slightly alkaline.

Therefore correct excretion by the cells and organs, clearing these waste products of protein synthesis, is fundamental to prevention of a sluggish system. The wholistic aim of all yoga is to clear a sluggish system so that not only the rods and cones of the eye but the cilia and other cells, which govern the release of ions in the body fluids, are super sensitive to incoming light radiations in all parts of the spectrum and not just to the normal spectrum. The entire body which has cilia in many parts of the organs of elimination and reception is polarised by oxidation. It is well known that in the absence of oxygen, radiation from atomic bombs, radium, etc. does not harm the human cells. The higher the threshold of unnatural radiation produced by man, the more we must extract oxygen from a system -- a very difficult task in a living being. To increase the threshold of natural light radiation by increasing the oxygen in yogic breathing immediately produces a higher ionisation count in the brain fluids and excites the cilia to a higher electrical potential, making the whole brain and nervous system far more sensitive to the total cosmic environmental signals and to its more efficient metabolism.

In the phenomenon known as dowsing researched by the author in "Supersensonics", the amplification of the nervous sytem by natural radioactive positive ionising sources is crucial to the detection of negative ions produced by water, plant photosynthesis, ozone, etc. To make the outer membranes of the cilia more positively charged instantly makes us aware of the presence of negative ions which have been proved to enhance consciousness, relaxation, etc. even in non-trained subjects in offices.

Now medical men are beginning to look at these processes and discover that what the author found in 1958 by 'Supersensonic' methods and published in 1968 is not so far-fetched after all. After another ten years the theory of Nuclear Evolution will be proved by medical physicists by their own methods.

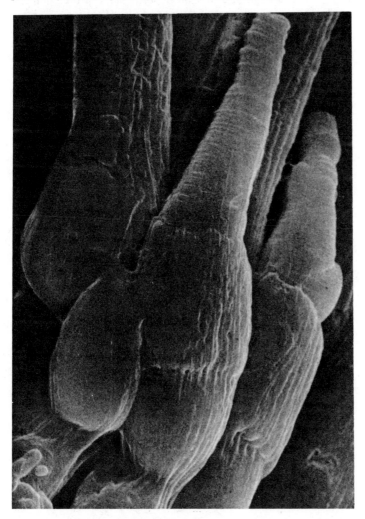

A micrograph of light sensitive cones from the eye of a mudpuppy.

The cone signal is more complex. There are three types of cones containing three different pigments sensitive to different parts of the visible spectrum of radiant energy. These send electrical messages which correspond to the perception of the three primary gunas which are received by our consciousness as blue, green and red colours. The pigments do not send any information about colours down the optic nerves, but colour is discriminated mentally as difference in potential between the three gunas.

This process, which is stimulated by ionising radiation of light, is the trigger for the sodium-potassium pump, which maintains an osmotic balance between the extracellular and intracellular fluids of the body. The system is not unique to humans since all cells, plant or animal, accumulate ions. The majority of cells maintain an internal concentration of sodium ions far less than the surrounding fluids in which they exist, while accumulating a higher concentration of potassium ions than their environment. These unequal concentrations on opposite sides of the cell membranes cause the cells to breathe and work off the excess energy by ion transport across the wall of the membranes. The process has not yet been scientifically validated although there are several models for the functioning of the sodium-potassium pump. The Nuclear Evolution model just described uses water and cytoplasm as an electrolyte causing oxidation of the metabolic compounds in the body.

MODEL OF SODIUM-POTASSIUM PUMP

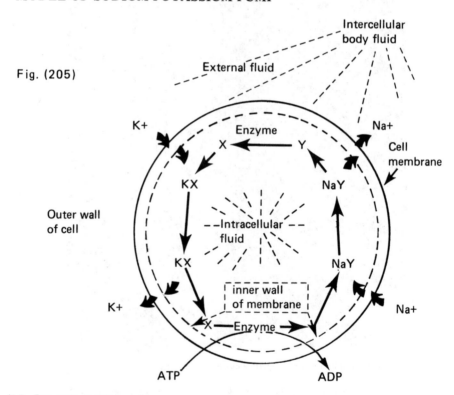

Fig. (205)

N.B. For more detailed explanation of the process, see Part III "The Physics of Consciousness".

The current theory in biology at this time is that a carrier compound which exists at the outer surface of the membrane unites with potassium ions K, to form a new compound KX. This is in a higher concentration on the outer surface so that electrons tend to diffuse towards the inner surface of the membrane wall. Once a molecule of the KX reaches the inner surface of the cell it releases its potassium ion K into the cell interior while the carrier compound X is converted immediately into Y. This readily unites with any sodium ions at the inner surface. Through an energy reaction with ATP, a chemical in which the cell stores energy like a savings account at the bank, any sodium ions which unite with Y form a new compound NaY which diffuses from the inner surface of the membrane wall to the outer surface. When such a molecule of NaY reaches the outer surface, which is bathed in the extracellular fluids, it releases its sodium ion into these fluids and Y is immediately converted back into X by an enzyme reaction.

The carrier molecule X is then ready to pick up any other potassium ions to form KX again and thus start the cycle all over again. Thus the carrier molecule has two identities X and Y which act as a shuttle for the membrane transport of ions, bringing potassium into the cell and taking sodium ions out into the surrounding cytoplasm electrolyte. The energy which operates the sodium-potassium pump X-Y is provided by ATP stored in the cell from cell respiration and oxidation. This model is not yet proved as a fact and does not explain the action of photoelectric light interactions with human cell matter. In fact it is purely a chemical model which hypothetically omits any interaction of cosmic rays or environmental radiation in which all cells exist. The actual process is described in greater detail in part III of this book - The Physics of Consciousness.

THE PERIODIC TABLE

On the following pages we can see the connection between sodium and potassium as they combine with the oxygen atoms in the water of the body. The fluids between the cells and the internal fluid of the cells are very finely balanced by the exchange of one electron. In the periodic table we can see how all elements move up in the spiral of life through gaining a proton or they move down through weak interactions with certain other elements by losing a proton. The question is what makes the elements move from an existing structure of building blocks of proton, neutron and electron to another structure in the spiral of life? The answer is the penetrating power of cosmic radiation and light. The entire galaxy is involved in the process of transmutation of the physical elements into energy and light. We must now see how these elements of which we are made act as an antenna for "proticity".

601

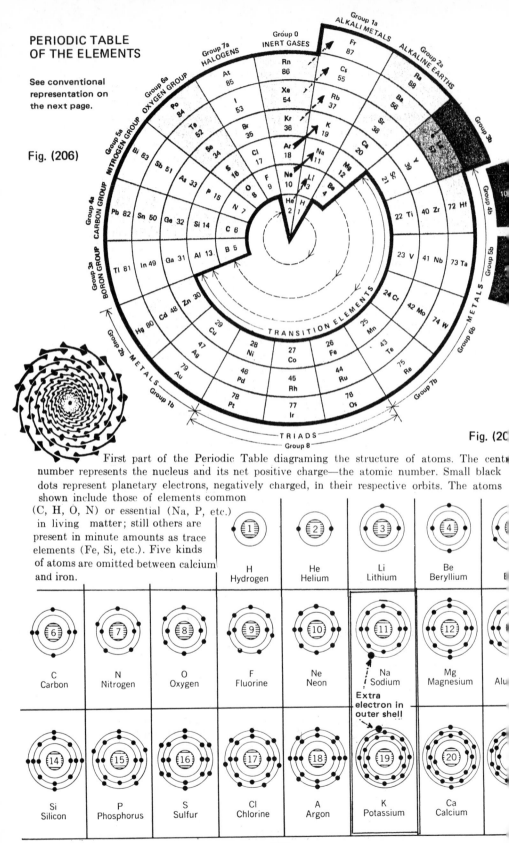

PERIODIC TABLE OF THE ELEMENTS

See conventional representation on the next page.

Fig. (206)

Group 7a HALOGENS
At 85
I 53
Br 35
Cl 17
F 9

Group 0 INERT GASES
Rn 86
Xe 54
Kr 36
Ar 18
Ne 10
He 2

Group 1a ALKALI METALS
Fr 87
Cs 55
Rb 37
K 19
Na 11
Li 3
H 1

Group 2a ALKALINE EARTHS
Ra 88
Ba 56
Sr 38
Ca 20
Mg 12
Be 4

Group 3b
Y 39
21 Sc

Group 6a OXYGEN GROUP
Po 84
Te 52
Se 34
S 16
O 8

Group 5a NITROGEN GROUP
Bi 83
Sb 51
As 33
P 15
N 7

Group 4a CARBON GROUP
Pb 82
Sn 50
Ge 32
Si 14
C 6

Group 3a BORON GROUP
Tl 81
In 49
Ga 31
Al 13
B 5

22 Ti 40 Zr 72 Hf **Group 4b**
23 V 41 Nb 73 Ta **Group 5b**
24 Cr 42 Mo 74 W **Group 6b**
25 Mn 43 Te 75 Re **Group 7b**

Group 2b METALS
Hg 80
Cd 48
Zn 30
29 Cu
47 Ag
79 Au

Group 1b
28 Ni
46 Pd
78 Pt

27 Co
45 Rh
77 Ir

26 Fe
44 Ru
76 Os

TRANSITION ELEMENTS

TRIADS Group 8

Fig. (20

First part of the Periodic Table diagraming the structure of atoms. The cent[r] number represents the nucleus and its net positive charge—the atomic number. Small black dots represent planetary electrons, negatively charged, in their respective orbits. The atoms shown include those of elements common (C, H, O, N) or essential (Na, P, etc.) in living matter; still others are present in minute amounts as trace elements (Fe, Si, etc.). Five kinds of atoms are omitted between calcium and iron.

1 H Hydrogen	2 He Helium	3 Li Lithium	4 Be Beryllium	
6 C Carbon	7 N Nitrogen	8 O Oxygen	9 F Fluorine	10 Ne Neon	11 Na Sodium	12 Mg Magnesium	Alu
14 Si Silicon	15 P Phosphorus	16 S Sulfur	17 Cl Chlorine	18 A Argon	19 K Potassium	20 Ca Calcium	

Na Sodium — Extra electron in outer shell

602

A PERIODIC TABLE OF THE ELEMENTS

Elements above and to the right of this line are nonmetals.

Elements below and to the left of this line are metals.

TRANSITION ELEMENTS

PERIOD \ GROUP	IA	IIA	IIIA	IVA	VA	VIA	VIIA	VIII	VIII	VIII	IB	IIB	IIIB	IVB	VB	VIB	VIIB	VIII (O)
1	1 H Hydrogen																	2 He Helium
2	3 Li Lithium	4 Be Beryllium											5 B Boron	6 C Carbon	7 N Nitrogen	8 O Oxygen	9 F Fluorine	10 Ne Neon
3	11 Na Sodium	12 Mg Magnesium											13 Al Aluminum	14 Si Silicon	15 P Phosphorus	16 S Sulfur	17 Cl Chlorine	18 A Argon
4	19 K Potassium	20 Ca Calcium	21 Sc Scandium	22 Ti Titanium	23 V Vanadium	24 Cr Chromium	25 Mn Manganese	26 Fe Iron	27 Co Cobalt	28 Ni Nickel	29 Cu Copper	30 Zn Zinc	31 Ga Gallium	32 Ge Germanium	33 As Arsenic	34 Se Selenium	35 Br Bromine	36 Kr Krypton
5	37 Rb Rubidium	38 Sr Strontium	39 Y Yttrium	40 Zr Zirconium	41 Nb Niobium	42 Mo Molybdenum	43 Tc Technetium	44 Ru Ruthenium	45 Rh Rhodium	46 Pd Palladium	47 Ag Silver	48 Cd Cadmium	49 In Indium	50 Sn Tin	51 Sb Antimony	52 Te Tellurium	53 I Iodine	54 Xe Xenon
6	55 Cs Cesium	56 Ba Barium	57-71 Lanthanides (see below)	72 Hf Hafnium	73 Ta Tantalum	74 W Tungsten	75 Re Rhenium	76 Os Osmium	77 Ir Iridium	78 Pt Platinum	79 Au Gold	80 Hg Mercury	81 Tl Thallium	82 Pb Lead	83 Bi Bismuth	84 Po Polonium	85 At Astatine	86 Rn Radon
7	87 Fr Francium	88 Ra Radium	89-103 Actinides (see below)															

INNER TRANSITION ELEMENTS

	IIIA	IVB	VB	VIB	VIIB	VIII	VIII	VIII	IB	IIB	IIIB	IVB	VB	VIB	VIIB
Lanthanide Series	57 La Lanthanum	58 Ce Cerium	59 Pr Praseodymium	60 Nd Neodymium	61 Pm Promethium	62 Sm Samarium	63 Eu Europium	64 Gd Gadolinium	65 Tb Terbium	66 Dy Dysprosium	67 Ho Holmium	68 Er Erbium	69 Tm Thulium	70 Yb Ytterbium	71 Lu Lutetium
Actinide Series	89 Ac Actinium	90 Th Thorium	91 Pa Protactinium	92 U Uranium	93 Np Neptunium	94 Pu Plutonium	95 Am Americium	96 Cm Curium	97 Bk Berkelium	98 Cf Californium	99	100			

HUMAN LIGHT SYNTHESIS

The human body is a very complicated organism living not only on food but air, water and light. The way it splits water and metabolises the bio-energy depends on the inputs it receives from all sources. The following diagram is not intended as a strictly accurate picture describing these inputs but gives an idea how human organisms absorb light energies of a radio-magnetic and ionising character through different thicknesses of the galaxy.

THE GALACTIC DISC ACTING AS COSMIC LENS

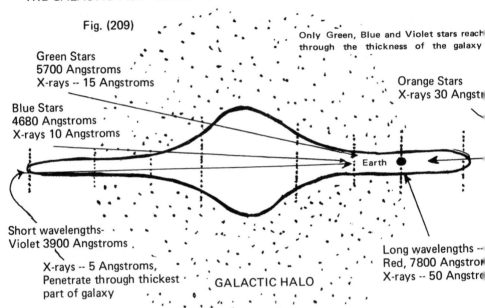

Fig. (209)

Only Green, Blue and Violet stars reach through the thickness of the galaxy

Green Stars
5700 Angstroms
X-rays -- 15 Angstroms

Orange Stars
X-rays 30 Angstr

Blue Stars
4680 Angstroms
X-rays 10 Angstroms

Earth

Short wavelengths-
Violet 3900 Angstroms

X-rays -- 5 Angstroms,
Penetrate through thickest
part of galaxy

GALACTIC HALO

Long wavelengths --
Red, 7800 Angstrom
X-rays -- 50 Angstr

X-rays of very short wavelength are emitted when the inner shell of an atom of a gas o element in nature is filled by an electron from the outer shell. Other microwave energ with ionising power comes from stars outside our own galaxy as well as cosmic ray loaded with ionising power are sometimes scattered by the low density gas of the galacti halo; passing through the dense part of the galaxy only the high frequency short wave lengths penetrate to the earth from the edge of the galactic disc. The disc is a spiral an therefore transparency varies with the direction in the galactic plane zodiac.

Radiations from stars excite molecules of air and ionise the surrounding air as well a penetrate the fluids of the human body. These oscillations in the air are well known t water diviners because they create a radiation from colliding atoms and molecules whic affect the divining ability. These oscillations and ionisations create the growth of crysta and cause chemical changes in the air and all living substances. Molecules of air vibrat normally at indoor temperatures at individual velocities equal to the speed of a rifle bulle The interacting fields of all solids and liquids with the vibrating air gases causes an excita tion around each object on the surface of the earth including the liquid crysta (chloresterol) in the body which can be detected by dowsing instruments. These motior make the oxidation process in respiration and disintegration of protein molecules activ Exclude air and we exclude ionisation process.

604

Fig. (210)

The figure shows the glands and nerves which absorb the main ionising wavelengths of cosmic rays in the form of radiation in addition to the visible spectrum and also weak X-rays coming from neutron stars in most parts of the galaxy. These three kinds of light are constantly bathing the earth and everything on it with octaves of vibration which excite the nervous system and its psycho-physical centres.

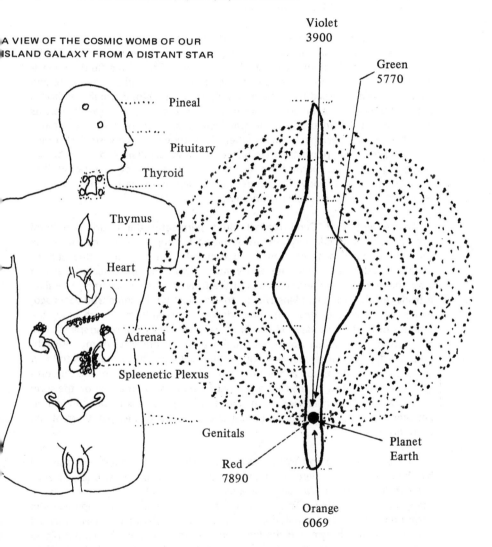

A VIEW OF THE COSMIC WOMB OF OUR
ISLAND GALAXY FROM A DISTANT STAR

Violet
3900

Green
5770

Pineal

Pituitary

Thyroid

Thymus

Heart

Adrenal

Spleenetic Plexus

Genitals

Red
7890

Planet
Earth

Orange
6069

Waves of radiant energy from different parts of the galaxy penetrate from other stars and universes into our own island galaxy. The shorter the wavelengths, such as 5 and 10 angstroms, the better they penetrate to the earth. The larger waves, 50 angstroms and up, only get through where the galaxy is thinned out. Therefore a greater amount of shortwave radiation reaches us on the earth when it is facing the thinner, less opaque part of the cosmic lens.

Here is the statement of Aaron Friedell, M.D., who agrees fully with Nuclear Evolution.

The body is composed largely of three different types of fluids. These are: the Intercellular fluid accounting for 15-20 liters, blood accounting for 5 liters and Cerebrospinal fluid - less than ¼ liter. Together these three fluids make up 70-75% of our physical form.

The Cerebrospinal fluid is the intercellular fluid of the brain cells and of all nerve tissue elements throughout the entire nervous system. The Cerebrospinal fluid is the latest in the evolution of the three fluid compartments. One of its major functions is to carry nutrition and elmination to and from the brain. Formed from the blood plasma as the blood circulation brings blood plasma to the capillaries in the charoid plexus in the brain ventricles, its activity is not confined to just the brain cells or spinal cord, but perfuses into and through the peripheral nerves where it is known as axoplasm. The fluids of the three components interchange via the capillaries of the blood, branching out and permeating all parts and nooks of the body. The branchings of the body fluids are in contact with each other, but are separated by semipermeable membranes.

The extent that Cerebrospinal fluid permeates the entire peripheral nervous system is relatively new information to modern medicine. All of the three interchanging fluids can be consciously guided and influenced to increase or decrease their rate and volume flow. The yogic techniques can alter the volume, rate and pressures of the flow. An Italian scientist, Valsalva, introduced the Valsalva Maneuver to the medical world some 300 years ago, which also modifies flow, to some degree. It is still made use of in the practice of medicine today. However the method by which we can specifically guide the Cerebrospinal flow effectively is the main objective of my research. Since all the fluids interchange through the blood circulation we need to learn to guide at will the blood as the first step in learning guidance of the Cerebrospinal fluid. Control of the Cerebrospinal fluid has a direct effect on the state of relaxation of the nervous system. There definitely seems to be a connection between the state of bodily and emotional stress, and the operations of the body fluids.

The 5 liters of blood in the body are centered in the chest and pumped by the heart. Thirty percent of the blood volume is in the arteries, seventy percent in the veins. We can influence the venous blood flow more easily than the arterial flow. This is done through guiding our diaphragmatic breathing. With a deep inhalation we compress the inferior vena cava (located between the diaphragm and the liver) and we thus increase the venous blood pressure below the diaphragm. As we continue and lengthen inhalation time we distend the upper chest. This distension compresses the two subclavian veins that bring blood back from the brain. That increase of blood in the brain helps to profuse circulation to the brain and, on the exhalation, will increase the flow of the Cerebrospinal fluid into the peripheral nerves, relaxing the body, reducing acidity in the system and tension by calming the nerves.

24

NUCLEAR EVOLUTION
METHODS OF KNOWING
BY NATURE'S LAWS
NUCLEAR EVOLUTION
OF COLOUR
RAINBOW BODY
IMAGINATION BARRIER
FOURTH FORCE
AND THE CHAKRAS
SHAKESPEARE'S
HOW DO HUMANS
INTERNAL & EXTERNAL
METAPHYSICS OF
IS KUNDALINI
PRIMORDIAL
SPACE AND
THE CONTRACTION
SOCIOBIOLOGY
OF RELATIONSHIP
SPIRITUALITY
LEVELS

INFLUENCE OF COLOUR AND LIGHT ON PERSONALITY

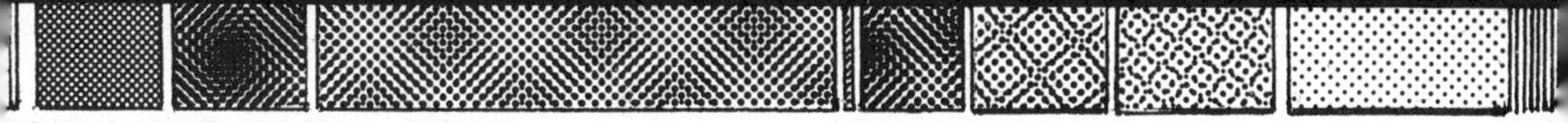

13 Red 19 Orange 25 Yellow 50 Green 55 Blue 62 Indigo 68 Violet 80

THE INFLUENCE OF COLOUR AND LIGHT
ON HUMAN PERSONALITY

In the Introduction to Chapter 8 we referred to the effects of colour on the time worlds of the introvert and extrovert and the way they both process the incoming energies of the cosmos. Now we must look deeper into what this means in terms of the structure of human personality.

Psychologists have been industrious over the last fifty years in producing several theories of personality, many of them still in use in therapy. From Freudians to Jungians, Adlerians to Psychosynthesis of Assagioli, which brings in the eastern philosophy of self, we are today presented with systems which all emphasise one aspect or another. Freud relates everything to the Libido (the bottom, Red chakra function) and Assagioli approaches from the Imagination and Will (the top Violet chakra function). In between the two extremes we have Adler relating his drives to insecurity (the Green heart chakra) and Jung to the Intuitive dream life (the Indigo brow chakra). No one seems to have a comprehensive system which accounts for the many types of people and the enormous variety of human personality. The fact is that the catagorising of human types in any set, fixed way or the establishing of standard types in some already delineated fashion leads not to a clear picture of the inner world, but merely to a caricature. We are left with a cardboard copy of a person which falls down like a pack of cards the moment the person is free and spontaneous and does something out of line with his typical characteristic behaviour. Prediction of behaviour becomes chancy with these early methods and not only is it difficult, but the work of analysis becomes long and expensive.

The method of typing the structure of our own human personality in Nuclear Evolution is only a matter of thoroughly learning the nature of eight drives and with these we may type any human being in terms of numbers 1 to 8, in any number of permutations, by giving weights or percentages to the levels of consciousness.

Let us illustrate with our own self. If we functioned on every level of consciousness as most of us would like to do then we would be a 1 2 3 4 5 6 7 8 or R O Y G B I V Bl/Wh type, but if our main drive was the Yellow intellectual, then we would begin with that number 3, and follow with 1 2 4 5 6 7 8 . If our second colour preference was Indigo (colour Number 6) then we would lead with 3 and 6 and follow with the numbers 1 2 4 5 7 8 and so on in the correct order of our colour choices. By weighing each of the colours with, for example, a percentage of Green in the colour Blue, or of say a Magenta of 55% Red and 45% Blue, we can make an exact record for future testing. Thus any number of combinations of colours produces an instant understanding of the different subtle shades of human personality in terms of the total being and its interaction with all levels of consciousness in a holistic sense.

Thus Nuclear Evolution is the most accurate and most detailed way of mapping a personality and its overlapping drives hidden at the very depths of the unconscious. Furthermore this labeling can be done with numbers, so that the reading of a person can be instantly formulated as a 1,3,6 or a 3,6,4 or any combination of chakra functions up to 8^8 to produce the most detailed information map of a person's relationships to time, the physical world, the intellectual, imaginative and intuitional worlds, as well as their sense of certainty and insecurity, all in the space of eight numbers. These eight numbers represent colours which in themselves represent whole books of information. To continue studying Nuclear Evolution, therefore, without taking time to digest and familiarise ourself with the meanings of these colours 1 through 8 would not be profitable. The meanings of each colour have only been lightly touched upon in Chapter 8 (Red) through Chapter 16 (Black) and whole books could be written about each one. As we have said already, since all of Freud is Red orientated and Jung Indigo orientated, one would need only to read their works to see what these two colours meant. Though Freud attributed all psychic activity to Red level (No. 1) functions he wrote of it from the Yellow level (No. 3) on which he himself functioned as an intellectual. The Red level, as seen from two levels above it (the Yellow level) is viewed entirely differently from the way in which the Jungian Indigo level (No. 6) would view it.

To understand these different viewpoints of how each of the levels appear from the levels above or below it, we must go back to the introvert and extravert and see how they feed off light and colour unconsciously. We must now begin to probe deeper and deeper into the psychic functions of the total self and discover its rainbow structure.

Fig. (211)

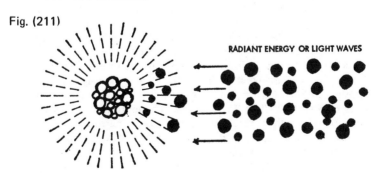

RADIANT ENERGY OR LIGHT WAVES

The diagram shows the longer waves of light represented as large black dots absorbed at the outer bands of consciousness. The shorter wavelengths penetrate to the core of the nuclear centre of being.

It has been stated that the positive energies of red, orange yellow, are expressive and are all on the outside of the neutral green band. They are absorbed in reverse order to those being expressed in Fig. 196. Outputs and inputs are viewed as complementary opposites.

THE EXTRAVERT

Fig. (212)

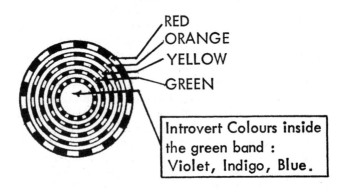

RED
ORANGE
YELLOW
GREEN

Introvert Colours inside the green band : Violet, Indigo, Blue.

The figure shows the personality of the extravert absorbing Light into the outer shells according to its resonance with the type and colour wavelength of the radiation being absorbed.

At the lower energy levels the longer wavelengths do not penetrate the psychic layers inside the neutral Green band of consciousness and are re-emitted with a time lag which is dependent on the inner time world of the individual personality.

All those persons whose output is in the Red band will absorb that colour and express it, unless there is a conflict which makes the intensity of the colour Red unbearable to the organism. In this case they will reject red and it will remain unabsorbed, and by their intolerance of the Red, their need for inner peace will indicate the lack of Blue or Indigo. As there may be a combination of several colours lacking in the personality, and the same Rule of absorption applies, it can be seen that penetration of any energy will depend not only on its wavelength but on the absorption layers it has to pass through. This will depend on whether the human entity is outgoing and extravert or ingoing and intravert. In the intravert the outer layers of Red to Yellow do not exist. The extravert will reflect energies before they reach the inner layers surrounding the nucleus ; he will not generate the energies from within but reflect them from the surface.

SHELL MODEL OF PERSONALITY

The brain has **100** billion cells, about the same number of stars in our galaxy, with 10 billion neurons which trigger its activity. Medical authorities believe the pituitary and pineal are under the control of the hypothalamus and that this connection regulates the nervous system and endocrine system. To determine our extrovert/introvert personality we must look to control of the endocrine secretions. In Nuclear Evolution theory the chakra system controls the function of the endocrine glands and in turn the chakra system is controlled by the hypothalamus depending on a person's attitude to the taking in of light (absorption) or the giving out of light (radiation).

There is evidence that there are blackholes of a million times the sun's mass at the galactic centre which are fueled by capturing gas light and even whole stars. Blackholes form out of super massive star clusters in galactic centres and intense gravity increases the density of stars around the centres.

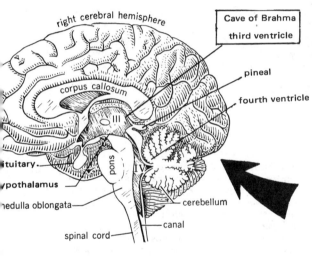

right cerebral hemisphere

Cave of Brahma

third ventricle

corpus callosum

pineal

fourth ventricle

pituitary

pons

hypothalamus

medulla oblongata

cerebellum

canal

spinal cord

Extraverts respond to radiation as a mirror to cosmic reflection of light.

EVERY PERSON'S CONSCIOUSNESS IS ANNIHILATING ITSELF IN A BLACK HOLE INTO WHICH THE UNIVERSE CONTRACTS SPIRITUALLY AS IT EXPANDS MATERIALLY.

The ventricles are the key to personality as they control (through ionisation processes) the functioning of the chakras in their intake of radiant energy. The lateral ventricles are caves separated by a vertical partition but connected with each other through the third ventricle (the Cave of Brahma). The ventricles are each lined by a thin diaphonous membrane which is covered by cilia. The lateral ventricles come forward and outward into the frontal lobes, backward into the occipital lobe and the middle descends into the temporal lobe. The roof of these three is formed by the undersurface of the corpus collosum. Their floor is formed by many of the major parts of the brain including the charoid plexus, the optic thalamus, and the hypothalamus and links both hemispheres with a thin semi-transparent vertical membrane -- the septum lucidum.

The interbrain is connected to all other parts by the third ventricle, the Cave of Brahma, which constitutes its side walls. From its roof hangs the charoid plexus. Its floor extends along the hypothalamus from the pituitary body in front to the pineal gland at the back. Its sides are formed by the optic thalamus. The pineal gland is larger in the child than in the adult and larger in the female than in the male. Its structure is similar to the pineal eye of lizards. In these reptiles the pineal is attached by a long stalk which projects through the brain and lies immediately under the skin. Microscopic examination reveals light sensitive structures similar to those in the eyeball.

It is obvious that we can radiate outwards in expression only that which we reflect or have absorbed. Out of a wide range of frequencies of colours hitting an organism, only those colours which have significance to the goals of that organism, will be absorbed and stored. The greater ability of those people on the inner layers inside the green band to absorb stimuli of all frequencies and colours indicates they are more peaceful, less reactive. But this also means they take a longer time to process stimuli so as to decide on their significance to the needs of the organism.

THE INTROVERT

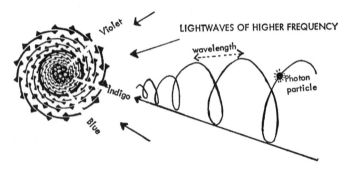

Fig. (213)

The figure above shows microwaves or Light penetrating through to the nucleus inside the green band when the higher energy photons in the Violet, Indigo, and Blue wavelengths spiral into the radiant energy field of consciousness. In the introvert the energy is held longer by gradually distributing towards the more external orbits but is not quickly scattered as in the case of the extravert. The introvert acts more like a prism with the psychic energies from within radiating outwards in reverse order to those absorbed by physical matter. The extravert, being more reactive, acts more like a mirror than a prism.

It will be obvious that as the energies passing to the inner side of the green layer are inward working and the colours on the surface are outward working, the types of personality absorbing energies from different ends of the spectrum will conflict unless they both understand their inner worlds of time and colour.

We have shown that the contractive forces of the universe such as the coldness of space which are inward working are balanced by the expansive forces of creativity. However we can see in the social sense that both these positive and negative forces can be misused and misdirected. The two-page sketch gives a few key words which will enable us to check against the realities of life before we go on to interpret the reasons for our basic drives.

Fig. (214)

THE STRUCTURE OF PERSONALITY IN NUCLEAR EVOLUTION
A THUMBNAIL SKETCH OF INPUTS AND OUTPUTS

Kind of Love or Self-regarding sentiments	General qualities of both the positive and negative types	Positive result in creativity and the individuality of expression.	Negative results in self-centredness disintegration of personality and inner conflicts.
DRIVE (1) RED	Sensation type : Orientated to transient external stimuli; the impulsive manipulation of objects affecting touch and experience in the immediate now, without much awareness of past or future events. His concrete reality is not related to flow of time which is always now. Relates all sensations to self pleasure or self pain and is unaware of inner worlds of others unless they are useful for purposes of self-esteem. The colour red brings on reactiveness and physical excitement, related to anger, pugnacity, aggressiveness, sensation, intensity, physical bully.	Wants to experience intense mental and physical excitement. Highly reactive to stimulation. Expresses energy through sex. Emphasis on the mating instincts and the bio-chemical experience of Love. Responds quickly to approval. Direct action preferred.	His attitudes bring inner conflict between the desire to conquer society or the opposite sex and the need to be left alone to experience alone. This produces ignorance of environment, feelings of flight and home to mother attitudes. Cannot take disapproval. Expects action from others on demand.
DRIVE (2) ORANGE	Optimistic type : A sensation type who is orientated to the future and contact with the community. Hopeful and optimistic at finding his real place in society, living intensely and meaningfully in the concrete world. Expansive and always seeking wider fields of experience. Experiences time as sensation in the present but applies it to the future instead of the immediate now. The colour orange relates well to herd instinct, ambition, agitation, restlessness, exploration and busyness. Movement of sexual energies towards thinking processes causes interest in politics and pride.	Seeks energetic social contact and acceptance, ambitious community nation or business. Likes big projects of world-wide scope and would love to expand. Quietly proud of his own dynamism but is introspective and aware of his own compulsions. Desires hope, social work and do-gooding.	Selfishly proud and ambitious for growth of business, political reputation or his social climbing. Drive belong gives him conflict with the desire to elbow his way around the community more effectively, using gifts of education, etc. for this purpose. Harbours foreign feeling and mistrust of others.
DRIVE (3) YELLOW	Intellectual thinking type : This type analyses everything and must know what and where. Uses intellect to cut up events into true or false, past or future and remains detached from the immediate now. Must know logical framework before capable of understanding anything, yet seeks originality and change. Weop as concepts based on theoretical content and temporary proofs in order to justify putting content into an ideal or hypothetical form. Often feels emptiness and coldness in relationships and develops zealousness to compensate. Experiences time as continuous flow of process. Insists on details and logical supremacy in all matters. Is self-assertive and relates to intellectual thinking, drive towards change, Love of novelty and mental excitement.	Seeks a liberating key thought and is constantly searching for new ideals, novel solutions, etc. in hope that his many expectations will be fulfilled. Needs sympathy and warm response from others and self-expression in his Ego. Has creative expression in art, literature, music, etc. Heightened sense of individuality causes separation from community.	Feels deprived of recognition. Conflict is generated within by the drive for fulfilment through constant change, and a vague feeling of emptiness. Woof and expecting critical rejection. Worries over insecure thinking, fear, and becomes mental bully. Dogmatic. Isolates self from activities of others and fears group power.
DRIVE (4) GREEN	Self-assertive type : The desire for power to survive and store up energy and "vital force" causes individuals to expend energies to get them. The need for emotional and spiritual security leads to feelings of lack. Such individuals seek the effectiveness and power to assert themselves in the community. Jealousy caused by loss of control over the love object need to be dealt with when arising from the possessive instincts. This type relates to self-centred love fixations, Love/hate emotions, power and feelings of absorption and retention. Self assurance and confidence may camouflage unacknowledged self-doubts. Experiences time as past present or future depending on each situation and its threat to security.	Strives to assert himself to obtain vital-force, money, love and to have his own ideas confirmed by others in order to establish inner security. Drive for vitality, stamina, wealth and security causes constructive effort to be made to solve problems. Adopts independent attitude and wants to overcome obstacles and assert himself on his own.	Expects confirmation to come from others but is unable to enforce his will and therefore puts blame for his failure on others. Conflict comes from the determination to assert his own ideas and a need to free himself from self-restraint and the restraints of society. Needs to free himself from limitations generally. Suffers from jealousy, hatred and selfishness.
DRIVE (5) BLUE	Feeling-satisfaction type : This type lives in a mental world of his own commitment to idealistic feelings. He is hindsighted and historical, living in a present composed of memories of the past. Existing concepts family values, recognised authorities and situations are all bound into his ideals and accepted as images of reality. His feelings for family and community, traditions and fixed sense experiences are imprisoned in an objective time so as to relax and feel satisfaction. He experiences time as binding all events into memories of emotional and mental concepts. Loves established ways, principles, ethics, morality.	Has a deep longing for fulfilment of his clearly worked out ideals and defined thoughts so as to find contentment and peace of mind, is satisfied when conditions settle, loves small children, judgement, love of commitment, reverence, devotion, fixed groups, idealism, etc. Reacts strongly to disturbers of the peace.	Conflict develops between the strong desire for contentment and the tense condition of discontent, caused by dissatisfaction with stagnating smugness of accepted authority of the status quo. Seeks dominion over inferiors and surrenders to superiors and suffers from his inability to be free from fixed ideas.

613

DRIVE (6) INDIGO	Intuition type: Discontinuity with the past and present gives this type a personality which is always living in the future. He appears to be divorced from concreteness because he does not identify reality with the senses. Is continually impatient for the present to catch up with the future already perceived. Not punctual and difficult to tie down to details, fixed concepts, ideas or plans. Instinctive need for communication, sensitivity, telepathy, intuition, integration, etc. Places his Faith in the future, in the not-yet-manifested; and experiences time as a telescoping of the future into the present, and the past as a dim mist.	Needs a conflict free relationship. Seeks sensitivity to the internal condition of others which brings out the faculty we know as taste. The great task is the discrimination between human intelligence and that which is extra-cerebral/supramental. Given to admiration, high inspiration, passiveness, and is quietest, visionary, anticipatory.	Conflict within is triggered by an inborn sensitivity to the impressions of others. This person fears the dark unconscious on the one hand and has a fascination with external intelligences and power for selfish ends on the other idol relationships are common, there may be envy of others talents, belittling others, and a tendency to be easily fascinated.
DRIVE (7) VIOLET	Imaginative type: This type seeks for an ideal state of harmony and enchantment as seen in the drama or the stage and is therefore out to make a good impression and become popular as a result of his charm. Tenderness he skilfully makes himself indispensable in situations. Is basically concerned with time and its annihilation orientated to the healing power of poetry and literature and its transforming effects through highly original metaphors. Needs an archetypal image of the Cosmic Intelligence otherwise conflict between "will" and the "imagination" develops. Tries to create a pattern of life and sets out an example of goodness. Experiences time in his imagination and is able to distort it in drama, art forms, poetry and imagery.	Has a deep sense of wonder, ecstasy bliss and self-surrender. Has a deep desire to integrate through tenderness and to be charmed by tenderness and the sympathetic emotions. Has a desire for magical transformation of chaos into bliss. Strives to make a good impression and influence others with the power of spiritual and magical images. Love of withdrawal, self humiliation, absolutism and has an instinct for divine order and enduring patterns.	Conflict between the desire for tender charm or sympathy on the one hand and an unconsciousness on the other of a tendency to criticise others for not understanding his own need for tenderness. The drive to imagine a heavenly state of bliss conflicts with the personal reality. Feels misunderstood through his inability to have enduring relationships at deep levels of being. Experiences shame, intense erotic imaginations, magical practices, self-denial and self abasement.
BLACK NUCLEAR CENTRE OF BEING:	Absolute type: Cannot compromise with uncertainty and hazard in the universe without self-surrender to Cosmic Intelligence and an "eternal now" as the real state of being. The annihilation of the "real external world" occurs when the individual ego unites with the self-consciousness behind all of the manifested creation and notions of bodily objects. This type has a desire to bring order out of chaos by the "willing" of eternal events in time—the function of prayer. The drive of self-annihilation creates a stubbornness and desire for absolute freedom to be a law unto oneself. Self mastery involves coping with this secret desire to play God at the heart of all being. Unyielding, certain, over-confident, hard of heart, spiritually ruthless, self-defeating, and on rare occasions completely broken in "will" and lost in the dark night of the soul. Must surrender to ultimate self or becomes destructive instead of creative. Is often grateful for small recognitions and does not expect rewards. Will serve only what he feels is a universal or cosmic will. Messianic pretensions must be coped with for psychic health as they are driving forces in the secret desires of many more men than is believed.	Seeks to become Godlike and will obstinately resist currently accepted ideals like a John the Baptist and rejects any encroachments which may impede his own actions. Becomes his own authority and tries to master his dark unconscious in order to achieve a certainty and lasting order. Is defiant of temporal authority and feels often to be terribly alone. Is in love with Love itself. May be in contact with the supramental Self but cannot easily surrender to it without passing through the divine without demand unasked. Can love without reward, ing in return. Once liberation from Self is achieved enlightenment follows the struggle.	Conflict arises in facing the much needed self-annihilation of Ego which is his unfulfilled desire. This desire stimulates attitudes of obstinate and defiant absolutism. A stubbornness which will conflict often with the desire for absolute freedom to fulfil his own will at any cost to himself or to others, may result in anarchy and chaos. Many adolescent students pass through this phase briefly as they compromise with worldliness. Divided against self, they can become suicidal, self-destructive, paranoiac and sometimes an Ego-maniac who tries to conquer the world instead of himself. In extreme cases mental health breaks down into psychoses.

NOTES: The human fear of "Voidness" (empty space, totalmind, God, etc.) is in depth the fear of absolute and total dominion which life has given over ourselves so that we may experience God Consciousness (I AM ness). Such pure selfless awareness, which has to live with itself by seeing itself in all things, removes the duality of subjective and objective, good and evil, self and not-self, and penetrates beneath the separative and different styles in which Truth appears to dress itself. In fact Truth has no style, may appear oversimple and naive or extremely complex. It is the Self that clothes it in different styles. Ultimately we reject God (total I AM ness) when we reject our awareness of that which is unaware in us. When we become aware, when we meet another self who is more aware, we increase our awareness. There is no other way. Meditation alone cannot give awareness of THAT which lives only for others and loves all things great and small as itself. Hence man incarnates in the flesh for the purpose of soul-making.

There is an elaborate balance between all the above primal drives whose functions overlap. Each personality is a time-space bubble inhabiting several worlds of time.

If we followed the suggestion a little way back to take an eight-colour Luscher Test, then we have ready-made material to use here and to apply to the discussion of the worlds of the introvert and the extravert. Suppose we selected blue as our first choice, which puts us among the introverts, among those who take time to respond. Even if we give a spontaneous response on the spur of the moment, that is not the end of the matter for us. We continue to reflect and turn over in our minds what has been said or done. In other words everything is taken to heart and if the experience has been hurtful to our ego, we walk around in a fit of the "the blues." If we are living with a red, orange or yellow level mate, our emotional churning and gloomy silence will not only be depressing but also bewildering. "What's eating you?" they say, "Why don't you come out with it? Say something. Express yourself. Be spontaneous!" In other words, your yellow level mate is asking your blue level to behave as he/ she would in your situation.

The ancient Hindu Samkhya system behind all Yoga attempts to get conscious control over the different levels of awareness by the following techniques: YAMA: the will to investigate our mental nature by following specific resolutions; and abstention from: stealing, covetousness, attachment, twisting of Truth and anger. NIYAMA: Study of reactions of the body and mind, such as the purifying of thoughts; inward observation of restlessness and of self study. ASANA: Control of intellect and body to allow the free flow of psychic forces through the physiological mechanism. Control of physical postures and nervous energies. PRANAYAMA: Control of Prana (*vital force*); controlling the expansion of individual energy into cosmic energy. Techniques of breathing inwardly rather than with the lungs. Sending of psychic breath (psychic electricity) through the body. PRATYAHARA: Raising of lower psychic feelings from the mental and sensual levels to the higher levels. Withdrawal of energies and consciousness from all bodily sensations. DHARANA (*Concentration*): Fixation of total attention on an object or idea. Union of the self with an object or idea so that it becomes Self in self-concentration. CONCENTRATION of Self on the object of attention while visions come and go—light, sounds, etc. DHYANA (*Meditation*): Focussing of attention on supreme spiritual goal or archetype so constant that other thoughts do not enter, and sending 100% suggestion in continuous meditation. Vision of supreme Lord of Body (Self) in the heart like a lamp, which shines everywhere but burns in a limited region like the sun. SAMADHI *(Contemplation)*: State of superconscious. " I " identifies with supreme consciousness in union of individual with Cosmos. State of suspended animation in deep trance; not aware of awareness; like a deep sleep, out of time where Self is free of material conditions and of self-orientated sensations.

615

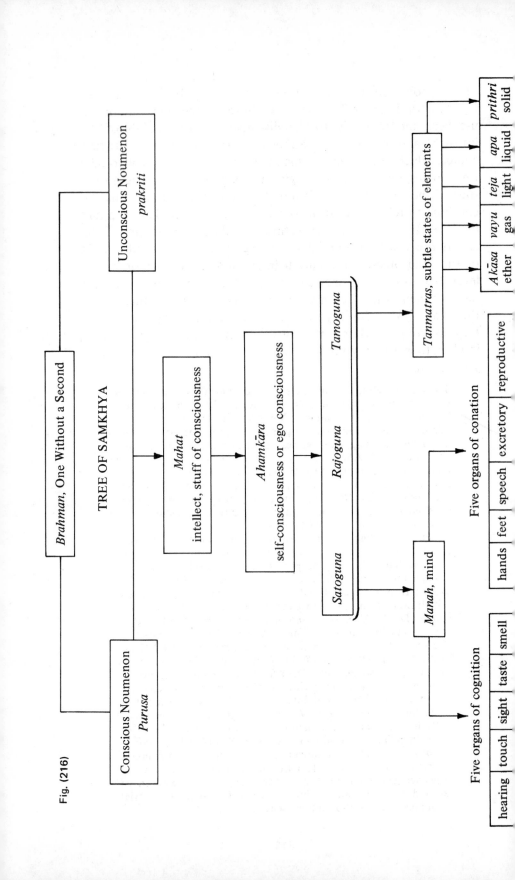

Fig. (216)

TREE OF SAMKHYA

Brahman, One Without a Second

Conscious Noumenon *Purusa*

Unconscious Noumenon *prakriti*

Mahat intellect, stuff of consciousness

Ahamkāra self-consciousness or ego consciousness

Satoguna   Rajoguna   Tamoguna

Tanmatras, subtle states of elements

| *Akāsa* ether | *vayu* gas | *teja* light | *apa* liquid | *prithri* solid |

Manah, mind

Five organs of conation

| hands | feet | speech | excretory | reproductive |

Five organs of cognition

| hearing | touch | sight | taste | smell |

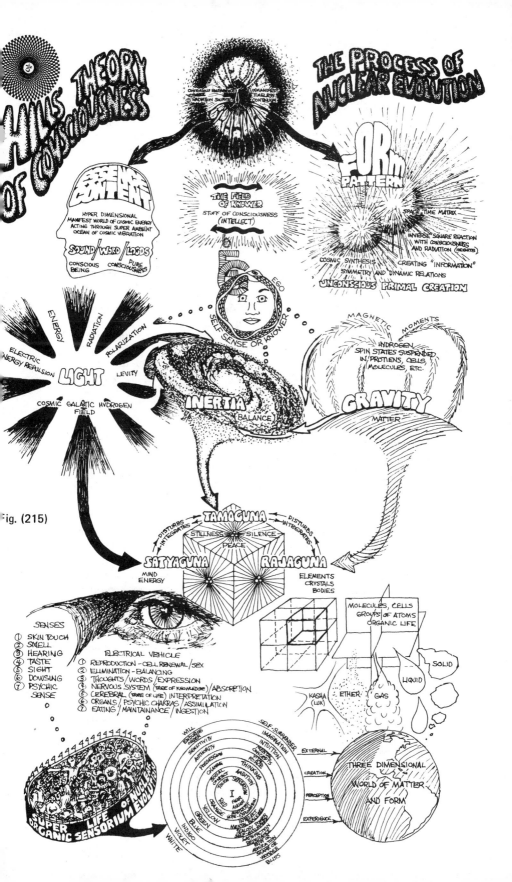

HILLS THEORY OF CONSCIOUSNESS

THE PROCESS OF NUCLEAR EVOLUTION

Fig. (215)

ESSENCE CONTENT
HYPER DIMENSIONAL MANIFEST WORLD OF COSMIC ENERGY ACTING THROUGH SUPER AMBIENT OCEAN OF COSMIC VIBRATION

SOUND / WORD / LOGOS
CONSCIOUS BEING   PURE CONSCIOUSNESS

THE FIELD OF KNOWER
STUFF OF CONSCIOUSNESS (INTELLECT)

FORM PATTERN
SPACE - TIME MATRIX
INVERSE SQUARE REACTION WITH CONSCIOUSNESS AND RADIATION (HEIGHTS)
COSMIC SYNTHESIS   CREATING "INFORMATION"
SYMMETRY AND DYNAMIC RELATIONS
UNCONSCIOUS PRIMAL CREATION

SELF SENSE OR KNOWER   EGO

ENERGY   RADIATION   POLARIZATION
ELECTRIC ENERGY REPULSION   LEVITY
LIGHT
COSMIC GALACTIC HYDROGEN FIELD

INERTIA
BALANCE

MAGNETIC MOMENTS
HYDROGEN SPIN STATES SUSPENDED IN PROTIENS, CELLS, MOLECULES, ETC.
GRAVITY
MATTER

DISTURBS INTEGRATES   **TAMOGUNA**   DISTURBS INTEGRATES
STILLNESS   SILENCE
PEACE
SATYAGUNA   **RAJAGUNA**
MIND ENERGY   ELEMENTS CRYSTALS BODIES

SENSES
① SKIN TOUCH
② SMELL
③ HEARING
④ TASTE
⑤ SIGHT
⑥ DOWSING
⑦ PSYCHIC SENSE

ELECTRICAL VEHICLE
① REPRODUCTION - CELL RENEWAL / SEX
② ELIMINATION - BALANCING
③ THOUGHTS / WORDS / EXPRESSION
④ NERVOUS SYSTEM (TREE OF KNOWLEDGE) / ABSORPTION
⑤ CEREBRAL (TREE OF LIFE) INTERPRETATION
⑥ ORGANS / PSYCHIC CHAKRAS / ASSIMILATION
⑦ EATING / MAINTAINANCE / INGESTION

MOLECULES, CELLS GROUPS OF ATOMS ORGANIC LIFE

SOLID
LIQUID
KASHA (LUX)   ETHER   GAS

SUPER ORGANIC SENSORIUM   LIFE OF NUCLEAR EVOLUTION

WILL   SELF-SURRENDER
ENDURING FORM   IMAGINATION
SENSITIVITY   INTUITION
AUTHORITY   SECURITY
POSSESSION   PEACE
CHANGE   THINKING
CONTROL   AMBITION
SENSATION
I
EXTERNAL
CREATION
PERCEPTION
EXPERIENCE

THREE DIMENSIONAL WORLD OF MATTER AND FORM

RED   ORANGE   YELLOW   GREEN   BLUE   INDIGO   VIOLET   WHITE

Explanation of the Samkhya system can be shown in diagram form as it developed through thousands of years of clairvoyance and mathematical genius of the ancient researchers. It was embellished by many who added and subtracted from it by whim or by penchant of those without direct perception or ability to do research. It is given here in the pure form as detected by the Supersensitive faculty of these mystic researchers who used Supersensonic methods to detect the different lokas or worlds of existence. The diagram is given here merely for students of the Gita and Vedanta to relate the findings of Nuclear Evolution which concur with its seven levels of manifestation.

REFLECTED COLOURS AND PRIMARY LIGHT

In the Luscher test there are 12 tables which give the special nuances of shade which are accurately "tuned" to psychological criteria where accuracy is an essential factor in carrying out the test. Anyone who wishes to study the effects of *reflected colour* will find the Luscher tests indispensable (see references given for this purpose). Complete understanding of this enables accurate diagnosis. However the detailed study of effects of *primary light* and colour on the person when using an energy source such as a lamp tuned to a specific frequency with colour filters, is a different and more potent proposition since the primary source of the colour is a form of raw radiant energy of photon particles which have not been reflected from an absorbent surface and are therefore not "polarised" by partial absorption, or by the angle at which they are reflected to the eye or skin. These photons are "invisible" colour rays since the energy cannot be "seen" except when it strikes its receptor.

The science of Supersensonics involves the external psycho-physical perception of radiations of subtle energy and primarily deals with the polarization of wave-fields sent out and received by the vehicle of consciousness, while this book on the rainbow body deals with the nature and evolution of consciousness and the way the kundalini manifests internally through the chakra system.

In both external and internal perception the primary light of radiation and the light of consciousness are identical, differences only arising in them according to sensory discrimination of the change between one object of sensation and another. Light strikes the psycho-physical receptors which themselves are just as invisible to ordinary eyesight as the chakra energies themselves. Light energies are invisible and their effects can be seen by our senses only when absorption of light by the receptors and the antenna of the nervous system takes place. The resulting stimulation of nerve currents from the receptors is what we describe in Supersensonics as natural biofeedback signals. The person's body and the environment are a natural biofeedback loop which responds to internal and external sensations from the receptors. All dowsing and psychic sensations are an elementary form of feedback signal from some object or energetic system on the subtle energy levels of perception, which then interacts with our receptors.

The receptors in this case are not merely the light sensitive rods and cones of the eye but the residual " memory " in the cells of the skin and at the " nuclear " level of the neurons and the dendrites which shoot out to receive it. The " need " or the deficit of the nucleus causes the dendrites to grow towards the point of greatest stimulation. There is the analogy of the plants and their shoots growing towards the source of the Light.

The more the inputs of a specific frequency, the more stimulation is required for " growth "; the wider the " rings " in the tree, the bigger the pipes grow for the streaming sap. Hence a large tree is soon lifting tons of water to its top. Similarly the receptors of Light and colour in the human body are in deficit the moment they are " attuned " to a much needed input, when there is no opportunity for " output ". The sap in the tree must have somewhere to go for the roots to continue drinking in large quantities of water. Hence lack of expression and " engagement " with the Cosmic Source of Light is just as much " deficit " as the lack of " attunement ". Nuclear Evolution is finding both input and output. In the use of PRIMARY Light as compared with REFLECTED Light we excite and stimulate the " feedback " required by the Nucleus of the cell for real " growth " of the sensitive dendrites. Because of this the colours selected and rejected by the personality will be more accurately determined; and with a proper range of filters the colours can be mixed to give frequencies of light which can give any subtle colour radiation. Instead of a " diagnosis " the attunement becomes a " treatment ".

THE FAVOURITE COLOUR selected by a person in a test at our Centre indicates the drive required to compensate for the person's deficit. *An example* can be shown in the choice of Red by a person who is suffering from Cardiac deficiency. They will choose Red as their least favoured colour. This colour means high pent-up excitement with a passionate intensity and the rejection of Red shows that the subject is suffering from a bio-energetic deficiency in spontaneity, lacks the much needed will to conquer his environment. The effort is too much, he suffers from his excitement, impulsiveness, fear, and any exciting intensity. At the same time as rejecting Red, heart cases usually choose primary Blue or Indigo as a favourite colour. This colour means Peace, contentment, the satisfaction of settled defined thought, and quiet. The condition therefore required by the personality to compensate for the deficit of pathogenic excitement and his fear of impulsiveness is "Peace and quiet". A person may look for peace in quietness and never find.

Using Fig. 196 and the table in Fig. 214, it is possible to establish the positive and negative expression of the drives in each individual person as it manifests in their fulfilment or lack of it. Similarly it is now possible to find out how they project, each in his own way, their deficit into the psycho-social atmosphere. The total sum of all these individual tensions and conflicts develops into a mass neurosis, and this aggregate condition can only be cured at the level of each person. Only when each individual person knows how to handle the energies in the basic drives within, can there be any real evolutionary advance. The testing of personality patterns in industry, in politics, in art and in science, is fundamental to the understanding of Nuclear Evolution and its penetration into the dense material fabric of the social scene.

In the past, grand schemes for the improvement of mankind in any or all of these areas have failed or at most succeeded for only a limited period of time, because the essential dynamic and premise of Nuclear Evolution has been ignored, namely that it is impossible to change the world unless each and every man faces the challenge of first changing himself. You may be saying inside yourself that this is an impossible dream, but experimentation is already being done in banks and other large corporations, using colour tests to determine the suitability of certain employees both for their job and for their relationship with other employees. Other techniques are also available, such as aura balancing, which is outlined in "Supersensonics" and "Alive to the Universe". The practical value of detecting the aura colours is described, revealing methods of direct .perception which most people have thought of as psychic but which anyone can use once shown how. To operate effectively it is necessary for most people to have these tools which operate below the conscious mind. The results are just as accurate as conscious signals and the fact that information is received unconsciously does not make it any less valid. The truth is that the conscious mind is just as inaccurate in perceiving the ultimate nature of reality as the unconscious. It will be some time before mankind recognises the low state of its conscious faculties and begins to use the gifts of its unconscious perceptions. It is not often realised how many successful businessmen operate just as much from hunches as they do from cold calculating reason. Now it is only a matter of time before our present civilisation realises the psychophysical nature of divination and applies more sophisticated research to the phenomenon at all levels of life.

LOOKING AT CONSCIOUSNESS

The onion-skin layers (or shells) of the orb of consciousness shown in Fig. 196 by the rings of colour are a reversed order "mirror-image" of consciousness as it might look from an enlightened "self-observer" from the outside-in. This means that Light absorbed by the entity from outside-inwards has the colours reversed in order as in a reflected rainbow. The sages of India likened these layers of consciousness to seven different kinds of Yoga into which the light penetrated in different ways —some as wisdom, some as thought or mind, some as devotion, some as intelligence, some as intuition, some as imagination, and some as the physical body. The light was blocked by the mis-chanelling of passion or excitement at every level. The Sages compared the passions to those heavy clouds which sometimes shut out the view of the sun's light entirely, or obscured the true brilliancy of its Light. The Vedas describe the mis-direction of the manic-type energies of the personality (the need for external objects and restlessness and impatience to reaching a goal object) as a violent wind, which agitates the surface of the water so that it cannot reflect the splendour of the sky above. If the individual absorbs into all the layers, the full spectrum of colours (white light) this is a full "input" into the orb of consciousness. If however he "ingests" them totally and radiates nothing outwards, he has no outputs and his deficit of consciousness would *desire* the colour Black. This would turn the energies inward into depressive states. If however we "digest" them and channel them all properly through our endocrine system we become Self-giving and radiate them back to the source; our consciousness then tends to reject the Black. We reject annihilation in favour of Being and Creativity.

On the heroic journey towards the Creative Void (the complement of the Black) we can only see this reality from inside-outwards from the sphere of consciousness we ourselves have reached. On this journey we tend to reject the Void because it is an unfulfilled desire. After, and only after, we have reached the Creative Void can we look back (outside-in) at all the bands of colour which represent a frequency response in consciousness to the absorbed Light on which we feed. We then see that these colours ingested which create our psychological dispositions and channel our bio-energy, are complementary to the ones we radiate. When we understand the true goal of the personality is to reach the Creative Void then we tend to surrender to it, not by accepting the Black but by going through it. This is the well-known terror of the " Black night of the soul " of self-annihilation, and represents the great difference between the positive expression of self-fulfilment and the negative emotion of self-negation and false humility.

To read the two preceding paragraphs without relating them to experience or at least bringing to them the full concentration of an insightful intuition and imagination, is to fail to comprehend one of the fundamentals of Nuclear Evolution. So it is well to pause here and to question the depth of our own understanding. If we have already made drastic changes or leaps in consciousness then we can use them as validation of what has been said here by asking ourselves a few self-confronting questions:

1. What was the change and when was it made?
2. Was it easy to make?
3. If so, was it a REAL CHANGE or an acting out of a change that was expected of us? Was it pressured by events or was it some change we chose freely to reach reality?
4. If it was REAL was it preceded by an experience of being "at the end of the road" or "with our back to the wall"?
5. What finally compelled or impelled us to make the leap or change?

If we have answered these questions honestly we have put ourselves in touch with the real dynamic of genuine change. At the University of the Trees in Boulder Creek, California, resident faculty and students have an opportunity to accelerate the growth and change process by means of "creative conflict" in a group held together by love and trust. When it seems that one of the group is avoiding change, in spite of many patient confrontations and "mirroring" of him/herself, then the challenge becomes stronger and stronger, sometimes reaching the point of "change or leave", but whereas life in its ordinary course also offers these ultimatums, in the group situation they are recognisable and understood. In the so-called "outside world" our battered personality is often bewildered by what life is trying to tell us; we stay in the black state of despair and after a period of acute depression drop back into the old patterns and the whole process starts over again.

Two of the editors of this book have been through this experience. Both have reached the end of the road through their refusal to let go of their attachments and both ultimately got to grips with their negative doubts and fears about losing the object of their attachment. The final breakthrough for each of us came after much pain, but although we are still aware of the old patterns we have, with the encouragement of the group "creative conflict",* broken through to a new level of seeing that makes our old apprehensive and fearful state look shabby and very small. We feel that the current appalling divorce rate could probably be halved if married couples had the opportunity to face their attachments, doubts, fears and jealousies as we were compelled to do.

MANIFESTATION THROUGH CONSCIOUS NUCLEAR EVOLUTION

There is no proof of consciousness except "Life" itself; which to a convinced materialist, can be seen as a constant random change in the structure of matter without any need for something called "life". But there are definite proofs in the way consciousness as "life" expresses itself in the body which can be verified in the way the seven shells of consciousness react physically to the spectrum of Light.

What follows here is not easy to grasp mentally because it is so simple. Because of the structure of personality it will appear simple to the simple-minded and complex to the complex-minded. Those who can understand it can class themselves as a "Divine Fool" who can see that indeed the Emperor has no clothes on! I say this because of a general awareness of the trend in our universities today to think that the "pure" consciousness, which cannot be separated from anything, grasped by the mind, or defined to the western mind, is not worth talking about as there can be no "meaning" in it for philosophers to dally with. Intellect cannot experience *wholes*, and cannot observe the observer who sees all the outer life with the eye of the seer within. Every outer act of a man has an inner man pushing him into action who is both absolute Self and self-regarding.

Man who is not liberated from *conceptions* (level or drive No. 5) and is still imprisoned in imaginations (level No.7) will quite naturally experience and manifest a "time-bound" consciousness of Cosmic events in which he has no power to CHANGE in a fundamental way, his own energy states. Self-limitation acts throughout the total self-hood and its physical embodiment.

---

* See "What is Creative Conflict?" at end of this chapter, and also Part III.

At level 7 the love of Absolutism is born which proceeds on to an 8th domain (not a level or shell or limited system but a domain over which dominion is exercised) of pure Being which enables us to see that the hazards and uncertainty in Life (if any are experienced) are merely a man's inability in lower states of consciousness to change " life " or to become complete master of himself. He therefore surrenders in his Self-humility before God (and not necessarily before men) in his own desire to surrender to the *Cosmic Will* and to serve the Absolute Self. He is then ripe and ready for Conscious Nuclear Evolution because the master becomes the servant, and he interprets the Cosmic Will as his own will. The next step after this surrender is embodiment of this will as exemplified in the untiring efforts and total commitment of all Saints, Prophets and Messengers.

INTERPRETING THE " COSMIC " WILL

The higher Wisdom behind the directive intelligence of the plan we have called the " Cosmic Will " is more than just a knowledge and an understanding of the programme for the conscious evolution of humanity. It is absolute Self-Mastery in action, reconciling all the levels of Love in the drives of humanity through the use of Light. Here I do not refer to Light in a metaphorical sense but those specific frequencies of " LIFE " which resonate with the personality in a direct experience of individuality in which the whole of humanity shares. It may be colour, sound, radiation or pure conscious-ness of Truth. Such an expression penetrating into the heart of a positive nucleus of only a small group of men, changes the course of history. The man or woman who brings this Reality into active manifestation can do nothing but obey, for they *are* the channel of the power of Consciousness and Supreme Will.

DEFINING THE INDEFINABLE ABSOLUTE

The essence of consciousness is returning to the beginning. All action in Nuclear Evolution is only the motion of returning to THAT which made us. The whole earth and our bodies and that which we eat in the form of "life" is made of some form of Light. To experience that outer Light and return to the inner is the purpose of LIFE on earth. The next few words will be easily understood by those who already "know" but for those who may consider all this an intellectual exercise, the reading of this book from Fig. 190 onwards relating the spheres of consciousness to the actual spectrum, will make a second attempt more profitable. The way of return to the original Self is not new but it can only become intelligible to man when its expression is in accord with the time and place, as it has been at certain periods down the ages.

The energy of the pyramid was researched by Christopher Hills after discovering the divining methods of L. Turenne for probing unseen energies in 1958. The work of Chaumery and Belizal with these forces inspired by Mr. Bovis in France caused Christopher Hills to purchase many different types of divining equipment and to collaborate with Noel Macbeth of England who privately translated over one hundred books on the subject. These works are now in the author's collection at his London centre. The work to validate the Pi ray and its connection with the "life force" generated by pyramid forms and other radiesthesia devices is written up in the book "Rays From The Capstone" by Christopher Hills, published in 1976. A deeper study of this divining research done in 1958/1959 including pyramid radiations and their connection with the psycho-physical field of consciousness and the rising of kundalini was published in 1975 under the title of "Supersensonics". The connection of the pyramid with the "Rainbow Body" can be researched by anyone with the tools of radiesthesia and radionics. The construction of psychotronic generators such as the pyramid and its relationship to the half sphere is related to the radiation of harmonic vibrations which resonate with certain angles and colors. Since this is outlined in great detail in "Supersensonics" there is no purpose in repeating it here.

The Pyramid and the Greek transcendental number Pi preserve for posterity a certain knowledge acquired by man from the beginning. Pyramus means "to rise at birth" and mastery of the shells of consciousness involves a rebirth of the individuality.*

From the beginning this knowledge has been hidden at some times and shouted from the housetops quite safely at other times. It has been passed down through the ancient Rishis, disguised as a hierarchial priesthood in the Druids and initiates of Mycenae, hidden by the Sufi traditions, shot through the healing and divining abilities of the Essenes and released through Jesus of Nazareth, imprisoned in the structure of the Great Pyramid, carved in symbol on the rocks of Tintagel, enshrined in the Arthurian legend which can be seen today in the pathway of initiation around Glastonbury Tor, and all contained in the seven spheres of consciousness shown in Fig. (217)

Fig. (217)

Symbol found carved on rocks at Tintagel Cornwall England from Pre-Roman times representing Consciousness.

---

* See pages 580 et seq. "Supersensonics"
pub. University of the Trees Press

Humanity has walked the path into the Centre towards the Holy Reality of the Grail through the higher Wisdom of many cultures and for those who have the eyes to see and the ears to hear they are all saying the same thing – "I shall return" and "I shall rise again" and the rainbow is God's promise and a sign, not to a stupid and illiterate tribal group, but a symbolic covenant hidden for those who can accept the words that follow as Truth.

After illumination and the experience of total unity of Self at the 8th domain of self-surrender one does not stop growing in awareness. No person has " arrived " at pure self-hood without becoming " non-person " and one goes to the bottom of the class in a new domain of Being. One becomes progressively nothing, so that the something " Centre Within " we have called LIFE emerges as pure changeless consciousness of " I " standing securely in the midst of all changes. Even the very elect are not given to seeing clearly " at once " that it is the ultimate subject willing all changes for the Lord of the body, who is Self-existent, Self-luminous and Self-satisfied, and absolutely in charge of the whole body (and of creation). All sensations and dissatisfactions are conscious communications of Ego to Ego, Self-consciousness to Self, therefore the way to change the creation if one is not satisfied, is to stop all the divisive thinking and return to the one consciousness who is master of the body and soul-stuff.

The universe is the body and seat of consciousness together and it can only be known by indwelling consciousness itself looking outwards from its centre. Consciousness is all, both subject and object ; the total mechanism of perception and the perceptions themselves are objects of consciousness which change only with changes of " I ".

These are the words which mean very little or nothing to anyone who has not been able to recognise their own levels of consciousness through the use of Fig. 196, but to him who is at the portals of the obscure black night of the soul and has surrendered without fear, it says along with all the messengers, I AM THAT, and there is to be no change in the Absolute " I " unless it so wills it in the state of conscious Nuclear Evolution ; this individuality has the power given to it from the Absolute to change its own creation through incarnation into matter as the Human Self-luminous reflection of the Lord of Creation.

Those who are truly Messengers of God upon earth are wholly united with the Will of Christ and receive all other men who seek this Holy Grail, into them as they would receive a Christ.

WHAT IS CREATIVE CONFLICT?

Creative Conflict is a technique developed by Christopher Hills at Centre House in London over a period of six years and later used and taught by the student/faculty at the University of the Trees in California. It is a method whereby conflict, disagreement and the normally destructive human interchange becomes creative and growth-producing. The first basic requirement for its successful functioning is total openness, which does not mean total exposure of all one's mental and emotional garbage, but rather both openness in sharing real feelings and openness to others in a state of receptivity.

The second requirement is a full understanding of the levels of consciousness described earlier in this book, so that there are no basic assumptions that other people function, think, feel or act as you do. In other words, for conflict to be creative and to reach a positive and beneficial outcome, the Yellow intellectual has to allow for the Red level man of immediate action to become restless over meticulous and lengthy planning. The Red level activist on his part has to accept that the Blue level group member may be seeking an authoritative basis for his decisions, while the Yellow level planner is trying to fit everything into a logical framework. All these differences and many more have been and still are the cause of unresolved conflict and of tension in groups, committees, company boards and, on a larger scale, international conferences.

The advantages of working in a group with a range and variety of personalities far outweigh the temporary irritations and frustrations, once creative conflict is understood and skilfully practiced. To have ourselves mirrored back by others is one of the surest and most effective ways of discovering what we manifest in reality so that it becomes increasingly difficult to fool ourselves with false self-images and ego-salving concepts of who we are or even of what our potential is. In creative conflict our "blind spots" become blatantly apparent and once these are seen and recognised then the real growth work begins and Nuclear Evolution for the individual and the group becomes an exciting prospect. One of the most rewarding experiences for students at the University of the Trees is to see someone freely grow and change, not superficially but basically and permanently. A number of examples come to mind. There was the Red level, reactive, egotistical man who, because he had a highly paid job and contributed generously to the work at the University, felt that he deserved more attention and recognition than anyone else, and became indignant and resentful when others seemed more highly favoured. One of the women students, an intelligent Yellow level intellectual who had been a spiritual seeker for several years and felt herself to be advanced in comparison with the other members of the group, separated herself from others by her superior spiritual attitude. After two years of creative conflict the man is one of the most open to group feedback and has written a book about his evolutionary experiences. The woman, after some heavy confrontations in which the group showed her how her ego was operating, now has become more humble and more human and has ceased to make the rest of the group feel like second-class citizens. Many more examples could be given of change that has gradually taken place with the skilful aid of the Director, Christopher Hills, and the persistence of a group committed to love and to growth.

BASIC PRINCIPLES OF CREATIVE CONFLICT

- We are whatever disturbs us (we own that the disturbance is our problem).

- We come in with "total openness", which means that we are receptive both to feedback and to the inner worlds of others, and are willing to share our real feelings.

- We agree to disagree, recognising everyone's uniqueness, and working from there to get to the real cause of any disturbance.

- We go beyond the words (language barrier) to the essence of the being that is trying to express.

- We agree that everyone has truth from their own viewpoint.

- We do not make speeches or toss in opinions.

- We avoid "red herrings" and quibblings, i.e. observations, opinions, etc. that divert the energy from the mainstream.

- We check ourselves and others for projections.

- We make sure we have heard words correctly by deep listening and obtaining confirmation from the speaker of their meaning before replying. (Mirroring)

REFERENCES

PART I

Aaronson, Bernard "HYPNOTIC INDUCTION OF COLORED ENVIRONMENTS", Perceptual and Motor Skills, 18, 30, 1964b.

Aaronson, Bernard, "HYPNOSIS, TIME RATE PERCEPTION, AND PERSONALITY," Journal of Schizophrenia, 2, 11-1 11-14, 1968a.

Aaronson, Bernard, "HYPNOTIC ALTERATIONS OF SPACE AND TIME," International Journal of Parapsychology 10, 5-36, 1968b.

Aaronson, Bernard and Osmond, Humphrey (Ed.) PSYCHEDEL—ICS, Anchor Books, (Doubleday & Co. Inc., New York) 1970.

Aaronson, Bernard, and Mundschenk, P. SOME SPATIAL STEREOTYPES OF TIME. Presented at Eastern Psychological Association meetings, Washington, D.C., 1968.

Abrams, Albert, M.D. NEW CONCEPTS IN DIAGNOSIS AND TREATMENT, The Philopolis Press, San Francisco, 1916.

Assagiolo Roberto, PSYCHOSYNTHESIS, New York, Viking Press, 1965.

Abell, George, EXPLORATION OF THE UNIVERSE, Holt, Rinehart and Winston, New York, 1969.

Bagchi, B.K. and Wenger, M.A. "ELECTROPHYSIOLOGICAL CORRELATES OF SOME YOGA EXERCISES" International Congress of Neurological Sciences, First Session, 3, 141-46, 1957.

Beasley, Victor R. DIMENSIONS OF ELECTRO-VIBRATORY PHENOMENA, University of the Trees Press, Boulder Creek, CA, 1975

Best, C.H. and Taylor, N.B. THE HUMAN BODY, Henry Holt and Co., New York, 1932.

Bethe, Hans A. "WHAT HOLDS THE NUCLEUS TOGETHER?" Scientific American, Sept. 1953.

Bethe, Hans A. and Morrison P. ELEMENTARY NUCLEAR THEORY, Wiley, New York, 1967.

Boring, Edwin G. SENSATION AND PERCEPTION IN THE HISTORY OF EXPERIMENTAL PSYCHOLOGY, Appleton-Century-Crosts, Inc., 1942.

Brown, Barbara B. NEW MIND, NEW BODY, Bantam Books, 1974.

Burr, Harold Saxton, PhD. BLUEPRINT FOR IMMORTALITY -- THE ELECTRIC PATTERNS OF LIFE, London Neville Spearman, Ltd., 1972. American edition: THE FIELDS OF LIFE. OUR LINKS WITH THE UNIVERSE, New York, Ballantine Books, Inc. 1973.

Capra, Fritjof, THE TAO OF PHYSICS, Berkeley, CA, Shambhala, 1975.

Carlson, A.J., Johnson, V., and Cavert, H.M. THE MACHINERY OF THE BODY, University of Chicago Press, 1961.

Clark, Ronald W. EINSTEIN: THE LIFE AND TIMES, The World Publishing Co., New York and Cleveland, 1971.

Dass, Baba Ram, THE ONLY DANCE THERE IS, Garden City, NY, Anchor/Doubleday, 1974.

Day, Langston, with de la Warr, George, NEW WORLDS BEYOND THE ATOM, Vincent Stuart, Ltd., London, 1956. MATTER IN THE MAKING, Vincent Stuart, Ltd., London, 1966.

De Chardin, Pierre Teilhard, THE PHENOMENON OF MAN, Translated by Bernard Wall, Harper and Brothers, New York, 1959.

The De la warr Laboratories Ltd., "MIND AND MATTER", A quarterly journal. The Radionic Centre Organisation, Raleigh Park Road, Oxford. (Newsletter.)

Fox, C.F. "THE STRUCTURE OF CELL MEMBRANES" Scientific American, 226(2) 31-38, 1972.

Gaierluce, Gay, BIOLOGICAL RHYTHMS IN HUMAN AND ANIMAL PHYSIOLOGY, Dover Books, 1971.

Gallert, Mark L., N.D., M.Sc., NEW LIGHT ON THERAPEUTIC ENERGIES, James Clarke and Co., Ltd., London, 1966.

Goldsby, R.A. CELLS AND ENERGY, Macmillan, New York, 1967.

Gray, Henry, ANATOMY, Bounty Books, New York, 1977.

Gray, H.J., and Isaacs, A., A NEW DICTIONARY OF PHYSICS, Longman, London, 1975.

Green, D.E. and Bruckner, R.F., "THE MOLECULAR PRINCIPLES OF BIOLOGICAL MEMBRANE CONSTRUCTION AND FUNCTION", BioScience, 23(1) 13-19, 1972.

Hameroff, Stuart Roy, "CH'I: A NEURAL HOLOGRAM? MICROTUBULES, BIOHOLOGRAPHY, AND ACUPUNCTURE", American Journal of Chinese Medicine, Vol. 2, No. No. 2: 163-170, 1974.

Hasler, A.D. and Larson, J.A., "THE HOMING SALMON", Scientific American, 193: 72-76, offprint No. 411 Freeman, San Francisco, 1955.

Hewitt, Paul, CONCEPTUAL PHYSICS: A NEW INTRODUCTION TO YOUR ENVIRONMENT", Little Brown, San Francisco, 1976.

Hewish, Anthony, "PULSARS AND HIGH DENSITY PHYSICS", Nobel Prize Lecture, 1974. Science 188 (June 13, 1975), 1079-1083.

Hills, Christopher, RAYS FROM THE CAPSTONE: HARNESSING PYRAMID ENERGY, University of the Trees Press, Boulder Creek, CA, 1976.

Hills, Christopher, SUPERSENSONICS: THE SPIRITUAL PHYSICS OF ALL VIBRATIONS FROM ZERO TO INFINITY, University of the Trees Press, Boulder Creek, CA, 1975.

Kaufmann, William J., III, RELATIVITY AND COSMOLOGY, Harper and Row, New York, 1973.

Hoyle, Fred, ASTRONOMY AND COSMOLOGY, W.H. Freeman and Co., San Francisco, 1975.

Jastrow, Robert and Thompson, Malcolm, ASTRONOMY: FUNDAMENTALS AND FRONTIERS, 2nd ed. Wiley, New York, 1977.

Karagulla, Shafica, M.D., BREAKTHROUGH TO CREATIVITY -
-- YOUR HIGHER SENSE PERCEPTIONS, DeVorss and
Co., Inc. Los Angeles.

Katz, B., "HOW DO CELLS COMMUNICATE", Scientific
American, 205(3): 209 offprint No. 98, Freeman,
San Francisco, 1961.

Kendrew, J.C. "THREE-DIMENSIONAL STRUCTURE OF A
PROTEIN MOLECULE", Scientific American offprint No.
121, 1961.

Krishna, Gopi, WHAT AND WHAT IS NOT HIGHER
CONSCIOUSNESS", The Julian Press, Inc. New York, 1974.

Land, Edwin H., COLOR VISION AND THE NATURAL
IMAGE. PART I, in Proceedings of the National Academy of
Sciences, Vol. 45, No. 1: 115-129, Jan. 1959.
COLOR VISION AND THE NATURAL IMAGE. PART II,
in Proceedings of the National Academy of Sciences, Vol. 45,
No. 4: 636-645, April, 1959.

Land, Edwin H., EXPERIMENTS IN COLOR VISION, Scientific
American, May, 1959.

Lehninger, A.L., BIOENERGETICS, Benjamin, New York, 1965.

Lehninger, A.L.,THE MITOCHONDRION, Benjamin, New York,
1964.

Levey, R.H., "THE THYMUS HORMONE", Scientific American
211(1): 66-77, offprint No. 188, Freeman, San Francisco,
1964.

Loewenstein, W.R., "BIOLOGICAL TRANSDUCERS", Scientific American, 203(2): 98-108, offprint No. 70, Freeman,
San Francisco, 1960.

MacNichol, E.F., Jr., "THREE-PIGMENT COLOR VISION",
Scientific American, 211(6): 48-56, offprint No. 197,
Freeman, San Francisco, 1964.

Mann, Felix, ACUPUNCTURE: CURE OF MANY DISEASES,
Boston, Tao Books, 1972.

Massy, Robert, HILLS' THEORY OF CONSCIOUSNESS: AN
INTERPRETATION OF NUCLEAR EVOLUTION,
University of the Trees Press, Boulder Creek, CA, 1976.

Massy, Robert, ALIVE TO THE UNIVERSE: HANDBOOK FOR
SUPERSENSITIVE LIVING, University of the Trees Press,
Boulder Creek, CA, 1976.

Mazia, D. "HOW CELLS DIVIDE", Scientific American, 205(3):
100-120, offprint No. 93, Freeman, San Francisco, 1961.

Mishra, Dr.Rammurti S., YOGA SUTRAS (PATANJALI'S
YOGA SUTRAS), Anchor Press (Doubleday), 1973.

Mishlove, Jeffry, ROOTS OF CONSCIOUSNESS, Random House,
1975.

Moss, Thelma, THE PROBABILITY OF THE IMPOSSIBLE,
J.P. Tarcher, Los Angeles, 1974.

Muses, Charles and Young, Arthur, CONSCIOUSNESS AND
REALITY: THE HUMAN PIVOT POINT, Avon Books, New
York, 1972.

Ornstein, Robert E., THE PSYCHOLOGY OF CONSCIOUSNESS,
The Viking Press, New York, 1972.

Ostrander, Sheila and Schroeder, Lynn, PSYCHIC DISCOVERIES
BEHIND THE IRON CURTAIN, Prentice Hall, Inc., 1970,
Bantam Books, Inc., 1971.

Ostrander, Sheila and Schroeder, Lynn, HANDBOOK OF PSYCHIC DISCOVERIES, Berkley Publishing Corp., New York, 1974.

Ouspensky, P.D., THE FOURTH WAY, Vintage Books, 1971.

Penrose, Roger, "BLACK HOLES", Scientific American (May, 1972), 38-46. Pike, J.E., "PROSTAGLANDINS", Scientific American 225(5): 84-92, offprint No. 1235, Freeman, San Francisco, 1971.

Porter, K.R. and Bonneville, M.A., FINE STRUCTURE OF CELLS AND TISSUES, Lea and Febiger, Philadelphia, 1968.

Presman, Alexander S., ELECTROMAGNETIC FIELDS AND LIFE, Plenum Press, New York, 1970.

PROCEEDING OF THE SCIENTIFIC AND TECHNICAL CONGRESS OF RADIONICS AND RADIESTHESIA, London, Markham House Press, Ltd., London, 1950.

Rabinowitch, Eugene L., "PROGRESS IN PHOTOSYNTHESIS", Scientific American, Nov. 1953.

Rasmussen, H., "THE PARATHYROID HORMONE", Scientific American, 204(4): 56-63, offprint No. 86, Freeman, San Francisco, 1961.

Reidman, S.R., OUR HORMONES AND HOW THEY WORK, Collier Books, New York, 1962.

Reiser, Oliver L., THE INTEGRATION OF HUMAN KNOWLEDGE", Porter Sargent, Boston, 1958.

Rendel, Peter, INTRODUCTION TO THE CHAKRAS, Samuel Weiser, New York, 1974.

Richards, W. Guyon, THE CHAIN OF LIFE, John Bale, Sons and Daniellson, London, 1934, Rustington, Sussex, England: Health Science Press.

Rossi, Bruno, "WHERE DO COSMIC RAYS COME FROM?" Vol. 189, No. 3, Sept. 1953.

Russell, Edward W., REPORT ON RADIONICS, Neville Spearman, London, 1973.

Sauer, E.G.F., "CELESTIAL NAVIGATION BY BIRDS", Scientific American, 199: 42-47, offprint No. 133, Freeman, San Francisco, 1958.

Erwin Schrodinger, "WHAT IS MATTER? ", Scientific American, Vol. 189, No. 3, Sept. 1953.

Shipman, Harry L., BLACK HOLES, QUASARS AND THE UNIVERSE", Houghton Mifflin Co., Boston, 1976.

Sienko, Michell J., and Plane, Robert A., CHEMISTRY, McGraw-Hill Book Chemistry, 1957, 1961, 1966.

Solomon, A.K., "THE STATE OF WATER IN RED CELLS", Scientific American, 224(2): 88-96, offprint No. 1213, Freeman, San Francisco, 1971.

Snider, R.S., "THE CEREBELLUM", Scientific American, 198(2): 84-90. offprint No. 38, Freeman, San Francisco, 1958.

South, John, "NEW TECHNIQUE CAN DETECT PIN-SIZED CANCERS YEARS EARLIER THAN PRESENT METHODS" National Observer, Nov. 2, 1976.

Staff, New York Times, "FLUORESCENT LIGHT'S EFFECTS ON CELLS", San Francisco Chronicle, April 28, 1977.

Tyberg, Dr. Judith M., THE LANGUAGE OF THE GODS, East-West Cultural Center, Los Angeles, 1970.

Van Nostrand, SCIENTIFIC ENCYCLOPEDIA, Ed. Douglas M. Considine, Fifth Edition, Van Nostrand Reinhold Co., 1976.

Walker, Kenneth, A STUDY OF GURDJIEFF'S TEACHING, Jonathan Cape, 1957.

Ward, Ritchie R., THE LIVING CLOCKS, Alfred A. Knopf, New York, 1971.

Weaver, Warren, "FUNDAMENTAL QUESTIONS IN SCIENCE", Scientific American, Vol. 189, No. 3, Sept. 1953.

White, John, EVERYTHING YOU WANT TO KNOW ABOUT T.M., Pocket Books, New York, 1976.

White, John and Fadiman, James, RELAX, The Confucian Press, 1976.

White, John (Ed.), THE HIGHEST STATE OF CONSCIOUSNESS, Anchor Books , Doubleday & Co., Inc., New York, 1972.

Whittaker, Sir Edmund, "G.F. FITZGERALD", Scientific American, Novémber 1953.

Wilcox, John, M.A., RADIONIC THEORY AND PRACTICE, Herbert Jenkins, Ltd., London, 1960.

Winchester, A.M., GENETICS: A SURVEY OF THE PRINCIPLES OF HEREDITY, Houghton Mifflin, Boston, 1966.

Wurtman, R.J. and Axelrod, J., "THE PINEAL GLAND", Scientific American, 213(1): 50-60, offprint No. 1015, Freeman, San Francisco, 1965.

Zweifach, B., "MICROCIRCULATION OF THE BLOOD", Scientific American, 200(1): 54-60, offprint No. 64, Freeman San Francisco, 1959.

Zuckerman, Sir S. "HORMONES", Scientific American, 196(3): 76-87, offprint No. 1122, Freeman, San Francisco, 1957.

SUPERSENSITIVE LIFE OF MAN SERIES

Volume 1: "Dimensions of Electrovibratory Phenomena", by Victor Beasley

Volume 2: "Energy, Matter and Form", by Phil Allen, Alastair Bearne, and Roger Smith

Volume 3: "Supersensonics", by Christopher Hills

Volume 4: "Divine Mathematics", by Christopher Hills (to be published 1978)

Volume 5: "White Magic: Spiritual Mastery of the Powers of Consciousness", by Christopher Hills, edited by Robert Massy

Volume 6: "Alive to the Universe", by Robert Massy

I.R. 13 Red 19 Orange 25 Yellow 50 Green 55 Blue 62 Indigo 68 Violet

PART 2

SOCIOBIOLOGY
AND
PSYCHOPOLITICS

EDITOR'S NOTE

To provide the link between Part I and Part II, as we move from the individual person to the social unit of which each individual is a part, we quote one of the author's key sentences in Part II:

> "Planetary Man is evolving through what actually happens in the consciousness of each individual in the Nuclear Group, since it is this which spurs a man to action . . ."

Whether this group is a family, a community or a nation, its overall image, its effectiveness and its fulfillment will be enhanced or dragged down in proportion to the awareness and positive will for evolution in the individuals that make up the group. If we take this as our premise for the study of Part II of this book, we shall be a long way along the road to eliminating from our consciousness once and for all the idea that what happens in the group or the community or the nation is "somebody else's fault"!

Running like a continuous unbreakable thread through this book is the insistent message or theme that each one of us creates our own life situation and all that it entails, by the power of our own consciousness. So in this section of the book the renewed study of the seven basic drives is now extended to the manifestation of those drives by men and women in the social, political, scientific, religious and commercial fields.

Nearly ten years ago, when this book was first written, the book opened with what is now Part II, because Christopher Hills believed that until the sociological manifestations of consciousness could be seen by enough intelligent people, the likelihood of world transformation at the political and institutional level of life on the planet could not take place; moreover the individual would not even feel inspired to perfect his or her nature without the incentive and the vision of a new society. However, as the consciousness revolution has emerged over those ten years, it has been evident from the first two editions of the book that Part II, with its profound insights into the nature of the individual levels of consciousness, has played a significant part in awakening people to a totally new awareness of their own inner beings. The book and Christopher Hills' lecture series on Nuclear Evolution have helped to jolt people out of their basic psychological assumptions, which have for centuries determined man's progress and which even today continue to form the basis of decisions and actions for a large number of the world's population. By placing the section dealing with the individual drives of the personality at the beginning, we have now given additional emphasis to what has proved to be the most challenging and potentially the most transforming part of the book.

One of the major reasons for producing this new enlarged edition of *Nuclear Evolution* is to bridge the gulf between old religious and psychological assumptions about self and the new revelations that come with the understanding of the nuclear self. Through the study of the colour levels and the way consciousness works, we explore the very stuff of life, namely relationships, communication and understanding of others, and so eventually we find our true selves. Lovers, families, groups and nations will discover that their joy or their misery is in proportion to their ability to relate and to understand where others are coming from. Then the greater realisation may dawn, that there are in Reality no "others", that in our essential beings, in our Rainbow Bodies, everything and everyone is an acceptable part of the ONE PURE CONSCIOUSNESS.

N.H.

INTRODUCTION TO PART TWO

The question we now have to ask ourselves is "What is the relevance of this research into the nature of consciousness in a world of social problems, politics, crisis and revolution?" For the author, Christopher Hills, an evolutionary revolutionary, the answer lies in his conviction that by changing individuals we can change the world, or, conversely, as he says in Part One of this book, it is impossible for man to change his world until he has changed himself. To achieve permanent change in society he encourages the development of heightened perception and awareness of self in the universe, a development that could have a profound political effect.

The logic of his answer is simple and undeniably valid and can be proved over and over again if we search out the cause of social and national tensions. What are they but the aggregate of personal tensions? And what is international tension other than the accumulation of national tensions which lead to war, defense spending and threats to world security? Since the root cause lies within individuals it is there that we must begin, otherwise we shall never have lasting peace.

Christopher Hills' approach to this problem is not to stress political theories about the best way to compel people to become selfless and altruistic, but rather to encourage integrity in communication. At every level of relating from marriage to the international conference table there is this need to revitalise and clarify human communication so that words begin to mean something again. We have to start with the individual and get beneath the social veneer, the endless platitudes and clichés, to a level of more direct communication.

One of the techniques developed by Christopher to accomplish this improvement in a breakthrough in communication is "Creative Conflict" which has become an integral part of life at his University of the Trees.

"You have to come in psychologically naked" he says "with all the defenses off. It can be more frightening than taking off your clothes, but you have to learn to expose yourself without feeling threatened."

The difference between his method of creative conflict and the encounter session is that it ensures "constructive continuity" and by compelling people to be "real" it avoids the "narcissism" of most growth and guru-orientated groups in the consciousness movement. To engage in creative conflict one must

1) be prepared to change;
2) agree to disagree, respecting differences;
3) play back what you think you heard, so that the other person can correct or confirm it before responding;
4) respond.

One of Christopher's students, Roger Smith, describes this experience of creative conflict and its effect on communication:

"You argue one-to-one but the others in the group act as a mirror in which you begin to see inconsistencies or distortions of truth. You filter out the 'bull-shit' to get at the truth, and then you face the choices. In the process you develop trust by working together; it's a really changing experience."

Roger voices here the typical enthusiasm of students at the University of the Trees in California and at the Centre House Community in London, where creative conflict is used regularly as a method to prove the theory of Nuclear Evolution.

The whole three-year consciousness study program at the University of the Trees is geared to mind expansion and development and the students work for their bachelor's, master's or doctorate degree and at the same time work on themselves as potential world changers and peace-makers. The work must, above all, find some way of withstanding ego-tricks that keep us from clearly seeing the real nature of man, his place in the universe and the potential of his higher sensory perception as yet mostly untapped and undeveloped.

The nearer we come to an awareness of our latent powers the further we move away from the old ego-centric, restrictive and conflict-producing methods of communication that divide rather than unite men and women. As a means of tuning in to this latent perceptive power Christopher has developed and introduced his students to a range of "Supersensonic" devices which are refinements of the ancient divining tools and which provide us with a supersensitive antenna for getting in touch with the world of nature and with the inner worlds of fellow human beings. Not only is it possible to dowse for water and minerals but we can also determine what parts of the body are in conflict and read nutritional signals from body cells by means of these simple biofeedback instruments. Moreover, a device as simple as a pendulum can give a reading of the unconscious mind.

As with creative conflict so with these Supersensonic tools, the main purpose in devising the technique and the instruments has been to give mankind things that he can use to know himself and his fellows more thoroughly so that communication operates at a deeper and a more meaningful level.

"We need tools that can reach into the unconscious mind like a juke box arm," says Christopher, "to do things that have not yet been done except by the psychics." He believes that the ability to dowse or divine is not a rare but an inherent gift, use of which has been blocked by too much intellectualising about it. Just as swallows can find their way to Capistrano, California, from their winter homes in Argentina 10,000 miles away, and animals can sense and predict earthquakes, so human beings have latent sensory powers, and it is by developing these powers that we can become supersensitive, extra aware and better able to sense what is going on in others and in the world around us. Inevitably this will lead to better communication and a relaxing of tension at the personal, group, national and even international levels. The inability to communicate even at simple levels between man and woman, child and parent is the real world problem.

N.H.

WHAT SUSTAINS
SELF-PERPETUATING
SOCIAL ORDER?

Evolution of democratic ideas have added nothing since the ancient Greeks who had a better understanding of the weaknesses of the system. In the democratic capitals of the world the elected representatives are the power brokers who do nothing to evolve the system but perpetuate the weaknesses. What was good for small Greek city states is no good for large populations. The Greek Federation at Delphi was a spiritual union of secular states.

The final authority for the representatives of the Greek secular states at the Federal Center was the temple of the oracle (divination of Cosmic will).

INTERNAL AND EXTERNAL POLITICS

Within every being there is a minor political election going on in which the candidate for president is the Self. This internal political campaign is expressed on the outside in man's social environment in the form of politics. The nature of this internal campaign is known only to a few people because it is going on in the unconscious. Ordinary politics is the tribal ritual by which we express vicariously our deepest drives for dominance on the battlefield of life. The subliminal urges and drives which work themselves out of the system through the vicarious participation in sports, wrestling matches, TV violence and various staged fights has its direct counterpart in the ritualised contests in political life. Man's aggressive red level is worked out in a democracy in the verbal fights on the floor of the council chambers of the world. In the power struggles within the communist system the red battle of the revolutionaries eventually turns into the anti-radical consolidation of power in the blue conservatives and their rigid maintenance of the status quo. In capitalist countries the blue conservatism of those who cannot tolerate too many sudden and unpredictable changes takes the form of resistance to radical and liberal forces which would sweep away the established order. The result is a kind of dis-ease in the body politic and a corresponding sense of disease in the private individual who longs for the security (Green) of a more certain and just social order. The condition of the nation is the result of the malfunctioning of the social (Orange level) sense and the intellectual confusion (Yellow negative) working through the lack of understanding of governance (Blue authority drive). The interplay between these three dominating levels of consciousness in man becomes more complicated as the public mind becomes more confused as to the real causes of political disease.

The leaders and flag wavers who live their lives out front of the social milieu and affect its future course with their insights or ignorance (Indigo intuitive) pretend to know the outcome of social action. They arrogate to themselves the seeming authority of certainty for those members of society in the green and blue levels which crave it. If they are true visionaries and see penetratingly into the cosmic plan for man's evolution then a golden age follows. If they follow some unspoken secret messianic urge to lead and sit atop the social pyramid, then their fellows at the base merely feed the ego and become the pawns in a huge political game. The tragedy is that real people are the pieces and real lives are lost and ruined in the contestants' drives to realise their purposes. In order to communicate with the people from the high political capstone which rests upon the base of the social pyramid, there must always be deceptive simplification of political issues. This very simplification ignores the context of human levels of consciousness and reduces all political substance to a kind of moralising politics which hinges on the personal character of individual politicians. Therefore the great issues are secondary to such considerations as to whether a politician takes bribes or indulges in extra-marital sex. What is said and done during the election fight in the external world seems to have little to do with what will happen during the reign and exercise of power which springs from the internal world of the political candidate. The sterility of political campaigns is not the fault of individual politicians but the absence of public awareness of the real determinants of social change. The idea that everyday government can be transferred to some remote power seat is very old in mankind. Whether it is a president or a king, a dictator or a powerful party boss, the tendency of the public to believe they are participating in the absurd notion of government through the conduct of public affairs, completely blinds society to the real issue of the human drives. The deflection of consciousness from these drives, which dominate all social conduct according to the levels of consciousness in each individual, is the skilled work of a politician, the manipulator of public opinion, and the media which gains its very existence from the resultant controversy. Without this footling controversy to whet the readers' appetite for vicarious identification with well-known personality figures (whether film stars or politicians) the magazines and newspapers would not sell and the lives of journalists would be empty and worthless. What journalist is going to honestly support any worthwhile system which will eventually lead to his own redundancy? What writer and originator of public controversy is going to expose the worthlessness of all human opinion and return man to the direct perception of nature's own knowledge and ways of governance? For a complete review of these social blockages to the manifestation of the idealistic (Blue) and utopian (Indigo) drives the reader is referred to the author's book "Universal Government By Nature's Laws" published 1977. The difficulty with the simplification of complex issues when looked at through liberal and idealistic eyes is that their view of life is based on certain invalid assumptions. Many of these basic assumptions and personal opinions belong to social life because their owners feel so possessive about them. They truly believe everyone else should or ought to hold their pet assumption because it fits with their own drive and temperament. The inability to see this moral self-righteousness is evident in most politically conscious beings which means 90% of the people.

Let us take the example of the scientists chasing government money or the radicals and liberals who believe that a mere readjustment of wealth or a wider distribution of education, services and material goods will improve the status of everyone as a whole. Firstly they are generous with the social captital raised

$5,000 X 1,000,000 for a few rocks while $100 X 1,000,000 would feed the world from Algae Farms

by the uncomplaining taxpayer, who must by edict of the law-abiding money-spending politicians, part with up to forty percent of the hours he works or the income he receives. So that others may benefit from science or welfare and to make sure he feels securely defended by the state against enemies, the average tax-payer in a modern democracy must pay more tithes and taxes than even was demanded by imperialists, kings, and other historical extortioners. In the name of the "great ideal" we are told by generals, politicians, scientists and social do-gooders that even bigger budgets and expenditures are needed to cure the national diseases and world problems.

To spend $5000 million to go to the moon and not to have any way of effectively converting the mass sewerage of cities into energy or fertiliser and continue to pollute the planet is an example of government waste. The enormous difficulty of obtaining even one million for basic projects like algae development which would clean up the polluted waters of our rivers and oceans has been for several years the first-hand experience of the author. To compete with the imaginative promises of "spin off" research and the space age science fiction of "progress" through appealing to the enhanced school–child fascination of rocketry is impossible with the lowly and humble algae which were the very first forms of life on earth. The fascination with the last and supposedly most evolved forms of life in space is an example of man's total blind-ness to the fact that the entire life cycle of the planet depends everyday upon its most basic links in the food chain. The subtle balance of life in the oceans, so essential to the climatic conditions on land masses, are ignored in favour of two-week television dramas walking the face of the moon. To speak like this is unpopular and is shouted down by the so-called idealist who knows better. Yet the planet will teach them their ignorance; if we continue in our present course the pollution of the planet through the madness of the scientific imagination is certain and uncontrol-lable. The spending of vast sums on oil and nuclear fuels is another example of ignoring nature's own way of making these fuels. To grow algae in mass cultures not only by-passes the fossil fuels which are made by nature from them, but ties in with the cycle of life. It is through the mass photosynthesis that man has already learned to harness the sun's light, but deaf ears and blind eyes do not want to know that small algae factories already exist. Humans eat fish, big fish eat little fish, little fish eat very small fish, and small fish eat plankton and organisms. These organisms eat algae and the algae harvests the elements which pollute the waters and change it into protein. The purification of the waters of the planet rests with algae and water is the universal medium of life. For man to understand his part in the environmental cycle is far more important than getting to the barren moon in spite of the space buffs who do it at the expense of every working man. The liberal spending of man's resources on fanciful projects and the complete neglect of less glamourous but more vital and essential ones, is the result of misplaced idealism. Why is it that this is so? There is no credit for a politician to work for something unless it's new and exciting and can attract attention to himself. It is no value to a scientist to get a research grant to rediscover what others have already done in other lands. Even if it is done already the tendency is to repeat it all again to get the grant money voted on a supposedly new project. It is important to see this because the internal politics which motivates both scientist, politician and do-gooding liberal alike lead to identical and inevitable (remorseless) consequences for man, blinding the self thereby creating social blindness.

The generosity of politicians and liberal spenders of public wealth who rip off forty percent of the working man's time, energy and money is justified by two naive assumptions in the public mind. The first assumption concerns the superabundance of Nature. Because we assume idealistically and ignorantly that there is an inexhaustible abundance in Nature to fill all man's requirements and to satisfy his rapacious appetite for energy, then we are prepared to work and even to be taxed to supply those selfish needs. So we go along with the politicians and their extortionate demands for more grand multimillion dollar schemes.

The second concerns the nature of man. If one believes that the lack from which many suffer is not imposed by Nature but by lack of man's productive inventiveness, then one must believe that the world's deprived millions are the victims of the creed of others or general indifference, or is brought about by some mysterious force called imperialism or is the result of institutional failure, lack of education, or temporary underdevelopment.

In all this projection of blame or lack upon external conditions and the accidents of nature's beneficence or bounty apart, people the world over are idealistically conceived of as being more or less equal in capacity of work, and skill.

If nature is not bestowing her gifts on all or if the capacity and gifts of individual people are not as equal as we assumed idealistically then equality and uniformity must be enforced on all members of society. Theoretically this is the socialist and communist ethic, but because humans are human and do not conform by nature to equal capacity, a distinct hierarchy of rulers, privileged power wielders, members of the communist party or politburo members harass and enforce their idea of equality upon any individual with dissident views. To the extent that literally millions of Russians, millions of happy Tibetans, and millions of Chinese have been murdered, imprisoned or worked to death in camps, this idealistic ethic has been forced on mankind

The Berlin Wall is symbolic of the repressive politics of the self-righteous who know what is best for everybody. They are prepared to kill if you put one foot outside their mental walls.

The Wall was created in 1961. On one side of the Wall is the grey regimentation of the human spirit; on the other the democratic freedom which lured thousands every day -- until the Wall. Yet democracy must evolve its selfish self-centred philosophy in order to survive.

without choice in the name of society itself. The spokesmen for mankind who judge all by these basic assumptions are so-called liberals who derive their philosophy from liberty.

The ethic of conservative politics is harder to discriminate. More than the conservation of traditional values it appears to be the conserving of the free enterprise system as the dynamic agent of transformation. The philosophy that by conserving commercialism and economic growth and pursuing our enlightened self-interest everybody will get what they deserve seems to be a sacrifice of all that is small. The small enterprise, the small village, environmental preservation and the small craftsman cannot compete against the remorseless, cost conscious commercialism which destroys the sense of community. Unless big business can find some way of common ownership which converts its reason for existence from profit-making to other levels of humane living, it would seem that it has its own in-built destruction since corporations will eventually swallow up all that is small until the government has to nationalise it to prevent exploitation of the people.

To govern one must have a philosophy since all living systems have some mode or purpose. If the philosophy of conservatism is merely that of conserving "free enterprise" which merely has self-interest or profit as its goal, then to impose this collective will on others will be to restrict the process of change and preserve the exploitation of the small. This philosophy leads merely to the competing of private interests for a share in the social capital and wealth of the whole. Such a politics is not within the aspirations of much of our youth and encourages the very disease of politics and enables powerful interests to lobby against the common weal.

Politics should be based on a community which shares all values, that agrees to disagree because men express themselves on different levels of consciousness and are not equal with their talents and gifts. Politics has become a disease. Instead of a method of keeping order and being a cure for the anarchy of self-interested and unwilling anti-social people, it has become the sickness itself. Cancer is riddled through the body politic.

There is no evidence that the world wants a more evolutionary system if we look at public apathy for change. Such an attitude can only change when there is a method for testing man's motives and for understanding the powerful drives which underlie all their social actions.

WHY DO YOU STAND AGAINST COMMUNISM?

Young idealistic people who read the first edition of this book often said that by bringing politics into my work I had made them want to put the book down. They resented my stand against Communism. To them, the evils of the Communist manifestation did not invalidate the Marxist theory which, given the right people to make it work, would be wonderful. My answer to these young people is that I speak out against the Communist system and Marxist thought for the same reason that Communists Sakharov and Solzhenitsyn speak against it. My negative stand against actual real life manifestations, such as the Communist state, does not spoil the positive idealistic thrust of my work but is an indispensable complement to it. Unlike Communism, Nuclear Evolution is not an impractical theory made out of words. It has existence only in so far as someone is willing to become the theory and manifest it. Without such persons, who have the courage and tenacity to change themselves and to live out their own vision of truth before trying to change or advise others, there is no Nuclear Evolution.

The appeal of Communism is its selflessness which calls on the world to recognise the selfishness of other systems which allow vast wealth to exist uncaringly alongside extreme poverty. On this factual and undeniable point I reply that until the finger of blame can point to itself first before it looks "out there" for selfishness, there will be no caring in the world. The Communist party is itself the best proof of this spiritual axiom, for its inhumanity to man is glaringly visible. The selflessness of Communism is the destruction of individual selves and the repression of freedom of self, while any genuine spiritual selflessness consists in the realisation that we are one with all selves. The fervor of moral accusation by which Communism attracts its main worshippers is misplaced idealism. Simply put, Marxism is based on a false idea of human selflessness and can therefore never work because the power seekers will benefit even more ruthlessly than the money seekers benefit in the Western Democratic system.

I have been told that I am swimming against the main ideological tide of thought in our universities and that if I stand against Communism, people will write me off. So be it! I can surely risk that much if Solzhenitsyn and Sakharov have risked death, imprisonment and repression of all their lifework in order to speak about what they see as a basic flaw in human nature -- the absolute self-righteousness of the blind, who are so convinced they are right that they would imprison millions or kill those freedom lovers whom they regard as enemies of their system.

I, too, stand against selfishness, but my philosophy calls for total realisation of one's **own** selfishness and a realisation that we are projecting our selfishness out onto others in society. I believe in dying, if necessary, for freedom of self, but not in killing others in its name. I believe that one has to be spiritually blind not to see the flaw in Communism's disregard of human freedom, but to see that flaw without questioning our own selfishness (whether it is the selfishness of big corporations and private industries which do not become cognisant of public health or moral corruption until forced by law or whether it is some personal selfishness) is the same spiritual blindness. This almost automatic mechanism, which causes every human being to see evil "out there" while blurring out of focus the selfishness within, is the stumbling block of all ideologies, Communism not excepted.

In short, I believe that Marxism is based on the big lie. Even if it were perfectly practiced as desired by its youthful followers, that lie would still prevent the total realisation of Self and still foster the selfish idealism of those arrogant insensitive people who think they can say for another what he should do with the precious gift of life. Those who cannot relate to such a perception in political terms can look around them and see it in the eight out of ten parents who try to govern what their children will do with their unique individual potentials. Or in the spiritual movements where false gurus prefer disciples dependent on their authority and do not build in their followers that centred self-reliance which is the mark of genuine spiritual evolution. The prevalence of such teachers proves that people who claim they are selfless are not always as selfless as they believe themselves to be and in fact are often **more** selfish than others just by virtue of the self-deception. Small wonder that Christ called the sinners to repentance and left the righteous to go their way.

To adopt such a cynical attitude does not necessarily throw cold water on the emotional enthusiasm of a revolutionary mentality. I believe there is a bigger revolution coming than a political one -- an evolutionary breakthrough that will show mankind how selfish he really is. But the egocentric person will not welcome this revolution in perception any more than the selfish rich welcome those who care about human poverty and make them look at it. Political commissars, who kill and exterminate those who have this determination to see past the words and concepts of false idealism to the core of man's actions, are the real selfish and self-righteous ones who need to work on the purity of their own minds. Nuclear Evolution therefore begins at this unpopular point (both politically and privately): that the demons are not all "out there" but reside behind the comfortable smugness and misguided opinions in our own minds, no person excepted.

I believe that self-centred people, rich or poor, bigotted or liberal, are the same everywhere and exist behind the claims to selfless ideals in every race and culture. I want to see a system evolve where selfish people cannot come to power, either here in the West or under Communism. I have not been content to point the finger and do nothing, but, to make my ideal a reality have invented such a system which is being practiced by small groups of people before being foisted on the world as the answer. Whenever I look at Communist nations I see that the system is imposed on the proletariat by violence. Critics of the West claim that our police system does the same, but this view is terribly naive since the police can only work subject to law. A better analogy would be the Watergate scandal in which most of the American people thoroughly enjoyed pointing the finger of blame at their leaders while only a few had the perception to realise their own responsibility, by default, for that corruption. Whose selfishness was it that said "The system is too big, what could I hope to accomplish?" Who preferred to bake cookies, play golf, buy stocks, rather than put his or her consciousness on the deeper issues of human life and wonder where it was all going? Who played the liberal role in public while in private matters was an arch conservative? And who was inspired by ideals of selflessness on Sunday but assumed there was no workable way to actually become selfless in the "real world"?

Nuclear Evolution is the tool designed by nature to take this journey into the selfless state of human life. It does not blame others for the state of life or society but says if you don't like what you see around you, form your own system, make it work better, and keep your freedom too. Do not believe that you have to give away your freedom for a promise or a big lie. Wake up to what Solzhenitsyn is saying. Study his life and his record and look deeply at your own mendacity and idealistic excuses which allow any decadence to exist. Do not let the authorities anywhere in the world confiscate your entire truth, and rule by lies and half truths. If you examine yourself and the true nature of selfishness, you will understand my stand against Communism which claims to be selfless but demonstrates and legislates its opposite, and you will understand why only that which is manifested and visible can claim any worth at all. There is much idealistic fervor today about meditation, but even with meditation, if it all happens inside the head with no outward expression, it is worthless. Real meditation is "**doing** the wisdom." Therefore to speak out against the big lie in the political arena strikes also a blow at the little lie and furthers the evolutionary process in every individual person, regardless of whether he is brainwashed by Communism, Capitalism, some materialistic guru, his own mother, or just by life. There is only one doorway to freedom.

THE NEXT STEP –
SITTING AT THE CENTRE OF PEACE

The only real utopia is the one we create inside our own hearts. It is there that we make our heaven or hell. But if a group of people were to work on themselves with enough dedication to attain that inner peace, then it would be possible to begin a plan for that larger utopia in which all the hearts become one and sit together at the centre of peace. Having built foundations for this kind of utopian community at the University of the Trees in California, the group which is living and working there now wishes to share its vision and join with others who may be interested in building on the same principles and foundations. In our living expression of the nuclear model of Nature, we have an inner nucleus of dedicated people, including protons (leaders) and neutrons (milder people who are very necessary to the dynamic of the whole). In this model in which we live according to Nature and her laws, there are also rings of orbiting electrons, people whose commitment to the community might begin with no more than a willingness to give materially to the building of a future in which they would have a share. If you are such a person, who is wishing for a way to live more in tune with Nature and with the Cosmic Intelligence, we invite you to consider what part you might play in the unfolding of a new pattern of life: the evolutionary yeast which will someday lift the whole of society to a new level of relating.

There is only one stipulation which I must make totally clear at the outset. If you are excited by the idea of a world peace centre, or a village of peace, now is the time to become part of it. We have no patience with those who say "you do all the work to establish utopia and then I will come and join you later." We can have no place in our vision for such a person. Until they have the attitude of a doer he or she will never find a place with us. Only those who are prepared to invest **NOW** some part of themselves (whether land, money, energy, talent, or some other thing) will find their place on one of the electron shells of commitment not only to their own tranquility but to a unique opportunity for giving to the world. Rarely do we find some work or cause that is pure enough to give meaning to our lives! Our giving to this charity or that seems to ease our conscience a little but never enough. We give, but we do not feel connected to the thing we have given to. No one seems to offer a chance to really give, to become part of something. Our dynamic resonates with those who do not wish to remain on the sidelines waiting for someone else to make it happen. We have found by experience that 90% of the world's people are fencesitters and 10% carry the rest in their motivation towards higher consciousness.

The widely diverse experimental group of people at the University of the Trees has researched the nature of Group Consciousness (the ways by which a group of people can function as one organism, co-operating within a framework in which the manifested realities are building toward the ideals rather than trying to make an as yet impractical ideal the basis for our manifestation). Now there must be an on-going vision which creates the new social unit as a demonstration of these evolutionary techniques at work in the world at large. In other words, the yeast must leaven the bread or its value is only potential. But we begin not with a collection of theoretical ingredients. Our yeast is a living expanding essence which will permeate the whole and lift it up. In the past, utopias have failed because the human personality and its ego-centric viewpoint has never been tackled from inside - out but has always depended upon "the system" to mold and shape selfless people who are great enough in being to operate a model self-governing constitution. All these utopian groups have eventually succumbed to the violent power struggles of a few individuals or the seeds of division have been allowed to grow to the point where the utopian vision deflates into the status quo. Because these groups are centred around some charismatic leader who does not teach people to think for themselves but to be good "followers" their new age schemes finish up as enclaves within the existing society, which runs on the same "personality" principle.

How can we establish a community which not only governs itself but is self-financing and does not depend on economic handouts from its predecessors? Is there an opportunity anywhere today where a concentrated attempt at establishing an alternative way of life, alternative energy sources, alternative states of economic and spiritual existence can be tried out without interference from entrenched hierarchical authorities or even some dictatorial authority from within? To be a viable project, the experiment should be capable of being funded and owned by those who contribute work, time and energy. To get started the group must build up some social capital for purchase of land, buildings and utilities. Here the ideas advanced by the author in 1963* on the joint Democratic ownership of industry can be a starting guide until the nucleus can take over the full responsibility for the operation and providing of leadership of a group which has solved the problem of economic and spiritual existence, without the age old split between the priviliged few and the "workers". To build a community which is neither communistic (robbing the individual of the fruits of his work for the good of the whole) nor capitalistic (allowing the fittest to survive without enough regard for the good of the whole nor any caring for one's neighbor) is the next step of Nuclear Evolution.

---

*Now part of "Universal Government by Nature's Laws", published by University of the Trees Press, 1977.

THE VISION – A PEACE VILLAGE

This community will not only be a centre from which peace can enter the world at large but will be a centre of peace in itself, built upon tested principles of creative conflict and spiritual laws which are drawn from nature: for example, the law of humility which requires that every person share in the donkey work, not leaving it all for the less talented or less aggressive ones, or the law of consideration which requires that every person clean up his own mess. The peace village project will be a cooperative spiritual community providing pure nourishment for the body and spirit and dedicated to practical research into consciousness to achieve a fulfilled life. For those in the outermost rings of the electron shells, it may be nothing more than a beautiful setting of tranquility in which they retreat once or twice a year, but the beauty and tranquility will stem from a wider vision in which all play some part.

The policy behind the starting of this community and school of wisdom is to provide the nourishment of the highest state of consciousness. This cannot be achieved, however, if through weakness of the spirit people cannot support themselves in some useful work or service, for then a feeling of uneasiness overtakes them (a darkening of the light of their spirits), particularly if they have to seek support as a favour from the government or become dependent on the society around them. The new society must evolve an income-producing energy exchange, some non-taxable barter system to avoid paying income taxes to support the existing system. Obviously land taxes and road taxes and taxes levied for hospitals, fire fighting, etc. must be paid, but in as many ways as possible we would become self-supporting. To achieve this, the community members must support themselves from the land or tap new resources so as to be totally free from accepting welfare handouts in any form. The means by which we can achieve these utopian conditions is set out in "Universal Government by Nature's Laws." We must not feel ashamed of starting materially small or beginning in simplicity for this is the very thing needed to build inner strength for bigger undertakings in the world community. Only by the realisation of pure consciousness and clear seeing can human rights be preserved. The beautiful environment which we will then create will not be a mask to cover selfishness and hard-heartedness but will be a natural by-product of the harmony we have built within.

AN EVOLUTIONARY PLAN
FOR COOPERATIVE OWNERSHIP

The design of the legal machinery for developing the community is to use the existing University of the Trees and its campus as a non-profit organisation to operate and manage the land acreage until the project has established its own effective government. Roads, mobile homes, domes, home-sites, meditation huts, areas for craft industries, farm and vegetable growing, algae cultivating and all other improvements to be decided by the members, are either now being planned or will be put under construction as soon as there are enough down payments to secure the property and acreage. The community is expected to be part of a 1,000/2,000 acre ranch in California or other frost free area.

This campus experiment for the evolution of a new society will have an autonomous government and membership, not necessarily involved in other branches of the communal projects but working in cooperation with them. Once accepted by the nucleus and upon making the down-payment, the incoming member is immediately entitled to full rights in the government of the campus experiment, including ownership of an undivided interest in the acreage acquired. The books of account and the prospective properties will be open for inspection by members wishing to investigate this new design for creative living. As owner, each member will have full use of all the cooperative group facilities or of any that may be added in the future. He or she will also have a vote in the management and government of the community, and the privilege under the special by-laws of the constitution of electing or serving on the policy-making board of directors, i.e., the non-dictatorial leadership nucleus. By qualifying for membership, one acquires the right to build a mobile home or some other approved structure on a site in the community for personal use. All such matters of use, operation, and development will be governed by the constitution created and shaped by each member, the cooperative joint ownership by-laws as set out in "Universal Government by Nature's Laws". Sites for homes and small industries will be leased from the non-profit corporation by individual members for personal use on a first come first served basis at a fixed low fee of one dollar per month, hence there is no rent to pay. The installation and ongoing costs of water, sewage, electricity, telephone, other utilities, the observance of local health regulations and taxes will be borne at cost by the members. The home sites will be clustered and separated by wide areas of natural tree life.

THE CONCEPT OF A HIGHER CONSCIOUSNESS COMMUNITY

Although simplicity is the theme and starting small is the method of carrying out the undertaking, this does not mean we need to restrict our vision of the ultimate potentials of expansion within a specific acreage. Many such communities can be sponsored in any part of the world. First we must get the right people and then the land. To get land and then acquire people is the way to attract people who have not digested the implications of Nuclear Evolution and its revolutionary concepts of "**creative** conflict." But it is people, not places, that make a scheme succeed or fail. Clarity of vision before acquiring property is essential for tranquility. Once the land is acquired, it will be divided into several separate sections so that persons at different levels of consciousness and commitment may experience the full spectrum of consciousness growth.

THE NEXT STEP

Having shared with you our full vision for that peaceful community which will, by its own example shining as a light, change the world, I want now to clarify that we are still at stage one: the consciousness research work in which we transform first ourselves before trying to transform society. The University of the Trees' physical location at present consists of eight contiguous houses on Pine Street in Boulder Creek, California. Though these are a simple and modest beginning, they are suited to our present needs. Our next step is to find a piece of land on which to expand. Such a piece of land, if you know of one that is suitable, is tax deductable as a donation to a non-profit organisation, or the purchase could also be financed from membership fees right now. Until the right person with the right property appears, we are happy to continue to expand organically from where we are, but we keep our minds open to whatever is possible because we know that sometime, the next step will begin, and the evolutionary expansion of our work will reach out to include spiritually hungry people everywhere.

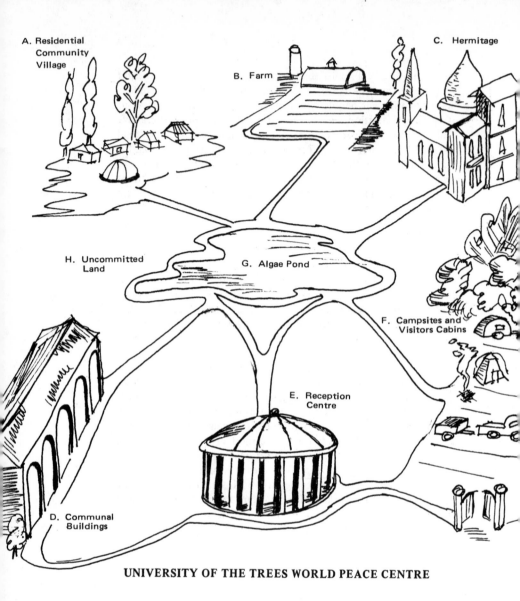

UNIVERSITY OF THE TREES WORLD PEACE CENTRE

A. Permanent Residential Community Village.
B. Centre Farm Cooperative, Small Craft Industries
C. Hermitage for Study and Renunciation
D. Communal Buildings for use as Growth Centre, ashram facilities,
shrine, meetings, library, sauna, hot spring, etc. etc.
E. Reception and Educational Centre for Orientation of New Visitors
and Members, tours of the village, and courses, talks on the community,
etc. etc.
F. Campsite and Visitors Cabin Building Project
G. Algae Pond for growing edible algae, usable for food, building material,
fuel, etc. etc. Also Lakeside Gardens and building of houses for temporary
resort use as visitors cabins.
H. Uncommitted Land -   available for new experiments in creative living
with synergistic possibilities, e.g. the World Yoga University, University of
the Trees, Institute for Therapeutic Energies, Meditation School for
Children, Wholistic Health Centre, etc. etc.

SITTING AT THE CENTRE OF PEACE

The ONE I love
is an infinite
ever-welling spring
of joy-saturated love,
The source of
never failing guidance,
The centre of
all-sweetening grace,
The stillness of
the all-penetrating gaze.

When the centre is still
the ultimate Being,
whose goal is the
gathering of all hearts,
guides us to the
God of Supreme Joy.

Could I be found not willing,
to work for such a wondrous ONE?
Could I begrudge the time
to sacrifice myself for love?
Could I be weighed on
my own scales,
and judged still wanting?
Could I be found out,
by my own heart
to be unwilling?

For the gift of love
is given to every temple
and the joy of life
is hiding in every heart,
and the sacrifice of the selfless ONE
is seen in every Self.

When the centre is still
the Self that sees is Pure Consciousness,
ultimate,
all aware,
all-joy saturated Being,
melting the icy walls
of all separation
from the Love-crowned King,
Who is the ONE I love.

I.R. 13 Red   19 Orange 25   Yellow   50 Green 55 Blue 62 Indigo 68 Violet

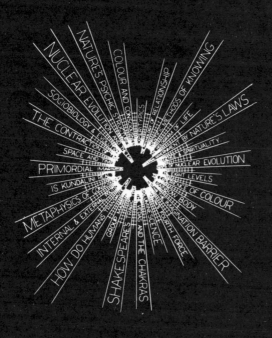

WHERE IS
EVOLUTIONARY INTELLIGENCE
TAKING US?

THE MILLION-YEAR LEAP – NOW!

Evolution works slowly and its influence cannot be felt by any one individual person. A hundred thousand generations may pass before a big change becomes obvious. Yet there are times in the billions of years of our history where the subtle advance has been dramatic and sudden, where the preparations over a million years provide the ground for a million-year jump which takes place in one event, in one generation. This leap ahead represents a change in the nuclear structure of the guiding field of the organism. The physical changes follow this nuclear change by releasing the intelligent energy accumulated over a million years into one moment of realisation, one great moment of thrust into new understanding of man's role in the vast cosmos, one great change in his purpose.

Do we look backward to the fossil record of the planet to mark the path of the future? Do we look at the path which life has climbed up the mountain and confuse it with the vision from the peak? For years the human race climbs upward with only one view of the mountainside. Then suddenly we are there on the top, and the view of 360 degrees is nothing like the view from the pathway up the mountain. Such is the path of Nuclear Evolution. The fossil record gives no more clue than the mountain path gives of the view from the top; and the millions of years of the climb are a totally irrelevant memory compared to the new sweep of vision. The profusion of living forms along the path becomes suddenly the view of the vast cosmic ONE at the peak, who sees the purpose from the highest to the lowest, the biggest to the smallest.

The galaxy of 100 billion stars is suddenly our home with a garden of ten billion galaxies, each with a 100 billion stars to roam. To a material scientist the discovery of other life in the cosmos is important, vitally significant. To another, who accepts it in the peace of his heart, the excitement of such a discovery will last two weeks, three weeks, a year at most.

Life has been waiting a million years for the climber to reach the peak and sit at the centre of peace. Let us look at our future home with the wide angle lens of the liberated mind and know that although this lens took a billion years to fashion it takes only a moment to peer through it at the nuclear centre of life.

NUCLEAR EVOLUTION AND
NATURE'S PSYCHIC STRUCTURES

Once a scientist or an artist has an insight into nature's structures or sees a vision of her marvelous beauty, there immediately arises the problem of how to convey it to another human being. It is exactly the same for the yogi or mystic since the territory which exists in other dimensions of being is often beyond the power of imagination to describe. Nuclear Evolution in its written form is a verbal description of a model seen directly in nature and, in this sense, it is being written backwards towards the original vision. The development of "Supersensonics" provided the psychotronic science of perception which enabled the author to feel and sense the structures of the different spheres of consciousness, just as anyone else would trace the invisible fields of a magnet with iron filings.

One of my London students thought that "Supersensonics" was a development of the Nuclear Evolution Theory from its first appearance as a booklet in 1967. Actually these images were developed in lectures and put on tapes long before the booklet was written. The first edition of Nuclear Evolution was merely a reluctant verbalisation of what was already a complete research. It was in 1957 that I began to develop the psychotronic tools that enabled me to penetrate so many different fields of nature, but the task of documenting these discoveries in ordinary language became too formidable for any one man. Hence Nuclear Evolution was and still is a feeble expression of nature's own purpose on earth and a directly perceived account of the means by which she is achieving it. In that sense it was already a complete system before ever pen was put to paper. To pull something down from the more rarefied levels of human consciousness into everyday language of science is even more difficult when there are no words coined in our English like there are in Sanskrit to describe the countless aspects of consciousness.

The following account of evolution as it applies to sociobiology and the development of a new species of man is of course only a hint of where man is going with his inherited faculties. To get a wider picture from the phenomenal point of view, the student of Nuclear Evolution should read my other book "Supersensonics" in conjunction with, if not before, the reading of this one. To get an imaginative grasp of how the evolution of the microcosm interpenetrates the macrocosm we can take a look at society as a mirror image or a hologram of present-day man. To understand the social and political backdrop against which the drama of consciousness is played we can look at society as the product of human awareness rather than viewing each human as a product of the environment in which he lives.

THE MACROCOSM

It has taken the evolutionary intelligence five billion (5000 million) years to produce man in his present form of a positively and negatively charged cerebrospinal nervous antenna. The present radio telescopes which peer into other galaxies millions of light years away to detect extra-terrestrial intelligence are more sensitive on the physical sensory level but are not as sensitive on the six other levels of experience as the biological human antenna. The optical telescope concentrates rays of light and magnifies their images and even the radio telescope which creates different chart recordings gives images to the eye which must still be seen and interpreted by the consciousness which looks at the results through the telescope. So the **means** of our seeing has evolved, but the consciousness of the viewer is still the same self-separated entity and therefore the telescope, as with all other instruments, is only an extension of our existing limited state of consciousness. Although the man-made radio sensor took only 25 years to conceive and build, there is a good reason why the radio telescope is more sensitive than man's 5000 million years old physical eye which does not consciously respond to radio waves emitted by these distant galaxies. Why does not man's supersense and physical antenna make the use of such an external sensor obsolete? The answer is that it does as a biological dowsing instrument, but scientists feel they cannot trust these modes of measuring and knowing as they can their eyes and ears, even though these very scientists have proved our senses do not report the universe objectively as it is. It is difficult for many people to accept that our physically tested version of scientific reality is no more accurate than our properly trained intuition. The reason is that consciousness and radiation are inseparable from each other, just as light and our experience of it are inseparable, just as the observer's consciousness as the subject is not separable from the experience of an object.

Our exploration of the cosmos has extended as far as the limits of our senses can travel and therefore some new mode of knowing the many unexplored worlds is needed. For beings made of light and consuming the products of light, new ways of communicating with extra-terrestrial intelligences who also live off light are the next evolutionary steps for man. Yet most people still think in terms of physical communication of body to body instead of mind to mind, or spirit to spirit. Because our scientific culture is at present bound by the velocity of light travelling at 186,000 miles per (earth) second there are great problems in attempting physical communication over distances of 100 to 500 light years within our own galaxy which is approximately 100,000 light years across. The difficulty becomes even greater when communicating by radio waves or light signals over the vastness of extra-galactic space with objects millions of light years away. Anyone communicating with the physical sense of sight or using the various instruments our consciousness has built to extend it, e.g. optical and radio telescopes and photometric equipment, would be able to send a signal at the speed of light but it would not be received until 100 to 500 years in our human future on earth. Any response to this signal from outer space reaching us now would have to have been sent 100 to 500 years in our past. Consequently all these signals and responses would only have academic historical value to the extra-terrestrial beings who sent them or the humans who received them 500 years from now.

Yet all these limits are not limits within reality itself but are created by our sensory perceptions of reality. Earth time is measured by arbitrarily marking off periods determined by the revolutions of the earth on its axis, then applying them to the revolution of the earth in its orbit around the sun, then extending these units out to measure the passage of light from imaginary, fixed still points in space to another fixed point in space which has in fact already moved in the galaxial rotation before the light gets there.* As we said, present scientific measurements estimate that our own galaxy measures about 100,000 light years across and we are approximately 30,000 light years away from its centre. To travel this distance by space craft at our present speeds it would take about 300 million years for intelligent life to reach the centre of our galaxy. This is a much shorter time than the 5000 million years it has taken the evolutionary intelligence to produce man. It would in effect be much quicker to spread the existing human intelligence through our galaxy by space travel than for new intelligent life to originate physcially somewhere else at the same evolutionary rate as mankind. However, the mistake of all our physical sciences is to see the spread of intelligence only taking place at the physical level of consciousness. Astrophysics relates all its reality to those sensations vibrating in the physical spectrum and completely ignores the speed of thought, rules out the "all-pervadingness" of consciousness and the formative power of imagination and does not study the nature of perception on levels of consciousness more sensitive than the physical cell life of biological receptors such as eye and ear, etc.

---

* A series of Nuclear Evolution lectures touching on these complex problems of reality were given in London in 1967 and again in 1973, also in Boulder Creek, California during 1976; these are now being put into book form by various students of the author. See references at the end of the chapter.

By Supersensonic means we can step outside of time, send an instantaneous signal across our galaxy, receive the answer back with the speed of thought, and our nervous system will react with the customary diviner's reaction. But if we are not open to this possibility then the world we live in will be bounded by the very real barrier of the speed of light and the limited response of the senses. Depending on the logical code or language we have programmed into us, so will be our experience of the universe. If we limit consciousness, then we are not aware that the stars are enclosed in our consciousness which is already "out there" all-pervading the whole. In actual fact we do not experience radiations of stars "out there" because all signals from the external environment actually finish up "in here" where they are truly experienced. In that sense, the galaxy -- even the whole universe -- is inside us. To separate oneself from the whole and become a part is not possible. We are the **whole**, whether we like it or not -- perhaps a self-limited image of the whole or perhaps a whole dreaming it is a part, but nevertheless we are that image in our consciousness. This universal hologram of consciousness which creates the experience of this three-dimensional universe is only limited by our self-programmed thoughts and whatever limitations the thinker is imposing on his senses.

THE MICROCOSM

Even our biological sciences do not study the psychic perception of biological cells. Obviously the individual cell must have considerable intelligent discrimination to choose from the human blood stream only those chemical nutrients and vitamins which it needs from a whole mass of chemical elements. To argue that the making of these chemical choices is purely dependent upon the selective mechanistic arrangement of genetic materials in the cell is rather naive. It is the equivalent of saying to a human being that your choice of radio or TV show is determined biologically from your father or your mother. Even more ridiculously it is analogous to saying that out of 100 radio shows broadcasting on different frequencies of radio energy you will always pick a show because of the wavelength of the station, not the psychic content of the program! As important as it is, the genetic material is only the **carrier**, like the radio wave. The evolutionary program is something else again.

The evolutionary intelligence both in the cell and in the macro-cosmic sense of extra-galactic intelligences is already here in each of us; the fact is that consciousness does not depend for its ingestion into our nervous system on the physical receptors alone. To predicate our communication with extra-terrestrial intelligences on the physical sensory level alone, limited as it is to the speed of light, is as silly as limiting our microcosmic intelligence of inner cell life to dependency on the things we eat. Certainly a healthy body depends on certain basic dietary intake of water, protein and so forth but you can get enlightened on rice and lentils just as well as you can on wheat sprouts and beefsteak. To think that consciousness is improved by eating is to make the same error as the astro physicists and the biological scientists make when they state that somehow the quality of intelligence is dependent on the material ingestion of energy. Certainly we must have energy, just like a radio station has wattage, but the power of the radio station has nothing to do with the quality of its program. For evolution to thrust itself forward, mankind must know what that program is.

NUCLEAR EVOLUTION AS THE PROGRAM

If the evolutionary intelligence has been busy so many millions of years to give mankind a cerebrospinal nervous antenna sensitive to fantastic subtle radiations of intelligence from the macrocosm and microcosm, we can then ask why don't people know more about it? You may as well ask the same question of the extra-galactic intelligences! Why do we petty humans, sitting in our ego-centric consciousness of the universe, know so little about the intelligence levels of our own galaxy? Or the micro-cosmic selection devices of our own cell life? The reason is not difficult to understand but the acceptance of the fact is difficult. Man has literally been asleep for 5000 million years in a state of consciousness on which he has not really known, except in a few occult instances, any contact at physical levels with intelligences on higher levels of conscious evolution. A few sages, holy saints and a small sprinkling of philosophers appear to make up the sum total of these remarkable enlightened ones.

These few have all stated clearly that the evolutionary intelligence knows what it is doing and is concerned with the human readiness for receiving higher inspiration as much as it is with general progress. It is now obvious that progress will depend on prior preparation of maps and exact blueprints for the conceptual, ideational and inspirational discovery of man's next enterprise.

NATURE'S OWN MAP

Nuclear Evolution is an existing mental map of the hitherto unknown territory from which no traveller has ever returned. The human race has inherited this map not only in the blueprint genes of each cell but directly from the higher levels of the cosmic intelligence in each person. The qualities of the biological electro-physical wave-fields which surround man as an aura consist of wholistic systems of energies. These wave-fields are definitely determined by those energies of consciousness which program the wave-fields from the heart of every cell. At the nuclear centre of every cell there exists the central broadcast station sending out its aura, like a program on certain frequencies. These carrier waves broadcast on biological radio frequencies and are picked up by the tuned circuit of the human chakra system like a radio receiver. But until the aura/cell program is made and sent out on the radio carrier wave-field there is no actual intelligence in the carrier signal to be communicated. The carrier wave itself carries no intelligence in the signal; therefore no communication with anything in the immediate environment is achieved nor possible without the program. Intelligence is the program in the evolutionary sense. This intelligence is resting potentially in memory (soul). In the tuning and refinement of the carrier wave-field (consciousness) we are enabled to step up the thresholds of manifestation and perception to wider evolutionary goals.

WHERE DOES EVOLUTION
ACTUALLY TAKE PLACE?

All evolution of biological cells begins with the structural patterns in the central nucleus of the seed. According to current theory this pattern is not changeable by mental means but is strictly inherited from parental genes. Such a belief in the unchangeability of the nuclear centre is **not** backed up by any experiment whatever to prove that mental forces **do not** affect its inherited structure. No biologist has ever published to our knowledge at this time in any reputable journal any experiments which disprove psychic effects on genes. Neither has anyone published a proof of these effects, because no reputable scientific journal would accept it as possible without a great deal of replication of the experiments at distinguished universities. This does not mean that theoretical papers have not been written or that no work has been done, but to the writer's knowledge all such papers have been rejected by academic institutions as inconsistent with known facts. Yet nowhere are these facts to be found which disprove the effects of consciousness on inherited genes.

For example it is possible to grow a simple culture of bacteria in milk and demonstrate in a few hours the effects of consciousness on the growth of organisms and their ability to acquire such new characteristic strains as sweetness, sourness, etc. Take a flask of yoghurt culture and divide it into three equal flasks and label them A – God's blessing, and B – neutral control, and C – Devil's curse. Keep them all in the same constant temperature. Curse culture C with all your being and bless culture A with all the love you can muster. Leave culture B alone to its own process. Check the times when the culture becomes firm and taste it. Culture C will finish several hours before A and will taste bitter/sharp; and culture A will finish long after B control and taste sweet. Use the culture again and we find the bitterness or sweetness of the bacteria culture is transmitted to the following generations. It is well-known also that the presence of certain people will spoil development of these cultures in a cheese factory, particularly the aura of a menstruating woman, who does not have to be handling the cheese but merely in the same building; hence these women are always sent home from the factory. It is possible to try a number of variations of this experiment with other cultures both human and animal including the coagulation of human or animal blood. The period of coagulation can be varied in different flasks with the projection of consciousness on different samples showing that coagulation time is not merely a genetic factor of the type of blood. Somehow the nucleus of the blood cell is able to pick up the signal and respond to it on non-physical levels of communication. Perhaps the blood cell is just as sensitive as humans are to cosmic intelligence acting through the different sections of the heavens called the zodiac. Obviously the energies and carrier waves of light from different galaxies contain varying inputs and types of intelligence which may account for blood cells working with different levels of efficiency, different thresholds of absorption and excretion.

That consciousness does affect the central nucleus of the seed in such a way that evolution is achieved in its replication is far more probable than the concept current today that it is the survival of the fittest which determines man's evolutionary progress. Over 5,000 million years, if this were true, we would now only have humans on earth with the kind of intelligence which is obsessed with survival and fitness. Yet we see almost a deliberate ignoring of survival issues by psychologically blind and pollution prone mankind. His fitness both physically and morally seem to have degenerated beyond any previous level in history until there is total dependence on weapons which can only bring about almost total extinction of the race. We could say that man is so obsessed with survival, yet he builds atomic suicide weapons. This drive towards annihilation on the physical level is also matched with a spiritual drive for annihilation of the Ego and we can see today that the violent fighting man, who was always the hero of those genetically disposed towards aggression and survival is gradually losing all glamour. Soldiers, police and violent authorities are looked down on by many cultures today as cannon fodder, who perform ugly social tasks like a garbage collector. Therefore the survival of the fittest concept does not seem valid. Something else is guiding the developing awareness of man's cosmic existence on the planet. Man is about to discover the laws which govern the intergalactic flow of living energy at the heart of every nucleus.

It is this possibility that we can influence the nuclear seed, not only physically by psychic means, but spiritually re-create the cell structures that will determine the whole future of mankind. The future state is not only contained in the seed in the form of genetic material for the reproduction of itself but also in the surrounding aura which contains the intelligent guiding wave-field which decides the program of its development. Not only is there a nuclear centre at each level of the cell, molecule, atom, etc. but also each functional system has its own government, laws, customs, habitual responses, etc. Each organ and the total system which contains the organs, has a group force or intelligence which must be present around the nuclear centre of all systems if the whole person is to avail itself of the full potential of the genetic material it utilises.

The genetic material alone is only the ladder which an evolutionary being climbs – it is not the climber of the ladder. In the same way the genetic material provides the drives which are only carrier waves requiring to be fleshed out with specific programs, actions, decisions, choices, etc. which can be used for the good or ill of the organism. The drive from the genetic material will provide the natural temperament, will condition the functioning of the endocrine secretions and thereby affect personality, but it will not provide the specific program. How we respond to the drive and how we utilise it will depend entirely on the program written on other non-physical levels of consciousness. Therefore the genetic material is the tool of the spirit and not vice versa as academia would have us believe.

All humans present in a physical incarnation upon this earth have, without exception, inherited potentials from millions of years of evolutionary development which cannot be used until evolutionary intelligence is there. If this intelligence or cosmic program is swamped by the cares of life, by sickness, starvation or self-ignorance, this does not mean that it is not instantly available with a radical change of consciousness.

Over and over again it has been demonstrated that criminals and sex maniacs can turn into saints, that schoolboys considered dull and stupid for not knowing stock answers turn into Einsteins, that the murderous aggressiveness of a St. Paul can be channelled into love and ambitious church projects. It is in the crippling environment of the slums, with their violence and human degradation, that the boy with the potentials of greatness can be born to prove again and again that man progresses in spite of the environmental brainwash.

All humans have incredible computers but not everyone has the intelligence to search for an instruction book as to how that genetic inheritance of millions of years really works. The chance that any given human being will discover such instruction books either hidden in allegories by our forefathers who also found the keys of its construction, or because the cosmic program is already within them, will not depend on his or her station in life. Men who are born in luxury can be notoriously decadent and stupid and men born into suffering or in a stable can be in direct contact with the evolutionary instrument and mount the genetic ladder to its creator's feet.

In this total sense the biological ladder is the end product of a long line of unions at every level of consciousness, although the physical transfer of the seed from one organism to another cannot have one sperm or ovum missing in that long chain of events. Consciousness has been writing itself into that long line of continuous flesh for millions of years and it is only the ignorant who think of themselves as separate beings independent of all that long inheritance. Survival of the fittest implies that evolution favours success, but success and failure are equally important in the development of the species. To see value only in successful maintenance of survival is to misunderstand evolution, since failure is as much a determinant in future actions of the cosmic program as success is. In fact, failure may be a more persistent teacher and evolver of man than the occasional successful model or embodiment. It is doubtful how many humans have become as evolved as Christ because of his positive example. From the standpoint of survival, the crucifixion was a failure and only the "risen Christ" who triumphed over physical death was the success.

Is it part of the evolutionary design that we should all rise from the dead and if so what does this mean? The number of people who have risen from the dead, even if this were the evolutionary plan, seem to be remarkably lacking in the last 2,000 years. What did Christ and the prophets mean by this expression? Obviously it was not a physical rising of the dead bodies from all the graves, as has been prophesied for the end of the world, but it referred to the spirits of men who live on after death. The secret of eternal life is to live in the state of timelessness which is not a physical rising but the very opposite of time-bound, space-bound physical existence. It is not that a person rises into some heavenly state but that this state of divine consciousness rises in him! This rising entails nothing less than the complete peeling of the scales off the eyes of the blind as prophesied by Isaiah:

Arise and shine! Thy light has come! The radiance of
the eternal One has dawned in thee.

For a being in this state of clear-seeing, in which the separate self-sense that creates the limits of time and space is let go, the spirits of all people can "rise" in his consciousness from out of the Akasha regardless of what time they lived on the earth. But although these souls have survived the physical death of the body, they are not risen into eternal life until they too have felt the radiance of the eternal One dawn in them:

> Lift up thine eyes! Look around and see the gathering together of the universe to come to thee. . . . . Then your enlightenment shall see the flowing together and thy pure heart shall unfold within thee . . . . . No longer will the sun be your light by day nor the brightness of the moon by night, for Pure Consciousness has become thy God and everlasting light to glorify thee.
>
> (Isaiah 60, vv. 1-5, 19, 21)

The early Christians up to the year 400 and occasionally amongst Christians after Christianity became an organised religion at Rome, actually believed in a physical revisitation by the historical Christ. Nowadays only a few fundamentalists believe this. The more esoteric believe in Christ more as a principle or essence inherent in everyone. That Christ's spirit did impregnate the psychic atmosphere of the planet most powerfully on the intuitional level, however, was not in question amongst the early Christians. The question was the physical embodiment of Christ. The faith was that there is to be again a living Christ, an incarnation as an avatar, or the coming of someone who manifests the wish fulfillment of the new age. Even today there are new sects springing up on this messianic expectation with boy teachers and messiahs and places out in the desert for believers to visit. The belief in some magical wonder which will automatically solve humanity's problems is strong. Amongst religions and science fiction adherents, the visitation of some super-intelligence who will transcend the physical earthly condition is a common belief shared down the centuries by Christians who believed Christ would reappear in the same form and image as He did so long ago. To expect Christ to appear in modern clothes and without long hair and a beard is almost unthinkable to those who think they would recognise him instantly. Undoubtably there is always a living Christ and he would be the most advanced human on the face of the earth at any one time. Whether we would recognise his stature with our own limited consciousness, or instead be fascinated by a personality drama of those making gross claims to avatarhood depends on our drives, expectations and wish fulfillments originating in the Indigo level of the sixth chakra.

Repeatedly certain types of people dream of escaping earth by creating communities in outer space or being lifted off to more evolved planets in flying saucers. They are so obsessed with physical transcendence, they cannot see that "salvation" will happen right in our own consciousness once we open the imagination chakra. Whether the early Christians were as gullible as today's cult adherents who flock to gurus, who claim to have "powers", is not the point. The point is, what does this preoccupation with physical transcendence of the body do for the evolution of mankind? The answer is it does nothing, because the failure of the Christian religion to see what Christ was really talking about is almost equal to the failure of the Marxists to see anything evolutionary at all in religions.

Christ was indeed talking evolutionary language but as it is translated and understood in ordinary language it is comic, not cosmic, that we should practice the opposite of what he says. Do not set me up as a personality cult, he keeps saying -- there is only ONE. Yet the Christian religion is personality cult Number One, even greater than that of Mohammed as sole and last prophet of God's cosmic plan.

God must be wondering why these people of the earth cannot even see the tricks of their own consciousness and ego structure, yet they talk of God with every breath as if they knew his evolutionary purpose. What arrogance! But how devout they are and how regularly do they pray in vain.

By contrast Nuclear Evolution is the cosmic program as revealed in nature's own intelligence hidden in the human body. If man is ever to understand his own social evolution he must first know what a human being is, in order to see how his unconscious drives are projected out into society. Nuclear Evolution is a crude typology which mankind will continue to refine for eons to come. It is a way to transcend personality cults. The human biosphere and seven levels of consciousness vibrating in different worlds of time and being is the radio station which communicates the cosmic program to the total environment around us. It is on these planes of consciousness that we shall rise from the dead state of being and transcend the physical consciousness and enter the many mansions which Christ talked about.

BOOKS ON NUCLEAR EVOLUTION
SUGGESTED FOR FURTHER READING

REFERENCES

See:

HILLS' THEORY OF CONSCIOUSNESS (a physicist's view) by Robert Massy, PhD, Publ. 1976.

JOURNEY INTO LIGHT (a viewpoint from a dream analyst) by Ann Ray, PhD, Publ. 1977

THE ARCHITECTURE OF CONSCIOUSNESS by Michael Hammer, Publ. 1977

THE MIRROR OF CHANGE by Norah Hills (a practical course) Publ. 1978

DIRECT PERCEPTION by Deborah Rozman, PhD, (a psychologist's view) Publ. 1977

EXPLORING INNER SPACE by Christopher Hills, Edited by Deborah Rozman and Susan Welker, 1977

ENERGY, MATTER AND FORM by Phillip Allen, Alastair Bearne and Roger Smith, Publ. 1977

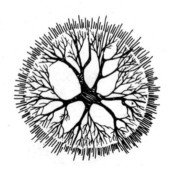

The forthcoming titles on the subject of Nuclear Evolution are in preparation and are to be published in 1977/78:

BREAKING THROUGH THE LIGHT BARRIER by Richard Welker

METAMORPHOSIS OF A HUMAN BUTTERFLY by Jeffrey Goelitz

THE COSMIC CIRCUS by Susan Welker

LOVE'S SPECTRUM by Susan Belanger

IM-PRISMED by Roger Smith

THRESHOLDS OF LIGHT by Rod Glasgow

THE WORLD IS A MIRROR by Wendy McFadzen

EVOLUTION OF
CONSCIOUSNESS
AND GENETICS

SOCIOBIOLOGY AND EVOLUTION

There have been endless debates from ancient times on the origin and evolution of mankind. Even in this "New Age", the old controversy between heredity and environment carries on: are we really who we are because of biological inheritance from our parents or are we shaped by the environment we grew up in? The debate upon these external questions prevents our searching in the nature of man's being for some inner structure of consciousness which shapes his **response** to the givens of his heredity and environment, some deeper part of him that is not merely influenced but which in itself knows the secret of evolving and which evolves not only physical strength and mental cleverness but can actually unfold into a higher kind of being.

Sociobiology implies that there are genetic influences in human social behaviour, inherited from our animal background in the long evolutionary spiral: animal instincts such as aggression, mate selection, reproduction and social competition between species. But even though the human animal has the same organs, eyes, excretory systems as animals and similar nervous systems, there is something about a human being that so far transcends such similarities as to make the comparison with animals very naive. The evidence is strong that the human brain contains a bio-program of potentials built into the species by some evolutionary intelligence and that these faculties are evolved long before they are needed. In other words, the bio-energetic equipment for Nuclear Evolution has already been given each individual person and is just waiting to be used. The human brain is so constructed that only one tenth of it is necessary for life purposes on the planet at the material biological level of existence. Barely another tenth is needed for all the social and human knowledge, which leaves eighty percent of its potential use available for higher functions. The nature of these higher faculties is not culturally determined but is realised only by the very few individuals who are imaginative enough to open to new possibilities. In fact, cultural determinism works against it.

Most social biologists still hold to the idea of natural selection through countless centuries of trial and error. This dated theory can explain biological structures such as the capacity of the eye to take in light through the pupil, but it does not even attempt to deal with the really crucial issues like the experience of light as internal brightness in the brain. It may explain the way people and animals band together in groups but it does not look at mankind through other comparisons like the way birds navigate a distance of ten thousand miles or insects find food or a mate by E.S.P. Scientists are willing to use the well-known behaviour of animals in a zoo a few days prior to an earthquake as a means of

*"Freedom is indivisible . . . One must take a moral
attitude toward it."*

prediction, but to use similar human potentials for divination of a critical evolutionary pathway is not considered scientific. Man's use of telepathic and intuitive modes of knowing are more accepted now than they once were, but scientists have yet to recognise the wider thresholds of that physical body which they treat as merely a sensory detector of environmental signals. When they do, they will come face to face with the fact that natural selection is too limited to explain the ultimate guiding intelligence which has created unused dormant faculties to probe the unknown vibrational worlds beyond the narrow range of the senses.

NATURAL SELECTION IN REVERSE

Every major social advance in the world has been made by individuals who obtained their predictive abilities from higher abstract levels of consciousness than the sensory information levels of perception. Whether we speak of Moses, Christ, Krishna or any leader of a cultural or scientific development, such as Einstein, we see a certain factor present in the originators. Whether the Chinese use the I Ching, developed over thousands of years by men of paranormal perceptions, or revert to purely mental, idealistic and conceptual thoughts as they have done under Mao Tse Tung, the moulding of a culture has been determined by the intuitive vision of the governing individuals. Where natural selection has weeded out the sensitive, caring and highly critical and individualistic members of society who might hold dissident thoughts toward the ruling oligarchy, there has always been a revulsion or reaction from later generations, however ruthless the annihilation of the troublesome genetic materials from the species.

Stalin consistently murdered millions for nothing more than disagreement with his methods. Peasants and intellectuals alike who got in his way were trampled ruthlessly underfoot in more savage ways than anything Hitler did if we are to believe the documentation of Solzhenitsyn. Yet we may still see the ruling clique overturned in years to come by more enlightened people. Even the revolutionaries have now become conservatives and the dissidents may yet rise above the millions of dead reactionary genetic material now lying beneath the earth. In other words, there is some spiritual essence or qualitative leap in the human soul that transcends the workings of socio-biological laws and, despite attempts to stamp out these genetic qualities of so-called reactionaries, the human spirit seems to have its source in another framework entirely and therefore always springs to life again.

Democracy evolved more human ways of killing those who transgressed its social laws. The electric chair was eventually scrapped when the death penalty was abolished. Now the number of murderers is increasing so rapidly at public expense that the jails are crammed. The taxpayer bears the brunt of their crimes both ways, once as victim and again as provider of T.V. shows, rehabilitation programs, food and wages. The laws of a democracy protect the individual even when the individual commits criminal acts. The laws of a socialist country do not even protect the individual against thinking the wrong thoughts. Sakharov and Solzhenitsyn risk worse than death in the bestial conditions of the Russian slave camps. Who cares? The Russian dissidents say freedom is indivisible.

However I realise that it is not good enough to speculate that there is some higher evolutionary program written into the brain and its connected nervous antennae. More specific evidence of higher perception must be offered if we are to study human behaviour using less speculative, more vigorous research into the evolutionary thrust towards higher and more complex organisation. This need has now been filled in "Supersensonics" (published 1975) which sets out the methods and faculties which all human beings can develop to get in direct touch with nature's own universal laws of behaviour.

These laws are working out through specific patterns of consciousness and are built into every organism. Not a single cell of biological material on earth can be separated from the total environment which moulded it. To look at evolution purely from the micro level without knowing the macro view through the faculties used in Supersensonics, is to see only a worm's eye view of the creation. To divine what the remaining eighty percent of the brain is for may appear miraculous to such a worm but to the evolutionary intelligence such methods of tuning in to environmental conditions are only a beginning. It is a fact that many insects and animals already have higher faculties of communication which are not always used for survival, e.g. dolphins, whales, seals, who have no fear of man and his aggressiveness. They seem to accept physical death at the hands of their enemies with a forgiveness equal to that of a Christ.

The higher functions of telepathy, other intuitive modes of knowing, and clairvoyant images do not seem to be very useful as a survival instrument but function instead as faculties for selection of mates and for envisioning and setting out the path of evolution. This capacity to envision makes it possible for a human being to step outside the picture frame of evolution and by-pass whole segments of this long arduous process, making leaps into higher states of consciousness even within one lifetime. Anyone who can let go his sense of identity long enough to envision something larger can begin a new evolutionary spiral into vast areas of being that are not comprehensible at the level where fins become feet and a sea creature emerges onto the land. It is the visions of our most imaginative people today which will determine the shape of the future. How we respond to those images of ourself and the future will depend on how well we know the imagination which controls the social behaviour patterns of individuals.

Altruistic behaviour is not the unique property of humans and is common among animals. The idea that natural selection works only for the selfish advantage of an individual cannot be true since altruism, which is giving to society and others more than you get back, would long ago have disappeared off the face of the earth. Such altruistic individuals would be less fit to survive against selfish and ignorant competitors, and evolution would be disproved by breeding only the favoured selfish people. Also the future would promise no hope of less egotism, and natural selection's corollary of a continually advancing civilisation would be impossible.

PRIMAL DRIVES AND NUCLEAR EVOLUTION

It is difficult to make general statements which apply to all the nonhuman primates, much less to infer behavioural similarities between them and humans. To some researchers it seems inappropriate to use the patterns of nonhuman primates to justify our own patterns in very different, strictly human environments. They argue that there are specific human problems which need to be viewed in human psychic environments such as nationalism, poverty, economic conditions, racism, etc. But all these kinds of human social phenomena are only effects, whereas Nuclear Evolution looks at causes: those primal drives which are present in all organisms, in animals, mankind and even in some species of plant life. In other words, Nuclear Evolution recognises the drives which mankind has in common with the rest of nature, yet sees also his vast evolutionary potentials which far surpass what sociobiology sets forth. After twenty years of research into colour psychology, I believe it is these drives which shape society and determine the level of communication between humans, between human bodies and their environment, and even between other species and intelligences.

Since primal drives in nature are determined by the unconscious control of the chakra system, the human aura reveals remarkable psychological correlations to the spectrum. There are specialists today, as there have been throughout history, who are as yet unaware of psychic effects which ordinary people without any scientific experience can confirm as easily as looking at a rainbow. The facts are already written unconsciously in the language. From ancient times references to colour, such as red with action and anger, black with resentment, grey with fear, green with envy, jealousy and insecurity, blue representing conservative authority and nostalgic history, and purple linked with power, are hidden in the language of many cultures. To some people, however, black may represent annihilation in death and to others annihilation of the ego, as with a priest. But in spite of cultural preferences, the effect of black on the psyche is the same the world over. For example, in primitive cultures, black has a positive cultural meaning but its effect on the cells and psychic equipment of a pygmy in Africa is the same as on an Eskimo in the arctic. When a Londoner shows red anger in his aura the same colour is seen in the angry revolutionary Chinese in Peking. The theory of Nuclear Evolution looks from the viewpoint of how light is absorbed and interacts with all cell life in terms of the total light spectrum of cosmic forces from surrounding stars and not just our local sun. It is these more subtle primal ingestions of light energy which control the evolution of the planet and the environment well below and above the conscious mind of most of mankind.

The study of Nuclear Evolution is therefore a way of penetrating the chemical reaction of the endocrine glands to light and colour and penetrating the human personality at the deep unconscious level at the same time. Consequently, we can use colour responses to predict behaviour of groups of conservatives, intellectuals, manics, schizoids, poets, scientists, religionists, pacifists, etc. But prediction at the group level, although possible, is not the main purpose of this approach. Nuclear Evolution is most fruitful when individuals, one by one, use it to understand themselves and to deepen communications with other human beings. At this level, the theory has enormous implications for mankind, because no solution of international disorder can be achieved until the tension within individuals is lessened, since it is the aggregate tensions of individuals which make up national tensions. Far greater than any nuclear threats or external pollution of the planet is the pollution of man's inner mind and heart from which all the fears and shadows about the intentions of others originate. The arming of great nations with weapons is only an effect of this cause.

These fears originate in uncertainty and mistrust of conflicting ideals in groups whose ideals and values are different. When some people speak of Communism, for example, they infuse the word **they** with an energy that vibrates with a total inability to get into the Communist mind and see how it works. Instead there is a clinging to their own values in a fearfulness which is directly proportional to the unwillingness to look. Ignorance of the invisible inner worlds is the root of all human fears. Obviously the individual can never master his fear without some mapping of the unknown territory, and yet the same psychic filters that we are investigating colour our findings. This applies particularly to Yellow level scientists who tend to think they are objective and hardnosed and logical, but it also applies to Blue level religious people who suffer from self-righteous pride in their doctrine or teacher. More than to any group it applies to politicians and idealists who are prepared to murder millions of people who happen to have other chakras functioning and whose reality is therefore different.

RATIONALISM AND EMOTIONALISM

For the Yellow level rationalist to acknowledge the real essence of new knowledge and really look deeply enough so that he can see it, is rare. Usually there is a gut feeling against certain evidence which conflicts with accepted entrenched consensus knowledge and then out comes the sword of reason to destroy it. Eddington saved Einstein's theory of relativity from oblivion because he was able to see it not as threatening but wonderful. He was one of only six men on the planet who could have understood it enough to test its validity in 1917. But for many years after proof of the theory, there were anti-Einstein societies and letters to editors by prominent scientists rationalising him away as an addle brain. Sir Isaac Newton had a similar experience and refused to publish for fear of having to answer a host of smatterers who refused to look at the evidence in any depth. Einstein wrote his proton theory in 1905 but did not get the Nobel Prize for it until 1921, because many hardnosed scientists refused to accept it, even though it had been experimentally proved five years earlier.

This same threatened feeling but in magnified form is behind the military-industrial complex, and these same deep fears are common to other creatures. Birds fly away from imaginary enemies, wild animals are insecure in the presence of humans; some freeze and others take flight. Humans feel no different on these levels and only their methods of handling fear are different. It is one thing to argue that there is no counterpart among the nonhuman primates for such particularly human afflictions as political idealism or massive military threats of annihilation, but it is quite another to realise that this rational way of looking at man's evolution is merely a superficial approach. Whether you die by the atomic threat or an African spear has not much relevance to someone confronted with imminent death. Perhaps the fear of the spear is even greater in the moment of Truth for a rationalist. Therefore we must penetrate much deeper into the structure of human personality and its unconscious drives if we are to understand the forces which dominate society.

The approach of ninety-five percent of modern man at this time in history is not wholistic. It is much easier when ideas get complex to rationalise in an either/or framework, but knowing Truth is more a matter of the observation point and the observer's methods of perception. The university approach polarises itself between environmentalists and geneticists. Out of seven possible levels, it limits man to only two levels of consciousness: on one hand the physical cell-like biological basis of primal urges (Red), and on the other hand the controlling effects of social environments (Orange).

Undoubtedly a considerable amount of brainwash takes place in every culture as to how we should think. In countries where absolute control is exercised over knowledge and where public news information is withheld, it is impossible for the residents of the community to make intelligent decisions or assessments. Political indoctrination from youth can enslave the mind to one method of thought, and society no doubt can be built to produce economic wealth in the image of a certain doctrine. But this does not stop people's fears, hatreds, insecurity, doubts or bigotry on the five other levels of the intellectual (Yellow), acquisition (Green), conceptual (Blue), intuitive (Indigo), and imaginative (Violet) functions of human life. To legislate these areas of human interaction is a cosmic pipe dream of enormous size and can only be the product of total self-delusion in the holy name of reason and thought.

The facts are that humans, and to some extent other primates, operate on seven levels of consciousness which make up all the functions of Being. To omit any one drive is to give only a partial picture of reality, and to omit five and operate on only the two levels of biological (Red) and social (Orange) reveals that only the lowest and most limiting of nature's drives are presently functioning in most people. To be able to analyse on the Yellow level and see that society is influenced unconsciously by the other six, even more profoundly because it is unconscious, is to be liberated from the limitations of the first two levels that monopolise the socio-political ferment taking place on the planet at all universities. The fact that any level can always see the levels below it or opposing it but never understand completely all the levels above it, is a profound insight in Nuclear Evolution. Suddenly we see why things are as they are. We stand up and see down the centuries how social conditions have emerged out of this dualistic framework, this either/or thinking which man has continually projected upon the vast scene of evolution. The inability to learn the Blue level lessons of history, because of crude Yellow level intellectual blindness, has dominated the political and philosophical climate from the time of Plato's Republic to the present day. Mankind has swung back and forth like a pendulum between opposites instead of going round and round in a spiral.

The passionate embroilment of behaviourists of all schools and the geneticists alike, suggests that humans, even at the Blue and Yellow scientific levels of conceptualisation, are driven from some other vaguely unconscious level of consciousness. In the same way international terrorists unconsciously rationalise the murder of innocent people for their causes, so do nations and their leaders unconsciously validate reality from one or two levels

– their own. Among scientific, spiritual, and social politicians equally, this subtle blindness to the real structure of consciousness and its levels of functioning serves to create a natural barrier to the development of individual awareness and thence to an enlightened mankind. We see this blindness in the traditional Blue level guru trapped in his culture just as much as in the Western priest or scientist, fighting the last-ditch battle for well-entrenched Truths. The guru who becomes an authority figure and teaches dependence rather than thinking for oneself, rationalises his desire for many disciples by feeling virtuous over Blue level ideals. This kind of self-deception at the Blue or any of the seven levels is part of being human and is not to be condemned but to be clearly seen. The whole purpose of studying the levels of our consciousness is to become aware of their drives at work in us, for only by making them conscious can we begin to gain mastery of them. To understand what is controlling our behaviour unconsciously in each of the seven levels is to gain the power to advance our own evolution tremendously through conscious redirection of the energies.

OPENING TO NEW AWARENESS

Everyone likes to think he is seeing with clarity and, to one who is looking at the world through the narrow window of one chakra, his perception of life seems a true picture of reality. But in fact his tunnel-vision blocks clear seeing on all the other levels. Only constant mistakes and failures convince people they are lacking in perception, and even then it is difficult to let go of the idea that one's own reality is truth. This constant blindness reflected in all schemes for social evolution is directly connected to this mechanism in each individual person which convinces him that the perception of life -- as created by his own assumptions, opinions, past experiences, preferences, hopes, and fears (to say nothing of the limited range of his senses) – is the truest possible view of reality. He believes he already knows, and this prevents him from being receptive to that evolutionary intelligence which is working through him. If he is locked in the Red, Orange, and Yellow levels, he cannot be convinced that the others are really there, not even if he reads about the seven colours which offer a psychic thumbprint of our souls. He may believe it in theory but in his life he will continue to feel that he is seeing true, because his own direct experience is his only universe. The theory of Nuclear Evolution teaches that we live not only in different personalities but in entirely different worlds. Nonrecognition of the real enormity of this fact is the source of all tensions and misunderstandings among people, whether between husband and wife or between nation and nation.

685

The Independence war in East Pakistan caused an estimated million of Bengalis to be massacred by troops of West Pakistan. These bodies of three women, three children and an old man along with thousands of others in long pits were found dead after the Pakistani troops withdrew from Jessore city. Millions of other Bengalis fled to India to escape the brutality of their fellow countrymen. The senseless killing was done by guns. Years earlier, at the time of partition in 1947, the killing of ten million in communal riots was done with knives.

The beginning of clear seeing is nothing dramatic. It is only a matter of allowing ourselves to become aware of more factors than our viewpoint normally includes. If someone has hurt us, we can focus not only on our hurt but stop to wonder what is happening in their world to make them treat us badly. Seeing the causalities frees us from taking umbrage personally at the behaviour of others. Then we can let them be and this is in itself a very large step in evolution. The words sound simplistic, but how many of us actually bother to control our consciousness in this way? How many of us even notice what our consciousness is doing as it moves around inside us responding and reacting to life? We can step outside ourselves and see, for instance, that if we as a society really believed that we have the power to change reality by planting an idea in our imagination (the order orientated level Violet), then we could not continue to blame the government as we do now but must see that we alone are responsible for our destiny. If enough people functioned from the intuitive knowing of essence (Indigo), our society would then communicate more by what is **meant** rather than by what is said, and the whole political structure would have to evolve and become more ordered.

In opening to new awareness, we begin to notice a difference between how things ought to be and how they really are. We notice, for instance, how the seven drives shape society even at the highest scientific and religious levels of human endeavor. Religious fratricide in Northern Ireland between Catholics and Protestants differs little in the final results from the communal riots between Hindus and Muslims at the time of partition of India and Pakistan. Ten million people were butchered by fanatic zealots in various states along the borders of India and Pakistan without any sophisticated military-industrial complex or weapons other than knives. So we also see through the false argument that wars, violence and oppression arise out of the making of armaments or from the industrial-economic complex or from any other aspect of the external environment. We perceive that aggression is often deliberately cultivated among communities which were formerly loving, generous and unselfish, by political activists among whom the physical Red drive for dominating others is the major chakra function. And seeing clearly in this way brings us to realise that we too have the power to rechannel these very same drives in ourselves.

LEGISLATING CHANGE

To evolve society, we must first evolve ourself. The Dean of one American college used to say he had no use for yogis because they only sat in caves, whereas he was changing the world. His field was Sociology and his way was to gather people together in

687

groups and to legislate change. But after a while, as each of his projects began to lose force and people slipped back into their old ways, he saw that he was old and had really accomplished very little. He was disillusioned with his ideals and yet had nothing to put in place of them. Even though he was a pedant, there was something in him that made him try. And perhaps this same impulse could really have accomplished something if he had had other levels of awareness beyond the Orange, Blue and Yellow. He felt virtuous because he had done his best and because his ideals were high, yet his stubborn blind spots made him a small person. It is an odd paradox to think that ideals could be a stumbling block to evolution, but often the very striving of an idealist blocks the thing he is striving for from happening.

To determine where man is on the spiral of evolution, using the spectrum as a yardstick, we can see clearly that mankind is still mainly at the Red level, materialistic, concrete awareness of reality, using the idealistic level of consciousness in the service of materialism. So we must make a clear distinction between thinkers who want to evolve society by external manipulations and the Nuclear Intelligence which simply unfolds. Man's belief that evolutionary developments can be legislated irrespective of the inner thoughts and feelings in the hearts of men, is an hallucination, an extension of his other false belief that ideas and products can be sold indefinitely by advertising if only enough money or resources or control over the media is obtained. This idea stems both from the temporary success of big business which controls the sales of certain products and services to large populations by persuasion and from the supposed fact that a government can influence the evolutionary thrust by forbidding competing newspapers and censoring dissident publications. But in fact, this social brainwashing does not change the inner nature of mankind. Man loves, hates, relates and climbs into positions of social power in exactly the same way as ancient times; only the scenario and external trappings are changed into a new illusion, a new drama. However, Nuclear Evolution does not depend on the continuous propaganda of parties or governments to keep it alive or promote its eventual takeover of man's thoughts, simply because Nuclear Evolution is already within each person in the structure of the Self. It is the basic structure of man's evolutionary being which he cannot escape from by putting on little sideshows and dramas which ignore reality.

Many of the greatest schemes of men have fizzled with heavy financial or government backing while the young inventor or social originator has flourished for good or ill. Take the two examples of Einstein and Marx. Both were almost poverty-stricken whilst writing their world-changing theses. While Einstein's ideas took 70 years to be fully understood at the high school level, they influenced the whole of electromagnetic man's achievements. During the same period Marx's totalitarian social concepts of the supremacy of the state over individual life have dominated by force half the planet. And again, this happened through the filter of the individual level of consciousness, as it was always certain individuals like Lenin, Mao Tse Tung, etc. who were responsible for the interpretation of Communism as well as its execution. Had their consciousness been functioning at a higher level, then history would be happening in a different way, and the same is true of the use men chose to make of Einstein's discovery of $E=Mc^2$. Despite the effects on society, one can still see an invisible hand behind the efforts of Einstein and Marx, who put some essence into the headwaters of the stream before it became the mighty rivers of science and politics respectively. But unfortunately, the presence of an invisible evolutionary spirit at work is discernable only to those who develop the higher faculties of direct perception.

SUPERSENSONICS

Nuclear Evolution even now is working in a similar way towards transformation of the planet through the structural composition of consciousness expressing itself in a seven-level sociobiology beyond the conscious mind of man. Almost eighty-five percent of all people already have, in dormant state, the supersensitive faculties of dowsing and divining their untapped levels of consciousness with biofeedback tools. The blueprint of evolution is therefore within their grasp. By biofeedback, I do not mean expensive EEG machines which hook electrodes on your head, but simple biological feedback instruments which give neuro-muscular response from the unconscious awareness of the more subtle wave-fields of the human aura. The book "Supersensonics" explains these subtle energies which interpenetrate the biophysical nature of man. I wrote it to set out a method by which anyone who had the will or the time to do some simple experiments could easily prove for themselves the existence of the different levels of consciousness. The purpose in this present book is to outline the theory; Supersensonics is the practice and technique of Nuclear Evolution. Because Supersensonics provides self-validating results which can be checked by our peers and not some special "expert" authority, the theory and practice together put the power over our own lives back where it truly belongs — in our own consciousness. Supersensonics can be used for divining the state of consciousness of our own selves or of the highest representatives of humanity, checking on the integrity of our representatives in the House of Representatives or negotiating at the peace table or deciding whether a violent criminal will commit another crime before releasing him on parole. With Supersensonics we can determine the hidden intentions of those who are racing to place nuclear warheads in the rockets that are pointing at us. It is not only a tool for investigating behaviour but an instrument of survival. By employing the knowledge of the human personality in Nuclear Evolution, Supersensonics allows us to gain some understanding of the subtle·but potent images which lurk in the dark unconscious of certain key people in power. We can test the ability of the imagination (Violet level) to twist reality or the way complex theories from the Blue level of consciousness are foisted upon us (from many different motives) by political radicals who do not test their concepts on themselves before trying them out on the large social scale. Similarly, we can test the rationalisers and their basic assumptions about facts.

AWARENESS: THE EVOLUTIONARY THRUST

Explanations, rationalisations and theories which use natural analogies to boost the validity of social ideas are often based, for better or worse, on scientific assumptions which are later found to be totally false. These logical intellectual fashions of our society which are constantly changing and fermenting on every university campus are really of little importance against the back-drop of cosmic evolutionary time. The notion that there is a biological or genetic component in human behaviour calls into the social arena the dualistic battles of human versus animal, spirit versus matter, mind versus body, when none of these is relevant to the vast marching on of evolution, which ignores these idealistic conceptual levels of human activity and manifests itself at much deeper and more profound levels of Being. The forces of social upheaval and change in human history are natural consequences of Man's awareness and transcend the genetic differences between one class and another, if any.

Although the majority of society is composed of individuals who are territorially minded, physically possessive and acquisitive, which may be good for the survival of the fittest, the masses do not evolve much in reality because their greater love of authority, conformity and stability holds them back from real change. These masses become passive instruments in the hands of the more imaginative, more aggressive leaders. It is a fact that mankind rises above its animal origins and acquires noble, compassionate and altruistic traits not by genetic or culturally determined behaviour patterns, but in spite of them. The reason is that the manifesta-tion of all higher faculties is not learned second-hand from others but through the natural unfolding on higher levels of conscious-ness. Compassion or love cannot be learned, legislated or acquired; it is the direct result of the natural goodness which emerges through the practice of self-improvement, meditation, contempla-tion of consciousness itself, and understanding the ego conflicts. It is not the property of the genes nor is it culturally determined.

690

Compassion, mercy, and divinely inspired intellect come to those who work on themselves; these qualities do not come through hereditary transmission or by eating certain foods or even via religious beliefs and scientific philosophies.

In India where prayer, chanting and devout spiritual practice have been the greatest expression of the culture for thousands of years and where belief in preserving life of animals and even insects is culturally determined, there can be the most horrifying bloodlettings and civil disturbances with literally millions of deaths, as at the time of partition. The number of deaths and mutilations over one year far exceeds all casualties during the two great wars. The genes of these people are definitely passive and peace-loving if one regards their history and long spiritual practice. Yet over ten thousand people died in a commune riot over a relic of the prophet's hair in two days while I visited Chandigarh. The view that evolution programs higher impulses and noble actions into human behaviour as a practical strategy for survival is also wishful thinking. These nonphysical traits only emerge in highly evolved beings who set examples of behaviour which people generally do imitate idealistically, but without actual work on themselves, these acquired and learned high level responses of people disappear at the first real threat to survival. The great tenets of the Sermon on the Mount are livable only by a dedicated few, for though many profess belief in them, the quality of life in Christian communities betrays the real mediocrity of mass thinking on these high teachings. Only a very few people become saints and provide the models for human behaviour and its evolution to higher, more caring and compassionate levels of consciousness. By practicing spiritual breathing and yogic techniques, many human behaviour patterns such as those attributed to genes can be changed and overcome. This applies to male/female unbalance such as homosexuality, male dominance, power-seeking, or sexual appetites. Changes in the pH of the cerebrospinal fluid* due to yogic breathing are much more likely to affect behaviour and thought processes than a person's genes, because they evolve potentials in him which transcend the limits of just one incarnation.

THE TREADMILL OF HISTORY

The theory of Nuclear Evolution is predicated on the fact that changes at the nuclear centre of being do not take place through superficial or external pressures from the environment, but in

---

* Aaron Friedell, M.D. "May You Live In Health", available University of the Trees Press.

spite of it. The changes which take place in individuals at the idealistic level do not necessarily bring about evolutionary changes in man's social world but merely produce an exchange of roles. Revolution is going round and round. Hence the czars and baronial rulers who established the social pecking order in Russia were replaced fifty years later by a system of power struggles within the Communist party and the governing polit-bureau which erects a new baronial tree in place of the old one, the new barons having even more power over the resources of the proletariat than the old. This power extends to dictating where they shall work and what they shall say and holds more chance of arrest for them than ever existed under the original baronial order.

The facts given by Alexander Solzhenitsyn that the czar needed only to execute about 400 in the final year of his reign while Stalin liquidated 40,000 helpless dissidents per month, should give some of us the understanding of the vast difference between external and idealistic communist or political revolution and the internal and nuclear permanence of evolution. The revolutionary fervour which has marked most of the political changes of human society cannot be given any other name except that of "Self-righteousness" of those who believe they know the answers to human existence. The fact that they have had to murder millions of their Russian, Chinese and Tibetan brothers and sisters in order to satisfy this self-delusion that they themselves are the agents of evolution, should give mankind some sobering thoughts about the level of man's social knowledge.

Even if the theory of man's levels of consciousness were widely accepted, it would be a political hot potato which no leader would want to get into for fear that he might personally measure rather low down on the scale of evolutionary intelligence. Yet any formulations of human nature, setting out its real needs and evolutionary potentials and the structures of consciousness which shape human social interaction, is a political issue of the highest importance if mankind is to get off the treadmill and stop repeating the age-old patterns of history.

THE NECESSITY OF GROUP CONSCIOUSNESS

What is the true essential nature of our species? This question most urgently needs an answer if individuals and the societies they create are to understand each other. The Darwinian concept of evolution is that organisms compete against their fellows for survival, with the "successful" competitors surviving at the expense of others and producing more progeny of their own ability. For single organisms this may be true but for social animals who live together in social groups the most harsh

692

competition for power and resources usually produces a reaction or revolution which prevents them from competing too well against their own species. The history of all kings and emperors and big business corporations and other special groups has often been greatly modified by their governments who have stripped them of absolute power. Because of this, evolution of social animals often favours the success not of individuals who are highly original or who break through to other levels of human consciousness, but of groups of those individuals who, for various motives, give up their self-interests in favour of the social group. As such they can abdicate their spiritual responsibility to evolve in order to perform unpleasant tasks in the name of the group which other individuals would not wish to perform. For example, companies which kill other species like seals and whales are owned in part by shareholders such as churches. Other examples are groups, such as political parties, who set out to win and elect individuals who will serve the power interests of the group above the interests of Truth and of their own soul.

This amalgamation of low levels of consciousness into group solidarity makes for survival not of the fittest but often of the least fit. People with the least individuality and least spirit become the genetic backbone of the human race. Therefore the implementation of Nuclear Evolution must depend on those few beings who will daily invest consciousness and caring into the changing of human behaviour patterns in themselves as they interact freely with groups of like-minded souls. Even when negative patterns are inherited biologically and enforced culturally, such caring persons can transcend these external limitations by modifying the structure of consciousness. The way this works in the evolution of human social organisations is described in my book, "Universal Government by Nature's Laws", formerly published as "The New Book of Changes" in 1963 and reissued in 1978. After fourteen years of direct experiment in two communities, one in London and the other in California, these theories of government and human change have proved to be socially possible alternatives, not just idealistic words.

WHO WILL MAKE IT HAPPEN?

Being people, like any other part of society, scholars are subject to the same problems, the same self-deceit, the same ignorance of Self and the same blindness to the obvious as humans always have been. Therefore the next step in the cosmic drama will not flow forth from universities or seats of learning but, when nature reveals her evolutionary instrument of the Rainbow Body, it will obviously be the universities which will research its validity and test it theoretically. Although it is clearly the business of the university to study all social changes and to provide the scientific rigour of research, it has always been certain uncompromising individuals who have changed society or brought illuminating Truths. We need only to mention the names of Einstein, Jesus, Galileo, Newton, Lao Tse, etc. who have not compromised with the prevailing thoughts of contemporaries. Institutions representing the establishment have always resisted real change and we can see that ideas, philosophies, new viewpoints of cosmic events happen in spite of them. In other words, the traditional seats of learning study something deeply only after it has become meaningful to an expert few.

The role played by Eddington in the proving of Einstein's thought experiments and predictions is perhaps the same role played by the gatekeeper in preserving the wisdom of Lao Tse for the generations which follow. Without this help Einstein would have probably been still a very poor patent clerk in Switzerland and Lao Tse some unknown recluse whose knowledge died with him. Newton's most brilliant work, which set the tone of scientific enquiry for several hundred years, would never have been published during his lifetime but for Halley, who badgered him to publish for ten years and eventually paid for its printing out of his own pocket.

For us with hindsight it seems unlikely that the destiny of movers and changers of the world's millions would hang on such slender happenings whilst the great debates rage over current fashions of thought. The next cosmic unfolding, hanging perhaps by some slender subtle thread which decides whether it will or won't happen in the world, will come in one of those rare individuals, while the more heavy-footed investigation of this unfolding (after the fact) will take place in the schools and universities. Like a completely saturated solution which needs only one tiny crystal dropped into it to completely transform itself according to the pattern of that crystal, the world too comes to a state of readiness in which an Einstein can lightly touch the fabric of things and all human life is suddenly transformed. The wondrous thing about evolution is that it only takes a very few highly evolved people to create the state of readiness into which a Christ can come and crystallise a whole new order of Being. Those who read "Nuclear Evolution", and by applying its truths **become** those truths, will bring about the next step in the evolution of all mankind.

CAN CREATIVE IMAGINATION
CHANGE
MAN'S SOCIAL NATURE?

CAN IMAGINATION CHANGE MAN'S SOCIAL NATURE?

THEME:
> The Self-transmutation of each person
> as an instrument of evolutionary change . . .
> in celebration of Good in the World.

THE POLITICAL AND ECONOMIC IMPACT ON THE FUTURE WORLD SOCIETY OF THE " CENTRE " CONCEPT

It is not sufficient to have bright ideas about the future. It is not even sufficient to be a modern prophet analysing what is wrong with our society. It is no use holding seminars and conferences or lecturing about beautiful changes to be brought about in our new civilisation. These discussions do not prove that we have the answers, or that we even have a realisation of the true human potential for developing vital instruments of CHANGE.

What is needed is an aspiration towards the complete change of life itself. By this I mean bio-energetic changes in man that go far deeper into his material being than any technological system or scientific materialism. With that little bit of consciousness that we have inherited from the Great Creator of Life itself, evolution now expects everyman to change his environment, or stagnate and die unfulfilled. The fact is that more than ever man does change his present environment and he is the agent of new evolution, responsible for each step into the future.

There is no question that man is approaching a crunch point in his evolution. Over-population, insufficient food and fuel supplies, and the increased possibility of global annihilation are as yet unacknowledged symptoms indicating deep and obscure causes in the hearts of men. The failure of science, technology, religion, and government to penetrate these causes shows all the more clearly that the solutions offered by these agencies are of a superficial order, and not necessarily a potent reflection of the vast potential that exists within the human consciousness. Man is like an iceberg in an ocean of consciousness, his visible self being but a small part of the total which lies hidden in subtle fields of radiation. Because of this, attempts to respond only to what is seen has left vast areas of being untouched. These are precisely the keys that will enable man to transcend his present limitations and evolve totally new cultures and civilisations. However, until man can accept the possibility of himself as a being of unlimited potential with a will to match, he will find himself stuck in the ruts of ignorance, atttempting to remedy the symptoms rather than understanding the cause. To admit to causes far beyond our present level of awareness necessitates a fundamental shift in our attitude about change itself, as well as the one who is making the changes. It is the incredible admission that we do not know what we do not know.

> The first question I ask myself is: — How do I see this basic change in LIFE taking place, and even when I do see it, understand it, analyse it, then HOW do I go about doing my part to achieve it?

> I can best give an analogy of this move into the unknown from Nature herself, when she stepped up her social organisation of atoms to the higher government of the molecule. So that when the molecule united in a new federal structure with other sovereign and different molecules there emerged the government of the cell. And when different cells merged in their biological unity, they became sensitive to the tremendous communication network of the whole complex system of organs, and when all the organs perceived that nutrients would not flow efficiently without some new government in which power could be shared and stabilised, we grew the bi-cameral government of the two-hemisphered brain. We have been told by all the great teachers that the next step is Immortal planetary-thinking Universal Man.

The Great Ones like Krishna, Buddha, Jesus, and Lao Tsu have all said the same thing. To him who can hear the message, that message is the eradication of the ego consciousness.

> I see several fundamental changes in Man and his social and political systems that must come about first before this destiny of the body and its surrounding physical energies can ever inhibit the ageing process or arrest the disintegration of his personality. The very first of these changes, described in the first half of this book is to become sensitive to the influx of psychological supra-mental forces which will transform and transmute our present biological functions. Perhaps there are many who will disagree, who feel no dissatisfactions with their physical limitations, whose needs can be gratified without effort, and who would be quite happy to leave things as they are. I represent those men who do not wish to tinker with the Earth and spoil it the way man has done in the past, but who wish to

come closer to Nature and work *with* Life as the evolutionary intelligence at work in all matter. In this sense Supra-mental energies must liberate us not only by penetrating deeper and deeper into material events but by transcending the physical consciousness brought about by the process of ingestion, digestion and excretion. This does not mean we must negate physical well-being but intensify it with our spiritual knowledge. This is what men of goodwill are trying to do the world over. Unfortunately most of humanity gets stuck at this level and " settles for " a conceptual or physically pragmatic satisfaction of this drive for liberation. Like a radio receiving apparatus the human being can only receive those frequencies of thought and consciousness which are within his range. Until Man can transcend his physical incarnation in this world, he remains of it. Planetary Man remains in this world but not of it.

In spite of the idealistic efforts of environmentalists, social organisers, philanthropists and others, their work will not fundamentally alter man's conviction that he is a physical body. Hence a man with this belief must settle for a freedom that is not a true freedom, because he is still trapped in the notion of physical existence. Even if he lives in the greatest democracy and can obtain all his material wants with ease, he is still tied down to the physical level and will be totally unable to evolve to those new levels of awareness which take their direction from a Higher Intelligence.

What is the unused organ of perception for ordinary man which will enable him to perceive the guiding Logos and take the next step to Planetary consciousness? How can he now develop the extra biological supersense so that he can tap the contents of a World-wide Sensorium in which each individual brain is a cell in a giant world cortex?

We have a prize example of this self-perpetuating dilemma at the physical level in the current energy crisis (1976/77). The Oil companies, by persuasive and often blatantly deceptive advertising, encourage us to continue our dependence on them, while the Oil Sheiks of the OPEC cartel greedily increase their demands for higher and higher prices. Meanwhile aware people know that the answer lies in a bold leap off this self-destructive merry-go-ground and a daring and decisive plunge into serious development of Nature's own gift of solar energy. This is only one example out of hundreds in which man allows vested interests and established authorities to hold him back from experiencing a breakthrough to his own unused and untapped potential. On other levels than the physical and material we can cite the stifling influence of the Church which was for centuries an impregnable fortress of conservatism; or Science and the Arts, with their set and conventional standards which have discouraged all but the truly brave, whose unique genius demanded expression in spite of the antagonism and ridicule from the establishment. The very fact that later years have brought these people acceptance and acclaim points to the rigidity and blindness of their own generation. Names like John Wesley, Edison, Van Gogh and even Einstein, in the fields other than his Relativity Theory spring to mind. We could well ask ourselves right now whether we are still stifling real originality, not only in the areas of research and innovation at the national and international levels, but also in the less spectacular and obvious areas of our own social or family circle. Do we cold-shoulder the men and women who are "different" because they seem to be in touch with a totally strange source - with a new understanding of what life is all about? Do we stifle the oddity in our family because he or she embarrasses us and fails to fit our accepted, comfortable and limited norm? Are we also killers of the vital "sensitivity"?

> So far in man's history he has developed no revolutionary system of order which can even imitate the natural process, neither in politics nor in business nor in most organised religion. The Communist revolution appears to any deep thinker as a sham in which one set of baronial masters has been exchanged for another. Neither can the feudal system of Capitalism in its present form begin to manipulate the baronial charts of big industrial complexes in order to become the instrument of change; simply because the selling mentality holds the society on which it feeds in a vice-like grip of skilled and psychologically-tested techniques of persuasion. By its own admission it has become the killer of " sensitivity ", which is the very first aesthetic biological sense needed to perceive the next step ahead. It is this sensitivity that can prick the veil preventing communication with those supra-mental energies which will spearhead man through the stagnation point at which he has now arrived.

As we continue to ask the question, "How can man be encouraged to tune in to a higher guiding consciousness and throw off the shackles of a brain washing culture?", we become aware that we are up against not only a prevalent apathy, but a more aggressive attitude expressed in post-war England by the phrase "I'm all right,Jack." Any suggestion that a fundamental, radical change is needed in an individual is scorned and even belligerently contested, particularly by those whose sensitivity to anything but their own "wants" has long been blunted and dulled by the batterings of social and political indoctrination. "Change the government, investigate the C.I.A. and the Oil companies, prosecute the polluters but don't confront me. I'm all right as I am," seems to be the current cry.

Even within academia there is this same resistance to change that might conflict with their consensus views. Not only is there resistance but an active persecution and even prosecution of any so-called "upstart" who might have a new and original idea. For a non-degreed and self-taught man like Buckminster Fuller it took over fifty years to become recognised by the scientific establishment as having anything worthwhile to say; but he rose above them, in spite of their original ridicule and "cold-shouldering," in spite, too, of their inability to understand his concepts and his powerful confounding of the conventional in Geometry, Maths, Physics and Education. This is a typical condition of the human situation which has existed throughout time and which is at the back of all heroic myths, including the crucifixion of Christ, which the early Church used to promote its resistance to the establishment until the Church itself became the establishment.

THE IDEOLOGICAL PRECIPICE

Change in mental concepts such as Capitalism and Communism and all the other Isms which call for faith now and the good life later, have no power to change and transform the social system deeply, simply because men can only change any system, or write out a constitution, to the extent that they know themselves. What *does* change society is a general feeling of liberation, an emancipation of Man from fixed ideas in the Religious, Political, Economic and Scientific authoritarianism into which he happens to be born, and a sense of great enterprise afoot with every individual an active part in a universal plan. Such social feelings give rise to the birth of new logic, wide vision and a keen intellectual ferment which may at times transcend the semantic reactions of words. But such idealism and progressive feeling cannot be sustained without there being continuous transcending of mental concepts through deep penetration into the nature of man himself.

In order to keep pace with reality even the most die-hard Soviet ideologist must quickly acknowledge the external changes in Western Capitalism, for he can no longer insist on the infallibility of the prophet Marx and his classical picture of Capitalism as economic stagnation, contradiction and exploitation of the workers. Obviously the proletariat is no longer the fountainhead of the revolutionary movement (if it ever was) and the traditional working class engaged in physical labour is shrinking as a political force; with automation it may even disappear or become so insecure psychologically as to increase its basic drives for durables, refrigerators, motor cars, television and other status symbols. The workers in the Capitalist society can now be regarded by communists like the former bourgeois, completely caught in the rat race, the status and pleasure of possessions, and the pursuit of material satisfactions. While the search for the ideal system goes on inside men's heads, Nature's enduring order, much neglected by our economic and political activists, silently acts as a reproach to man.

Why do men repeatedly insist and argue that the existing political systems are the last straw in the lives of men? Have we really got such holy cows that these imperfections cannot be seen for what they are? Is it not absurd for the Communist to insist that Marx was right about Capitalism when Capitalism has outproduced, outgraded, and outdistributed Communist coercive economics? And is it not plain that Capitalist Man is far more concerned with getting "his daily bread" than with being delivered from evil? The fact is, Capitalist Man spends 36 to 40 hours per week, year in and year out, getting *things* and that doesn't leave him time to consider the nature of government or himself. Yet in front of our very eyes lies an order that has survived longer than man himself, let alone his petty changes in government. This is Nature herself, a living, proven, workable system of adaptability in the face of *all change.*

The huge and ominous gap between the bulk of mankind's materialistic, selfish, ugly and grabbing approach to life and Nature's cyclic beauty is fast becoming a chasm into which the exploiters must inevitably fall, dragging even the sensitive souls with them, unless those with tremendous vision and equally tremendous courage and persistence can produce and put into operation a totally new and viable constitution for man's self-government. It will have to start with small groups and communities, so that when they have proved its workability it can be extended to larger units and eventually to nations and international organisations. What will provide the model? The answer would seem obvious. Since man has made such a mess of it so far by relying on his own ingenuity, he must turn now to Nature for his model. If he looks no further than his own body he will have a marvelous prototype.

THE DEATH OF THE ISM

The new method or framework should contain laws for living which reflect the vast difference between Group Law and Individual Law. Its constitutions should represent the new knowledge of man's personality which science gives to the human situation. It should foster all the opposites of the present system, namely concepts of sharing, cooperation, creative conflict, practical ethics, the good life in a Global Culture ever open to newness, in order to avoid the need for violent revolutions. CENTRE (see footnote) has such a method in crude form awaiting the nucleus of those who will refine it. No vast claims are made for it, except that it is something to begin with, perhaps tear apart and change by the method provided in it, perhaps study as background for the next jump. Gradually in concept-form it is infecting the minds of the human planners, the moulders of opinion and philosophers in waiting. In some parts of the world it has gone beyond the concept and is manifest as the direct action of a yeast and leaven in society. There is a nucleus in every person with the will to unite with others in an emergent group of highly individualistic people. With such groups there is the possibility to penetrate society in the same way that the Founding Fathers did with their concept of Federal Union.

Such a diverse group is at present working at the University of the Trees in Boulder Creek, California, using the constitution set out by the author in his book "Christ Yoga of Peace" (soon to be republished as "Universal Government by Nature's Laws"). Using Creative Conflict and other techinques of growth, the group is exploring ego confrontation as a method of transcending the natural human propensity for self-interest and self-obsession. By seeing themselves reflected back by others in the group, people find an incentive to change and grow. The ultimate aim of every confrontation, however disturbing and ego-reducing, is to discover and experience the nuclear centre of being, so Creative Conflict becomes one of the tools of Nuclear Evolution and produces a "hothouse" for the growth process, leading to the discovery of the oneness within the diversity not only of the group but of the wider community. Thus self-awareness and self-mastery, rather than intellectual brilliance, are set as the ultimate goals.

---

* Centre is the name given to groups of individuals who are working out these concepts in the Centre community in London and at the University of the Trees in California.

702

HOMO PROGRESSIVUS

We must never confuse complexity and the world of thought with spiritual advances. Some of our modern prophets see signs and wonders in the flowering of man's intellect, his power to think, and the potentiality of science to make the world of one language. The phosphoresence of thought has been with Man from the beginning and the surge and flux of his enquiry in the past have even transcended our present wisdom in areas where modern man is basically ignorant. Everyday we rediscover what has been old hat for several thousand years and are struck with awe at our own cleverness. Some of our modern complex systems, computers and expensive techniques contribute little to man's knowledge of himself. A man on the moon will not enhance the spiritual condition of the Earth one bit. The window on the world of modern T.V. may very well widen the vision of fellowmen everywhere and introduce, expose and educate us to people we could never meet. It can also blunt the edge of perception of subtle truths. Man behind the controls of the fast jet plane is no wiser nor spiritually enlightened than the man driving his horse and buggy. Man has arrived at the modern Cybernetic revolution with a vast communications network—sensitive only to the radio frequencies of electromagnetic man (e.g. the mass society of T.V. millions) and without anything much new to say on its Laser-beams except " Hello Mother " or more accurately, as the first words in and from extra-terrestrial space are recorded in official history books, " GO, GO, GO "—All systems Go!

In order to illustrate the point that cleverness is not evolution, let us examine briefly some excerpts from a west coast newspaper. Next to the announcement of a new mechanical ear is the revelation that the U.S. Army released some harmless germs and "possibly" infected the local area, since it now boasts of the highest incidence of infection anywhere in the U.S. Next to Presidential appeal for world human rights, broadcast on the most sophisticated electronic equipment available, a Ugandan dictator murders his opposition in the same bloody tradition that has characterised strong-arm politics for centuries. The fact that murder can be accomplished with germs, highly engineered weaponry or even radiation does not mean we are wiser. Only more clever. The fact that we wear the most advanced in synthetic fashionry does not counter our spiritual nakedness.

GROUP v INDIVIDUAL

Just as nature has proceeded step by step from one form of government—through the positively charged nucleus and the negative electron to the step (2) molecule, the step (3) cell, step (4) organ, step (5) body, step (6) brain—so I believe there are facts as evidential as the vibrating molecules of a gas are shown by the spectroscope, that there is a step (7) which parallels all these leaps towards more complex groupings, on a higher level of consciousness. It is not the complexity which is marvellous but the fact that the leap can take place at all, since no man can say How. What is the hierarchic intelligence which has organised these leaps science cannot say, anymore than Adam could say when he woke up from his deep sleep, and found one of his ribs had been made into a woman. Man is now at the threshold of contact with this group intelligence in the thrust of evolution at the Nucleus of all Life. In a thousand years from now, the new aesthetically and biologically sensitive Man will wonder how on earth we endured our selfish and precious individuality, the cause of all the nasty smells and noxious influences at work in our so-called civilisation today.

Living in the transition period, before this new realisation spreads like a benign plague across the planet, we can count ourselves privileged to both watch and take part in the process, even though it is often painful and invariably challenging to our pet attachments and our dearly cherished Egos. Periodically we catch glimpses of a group consciousness that eventually will stop flickering on and off like a defective lamp and give out a bright and steady beam, and we know that the current is the *One* consciousness that flows through us all; with this realisation comes also the awareness that we have at last found Life's common factor and it far outweighs in beauty and in truth the habits and the life-styles to which we attached such tremendous importance. However, none can pretend that the road to group consciousness, if exciting, is not rough and often disheartening. To relinquish or even to share our cherished "private lives" and intimacies is for some of us a process of slow torture. For others the gradual whittling away of a long standing self-image is like being stripped naked and left to die on a cold mountainside! For yet another, dreams and expectations that gave life its dynamic have to be released and given up and the painful reality of the immediate present has to be faced. For each individual the struggle is unique, but finally the worst fear, namely that in relinquishing our attachments, self-images and dreams, we lose our individuality, proves to be a myth. We discover that unity is only valid if it has within it the full spectrum of diversity to keep it alive.

Let me answer my second question: I have asked myself HOW this new man is likely to arise and benefit from the fertile manure of a decadent society and a dying age. If man is to redeem his planet he must arrive on it and incarnate when there is work to be done. The question is WHAT is the work and HOW do we get the aesthetic insight and sensitivity to know the way our Planetary Brain wants us to go? And having got this sensitivity so ingrained into our conditioned biological nerve trunkways, how do we insure that it is incorporated into our social and political systems of local and national government, to prevent our being enslaved by an insensitive society and its moronic drives which lead to wars, fratricide, industrial bigotry between labour and capital, and all the patent stupidity and impotence which we allow ourselves to wallow in day after day. It is obvious from the state of the world that the sensitive, because of its very nature, is ruled and dominated by the insensitive.

The trials of Soviet writers and students are an attempt to enslave the intellectual freedom of millions of Russian youth. Russian music and poetry reveal its sensitive heart. Easily dominated by past and present masters of persuasion the people feel the great need for liberty and are wondering who can lead them towards the free society. Will it be the old style Marxist revolutionaries or the new technocrats? Obviously these elements of society are no more capable of self-liberation in its ultimate sense or its political counterpart than are the entrenched Capitalists and Proletariat of the affluent Western Democracies. The underground intelligentsia of Russia can ask for full public information about the charges against these writers who are entitled to be tried under the constitution in an open court. It can excite the deeply disturbed public opinion outside of the sole official newspaper which exists in an atmosphere of society which until recently was the impotent witness of mass rehabilitation of political deviates. It has not yet recovered from the crude repressions by the labour camps of Siberia under the tyranny of Stalin. It can call for full public ventilation of hushed up court cases for those condemned on false accusations; but can it liberate itself? No more than the intellectual climate in the west can liberate itself from its own division and fragmentations or its dependence on Logic, words, definitions and ideals which make up its current ideological concepts. The intellect as an instrument of change is subject to subtle enslavement and tyranny and can be used in service of repressive techniques and is therefore incapable of leading youth to liberation, to the self-governmental system which has become an Art-form. We do not decry the intellect which is the source of man's power to discriminate, we merely say it is not enough.

The function of the intellect is discrimination. It cuts up, dissects, analyses, and organises the manifold bits and pieces. It is the separator and the fragmentor, finding differences in things in order to make logical categories. It is not, however, capable of discriminating wholeness because the vision of wholeness is so by virtue of the fact that there is no separation between parts and whole! The incredible "red tape" that is often the accompaniment to governmental service is indicative of the intellect. Thus, intellectual processes applied to the problem of red tape often produce more of the same. Only when imagination is applied is there any progress.

The answer is to be found ironically enough, in a subtle mirror-image of present reality, in a glimmer of a new revolution now imminent in the total management of human Imagination by both the Capitalist and Communist systems: here the vitality of the whole society is used unconsciously by the masters of existing opinion to self-destructive ends. This can be seen in the desire for domination of the Earth's space envelope, the calculated manufacture of fear, useless nuclear overkill, biological germ warfare, national narcissicisms, the deliberate pollution of thought and news. These are the techniques of grasping political imperialisms which blind people with hate, arouse strife and confusion in every headline; all these bring tensions in individuals, which cannot help but bring chaos and create a mass neurosis, setting up an atmosphere in which the aggregate sum of individual tension is the cause of war, hysterical killing and eventually mass human suicide. The drive to self-annihilation is beyond the reason and rationalising faculty of man; it is even beyond the imagination of man, lying latent in his dark unconscious.

This mirror image of man's present negative use of the human intellect can be seen in the positive vision of a golden age where people do not worship the authorities of state or the expertise of science, nor praise the spin-off from wasteful trips to the moon as a special virtue. It is this reverse image in the mirror which gives man the ability to see that logically it is foolish to go on polluting the planet and then escape into space. One thousand billions are spent on space moonshots, when the polluting sewage of cities in the rivers could produce green algae for use as cattle food, for investments of only a few million. Another example is when energy is obtained from exploiters who control sources of fossil fuels while the free energy of sun, wind and sea is hardly used or researched by our public utility cartels lest it escape their metered control. The statement that the technology is not yet developed is not true. When man's intellect is sufficiently aware of its subtle justifications for wasting billions on science fiction space age boondoggles, the overtaxed citizen who foots the bill will get the less spectacular but more imaginative answers to the real world problems. The "real world" is not the wars, rockets, bombs and mechanical devices for defense but the discovery of methods of deep human communication and purification of fears and polluted thinking processes which spawn the need for these horrors. Research on the nature of consciousness is not voted on by politicians or governments and at this time is non-existent. Except for brainwashing techniques, the enslaving power of truth drugs, nerve gases and sinister uses of science, there are no programs in the real world concerned with such problems as solving human conflicts rather than fighting them out.

However, the mirror image of the trend is to be found now in the unfinanced attempts of wholistic groups and private researchers and the challenge is to come up with original and more fulfilling methods of communicating.

CANCER OF THE IMAGINATION

In the Tower of Babel story in Genesis 11 which is obviously not meant to be taken literally, there is an interesting symbolism which shows that the ancients were aware that excellent communication is not enough. In this fable the whole world was of one language and of one speech and the children of men were in a fine mood for real international cooperation, but the Creative Intelligence had other ideas and began to think " nothing will be restrained from them which they have IMAGINED to do ". The children of men were busy building their city to make a name and a big reputation for their own cleverness, without really understanding their own imaginings; the Creative Intelligence which could foresee the abominations which would emerge, thought that the best way of fouling up the communications system was to bring confusion in the language of all the Earth. The parallel situation exists today, wherein man's nefarious uses of atomic energy, biological warfare, pollution of the mind by poisonous propaganda, etc. may well bring self-destruction.

Since language is the medium for conceptual thought, it is easy to see that if the user of the concept-tools does not understand concept-making, he will forget WHO is the concept maker. People who forget themselves, wallow in apathy, think that Self-government is leaving decision-making and concept-making to the government, and are happily satisfied with existing authorities, soon find that in her Divine Wisdom nature has not only provided the tax man, but puts the confuser and general " mucker-upper " into their lives.

The management of the Creative Imagination is not only the next step in political persuasion but it will become an economic factor and be calculated as part of the cost of production. Already the larger part of the expense of all research in space and technology of nuclear fission and its " tower to heaven " and of government planning is payment for the cost of " Imagination ". The cost of marketing a product in terms of modern advertising, sales force, and promotional aids for mass T.V. audiences is the cost of Imagination in the product. The failure of the Marxist revolution can be now traced to the fact that Marx *believed* that the cost of a product was the *labour* involved in producing it. Like the tower builders he forgot the most important thing!

The "Imagination", we can so easily see in that sham freedom of the Marxist concept and the confused revolutions it has spawned, is so tightly held down as a servile slave, that Berlin walls, iron curtains, party denunciations and now mock trials of scientists, writers and poets have to be engineered to contain it. So when people claim "sensitivity" they are in no position to make a critical judgement until they have done several years' work on themselves and discovered what the Creative Imagination is and how dangerous it can be, when perverted to erotic expression in advertising or applied to systems of repression. Certainly the ancients knew what happened when man ignored the fact that the power to create, preserve or destroy lies dormant within the Imagination. Whether the society is Capitalist or Communist, the mental prostitution of our drives by potent Madison Avenue techniques leads to the employment of the best psychologists and behaviourial scientists as effective consultants in enslaving the subconscious minds of millions of unsuspecting people.

To gain a temporary insight into how the Imagination works in our lives, recall an occasion when you have exclaimed, "I never imagined that such a thing could happen to me, not in my wildest dreams!" Now ask yourself to be quite honest and to consider whether the truth is really that you *had* imagined this thing happening. In fact in your daydreams and aspirations you had actually produced images of this very situation that has now materialised. Isn't that true? Didn't the event fulfill one of your deepest desires? Moreover, didn't some of your actions or fears unconsciously lead toward the final outcome? In the spiritual life this process can apply to our enlightenment or to the programming of our own downfall.

SENSITIVITY CENTRES EVERYWHERE

The books of the new planetary future "Supra-mental Man", which are not yet written, will have to describe a way of overthrowing the domination and authoritarianism of concepts of capitalism, of the ideologies of communism and of religious dogmas by some form of peaceful revolution. Whereas all other revolutions have been misnamed, this one will affect the "biological sensitivity" of the new mental organs of perception, through the power which the "Creative Imagination" has over the intelligence in the human organism at all levels of its Being. (see **Fig. 196**) The newest research on human brain potentials reveals this "sensitivity" *as an evolutionary instrument*.

The CENTRE movement, which I see at the spearhead of this break-through in the new scene emerging everywhere, has been conducting research since 1957 into the influence of Imagination on our faculties to perceive, sense and CHANGE Life. We learn to rejoice in change and understand it, not to resist it. The

"CENTRE" is a *way of looking* at each Self as a pivot of evolutionary progress. Its symbol is that of Nuclear Evolution which is the grouping of several human cells into a group mind which becomes *sensitive to and attracts the new species* of Planetary Man. Its ultimate goal is the contact with Supramental consciousness in a voluntary open community; not open to all and everything but a community of great *sensitivity* and ruthlessness in the weightier matters of the laws of living. CENTRE is not a unity of ideas in the head but the actual unity found in lovers of the world: an infection caught up by inward joy.

THE HUMAN MATERIAL

In the first part of this book we find that man's personality operates from seven basic drives from which all others are derived. Minor drives, such as curiosity, etc., do not affect the main expression of our vital forces, but these primal seven layers of our psychic and social beingness influence every thought and every concept.

These seven spheres of consciousness are also essential, as we saw in Part 1, for the attainment of a new level of experience. Throughout history the greatest heroes have talked about the existence of new dimensions and today this same awareness of greater possiblities for man is emerging everywhere. What is needed is a technique by which this awareness can be encouraged and evolved. To sum up the particular technique offered in Part 1 we could write it as an equation: "Freedom to change" + "Creative Conflict" = "Nuclear Evolution". Within the context of this evolutionary process there is an infinite variety of possibilities for the individual, since each of us manifests the "drives" in different proportions and they modify the intensity of each other to produce totally unique individuals.

Only two of these drives, namely the sensual and the herd drives, are presently being exploited by the mass persuaders. It might appear that they also use the acquisitive drive, but, in fact, society ostracises excessive wealth and deliberately taxes this drive in order to repress it. This leaves a vast potential for emerging Planetary Man to liberate himself from power structures and the impotence of the status quo, and so through his Imagination transmute his conscious life and environment on this planet as well as the life in his physical body.

Each of these primordial drives is revealed in the full spectrum of personality as a very definite positive or negative manifestation. This is then projected into our view of society. In every work of art, philosophical system, civilisation or culture, these seven drives are represented by mirror reflections of the basic needs of human consciousness.

I.R. 13 Red 19 Orange 25   Yellow   50 Green 55 Blue 62 Indigo 68 Violet

LEVELS OF
CONSCIOUSNESS
AND BASIC DRIVES

Editor's Note

Change cannot occur until two conflicting tendencies in the human psyche surface consciously and reveal themselves. The penetration of this Conscious Conflict is therefore creative, since the resolution automatically propels one forward on one's evolutionary journey. It is called NUCLEAR EVOLUTION because this movement does not occur outside one's own being, but on the contrary, it has its origin at the very heart and source of the nuclear personality.

THE BASIC HUMAN DRIVES:

Our link between consciousness and the seven different kinds of Love we experience as "drives", and their manifestation in the psycho-social atmosphere has been dealt with quite extensively in Part 1. The eight factors which emerge in this system (7 drives plus a dimension of self-annihilation) must, however, be briefly referred to in order to understand how they influence changes in the human personality and its projection into a healthy or unhealthy society. They can be referred to as 8 need systems or drives that resonate positively when they are selected by an individual. On the other hand when a drive is rejected it is related to the same area of the personality which may be negatively projected into the political, social or economic environment as the opposite aspect of the area of need in any person.

Industry makes use of this aspect of human personality when it makes a " product " and also makes its " anti-product " with all the drive-need factors which the customer dislikes in the first, built into the second; it then cannot lose. Large corporations have already caught on to this through their experimental market research provings from door to door feasibility studies. The different and opposite poles of each drive in the individual, bring the aggregate tensions and conflicts we experience in *society as a whole*. The full meaning of all these positive and negative factors can only be understood in relating their functions to each other.

The first two drives which are already exploited in our communication as individuals in the psycho-social sense are: (1) the MATING INSTINCT and (2) HERD INSTINCT.

DRIVE (1); Red. Obviously we can have communication at the sexual level even to the reproduction of the species, without any necessity for other types of communication at deeper biological levels or at higher spiritual levels of Being. We can easily have babies without getting married or even fulfilling ourselves sexually. The factors in this drive range from the

712

positive: a passive tenderness, yielding self-abandonment, encouraging the "femininity" component in every mature sexual
drive, in male and female equally, (Domination of this feeling in
males leads to Homosexuality) to the *negative:* aggressive
physical activity, the male "grabbing" instincts of the sadistic ;
(Domination by this leads to rejection of personalised affection,
frigidity, and to repression of the need for passivity) producing
longing for a love-object, without any release of tension, which
can be utilised by the skilled advertisers, and Bunny Clubs.

If we look at liquor advertisements with beautiful women,
cigarettes promising "Machismo", hair oil and after-shave lotion
ads that guarantee sensuous fingers fondling our faces, then we get
an idea of the kind of energy that is being aimed at us, to buy.
Any man who feels inadequate in the bedroom surely would want
something to strengthen his prowess. If he sees a superman
smoking nonchalantly on a filter king with a beautiful woman
waiting demurely in the boudoir, he learns very quickly to
associate the cigarette with that "He Man" image as being
attractive to a woman. In other words, he identifies himself with
the situation he wants to be in by associating himself with cigarettes. Now this is fairly obvious. What's not so obvious is that this
desire to identify is present in almost everyone to some degree or
other and is presently being used to control people's choices far
more than we are aware.

DRIVE (2); Orange: The drive which is also played on by
most of the masters of persuasion even more than the sexual
drive, is that of the herd instinct. This part of the human
personality which craves social contact, social acceptance, and
the group protection of one's property and rights, makes social
life of consequence to us. The drive to *belong* is found in man's
love of his own class, nation or community. It is his own "spirit
of community" which forms a man's emotions as a social
animal. Considerable research by professional persuaders and
psychologically respectable scientists shows that this "spirit"
so far developed in the majority of men, results from very
primitive psycho-social behaviour patterns many of which are
reflected in the growth of human organisations.

This herd drive is really a compulsive urge for some concrete
contact with reality. The *positive* reaction to it is a restless
attempt to extract the maximum pleasure from the world, which
leads to an increased interest in the immediate environment. If
this is dominant we have an exhibition of the manic tendencies
for keen rivalry, including persistence in reaching a goal, even
great obstinacy, and overestimation of the power of money,

reputation etc., while the *negative* brings depressive states due to lack of contact with this "spirit" of community with consequent feelings of frustration and deprivation through loss of reputation or position. It may apply to loss of possessions if they bring influence. If this is dominant and negative it produces the real conservative who shrinks from all innovations and political CHANGE.

The second drive is often prostituted as we see in politics, and then again by the constant encouragement we receive from big business to "keep up with the Joneses". It is this drive which leads in its extremes to the Rat Race. The herd drive is also played on in Communist society as the need to conform, to sacrifice oneself for the revolution or posterity, to obey the dictatorship of the few for the economic salvation of the many and finally to submerge one's individuality in the State by holding in one's Imagination the prime idea, concept or belief that Man is made for the State, not the State made for Man.

The fact that there are still five more drives in Man as yet not developed to their full potential by either the Intelligentsia or the Proletariat, shows that neither of these agencies of potential change is yet fit nor qualified to be the instrument of fundamental CHANGE that will bring about the arising of a new species of Man in the Universe. I would not care to make such a categorical statement unless I had had much experience of both of them and could equal their arrogance with my own! Pride, which belongs to the second drive and is the common link between these two classes, often makes them think they are the most intelligent members of society. Certainly neither can be found to go in search of the "wise man" if they believe such a person exists. We must contrast this herd drive with its complementary one (Drive 6) which in its positive expression is in constant search for the sage, if necessary going far afield to India or overseas to find one!

The following *five drives* through which leaps in consciousness will take place, will develop and expand into a completely different reality from the one we live in at this moment. This leap from the primitive behaviour patterns to conscious understanding of man's personality, will give Man some idea of the existing primitive psycho-social ecology surrounding some of the most respected and powerful institutions. This will include such complex organs as the United Nations and many deeply cherished concepts of free enterprise and democratic Government.

It is not within the realm of subversive activity that institutions like the U.N. and democracy are referred to here as "primitive." Rather, the level of consciousness from which this statement originates is beyond the senses, beyond the intellect and even beyond the mind. It comes from an awareness of the vast human

714

potential of man unfolding, as well as a keen hindsight as to where he's been. It is an unimpeded perception of where we stand now, collectively on this earth, and where we can go. Just as our forefathers had the imaginative vision to create a new constitution and inspire within the people an allegiance to a democracy, so do we now find men whose vision extends beyond the geographical frontiers to the barriers of consciousness itself, inspiring within the people the will to secure their own salvation, to be free of nationalisms and to think for themselves.

I will now outline these drives and their domains for advancement in the human race so that we can see that if we are to take these potential leaps at all, it must be from where we are now, with two feet placed firmly on the ground on which we stand, i.e. the present world situation. We must accept our predicament under the overlordship of all that is gross, material-minded, self-interested and affluent, highly reactive, and conservative in the sense of fearing fundamental CHANGE.

EXAMPLES NOT GENERALISATIONS
MUST BE GIVEN

Specific examples can be found within any society as the drives are cross-cultural and apply to a village of pigmies as much as to a highly sophisticated culture. Using the method of over-lapping the drives described in Part I these examples can be seen to emerge quite clearly in ownership, scientific and religious authority, aesthetic values, our present political system and ideas of lasting order.

Here the idea is expressed that regardless of the culture, the drives exist within all humans and can be identified in the most primitive of men as well as in the most civilised. On first thought one wonders how this could be, but the language of the personality drives as translated through the human organism is universal, irrespective of language, reality perception, or cultural conditioning. Consequently the same drive to mate that occurs in the eskimo occurs also in the Pope, although it could be said that what each does with this drive might vary a great deal. In the same way, the drive which regulates a tribe of nomads in the Sahara with a structure of authority is the same drive that leads a highly developed nation like Britain or Israel to adopt a parliamentary system or a country like Russia to establish a dictatorship of the party secretary.

However, negative conservatism and resistance to change is not always found in forward-looking corporate thinking at the gross material level. Whereas the leaders of communism have one foot on the moon and the other still in the dark ages there are enlightened capitalists whose idealism looks for new spiritual answers to economic problems, and, in their search for the " good life ", often give birth to Homo Progressivus, who goes on to become Planetary Man, sensitising himself by virtue of his very openness and humility in the face of a vast incomprehensible complexity. On the other hand, the Labour Unions are an example of the inability to accept a share of the responsibility for the security of the industrial means of production. So far they have failed to see completely that some revolutionary concept of Co-Ownership between Labour and Capital is essential to the management of the productive vitality of society.

So long as there is a faction of people called "labour" and a faction of people called "management", there will be separation, division and conflict. If the present system of unionism and capitalism really worked efficiently, there would be no need for strikes, for deplorable safety conditons, and the oft expressed suspicion that is even today being generated between these two forces of production. A major cause of industrial conflict is based on the fact that labour is thought to be a separate entity from management. Shop foremen are usually company men while the stewards are union men. This way of looking at the whole production has its divisive effects, since the one party can always point to the other as being inflationary, uncooperative, and self-interest oriented. The constant argument by management is that it owns the stuff of production and if labour doesn't like it they can go find someone else to work for. Similarly, unions reserve the right to cripple and prevent an employer from seeking other labour in the marketplace freely.

The key does not lie in higher wages and better organised unions, but rather in more "inclusive" unions that are a synthesis of labour and capital in cooperatives in which the worker finds himself up-leveling his part of the whole operation to an active participation in all areas of responsibility. Thus, a labouring worker who perceived inadequate lighting on his job would no longer be required to call the safety board and make a report, thereby jeopardising his job, but would be given the responsibility himself for getting adequate lighting at the cheapest price possible since ultimately his share of the agreed wages would depend on it!

This is *not* communism nor is it capitalism nor is there yet any system of government on the earth which has devised a means of essential co-ownership without dictatorship. However, the techniques are already here and there are several successful examples, such as the Scott-Bader Commonwealth Company in England, as well as several others.

SHEPHERDS OF THE FLOCKS

There is a tendency to confuse socialist pragmatism in Russia with the profit motivation of enlightened capitalism in America. With the introduction of profit incentives into Socialist planning it would appear that the systems are meeting each other half way, but it would be folly to confuse the prostitution of the herd drive by the Soviets in Drive 2 with the dominating all-acquisitive influence which preys on the herd for profit under the free enterprise system (see drive 4). We cannot confuse these drives because it is obvious that the first is forced on the people who are ruled by the state who is the real owner, while the second is permitted by the state because it is the philosophy of success held by the people. Whenever the capitalist cartel becomes the oppressor the state steps in to protect the people, whilst in the communist system the state is the oppressor. While the Capitalist State (America) can bring guilty verdicts in court against the three largest drug companies for deliberate conspiracy to monopolise production and sales of antibiotics, it is unthinkable in the Soviet State that the government should prosecute its own state industries and, in fact, it suppresses any criticism whatsoever of state policy in industry. The consumer is quite unprotected against overpricing or criminal negligence in the Soviet state. This socialist control of the herd drive affects not only its own industries but the liberalisation programmes in neighbouring countries e.g. the invasion of Czechoslovakia with military force in August 1968 and the bloody suppression of Hungary in 1956.

Many captains of industry regard their shareholders as faithful sheep and the workers as donkeys awaiting the "Carrot" but obviously merely giving the workers a few shares in the enterprise only turns them into minor capitalists, tempted into Drive 4 which in its negative expression, gives them a desire to watch the daily market value of their shares. This gives them no more responsibility for the security of the enterprise than the faithful sheep. Responsibility for decision-making at shop floor level and the evolution of new corporate structure as an Art-form in industry is a sign of Planetary Man at work. Mastery of the herd drive leads to fundamental change in society.

The birthing of harmony instead of the current industrial conflict is the next step to achieving any change in the political system conceived as an Art-form. Rather than a fixed methodological concept of government we must work for a nuclear constitution which allows constant revitalisation and CHANGE to satisfy Drive 3, and at the same time preserves a method whereby those members of society who are led, transfer their power to the leadership by an orderly process.

Fundamental changes in society occur when men overcome their fear of the consequences of speaking out and expressing themselves as men alone against the tide of prevailing public opinion. Certainly Einstein was scoffed at, Galileo villified, Alexander G. Bell disbelieved, and Christ crucified. Yet the herd was wrong and these men right. Time after countless time this same barrier must be broken in order to accomodate new discoveries in all areas of human life. Ghandi was popular enough with his outspoken ideas of pacifism yet he was shot; today very few carry out his ideas in practice yet he has left a lasting mark on the hearts of millions. Now too, we find that our next step in government is to up-level our concept of constitution and political decision-making to a beautiful art form, one that can be changed and modified to fit the needs of the time, and yet still provide a system whereby the transfer of power is peaceful, orderly and with the full consent of the people. Whenever money, power or force is used to achieve leadership, there is separation and discontentment. What is being expressed in Nuclear Evolution is the dawning of a new age from within the soul of mankind, where government will be an expression of the hearts of people, like a beautiful statue is of a sculptor or a painting is of an artist. It is not to be brittle and grey like a dead tree but alive and supple to the changing winds of circumstance. In other words, man for the first time in history will really have the privilege and freedom to paint, sculpt, mould or carve his constitution, into his own mirror reflection in the environment he perceives. Were this not a valid endeavour then men would still be saddled with the Magna Carta, the Code of Hammurabi or the Jewish Torah. Had the founding fathers been aware of the vast technological civilisation that would emerge from a little tea party, they might have planned an entirely different kind of democracy. Thus, as man's environments and perceptions change, so too should his constitutions.

DRIVE (3): yellow. The evolutionary process we have been working on for many years must now expand into Centres everywhere. We continue working at it within our small community at the CENTRE. The willingness to experiment with techniques of group formation gives each member the right to become his own constitution maker. It requires a revolution in thinking about CHANGE itself and the nature of the power-urge in man.

To be able to see the deep implications in the ultimate liberation of Man from his own ignorance, everyman must first understand the basic drives in his own personality. If the second kind of love was the *Herd Instinct*, the THIRD DRIVE is the love of CHANGE, newness, novelty, self-assertiveness, Self-expression, intellectual freedom, and the freedom to travel anywhere to any country, and to enjoy all human rights with their commensurate responsibilities all over the Planet. This drive is concerned with Ego development. Its *positive* expression creates the self-expansive needs of each individual Ego and its need to fuse into the environment which in turn leads to the need to move from one situation to another and for positive CHANGE. The *negative* expression of this drive brings a need to keep one's individual separateness from the objective environment and creates the tendency for holding on to a narcissist integrity of the personal Ego. One finds this in people who always insist they are doing something quite different from everyone else even when one knows at least three people who are doing exactly the same thing. The function of the intellectual process is the dividing of everything into neat categories and discovering division where there isn't any. In its extreme it even divides the Ego in schizophrenia.

WHAT SHALL IT PROFIT?

DRIVE (4) green, is *possessiveness*. The ushering in of a New Age of Habeas Proprietor as well as World Habeas Corpus would bring some understanding of this drive for feelings of security of property as well as security of body. It is a prime drive to possess what we love, to get fixed on the love-object, and to ignore this love of possession brings much hatred in the social feeling. It is a razors-edge on which only the spiritually awake man can walk. It should be obvious to all Christians as well as to all Hindus and Islam, that their Messenger had a subtle understanding of how possessions make a man self-satisfied but unhappy when they are told that one must lose one's life for reality's sake in order to find it. The Christos included the laying down of his own life perhaps as an example of this. Whatever we may personally believe about the scripture writers and the origin of the message, we know it is talking of this same drive for possession when the prophet speaks of the difficulty of the rich man in rejecting his possessions in order to receive the treasure of the kingdom of Reality.

The story of the Rich Young Ruler, who turned sorrowfully away after Jesus asked him to sell all he had and then take up the spiritual search, has usually been taken to refer to those of great material wealth. However, the desire to possess and to experience the power and security that possession gives, although it originates at the Green level of consciousness, permeates all the chakra levels. We cling to many things besides money and material goods. For example, the Yellow level intellectual is very possessive of his acquired intellectual knowledge and well-reasoned theories; the Blue level scientist or theologian is strongly attached to his scientific or religious "Truth" as he sees it or conceptualises it. Even the intuitive Indigo level finds it hard to let go of his glimpse of a fabulous future and return to present reality. At every level possessiveness operates and it is to this mental block or attachment that Christ refers; it is this desire that we have to let go "for the Kingdom of Heaven's sake."

> The desires for money, power and importance must be regarded with great sympathy for they are fostered in us by human society. Obviously the Christos says we must reduce these desires or needs, not only because wealth and pride bring about their own downfall, but because they leave us no time for self-cultivation or pursuit of ultimate reality. They distract us from our highest expression. Competition is often needed in order to get them, and such social competition leads to ambition which endangers the whole community, creating envy that was never there to begin with, and hatred of those people who do have the aggressive ambition to go out and win the top prizes. To understand this we must go back to the formation of the Ego in early childhood, to the untarnished pure consciousness of our own identity.

> The persuaders exploit our *drive to possess* material power rather than spiritual things. But we can also develop our drive to possess, and express it as the search for Light. If we could return consciously to the state of the infant where each need is gratified without search for an outside object there would be no frustrations experienced. If the mother's breast is available before he experiences hunger, the infant is not aware that his body has limitations of movement and there is no need to repress these needs.

> So long as need-gratifications are not frustrated in real life, there is no boundary between the person and his environment or his inner and outer life; nor does such a person develop any critical faculties of value since he does not strive to organise any needs. Nor do we find such functions as taking sides or a position.

It is rare to find ambition and possessiveness in a baby. This is because he has not yet learned that he cannot get whatever he needs the minute he needs it. And in addition, his needs are few. But as we grow older we begin to feel separated from the things we need. Our bottle is on the other side of the room and we cannot yet crawl. We must make efforts and when we fail, we become frustrated. We need love and attention and our parents haven't the time. They give us pacifiers and teddy bears and swings with little motors and springs in them to help us be happy. We begin to crave bigger and better editions of these things and when we do not get them, we become frustrated. Later, as our insecurity grows we begin to protect our things and find it difficult to share them. If it's love we need, we try to possess the person; when we cannot we become frustrated and feel cheated. If it's recognition we need we become ambitious and try to be somebody. When we cannot reach the top we become frustrated again because our need is so great. If we feel insecure and impoverished we work and work to save and hoard stockpiles against the time when something may happen and we can survive. But somehow, we never get enough or we manage to spend and spend as fast as we earn it, so that we daren't look around us to see if we really are getting what we think we are.

These are the familiar words of Christ: "Consider the lilies how they grow? they toil not, they spin not: and yet I say unto you that Solomon in all his glory was not arrayed like one of these. If, then, God so clothes the grass, which is today in the field, and tomorrow is cast into the oven, how much more will he clothe you?.....seek ye the Kingdom of God, and all these things shall be added unto you." He gives us here directions for a way of life that he himself followed and which, down the ages, has proved to be viable for those men of wisdom and understanding who have put their whole trust in the One Supreme Intelligence.

This paradise state of Being was seen by the Christos as a total dependence on the ultimate Reality (God) to deliver what we merited at or before the time it was needed. Frustrations, ambitions, and possessive drives begin the moment we are separated from something we love.

Take no possessions when the moment of liberation comes, the Messenger says; trust in Reality rather than physical things and possession stored up. He is not making the false promise of the tempter within who tries to convince us that we can possess the world *and* Reality! That we can enjoy *two* value systems, is not in question; but whether one of those systems has the value in Reality that we think it has is another matter! Obviously he is not talking to those who have no choice, but to those who really have something to reject. Everyman's treasure is what he really desires. If he *has* wealth but does not need or desire it, he is free; but it is of no value to reject what we have never had. If we *need* the money and fame of this world, whether we have it or not will make a difference when we come to reject its values. The Christos says that any man who leaves what he has for Reality's sake, he shall receive much more *in this life* and in the immortal life of Reality.

Certainly the Buddha as a young prince had a palace to reject. We do not know if Jesus had been a master of money in his thirty years before he began his mission. He certainly talked with the authority of one. The master of money should be able to burn it and not become its slave. To burn good money would be to burn some people's God, to commit a sin of wastefulness, to show off, or to become a fool. But the Master does not burn it for the sake of burning it, but forgoes it for Reality's sake! It becomes a burnt offering, a sacrifice of worldliness. The Master of himself knows that to reject something he does not possess shows a need, and to reject something he has shows liberation from it. He need only show himself that he can do it, but he cannot show himself without actually doing it. That would be a sham!

The supreme test given to Abraham by the God-self within him was to sacrifice the thing that he loved most in all the world. When the horrific realisation dawned that this 'thing' was his own son, he still went ahead and was prepared to plunge in the knife. For the Divine Intelligence the readiness was sufficient, as it always is; an alternative sacrifice was provided. We are all Abrahams at some point in our lives, when the supreme test of giving up the last and greatest attachment has to be faced and overcome if Self-mastery is to be ours.

The positive expression of this drive toward a love object lets go of attachment to objective material things, although a person may conquer possessiveness towards the love object by integrating it with his ultimate goal or, in the case of the sex drive, with practice of Tantra Yoga. Possession of the body as a sexual love object is taken to the height of abstraction as an object of adoration. Another example can be the multi-millionaire and his attachment to money, when he gives it away to some foundation whose goals he has created out of altruism. However, this may mean that in spite of his worldly wisdom and good intentions he may not have any real discrimination when it comes to deciding what is really worthwhile. The **negative** reaction to this drive is a basic need for concrete objects and a general interest in an **outside reality** as the source of all manifestation, whether it be of material things or one's view of Reality. This need would be accompanied by a tendency to pursue and manipulate real objects, and the inability to understand one's own possessiveness.

This was the dilemma of King Lear and the cause of his downfall. His intense need for confirmation in the shape of protestations of love and devotion from his children, caused him to lose all discrimination and judgement and to fall for the specious and false glitter of Goneril's and Regan's words and to reject the quiet sincerity of Cordelia's true and honest love and the selfless devotion of his trusted adviser, Kent.

The ownership of Capital and the means of production and the storing up of the vital forces of the community in the form of money in the banks and other financial institutions cannot be really understood without reference to this prime drive in man's own personality. Any attempt to do so will fragment his view of society since this drive affects his whole idea of security, obtaining sufficient vital force and nutrition, and also need for lasting order. The power urge in man in Drive 3 is not only to retain the results of his own creativity in Drive 4 but to assert himself without restraints like a God who resists any attempt at impeding his actions as if it were an encroachment on his liberty. Hence the man dominated by this drive strives to have his own ideas confirmed by others so as to establish his own inner authority.

We can take as an example of this a Yellow level (Drive 3) intellectual with a strong Ego, who, having assimilated the wisdom and teachings of a Master then proceeds to use them not only to build his own philosophy but to found a material organisation that will bring him both reputation and financial reward (Green Drive 4). This he does without any acknowledgement of the source from which he drew the truths on which his whole project is founded. Moreover, he professes to be both the originator and the promulgator of those basic teachings.

DRIVE (5) Blue. The next human drive is the *love of authority* in the family, in religion and in science. Down the ages Family Love has depended so far on blood links. The New Age Family consciousness will bind itself with Spiritual Love in a new covenant with Life. All covenants whether written with blood or spirit represent authority. The human need for authority is a reflection of the unifying force at the centre of every Nucleus over its constituent parts. Deep in the heart of Reality only the Mystic can understand the ultimate Fatherhood or Motherhood. If awareness of Being (Self) and delight of Being (Self-replication) are the first parents of LIFE (Consciousness) then they are the very last states of a transcendental Creative Being. The manifest result in the created world of these two unconditioned and complementary states of Being is the drive to bring out Self-replication in others; as we see in nature around us, it is biologically and psychologically projected into the Family as the formal unit of procreation, of self-satisfaction and contentment, and of a stable and fixed reality of Being. Motherhood *can be* fulfilled in the family contentment, Fatherhood in creating its form. It is the complement of the sex act where the roles are reversed and the Mother provides the *form* while the male provides the *content.*

The family is in itself an expression of the natural order of the universe. Within the family exist relationships that must reflect this Cosmic order to become a unifying nurturing force, else chaos and remorse are the consequences. From this need for things to assume their proper places there comes the drive for authority. Authority in this context means something that has the power to bind so that elements can assume their correct relationships. Just as the nucleus of an atom exerts authority and binds its electrons into orbits around the center, so too does the human being achieve stability first by the binding influence of his family. When the roles of father and mother correctly mirror this natural process, satisfaction, contentment, and stability are the result.

All parents who are mature want the child to compensate for their own self-deficit; they all desire the child to achieve what they did not. They also want them to enjoy what they delighted in during their own youth. Here we see both lack and fulfilment are projected into the family preferences, thereby structuring the guiding field of authority.

Those readers who have first-hand experience of experimental communities can arrive at their own decisions and conclusions as to the viability of a totally leaderless group. Is there even such a thing at all? Or, if there is, how long does this leaderless state last? It seems that eventually one of two things happens. Either the group disintegrates, falls apart from the lack of direction or even from a failure to resolve the problems of conflicting egos. Or there arises within the group or community a natural leader, not through a will to dominate others but through the individual's innate quality that draws respect and a willingness to be guided into a productive and fulfilling way of life for the group. In the case of the second alternative, Nature's own law is being fulfilled and the nuclear force is naturally manifesting its unifying power.

> Although it may be thought superficially that only the Father wants authority in the Family, and that domination is *his need* only, mother and children also have a secret need for mastery. Authoritarianism and tyranny is indeed two-edged and very few members of the modern society understand it. It is certainly true to say that in its very deepest expression it is the tyranny in people's hearts that allows tyrants to rule them with a handful of ruthless men. People just love authority and stoically accept domination and no other evidence than the facts of today's world or the present human situation is needed to bear me witness. Radicals question this in the modern Utopias; they feel this is conservative doctrine and that " authority " is not a genuine need for adults. I wish this were true for those who *demand* " authorities " for the contents of this paper. The writer at one time concurred with this radical wishful thinking, but found by actual experiment with New Age group leaders in many parts of the world, that real CHANGE only results when the " leadership " is so subtle that the whole operation appears to be leaderless. He postulates a "guiding Logos" within; this does not support theories of the leaderless community, group or Utopia.

If we look at the whole question of authority, we must look at the world situation as well. For example, in Uganda, one man, a dictator, terrorises thousands of innocent people. In Russia, a score of men inhibit the intellectual expression of millions. Why? Because they have taken the authority of the people.

The same thing applies to knowledge. We cannot accept knowledge until religion has blessed it, science probed it, medicine approved it, the government taxed it, business mass-produced it and the advertisers packaged it in such a way that if we don't buy it we're damn fools.

> People who feel dominated by the existing system reveal that their childhood needs for dominion and self-dominion have not been satisfied once and for all. A strong Father or Mother will bring out the need to conquer oneself. It is more difficult for a man to conquer himself than to start conquering others. The will to dominate others physically is to be found in DRIVE 1, while the need to side with established might and authority is in Drive 5.

Our need to gratify desires, such as a " clinging to the family " (or society, group, club, etc.), is often frustrated by the absence of a feeling of personal authority in the family infra structure ; in Freud's system these frustrations can be traced back to the unsatisfied infant drive to cling to another's breast in the oral types. The deep reality of needs created by lack of sensitive parental love in childhood shows itself in a complementary way in the need of youth to give Love of an idealistic kind (the flower children) as well as emotional support to the object loved or identified with e.g. Father/Mother figure, Beatles, Hippy heroes, convention breakers, etc.

The *positive* reaction to this drive is more of a sublimation and a warm group feeling for those who have found their place in society or within a smaller in-group such as a family, a group of close friends, or such as CENTRE which is founded as a New Age family where Christ Consciousness, Krishna Consciousness, Buddha Consciousness and Cosmic Consciousness can be given birth. It shows a need of positive emotions from others as well as the ability to give love and affection to others.

In addition to the New Age family or community founded by the author in London in 1967, there is also the University of theTrees in California, where the student-faculty works together as a nuclear group to study consciousness and to discover the dynamic which unites a diverse group of people, and brings them to an intensifying sense of purpose and commitment. Focussing this commitment on the need for change and growth to a higher, non ego-centered level of awareness, the group seeks to demonstrate Nuclear Evolution at work. It also works to achieve group consciousness by releasing attachment to personal desires and by tuning to the inner worlds of others in the group or family.

The *negative* expression is a denial of the personality of the need to cling and lean on others or participate in the group spirit. It brings frustration for those who have given up any hope for compensating for earlier childhood frustrations through new group contacts. There is a wistful withdrawal and sadness in group relationships. Persons who are experiencing this Drive 5 predominantly in its negative aspects feel a great loneliness and unhappiness, with individual feelings of isolation from the family in-group. They often feel they are " helpers " when they themselves are in the greatest need of support and love. They feel they could help mankind, but in reality they cannot help themselves. They complain of domination but have no self-mastery.

If this drive is for contentment in its positive manifestation, the extreme negative of it is expressed in the mental bully or the fanatic ; unfortunately the extreme drive for contentment and " peace and quiet " tends to tolerate the bully indefinitely because of it. The lack of " authority " in family life often fails to turn out men who really do " will-to-be " masters of themselves. If this were not so we would have heaven on earth without any need for DRIVE 6 or 7 to complete the picture of the human drive for extreme discontentment so common today.

THE BULLY

The physical bully drive (1) Red negative plus mental bully breeds the conservative revolutionary dogmatists.

The military invasions by Russia of iron curtained satellite countries has finally exposed the inability of the gullible idealist to form valid concepts of reality. This destroys all hopes of the human mind to defend the world against man's stupidity. The answer lies not in the mind, but elsewhere. As will be seen from Part I, the mind is as much the instrument of an ignorant self, as it is the tool of those already enlightened ; of itself it can provide no wisdom or reality.

It is obvious that the Russian leaders are frightened men. Spectres arise in their imaginations even with their brother communists and fellow idealists with exactly the same goals. Today one of the greatest heroes of Russian Society exposing himself to liquidation is the present head of the thermonuclear programme in that country. He is an active critic circulating an illegal document reviewing " a blindly cruel criminal domination by dogmatically narrow-minded men compounding crimes with criminal negligence."

I repeat in his own words : " after 50 years of unrestricted domination over the minds of a whole nation our leadership apparently fears even the slightest hint of any discussion. A party with such methods of persuasion and education can hardly claim to be the spiritual leader of mankind." Academician Sakharov may think his reputation and position may protect him and he will be lucky if he is not liquidated, but how he could even dream in his wildest moments of idealism that Russia has ever represented spiritual leadership to mankind, when every act of the state from its inception has been a negation of the spirit of man, is one of the mysteries of mental gullibility.

The brutal aggression and massive invasion of Czechoslovakia against the united will of the people [as this book went to its second printing] involving as it does the physical liquidation of all those politicians and people who wish liberation from the repressive methods of press control and freedom of speech, is indicative of the terrorising power of the imagination, its power of liberation and its misuse. The bloody and vicious murder of over 100,000 Hungarians for wanting a democratic version of socialism in 1956 was an attempt to murder the free use of the imagination. Twelve fateful years have passed while the idealists, blind to all but their own emotional feelings, living in a band of consciousness which must experience reality in metaphors and ready-made concepts, have daily argued for compromise with the totalitarians. There can be no compromise with the things of the spirit. Totalitarianism is an affirmation that the State is supreme and that God is dead. Man is made for the state not the state for man. In the Soviet system Man is dead !

Since this book was first published nearly ten years ago in England, there have been reactions to it from people who seem to be quite unaware that politics is the outcropping of the unconscious drives of millions of people. Apparently the politically-minded do not realise that ninety-nine percent of the human race is suffering from a disease of social and political blindness. Moreover, they actually consider politics to be the solution and remedy for the problems of the world!

Important events, which strip whole nations of their human rights, in time wear off in their importance to the future generations, and those who were fifteen years old in 1968, when this book was first written, have hardly heard of the invasion of Czechoslovakia or the bloody slaughter of hundreds of thousands of people in Hungary in order to support repressive totalitarian regimes. These ex—teenagers who are now twenty-five years old even wonder why we use the Russian invasion of Czechoslovakia as an example of political blindness, since the event is far distant in time and for them it seems of little relevance to include such politics in a book about the spiritual nature of man. However, they ignore the fact that spiritual freedom for man is in essence the freedom to think and to live out his own life, and for good or for ill, to create his own destiny. Whether he does this within the communist or the capitalist system is irrelevant. What is important is that there should not be brutal repression of the right to dissent peacefully and to speak out freely without risk of coercion and threats of imprisonment or banishment. We have already referred to the blatant example of the invasion of Czechoslovakia when the full might of thousands of Russian tanks and troop transport planes overwhelmed the free spirit òf a fellow communist country headed by a popular Prime Minister, Dubjek. This total violation of human rights was then followed by the installation of a handful of puppets sympathetic to the Russian methods of coercion, and they in their turn proceeded to strip all freedom of thought and action and speech from every citizen, thus crowning the physical violence with attempted murder of the spirit. What lay behind this invasion was obviously the Russian fear of the ghosts which continually attack in their imaginations; they could not stand the spectre of a free society.

Andrei Sakharov, the Soviet physicist and inventor and former head of the Soviet H-bomb project, joins with three other Nobel Prizewinners Albert Einstein, Niels Bohr and Bertrand Russell in a feeling of responsibility or guilt for their roles in the scientific development of a possible thermonuclear catastrophe in which the extinction of mankind would be total.

Professor Sakharov turned to the civil rights movement as a result of his repeated warnings to Soviet leaders being totally ignored. These dissidents have been put on trial repeatedly as traitors and the Kremlin has increased its persecution and arrests of prominent dissenters in spite of signing a new Helsinki agreement with civil rights guarantees with 33 other countries in 1975, nearly 2 years ago.

Sakharov: Soviet scientist urges 'saving mankind from . . .thermonuclear catastrophe'

In 1968 when we mentioned Sakarov in the first edition of this book he was virtually unknown in the West. On visiting Moscow in 1970 I was not allowed to go freely around but was assigned a professor of philosophy who was a trusted party interpreter who showed me around. I asked what about Sakharov? She replied,"we know nothing of him here; he is never mentioned in our "Pravda". Who is he?"There are only five million party members who rule the proletariat of 248 million people who know only when they are told.

Does Sakharov have a chance?

This same blindness is not unique to the small clique who rule in Russia; it is also typical of the unconscious mind of an individual, but socially and politically it appears on a much wider scale and therefore is more difficult to see. Just as individual men and women can neither recognise their own unconscious acts nor see that their conscious mind is actually embodied in their unconscious actions, so is society as a whole unable to see the causes of its predicament and therefore occupies itself only with effects. The unconscious drives of politicians, communists, capitalists and armchair philosophers alike, are totally responsible for their conscious actions, thoughts and imaginings. The ghosts that lurk in individual minds in the invisible corners of the unconscious selves of millions of people, are projected out onto the movie screen of life, where they identify with the heroes in sport, politics and crime, vicariously obtaining satisfaction for these unconscious drives. In surface contact with such people we hear the mouthings of great ideals, the expression of concern for humanity, the excusing of political acts in the name of expediency, and most of all the thunderous roar of their silence on real matters of freedom of human expression. Only a few real heroes speak out, men like Sakharov and Solzhenitsyn and others willing to risk their necks without fear of imprisonment, torture and exile.

In the everyday lives of individuals there is this same separation between conscious and unconscious living, when in actual fact there is none. So it seems most people lead double lives; one is the life that they think might be acceptable to others and the other consists of their real feelings and hurts, aggression and fears. To acknowledge these dominant but subterranean drives is difficult so long as we are blaming others for our woes, while at the same time demanding that others shall fit the ideals, patterns and thoughts that we are not even living out ourselves. If the individual is unaware of this double-bind in his life, he is even less aware of it in society as a whole. We humans cannot see that we always regard our conscious acts, decisions and opinions as somehow separate from the consciousness which expresses them and not as what they really are, namely mirror reflections of the group unconscious life of individuals.

Thus the problem of humanity is not war or armaments, not oppression, not government or nationalism, not massacres and genocides, but the more important cause of all these monsters - our inability and impotence to show the ignorant any insight into their own self-righteous attitudes to others. In short, man is incapable of communicating at levels deeper than words, concepts, ideas and theories. The fact that real life goes on at far deeper levels than such means of communication and has done so for thousands of years of evolution, but is not recognised by the mass of humanity, does not mean that it must always go unrecognised. Nuclear Evolution reveals that when the inner worlds of men become consonant with their external worlds, when the mouths utter the thoughts of the heart, when they recognise that relationships and not language are the real basis of communication, then a golden age ensues.

DRIVE (6) indigo. The sixth drive is intuitive sensitivity or taste. Only by understanding the previous five drives in the human personality and channeling its energies constructively into a new image of Man, can we avoid their development into combative energies. If the individual fails to widen the horizon of Self these energies conflict with the ultimate biological goal of Man. This goal of the nervous system and the frontal lobes can be shown as man's journey towards total sensitivity to the Will of the Planetary Logos which has designed the brain and its antenna for a specific purpose. It is well known in Cybernetics that if man could utilise ALL the billions of neurons functioning like tiny crystals called transistors, the brain could act as an amplifying system which can govern the movements of charged particles in the membranes and nerve fibres, creating bio-electric currents which resonate with some all-inclusive brain-field in the Earth's total intelligence. Drive 6 is towards a sensitivity to this wider than human intelligence and the way it wants to go.

The body-politics in the overall organism which cause these conflicts and decide where these supra-mental psycho-social energies manifest throughout the sensing faculties of human perception, correspond exactly to man's knowledge of the seven basic drives within himself. He cannot possibly understand that what is observed is not important; what is important is the point from which it is observed and WHO is the perceiver of the perceptions which bring the conflict. Man will continue to project his spiritual pride and thus point his finger at his own reflection in a sick world until he reaches the sixth layer of his own consciousness. Until then he cannot reconcile man's inhumanity with a God who created it that way; he cannot bear to think of any intelligence superior to Man who would allow such suffering in the world. Until then he cannot see that in the Kingdom of Heaven on Earth, " All is Well " and that pain, suffering and dis-ease have a purpose in the evolutionary push. That these outer manifestations are in effect symptoms not causes; they are messages to our sensitivity which say that there is something needing attention which has been left undone.

Many philosophers have dealt with the problem of evil on earth. But perhaps if we look at our own lives, we can see how times of loss and suffering were really periods of growth. Sometimes for example, when we experience the shock of divorce, we are propelled forward to find out the cause. A great illness might cause us to begin searching for something meaningful in life. The loss of a loved one may cause us to wake up and begin living.

In the world there are earthquakes, famines, and wars. It doesn't mean God is mad or dead or even silently approving. But every short-term wrong inevitably leads to its opposite, for pain causes men to open their eyes. This awakening is human evolution.

In the positive expression of this drive lies the need to include the pain of the world within the boundaries of the Self, by sensitive contact with THAT outside of the Self. It is a deep feeling within the Self to expand in a dynamic need to widen the radius of the Self. It corresponds to the need for a more inclusive order rather than a more enduring order which is characteristic of drive seven. The feeling is not stemming from any specific need of the Ego and its inner contents as in Drive 3, but is an overall need which can only be expressed as a vague feeling of the personality as a whole. It is none the less real and valid, though it is indefinable to the personality experiencing this drive predominantly. The *positive* manifestation in society is an identification with and acceptance of man's need for emotional contact with his fellows, a " falling in love " with an idea, a leader in thought, or union with humanity. It is an identification with " fusion " itself, and this is felt even in its negative expression. However, the *negative aspect* of this drive 6 is the tension developed by the frustration encountered in the expression of this need to abolish the boundaries of separate and self-centred individuality and to become sensitised to the outer world. If this need is not recognised by the person, the group or community in which these tendencies originate, then the tension mounts up and can only be discharged through conflict. So that if the individual person is unaware of several of these drives within himself, to that extent he will be enslaved by Self-delusion and perhaps experience great personal difficulties in overcoming the prevailing ideas of the intelligentsia, or the dominion of accepted authority. He will also find it difficult to wrest himself free from the blind reactions of planned hate so prevalent in present day politics. If he is socially aspiring such a person will be unable to rise above the mental snobbery of deliberately calculated newspaper controversy.

TRANSCENDING THE THOUGHT FORM

Thoughts are transmitted through concepts and clearly defined words. Through the constant use of Drive 6 these hard and fast definitions are transcended and the usual thinking process is transformed from its horizontal patterns to a vertical process. The vertical thought process views the personality as a hierarchial system, more as an Art-form than a thought form, and it projects the products of consciousness into the environment against a tide of skepticism flowing towards it from the five lower drives in the system. Though it may be more at home in the realm of images, the personality cannot often understand what the true imagination is, and is often unable to make a careful discrimination between fancy and the Creative Imagination. Hence intuition meets with skepticism both from the level above it and all the levels below, since the level above is much more ruthless with the products of its own imaginations. In its attempt to express itself the personality dominated by this drive will meet up with two kinds of skepticism in the political and economic life of society which are both completely self-negating. There is a third kind which is positive but does not recognise the difference between utilitarianism and activity as an Art-form and is therefore sympathetic but ineffective criticism of intuitional knowing.

The first kind is the unbridled pragmatism that goes skeptical on the grounds that most of humanity is insensitive and difficult to persuade and that therefore nothing can be achieved in politics or economics without dealing with ground level activists for any reforms, or without attending ratepayers meetings, factory community associations, and local party and village hall agitation meetings to bring about CHANGE. Indeed such groups do make up society. It is groups of friends, families, clubs and churches which exert tremendous local pressure on the nuclear personality who would dare to break away from accepted authority. The domineering behaviour of people still imprisoned in Drive 5 towards their inferiors and submissive behaviour towards their superiors in society are complementary attitudes arising from the same tendency for respect of authority which the personality in Drive 6 is trying to escape. Therefore he suffers from the well-meaning skepticism of the political activist who cannot see further than the limitations of the horizontal thought-form system. Before we can restructure government as an Art-form we first have to see that bad government always results from looking at pressures first and allowing them to shape the policy. We must first study policy, then study government and politics; then work at the Art-form with the feasibility of the best solution. Planetary Man who emerges from his battle with Drive 6 knows that the solution lies in the human personality itself. First then study personality, then policy, then government.

It is good to pause at this point and to apply what has just been said to actual situations in our own lives, to actual groups, associations, committees or even government departments of which we have first-hand personal experience. Otherwise the danger is that what is being said can always apply to "the other guy" but not to us! Let us ask the question: "What governs the decision making in these organisations? Is it overpowering respect for authority however restrictive and outdated? Or is it pressure of immediate needs rather than a vision of a totally new shaping of the whole system?" We can also ask ourselves how we treat those who dare to bring up the question of a need for total reorientation of policy and then present ourselves with the challenge that we may be among those who strongly resist any idea of reshaping not only in society, but more basically where it is most needed, namely in our own personality.

> The second kind of negative skepticism is the Ivory Tower isolation of the man with a special mission, perhaps self-chosen rather than elected or eligible, who insists that messing about with politics, business reforms, corporate growth, biological and material matters, is unwittingly tainting one's spirituality and putting Mammon before God. His main philosophy of life is that we should not engage in activity but pray, withdraw and remain apart, make contact with the higher spiritual inspiration and pass on the benefit of Absolute Truth in word form so that others can put his message into action on Earth. We know, however, that the real teacher is the one who does.

If theories and philosophies and spiritual teachings could change the world without their originators and disciples becoming involved in the world, then we should not be in our present mess. Look at what has been done with all the teachings so far, from Buddhism to Christianity to Taoism. The only effective use of these magnificent programs for man's enlightenment has been by those who lived them day by day. Christ's demand of his followers was that they test out the teachings in real life. Instead we have built thousands of churches, in which priests can sermonise and theorise to captive audiences about what Christ said. Or we have retreated into monasteries or the Himalayan caves to meditate and to pray for the world of men, which is meanwhile sliding faster and faster into self-destruction. The only effective ones have been the teachers and saints who have stayed in the thick of things and have encouraged their students to face life as it is and themselves as they really are. Then, before allowing them out into the world to start "helping" people and "doing good", these teachers have insisted on real change, which involves the conquering of the Ego.

The third kind of skepticism is positive but ineffectual; it says that anyone who wants CHANGE must first make changes in the consciousness of individuals before it can manifest on Earth, therefore any higher wisdom has to result in the full ability to control one's environment; to this kind of skeptic, the world-changer, must immediately demonstrate spiritual and economic Reality in a practical way. In other words create Utopia now so that we can go there and live in it! One of the two thieves who asked Jesus to get them all off the Cross is an example of this kind of skepticism of Planetary Man. All of these skeptics are merely projecting their own inability to perform, and their views have little or no Reality at the level of Nuclear Evolution.

Here again we can support and illustrate our understanding of this type of skepticism with examples from our own experience. If we ourselves have ever tried to start a new community that will demonstrate a new life style and a positive example of how men and women can live together in harmony in a growth-producing situation, we shall have encountered these skeptics. They are the people who want to see us do it first and then, when we have born the financial and practical load and ironed out all the initial snags and problems, they will condescend to participate in our experiment. Search out your own examples and you might even have to confront the fact that you yourself fall into this category of those who doubt the feasibility of anything new and original until someone else has manifested it, tested it and shown it to be viable.

Planetary Man is evolving through what actually happens in the consciousness of each individual in the Nuclear Group since it is this which spurs a man to action; in reality it has nothing to do with theoretical possibilities, speculative thoughts, or the outcome of practical action. It has to do with the role of beauty as an instrument of evolution—the Art-form. The colours in the butterfly wing are part of its survival, its ability to find a mate. There are many practical projects which if projected forward to their accomplishment, can be seen to be stillborn. Down to earth buildings, churches, centres, institutes, etc. are practical activity, but without the head-in-the clouds thesis and metaphysics of a Jesus, the churches become expensive and useless derelicts suitable for conversion into Bingo Halls. But the Cathedral that was built with love, where the craftsman has created a thing of beauty, where the Art-form has enshrined the spirit and ego of the group in His name, will live on its own. Skepticism cannot be justified until the work of building an Art-form has been completed. The building of a group committed to nuclear evolution must be considered as an Art-form.

735

This is really an extraordinary idea! The task of building fools into divine inheritors of the kingdom of God has always been the business of wise men. But it is a much more rare event when the wise man chooses to mould a group of fools into an art form that stands as a living tribute to the evolution of consciousness. In other words, he uses real people whose experience and dedication to self-government are effectively channeled through the positive drive of the intuition, to express beauty, and therefore to serve the larger purpose of evolution on earth.

Planetary Man can see that the unconscious manipulation of the political and economic environment in the affluent society at all local points is equalled in left-wing communism. It exploits the same *possessive* drive (Number 4) for material wealth (with the State acting as shareholder and board of directors on behalf of a theoretical owner) and then coerces the *herd* drive for political unity to be found in comradeship. The pollution of thought-forms at the mental level (Drive 5) and the techniques of persuasion are very little different. If persuasion does not work there is always the power of the ruling class in the form of the Communist Party or the mock trials of the State versus the intellectual. *Authoritarian* domination is man's inability to become his own authority.

Development of Drive 6 for an *aesthetic sense,* that can blend its insights for beauty, order, freedom and CHANGE into constitutional forms of Self-government, is an essential part of any leap in social evolution. To the man involved in the practical tasks of social service the question is always HOW. This however cannot become clear until we make *one more leap* in consciousness:

DRIVE (7) Violet. The last basic drive in the personality is for the *awareness of an enduring order.* The breakthrough in the form of Self-government which future man will evolve through bio-energetic sensing will depend on his own ability to use his power of internal vision (Imagination) to condition himself, rather than allow his natural environment to condition him. Understanding his " will " and " pure consciousness " will give him powers that work with nature to transform LIFE. The whole CENTRE CONCEPT which is described in Part I is specifically concerned with people who wish to make this break-through themselves; the world outside us will only change when we have changed ourselves within.

Developing our Drive towards ENDURING ORDER is the use of our power to directly " imagine " LIFE and its vital energies as they continually CHANGE and transform the human world and the human body. It is the power that awaits the insight. This is the drive in the human personality which will decide whether Man continues to stagnate without any

REAL revolutions in his psychic or biological ecology. It is the drive which will lead him to the discovery that he can speed up the process of evolution a million times. The price he must pay is the apparent loss of individuality as a small separate Self in order to gain contact with the Supra-mental intelligence of an all-present Overself. Man must first become Planetary Man and then begin his real work as a Cosmically Conscious Man, not in any mystical or psychic sensing of one's fellowship with other men and women unnamed, but in a Spiritual sense of indivisible Union of a specific group of inseparable people, a group which forms a new nucleus with its own Ego, its own soul and spirit. The technique for doing this is already hidden in nature, which has done it many times before. It is no use thinking of other "people" out there in the abstract world with similar ideas to our own. This is merely a "psychic" union in the head, whereas "spiritual" union is a real one with real people.

It is important to distinguish between the spread of ideologies and even religions by the methods of indoctrination, preaching and teaching, and the proliferation of an imaginative and world-changing dynamic that spreads of its own volition once the core energy reaches a certain intensity; this can happen both within the individual and within the nuclear group. It is of this that Christ spoke when he said: "When two or three are gathered together in My Name, there am I in the midst of them." Christians down the ages have distorted this to mean that the "risen Christ" is there in the religious group meeting, but what he really meant was that the Absolute "I" that is the Christos or the Nuclear Self in all things, once contacted, can transform the being from within out.

Another clear distinction has to be made between a type of sentimental or vaguely idealistic unity and the real stuff that involves the surrender of the self-sense or the separative Ego and the full realisation of the Greater Self, that permeates all life on the planet and is the guiding logos for those who gather together as a family or a community or a nation, in the name of the One.

It is in this word " spiritual " that difficulties in communication emerge. Yet in this seventh drive we find that better communication is only part of the answer, and that what is communicated is primal. Stripped of all sentimental feelings, the word which describes the " spiritual " drive for a technique of fusion with one's environment is " LOVE ". To the person at the seventh level of consciousness it is obvious that the *positive* aspect of a drive towards ETERNAL ORDER has to do with facing the IMAGE of one's Self as a reflection of one's needs in the universe as a whole. It is the strength of the boundary of individual consciousness which determines the degree of separateness of the Ego from the outer world and its many changing forms. The positive Ego-self in Drive 3 is dilated by its combining with man's HIGHER SELF in Drive 7; a technique of fusion into the objective environment breaks down the wall of tension between the subject and his environment. It involves a projection of Ego in its widest sense, into the entire universal process and not merely in the psychoanalytical sense of personal content which is projected outwards through being unacceptable to the subject himself.

The *negative* aspect of this drive is a binding back of the Ego upon itself without having faced its contents and this is experienced as a psychic impotence, as helplessness or internal unhappiness while on the surface all things may seem well. This is often experienced as loneliness in some phases of creative thinking, alternating with periods of inspiration, and this shows the connection between the super-conscious in Drive 7 and the intuitional thought process, or " vertical " knowing in Drive 6. If the negative expression becomes dominant there is a deep feeling of being completely abandoned by the Life forces as a result of a conflict between an imagined heavenly state of enduring bliss and the actual personal reality. The *need for* tender gentle Love contrasts with the *need to love* too much in the positive expression of this drive.

THE MEANING OF LOVE

The full meaning of all the positive and negative factors can only be understood in relating the functions of each drive to each other. It is obvious that all the foregoing drives are the " Love of Reality " in different ways of expression. Psychologically speaking we experience the ingestion of the Life Force as the consciousness of our integration with the universe. Life feeds off LIFE throughout the Cosmos. The cohesive force of " LOVE " is the Cosmic Force behind all Creation which creates the IMAGE of our Self, sustains the vital forces we call LIFE and destroys all that is unlike its own image in the end. The personality is made up of these drives called " LOVE " and when left undeveloped unconsciously it would destroy and annihilate everything unlike itself until it finished up with its indestructible Self. The pure naked consciousness when faced with itself is faced with what the Mystic calls " God " and therefore all thoughts about any " other Self " must die. That these " love " drives are destructive through human obstinacy and defiant self-will, at any cost to the personality and others, is made evident when they are in conflict with each other, or where the " will " and *imagination* of the subject are working in opposition.

If we understand our blocking of the cosmic process at the personal level we may be able eventually to grasp it at the planetary level. If we can see our will and imagination producing a double-bind effect in our own consciousness, we can expand that concept out to apply to what happens in families and in larger groups like corporations or even nations. The imaged state remains a latent dream, while the reality suffers at the hands of the perverse will that is regulated by the Ego.

As in the story of the Tower of Babel, LOVE and its drives created confusion when its presence was omitted by the builders of the Kingdom of Reality on Earth.

The secret of Planetary Man awaits the insight in this old fable, as ordinary man builds his tower to heaven in a towering mushroom cloud of nuclear energy. In addition to his building the edifice of U.N.O. and giving homage to the mandates of the Nations enshrined in its charter, or channelling his efforts into International Cooperation, or trying to make the world of one language, and striving to make a name at the council table, Man must now make LOVE and its drives the first authoritative mandate. What technique or system of government can allow for Love ?

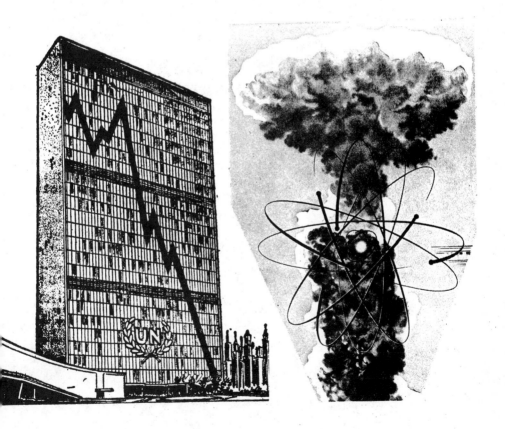

.R. 13 Red   19 Orange 25   Yellow   50 Green 55 Blue 62 Indigo 68 Violet   8

THE NEW IMAGE
OF COSMIC MAN

NUCLEAR EVOLUTION

The next step for Man is a direct unity with that Universal Spirit which in modern times we give the name of WHOLE-NESS (holiness) and the means to it must be the uniting of man's Creative Faculty with the whole of Creation. Only when we have made this first step and begin to manifest it can we talk about GOD. Secreted in the depths of the individual (real meaning: THAT which cannot be separated or divided) is the CENTRE "way-of-looking" at each Self as a pivot of all EVOLUTIONARY PROGRESS. When the power of this revolution in thinking beyond the seventh level of human consciousness takes place, a bio-energetic mutation follows. A "resonance" effect is created in the nucleus which absorbs energy from Light and sets up a "standing wave" within each cell. The absorption of ordinary Light by ordinary people is extra-ordinary but with training of the consciousness the positive charge on the blood cells is mirrored and amplified in all the other cells. In Nuclear Evolution theory all cells work to reflect the cosmic desire for union. A blood cell being the most reactive in responding to the "shells of consciousness", is the first **part** of the body to become conscious of the **whole**. As the medium for the carriage of oxygen, energy, vital chemical hormones, etc. blood is the first to experience a new **hierarchial** level of Being.

Every physics student knows that when sunlight passes through a rain drop, part of its energy is reflected back into the drop from the far boundary. Such reflections occur whenever waves of energy encounter a boundary between one medium and another, and the boundary of an atomic nucleus should be no exception. When "resonance" occurs between the energy being absorbed by the nucleus at the atomic level and Light being absorbed at the nucleus of the cell, a "standing wave" is thereby set up throughout the entire body. If the rain drop (or nucleus) in our analogy is of the right size to allow the incoming waves of energy and the reflected waves to reinforce each other, they will form the standing wave which contains so much energy that even a very poor absorber will soak up considerable amounts of it. The size of the drop (or nucleus) must be in relation to the wavelength of the incoming energy in order to have a standing wave,* and therefore only certain frequencies of light will be absorbed. Nuclear Evolution is a process which opens the nucleus and annihilates certain boundaries. A transmutation then takes place in the *cell life* of the *whole* organism we call a body. It does not take place in the *cell* alone in isolation from other cells or in the nucleus at the atomic level alone. It is this mutation which I call the evolved nucleus in the process of NUCLEAR EVOLUTION

Although I refer to this as a " process ", in fact it is a leap in consciousness which brings about *change* at the CENTRE of all systems in the physical and mental well-being of that small Universe we call the human entity. We are enabled to clothe ourselves in Light and acquire a living Universe free from all sorrow, affliction and pain. This technique described in Part 1 has been separated from Part 2 because some of it needs deep study by those without the faculty of intuitive insight. In short it is a review of man's knowledge of Light and the way it is absorbed into his world and his own Self.

This brings us to the apprehension of the ultimate state, the goal of all living things in what I have called the 8th state of individual consciousness (see Fig. 190)   which is a transcending of all limitations or layers of being which divide it from the " whole " Universe . . . not definable or separable from any of the other Love-drives simply because it contains all of their positive manifestations just as white light contains all the colours of the spectrum.

It is in the eighth domain that the Rainbow Body is attained; it is here that the leap in consciousness is made that makes totally irrelevant all the distinctions, separations and limitations that belong to the other seven levels. The Red level leaps beyond the senses and the Orange finds itself merged in the total Being; the Yellow intellectual discovers the Heart and the Green possessor finds that the whole Universe belongs to him. For the Blue rigid conceptualiser devotion expands to serve All and the Indigo intuitive finally knows how he knows. At last the Violet imaginer discovers that the vision and the reality are ONE. Having transcended the limits of their levels, those who reach the eighth domain discover the ultimate perfection of all the spectrum levels of consciousness and the meaning of the words of Christ: "Ye are the Light of this world".

*A standing wave is one whose energy is contained within the wave. This restriction of energy or lack of energy loss allows the incoming energy to rapidly build up in the standing wave, as in a laser. A standing wave doesn't go anywhere. It is self-contained. Any transmission line such as a wave-guide or acoustic transmission system will exhibit the superposition of progressive standing waves, i.e. one standing wave backing up against another.

Working through to the seventh layer of consciousness leads to the 8th domain of pure Self-saturation in its positive expression while the negative results of the seventh layer lead to Self-intoxication. Both of these manifestations of this seventh drive of Love lead to a Self-annihilation in different ways ; the positive to integration with the living universe and society in immortality, and the negative through total disintegration and separation from it, to death. (See Fig.196)

Within a group committed to Nuclear Evolution, such as the one now working together at University of the Trees in California, examples can be found in all the unique individuals and in the group as a whole of the stages of build-up that come before the leap in consciousness is made. Doubts and fears fade and confidence grows as new potentials are discovered and put to use, so that the manifestation, whether it be in writing a book or organising a group project or dealing with finance or making a beautiful garden, reveals the potential of yet another evolutionary development. And as this spiralling process continues within the individual and within the group we see that it is analogous to Nature's own pattern.

Every manifested state of being or existence in Nature springs from a potential state which has to be actualised. This actualisation is a process which prepares each organism in Nature for a leap to a new threshold in the evolutionary spiral, a leap that cannot take place until the build-up of the prior potential state has been completed.

Subtler but even more vital to Nuclear Evolution in the group is the link between two processes: (a) the transformation that takes place on all levels within the consciousness of individuals, and, (b) the gradual emergence of a group consciousness, in which the individual Ego or self-consciousness has to let go when faced with the group's growing strength and expression of selfless love and surrender to a higher guiding intelligence. At this point, when the potential state has reached its maximum, it can be likened to a saturated solution which is about to crystallise into another form. However, to go from liquid to a solid crystal is an example of Nuclear Evolution in reverse; what happens with man is that he evolves from a solid state to a more rarified state once his maximum potential has been totally saturated. Therefore it would be more like proceeding from a crystal to a liquid and thence into a gaseous state.

An equivalent development in an individual could be his or her relinquishing of bodily attachment with all its sensory and sensual trips, and the realisation of potential in the areas of the mind, the intuition or the imagination. In other words to clarify it further since each manifested state of any organism or being has latent within it the potential state of its next higher manifestation, it can be seen that a leap to the next threshold of existence cannot take place until the potential of each individual part of the whole (each molecule in a saturated solution ready for crystalisation) has been totally saturated with the group readiness. So in a group of people the spark of enthusiasm for change and growth towards the selfless state has to catch fire right through the group before a genuine evolutionary leap to another level of consciousness can be made.

A seed cannot maximise its potential without the addition of water to germinate its chemical structure and will lie dormant in the earth for thousands of years, like the wheat that was taken out of the pyramid and which sprouted several thousand years after it was put there. So in the group there must be a seed crystal of a particular form and pattern which guides the formation of all the other crystals and acts as a trigger. So does Nuclear Evolution act as a seed or seed crystal which is germinated by the addition of the Living Water in each individual person. That "living water" is the realisation that consciousness, which validates every act of perception and lives at the heart of this agglomeration of cells called a body, is the same thing as Light as it courses through space. The next step, which creates the actual crystalisation or leap on to the next threshold, is the realisation that this same consciousness within every living thing is not only Light but the Living God.

Nuclear Evolution is shot through with universal fulfillment while any state inferior to this is riddled with constant self-limitation, separation and repulsion from absolute wholeness in one's incarnate form. The state of Nuclear Evolution into which the Christos is born is the formal unit of procreation, the family of man, raised up into an exalted state of physical manifestation at higher energy levels of Being. I have been impressing this thought into my own cell life and radiating it into the psycho-social atmosphere now over many years as a full time job. My work as Director of the Commission for Research into the Creative Faculties of Man has led me to every part of the world where men of insight have been probing the inner sanctum of Man's full potentialities.

The work of the Commission since 1962 has been to provide a forum for exchange of ideas, facts and researches among persons professionally concerned with economic, spiritual and scientific development of man's environment, and with the regeneration of human society specifically in terms of a real CHANGE in the individual person and his attitudes to the group mind. Much of this work has proceeded at such a pace that there has been no time to stop and type out the many lectures, tapes of seminars, papers on basic research and most important, a polished account of all the experimentation which can be repeated by others. We have already formed embryonic groups among aware philosophers, thinkers, planners, business consultants and scientists who can feed and redesign the human world e.g. The Chlorella International Union, a consortium of scientists with the aim to exchange knowledge and technique with researchers in the microbiology of Algae for growing food from the sun's Light.

There is also the Centre project in London, where a group of people from all walks of life live in a six-floor building and dedicate themselves to conscious Nuclear Evolution, not only within the group but as it relates to a wide range of teachings, including the I Ching, astrology and yoga.* In USA the University of the Trees in Boulder Creek, California, has already been mentioned in connection with work being done by individuals and by the group to transform consciousness and to manifest Nuclear Evolution in action. The University, which offers degrees in consciousness research, functions as a training ground for potential founders of similar groups and centres for people who are seeking the regeneration to be found within free and unstructured Nuclear Evolution.

---

* See article on Nuclear Evolution and the I Ching by Regan Power of Centre House, London, in Part IV of this book and "Wholistic Health and Living Yoga" by Malcolm Strutt, also of Centre House, London, to be published by University of the Trees Press in September 1977.

A FEW OF THE NUCLEAR FAMILY AT UNIVERSITY OF THE TREES: (Back row left to right:) Christopher Hills, Norah Hills, Ann Ray, David Edwards, Jeff Goelitz, Gary Buyle, Roger Smith, Phil Allen, Ted Saunders, Michael Hammer. (Middle row standing:) Dan Hime, Susan Welker, Susan Belanger, Wendy McFadzen, Diane Vandewall. (Front row:) Pamela Osborn, Robert Massy, Rod Glasgow, Richard Welker, Stephanie Herzog, Deborah Rozman.

Crystallisation has yet to take place in similar efforts the world over for there to be a coming together of the forces of Good. A network of awareness for the people who can offer humanity creative energies was the first objective of the founders of the Co-mission and now specific Centres are ready to crystallise everywhere. The seed-crystal is the nucleus group of several human Egos forged into a group sensorium so as to become sensitive to the new species of COSMIC MAN. This is a step as big and as difficult as the step from the atom, with its shells of electrons moving around the central nucleus of its group being, to the next molecular level of Being. Such a jump for each man should not be underestimated, for it is as difficult for Nature to achieve as the jump from the molecular level to that of the cell. It is as difficult to accomplish as it is for human body cells to feed directly from Light and radiation, as do atoms and plant cells.

The nucleus of the cell, which causes it to group, found it just as difficult to jump from the cell level to the destiny of the body as a whole. It is obvious therefore that men will find it difficult to group together in a Nucleus which is sensitive to the level above it. As Part I shows, Man is partly already there in his limited sensitivity to light and radiation which is taking place in his body constantly. Extra-terrestrial cosmic intelligence, which merely uses the cerebral instrument as an organ of perception on earth, is the next leap in evolution which will smash through the crisis to which the world has now come. CENTRE is constantly seeding a nucleus in scientific groups, spiritual groups and political groups, because its members are expecting total and inevitable saturation of the human mind with the mere communication of information, which must precipitate its contents in *a new form* of Being. This new form must now include a mixture of the different varieties of human experience, preparatory to its crystallisation in Nuclear Evolution.

It will be seen from a study of Part I, that if all men were aware of the great influence of all seven drives in the self-regarding sentiment which makes up their own personalities the human race could attain a million years of evolutionary growth in 50 years. The next 50 years ahead in our thinking for the world's future society should include those " philosophers-in-waiting " who have not only analysed and seen the way HOW, but have worked out specific answers.

ANSWERS ARE NOT ENOUGH

The real trouble with knowing the answers is that they are all *answers for other people* to carry out, for if they are answers to our own problems we would have already carried them out in order to solve our own problems; they can only be proved answers when they have been tried and tested by time.

748

The technique and method of Self-evaluation which helps us to make those decisions in the spheres of action in which we must fulfill ourselves, are given in the first half of this book because unless the human personality can relate itself and its love-drives to a real yardstick in nature such as Light and colour and their psycho-physical reactions and interactions between the levels of experience, we can never arrive at a common standard for judging ourselves. Truth which needs long lists of academic authorities to back it up will never eclipse the truth of first-hand experience of a Jesus, a Buddha or a Lao Tse. The test of any method is in the direct experience of its efficiency.

The method is based on drives which feed on colour because the objective and subjective expressions and impressions of the colours are well known in society and are unconsciously incorporated in all the different languages of man. It is well known that manic patients at the asylums preferred red colour and this drive is reflected in responses of the crowd and the herd. Depressives prefer blue and schizophrenics are sensitive to yellow. Selfishness and acute paranoia are brown in colour preferences, showing a mixture of red and green. Man's words enshrine these experiences over the entire Planet and incorporate his innate subconscious knowledge of colour and its relationship to consciousness over thousands of years. We talk of Blue as subduing, cold, contemplative, conservative and sober in its expressions. Its impressions are gloomy and fearful and subjectively calming in very tense subjects. We know Red is passionate and exciting and active in its expression; while the subjective impression of it is intense, angry, inflamed and disturbing to the anxious and tense subject. No one would argue about the validity of our colour susceptibilities which have been proved by large business corporations in their marketing techniques.

Green is quietly refreshing, seeking security and vitality in its expression. Subjective impressions of green are ghastly, sickening, envious and possessively jealous. The objective expression of black is commonly known as spatially annihilating—seen at funerals, ominous, depressing; in its subjective impression the colour Black is angry hatred, suicide, self-annihilation and death, the total negation of the human spirit. The royal colour of purple is pompous, dignified, religious and mystic in its expression, but its subjective impression is lonely, mournful, full of desperate shadows. The colour of centrifugal action radiating outwards from the centre is Red/Orange/Yellow, which are conducive to expansion, spontaneous expression and active, extrovert activities working from the CENTRE within. The colours coming towards the CENTRE are those of centripetal action; violet or purple, blue, green and grey. Our friends say we are " off-colour " and grey when we are thrown off-centre. These colours reflect our drives and affect our moods, our business and our lives, and are invaluable for testing our own physical and psychological states of Being. They provide answers on which we can act.

The difficulty in society as in any other form of activity is finding the "know how" and then acting on it. The trouble is that people in general are not "self-acting"; they make suggestions for others without carrying them out or knowing anyone else who can carry them out. This usually involves rationalisations of their own inadequacy but never the putting of one foot forward on the long journey. Those who do make a start by working first on themselves are the new heroes who create the *Now* Generation, the moulders of the new Image of Man that we must now form. They are writing the constitution of Man as the instrument of political and social CHANGE which can be put to work *Now,* incorporating LOVE and its drives in the mechanism for Nuclear Leadership, which draws upon its own group membership for vitality by a natural method of CHANGE such as we find in the ancient Chinese "Book of Changes" and modern scientific knowledge. *

Such a Nuclear Constitution NOW can follow a process of ingestion, digestion, and excretion of imaginative ideas of the way ahead.

This will allow the PHOENIX to rise and this will ensure that the next CHRISTOS is not sent to the cross for daring to suggest that the key to real revolutions in Being is SENSITIVITY TO THE GUIDING LOGOS.

---

* See Universal Government by Nature's Laws to be published late 1977 by University of the Trees Press.

THE ANSWER TO
THE SOCIAL DILEMMA

I have undertaken two practical experiments in creating a new kind of group consciousness, a higher level of integration than has been sought in the world even by religious groups. These two communities, one in London and one in California, are based upon an in-depth spiritual commitment which is nothing less than a divine marriage, a union of hearts. If we ask what is the purpose of seeking this unitive experience, an idealistic answer might say that it is to teach how one can escape from illusions of the separative self-sense by entering into healing relationships to discover the presence of love at the centre of the Nuclear Being. But in practical experience, what could motivate people to stay with such a commitment, especially when they begin to see what it really entails? The following is an answer to this question from one of the members of the Nuclear Evolution group at the University of the Trees.

Since no ego wants to die into selflessness, what is the lure that draws anyone to attempt group consciousness? What makes a person want to give freedom as much as to get it? What makes anyone care about fusion when fission is so much easier to achieve? Group consciousness requires an incredibly large commitment. Why did we do it?? We didn't do it overnight. We made a very small commitment, then a slightly larger one, then another and another until one day we had before us a choice to make Nuclear Evolution our life's work and to be together (whether geographically or not) for as long as it might take—even to eternity. Our marriage would be a covenant, like the covenant Abraham made with God, pledging the Jewish nation to be guided by God alone. In the same way, we would be a political unity guided by attunement with something larger than ourselves. These were lofty thoughts and they appealed to our idealism and our need to do something worthwhile with our lives. We did not think much about the amount of dying that our egos would have to endure before we could manifest our ideal. Sometimes in the painful process of stretching to become bigger people, we ask ourselves "What am I doing here? I must be crazy. Why don't I just leave?" But if we really think of leaving, suddenly it seems impossible. To go back to the ways of the world seems out of the question. Nothing would ever seem meaningful to us again. To just work for ourselves would feel so pinched and small. We have the feeling that some nameless depression—some unfulfillment, some void—would be with us the rest of our lives. Knowing that to be part of the group marriage is in tune with the universe and its evolutionary thrust, we also know that if we left, once having joined, we would be out of tune and life would reward us accordingly. Things would go wrong and some light would be gone from us. So the thing that makes a person care about fusion is the same light, the wonderful feeling that you get when for just a moment you let go of small personal cares and let in the Truth."

WHAT IS A NUCLEAR MARRIAGE?*

When we talk of a divine marriage or a union of hearts in a group situation, does it mean that all the participants must hold the same ideas in the head? Must the concepts of union be identical with each person in order for the group to survive? If we look at religious groups, we can see differences in various sects within the whole of Christianity, Buddhism, etc. In the Roman Catholic orders the Jesuits are scholars and teachers, the Benedictines are contemplative, the Franciscans serve the sick and destitute and declare poverty a virtue. Yet in the heart there is a common bond through Christ, which transcends the differences in concepts. Similarly in Buddhism, there are countless approaches and even in one branch of it we call Tibetan Buddhism there are four major orders all practicing different approaches to the Hinayana, Mahayana: (1) the Nyingmapa, (2) the Kagyuptas, (3) the Gelugpas, and, (4) the Sakyas. Yet they are all united by one common thread at the core, which is the death of the ego and the realisation of oneness or total openness with all sentient beings. To the extent which the sects of any religion dwell upon their separate concepts, they become dry and dead, a union of the head. And even if they keep alive the deeper bond, their drive for perfection, how do they become more than just an association of people who want the same goal? Is this what we mean by group consciousness or do we mean something on a higher level of integration? How can a union of love, which is the embodiment of their ideal, ever actually manifest? How can we remove the blocks to awareness which alone can bring love into the larger social unit and so heal the world?

So many differences exist between two people, let alone between whole nations of individuals, that the task seems tremendous. The task only awaits the understanding of man's real inner being to discover what blocks and what liberates the soul in millions of lives. Because Nuclear Evolution is not anything different from what man actually is, nothing but an understanding of the different levels of consciousness is needed to see the

---

* A series of tapes on "Group Consciousness" given to an actual group working together to consider the questions involved in a group marriage, available from the publishers. (12 tapes of 2 hours each.)

vision and to activate the cosmic program already projected into the hologram of the human brain with its resultant effects on genes. (See page 748) The two group experiments in London and in California, founded several years ago on the principles of the levels of consciousness first described in the earlier editions of this book, is a commitment not only to share a common ideal but to become one soul, married in the highest sense of the word.

For many older people, the idea that there can be closer and more dynamic relationships, similar to marriage but in a group sense, is an intolerable one. The institution of marriage between two people is a deep-rooted ancient tradition, though the two mates may be living in totally different worlds of Being. While speaking the same language and sharing the same bed and in a domestic sense getting along, the interests, drives, thoughts and needs can be worlds apart. Legal marriage may have nothing to do with real love (as the fifty percent California divorce rate shows) but only with what each partner can "get" from the other in terms of security, confirmation, love, status, companionship, etc. The commitment of the Nuclear Evolution group is a commitment to build and manifest a true bond of love, but love means many things to many people and in the context of Nuclear Evolution can mean seven different kinds of experience, including the level of physical love. To share all things in common was an early Christian practise but did they share each other's bodies or was the union limited to the idealistic level only? How does Nuclear marriage work out in the nitty gritty sense of you and me, him and her, and does it mean that there is a separation say at the sexual level and a divine marriage at another level? Does it mean that we possess each other as in earthly marriage, to have and to hold and worship each other with our bodies? How far does Nuclear Evolution go beyond these primitive and personal and very human ideas of marriage? What kind of power binds the nucleus together with such force that it does not fall apart? If it is not just ideals and philosophy in the head, then what is the bond in the heart and how is it created? How does this union differ from all the religions and all the spiritual groups through-out history?

The answer is that the unity of the Nuclear group has very little to do with ideas and concepts in the head but hinges more on the feeling in the heart. This has been the teaching of all religious leaders such as Christ, Buddha, etc., but the religions have made the teachings into learned concepts, creeds, doctrines, laws, rules and commandments. Therefore the answer must in some way differ from the idealistic level of belief and shift to the level of direct knowing.

Who establishes the physical limits of consciousness? It has in the past always been the group which manifests a leader at a particular time who says what is moral and what is sin. What was sinful yesterday is not sinful today in ordinary relationships, although murder and stealing and hurting others have in past history always been sinful, yet there are societies built upon such murders of innocent people, who did not believe in the same ideas. Both Stalin and Lenin murdered millions of dissident peasants and Stalin and his henchmen at one time were killing 40,000 per month. Obviously it was not regarded as sinful by Hitler that he should murder millions of Jews or that Mao Tse Tung's revolution should sentence millions of peasants who did not agree with its concepts to death in the people's courts. Millions of Tibetans were murdered in cold blood by the Chinese army and it is all documented by an official team of jurists from the Hague international court.

These international issues of ideological murder lose their significance as crimes and the sins pale against the more subtle nearby separations we make everyday of what is right and wrong in our closer relationships.

The Truth is that all limits are set by Consciousness and that to unite with others at the physical sex level and the spiritual level at the same time is sin to one person and liberation to another. Within a nuclear grouping at the level of pure consciousness each group must in freedom work out its own natural levels of sharing. When most people truly love someone they do not wish to share that person intimately with others; yet at another level, real love means allowing a person to be free to associate in any way without creating a cramping restrictive vibration of possessiveness. For any group to give indulgent people a licence by making an agreement for sexual union without a corresponding spiritual union, would automatically restrict any real union on the other six levels because of the expectations at the sensory skin level.

The nuclear marriage could not make any hard and fast rules for personal morality but would instead put all its energy into the minimum number of rules for confronting any situation that was hurtful to the group's evolution. To be able to bring up issues that are sensitive without fear of reprisal is the essence of the group marriage. It does not mean any physical limits have to be drawn by its members as to what is the good and wholistic living process. Each individual is free to innovate, with responsibility to the entire membership for the consequences. Partners in an earthly marriage are responsible only to each other whereas a Nuclear marriage of the wider spiritual group is responsible for the thrust of evolution and the new shape of the entire future whole. Its morality by rules is only an aspect of its virtue

Picture shows bodies of executed peasants thrown into the Yangtze River. They disagreed with the political views of the local commissars of the people's courts. Millions were executed because they could not believe and accept the doctrines of Marxism.

because the virtuous person makes sure he is not hurting anyone before acting selfishly. Therefore he is not bound by sex codes or man's laws if he sees these laws are themselves restrictive and criminal or sinful. Many sex taboos, for instance, are ignorant of the fact that sex is God's creation. The answer to group marriage is, then, that each separate nuclear group itself decides its life-style and what it considers to be non-hurtful of others. The Nuclear group does not allow the beliefs of non-members to dictate what the marriage commitment is or should be. The bond which exists must be forged at another level of being so that marriage as a formality only becomes a ceremony which confirms the already existing bond which has already taken place in the hearts of the group members.

Does such a marriage mean that Nuclear Evolution is some clearly defined concept that binds each person into the nucleus so that they are forever tied to certain roles and they lose their individual freedom to the group soul? Of course not. The Nuclear group insists that all its members have the total openness of real freedom to express themselves at any level.

The group energy mirrors back the Truth of a person's being. However painful it is to accept, each ego must face its own blindness if the group purpose is the nuclear consciousness of the One. The first experience of the deep-rooted self-sense is self-preservation from the Red level chakra. Particularly when the energy of the libido is not finding any release of its drive in a mature way, then the drive is transferred from the urge for self-replication (sex) to self-preservation.

The thought energy locked up in the image of the self-sense panics at the possibility of all the demands a group might make upon us. The ego feels like it could be swallowed up by peer pressures. This is how we discover our fears in the group situation when the energy of the whole sweeps up each individual ego and each member agrees to do something because each is thinking the others are expecting it. But who is expecting it? Each one is expecting it himself but transfers that expectation to the others acting as mirrors of his own psyche. Thus their fears make each one afraid to voice his negative feelings to the group. This kind of so-called "Truth and openness" which holds back its real feelings and thoughts for the sake of its own image is most quickly revealed in the nuclear group. The threat of being swallowed by the group or of being criticised operates powerfully, so that the truth does not set one free to be himself or herself in a negative way without being challenged for one's own selfishness.

757

For example, one member of the group marriage simply could not share his honest feelings with the entire group. Even after three years of kind encouraging, and finally intense confrontation, the fear of having his secret self-image challenged still kept him bound and emotionally constricted. When the pain of separation became very great he at last came to the group with his real feelings about himself all written down on paper and he shared them beautifully. The group was appreciative and mirrored back his own openness. After an hour or so he became defensive and began to express his fear of the group and the ring of truth left his voice. When we mirrored that back to him he shut up like a clam again, admitting that he was afraid to go further, because we were now talking about deeper things he had not already figured out and put on his piece of paper. He also expressed a fear of sharing deeply because the group might swallow him up. What he really wanted was to fall in love with a woman and if he were to be more open and relate more closely with the group he might not have the time or energy to give to finding a woman. Yet all the women he had met were turned off by his emotional inhibitions and his holding back. He knows the group feedback is for him to open up and listen to the group he is married to and then he will be open "out in the field" as well. But his fear of changing his self-image and his old ways of thinking keeps him struggling with his ego and suffering with psychic pain.

The more any group member identifies with his ego, the more he experiences the loving help of the group as something inimical and harsh, so the natural reaction is to withdraw and hide his negatives. But the resulting lack of integrity causes an exquisite kind of pain which ultimately hurts more than to face the group mirror. If one chooses **not** to be open, then life itself does the mirroring because the self-obsessed ego is repellent, in or out of the group. The fear of being criticised by the group is a fear that life or the universe won't fall in line with the ego's position, and this natural fear of the ego is terrifying. Yet once a person lets go of the ego position (what it wants; what it doesn't want), the fear of the group vanishes; the ego reevalutes itself and a more solid, free, and wholesome feeling takes its place. The sense of freedom comes in knowing that our ego fear is illusory and that the nuclear group is not a threat to our individuality but an opportunity to grow into greater individuality and to gain the greater freedom in our realisation of the Truth of the oneness of all things. Not all people will experience this in the same way. Here is one member's account:

> First we made the commitment to work toward group consciousness and then it remained for us to manifest that marriage or union, but it did not happen overnight. We were so far from being able to

think of sharing our mates and sweethearts, we were not even able to put the group's tasks before our own plans in simple everyday matters. Life since the marriage has been a constant stretching so that more and more selfless input into the group effort is taking place as a matter of routine. Tasks that formerly took an act of will and self-discipline and conscious sacrifice to do, gradually became an assumed part of our lives, just as one assumes he will take some time each night to sleep or take time to eat during the day – a matter of course. Even so, there were always new resistances arising and always there was grumbling, though when we looked back over the months behind us, we were proud to have grown and proud to see our own input as part of the team, part of the achievement. Selflessness was contagious, just as selfishness is contagious. The more some individuals threw themselves in (or used the last of their savings to pay for a sales trip for the group business), the less the others felt they must be cautious and self-protective. So we learned to risk what the world would call "being a fool". We did this in little ways, but we knew that some day we would arrive at that ultimate selflessness expressed in Christ's words: "Greater love hath no man than this, that he lay down his life for his friends."

To paraphrase another of Christ's sayings: "The Truth shall always set you free, not bind you into some constraining commitment." Therefore the commitment must also be to freedom of spirit and that means freeing everyone in the group to be themselves. If we were truly ONE, would we get uptight if another member of the group was intimate with our mate at the physical level? In other words, is the marriage okay in theory in the head but when it comes to practical things, like money and sex and food and sharing time and other things which humans hold as precious, does the love which binds the idea become tarnished with selfish thoughts? Would certain people freak out in the group if someone they wanted to possess for themselves was giving attention to others as well? These very human feelings are all the nitty-gritty energy which normally divides groups and prevents the binding in marriage of each ego in freedom to BE whatever they are in essence.

FROM SELFISHNESS TO SELFLESS SELF

Nuclear Evolution must always appear different to different people; the group must be sensitive to those who may differ in temperament and feelings and who conceptualise the unity of divine marriage differently from ordinary marriage. How do we attain this binding energy, without the explosiveness of different forces in the nucleus unleashing the power of consciousness divisively? The Christ-Yoga system, being edited and republished as "Universal Government by Nature's Laws" by University of the Trees Press, is designed solely to understand what this divisiveness really is in the working situation of a group living and governing themselves. Until the divisive forces in our consciousness are recognised and we can handle them, we cannot effectively aim at unity itself. We can only be what we are in essence, hence we must discover what we are and work with that. Nuclear Evolution creates a new state of human Being that has nothing to do with religion or any ideas or concepts. It is not centred around a person, a sacred place or a priestly vocation. It is centred around the experience of Pure Consciousness in each individual: to be able to look at someone clean without dirtying them up with our minds. By this I do not mean that people are not already dirty, but we let them do the dirtying rather than throw our own dirt on top of theirs.

To have pure consciousness we must practice daily the techniques of cleaning our consciousness up by realising that every thought is not only put there by us but also projected out into the family or group or community. We can only see others and the situations in society in terms of the quality of our own consciousness. There is no better place to refine our Being and test the validity of our thoughts than in a spiritual community or group marriage. The thoughts we entertain may be those of Christ or Buddha but we may not live those thoughts, we may have the thought of love, but have no love. We may talk of caring for others, but by our actual example of life, show that we do not care. We may project the contents of our minds out into society and from some secure haven see only our own shortcomings in others. A group life will correct this type of narcissist seeking that is purely for self. There will always be problems with groups but they are growth-producing for everyone in the group consciousness. Any number of conflicts may arise but to resolve them requires skill on the spiritual level and makes the community a nursery school for saints. In any community, people will take sides in a conflict and project their own values, morals, etc. out into the conflict. Whether these are positive or negative we soon find that in the group life we cannot add our own selfish desires onto the group life-style without some reaction from others who are trying to be unselfish.

For instance, there will always be romance and sex desire in any community. How does the group deal with this? Supposing a young woman allowed her erotic cravings to destroy the group unity by dividing one fellow against another? Or suppose a young man, competing to enter an already existing relationship, disregarded the feelings of his fellow group member. If the group has no way to resolve the conflict openly, these situations could destroy the cohesiveness of the group soul. To deal with the blindnesses of others the entire membership cannot be blind to that which subtly divides. In love the natural urges are dealt with by different people in different ways. If someone chooses to deal with these feelings selfishly, without consideration for others, then we do not close our eyes to this dirtying up of their consciousness but instead we acknowledge it as the quality of what they are. We do not judge them for their urges but confront the manner in which they have dealt with them. We do not compare these persons to ourselves and point the finger of blame, because we acknowledge that they are unique individuals, yet we do not permit them to lower the vibration of the whole group by ego-centric ways. We try to get beyond our own filters and hang-ups in order to see their dirt clearly and impartially. If we cannot manage this objectivity, then we are obliged to see our own bias with the same clarity that we are expecting from the other. In short, Nuclear Evolution and its techniques of creative conflict and meditation, Supersensonics and the detection of each other's aura levels, is the coming together and the sharing of what is.

Working on ourself in terms of the community or group consciousness is hard work because hardly anyone accepts himself as he is. Most people have some private image which they cannot live up to and then, at the opposite extreme, they struggle with a negative self-image which is not accurate either. The secret of working on oneself is to find that middle ground between extremes, which is what we truly are. From this balanced middle point real growth can take the place of compensation; instead of blowing up big to make up for feeling small, one can afford to see things as they are. This subtlety is the essence of the spiritual life. It would be smug and self-righteous to think we cannot always improve our Being and the way it manifests. Yet we are often told we are sparks of the Divine and therefore perfect; the distinction between the potential perfection and the actual is never made. Accepting what we are and what others are requires love and compassion but does not mean we immediately stop work on what we can potentially become. On the contrary, the first step in the group marriage is to accept what you are and apply it to the next step of Nuclear Evolution. We may, for instance, be a sex kitten trying to be spiritual. To repress the biological urge is the opposite of spirituality, but that is how people with spiritual aspirations usually handle it. To accept the biological fact means that it can begin to be dealt with and channelled into constructive energies.

The first question people ask when faced with changing themselves from sex kitten to saint or from a self-righteous judgemental person to one who accepts people as they are, is the question "how?" There are many disciplines which tell how, but this is not the problem. We already know how; we have been told a thousand times between messiahs to put all our consciousness on God or to put all our consciousness on the search for the Self, but always the question comes "how?". The reason is in the heart, not the head; we don't want to change; we think it would be easier and more pleasant either to do something more exciting or to drift along until life's emotional earthquake shakes us loose from the question "how?". The answer is you just do it. Begin first and you will find all the ways and means how! We hear the "how's" everyday with trap-door ears which filter all seemingly difficult things out. First we must understand the question is not "how?" but "why should I?" Once convinced, we then find out **how** to change ourself by accepting the fact that we don't want a change or we do not have the will. If you were greedy and had appetites which you could only secretly indulge in then you would have to come to some understanding in your heart of your motives. You must know your own will and accept that part of yourself before you can begin gradually to master those resisting forces. If we think we are more important or more pure or more advanced without still recognising that what we don't want to accept about ourself is really there, then we will become divisive not only in ourself but will bring divisiveness to the nuclear group even without our knowing it.

So Nuclear Evolution is not only acceptance of what is, but also the working of what is into something more mature and more integral in the same way that our bodies are a more mature system of cells than individual organs are, in the same way that our cells are complex organisations of molecules bound together, not only for the sake of the whole organ and body but also out of self-interest motives such as survival, satisfaction of basic needs of food, nourishment and love on every level. This self-interest is actually programmed into the universe, but this does not mean we just go out and get what we want or that it becomes a licence for gluttony by some rationalisation which says we unite to get our appetites satisfied. What we unite for is not only to **get** more freedom but to give it; to do this we must feel that not only the giver but those we give ourselves to are worthy of the gift. Without this feeling we would feel the whole thing is a sham and an hypocrisy, a mere idea in name only. The words and language of unity, comradeship, and all the other cliches we hear everyday would be used, but without giving everyone in the group freedom it would always become coercion that was the binding power of the marriage.

The marriage of the forces in the Nucleus is achieved in Nature in the same way that it is achieved internally in human nature. The fact is that man's love and understanding is always several thousand years behind nature. In order to achieve the binding of a nucleus at the atomic level there must be a natural acceptance of the roles that each member particle of a nucleus plays. The Nuclear force in nature is only divided in man's world by unbalancing the energies of the atom with a fast stream of neutrons and causing an explosion through the intensive division called fission. Fission is not natural and does not occur in nature. Only man's consciousness and understanding of the unbalanced forces in the atom can cause the divisive fission to take place. In that sense nature's binding force has been perverted by the divisiveness of man's mind which is continually splitting apart. The fusion process is a natural way of releasing the same energy but man has not yet fully mastered controlled fusion. The fusion process is similar to Nuclear Evolution at the human level of society. It is the next step for man to understand the energy of social fusion or unity. First, the different parts of the nucleus must be identified, not only by the surrounding entities in the environment such as electrons and other atoms, but within the atom itself; its needs must become communicable and clear and so it is with human entities who would fuse their individual egos into one. The identification of these parts of humans can be called the physics of consciousness.

REFERENCES

PART II

Allport, G.W., PATTERNS AND GROWTH IN PERSONALITY, Holt, New York, 1961.

Andrews, L.M., and Karlins, M., REQUIEM FOR DEMOCRACY, Holt, New York, 1971.

Arnhoff, F.N., "CONCEPTS OF AGING" in P.H. Hoch and J.Zubin (Eds.), PSYCHOPATHOLOGY OF AGING, Grune & Stratton, New York, 1961.

Asch, S.E., "EFFECTS OF GROUP PRESSURE UPON THE MODIFICATION AND DISTORTION OF JUDGEMENTS", in H. Guetzkow (Ed.), GROUPS, LEADERSHIP AND MEN, Carnegie Press, Pittsburg, 1951.

Bach, M. STRANGE SECTS AND CURIOUS CULTS, Dodd, Mead, New York, 1961.

Bales, R.F.,PERSONALITY AND INTERPERSONAL BEHAVIOR Holt, New York, 1970.

Barber, T.X., HYPNOSIS: A SCIENTIFIC APPROACH, Van Nostrand Reinhold, New York, 1969.

Barber, T.X., MARIHUANA, YOGA AND HYPNOSIS, Aldine, Chicago, 1970.

Barron, F., "THE CREATIVE PERSONALITY AKIN TO MADNESS", Psychology Today, July, 1972.

Bass, B.M., LEADERSHIP, PSYCHOLOGY AND ORGANIZATIONAL BEHAVIOR, Harper, New York, 1960.

Berkowitz, L. THE FRUSTRATION -- AGGRESSION: A RE-EXAMINATION OF THE FRUSTRATION -- AGGRESSION HYPOTHESIS, Atherton, New York, 1970.

Brodeur, D.W., "THE EFFECTS OF STIMULANT AND TRANQUILIZER PLACEBOS ON HEALTHY SUBJECTS IN A REAL LIFE SITUATION, Psychopharmacologia, 1965.

Dolgun, Alexander with Patrick Watson, ALEXANDER DOLGUN'S STORY, Alfred A. Knopf, New York, 1975.

Dunlap, R.E., and Gale, R.P., "POLITICS AND ECOLOGY: A POLITICAL PROFILE AND STUDIO ECO-ACTIVISTS," Youth and Society, 3, 379-397, 1972.

Fiedler, F.E., "STYLE OR CIRCUMSTANCE: THE LEADERSHIP ENIGMA", Psychology Today, March, 1969.

Fiedler, F.E., "THE TROUBLE WITH LEADERSHIP TRAINING IS THAT IT DOESN'T TRAIN LEADERS", Psychology Today, Feb., 1973.

Flacks, R. "THE LIBERATED GENERATION: AN EXPLANA—TION OF THE ROOTS OF STUDENT PROTEST", Journal of Social Issues, 23, 52-57, 1967.

Foucault, M., MADNESS AND CIVILIZATION: A HISTORY OF INSANITY IN THE AGE OF REASON, Pantheon, New York, 1965.

Gordon, William J.J., SYNECTICS, Collier Books, 1961.

Hampden - Turner, Charles, RADICAL MAN: THE PROCESS OF PSYCHOSOCIAL DEVELOPMENT, Doubleday, Garden City, New York, 1970.

Hills, Christopher, UNIVERSAL GOVERNMENT BY NATURE'S LAWS, University of the Trees Press, Boulder Creek, CA, 1977.

Pettman, Ralph, HUMAN BEHAVIOR AND WORLD POLITICS, St. Martin's Press, New York, 1975.

Pye, Lucian W. and Verba, Sidney, ASPECTS OF POLITICAL DEVELOPMENT, Brown, Little and Co., Boston, 1966.

Solzhenitsyn, Alexander I., THE GULAG ARCHIPELAGO, Harper & Row, New York, 1974.

I.R. 13 Red   19 Orange 25   Yellow   50 Green 55 Blue   62 Indigo 68 Violet

PART 3

THE PHYSICS OF CONSCIOUSNESS

INTRODUCTION TO PART III

I feel very privileged to be the editor of Part III in this presentation of NUCLEAR EVOLUTION. The enormous implications of this book on the whole of scientific method and spiritual understanding are yet to be realised by the world. Every time I read Part III of NUCLEAR EVOLUTION I experience an awe-inspiring glimpse into the Cosmic Consciousness of the interconnectedness of life. I find it humbling and at the same time mind-expanding to peer into nature and realise that the stuff which programs our DNA and all of the bio/chemical/electrical reactions in the nucleus of all life forms, is the same stuff that flows through us which man calls awareness. It is the very same stuff we experience as "I" even though we cannot see it because we are using it to see with. It is the foundation of perception and intelligence which we call our self – consciousness.

To realise that in consciousness lies the link between our sense of being a personal self and all other forms of life in Nature, brings us to the challenge of penetrating our own consciousness to enter into our own DNA, atomic and cellular programming, perceive into Nature's Nuclear processes from *inside -- out,* and work in harmony with the Cosmic Intelligence-Will for consciously fulfilling its amazing plan of Nuclear Evolution.

Nuclear Evolution ushers in an age where man can cooperate consciously with God, hand in hand, to fulfill the purpose of life, not through blindly obeying ethical codes and laws from an external authority, but through direct knowing and conscious awareness.

Nuclear Evolution penetrates the very foundation of life itself. Physics, Psychology and Spirituality come together as One. The scientists' incessant search for Nature's secrets, the philosophers' and psychologists' study of human experience and the spiritual persons' tuning into the ways of God, the Founding, Guiding Intelligence - fuse in One.

By tapping the Nuclear powerhouse within our own Self we can transform cell life and release dynamic energy for personal growth. To clear the filters of human consciousness and make way for the unfoldment of the Nuclear potential, requires a vehicle that can sustain the energies induced by a heightened state of awareness. Part III takes us into the inner world of the vehicle of consciousness in the atomic, molecular, cellular, individual and group life.

By using visual models of Nature's patterns of growth to seek the glue that binds these various vehicles together, we gain access to Nature's own handbook of instruction for our evolution. The real Bible is Nature and by reading this Handbook we can evolve consciously and more rapidly through learning how to tap into the evolutionary energy in the heart of the nucleus of all life forms which are all part of our Self! We can observe underlying similarities in the way atoms come together to form molecules in an evolutionary thrust and the way molecules make a leap to organise as cells, cells as organs and organs as bodies. So too, a group of individuals and the whole of humanity can potentially come together to form a body that functions as unitedly as does a normal cell composed of molecules.

NUCLEAR EVOLUTION AND SPIRITUAL REALISATION

When these archetypal patterns observable in nature are applied to human levels of consciousness we experience a REVELATION as to the evolutionary direction of humanity and the purpose of life. It is this *revelatory* message that Christopher Hills has brought to mankind in NUCLEAR EVOLUTION. I have had the opportunity to study closely with Christopher Hills and a wonderful group of people at the University of the Trees in Boulder Creek where we are applying the Nuclear model to the individual and the group consciousness. The theory outlined in this book has become a vibrant reality in the hearts of many of the Nuclear group members as we watch the Cosmic drama of evolution unfold as in a time-lapse film, right before our eyes. It brings a great sense of conviction to see the theory become practical, the ideal real, in a live situation.

Our work on evolution combines both the spiritual, subjective point of view (inside – out) and studying the so-called objective models (outside -- in) revealed in natural phenomena. One advantage of bringing science and spiritual self-study together is that the scientific approach provides for a means of concensus to include those who are not yet experiencing the vibrant contact from within with the evolutionary dynamic of life. The objective scientific model of Nuclear Evolution provides us with a map which clarifies the spiritual path and also eliminates many of the potential ego diversions, the trips and traps that we usually encounter and have to wade through in our subjective work on ourselves. If we can learn to read and follow the map our spiritual course will be straight.

Normally the ego is blind to itself and when we confront ourselves subjectively in trying to deal with life we grapple and struggle to understand our inner confusions, feelings, drives and those of others. Any light shed from the model of Nature becomes a guide for understanding the labyrinth of our inner being. Nature serves as a mirror of ourself which we can peer into and see the way ahead. The mirror has been there all along, throughout eons of evolution. Modern man is only now beginning to read it with some depth.

From the enlightened level of unitive consciousness all is ONE and there is no separation between how energy works inside us or outside, so the study of the atom and Nuclear energy in this Nuclear age was destined to lead to a model for practical growth from self-consciousness to group consciousness to planetary consciousness through Nuclear Evolution. However, it takes a seer of the same order as Einstein to be able to penetrate the various dimensions of the energies of consciousness and present a theory as workable as $E=Mc^2$. Through conscious Nuclear Evolutionary techniques, taught by Christopher Hills in various courses of study, we too can experience the causal levels of energy, light, and consciousness, and perceive the entire universe as One, emanating from a single energy source in the nucleus of our own self. We can actually feel the release of Nuclear energy in our being as a result of inner contact with that source and can observe its effects on our behaviour, on our perceptions and in our relationships with others. Our experience of life takes on a whole new dimension.

THE NUCLEAR MODEL

How this Nuclear process works out in human beings can be seen in the model depicted for cells (and all other life forms) shown in the diagram on page 785. By creating a positive charge at the centre of each individual cell in the nucleus of our personal consciousness, we create a corresponding repulsion in our personality. Christopher has labeled this conflict "creative conflict". It is conflict in that the repulsion is a disruptive force, a natural electro-magnetic effect, and it is creative in that the final outcome of all conflict is growth. By studying this model we learn to see that our pain is for our growth and we can begin to use conflict and pain creatively instead of resenting it. That mankind grows and evolves to love through conflict should be obvious. We can see a conflict of polarities as part of the positive-negative electrical dynamic of Nature working out everywhere and as the foundation of relationships from atoms to humans. The male-female relationship is the most apparent example in human society. The handling of creative conflict which is occuring in everyone can be optimalised when we share openly together in a conscious creative conflict group. We practice conscious creative conflict effectively in a group at the University of the Trees and have applied it successfully with couples, with children, in business situations and in politics. Just about any group can resolve conflict creatively if they could only understand Nature's own method. The implications for unions and governments are enormous.

PREPARATION OF THE OPTIMAL CONDITIONS

As an individual or as a group we have to recognise that the essential ingredient to achieving unity and the creation of a positive charge in ourselves or in a group is our positive will to unite in a common purpose, and commitment to carry it through despite the challenges that come. Our will and commitment evokes dynamic energy which creates the positive charge at the centre of our Nuclear self, and pulls us along through the conflicts until a creative resolution and synthesis is found.

Without commitment it is impossible to achieve the positive energy level necessary to neutralise the negative surface tensions - our separate ego self (selves). Without neutralising the ego (egos) the person or group cannot form a true nucleus at the next level of consciousness. Instead it will remain in a state of vibrating tension until it later succeeds in achieving the necessary selfless unity or it will retain within itself the seeds of its own division and will fail. Ego divisiveness has made Nuclear Evolution unusual in individual humans and, on a group level, exceedingly rare in all human history. Neutralising ego, however, is not neutralising the individual but heightening it to cosmic consciousness.

GROUP CONSCIOUSNESS

Group consciousness as envisioned by Christopher Hills at the University of the Trees and based upon the Nuclear model is not just a gathering of people for a common goal, as there are many such groups around. It is not just a family living and working together. Rather it is a group of people who are committed to surrendering their separate egos - the self-sense that says I am here and you are there - for the purpose of becoming a greater whole. Losing one's personal identity seems like a huge sacrifice to most people and an impossibility since so many are craving to build identity and personal self-esteem. Even in our committed group it is not easy to let go of the self-image that we have built up for so many years. This order of sacrifice requires us to break out of the limitations that the self-sense presents in order to realise the greater Self. Then true individuality can manifest - not as a separate self but as one who is indivisible from the whole Self. One does not give up self-respect or self-esteem, but rather builds it on a solid base.

PRACTICAL MANIFESTATION

I feel grateful and fortunate to have the opportunity to be a member of a pioneering group of selfless, bright people working on conscious Nuclear evolution together. Our application of Nuclear Evolution is revealed in the increasing, evolving commitment of the entire group. The creation of the positive charge at the centre of each member is enhanced through meditation and awakening to the source of the inner light of consciousness. As we develop resonance with pure light, which some call spirit or soul, we intensify the repulsion at the same time in our ego personalities which generates and magnifies internal conflict. The acquired self-image, concepts, memories of incarnations, crystallised mental patterns and self-limitations are challenged by the incoming light of awakening awareness and our personalities go through mental, emotional, and physical conflict as the old patterns are dispersed to prepare room for new light. Since we are open about our conflicts with each other, they are brought to the fore so we can confront our basic assumptions about ourself and others. Group feedback confronts us with ourself, intensifying the conflict in a creative, loving, supportive and often humorous way. We meet frequently, according to need and desire, to express any difficulties we are having internally or with others. After several years together, the group members are now highly trained and perceptive and can cut through to the bare-bones cause of our conflict swiftly to help us penetrate the nature of our ego position. It isn't always easy to face and the ego tries everything to wriggle out of facing itself. But the reward is great when we finally receive the truth as love, and the glow on the face and in the being of the one who has truly received makes it all worthwhile and is motivating to everyone. As our positive wills gradually coagulate in united purpose and realisation of higher states of awareness, our negative charges (separate egos) lose their negativity. (See model on page 785)

The often unconscious negatively-charged surface tensions of our ego conflicts are brought into more intense contact with each other by the very positiveness of the energy dynamic generated in our group or by the infusion of light from our work on ourself. The intensification of contact brings turmoil within our minds and emotions since the negatively charged particle's nature is to repel a negative, not brush up against. This pressure brings more rapid growth and continues until the positive energy has worked the process through to a creative end. The process does the work in cooperation with the will in the heart. We have to keep our heads (egos) out of the way to let it happen with the least amount of resistance. Gradually the surface tension of ego-personality is neutralised in selflessness, and an evolved positive nucleus – the radiant inner light of the soul – appears in the individual and in the group organism as a whole.

If there is too much negativity in the group it overpowers the positive, coagulating force and the group will divide. We have had to be very careful and become very aware of how the negative, often unconscious, energies of personality function in people and to skillfully point them out so all may see where the weak links lie. Often one person becomes the seat and focal point of the negative due to a hardened attitude. Unwillingness to change is at the root of inability to change. "I can't" really means "I don't want to". Unwillingness has many causes – fear, desires, self-doubt, etc. which we probe in ourself and together. The group is very patient with those who are sincere. When the unwillingness repeatedly deflects the group energy away from its evolutionary purpose it must be confronted and its cause removed or the group will remain divided against itself and fail. We don't reject people, but we allow them to describe themselves. They feel uncomfortable and excuse themselves when they see that they don't really want to change. As we grow together the positive energy works in all of us throughout our daily activities – bubbling away with life. Often we become aware of its potency by looking back at big changes we have made and the pattern of our growth. Then there is a real joy of accomplishment.

In our group evolution we have had an ongoing, expanding Nuclear group for three years. The group has grown entirely spontaneously and organically of itself. As in Nature, authority comes from within each individual, not from outside. As we evolve we awaken to the authority and organisation inherent in Nature. The self-organising growth and reliance on the inner free will of each member distinguishes this group from the all-too prevalent "Moonie-type" spiritual groups which dwell on obedience to an outer authority, always quoting the authority as proof of their philosophy rather than presenting practical examples or their own direct experience. Nature's patterns are ordered for optimal growth for all forms if we can only tune directly into them. Neither is our form of government anarchy. It is self-governing based upon organic models of growth using Nature's system of checks and balances. This process is felt and experienced as a positive-negative electrical dynamic working through all the members but is difficult to describe to non-participants. The checks and balances are dealt with in another book by Christopher Hills on natural government.*

---

*"Universal Government by Nature's Laws", formerly published in London by the Centre House Community which Christopher Hills founded in 1966. It was then entitled "Christ-Yoga of Peace" but has since been brought up to date in the new title, published by University of the Trees Press, 1977.

HOW IT ACTUALLY WORKS IN PRACTICE

Initially the positive will to unite in our group was very idealistic or theoretical, and only slightly manifested. The group members were all normal, self-centred people and the negative surface tensions of doubt, personal desire and inexperience inhibited group unity. These assertions of ego also block contact with the Nuclear centre from taking place within each person. Even a bit of the self-less, positive will to unite, genuinely experienced, creates a flow of intensified light coming from the charged centre of our group will. The positively charged nucleus is enhanced by the added dynamic energies of an enlightened teacher. The result of more light added to light is more awareness, deeper relating and deeper intensification of the creative conflict as much as is beneficial to the organism. When there is too much intensity coming from the Centre, the personality conflict can become destructive, not creative. The challenge in order to be creative must not be more than the capacity to answer it.

I saw this pattern in my own life at a time when I went off on retreat to meditate. After charging up with life-force, I felt sensitively aware and in tune with Nature – a nice high good feeling. I came back into the group and immediately began to see some people were resisting changing their inner negativity. They also seemed to be unaware of others' worlds, my own included. I confronted them on separate occasions and received feedback that even if what I said was true, I was not caring about them and coming on "like a Mack truck" and a know-it-all. They were hurt and felt that the way I confronted them was not compassionate. And furthermore, if that forceful way was my manifestation, how could I be having such great meditations? I reacted and defended myself. It wasn't until after much confrontation that I was able to see how my old ego pattern of lifting up to a "high" vibration from which I looked down on others with superiority had been reinforced, blown up and intensified during my meditation retreat. It had come out again in full regalia. The intensity of the "high", the light, brought an immediate corresponding intensity of the ego conflict and plummeted me into a low of equal power as the high. The low was perhaps more enlightening than the high, however, because it made me confront myself, and as a result I had a tremendous insight into my real being which has released me into a greater love, compassion and positivity than I have ever demonstrated in the group. Christopher acted as a mirror for my state and showed me how I treat others by treating me that same way for a short period. That was painful to see and face, but after grappling with my stubborn resistance and remembering the purpose of creative conflict I was able to release the self-image of wanting to be holy which supported my ego, and just be the real me. Now I see others (including those who were heaviest with me) being confronted on their own attitudes of self-righteousness, and because of what I struggled with myself I can now feel compassion for them. So often what we see so well in others is a mirror of ourself. All of this openness leads to bringing us more into the heart where we can experience all as One. We work with our ego reactions to others in solitude as well to change them into the positive by turning our thinking around, and by affirmation as most spiritual groups do. But we also recognise as reality the process of creative conflict and that only by bringing this conflict into the open can we see what we are really able to manifest in love, not just what we act out or idealise in the head.

Gradually we become aware of a resonance with each other and we stay attuned to the energy requirements of the group as a whole. Sometimes we need more heart-to-heart contact, sometimes more meditation, sometimes more open sharing, sometimes more writing or physical work to manifest, serve and eliminate what we've digested and absorbed. When the heart guides, the simplicity of natural, rhythmic life is revealed to us. We can unite permanently only when there is complete selflessness - when penetration of the veil of separateness occurs. A great deal of self-confrontation is needed before this happens. Selflessness means real egolessness, tested in the fires of life and relationships - not a sentimental or false humility.

God's Mills Grind Very Slowly
but Very Fine.

As we come together in meditation, sharing inner worlds, presenting conflicts, and giving and receiving feedback we can actually feel the positive energy as a pool of life and consciousness working as a solvent of our separate membranes of self-sense. Deepening experiences of unitary consciousness gradually evolve, revealing the oneness of life, inner and outer. Only when all the Nuclear group members embody this selfless unitary consciousness can the nucleus fuse in actual Nuclear/soul consciousness to form a group at the next level – PLANETARY AWARENESS AND IDENTIFICATION.

Through a three-year meditation course on direct perception entitled "Into Meditation Now" we learn step-by-step practical methods to tune to our cell life and contact the Nuclear energy within for conscious Nuclear Evolution. We practice our success at direct perception in the group to see if we are perceiving purely, seeing things as they really are. Direct perception opens the ego filters and allows for the transformation of our interlocking bodies of energy. Take any situation, inner or outer, and put the attention on seeing it as it really is, beneath all the ego filters, and you will be wielding the tools of Nuclear Evolution. Total openness to the inner worlds of others as well as our own is absolutely required to achieve pure perception. We come to recognise that a Doctrine of Total Openness to Truth with one another is essential to enlightenment and is the answer to resolving differences as well. Total openness does not mean having to tell all one's inner thoughts, but rather being open to sharing our real feelings and being open to receiving the inner worlds and feelings of all others. It is the answer to bringing together divergent groups, leaders and individuals to arrive at Truth.

CONSCIOUS MIRRORING

Just as Nature is a mirror for the human condition so we are all mirrors of each other. The entire universe is a mirror and we use conscious mirroring in our group work with each other to get beneath the ego filters and reveal open truth which allows the positive energy to release for unity. We mirror by learning how to fully listen to another and then feedback what we feel their being is really saying, to their satisfaction, before we express our own point of view, which they then will listen to and mirror back to us. It is always amazing how this technique reveals that 90% of the time people cannot hear or mirror properly, and colour what is being said with their own personality assumptions and filters. Only when the ego is out of the way does perfect listening and perfect mirroring take place -- then oneness in being is experienced.

777

PLANETARY AWARENESS

Eventually through openness the Nuclear "I" may be expanded to include the entire planet, illustrating a divine symphony of how life feeds off life. The activation of this Nuclear dynamic life ray, in conscious Nuclear Evolution in people, transforms our evolution into a more rapid, direct process traversing the time dimensions. We can transcend the slow, spiral motion of evolution on all separative personality levels by patterning our life after the Nuclear model which operates within the laws of light.

The thresholds of light synthesis on different levels of conscious-ness in the group show us how nature traverses dimensions of time. By tuning to various resonances we too can subjectively experience the telescoping of evolutionary time from its apparently slow, spi-ralling cycles, direct to the void–the Absolute–where Oneness in eternal time lies. An act of Divine Will at the centre of the Void within responds to our light-releasing selfless will, bringing a Nuclear transformation of consciousness which makes the "part" or person into a "whole", brings awareness at every level of Being and brings God back full circle to God.

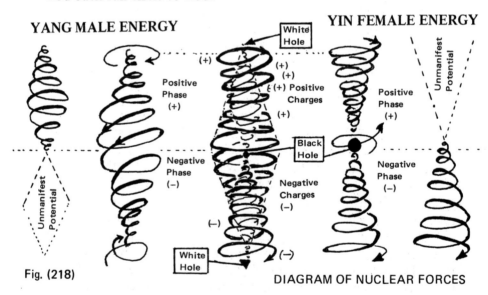

YANG MALE ENERGY　　　**YIN FEMALE ENERGY**

Fig. (218)　　　　　　DIAGRAM OF NUCLEAR FORCES

The POSITIVE DYNAMIC OF EVOLUTIONARY THRUST, sweeping up the negative conflicting energies which get jostled around in the process is illustrated in the above diagram. The positive energies coagulate in the nucleus and enter the VOID of unity and eternal time beyond the slow, multi-billion year pain/pleasure evolutionary process.

THE NEW AGE

Many of today's spiritual and religious leaders forecast a New Golden Age dawning in the consciousness of mankind preceded by a breakdown and destruction of the old forms. Few have offered any concrete evidence of what form this new age will take and have hopefully pronounced it as a utopian age where peace, harmony, spiritual realisation, universal love and enlightenment will reign. How we are going to get there, the link between the age of self-ishness/materialism and the new age, is left to each person to divine and work out in his own way, through various spiritual disciplines, religions, science and other panaceas which have all been tried for millenia.

Nuclear Evolution provides a clear understanding of the transition stage humanity is confronted with in this 20th century. By applying Nature's Nuclear model to the larger social group of humanity we can see the same evolutionary dynamic working out in society as a whole as we see in atoms, cells, molecules, individual people and in our group work at the University of the Trees.

Increasingly people are thinking more for themselves and rejecting the old philosophies and institutions they find confining. This is occuring today in present patterns of education, traditional life style, politics, religion and science, all of which in their existing forms are felt by many to be too limiting. Few people have been able to offer new viable solutions, and those that have been pre-sented have been quickly squelched by the traditional authorities in power. Even the new spiritual groups which depend on the external authority of a guru for their reality do not seem much different from the old age, seeking authority in religion, science or political leaders. How many times do we hear members of these new groups unthinkingly say, "It's right because Guru says," or "Jesus says," or "So and So says?" A true Nuclear model for living, based upon Nature's own blueprint may still be centuries away in awakening to the planet as a whole. Mankind loves to hang on to its old ways of doing things, until some catastrophe occurs to shake us into seeing

779

our own self-will that has departed from Nature's cosmic will.

On a large social scale we can see the positively charged particles in the Nuclear model are those selfless humanitarians and spiritually aware individuals who are attuned to unitary consciousness and are working for the spiritual union and evolution of the planet.

As they slowly coagulate into Oneness they slowly neutralise the negative personality tensions between their own egos first and then throughout the world. However, as the positive will to unite increases in potency, so does the intensity of the conflicting energy which breaks down the egos and the old social forms. The positive always attracts the negative to neutralise it. The challenge to make the resultant conflict on a world-wide scale creative, rather than destructively killing off of the entire organism of humanity through abuse of Nuclear energy, is now before every individual and group. It will not go away by ignoring it, hiding it or trying to put it back into Pandora's box.

In fact, as a thousand years pass by us, the knowledge of the Nuclear fire ball in the heart of Nature can only advance and become more sophisticated in its lethal path or become more beautiful and awe-inspiring. Conscious Nuclear Evolution is perhaps our only choice.

D.R.

THE PROCESS
OF
NUCLEAR EVOLUTION

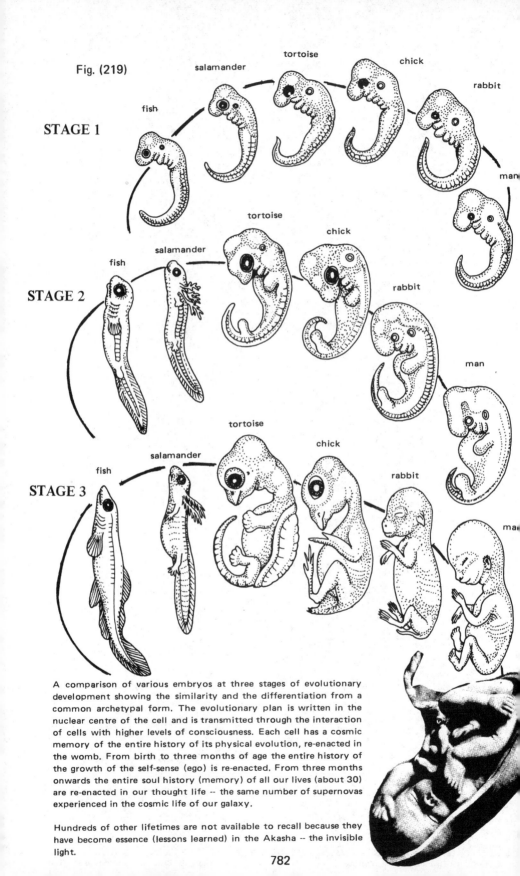

Fig. (219)

STAGE 1

fish · salamander · tortoise · chick · rabbit · man

STAGE 2

fish · salamander · tortoise · chick · rabbit · man

STAGE 3

fish · salamander · tortoise · chick · rabbit · man

A comparison of various embryos at three stages of evolutionary development showing the similarity and the differentiation from a common archetypal form. The evolutionary plan is written in the nuclear centre of the cell and is transmitted through the interaction of cells with higher levels of consciousness. Each cell has a cosmic memory of the entire history of its physical evolution, re-enacted in the womb. From birth to three months of age the entire history of the growth of the self-sense (ego) is re-enacted. From three months onwards the entire soul history (memory) of all our lives (about 30) are re-enacted in our thought life -- the same number of supernovas experienced in the cosmic life of our galaxy.

Hundreds of other lifetimes are not available to recall because they have become essence (lessons learned) in the Akasha -- the invisible light.

782

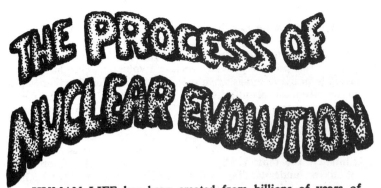

THE PROCESS OF NUCLEAR EVOLUTION

HUMAN LIFE has been created from billions of years of absorbed stimuli pouring down on the Earth in the form of light and Cosmic radiation. The cell life and the nervous system have a residual memory of THAT which has built it from the first primal Algae. The CENTRE method of creating a positive charge at the *Centre* of each individual cell in the nucleus of personal consciousness, creates a repulsion which we call CREATIVE CONFLICT. True unity and harmony occur when the cells come together in the 8th domain of Self-surrender. The positive " will " to unite creates a coagulant of the opposite polarity to the surface tension of each group of cells and this in turn acts as a solvent of the thin membrane which separates the inner and outer life of the whole organism. A special unitary consciousness must prevail at the CENTRE of this Nucleus in order to penetrate the veil between it and the next sphere of consciousness, and become part of a nuclear grouping of individual cells. If this special virtue is not manifested by ALL its members, the group cannot form a nucleus at the next level of consciousness ; it would retain within it the seeds of its own destruction and division. The separative functions of a divided house are well expressed by the Christos when it said that anything that is divided against itself, has its own death sealed within it, and therefore that is the end of it. Nuclear Evolution looks on each human being as a brain cell in a huge planetary brain which is constantly scanned by the Logos which unites them together not only in thought but an intelligence interpenetrating all life. Cells coagulate when the charge on their surface is neutralised. They repel each other, retaining their separate identity until a coagulant of opposite polarity to the surface charge comes into contact with them. Our individual intelligence interpenetrates every cell in our body even when we are not aware of it ; blood and nerve unites all the body cells, but the link between individual human entities is the spirit of *Life* itself. Only when there is LIFE, is there Conscious " knowing "

N.B. In Nuclear Evolution the neutralised surface tension occurs when each individual cell of the nucleus in the group has a special positive unitary consciousness of LIFE.
The CENTRE method of creating a positive charge in each ring of consciousness around the nucleus and then radiating it outwards from the CENTRE brings creative conflict and intensified attraction and repulsion.

in the human sense (see Fig. 220. DIAGRAM OF NUCLEAR EVOLUTION). The positive LIFE-FORCE in every seed, in every nucleus, in every cell, can neutralise its external surface shell by the process we call Nuclear Evolution. This happens naturally in living things when they begin to oxidise, breakdown, rot or ripen, or disintegrate and return into Life. Under the pressure of this positive inward Life-ray, the consciousness within, the personality at the nuclear level breaks down if it cannot hold its positive charge at the Centre. Death always ensues when "Life" is negated in consciousness. Ultimately the most vital and revealing concept of self observation for understanding Nuclear Evolution is the way each personality deals with the illusion of its separated self, the entity which we call "I". It is without question that real self-observation is almost impossible for physicist, bench worker or pigmy in the jungle alike, because of the lightning speed with which the "I" constantly flickers from one level to another. It is so deceptive that anyone who is not aware of this and who attempts to persuade another self, may unwittingly become both the deceiver and the deceived.

The "I" moves from bodily awareness to awareness of space (the void). These are the two extreme levels of consciousness in Nuclear Evolution which create the illusion of time, sensory reality and Self. The "I" moves with such effortless rapidity that it does not perceive that the seer of the separation between an object and space, is the witness of an illusion. The ordinary observer sees individuality as a common property of all the separate entities and as a fact of nature. It is only an apparent fact at the physical (Red) level because the vibrating cosmic energies pass through the body and space alike and yoke them together on unperceived physical levels. This is why yoga, meaning yoke or union, is an empirical science which begins its research with the physical body. In reality there is no separation between body and the energy field it lives in. The awareness of "I" jumps between one framework and another without any apparent motion of psychological energies within the observer. In exactly the same way the separations in nature are *not* experienced between the cell and the body, the molecule and the cell, the atom and the molecule, the electron and the atomic nucleus, which all make up the human entity, even though bio-energetic transactions between them are very real indeed.

THE PROCESS OF NUCLEAR EVOLUTION

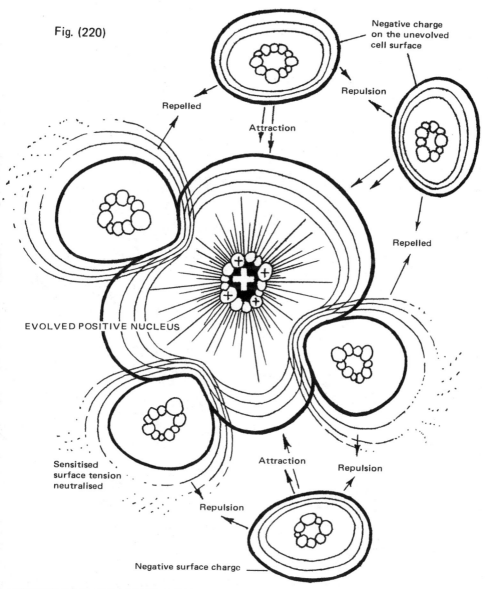

Fig. (220)

Negative charge on the unevolved cell surface

Repulsion

Repelled

Attraction

Repelled

EVOLVED POSITIVE NUCLEUS

Sensitised surface tension neutralised

Attraction

Repulsion

Repulsion

Negative surface charge

DIAGRAM OF NUCLEAR EVOLUTION

The diagram gives a figurative explanation of how individual cells are polarised by neuro transmitters which constantly send messages as to the inner state of being in the Cave of Brahma. The peptides released into the third ventricle determine our fear of darkness or our love of light. The entire nervous system is constantly bathed with this continuous signal to polarise and coagulate the cell life into one wholistic vehicle. Individual cells experience separateness until they are permanently charged with positive ionisation at the centre of each nucleus. Normally cells are charged positively at the centre and negatively at the surface, thereby attracting positive ions to the membrane. When the whole cell becomes positive, the negative surface charge is annihilated and the membrane is neutralised in respect to other cells and proteins adhering together. The membrane then attracts negative ions from the total environment. The cells no longer repel each other as separate entities and become united permanently.

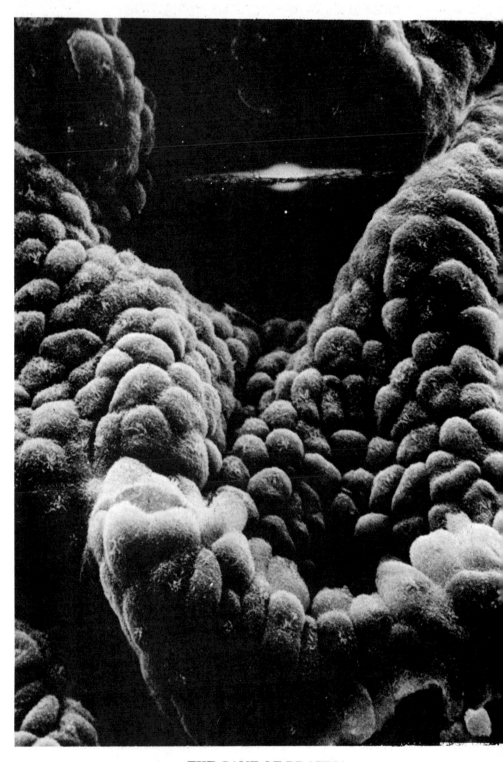

THE CAVE OF BRAHMA

whose walls are the thalamus and whose floor is the hypothalamus and whose roof is the choroid plexuses of the third ventricle in the human brain.

To summarise briefly, Part III deals with the four basic concepts of force and interaction in matter which account for all "scientifically" known facts and phenomena. We present these concepts as a basis of our discussion on the Physics of Consciousness.

First there is the *Nuclear force* which is the most strong and powerful of the four interactions. The next force in order of strength is the *Electromagnetic force*; this is about 1 per cent as powerful as the strong force, and its range is unlimited. This force acts on all particles that are an electric charge, including the photon of Light which is the neutral carrier of the electromagnetic force field; this force binds electrons to the positively charged NUCLEUS to form the atoms, it binds the atoms into molecules, and is directly responsible for all the manifestations in biology and chemistry. Next are the *Weak Interactions* which govern the decay of matter and the breakdown of the radioactive nucleus; they do not bind anything but are responsible for the CHANGES in the many kinds of strong interactions between atoms; they are not sensitive to the strong Nuclear Force even though they are responsible for its decay.

The fourth and weakest force is *Gravitation* which produces large-scale effects because it is always attractive. It operates at long range but on the scale of the atomic nucleus it is undetectable. Many particles of matter are "yoked" to all four of these interacting forces. The protons which make up the atomic nucleus are strongly interacting particles which can "feel" the electromagnetic force and also participate in the weak interactions. Like all other matter they are attracted by *Gravity*. The least "reactive" particle of matter is the Neutrino, which is only coupled to weak-interacting forces and to gravitation; it shares with a few other particles a complete immunity to the "strong" nuclear force which man knows in the popular sense as "Nuclear Energy". The purpose in writing the next few pages, before coming to the question of "Nuclear Conscious Evolution", is to show how these basic forces can do much more than bind things together, and that there is in fact another "glue" that openly exists, and, while it may not be directly measurable with scientific methods, is just as observable as Gravity, Radiation or Light.

This fifth power of the universe is *Levity*, sometimes described by astronomers as "radiation pressure" inside a star which begins when the forces of Gravity have compressed it into an intense, excited and dense mass of whirling gas. The laws of thermodynamics and entropy cannot be true if they hold that the universe is running down and losing energy. This treats "space" as some cold absorber of heat and radiation as if it had no other function. Cold we all know compresses and heat expands. The function of " space " is to attract all energy and radiation, all heat and matter, and compress it into a formal CENTRE ; and to achieve this it uses *Gravitation*. Once achieved with a sufficient intensity, then it produces *Levity* and pressure within. The obvious proof of this hypothesis is that intense cold will bring forth Levity. It is now scientifically possible to demonstrate Levitation at temperatures near Absolute Zero.

We can look at all of the force fields from the human microcosmic experiential view as well as study the bio-physical macrocosm. The *nuclear force* is that positively charged energy that comes direct from the centre of our Nuclear Self -- leading, guiding, inspiring -- which few people are in touch with consciously. It exhibits itself in behaviour such as the positive will to unite with others for an evolutionary cause. This positive will comes from a true commitment in the heart, not from an idealistic feeling in the head. The idealistic feelings and other responses from the various personality drives, described as the colour levels, are subtle *electro-magnetic* energies, and we all know that colour is part of the visible *electromagnetic spectrum*. Emotions are *electromagnetic* chemical effects felt by human beings due to reactions on a feeling level to some stimulus, whether from other people or from our own inner thoughts and senses. Emotion is actually produced by a biochemical reaction in the body that responds to conscious or unconscious thoughts in the mind. We gradually learn to get in touch with all processes and forces within by working on ourself consciously.

The *weak interactions* break down the old nuclear blueprints and crystallised forms to make way for something new. The *weak interactions* are due to the death ray in consciousness, that disintegrating, underlying force of *change*. They manifest in human form in such excreted light as thought waves. The *gravitation force* draws all of life along the path of evolution, drawing everything towards the centre slowly. The fifth force, the radiation of *levity*, comes as the result of spiritual contact with centre and the need to re-radiate what has been absorbed and compressed by the *gravitational force*. The *levity* of a divine being who has contacted the centre of Oneness in the nucleus is a brilliance and radiance surrounding the aura.

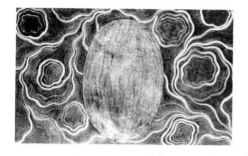

The ancient Hindu seers in deep meditation saw the cosmic egg forming in the primeval waters of the akashic sea of radiation and light. The Hindu view of creation shows the forming of the spiral galaxies from the big expansion of Brahman.

Throughout Part III, editor's notes have been added at points where I have felt a correspondence could be made between the human psychological experiences, both individually and in groups of people, and the processes occuring in matter. Many, many more correspondences are indicated, hidden in between Christopher Hills' words, awaiting only the insight of the attuned imagination. As we proceed, we can gain a deep psychological understanding of the nuclear processes if we remember to substitute soul for sun or centre, body for earth, and aura for earth's environment. We can also interchange the word individual (as a group of energies) with the word group (as in a group of atoms, or cells or people), and particles for persons. It is also very important to keep in mind the correspondences between atomic, cellular, molecular, organic groupings and human social evolution for insight into the evolution of humanity.

THE PROOFS OF NUCLEAR EVOLUTION

Around this Earth scientists have found a highly energised envelope of positive ions and protons which sends showers of negative electrons down upon us. These are caused by the collision of a cosmic ray with the nucleus of atmospheric atoms. Cascades of cosmic particles come from our Sun in solar flares along with much higher energy from other more intense stars (Ref. 1). These high energies are checked in space and trapped in the earth's magnetic field which forms a skin or membrane that lets in some of the sun's light (Ref. 2). Every cell of all living tissues, whether animal or vegetable, is subject to a continuous rain of these cosmic wave-particles which leave a positive charge of bio-electricity at the nucleus of the cell and a negative charge on its surface skin (Ref. 3).

The difference between live and dead matter is in consciousness; but I do not mean by this word *human* consciousness. This *consciousness* is the ability of the nucleus to create a surplus positive charge, thereby negating its surface charge and causing a movement of electrons to be induced into the cell from the negative surrounding free electrons cascading down into the earth's environment. This makes each cell of the blood repel each other so that they do not actually touch; space between them is induced and they will not coagulate together.

At its greatest intensity this experience of expansion of " space " in each cell and its electrical force field is transmitted to all cell life in that bundle of vibrations we call our body. When these enter into homogenous vibration with " Life " we are in a state of nuclear evolution. The ancient sages of India described this as a soft rain of dew when they were receiving inspiration (Ref. 4). The real meaning of their words, however, was not dew or rain but a sensitivity to the gravitational flux, the " glue " which holds the universe together. This was physically experienced as an " attractive " tugging feeling at the skin, as if the flesh were gently swirling with vibrational life. *Gravity* is the most subtle of all forces and draws all energy into the CENTRE of every system, condensing all cosmic dust and matter into planets and stars. It is balanced by *Levity* which produces outward expansion and Light.

Individuals attuned to Life, the Nuclear Self, will not become so embroiled in negative mental or emotional energies, yet they are open so they absorb more negative electrons the more the positive charge increases at the centre. When we walk by the sea or in a forest where there is a high concentration of negative ions we feel uplifted and expanded. Since our inner intelligence is informing the cell life in our bodies as well as our personalities, whether we are conscious of it or not, any expansion of space in our conscious awareness or in our cells is transmitted to the rest of our being. When the entire organism is attuned to Life we can feel it as a wholeness, our cells tingle, as does our awareness, in harmonious attunement to all the forces of nature. Thus the positive charge is sensitising us to the "glue" of the negative electrons that bind matter and of gravity that holds the universe together in a universal field--- love.

To achieve this enhanced flow of energy one must learn how to consciously work the little electron pumps which move the free electrons into the cells so as to oxidise and synthesise the nutrients in the cell and store the energy. All living things have these electron pumps ; in the human cell it is the Mitochondrion which collects and attracts electrons from the earth's surrounding sea of electrons which we call " static " or free electricity. This has been known by special people called prophets and initiates for a long time but now science is making this knowledge available to everyone. Before we go on to say how our cells " feed " off this kind of Light we must state our hypothesis for those who think in a certain way. It is that each cell absorbs Light and radiation when the wavelength of the Light corresponds with the handful of wavelengths which are themselves characteristic of the structure of the potassium, sodium, calcium and magnesium molecules of the nutrients, and the way in which the atoms of these larger molecules vibrate. In other words if we can consciously attune the wavelength just right, the molecules, and of course the cell, will radiate at an excited state.

Through the science of Supersensonics and radiesthesia we can train our nervous systems to detect the wavelengths of these essential nutrients that form our cell life for conscious attunement. The author of Nuclear Evolution has also originated a new form of yoga techniques to practice attuning the cell life. It is "The Science of Vibration and Transmission of Life Force" and includes control of the life force over the bioelectrical fields so all may enter the "prophetic state." Certain yogic breathing exercises and meditations are orally transmitted and designed for the purpose of increasing the oxidation and enhancing the response of the cell life to the field of consciousness by ionizing the body fluids.*

THE HYPOTHESIS

The hypothesis advanced in this book is based on actual observation and subsequent experiment (Ref. 5) and it says that the human cell-life can absorb energy at a higher vibratory rate than that considered possible by present day biological theory, although there are some Professors of Botany who have set out the hypothetical arrangements for those chemical compounds which are responsible for the transport of the electrons (or the Hydrogen atoms) in the photosynthesis process (Ref. 6). The absorption of Light by the human cells brings in fundamental problems in physics and chemistry which are related to fluorescence and resonance, but every day there is new evidence that Light energies at specific frequencies have profound effects on body chemistry. Our hypothesis is gradually being confirmed by other workers; since 1962 when it was first published, a great many discoveries have been made concerning the magnetosphere around man.

---

*The whole series of 24 tapes links modern scientific understanding with the Sanskrit Yoga Sutras of Patanjali. (They await publication by an enterprising editor who wishes to undertake a major work.)

Like any Art-form it is certain that the attunement possible cannot be attained without enough practice to transcend its own concept form. However, the common view of the scientific method is oversimplified and erroneous and does not take account of less predictable factors such as intuition and imagination which are important features of scientific investigation. Concept-making is often grossly over-simplified by step by step mechanical thinking which is mentally binding on the physical faculties of perception. A star pianist does not have to think how to play notes or the artist stop to think how to mix colours. To do so would interfere with his performance. He is concerned with the " something " beyond thinking which transcends mechanisms. Of course he must first start at the bottom of the class and learn what these mechanisms are in order to go beyond them. Sense experience so easily cramps and inhibits the creative faculty that often it becomes impossible to make an imaginative leap.

We have to practice attunement techniques to comprehend the power of our own intuition and imagination before we can affect our cell life in order to attain the state of Nuclear Evolution, which is beyond all our concepts about it. Hence the ability to practice rather than theorise makes the difference between direct knowing and knowing about.

Without knowing experientially (not just in the head) our personal reactions to colours, which are precisely tuned wavelengths or frequencies, we are no more capable of re-emitting absorbed radiation from the positive nucleus, than the man who sings in his morning bathtub is of getting the leading part in the La Scala Opera. We must continually reform and rethink our preconceived ideas about sound and colour.

If we reject certain colours or are attracted to others we also are rejecting or are attracted to the psychological state that colour represents. Our choice of colour indicates how we absorb light and filter it through our egos.

The UNIVERSE is not *matter* but music and colour. Its basic building blocks are made of dynamic waves which have consonant form (Ref. 7). The new physics says that even though our senses cannot always perceive it, we are surrounded by evidence, at every moment of our lives, of the unheard melody and harmony of the Music of the Spheres. The scientists tell us that the walls of the room in which we are sitting and the entire environment around everyone, are all vibrating at this very moment with millions of tones; and within your own body the atoms are radiating outwards a throbbing symphony, its billions of cells all singing their own songs with special harmonies. In this body are fifty billion neurons in our nerves and brain acting as receptors of protons, neutrinos, and electrons, particles with indestructible and immortal lifetimes, all made from high speed photons (Light) falling onto this earth. Let us rebuild the py-ramid of man's knowledge as he has constructed it so far, like a raft on a sea of thought, from which he can look out at new vistas of the Universe within him.

All of the force fields, wave particles and their interactions, and colour frequencies, affect human perception. By experiencing them consciously we expand awareness evolving ourself and them into a higher resonance with Life. First hand experience of direct perception is essential to our complete understanding.*

The author merely wishes to stimulate those who are on the path to Cosmic Consciousness and asks them to do no more than check out these few facts for themselves and become their own authorities. He has been privileged to travel extensively and meet leading researchers in all the fields discussed, but does not believe in personal reputation building, therefore will not inflict his background on the reader or make detailed accounts of his travels, teachers, or personal experimentation. It is sufficient to be still and know!

In a group or individual, the entrance of a new high energy idea or person (pi-meson) confronts the existent group of energies (atomic nucleus) which sets change in motion in the group (decay of weak interactions) releasing Nuclear energy potential (room for new inspiration, direction, power) to the new group (daughter atom) which now includes the new person or idea. At the same time new unstable feelings and thoughts (weak interactions-beta and other particles, and electro-magnetic waves) are created. Weak interactions decay and are reabsorbed consciously or unconsciously depending upon how they are dealt with by the group and by each member. Will it bring fear, doubt, outward conflict to the ego or will it be handled with skill and bring harmony and integration? Are the group interactions weak or strong?

---

*There are several books now published by students of Christopher Hills which go more deeply into the effects of colour and light on our personal lives. A list of these books, written from his oral teachings on colour and consciousness and from personal experience, can be found in the back of this book.

In our Nuclear group, new high energy persons have entered with fresh ideas, ready to fill some obvious gaps in leadership (obvious to some). Some of the older members reacted with jealousy and self-doubt at their own abilities. Their feelings were shared and dealt with openly, so negative waves were minimal. These reactions are typical for any social or political group, but usually they go unspoken and come out in power plays and negative attitudes toward other group members. Our will can change and transform these reactions and internal energies or allow them to run their course through us. We have the choice as to how to direct our energies.

Psi and Pi, THE FORCES OF WEAK INTERACTION

The cement which holds the universe together is the force of *Gravity*. The glue that holds the parts of the atom together is *electromagnetic attraction*. The *nuclear* energy that holds the *nucleus* of the atom together is the strong interactions. The Pi meson is a high energy cosmic particle that hits the earth by collision with the *nucleus* of an atom that decays and releases vast energy to the *nucleus* of the daughter atom in a very strong interaction, but at the same time creates new particles and waves which are unstable and therefore decay with weak interactions; they are then re-absorbed into the material atoms of our world, our bodies. They can only be described by physicists as packets of wave-energy. In a flash they can be transformed from bits or particles of energy into waves of energy. Man has known this from the beginning by other means of sensing than our scientific instruments of today, but this knowledge has been personal and not communicable in objective ways. Now man has instruments sensitive enough to measure deliberately "willed" changes in these waves; the author along with other Yogis, healers, and medical men, has participated in the use of these different methods.

These packets of wave-energy make up the cells of our body and are surrounded by one to seven shells or orbits of rotating electrons, depending on the availability of oxygen and how much of this cosmic energy we can absorb by attuning our cells to it.

Cosmic radiation and its high energy vibrations are constantly creating tremendous changes in mankind even though our normal senses do not perceive it. Handled the wrong way it can cause disintegration and fear at the heart of each nucleus of the atoms in our body and bring chaos into the nucleus of each cell . . . and handled the right way we can avoid chaos and confusion and plug into harmony and joy.

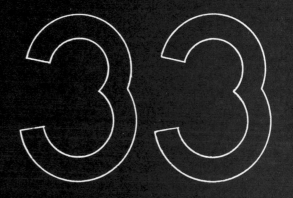

INSIDE THE NUCLEUS

Fig. (222)

Wrong way ? Right way ? Whose way ? It may be thought that wrong and right depend on the individual viewpoint and therefore we shall use nature's rule book to discover the group law by which she governs the lifting up of individual separate members of a nucleus to a higher energy level. In the following description of Nuclear Evolution we return to the resonance of light waves on page 742 in Part II which makes each cell receptive to lower and higher levels of energy so as to become an absorber of Light. As nature organises each nucleus along the same general lines we will use an analogy of "conscious knowing" within the atom which can be applied to groups of people, as well as groups of molecules, groups of atoms or particles inside atoms. If we can stretch our imagination to think of the individual particle as a person, or as an individual

796

within a group of persons, then we can see the "jump" we have to make from individual law to the group law. For those who know nothing of atomic physics we will say in the next few paragraphs what actually goes on inside a nucleus.

We must now build an image of ourselves sitting inside the nucleus of an atom and must pretend that in that atom we are also inside the nucleus of a human cell and that we are now in touch with an "order of being" which can at the same time project this image into a group of people who can think and feel as a whole unit or as a single body—a body of people such as CENTRE is. Holding this thought in our minds we can now look at some useful models of the nucleus in physics and biology so that in describing a few of these conceptual pictures, our minds will grasp the conclusions about the effects of colour and consciousness which follow later on.

There is the "shell" model which conveniently groups together the particles moving in their orbits around a common CENTRE but correct understanding of the forces between them and the saturation of these nuclear forces within the atom requires some careful thought. The nucleus is the dense central core of an atom or cell in which most of the mass and all of the positive charge is concentrated. When stable, it exactly balances the charge of the electrons which circle around it in orbits. The nucleus itself is made up of tightly packed protons and neutrons in roughly equal quantities which we call individual particles.

Fig. (223)

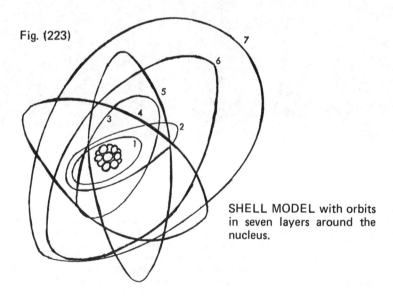

SHELL MODEL with orbits in seven layers around the nucleus.

The shell model of the atom above indicates the orbits which can be occupied by the negative particles such as electrons

All the intricate patterns and colours of this magnificent display are written in the peacock's egg. The ancient vedic seers likened the real nuclear self of man to be like a cosmic egg containing all the parts of his being in the homogeneous limitless state of consciousness. Just as the yolk of a peacock's egg contains the DNA message to produce all the arrays of cells in the construction of the feathers which extract the colours from light without having any fixed colours of their own, so the seers reasoned with the construction of man's nature in relationship to the One intelligence at the heart of all existence.

at different levels of excitation. Similarly the nuclear shell model involves the idea of orbits for the protons and neutrons which absorb energies at sharply selected resonances which correspond to seven states of intensity and excitation. Spiritual consciousness has seven layers, one of which is physical consciousness. **All are controlled, guided, separated, and experienced by awareness of a self-limiting ultimate " I " sense, pervading all matter and Light energy.**

In the shell model, applied to a group of people, each person has protonic, neutronic and electronic qualities corresponding to the three gunas of sattva-knowing, tamas-inertia, and rajas-activity, which are the three intertwined creative forces in all of nature. How "I" responds to these creative forces determines which force we manifest predominantly. The protons in the group and in ourself are the positive, creative leaders, the neutrons are slower to respond and are a necessary stabilising balance to the leaders who might push too far, too fast, with their dynamic energy and throw the system into too rapid development. The electrons which orbit around the protonic-neutronic nucleus are the active members who mediate with the larger community carrying the inspiration and messages of the nucleus into the world. In the group they are often people who are in the process of learning to tune to the centre and are less committed due to newness or other obligations than the totally committed nuclear members. The "tightly packed" nuclear members are united in a divine marriage of purpose and partnership.

The seven colour levels, referred to in Part II, orbit around the Nuclear Self-soul with the same pattern as the shell model depicts, showing another correspondence in Nature.

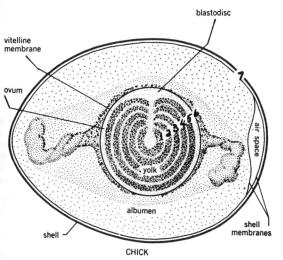

blastodisc

vitelline
membrane

ovum

air space

yolk

albumen

shell

shell
membranes

CHICK

Fig. (224)

The shell model has many examples in nature. The chicken egg for instance has one hard shell to protect its nucleus in the homogeneous mass of yolk. But once fertilised a growth pattern of seven clearly distinquishable layers form around the nucleus of the ovum. The shell analogy of an atom may be likened to a yolk all smeared out through space yet containing the blueprint for its interactions like the yolk has a full blueprint for every chicken feather, bone, etc.

799

In an attempt to get inside the invisible world of the nucleus without some form of clairvoyance we are like a blind man examining an elephant. We have to side step the way the individual particles of the nucleus interact to look at the " whole " gross structure of the nuclear concept. In nature the dense impinging energies from the cosmos collide with the nucleus and get trapped, creating neutrons which interact with the nucleus and radiate their excess energy outwards in the form of radiating Light. There are a large number of resonances i.e. sharply defined wavelengths of energy at which neutrons are sure to be picked up by the nucleus of an atom. Once a neutron gets into a nucleus under conditions of exact resonance it will stay there a long time. The liquid-drop model of the nucleus we referred to on page 742 handles this extra energy by distributing it to other resident particles in the nucleus. If we as individuals could join a group and merge in the way a molecule of water hits a drop of water, we would become selfless. As is explained in the ancient Vedas, the universal " knower " is like the drop of water that enters the ocean and becomes the " whole " ocean. This gives a good idea of one model of the nucleus confirmed by modern science.

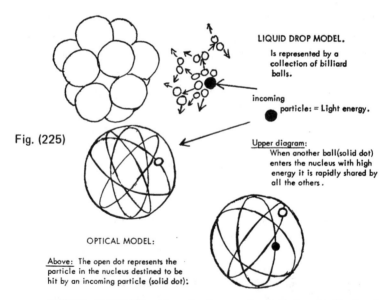

LIQUID DROP MODEL.

Is represented by a collection of billiard balls.

incoming
particle: = Light energy.

Fig. (225)

Upper diagram:
When another ball(solid dot) enters the nucleus with high energy it is rapidly shared by all the others .

OPTICAL MODEL:

Above: The open dot represents the particle in the nucleus destined to be hit by an incoming particle (solid dot):

LOWER DIAGRAM: After the impact the incoming particle has lost energy and taken up a vacant orbit in the nucleus. The target particle has absorbed the energy and jumped up to a higher energy level in another orbit. The transaction is possible only if there are vacant positions within the nucleus for both particles. The tendency to absorb energy increases with the power of the bombarding particles because the inputs of high energy impacts (such as Cosmic rays of light) raise up both particles to domains which are sparsely populated, while low energy particles do not force the resident particles out of the lower regions where there are less vacancies.

A low-energy person coming into the group does not usually stay because the low-energy positions are usually all taken up. He may just pass right through without leaving much impression. It depends on his attunement with the centre and his commitment to growth. Vacancies and needs are most pressing in the higher "sparsely populated" orbits where greater talent and skill is required to function at those energy levels. If Joy, Mary, Jack and Bill are low-energy members, another low-energy person seeking admittance, George, may be a drag on the group dynamic with little to offer. Normally he won't even feel attracted, there will be an invisible repelling or a neutral vibration from the group, which only expands when there is readiness. Since the entire Nuclear purpose is to be in resonance with each other in the ONE, only people of accurate resonance find places. A high energy person, Lois, whose awareness vibrates in deep resonance with the purpose, is also more likely to have a great deal to contribute which will further the entire group. The group never rejects any potential member. Those incoming persons, in describing their own wants and needs will excuse themselves when they find their personal needs and desires differ. The most telling criterion of a person's readiness is his ability and willingness to work on himself and give selflessly.

> The optical model of the nucleus shows us that the strength of this absorption of the cosmic energies is related to the collisions which occur inside the nucleus. It is somewhat like a cloudy crystal ball, and the cloudiness represents the tendency of bombarding neutrons from the cosmos to be absorbed by the nucleus at certain atomic numbers of protons and neutrons. One is reminded of the magic numbers of the ancients! *

When a high energy, creative person enters the nucleus, his energy is rapidly shared by all other members. When the high energy person has shared himself and found acceptance and a place for his creativity, he merges with the group, filling a need or role which the group may have not even been aware was vacant before he presented himself. The rest of the group, and maybe one or more persons especially, are lifted up to a higher energy level in another orbit of consciousness. Only if the new person's energy is really needed by the group will this transaction take place. An incoming potential member who is on a power trip or who has great ideas that cannot manifest, or someone who is not in tune with the group needs, will find difficulty in putting them over and their energy will not be readily absorbed.

---

* See Atomic Table Chapter 23.

The mutation referred to on page 785 is only possible in a group where people are in resonance. The standing wave of energy absorbed directly from the cosmic centre of intelligence is powerfully felt and shared by all. Here the central theme is "Readiness is all".

HOW THE NUCLEUS ABSORBS LIGHT

Having no method of investigating the consciousness of the atom from within, science has to discover the attitudes of the separate particles to the whole nucleus by subjecting it to attack from without. In nature however, where freedom of choice may depend on "ripeness", the nucleus may have some say on whether it is destined to be hit by an intruding cosmic ray. In science one cannot observe the behaviour of an atom without disturbing it with unnatural beams of energy. The social behaviour of the individual particles under such stresses from outside can give us some picture of the group force of the "whole" assembly. In physics this is done by bombarding the inner nucleus of the atom with the energy of a beam of light made of neutrons; these are wave-particles which have no charge of positive or negative electricity; they are neutral and can therefore easily enter the nucleus of an atom without being repelled by the electrostatic charge of positive electricity on the nucleus. (Ref. 8). In a human sense we could relate these neutrons to a procession of uncommitted people travelling through a group of dancers engaged in a choreographic session. One individual might try to cross the floor; in doing this he might be grappled by a partner. But on the other hand he might avoid the individual dancers and emerge on the other side without losing any time or energy. So each neutron in the beam of light may be swung away from individual contacts with protons in the nucleus by the group force of the whole assembly and pass through it as if it were transparent. Now if we try to think of these individual particles of energy as wave-energy we can find out by experiment that the frequency of a wave measures the energy of its particles i.e. a high frequency or short wavelength gives us a fast particle and a low frequency or long wavelength yields a slow particle.

If the scientist aims a beam of neutron light at a group of particles bound into an atomic nucleus the scattering and absorption of these neutrons can be measured by the dimming of the brightness in the beam in its passage through the group of particles which make up the nucleus. Thinking in terms of the optical model we know that the amount of absorption will depend on the wavelength of the neutron-light used. We can imagine easily a beam of light made to pass through a model nucleus consisting of a group of transparent glass-balls which would of course be dimmed, just as if we passed it through the atoms and molecules of glass in a crystal ball. Some of this light would be lost by the bending of the rays depending on the refraction of the glass and some of it would be lost by absorption within the balls depending on the absorption power or cloudiness of the glass. By means of certain experiments with light (Ref. 8) the refraction and absorption power of the nucleus has been discovered. We know that the emerging waves of light may change their direction but not their wavelength, which means that some of the neutrons get out again without changing their energy. We might then ask how can these particles (individuals) pass through the group without interacting with the other particles in the nucleus (society) and exchanging their energy with the other partners in it?

When we relate the intensity of the wave particle (the frequency of the light energy) to the intensity of a person in a group, we could say that only when an individual person passes through society (the medium of exchange) with life vibrating at a very high frequency and at great intensity, does he leave any impression on its members; at a low energy state he passes through society as if it were transparent.

Now to get another picture of the " social behaviour " of the individual particles we can turn to the " shell " model of the nucleus. (Ref. 9). We can see in this model that the protons and neutrons inside the nucleus are arranged in rings in a system of seven concentric shells or orbits, just as the electrons around the outside of the nucleus are. Each orbit corresponds to a *specifically attuned* hierarchal level of energy, so that any one particle in the nucleus can pass from an inside energy level to another level only by an abrupt " jump " towards the outside rings. It is this expansion and inner *radiation of energy* in the " group force " towards the outer surfaces of the atom and the cells, and from each member of a group, that we have called Nuclear Evolution. Let us now consider *how* this " jump " in intensity is made in nature.

It is especially interesting to note that the only way a jump can be permanently made to a higher attuned hierarchical energy level is by expanding and levitating the group force outwards toward the surfaces of the group in an ever-increasing rising spiral to absorb and include all who are ready in society. The group must grow and expand. Only through radiation of light and love can Nuclear Evolution be fulfilled by growing and attracting and drawing all into the positive centre.

THE GROUP LAW OF THE NUCLEUS

Nothing can be absorbed into a nucleus until it is " ripe " or until a place has been made for it. The famous exclusion principle says that no more than one electron can occupy the same orbit around the nucleus at the same time. The same principle is at work inside the nucleus and these " occupancy rules " mean that when the nucleus has filled each of its nuclear orbits the particles in it exhibit a " social behaviour " which prevents any newcomers because the places are already filled. The latecomers find no place and pass right through without being absorbed. The consciousness at the heart of the atom " knows " the over-all situation and each of the particles stays in its proper place. The force therefore enjoyed by *each indivi-duel particle* is a " group force " *coming from the " whole" assembly of its neighbouring partners* in the nucleus acting as a single body.

In remembering that the purpose of form is growth of awareness, the nucleus would never grow in energy level if all the new potential members were actually absorbed. The reason for hierarchichal levels is to further evolutionary growth by setting up a system of energy transformers. The social group evolutionary process proceeds under basic energy laws.

In the human group working for Nuclear Evolution we have to learn how to absorb and emit light under the influence of some exciting agent, which in this case is cosmic radiation, and achieve flourescence. The group involved in Nuclear Evolution is working on the cell-life so that emission persists even after the contact with the exciting agent has ceased, thereby achieving a heightened phosphorescence that continues to use the phosphorous compounds in the cell after flourescence has taken place, very much like the fire-fly has the power to generate its own light. The Light we speak of here may not be visible to the ordinary eye and may be as invisible as heat rays, ultraviolet rays, or radio waves are. Ultimately the group would be working towards lumin-escence in the visible spectrum of Light, that is towards a condi-tion very similar to that described as the "transfiguration", which is a state of bioluminescence. (See p. 806)The writer has actually seen this aura surrounding one person in high spiritual ecstacy. The group nucleus must have a unitary consciousness which understands that the power of "union" of the "group force" can only be absorbed, to raise it up to its next level, when they can think and act as a unanimous single whole consciousness.

The transfiguring power of group force is successfully absorbed only as the group can demonstrate this wholeness in its *manifesta-tion,* not just in its head. Christ's first disciples are an example of this successful absorption when they all received the holy ghost at the same time at Pentecost. They had attuned themselves to the positive Christ-soul-nuclear force and were ready for the "jump."

Any light-energy (individual particles or persons) entering the group or nucleus from outside is immediately confronted by these "rules" in the form of the *single force exerted by the entire population* of individual particles resident in the nucleus. Because this group force "knows" that all the orbits are filled at the *lower energy levels* the neutron particles in our example will avoid contact with the individual particles in the nucleus as if there were a repulsion or non-acceptance, and they will come out the other side quite unchanged. If, however, we think of rushing through our dance group with *high energy*, it becomes excited and makes a place vacant so that the incoming individual particle (or person) is grabbed by a partner to share a new orbit and so lose its energy in the group. If the group is highly excited, several more orbits in the shells within the nucleus are made vacant, and then the potential exists in the nucleus to absorb much more energy and more individual particles from the Light beam. It has been found in these experiments that when a nucleus absorbs a *particle* from a light-beam and it drops into its vacant orbit, the effect of entry is to cause partners to jump up to a *higher energy* level orbit in order to share its energy. The energy exchange is only possible when the vacant space in the outer orbits has raised the partners in the group together to a new "ripeness" for new life *to enter in to all the individuals* in it. Cloudiness of the glass balls, or the tendency for greater absorption increases with the intensity of the energy level or frequency of the bombarding light-beam; this is because higher energy impacts on the target particle in the nucleus and the incoming neutron particle puts both of them in the upper more sparsely populated orbital regions, making the nucleus larger and more absorbent, and more intensely charged.

If some thought enters our individual awareness, or if someone enters the group with high intensity stirring up the energies (of the group members or of our minds) the excitation opens the awareness, decrystallises its present form and makes space for more new ideas or members to join. This grouping of energies is not random but occurs according to laws of attraction and repulsion as well as in an orderly process.*

The transparency of the glass balls in our model will also depend on their potential absorbing power and the intensity (wavelength) of the energy which is attempting to pass through it. The lower the energy of the light beam (neutron particles) the more transparent the nucleus made up of glass balls becomes. On the human level the more power the prophet has, the more cloudy will be his vital message, and the more mud he will stir up! This is because the more snug the particles

---

*See UNIVERSAL GOVERNMENT BY NATURE'S LAWS" published by University of the Trees Press, for actual process of admitting new members, challenging leadership, etc.,etc.

are in the nucleus the tighter they are packed in the lower regions and the greater the energy required to impregnate them and find vacancies. Other experiments with wave particles such as protons yield the same results (Ref. 8) and it is our view in Nuclear Evolution that a photon of Light, which like a neutron, has no charge, is also confronted by these rules of social behaviour in the over-all nuclear group consciousness. If we have taken pains to paint this complex picture it is because with these models in mind we can now return to what we said on page 742 about resonance.

The group grows towards the state of Conscious Nuclear Evolution by building up its nuclear resonance. The nucleus can be tuned to receive incoming persons which reinforce each other with the reflected waves of the group interaction and create a resonant standing wave. This makes the group even more absorbent of light energy and people. Thus the group potency can reach a height where it can sweep up and carry incoming weaker individuals as well as more powerful radiation intensities of light. The group power can absorb logarithmically as the standing wave increases potency, which is much stronger and more absorbent of light and consciousness than the sum total of the individual persons. Individuals of all energy levels are needed for the evolutionary growth of a Nuclear group. The high powered individuals require both higher potency individuals and lower potency individuals in order to make that jump up to a higher energy level. The tendency for greater absorption increases with the intensity of the energy level or frequency of the bombarding light.

In this reference to Nuclear Evolution we mentioned that it was possible for a state of resonance to occur within the nucleus which would make it even more absorbent of light energy of a resonant standing wave. This was because the nucleus could be tuned to receive incoming waves or particles which reinforce each other with reflected waves which soak up the lower energies of visible light as well as the weaker and more subtle interactions. It is the group power within which makes the "group force" control the receptivity of the nucleus to incoming energies from outside.

TRANSFIGURATION OF THE CELL NUCLEUS

The foregoing examples have related to the nucleus of the atom but we must now " jump " up to the next hierarchal level of the molecule and the cell nucleus. When we look at the electric polarity of the cell and correlate it with electric currents which accompany the *cell oxidation* of its nutrients, we find that oxidation-reduction depends basically on the action of its electron pumps (the mitochondria). The supply of electrons in this case is regulated by the " group force " which, enjoyed by each individual molecule, comes from the " whole " assembly *of its partners in the cell* acting as a single living entity. This " cell " consciousness is in turn part of an *all-inclusive brain field* which interpenetrates the total organism and guides the development of each individual cell. This " brain field ", normally referred to as an *individual person,* is also " in resonance " with a *Cosmic brain field* and its electromagnetic integrations which unconsciously cause *absorption of the energies required* for the chemical reaction of the cells to trap and re-emit radiation (Light).

There are thirty different processes known to science by which energy is introduced into or released from luminescent systems in nature (Ref. 10) and there are at least four thousand papers written on the excitation of the Earth's plasma skin (ionosphere), that membrane of highly excited particles which surrounds the earth planet with a brilliant aura of blue light. (Ref. 11). When this ionospheric plasma skin lets through a high energy particle it collides with the nucleus of atoms in the upper atmosphere and scatters into the molecular plasma of the ionosphere (Ref. 12). This creates showers of ionising radiations in the atmosphere which are absorbed at certain frequencies and at certain resonances with the oxygen atoms in it; this then creates *resonance radiation.* (Ref. 13). These resonances and frequencies have been determined by experiments in the splitting of water, which cannot be given here.

Part of the three year course includes yogic techniques for tuning our cells to the resonance radiation to create a surplus positive charge which tunes our awareness to the nuclear force and the universal link–consciousness. When the resonance is achieved there is an awareness that makes the human being into a "Whole" at every level of being–atom, molecule, cell, organ–all are realised as part of one field and conditioned by our own field.

It is this resonance radiation to which we can tune our bioelectric fields in the body cells and create a surplus positive charge at the nucleus (Ref. 5). The attraction of electrons to the surface of the cell and towards the outer surface of the electron pumps in the powerhouse of the cell, is achieved by its absorption of Light (resonance radiation in the electro-magnetic radio spectrum) as mentioned on page 743 in Part II.

I.R. 13 Red   19 Orange 25   Yellow   50 Green 55 Blue 62 Indigo 68 Violet

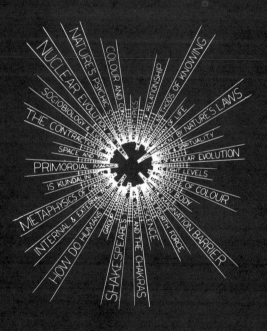

Inside the starburst:
NATURE'S PSYCHIC... · COLOUR AND CON... · ...RELATIONSHIP · ...THODS OF KNOWING · NUCLEAR EVOLUTION · SOCIOBIOLOGY & ... · ...RAM OF LIFE · ...NT BY NATURE'S LAWS · THE CONTRACTION ... · ...RITUALITY · SPACE AND ... · NUCLEAR EVOLUTION · PRIMORDIAL IMAGINING · ...IGHT LEVELS · IS KUNDALINI · ...OF COLOUR · METAPHYSICS OF ... · ...OW BODY · INTERNAL & EXTERNAL ... · ...AGINATION BARRIER · HOW DO HUMANS ... · ...ORTH FORCE · ...ENCE · SHAKESPEARES ... · AND THE CHAKRAS

THE INNER SANCTUM
OF LIGHT

Dr. Maurice Wilkins, a British biophysicist, examines a model of the DNA molecule. Along with Dr. Francis Crick and Dr. James Watson he received the Nobel prize for working out its arrangement at the nucleus of the cell.

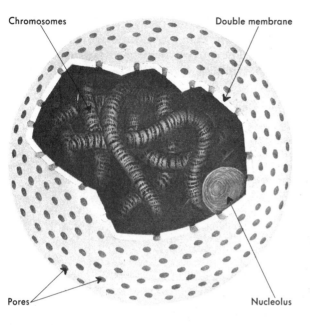

Chromosomes   Double membrane

Pores

Nucleolus

Fig. (226)

The nucleus of a cell is usually a spherical envelope composed of a double membrane with perforations to permit nutrients to pass between the nucleus and the cytoplasm. The nucleus contains the chromosomes which direct all activities for the whole cell through DNA. It is the nucleus which evolves and contains the nucleolus which synthesises RNA to move the DNA message of life into the rest of the cell.

MUCOUS CELLS

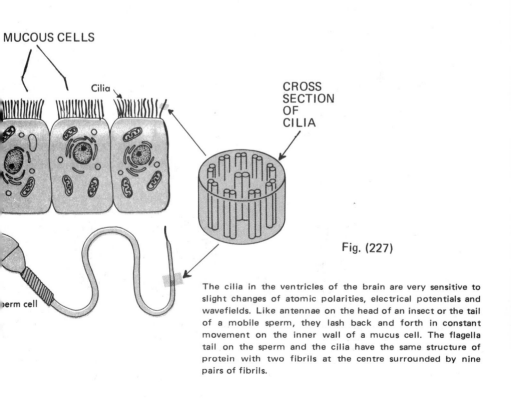

Cilia

CROSS
SECTION
OF
CILIA

Sperm cell

Fig. (227)

The cilia in the ventricles of the brain are very sensitive to slight changes of atomic polarities, electrical potentials and wavefields. Like antennae on the head of an insect or the tail of a mobile sperm, they lash back and forth in constant movement on the inner wall of a mucus cell. The flagella tail on the sperm and the cilia have the same structure of protein with two fibrils at the centre surrounded by nine pairs of fibrils.

The nucleus transfers genetic information in the DNA and sends orders to other parts of the cell by means of a messenger substance (RNA). Picture shows the beginning of the process inside the nucleus. The central backbone of each carrot-like structure is a chain of DNA which acts as a template. Each DNA strand is synthesising about 100 RNA molecular strands. The process is begining at the narrow pointed ends of each "carrot" while the longer fibres at the thicker end are almost completed strands of messenger RNA.

BIO-ENERGETIC TRANSMUTATIONS IN THE CELL NUCLEUS

The proteins and nucleic acids provide the principal constituents of the living cell which organise themselves into higher structures of cells and tissues. The protein called keratin forms the principal structure of hair, horn and fingernail. The protein collagen serves a similar purpose in skin and tendon. Elastin is a springy protein ; it occurs in ligaments and the elastic fibres of connective tissue. These three types of protein are more passive ; others are very active and react quickly to changes in their environment. Proteins of muscles contract. Contraction is a property of many other biological protein structures ranging from the rapidly oscillating tail of a sperm cell to the waving arms of the amoeba. Contractability is an essential feature in all living cells and they appear to employ a common molecular mechanism in the " group force " of the whole assembly of proteins which make up the single cell. What makes these molecules contract and is there any connection between the " social behaviour " of the various individual particles of the atom? The protein transmits to the connective tissue " tension " which is caused by the quick CHANGE in the relationship between two different proteins, just as the " energy " in the atom's nucleus was absorbed by the CHANGE in the relationship of two different wave-particles. The relationship in the cell is influenced by the ionisation of potassium, sodium, calcium and magnesium and by A.T.P. (Ref. 14). The function of ATP is then regulated by an enzyme ATP-ase which is sensitive to radiation and light and helps in photosynthesis and other energy transductions.

DNA AND THE CHEMICAL MESSAGE OF LIFE

The DNA molecule and its protein partners in the threadlike chromosomes of the cell nucleus, maintain the specific linear sequence of the genes in passing on their hereditary message of evolution. But the DNA can be easily dissolved out of the nucleus of the cell by weak chemical treatment which breaks the bonds that link DNA to its own protein molecules. The fact that these bonds can be broken so easily makes it very likely that the chromosome when exerting its bio-chemical effects in replication is NOT an indivisible unit with all its many constituents in a precise unchanging hereditary chemical pattern existing from one generation to the next. It is of course subject to evolutionary CHANGE. Yet in their function these chromosomes have to be capable of precise replication, so they must spontaneously aggregate into the patterns of LIFE (consciousness of form) which is characterised by the chemical environment in the nucleus of the cell. Any change in this immediate environment, such as a change in the specific frequency of a sharply selected energy, of radiation, of light, of electromagnetic waves or of sound, may alter not only the structural relationship of the molecules in the cell nucleus, but also their bio-chemical and genetic activity.

RNA is the messenger of that message contained in the DNA at the nucleus of the cell. Obviously the message can be modified in its transmission, since all people are differentiated by the unique way the nucleus of the " I " interacts with the biological functions of each cell nucleus. Though the Self is the same " I " in its undifferentiated form of pure conscious-ness, the carrying of its message to its component cells in the body is achieved through replication in living cells which are differentiated. These self-renewing cells are passed on down history's time-line as immortal protoplasm in the ovum and sperm. At no time is there a break in the physical chain of cells which carry the message of life and consciousness. All our cells we inherited from living cells whose DNA message was mingled with other DNA's which have been modified by consciousness.

Only consciousness is aware of the needs of the organism as a whole. It forms its goal and is the selector of the environ-mental stimuli for the cell life. It is the absolute dictator of their biological and psychosomatic attitudes to all stimuli even though the cells are not aware of it. In the same way the person who has not found the absolute nature of " I " Self, is not aware of his unconscious choices. If DNA is the message and the RNA its runner and messenger, who writes the message in the DNA and modifies it? If it is now an intelligence that asks who and declares it an unscientific question, then our objectivity which is limited by " I " and its vision, must ask the question " what guides the process? "

The consciousness of the nucleus of "I" interacts with the biological functions of each cell nucleus. One who has awakened to the pure consciousness of I, whose self-will has become the Divine Will, has the ability, through penetrating the imagination, to enter into and effect changes in the DNA and enable the RNA messenger to carry the next evolutionary message from the Cosmic blueprint stored in the DNA. That One can cooperate with evolution. Humanity's level of awareness, evolution of consciousness, is impregnated in the DNA of his cell life. The awakening to expanded awareness in man is not separate from the processes in his biological life. The transmutation of energy through oxidation and ATP, the functioning of the mitochondria which governs the energy supply and all of the processes and activities in cellular life, are all vehicles of consciousness. By enhancing these activities through various methods, consciousness is expanded. As one meditates properly, one begins to experience changes in the body both in the experience of communion with its cellular functioning and in actual physical appearance.

A photo and a diagram of a mitochondrian shows the structure of the interior walls of the membrane. The outer membrane is smooth but the inner membrane is convoluted like the plates of a wet cell battery.

Photo by J. F. Gennaro, Jr./NYU Biology

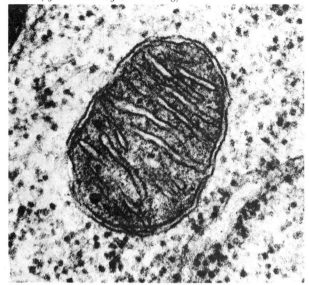

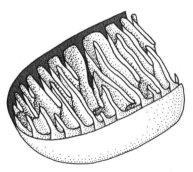

Outer membrane

Inner membrane

Cristae

(229)

The structure of the mitochondrion shows the inner membrane folded into cristae which project into the intracellular fluid of the interior. Very active cells have more cristae than less active cells. The charge on the inner walls is negative and the outer wall is positive.

NUCLEAR ELECTRON DISCHARGE

The molecular architecture of the Mitochondrion, the small body within the living cell which governs the supply of bio-energetic power to the cell, is all summed up in the DNA nucleic acid with its message of replication *and* the ATP molecule which supplies the energy for that replication, including all the other processes of LIFE in the evolutionary thrust (Ref. 15). Obviously the replicating process is shaped by the guiding field of the *resonance radiation with oxygen atoms* in the total environment. The energy-generating systems of all living things depend on two related actions in nature: oxidation plus synthesis of ATP. The action of *oxidation* releases electrons which act as agents for transformation of energy (Ref. 16). The action of ATP acts as a storage battery, feeding the cell with energy as it is needed. The Chloroplast makes the ATP in the world of green plants and the Mitochondria make it in the animal cells. Similar electron-pump systems exist throughout all the cells in the body for the transportation of materials through membranes, for contraction of muscles and for all energy-transforming processes in the cells. There are several hundred mitochondria in each cell—each shaped like a sausage with a thermos-like two layered wrapping, an inner and outer membrane with a watery fluid filling the space between them. Each membrane is made up of two different materials—a protein and a fatty lipid. The electron transfers occur on the inner membrane to synthesise ATP, while oxidation reactions are carried out on the surface of the outer membrane to supply the electrons to the inner membrane

If we take the analogy of this picture of the energy transfers between the outer ionosphere and the inner envelope of the earth's mantle where oxidisation of cosmic radiation occurs,we may be able to see why low-energy radiation does not effect the biology of cell life in the absence of oxygen. The well known sensitivity of almost all biological systems to the damaging actions of ionising radiations becomes much less, as the oxygen present in the system is decreased below that contained in air (Ref. 17). The air contains about 20 per cent of oxygen and the sensitivity of the cell depends on the amount of oxygen removed from the air. If we regard the ionosphere as an outer membrane, and the inner atmosphere as the absorber of resonance radiation, we shall see that the presence of oxygen in both cell and atmosphere influence the metabolic processes as well as radio-sensitivity of the nucleus. The mechanism of resonance radiation would explain to radio-biologists why man has little protection from the biological action of densely ionising radiations such as high energy cosmic particles, alpha particles or fast neutrons, which have not been filtered through the outer membrane of the ionosphere.

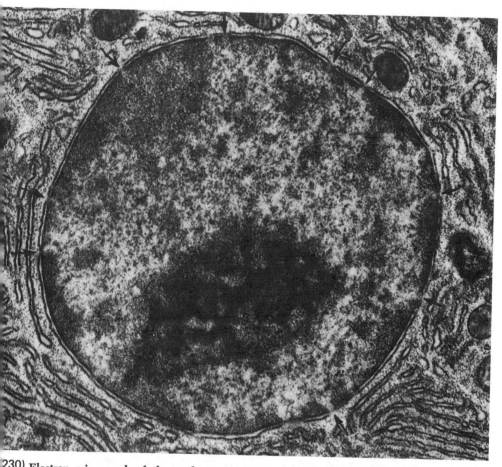

230) **Electron micrograph of the nucleus of a pancreatic cell.** The dark area inside the nucleus is a nucleolus. Numerous "pores" (arrows) can be seen in the double nuclear membrane. ×17,100. [Courtesy D. W. Fawcett, *A Textbook of Histology*, Saunders, 1962.]

If man can learn to enhance the action of oxygen in his body cells, as some yogic techniques teach, he will be able to withstand the absorption of greater intensities of radiation from the atmosphere, which may at sometime prove essential for survival of human life on the planet. This yogic ability may enable trained individuals to survive what would otherwise be a deadly dose of radiation. We can see from the practical experiments yogis have performed with respiration control, thus altering brain and nervous system functions (see Ch. 20), that oxygen is indeed the fuel of consciousness. Control of oxygen intake combined with a trained imagination is the key to *conscious* transmutation of cell life and genetic programming. A detailed study of the vitally important oxygen consumption and transfer system is presented in this chapter to illustrate and illumine nature's intricately designed processes for converting light into human consciousness.

The mitochondria, with their charge of negative electrons supplied by oxidation, are the electron pumps whose main function is to synthesise ATP, exporting it as packaged energy for many life processes in the body and its billions of cells. We must now ask how this metabolism is affected by Light and radiation, how the discharge of electrons in cell and membrane is accomplished, and why.

SENSITIVITY TO LIGHT AND VIBRATION

The bombardment of mitochondria in the cell with ultrasonic frequencies, cosmic rays and ionising radiations will dislodge most of the electrons on the *outer surface* membranes but will not disturb the electron transfers on the *inner membrane*. Perhaps we should look deeper into this disturbance of the oxidation process when it is subjected to *higher levels* of energy. How does nature switch the electron pumps off and on? Structurally speaking the mitochondria are very much like the virus particles, with a protein coat and a nucleic acid core. When these two are separated they are inactive ; when they are combined again they recover their ability to infect. In exactly the same way the mitochondrion loses its ability for transferring electrons in the making of the ATP when its protein is separated from its phospho-lipid. The two partners are incompetent when alone, but become active when coupled. Here we have the answer to the sensitivity of the membranes and their ability to discharge *high bioelectric fields* under excitation and ionisation.

The production of energy through ATP synthesis is by joining a phosphorus atom to ADP, and the hormones of the endocrine glands can switch off this synthesis and turn on the electron oxidisation process which governs the movement of ions (Ref. 15). Here we have an instance of the regulation of the electron pumps in the mitochondria by the secretion of a hormone. The ability to control the electron discharge of the cell in this way is even more important when we come to consider the action of light of specific frequencies (colours) on our glands and hormones.

Certain frequencies of light, including color, induced into the chakras depending upon the psychological level of awareness, create different psycho-somatic reactions in the glands and hormones. These hormonal responses in turn regulate the energy transfer systems in the cells, governing the functions of the body and the replication of DNA—the working out of the evolution of consciousness.

Conscious Nuclear Evolution is making contact with the internal energy systems and perfecting their resonance and attunement with the blueprints of life for enhancement of growth and awareness.

Most of these processes of bio-energetic cellular transformation, DNA-RNA function, ATP synthesis, etc., can be experienced inwardly in consciousness in certain meditative states. Since consciousness permeates the entire organism, it is possible to tune up the etheric vehicle to experience altered states of consciousness and correlate them with the biological energy transfers. To get inside the DNA patterns in our awareness is one step removed from consciously-willed changes to the DNA, so that primordial imagination can unlock great transmutational forces within ourself.

Membrane systems generally show the same features as those described for mitochondria which is the characteristic blue-print of all the membrane systems and energy transfer systems in all the cells of the body. The double membrane seems to be universal in all living systems. In the study of the human personality and colour conducted by the present author it has become apparent over and over again, that there is a psychic membrane surrounding the physical skin, which is not only light-sensitive, but sensitive to radiations from water-tables under the ground and highly charged clouds floating above. The relationship of these water-held fields of energy to the bio-electric and bio-chemical storage of electrons in the cell is controlled by our conscious or unconscious reactions to specific parts of the spectrum of light (colour) as we show later. The ionisation of membranes when specific resonances occur determines the psychic causes for functional psychosomatic disturbances as well as the emotional differences through our glands and hormones.

Control of the mitochondrion works in a similar way in the Chloroplast, within which the photosynthesis of light takes place in plant cells; we see this the moment the sun touches the horizon, when the protoplasm starts streaming in the opposite

Fig. (231)

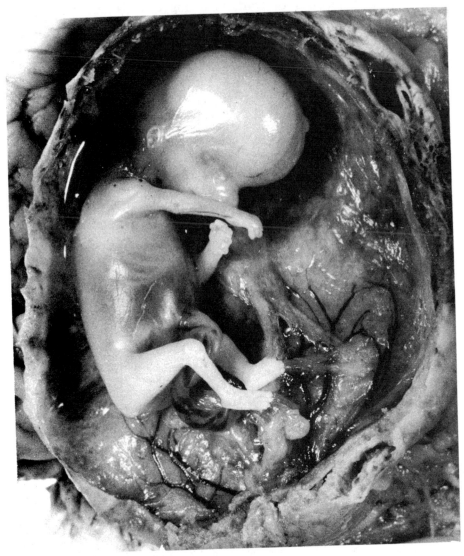

Evolution of the human egg takes place in the liquid-filled space of the womb where it relives the whole evolution of the human race in nine months. When the hollow-sphere, fertilised ovum containing the embryo is implanted in the wall of the womb only the inner cell mass or yolk develops into a human being; all other parts form the membrane and placenta which protect the foetus and filter its nourishment. Until contact with the umbilical food supply is established from the bloodstream of the mother the embryo gets nourishment by digesting the cells of the uterine lining. The double membrane system is common for the foetus as it is for every cell in the body. Psycho-physical enhancement of the electrical potentials between the outer and inner membranes creates high bioelectric ionisation of body fluids. Awareness of Cosmic Being is also prepared in the womb by the unconscious polarisation of the fluids between the inner and outer membrane of the developing skin.

direction; whether or not the light is obscured from the plant does not matter, it just knows the exact moment when twilight begins! This is not accidental. Photosynthesis is the source of all living matter on Earth and the origin of all biological energy. The chain of oxidation in the reduction of hydrogen atoms has links that involve electron transfers, just like those in the mitochondria, which can be measured in terms of electro-chemical potentials (Ref. 6).

The microcosmic universe of a cell is a mirror reflection of the macrocosm of the whole *human* cell which is in turn a microcosmic universe, a mirror reflection of the larger macrocosmic energy system of the planet, and so on, on all hierarchical levels. The analogy can be extended even to seeing "a universe in a grain of sand". All life forms exist within greater life forms and all are interlocking and interconnected with consciousness.

The electron donor to the energy pump in the case of plants is water, and the electron acceptor is carbon dioxide. The respiration and oxidation of plants provides a link with the oxidation in mitochondria which both synthesise ATP and the phosphate molecule. This supplies enough energy to the plant cell to provide the electron potentials needed to reduce carbon dioxide to carbohydrate in photosynthesis. The pumping of the electrons is a two-step electron transfer process for storing up the energy which is activated by the Light falling on the chloroplasts (Ref. 18).

THE INNER SANCTUM OF LIGHT

Most people react to light as something we can see, but like all invisible radiations we can only see it when it strikes something that gets in its way and is absorbed or reflected into the light-sensitive pigments of our eyes. We can observe its passage through a medium, even though we cannot see light itself; we "see" it as a beam in the dark or as heat waves moving the air, or when it hits specks of dust particles, or when it casts a shadow. Daylight is the sun's rays intercepted and absorbed by the atmosphere and reflected from the clouds, and so forth. But science tells us that visible Light is only a small part of the total spectrum and that all radiant energy is light in some form or another. The important thing about Light of all kinds is that objects which we sense absorb it according to their form and pattern. An object made of iron atoms with 26 protons packed into its nucleus will absorb a different amount to Lead with 82 protons. High energy emission of gamma rays, electrons which shower down on earth together with mesons, are all absorbed into our bodies according to the chemical constituents. Pions (Pi-mesons) are emitted and the re-absorption takes place so rapidly that we cannot detect it (Ref. 19). Since any phenomenon that is undetectable cannot be ever regarded as

" real " in the strict sense of a scientific reality, we can speak only of a " virtual " emission and absorption with their consequent exchanges of energy. In this same way the absorption of colours (specific frequencies of light) is to be observed in the actual results of personality changes in a " virtual " way of measuring, very much like the artist drawing " virtual " space into the lines of perspective of his picture rather than putting in " real " space. Yet the laws of perspective which make things smaller when they are far away and bigger when they are near, can be used for calculating our distance away from a lighthouse when at sea, and are reliable for navigating ships, and for taking angles of stars, even when we know that objects in reality do not grow bigger as we approach them. The **laws of optics and geometry are good for " seeing " even though** they contradict physical laws of reality and make things " grow " bigger. This is a very difficult and subtle point which can only be lightly dismissed by insufficient thinking, since the interference of psychological laws of vision in observing facts must be taken into account (ref. 20).

If the absorption of Pions *cannot be observed in reality,* there are still many particles and waves of light-energy that are not measured by their " virtual " exchanges of energy but by their very potent and intense " tracks " which are visibly recorded in photographic emulsions and in images of collisions. When a highly charged particle (i.e. a Cosmic ray) travels through the emulsion it forms a latent image of its path in the silver bromide grains, just as light does in an ordinary camera photograph. This results from the ionisations by the wave-particle on its path through matter and the same penetration is recorded in the cells of the body. Each constituent of the atoms in the cells is characterised by the path the light particles take as they decay and disintegrate.

As the wave-particles decay it follows that our bodies will absorb Light (radiation) according to the chemical balance in our cells and hormones. (Ref. 17). Cosmic rays i.e. particles of intense light, are continually breaking up matter and disintegrating in our membranes, brain and nerve trunkways, and endocrine glands, which become ionised and cause oxidation, thereby producing bands of re-emitted energy, radiation and colour in the same way as minerals such as mica, silver, vanadium, are often surrounded with coloured halos of Light when they are irradiated with intense sunlight. Science believes the correct explanation of these coloured bands is that alpha particles radiating from radio-active atoms at the centre of each tiny sphere, can ionise the iron atoms in the mica near the end of their path, which then causes the iron to become oxidised and thereby produce the coloured bands. (Explanation by Herman Yagoda in " The Tracks of Nuclear Particles " published in Scientific American, May 1956). However, there are other explanations not so well accepted by quantum physicists, which account for these phenomena by resonance bands of radiation. (See Ref. 5b The Search for the Universal Link, published 1962).

It is a fundamental point in Nuclear Evolution that consciousness or the "group force" within every atom in its chemical environment, has something to say about its own acceptance of intruding particles. Just as the earth's atmosphere acts as a membrane which lets in only *some* particles of Light and functions as a giant cell, so there is *some* decision making and selecting of the nutrients which pass into the body cell, and also, at even more subtle energy levels of the weak interactions, there will be the "social behaviour" between atoms and the attraction and repulsion of particles of Light. Positively charged Pi-mesons decay into more subtle radiation energy, are quite immune to capture by human cell matter and plunge deep into the earth, but negatively charged Pi-mesons react strongly with the atomic nucleus and cause disintegration in the nucleus of the cell. Neutral particles of light are also absorbed by the nucleus of each atom in the body, just as neutral chemical substances are ingested through the membrane into the cell nucleus.

It is well known that the colour of matter changes with the frequency of the energy absorbed by it. Experiments with luminescence show that coloured light can be created merely by exciting a phosphor embedded in a non-conducting material; and the key to this is the propensity of the electrons to jump from one energy state to another. (Ref. 21). Upon absorbing some energy from an outside source, the electron particle spinning around the surface of the atom, "jumps" to a higher or "excited" state. It then jumps back to its normal state to occupy its normal orbit around the nucleus, at the same time re-emitting the absorbed energy. When cells containing these phosphorous atoms get overcharged with this re-emitted energy, a halo in the human aura is produced which is slightly beyond the visible spectrum, yet it is quite clear to anyone who has conditioned his visual pigment in order to see it.

This is not surprising since some plants when illuminated, have cells which fluoresce i.e. the pigment molecules which are energised by the absorption of light, re-emit some of this energy absorbed, which we call *fluorescent* light. The main fluorescing source here is the green chlorophyll and the transfer of electrons is effected by a "resonance process" which creates an *enhancement* effect so as to collect all the energy needed for the photochemical process. Nuclear Evolution follows this natural transmutation of Light energy as it penetrates into every part of the body; each cell being submerged in an ocean of Cosmic energy which acts as an "exciting agent" which cannot be removed once the fluorescent enhancement effect has begun.

THE UNIVERSAL LINK—LIGHT

In Nuclear Evolution the nucleus of each of our *cells* as well as the *atoms* in them should be able to absorb the Light and radiant energies from the Cosmos by a *resonance transfer* of their excitation energy. This transfer of energy which is pumped up to an enhanced level is very similar to that attained by the mitochondrion in the human body and the chloroplast in the plant life. The physical atom which is made up of wave-particles of energy (as opposed to the empty spaces in it awaiting a new impregnation) undergoes oxidation in the body. We can refer particularly to the nucleus of the iron atom which is found in the proteins called cytochromes which are part of the mitochondria and chloroplasts. In the photosynthesis process it is the iron in cytochromes which might act as intermediate carriers of electrons, and link the two systems of oxidation together and connect the photochemical reactions to light. In photosynthesis there is a second-stage pumping of electrons in the submicroscopic structures of the cell, in which the molecule of ATP is formed by the oxidation of a cytochrome; where in the *first stage* the absorption of light causes a reduction, the *second stage* excites it by the reaction of light; it then readily transfers its new excitation to a neighbour by *resonance*. (Ref. 6).

This resonance can be felt in a group as excitement and energy get transferred from person to person. At times one individual's insight bounces to another, then another, and like telepathic pinball, flashes through the whole group.

This energy goes on bouncing through the entire " group force " which makes up the cell just as a pinball machine turns on one light after another. Eventually the migrating energy arrives at an enzymatic membrane at the outer surface, where it is trapped and utilised by a molecule waiting for impregnation at a lower excited state. The inner consciousness of the " group force " of each *cell assembly* is also reflected in the way it attracts and accepts *the atoms* it uses for its own replication. Similarly the inner consciousness of the *atom* is reflected in the way it attracts and accepts the destructive or integrative *cosmic energy* of weak interacting or strong interacting wave-particles. At every hierarchal level there is *choice* and *will* in nature, if only we can look deep enough!

The consciousness of the mind and body relationship is attuned, through resonance transfers, with the consciousness of the whole system, acting as a single unit which is the Lord of all individual cells–You! This consciousness of "wholeness" descends into the dense material fabric of the universe until it reaches the Void at the CENTRE of all rotating systems. It demonstrates itself in nature in the gyratory nature of wave-propagation in cones of energy, and then binds back on itself in order to redeem and lift up the energy we know as matter, into the Self-awareness at the central point of the cone, and with super-reason says to itself: "If I am part of a 'field' of energy and exist, then somewhere the 'whole' field must exist". (Ref. 5b). An act of will, at the

CENTRE of the Void within, brings a NUCLEAR transformation. It is the peculiar arrogance of the human mind and intellect, that thinks this can *only* be done at the *human* level of being, not at the level of the atom, the molecule, the cell, or the individual organ or gland. Yet no one has seen any of these in their natural states, every one of them having been grossly disturbed and attacked by light in order to observe them, or smothered by ionising emulsions and gases in order to record their death pangs. First of all, in order to transcend the prison house of the mind and the limitations of the seer of what IS seen, we must know WHAT we are transcending. This is more difficult to achieve than most people imagine because of the pyramid of knowledge which Man has built up in concepts from the beginning. There are many " realists " who feel that if any foundation stone in this conceptual pyramid is destroyed, the whole edifice falls—and this fall of " defined " reality, like Columbus sailing off the edge of a " flat " world, produces fear and even neurosis.

NUCLEAR TRANSFORMATIONS

The transformation which makes the " part " into a " whole ", brings the awareness at every level of Being, that every atom (also cell, organ, molecule) which makes up a " field " of energy or radiation, is conditioned by its own field; therefore it requires all of us to develop a new logic to transcend our objective and discontinuous personal consciousness. (Ref. 22). Typical of our discontinuous thinking is the current knowledge about the *interactions* in the atomic nucleus and its absorption of Light, which leads eventually to the need to find a particle with " zero " mass and an " infinite life " such as the " photon " and " neutrino ". Surely all theoretical work must come to an end in the invention of such concepts; surely we are spinning our mental wheels when we find the proton can be annihilated completely by the anti-proton, matter annihilated by anti-matter, the universe annihilated by an anti-universe, the person annihilated by an anti-person. If these observations are true in fact, and experiments appear to show that they are, then there must be anti-observer, an anti-body, and such a blissful condition as anti-consciousness. Perhaps some would say this is just another way-of-looking at the " unconscious " since that which is not " conscious of itself " is divided against itself. Because " self-annihilation " has been the road of all the great spiritual prophets, and the most difficult thing for man to master and understand, we might be unconsciously chasing it, even being driven by some primordial drive to chase it, in the search for the self-evident, without being aware that there is nothing in this universe which can or ever will be " self-evident ", excepting consciousness itself.

Let us briefly review WHAT we have to transcend in order to be fully "conscious" of the observer as well as what is observed. We must begin with the so-called nuclear transformations if we are to prove that the UNIVERSE is not matter but music and color.

The *weak interactions* are now recognised as a fourth force of nature. The other three are GRAVITY, ELECTRO-MAGNETIC RADIATION (light), and the STRONG INTER-ACTIONS which hold together the particles of the Atomic Nucleus. The weaker forces associated with the decay and transformation of most of the newly discovered particles of energy, absolutely confound the structure of physical theories, but men being what they are, having built their reputations and made their names, are very frightened to admit that they have built their knowledge on foundations of sand. Just as we cannot see or *observe* Light (we can only observe its inter-actions) so we can only deal with (Ref. 23) the interactions of substantial bodies such as planets, galaxies, etc. through the force of GRAVITY, the strong interactions of NUCLEAR forces, and the fields of energy we call ELECTROMAGNETIC RADIATION, and now the WEAK INTERACTIONS of sub-atomic particles.

At present the list of theoretically inferred particles stands at over thirty–three, but few of the latecomers on this list have any REAL part to play in the constitution of "matter" as man directly experiences it because all of them are unstable, and most of them decay slowly by weak interaction processes which can only be observed in cloud chambers and photographic emul-sions, or "seen" subjectively by mystics with "hidden" senses. The scientist constantly extends his normal visual cortex and nervous system with more sensitive electromagnetic devices such as the ion microscope and radio-telescope, but the images and noises they make are no more " real " than the ordinary senses are. Training of these " ordinary " senses to " feel " and " see " better than " normal " is not yet scientific since the results cannot be effectively published. However, The Institute for the Achievement of Human Potential in Phila-delphia is rapidly bridging this gap.

Until these " hidden " senses such as radiesthesia, divining, clairvoyance, telepathy, etc. are investigated by physical scien-tists with the same diligence which they employ in the search for objective self-evident truths, they will always be dismissed with arrogance through an obsession for a clearly defined reality. Many thousands of years ago, Man, " searching in his heart with his intellect, found the link to the existent in the non-existent " (Ref. 24) and realised that all definitions, although useful tools and builders of concepts, were merely artificial self-projections, throwing out of the subjective imagi-nation and image-making faculties of the human mind. Having gone through the dark ages in between, Man is now discovering again that he can only see in Nature, what is potentially in himself. The sages of ancient China encapsuled this supreme knowledge of the " hidden " world of nature, its rhythms and phases, its CHANGES and mutations, in the book known as the I CHING, often translated as " The Book of Changes ", or " The Book of Mutations ".

Some years ago two brilliant young scientists were awarded the Nobel Prize for the discovery of two wave-particles which shocked physicists into completely new and unusual approaches to the constituency of Matter and the world of form. The law of the conservation of energy was violated and found inoperable in nature when the re-discovery of Tsung Doa Lee and Chen Ning Yang using the hexagrams of the old Chinese Book of Changes, demonstrated that the laws of parity in physics were toppled by the *weak interactions*. The equally fundamental symmetry law was proved untenable at the same time; the symmetry between Matter and Anti-matter had been found to be disregarded by nature. It must be true after all this time, that the very *enduring order* in nature, must rest upon more subtle knowledge than all our theories have *imagined* with our intellects.

The term WEAK interactions as compared to STRONG nuclear forces is of course a dualistic term which means exactly nothing except in a " time bound " domain related solely to the reactions of other particles, and their waves of energy. Strong interactions predominate in high energy collisions such as a proton with a pi-meson, the proton being a stable particle of the atomic nucleus, and the pi-meson being an unstable particle that reinforces the STRONG forces within the nucleus. But the product of such a collision yields two new unstable particles, which, on the time scale of the STRONG interactions in the central nucleus, are incredibly slow. Scientists think of the *electromagnetic* forces as being very weak compared to the STRONG nuclear forces, but the energy of the WEAK INTERACTIONS is about 12 decimal places weaker. This energy is so incredibly weak that its power is nearer to thought energy than anything material; it is now recognised as less material and more mental. (Ref. 25)

A typical WEAK interaction is the decay of a Beta particle; defined as having no independent existence inside the nucleus but created at the instant of emission; the Beta ray is a positively charged electron (new name positron) and the negatively charged Beta ray is identical with an electron. The emission of an electron from the atom entails the change of a neutron into a proton inside the nucleus. (Ref. 10). This type of interaction was first observed to be naturally occuring at the turn of this century by the Curies in the discovery of Radium, which demonstrated the instability of the radioactive elements. Normally when a neutron (which is a non-charged neutral particle) breaks down spontaneously it forms into a positive proton and a negative electron; this electron flies off freely while the positively charged proton stays bound tightly in the nucleus; as a result of this the atom concerned is now transformed into a new species of atom with one more unit of charge. However in the radioactive nucleus the inherent instability of the neutron is allowed to manifest itself and it throws off a positive Beta ray electron because the " group force " of the nucleus creates a surplus positive charge, and negates some of the tension on its surface. It therefore "radiates" its surplus as it decays into the element at the next level.

What else happens when such a spontaneous neutron decays? A new unseen and intangible particle is emitted in the disintegration of the neutron along with the Beta ray, and this is called a neutrino. At this moment there are neutrinos from the Sun and other radioactive stars coursing through our bodies and all of matter, but they are in no scientific sense a part of matter. According to the best scientific authorities (Ref. 25) the neutrino goes off on a journey out of our spontaneous atom to the end of the Universe and does nothing more once it is produced! It passes unreacting through our bodies, through the earth and out the other side without slowing down and is unstoppable; it has a mass of exactly zero! Perhaps all the more easy for the "will" or "thought" to influence it; after all it has no charge, no mass, and infinite lifetime, and therefore no identity or self-hood of its own.

If ANY wave-particle (such as a neutrino or photon) can be said to be "zero" mass with an infinite life (immortal) to go anywhere in the universe and keep on going, then perhaps it is not making much of a claim for a "whole" Man to say humbly that "consciousness" (which is the observer of that wave-particle) can also do the same. Perhaps the ultimate consciousness can also annihilate our timebound limitations and like the little "neutrino" become immortal too.

THE IMPOTENT MIND OF MAN

Perhaps we can now ask on logical grounds how Man can become one with the *ultimate consciousness* in all things, while being so puny a creature he cannot even equal the rays of the Sun, which is but a small micro-star in the manifestation of the great Being of the Universe. To understand this "contact" with an ultimate reality we must take a leap from the type of consciousness which has written the previous fifteen pages. The "jump" must transcend the level of knowledge which depends on past "authorities" and concrete objects. It means going beyond the need for an *outside reality* as the source of all manifestation.

It means direct perception of the link between "matter" and the spheres of consciousness which manifest it. The mind is a labyrinth; we can only come out of it by following the thread of "Life"; a man who has lost this thread is lost in the maze of mind. Such a man is impotent; he builds his tower to heaven with mental promiscuity, forever discovering more building bricks and particles, while the secret constituents of the "glue" which holds them together, lie forgotten or even dismissed in the conceit of the intellect, which says that anything which cannot be defined is not worth talking about. It could be the *only* thing worth talking about, since it is the very source from which all ideas come into our *Consciousness*.

REFERENCES

REFERENCES :

1. Cosmic Rays, by C. B. McCusker, Prof. High Energy Nuclear Physics, Sydney. Publ. Science Journal, Vol. 2, No. 12, Dec. 1966.

2. United States Coast & Geodetic Survey.

3. A Bi-polar Theory of Living Processes, by Dr. George A. Crile, Head of Cleveland Clinic. Publ. Macmillan Co., New York, 1926.

4. The original name of Sarnath was MRIGDAVA or "Deer Park", and is derived from SARANGANATHIA meaning "Lord of the Deer". However the Vedas which were written there call it RISHIPATANA meaning "The place where the rain of the Rishis fell". The Buddha rejoined his disciples at this holy spot to give his first sermon after he was enlightened at the Bo Tree in Bodhi-Gaya, India.

5. (a) Theoretical, experimental and primary work on the foundations of physics and chemistry, by Ludwig Zender, Prof. Extraordinary Physics, Basle University, 1935-38 (Rontgen's collaborator and first constructor of the Rontgen Tube). Publ. Commission for Research into the Creative Faculties of Man, paper No. 6, 1963.

   (b) The Search for the Universal Link. Paper on East-West Flow of Electrons, 20 pp., by Christopher Hills. Publ. Commission for Research into the Creative Faculties of Man, 1962 (private circulation).

   (c) The Duality of Light, Resonance & the Sight-Beam, Paper No. 4. Publ. The Commission for Research into the Creative Faculties of Man.

   (d) Py-Waves, the Cosmic Sound and its relationship to the Spectrum. Publ. The Commission for Research into the Creative Faculties of Man, Paper No. 5, 1963.

6. The Role of Chlorophyll in Photosynthesis, by Eugene Rabinowitch & Govindjee. Publ. Scientific American, July, 1965.

7. Consonant Form in Art & Music, Dr. Donald H. Andrews, Prof. of Chemistry, University of Florida. Publ. The Symphony of Life, Unity Books, U.S.A.

8. A Model of the Nucleus by Victor Weisskopf & E. P. Rosenbaum. Publ. Scientific American, Dec., 1955.

9. The structure of the Nucleus, by Maria G. Mayer, Scientific American, March, 1951.

10. Handbook of Chemistry & Physics, 44th Edition. Publ. The Chemical Rubber Publishing Co., Cleveland, Ohio, U.S.A.

11. Bibliography of the Ionosphere. A Survey by Lawrence A. Manning. Publ. Stanford University Press, 1962.

12. Lebedev Physical Inst. Academy of Sciences of U.S.S.R., Radiofiz : 1.V.42. 2N3. 355-369 by A. V. Gurevic, 1959.

13. Technical Research Institute. National Defence Agency, 1959, Tokyo, Japan, by Y. Inoue. J. Atmos. Terr. Phys. 15 N2 85-88.

14. Giant Molecules in Cells and Tissues, by Francis O. Schmidt. Publ. Scientific American, Sept., 1957.

15. The Mitochrondrion, by David E. Green, Prof. Enzyme Chemistry, University of Wisconsin. Publ. Scientific American, Jan., 1964.

16. Symposium on Oxidative Phosphorylation. Proceedings of F.A.S.E. Biology, Vol. 22, No. 4, Parts 1 and 2, 1963.

17. Atomic Radiation and Life, by Peter Alexander. Penguin Books, 1959.

18. The Role of Light in Photosynthesis, by Daniel I. Arnon. Publ. Scientific American, Nov., 1960.

19. Pions, by Robert E. Marshak. Publ. Scientific American, Jan., 1957.

20. *Do we really see what we think we see? by Prof. Vasco Ronchi, Head, National Institute of Optics, Florence, Italy.

* Supersensonics, Christopher Hills, see Chapters 14-17 on Vision and the Laws of Perspective, University of the Trees Press, 1975.

21. Electro-Luminescence, by Henry F. Ivey. Publ. Scientific American, Aug., 1957.

22. The New Logic, by Christopher Hills. Publ. Commission for Research into the Creative Faculties of Man, Sept., 1963.

23. Models of the Nucleus, by R. E. Peierls, Scientific American, Jan., 1959.

24. Rig Veda X, 129. The Hymn of Creation.

25. The Weak Interactions, by S. B. Treiman. Publ. Scientific American, March, 1959.

LECTURE TAPE REFERENCE LIBRARY
at Centre House, 10A Airlie Gardens
Campden Hill, London W.8

Interview between Dr. F. Woidich and Christopher Hills on Endocrine Glands and Colour Absorption.

Lecture on Meditation by Christopher Hills. (No. 1.)

Lecture on the Inner Mind and Inner Voice by Christopher Hills given at College of Psychic Science.

Lecture on Yogic Trance by Christopher Hills at Caxton Hall, London.

Colour Effects on Psyche by Christopher Hills at Caxton Hall.

Scientific Method and Radiesthesia by Christopher Hills at British Medical Society Radiesthesia Group.

Talk on the Practice of Meditation by Robert Dolling Wells, Encompass Institute.

Evolution of Groups, Seminar talk by Dr. T. Maughan.

The Practice of Homoeopathy and the Way it Works by Dr. T. Maughan.

Gifted Children, Seminar talk by E. J. Burton, M.A.

The Gifted Child, Conference lecture by E. J. Burton, M.A.

The Personal and Impersonal-Universal, by Christopher Hills.

The Annihilation of Time, Seminar talk by J. G. Bennett. Given at Centre.

The Place of Hazard in our Lives by J. G. Bennett. Given at Centre.

The Place of Certainty in Life by Christopher Hills.

Telepathy by Christopher Hills. Given at Caxton Hall.

I Ching or " the Book of Mutations " by Christopher Hills.

Supramental Energies by Christopher Hills.

In Celebration of Good by Christopher Hills. Seminar talk.

Integrating Groups by Christopher Hills. Lecture at Joint Conference.

Reading Faces by Christopher Hills. Lecture at Centre House.

The Lost Word by Christopher Hills. Lecture on the Music of the Spheres.

Deep Meditation and Self Hypnosis by Christopher Hills. Given at Caxton Hall.

Thresholds of Consciousness by Christopher Hills. Lecture Course.

Plugging into the Ultimate Source by Christopher Hills. Lecture Course.

Contacting the Life Force by Christopher Hills. Lecture Course.

Revolution in Thinking by Christopher Hills. Lecture Course.

Imaginative Trip into the Personality by Christopher Hills. Talk at Centre.

Transmitting the Love Instincts by Christopher Hills. Talk at Centre.

Meditation Music by Christopher Hills. Talk at Centre.

Meditation and Telepathy by Christopher Hills. Talk at Centre.

Lecture on Meditation (No. 2) by Christopher Hills. Talk at Centre.

The Sovereignty of the Individual and Nation by Christopher Hills.

The Science of Symbols, Seminar Talk by Dr. T. R. Henderson.

Symbolism, a Lecture by Dr. T. R. Henderson.

Towards Unity in Being, Conference talk by Dr. T. R. Henderson.

Colour Testing of Personality, Lecture by John Damonte.

Radionics and Radiesthesia for the Beginner, Lecture by John Damonte.

The Philosophy of Martinus by Mogens Moller, Martinus Institute, Denmark.

Opening of " Centre " Concert, Introductory Speech by Peter Rendel.

Communication Across Time, Seminar Talk by Dr. Andridja Puharich.

The Basic Tools of Evolutionary Leaps by Christopher Hills.

Biological Radio and the Reception of Nature's Vibrations by Christopher Hills.

The Next Development for Man by Christopher Hills.

The Influence of Imagination on Water by Christopher Hills.

The Management of Imagination in the Growth of Biological Form by Christopher Hills.

Rituals, Divination and Spells and Talismen by Christopher Hills.

Radionics in the World Today by Mrs. A. L. G. Dower, Radionic Association.

The Work of Rudolph Steiner, Lecture by Dr. Alfred Heidenreich at Centre.

The Place of Yoga in the Western World by Peter Rendel, Lecture at Centre.

The Principles of Homoeopathy by Dr. M. D. McCready, Talk at Centre.

The Power of Sound and Mantra by Christopher Hills and Dr. Rammurti Mishra.

Integrative Thinking and Corporate Growth, Lecture at Centre by James McCay.

The Integron Project and the Revitalisation of Industry by James McCay.

LECTURE TAPE REFERENCE LIBRARY
University of the Trees, P.O. Box 644
Boulder Creek, California 95006

PUBLIC LECTURES

TAPE NO.	SUBJECT
O-11	Attachment to Beauty
O-18	Healing
O-19	Drugs
O-20	Habits
O-23	Letting Go
O-27	Skill
O-28	Tantra
O-33	Readiness; Mantra
O-34	Thankfulness
O-35	Psychic Knots
O-38	Initiation
O-39	Ways of Self-evaluating
O-43	Working on Our Patterns
O-47	Chanting & Non-verbal Communication
O-48	The Tree of Life
O-49	The Tree of Life
O-50	The Few Who Get Through
O-55	Good Friday - Crucifixion
O-57	Mother & Father
O-58	Blocks on the Path
O-60	Surrender; Imagination; Ideals; Relativity; the Absolute
O-61	Praise; Purposes; Sincerity; Faith; Moksha; Discipline; Tolerance & Responsibility.
O-62	Doubt; Breath; Light.
O-63	Samadhi; Love & Giving.
O-64	Stubbornness; Desirelessness.
O-65	Real Love; Motives.
O-66	Soul & Being; Use of Emotions.
O-67	Adoration; Foolishness; The Darkness; Intellect.
O-68	Grace; Devotion; Stimulation.
O-69	Suffering; Criticism; Discrimination; Confidence; Arbitrariness; Guilt; Personal God; Love & Caring; Non-Attachment.
O-71	Detachment & Non-attachment (Continued).
O-72	Maintenance; Ruthlessness; One-Pointedness; Proselytizing.
O-73	Humility; Anger; Service.
O-74	Confusion; Time-Saving & Eternal Time.
O-75	Openness; Acceptance.
O-76	Aesthetics; Resignation; Complacency and Contentment; Timing.
O-77	Devotion & Worship.
O-78	Change & Self-mastery.
O-79	The Heart; Sympathy; Empathy Compassion.
O-80	Revolt; Meditation; Intelligence.
O-81	Karma; Duty; The True Nature.
O-82	Dispassion; Emotion; Devotion; Wu Wei.
O-83	Synthesis; Generosity of the Spirit.
O-84	The Rainbow Body.
O-85	Prime Imagination; Space; Universal Consciousness.
O-86	Self-righteousness; Right Action; Change.
O-87	Laws of Probability; Ruthlessness.
O-88	Children; Friendship.
O-89	Christmas; Wonder; Light of Consciousness; Christ's Message.
O-90	Renunciation; Nutrition.
O-91	Honesty; Feeling; Sentimentality.
O-92	The Now; Heavenly Father; Judgementalness.
O-93	Appreciation.
O-94	Acknowledgement.
O-95	Tamas; Living Waters; Harmony.
O-96	Vision.
O-97	Dying Daily.
O-98	Creative Impulse; Music of the Spheres.
O-99	Conception; Centre; Communication.
O-100	Desire; Hare; Responsibility; Work; Rebirth.
O-101	Challenge; Tension; Attention.
O-102	Self-reliance; Faith; Efficiency; Universal Field.
O-103	Resistance; Release; Jealousy;
O-104	Christopher's 50th Birthday Message - Tests of his 1st 50 yrs.
O-105	Our Crucifixions.
O-106	The Nature of Fire; Karma Yoga.
O-107	Aspiration; Adoration; Practical Radiesthesia.
O-108	Delight; Knowing; God's Will.
O-109	Inner Truth; Joyfullness; Emptiness; Entropy; Vitality.
O-110	Contraction; Concentration; Still Small Voice.
O-111	Duty; Guru; Diffusion; Selflessness.
O-112	The Levels of Consciousness.
O-113	A Message for the Press.

LOVE

LOVE AND HEALING

PART 4

ANCIENT AND MODERN SEERS

SHAKESPEARE'S
TRAGIC TYPES
(HAMLET)

SHAKESPEARE'S TRAGEDIES AND THE NUCLEAR EVOLUTION COLOUR LEVELS OF CONSCIOUSNESS

Norah Hills

Our reason for moving from so-called 'real life' to drama is that the great geniuses who wrote the eternal dramas were all clued in to the dynamic of Nuclear Evolution and, with their discrimination and skill, were able to select from the whole lifetime of a character those significant events that were the milestones on the evolutionary journey. Within the span of a three-hour play Shakespeare unfolds for us the whole karmic history of a king and, by virtue of the selectivity involved, we are made aware of the salient qualities, blocks and blindnesses from which the tragedy springs.

We shall use Hamlet, Othello, King Lear and Macbeth to discover how the levels of intellect or the emotions or pride or ambition work, not only in the characters but in ourselves. Some of these drives we may not even have acknowledged before, but when Othello smothers the woman he loves, what is happening inside us? Are we saying, "What a fool, to destroy what he loves and values most in life out of suspicion and jealousy!" Or do we look deeply into ourselves and remember the gnawings of jealousy in our own guts that made us withdrawn, morose and unattractive, helping to destroy a relationship that we held most dear?

In each of the four major tragedies, the central figure has a tragic flaw or failing or blindness which makes it well-nigh impossible for him to deal with the situation in which he finds himself, and the flaw or the block is always related to the level of consciousness from which he is operating. King Lear's pride and his desperate need for confirmation within the context of his court leads him into the folly of hinging his whole future and the division of his kingdom on the expressions of love and devotion from his three daughters. The result is that he is hopelessly duped and exploited by Goneril and Regan, with their eyes firmly fixed on their shares of the realm, and he rejects Cordelia, whose honesty makes it impossible for her to "heave her heart into her mouth" in a specious and false declaration of total devotion. Similarly Othello's Blue level idealism and his readiness and need to believe that all is well make him an easy prey for the wiles of Iago, whose negative Green energies produce a bitter and malicious determination to pull down the Moor by

practising upon his peace and quiet,
Even to madness.

Just as Goneril and Regan exploited their father's need for adulation so Iago, in his own words, admits to exploiting Othello's need for satisfaction and peace.

These examples are just a minute sampling of the rich fund of material for research into the levels of consciousness that lies in the dramas of Shakespeare. These slices of life, from which the petty and confusing details have been eliminated, throw into relief all the basic drives, motives and passions of men and women, in an artistic form which entices us into a world that is larger than life but which is, at the same time, often more graphic, more meaningful and more relevant than the confusing events in our own lives.

Let us dispense with any limited notion that we are dealing with fictional plays. The greatest of all dramatists was in tune with the originator of the Cosmic drama Himself, whose stage is the Universe, and thus he had that sure knowledge that every genius has, that the whole of creation is at his command as dramatic material. The four great tragedies of Shakespeare that will provide our working material in this brief study are soul mirrors for us all and it is as such that we have to use them in exploring the levels of consciousness from which the characters operate. Our own gut level responses to the play's events will be our guide and where we respond most or react most strongly, where we lay our emphasis when we recall the play, there will be our own truth. It is this recognition of our own reality in another that shows us who we really are.

Shakespeare held "as it were the mirror up to Nature - to show virtue her own feature, scorn her own image, and the very age and body of the time his form and pressure;" in other words, he did not expect us just to sit back and be entertained, but to experience with the characters in his plays our own drives and urges, our own fears and failings, our insights and our joys. By making our study of a play a deliberate and conscious exercise in identification, we experience parts of ourselves that we might not have even been in touch with without this particular method of study. Moreover, because the great dramatist lends his characters his own expressive skills, they not only speak in character, but they speak with that additional flair for semantic truth that embellishes their thoughts and emotions just enough to penetrate our understanding more forcefully and more vividly than most of the words that daily pour into our ears and out of our mouths. So it is on account of both their selectivity, their sifting of the dross of life, and their gift of intensely imaginative and colourful speech that we can use great works of literature as research material in our study of Nuclear Evolution.

THE FOUR TRAGIC HEROES

What is a Tragedy, in Shakespearean terms? It is the dramatisation of that part of a person's life in which the karmic lessons are finally learnt and the breakthrough is made to a totally new understanding of the purpose of life and, in particular, of his own life. At the core of the tragic problem is what has been called the "tragic flaw", the area of consciousness where we are not in touch with Reality. In terms of Nuclear Evolution the tragic flaw is the level of consciousness on which we do not function at all, together with a negative functioning from one or more of the chakras which are open. This results in total blindness in certain areas and it is this area of blindness that becomes more and more apparent as the play moves along. We sit in our seats in the theatre and groan and writhe because we can see so clearly that the great protagonist of the tragedy is "digging his own grave", which ultimately he literally does. None of Shakespeare's tragic heroes is alive at the end of the play, which brings us to another element in Shakespearean tragedy. Not only does the hero, in the course of working out his karma, bring about his own downfall or death but he drags numbers of others down with him. By the end of the play the stage is usually strewn with corpses! So Shakespeare chooses for his central figures men and women whose actions and destiny affect a wide spectrum of people and thus the dramas reach a grandeur and a cosmic significance that domestic drama rarely achieves. Macbeth's series of murders involves the whole of Scotland in civil war. King Lear's pride, stupidity and blindness bring suffering not only to those close to him but involve the country in war with a foreign power.

This blindness or tragic flaw is in all of us and although the repercussions of our actions may not be so disastrous as for these kings and princes, we too can spoil the lives and destroy the happiness of others by our refusal or our inability to see ourselves and to change. It is always easy to see someone else's problem and to give advice but do we really penetrate our own? By watching these four great tragedies unfold and observing how the actions and non-actions of the heroes escalate a disastrous chain of events, we are giving ourselves a wonderful opportunity to check our own track record. It does not matter whether we are kings or carpenters, queens or housewives, the basic problem is always the same. Here we are on this planet in a set of circumstances with which we cannot always cope. And why can't we cope? Because we have a blind spot, a tragic flaw.

Take one example from Hamlet. We have two young men with murdered fathers. One takes a matter of ten minutes to discover who his father's slayer is and to draw his sword to kill him. This is Laertes. The other, Hamlet, proceeds to soliloquise, rationalise and torture himself (and others) for the length of the entire drama, until he has dragged himself and six other people into a series of fatal killings. Although he lashes himself verbally for his delaying --

> Why, what an ass am I! This is most brave,
> That I, the son of a dear father murdered,
> Prompted to my revenge by Heaven and Hell,
> Must, like a whore, unpack my heart with words
> And fall a-cursing like a very drab,
> A scullion!

the yellow intellectual drive is strong and he has to prove to himself the validity of the source of his information, the ghost, and even then, having decided that "it is an honest ghost", he fails to act. At one point he even rationalises his unwillingness to get the deed done when he is standing behind the king with the sword in his hand. He uses the argument that if he kills the king as he seemingly kneels at prayer this would inevitably send the king's soul straight to heaven! Picture Laertes in Hamlet's shoes and we would have had no drama. Claudius would have been dead in Act One!

Like Shakespeare's tragic heroes we incarnate on this planet to transcend our own level of consciousness, to discover our particular "tragic flaw" and to open those chakras or centres that are not operating. By watching this opening up process in the plays and by realising the suffering that the hero and others go through in this process, we may glimpse parallels in our own lives. Are we dithering intellectuals or are we nostalgic and stubborn conceptualisers relying on basic assumptions? Or are we caught in the tentacles of jealousy, possessiveness and attachment? The slow and painful deterioration of Othello as these tentacles close about him can make more vivid for us what we may be allowing to happen to ourselves.

If pride and the need for confirmation is our "trip" what happens when we are confronted with these weaknesses in Lear? "What me!" do you say, "Like that arrogant old man trying to get his daughters to make a public demonstration of love just to feed his Ego?" But can you accept that in many subtle ways we do often try to get our loved ones to confirm their love, both in the presence of others and when we are alone with them? Have you ever glowed with satisfaction and pleasure when your child proclaimed, "My Dad's a great guy!" or "I've got the best Mum in the whole world!" Can it be that we, like Lear, look for reassurance and Ego food from our children? Blind and excessive pride in King Lear shook a whole kingdom and brought a foreign army in. The same pride in a domestic context could cause our sons to drop out and our daughters to leave home. The scene is more limited but the repercussions of the "tragic flaw" are just as disastrous.

In the study of the four heroes which now follows, Hamlet will be considered in some detail while the other three studies will be in the form of guidelines for the student's own research into the levels of consciousness as they manifest in the tragedies.

HAMLET

Since 1600 when Shakespeare's "Hamlet" was first performed on the stage, every actor has felt that he could portray Hamlet better than any actor before him, that he had a special insight into the role. This fact may be a clue to understanding the levels of consciousness or the drives that motivate Hamlet's words, actions, and non-action. Hamlet swings and fluctuates between the Yellow, separative, Ego-conscious intellectual level and the Blue, idealistic, conceptual judgemental level, with flashes into the intuitive Indigo level, the image-forming Violet level that colours the expression of his varying moods, and even the impulsive Red and the social Orange levels of consciousness. For some actors the all-important motivating force in Hamlet, that inspires his eloquence but defeats his action, is his intellect that, as Hamlet himself says, causes him to think "too precisely on the event" and so "lose the name of action". For another actor, to whom the emotional content of drama is all-important, the emphasis will be laid on the utter disillusionment that the idealistic (Blue level) Hamlet suffers after his father's death and his mother's "o'er hasty marriage". Such an actor will gear his whole portrayal to a young man who is compelled to go on living in a tasteless, sullied world and, worse still, to have hanging over him a crude Red level task, for which the lethargy of Blue level melancholia makes him totally incapable. So we will see the role played, as it were, behind a dull Blue veil of depression which he disguises by feigned madness, and through which his enthusiastic and responsive intellect breaks occasionally in response to various stimuli, like news of the ghost's appearance, and the coming of the troup of Players. Yet another actor functioning on another level of consciousness, thrilling to the infinite variety, freshness and vividness of the imagery might see Hamlet as a man with a powerful imagination (Violet level) that not only gave eloquence and imaginative colour to his speech but also accounted in part for his dilemma. Those who live on the Violet level experience a terrible conflict between a yearning for an imagined state of bliss and the harsh reality of their actual situation. Hamlet's intense feeling of being misunderstood and condemned to live in an environment totally alien to his true being is hinted at in his opening words:

A little more than kin and less than kind.

It is bitterly expressed in his disgust with the crude sensuality of the court and the current modes of behaviour in Denmark, and it could also be the basic cause of his feigning madness to avoid the exposure of his vulnerable self to insensitive individuals, like Polonius, Rosencrantz and Guildenstern.

There has been much speculation about Hamlet's feelings for Ophelia and here again it seems that Shakespeare has given the actor more latitude than he did with any of the other tragic heroes. Has his mother the Queen's behaviour sickened his attitude to all women? Or had he the Violet level yearning for a greater depth in relating that Ophelia could not give? In sending her "to a nunnery" was he dismissing all women from his life as shams and tricksters, falling far below his Blue level ideals? Or was he prompted by the despair and revulsion against himself that haunts the negative Violet level? This harrowing conflict happens when the gap is experienced between the imagined state of things and the reality.

Whichever way we throw the emphasis, it is clear that we have in Hamlet a unique piece of characterisation and it will be for each one of us, as for the actor, to decide what was in Hamlet the "tragic flaw" that made him unable to face either life or death, unable to act or to tolerate his own inaction, unable to love or to forget love, until life forced him, as it forces us all, to find our real Centre, our True Self and the meaning of life and death.

As with all the other tragedies, the scope of the play is only a small slice of the hero's life, that final phase in which the karmic lessons are finally and painfully learnt, so that by the end of the play the inner eye is opened and all the blocks are cleared away, and at last at the moment of death, consciousness becomes pure. We do not know how often in his earlier life, or even in other lives, Hamlet had reached a similar dilemma. All we know is that when all the torturing mental debating ceases and acceptance takes the place of bitter recriminations, he knows that "the readiness is all"; it is of little importance to him that when death, or "felicity" as he calls it, finally comes, it also brings the accomplishment of the ghost's command.

Before we start our detailed study of Hamlet's evolution as the play unfolds, let us remind ourselves that we have to look for the working of the various drives as not consecutively operating but rather as spheres within spheres within spheres that are all inter-related and intermingling. So we must beware of saying "Now he's being intellectual, now he's Blue level —" and so on. Often within the scope of a single sentence we can, any of us, switch from level to level. Take Hamlet's response to the ghost:

Haste me to know it (my task), that I, with wings as swift
As meditation or the thoughts of love,
May sweep to my revenge.

In three lines he has manifested this urgent need to act in Red level response to a stimulus, the vivid imagery of the Imaginative Violet level and the Blue devotional and emotional urge to avenge a dear father's death. It is true that Hamlet does operate mainly from one or two levels but there is never a rigid dividing line between them. If we immerse ourselves in his world by process of deliberate and conscious identification, we shall experience this non-linear, simultaneous flowing of the basic drives.

We referred just now to Hamlet's state of melancholy and to how it coloured not only his view of life but his mode of expression. This is the negative aspect of the Blue chakra that reveals itself when ideals are shattered. We know ourselves that in a fit of "the blues" everything we see and hear has a tinge of gloom. A dull torpor destroys our dynamic and if we act at all, it is without enthusiasm, if we socialise it is with effort, and our humor tends towards sarcasm and caustic wit. So it is with Hamlet.

Two alternative methods of approach present themselves. One is to show how at different times Hamlet operates from each of the levels and to follow the spectrum through, supported by various examples. The other is to follow the actual sequence of the play itself and to watch the prismatic colour effects as Hamlet draws on different levels of his consciousness. It is the latter method that I have chosen, since it is more in keeping with our study of Nuclear Evolution.

In the opening court scene Claudius, the murderous usurper, has dealt swiftly and diplomatically with various matters before he turns to the solitary figure dressed all in black:

Claudius: But now, my cousin Hamlet and my son . .

Hamlet: (aside) A little more than kin, and less than kind!

Claudius: How is it that the clouds still hang on you?

Hamlet: Not so, my lord, I am too much i' the sun.

Here in four lines lies the clue to a large part of the tragedy's dynamic. The smooth villain confronts and cajoles his mourning nephew, whose grief and possible suspicion can be dangerous and whose uncomfortable wit is an embarrassment for Claudius in an otherwise near-perfect situation. Not only does Hamlet refuse to cast his "nighted colour off", so that he stands out like a sore thumb in the colourful court, but he insists that his black garments are but "the trappings and the suits of woe" and that deep in his heart is a grief that cannot be expressed or demonstrated. Here, as a mere hint right at the start of the drama, is a glimpse of another level that runs like a deep tide beneath all the other colour drives. This is the level of the black, with its desperate desire for self-annihilation. It is to this that Hamlet refers when he talks of "that within which passeth show" and it is this deep and dark area of his consciousness that surfaces only in the soliloquies. Not until the stage is empty can we listen in to Hamlet's agonised despair as he pours it out in the silence:

> O that this too too solid flesh would melt,
> Thaw and resolve itself into a dew!
> Or that the Everlasting had not fixed
> His canon 'gainst self-slaughter!

Here, as in all the soliloquies, is an opportunity as actor or audience to get inside Hamlet and to try to discover why he longs for self-annihilation. Is the sight of his mother with the "satyr" king so painful that he wants to obliterate it forever, and does the shattering of his concept of an ideal marriage warrant this desperate step? Is the complete turning upside down of one of the most stable and beautiful things in his life, his parent's marriage, responsible for his disillusionment with the whole world?

> How weary, stale, flat and unprofitable
> Seem to me all the uses of this world!
> Fie on't, ah fie! 'Tis an unweeded garden
> That grows to seed; things rank and gross in nature
> Possess it merely.

If so, we can see him as a "feeling" type, to whom any change is abhorrent and such a total upheaval quite intolerable. This would put him on the Blue level, but the cry of the shattered idealist could also be that of the Violet level with its aspirations toward certainty in a hazardous world. His mother's act could seem like a betrayal of the dream of a greater union, of which the parents' marriage was only a human prototype. What secret images of man's divine nature were destroyed for Hamlet by his mother's "most wicked speed, to post with such dexterity to incestuous sheets?"

The arrival of his fellow student, Horatio, from Wittenberg swings Hamlet into his social centre which, as a prince, he has obviously had to cultivate, but it is the Orange level tinged still with the bitter feeling of betrayal of the idealistic negative Blue, so that his geniality emerges as sarcastic wit. The wedding of his mother, he tells Horatio, followed close behind the funeral of his father to save expense:

> Thrift, thrift, Horatio! The funeral baked meats
> Did coldly furnish forth the marriage tables!

As soon as Horatio introduces the subject of his father's ghost, Hamlet's keen intellect comes into play and his shrewd and detailed questioning betrays the need of the Yellow level to have everything clear and sequential before a plan of action can be made. His questions come out rat-a-tat like machine gun fire:

> "But where was this?"

> "Did you speak to it?"

> "Hold you the watch tonight?"

> "Armed you say?"

> "From top to toe?"

> "Then saw you not his face?"

"What, looked he frowningly?"

"Pale or red?"

"And fixed his eyes upon you?"

"Stayed it long?"

"His beard was grizzled -- no?"

This is typical Yellow level stuff. If you tell an intellectual any piece of news, be prepared for such a cross examination. For the Indigo intuitive, the news that his father's ghost had appeared would have been enough for him to fill in the rest of the picture without the details; for the Red activist Hamlet's final decision: "I will watch tonight", would have been his first. But the Yellow has to have it all spelled out in sequential order without a single item missing.

The excitement of the news propels him out of his depression into an almost feverish urge to get going:

Would the night were come!

He is in the same excited state when he reaches the battlements and in his ranting, in true Yellow level style, about the depravity and over-indulgence of contemporary life in Denmark, he loses track of himself in an avalanche of parenthetical phrases which are delivered with a nervousness that betrays his apprehension. With the ghost's entrance he becomes a desperate man of action, defying anyone to prevent his following the ghost, but Hamlet is never operating solely from this Red level.

The aftermath of the ghost's full story is sheer horror and a tottering of the rational mind, so much so that Hamlet grabs his tablets to steady himself by writing down an intellectual observation on his uncle:

That one may smile and smile and be a villain.

This way of imposing order on the chaos of emotion is typical of the intellectual, who cannot bear for long to be caught up in a blurry uncontrolled state of mind. By putting the feelings into words and concepts, the mind lays claim to what, a moment before, was the province of the feelings.

Thus reeling under the shock of what he has heard, Hamlet attempts to galvanise himself into a total commitment to revenge. But already the crude physical aspect of the task gives way to idealistic rejection of the old delights in books and study and a reiteration of the ghost's command "Remember me." The Red level urge for action Now, gives way to Yellow level formulation of a plan.

Both of Hamlet's main drives (Blue and Yellow) are inhibitors of action. The Yellow intellectual level must always plan before acting and often spends so long on the precise planning that nothing manifests. The Yellow also always sees everything as a "problem" and even though Hamlet's disenchantment with a previously idealised world comes from the Blue level, his elaboration on the problem to Rosencrantz and Guildenstern arises from the Yellow intellect. Melancholy and Black depression are also inhibitors of action and Hamlet's initial burst of enthusiasm for immediate action gives way first to bitter regret that the onus of revenge has fallen on him. Then, sensing his own instability, he elects to put an "antic disposition" on and to feign the madness that so nearly engulfed him after the meeting with the ghost. Here Hamlet is showing an awareness of how the Black undercurrent that is affecting all his thoughts and actions could easily throw him into a state of real madness. So it is with all those who sense the imminence of the Void, until the realisation dawns that to go through it is to be eternally free.

Psychologically what we are witnessing here is a sensitive soul highly evolved in the higher centres of the intellect, the conceptual idealism, the intuition and the imagination, (that is on the Yellow, Blue, Indigo and Violet levels) being confronted with a task that demands crude Red level physical action, a killing in cold blood, something of which a man of this nature is practically incapable, except on the spur of the moment before thoughts or doubts or qualms have had a chance to operate. So his head may tell him "This thing's to do", while his finer feelings and his sensitivity make the task utterly repulsive.

This is the situation that occurs in all the tragedies; the hero inevitably finds himself in a set of circumstances with which he cannot cope. Put Laertes in the same situation and the clear-cut issue of revenge is not a problem at all.

Hamlet's words to Rosencrantz and Guildenstern describe his state:

> I have of late - but wherefore I know not - lost all my mirth, forgone all custom of exercise; and indeed it goes so heavily with my dispositon that this goodly frame the earth seems to me a sterile promontory; this most excellent canopy, the air, look you, this brave o'er hanging firmament fretted with golden fire, why it appeareth no other thing to me than a foul and pestilent congregation of vapours.

Was there ever a more perfect description of Black depression expressed as an intellectual problem by one whose idealised view of life has suddenly been shattered? Here again, however, it is possible to ascribe to Hamlet a vision of Man's divinity that outstrips idealism and gives him the Violet level's insight into the eternal order and enduring nature of existence:

> What a piece of work is man! How noble in reason! How infinite in faculties! In form and moving how express and admirable! In action how like an angel! In apprehension how like a god!

Since Shakespeare himself worked from this level of consciousness it is inevitable that his own grand image of reality should find expression from time to time in his dramas, through a sympathetic character. And this greater cosmic view of existence could conceivably have been glimpsed if not sustained by Hamlet, and so have caused him the despair at the obvious disparity, in his own life, between the vision and the reality, a despair that put him constantly in touch with the "sacred space" of the Black level.

Hamlet's first encounter with the strolling company of players rouses him into temporary enthusiasm. This is the Yellow level love of change and novelty. Blue level recollections of the past spark off his recitation of a dramatic speech and for awhile his horrific task is forgotten and we glimpse the buoyant young man that could have been Shakespeare himself. But as soon as he is alone the very cause of his temporary pleasure becomes the trigger of his anguished self-abuse. The player can weep for Hecuba, a queen of a thousand years ago, but Hamlet has done nothing to avenge a murdered father.

> What's Hecuba to him, or he to Hecuba,
> That he should weep for her?

From what level is he coming now? Great floods of banked-up frustration and Blue level emotion, the effects of grief, remorse and disillusionment, pour out in gushes of graphic images that draw on the Violet level imagination for expression. Experience with Hamlet the revulsion that he feels for his uncle, coupled with disgust that he cannot galvanise himself into Red level action, only "unpack (his) heart with words." Can you link this self-torturing with any experience in your own life when, knowing what has to be done, you still delay?

By pausing at this point to ask ourselves a few self-confronting questions, we may avoid the pitfall into which many self-righteous critics of Hamlet's so-called "procrastination" have fallen. They join him in his self-condemnation, but neither they nor he himself are really in touch with what is operating within the psyche of a person who cannot galvanise himself into action. Honest answers to these questions may give us a greater empathy with Hamlet's deep-rooted problem and greater patience with his futile verbiage:

1) What in your life has needed action which you have not taken?

2) Why have you delayed?

3) Is there a deeper reason for the delay, that stems from a conflict between your will and some inhibiting, half-understood fear of the consequences?

Although by the end of the soliloquy Hamlet has at least a plan of action, he is still exasperated at his own ineffectiveness, and he is obviously undergoing that self-torturing regret that we feel when we have avoided an obligation. The total commitment and involvement of others in their calling or their cause reproaches him and we sense the Indigo level of his consciousness at work that so vividly envisages a future action that it feels the act to have been already accomplished. The result is this self-torturing anguish at his inability to come to grips with the demands of the immediate need of manifestation now, in the present.

At the end of the soliloquy Hamlet devises his scheme to trap the king. Here the Yellow intellectual planning level comes into play and not only rationalises his dilatoriness with doubts of the ghost's authenticity, but is stimulated by the cleverness of his own brain in contriving the trap.

In the famous "To be or not to be --" soliloquy, Hamlet himself not only describes the inhibiting effect of too much thinking:

> And thus the native hue of resolution
> Is sicklied o'er with the pale cast of thought,
> . . .

but he actually demonstrates it by swaying back and forth between disgust with life and fear of the unknown.

Much has been written on the interpretation of this soliloquy, but whichever way we take it "the dread of something after death" stands as the inhibiting factor that "puzzles the will" and numbs the power to act. What is it in Hamlet and what is it in us that holds back the creative initiating thrust of positive action and causes

> . . . enterprises of great pith and moment
> With this regard their currents (to) turn awry
> And lose the name of action?

Fear and doubt can affect and negate every level of consciousness, as we have seen in an earlier section of this book. But is Hamlet's expressed fear of the unknown used here as yet another excuse for doing nothing? Another Yellow level rationalisation for inaction?

Or is "the undiscovered country, from whose bourn no traveller returns" the Black level's fear of its unknown self that paralyses all action?

It is interesting at this point to compare the Hamlet of the soliloquies with the Hamlet who jibes at Polonius or who entertains the players or feigns madness in his rantings at Ophelia. Perhaps his words to Horatio give us the best clue to his state of being and to our own when life's batterings make us swing from mood to mood, and the real challenges cannot be met from a calm centre within. When he tells Horatio,

> For thou hast been
> As one, in suffering all, that suffers nothing;
> A man that Fortune's buffets and rewards
> Hast ta'en with equal thanks?

we are reminded of Kipling's poem "If":

> When you can meet with triumph and disaster
> And treat those two impostors just the same . . .

and the message seems to be that the all-important factor is detachment. Horatio has this detachment and so he provides an excellent example of the positive Green level of consciousness with its sense of inner security. This Hamlet lacks. He is terribly attached to his own egocentric intellect, to the memory of a dearly-loved hero father and to the idealised picture of the relationship between his mother and father, which has been totally destroyed by her rush into marriage with his bestially sensual uncle. As he talks to Horatio before the play, he speaks of himself as a pipe, played upon by Fortune's finger, "to sound what stop she please."

This is a perfect image for that state of consciousness in which inner peace is lost and we become "passion's slave", or, in other words, we flounder at the mercy of conflicting emotions, resolves and revulsions, out of touch with the nuclear centre that is our real being. In the tumult of this tragic drama of "Hamlet" only Horatio remains "on centre", like the eye of the hurricane. There is a clue to Hamlet's essential nature here too when he tells Horatio that he has always been drawn to his honesty and stability, so we catch a glimpse of a Hamlet that may again and again have been "thrown" and disturbed by "problems" that shook his emotional being and could not be solved because his brilliant intellect fed on their analysis. This present situation is the culmination of a string of "tests" that have challenged Hamlet to find his own inner certainty and to operate from a still centre which he yearns to discover.

Soon the play within the play confirms Hamlet's suspicions: the king rises and calls for "lights!" as he witnesses the replay of the murder he committed, and Hamlet, in a state of delirious excitement, leaps around in jubilation composing trivial little rhymes. His ecstatic bravado is thrown into relief by Horatio's contrived calm with which he tries, ineffectively, to steady Hamlet. So Horatio stays with reality and Hamlet allows himself a release of nervous tension, drawing on his fertile imagination and his intellectual wit, but at no point showing any inclination to follow up in sober fashion on the confirmation of the king's guilt that he has just gained.

Guildenstern comes to tell him that his mother wishes to speak with him and then unwisely tries to probe the source of Hamlet's deranged behaviour and his inner sorrows. It is then that Hamlet hands him the recorder and tells him to play it. When Guildenstern protests that he has no idea how to play it, Hamlet in his response gives us a glimpse into his suffering . . .

> "Why, look you now," he says, "how unworthy a thing you make of me! You would play upon me; you would seem to know my stops; you would pluck out the heart of my mystery . . . and there is much music, excellent voice, in this little organ, yet cannot you make it speak. 'Sblood do you think I am easier to be played on than a pipe? Call me what instrument you will, though you can fret me, you cannot play upon me."

This speech of Hamlet's that springs from the Violet level both in its imagery and in the despair at finding no one to understand his deeper being, is quoted in full because it not only reveals the pain that non-communication can bring to a sensitive soul, but in these words lie the essence of much of the world's pain that is caused by total unawareness that we all live on different levels of consciousness. We talk *at* each other, probe each other, bully each other, but rarely listen to the music of each other's souls. Rosencrantz and Guildenstern are typical of thousands of people who function only on the Red and Orange, physical and social levels, yet assume that they can make deep contact with others whose beings express and resonate with the finer and deeper idealistic Blue, intuitive Indigo and imaginative Violet levels. For years, in my own marriage, I, with my firmly established Blue level concepts, failed to listen to the sweet inner music that was playing from my husband's soul that was at home in the realms of the intellect and imagination. I just assumed that I knew where he was coming from. In the whole court of Denmark only Horatio is in tune with the "sweet prince -". When Nuclear Evolution becomes not a theory but a daily practice in our lives, then great and sensitive beings will no longer suffer at the hands of those who ignorantly believe that what they themselves experience is all there is to know.

To return to the sequence of the play, Hamlet is on his way to visit his mother when he comes upon Claudius ostensibly praying and draws his sword ready to kill him, but once again something holds him back and he does not act. Is it revulsion at the crude physical act, backed up by rationalisations that Claudius murdered his father without his having a chance of confession, while he was sleeping off a heavy meal? According to current religious beliefs this meant Hamlet's father would have suffered the pangs of hell. If Hamlet now kills Claudius in the act of prayer, his soul could go straight to heaven. As it happens, the Yellow level rationalisation is unwarranted; the king is incapable of real prayer:

> My words fly up, my thoughts remain
> Words without thoughts never to heaven go.

says Claudius after Hamlet leaves.

The interview with his mother opens for Hamlet the floodgates of resentment against the woman he once idealised and set up on his conceptual pedestal together with his father as the perfect example of marital bliss. So threatening and ominous is his behaviour when he enters her room that Polonius, who is spying on them behind the curtain, shouts out for help and attracts the deadly sword of Hamlet. In one surging moment Hamlet hopes that he has killed the king, for by now he knows himself well enough to realise that for him the Red level act will only be done on the spur of the moment, without the inhibiting doubts, fears and excessive analysis of circumstances, that have had him hamstrung so far. But he is not to be diverted from his outpouring of disgust and resentment against his mother. The disillusioned and judgemental Blue level, whose devoted love and peaceful satisfaction have been shattered and sullied by such an act

> That blurs the grace and blush of modesty,
>   makes marriage vows
> As false as dicer's oaths,

now draws on all his eloquence and imagination to confront the cause of all his misery. Image after image, drawn from his very vital Violet centre, crashes down on the head of the horrified queen. Forcing her to look at portraits of her two husbands he demands:

> Have you eyes?
> Could you on this fair mountain leave to feed,
> And batten on this moor?

And when she squirms and implores him to stop, he spits out the final words of disgust against the woman who has tainted all womanhood for him:

> Nay but to live
> In the rank sweat of an enseamed bed,
> Stewed in corruption, honeying and making love
> Over the nasty sty . . .

The ghost's express commands were to avenge his death and to contrive nothing against his mother. And what is he now doing? Lambasting his mother, from the Blue, judgemental level, with his own revulsion, and leaving "the dread command" unheeded. The appearance of the ghost at this point, "to whet thy almost blunted purpose", represents Hamlet's own returning self-reproach, and out of it comes a compassionate reasoning that combines a sweet tolerance with a soundness that could have been his normal regular state of being in less stressful days. There is understanding and quiet forebearance now, as if the earlier violence of deed and words had purged his soul and clarified his awareness. He advises his mother to abstain from her sensual indulgences:

> Refrain tonight
> And that shall lend a kind of easiness
> To the next abstinence.

There is a gentle persuasiveness in his tone and real regret at Polonius' death. But the mere thought of his uncle renews the bitterness, especially when he realises that the queen will tell Claudius everything, in spite of her protestations; sarcastically he counsels her:

> 'Twere good you let him know;
> For who that's but a queen, fair, sober, wise,
> Would from a paddock, from a bat, a gib,
> Such dear concernings hide?

This scene with his mother could unlock Hamlet's soul for us and throw light on something deep within us all. When we pour out vituperation, scorn, disgust, anger or recriminations on the head of another, what is really going on? When we shout at a child for doing something that we have already asked him not to do many times, who are we shouting at? Where is the frustration? Is the child a part of our own consciousness and is it our own inability to communicate effectively that makes us scream? Or do we see our own rejected traits mirrored for us by the child?

When Hamlet hurls abuse at his mother, is he bawling at the woman who bore him or at some part of himself that has never experienced fulfilment in the physical expression of love? Has the Red sensory, sexual drive in Hamlet been so inhibited that it surfaces now as sensual garbage hurled at his mother? Having brought his mother to a state of seeming penitence and remorse, he says goodnight and she asks him what she shall do:

Hamlet: Not this, by no means, that I bid you do:
        Let the bloat king tempt you again to bed;
        Pinch wanton in your cheek; call you his mouse;
        And let him, for a pair of reechy kisses,
        Or paddling in your neck with his damned fingers,
        Make you to ravel all this matter out . . .

His obsession with crude sensuality came out in the short dialogue with Ophelia before the play and probably motivated his rejection of her and coloured his bitter words in the "Get thee to a nunnery" scene.

If we are whatever obsesses and sickens us, what was latent in Hamlet that produced these crude Red level verbal insults? Suppressed and thwarted sexual desire? Are we to add now to the complex fabric of Hamlet's personality those very same sensual urges that he condemns in Claudius and is repulsed by in his mother?

This seems a good point at which to confront and examine a little further Hamlet's handling of his sexual energies and his relation to the Red level of consciousness. We have said that he was only capable of Red level action on the spur of the moment; but there is something deeper at work in his pounding of his mother and in his scorn and disgust for the sensuality and indul- gence that goes on at the Danish court. Then there is his relation- ship with Ophelia, which he cuts off on the excuse, to himself, of dedicating all his energies to the task of revenge. But in rejec- ting her he has to slander all womanhood. Why? Perhaps if we recall that his state of melancholy started before his meeting with the ghost, it will become more evident that the cause of his depres- sion lay mainly, as his mother knew, in the "over hasty marriage". What was the relationship between Hamlet and his mother? Was there an Oedipus complex at work that allowed him to tolerate the tasteful and romantic relationship between his mother and father, but not the powerfully sexual and, as he saw it, incestuous mating with his uncle?

Flowing deep beneath the more obvious fluctuations between the Blue and the Yellow and the Violet levels of his consciousness, there seems to be in Hamlet that volcanic energy that for any human being can either give meaning and manifestation to all the other levels or, if suppressed, can sour the whole of life and love. This leads us to ask ourselves whether it was not only the Yellow and Blue level inhibitors that prevented action but also this submerged and seething anger and disgust, which is finally poured out, like waters from a dam, in the interview with his mother. This scene offers another catharsis, too, when he plunges his sword into Polonius, thinking it is the king. As he "lugs the guts into the neighbor room" we experience something more real and more in touch with the undiscovered country not of death but of Hamlet's "other Self". It is this unknown Self that we all have to face if we are to go through the Black or "the dark night of the soul", and Hamlet is confronted here first with his own blatant defiance of the ghost's command to leave his mother "to heaven," and then with himself as a murderer of old Polonius. From this point on there is a ruthlessness and a greater decisiveness in Hamlet:

> From this time forth
> My thoughts be bloody or be nothing worth.

he proclaims as he leaves for England, and all his actions on the trip are manifestations of this decision. On his return from England, having discovered that he is capable of effective action, Hamlet makes straight for the court to take his revenge on Claudius, for which, he now tells Horatio, he now has ample cause:

> Does it not, think'st thee, stand me now upon—
> He that hath killed my king and whored my mother,
> Popped in between the election and my hopes,
> Thrown out his angle for my proper life,
> And with such cozenage -- is't not perfect conscience
> To quit him with this arm?

Not only is there this new awareness of his Red level drive for action, but we sense too a mellowness, a discovery of his Green level heart that has only been glimpsed in his warm praise for Horatio and in his rather pathetic little poem and letter to Ophelia. Although the critical, intellectual Yellow is there in his graveyard speculations there is a wistful warmth in his recollection of Yorick, the court jester, and although he "forgets himself" in the grave with Laertes, he is swiftly to regret his actions and his words:

> But I am very sorry, good Horatio,
> That to Laertes I did forget myself;
> For by the very image of my cause I see
> The portraiture of his.

Most poignant of all are his outpourings of his love for Ophelia:

> I loved Ophelia. Forty thousand brothers
> Could not (with all their quantity of love)
> Make up my sum.

This expression of love has been dismissed and questioned as ' Yellow level verbiage ', but if we allow ourselves to get into Hamlet's world we experience here an outburst of deep and genuine feeling that he had forced himself to suppress and which Polonius, by his meddling, had forced Ophelia to doubt. Looking back at his little poem to Ophelia we find the same anguished expression of deep feeling: "O dear Ophelia, I am ill at these numbers (verse); I have not art to utter my groans, but that I love thee best, O most best, believe it . . . " At last we have a Hamlet who is in touch with his real feelings, a Hamlet who is no longer contorting himself to fit an obligatory pattern, and as he gets more and more in touch with his real self we lose our irritation with his vacillations and respond to his new certainty. He knows that he must confront and destroy Claudius and he knows that his fears of the "undiscovered country" are unfounded. Talking to Horatio of his instinctive doubts about Rosencranz and Guildenstern on board the ship to England, he tells how he could not sleep and how this prompted him to sneak a look at their commission from King Claudius. He sees in this a prompting beyond his own intelligence:

> There's a divinity that shapes our ends
> Rough-hew them how we will;

and it is to this divinity that Hamlet now surrenders as he consents to what he intuitively knows will be the fatal duel with Laertes.

We move now into the final scenes of the play and also into the final breakthrough in Hamlet's awareness of the real meaning of life and death and of his own part in the cosmic drama. What has brought him to this awareness? Is it his own escape from death, once by foiling the king's plot to have him killed and again in his survival of the pirates' attack on his ship? Or is it that he has reached the point that we all have to reach when there is no choice but to change, when our will *has* to become one with the cosmic will? All his attempts to do what the ghost (his conscience) urged have ended in nothing, but he senses now a guiding intelligence and is prepared to submit to it. Yellow level rationalisations, Blue level disillusion, Indigo level detachment from the Now and even the Black despair fall away from him now. That the realisation of the need to surrender comes too late to save the physical lives of himself and the others who die in the final imbroglio, is the essence of the tragic dilemma, in which the transformation of consciousness or the breakthrough in the soul's awareness involves the death of the physical body.

In the final scene, Hamlet's old "resting" colours -- the Blue and the Yellow, are expressed in the tender reminiscences about the court jester and in his witty word play with Osric, the king's messenger. But the real change is most clearly seen when he and Horatio are alone and Hamlet's intuition (Indigo level) tells him that the duel with Laertes has more to it than sword play. Horatio tells him to follow his intuition and call off the contest, but Hamlet has come to terms with his fears and sees only the need for acceptance of what must be:

> If it be now, 'tis not to come; if it be not to come, it will be now; if it be not now, yet it will come: the readiness is all. Since no man has aught of what he leaves, what is't to leave betimes? Let be.

This is a far cry from "the fear of something after death" and the cowardice for which he has reproached himself throughout the play. From a quiet center within himself he asks for Laertes' forgiveness, blaming his distracted state of mind for his sudden slaying of Polonius and his treatment of Ophelia:

> Sir, in this audience,
> Let my disclaiming from a purposed evil
> Free me so far in your most generous thoughts
> That I have shot my arrow o'er the house
> And hurt my brother.

At what point did the change take place in Hamlet? That is a question as difficult to answer as it is when the change takes place in ourselves. Suddenly there is a freeing of the spirit; despair falls off like a black cloak and the futility of past doubts and fears is blatantly apparent. The "dark night of the soul" has passed and the dawning of a new consciousness is upon us. So it was with Hamlet. We can theorise about the cathartic effect of his confrontation with his mother or the reestablishment of self-confidence that resulted from his thwarting of the king's plot to have him killed, but ultimately, for Hamlet, as for everyone, the cause and nature of the breakthrough remains a part of the mystery and beauty of the Cosmic Intelligence working through us all.

If we follow step-by-step Hamlet's interchange with Laertes in these last minutes of his life, we sense a quiet serenity that comes only from awareness of a vaster context of life and death which dwarfs the paltry tricks and contrivings of men until they appear of no account, even though they may bring about death.

Not only is there a calm acceptance of his own death, but a dignity and strength that sees all the levels of consciousness clearly and prevents Horatio from drinking of the poisoned cup, so that he may tell the true story behind what must seem bewildering events to those who know nothing of the reality of how his father died. Note that death itself is now "felicity" or blissful joy. "Absent thee from felicity awhile," he says to Horatio, and in his final words his concern is not with his own dying but with assuring a wise succession to the throne of Denmark.

At the last the slaying of Claudius is an unimportant incidental event, although it has monopolised so much of Hamlet's thinking during most of the drama. So what is the main dynamic of the tragedy? It is the same dynamic that governs the life of every man and woman in their search for the rainbow body. Blocked on his journey of self-discovery by Blue level disillusioned idealism and Yellow level prevarication and rationalisation, he finally breaks through to a clarity of total vision and self-integration with the Cosmic impulse. And here not only Shakespeare's dramatic genius but his insight into the enlightened experience becomes clearly evident. Note how this self-realised Hamlet no longer unpacks his heart with words, and when for a moment he does rant at Laertes in the grave and, as he says, "forgets himself", he knows what he has done.

Through identification with Hamlet or Lear or Othello, but most of all with Hamlet, we live through the spiritual transformation of different levels of consciousness that is the essence of Nuclear Evolution and of all the great artistic creations of genius that have as their high motive the dynamic behind the oracle at Delphi:

Man, know thyself.

FOOTNOTE: If this work on Hamlet and on ourselves is to have real value it would be well to reread the play at this point, or at least to reread those scenes in which Hamlet himself appears. We need to become the potential actor of the part and to decide now on our interpretation of the role. Hamlet, more than any other character in Shakespeare, holds the mirror up to us all and we identify with him according to our natures. If I have stressed the disillusioned Blue level idealist it is because I function mainly from the Blue level. You may feel a stronger identification with Hamlet the intellectual, who prevaricates and rationalises himself into a fatal series of procrastinations; or with Hamlet the Violet level cosmic imaginer, whose vision of the world and of man's spiritual potential has been devastatingly destroyed. Is Hamlet one of those characters through whom Shakespeare himself speaks most clearly and is Hamlet voicing for him the exasperation of every visionary genius for whom the vision and the reality remain forever far apart? There are some who see Hamlet as a dithering self-obsessed philanderer, indulging himself in verbal and emotional orgies, and he sees himself this way too at times as operating from the Indigo level that fails to bring the intuited event into present reality. Then there is the Black level's desire for self-annihilation that first presents itself to Hamlet as an urge to kill his body, but is later understood for what it is, "the dark night of the soul" that precedes the death of the Ego and the birth (for Hamlet at the end of the drama) of a new and fearless being. Whatever we see in the other is in ourselves. "You are whatever disturbs you," says Nuclear Evolution, and we look at everything from a flower to a tragic hero through the filter of our own level of consciousness.

SELF STUDY USING
KING LEAR
MACBETH
OTHELLO

THE NUCLEAR EVOLUTION PROCESS

A Practical Method of Research and Self-Study
Using Three of Shakespeare's Tragedies:

> King Lear
>
> Macbeth
>
> Othello*

In our exploration of the character of Hamlet we used the method of travelling with Hamlet on the last stage of his evolutionary journey, step-by-step. In our study of the other three great tragic heroes we shall use a method that throws the onus of the study onto the student, and provides guidelines in the form of references to the text with brief commentary and particularly salient quotations.

This is not an academic study and its purpose is not to enable students of English literature to get better grades in that subject, but to use the characters as mirrors for the experience of their own evolution, to spark off responses in the psyche to the motivations, actions and words of these larger-than-life, yet extremely life-like, tragic heroes. In so doing we fulfill Shakespeare's original purpose in writing the plays, "whose end, both at the first and now, was and is, to hold as it were, the mirror up to nature: to show virtue her own feature, scorn her own image, and the very age and body of the time his form and pressure." In re-quoting these words of Hamlet that gave Shakespeare the chance to voice his own ideas, I want to stress that just as Shakespeare felt that the actor's job was to give a recognisable portrayal of the human virtues and vices and emotions, so the purpose of the study program outlined here is to encourage the student of life to use the dramatic material as a typological tool for self-discovery. In order to make this identification exercise effective we have to rid ourselves once and for all of the misconception that because these characters are kings or generals and their lives and actions affect whole nations, their situations cannot be in any way comparable

---

* Although it will have been possible to follow the essay on Hamlet without having studied the play, it will not now be possible to use the Guidelines on King Lear, Othello and Macbeth if you have no acquaintance with these three plays.

with our own. Only the context of their lives is remote from ours, not the motivations, emotions, fears and follies. Lear could be any old father who thought his children loved and respected him enough to take over his business and home in exchange for looking after him for the remainder of his days. Macbeth's ambition, his fears and his scruples could be those of any man tempted to commit a crime of any size against his conscience for selfish gain. "Othello" comes nearer to the classification of domestic drama and it is easy to identify with his jealousy and self-torture once Iago has planted the seeds of suspicion.

Behind the stories of these dramas lies an evolutionary pattern that can be traced in the life of nearly every man and woman, and if we can get in touch with this pattern in our own lives we can recognise it at work in the dramas and conversely by seeing its tragic consequences there, we can confront our own pattern at its present stage. Macbeth did not suddenly become power-seeking and Othello's jealousy does not belong only to the part of his life covered by the play. Lear, in the words of one of his daughters, had "ever but slenderly known himself." As a result of these patterns and the blocks or blindness that cause them, we move nearer and nearer to the crunch point or ultimate self-confrontation in our lives. Hints of possible consequences of our actions and non-actions are dotted along our evolutionary journey, but we ignore them until their accumulating strength forces a confrontation. It has actually been said by wise men that we get three intuitive promptings as to the right course of action in any situation. This you can check out in your own life. We shall look for these patterns in the three heroes, but it is even more important that we search them out in ourselves if we are to recognise the process. Then we shall bring our own validation to the Nuclear Evolution process as it works itself out in the tragedies, for we are all potential tragic heroes. We all have a tragic flaw, a blindspot uniquely our own, which others can easily recognise but which makes it seemingly impossible to deal with the circumstances into which life propels us. For some it is a minor defect that only slightly disturbs their life and other lives around them. For others it is a deep-rooted fault that has to be agonisingly confronted when it brings them right up to the brink of disaster. To get in touch with this flaw in ourselves, as we vicariously experience it in the tragic hero, is to use the drama as an evolutionary tool in our own life's work toward achieving self-mastery.

Taking each play in turn we shall now ask certain questions which will act as guidelines for our research into the tragic process and into the working out of Nuclear Evolution, which is the stripping away of the Ego or the lower self until at last the Nuclear Being or the True Self is revealed. For Hamlet this came with his recognition that

> There's a divinity that shapes our ends,
> Rough-hew them how we will,

and since we all struggle through innumerable incarnations to carve out or "rough-hew" our destinies, he voices the realisation that in the end comes to us all, namely that "if it be now 'tis not to come, if it be not to come it will be now; if it be not now, yet it will come. The readiness is all."

To set the scene for our study we shall compare and contrast two pictures of the tragic hero in each play. One will show him at the start of the play, the other as he is at the end. In between is the evolutionary process at work, whereby the layers of Ego and personality are relentlessly shredded off to expose levels of consciousness not known before and the essential being, the "other self" that we all fear to face. For Hamlet it is exposed in the scene with his mother; for Lear, his blind folly and his arrogance are flung back at him by the storm winds, until he is driven to madness. Macbeth confronts his towering ambition too late, but it puts him in touch with what he has lost, namely peace in this life and his immortal soul. Othello, caught in the toils not only of Iago's wiles but of his own fatal tendency to believe that men are what they seem, allows "honest Iago" to play upon his credulity until he kills what he most loves.

KING LEAR

When Charles Lamb said "King Lear is essentially impossible to act on the stage" he voiced the feeling of many who, while not agreeing with him, yet see this tragedy as larger that life-size and perhaps the most painful to witness. The earlier pre-Shakespeare dramatic versions of the story gave the play a "happy ending", showing Lear reconciled with Cordelia and regaining his throne. Shakespeare has relentlessly allowed the tragic sequence to reach its inevitable conclusion and in his non-avoidance of the final calamities has given depth and beauty to the real message of all his tragedies, namely that physical death is insignificant in the vaster context of man's evolution toward full realisation of his nuclear self. In other words Lear's physical death, like Hamlet's or yours or mine, is of little importance compared with the breakthrough from negativity to positive perception, from blindness to sight and from darkness of self obsession and self pity into the light of a purified and selfless consciousness.

Using the play "King Lear" for our research into the levels of consciousness and the process of Nuclear Evolution, we are presented with mainly Morality style prototypes in the other characters who contribute to the unfolding of the story, for the most part, from an inflexible, unchanging and relentlessly uncompromising part of their being. So Lear himself, as he goes through the process of transformation, stands out like a huge giant among these types who remind us of the Virtues and Vices in the old religious dramas. For example, in the opening scene of the play we have the virtuous truth-speakers Kent and Cordelia on one side and the vicious flatterers and manipulators Goneril and Regan on the other. Like an archetypal representation of Man himself Lear strides the stage and the other characters with whom he interacts seem almost like externalisations or mirrors of his changing moods.

For purposes of this study we shall concentrate only on Lear and the refining that he goes through. His first appearance in the play, heralded by trumpets and holding in his hand a map of his vast territories, presents us with a bold portrayal of the Orange level of consciousness. Tremendously conscious of the power, prestige and authority represented both by his throne and by his lands, he proceeds to arrange to maintain his kingly title but to hand over the burden of government for his remaining years. His three daughters and their husbands will take over the management of his kingdom and provide him with a place in their homes for the rest of his days. In return for their expression of love and devotion in the full court he will dispose at a stroke of his kingdom and estates:

> With shadowy forests and with champains riched
> (plains enriched)
> With plenteous rivers and wide-skirted meads . . .

Here on a grand scale is the Orange level awareness not only of the value of great possessions in the social and political context, but also of dramatic demonstrations for the benefit of the assembled court. In his demand for the declaration of love from his daughters is the insistence on their conforming to the norms of filial behaviour, and this insistence on obedience, respect and gratitude as a valid expectation for a father to have of his child becomes a recurring refrain as the play continues. The fact that his plans go awry and, through his failure to know himself or his daughters, the confirmation that he expects turns sour, brings out the negative aspect of this Orange level and even within the opening scene Lear's mood changes from confident arrogance to outraged frustration and Red level anger. One could find a modern analogy here in the reaction of some parents to a generation of "hippie" children, who have flouted the social norms and even their filial obligations, like Cordelia, in an attempt to be honest and to carve out their own life-style.

From the moment when he dismisses the devoted Cordelia and Kent and leaves himself at the mercy of the unscrupulous Goneril and Regan, he begins to reap the karma of his stubborn will and total ignorance of other levels of consciousness. "He hath ever but slenderly known himself" says Goneril, who already knows that her father has done a stupid thing in leaving himself at her mercy! Is this then the tragic flaw, that he was blind both to himself and to the real nature of others around him? Is there here also some of the Blue level that idealises a situation, sees how it could and should be? Perhaps the Blue idealism joins here with Orange level social conformity to accentuate Lear's obsession with the obedience, respect and gratitude to be expected from one's children.

Our purpose here, however, is not to pass judgement on Lear, but to follow the last days of his life and to watch what happens to the consciousness and awareness of this old bewildered king who, seeking rest, peace and security for his closing years, found suffering, turmoil and a torturing realisation of his own blindness and folly. The extent of the transformation that takes place within the short span of time covered by the play becomes strikingly apparent when we set side by side two pictures of the king, one in the opening scene and the other from the final scene. Flash these two pictures on the screen of your mind and you will have a prototype of the change that we all have to make if we are to evolve from the ego-centred to the selfless state. In the first picture we see a fully robed and attended king enter, with a realm to dispose of at his will. In the second the poignant stage directions tell their own story: "Enter Lear with Cordelia dead in his arms." In the opening scene his words are powerful and not to be contradicted or questioned; "Peace Kent" he shouts, when his loyal retainer tries to point out Lear's folly, "Come not between the dragon and his wrath." Contrast this with his words at the end: "You must bear with me . . . I am old and foolish . . . Pray you undo this button. Thank you, sir." Between the two is the whole substance of the Tragedy and of that part of Lear's evolution that brings the compulsory change and the breakthrough to a new seeing that is Nuclear Evolution. The Ego is shredded away from the arrogant ruler who is answerable only to God in his spacious realm, until he becomes the gentle, considerate old man, whose prison cell is his kingdom and whose sweetness at the end moves us all to tears.

GUIDELINES FOR STUDY OF KING LEAR

Below we present a series of basic questions relating to the process of change and Nuclear Evolution as it takes place in the tragic hero. It will be up to the student of consciousness to decide how much further he or she wishes to take this research. References are given and some specific quotations, but there are many more to be found, both in the text of the play and in parallel examples from our own lives.

QUESTION ONE: What is the resting colour or basic drive in King Lear?

For kings and princes and leaders whose words and actions affect the lives of many, the basic drive is inevitably Orange since consciousness will be focussed on the relationship with those whom they lead and govern. How this supremacy and responsibility affects the individual will depend on his state of evolution and primarily on his understanding and command of his own Ego. There have been selfless rulers who, though proud of their achievements, never lost sight of the needs of their people; and there have been those whose pride became arrogance which resists all opposition and advice, and is aware only of what is owed in terms of respect and even love. This latter is the negative Orange and it is from this type of pride that Lear is brought crashing down in the course of the drama. Together with this negative Orange that is centred in the Ego's pride in its position, prestige and authority there is a Red level reactiveness that shows immediately Lear is frustrated or opposed, so that he even draws his sword on the loyal Kent. When his plans are thwarted there is no reasoning with him. Both negative Orange and reactive Red manifest when Cordelia's uncompromising honesty upsets his whole scheme for the division of his kingdom. When she protests that she is young and true he rails at her:

> Let it be so; thy truth then be thy dower . . .
> Here I disclaim all my paternal care.
> . . . Hence and avoid my sight!
> *(Act 1, Scene 1)*

and when Kent attempts to point out the error of his judgement he is exiled forever. By one stroke of his Ego-centred stubborn pride Lear loses the only two people he can really trust.

This same arrogance he takes with him to Goneril's house, but what was tolerated in an obsequious court now meets with resistance and rational objections. Lear, returning from hunting, shouts as he enters the house:

> Let me not stay a jot for dinner:
> go get it ready . . . . . Dinner,
> ho dinner!
> *(Act I, Scene 4)*

but no one runs to do his bidding, no one even answers his call. Watch now what happens in the scenes that follow, how egotistical pride struggles to survive, as his daughters persist in their efforts to pare it down. Ruthlessly they confront him on his need for attending knights and relentlessly they work together to cut the number of those knights from one hundred to fifty, then to twenty-five and finally to none. (Study in detail how Lear turns from one daughter to the other and back again in desperate hope of saving some of his retinue that symbolises the last vestige of his Ego investment and his kingly power. Act II, Scene 4.)

What happens to the proud Orange level king when all his assumptions and expectations are destroyed? His first Red level impulsive reaction is to salve his insulted ego by riding out in a towering rage from the unbearable situation in Goneril's house:

> Darkness and death!
> Saddle my horses, call my train together!
> *(Act I, Scene 4)*

But this is followed by deeper and more heart-rending realisations that are the beginning of an opening up in Lear to new areas of understanding, new levels of awareness: "Woe that too late repents!" he cries out as he thinks of his treatment of Cordelia. Then back he swings to furious indignation and bitter hatred for the perfidious Goneril, on whom he lays a terrible curse. This swinging between remorse, that involves facing himself and what he has done, and the other extreme of blaming his children for his misery, is the start of the ego-stripping process that we all have to go through. The old patterns of thought and speech and action are still with us and we cling to their familiar forms, but as they start to be broken down we alternate between mourning the death of what seemed such a real part of our being and rejoicing at the glimpses of whole new areas of perception.

For Lear the conflicting emotions shake his ageing mind and he beats at his head as he feels himself going mad:

> O Lear, Lear, Lear!
> Beat at this gate that let thy folly in
> And thy dear judgement out!
> *(Act I, Scene 4)*

As his mind staggers under the shattering blows of remorse over Cordelia's banishment and rage at Goneril's and Regan's betrayal, the frustrated Orange drive for power and prestige first lashes out in curses on Goneril (Act I, Scene 4, Lines 284-298) and then in vague threats of revenge:

> I will do such things,
> What they are, yet I know not, but they shall be
> The terrors of the earth.
> *(Act II, Scene IV)*

We all at some time go through this "I'll show them" reaction, but in a king, used to having great power at his command, the ego is writ large. Yet a king is no different from any other human whose only real power is to change himself, not the world "out there", and once life begins to work on Lear, his Titanic curses serve only to delay the inevitable facing of self.

From this point, when he goes out into the storm on the heath, to the end of the play there is a gradual refining of his consciousness. The ego-centred Orange drive is compelled to take into account others who also suffer and the compassion and magnanimity that characterise the Orange in its highest expression now creep into Lear's awareness and his words. In the agony of his own self-torturing thoughts he finds space in his mind for others who have no defence against the storms of life, and so he now at last manifests the positive Orange with its concern for humanity:

> Poor naked wretches, whereso'er you are,
> Who bide the pelting of this pitiless storm
> etc.
> O! I have ta'en
> Too little care of this. Take physic, Pomp;
> Expose thyself to feel what wretches feel,
> . . .   *(Act III, Scene 4)*

So Orange is the basic drive that starts as negative arrogance and is purified by the end of the play to a beautiful humility and self-lessness. (Note particularly his words to Cordelia "Come let's away to prison," Act V, Scene 3, Lines 8 et seq..) Other levels flash in and out of Lear as they do in us all. In a final flash of the old Red reactiveness he kills the man who was hanging Cordelia. In his railings against the gods who would seem to have sided with his pernicious daughters there is a Job-like, Blue level, self-righteous confrontation with the universal will. Things *should* go according to one's own concepts; gods *ought* not to let such things happen; reality does not bear out one's assumptions and mental models.

QUESTION TWO: How do you relate to the drives and the transformation in King Lear? Have you experienced:

1. Stubborn pride?
2. Strong expectations of other people?
3. Violent reaction to criticism of your judgement?
4. Impotence in the face of life, unable to make reality conform to your will?
5. Self pity and bitterness, which blames others and even God for the situation?
6. Remorse at some error realised too late?
7. Humiliation resulting from the stubborn pride?

QUESTION THREE: What is the tragic flaw or Ego blindness in Lear?

This has been partially dealt with in the section on his basic drive. All that is needed now is to follow the course of the unfolding tragic events that stem from Lear's initial folly of believing in his own infallibility and his arrogant assumption that everyone will fall in with the requirements of his scheme. Add to this his failure to "know" either himself or those near to him and we find him accepting the hollow and specious words of Goneril and Regan and rejecting the total honesty of Cordelia and Kent. If he had developed his Indigo intuitive centre he could not have made this terrible blunder. His awareness of others, even his own children, is crude and sees only the outward appearance, not the reality behind. He listens to the words spoken by his daughters but cannot tune in (through the Ajna chakra) to the vibration of genuine love in Cordelia and the vibration of total selfishness in her sisters. Only on the heath, when he has been stripped of all the physical and social trappings of kingship, does the realisation of his former blindness literally drive him mad and allow the real innate nobility and royalty of his nature to emerge. The self-image of himself as a king, and all that this implies in the social context (Orange level), has always blocked him from being in touch with his real feelings. Now this is removed; stripped of "the King" he becomes "the man".

QUESTION FOUR: Man's greatest dilemma is his attachment to the workings of his mind and intellect, while he neglects the promptings of his heart. Nuclear Evolution involves combining the functions of head and heart. How does this apply to Lear?

The Ego uses the Head and reasons its way through life. Lear's head, governing his sense of propriety and dignity as a king, contrived the farcical device of getting his daughters to proclaim their filial love in the open court. His heart had always valued Cordelia most:

Lear (to Cordelia) . . .

> Now, our joy,
> What can you say to draw
> A third *more opulent* than your sisters? Speak.
> *(Act 1, Scene 1)*

When she could not speak her love, his head cast her off. In the same way his heart knew the sterling quality of Kent's devotion and loyalty but the egotistical prideful head sent Kent into exile for daring to contradict.

In relation to the levels we have here an example of negative Orange pride and stubborn attachment to the rational prerogatives of kingship and fatherhood; while his positive Green heart energy is stifled. At one point he actually tells his rising heart to get down:

> O me! My heart, my rising heart! but down!
> *(Act II, Scene 4, Line 1-21)*

When they try to get him to shelter from the storm he tells them:

> ... where the greater malady is fixed,
> The lesser is scarce felt.
> *(Act III, Scene 4, Line 8)*

The "greater malady" is the pain of getting in touch too late with his great heart and his real being.

QUESTION FIVE: What are the circumstances that make the tragic sequence of events inevitable? What is Lear's karmic context?

Goneril: ...   he always loved our sister
most; and with what *poor judgement*
he hath now cast her off appears
too grossly.

Regan: Tis the *infirmity of his age;* yet he hath ever but
slenderly known himself.

Goneril: The best and soundest of his time
hath been but *rash* ...
(Act I, Scene 1)

Speaking these words about their father the two villainous daughters present for us both the cause within Lear and the tragic context of his earthly downfall. Lack of judgement, and discrimination, combined with rashness when he is thwarted, inevitably lead to disaster, when knowledgeable schemers are there to take advantage of his folly.

So it is with all the tragic heroes. They find themselves in a set of circumstances with which by virtue of their nature they cannot cope. This too is the whole story of Nuclear Evolution and the enlightenment process. We incarnate with a particular flaw or failing built up over previous incarnations and are placed in a set of circumstances where it must "come to question," where we must confront ourselves and break through or continue to live in a self-created Hell.

QUESTION SIX: What is Lear's "dark night of the soul"? What is the nature of his ultimate surrender?

The Hell just referred to is this "dark night" or the Black level of consciousness which all the tragic heroes and all men and women must go through before they graduate from this karmic school of earthbound existence. For every human being the "dark night" involves a total upheaval and releasing of all attachments, whether it be to ways of life or to doctrines and beliefs or to people or to all of these. All one's powerful emotions rise to the defense of the Ego in its death throes and self-pity, bitterness, remorse, anger and despair all clamour for expression. For Lear this confrontation with his own negativity and his powerful Ego never really tested by life until now is coupled with a growing madness which frees him from the inhibitions that temper the sane man's anguish, so that what most of us suffer in silent self-torture, Lear shouts out into the storm winds or the ears of Kent, the fool and Edgar in the hovel on the heath. To add to the poignancy we are presented with a double turmoil for, as Lear himself says, the tempest on the heath is paralleled by the tempest in his mind.

Everything in Lear is on a grand scale; everything is extreme, all or nothing, a kingdom or a hovel, sanity or madness. For Lear the madness creeps up on him and finally takes over in the hovel and as the storm mirrors his growing madness so the growing madness both parallels and intensifies the agony of this battle with his other self. Of all the tragedies only "King Lear" shows the whole self-destroying process in such detail, as the Ego in its death agony struggles to lay blame anywhere out but on itself:

> I am a man
> More sinned against than sinning.
> *(Act III, Scene 2)*

But he cannot avoid reality and his own words condemn him as a selfish king:

> I have ta'en
> too little care of this. Take physic, Pomp;
> Expose thyself to feel what wretches feel,
> *(Act III, Scene 4)*

The Ego thrashes around like a wounded snake and Lear, caught in its coils, lashes out at life cursing Goneril, blaming the gods for siding with the elements against him and for turning his daughters' hearts against their father. Then he identifies with the storm and bids it seek out all criminals and strike them down. But even in his maddest moments he knows that the real battle now is against his own blind arrogance and total selfishness. He even has insight into the cause of it all. As a king his chances of self-knowledge and understanding were, he says, nullified by the very fact of his being a king to whom everyone gave way and whom they flattered as wise before his time:

> They flattered me like a dog, and told me I had white
> hairs in my beard ere the black ones were there. To say
> 'ay' and 'no' to everything I said . . .
> *(Act IV, Scene 4, Lines 97 et seq.)*

So Lear bears out the truth of the sages' teachings that to know reality involves going out of one's mind. The further out of his mind that Lear goes the nearer he gets to real self-knowledge and the selfless state. From the fluctuations in the early stages between furious indignation and a striving for patience (Act II, Scene 4), he moves to real madness in which, though still obsessed by the villainy of his daughters, he yet treats his companions with courtesy and kindness. And after the storm is over we have a man, still out of his mind, but with a new insight into the ways of the world. (Act IV, Scene 6)

When Cordelia returns to him, a gentleness and humility confirm the total transformation that he has gone through. This is the total revolution that is involved in going through the Black or "the dark night of the soul" and this is the breakthrough of the Nuclear Evolution leap to another state of consciousness. Although it does not involve for everyone the loss of sanity that came to Lear, it does involve the total upheaval and reversal of all the old ways of being, living and thinking. When the breakthrough is finally made and the dark night has been gone through, all the negative has become positive. In Lear the negative Orange arrogance and selfishness becomes positive dignity and concern for humanity and its twisted view of reality. (See Act IV, Scene 6, Lines 148-164.) The negative Red, that flares up in reaction to any affront on the Ego, shows itself now in righteous anger that kills the slave that is hanging Cordelia.

We could ask in closing what was the cathartic agent that brought Lear through. Was it the remorse at his blind folly that had exiled love from his life?

Woe that too late repents!

he cries out and echoes thousands of such cries from human hearts. For most of us (and you can check this out in your own life) when the final test comes, it is remorse at our own past blindness that is both the salient factor and the purgative agent in the agonising self-confrontation that we call "the dark night of the soul".

Note: As a commentary on Lear's progress through the stages of his growing awareness of his error and as a mirror of his soul's agony, follow the Fool's comments from Act I, Scene 4 to his final exit in Act III, Scene 6.

MACBETH AND OTHELLO

In the study of the last two of the tragic heroes the whole emphasis will now be shifted on to our use of Macbeth and Othello as sounding boards for our own Ego confrontation. What is important in all these studies is not so much what happens to kings and generals but what happens in our own consciousness when we applaud or condemn their words and actions. We have two options; either we separate ourselves from their failings and blunders, their blindness and their suffering, or we say in our hearts: "There but for the grace of God go I." By taking the second attitude we get inside the tragic hero, look out of his eyes, experience his emotions and conflicts and in so doing get new insight into our own potentially tragic state of being on the evolutionary spiral.

Macbeth is unique among the four tragic heroes for several reasons. He commits a deliberate, totally unjustified murder for totally selfish motives. He is haunted by a colossal imagination which he can neither understand nor master. No really deep evolutionary transformation takes place in Macbeth other than the inevitable realisation that he has sold his soul to the devil for nothing and has lost his peace of mind, together with all hope of "honour, love, obedience, troops of friends."

At first glance we recoil from identification with a bloody murderer, but if we have any real perception we see that the pattern of Macbeth's life is the pattern of thousands of lives on the planet, lives in which the pull of the "dark and deep desires" of the unconscious will is stronger than the promptings of the Higher Self. Often we are not fully in touch with the deep heart feelings and urges but they are traceable in our unspoken thoughts. Mainly it is our self-image that keeps them dark, but they are still a strong motive force for our actions. We do not resort to murder to fulfil those desires but our Ego propels us into actions and utterances that our True Nature often abhors. If, as with Macbeth, our Violet chakra is open, our imagination will speak to us in mental pictures, first as hints of dire consequences, which we ignore, and then in haunting images that call for remorse and repentance and total surrender and change. We can either ignore these promptings of our higher faculties, as Macbeth did, and plunge further into cover-up actions, or we can, in all humility, admit our error and go through the "dark night", as Lear did, so that the Ego is stripped away and the Real Self is revealed as a free and still evolving selfless spirit.

GUIDELINE QUESTIONS FOR THE READER

(a) At this moment in time what do you really want? What are *your* deepest, most secret desires? Would their fulfilment involve any suffering for others? Can you imagine the consequences if you set out ruthlessly to fulfil them? From what level of consciousness do they arise?

> Red? (sexual, sensory, physical)
> Orange? (ambition, pride in social achievement)
> Yellow? (intellectual)
> Green? (acquisitive)
> Blue? (idealistic or authoritarian)
> Indigo? (realisation of potential)
> Violet? (imagined perfection)

(b) What is holding you back from going out and getting what you want?

(c) How much are you affected by other people's persuasion or example?

(d) Have you already compromised your conscience (in business? in love affairs? in politics? etc.) If so does your unquiet mind bring haunting and reproachful images calling for remorse and restitution?

(e) Is your Ego refusing to admit that you ever took a wrong step? Are you preparing to take some action now to cover up the effects of the first action? If this does not apply now does it apply to the past?

(f) Have you, right now, got peace of mind? If not, what destroyed it?

(g) Are you fighting to preserve your Ego at any cost or are you ready to admit faults and failures, to be humiliated and to surrender and start again?

Your answers to the above questions will now be the context in which you look briefly at Macbeth's life and death. So each of you will view him as a man on the evolutionary spiral, having to face choices and deal with a powerful Ego, rather than as someone to be judged and condemned as a being totally separate from you.

For Macbeth and for Banquo the witches act as a trigger for the voice of inner temptation but the response of the two generals is widely different. Whereas the witches stimulate in Macbeth urgent and ambitious desires for kingship (Orange level) and stir up thoughts that make his hair stand on end, in Banquo they probably only confirm a long-held hope that his descendants may one day be kings of Scotland. He is prepared to wait. In Macbeth's mind there is already a churning confusion of fears, hopes and "horrible imaginings" and the mere thought of murder throws him into a state of chaos:

> My thought, whose murder yet is but fantastical,
> Shakes so my single state of man, that function
> Is smothered in surmise, and nothing is
> But what is not.

What actually makes Macbeth hesitate to commit the murder? Mainly it is his imagination running rampant with fear. If he could get the deed done and be sure of instant success and no consequences, he would risk his immortal soul, or, as he puts it "jump the life to come." He gives all the obvious arguments against murdering Duncan, who has been a noble king, and who is also Macbeth's kinsman and guest, but there is no heart in his reasoning. Never once do we sense that concern for Duncan as a human being holds him back. His powerful imagination conjures images of Duncan's virtues as angels "trumpet-tongued" crying out to the world the horror of the crime, but it is fear of discovery, rather than shame at the deed that holds him back.

However, there are always warning hints of what we may lose by taking the left-hand path, and Macbeth tells Lady Macbeth that he has decided to proceed no further with the murder plan. Out of pity for Duncan? No. He has just received new honours and titles and he would like to enjoy them for a while, together with "golden opinions from all sorts of people." Subconsciously he must know that once the murder is done and suspicion is seeded he will swiftly lose all his friends and the joys of relationships based on trust or respect. A little before his death he actually voices this regret that these pleasures can never be his.

Neither these qualms nor the "horrible imaginings" of consequences are strong enough to counteract the powerful influence of Lady Macbeth who not only knows how to goad his Ego but is also fully aware of his moral duplicity:

> What thou wouldst highly
> That wouldst thou holily - wouldst not play false,
> And yet wouldst wrongly win.

It is from this shrewd knowledge of her mate that she works to persuade him to murder Duncan. This two-faced approach to life, so typical of the negative Orange level, is rampant in those areas of society where it is permissible, even acceptable, to cheat and lie and manipulate during the week, so long as you conform to the social and religious standards in formal situations like club and church attendances at the weekend! So Macbeth is far from unique in this area!

Such superficial double standards do not make for strength or stability, so Macbeth is easily persuaded, since he has no firm centre from which to view life and its challenges and temptations. This is made even more obvious by the contrast with Banquo, who will do nothing that will lose him his honour. His heart must be free of all guilt and his allegiance to the king cannot be shaken, whatever the rewards of treachery may be. So the Blue level solidity of Banquo throws into relief Macbeth's unscrupulous Orange level desires.

Once the murder is done the consequences are upon Macbeth and the same Violet level imagination that made his "seated heart knock at (his) ribs" in anticipation, now produces a voice that shouts "Macbeth shall sleep no more!" He has not only murdered his king, but he has killed his peace of mind - ("Macbeth hath murdered sleep!") What is worse Banquo, who heard the witches' prophecy, is now suspicious and must therefore die, and from this point Macbeth begins his series of bloody cover-up deeds, that fail totally to bring the desired results of peace and security. Why? Because Macbeth fails to see that his enemy is within himself, that the attack now has to be made not on external foes but on his own Ego that led him, with Lady Macbeth's skillful manipulation, into the trap of self-destruction.

This is the point at which, when the big error has been committed, the Ego can either be confronted as the major cause of disaster or it can continue to protect itself by more and more foolish, self-defeating acts and by continually laying the blame for failure or suffering "out there". This is the point in Nuclear Evolution where either the breakthrough is made, the blindness is admitted and self-mastery is achieved, or there is a stubborn refusal to change and all hope of transformation in this lifetime is lost.

Macbeth took the second course of stubborn persistence on his fatal course. Clinging to his much vaunted physical courage, one of the main buttresses of his Ego, he defies the whole world, bolstered by the witches' quibbling promises of safety from all but a man not born of woman. (We are reminded of his modern counterparts who rush around to "psychics" for Ego support!) So having separated himself from the whole universe Macbeth still struggles to manipulate and control events, although with a dim sense that all his efforts are doomed.

When he does pause to consider where he has got himself, or, as he sees it, where life has put him, he experiences "a tale told by an idiot". Life creeps in its petty pace from day to day on the road to "dusty death". From the moment when he kills Duncan he knows that he has sold his soul, "his eternal jewel", to the "common enemy of man", but he has no idea how to retrieve it, nor any will to make amends and change. Lady Macbeth sees it too:

Naught's had, all's spent,
Where our desire is got without content,

she muses and her thoughts and memories drive her insane. The same realisation of total futility drives Macbeth on and on to the very end when he goes out to die in battle, with a courage rooted not in certainty but in desperation:

Blow wind! Come, wrack!
At least we'll die with harness on our back.

As an example of the failure of a being to respond to the natural process of Nuclear Evolution because of a totally stubborn Ego, "Macbeth" provides an invaluable bit of spiritual teaching.

OTHELLO

For many years when I re-read this play I came away with a feeling of dissatisfaction. I put it down to the limited nature of its scope, confined and concentrated as it is within the limits of Iago's plottings and manipulations to destroy first Cassio and then Othello. The play seemed more on a par with some recent domestic dramas than with the other tragedies of Shakespeare, which all tap into wider, more universal themes. Now, after some years of study of Nuclear Evolution, I have come to a new realisation about this slice of life that Shakespeare chose as a theme for one of his tragedies and it has given me a whole new appreciation of an underlying purpose in his writing the play. I had always felt too that Iago was a more interesting character than the hero, Othello, and wondered why Shakespeare had not given Othello more depth and more subtlety, but now I see that Othello is completed by Iago! After Iago has sown the first doubts in Othello's mind about Desdemona's fidelity, Othello says to him, "I am bound to thee forever;" strange words to speak to a man who is undermining your trust in the woman you love! But they are not so strange if that man is verbalising your own darker thoughts and fears and suspicions, that negative side of your being to which you are certainly "bound" until you face it and dismiss it forever.

We can look for verification of this psychological phenomenon in our own lives. When we latch on to a negative suggestion made by another person, even though we know it is destroying our peace of mind and threatening a much valued relationship, what are we really doing and why do we do it? Are we just allowing ourselves to listen to someone else's tittle-tattle and malicious gossip? Or are we allowing the negative part of our own being to soak up the disturbing words because they echo thoughts which are inside us already, like seeds waiting for a drop of water? Search in your own recollections or even in your present situation or that of someone near to you and ask this question -- why do we listen to disturbing suggestions about those whom we say we love and trust, and why do we even ask for more, as Othello did? We say we want proof, we will not believe anything until we are absolutely certain, but isn't it nearer the truth to say that we want more fuel for the little fire of doubt that we ourselves have lit in our own minds? Maybe our partner has not given us so much attention lately or has seemed less amorous: "I wonder whether he/she is as loyal as I thought," whispers the Ego, which is the part of us that will suffer if the suspicions are true. "Supposing there is a secret liason. How would I know about it?" says the voice of the doubter, and from that point we are ripe and ready to have our doubts confirmed either by harmless incidents (like Cassio's leaving the room after a talk with Desdemona, just as Othello walks in) or by the insinuating words of another. We may not have to contend with an external Iago, goading and provoking us into suspicion and resentment and ultimately revenge, but we may still have the same "agent provocateur" within us, functioning as the powerful self-protecting Ego.

The tempter or the "adversary" is beyond all doubt a part of our consciousness, and whether it manifests in the form of thoughts in our own mind, such thoughts as are voiced in the soliloquies of Hamlet and Macbeth, or as resonance with another human, as in the case of Lear and the Fool or Othello and Iago, the relevance to our evolution is the same. There are always two ways to go: we can either switch off the mental tapes, quench the fire of doubt and forcefully confront and reject the person who is pouring the poisonous words into our ears, or we can become the willing victim of the negative promptings from our mind or our human betrayer.

When we defy the tempter we stand firm in our own nuclear centre. Banquo did this and the witches' words had no effect on him. Macbeth himself stood out against the damnable suggestions at first, but weakened under the powerful persuasions of his wife. Note too the occasions when, in the earlier stages of Iago's undermining of Othello, he resisted the sinister suggestions, protesting the purity of Desdemona and demanding absolute and undeniable proof. At those times Othello was his true, noble and trusting self, operating from the strong central core of his being that made him loved and respected by heads of state and his colleagues on the field of battle.

What was it then in Othello, and what is it in us that makes him and us an easy prey for haunting thoughts and beguiling and deceptive words? Othello operated from the Blue, idealistic authoritarian and conceptualising level of consciousness. He set his standards of warlike soldierly behaviour at a peak of perfection and his loyalty and service to his state were impeccable. He also projected his own integrity out on to others who professed honesty and integrity; "Men should be what they seem," he says, and here for him lay the danger. Men are *not* always what they seem and deep underneath his protestations of what "should" be, lay his smouldering doubts. They found their focus, as doubts and uncertainty always do, in the area where he was least sure of his ground, in his relationship with Desdemona. For a Moorish soldier, unused to the sophistication of Venetian society, he took a risk when he married an aristocratic young woman. So when Iago talked of the wiles and tactics of Venetian ladies who deceived their husbands, he was surely voicing Othello's secret fears and fanning the smouldering flame of suspicion. Until we discover our nuclear centre of being, our True Self, we all have our own vulnerable area of uncertainty and doubt, the "Achilles heel" of our consciousness, and it is here that the Ego sees the greatest need for self-protection. What's more, the Ego always understands very well how to turn everything, even virtues, to its advantage. Not only does Iago exploit Othello's lack of assurance in the relationship area but he knows Othello's true nature and is prepared to take this into account in his manipulations:

> The Moor, howbeit that I endure him not,
> Is of a constant, loving, noble nature.

So he gives all his insinuating and destructive warnings to Othello as one who loves him dearly, and in return Othello is duped into trusting the "honest" Iago. In the same way, the certainty of our own virtue in some areas can blind us to our faults in other areas. Like the Moor, we pride ourselves on our valour or our generosity or our loyalty or whatever our prime quality may be, and we fall for our own self-image, while the Ego uses our blindness to our faults to ensnare us. The generous father doesn't see that he is also a bully with his children and the loving mother fails to realise that her possessiveness smothers the children's freedom. So the mind, or the Ego, flatters and traps us. Our children have to leave home before we see what our bullying or possessiveness has done to them. Othello has to murder the woman he loves before he wakes up to ask the question:

> Will you, I pray, demand that demidevil (Iago)
> Why he hath thus ensnared my mind and body?

Too late we look back in horror and wonder what has lost us the thing we treasured most.

Why did Othello and why do we have to come to the point of disaster before we are willing to actually face up to the Ego? The answer lies in our tremendous attachment to our own self-image and identity. The noble respected general, Othello, could not face the prospect of seeing himself a cuckold. Anyone who has ever actually confronted his own Ego knows the agony of accepting himself as he really is. This is why the process of Nuclear Evolution so rarely takes place, because it demands that we transcend the blind spots and the limitations of our particular and much loved level of consciousness and totally eliminate the permissive Ego. Othello's surrender to Iago's devilish promptings or our surrender to the Iago within us, the Ego, leads inevitably to tragic results. Iago has to be ruthlessly confronted. Just as Othello seems to have had a powerful identification with Iago, ("I am bound to thee forever ... "), so we nurture the bond with our inner "tempter" and to destroy it is like killing our own flesh and blood. Just as Krishna in the Bhagavaad Gita had to force Arjuna to kill his own kindred, symbolising his inner demons, in the battle of Kurukshetra so, if we listen to it, our higher self (Krishna) can thrust us into a confrontation with the beloved seducer within us. In the same way that parents are blinded by their attachment to children, whose outward charm and plausibility masks ego weaknesses and character deficiencies, so we do not see these deceptively appealing parts of ourselves that have to be rejected. If we can actually bring ourselves to kill our inner kindred, as Arjuna does, then instead of a tragic defeat, we achieve a triumphant breakthrough, a leap in our level of consciousness that is Nuclear Evolution in action.

37

NUCLEAR EVOLUTION --
A FOURTH FORCE

MODERN PSYCHOLOGY AND NUCLEAR EVOLUTION–
A FOURTH FORCE

Deborah Rozman

The field of modern psychology has had a number of observable waves of insight, each of which carried the tide for a good number of years until some perceptive mind came along with a new thrust. Psychology, the systematic study of the conscious and the unconscious in man, has been around for thousands of years disguised in ancient religious and philosophical forms. It wasn't until Sigmund Freud introduced his theories of the libido, id, ego and superego that the field of psychology began to develop with some breadth and depth in the western world. Freud is often considered to be the first force in modern psychology. There are many "Freudians" in these 1970's, mainly psychotherapists, who still cling to riding the first wave and lend little support to the later directions psychology has taken. Jung and Adler, both students of Freud, built upon his work on the unconscious and departed from some of his tenets to develop their own theories. Jungian symbology and Adlerian expansion into social awareness and creativity added new levels of consciousness to Freudian psychology. Rank, a student of Adler, thoroughly rejected Freud's "original sin" views that man is primarily an instinctual, sensual being and if left to his own devices would become more animalistic. These later psychologists proposed that the spark of creativity in man proves that man is in essence a spiritual being, and that with the proper environment can have the creative spark nurtured. Jung proposed the idea of the collective unconscious and dipped into the intuitive realms of consciousness. While this unfoldment and dialectic between the psychological "Marxist-Hegelians" was occurring, a second wave arose in psychology -- the objectivist-behaviourists. The behaviourists maintain that man is unconsciously conditioned by his environment anyway so why not condition him consciously by stimulus-response methods to train his behaviour. The Russian Pavlov and American B.F. Skinner, promoted behaviourism with its statistical measurements, and this mechanical approach gripped the field of psychology for twenty to thirty years as a second force.

Abraham Maslow was one of the greatest spokesmen for the third wave which arose out of Adlerians, Rankians and Jungians, as well as out of a severe reaction to the sterile, dehumanising methods of the behaviourists. The third force is the humanistic, ranging from Gestalt to Primal scream therapy and including all the many, many growth groups so prevalent today. Maslow's outspoken theories of humanistic psychology were subject to severe attack during most of his lifetime and it wasn't until his last years that his work, and that of humanistic psychology, became generally accepted as valid and valuable to the field of psychology. Prior to mid-1960, Maslow was a black sheep amongst the behaviourist dominated scene. Towards the end of his life Maslow predicted that a fourth force would emerge and usher the field of psychology into totally new territory, and that it would be a spiritual force. In Maslow's own words:

> I should say ... that I consider Humanistic, Third Force Psychology to be transitional, a preparation for a still "higher" Fourth Psychology, transpersonal, trans-human, centered in the cosmos rather than in human needs and interest, going beyond humanness, identity, self-actualisation and the like ... These [new] psychologies give promise of developing into the life-program, the religion-surrogate, the value-system, the life-philosophy, that these [young] people have been missing. Without the transcendent and the transpersonal we get sick, violent and nihilistic, or else hopeless and apathetic. We need something bigger than we are to be awed by and to commit ourselves to in a new, naturalistic, empirical, non-churchy sense, perhaps as Thoreau and Whitman, William James and John Dewey did.

Maslow and Christopher Hills communicated by letter prior to his death and discussed Maslow's typology in "Towards a Psychology of Being" in relation to Hills' research on the colour levels and personality. Maslow expressed great interest in Hills' work, but died before any real bridging could take place. Maslow's own work is only now, in the 70's, receiving popular acclaim. The third force, humanistic approach to "affective" learning as the basis of "cognitive" learning, is gradually gaining respect in education and in business.

A good number of young people are now merging humanistic psychology with spiritual disciplines, psychology with parapsychology, and out of this merger transpersonal psychology has been born. The 1970's has seen a boom in bringing the spiritual psychology of the East together with the methodology of the West, creating a more wholistic view of man's being. The quantum leap to a fourth force that penetrates the spiritual nature in man to the cause of his being, is a leap to Pure Consciousness itself. Pure Consciousness is behind all perception and understanding, behind all scientific method, all spiritual or religious experience and behind all concepts and theories in psychology.

Nuclear Evolution is the most in-depth penetration into the nature of consciousness and all its effects, both in the universe and in man, yet to be presented. As the universal field, it includes and synthesises all methods and typologies revealing their relative value in relation to the greater whole.

Nuclear Evolution, as an embodiment of Pure Consciousness, and all its manifestation in man's psyche, includes Freud, Adler, Jung, Rank, gestalt, behaviourism, Maslow, parapsychology and transpersonal psychology, as reflections of the seven different levels of consciousness and different modes of knowing. Its scientific empiricism and authority, taken direct from nature, give it the credibility of the predicted fourth force in psychology–the evolutionary thrust.

Just as it has taken years of struggle for humanistic psychology to begin to gain acceptance, so it will undoubtedly take years for the depth of Nuclear Evolution to become recognised, especially since it challenges every individual to confront his own ego which separates him from his environment, and to seek his Self in the Whole.

EXPERITYPICS
ANOTHER
OF THE NEW TYPOLOGIES

13 Red   19 Orange 25   Yellow   50 Green 55 Blue   62 Indigo   68 Violet   80

Editor's Note:

Parallel to the development of Nuclear Evolution, other methods of probing the different experiential inner worlds have been originated by psychiatrists and physiologists. One of the most remarkable correspondences has been with the meanings of the eight types in the typology developed by Dr. Humphrey Osmond and his colleagues Dr. Richard Smoke and Dr. Miriam Siegler. The following abbreviated account of this method of mapping the inner worlds of consciousness is included here because it not only provides an independent proof of Nuclear Evolution arrived at by a totally different means, but it shows also that the inner time-worlds that exist subjectively with different states of consciousness are responsible for certain types of human behaviour. The fact that Christopher Hills was able to read the inner worlds and the experience of time at a conference in 1969 and to obtain the same results as were independently worked out by Experitypics shows that Nature is the real source of both systems.

For the convenience of the reader we set out below the corresponding terms in Nuclear Evolution and Experitypics:

COLOUR PREFERENCE	NUCLEAR EVO-LUTION TYPE	NORMAL DIS-TRIBUTION %		EXPERITYPICS TYPE	DISTRI-BUTION %
		Child	Adult		
RED	Sensation		21	Sensation	
ORANGE	Social	35	16	Sensation/ Thinking	35%
YELLOW	Intellectual/ Thinking	11	12	Thinking	20%
GREEN	Acquisitive/ Security	15	10	SPATIAL UMWELT - made up of structural/ oceanic; aetherial/ experial	
BLUE	Conceptual/ Feeling	12	16	Feeling	30%
INDIGO	Intuitive	11	11	Intuitive	15%
VIOLET	Imaginative	16	15	Intuitive/Feeling	

Note: The above results show that the child's need for security (preference for green) is actually greater than adult's who preferred peace and quite (Blue). Adults, whose emotional satisfaction drive is for more leisure and relaxation (Blue), feel more secure and stabilised financially than children. Children chose 50%

more green because they are insecure and uncertain environmentally. However, both prefer stimulation and intensity of experience in the sensational (Red) and social activity (Orange) as shown by 35/37% colour preference. Colour preferences of returnees from Viet Nam showed the emergence of hope and fear by choice of Green as first preference and placement of Yellow (expectation and hope) to a back place. In returnees the normal first choice, Red, was displaced by Green, and Violet (50% Red, 50% Blue), the color of erotic magical identification, was displaced by Grey, the colour of fear.

The following is a brief account of the four main types with their four overlapping combinations which make eight types of time-world, plus an "umwelt" or attitudinal sphere of consciousness which Christopher Hills refers to as an "ego bubble" in the Nuclear Evolution oral teachings. The editors are indebted to Dr. Richard Smoke for specially condensing a book-length manuscript into a few pages for this edition of Nuclear Evolution.

EXPERITYPICS – ANOTHER OF THE NEW TYPOLOGIES

Introduction

As humanity begins to enter the Aquarian Age, a major expansion is occurring in many spheres of our comprehension of life, the universe, and our own nature. Such new dimensions as Nuclear Evolution are opening up, above all showing our apprehension of the richness and complexity of human consciousness and its possible height and breadth. We see new vistas of possibility for any individual, and we are also learning—what is the other side of the same discovery—how profound can be the *diversity among individuals.* People can be found who already embody and exemplify, if not all, at least many of the strands of the vast fabric of human consciousness. We are learning a whole new appreciation of how different one person may be from the next, and how deserving of respect for the uniqueness of his or her own perspective from the Nucleus of Being is, while still remaining part of the fundamental unity of humanity.

As this awareness dawns, new concepts (thoughtforms) emerge that identify in words the different colors and shadings that make up the fabric of human consciousness, or to change the metaphor, the different "places" or "spaces" an individual may occupy within its folds. Each of these new concepts cuts through this fabric, as it were, from a different angle; hence each yields a different set of human types—a different typology of human consciousness. The

The material on Experiential World Typology presented in this appendix was prepared by Humphry Osmond, Miriam Siegler, and Richard Smoke. This material is contributed to supplement the principal subject of this book with another, not wholly unrelated, perspective; but in the available space cannot, of course, offer a full statement of the substance or significance of Experiential World Typology. For a fuller rendition, see "Worlds Apart" (tentative title), a forthcoming book about that typology by Osmond, Siegler and Smoke. The important contributions to that typology of Dr. Harriet Mann are gratefully acknowledged, as are the valuable suggestions of Dr. Bernard Aaronson; many others too numerous to mention here but acknowledged in "Worlds Apart" have also played contributory roles in the development of Experiential World Typology. Preparation of this appendix was supported in part by a grant from the Huxley Institute for Biosocial Research.

process of Nuclear Evolution, as explained in this book, gives rise to one of these new typologies. Another, which adopts a different viewpoint on the diversity of individuals, is astrology—an ancient art now enjoying a rebirth, with its own typology of 12 main human types. A third is the typology of the seven personality rays, similar to Nuclear Evolution's seven levels of consciousness. This was introduced in the esoteric writings of Alice Bailey (Djwal Kul) and is now gradually becoming better known. A fourth was introduced over fifty years ago by Carl Jung, but is only now beginning to be widely understood.

Jung's book *Psychological Types* (Zurich, 1921) suggested two major ways in which people differ. One, which has become famous, is the difference between extraversion and introversion. This simple duality hides some important distinctions, but broadly it is the difference between being oriented mainly toward the outer world or toward the world of inner experience. The other major way in which people differ which Jung suggested has remained obscure. He believed that the human mind possessed four principal "functions," which he called "thinking," "feeling," "sensation" and "intuition" (as compared to Nuclear Evolution's seven). In any one individual, however, only one of these functions predominates; the others are wholly subordinate to it and may indeed be partly or entirely unconscious. Accordingly, there are four major kinds of people: thinking types, feeling types, sensation types, and intuitives. A refinement was added to Jung's four types by the suggestion that each major type could enjoy the support of either of two of its subordinate functions (but not the third) in a secondary role. A thinking type, for instance, could have sensation or intuition, but not feeling, as his or her secondary function. This created a total of eight types or, since each type could be either extraverted or introverted, a final total of sixteen.

There seem to have been a number of reasons—apart from the question of its ultimate validity—why this typology has not been widely understood in the decades following its introduction. *Psychological Types* is a difficult and not wholly coherent book. The Jungians themselves have employed the theory of the functions more in plumbing the relationship of unconscious forces within any one individual (for instance in dream analysis) than in typologizing individuals or in exploring the ways different types participate in social life and relate among themselves. No typology can be very useful until it can offer fairly reliable tests* by which one can identify any individual, or at an absolute minimum, can offer agreed-upon lists of representatives of each type; and these things were not provided. The words used to name the four functions are very broad and ambiguous. And finally, most people experience themselves doing all four things all the time, and not just one most of the time.

Another idea was coined, though, in the years following Jung's book, which offers a powerful hint for refining and utilizing this typology. Curiously enough, its author lived not far from Jung and was well known in his field, yet so far as we know, the two men never met. Jacob von Uexkuell was one of the first generation of ethologists, a predecessor and teacher of Konrad Lorenz. In a charming but little-known essay, "A Stroll Through the Worlds of Animals and Men," von Uexkuell described some of the ways that different species perceive and experience the world, because of their very diverse sense receptors and other organs. He used the term *umwelt* to name the "bubble" of space and time surrounding each organism, and pointed out that the experience even of these fundamentals must differ enormously among the species. An insect, for instance, that lives its entire life cycle in a few days must have a wholly different experience of time from that of a human being.

Here is an idea which may apply to more than ethology. Supposing there are also such differences *within* a species, such as *homo sapiens,* subtler no doubt than the differences among species and hence, perhaps, showing up psychologically rather than in gross behavioral differences? Supposing there are several, slightly different space-time bubbles, or umwelts, possible for human beings, with different individuals finding themselves in different umwelts for genetic or other reasons? To identify the different types of personalities and psychologies resulting, one would need an *experiential world typology.* [Nuclear Evolution provides one such map of the inner world and may be compared to actual human experience with other typologies.]

---

* [Nuclear Evolution offers such lists and color tests which agree with those results obtained by Experitypics — Ed.]

Such a typology, sometimes called Experitypics for short, has been developed and seems to identify more closely and more usefully the categories that Jung was apparently driving at. The remainder of this appendix describes, first, the major time umwelts; second, the major space umwelts; and third, these umwelts' relationships to each other and the structure of the overall typology. The descriptions must, naturally, be extremely terse and omit many subtleties. To avoid introducing more new terms than strictly necessary, we will use the Jungian terminology where possible here. [They can be compared and interchanged with those of Nuclear Evolution in the first part of this book.]

Time experience

The easiest experiential world to understand, for those who do not share it, is the one in which time is linear. Past, present and future are connected by lines of time, along which the present marches steadily and continuously. This is time as it is conceived by the scientist and the historian. It is time as we are all taught to believe is "the real" time, and hence is comprehensible to a considerable extent by everyone.

For *thinking types,* though, this is the only possible experience of time; it is necessarily and invariably linear. This type will often remember and identify events in their own personal past by what year and month they occurred, not by surrounding events, and they linearly extrapolate their personal future, so that what they expect to be doing 6, 12, 18 months from now (and often much longer) is very real to them. For this type, an event cannot be understood or discussed without being conscious of when and how it originated, how it developed, and when and how it concluded (or where it is leading if it is still ongoing). Discrete, spontaneous and tangential events are ignored until they can be fit into this continuity; this type is unwilling to recognize things which come from nowhere or "out of the blue."

Because this experiential world is occupied mainly by ongoing processes, thinking types often seem to be cool, detached, a bit remote. In fact their involvement in any situation is with the process as a whole: if one sees a situation constantly as stretching over years or even decades, it is not hard to be detached about what happened with it this morning. In the same way, for this type every event finds its place, almost effortlessly, in some overall, orderly pattern, so it is not hard to disengage from its immediate tangibility by seeing it in broader frameworks.

Since their experience of all things is temporally organized this way—automatically, as it were—thinking types are natural planners, systemists and theorists. Ideas, theories and principles, not always articulated or even conscious, provide the coherence by which the equally real past, present and future can be grasped and manipulated, and by which the type can be confident their actions will be consistent over time. Nearly always they can explain their behavior in a way that is logical and rational with respect to *some* set of principles.

History is full of logical, determined thinking types who tried to build a better (that is, more rational) society—for example Thomas Jefferson, Woodrow Wilson, Franklin D. Roosevelt, John F. Kennedy, and Lenin. They are also well represented in literature, partly because the type is an easy one to parody, though there are good sympathetic portrayals as well. Among these are Joseph Knecht (Hesse's "Magister Ludi"), Shakespeare's Portia and Cordelia, Jane Austen, and Meursault (Camus' "stranger"). Possible negative features of the type are displayed in Shakespeare's Lady Macbeth, Shylock, and Coriolanus.

Time for the *feeling type* is also continuous, but in a quite different way. It is circular or cyclical. The past develops into the present, which immediately becomes past again by becoming a memory. The present, though experienced as vividly real, becomes part of the past with each instant that passes; at the same time the past keeps re-echoing and ramifying in the events of the present, and also is re-experienced often, by treasuring and reliving memories. The future is a realm for hope, but is not truly real until it becomes part of the ongoing cycle of present and past. Though feeling types can and do learn the socially-approved doctrine of linear time, the time that is really real to them—time as it is experienced—is like a spiral tapestry, constantly growing outwards from the center, in which the same basic threads and colors repeat themselves (usually in new combinations) over and over again.

Not everything makes equally strong and rich memories. Events of the kind historians chronicle do not, and ideas still less so. The memories that are best able to live are memories of people and one's relationships with people, and memories of the events (external and internal) of one's own life. It is the *emotional* meaning of these things which gives these personal memories their strength and richness, and it is these kinds of feelings, not necessarily all feelings, of which "feeling types" are deeply aware. (They are not necessarily more conscious than, say, thinking types, of the feelings associated with intellectual discovery, for instance, though even these they may remember better.) Feeling types are aware almost automatically of how valuable a memory any ongoing event will make, and sometimes they evaluate events consciously in those terms—something no other type does. They act to increase as much as feasible the emotional side of situations, therefore, in order to expand and enrich their past and present. It is a distinctive characteristic of this type, for instance, that although they prefer positive feelings to negative ones, they will sometimes act to create negative feelings—picking fights, etc.—in a personal relationship that is important to them, rather than allow all feeling in it to drain away into sterility.

Because the feeling type's experience of time is cyclical, they do not need to be concerned, as thinking types do, with consistency over time. Memories of the past are always present, providing guides. But because their experience of time is also a continuous one, they too are good at organizing things, especially at all aspects of organization that involve interactions with people. Where a thinking type, for example, often treats people impersonally, as just another factor in the overall pattern, the feeling type is incapable of relating to a person in any way except personally, and skill in all kinds of interpersonal relations is this type's forte. Men as well as women of this type are warm and empathetic—when the men allow themselves to be, as increasingly in today's society they do. Good with children, to whom (unlike other types) they can give attention for long periods, feeling types bring loyalty, companionship, conviviality and cohesion to every social interaction and every relationship.

Prominent feeling types include: Gerald Ford, Dwight Eisenhower, Winston Churchill, Robert Kennedy, Hubert Humphrey, Franz Schubert, Marcel Proust, Konrad Lorenz, and in literature, Othello,

Lear, Desdemona, Anna Karenina and David Copperfield.

For the *sensation type,* time is not continuous. The past and present are not experienced as being related in any primary way. And neither the past nor the future is experienced as real. What is real is what is current and immediate. In no other type is the ability to perceive the present in all its shadings and ramifications so well developed. Sensation types meet events as existential realities, with little concern for how they got to be what they are and equally little concern for where they are going.

Because awareness is concentrated in the present, sensation types are superbly effective in dealing with concrete reality. Nothing distracts them from perceiving the object before them in all its aspects and dealing with it. Usually they respond without hesitation to environmental stimuli, responding as the stimulus itself suggests, not by a pre-existing conceptualization or personal commitment. Rarely volunteering an explanation for their behavior, if pressed for one they will say that a door ajar, an odd sound, or a change in the air "told them what to do." This is how they experience it. They are not aware of an event's logical ("thinking") or psychological ("feeling") implications. That intervening step does not exist. The event occurs and instantly they know what to do.

In this experiential world, time is not experienced as flowing. This type learns that it moves; they can read the clock; and as keen observers they quickly discover that the socially correct thing is to say that it flows. But they do not experience it so, in the way the two continuous types do. Their inner experience is of a present which is rich, full, deep, and always there. They are carried from one moment to the next by their own and others' activity; by connecting their inner sensations and needs to some behavior, like going to get food when they feel hungry; and by learning to read the present "in depth" to spot things in it that mean that something is about to happen that they must deal with.

Living in the umwelt of the absolute present, sensation types are highly effective in emergencies, in crises, and in all situations where success depends upon physical action. By the same token it is difficult and even painful for them to wait. Waiting—unless it be for an already-emerging situation to take shape sufficiently to act —

is the equivalent of denial. A sensation type told to be patient and wait a few weeks or a few months finds the suggestion dubious at best and in many situations, literally meaningless. Often what follows is premature action or an equally premature walking away from the whole problem. But conversely, when the situation changes it is, for the sensation type, a totally new ball game which he can deal with unencumbered by awareness of what it was or might have been.

Focussing their full energies on the present, sensation types create an impression of vitality, immediacy, and "presence," compared to other types who at any moment may be experiencing wisps of past or future in the back of their minds even when they are trying to attend to the present. Sensation types also find, or if necessary create, challenges that will demand and absorb their immediacy and full attentiveness to the present: for much of their lives, many of them enjoy games of power, status and sex, of kinds which often do not hold the interest of other types for very many years. But sensation types play them for the challenge of the game and the fun of gamesmanship as much as for tangible goals.

Prominent sensation types include: Lyndon Johnson, Harry Truman, Richard Nixon, Teddy Roosevelt, Jack Nicholson, Robert Redford, Humphry Bogart, Charles Lindbergh, Henry VIII, Stalin, Louis Pasteur, both Richard Burtons; and in fiction, Iago and Goldmund.

The intuitive type, perhaps even more than the other Jungian types, is poorly named. The intuitions he or she experiences are *not* the same thing as insight, empathy, depth of understanding, or hunches, and are not to be confused with having inklings or with psychic sensitivity. People of all types experience many or all these things. The intuitions of the "intuitive type" are of a particular kind—they are perceptions of potentialities.

The time experience of the intuitive, like that of the sensation type, is discontinuous. Like that type the intuitive does not experience any profound relationship between the present and the past, and for the intuitive too, the past is unreal. For the intuitive, though, the present is also unreal, except insofar as it contains the future within it. The time experience of the intuitive is one in which every event is perceived, as it were, in its futurity: events are perceived not only as significant, but as *real,* to the extent that they embody or contain the emerging future within themselves. The more of the future they carry, the more real they are. Events bear no necessary relationship one to another because of the order in which they occur; rather each new event, each new moment, bears its own, discrete relationship to the future to a greater or lesser degree.

Intuitives experience the degree of futurity in an event not only by how real it seems, but also by how much excitement it generates in them (and others). Unless strongly introverted, in which case the excitement remains inside them, they have a standing need to create more excitement in situations, analagous to the standing need that all but strongly introverted feeling types have: to create more feeling. (To be exact, others experience these types *creating* the excitement or feeling; they themselves experience themselves as *developing* excitement or feeling that is already there.) The excitement, like the feeling, is created or developed in order to expand and enrich the world they experience. Increasing the excitement in a situation makes it more real by enhancing its relationship with the future; people who are excited by something give it their energy and their awareness, and this ensures that its full possibilities are realized.

In addition to this discontinuous perception of the futurity in all events, many though not all intuitives also possess an overarching image of *the* future—a vision, although it is not always called so. Where this exists, all things that could conceivably have any relationship with the vision are perceived in relationship to it; and every effort is exerted that bears any chance of bringing the vision a step closer to manifestation. No opportunity is lost to inspire anyone and everyone with the tremendous importance of the vision, and the intuitive may work tirelessly for years, perhaps for a lifetime, to bring it to fruition.

Some examples may illuminate the intuitive experience of time, for it is by far the most difficult to understand for those who do not experience it. Consider Joan of Arc, Adolph Hitler, Leon Trotsky, Marshall McLuhan, and Timothy Leary. Each of these intuitives found an overarching vision: the liberation of France, the 1000-year Reich, the permanent revolution, the new consciousness created by electronic media or LSD. In each case, the present offered, or seemed to offer, the possibility of the vision's fulfillment, but in an emergent, half-formed, precarious state. To the intuitive, however, the vision was exceedingly vivid and real: it already existed, vibrantly alive, embedded within the present. Seized with the transcending vision, the intuitive resorted to every possible means to inspire everyone with its power, excitement and importance, so that they would experience the vision as the intuitive himself did—thereby guaranteeing its triumph. Although few intuitive visions are, in fact, as grand as these, the experience of being seized by a vision of some form and degree, and then attempting to inspire others with it, is broadly similar for all intuitives who have experienced it at all. Those who have not are usually searching restlessly for one, unhappy until they find it.

This description, and almost any description, of the intuitive experience of time does not communicate it fully, however, because the linear, past-present-future axiom of thinking type time is built into our very language. The intuitive actually experiences present and future in the reverse of their "normal" sequence. He experiences *first* the futurity of any event or situation—what it can be or will be when it is fully realized—and only *then* does he recognize what its present, limited, unfulfilled status is. Every intuitive is grimly familiar with the experience of having to wait, then, while factual reality catches up, often at an agonizingly slow pace, to the point that he has already experienced its essence to be. Impatiently he must wait for time to catch up to where he sees that, truly, it already is. This unique experience of time is characteristic of the intuitive world and is all-but-unheard-of, as a common experience, in any other type.

In fact intuitives, like sensation types, experience themselves to be living in the *present,* and are often puzzled why everyone else thinks—if they understand them at all—that they have their eyes on the future. It is an artifact of the language that intuitives, in order to talk about potentials, must talk about what is "going to be." They, however, see the potentials as already existing, in their full form, right now. From the intuitive's viewpoint, it is not that he is seeing the future and everyone else is seeing the present; his experience is that he is experiencing the present and everyone else is stuck in a past that is already dying or dead. To rescue the living present from the clammy hand of the corpse of the past is, for the intuitives of the earth, a never-ending battle.

Besides those already mentioned, other intuitives include Zero Mostel, Woody Allen, Albert Einstein, Admiral Lord Nelson, Che Guevera, and Hamlet.

Space experience

The spatial umwelts, of which there are also four, are richer, more complicated, and even more far-reaching in their consequences than the time umwelts. Only a few highlights can be sketched here, taking them in pairs.

Space may be experienced as inherently structural in quality, or inherently undifferentiated. Structured space is like geography, broken up by rivers, mountains, farmlands, and also artificial lines and boundaries. Undifferentiated space is like the ocean, which has currents but no demarcations, and indeed we term this experience of space "oceanic" as opposed to "structural." As a primary backdrop or space within which, or upon which, all experience occurs, each excludes the other. One or the other but not both are possible "grounds" or "textures" for the stuff of human consciousness.

The structural umwelt imposes order upon all experience to a greater or lesser degree. Grossly or subtly, the structural type experiences things as mutually distinct, as arranged, as frameworked. The static backdrop creates the possibility for comprehensible change. Grossly or subtly, the oceanic type experiences things as mutually permeable, as fluxes, as gestalts. The underlying flow provides the possibility for temporary, relative, and comprehensible coalescences. In the structural world, distinctnesses occur naturally and unification may be an act of creation; in the oceanic world, unity occurs naturally and particularization may be an act of creation.

People of other types may perceive structurals as orderly, reasonable, capable, skillful, responsible, dependable, and protective. Or they may perceive them as dry, lifeless, rigid, domineering, sterile. Rarely are they perceived as frivolous, deeply sensitive to mood, overly imaginative or mystical. Not surprisingly, structurals may perceive people of other umwelts simply as faulty or mediocre structurals—sloppy, unprincipled, stupid, ineffectual, unrealistic, or crazy. Or they may be greatly attracted to the warmth, spontaneity, flexibility, imaginativeness or freshness of viewpoint that they find in others but not in themselves. (People of all types tend to see those of other umwelts either as inadequate representatives of their own umwelt, or else they over-value them in a romanticized fashion.)

Sigmund Freud was a structural who strove to impose—or as he experienced it, discover—a structure for the psyche. His comments about the id are revealing. He said "it is chaos, a cauldron . . . it has no organization . . . the logical laws of thought do not apply . . . contrary impulses exist side by side without cancelling each other out." Freud's id was the exact opposite of his conscious world, the antithesis of structure; and by defining it so he made it something to be feared and conquered. (Jung, not being a structural, did not need to define the unconscious as non-structure. He was able to people it with coherent, though not rigidly organized, forms such as the anima/animus.)

The chaos that Freud feared, though, does not seem so frightening to people in the opposite umwelt. Mao Tse-tung, an oceanic, seems to have found it positively exhiliarating. His phrase "luan, laun ti"— chaos, more chaos—summed up his formula for preventing the bureaucratization and over-organization of society, thereby preserving dynamic change. The Cultural Revolution he launched in the 1960's was a deliberate attempt to introduce chaos, which Mao saw as creative, into China.

What oceanics have in common is that they experience life as a seamless whole; all events which seem real to them come together effortlessly. Where structurals tend to see phenomena and even people hierarchically, deferring to those above and instructing or directing those below, oceanics tend to see all people as equal. Toward those they admire they may feel reverence, but rarely deference. Where structurals tend to see all phenomena as objectified (because there is a structural relationship between self and all other things) oceanics are absorptive, making all things part of themselves to a greater or lesser degree.

People of other types may experience oceanics as receptive,

flexible, nonjudgmental, romantic, mystical, inspiring, charismatic, or empathetic. Or they may be seen as helpless, moody, unpredictable, disruptive, irrational, or despotically egocentric. Oceanics, who are sensitive to others' personalities and see others' personalities—not their abilities, talents, deeds or standing in society—as important, often find people of other types to be unresponsive, unfeeling, rigid, alienated, overorganized, silly and, above all, impersonal.

Winston Churchill was an oceanic who revelled, in his youth, in what at that time was still the romance of war. He searched out skirmishes on the frontiers of the British Empire, in India, Egypt, and South Africa, and with his charm and charisma managed to worm his way through and past the usual (structural) rules to take part in military engagements where, technically, he did not belong. With the usual oceanic flexibility he returned home to England, ran for Parliament, switched parties after awhile when he no longer liked his original one, added one or two careers on the side, and then later switched parties again (a thing unheard of)—along the way collecting an unusual assortment of the warmest friends and bitterest enemies. Then, in Britain's dark days of World War Two, he tapped the depths of his charisma and almost mystical grasp of the true significance of the Nazis, and created some of the most profoundly inspiring addresses ever to come forth in any language. He fused his countrymen into a single whole, a depth of unity few nations have ever experienced.

Malcolm X, by contrast, was a structural who spent his early life maneuvering and manipulating his way through the criminal order. Rising step by step in the hierarchy of the underworld, he was eventually caught. In jail he discovered the prison library, began to read about philosophical systems, and was converted to the Black Muslim doctrine of Elijah Muhammed. Studying every Muslim document he could find, he presented himself to Elijah after being released, and proved that he had thoroughly mastered the doctrine. Quickly he proved himself to be a master organizer as well. Starting at the bottom of the Muslim organization, he moved up at express speed by reorganizing, expanding and developing each successive level he directed. Elijah made him his right-hand man, in charge of all organizational matters nationally, and for years Malcolm crisscrossed the country by jet several times monthly, directing, instructing, arranging, coordinating, regulating. Rarely liked or disliked intensely, he was respected. For a long time he made few friends and refused to marry, because such things would interfere with his organizational work. By the time of his assassination he had twice changed his system of belief and action, always a difficult and painful thing for a structural to do. First he broke with Elijah and established his own organization, because he became convinced that the top of the Muslim hierarchy was impure; to him they were not acting consistently with their doctrine. Later he visited Mecca and found that some blue-eyed white people worshipped the same Allah he did. However painful it may be, structures are changed when an inconsistent fact appears. He was developing a new doctrine, in which whites were not necessarily devils, when he was killed.

Other structurals include Aristotle, Johann Sebastian Bach, and Thomas Aquinas. Other oceanics include Gandhi, e.e. cummings, and Rousseau.

The other pair of spatial umwelts concern a wholly different aspect of the "space" of consciousness. They also exclude each other, in much the same way that the structural-oceanic pair mutually exclude each other, but neither of them excludes either the structural or the oceanic experience.

Space may be experienced as rarefied or condensed. Rarefied space is like the upper atmosphere or the Ptolemaic conception of outer space—a realm of intangible auroras and transparent spheres. Condensed space is like a walk through the woods—a realm where every step brings something tangible to see and touch.

As a primary backdrop or "stuff" upon which, or within which, all consciousness and experience occurs, we term these aethereal and experial space. In the aethereal umwelt, all things are mentally *apprehended,* to a greater or lesser degree, as essences. In the experial umwelt, all things are *experienced,* to a greater or lesser degree, as manifestations. Grossly or subtly, the aethereal perceives things as abstract, hypothetical, conjectural or symbolic; in a word, as ideational. Grossly or subtly, the experial perceives things as concrete, actual, substantive, specific; in a word, as palpable. The keynote of the aethereal world is detachment. Aethereals stand outside things and, as they experience it, above them, comprehending them theoretically and verbally. The keynote of the experial world is involvement. Experials engage things directly and, as they experience it, vitally, living in and through them.

Tangible realities are important to aethereals, to the extent that they are related to ideas. Conan Doyle's great aetherial character, Sherlock Holmes, paid great attention to concrete details that are generally ignored by others, when they are of potential relevance to solving a crime. He has no intrinsic interest in where a lady's glove was purchased, but it may prove or disprove a theory. Details that bear no possible relationship to his hypotheses are simply omitted from his awareness; if Watson brings them to his attention he evinces impatience or irritation.

Ideas are important to experials, to the extent that they are related to concrete, vital experience. Konrad Lorenz made hundreds of observations of his ducks and geese before even beginning to hypothesize. The birds were intrinsically interesting in themselves, almost like pets. He would have enjoyed watching them, and his observations would still have been valid, even if no ideas had developed at all. Ideas which bear no possible relation to experience simply drop out of experials' awareness; if such ideas are pressed upon them, experials eventually show impatience and irritation.

Reality for experials is what happens day by day. One experial was astounded to discover that people of other types were willing to spend large sums of money in encounter groups and other kinds of therapy to learn to do what she could not avoid doing: relating, responding, getting involved, experiencing the richness of the here-and-now. The other side of the coin is that experials often have difficulty disengaging themselves from the environment in which they are involved so thoroughly.

This involvement gives experials mastery of social interaction, of "how things are done." Happy is the anthropologist who has an experial informant! Experials always know (usually without thinking about it) what is the right thing to do in social situations, and most of them spend considerable time noticing and talking about how others are behaving—an awareness from which they derive a quick sense of how fashions, subcultures, and "the times" are changing.

People of other types perceive experials as socially adept, warm and sensitive in human relationships, practical, dependable in social situations, "down to earth," fashionable, and morally authoritative. They may also be seen as unimaginative, highly conventional, intolerant, stubborn, less than intelligent. Not surprisingly, experials may perceive others as kooky or downright crazy, unobservant, unfashionable, impractical, overintellectual, or aloof. Anthony Quinn and Marlon Brando are experials, as was Emily Dickinson, and in fiction, Macbeth, Othello and Lear.

George Washington, the first president, was an experial who conceived his task to be not the creation of specific government policies or programs, but setting an example of what the presidency should be. No one knew. Many thought the president would turn out to be a sort of a king. Washington was determined to give the role a great dignity, but to remain a citizen wholly subordinate to the law like other citizens. At no time did he develop a theory of the presidency; he wrote no articles and gave no speeches about it, then or afterward. Rather he demonstrated what the presidency should be, by simply being it. He neither curried nor granted favors; he pulled no wires and refused to be pulled by any; he neither maneuvered nor manipulated. He exercised his powers as president so very frugally that for a whole century thereafter the Congress, not the Executive, was generally considered the strongest branch of the government. Thomas Jefferson remarked of him that "so far as he saw, no judgment was ever sounder. It was slow in operation . . . but sure in conclusion . . . His integrity was the most pure, his justice the most inflexible I have ever known." He contributed few ideas to the Constitution, the Federalist Papers, or other original documents; his tremendous strength lay, rather, in the moral solidity of his personality. In Jefferson's judgment, "the moderation and virtue of a single character probably prevented this revolution from being closed, as most others have been, by a subversion of that liberty it was intended to establish."

The primacy of ideas in the aethereal umwelt means that aethereals live in a world of books, magazines, journals, lectures and intellectual conversation. Aethereals of all degrees of intelligence are verbalists. So are intelligent experials, but the difference in the way the two types use words is distinctive. Experials converse to exchange information about the latest things the people they know are feeling, thinking and doing. Conversation is used to explore and share their own lives and the lives of specific friends and acquaintances, and is rich in detail. Aethereals converse to exchange abstractions: novel ideas, intellectual interpretations of events, hypotheses about the social, psychological and other sources of national events or peoples' behavior. Factual detail arises only as it provides the "nodes" around which the field of ideas orients itself like a magnetic field around a magnet. A social conversation between aethereals may go on for hours exploring various alternative perspectives on a single event or fact.

People of other types perceive aethereals as logically adroit, brilliant, witty, imaginative, playful, highly principled, detached, amusing. They may also be seen as impractical, indecisive, remote, heartless, inhumanly intellectual, and living in an ivory tower.

Karl Marx was an aethereal who spent his life creating, fashioning, elaborating and refining a new intellectual understanding of human history. A newspaper editor as a young man, he abandoned his trade in order to be able to devote more time to research, thought, and writing. The most comprehensive and far-reaching of revolutionaries in theory, he never took part in a revolution. During the dramatic uprisings in Europe in 1848, he stood on the sidelines, watching and assessing; the result was a series of brilliant historigraphical analyses. In the following decades there was a revolutionary socialist underground in every major nation in Europe, save England, any one of which would have been thrilled to have enjoyed his participation or even active support. Where did Marx live? In England, where he could lead a quiet life, undisturbed by alarums and excursions, and where he could spend his time in the British Museum library. Caring nothing for the material amenities of life, he lived and died in poverty and is buried in a crowded commoner's cemetery. Marx was powerless and relatively unknown, except among his ideological comrades, through most of his own century; in the century following he has been revered by half the world and his writings have influenced, to a greater or lesser degree, the course of every nation on earth.

Aethereals have their influence through their ideas, not their persons or their actions, so this kind of delayed impact (though on a lesser scale) is almost common among them. To have far more influence after their lifetimes than during is a not infrequent aethereal destiny—and a not particularly uncongenial one. Besides those mentioned, other aethereals include Darwin, Einstein, Plato, Galileo, Aldous Huxley, Martin Luther King Jr., Virginia Woolf, Mozart and Shakespeare.

The Relationship of the Types

The experial/aethereal polarity defines an individual's space in one way; the structural/oceanic polarity defines it in a different way. Both are required to create one complete spatial umwelt. Schematically, we visualize the aethereal and experial worlds divided by a horizontal line, as at left, and the structural and oceanic worlds divided by a vertical line, as at right. The combination of the two polarities yields a quaternia design, as below. (Be sure to observe that this design does *not* define four "quarters," but rather two sets of two halves, one set superimposed upon the other.) For

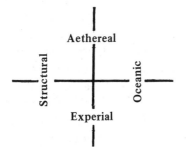

reasons too complicated to explain here, however, the two types of spatial experience comprising any one umwelt cannot be co-equal. One must be more fundamental than the other; it completely dominates in all circumstances where there is any tension between them.

Accordingly, there are not four basic spatial umwelts possible for human beings, but eight. An individual's umwelt may be primary aethereal, secondary oceanic; another's may be primary oceanic, secondary aethereal. One individual's may be primary experial, secondary structural; another's may be primary structural, secondary experial. One way of visualizing this relationship of umwelts is suggested at right, in which the darker cross-hatching indicates the primary experience of space, and the lighter lines indicate the secondary experience. The example illustrated is that of the primary aethereal, secondary oceanic.

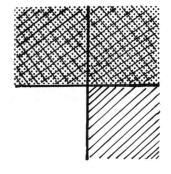

The time umwelts, discussed earlier, are not connected randomly with the space umwelts; there is an intimate relationship among them, in which spatial, not temporal, considerations are the controlling factor. Demonstrating why this is the case, and showing the necessity of the particular relationships that exist, unfortunately is beyond the scope of this paper. The easiest case to see "intuitively" may be that of so-called thinking time. The linear past-present-future of this type comprises a combination of structural consciousness and aethereal consciousness, applied to temporal experience. Structural consciousness: the linearity structures the apprehension of time. Aethereal consciousness: past and future, and for that matter present, are experienced predominantly as "idea," not personal experience. Thus this type remembers the *idea* of, say, something important that happened three months ago, not the *experience* of it, and the totality of such memories are structured. The other relationships are these:

absolute present ("sensation")	— structural + experial spaces
present and past fused by memory ("feeling")	— oceanic + experial spaces
present and future fused by potentiality ("intuition")	— oceanic + aethereal spaces

Thus the time umwelts half-overlap the space umwelts, and there are still only eight types of consciousness. Each type can, however, be labelled several ways. The example illustrated on the previous page, for instance, can be called a primary aethereal/secondary oceanic; or simply "an oceanic aethereal;" or an "intuitive aethereal." (In assigning time umwelts to combinations of space experience, the order of predominance of the two space experiences being combined does not matter.)

Perhaps the biggest difference between this experiential world typology and the Jungian typology from which it evolved, aside from the addition of new concepts, lies in the much greater flexibility it grants to the deployment of energies within an individual's psyche. The experitypic view is that the space-time umwelts define a "bubble" of consciousness within which all experience occurs. *Within* that bubble, however, an individual may deploy his energies or "functions" in many ways. For instance, someone in the structural-aethereal space umwelt — hence the linear ("thinking") time umwelt — may fall in love and for a long period enjoy predominantly feeling, not thinking, experiences—without in any way departing his own space-time umwelt. There is no necessary connection, at least at any particular time, between the umwelt and the energies within the psyche.

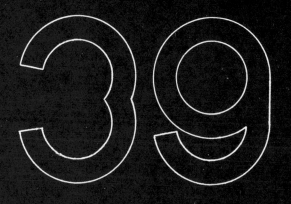

THE EXPERIENCE
OF COLOUR

THE EXPERIENCE OF COLOR

by Vasco Ronchi
Director, National Institute of Optics, Florence.
Edited and condensed by Carolyn Hill.

The third and last subject we want to treat is that of color.* Although there is a large body of literature devoted to its study, the subject of color cannot be considered at all exhausted.

Since ancient times, the man-in-the-street has thought of color as something set inside luminous sources, either adhering to body surfaces or, in the case of transparent substances, contained within their mass. Thus a flame is red, a leaf is green, a glass is red. In addition to this popular conception however, was another known to the ancient Greeks and Romans; philosophers had concluded that color is a psychical subjective entity which could not be objectified. No one, they said, could define absolutely how he sees a color; the only way that one can communicate about his experience of color is to show and name samples one by one. The person to whom these samples are shown might see certain color nuances and agree to the names used, but there is no proof that both people see the same colors in the same way.

Thus the problem arose of individuating the way in which the psyche could know the color of objects.

The visual-ray theory did not answer the question. Color was considered as something akin to the shape of objects or bodies looked at: it was customarily said that the task of sight was to know the "shape and color" of bodies. The visual rays, which had the task of exploring the external world and indicating to the eyes the shape of the explored bodies, also had the task of exploring their colors. But mathematical exactitude was lacking.

The theory of *eidolas,* or images, was more explicit in this regard: eidolas, which continuously detached from body surfaces, had not

---

* The first two subjects in the "New Optics" are the "Mechanism of Vision" and "Radiation and Light", covered fully in SUPERSENSONICS by Christopher Hills, published 1975 by University of the Trees Press.

only shape, but also the colors of bodies.

But complications and difficulties were already beginning to arise. One of the best known was that of the rainbow, an imposing and striking phenomenon, which had always raised problems to people who tried to explain it. It was clear that it was a result of small water drops suspended in the atmosphere during or after a rainfall. What was a mystery was why those drops of transparent water, so small in size, should give rise to that finely-colored bow. The same question could be asked about soap bubbles; a very thin layer of transparent soapy water takes on vivid colors: where do they come from? This was a question which no one could answer.

However, the observation of these phenomena yielded a classification: colors which remained in objects (e.g. in flowers, leaves, or stones) were called *permanent colors*. Colors which appeared unexpectedly (in rainbows or soap bubbles) were called *apparent colors*. There was not much discussion of the matter however, even though it did interest such people as painters and decorators.

Thus one arrived at the seventeenth century with the conviction that light was white and colorless and that it was corrupted with colors when it was altered by contact with objects.

But a new point of view appeared in 1638 in the book *Dioptrique* by Réné Descartes. As previously mentioned, he raised the hypothesis that *lumen* consisted of spherical corpuscles of matter, possessing a very high velocity (not as yet measured) and at the same time a rotation movement around an axis passing through their center. Descartes affirmed that color was the subjective representation of this rotation movement. In other words, he "transferred the color to the radiation, though explicitly saying that the radiation is not colored, but the observer sees different colors because of the different movements of the various corpuscles." However, he did not treat the question very deeply, and his ideas did not influence the history of color theory very much.

Meanwhile, the number of cases noted of *apparent colors* had increased. When a beam of radiation was refracted at the surface of a container of water, colors projected on the bottom of the container were noticed. The vivid colors seen by looking through

917

a transparent glass prism were observed, as well as the colors of the thin layers mentioned previously (due, as we know today, to interference phenomena).

During the seventeenth century, while scientists enthusiastically dedicated themselves to researching the nature of the "something" responsible for vision, phenomena were becoming evident in the field of light and radiation which were complicating the work of physicists and philosophers.

Important progress was made by F. Grimaldi in his book of 1665 entitled, *Physico-Mathesis de Lumine, Coloribus et Iride.* He discusses color extensively in this book, investigating its formation in the phenomena of reflection, refraction, and diffraction (noting the colored fringes formed during diffraction). He concludes from his analyses that color is something inside the *lumen,* and that it is a modification of radiation which causes one to see colors.

He also suggests a hypothesis about the nature of this modification. In the first part of his book where he has supported the substantial nature of radiation, he also assumes that the trajectories of the corpuscles are sinuous rather than straight lines. The color which the eye sees, he claims, depends on the frequency of the logarithmic spiral of radiation. "This hypothesis, clearly, must be dropped nowadays, because, by virtue of the inertia principle, we know that sinuous trajectories are not possible." Although he cannot support the idea of the sinuous trajectories, Grimaldi proves that color must be considered an effect in the observer of a modification of radiation. This idea, in a different form, was to later prove quite fruitful.

F. Grimaldi's book had just appeared when Isaac Newton began his series of important and elegant experiments on color, those which immediately earned him a place of renown in the scientific world. Newton had enthusiastically accepted the much-discussed corpuscular theory of radiation. Associating it with the principle of attraction of material bodies, he succeeded in finding the explanation of refraction: it was the effect of the attraction of the refracting body on the particles constituting the radiation. He then arrived at the explanation of optical dispersion, simply by assuming that in the impinging beam there were particles with different masses. Since in dispersion, especially of solar radiation, colors are seen in well-defined succession (from the least deviated seen as red to the most deviated seen as violet), Newton deduced that in the impinging beam of white light there were mixed all types of particles. Singularly taken, these particles made one see single colors, and refraction selected and conveyed them in different directions due to the different attraction on the particles of different mass. According to Newton, therefore, color is not due to a modification of radiation as his predecessors had said, "but is due to the nature of the radiation." The particles with different mass do exist; one has only to select them or to mix them in different ratios to obtain different colors.

In order to check these points of view, he carried out a number of elegant and convincing experiments, two of which had decisive importance.

The first consisted in proving that if a beam is composed of identical particles, it does not split (experience dispersion) when it crosses any number of prisms. In his experiment, he obtained what is today called *monochromatic radiation,* and he obtained it in the same way that it is obtained today with the apparatus called the *monochromator.* If a beam of white light is sent into a prism, a *spectrum* is obtained. By means of a narrow slit, only a very narrow portion of this spectrum is allowed to pass, and if this narrow beam is made to cross another prism or many other prisms, it does not experience any additional dispersion.

The second crucial experiment carried out by Newton consisted in superposing again all the beams of radiation emerging from a prism. He thus obtained the white light which had been sent onto the prism and which had been dispersed by it.

However, even Newton emphasizes that he does not believe that the material corpuscles are colored, as if they are red, green, or yellow dust. He says that he would call his rays rubrificent (i.e., reddener) rather than *red,* because they are not really red, but only make one see the object from which they are emitted as red. He adds that if, in the sequel to his book, he should use the terms "red rays," "green rays," or "violet rays," he will do so in order that the "common people" may better understand the experiments he will describe . . .

Newton's corpuscular theory proved completely powerless to explain colors of thin layers, and the colors which occur in diffraction, or as he called it, inflection.

Moreover, Newton himself had made certain important reservations. He had explicitly realized that some colors seen under certain conditions cannot be explained in terms of the size of the corpuscles constituting radiation (e.g., in dreams, hallucinations, compression of the eyeball). He concluded that under such conditions particles with certain refraction properties act on the eye in a way that is connected with color vision. This reservation hindered the construction of a unified corpuscular theory.

However, Newton's ideas completely conquered the scientific world of the eighteenth century. The growth of positivism influenced the study of color, and the reservations made by Descartes, Grimaldi, and Newton were forgotten. People began to say that colors were in the radiation, and the role of the observer completely disappeared. Colors became physical entities which could be measured by means of physical devices.

Thus when the wave theory replaced the corpuscular theory at the beginning of the nineteenth century, any questions about colors were readily answered. Measurements of wavelengths easily proved that the longer waves (those with $\lambda = 0.7$ micron) make one see red, while the shorter ones (with $\lambda = 0.4$ micron) make one see violet, and those with intermediate wavelengths make one see the spectral colors intermediate between red and violet. Moreover, waves with λ larger than 0.8 micron or smaller than 0.4 micron, by which nothing is seen, were said to cause vision of the color black.

Actually, nobody spoke of rays *causing* vision of certain colors; rather, everyone said that the waves with $\lambda = 0.8$ micron *are* red, those with $\lambda = 0.4$ micron *are* violet, and so on. The same way of speaking is used today, disregarding its logical absurdity. It is evident that electromagnetic waves are not colored; as they have no appearance, they have no color.

The wave theory only complicated the understanding of color. As a matter of fact, the particles assumed by the corpuscular theory had never been directly and singularly observed. On the contrary, the wavelengths of optical radiations were now easily measured, and as λ was measured, the corresponding color was seen. With the positivistic tendency of the age, it was inevitable that waves and color should be connected objectively.

The understanding of color has always paralleled that of light, of course, but the two have not always been studied together. Thus, when the wave theory demolished the corpuscular theory at the beginning of the nineteenth century, physicists were studying only light and ignoring the question of color.

A ferocious attack against the color theory proposed by Newton was instead launched in 1810 by a famous literary man, Wolfgang Goethe. No one, however, took it very seriously, because the Newtonians were too busy with the serious attacks of physicists to defend themselves against a literary man. However, Goethe's reasoning was worth considering. He was objecting to those who insisted on considering colors as physical phenomena and ignoring their physiological aspects and other complications. But no one agreed with him, except another philosopher, A. Schopenauer, who went even further and concluded that in his opinion colors were only physiological because they originated at the retina of the observer's eye. He was also ignored.

Thus the prevalent opinion remained among physicists that the question of wavelength solved the problem of color.

However, at the beginning of the nineteenth century the mechanism of *trichromia* was being defined more and more precisely, mainly because of Young's work. From time immemorial it had been known that when mixing certain colors for painting, other colors were obtained. Moreover, it was known that many colors could be obtained from only a few, just by varying the ratios of the components. However, now it was discovered that by means of only three colors, called *fundamental,* all other colors could be obtained.

The theory was then proposed that there was a retinal correspondence to these fundamental colors, that is, that there were three types of receptors in the retina, each sensitive to one of the fundamental colors; the seen color supposedly resulted from the ratios of the excitations of these three types of receptors.

Thus, even in the field of color a split was occurring between the physical and the physiological factions. Both factions ignored each other, or nearly so. The physiologists, indifferent to the convictions of the physicists, devoted themselves to research of the retinal receptors specialized for the three fundamental colors. But they found nothing. Next, the theory was proposed that there were substances presenting a selective absorbing power for these colors. But even these substances have not been clearly isolated. Next, it was thought that there were selective filters, but the problem is still open. Many physiologists have carried out countless experiments in this field and proposed many theories, but a definitive layout does not seem to be forthcoming in the near future.

Meanwhile, a new science was acquiring a certain uniformity: *colorimetry*. Color was becoming more and more important industrially both in the production of paint pigments and dyes. A mechanism had become necessary that would allow an exact definition of a given color. Once again, the conviction that colors were inherent in objects, well-defined, objective, and constant for all observers, led to posing the problem of measuring them with physical methods and apparatuses. Colorimetry seemed fit for the task.

But colorimetry raises the same problem as we find in photometry. Since colors are a purely psychic entity, it is impossible to measure them by physical means and procedures. Measurements of this type can be carried out only on radiation. Accordingly, the problem should be posed in the following terms: how can the composition of radiation which makes one see a given color be determined?

Unfortunately, the answer to this question is not yet possible. The phenomena elude exact definition. The common opinion may be that objects have certain constant colors, but things appear very different to anyone who would try to determine those colors.

It is one thing to consider the color of light sources, another to deal with the color of opaque bodies or that of transparent bodies. The fact is that radiation, as emphasized in the preceding chapters, is neither luminous nor colored. It is capable of acting on the retina, giving rise to the transmission of nervous impulses to the brain. Now the information which has arrived there through the optical nerves is represented in the psychical center. Earlier we studied the representation of shapes and their localization in apparent space. We only briefly mentioned that these stimuli bring additional information to the retina, which registers both the photometric and colorimetric aspects. In other words, the internal effigies created by the psyche are given a certain *brightness* and a certain *tone of color.* A third characteristic must be added to these two, *saturation,* which is necessary to define the other two.

The term "brightness" denotes the stronger or weaker clarity of an internal effigy. Among photometric quantities, we noted *luminance,* a very recent name of that quantity which represents the luminous intensity per unit surface of a body in a given direction (i.e., that quantity expressed by giving the number of candles emitted by one cm^2 of the body surface in the chosen direction). This is a photometric element, which corresponds to the radiance in the group of radiometric quantities. It is a very important element which is widely used in the study of the luminosity of optical systems, and until very recently it was called brilliance. Recently however, the International Commission for Illumination had to admit that convenience dictated two different names to indicate physical cause and psychical effect. The above-mentioned photometric quantity, even if evaluated with a conventional criterion, is undoubtedly the element which determines the clarity of the seen figure (effigy), but the two things are best distinguished from each other. Accordingly, the photometric element has been called luminance, and the name of brilliance has been passed to the psychical element.

Thus, in modern terminology, it must be said that the solar disc as seen in a clear sky at noon has a higher brilliance than that of the moon disc, seen also in a clear sky.

The tone of a color is that aspect of the effigy created by the psyche, indicated with the words red, green, blue, etc. As we have already noted, there is no means for describing this aspect, other than by showing a sample. The tone of a color is usually named from the object on which it is found; thus orange is the color of the peel of the oranges, sky-blue is the color of the sky, and so on.

The concept of saturation has been introduced to indicate that a given tone of color can be more or less intense or attenuated. Thus one speaks of pure yellow or of more or less soft yellow. There is vivid red and there are several pink gradations; there is green and soft green, azure and soft azure and so on. The more vivid colors are said to be saturated, those that are attenuated can be considered as mixtures of saturated colors, with a certain quantity of *white.* The amount of saturation is indicated by the ratio of the quantity of pure color and that of white, with which the former is mixed.

Now the problem becomes the following: which of the elements of radiation that arrive at the eye are represented by the psyche as brilliance, color tone, and saturation?

As to brilliance, the answer is rather easy. To a higher luminance, usually corresponds a higher brilliance. The answer may seem evident, but things are not quite so simple. The psyche creates effigies on its own judgment. In certain cases it creates them even without receiving any stimulus along the optical nerves; in other cases it creates them by receiving nerve impulses along that way which do not originate by a radiant stimulus arriving at the retina. Rather they originate from a completely different cause; the beams seen when one is punched in the eye, or when one presses on the side of the eyeball with a finger are examples.

Even without considering cases so far from ordinary vision, adaptation to surrounding luminosity must be considered. This refers to the fact that with the same luminance one sees effigies with different brilliances, depending on retinal conditions, which can change depending on the surrounding luminosity. Because it has been ascertained that there is not a constant relation between luminance and brilliance, it has been thought better to indicate the two elements by two different names. . . .

For now, to avoid confusion in our argument, let us assume that brilliance is strictly related to the luminance of the object.

To proceed, which characteristic of radiation is represented by the psyche as a given tone of a color? This is still an open problem. Physicists, as we have seen, think they have solved the problem and assert that wavelength is that characteristic. But we cannot completely agree with them. There is not always a one-to-one correspondence between the wavelength of the radiant stimulus at the bottom of the eye and the color tone of the effigy.

Every now and then some circumstance is noticed which shows that the color of the effigy changes if the spectral composition of the radiation remains constant. Among the best known can be recalled the Purkinje effect, which consists in an increase of retinal sensitivity to the optical radiations of shorter wavelengths, when luminance decreases. This phenomenon explains, among other things, the fact that moonlight, though it is due to solar radiation and lacks short wavelength radiations, appears markedly more blue than daylight, while it should appear more yellowish. The reason is that daylight is much more intense. But it should also be noted that effigies created under moonlight are all gray, without color tone, though objects seen at night send radiations to the eyes with almost the same spectral composition as during daytime, only much weaker.

Moreover, many experiments have proven that the color of an effigy varies when only the surrounding field is varied. For example, the color of an object appears to change if one has adapted his eye for a length of time to an object of a different color. Or a perfectly normal psyche might apprehend a color differently from what the accompanying radiant stimulus would be thought to determine. Thus, a black cat will send to the observer's eye a radiation much more intense during the day than a white cat will send at night; nevertheless, the former is seen as black, the latter as white. Similarly, the radiation sent by the national flag into the eyes of observers at sunset has a decidedly different reddish spectral composition from that sent by the same flag at noon. Nevertheless, the same flag is usually seen, with the same color tones.

It has even been proven that a figure, for instance a colored disc, is seen with a different color from that of the same disc of equal size, and equally illuminated, but with a tapered edge instead of a sharp edge.

On the other hand, the opposite observation can be made. Not only can effigies with *different* color tones be created when the eye is stimulated by a given spectral radiation, or wavelength, but the *same* tone can be seen when either a radiation of a well-determined wavelength (that is a monochromatic radiation) enters the eye or when a mixture of radiations enter the eye with completely different wavelengths, suitably proportioned. As previously mentioned, this is just one of the bases of trichromia. The phenomenon is so well-known that two colors seen as equal when beams of radiation of different spectral compositions enter the eye, have been given a particular name: *metamerical.*

If there is still such uncertainty about color tone, the same must be said for saturation, which is substantially a particular tone of a color.

If one then adds the fact that several well-known anomalies exist in observers' eyes (usually attributed to eye structure), in which sensibility to various wavelengths is markedly different from that of the most common (and therefore called normal) eyes, one must arrive at the conclusion that "color is the psychical representation of a characteristic of radiation, to which we cannot yet give a name."

This is the situation, after thousands of years in which the nature of color has been studied.

* * *

Let us now return to colorimetry. What meaning can carrying out measurements on colors have, if these are hermetically sealed in the subjective world of observers, and if the correspondence to physical stimuli is so loose that we do not even know what physical characteristic they represent?

This question will be answered after we have seen what colorimetry mainly consists of.

For the sake of simplicity, let us limit ourselves to the case of opaque bodies which reflect impinging radiation. This will cover paints, cloths, papers, and all other objects usually termed colored.

After what we have said, it is clear that they do not "have" a color in themselves, but that the effigies by means of which they are represented in the psyche of the observer are colored, on the basis of the spectral composition of the radiation which arrives from the objects to the eyes. Since such radiation is not emitted by the objects, but arrives onto objects from another source which lights them up, one soon concludes that the final result will depend also on the spectral composition of the radiation sent from the source onto the objects being considered. The objects themselves have only one task: that of *selectively* reflecting the radiation which illuminates them.

In order to determine the actual intervening color absorption of the object, it is first necessary to fix the spectral composition of the enlightening radiation. This is an extremely difficult problem, since all the surrounding available sources in nature are extremely variable.

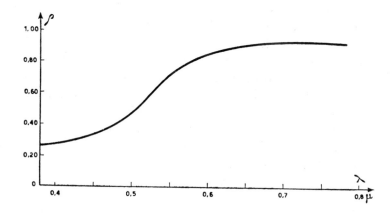

The ICI* solved the problem by an *international convention:* it defined three special sources, which are termed *illuminant A, illuminant B* and *illuminant C,* and also gave the rules for their realization. Roughly speaking one can say that these sources emit radiations which correspond to that of incandescent lamps, of the midday sun, and of the daytime sky toward the north, respectively.

Once the illuminant is chosen, one determines in a spectro-photometric way the reflectivity factor of the object under consideration, at the different optical wavelengths. The reflectivity factor indicates the percentage of the radiation which is reflected. The result of the measurements is represented by a diagram of the type in Fig.

By combining the characteristics of the emission of the chosen

---

*International Commission for Illumination

illuminant with this diagram, one obtains the spectral distribution
of the radiation reflected by the object being considered.

Now one must determine the effect of this radiation on the eye of
the observer. Even here, as in photometry, one must give up real
"observers, which are too variable and inconstant, and replace them
with a standard observer: the normal eye."

"In this way one obtains a diagram which should indicate the
answer of the normal eye to the radiation of the chosen illuminant
as reflected by the body."

After lengthy studies were made on the choice of fundamental
colors, a procedure was finally determined, which gives up direct
determination but makes use only of the spectrophotometric diagram of the reflectivity factor of the object under study. Thus,
three fundamental colors have been selected, nonexistent but mathematically derived, and with a numerical and conventional procedure,
where the characteristics of the chosen illuminant and the visibility
curve of the normal eye appear in the form of coefficients. And one
arrives at determining three numbers, whose sum is equal to 1, which
are termed the *trichromatic coordinates* x, y, and z of the measured
color.

Everytime the measurements give the same coordinates as a result,
the observer should see the same color.

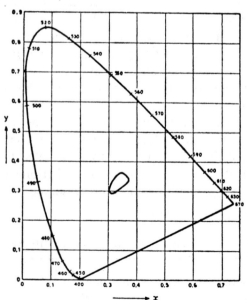

' "Does one measure the color in this way? Clearly, one does not. A numerical manipulation has been devised of the experimental data of the selective reflectivity of the surface under study, and one has arrived at representing a certain physical condition, under which a mean or normal eye should see a given color, when looking at that surface enlightened by the chosen illuminant."

The fact that it was necessary to crystallize the spectral composition and the intensity of the enlightening source radiation as well as the characteristics of sensitivity of the eye of the observer proves that the experience had demonstrated that color is continuously changing in the ordinary conditions of observations. This would be true both when the illumination changes and when the observer (or the conditions under which the observer operates) changes, as emphasized above.

BIBLIOGRAPHY

EUCLIDE, *Ottica e Catottrica*. Trans. by F. Egnatio Danti, Firenze, Giunti, 1573.

ALHAZEN, *Opticae Thesaurus Libri septem*. Trans. by F. Risner, Basilea, Episcopios, 1572.

F. MAUROLICO, *Photismi de lumine et umbra. Diaphaneon seu transparentium*. Napoli, Tarquini, 1611.

G. B. DELLA PORTA, *Magia Naturalis*. Napoli, Salviani, 1589.

G. B. DELLA PORTA, *De Refractione*. Napoli, Salviani, 1593.

J. KEPLERO, *Ad Vitellionem Paralipomena*. Francoforte, Marni, 1604.

J. KEPLERO, *Dioptrice*. Augusta, Franci, 1611.

R. DESCARTES, *Dioptrique*. Paris, 1638.

F. M. GRIMALDI, *Physico-Mathesis de Lumine, Coloribus et Iride*. Bologna, Benazi, 1665.

R. HOOKE, *Micrographia*. London, Martin, 1665.

G. GALILEI, *Sidereus Nuncius*. Venezia, Baglioni, 1610.

I. NEWTON, *Optice*. Lausanne, Bousquet, 1740.

Ch. HUYGENS, *Traité de la lumière*. Leiden, Vander, 1690.

V. RONCHI, *Storia della luce*. 2ª Ed., Bologna, Zanichelli, 1952.

V. RONCHI, *Optics, the science of vision*. New York, New-York University Press, 1957.

V. RONCHI, *Il cannocchiale di Galileo e la scienza del '600*. Torino, Boringhieri, 1958.

V. RONCHI, *Critica dei fondamenti dell'acustica e dell'ottica*. Roma, Ministero della Pubblica Istruzione, 1963.

V. RONCHI, *Sui fondamenti dell'acustica e dell'ottica*. Firenze, Olschki, 1967.

V. RONCHI, *The nature of Light*. Harvard University Press, Cambridge, Mass. 1970.

The radiating text in the image includes:
NATURE'S PSYCHIC
COLOUR AND CONSCIOUSNESS
RELATIONSHIP
WINDOWS OF KNOWING
NUCLEAR EVOLUTION
OF LIFE
SOCIOBIOLOGY
BY NATURE'S LAWS
THE CONTRACTION
SPIRITUALITY
SPACE
NUCLEAR EVOLUTION
PRIMORDIAL IMAGINATION
LIGHT LEVELS
IS KUNDALINI
OF COLOUR
METAPHYSICS OF
BODY
INTERNAL & EXTERNAL
RADIATION BARRIER
HOW DO HUMANS
GROUP
SCIENCE
FOURTH FORCE
SHAKESPEARES
AND THE CHAKRAS

NUCLEAR EVOLUTION
AND
THE I CHING

NUCLEAR EVOLUTION

&

THE I CHING

Correlations between the unconscious time-worlds of the seven energy levels of consciousness and the eighth domain of the Tao.

BY REGAN POWER

An explanation of the past, present, and future in the rainbow of consciousness as seen by the ancient seers and diviners of nature's laws in the I Ching.

EDITORS' NOTE

When Regan Power came to Centre House Community in London in 1967 he was studying for his psychology degree and about to get married and give up psychology. Christopher Hills persuaded him to continue with his degree but strongly discouraged the marriage in view of the future.

In order to back up the effectiveness of this seeming interference in someone's life, Christopher introduced Regan Power to the I Ching and showed him its profound accuracy in divining the psychological tensions between the conscious and unconscious states of Being.

Regan thereupon agreed to make a deep study of the I Ching and as one of the longest residents of the Centre House Community founded by Christopher in 1966, he has spent the last ten years of his life there becoming an authority on this remarkable book of wisdom.

The following outline of the relationship of time with consciousness and the experience of Nuclear Evolution as taught orally by Christopher to all his students who use the I Ching as an instrument of knowing, was specially written for this third edition of NUCLEAR EVOLUTION and the editors are grateful for Regan's timely contribution to the work.

BACKGROUND FOR CONSULTING THE I CHING
IN RELATION TO NUCLEAR EVOLUTION

The I Ching, or "Book of Changes" is an ancient Chinese book of wisdom that is constructed in the form of an oracle. A person can ask it any meaningful question and receive an answer, which is obtained by building up a Hexagram, or six-line figure, according to the outcome of the casting of some yarrow stalks, or alternatively, the throw of three coins. The I Ching has at all times, it would seem, been generally considered to be one of the profoundest books in the world. The most eminent Chinese thinkers and philosophers gave it their attention, including Confucius and Lao Tzu. Prominent westerners who took up study of the I Ching were Leibnitz, the mathematician, and more recently, C.G. Jung, the psychologist. The book is also one of the oldest in the world, its origins antedating recorded history. At least some of the ideas which comprise its content were recorded in about 2,000 B.C.; it is in this century, however, after four thousand years of maturation in Chinese hands, that the I Ching has been rendered appealingly to the western mind by the late Richard Wilhelm, whose edition includes a foreward by C.G. Jung. Wilhelm did the monumental job of assembling, editing and organising the mass of texts and commentaries on the I Ching into a single clear and coherent synthesis. In so doing, however, he also captured the beauty and the essence of the ancient Chinese wisdom, which always rests upon the natural and the self-evident, yet is nonetheless mysterious. Nuclear Evolution has its roots in the same natural source and is a further development of the I Ching.

The subject matter of the I Ching (the way of Nature or the meaning and the eternal laws of life), is universal, transcending all barriers of culture, of religion or whatever else may separate the minds of men. Of course, like Nuclear Evolution, not everyone takes to it, nor does everybody make sense of it. But increasingly, the I Ching strikes a deep chord in people's breasts and today there are large numbers of people, old and young, who keep a special place for this friendly old sage in their lives as a source of illumination and guidance. The form in which the subject matter of the I Ching is presented is very systematic.

Firstly, it posits the existence of an eternal life-principle: the monad, which underlies all creation. This unified state of ultimate reality is pure spirit and is conceived to be ever-present everywhere. Corresponding with the "Chaos" of the ancient Greeks, the "Unmanifest" of the Hindu, and the "Void" of the Buddhists and of Genesis,* this fundamental level of the Universe is considered to contain everything, consciousness and energy, within itself in undifferentiated unity. Since this level of existence remains ever the same, it lies outside of time and change. The I Ching says that this domain cannot be apprehended through words or thoughts, but can be experienced in the silence of inner stillness. It represents this domain by the term "T'ai Chi T'u," meaning the "Primal Beginning" and symbolizes it as "the Great Ridgepole," i.e. that which supports the Heavens, the roof of the world.

Although the T'ai Chi T'u does not itself enter into change, it gives rise to creation and its being permeates the whole Universe transcendentally, thus determining the law that governs all movement in time and space. This law was called "Tao," meaning "The Way." Hence, to apprehend and express the Tao in every situation is equivalent to entering into unity and harmony with life at its most fundamental level. Thus, the I Ching is concerned with describing the nature of the Tao as it appears in every possible situation, and with describing the kind of practical action that conforms with the Tao in the given situation. The I Ching uses sixty-four archetypal situations that are complementary to one another, like spokes of a wheel, and which collectively exhaust the full spectrum of possibilities of expression of the ultimate Tao. Each of these archetypes is represented by a Hexagram composed of a specific combination of broken and single lines.

As the creation emerges from the primaeval state, the T'ai Chi T'u, two fundamental aspects of Being appear: the light and the dark.**

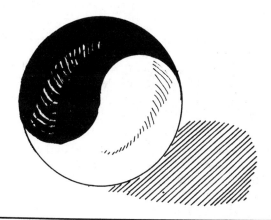

The light principle, called "The Creative" and symbolised by Heaven, is the generative, life-giving force of consciousness; while the dark principle, called "The Receptive" and symbolised by the Earth, is the reflective, form-giving force of mind and of matter. These two world principles are not thought to be antagonistic but rather to mutually complement each other, as the archetypal male and female. Out of the union of these two principles, the universe of created things is said to derive. Hence, Heaven, the procreative force which supplies the seed of individual consciousness, is called the Father, and Earth, which receives the individual seeds of life from Heaven and gives them material form, is called the Mother. In Nuclear Evolution this duality of Heaven and Earth is represented by the colors orange (expansion) and indigo (inward contraction) in one phase and white and black in another phase. The "Tao", the law of movement, of the white light principle is expansion and its attribute is strength, power or energy. The I Ching represents this force as an unbroken line, ———. This line signifies the unified nature of the Creative, from which its strength derives. The Tao of the dark principle is contraction and its attribute is yieldingness or adaptability. This is represented by a broken line, —— ——, signifying duality and inner emptiness, from which the yielding quality derives.

In the manifest Universe, every naturally created thing is conceived of as being composed of elements of the Creative and Receptive principles conjoined together. The light principle, the spiritual element, is the creature's individual soul. The dark principle, the maternal element, is the body. In Nuclear Evolution, the individual soul is depicted as having seven bodies, or seven energy levels with an eighth domain of the absolute Self. Likewise, the I Ching describes seven forms of energy plus the eighth homogenous form of purely spiritual energy from which all the others are divided. These are represented by the eight "Trigrams" or "Pa-kua", which are three-fold combinations of the lines of the light and dark principles. As with the original light and dark principles, the Trigrams are represented as complementary opposites, having overall affinities with either the light or the dark principle, but differentiating the "Tao" of each yet further. The I Ching presents these according to the following circular scheme, which is related to the points of the compass.

936

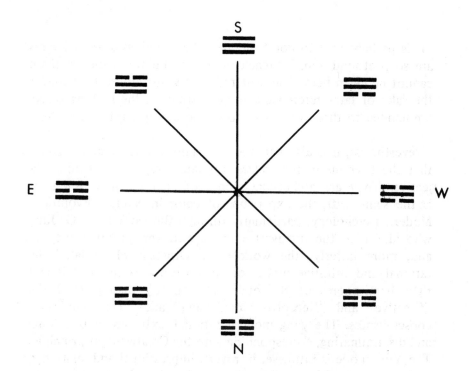

Each Trigram is symbolised by some part of nature. Ch'ien, ☰ , the Creative, and K'un, ☷ , the Receptive, are symbolised straightforwardly, by Heaven and Earth respectively, being essentially identical with the original Creative and Receptive principles.

Li, ☲ , called "The Clinging", is symbolised by Fire and its attribute is dependence, just as a flame depends on a source of fuel for its existence. Its opposite, K'an, ☵ , called "The Abysmal" is symbolised by water, and its attribute is danger or obscurity. These two are obviously related to the primal light and dark principles, Ch'ien and K'un.

Chen, ☳ , "The Arousing", is symbolised by Thunder and its attribute is shock, energy, vigour. It represents a rushing forth of life-energy. Its opposite is Sun, ☴ ,"The Gentle, The Penetrating", symbolised by wind or wood, and represents organic development. Chen belongs to the strong, light principle and Sun to the weak, dark principle.

Finally, Ken, ☶ , called "Keeping Still", is symbolised by the Mountain representing tranquil but lofty contemplation. Of the things of nature, this comes closest to Heaven. Its opposite, Tui, ☱ , called "The Joyous" is symbolised by the Lake, whose surface reflects the light and beauty of Heaven. Ken belongs to the light principle and Tui to the dark.

937

It is perhaps well to point out that the meanings of the trigrams are so profound and far reaching that a full treatment of them cannot be given here. The reader is merely introduced to them for the sake of later reference and some study of the I Ching is recommended to those who wish to go more deeply into these ideas.

Nevertheless, it is also perhaps important for us to remain aware that the trigrams in themselves ultimately represent nothing objective. They are archetypal modes of energy-consciousness. It is the same with the experience of color in Nuclear Evolution. Modern psychology, particularly through the work of C. G. Jung who identified the Introvert and the Extravert personality types and, more latterly, the work of B. Ornstein who related the rational and intuitive modes of consciousness with the left and right hemispheres of the brain, has already distinguished the "Creative" and "Receptive" or "Yang" and "Yin" modes of consciousness. The yang mode is rational, extravert, expressional and discriminating, corresponding with the Creative light principle. The Yin mode is intuitive, introvert, impressional and relational, corresponding with the Receptive, dark principle of voidness. In Nuclear Evolution the colors represent thresholds of energy in the psyche. However, modern psychology does not yet recognise these forms of consciousness as also corresponding with specific forms of energy. The authors of the I Ching apparently saw no ultimate distinction between energy and consciousness and therefore to evolve a system describing one was automatically to describe the other. Hence, we find that the patterns and images in the I Ching relate equally to states of consciousness and forms of energy - hence, to objective events in time and space. The Theory of Nuclear Evolution attempts to bridge this same gap in consciousness. Furthermore, the originators of the I Ching, in generating the trigrams from the simple Yang and Yin, differentiated these two basic modes of energy-consciousness into a more refined eight-fold order. These readily formed a viable bridge between the subjective world of consciousness and the objective world of things, forces and events. Thus, the eight trigrams were readily applied to the divining of minerals and natural force-fields, geomancy, magic, healing and medicine, philosophy, numerology, self-development yoga exercises (some of which later developed into martial arts), psychology, agriculture, astrology and astronomy, meditation, and in consulting the Gods. In short, there seems to be virtually nothing to which the eight trigrams could not be applied. In the same way in Nuclear Evolution the seven domains of color and the eighth domain of the creative void can be applied to all of nature. Out of the combinations of trigrams in the I Ching, two at a time, the sixty-four hexagrams arise. The hexagrams, like trigrams, have meanings of their own, but these can also be deduced by reference to the component trigrams. While the single trigram can only relate to a single force, pattern of movement, or state of energy, etc., the hexagram, consisting of two trigrams, can depict the relationship between things. Thus, by reference to a hexagram, a man may assess himself in relation to his environment and hence determine the possibilities for action. In general, the lower trigram represents the "inner" world of content and causes, while the upper trigram represents the "outer" world of form and effects. Also, the upper and lower trigrams usually represent differences of elevation in terms of power and influence, the upper trigram occupying the place of Heaven and the lower that of the Earth. However, these general rules are by no means rigid and every hexagram is finally interpreted according to its own inherent rules. It is thus the same with each color in Nuclear Evolution which can be represented equally as a trigram.

In each hexagram, the meaning of the situation represented by the hexagram as a whole is explained under a section entitled "The Judgement", which includes an assessment of the prospects for good or bad fortune in the situation and the kind of action which is appropriate for it. Also in each hexagram another section, entitled "The Image", shows how the component trigrams produce the meaning of the hexagram as a whole and, using the images associated with the trigrams, portrays a scene from Nature which, as the very embodiment of Tao, or natural law, is used as a model for human behaviour, from which directives for the action of the "Superior man" are derived. A third section under each hexagram attaches a judgement to each individual line. These render the I Ching's answer yet more pertinent to the specific question put to it as well as explaining the meaning of the hexagram in more detail. In the same way "divination" in Nuclear Evolution can be achieved by using the colors as components of a complex energy field in place of trigrams and hexagrams.

For those who are unfamiliar with the technique of consulting the
I Ching, the coins method of building up trigrams and hexagrams
will now be described. Three similar coins, having clearly distinguishable "head" and "tail" faces, are taken and the numbers 2 and
3 are ascribed to the heads and tails. It does not matter whether one
makes heads 3 and tails 2 or heads 2 and tails 3 so long as one is
consistent in sticking to the arrangement chosen.

Next, the questioner frames his question in words, preferably
writing it down on a piece of paper. This small discipline is highly
useful for two reasons: firstly, it often makes the question clearer,
and secondly, it provides a tangible record of the question throughout the interpretation. It is remarkable how easily one's idea of a
question can change in so short a time.

Having composed his mind on the question, the enquirer mentally
presents it to the I Ching and throws the coins onto a flat surface.
Then he adds up the values shown by the coins as they have landed.
He may thus obtain a total of 6, 7, 8, or 9, and he draws the first
line of his hexagram according to the following scheme:

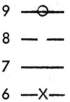

The small circle and cross in the middle of the lines associated with
9 and 6 indicate that these lines are "changing". This will be
explained shortly.

Let us suppose that the questioner obtained a 7. Then he would
simply write down an unbroken line ———— . Then he throws the
three coins again, and let us suppose that this time he gets 9 as his
total. This time he writes a solid line with a circle in the middle,
placing it above the first line, thus:

He throws the coins four more times, and puts down a line for each throw, placing each new one above the others until the hexagram is completed, which could look like this:

Ignoring for the time being any crosses or circles on the lines, he refers to the table at the back of the Book of Changes and finds the number of the hexagram.

Finding now the appropriate hexagram (the above example is No. 61) in the front part of the Book he simply reads the interpretation that is given there. The Judgement and the Image interpret the general meaning of the hexagram. The Judgement on "nine in the second place" (the places are numbered from the bottom of the hexagram) should also be read. The fact that this is a "changing" line in this hexagram designates it as having a special significance in the answer. The idea of the "changing" line is as follows: The broken and unbroken lines represent Yin and Yang forces respectively. When either of these reaches its extreme, it turns into its opposite. Thus, when something has become fully expanded (Yang), it starts to contract (Yin), and once it has fully contracted, it starts to expand again. The numbers 6 and 9 represent the extreme values of Yin and Yang and so are considered to be about to turn into their opposites. Thus, the yin line of the number 6 becomes a yang line (———), and the yang line of the number 9 becomes a yin line (— —).

The questioner may obtain a second hexagram, describing the conditions when those changes represented in the first hexagram are completed, by carrying over all the unchanging lines of the old hexagram into the new and by writing in the opposites of the changing lines in their appropriate places. Thus, in our example of Hexagram 61 with the second line changing, the new hexagram would be:

(Referring again to the table at the back of the Book of Changes, one finds that this is Hexagram 42.) One might simply write all this down as:

61   42

Again looking up the interpretation of this hexagram in the front part of the book, one reads the Judgement and the Image. However, no individual lines are to be taken as specially significant, for none are now "changing".

In interpreting the I Ching's words, I have invariably found that the best results are obtained by having a completely open mind, without preconceptions or expectations. In spite of all one may have learned about the meanings of trigrams, hexagrams and images, the real message may lie in some phrases or passages that would normally appear quite insignificant or even superfluous. On the other hand, it can be helpful in some cases to have a general understanding of the meanings of at least the trigrams, for in difficult instances, these can help one to see what the I Ching is getting at. Should the oracle's answer be somewhat baffling, reference to the commentaries on the hexagrams, in the last section of the book, can often give the vital key.

A note of complexity arises when we consider the significance of the second hexagram, derived from the changes present in the first. Although, as stated above, the second hexagram is generally thought to relate to future conditions when the changes represented in the first have occurred, what happens in the case of a question that has nothing to do with time, so that the question of past, present or future conditions is inapplicable?

This presented no small stumbling block to my understanding of the I Ching's answers until it eventually became clear to me that the second hexagram in fact represents a deeper lesson, something more basic, causal and fundamental than the first. In fact, the ancient Chinese word for change, as applied to the lines of the hexagram, really meant "decay".

Thus, the lines of the second hexagram represent a kind of skeletal structure on which the first hexagram is built. While the first hexagram may show what action is appropriate in a particular situation, the second hexagram will impart a deeper, more enduring meaning, often showing why the situation in question arose in the first place.

Finally, in spite of the I Ching's mystery and the frequent uncanny correspondences between the wording of the text and the nature of the question that is asked, the I Ching holds firmly to law and order. No statement is made without explaining this by reference to the operation of some natural law or principle, so that the questioner is given a revelation into the nature of the real forces at work in life. An actual example will perhaps render this most clear.

Some years ago, I detected a cavity appearing in one of my teeth. It was very small, but it was right on the base of the tooth, where the root begins, and I had heard from a dentist friend that if the drill should penetrate through the surface of the tooth at this point, the tooth would be lost. So I was unsure about having it filled. I sought the I Ching's counsel on the matter, and obtained Hexagram No.2, "The Receptive", with the first line changing. The judgement on this line was as follows:

Six at the beginning means:
When there is hoarfrost underfoot,
Solid ice is not far off.

"Just as the light-giving power (Yang) represents life, so the dark-power, the shadowy (represented by the Yin lines of this hexagram) represents death. When the first hoarfrost comes in the autumn, the power of darkness and cold is just at its beginning. After these first warnings, signs of death will gradually multiply, until, in obedience to immutable laws, stark winter with its ice is here.

"In life it is the same. After certain scarcely noticeable signs of decay have appeared, they go on increasing until final dissolution comes. But in life, precautions can be taken by heeding the first signs of decay and checking them in time."

The choice of the word "decay" in that last sentence could not have been more apt! Needless to say, I lost no time in getting the tooth filled.

However, the reading shows how the I Ching takes a small mundane situation and in answering the question, reveals an eternal principle that has possibilities of application far beyond the situation at hand. This particular reading also illustrates the I Ching's attitude to human destiny and free will: it is not fate that is immutable, only the laws that govern it and by acting in consciousness of these laws, man becomes master of his fate. The Book of Changes itself is widely considered to be a complete exposition of natural law. It is from this root that Nuclear Evolution has evolved into a modern scientific explanation of the structure of nature's levels of consciousness.

This scanty introduction to one of the world's most ancient, profound and mysterious books of wisdom ends here. Let us now take up the main theme of this work, which concerns the I Ching as a book of Time and its relationship to Nuclear Evolution.

SOME PRELIMINARY THOUGHTS ON TIME AND NUCLEAR EVOLUTION

In investigating the nature of time, it is important for us to recognise that there is more than one kind of time. Time can, of course, mean the position of the present moment in relation to the past and the future, as suggested by the hands of a clock. Time can also mean duration, as when we speak of an interval of so much time. Here the idea of time as a uniform continuum composed of identical time-units, which we may label seconds, hours or whatever, is implicit. This assumption is a mental one, enabling us to make our experience orderly and hence, sane and reasonable. It is, however, questionable. The fact that the passage of time can appear to speed up or slow down according to our level of interest or boredom points to the ultimate subjectivity of time. This subjectivity of time is further confirmed by the fact that everyone can experience at least three completely different kinds of time during a single day, namely that of wakefulness, of dream and of deep sleep. During wakefulness, time is the implicit order of experience that gives rise to the appearance of cause and effect. During dreams, time is not so orderly and effects do not necessarily need causes to bring them about - we may find ourselves hopping between present, past, and future. In deep sleep, we have no awareness of any particular instants of time, but when we wake up, we are aware of having been in deep sleep. (See section on Color Black, Part 1-Time, Space, and Colors.)

Another variable in the phenomenon of time arises from the different grades of life-time that are present amongst creatures in the universe. Man lives for about 70 years of Earth-time, but what of the may-fly, who lives for a day? Does he experience at the same rate as us? Or what of the chirrupping sparrow, whose melodic tunes are so condensed in time as to sound to us as mere twitters, and who can adjust his path of flight quicker than we can see him do it? Anyone who has tried to swat a wasp in flight will appreciate the speed of perception of small creatures. Evidently, time is very subjective. Psychologists have discovered that a person's experience of time may be distorted in hypnosis and if the distortion is retained by the subject on coming out of the trance various forms of psychosis start to appear in him. Apparently, having an orderly experience of time fulfils a very deep need in us and is basic to our sanity.

Since the days of Einstein and Minkowski, the relativity of time has been recognised. The idea of time as a dimension, like a distance in space, became popular in the latter part of the 19th century and out of this, the idea of the four-dimensional manifold of space-time developed. The Theory of Relativity which developed out of this milieu, apparently posits that a man who goes off on a long space journey will, when he returns, be younger than those who remained behind. Furthermore, the idea of time travel has also become very popular since the days of H. G. Wells' "The Time Machine". This idea, which was so controversial amongst scientists and philosophers, is today commonplace in children's science fiction television programs and magazines. Clearly, our concepts of time, have, in recent years, undergone some radical revisions. What has been gained in terms of freedom and scope has, however, been lost in terms of simplicity. The physicist's concept of time may be very different to the biologist's, which may in turn be very different to the psychologist's, and none of these need have much to do with the individual who rushes his breakfast in order to be able to catch the train that will get him to work "on time".

CONCEPTS AND EXPERIENCE IN NUCLEAR EVOLUTION

By definition, our concepts of time are mental creations. But what of our experiences of time? All the forms of time mentioned above are also mental creations. The past exists in the mind as memory. The future exists in the mind as imagination. Even the present moment of awareness of the "objective" universe, is a mentally created experience. However complex or paradoxical our experiences of temporal relations may become (as with the hypothetical space traveller of Relativity Theory), time remains a mental ordering principle which we use to make sense out of our experience of change. If we view it closely enough, we see that perception is always now. Our memories, which form the past, are experienced now. So are our imaginations of the future. So, too, are our sensations of light, sound, feeling, taste and touch that make up our impression of the objective world. All our knowledge about the world is perceived in the "Now" and so are all our ideas, including those about time, relativity and perception. The self is now.

946

Time, then, in Nuclear Evolution is a self-created abstraction, perceived, not in sensory experience, but as the relationship between experiences. Whilst on this philosophical note, it is perhaps worthwhile to draw two conclusions from the discussion so far. Firstly, because time is a mental construct, it is erroneous to think of oneself as existing in time. The correct standpoint is that time exists within oneself. (Incidentally, the same argument applies to space.) Secondly, because the self exists always now, and because time exists within it, the self exists outside of time; that is, it is eternal. This last statement is no mere abstraction far removed from experience by some subtly disjointed logic. The life of everyone confirms it. The "I" that is born into the world is the same "I" that leaves it, however, the body and mind may change.

TIME IN THE I CHING

We have seen then that time does not apply to the ultimate subject, the "I", which is unchanging. Time applies to the changing phenomena of experience, the forms which appear and disappear in the mind, some as sensations of light, color, sound, etc., some as objects of the world and some as our own "private" thoughts which do not appear in the objective world. Obviously the mind has an organised structure, for, in a clear mind, one's sensations, thoughts, feelings, etc., are not all mixed up together but are distinguishable planes of experience. Correspondingly, time on the sensation plane may be somewhat different to intellectual time, which may again be different to time on the emotional plane. Whatever different forms of time may apply to the different planes of the mind, we may reasonably affirm that the process which we call "life" is the experience of mental forms, or "images". Change is the appearance and disappearance of these images.

Time, then, must be that process by which mental images take form and dissolve, or arise and subside in consciousness. Time is the process of becoming and annihilation, growth and decay, life (experience of images) and death (non-experience). The self and the mind endure eternally, so there can be no final death, only a return to the unmanifest. Time in Nuclear Evolution turns back on itself and becomes spirit. This process is also described in the I Ching, and is to be understood as applying to everything, the individual and the universe alike. Thus, in every moment of experience, the individual reproduces in himself the original act of Cosmic Creation.

In the first hexagram, Ch'ien, representing the creative power of the spirit, we read:

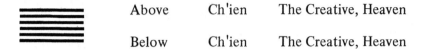

| | Above | Ch'ien | The Creative, Heaven |
| | Below | Ch'ien | The Creative, Heaven |

"The first hexagram is made up of six unbroken lines. These unbroken lines stand for the primal power, which is light-giving, active, strong, and of the spirit ... Its image is Heaven ... The hexagram includes also the power of time and the power of persisting in time, that is, duration ...Confucius says in explaining it: "Great indeed is the generating power of the Creative; all beings owe their beginning to it. This power permeates all heaven" ...

"The beginning of all things lies still in the beyond in the form of ideas that have yet to become real." Here we are told that the state of the Unmanifest, the origin of the Universe, is stillness and that the forms of Creation already lie latent within it as ideas. Continuing, we read "But the Creative furthermore has power to lend form to these archetypes of ideas . . . and the process is represented by an image from nature: "The clouds pass and the rain does its work, and all individual beings flow into their forms."

The hexagram of the Creative represents the spirit, in the Universe and the individual alike. The creative process is compared to the discharge of rain from clouds. The clouds symbolise the diffused, formless ethers of the spirit. These give birth to individual spiritual seed particles. However, in order to understand what is meant by "the rain does its work, and all individual beings flow into their forms", we must refer to the hexagram of the Receptive (No. 2) which represents the reflective, form-giving complement to the Creative. In the Universe it represents Nature. In the individual it represents the mind. Here we read:

| | Above | K'un | The Receptive, Earth |
| | Below | K'un | The Receptive, Earth |

"This hexagram is made up of broken lines only. The broken line represents the dark, yielding, receptive primal power of yin. The attribute of this hexagram is devotion; its image is the earth. It is the perfect complement of the Creative - the complement, not the opposite, for the Receptive does not combat the Creative but completes it. It represents nature in contrast to spirit, earth in contrast to heaven, space as against time, the female-maternal as against the male-paternal . . . Indeed, even in the individual, this duality appears in the coexistence of the spiritual world and the world of the senses." (Perhaps we should note here that the "world of the senses" (red level) is in fact part of the body/mind.) . . . "The Receptive connotes spacial reality in contrast to the spiritual potentiality of the Creative." . . .

"Only because nature in its myriad forms corresponds with the myriad impulses of the Creative" (these are the raindrops of the earlier image) "can it make its impulses real . . . It is the Creative that begets things, but they are brought to birth by the Receptive."

Thus we see that in the Cosmos, nature, the maternal principle, completes the work of Heaven by taking up the spiritual nuclear seed (the individual soul) and giving it corporeal form. This work is aptly represented in the image of the Earth, which receives wriggling seeds of light from the sun, moon and stars, and brings forth living creatures. Indeed, all nature reflects this image in the process of sexual procreation. The impregnation of the female egg by the masculine seed is paralleled by the stimulation and impregnation of the mind by the light of consciousness. We even speak of "conceiving" an idea, of "mentally brooding" and of thoughts "germinating" in the mind, which may be described as "fertile". These terms betray our unconscious recognition of the creative process by which images form in the mind. Viewing the creative process from this aspect, we might refer to hexagram 61, called Chung Fu - "Inner Truth", which describes the bringing forth of life by the spirit.

Above   Sun   The Gentle, Wind

Below   Tui   The Joyous, Lake

"The wind blows over the lake and stirs the surface of the water. Thus visible effects of the invisible manifest themselves. The hexagram consists of firm lines above and below, while it is open in the centre. This indicates a heart free of prejudices and therefore open to truth." ...

The idea of wind blowing over water bringing forth vibration reminds us of the account of creation in Genesis: "And the spirit of God moved upon the surface of the waters", and also of the Indian Vedic cosmology, in which the Creator, Brahma, breathed upon the waters of the Unmanifest, also in Nuclear Evolution the infra black akasha of the creative void. The lake may also be taken as a symbol of the mind, whose face is stirred by the movement of the spirit. Let us return to the I Ching's thoughts on the meaning of this mysterious hexagram:

"The character "fu" (truth) is actually the picture of a bird's foot over a fledgling. It suggests the idea of brooding. An egg is hollow (like this hexagram). The light-giving power must work to quicken it from outside, but there must be a germ of life within, if life is to be awakened. Far-reaching speculations can be linked with these ideas."

The lake symbolises the mind, which is like a fertile egg because the individual spirit, the germ of life, is already inside it. Thus, the individual in this state is receptive to the influence of Heaven. It is the state of potentiality, of the unmanifest, which is stillness, like a lake whose surface is calm and clear. This is the state described in the hexagram of the Creative where it is said, "The beginning of all things lies still in the beyond, in the form of ideas that have yet to become real." In the hexagram of the Receptive, the individual is advised to get into this receptive condition in order to receive Heaven's guidance. In this state of mental quiet, the intuition (indigo level) is born. In this state of inner repose it is possible to conceive anew. But to be in this state, one must have no preconceptions, and so in the hexagram of Inner Truth, the advice is to put aside any that one may have. Then there is nothing to obstruct Heaven's work of stimulating and awakening one's inner potential.

This same message was imparted to me once when I besought the I Ching's instruction on how I might attain the state of spiritual consciousness of the Creative. The answer was hexagram No. 2, the

Receptive. Not only did this answer my practical question, but it also suggested that the work of the Creative is to lead man into its own supreme state of consciousness, for the Receptive only follows where the Creative leads. Thus the purpose of experience in time, which is activated and directed by the spirit of Heaven, the Creative, is the realisation of the Creative within oneself. This supreme revelation is brought about through Receptivity, through emptiness. In Nuclear Evolution this is referred to as returning through the endless orb of sight, to the creative void in an eighth domain of pure consciousness. There lies hidden the rainbow body in everyone.

So far, we have been considering the dawning, the germinal beginning of manifestation. The creative process is an expansive one that releases energy. We may observe how the creation proceeds by considering an example from nature, the development of an embryo. After germination, expansion of the nucleus proceeds, at the same time being a process of differentiation. The egg, or unfertilised ovum, is homogeneous, like water, but once it is fertilised, differentiation sets in, producing diversity of forms within itself. In the same way, on the cosmic scale, the individual worlds which comprise the Universe were considered by the ancient Chinese to have developed out of the Unmanifest by a process of differentiation, and they even symbolised the Unmanifest, the Primal Beginning (T'ai Chi T'u) as the "Cosmic Egg". Likewise, the appearance of diverse forms within the mind depends on mental differentiation and discrimination. Thus, the One becomes many. The experience of time also depends on the discrimination between moments of experience. Space, as well, depends on the differentiation of one place from another. This aspect of the creative process is, of course, mentioned in the hexagram of the Creative: under the Judgement we read,

"The act of creation having found expression, ... the work of conservation is shown to be a continuous actualisation and differentiation of form."

We also meet the idea in hexagram 38, K'uei/Opposition: Under the Judgement here we read "The oppositions of heaven and earth, spirit and nature, man and woman, when reconciled, bring about the creation and reproduction of life. In the world of visible things, the principle of opposites makes possible the differentiation by categories through which order is brought into the world." The alternation of light and dark, day and night, summer and winter, is the basis in our experience for constructing a time order. The Book of Changes, based on the polarity of light and dark principles, is an aid to man in bringing order out of Chaos. In Nuclear Evolution we can understand this chaos through the primal drives which make up the positive and negative, light and dark energies of consciousness as it manifests from potential states.

As the creative potential in something unfolds, we see opposition emerge also. An embryo differentiates head from tail, right and left organs and limbs, male and female components, which all reflect the primal opposition of Yin and Yang. While in nature the emerging opposites do not separate but remain harmoniously integrated within the whole, in human society, and in the human mind too, opposition can become conflict and separation. For example, brothers and sisters in the same family may end up at loggerheads, and society is largely a collection of competing factions rather than an organically ordered whole. In the human personality too, there is always the danger that the discriminating intellect will divide every experience into tiny bits of information and split so many hairs that the mind loses its coherence. The hexagram of Opposition warns us that differentiation should not go too far.

The Judgement reads: "Opposition. In small matters, good fortune." Left to itself, the differentiating power of the Creative would fractionate the Universe until it completely disintegrated. Therefore, it must be balanced by another power - a cohesive force which binds everything together in oneness. This is the power of emptiness, or void, into which all things are drawn. This is the power of the Receptive, which contains, shelters, and protects things. The I Ching describes the condition of unity in hexagram 8, Pi/Holding Together (Union).

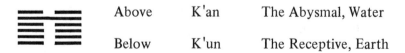

	Above	K'an	The Abysmal, Water
	Below	K'un	The Receptive, Earth

"The waters on the surface of the earth flow together wherever they can, as for example in the ocean, where all the rivers come together. Symbolically this connotes holding together and the laws that regulate it". Under the Image, we read: "Water fills up all the empty places on the earth and clings fast to it . . . Water flows to unite with water, because all parts of it are subject to the same laws."

In this hexagram, we are shown the natural elements (water) being drawn together by the earth's emptiness. However, they are bound together by the single law of their nature. This idea is also expressed in the hexagram of the Creative. The Creative's power to bring its creations into full and complete manifestation is indicated by the word "success" in the Judgement. In the following words, we are told the secret of this success: "Here it is shown that the way to success lies in apprehending and giving actuality to the way of the Universe (Tao), which, as a law running through end and beginning, brings about all phenomena in time. Thus each step attained forthwith becomes a preparation for the next. Time is no longer a hindrance but the means of making actual what is potential." In Nuclear Evolution "time" is regarded as an instrument of the spirit of evolutionary intelligence.

The unfoldment of the embryo, the unfoldment of the Cosmos and the unfoldment of the spirit in man, follow the law of the Tao in every detail and so all parts hold together in a dynamic order as the differentiation goes on. The Tao, which is unified and harmonious in itself, guides the harmonious unfoldment of the whole universe. However, it does this from within things, as well as from outside, for the Tao is the unmanifest potential in all things. Thus, in the hexagram of union, we are shown the receptive power as lying below (that is within). By becoming inwardly receptive to the spirit within oneself, one apprehends the "way of the universe" and by following the directives of this inspiration devotedly, one gives expression to it. Thus, in unfolding one's own potential, one manifests the hidden order of the Universe. These ideas, enunciated in the hexagram of the Creative, are elaborated in that of the Receptive.

Thus we see that the first aspect of time, the creative process, is a manifestation of inner potential and this is a process of expansion and differentiation. Within the individual, this implies that the forms and images which exist in our minds are manifestations of our own individual consciousness. Hence, every experience in life is really the experience of one's own nature. This creative process, then, is one of externalisation. However, once externalisation and differentiation are completed, a reversal sets in. Differentiation gives place to unification. Expansion turns into contraction. Externalisation is replaced by absorption. Form decays back into the formless. This is the receptive phase that completes *the cycle of time,* returning effects back to their causes and energy back to its source, thus making the cycle self-renewing. This rhythmic *nature of time* is mentioned in the hexagram of the Creative. Under the Image, we read:

> The movement of heaven is full of power.
> Thus the superior man makes himself strong and untiring.

"Since there is only one heaven, the doubling of the trigram Ch'ien, of which heaven is the image, indicates the movement of heaven. One complete revolution of heaven makes a day, and the repetition of the trigram means that each day is followed by another. This creates *the idea of time.* Since it is the same heaven moving with untiring power, there is also created the idea of duration both in and beyond time, a movement that never stops nor slackens, just as one day follows another in an unending course. This *duration in time* is the image of the power inherent in the "Creative".

Here it is clearly indicated that in the Book of Changes, *time* is regarded as a cyclic, not a simply linear process. The idea of the cycle implies return to the origin. This theme is elaborated in the hexagram of Duration (Heng, No. 32) and shows us why the Creative, the spirit, is untiring and enduring in its influence:

	Above	Chen	The Arousing, Thunder
	Below	Sun	The Gentle, Wind

Under the Judgement, we read:

"Duration is a state whose movement is not worn down by hindrances. It is not a state of rest, for mere standstill is regression. Duration is rather the self-contained and therefore self-renewing movement of an organised, firmly integrated whole, taking place in

954

accordance with immutable laws and beginning anew at every ending. The end is reached by an inward movement, by inhalation, systole, contraction, and this movement turns into a new beginning, in which the movement is directed outward, in exhalation, diastole, expansion.

"Heavenly bodies exemplify duration. They move in their fixed orbits, and because of this their light-giving power endures. The seasons of the year follow a fixed law of change and transformation, hence can produce effects that endure."

"So likewise the dedicated man embodies an enduring meaning in his way of life, and thereby the world is formed."

We are shown, then, that every cycle of time is an expansion from the unmanifest potential state and a return to it again. This cyclic pattern of change and renewal is shot through the I Ching. It underlies a saying in hexagram 48 (Ching/The Well), which symbolises "an inexhausible dispensing of nourishment". Here we read:

"Life is inexhaustible. It grows neither less nor more; it exists for one and for all. The generations come and go, and all enjoy life in its inexhaustible abundance." This self-maintaining, self-regenerating function of life is also inferred in the ancient alchemical symbol of the snake or dragon eating its own tail. In Nuclear Evolution this is the cyclic backflow of time becoming once again the creative spirit.

However, although time may be cyclic, it is not entirely circular. The return to the unmanifest does not mean the absolute negation of the effects produced, although the forms which once embodied the spirit have decayed. Some inner growth is produced. In spite of its cyclicity, *time is forward moving*. This is inferred in the hexagram of the Creative, where Confucius comments: "The course of the Creative alters and shapes beings until each attains its true, specific nature, then it keeps them in conformity with the great harmony. Thus does it show itself to further through perseverance." As well as the form-giving, differentiative aspect to time, by which individual beings are created, there is also the harmonising, evolutionary aspect, by which they are related together as one whole.

As each stage of creation in time is completed by bringing its elements into harmony with the whole, it gives rise to a new stage of creation and manifestation. Hence, if we examine the heirarchy of nature's kingdoms, we see that individual atoms were formed and shaped, then harmonised and united. Out of this harmony, the molecular world developed. However, refinement and shaping had had to take place on this level before the next level of unity and wholeness, the cellular, could take form. In turn, the organic cells, at first amorphous, took diverse shapes and eventually were able to unite, thus creating another order of beings: the multicelled organisms. These have been developing and refining themselves for thousands of millions of years: first through the vegetable stage, next the animal, and finally man. Here we come to the *synthesis of Nuclear Evolution*. The next evolutionary stage of creation will begin when human beings can achieve such complete harmony with one another that they unite in a group soul. The development of the cosmic manifestation of God is the continuous process of time.

THE UNIVERSAL PROCESS

Why, one might ask, is God, the Creative, heaven, doing all this? Why did the Creator make the Universe?

This hoary question arose one evening when some fellow students and I were discussing the I Ching. Someone wanted to know why the Cosmic Process was necessary, so we put this question to the Oracle. The I Ching's answer was Hexagram 63,"After Completion" with the top line changing.

Above	K'an	The Abysmal, Water
Below	Li	The Clinging, Fire

This was an example of an answer that would have hardly been understandable had we not already known something about the meanings of the two trigrams Li and K'an, for the text is concerned chiefly with giving practical advice to man as regards what he may do in a life situation of the type represented by this hexagram. However, we understood Li and K'an to refer to the energies of the light and dark principles and in this hexagram, they are shown as being united in a state of rather unstable equilibrium. The key sentence in the text seemed to be that directly following the Image: 'When water (K'an) in a kettle hangs over fire (Li), the two elements stand in relation and thus generate energy (cf. the production of steam)." Another important statement, drawn from the Judgement, seemed to be: "Everything proceeds as if of its own accord."

We were being given the picture of the creation of the universe happening apparently spontaneously, by virtue of the primal elements of life having been brought into relation. The Judgement on the changing line reads: "He gets his head in the water. Danger." and the text interpreted this as follows: "After crossing a stream, a man's head can get into the water only if he is so imprudent as to turn back. As long as he goes forward and does not look back he escapes this danger." The attaining of the unity and equilibrium between the two primal elements was being compared to the dangerous enterprise of crossing a great stream ("crossing the great water" is the corresponding term used elsewhere in the book). It is the step of bringing the primal elements out of confusion into the order in which they belong. The hexagram as a whole portrays the idea of this step having already been completed and in the Judgement on the top line, we are warned of the possible mistake of turning back. The unfoldment of the Universe has begun and we are part of the process. To not go forward with it would mean a reversion to the darkness of confusion and disorder.

This hexagram through the change in the top line, becomes hexagram 37 (Chia Jen/The Family), the upper trigram changing from "Kan"/Water, to "Sun"/Wind, Penetration. Under the Image we read:
> Wind comes forth from fire:
> The image of the Family...

"Heat creates energy: this is signified by the wind stirred up by the fire and issuing forth from it. This represents influence working from within outward." And earlier in the text on this hexagram, we find:"The Family shows the laws operative within the household that, transferred to outside life, keep the state and the world in order." Hence, the hexagram suggests that the unmanifest Being of the universe is really a family that is already in order, yet the Cosmic Process, about which we had asked, was necessary so as to manifest this inner order outwardly. Both the I Ching and Nuclear Evolution Theory view the universe as a flower unfolding from a seed. The upper trigram, Sun, the Gentle, which is symbolised by the wind, has the alternative symbol of wood, representing organic growth. The lower trigram, Li, whose symbol is fire, stands also for radiant light, clarity and consciousness. Thus we are given the image of the cosmic family as a tree growing from a *seed, a centre, a nucleus of clear, radiant light or consciousness.* This image may be applied not only to the universe as a whole, but also to the individual, for everything in nature grows organically from an *individual seed of clear intelligence-stuff* and the outer, visible structure of the organism reflects the inner order or pattern of structure of the nucleus. Again, if we contemplate the structures of nature's myriad creations, we see that at the atomic level, the individual atom has at its centre, a nucleus whose inner *structure of harmony determines the outer structure of its electron shells* as well as specifying the individuality or species of the atom.* Likewise, at the molecular level, the more complex molecules develop definitely centralised structures which serve to order the molecule as a harmonious whole.** The so called "organic" molecules demonstrate this most visibly. On the next level of Creation, we see that the refined organic cell is a *nucleated structure* and again, it is the structure of the nucleus, containing genes, which determines the individuality of the cell. Likewise on the multi-cellular level, the central nervous system, which connects the physical organism with the governing intelligence, stands as a *nucleus* of the body. Turning now to higher levels of creation, we may observe that the sun, the radiant *nucleus of light* at the centre of its universe, determines, by virtue of its own individual nature, the structure of the solar system.

On a yet larger scale, we may observe that even stars can be members of a larger organism, a galaxy, which has its own *nucleus* of organisation surrounded, in halo formation, by the very oldest stars. Galaxies, too, cluster in groups, but things on this scale are hard to determine even with the aid of our largest telescopes. Returning,

---

*For example, a hydrogen atom is a hydrogen atom rather than, say an oxygen atom, because it has only one unit of electrical charge in the nucleus instead of the eight units which oxygen possesses.
**For example, the water molecule consists of an oxygen atom in the middle of two hydrogen atoms.

then, to the human level, we may consider the human organism as a structure whose order reflects the inner order, or pattern, of *the nuclear intelligence:* the individual human soul. In Nuclear Evolution, we are shown the central nucleus of light, the individual soul, surrounded by seven spheres which differentiate the light of the *nuclear consciousness* into different energy levels. This image corresponds completely with the I Ching's portrayal of the pattern of organisation of the individual world as revealed in the hexagram of the Family.

THE TRIGRAMS AND LEVELS OF CONSCIOUSNESS

A significant idea in Nuclear Evolution is that when the eighth level (Black) of the *nuclear intelligence* wills some event into manifestation, the seven levels of consciousness process the information content of the event in turn, firstly on the Imagination layer and lastly on the Physical. We may note that the *nuclear intelligence* lives in a *zero time domain,* that is, it is eternally now, while the physical-sensation (Red) level of consciousness exists as a fully *time-bound domain* in which "now" is a unique instantaneous experience discontinuous with any other "nows". The intermediate levels, the emotional (Blue), intellectual (Yellow), etc., constitute different time-domains and the will must be processed through each of these in turn if it is to emerge finally as an event on the physical plane. This process is identical with the organic development of creation from the seed of the unmanifest mentioned earlier. The I Ching represents the different planes of "being" by the eight trigrams. The diagram below, called the Primal Arrangement, shows the trigrams as they are harmoniously ordered within the *nuclear seed of light* (represented by Li, ☲ , the Clinging, Brightness) in the Family.

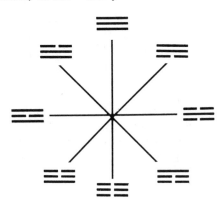

In the harmonised relations shown above, they together show us the implicit family order of the unmanifest. The following table shows us the places of the trigrams in the universal family:

☰	Ch'ien,	Heaven,	The Creative	-	Father
☷	K'un,	Earth,	The Receptive	-	Mother
☳	Chên,	Thunder,	The Arousing	-	Eldest Son
☴	Sun,	Wind/Wood,	The Gentle	-	Eldest Daughter
☵	K'an,	Water,	The Abysmal	-	Middle Son
☲	Li,	Fire,	The Clinging	-	Middle Daughter
☶	Kên,	Mountain,	Keeping Still	-	Youngest Son
☱	Tui,	Lake,	The Joyous	-	Youngest Daughter

The trigrams may be correlated with the seven levels of consciousness plus the *nuclear domain* according to the following scheme. This is also made to portray the organic progress of the will, the influence of the nuclear essence, through the levels.

Firstly, the *nuclear being* itself, the seed of the will, is symbolised by K'an, the Abysmal (☵). Here, we are shown the light principle enclosed by darkness, that is: "the soul locked up within the body", to quote from hexagram 29. K'an represents the *seed* of individual consciousness that has dropped to Earth as rain from Heaven. Consciousness is as yet unreflected in any image. The color is therefore black, but potentially it is white, for the light is contained in it. The will begins here, although it is still obscured in darkness. It is purely an impulse of the spirit.

As the impulse of the will is received in the mind or psyche, an image is formed. Non-personal and primal, the image reflects the nature, the law of being, of the will-impulse. This is the Violet, *Imagination level* of consciousness.

Thus, the impulse of the spirit is given form as an *image* reflecting the eternal law inherent in its nature. The trigrams themselves may be thought of as such archetypal images. However, on this level, the will has not yet entered into time. Hence, the next level, that of the *Intuition,* is needed to conceive a specific form of the archetype as the image of a future manifestation. This level of consciousness corresponds with the trigram K'un, ($\equiv\equiv$), the Receptive/Earth, which receives the impulses of the light and envisions a goal to be actualised. K'un is the maternal womb, the empty void, yearning for the impregnation of the light principle. Its color is midnight blue/indigo, the color of deep space.

Once the idea to be realised has been received, the next step is to mobilise all available energies for the execution of it. On the *Intuitive-level,* the impression received is purely idea. This will not manifest if it does not meet with emotional conviction. It will merely slip away to be replaced by some other intuition of what the spirit is wanting to manifest. Thus the next level, the *Mental-Emotional,* (Blue), fixes the image firmly in the mind and checks its authority by reference to past experience. If the new image proves to be authentic, then emotional conviction is given, enthusiasm aroused, and the idea is given expression with *authority* and vigour. The next level (Green) provides *life energy* in motion.

Once the energy for doing the job has been secured, a plan of action is needed if the willed idea is to be executed. Events must be made to unfold in sequence to eventuate in the desired effect and so how this process is to be organised must now be thought out. Hence the next level of consciousness is the *intellect*, which discriminates stages of development in the process of actualising an idea with the resources at hand. Thus *time* on this plane is *linear and sequential,* a string of separate events extending logically from the past through now into the future. The intellect cuts up experience into "bits" of information or separate events in time, thus destroying continuity and the overall meaning of the whole (the "gestalt"). This has a useful function in regard to formulating plans. The color associated with this level of consciousness is Yellow.

After becoming a plan, the willed event is in principle ready for its execution. However in Nuclear Evolution the question now arises as to who is going to actualise it. The social factor becomes significant. Also to be considered is how the changes that have been planned will affect other people. Society is resistant to change and social authority will promptly squash any plans which threaten to upset the status quo. An individual who wants to change anything at all in the world will need everyone else's permission to do it or he will quickly find that either his action is blocked or it is soon superseded or negated by someone else's action. He needs to be able to exercise influence in society and thus he needs connections. Vital wheels can be made to turn if one knows the right people. The next level of consciousness after the intellectual is the *social,* in which intelligence is directed towards finding out who's who and gaining social prominence. This is correlated with the trigram Ch'ien ☰ the Creative, Heaven, the strong, expansive principle whose motion is powerfully upwards. The individual lines of the hexagram Ch'ien (No. 1) show the progressive stages in the rise of the "great man" to power and influence. The *time-world* of this level of consciousness is future-oriented towards the materialisation of the will when sufficient social status will have been attained. The color associated with the social level of consciousness is Orange.

When the creative individual has attained the place in society that accords with his nature and has organised his helpers so that they can work together as a concerted unity, the idea conceived so many stages back can now be materialised. Here, however, another level of consciousness is called for: that which will act upon physical matter and move it or shape it. This is the level of *"physical" consciousness,* of sensation and reflex action.

EDITOR'S NOTE: King Wen's arrangement of the colours and hexagrams differs from later periods in the evolution of the I Ching. The correlation between the hexagrams and colours is complex because there is a horizontal sequence and a vertical sequence which changes not only with the seasons (the angle of the sun to the earth's ecliptic) but also during the day as the sun changes its angle to the observer's consciousness. A colour extracted from light is a subjective experience of radiation which varies with the thickness of the medium it passes through. The correlation between colour and the I Ching phases is fully explained in "Supersensonics" pages 548-570.

The time-world of this physical level of consciousness is confined to the "now" of sensational experience. Its color is Red.

The correlation between the colors of the spectrum and the primal arrangement of the trigrams was suggested by Christopher Hills in the original edition of his "New Book of Changes." (Now republished in part under the title "Universal Government by Nature's Laws,"University of the Trees Press).

Let us view the primal arrangement again.

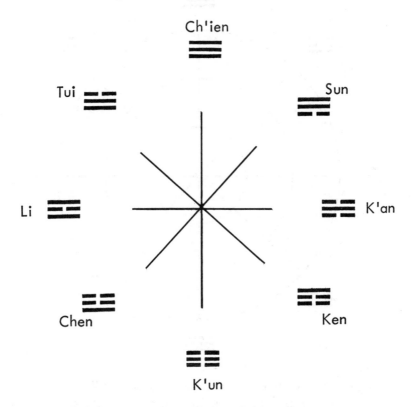

It is notable that the trigrams are arranged here as pairs of complementary opposites (cf. The I Ching, "Discussion of the Trigrams"). Hence, we are also given here the complementary relationships between the levels of consciousness. We shall return to this idea shortly when we have seen what is known as the "secondary sequence" of the trigrams.

Meanwhile, let us perform a transformation on the primal arrangement of the trigrams as follows, to obtain a representation of the underlying pattern.

Let us take the eight "spokes" which indicate the directions of the trigrams as above, but let us now draw three concentric circles about the centre, as below. These are to represent the three places of the lines in the trigrams, the innermost circle representing the lowest place in the trigram.

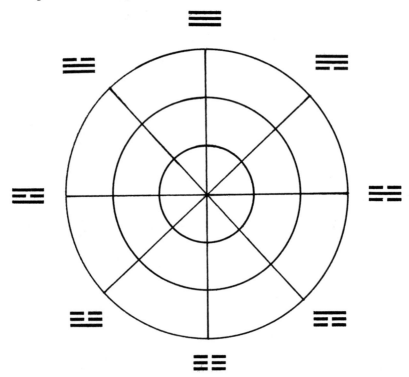

Ignoring for the moment the trigrams Li ☲ and K'an ☵ , let us place open or filled circles along the appropriate spokes where these intersect the three concentric rings to indicate the light or dark characters of the lines of the trigrams. This is done in the following diagram:

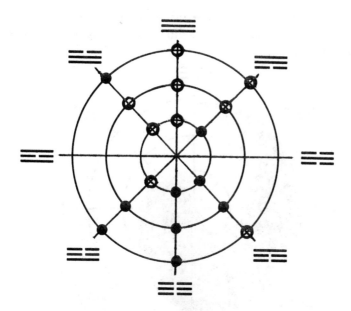

Let us now draw in two contours demarcating the interface between the light and the dark forces as follows: draw one smooth line from the centre through the uppermost open circle of Chen, through that of Tui and on to that of Ch'ien; draw the other contour smoothly from the centre, through the uppermost dark circle of Sun, through that of Ken and on to that of K'un. The diagram now appears as below:

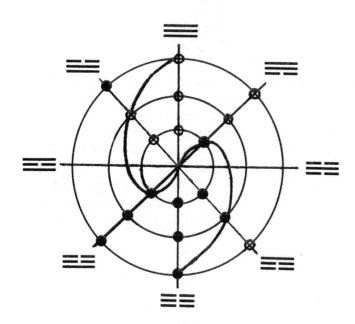

Leaving out now the black and white circles and shading in the space which contains all the dark lines of the trigrams, we obtain the following diagram:

It is now apparent that we have produced the symbolic form of the T'ai Chi T'u, the Great Primal Beginning, which became stylised over the years into the following popular form:

If we were to take an axis from the centre and rotate it about the centre, then as it turned we would observe the light force and the dark force growing up into it alternately from the centre. This idea is also used in interpreting the meanings of some hexagrams, specifically those twelve which are correlated with months of the year. In hexagram 11 (T'ai/Peace), under the Judgement we read: "The individual lines enter the hexagram from below and leave it again at the top. Here the small, weak and evil elements (dark lines) are about to take their departure, while the great, strong and good elements (light lines) are moving up."

By performing on the twelve monthly hexagrams the same operations that we performed above on the trigrams, one arrives at the following identical picture:

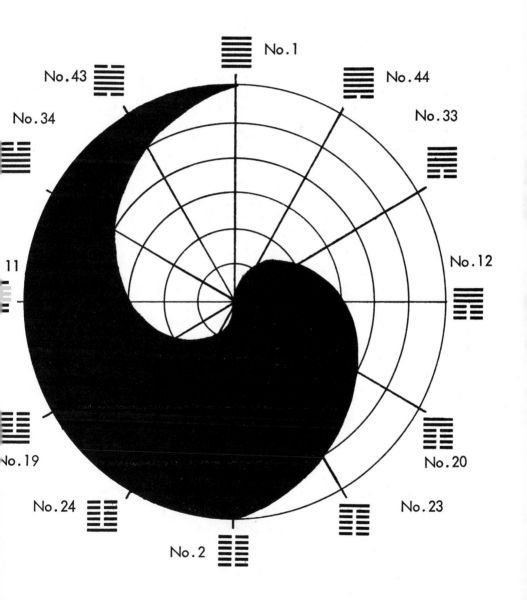

Returning to the pattern of the T'ai Chi T'u in the primal arrangement of the trigrams, we may observe that the contours dividing the light and dark principles cross the axes of Li and K'an precisely at their mid-points. Hence Li represents the ascendence of the light principle over the dark in which the dark principle is subordinated to the light and becomes hidden. In this sense, Li corresponds with the meaning of the hexagram of Peace (T'ai, No. 11) in the monthly sequence of hexagrams. Similarly, K'an represents the ascendence of the dark principle over the light, in which the light principle is subordinated to the dark and becomes hidden. In this sense, K'an corresponds with the meaning of the hexagram of Standstill (P'i, No. 12) in the monthly sequence of the hexagrams. We may also observe that the T'ai Chi T'u figure is symmetrical about the Li-K'an axis. Above this line, the light force is larger and below it the dark force is larger. Thus, the trigrams above this axis have more Yang lines and those below it have more Yin lines, while Li and K'an represent transitional stages between Yang and Yin predominance. Applying this dichotomy to the levels of consciousness, we may say that the Red, Orange and Yellow levels (corresponding with trigrams lying above the Li-K'an axis) preponderate in the expansive, expressive, externalising, out-going, extravert Yang energies; while the Blue, Indigo and Violet levels (corresponding with trigrams below the Li-K'an axis) preponderate in the contractive, impressional, internalising, in-going, introvert Yin energies.

The Green level, the level of the heart, is mobile between introvert and extravert functions. The Black domain of consciousness constitutes an unstable personality condition which ends in some form of death, changing from a Yang, *causative* state into a Yin, *affective* one. The borderline between Black and White is the eighth domain of Nuclear Evolution where death of Ego leads to rebirth in the Rainbow body.

Death is the necessary complement to life, just as decay is the necessary complement to growth and night is the necessary complement to day: it is this which makes the cycle of life self-renewing by returning everything to its origin.

We have considered the levels of consciousness as they stand harmonised in complementary relationships within the individual and these were represented by the trigrams in the "Sequence of Earlier Heaven" or the "Primal Arrangement". This order represents the formation within the seed, or *nucleus,* of the individual, although we have also used it to demonstrate the order of stages in which the will takes form on earth and thus to identify the levels of consciousness of *Nuclear Evolution.* The Book of Changes re-arranges the trigrams into the "Sequence of Later Heaven" or the "Inner-World Arrangement" to show the cyclic temporal progression of the effects of the trigrams in the world. This arrangement is shown below, correlated with the points of the compass as was the Primal Arrangement:

DIAGRAM SHOWS
SECONDARY ARRANGEMENT
OF THE "INNER-WORLD".

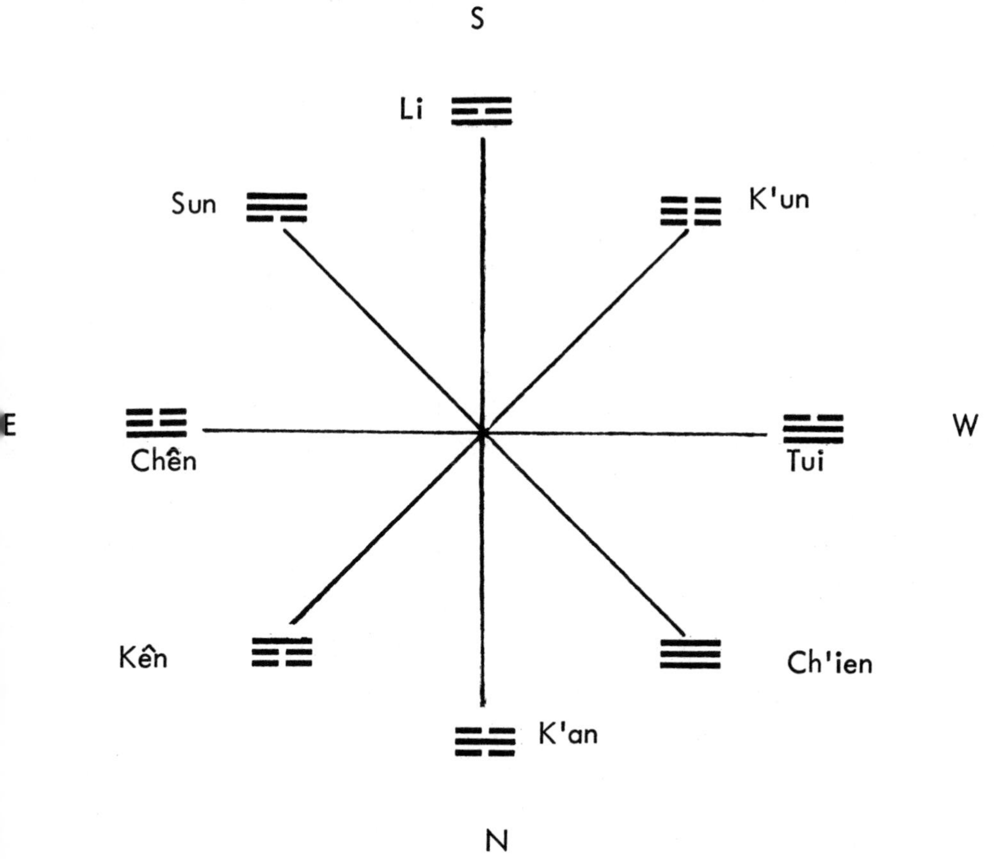

Since this sequence is explained in the I Ching under "Discussion of the Trigrams", only a brief description is given here. The beginning of activity is symbolised by Chen, the Arousing, Thunder, which stands in the East where the sun rises. This also represents Dawn and Spring, the times of birth and awakening in nature's cycles. This gives way to a time of organic growth and development as living beings flow into their forms. This stage is represented by Sun. Then organic development gives way to perception and clarity as the sun stands at its highest place in the South at noon and mid-summer. This stage is represented by Li. Next comes the work of bringing things to completion as nature brings fruits to ripeness. This is symbolised by K'un, which works devotedly. In the West, in the place where the sun sets, we have Tui, symbolising the joy of harvest and also death, for Tui means sacrifice. This corresponds with sunset and Autumn in the cycles of the day and the year. Following Tui is Ch'ien, symbolising judgement and decision: the effects of the year's activity have come to fruition and the good and evil are separated. Next, the fruits are gathered into barns and the life energies are gathered into their seeds. This stage is represented by K'an, which stands in the dark North, the place which corresponds with Midnight and Mid-winter, the times of maximum concentration. Finally, the trigram Ken represents stillness, in which the old cycle is joined to the new.

Richard Wilhelm discloses a significant idea regarding the meaning of this sequence of trigrams. In the "Discussion of the Trigrams" he says "To understand fully, one must always visualise the *Inner-World Arrangement* as transparent, with the *Primal Arrangement* shining through it. Thus, when we come to the trigram Li, we come at the same time upon the ruler Ch'ien, who governs with his face turned to the South." Hence, the *Inner-World Arrangement* shows us the forms in which the corresponding trigrams of the *Primal Arrangement* appear in a complete cycle of time, involving the expansion of the life-force from a seed and the contraction back into it again. Retaining the levels of consciousness in their places as related to the *Primal Arrangement,* let us now ascribe the trigrams in the *Inner-World Arrangement* to them as follows.

In the place of Ken in the *Primal Arrangement,* we have in this sequence Ch'ien instead. Here Ch'ien shows us the manifestation of heavenly law - impersonal, impartial and perfectly just. Natural law is perceived from the Imagination (Violet) level of consciousness.

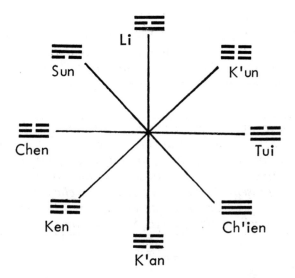

K'un, the Receptive, is here replaced by K'an, Water, representing the concentration of the life energies within the seed or *nucleus* of being. In this state of complete concentration, the intuition (Indigo level) operates freely.

On the Orange level of social consciousness, the expansive light principle, Ch'ien, appears in the form of the radiant centre of light, Li, whose symbol is fire. Orange is the color of flame. The radiance of the individual personality is a vital factor in nature's scheme of society, for by it the related opposites recognise one another and attract each other so that they unite.

Since the levels of consciousness, when arranged in this circular pattern, are related together as pairs of complementary opposites, we may view the levels as counter-balancing each other to maintain equilibrium of forces within the personality. Thus the excitability of the Red, sensation level, is pacified and tranquilised by its opposite, the calming Blue. The shallow and restless expansion of the Orange is tamed and deepened by the concentrating Indigo energy. The multifarious thoughts of the effervescent intellect of Yellow are brought into order and coherence by the generalising power of the imagination—Violet. The insecurity of green is counteracted by the self-reliance of Black/White and its attachments are released by renunciation and sacrifice. The cold gloominess of Blue is stimulated by the warmth of Red. The introvertedness of Indigo is lightened and uplifted by the expansiveness of Orange. The dreamy illusions of the imagination are dispelled by the discriminating power of the intellect. The capricious self-will of the Black is bounded and controlled by the recognition of one's dependence in Green.

> *Editor's Note: We are again reminded of the fact that the colours change from the primary sequence to the secondary sequence and from night to day in terms of overlapping cycles, and therefore cannot be fixed in time in any singular one to one arrangement. They can represent, however, alternating cyclic drives as shown in the few examples presented, and at any given moment the colour arrangements can be divined with Supersensonics.*

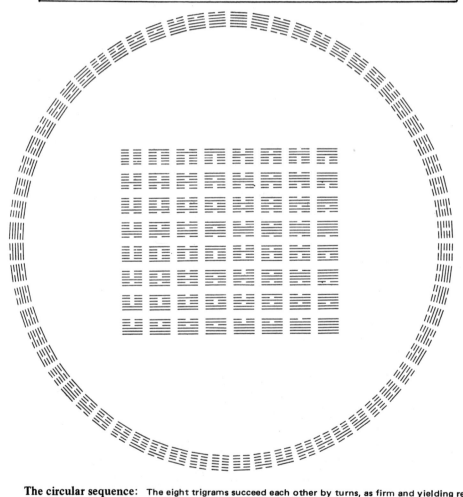

The circular sequence: The eight trigrams succeed each other by turns, as firm and yielding replace each other. The rotation of phenomena is depicted as circular. The nature of cyclic change and the alternations of the primal arrangement go in two directions, right handed and ascending and left handed descending. The receptive Kun starts from the lowest potential and builds and the creative Chien starts from the high point.

THE CIRCULATION OF THE LIGHT

When the creative energies, represented by the trigrams and the colors of the spectrum, are brought into perfect equilibrium within the personality, then the state of the original undifferentiated energy of life is re-created, just as when we combine the colors of the spectrum, we recreate the homogeneous white light from which they came. In this state of consciousness, which Christopher Hills calls the Rainbow Body, the experience of the objective world with its time and space conditions disappears. The equilibrium of the creative energies is described in the hexagram called "After Completion" (No. 63), where it is pointed out that this state, being a dynamic one, calls for the exercise of the utmost caution in maintaining it, for any change results in imbalance again. Furthermore, this condition of *dynamic equilibrium* is one which evolves energy: energy which can be applied to doing work in the world or which can, alternatively, be contained within the personality, where it automatically expands the consciousness. Such expansion is accompanied by an acceleration of the personality's cyclic processes, which, however, keep in perfect synchrony so long as the conscious mind does not interfere with them. The behaviour of the energy is conditioned by one's thoughts which are manifested with great force. It is therefore important, when in this state, to have only pure thoughts, for any harmful ones would manifest just as forcefully. It is also a significant point that the state of equilibrium arises and continues in the absence of thought, for thought, like the waves on the surface of a lake, is a displacement of the mindstuff from equilibrium. With the rise of the ego and its train of self-reflections, the *state of equilibrium* ceases and one arrives back in one of the seven levels of consciousness, with its particular time-world and specially filtered view of reality.

The creative energies in the personality are channelled through the seven "chakras", or *centres of consciousness* which are the origins of the *seven levels of consciousness*. The attaining of equilibrium of the full spectrum of the creative energies implies a balancing of the contributions of energy from the chakras. There are countless methods and techniques in existence that have been evolved for this purpose,* and they are to be found in the various schools and

---

* See "INTO MEDITATION NOW", a three-year course in self-mastery. (Details available from the publishers.)

systems of self-development, such as yoga and alchemy. The I Ching also provides us with an extremely simple method which I stumbled upon quite by accident, (although I no longer believe in accidents). Late one night, I was lying in bed going over in my mind the two basic sequences of trigrams, the Primal Arrangement and the Inner-World Arrangement. I associated them together by placing the trigram of the Primal Arrangement over its corresponding trigram from the Inner-World Arrangement, thus forming a hexagram for each of the eight places in the sequence. Hence the first hexagram, starting in the eastern place, was Shih Ho ("Biting Through", No. 21) and I imagined it clearly.

Then I moved on to the next combination and mentally placed that hexagram in the appropriate compass direction. So it went on, until I came to the trigrams lying in the North-West, which were Ken (☶) from the Primal Arrangement and Ch'ien (☰) from the Inner-World Arrangement. Immediately I placed Ken on top of Ch'ien in my mind's eye to make the hexagram called "The Taming Power of the Great" (No. 26), a wonderful feeling of tranquility and clarity came over me. My thinking was subsiding and I had a deliciously cool feeling in my head as though some psychic annular muscle had opened and was letting a cool current flow into me. I felt too as though all the parts of my being were holding firmly together - a condition which the hexagram describes. The effect was so immediate that there could hardly be any doubt that it was the visualisation of the hexagram that had induced it, but I tested the idea anyway by visualising a different hexagram. The result was conclusive: as I dropped the vision of the hexagram the experience subsided and taking up others in one or two cases produced very mild different effects, but mostly nothing at all. As soon as I came back to "The Taming Power of the Great", the original experience returned. I soon went off blissfully to sleep and awoke refreshed the next morning.

That following day, I was excited by this discovery and thought about it constantly. I remembered a healer telling me some years ago that he used the trigrams to project healing energies to his clients. I reflected too on the great extent to which they have been employed by dowsers and diviners down through the ages.* Now I had experienced them as not just *symbols* for psychological forces but actually as *psychological forces*. Two questions gradually were formulated in my mind: the first was the theoretical one of how the trigrams could achieve the effect; the second was the practical one of how to choose the appropriate hexagram to visualise, for the choice would have to be determined by whatever influence was needed to offset the particular direction of the psyche's imbalance, which could vary with time. The second question was in fact quite easily answered. Theoretically, one could, of course, run through all of the hexagrams mentally until the effective one was found, but since there are sixty-four hexagrams, such a procedure seemed rather cumbersome. The simple answer was to ask the I Ching for the hexagram.

However, during the course of that day, the two questions had not become fully differentiated in my mind, so I think I must have included them together when I consulted the I Ching on the whole matter. The question I asked was "Is it valid to consider the visualisation of the chosen hexagram as restoring the balance of the energies of the personality? The I Ching's answer was hexagram 27, called "The Corners of the Mouth", whose functional meaning is "Providing Nourishment".

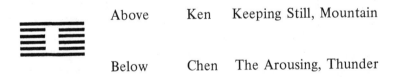

	Above	Ken	Keeping Still, Mountain
	Below	Chen	The Arousing, Thunder

Here we are told: "This hexagram is a picture of an open mouth; above and below are the firm lines of the lips, and between them the opening. Starting with the mouth, through which we take food for nourishment, the thought leads to nourishment itself." Obviously the I Ching could not be alluding to any physical mouth or physical food by this image, for I had asked about a psychological process: that of nourishing the personality on the energies of the

---

* See "Supersensonics", a 608 page book on the human faculty of detecting subtle wave-fields of Consciousness. Published 1975, University of the Trees Press.

hexagrams. The image of an orifice through which nourishment is taken possibly suggests the chakras. Chen, the lower trigram, means movement and the life-force. Ken, the upper trigram, means a gate. Hence, we have the idea of the life energy moving through a gate. The life energy may be conceived of as light, the energy of consciousness. The hexagram "I", like the trigram Li (☲) which also consists of an empty space between two light lines, represents the eye - that organ through which light enters the body. In the same way Nuclear Evolution views light as nourishment which enters the body through the psychic gates of the chakras. Each chakra can be depicted as a trigram and together as a hexagram.

The hexagram is hierarchically organised and so suggests the hierarchic organisation of the personality. The lower trigram, Chen, is associated with the body. This moves. The upper trigram, Ken, is associated with the higher, spiritual level of being, which is considered to be more fundamental and therefore more important. This keeps still. Hence the hexagram advises us to pay heed to nourishment of the most fundamental parts of our being and assures us that if one does this, the less important parts will also be served. Under the Judgement, we read: "In bestowing care and nourishment, it is important that the right people (i.e. the right elements in the system) should be taken care of . . . The great man fosters and takes care of superior men (the superior elements of the personality), in order to take care of all men (all elements) through them." Furthermore, the philosopher Mencius is quoted as saying: " . . . The body has superior and inferior, important and unimportant parts. We must not injure important parts for the sake of the inferior . . . " The chakras, those gates which regulate the inflow and outflow of the vibrating energy of consciousness, are the basic organic structure of the human constitution, while the life energies which they channel are the fundamental basis for the nourishment of all parts of the personality. The Judgement tells us "Perseverance brings good fortune", which therefore suggests that the activity in question, namely the visualising of the hexagrams, if properly done, will achieve the effect of nourishing the personality. Under the Image, we are given the idea of the in-going and out-going energies being regulated, which leads to the cultivation of character.

It was mentioned earlier that the bringing of the creative energies into equilibrium within the personality gives rise to the generation of energy. We could symbolise it by the trigram Chen (☳). However, if this energy is to nourish the personality, it must not be allowed to flow out immediately. It must be contained within the personality and thus made to circulate. This restraint on the out-flow of the energy could be symbolised by Ken (☶). Hence, the hexagram of Providing Nourishment, composed of Chen and Ken, suggests the creation of this circulatory process. A system of meditation practice, based on this idea, was developed in ancient China and given re-expression in esoteric circles in the eighteenth century. This was the practice of the "circulation of the light", described for us by Richard Wilhelm in his rendering of "The Secret of the Golden Flower". By virtue of the nourishment supplied by the circulating life-energy, the spiritual body was believed to develop or "crystalise". Nuclear Evolution determines the actual process of light ingestion and its crystalisation in the human body, thereby providing psychic nourishment. The process is organic, growing upwards from the lowest level of consciousness just as a lotus grows upwards from the earth to the surface.

This principle of circulation by which progressively higher energy levels of being are developed may be seen in nature in the process of evolution. The Earth is developing progressively higher levels of consciousness in the *evolution of life-forms,* by trapping the energy of sunlight and circulating it through the mineral, vegetable and animal kingdoms.

The principle may similarly be applied to society. Where a community is self-contained, the energy which feeds its most primitive processes, if conserved, is automatically re-cycled into progressively higher levels of organisation and function. If, for example, industrial waste heat were to be re-cycled, it could be made to nourish growing crops, to warm buildings and to drive electricity generators. These functions in turn support all the other levels of function in society. Instead, this valuable life-supporting energy is presently discharged as waste into the non-human environment, where it creates enormous pollution problems, while we look around hungrily for more energy resources to consume. In contrast to the natural world, the energy systems of human society are not self-contained and are therefore not self-renewing.

In the evolution of progressively higher levels of function in any system, we may observe a corresponding increase in the quality of intelligence or consciousness that is manifested. This implies an ability to process information relating to progressively larger spans of time and space. For example, we may say that man is more evolved and more intelligent than the fish. If we try to measure this difference in intelligence between the two creatures, we may find that only in a certain sense is man more intelligent than the fish and in other senses, we may find that the fish is actually more capable than man. Salmon and eels for instance, are able to navigate their paths of return to their birth places through thousands of miles of ocean, while a man would need sextant and compass and several years of training at a nautical school before he could navigate such a long journey. This is why Christopher Hills developed the new science of Supersensonics, to show that the salmon and the eel are able to perform this remarkable feat by use of a psychic homing device that man possesses but has not developed. Even so, man's reason, memory and imagination enable him to encompass and process the information relating to a greater span of events than can the fish, for when the fish at last returns to his breeding ground, man is already there waiting for him with a fishing net.

This evolution of intelligence continues in man and in the next few hundred years Nuclear Evolution will reveal to him the full spectrum of life. A man may indeed be able to anticipate the behaviour of lower creatures like fish so that he can catch them, but perhaps he may not yet have developed the awareness of the far-reaching consequences of his own behaviour: that is, he may not see that his overfishing and depleting of the fish stocks must have national, international and global consequences; or, if he does in fact see these, he may not see that the harmful effect he creates will be re-cycled back to him personally for readjustment, be it in five minutes or five thousand years.

The evolution of progressively greater spheres of awareness is portrayed in *Nuclear Evolution* as taking place according to the pattern of the seven levels of consciousness. On the first plane of consciousness, a man becomes aware of his own *bodily needs.* On the second, he becomes aware of society and its significance for him, that is, of his *social needs.* On the third, he becomes aware of the intellectual sphere and his *needs for self-expression.* Next, a person becomes aware of his dependence upon life and his need to find a dependable source of power or *vital energy.* Out of this, the next sphere of *family consciousness* develops, where he becomes aware of authority, tradition and his membership of a clan. On the next level of group or *community consciousness,* he seeks attunement with intelligences that are greater than human, sensing these to lie behind the formation and evolution of societies and groups. On the next level he becomes *globally conscious,* seeing the planet as a living organism of which man is a part, and perceiving those eternal archetypal images which life expresses in every individual manifestation. Here there is a drive to find *enduring order* in life and so awareness of fundamental principles and eternal laws of nature develops here. The next stage is *cosmic consciousness,* in which the individual sacrifices all separateness from Life and identifies itself with everything, seeing only the absolute reality - the Divine Being.

This evolutionary development of progressively wider spheres of consciousness in Nuclear Evolution seems, then, to constitute the returning arc of the time cycle, which began with the descent of the spirit into matter. The I Ching alludes to this process in hexagram 50, "Ting" (The Cauldron), where, under the Judgement, it says: "All that is visible must grow beyond itself, extend into the realm of the invisible. Thereby it receives its true consecration and clarity and takes firm root in the cosmic order." However, once this integration of the individual's consciousness with the ultimate reality has been completed, the movement again turns into its opposite and the cosmically enlightened man selflessly descends into the material world to raise it up through his light-giving influence. The hexagram of the Cauldron continues: " . . . the truly divine does not manifest itself apart from man. The supreme revelation of God appears in prophets and holy men. To venerate them is true veneration of God. The will of God, as revealed through them, should be accepted in humility; this brings inner enlightenment and true understanding of the world, and this leads to great good fortune and success." This same parallel is seen in the diagrams of Nuclear Evolution of each being reaching the absolute Self and acquiring the full rainbow body.

Because the sage has taken "firm root in the Cosmic order", his behaviour in the world is a pure expression of the Tao. Undoubtedly, his enlightening influence extends even to "pigs and fishes",* but to what extent he can bring the Cosmic order out of the chaos of human society depends a good deal on the general condition of the society at the time, for societies, cultures - even the whole human race - are subject to the cyclic alternation of the opposites. In the hexagram of Revolution ("Ko"/No. 49) we are told: "In the world cycle also there are spring and autumn in the life of peoples and nations, and these call for social transformations". The hexagram stresses waiting until the right moment, until conditions are favourable, before starting a great social transformation. This is the essence of Nuclear Evolution. Under the fourth line of the hexagram of the Receptive, which represents the world, we are told "The dark element opens when it moves and closes when at rest." Movement, when the dark principle is open and therefore receptive to the influence of the light, and rest when it is closed and therefore unreceptive to external influences, are the day and night phases of the cycles to which all created things are subject. In the case of society, this cycle can have a period of centuries, and in the case of the whole human race, it can be seen to cover thousands of years. At some times, a sage can stimulate his fellow-men to the creation of a whole new culture and the birth of civilization, and at others he can do nothing but carry the torch to the seclusion of the mountain tops while the world sleeps. However, the I Ching advises us not to be "confused by this universal law of fate" (hexagram 19 - "Lin"/Approach), for "Everything furthers": time is the instrument of the Creative. The "night" phase is as important and necessary to the world cycle as is the decay of autumn to the new growth of spring. And when the spring does come, the advice is to make as much use of the advantageous time as is possible, (cf: hexagrams No. 19 and No. 42 - "Increase").

---

* Cf: Hexagram 61 ("Chung Fu"/Inner Truth), in which pigs and fishes are used as images for "the most unintelligent of creatures".

THE ARCHETYPAL PATTERN OF CHANGE

The alternation of the light and dark forces which constitutes the basic pattern of nature's rhythms, is written through the twelve hexagrams that are correlated with months of the year. This pattern was presented earlier and was shown to represent the form of the T'ai Chi T'u - the union of the Yin and Yang principles. The pattern matches exactly with the astronomical sequence of the seasons, as measured from the Spring and Autumn equinoxes (when the sun crosses the earth's equator) and the Summer and Winter solstices (when the sun reaches its maximum northward and southward positions). It therefore also correlates point for point with the twelve signs of the zodiac, which are likewise measured from the equinoxes and solstices. Furthermore, the seasons of the year are reflected in the four major parts of the day, which are measured astronomically from sunrise and sunset, noon and midnight. The diagram below shows all these correlations. This is preceded by the following key to astrological symbols:

♈ – Aries (Ram)   ♎ – Libra (Scales)

♉ – Taurus (Bull)   ♏ – Scorpio (Scorpion)

♊ – Gemini (Twins)   ♐ – Saggitarius (Centaur-Archer)

♋ – Cancer ((Crab)   ♑ – Capricorn (Fish–Goat)

♌ – Leo (Lion)   ♒ – Aquarius (Water Bearer)

♍ – Virgo (Virgin)   ♓ – Pisces (Fishes)

Since the eight trigrams are also correlated with the four quarters of the day and with the four seasons of the year, we could, if we wished, show these too on the diagram following, but for the present purposes, it is only necessary for us to bear in mind that all these various symbolic schemes describe the same thing: the alternation of the influences of the light and dark principles.

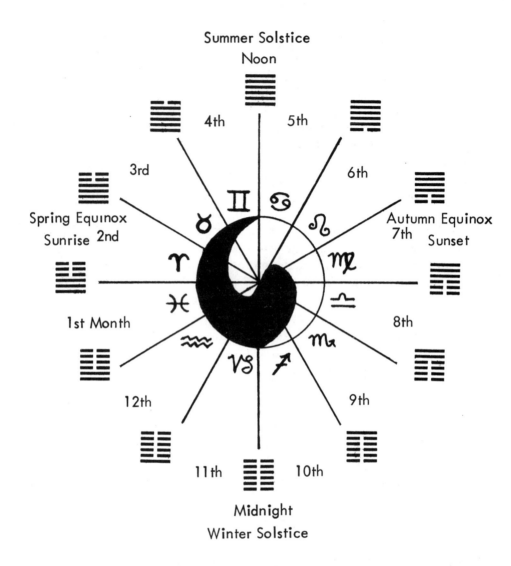

Summer Solstice
Noon

4th 5th

3rd 6th

Spring Equinox
Sunrise 2nd

Autumn Equinox
7th Sunset

1st Month

8th

12th

9th

11th 10th

Midnight
Winter Solstice

Some general observations about this pattern of nature's rhythms and cycles are as follows. Firstly, we may note that on the left-hand side, as we move around the figure clockwise, we see the light, yang lines growing up into the hexagrams from below, until the Creative is attained. Similarly, on the right-hand side we see the dark, yin lines growing up into the hexagrams from below, until the Receptive is attained. The yang lines represent the expansive, differentiative light principle, while the yin lines represent the contractive, unifying dark principle. Thus the pattern represents the cyclic expansion and contraction of the life-force in a seed which occurs in the course of the year with its seasons, as well as representing the daily rhythm of waking and sleeping.

Midnight and midwinter stand for contraction in the womb: the matrix from which all things come and to which all things return at the close of their life cycles. This is symbolised by the hexagram of the Earth, the Receptive, the maternal principle of space. Midday and midsummer stand for maximum expansion in the world, a time of creative action and radiance of light. This is symbolised by the Creative. The Spring Equinox and sunrise stand for the transitional time when the life-force expands out of its containment within the womb and unfolds into the world. This is symbolised by the hexagram of Peace (T'ai, No. 11). It is a time of birth and awakening. The opposite point on the cycle is shown by the Autumn Equinox and sunset, representing the time when the contractive power of the dark principle overcomes the expansive power of the light, so that action in the world is inhibited and life contracts back into the seed. This is symbolised by the hexagram of Standstill (P'i, No. 12). This is a time of retirement from the world, of sacrificing the fruits of action and the discarding of material forms. All this correlates with the idea of unfoldment of each individual from the nuclear centre of being - the nux or seed of consciousness.

The left-hand side of the diagram represents the unfolding of life from a seed. Following this line, we are told, leads to knowledge of the past for the pattern that unfolds from the seed was formed in previous times. The right-hand side represents the winding-up of the life energies into the seed. Following this line, we are told, leads to knowledge of the future, for the pattern of future unfoldment is being formed in the seed as the life energies contract. This is the essence of the I Ching and Nuclear Evolution which Christopher Hills further illustrates in his later book "Supersensonics" (Published 1975).

The traditional Chinese calendar with which we are familiar in modern times, measures the year from the time of a new moon in the early spring. Evidently, this lunar basis for the calendar is different to the basis of the I Ching's ascription of months to hexagrams, which involves only the earth's relationship to the sun at different times of the year. The solstices are specifically mentioned as key reference points in the hexagrams of "Coming to Meet" (No. 44) and "Return" (No. 24), but neither the time of New Moon nor that of Full Moon is mentioned in any of the twelve monthly hexagrams as reference points on the year's cycle.

These hexagrams, then, portray the increase and decrease of the light force through the year and the pattern is solar-based, not lunar-based. However, the pattern could be applied to the lunar month just as it is to the solar year, the equinoctial points being replaced by the moon's entry into its first and last quarters and the solstices being replaced by the times of the new and full moon.

Likewise, the pattern could be applied to the astronomical "Great Year" of about 25,700 years; the "Great Year" is the period of displacement around the astronomical zodiac of the sun's position at the time of the spring equinox. This phenomenon is called the "precession of the equinoxes" and in geological terms, it means that the earth's axis of rotation is gyrating about a central axis once every 25,700 years, so that the sun appears to be gradually shifting its spring equinox position with respect to the constellations of the stars. Thus, at the present time, we find that at the spring equinox, the sun is somewhere at the boundary of the constellation of Aquarius and will "precess" through this constellation for about the next 2,000 years. Hence, the world is said to be entering the "Age of Aquarius", when world conditions are supposed to take on an Aquarian character (since Aquarius is one of the zodiacal signs, its material, psychological and spiritual characteristics have long been identified and catalogued.*) Other methods of divination which may have been used by the ancient Chinese who evolved the I Ching are to be found in Christopher Hills' book on the subject called "Supersensonics".

For students of the I Ching and its relationship to Nuclear Evolution, Part Two of this article is available from the publishers at a small cost.

---

* Note for confused astronomers: The astrological zodiac (consisting of twelve signs) is measured anew every year from the position of the sun at the time of the spring equinox, this point being called the beginning of the sign Aries. The astronomical zodiac is ascribed to the twelve constellations of stars which lie along the ecliptic. However, the constellations are considered as sectors of SPACE, not as groups of stars, so that all are equal in size to one-twelfth of 360°, that is: 30° of the ecliptic. In astrological terms, each constellation is considered to have an influence that is characteristic of its corresponding sign in the astrological zodiac.

APPENDIX

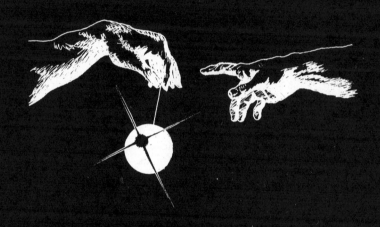

TOOLS of
SPIRITUAL
PERCEPTION

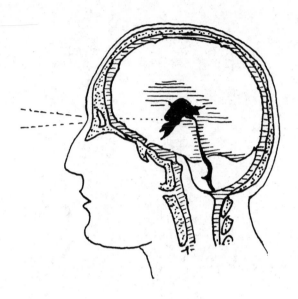

THE DIVINER'S REACTION

Much of the knowledge in this book has been obtained by divining the results from biophysical sources and by tuning the nervous system to receive very subtle signals from the total environment.

To detect the subtle wave-fields around objects the nervous system can be amplified by using various tools and a 608 page book, "Supersensonics" has been written on the phenomenon for those wishing to go beyond theory into the direct use of the Supersense themselves. The following appendix is to give those unfamiliar with the divining phenomenon an idea of how it works and what they can do with it. Unfortunately the author has no time for personal correspondence because he is engaged in producing materials which will answer all the questions one can ask on these phenomena but he will be pleased to guide those enquirers interested in developing their potentials to those who will answer correspondence and who provide divining services.

Learning to dowse for water, minerals and the subtle radiations of consciousness can best be done with some tuition from skilled practitioners but once the principle of biological ionisation has been mastered almost anyone can develop the Supersense.

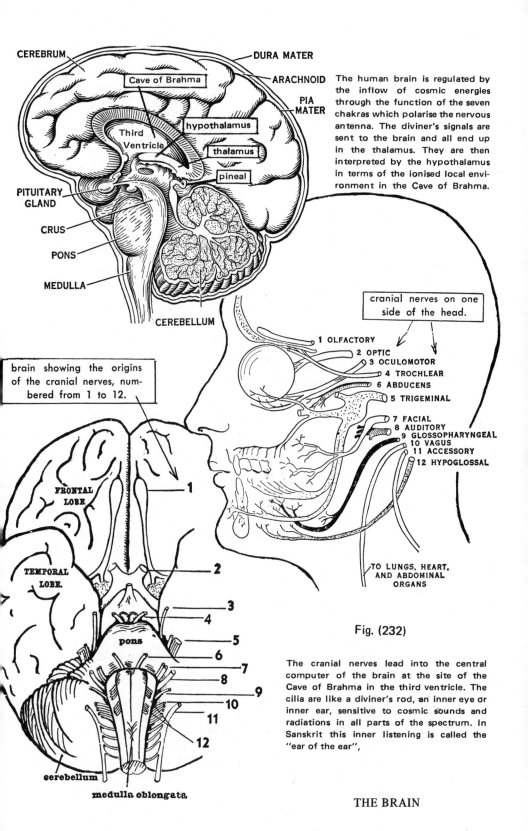

CEREBRUM

DURA MATER

ARACHNOID

Cave of Brahma

PIA MATER

hypothalamus

Third Ventricle

thalamus

pineal

PITUITARY GLAND

CRUS

PONS

MEDULLA

CEREBELLUM

The human brain is regulated by the inflow of cosmic energies through the function of the seven chakras which polarise the nervous antenna. The diviner's signals are sent to the brain and all end up in the thalamus. They are then interpreted by the hypothalamus in terms of the ionised local environment in the Cave of Brahma.

cranial nerves on one side of the head.

brain showing the origins of the cranial nerves, numbered from 1 to 12.

1 OLFACTORY
2 OPTIC
3 OCULOMOTOR
4 TROCHLEAR
6 ABDUCENS
5 TRIGEMINAL
7 FACIAL
8 AUDITORY
9 GLOSSOPHARYNGEAL
10 VAGUS
11 ACCESSORY
12 HYPOGLOSSAL

FRONTAL LOBE

TEMPORAL LOBE

pons

1
2
3
4
5
6
7
8
9
10
11
12

TO LUNGS, HEART, AND ABDOMINAL ORGANS

Fig. (232)

cerebellum

medulla oblongata

The cranial nerves lead into the central computer of the brain at the site of the Cave of Brahma in the third ventricle. The cilia are like a diviner's rod, an inner eye or inner ear, sensitive to cosmic sounds and radiations in all parts of the spectrum. In Sanskrit this inner listening is called the "ear of the ear",

THE BRAIN

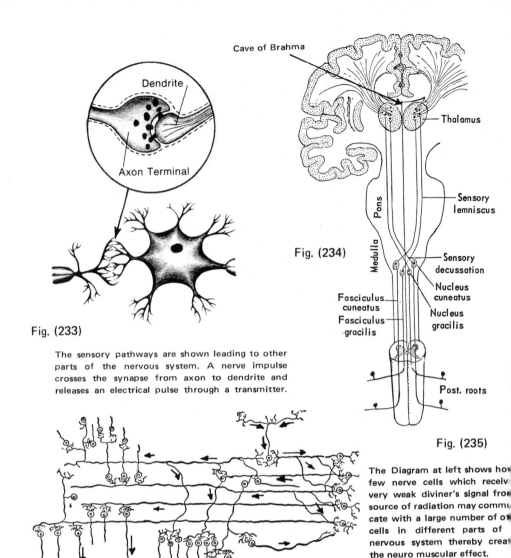

Fig. (233)

Cave of Brahma

Fig. (234)

Thalamus

Pons

Sensory lemniscus

Medulla

Sensory decussation

Fasciculus cuneatus

Fasciculus gracilis

Nucleus cuneatus

Nucleus gracilis

Post. roots

Fig. (235)

The sensory pathways are shown leading to other parts of the nervous system. A nerve impulse crosses the synapse from axon to dendrite and releases an electrical pulse through a transmitter.

The Diagram at left shows how few nerve cells which receiv very weak diviner's signal fror source of radiation may commu cate with a large number of ot cells in different parts of nervous system thereby creat the neuro muscular effect.

CAVE OF BRAHMA

The result of a signal from or to the brain is a synapse. A nerve impulse crosses the synapse in one direction only by releasing a neuro transmitter substance from axon to dendrite. The enlargement shows the tiny sacs filled with transmitter substance. Divining phenomena depends on the reaction of the nerve dendrites to an incoming signal from an object in the environment that is in tune with the image we hold in the Cave of Brahma which controls our imagination. These resonators in the third ventricle can be tuned by thought to respond to any question we can form in the mind. The answer "yes" or "no" comes to us in the form of a neuromuscular reaction with a diviner's rod or can come merely as a tingling sensation in the nerve − an answering glow from the wordless domain of pure consciousness.

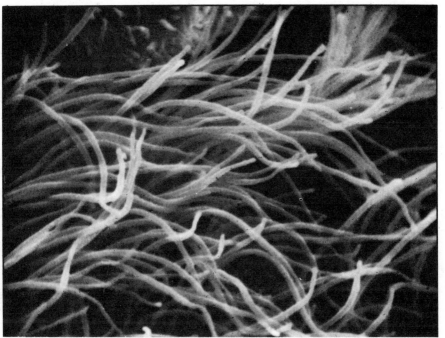

Cilia lining the brain's third ventricle, transport hypothalamic peptides.

CILIA

The hypothalamus is a cluster of special cells like villi and cilia that ooze small amounts of peptide hormones which signal the pituitary to release other trigger hormones to act on hormones in the endocrine system throughout the body. The hypothalamus and pituitary do not work only as hormone triggers in a chemical way, but also influence mental states, personality type and our ability to absorb light. Our behaviour is determined by the charges on ionised atoms which polarise the cilia lining the walls of the cave or ventricle and thereby control these peptide effects on memory and the power to improve visual retention as well as enhance attention. The voluntary control of these events reduces anxiety, causes bliss and makes us sensitive to different colours of the spectrum. These psychologically active enkephalins (peptides) not only influence the nature of personality throughout the chakra functions at the seat of consciousness, but enable us to be able to divine any answer to any question formed in the mind and asked of the cosmic intelligence. This is achieved by concentrating on the behaviour and ionisation of the cilia and tuning them with cosmic light/sound frequencies. The cells of the entire body, particularly blood cells, can be charged at their nucleus to become permanently evolved and positively charged to attract only the negative ions in the total environment.

Spherical bodies nestled among the cilia (fine hairs) lining brain's third ventricle.

The floor of the Cave of Brahma in the third ventricle of the brain is composed of the hypothalamus with the pituitary at one end and the pineal gland at the other. The walls of the cave are lined with the optic thalamus and many other interbrain functions.

SPHERICAL BODIES

The human being is basically an orb or sphere of resonating energies which are tuned by the cilia and small spherical bodies that react, like a rod or pendulum, to questions formed in the mind, thereby releasing a neuro transmitter which triggers a psychophysical response. Whether this reaction is biophysical or psychophysical is merely an academic exercise. The main cause can be divined with the tools of Supersensonics and an answer to any question can be obtained by developing an ionisation response in the rods (cilia) and spheres in the membrane walls of the third ventricle.

Fig. (236)

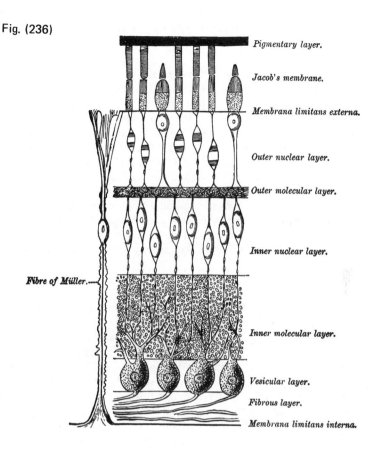

Pigmentary layer.

Jacob's membrane.

Membrana limitans externa.

Outer nuclear layer.

Outer molecular layer.

Inner nuclear layer.

Fibre of Müller.

Inner molecular layer.

Vesicular layer.

Fibrous layer.

Membrana limitans interna.

The cilia in the ventricles are constructed in exactly the same way as the rods of the eye which are light sensitive and send a signal to the brain. They are also similar in construction to the tail of sperm cells. The diagram shows the seven layers of retinal synapse as the nerve signal crosses through on its way to the brain. The cilia work in a similar way to these light sensitive rods, but these cilia are tuned to the ionising rays of cosmic radiation rather than rays of sunlight in the visible spectrum. The cilia in the eye are also sensitive to invisible energies of horizontal and vertical wavefields. As described in "Supersensonics", the eyebeam can be used as a detector in combination with a divining instrument. The cilia are that part of our nervous system which can be likened to the stimulated biological emission of a radar signal and the nervous system is the antenna which receives the answering echo signal to produce the diviner's psychophysical effect.

INSTRUMENTS OF PERCEPTION

The following photographs show some of the psychotronic instruments used to validate the wavefields around various objects including human beings and their thresholds of consciousness. It has always been asked, "How did you arrive at all this knowledge of the natural processing of light energy and color?" For the average scientist there is no way of checking the radiations of the human aura or the vertical wavefields above a water table several hundred feet underground. But to the twelve hundred members of the American Dowsers Association there would be no problem in getting consistent results. Most of them could not only tune into the vertical electrical field of water but also minerals such as gold, oil or any lost objects. However, as with any other science, conditions must be exactly right to get consistency.

The phenomenon of map dowsing or intuitional radiesthesia, as it is sometimes called, is the same for a lost person as a lost object. In fact, the map of the human brain or nervous system can be dowsed for mental events as easily as we can dowse for oil fields. To trace the pathways of a signal through the nerve ganglia is as easy from a map of the system, as it is for a mosquito to find blood or a swallow to navigate its 10,000 mile flight from Argentina. Insects and butterflies are much better diviners than human beings because their survival depends on their sensitivity. But humans have inherited from life a fantastic evolutionary tool in the sensitivity of the human nervous system. The tools shown on the last pages of this book are extensions of that tool. Essentially they work as biofeedback instruments to indicate when the unconscious reports a change in the internal state. In this sense it is no worse nor better than any EEG or any other biofeedback signal. These tools are the means by which anyone can prove for themselves what is written in this book without any chromium-plated gadgets whatever.

The skill in the use of these tools has been variously called Radionics, Radiational Physics, Radiesthesia, Reichian Orgone Therapy, Psychotronics, etc. The author has coined a new word "Supersensonics" to include all these terms and formulated a new science of perception with its own theory and methodology. This is the next step for man, to prove things for himself, so that he can become his own authority and get out of the hands of so-called experts. The means to measure and detect these wavefields of consciousness and thereby to communicate more effectively with our total environment are shown in the photographs which follow. The means to understand these instruments and to use them efficiently are to be found in the author's book "Supersensonics," available from the publishers.

992.

Fig. (237)

This Supersensonic kundalini device detects a person's aura colour and determines which of 44 natural elements is predominant in the physical body. Inside the unit there is a whole octave oscillator tunable from 200 cps to 400 cps as a physical exciting stimulus while the harmonics of the radio-magnetic field of the horizontal wave-field of the human emotional body are tuned by a magnetic dial at the centre of a Turenne disc. The "thought fields" of the vertical wave-field are patterned by an array of prefixed De La Warr permanently tuned dials set at the rate for higher creative intelligence in the east-west wave-field. The set was designed by the author and custom made to his specifications by George De La Warr of Oxford, England in 1960. The work of the De La Warr Laboratories is continued today by his wife and family who pioneered the field of radionics. The author's research proves that non-electronic equipment can be used to produce the psychophysical effect of the aura with radiative stimulators of Supersensonics.

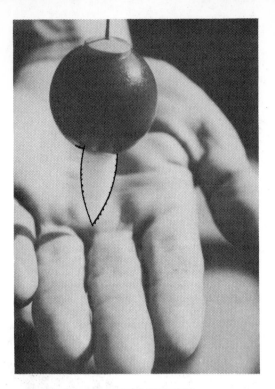

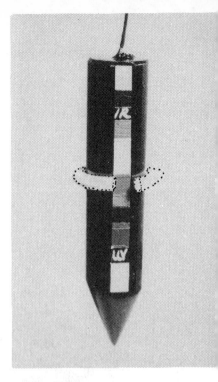

HILLS' POSITIVE GREEN

Is specifically tuned to life-force or prana and is therefore used for checking people's health and vitality, the nutritional value of foods and herbs, and checking positive or negative effects of pyramid energy. Can be used for charging up the body with vital energy.

AURA PENDULUM

A low cost pendulum for determining person's aura and the psychic atmosphere that surrounds them. Also detect the aura of objects, foods, and psycho somatic health conditions.

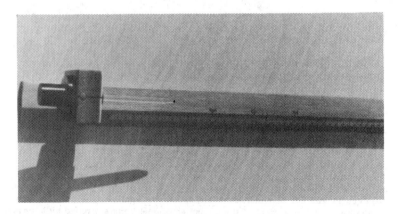

THE TURENNE RULE is an alternate version of the Turenne Disc for finding out abc your physical and emotional state of being. It is also a remarkable instrument for finding c your true health condition. Used by chemists and agriculturalists for detecting presence natural elements and soil conditions.

THE HEFIGAR amplifies the field so strongly that, using it, most people can beco divinens. It is a virtually indispensible instrument to be used in conjunction with a pendul or rod. Can be used as a pointer in prospecting or in archeology digs or finding lost peop

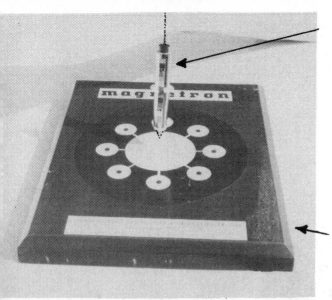

SPECTRUM MIRROR

An amplified pendulum for the professional diviner containing radium, a wave-guide tube and a silver mirrored surface to reflect off unwanted radiations including negative thoughts. Operates on several harmonic levels, atomic, molecular, cell and organ, therefore useful in analysis of foods, chemicals, musical vibration and tuning of sounds and colour of auras.

THE MAGNETRON

The Magnetron: This instrument is a broadcast healer and direction finder, allowing you to send healing vibrations to anyone whose photograph you place at the center. It can also be used to select which of eight homeopathic remedies is the best for the particular condition.

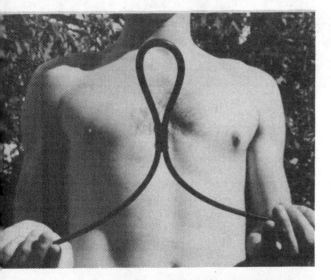

THE EGYPTIAN ANKH

The Egyptian Ankh is a type of divining rod that made the ancient Egyptians an advanced civilization. It is equivalent to the water diviner's rod and selects vertical positive fields same as those reflected from underground streams of water.

TURENNE MAGNET-FITTED PENDULUM

Called the "Rolls Royce" of pendulums because it has a wide range of selectivity and is specially suited for use with the Turenne Rule for detecting atomic and chemical substances. The researcher's pendulum sensitive to several different kinds of radiesthesic wave-fields.

THE ELECTIFIED PENDULUM

This incorporates the principles of the p
junction to create a permanent but subt
flow of electrons which act as a witness f
all electrical activity. Can be used in detecti
any discharge source, tuning the car, findi
trouble spots in electrical circuits, chargi
or discharging the electrical tensions
polarity in the nervous system, sexual polari
or tracing the electrical firing of nerve ce
Useful for detecting leaking bioelect
currents and charged static fields.

THE OSIRIS

A glass pendulum containing mercury which
is used to read people's thoughts and their
I.Q. Used also for intuitional readings of the
emotional and mental state of health from
photographs, blood spots from a distance.

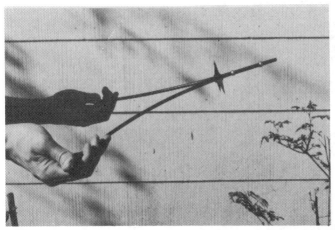

The Rolls Royce
of water divining
tools designed by
Louis Turenne, a
university lecturer
and radio engineer
and physicist who
took up dowsing.

THE TURENNE
MAGNET-FITTED ROD

A very selective divining rod,
used for outdoor work in
much the same way as Moses
and Jacob used their rods.
Can select three different
wave-fields instead of the
normal one.

THE PI-RAY ORGONE ENERGY ACCUMULATOR COFFER

This specially proportioned rosewood box combines the energies of the pyramid form with those of Reichian orgone accumulation. The right-hand spiral inside filters out the negative aspects of the downward disintegration flux called by diviners "negative green" and allows the Pi-ray to pass through the centre of a magnetic field thereby isolating its effect within a field of space. Experiments reveal that it actually "materialises our imaginings". Concentrates pyramid energy without any pyramid. Useful for healing plants, charging organic life and stones with the subtle energies of consciousness.

THE SPIDER PENDULUM

is an experimental pendulum for testing the nature of horizontal and vertical wave-fields, clockwise and anticlockwise vibrations, and east-west flow. Useful for detecting effects of vibrations on ourselves.

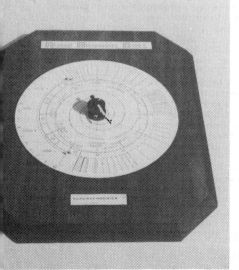

THE KUNDALINI ROOMPH COIL

is used to raise your kundalini in controlled fashion, until you begin to feel a bubbling sensation awaken a new quiet joy within your heart. Channels the fire of consciousness through the Nadis without burning the etheric vehicle.

997

SUGGESTED FURTHER STUDIES
IN CONSCIOUSNESS RESEARCH

NEW EVOLUTIONARY UNIVERSITY COURSES

The following are samples from the degree program of correspondence courses for credit or non-credit, which are not offered by traditional institutions. They offer a range of possibilities for students who can design their own path of study. Students not wishing to be evaluated or to have transcript records kept are not expected to submit workbooks and papers which credit students are required to complete.

CREDIT. Although University of the Trees is too new for accreditation by the Western Association of Schools and Colleges, certain institutions will accept credits for transfer. Students wishing to transfer credits and transcripts to other colleges should arrange transfer credits with their accrediting institutions beforehand, and copies of the University catalog showing the quality of the course material are available at $1.25 including mailing and handling. The University of the Trees is one of the independent California colleges listed by the Bureau of School Approvals to issue degrees under the State Office of Education code 29023 for B.A., B.Sc., M.A., M.Sc. and Ph.d. degrees.

SELF STUDY PROGRAM. These courses are a sample of those offered to the public and can be ordered without enrollment in the degree program by filling in the request form provided. Further details can be obtained by sending for the full catalog.

Course No.

A-1   LOVE -- 8 sessions on cassette tape on nine kinds of love from sexual, social, possessive, devoted to highest spiritual love.

A-2   LOVE AND HEALING -- 8 sessions on cassette tape on health, lessons of pain, tuning to perfect health and love, modes of healing.

A-3   THE LEVELS OF CONSCIOUSNESS -- 14 sessions on cassette tape on the seven levels of consciousness in Nuclear Evolution from the physical/sensory to the imaginative followed by talks relating the levels to chakras, auras, color, karma, communication, etc.

A-4   SPONTANEOUS WISDOM TAPES -- Tape course on the philosophy and psychology of consciousness. 25 different courses available from a large selection of taped lectures. Examples of tape headings include: Creativity, Patience, Purity, Emotion, Balance, Trust, Surrender, Imagination, Ideals, Relativity, The Absolute, Praise, Purposes, Sincerity, Faith, Moksha, Doubt, Discipline, Breath, Light, Samadhi, Love and Giving, Stubborness, Desirelessness, Real Love and Motives, Soul and Being. Use of the Emotions, Grace, Adoration, Foolishness, The Darkness, Intellect, Guilt, Devotion, Suffering, Stimulation, Discrimination, Criticism, Personal God, Confidence, Love and Caring, Non-attachment, Detachment, Maintenance, Ruthlessness and Patience, One-pointedness, Proselytizing, Service, Humility, Anger, Openness, Eternal Time, Worship, Change and Self-Mastery, Karma, The Heart, Compassion, Meditation, Intelligence, Duty, Wu Wei, Synthesis, The Rainbow Body, Prime Imagination, Space, Universal Consciousness, Renunciation, Laws of Probability, Light of Consciousness, The True Nature, Right Action, Self-Righteousness, Bliss.

A-5   PROGRAMMING CONSCIOUSNESS INTO SOUND & MUSIC -- Chanting and toning. Learning to use sound to influence the mind and bring peace and heightened awareness. 14 chanting session tapes with instruction, technique and practice of Troupad style chanting as a scientific method for stilling the mind.

-6   INTO MEDITATION NOW -- The three-year course of study for direct Enlightenment. Requires daily practice for achievement in direct perception. A scientific and simple method of achieving self-discipline over your thinking process, habits and faculties of perception. Not a religion or a Guru-centered learning program, it is "you-centered and you and your existing life situation become the Guru. The teacher is life. Compatible with other disciplines and teachings.

A-7   A THREE STAGE COURSE IN YOGA -- 12 weeks per stage. A practical step by step course in development and growth of understanding through yoga practice. Daily posture routines and study of diet, yoga philosophy, body awareness and theory of breath control.

A-8   ADVANCED COURSE IN YOGA -- A study in Wholistic Health and Living Yoga for those who have completed at least one year in basic yoga postures and philosophy.

A-9   INDEPENDENT STUDY -- This type of study is structured on topics of the student's choosing subject to written approval. Comparative studies between various consciousness expanding teachings are encouraged.

Suggested Consciousness Research Majors	RECOMMENDED FOR GRADUATE STUDY
Psychology of Consciousness	Consciousness and Healing
Methods of Knowing and Ratiocination	Awareness Levels, Receptivity Quotient
Physics of Consciousness	Wholistic Well Being
Philosophy of Consciousness	The Science of Yoga
Poetry of Consciousness	Communities and Self-Government
The Universe as Music	Light & Consciousness
Architecture of Consciousness	Social Systems and Consciousness
The Role of Consciousness in Art	Transcendental Science
Communication With Nature	Comparative Religion
Alternative Energy Systems	New Foods for Human Survival
Cosmic Mathematics	Natural Biophysical Feedback
Direct Perception and Meditation	Consciousness and Vibrations
Awareness Enhancement in Education	Evolution in the Family
Psycho-physiology	Colors & the Mind
Psychotronics - Supersensorics	Social Group Dynamics

Course No.

XB-1   PSYCHOLOGY OF CONSCIOUSNESS -- Research into the aura, light, levels of consciousness, group consciousness and the evolution of consciousness from the atom to man using NUCLEAR EVOLUTION: DISCOVERY OF THE RAINBOW BODY as a text.

YB-1   PHYSICS OF CONSCIOUSNESS -- Similar to XB-1 above only from a physics point of view.

B-2   HILLS' THEORY OF CONSCIOUSNESS -- A blend of the theory and practice of NUCLEAR EVOLUTION. There are a number of approaches to Hills' Theory available either published or to be published.

B-3   NUCLEAR EVOLUTION THROUGH CREATIVE EXPRESSION -- explore the color psychology of NUCLEAR EVOLUTION and master the art of writing at the same time. Course project is to get inside the inner worlds of each of the levels of consciousness and, looking through entirely different eyes, write a narration, argument, autobiography or some other rhetorical mode of expression.

B-4   ADVANCED NUCLEAR EVOLUTION -- 7 sessions on cassette tape, on the application of Nuclear Evolution to modes of perception and practical ways of penetrating the nature of ego.

B-5   THE SCIENCE OF VIBRATION AND TRANSMISSION OF LIFE FORCE -- Understanding the mindstuff and its processes of identification. Growing brain cells, in-depth study in the nature of the ego and self-transformation. INTENSIVE research into the nature of one's own consciousness, from the Rumf Roomph Yoga series of cassette tapes.

G-1   CONDUCT YOUR OWN AWARENESS SESSIONS -- Learn how to use and lead awareness games, psychological, sensory and extrasensory exercises, and ways to achieve a group consciousness.

G-2   UNIVERSAL GOVERNMENT BY NATURE'S LAWS -- Social/Political science for new age groups and communities. A practical application for higher systems of government.

G-3   GROUP CONSCIOUSNESS -- 20 sessions on cassette tapes for unfolding of group consciousness and the need for alternative political and social orders. Actual practice and discussion on the need for creative methods of solving conflict.

G-4   EVOLUTION IN THE FAMILY -- Family application for group consciousness. Studies in family psychology, children's evolution, problems in communication, and love. How to meditate together as a family and teach meditation to children.

G-5   AWARENESS EDUCATION FOR CHILDREN -- Practical work with groups of children using MEDITATING WITH CHILDREN and other methods of transpersonal education.

S-1   ALIVE TO THE UNIVERSE -- A practical handbook for supersensonic living using the new science of radiesthesia. Tuning the nervous system to subtle energies for divining, dowsing and training the intuition.

S-2   DIMENSIONS OF ELECTRO-VIBRATORY PHENOMENA -- Introduction to the electric and magnetic effects of human behavior, radionics, biofeedback and a survey of the field.

S-3   ENERGY, MATTER AND FORM -- For those interested in researching ESP, vibrations, pyramids, sound vibration effects, black holes, and the latest overview of the new science of consciousness.

S-4   PYRAMID ENERGY -- Studies in the architecture of inner space. The creation of a sensory deprivation quiet room or the energising of buildings, food, objects, etc. A study of the positive and negative uses of pyramid energy using RAYS FROM THE CAPSTONE.

S-5   SUPERSENSONICS --THE SPIRITUAL PHYSICS OF ALL VIBRATIONS FROM ZERO TO INFINITY -- INTENSIVE research into radiesthesia, physics and consciousness, learning how to validate the universal field for yourself.

S-6   THE BODY AS A SPIRITUAL FEEDBACK INSTRUMENT -- 8 sessions on cassette tape covering the instruments of Supersensonics, developing the nervous system into a biofeedback tool.

S-7   THE PSYCHO-PHYSIOLOGY OF THE CHAKRA SYSTEM -- Independent Study in experimenting with your own body and chakra network as a divining instrument.

- -

REQUEST FORM

University of the Trees, P.O. Box 644, Boulder Creek, CA 95006

Dear Registrar:
    I am interested in taking the following courses and request a catalog and further information. Enclosed is my $1.25.

COURSE NO: #_____   #_____   #_____   #_____   #_____   #_____
             #_____   #_____   #_____   #_____   #_____

PLEASE CHECK ONE:

I am interested in degree credit.   ☐
I am NOT interested in degree credit.   ☐
I am interested in being on your mailing list. ☐

NAME _____
ADDRESS_____
CITY _____   STATE_____ ZIP_____

1000

UNIVERSITY OF THE TREES PRESS

Publishers of practical spiritual guides, scientific books and Correspondence courses

INTO MEDITATION NOW: A COURSE OF STUDY, by Christopher Hills   45.00
This cost covers the registration and introduction to the comprehensive three-year course of study that enables you to make the philosophy of Nuclear Evolution a reality in your direct experience. Write for more details.

MEDITATING WITH CHILDREN, by Deborah Rozman   5.95
The first of its kind! A delightful teaching book that brings the great art and science of meditation and conscious evolution to children of all ages, this workbook is being used in classrooms throughout the country as a non-religious text in centering and awareness development.

MEDITATION FOR CHILDREN, by Deborah Rozman   4.95
A how-to-relax, concentrate, meditate and apply Nuclear Evolution book for the entire family. Awareness exercises deal with family psychology, problems with communication and openness, and ways to foster deep sharing and love. Published by Celestial Arts.

by Christopher Hills

"SPEAK TO US OF ... " SPONTANEOUS WISDOM TAPES

"SPEAK TO US OF – KARMA, DUTY, AND ONE'S TRUE NATURE" (Tape O No. 81) Realising one's true nature; karma as the duty to one's self; the gap between what we know and how we are living; making our desire the same as our true nature; the function of the ego. **$9.00 (2 Cassettes)**

"SPEAK TO US OF – CHANGE AND SELF-MASTERY" (Tape O No. 78) The place of change in the universe; man's striving for self-mastery; understanding creative forces; stillness; kundalini; changes on the seven levels of consciousness. **$6.00 (1 Cassette)**

"SPEAK TO US OF – THE UNIVERSAL HOLOGRAM" (Tape O No. 150) The universal hologram; finding and keeping centre consciousness; the distinction between lust and roomph; the cause of compulsions and self-absorption. **$9.00 (2 Cassettes)**

"SPEAK TO US OF – VISION" (Tape O No. 96) Physiological mechanisms; the roles that mind and imagination play; the vision of seers and prophets; Christ's meaning of "Ye are the light of this world." **$6.00 (1 Cassette)**

"SPEAK TO US OF – REAL LOVE, MOTIVES" (Tape O No. 65) The way Christ loved; the giving nature; parental love; the "do-gooder" contrasted with the person who is really good inside; purely motivated love without expectation. **$9.00 (2 Cassettes)**

"SPEAK TO US OF – LEARNING FROM NATURE, PROCRASTINATION, REBIRTH, MINDLESSNESS" (Tape O No. 136) Analogies from nature to describe the human condition: how to tackle problems; mental disturbances; how to nurture and unfold the flowers of inner being. **$6.00 (1 Cassette)**

"SPEAK TO US OF – THE RAINBOW BODY (Tape O No. 84) A transcription of this tape appears on pages 8/19 of this book. **$8.00 (2 Cassettes)**

MEDITATIONS ON THE ONE

For beginners and advanced students alike, these meditations create deep experience of the One, helping us to know that we cannot separate ourselves from the rest of the universe no matter how hard we try. The powerful chanting of Christopher Hills transmits the peace of meditation to the listener. Each tape is a C-60 Cassette, $6.00

Meditation No. 1 Riding on a Beam of Light; Habits, and a Journey Through the Body.
No. 2 Meditation and Chant for Dissidents in Russia; 360 Degree Awareness; and the Body as an Instrument.
No. 3 The Movie of Life; What We Want to Become; and Meditating by the River at Rishi-kesh.
No. 4 Does God Sleep in the Stone?; and The State of Flux.
No. 5 The Speed of Consciousness; and Merging with Brahma.

OTHER TAPES AVAILABLE IN SERIES OR INDIVIDUALLY:

THE CHAKRAS: This is the series from which the transcriptions were taken for Part I of this book. Series of 11 recordings.

THE NATURE OF LOVE: Sexual love; Spiritual Love; Self-Intoxicated Love; Love of Commitment-Devotion; Possessive Love; Perfect Love; Series of 8 recordings.

LOVE AND HEALING: Practical exercises for group use or for partners. Series of 8 recordings. Send for complete listing of tapes in the series on Love and Healing.

"THE ONE I LOVE"

Each cassette $6.00, $36.00 for the series.

T.O.I.L.-1 This describes the original meeting and gives the account of how the guru saw through concrete and steel as Christopher came up the path, and the Way the guru taught those with spiritual pride. Includes a meditation. The passing of the cosmic teachings.

T.O.I.L.-2 Account of an experience on the Mother Ganges with a peasant farmer. Some meditations of discipleship of the ONE Guru within and some chanting. The story of meeting the Prime Minister of Bihar state and at the bedside of the President of India.

T.O.I.L.-3 Side one gives an account of Christopher's experience of beauty in the slums of Calcutta. Side two is the experience of pure consciousness in the Guru's deformed son.

T.O.I.L.-4 This gives some teachings of transcendental Truth which is sheer poetry. . . . When the Center is Still, The Tunnel of Love, The Nature of Self, The Spirit of Christmas, The Pressures of Life, The Silence of Supreme Love, etc.

T.O.I.L.-5 Some of the poetic meditations and chants from the book "The One I Love"-- Represents some of the great inspirational chanting and accounts of Christopher's spiritual journey which provide deep spiritual insights and communicates his love to others.

T.O.I.L.-6 The story of how the happy Guru taught an ego lesson and showed how to talk to babies with some meditations on turning darkness into light, compassion & vision.

THE SCIENCE OF VIBRATION AND TRANSMISSION OF LIFE-FORCE

Rumf Roomph Yoga is the name given by Christopher Hills to a series of practical steps distilled from many different yogic techniques for heightening and purifying human consciousness. The words come from a combination of the Sanskrit word Rum meaning spirit and the American word oomph meaning the inner bubbling of life-force. These tapes cannot be effectively described as they are oral step-by-step instructions. Many people use these exercises for increasing the brain electricity and entering the Cave of Brahma.

RUMF ROOMPH YOGA

Available in sequence only

TAPE	SUBJECT
RRY-1	Introduction to the Series; the principle of Identification
RRY-2	Stimulation of Brain Cells; Expansion into Total Openness; Creation of Mudras
RRY-3	Tantric Union of Opposites through Shakti-Shiva Dance
RRY-4	How to Control the Chakra Forces by Looking at the Garbage
RRY-5	Radicalizing the Ego Sense; Meditation on the Center Symbol
RRY-6	Getting Control of the Ego
RRY-7	Meditation for Expanding the Self-Sense and Bursting the Ego Bubble
RRY-8	The Function of the Ego, The Super-Conscious Mind, & Imagination
RRY-9	Meditation & Breath Control for Protein Synthesis; Transmuting Sexual Energies
RRY-10	Understanding the Nature of Pure Consciousness
RRY-11	Practicing the Presence
RRY-12	Validation of Yogic Methods of Knowing, Washing the Mind Clear of Previous Concepts
RRY-13	Group Exercises for Dissolution of Separate SELF
RRY-14	Contacting the Tree of Life & the Tree of Knowledge inside Each Other
RRY-15	Evolutionary Group Interactions: The Low Seat
RRY-16	Principles of Creative Conflict; Mastering Self-Intoxication with Self-Saturation
RRY-17	Becoming a Soul Mirror - or Cosmic Television Camera
RRY-18	Anahata Nadam: Chanting through the Heart Centre; Gaining Control over Inner Forces
RRY-19	Group Discussion of Rumf Roomph Yoga Experience
RRY-20	Mahavideya: Super Penetration of the Mind stuff of Self & Others
RRY-21	Balancing Levity & Gravity; the Steps to Nuclear Evolution
RRY-22	Advanced Exercise in Shiva-Shakti; Surrendering All Your Being to the One Guru: Your True Self; Discovering Karma
RRY 23	Purifying the Chakras by Chanting the Om Overcoming Resistance & Inertia
RRY-24	Embodying the Avatar Consciousness

RRY No. 1, 8, 10, 18, 22, 23, 24 are $6.00 each (1 cassette) RRY No. 2, 3, 4, 5, 6, 7, 9, 11, 12, 13, 14, 15, 16, 17, 19, 20, 21 are $9.00 each (2 cassettes).

INDEX

* * *

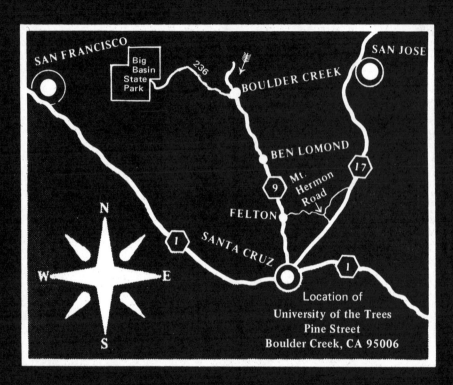